Jeni Wood.

/ 8 : VIII : 57 :

THE PLAYS OF J. M. BARRIE

Dear Brutus
Quality Street
The Admirable Crichton
Alice Sit-by-the-Fire
What Every Woman Knows

Peter Pan
Half Hours
The Twelve-Pound Look
and Other Plays
Little Mary, A Show Play
Mary Rose, and Other Plays

THE PROSE WORKS OF J. M. BARRIE

A Window in Thrums
My Lady Nicotine
Margaret Ogilvy
An Edinburgh Eleven
The Little White Bird
Auld Licht Idylls

Sentimental Tommy
Tommy and Grizel
Better Dead
Courage
A Tillyloss Scandal
The Little Minister

Uniform with these, Barrie's Early Days

THE PETER PAN BOOKS BY J. M. BARRIE

Peter Pan in Kensington Gardens
Illustrated in colour by Arthur Rackham

Peter Pan and Wendy
Illustrated in colour and line by Mabel Lucie Attwell

Peter Pan and Wendy
Illustrated in colour by Mabel Lucie Attwell

Peter Pan and Wendy
With drawings by F. D. Bedford

Peter Pan and Wendy
In the Happy Yellow Book of Pictures

The Nursery Peter Pan
Illustrated in colour, etc.

DOUBLAG: The Second Series to the
Stories of St. Andrews University

HODDER AND STOUGHTON LIMITED

THE PLAYS OF
J. M. BARRIE
IN ONE VOLUME

THE PLAYS

of

J. M. BARRIE

IN ONE VOLUME

Edited by

A. E. WILSON
Dramatic Critic of *The Star*

HODDER AND STOUGHTON
LIMITED   LONDON

First Edition	.	November	1928
Reprinted	. .	December	1928
Reprinted	. .	August	1929
Reprinted	. .	October	1929
Reprinted	. .	July	1930
Reprinted	. .	August	1931
Reprinted	. .	July	1933
Reprinted	. .	June	1936
Reprinted	. .	September	1936
Reprinted	. .	May	1939
Revised Edition		February	1942
Reprinted	. .	October	1943
Reprinted	. .	December	1945
Reprinted	. .	June	1947
Reprinted	. .	December	1948

Printed in Great Britain for HODDER AND STOUGHTON LTD., London
by T. AND A. CONSTABLE LTD., Printers, Edinburgh

FOREWORD

THIS definitive edition of the plays of J. M. Barrie contains the most important of his full-length works for the stage and the best of his one-act plays. It includes several plays which have not hitherto appeared in a collected form, notably *Walker, London*, *The Professor's Love Story*, *The Little Minister*, *The Wedding Guest*, *Little Mary*, and *The Boy David*. The principal omission is *The Adored One*, which was a failure on its original production in London in 1913 and again when it was presented in a revised version. Its first act was subsequently compressed into the one-act play *Seven Women*, and that, I believe, is the only form in which Barrie wished it to be preserved.

Thus forty-four years of active playwriting, extending from 1892 when *Walker, London* was first performed, to his last play, *The Boy David*, which was produced in 1936, is represented. Actually that was not the full extent of Barrie's work as a dramatist.

The playwriting urge, fostered by his visits to the little theatre in Dumfries, came early upon him. His passion for the theatre led him (as he has written) to form a school dramatic club for which he wrote that remarkable work *Bandolero the Bandit*, no page of which remains but, as he says, ' though it played for less than half an hour it contained all the most striking scenes which that boy (Barrie) had lapped up from his corner seat.' You will find references to this vanished juvenile masterpiece in his delightful dedication to *Peter Pan*. There was another play entitled *Bohemia*, dating from his Edinburgh days, and further there was *Caught Napping*, which was published in the *Nottingham Journal* where, before he ventured upon London as a free-lance journalist, he was engaged as a leader-writer.

His first plays to be publicly performed were the one-act *Richard Savage*, written in collaboration with H. B. Marriott Watson, *Ibsen's Ghost*, a one-act skit which was sold to J. L. Toole, and *Becky Sharp*.

His first full-length success was *Walker, London*, produced at Toole's Theatre on February 25, 1892. By the standards of its times it was a capital farce and it made a good deal of money for Toole, who bought it outright for £250. Barrie was not particularly proud of this achievement in after years. He once described it as ' an early indiscretion,' adding ' It is better dead.' In fact, when some years before his death an impresario wished to turn it into a musical comedy, Barrie threatened legal proceedings in order to restrain him.

I make no apology, however, for including it in this collection, for though it may have little artistic or literary merit it can be usefully studied by those who wish to trace Barrie's development as a dramatist. You will find little of the genuine Barrie in it, but, in the turn of certain phrases and in some of the oddities of character and twists of situation, the germ is undoubtedly there.

It is, at any rate, interesting to compare it with *The Professor's Love Story* (1894) and *The Little Minister* (1897), two comedies of charming sentiment which enjoyed considerable success. Here, undeniably, is the authentic Barrie touch. *The Wedding Guest* (1900) is one of his lesser-known plays. I include it, not on the grounds of its merits, but because it represents Barrie's only attempt at a ' problem ' play. It was clearly not his right medium. Only in the handling of minor characters is his touch sure. It has a theme which, one thinks, would have been much more expertly handled by Henry Arthur Jones. It is full of stage conventions. It poses a problem which is never satisfactorily solved ; indeed the issue is shirked.

It was in *Quality Street* and *The Admirable Crichton* (both in 1902) that the particular genius of Barrie fully flowered, and in *Peter Pan* (1904) there was introduced that element of

fantasy, that mixture of charm, sentiment, wisdom and tender-
ness, which Barrie brought so successfully into the theatre of
realism.

I have presented the plays in chronological order, giving the
dates of production as well as those of the most important
revivals on the London stage. The plays of Barrie's maturity
are given with his own introductions as they have appeared
in previous editions. In editing the first four plays I have taken
the liberty of slightly amending the stage directions in order
that the pleasure of the reader should not be hindered by the
constant repetition of such technical phrases as ' *Exit* L.C.,' ' *Enter*
R.,' ' *Crosses* R.C.,' and such other guides to the actor's movements
as irritatingly besprinkle the pages of ' prompt copies.' I have
made only slight changes in the wording and have allowed such
directions to remain as will enable the reader to follow the
action clearly. Would that we could have had Barrie's own
introductions to these plays and that linking together of the
scenes, those explanations of the motives and emotions of his
characters, which give such added charm and narrative interest
in the reading of his later plays.

The task of selecting the shorter plays has not been easy.
Barrie wrote a great many playlets for his own amusement and
for the entertainment of his friends. In the complete record
of his works we come across such items as *The Greedy Dwarf*,
' a moral tale by Peter Perkins,' a children's play in four scenes,
produced in the Barrie drawing-room ; *The Dramatists Get
What They Want*, a playlet introduced in a Hippodrome revue,
and a number of odds and ends, some of ephemeral interest,
some written for charity performances. Clearly, Barrie would
no more have wished such items to be preserved than he would
have cared to have that autumnal revue indiscretion *Rosy
Rapture, Pride of the Beauty Chorus*, included in any edition of
his plays.

But it has been a hard matter to discard other more ambitious
efforts. What I have selected represents the cream of his

miniature works for the stage. They include such little gems as *The Old Lady Shows Her Medals*, *The Twelve-Pound Look*, and *Shall We Join the Ladies?* which purports to be the first act of an uncompleted play, though whether it was just a brilliant *jeu d'esprit* or whether Barrie ever intended to complete it remains a fascinating unsolved mystery of the theatre.

I wish to express my thanks for help in preparation of this edition to the late Mr. R. Golding Bright; to Mr. John Parker, editor of *Who's Who in the Theatre*; to Messrs. Samuel French for permission to include *Walker, London*; to Peter Davies Ltd. for permission to include *The Boy David*; and to the *Fortnightly Review*, in which the full text of *The Wedding Guest* appeared shortly after the original production.

A. E. WILSON.

A LIST OF THE PLAYS

The plays are presented in chronological order, the year of production being given in parenthesis. Those indicated * are one-act plays.

PAGE

WALKER, LONDON (1892) 1

THE PROFESSOR'S LOVE STORY (1894) . . 53

THE LITTLE MINISTER (1897) 131

THE WEDDING GUEST (1900) 213

QUALITY STREET (1902) 273

THE ADMIRABLE CRICHTON (1902) . . . 341

LITTLE MARY (1903) 421

PETER PAN (1904) 487

*PANTALOON (1905) 577

ALICE SIT-BY-THE-FIRE (1905) 595

WHAT EVERY WOMAN KNOWS (1908) . . 665

*OLD FRIENDS (1910) 747

*THE TWELVE-POUND LOOK (1910) . . . 761

*ROSALIND (1912) 781

*THE WILL (1913) 809

*HALF AN HOUR (1913) 835

*THE NEW WORD (1915) 853

A KISS FOR CINDERELLA (1916) . . . 875

*SEVEN WOMEN (1917) 945

PAGE

*THE OLD LADY SHOWS HER MEDALS (1917) . 963

DEAR BRUTUS (1917) 993

*A WELL-REMEMBERED VOICE (1918) . . . 1061

MARY ROSE (1920) 1083

*SHALL WE JOIN THE LADIES ? (1921) . . 1149

*BARBARA'S WEDDING (1927) 1167

THE BOY DAVID (1936) 1183

APPENDIX : COMPLETE LIST OF PLAYS . . 1271

WALKER, LONDON

Produced at Toole's Theatre on February 25, 1892, with the following cast:

JASPER PHIPPS	. . . .	*J. L. Toole*
KIT UPJOHN	. . . .	*C. M. Lowne*
ANDREW McPHAIL	. . .	*Seymour Hicks*
W. G.	. . . . .	*Cecil Ramsey*
BEN	. . . . .	*George Shelton*
MRS. GOLIGHTLY	. . . .	*Effie Liston*
BELL GOLIGHTLY, B.A.	. . .	*Irene Vanbrugh*
NANNY O'BRIEN	. . . .	*Mary Ansell*
SARAH RIGG	. . . .	*Eliza Johnstone*
PENNY	. . . .	*Mary Brough*

The play ran for 511 performances.

ACT I

SCENE : A house-boat on the Thames. The blinds are down.
Time : morning. A canoe and punt on bank at the bow are
tied to house-boat. Someone in distance is playing a penny
whistle. W. G. is lying on plank lazily writing a letter. Presently he sleeps. Nanny is on deck fishing. Mrs. Golightly is
seen pulling up blind in saloon. The table is set for breakfast
on deck. The opposite blind is also going up, giving a view of
river and towpath. Mrs. Golightly sits at the window and
knits. Andrew is seen in the saloon with no coat, waistcoat or
collar. Bell is in the cabin. Nanny raises line. She has her
hair only partially done.

VOICE (*off*). House-boat ahoy ! Milk !
> (MRS. GOLIGHTLY *draws curtains of saloon.* BELL *draws
> blinds of cabin and dips jug out for water.* ANDREW *draws
> curtains.* BELL *drops jug into river and fishes for it with
> umbrella.*)

W. G. Breakfast ready, Mater ?

MRS. GOLIGHTLY. No, what are you doing, W. G. ?

VOICE. Hi ! Milk !

ANDREW. W. G., why don't you go across for the milk ?
> (*Noise of breaking dishes is heard.*)

NANNY (*to herself*). Penny breaking dishes again.
> (PENNY *enters through saloon, throws broken dishes into
> river. The splash brings* NANNY *to deck where she con-
> tinues fishing.* W. G. *takes piece of crockery and throws
> it down in front of* MRS. GOLIGHTLY. *She starts.*)

VOICE. Milk ! Milk !

NANNY. W. G., do go across for the milk. I do believe he

B

is asleep. (*Descends ladder and bends over him.*) I wonder if I could win a pair of gloves from W. G.

> (*She kisses him. He jumps up and pulls his hand indignantly across his mouth.*)

W. G.   Stop that ! Just think if anybody had seen you.

NANNY.   Pooh ! the time will come when you will be willing to give anything for a kiss.

W. G.   Rot ! You have no right to bring such charges against a fellow.

NANNY.   A fellow ! You horrid little boy.

W. G.   Little boy ! I 'm as tall as you !

> (*Turns and measures back to back. He looks to see if she 's tiptoeing and pushes her down.*)

NANNY.   You call yourself W. G. because you think you are a great cricketer and I can bowl you myself.

W. G.   You bowl me ! Oh, that time—because my foot slipped. (*Goes.*)

VOICE.   Milk ! Ahoy !

MRS. GOLIGHTLY (*speaking out at window*).   W. G. (*counts stitches*) 23, 24, 25, 26, 27, 28. W. G., do pull across for the milk !

W. G.   I 'll go, but it 's an awful swot ! (*Gets into punt.*)

NANNY.   And W. G., you needn't expect me to play in the cricket match on Saturday if you say I bowled you unfairly.

W. G. (*alarmed*).   Don't say you won't play, Cousin Nanny. I say, I 'm not angry with you for kissing me ; I know girls can't help it. And look here, read that letter I 've been writing to Daly Major, and you 'll see how I crack up your leg hits.

> (*Exit* W. G. *in punt. He is heard whistling after out of sight, until* NANNY *is on deck.* NANNY *looks at letter, laughs and runs on deck.*)

NANNY (*leaning over railing*).   Listen, you people !

> (BELL, ANDREW *and* MRS. GOLIGHTLY *put their heads out.*)

Do you want to hear W. G.'s candid opinion of you ? It is in a letter to a school friend.

BELL.   And very ungrammatical, I fear.

ANDREW.   Yes, I don't think you will have two B.A.s in your family, Mrs. Golightly.

MRS. GOLIGHTLY.   One is enough. 15, 16, 17, 18, 19. (*Goes on knitting while* BELL *puts finishing touches to her hair.*)

NANNY (*reading*). ' Dear old boy, I take up the pen to tell you we are in a house-boat this month, and it is the mater's house-boat, and she knits all day, like she does everywhere.'

BELL (*scornfully*). Like she does !

NANNY. ' My sister Bell is also here and you will regret to hear she has had the cheek to take a B.A. of London, and I am ashamed of her knowing all about the Differential Calculus and Greek verbs, it not being womanly ; but you were wrong in thinking she would wear blue spectacles.'

ANDREW. That 's one for you, Miss Golightly.

NANNY. ' There is another girl on board, my cousin Nanny, and we are to have a cricket match next Saturday in the village, men versus women. Nanny is good at high leg ones but I can always bowl her with a daisy cutter.' He can't !

ANDREW. One for you, Miss O'Brien.

NANNY. Yes, and here is one for you. ' There is a Scotch chap staying with us, called Andrew McPhail, and I 'm rather glad he is here—I 'm rather glad he is here, because he 's as bad a scholar as myself. He is an Edinburgh medical student, and is waiting to hear whether he passed his exam. to be a doctor, and he will hear by telegram on Saturday, but I don't expect he 'll pass ; and neither does Bell. She says he——'

BELL. Nanny !

NANNY. I 'll miss that. Hum—um—um ! ' McPhail is rather soft on my cous——' —hum ! (*With emphasis*) ' McPhail is rather soft ! ' Ah, Bell. Here is something about Mr. Upjohn. ' Who do you think is staying at the inn ? One of the greatest men of the day, namely Kit Upjohn who made 121 for Middlesex against Notts, and even then was only bowled off his pads.'

BELL. A poor kind of greatness !

NANNY. ' But though Upjohn is such a swell he isn't stuck up, and he treats Bell just like as if she was his equal. He comes to the house-boat every day, and lets her jaw away to him about choosing a profession, and sometimes the three of us go for a walk, and then he offers me a cane-handled bat if I can run the mile in six minutes.' Oh, Bell !

BELL (*indignantly*). It isn't true !

NANNY. What isn't ?

BELL. What you imply !

NANNY.   What did I imply ?

BELL.   That I——that Mr. Upjohn——that we——oh ! (*Retires from window.* NANNY *beckons to* ANDREW, *who saunters into saloon up ladder to deck.*) They all seem to think I 'm in love with Mr. Upjohn, a man who laughs every time I speak of woman's true position to him. I can't love him. I won't. (*Pulls down blind.*)

> (*A crash is heard.* MRS. GOLIGHTLY *raises hands in horror. Exits.*)

NANNY (*to* ANDREW *on deck*). And how have you slept, sir ?

ANDREW.   Badly.   I dreamt I had been plucked in the exam.

NANNY.   You have not got used to that dream yet ?

> (*Instead of answering* ANDREW *becomes rigid ; there is a horrified look in his face ; he draws a diagram in the air with his fingers and mutters.*)

Whatever is the matter ?

ANDREW.   I have just remembered——I believe—— Oh, Miss O'Brien, I think I gave the wrong answer to question five.   (*Continues to glare and mutter.*)

NANNY.   What was it ?

ANDREW.   ' Take a stomach ; remove the——'

NANNY (*putting fingers to her ears*). Disgusting !

ANDREW (*coming to*). We all have them, Miss O'Brien.

NANNY.   I suppose we have, but, sure, we needn't let on ! That 's the worst of being a doctor.

ANDREW.   I 'm not a doctor yet. Oh, to be one, to prescribe, to operate. To cut off legs ! (*Sits.*)

NANNY (*after looking over at* BELL's *window*). Mr. McPhail, did you ever propose to a lady ?

ANDREW.   No, but I want to——Nanny——

NANNY.   Hush ! If you were a lady and knew that a man was about to propose to you, and you meant to accept him, how should you——dress ?

ANDREW.   Dress ?

NANNY.   Or suppose you meant to refuse him, then how should you dress ?

ANDREW.   Really ?

NANNY.   Stupid ! I am quite certain from Mr. Upjohn's manner yesterday that he will propose to Bell to-day. Now if

I know it, you may be sure she knows it, and even you must see that she is taking twice as long to dress this morning as usual. Does that mean that she is to accept or refuse him ?

ANDREW. Accept obviously, because if she meant the other thing, she would not care how she looked.

NANNY. I think the reverse ; if she was to say yes, it would not much matter how she looked, because he would be seeing her so often afterwards. But if it is to be no, she would naturally dress carefully.

ANDREW. Why ?

NANNY. So that he should have her at her prettiest to remember her by after he goes to Manitoba !

ANDREW. But Miss Golightly despises dress—she told me so herself.

NANNY. Pooh ! I should like to see her wear a last year's frock.

ANDREW. Miss O'Brien, did you dress carefully to-day ?

NANNY. Awfully carefully ! (*Pause.*)

ANDREW. You 're a bonny wee lassie !

NANNY. No compliments, but I see you are a Scotchman now, and I used to doubt it.

ANDREW. Why ?

NANNY. Because you never say ' Bang went saxpence whatever,' and then you don't wear the national costume.

ANDREW. What national costume ? (NANNY *points to her skirts and to his legs.*) Oh, it 's only the English tourists that wear that ; besides, you 're not national either, for though you 're an Irish girl, you don't flirt !

NANNY. No, never. Oh ! there 's a fly in my eye !

ANDREW. Fly in your eye ! Oh, I must operate at once. (*They sit up back. He tries to get fly out of her eye.* BELL *pulls up blind and* MRS. GOLIGHTLY *speaks to her through saloon window.*)

MRS. GOLIGHTLY. Bell, the milk will be turned before W. G. comes across with it. He is so slow.

BELL. As we used to say at Girton, *tardus in rebus gerendis.*

MRS. GOLIGHTLY. Very likely, but that does not explain why the milk will not keep in this weather.

BELL. The reason is obvious—as the temperature rises, the *bacillus lacticus*——

MRS. GOLIGHTLY.   You will give me a headache, Bell.
(W. G. *heard whistling.* BELL *withdraws her head.*)

MRS. GOLIGHTLY.   Ah, I hear W. G. (*Goes to stern ;*
NANNY *and* ANDREW *are waving to someone.*)

KIT (*not yet visible*).   Good morning, Mrs. Golightly.

MRS. GOLIGHTLY.   Good morning, Mr. Upjohn.
(*Punt draws up with* UPJOHN *and* W. G. *in it.*)

KIT.   I happened to be on the towpath, so——

W. G.   So I asked him to breakfast.   Is it ready ?   We
can't keep Upjohn waiting.

MRS. GOLIGHTLY.   In twenty minutes.
(ANDREW *and* NANNY *go.*)

W. G.   Then we can go for a spin first.

KIT.   No, I—I——

W. G.   Oh, you don't need to do the polite.

MRS. GOLIGHTLY.   But perhaps——

KIT.   I would indeed.

MRS. GOLIGHTLY.   Take me instead, W. G. (*She steps
into punt, and* KIT *on to ledge of saloon door with milk can in his
hand.   Punt goes off.*)
(*Enter* BELL *into saloon.*)

KIT.   Miss Golightly !

BELL (*starting and putting her hand to her heart*).   You
startled me !

KIT (*entering*).   I am so sorry.   This is—the milk.

BELL.   Thank you. (*Puts it on table.*)

KIT.   When you saw me just now, you—you put your
hand to your heart.

BELL.   I was taken aback.   *Per torrita* would you say, or
simply *trepida* ?

KIT.   I did not come here to talk Latin grammar, Miss
Golightly, you were fourth wrangler and I am only a plain
man. (*Pause.*)   A plain man, I said.

BELL.   I did not contradict you.

KIT.   But last night I asked you a question and you promised
to give me your answer to-day.   Is it yes or no ? (*She
turns away agitatedly.*)   Do you care for me at all, Miss
Golightly ?

BELL.   How can I, when we are on opposite sides on every
question ?

KIT. Do you ? It is not a matter of logic.

BELL. It is—it ought to be. I don't see how I can love you. I have reduced love to syllogistic form——

KIT. Oh !

BELL. On an old examination paper.

KIT. And what was the conclusion ?

BELL. That it is absurd to think I love you.

KIT. What of that, if you do think it ! Where is that paper ? (*He comes near to her.*)

BELL. I—I tore it up, Kit ! (*They embrace.*) Don't !

KIT. Why not ?

BELL. It is so—unintellectual.

KIT. But if we like it ?

BELL. How can we ? There is nothing in it.

KIT. You quaint darling !

BELL (*stamping her foot*). No ! Promise, Kit, that you will never again call me such names.

KIT. But——

BELL. They are degrading !

KIT. Nonsense, child !

BELL. Child ! Do you not see that you are insulting me ?

KIT (*kissing her*). My beautiful !

BELL. You must never pay those infantile compliments to my personal appearance. If you love me, let it be for my mind alone, for all other love is founded on an ontological misconception.

KIT. We can settle all these little matters when you are my wife, Bell.

BELL. No, let us understand each other now. I must be your helpmate in all things. Should I seem unreasonable you must never humour me. No laughing me out of *my* arguments, nor kissing away *my* judgment. You will never yield to me for that most despicable of all reasons, because you think me pretty.

KIT. I will do my best to make you happy.

BELL. You will give up smoking ?

KIT (*after a pause—decidedly*). No !

BELL. Not when I ask you ? (*She follows and embraces him.*)

KIT. I have just promised when I think you in the wrong to say so.

BELL.   H'm ! You know how ambitious I am. You will stand for Parliament ?

KIT.   I mean to.

BELL.   But we are on different sides !

KIT.   Pooh ! Your politics only amuse me, dear.

BELL.   Amuse you, Mr. Upjohn ?

KIT.   Forgive me.   I suppose it would be better if we were of the same colour.

BELL.   Fortunately that can easily be remedied.

KIT.   You will join us, Bell ?

BELL.   Never ! But you can join us.

KIT.   Bell, how dare you ask me to——

BELL.   How dare you ask me ?

KIT.   Pshaw ! A woman's politics !

BELL.   Oh, very well !

KIT.   You are unreasonable !

BELL.   I !

KIT.   Be serious, Bell.

BELL.   You won't let me.   It is the last thing such men as you want of a woman.   Your heart's desire is a baby wife, to be fed on chocolates and has she been a good little girl to-day, and would she like another pretty bonnet to play with ? Oh !

KIT.   You are provoking !

BELL.   You are masterful—and a bully !

KIT.   —I will be master in my own house——

BELL.   But not of me.

KIT.   —You realise what you are saying, Bell ? It is my dismissal.

BELL.   If you will not listen to reason.

KIT.   You bid me go ?

BELL (*after pause*).   Yes.

KIT (*after looking at her*).   Very well.   Good-bye.   Please tell Mrs. Golightly that—that I have suddenly been recalled to London.   (*She bows.*)   I hope you will get a better fellow than I.   (*She turns away her head.*)   Good-bye, I suppose it is better as it is.   You and I could never—Bell, let us marry and risk it ! (*She seems about to assent.   Rushes into* KIT'S *arms.*)   They say a woman's No often means Yes.

BELL (*freezingly*).   It is a libel !

(*He looks at her, raises his cap, and exits along bank.*)

(*On bank.*) Oh ! he cannot love me or he would never have gone away like that. I did not tell him to go !

　　　　(W. G. *is heard shouting ' Ship ahoy ! ' The punt draws up.*)

MRS. GOLIGHTLY.　Be cautious, W. G.　(*Boards.*)　Bell, W. G. declares he saw Mr. Upjohn walking along the bank.

BELL.　He has been recalled to London.

W. G.　By telegram ?

BELL.　Yes.

MRS. GOLIGHTLY.　What a pity.　We shall all miss him ! (*Sounds of breakage.*)　Oh, listen to Penny smashing crockery for breakfast !

　　　　(*Exit through saloon.*)

W. G. (*in the punt*).　Bell, I believe that telegram was just an excuse to let Upjohn get away.　Have you been boring him again ?

BELL.　I—I hate him !

　　　　(W. G. *comes on bank.*)

W. G.　Hallo !　You are crying !

BELL.　I 'm not !　(*Sobs.*)

W. G. (*after whistling*).　Bell, I believe you 've gone and got too fond of him !　Oh, Cicero, you couldn't expect Upjohn to fall in what-you-call-it with the like of you !

BELL.　Don't talk nonsense, I have rejected him.

W. G.　*You !*

BELL.　Why shouldn't I ?

W. G.　Great Balbus, girl, why he made 121 against Notts. I say, I wonder what he saw in you ?　You are sure he wanted you ?　(BELL *slaps his face and jumps into punt.*)　Then I 'll go after him !

BELL.　No, I would rather die.

W. G.　Than what ?

BELL.　Than seem to ask him back.

W. G.　But you want him ?

BELL.　I don't !

W. G.　All right.　(*Is about to tie up punt.*)

BELL (*stiffly*).　You needn't tie up the punt, I am—going out in it.　(W. G. *whistles.*)　Only to practise punting for a few minutes before breakfast.

W. G.　You are going after him.

BELL. The idea ! (*Gets into punt.*)

W. G. You *are* !

BELL. Nothing of the sort. If I chance to meet him and he—apologises—I—W. G., am I a girl who could run after any man ? (*Punts out of sight in direction taken by* KIT.)

W. G. Balbus ! I 'm glad I 'm a man. (*Sits on plank.*)

(*Enter* MRS. GOLIGHTLY *through saloon with flowers which she puts on table.*)

Bell has gone out in the punt, mater. How long till breakfast now ?

MRS. GOLIGHTLY. A quarter of an hour at least, Penny has capsized the kettle.

(NANNY *and* ANDREW *come into view on deck.*)

W. G. I 'm famishing ! (MRS. GOLIGHTLY, *with knitting, follows him to stern.*)

NANNY. Come and feed the swans, W. G. Such beauties !

W. G. Greedy beggars, they are always eating. (*Goes on deck.*)

NANNY. Are you not coming, Auntie ?

MRS. GOLIGHTLY. No, dear, I have this to finish. (*She sits on plank and knits.*)

(W. G., NANNY, *and* ANDREW *are on deck flinging bread overboard.*)

NANNY. What long necks they have !

ANDREW. I should like to dissect them.

W. G. Chuck a crust at that brute. Oh ! did you see me hit him in the eye ?

(SARAH *enters along bank, and looking sharply into house-boat windows she jumps to see who are on deck.* MRS. GOLIGHTLY *looks up and sees her.*)

SARAH. Good morning, ma'am. (*Starts.*)

MRS. GOLIGHTLY (*wondering*). Good morning, who are you ?

SARAH. I 'm from London.

MRS. GOLIGHTLY. Yes ?

SARAH. And outspoken. You don't happen to have a villain on board ?

MRS. GOLIGHTLY. Gracious, no !

SARAH. I 've tracked him from London to this neighbourhood.

MRS. GOLIGHTLY. Who is he ?

SARAH. Jasper Phipps by name, barber by trade, deceiver by nature.

MRS. GOLIGHTLY. What has he done?

SARAH. Didn't turn up.

MRS. GOLIGHTLY. Where?

SARAH. At the church door.

MRS. GOLIGHTLY. You were to be married to him?

SARAH. I was, yesterday, and I waited an hour. Then this letter is handed to me. He is a scholar, is Jasper. (*Hands* MRS. GOLIGHTLY *a letter*.)

MRS. GOLIGHTLY. 'My dearest Sarah. You will be surprised at my not turning up to marry you, and I feel I owe you an apology.' (*Looks up*) I should think he did! 'First, my love, it is a startler to a man to wake up on his marriage morning and remember that in an hour he will be tied for life. Second, through shaving so many gents, I feel that I want to have a burst as one, myself. Sarah, it can only be done with the honeymoon money. Third, my sweet, I know a swell I am like in appearance, and I am going to pass for him, but he is a bachelor so it wouldn't be proper to take you with me. Fourth, it would be more difficult for you than for me to look like a swell. Fifth, there is not enough money for two at any rate. Everything considered, dear Sarah, I have decided to have the honeymoon before the marriage, and to have it by myself. Then, my girl, when my week's leave is up, I will come back and marry you. Fear not; I am staunch, and don't follow me. Your affectionate Jasper. P.S.—I love you! I love you! I love you!' The scoundrel!

SARAH. Nothing of the kind.

MRS. GOLIGHTLY. You said he was a villain yourself!

SARAH. I won't let others miscall him.

MRS. GOLIGHTLY. You are well rid of him.

SARAH. I ain't. I tell you I'll find him yet.

MRS. GOLIGHTLY. And then what will you do?

SARAH. Be revenged! Marry him!

　　(*Exit along bank*.)

MRS. GOLIGHTLY. Well, well, well!

　　(NANNY *comes to top of ladder*.)

NANNY. Bell, will you and Mr. Upjohn—why, Auntie, where are they? I thought I heard you talking to them.

MRS. GOLIGHTLY.   No.   Mr. Upjohn has been recalled to London and W. G. says Bell is out in the punt.

NANNY.   Recalled to London !   (*Turning to* W. G.) Do you know about this ?

W. G. (*eating a crust*).   Yes.   Upjohn went away in a huff, and Bell went after him.

NANNY.   After him ?

W. G.   You see he asked her to be his——

NANNY (*stopping him*).   Ahem !   Mr. McPhail, please get me my straw hat from the saloon.   (ANDREW *nods and goes down to saloon.*) Now, W. G., quick !

W. G.   Upjohn asked her to be his thingummy——

NANNY.   Yes ?

W. G.   And she wouldn't, so he went away and she went after him.

NANNY.   Oh, you silly !   What does it all mean ?

ANDREW (*coming on deck with a hat and basket rather like each other*).   Miss O'Brien, I know one of these is your hat, and the other your basket, and I brought both, because I 'm not sure which is which.

NANNY.   Thanks.   Take the basket back.   W. G., I shall be miserable until I know what has happened, and Bell is so proud, she won't tell me a word.

ANDREW (*looking off*).   I see the punt.

NANNY.   How many in it ?

ANDREW.   Two.

NANNY.   Good !   (*Begins to descend ladder.*)

W. G.   No, three.

MRS. GOLIGHTLY (*laying down knitting*).   Three ?   She went out alone.

ANDREW.   Upjohn isn't one of them.

NANNY.   Ben is punting.

W. G.   But who is that chap sitting beside Bell ?

NANNY.   I never saw him before.

ANDREW.   He is dripping wet !

W. G.   So is Bell.   There has been a spill !

MRS. GOLIGHTLY.   An accident !   (*Goes into saloon.*)

NANNY (*running down ladder to her*).   I am afraid so, but she is safe, dear Auntie.

W. G. (*hailing*).   Hi, what 's wrong ?

BEN (*invisible*). She fell into the river.

MRS. GOLIGHTLY. Bell !

(NANNY *supports her. The punt is drawn in.* BEN *is
punting,* JASPER *and* BELL, *both very wet, are sitting.*)

BELL (*boarding and kissing* MRS. GOLIGHTLY). No need for
alarm, mother, I am drenched, that is all. (*In saloon.*)

BEN. But it was a near shave. If it hadn't been for 'im !
(*Looking at* JASPER *who is modestly standing in bow, straw hat
in hand.*)

BELL. The punt shot away beneath me, leaving me clinging to the pole. I remember no more from that moment
until I opened my eyes and found myself safe on the bank.
Mother, this gentleman has saved my life.

MRS. GOLIGHTLY. Oh, sir !

JASPER. Oh, it was nothing !

NANNY (*aside*). How modest ! I wonder if he is married !
(*Aloud*) Bell, your teeth are chattering. Come inside, and
change your things.

BELL. Ben, do tell them what you saw him do. Mother,
Ben saw everything that happened while I was senseless in
the water !

JASPER. I only jumped in and pulled her out. That was
all.

(NANNY *and* BELL *retire into saloon.*)

NANNY (*in saloon*). Did you see Mr. Upjohn ?

BELL. No, I shall never see him again.

(*Exeunt.*)

BEN. It was this way, ma'am. The young lady, she falls
into the water as she has told you. It was at a ticklish place
just this side o' the weir, and before you could say Jack Robinson,
I sees her being carried towards it. Ma'am, my first thought
was, she 's as good as a corpse, for I didn't think there was a
man in England could ha' torn her out o' that rush of water.
But there was—this gentleman——

JASPER. Pooh !

ALL. Well ! Well !

(NANNY *returns and listens.*)

BEN. I just sees him flash by me and jump into the water.
It 's U P with both o' them I thinks, for by the time he gripped
her she were just on the point of being shot over the weir.

W. G. Balbus !

BEN. I shut my eyes, and when I dared look again, he had one arm around her and with the other he was fightin' agin the current. Three times, ma'am, it tore him back and I cries, ' Your only chance is to let her go.' He just shook his head and fought on and on, and inch by inch he brought her nearer the bank, till they both fell on it senseless.

ANDREW. Great Scott !

W. G. What a brick !

MRS. GOLIGHTLY. How can I thank you, sir ?

JASPER. Oh ! It was nothing !

NANNY. Ask him to have something to drink, Auntie.

MRS. GOLIGHTLY. You will stay to breakfast, Mr.—eh——

JASPER. With pleasure. My name is Colonel Neil, at your service.

NANNY. *The* Colonel Neil ? Africanus Neil !

MRS. GOLIGHTLY. Colonel Neil, the African explorer ?

ANDREW. Whose name is in all the papers ?

JASPER. The same, but I only did my duty in Africa !

(ANDREW *exits*.)

W. G. Great Caius and Balbus ! (NANNY *goes on to ladder*.) Colonel Neil, will you let me feel your muscles ? (*Feels them and then runs into saloon, shouting*) Bell, he 's Neil, Africanus Neil !

(*Exit*.)

NANNY. Auntie, Bell wants you.

(*Exit* MRS. GOLIGHTLY *through saloon*.)

NANNY. Colonel Neil, you are a hero and I could kiss you.

(JASPER *hastening to her*.)

If I were Bell ! (*Goes up ladder—to herself*) He is a bachelor —and yet I don't know—a married man might have wanted to do it too ! (*Sits on deck*.)

JASPER (*rubbing his hands gleefully*). Oh, this is better than the shop ! (*Is about to go on bank*.)

BEN (*still in punt*). A word with you, *Colonel Neil*.

JASPER (*assuming a high and mighty air*). Well ?

BEN. What does this 'ere rum go mean ?

JASPER. It 's all right, Ben. Go away.

BEN. 'Tain't all right, ain't I lied till my throat 's dry ?

JASPER. I paid you.

BEN. What for did you want to pretend as you saved the gal's life ? You knows as well as I that she fell into two feet of water, and I pulled her out with a boat hook.

JASPER. Quite right.

BEN. But she was senseless with fright, and before she come to, you made up them whoppers about saving her life, and teached me to say them ; and now I 'ave said them, what for ?

JASPER. Half a sov., Ben.

BEN. To make her think she had nearly been swept over the weir, you got me to carry her to the edge of it, what for ?

JASPER. Five bob.

BEN. And then you got me to fling some mud and water at you, so as you should look like one as had been swimming in his clothes. (*Wringing out clothes.*) Look here, Guv'nor, what for did you bring me into this ? 'Ow couldn't yer tell your own lies ?

JASPER. A gentleman doesn't brag about himself, Ben. And so I paid you to brag for me.

BEN. What are you going to do now ?

JASPER. Enjoy myself.

BEN. Blest if I believe you 're the Colonel chap you says you are.

JASPER. You can't prove I 'm not, Ben.

BEN. Are you ?

JASPER. I feel as if I was. (*Sits.*)

(*Cuckoo calls three times.*)

BEN. Do you hear that ? I tell you what, I believe you 're the cuckoo in the hen's nest and that 's your mate a-calling to you.

(*Cuckoo once.*)

There, it 's indignant it is. You see if it don't come aboard and claim you yet !

NANNY (*looking down*). You are not going away, Ben. I want you to tell us of Colonel Neil's bravery again and again.

JASPER. It was nothing. (*To* BEN) Crack me up !

BEN. Well, you see, Miss, she was drifting to the weir———

JASPER.   Desist, Ben.   (*To* BEN) Keep it up !
(MRS. GOLIGHTLY *enters on deck.*)

BEN.   When sudden like this brave gentleman——

PENNY (*entering*).   Tea or coffee, sir ?

JASPER.   Both !   (*To* BEN) Cut !

BEN.   I 'll be saying ' morning,' ma'am, if you can lend me
the punt.   Curious, ma'am, as some should be so wet when
others is so dry !

MRS. GOLIGHTLY (*on deck*).   Ah !   (*Gives him money.*) You
can drink the Colonel's health with that.

BEN.   And the young lady's.   The young lady's health,
ma'am, coupled with the name of her preserver——her *preserver* !
(*Exit* BEN *in punt.*)

JASPER (*aside*).   An impudent fellow !
(PENNY *enters on deck with dishes.* W. G. *follows with
tea and coffee. They place them on table.* PENNY *rings bell
and exits.*)

W. G.   Breakfast !   Come on, everybody !   (*Takes seat at
table.*)

MRS. GOLIGHTLY.   Come, Colonel !   (*Takes head of table.*)
(*Cuckoo once.*)

JASPER (*stumbles at stern*).   Confound the cuckoo !

MRS. GOLIGHTLY.   You are more exhausted than you said !
(*Enter* BELL *with* ANDREW.)

JASPER.   It is only a dizziness I am subject to.

BELL.   Lean on me——do.   (*Takes his arm. To* ANDREW,
who enters saloon) How forgetful of us.   You are wet !

JASPER.   It is nothing.

ANDREW.   Come to my bunk, and I 'll give you some dry
things, Colonel.   (*Exit.*)
(BELL *goes up ladder to deck.* JASPER *stands at window
with a grin.*)

NANNY.   He is middle-aged, but delightful !

BELL.   Not handsome exactly, but how modest !

MRS. GOLIGHTLY.   Perhaps a little wanting in polish——

NANNY.   Because he is no mere Piccadilly lounger.

W. G.   I bet he has shot lions !

BELL.   He is a hero !

ALL.   Yes, yes.

JASPER.   Oh, this is better than the shop !   If I don't spend

all my honeymoon in this house-boat, my name isn't Jasper
Phipps—I mean, Colonel Neil——

> (SARAH *comes along bank walking slowly, and in passing
> looks in at saloon window but none of them see her.* JASPER
> *sees her, gasps, and ducks head. She goes off. He looks
> after her in horror.*)

JASPER. Sarah ! (*With trembling hand he pulls down blind.*)
Oh, Jerusalem !

ACT II

THE house-boat at midday. There is a broiling sun. Jasper is lying in the hammock telling African stories. Bell is holding up sunshade to protect him. Nanny is fanning him. Mrs. Golightly sits at window knitting. Penny is listening at door. On deck Andrew is gazing at towpath through a telescope and W. G. is practising cricket, the ball being suspended on a rope, hanging from a sort of crane. The punt is on.

NANNY (*breathlessly*). And you killed him ?

JASPER. Yes, it was my life or theirs. They leapt upon me, brandishing their spears, but I lifted the chief in my arms and flung him with such force against his two warriors that all three were hurled over the precipice.

PENNY. Oh my !

BELL. And then you ran away ?

JASPER (*calmly*). Ran ! No ! I walked away, turning round every now and again to shoot another through the heart.

MRS. GOLIGHTLY. How brave !

JASPER. It was nothing.

PENNY (*aside*). He is a Nero. Haitch He Har Ho Nero. (*Exits.*)

ANDREW (*looking over*). Miss O'Brien, the telegram with the result of my exams. may come at any moment now. Do you think I have passed ?

NANNY. Bother ! Don't you see I am fanning the dear Colonel ?

ANDREW. What do you think, Miss Golightly ?

BELL. I am busy, Mr. McPhail.

ANDREW. What do you think, Mrs. Golightly ?

MRS. GOLIGHTLY. 31, 32, 33, 34, 35. Tell us about Lake Nyanza, Colonel.

ANDREW (*to* W. G.). W. G., the women can do nothing but gape over Neil's adventures. He has been here nearly a week

20

now, and what good has he done me, except that I have to sleep on a shakedown in the saloon, while he gets the best bedroom ?

W. G.   Isn't this a tip-top idea for practising batting ? (*Hits.*)   I say, I saw the Colonel spooning Nanny last night !

ANDREW.   No, no—it was your sister—I saw him too.

W. G.   About eight o'clock ?

ANDREW.   It was nearer nine.

W. G.   Eight.

ANDREW.   Nine.   I thought he had his arm round her.

W. G.   He has to do that, he says, when one of his dizzy fits comes on.

ANDREW.   Hum ! (*Continues to look through glass, and* W. G. *bats.*)

NANNY.   Of course you travelled with a caravan ?

JASPER.   A caravan ?   Not in *Africa* !

(PENNY *listens again.*)

BELL.   But I thought all explorers did ?

JASPER.   They do—yes, in a sense.

MRS. GOLIGHTLY.   What is a caravan like, exactly ?

JASPER.   Hum—ah—well, a covered-in van, you know, with brooms and baskets all over it and with two horses.

BELL.   I thought it meant the porters.

JASPER.   Yes, they march behind, except when they are in front, then of course they are not behind.

(W. G. *listens on deck.*)

NANNY.   And is it true that the ladies dress—ah—lightly ?

JASPER.   Mostly in telegraph wires——

NANNY.   What is the costume ?

JASPER.   Oh, it 's nothing.

W. G.   Fancy ?

MRS. GOLIGHTLY.   No, you mustn't.

(W. G. *goes back and sits.*)

BELL.   After all, these people are human beings—very like ourselves.

NANNY.   But, Bell, the women are sold to their husbands.

BELL.   So are most of our women, and they make willing slaves.

MRS. GOLIGHTLY.   But the native husbands are such bullies.

BELL.   So are all men naturally.

NANNY.   Yes, what a pity that all nice men are so nasty.

BELL. Show me a man, be he African or English, and I will show you a born bully.

PENNY (*aside*). She is a-hitting at Mr. Upjohn.

JASPER. It 's just the same, all the world over, the men run after the women—and the women run after the men. Oh, yes they do, I 've done it myself.

(*Exit* PENNY.)

W. G. I say, McPhail, wasn't it clever of me to rig this up myself ? I can do a lot of things on it. It is a way of getting into the punt, too. Look here, you hold this end, and I 'll show how it 's done.

(ANDREW *rises, holds end and* W. G. *clings to ball.*)
Mater, hi—all of you look !

(*They turn round, look up.* W. G. *is lowered to punt.* MRS. GOLIGHTLY *utters cries of fear, and coming out on plank.*)

That 's a handy way of getting into the punt, isn't it ? (*Boards and returns to deck.*)

MRS. GOLIGHTLY. I forbid you to do that again, you rash boy. You might have fallen into the river. (*Goes back.*)

JASPER. It is nothing.

W. G. Come up and let them see you do it, Colonel.

JASPER. Not just now, W. G., too comfortable where I am.

W. G. Well, don't forget any of you that we start for the cricket match, men *versus* girls, in half an hour.

ANDREW. I won't leave the house-boat till my telegram arrives.

W. G. You must play.

ANDREW. Do you think I have passed, W. G. ?

W. G. No. (ANDREW *looks through glass.* W. G. *tries to balance bat on his nose.*)

MRS. GOLIGHTLY. Who was the soldier that said the most dangerous thing he ever did was to cross Piccadilly Circus ?

BELL. That was nothing to Colonel Neil swimming the Congo with his hands tied.

JASPER. Yes, I did swim the Congo with my hands tied. A trifle !

BELL. Nor to his shooting the gorilla.

JASPER. Pooh ! When you meet a gorilla, what can you

do ? There 's the gorilla, and there you are—and—and—and there it is.

NANNY. Nor to his march through the forest of the dwarfs.

JASPER. My duty. Oh, I shot an elephant once ! Oh yes, I did ! I met the elephant in a forest, and I had an air gun with me, and I shot it. You can't shoot without a gun in Africa. You would have been surprised if you had seen the birds, the way they came down and pecked it. Hundreds of them !

BELL. What kind of birds ?

JASPER. Oh, there were eagles and snipe—vultures, sparrows, canaries, turkeys and bull-rushes, the oof bird—they ate that elephant up and left nothing but the trunk.

NANNY. And what did you do with the trunk ?

JASPER. Oh, I had it packed up. No, no, I had the trunk made into a portmanteau.

NANNY. Did you meet any lions ?

JASPER. I wrestled with a lion and sent a graphic account to the papers.

BELL. And then you saved me !

JASPER. *That* was nothing.

MRS. GOLIGHTLY. Strange that your experiences of the dwarfs should be so like Mr. Stanley's.

BELL. And that you shot the gorilla just as De Rougemont did.

JASPER. Yes, you see—there is only one way of doing these things. But, Mrs. Golightly, it sounds like boasting to be always talking of myself. Where have you been ?

MRS. GOLIGHTLY (*at window*). Never further than the Continent. I knitted half a muffler going up the Rigi—or was it in Notre-Dame ? Then I began a worsted waistcoat for W. G. in the Kremlin, added to it in Cologne Cathedral, the Colosseum, the Acropolis, and elsewhere, and finished it, I remember, in the Alhambra.

JASPER. The Alhambra ?

BELL. Yes, I was with mother.

JASPER. You ?

BELL. And I should like to live near it, so that I could go daily.

JASPER. What ?

MRS. GOLIGHTLY.   The Alhambra is in Spain, you know.

JASPER.   Oh, I thought you meant—oh !

(ANDREW *comes down ladder into saloon.*)

NANNY.   No sign of Ben with the telegram, Mr. McPhail ?

ANDREW.   None.

(MCPHAIL *goes into saloon and reads book.* **The cuckoo** *is heard once.*   JASPER *goes on bank.*)

BELL (*following*).   You are feeling dizzy **again,** Colonel ?

JASPER.   Just a little.

W. G.   Come up, Bell, and see me swiping.

(*Cuckoo is heard three times.*   JASPER *goes on plank and then into saloon.*)

NANNY.   Listen to that cuckoo.

MRS. GOLIGHTLY.   Yes, we never heard it till you came to us, Colonel, and now we hear it a dozen times a day.

(*Exit* JASPER, *retires to bedroom.*   BELL *goes on deck.* ANDREW *is watching bank in punt.*   W. G. *is on deck,* MRS. GOLIGHTLY *and* NANNY *at stern.*)

MRS. GOLIGHTLY.   23, 24, 25, 26, 27.   (*Looks after* JASPER.) How interesting a clever man is.

NANNY.   Yes, and even if he isn't clever.

(MRS. GOLIGHTLY *knits.   Cuckoo is heard again.*)

JASPER (*pulling up bedroom blind*).   Damn that cuckoo—it makes me nervous, I 'll get up early to-morrow and shoot it. (*He suspends little mirror at window and proceeds to brush his hair.*)

W. G.   Bell, I would rather take three wickets in an over than be Shakespeare and Homer and all these swells put together.   I say, what 's the matter with you ?   You haven't sneered at me for nearly a week—not since Upjohn went away.

BELL.   Mr. Upjohn !   I told you, W. G., that I dislike the very mention of his name—he has not even written !   I dare say he has forgotten me already.

W. G.   I dare say !

BELL.   W. G.

JASPER (*leaning out*).   If I 'm not Colonel Neil, I 'm the next thing to it, for I 've shampooed him, and I 'm very like him, and that was what made me think of being him.   It 's only for a week and I 'm doing no harm, and I *am* enjoying myself.

W. G.   You must have riled him by saying women are the equals of men, and all that rot !

BELL.   It isn't rot !

W. G.   It is tommy-rot !

JASPER.   I wish they wouldn't ask so many questions about Africa, though.   Good thing I read up the African books before I started on my honeymoon.

W. G.   Don't women's brains weigh less than men's ?

BELL.   Don't sixpences weigh less than pennies ?

JASPER.   What I miss here is the hair oil.

W. G.   How can you be a man's equal when you can't even find the pocket of your dress ?

BELL.   I can—usually.

JASPER.   It's a funny thing, but I 'm beginning to feel as if I had saved her life.   I like that girl.   Fancy her being at the Alhambra, though—even though it was a Spanish one.

W. G.   Look here, are you in thingummy with Upjohn ?

BELL.   Hush, dear.

W. G.   Dear !   You wouldn't call me that unless you were in what 's its name.

JASPER.   I like the other one too.

MRS. GOLIGHTLY (*in low voice and looking at* NANNY).   Nanny, (*Signs*) has Mr. McPhail *spoken* to you yet ?   You know what I mean.

NANNY.   I wouldn't let him, but some other body very nearly has.   (*Whispers.*)

W. G.   If it isn't Upjohn, it 's Neil.

MRS. GOLIGHTLY.   The Colonel.   (*She nods.*)   Well !   (*They whisper.*)

BELL.   I am not in love with Colonel Neil.

W. G.   Is he with you ?

BELL.   Yes.

W. G.   Balbus !

NANNY.   Yes, Auntie, the Colonel blew a ring of cigar smoke on to my engagement finger last night.

JASPER.   That dizziness has let me in for a lot of good things. I like being dizzy.   It is a good, good wheeze being dizzy.   I shall keep on being dizzy.

MRS. GOLIGHTLY.   I am afraid that wouldn't count in law. Besides, I thought he and Bell——

NANNY.   Whatever made you think that ?
> (ANDREW *is looking out of back window.* NANNY *goes to him. They go right off.*)

W. G.   Then it isn't Nanny the Colonel is fond of ?

BELL.   Oh dear no !

JASPER.   She 's a nice little girl that Penny.   I must keep my eye on her.
> (*Exit.*)

W. G.   I say, I 'll go out in the punt and see if I can spot Ben with the telegram.

MRS. GOLIGHTLY.   Ah, good boy. (*Goes into saloon.*)
> (W. G. *exits in punt.*)

BELL (*to herself*).   Yes, the Colonel does love me.   Conventionality says that a woman should never know whether a man cares for her until he tells her.   Well, perhaps she does not know even then, for Mr. Upjohn said he cared for me, and how much *he* cared he has shown since then.   Not a word from him !   But Colonel Neil's love for me is real, I know it.   He saved my life, he agrees with me in all my views as completely as Mr. Upjohn differed from me.   I respect the one highly, while I detest the other.   Then how is it that every time I try to think lovingly of Colonel Neil, my mind wanders to Mr. Upjohn ?   Bell Golightly, you might be some silly ninny in a London ballroom instead of a B.A.

ANDREW (*runs through saloon to deck*).   I see him !   I see him ! (*Runs up ladder to deck.*)   I see Ben coming with the telegram.   .
> (MRS. GOLIGHTLY *and* NANNY *hurry on deck.*)
Do you think I 've passed ?   Do you ?   Do you ? (*Draws diagrams.*)

NANNY.   Oh, I hope so ! (*Calling*) Quick, you two.

BEN (*not yet in sight*).   Coming.
> (W. G. *and* BEN *arrive in punt,* ANDREW *snatches telegram from* W. G. *and hurries on deck again.* BELL, NANNY *and* W. G. *gather round him.* BEN *remains in punt.*)

NANNY.   Open it !   Here is a hairpin ! (*Gives him hairpin from her hair ; he is nervous and lets it fall.*)

ANDREW.   I—I—ah—do you think I 've passed ?

W. G. (*on ladder*).   Look and see.

ANDREW.   I—ah—the examiners had a spite at me.

BELL. Mr. McPhail, I was perfectly calm when I took the fourth wranglership.

ANDREW. You see, to pass means giving up all one's old student life. What a loss that would be ! It would mean taking a practice and attending infectious cases, and very likely dying of small-pox.

W. G. Open it, you ass !

ANDREW. So I didn't want to pass. I purposely left several questions unanswered, because I didn't want to pass.

(NANNY *snatches telegram from him, rips it open with another hairpin and reads to herself.*)

ALL. Well ?

(*Enter* JASPER.)

ANDREW (*gazing at* NANNY). I did—didn't want to pass. (*She triumphantly hands him telegram. He looks at it, and slowly his face changes from fear to a transport of delight.*) I 've passed ! I 've passed ! Great Scott ! I 've passed ! (*Falls hysterically into chair and telegram drops on deck. They shake his hand, he jumps up.*) I 've passed ! (*Runs to top of ladder.*) Colonel Neil, I 've passed. (*Runs down ladder.*) Ben, I 've passed ! (*Rushes through saloon.*) Penny, I 've passed ! (*Goes into bedroom, dances wildly Highland fling for a moment, and into cabin, and then pulls down blind.*)

MRS. GOLIGHTLY. He is off his head. (*Sits down and knits.*)

BELL. About a common little medical degree. (*Sits and reads.*)

W. G. I hope this won't spoil his form for the cricket match.

(*Exit.*)

NANNY (*lifting telegram*). Dear, sweet telegram ! (*Kisses it, and puts it in her bosom.*)

(BEN *and* JASPER *have been looking quizzically at each other.*)

BEN. You—a colonel ?

JASPER. Go away, Ben.

BEN. You, Colonel Neil ! Read that ! (*Hands* JASPER *paper.*)

JASPER. What ?

BEN. Where my thumb is.

JASPER. Then take your thumb away. (*Reading*) ' I am

able to announce on the best of authority that Colonel Neil, the African Explorer, has decided to return to Africa immediately. He starts for Zanzibar next week. The gallant Colonel is at present residing with his relatives in Derbyshire.' (*Puts paper in his pocket, with an alarmed look round.*) Well?

BEN. Well?

JASPER. Well?

BEN. Well?

JASPER. It's a mistake, that's all.

BEN. What's a mistake?

JASPER. Saying I am in Derbyshire.

BEN. It don't say that. It says Colonel Neil is in Derbyshire.

JASPER (*weakly*). How much, Ben?

BEN. Ten bob.

> (JASPER *rises, sighs, and hands him the money, and exits on to bank.* BEN *is going off when* MRS. GOLIGHTLY *comes along deck knitting and speaks to him from top of ladder.*)

MRS. GOLIGHTLY. How cool you look, Ben, in this broiling heat.

BEN. Yes, ma'am, the midges don't bother me.

MRS. GOLIGHTLY. And I am a martyr to them. I wonder why that is.

BEN. P'raps you wash your face, ma'am. I don't. Afternoon, ma'am.

MRS. GOLIGHTLY. Take Penny across with you, Ben, as she has to go to the village. (*Down ladder into saloon.*)

BEN. Right, ma'am.

MRS. GOLIGHTLY. Are you ready, Penny? (*Exit.*)
　　(*Enter* W. G. *through saloon.*)

PENNY. Yes, ma'am.
　　(*Enters saloon and speaks to* JASPER *through window.*)
I am going shopping, sir, is there anything I can get for you?

JASPER. Ah! (*Whispers and hands coins to* PENNY.)

PENNY. Oh! Scotch or Irish, sir?

JASPER. Scotch.
　　(*Exit* PENNY *in punt.*)

W. G. (*on deck*). You girls, isn't it time you were dressing for the cricket match?

BELL. I am dressed, *simplex munditiis*. (*Exit.*)

W. G. Don't I know girls always have to change their dress before they can do anything ?

NANNY. Well, what shall I wear ? I have nothing fit to be seen in. The blue ? the pink ? the lace ? the check ?

W. G. What a lot you have !

NANNY. I haven't. All last year's things—nearly. No, I won't change my dress, but I must do something to celebrate Mr. McPhail's success, and I need your help, W. G.

W. G. Something to do with clothes ? (NANNY *nods yes.*) Look here, if you think I am to let you try your hats on me again, I *won't* !

NANNY. It isn't that, but in honour of Mr. McPhail's success I have decided to make my waist smaller.

W. G. Why, it 's too tight already.

NANNY. Nonsense—see there—W. G., there 's a darling, pull the belt tighter, won't you ?

W. G. Balbus ! here 's a pin. (*Pulls.*) How 's that ?

NANNY. Tighter !

W. G. (*putting his knee to her*). Iz ! iz ! iz !

NANNY. Tighter ! (*With difficulty*) I 'm sure I can stand another two inches.

W. G. Iz ! iz ! iz ! iz ! (*Lets go.*) Now see if you can breathe !

NANNY (*gasping*). Qu—quite—quite easily.

(W. G. *exits.*)

JASPER (*enters smoking pipe. Gloomily*). I 'm doing no harm—and yet if they saw that paragraph they would call me an impostor—just because I 'm a poor man. I wonder if Sarah went back to London when she couldn't find me here ? Sarah ! I am in a mess ! When I am in a mess my thoughts turn to Sarah. Sarah is the girl for me, and I 'll have no more dizziness on board this house-boat. (*Pulls himself together.*) I won't. (*Sits.*)

NANNY (*comes down ladder*). I feel like a stuffed doll. Papa —mamma—papa—ma—ma—— (*Sees* JASPER *and goes out to him on bank.*) Smoking again, Colonel ?

(JASPER *is about to pocket pipe.*)

Don't ! I like it !

JASPER. You do ? Then perhaps—— (*Holds out cigarette

case to her.   She signs caution, goes on tiptoe to saloon door, looks at MRS. GOLIGHTLY, *shuts door, comes back and takes cigarette which he lights for her, sitting on bank.*)

NANNY.   I am sure I look horrid !

JASPER.   Beautiful !

NANNY.   Is this the right way ?

JASPER.   So exactly right that if I did not know better, I should think you had tried it before.

NANNY.   Never !   (*Looks suspiciously at him.*)

JASPER (*looking sentimentally at* NANNY).   Miss O'Brien—ah—what a pretty name yours is !

NANNY.   Yes ?   But I 'm getting tired of it.

JASPER (*impulsively*).   Nanny !

NANNY (*calmly*).   Yes ?

JASPER.   Nanny, I—I—like you.

NANNY.   I am so glad.   Isn't this a lovely rose ?

JASPER.   Ah, there are two of you.

NANNY.   Two what ?

JASPER.   Two lovely roses.   I should like one of them.

NANNY.   Which one ?

JASPER.   Ah—ah—this one.   (*Pointing to rose.*)

NANNY.   You can have it.   (*Gives it to him, putting it in his buttonhole.*)   How long will you keep it ?

JASPER.   Till I die !   (*Aside*) Oh, Sarah, look after me, I 'm slipping.   (*Taking* NANNY'S *hands.*)   Nanny, what little hands you 've got.

NANNY.   Six and a quarter.   (*He drops hands.*)

JASPER.   You have little feet too.   (*She pulls them beneath dress.*)   Don't you ever have to light a candle to look for them ?   (*Sighs.*)

NANNY.   I believe you feel that dizziness again, Colonel. Lean on me.

JASPER.   I feel it coming on again now.

(JASPER *leans on* NANNY'S *shoulder.*)

I like being dizzy.

NANNY.   Is that better ?

JASPER.   Much.   I could do with a lot of this !   (*Putting fingers through* NANNY'S *hair.*)   Lovely hair you have.

NANNY.   Do you think so ?

JASPER (*dreamily*).   What do you use ?   (*Confused*) I mean—

I was thinking of the way they oil their hair in Africa. Same way as they do the caravan wheels.

NANNY. Oh, Africa? You must often have felt lonely there.

JASPER. Very lonely. No ladies' society.

NANNY. Dreadful! And a man needs it, doesn't he?

JASPER. He do——he does. I missed it so much that when I see a pretty girl now my first impulse is to put my arm round her.

NANNY. How strange!

JASPER. All the result of my solitude in Africa. (*Puts arm round her.*) Nanny, dear Nanny—I can't help it——I am turned on!—dearest Nanny, will you be my—— (*Comes to his senses.*) Sarah, I'm slipping.

NANNY. Your——

JASPER. You little beauty! My wife? (*Aside*) Sarah, I have slipped.

NANNY (*who has retreated from him—aside*). He has said it! I am so glad, for it *is* nice to be asked. (*Loud*) Oh, Colonel Neil, I am so sorry. You cannot say that I gave you any encouragement?

JASPER. No, I'll take my oath you didn't.

NANNY. I never dreamt of this. But you know, I can't. Mr. McPhail would be so hurt—not that he has asked me, yet I must say no.

JASPER (*aside*). Hurray! Jolly glad of it, got me out of a mess——

NANNY. Let me be a sister to you.

JASPER (*aside*). Capital! She'd make a scrumptious little sister!

NANNY. I feel so honoured, and of course I won't tell a soul, so you needn't go away.

JASPER (*aside*). Go away! Why should I go away?

NANNY. Dear Colonel Neil, I am so sorry to pain you. Do tell your sister that you know she is so sorry.

JASPER (*turning round*). My little sister! (*Is about to kiss her when she escapes from him and runs into saloon.*) I *am* going it.

NANNY (*at saloon window*). I might have let him kiss me. It would please him, and it wouldn't hurt me. (*Looks out.*) Colonel Neil, you may.

JASPER. May I ? I will—— (*They stretch their heads at window, kiss and withdraw heads.*) Oh, Sarah, I 've slipped. Oh, this is better than the shop. (*His pipe won't draw, he blows down it in vain, then puts stem of rose up to clear it, and flings rose away.*) Ah, that 's better !

(*Enter* MRS. GOLIGHTLY.)

MRS. GOLIGHTLY (*on bank*). Colonel, please tell W. G. that I want him to help me to wind this wool.

W. G. (*looking down*). Can't, Mater, it would tire me for the match. (*Sits on deck, whittling with knife.*)

JASPER. She 'd make a nice sister, too. May I ? (*Holds out arms.*)

MRS. GOLIGHTLY. Like playing at scratch cradle—isn't it. So good of you. (*Puts wool on his arms, kneeling on plank, and begins winding it into a ball.*) Just think, when I was in the village to-day buying wool I met that woman again.

JASPER. What woman ?

MRS. GOLIGHTLY. The London woman who is looking for a hairdresser. I told you about her coming here nearly a week ago.

JASPER. She hasn't gone back to London ?

MRS. GOLIGHTLY. No, she is searching for him still, and she thinks she saw him on the ferry two days ago, but she lost sight of him. (*Lets ball fall.*)

JASPER (*to himself while picking up ball*). I call this persecution, I do. (*Gives ball to* MRS. GOLIGHTLY, *who resumes winding.*) Perhaps she was mistaken ?

MRS. GOLIGHTLY. No, she recognised him from a distance by a straw hat he was wearing. It was one she had presented to him.

JASPER. Oh ! (*He is wearing a straw hat and touches it guiltily.*) Did she call him names ?

MRS. GOLIGHTLY. Yes. (JASPER *frowns.*) But she wouldn't let me say a word against him. (JASPER *smiles.*)

JASPER. You met her in a shop ?

MRS. GOLIGHTLY. Yes.

JASPER. What was she doing ?

MRS. GOLIGHTLY. Yes, and she seemed on good terms with the shopman. Thank you, Colonel. (*Wool is now wound.*)

(*Exit* MRS. GOLIGHTLY *into saloon.*)

JASPER (*aside*). Sarah carrying on ! I can't abide a woman that carries on. (*Enter boat.*) I 'll pay her out when I get her alone. And her engaged to me too.

(*Enter punt with* PENNY *alone.*)

PENNY. I didn't know you was here, sir. (*On plank.*)

JASPER (*sighing*). No ?

PENNY. You are sighing, sir ?

JASPER. Penny, do you know what it is to be deceived ?

PENNY. Oh, yes, sir.

JASPER. How did you get over it ?

PENNY. Tried another, sir.

JASPER. I like you, Penny.

PENNY. Oh, sir.

JASPER. You would make a nice little sister. Come here. (*He kisses her.*)

PENNY. Thank you, sir.

JASPER. It is nothing.

(*Exit* PENNY.)

There is something fascinating about young women, be their station high or low.

W. G. (*at top of ladder*). We start in five minutes remember, Bell.

BELL (*enters on deck ; —to herself*). I will marry the man I ought to love, Colonel Neil, and not Mr. Upjohn, whom I oughtn't to care a bit about. I will !

W. G. What did you say ? (*She does not answer and he looks at her.*)

JASPER. Sarah knew me by my straw hat ! (*Takes it off, looks guiltily around him, lays it down on plank, takes cap from his pocket and puts it on, sits on bow.*)

BELL. Ah, this is Colonel Neil. (*Looks up from book.*) *Pejus leto flagitium timet*—' A man who would rather die than act meanly '—that must be the man for me.

W. G. (*coming down ladder*). I say, Colonel, Bell is a bit queer, isn't she ?

JASPER. How ?

W. G. I suppose she is brooding about Upjohn. You know they are in a thingummy, and he wanted her to be his what-you-call-it, but they had a tiff, and he went back to London.

JASPER. She loves this Upjohn ?

B

W. G. No end.

JASPER. Are you sure?

W. G. Rather. (*Goes through saloon while* JASPER *stands reflecting.*)

JASPER. Then I'll ask her to be my sister—she's upon deck—the more the merrier.

BELL. *Justum et tenacem propositi virum*—'A loyal man and true'—Colonel Neil again. Yes, I will love him.

JASPER (*goes on deck*). Always with a book in your hand, Miss Golightly.

BELL. It is Horace.

JASPER. A cousin of a friend of mine—one of my favourites.

BELL. I like him too, but don't you think he is a little——

JASPER. Well, perhaps just a little.

BELL. This might be addressed to you. (*Reading*) *Quid terras alio calentes sole mutamus?*

JASPER (*aside*). This is very awkward. (*Aloud*) Miss Golightly—Bell—may I call you Bell?

BELL (*starting*). Do!

JASPER (*aside*). I'll bounce a bit. (*Aloud*) Bell, until I met you I never knew what a woman could be.

BELL (*aside*). How much nobler than Mr. Upjohn? (*To him*) What does one mean by an ideal woman? He means—man's helpmate; not his plaything, his equal in mind—no domestic drudge, no pretty-faced ninny, man's partner—not his mere housekeeper to be petted by him or bullied by him, a free human being to be argued with, not coerced, a sharer in the responsibilities of government, a thinker, a doer, his equal, in short.

JASPER (*breathlessly*). In short.

BELL. Colonel Neil, I agree with every word you have said.

JASPER. I haven't said many.

BELL (*aside*). Oh, I *must* love this man, I *must* despise the other.

(W. G. *comes to them.*)

W. G. Hi, everybody—time to start. (*Gets punt ready, puts cushions in punt.*)

JASPER (*looking down*). A moment, W. G. Run and play. (*Turning to* BELL) Bell, I love you.

BELL.   No, no, don't say that.

JASPER (*aside*).   It's all right, she prefers the other chap. (*Aloud*) Bell, will you marry me?

BELL (*swaying and then controlling herself*).   Colonel Neil, yes, I will. (*Rises—gives him her hands impulsively, then runs down ladder steps.*) Oh, what have I done? (*Turns back.*) Don't mention it to anyone—yet. (*Goes into saloon, where she meets* MRS. GOLIGHTLY.)

JASPER (*horrified and amazed—in chair*).   She will! Miss Golightly, come back. It is all a mistake. I was only asking you to be my sister. Whew! I must put a stop to this.

MRS. GOLIGHTLY.   Bell, Penny is anxious to see the cricket match. Do you think it safe to leave the house-boat without anyone in it?

BELL (*evidently thinking of other matters*).   Quite safe.

JASPER.   Sarah, I'll swear I never meant marriage to her.

W. G.   Come on! Colonel, slide down the rope.

JASPER.   Not if I know it—I'm not a slider.

> (MRS. GOLIGHTLY *and* PENNY *take their places in the punt.*)

BELL (*at saloon window*).   Kit, what have I done? (*Comes to stern.*) You horrid book! (*Enters punt.* NANNY *follows with banjo.*)

> (*Banjo plays,* ANDREW *pulls up blind.* JASPER *descends ladder, and* BELL *signs silence to him by putting finger on her lip. She enters punt.* NANNY *enters, presses* JASPER'S *hand significantly, and enters punt.* JASPER *enters punt, and* W. G. *is about to punt off.*)

NANNY.   Stop! Where is Mr. McPhail?

W. G.   Hi, McPhail!

> (ANDREW *enters. He is now dressed in frock-coat, silk hat, etc., with stethoscope sticking conspicuously out of his pocket. He walks with professional air.*)

Oh, Balbus! look at him!

ANDREW.   I see nothing to laugh at!

NANNY.   Nor I.

ANDREW.   But I am not coming with you. It wouldn't be professional to play cricket, and a physician must attend to medical etiquette.

NANNY.   Do come!

MRS. GOLIGHTLY. Do !

ANDREW. No.

JASPER. Come, though you don't play. There may be accidents, and a leg to set, or some stumps to draw.

ANDREW. Ha ! (*Enters punt.*)

JASPER. Stop ! (*Gets out of punt—takes hat and puts in drawer in cabin, returns to punt and exit.*)

(W. G. *punts off,* NANNY *playing banjo. Punt disappears to*)—

O'er the swiftly flowing tide,
  Gaily we row the boat along,
We wake the echoes far and wide
  With laughter and with song.
    Yeo ho, yeo ho,
    We gaily row,
Gaily we row the boat along,
  We wake the echoes far and wide
With laughter and with song.

(*After a pause enter* SARAH *along bank. She is looking about her suspiciously.*)

SARAH (*sitting on bank*). Oh, Jasper Phipps, if I could only find you, wouldn't I comb your hair for you.

(*The cuckoo is heard.*)

JASPER. Damn that cuckoo !

SARAH (*starts to her feet*). Jasper's voice—he's on board this boat. (*Has almost gone off.*) He is found ! Found, found ! (*Assumes fighting position and cries*) Jasper Phipps, hi !

(*Getting no answer, she looks about her. Then rushes into saloon, then into* JASPER'S *bedroom, where she sees his clothes, cries*)

His wedding clothes !

(*Folds them up, runs with them, reappears, runs through saloon with them, cries*)

He is gone ! (*Runs on deck, cries*) But he must come back. (*Puts clothes on lap, on deck, cries*) I'll wait !

(*Sits down on chair determinedly, with arms folded.*)

ACT III

EVENING, moonlight. The house-boat is precisely as when curtain fell on Act II, except that Sarah is now asleep in her chair on deck. From a distance is heard a piano with whistling accompaniment. Light splashes, as if of water rats, rustling in branches and ' wheep wheep ' of birds settling to sleep. Next the sound of oars and a Cockney voice, ' Look where you 're shoving your blooming canoe.' A shadowy boat with one light goes by, a bat flaps about, and disappears. A distant clock strikes nine. Next a punt passes, containing a male and female figure. Man exclaims, ' My darling, let us glide on like this for ever and ever ! ' The woman answers, ' But what would mamma say ? ' Then someone is heard singing a verse of a song in distance. The singing fades away into distance, then the sound of punting.

(KIT *and* BEN *enter on bank.*)

BEN. Here we are, Mr. Upjohn, but you see they ain't back yet ! Hi ! no, there 's not a soul aboard !

KIT (*boarding*). I 'll wait for them, Ben ! They must be back for supper presently !

BEN. I dunno, Mr. Upjohn. Penny, the servant gal, says as them are late for everything since the Colonel came. You have heard on him, sir ?

KIT. I heard of him at the Inn !

BEN. He saved the young lady's life—he did !

KIT. So I was told ! (*Sits on plank.*) But why should that make them late for everything ?

BEN. Penny says it 's because he do have such a way with him ! (*Lights lamp in bow.*)

KIT. The dickens he has !

BEN. It has even softened Penny, and I dunno as I ever knew a gal less easy to soften. You never seed him, sir ?

KIT. Never, but I know him by reputation !

37

BEN. He wouldn't let them put it in the papers about his saving the young lady's life !

KIT. Too modest, I suppose !

BEN. Modest ! Yes, he is very modest is the Colonel ! Gets quite riled, sir, when I praised him for his gallant action. (*On to plank—curiously*) Come here, sir, for another holiday ?

KIT. That depends !

BEN. Going to stay long, sir ?

KIT. You are inquisitive, Ben !

BEN. Yes, sir. Heard from any of the young ladies, sir, how they have been getting on here since you left ?

KIT (*sharply*). No !

BEN. Thought not, sir, they have been that busy with the Colonel !

KIT. Eh ?

BEN. He do have dizzy fits, sir, and needs to lean on the ladies.

KIT. He has ? Phew !

BEN. Yes, sir, that 's what I think too !

KIT. What ?

BEN. What you expressed just now in that whistle, sir.

(KIT *goes agitatedly to door of saloon and* BEN *speaks to himself.*)

He 's a deep one is that there Colonel—*Colonel !*—but I 'm not the kind to split on them as pays up. (*Aloud*) Good night, Mr. Upjohn !

(*Exits along bank.*)

KIT (*in bow*). Good night. Confound Ben ! he makes me quite uncomfortable. Though this Neil has saved her life, he can't have carried her by storm in a week—impossible ! Wonder if she told them the real reason why I went away ? I fancy not ! Hallo ! I am smoking and Bell dislikes it ! Never again ! (*Flings cigar into water and sighs.*) After all, it is an objectionable habit !

(*Produces cigar case, and flings away another cigar— sighs.*)

Making a chimney of one's nose ! (*Lights a cigar.* SARAH *wakes up, shivers, and wraps trousers round her neck and sleeps.*) It will be no deprivation to me—none at all. (*Takes cigar out of his mouth and looks at it.*) How did this come about ? (*Flings it away and sighs.*) Bell will be pleased. (*Takes another cigar from case.*) This is the last. (*Makes as if to fling it away.*) It—it seems to stick to my fingers ! (*Sound of singing in distance—rises and goes to bow.*) I hear their voices ! They are coming back ! Bell is coming ! (*Looks from cigar to place whence singing comes.*) Bell—cigar—cigar—Bell. (*Falters, then flings cigar into river, tries to catch it, misses, groans.*) It is nothing to give up smoking for the girl one loves !

    (*The singing ceases and punt draws up, all ablaze with coloured lights and the hood is on.*)

W. G. Hallo !

NANNY. You 've come back ?

BELL (*faintly*). Mr. Upjohn !

    (*Exclamations of surprise from all.*)

KIT. A surprise visit, Mrs. Golightly. I found I could take two days, and here I am !

MRS. GOLIGHTLY. So glad to see you again !

    (W. G. *gets out and goes at once to bank and begins to light up lanterns.* KIT *helps* NANNY *out, who goes into saloon.* MRS. GOLIGHTLY *remains outside.* NANNY *lights up inside.* BELL *gets out and talks to* KIT *in well. She then goes in saloon.* JASPER *and* ANDREW *still in punt tying up. Introduction of* KIT. ANDREW *goes on bank.*)

KIT (*drawing* BELL *aside*). Bell dear !

BELL. Oh, why did you come ?

KIT. Didn't you want me ?

BELL. Yes—no—why did you go away ?

KIT. You can't mean——

BELL. Not before them all ! (*Goes into saloon.*)

MRS. GOLIGHTLY (*who has been speaking to* JASPER *while* NANNY *is with* ANDREW). Mr. Upjohn, let me introduce you to Colonel Neil, who saved Bell's life ! (*Goes into saloon.*)

JASPER. It was nothing !

    (JASPER *and* KIT *shake hands.*)

KIT. It was a great deal. I seem to know your face, Colonel Neil, and yet I cannot remember——

ANDREW. Upjohn, look here !

    (KIT *goes to* ANDREW.)

JASPER. I have shaved him often !

    (*Exit to bedroom.*)

NANNY.   Auntie, I am dying to speak with you !   Did you see how white she turned ?

MRS. GOLIGHTLY.   Bell ?   I suppose she was surprised to see him !

NANNY.   Auntie, don't you understand ?   They quarrelled, and he has come back to make it up !

MRS. GOLIGHTLY.   Bell is so secretive !

NANNY.   You saw how she ran away from him ?

MRS. GOLIGHTLY.   Girls don't run from the man they love !

NANNY.   Oh, don't they ?   Sure, can't he run after them ?
          (*Exit* MRS. GOLIGHTLY *and* NANNY.)

KIT.   So that you are now a full-fledged medical man.   I congratulate you, old fellow !

ANDREW.   Oh, I was always sure I should pass, hadn't the least anxiety about it.   Have a cigar ?   (*Hands him case.*)

KIT.   Thanks.   (*He is about to take it, but draws back.*) No, I mean.   I have given up smoking.   It doesn't agree with me.

ANDREW.   Ha !   Heart ?   Liver ?   Pains here ?   (*Taps* KIT's *chest.*)   I 'll go over him to-morrow with the stethoscope. (*Exits.*)

JASPER (*with lighted candle in bedroom*).   I have not only shaved him—I have cut him !

KIT (*at bow*).   What can she mean ?   It cannot be that I am too late !

BELL (*at saloon*).   Oh, how is it that love and respect seem to be such different things !

JASPER.   This house-boat is getting too hot for me.   I 'll pack and be ready to bolt.   I would have bolted this afternoon but those two girls never took their eyes off me !

BELL.   Oh, that the Colonel had been content with sisterly regard !

JASPER.   She took me up wrong !   I only proposed to be her brother !   (*Proceeds to pack.*)

BELL.   But he loves me so !

JASPER.   But she was that keen about it !

BELL.   Kit—Kit !

JASPER.   I wish I was back with Sarah !   I wonder where Sarah is now !

          (SARAH *moves.*)

W. G. I say, Upjohn, what a pity you didn't come back in time for the match ! The men played with broomsticks, you know, but I was in tremendous form. I lifted Nanny twice clear over the pavilion !

KIT. Did you ? W. G., tell your sister quietly that I want to speak with her—quietly, remember !

W. G. All right—*Bell ! Bell !* Upjohn wants you !

BELL. Oh, what can I say to him ?

JASPER (*who has been packing*). Funny thing I can't see my best clothes anywhere ! (*Looks for them.*)

(*Exit.* BELL *leaves saloon and goes to bow,* W. G., *lying on plank, sits down and whistles.* BELL *and* KIT *look at him.*)

BELL. W. G. dear, go up and light the deck lanterns.

W. G. There 's no hurry !

KIT (*pause*). I have something to say to your sister, W. G.

W. G. All right—fire away !

(NANNY *enters saloon.*)

BELL. But alone, W. G.

W. G. Don't mind me !

(*They look at him helplessly.*)

ANDREW (*entering saloon*). Miss O'Brien, do you know what I have been thinking ? I have been thinking that I should like to have you for my first patient.

NANNY. But I am quite well !

ANDREW. Hum ! I am not so sure of that ! Have we had any headaches lately ? (*She nods.*) Ha ! has our appetite been—— (*She shakes head.*) Quite so. Let me see your tongue. (*She sits down and he feels her pulse, gets paper and writes a prescription, all in quiet by-play.*)

KIT. W. G., just before you came back, I saw a big fish jump over there—beneath the willow !

W. G. Balbus !

(*Seizes fishing-rod and exits along bank.*)

KIT. Bell—— (*She points to saloon.*)

ANDREW (*handing prescription*). Three times a day, Miss O'Brien, on a piece of sugar and we shall soon be all right !

NANNY (*curtseys*). Thank you, doctor !

(KIT *signs to* NANNY. *She goes to him, he whispers to her, she takes* ANDREW *by the coat and exits.*)

BELL. Oh, Mr. Upjohn, why have you come back ? (*On bow.*)

KIT. Are you not pleased to see me, Bell ? (*Sits on ladder.*)

BELL. Why did you not come sooner ?

KIT. I seem to have come too soon !

BELL. Why did you ever go away ?

KIT. You bade me.

BELL. No—no !

KIT. But, Bell, here I am at any rate, come back and humbled, dear, to ask you to be my wife !

BELL. Kit—you are too late !

KIT. What—Neil has—— ?

BELL. Yes, and I accepted him !

KIT. Bell !

BELL. Pity me, Kit !

KIT. Why should I pity you ?

BELL. Oh, Kit, he saved my life ! and he—he has precisely my views on every question of the day. I felt that he and I must have been made for each other. I felt that love, if it is a worthy thing, must be a matter not of mere sensation, but of judgment, and I drew up a paper to see, by the light of reason, whether I loved him or you. He got 90 per cent. for politeness, and you only got 50. For sweetness of disposition he had 80 to your 40. He got 85 for hard work, and you 30, and for largeness of view on the question of the sexes he had 100 to your 10. His total was 335 and yours 130. So I felt that I must prefer him, and oh ! I wish that I had never learned logic ! (*She cowers, sits, and he looks reproachfully at her.*)

JASPER (*looks out window*). I 'm wasting time looking for those clothes, and, after all, why should I cut the honeymoon short ? I suppose now that Upjohn is her brother. I wonder if he would change places with me ? But no—she wouldn't let him !

KIT. Damn logic !

BELL. Yes, yes !

KIT. Then you do love me, Bell ?

BELL. Yes, but——

KIT. It is not too late.

BELL. Is it not, Kit ? None of the others know.

KIT. I will appeal to him to set you free !

JASPER.   I 'll go to her and tell her flat that she took me up wrong !

KIT.   He is too much a man to insist on keeping you to your promise !

BELL.   He is noble ! But it will crush him, Kit !

JASPER.   I could break it to her gently, and I will, too !

KIT.   Go on deck, dear, until I have spoken to him. None of the others are there, are they ?

BELL.   No, there is no one on deck.

KIT.   Then wait for me there. (*She is about to do so*) Or get into the punt and push off a little !

BELL.   Yes. (*Gets into punt.*)

KIT.   And Bell, prove that your mind is made up at last by repeating the words I used.

BELL.   What words ?

KIT.   Damn logic !

BELL.   Oh !

KIT.   Logic has been the curse of our love. Bell, say it and be free !

BELL.   I can't *say* it !

KIT.   Yes, say it !

    (*She hesitates, then whispers in his ear.*)

Good !

    (*She pushes off in punt and he watches her.*)

And now for the poor Colonel !

JASPER.   I 'll tell her I was dizzy at the time !

    (*Leaves bedroom and comes to bow. KIT leaves bow to
    come to JASPER. They meet in saloon.*)

I want to speak with Miss Golightly.

KIT.   With me first, Colonel Neil, please.

JASPER.   I wanted Miss Golightly ! (*Sits.*)

KIT.   And I want her also !

JASPER (*turning back*).   Eh ?

KIT.   Colonel Neil, I have something to say that will give you great pain.

JASPER (*aside*).   Has he remembered where he saw me before ?

KIT.   You are a brave man !

JASPER.   No, he hasn't !

KIT.   And you saved Miss Golightly's life !

JASPER. It was nothing.

KIT. Nothing, I believe, to what I have now to ask of you. Miss Golightly has told me of your engagement to her.

JASPER. Mr. Upjohn, I never thought she would accept me—if——

KIT. You are too modest. But you know, sir, young girls often mistake their feelings, especially when they have cause for gratitude and—(*Turning into bow*)—and, in short, Miss Golightly has made such a mistake !

JASPER. What ? (*Rises, and follows into bow.*)

KIT. She has commissioned me to ask you to surrender your claims to her hand. (*Sits on bow.*)

JASPER. She wants to give me up ?

KIT. Yes.

JASPER. Say it again.

KIT. She does not love you.

JASPER. She told you to say this ?

KIT. Yes.

JASPER. She loves you.

KIT. She does. Do you liberate her ?

JASPER. Certainly !

KIT (*grasping his hand, rises*). You are a noble fellow.

JASPER. It is nothing.

KIT. A hero !

JASPER. Her happiness is all I think of.

KIT. No other person in the boat, I understand, knows of your engagement to her, and you may be sure no one will ever hear of it from me.

JASPER. Be good to her, Upjohn.
    (*Enter saloon.*)

KIT (*aside*). Poor fellow ! (*Signs to* BELL *to come back.*)

JASPER (*re-entering saloon*). Hurray ! That 's all right !
    (*Exit.*)

BELL (*draws up in punt and boards*). What did he say ?

KIT. Behaved magnificently. Bell, you are mine—forgive me for saying ' mine,' for it implies ownership. I have thought our quarrel over, and I see that you were right and I was wrong.

BELL. I am so glad to hear you say that—because it was I who was wrong.

KIT. My darling !—I beg your pardon !

BELL.   Why ?

KIT.   Because you don't like the word !

BELL.   I think I could get used to it !

KIT.   As for politics——

BELL.   Let us treat them as if—as if they were logic !

KIT.   And I promise never to call you pretty.

BELL.   Not before the servants.

KIT.   Nor to indulge in this sort of folly ! (*Kisses her.*)

BELL.   Except now and again.

KIT.   Our love shall be an intellectual exercise.

BELL.   Rational and adult !

KIT.   Why should men cease to be reasonable beings when they are engaged ?

BELL.   Or women behave as infants ?

KIT.   Let it be our part to prove that this is mere convention.

BELL.   As it assuredly is.

KIT (*taking her head in his hands and speaking with great solemnity*).   Does 'oo love me, 'ittle pet ?

BELL (*with great solemnity*).   'Es, me loves 'oo.   Does 'oc love me ? (*Nestles closer to him.*)

JASPER (*enters saloon*).   I feel as if I could dance.

        (KIT *on plank.*)

(*Aside*) I 'd better go on deck !

        (*They turn round.*)

BELL (*starting up*).   Colonel Neil, dear Colonel Neil, oh ! I cannot look you in the face !

JASPER.   Ah ! (*Pulling a long face.*)

BELL.   You will not leave the house-boat ?

JASPER.   Perhaps it would be better.

BELL.   Stay, dear Colonel Neil, and let me be a sister to you.

        (JASPER *sighs and ascends ladder.* BELL *and* KIT *then go on board and sit foot of ladder.*)

JASPER (*at top of ladder is swaggering along deck when he sees* SARAH. *He recoils and gasps*).   S—S—Sarah ! (*Retreats from her, then goes back on tiptoe.*)   She's asleep !   She must have come here when we were away.   Sarah, I 'll bolt !

        (*Hastens to top of ladder and comes to standstill at sight of* KIT *and* BELL.)

They would see me !   They may come on deck at any moment ! I can't get away—and I can't stay here !   I must waken her—

but I dare not ! She would tell them everything ! I must—I mustn't ! (*Goes in anguish between* SARAH *and ladder*—*groans*) Oh lor', what am I to do?

BELL. Kit, how selfish we are, not giving a thought to Colonel Neil; listen to him on deck in agony—agony I am responsible for !

KIT. Poor beggar—he is very hard hit !

BELL. Kit, the least I can do is to be nice to him. I will go up ! (*Begins to ascend ladder.*) Colonel !

JASPER. She's coming up. (*Gets to top of ladder to prevent her.*)

BELL (*stopping on ladder*). Dear Colonel Neil, it rends my heart to see you so miserable—for I know the cause !

JASPER. What—you *know* ?

BELL. I am the cause !

JASPER. Oh ! You !—yes !

BELL. Let me come up and talk to you, dear Colonel Neil.

JASPER. No—no !

BELL. You must be wretched up there, all alone !

JASPER. Alone—ah—yes !

BELL. You look so lonely !

JASPER. I 'm not so—so lonely as I look. I wish I was lonelier—I mean, I want to be left to myself. Go back, Miss Golightly, to Mr. Upjohn, don't think about me. I—mean I want to be left alone with my misery.

(*She sighs and goes back to* KIT.)

(*Looks at* SARAH.) My misery ! That 's you, Sarah ! Why, she 's got my trousers on and my coat and vest neatly folded —careful Sarah ! (*Stands looking at her.*)

(ANDREW *and* NANNY *in saloon.*)

ANDREW (*who has been feeling his pockets excitedly*). I have lost the telegram ! Left it on deck !

(*Hurries to bow, and is about to ascend ladder.*)

BELL. Don't go on deck, Mr. McPhail; Colonel Neil is there and he—he isn't well.

ANDREW. Not well? Caught a chill ? I 'll give him something for it. (*Steps on to ladder.*)

JASPER (*hearing him and running to top of ladder*). You can't come up here. (*Fiercely.*)

ANDREW.   I want my telegram !

JASPER (*fiercely*).   Go away !

BELL.   Mr. McPhail, Nanny has your telegram.   I saw her pick it up !

(NANNY *enters from saloon.*)

NANNY.   Who is that speaking of me ?

ANDREW (*re-entering saloon and shutting door*).   You have my telegram, Miss O'Brien !

NANNY.   See !

(*Produces it from her bosom.*)

ANDREW.   You kept my telegram there !   You darling ! (*Embraces her.*)

NANNY.   Are we engaged ?

ANDREW.   Great Scott !   I believe we are !   When will it be—next month ?

NANNY.   Without a trousseau !   It would be a tempting of Providence.

ANDREW.   But to have a wife would help me in my practice. Marry in an old frock, Nanny, and get the trousseau afterwards !

NANNY.   Marry in an old frock !   It wouldn't be legal.

JASPER (*groans*).   Oh lor' !

NANNY.   But what a shame of us to be so happy, when the Colonel is so wretched.   Listen to him on deck !

ANDREW.   That reminds me, Miss Golightly says he isn't well.

NANNY.   Not well.   That is all she knows, Andrew.   As you are my affianced husband I may tell you all, but you must never breathe a word of it to the others.   (*Whispers in his ear.*)

ANDREW.   No ?   (*She whispers again.*)   Poor chap ! (*Whispers*)   And you preferred me to him ?   I suppose he is groaning up there because you wouldn't have him ?

NANNY.   Yes, and I am so sorry for him !

JASPER.   Women never could resist me—never !

KIT.   I hear him muttering to himself !

BELL.   A man would not do that who was not suffering deeply.

(*Clock strikes* 10.)

JASPER.   Sleep on, Sarah, sleep on !   It is only a clock, sleep on !

NANNY.   This year, next year, now, never, etc.   Fancy !

I have been engaged for five minutes, and I haven't told Auntie yet. I must !

ANDREW.   And I 'll tell the others !

(*Exit* NANNY.)

Miss Golightly, I have something to tell you that will surprise you very much !

BELL.   Let me guess ! You and Nanny are engaged ?

JASPER (*looking down*).   A selfish lot that think of nobody but themselves !

ANDREW.   Yes, but how could you guess it ?

BELL.   I am so glad !

KIT.   And I too, old man, and just think——Bell and I——

ANDREW.   Engaged too ? I expected it !

(*Turns back into saloon and exits.*)

JASPER (*desperately*).   Miss Golightly, it is getting chilly. I think it 's going to snow——should you not go inside ?

BELL.   How thoughtful of you, dear Colonel. You will come too ?

JASPER.   Not yet.

(BELL *enters saloon, pulls down front blinds.*)

JASPER.   Mr. Upjohn, why don't you follow her ?

KIT (*reluctantly*).   I 'll come up and have a chat with you !

JASPER.   No——no ! I mean, you would prefer to be with her.

KIT.   Well, Miss O'Brien is getting up a dance, I believe I am needed. You are sure you don't mind ?

JASPER.   Not at all !

KIT.   You are a good fellow !

(*Enters saloon and pulls down blind.*)

JASPER.   At last ! (*Comes half down ladder and peers.*) Now then for Sarah ! (*Returns softly to her and wheels chair till it is beneath rope.*) The chances are she will fall into the water, but it is your own fault, Sarah, for coming here and putting me in a false position.

(*Music. Dance.* JASPER *ties rope about chair. Minuet danced in saloon by* KIT *and* BELL, ANDREW *and* NANNY, *during scene on deck. When* SARAH *is in mid air, cuckoo is heard three times. She wakens.*)

SARAH.   What is this——where am I ?

JASPER.   That damned cuckoo has awakened her !

SARAH.　You—Jasper !

JASPER.　S—Sarah !

SARAH.　Oh !

JASPER.　Don't scream, Sarah, or I'll drop you into the river !

SARAH.　You are murdering me !

JASPER.　Sarah, I saved a swell girl's life——

SARAH.　You, Jasper !

JASPER.　The way that girl and another one have run after me.　Called themselves my sisters.

SARAH.　The hussies !

JASPER.　They are, they are.　Why, one of them wanted me to marry her.

SARAH.　Jasper, you had no right to when you were engaged to me—Jasper !

JASPER.　But I refused.　And why ?　Because there's only one girl for me and her name is Sarah.

SARAH.　Oh, Jasper !

JASPER.　Yes, I trusted you, Sarah, but you don't trust me ; you followed me, and, Sarah, you have been carrying on with a shopman in the village.

SARAH.　No, I swear—nothing to speak of, Jasper.

JASPER.　You admit it !

SARAH.　Jasper, forgive me !

JASPER.　Yes, I do forgive you.　Now we'll slip away to London and get married.　We'll have a delicious honeymoon.

　　　(He lets her down and then descends ladder.)

SARAH.　You are sure you forgive me, Jasper ?

JASPER.　My own Sarah, I do !　(*Kisses her.　*W. G. *is heard shouting.*)　It is W. G.　Crawl in here, Sarah.

　　　(*She gets beneath awning.*)

I can't untie the ropes.

W. G.　Hi !　Hi !　Hi !　(*Comes along bank to* NANNY *and* KIT *at windows.*)　I had him out of the water—a three-pounder, and then the line broke.

　　　(KIT *and* BELL *come to saloon window.　*W. G. *notices*
　　　KIT'S *arm is round* BELL.)

W. G.　Balbus !　Why are you doing that, Upjohn ?

BELL.　Can't you understand, W. G. ?

KIT.　We are engaged, W. G.—congratulate me !

w. g. (*disgusted*). Engaged. Oh, hang it, you 'll be no more use for anything !

NANNY. And I am engaged to Mr. McPhail, dear, see !

w. g. You too ! What a confounded shame ! (*Flings down rod in a passion.*) Look here, all of you, I had better tell you this at once, if you should have any babies——

(*They pull down their blinds*—w. g. *is standing on bank.* JASPER *cautiously peers round corner at* w.g.)

or—or that sort of thing, you needn't expect me to hold the little beggars !

(JASPER *gets into punt, pushes chair beneath awning of it, pulls down awning so that* SARAH *is hidden from view, and is about to push off when* w. g. *crosses plank to stern.*)

w. g. Hullo, Colonel.

JASPER (*meekly*). Is that you, W. G. ?

w. g. If you are going out on the river, I 'll come with you !

JASPER. No, W. G., I—I—am going away !

w. g. Why ? Because you were bowled for a duck's egg ? Look here, I know why it is. It is because you are disgusted with those asses for going and getting engaged. Well, so am I !

JASPER. Good-bye, W. G.

w. g. I say, you are not going to leave me all alone with four engaged people !

JASPER. I must !

w. g. Do they know ?

JASPER. No.

w. g. I 'll go and tell them ! I say, the Colonel says he is going away !

ALL (*blinds up*). Going away !

JASPER. Yes, I—I—I——

MRS. GOLIGHTLY. But why, Colonel Neil ?

BELL (*going closer to him*). I understand !

JASPER. You understand—I wish I did !

NANNY (*to* ANDREW). Do you not see, he cannot remain here, when I am engaged to another !

w. g. It is because they are engaged !

BELL. Hush.

W. G.   But he told me it was !

MRS. GOLIGHTLY (*looking from one to another, and seeing that all seem to understand*).   Am I to understand, Colonel Neil, that you love——

JASPER.   Yes, that is it.   I love her and it is too painful to me to stay on in the circumstances.

(BELL *and* NANNY *are much affected.*)

MRS. GOLIGHTLY.   I see—I see !

JASPER.   I shall never forget your kindness !

MRS. GOLIGHTLY.   I am so grieved, but perhaps you act wisely in leaving us.   If it must be so, Colonel Neil, good-bye ! (*Shakes his hand.*)

JASPER (*aside*).   I 'll get off with a swagger yet !   (*With emotion*) Good-bye !

(NANNY *and* BELL *break down,* BELL *goes into saloon.*)

ANDREW (*on bow*).   Neil, (*In low voice*) Nanny has told me all.   Do you return to Africa ?

JASPER.   To-morrow, among elephants and caterpillars ! (*Shakes hands.*)

ANDREW.   I want to see you in London, what club do you belong to ?

JASPER.   I belong to the Toilet Club.

(ANDREW *goes on deck,* W. G. *follows.*)

KIT.   Colonel, Bell and I look upon you as a brother. Good-bye.

W. G.   I 'll punt you down.

JASPER.   No—no !   I mean, I had better go alone.   Ben will bring back the punt.   *Now* to escape !

NANNY (*on bank*).   Colonel !

(BELL *on bank ; they both beckon to him, he hesitates.*)

JASPER (*aside*).   Shall I go and kiss them ?   No !   Sarah 's behind !   I belong to Sarah !   (*Waves them good-bye.*)   I have enjoyed myself—and now for Sarah and the shop !

(PENNY *stands at cabin window.   He is now out of sight, distant music plays ' Home, sweet Home.'* KIT, W. G., *and* ANDREW *continue waving,* MRS. GOLIGHTLY, NANNY, *and* BELL *turn and face audience,* MRS. GOLIGHTLY *in centre.*)

W. G.   Hi !   Colonel, you 've left your hat behind !

JASPER (*off*).   Oh, it 's nothing !

MRS. GOLIGHTLY (*at window*).   And now, dears, I am dying
to know which of you it is !
  (*Both press her hands and sigh.*)
Which ?

W. G. (*on deck*).   We don't even know where to write to
him !

MRS. GOLIGHTLY.   He gave me his telegraphic address
yesterday.   Oh, I have lost it !   (*Runs to back of saloon.*)   Colonel,
what did you say is your address ?

JASPER.   What 's my what ?

MRS. GOLIGHTLY.   Your address ?

JASPER (*off*).   Walker, London.

ALL.   Walker, London.

THE PROFESSOR'S LOVE STORY

Produced at the Comedy Theatre on June 25, 1894, with the following cast :

THE PROFESSOR . . .	*E. S. Willard*
LUCY WHITE . . .	*Bessie Hatton*
DOWAGER LADY GILDING .	*Nannie Craddock*
HENDERS	*Royce Carleton*
PETE	*F. H. Tyler*
DR. COSENS . . .	*H. Cane*
SIR GEORGE GILDING . .	*Bassett Roe*
EFFIE PROCTOR . . .	*Mrs. H. Cane*
DR. YELLOWLEES . .	*Hugh Harting*
MISS AGNES GOODWILLIE .	*Mrs. G. Canninge*
LADY GILDING . . .	*Keith Wakeman*
SERVANTS	*Messrs. Moore and Maxwell*

The play was transferred to the Garrick Theatre. It ran for 144 performances. Revived at the Savoy on September 7, 1916, by H. B. Irving, it ran for 235 performances.

ACT I

SCENE : The Professor's study in London. Time : Half-past nine a.m. As the curtain rises Effie enters with the morning letters which she places on the table. There is a moment's comedy out of her reading inquisitively two post-cards. The first evidently amuses her. The second, to which she takes a magnifying glass, puzzles her. Enter Lucy White.

LUCY (*catching her at it*). Good morning, Effie.

EFFIE (*guiltily leaving letters*). Good morning, Miss White.

LUCY. Has the Professor seen his letters yet ?

EFFIE. No, he hasna come into the study yet. He 's no that length. (*Importantly*) The Doctor 's examining him again, tapping away at his chest as if it was the front door.

LUCY (*smiling*). Oh, the Doctor 's examining him again. Then I 'll run through the letters.

(LUCY *sits and opens letters.*)

EFFIE. I hope the Professor 's no very ill.

LUCY (*smiling demurely*). I hope not, Effie.

EFFIE. I dinna understand you, lassie ; I would say you was good-hearted, and yet you have just a queer smile on your face when I speak about the Professor's illness.

LUCY. I smile, Effie ? Oh no, I 'm crying gently. (*Wipes away a pretended tear with a handkerchief.*) And now that I have wiped away this insistent tear, tell me what sort of a man is this Dr. Cosens ?

EFFIE. Well, he 's no what I call good-looking.

LUCY. Poor lost soul ! Oh, I must do that again. (*Wipes away another tear.*) The Professor and he are old friends, are they not ?

EFFIE. I 've heard Miss Goodwillie say they were at the college at Edinburgh together, but they see little of one another now. You see, the Doctor married and the Professor didna.

LUCY. And after that, naturally they despised one another.

55

EFFIE. Why ?

LUCY (*laughing*). Well, of course, neither was quite certain whether the other hadn't done best. Is the Doctor Scotch ?

EFFIE. No, he's just English. But you dinna ask if the Professor's any better to-day.

LUCY (*smiling*). No, I don't.

EFFIE (*aside*). Laughing again ! (*Aloud*) Why not ?

LUCY. Because you couldn't know, Effie, unless you had been listening at the keyhole, and I am sure you would never do that. Just as I am sure you haven't read those post-cards.

COSENS (*coming half out of door*). Nothing to alarm yourself about, Professor—— I assure you I understand your case perfectly, perfectly ! (*Shuts door, sees* EFFIE *but not* LUCY.) Effie, what is the matter with the Professor ?

EFFIE. Have you no found out, Doctor ?

LUCY. Effie !

COSENS (*startled*). I didn't see you, madam. The Professor's secretary, I presume ?

LUCY. Yes, that's all. I'm Miss White.

COSENS. I hope you are very well, Miss White.

LUCY. Thank you, yes. I only wish we could say the same of the Professor.

COSENS (*professionally*). Ah !

LUCY. May I say I am so glad he is in your hands ? A sad case, Doctor. Effie, have you seen my handkerchief ? (*She dabs her eyes with it.*)

COSENS (*suspiciously*). Ho !

LUCY (*demurely*). Is the Professor's a very uncommon complaint, Dr. Cosens ?

COSENS. At first sight, Miss White, quite the reverse. He is suffering from a severe disinclination to work. One of the commonest complaints in the world.

EFFIE. But he never had it before. All his life he has been the hardest worker in London.

LUCY (*sitting down to letters*). And he has every incentive to work just now, for he is at the last chapter of his great book.

EFFIE. Ay, it must be a serious illness that keeps him frae finishing his great book.

LUCY. And so, Doctor, we are all so glad that you understand his case perfectly. I hope he said 99 nicely to-day.

COSENS (*frowning*). H'm ! Don't let me interfere with your work, Miss White.

EFFIE. What 's the name of his illness, sir ?

COSENS. The name ?

LUCY. We mustn't ask such questions, Effie. We may be sure the Doctor has an excellent reason for not telling us its name. Have you not, Doctor ?

(COSENS *winces*.)

And I think I know the reason, don't you think I do, Doctor ? Such a sad reason ! (*Gets out handkerchief*.)

COSENS (*exasperated*). Miss White—I—really—will you please to put away that handkerchief !

LUCY (*as if frightened*). Effie, have I been doing anything wrong ?

COSENS (*with a happy idea*). You talk too much, Miss White. You are not looking well. I want to know your temperature.

(*Puts thermometer into her mouth and chuckles*.)

Now, Effie, I want to ask you some questions. I suppose the Professor has been living his usual jog-trot life, eh ?

EFFIE. Oh ! Ay ! For the five years I have been with him, one year has just been like another. He has been six months here, lecturing and writing and making explosions in the laboratory. And then six months at Tullochmains in Scotland, writing and making explosions, but not lecturing.

COSENS. He still goes to Tullochmains for his vacation, I suppose ?

EFFIE. Yes, and though he 's such a great man now, he just lives on quietly in the cottage that used to be his father's. Miss Goodwillie, his sister, went there a month since to get it ready.

COSENS. Does she know of his illness ?

EFFIE. No, for if she did, she would come back to London by the first train.

COSENS. H'm ! I wonder if I should telegraph for Miss Goodwillie ?

(LUCY *taps on drinking-glass with paper-knife and makes inarticulate sounds with her mouth*.)

What is it ?

(LUCY *makes signs that she wants the thermometer removed*. COSENS *goes right to* LUCY *and takes it out*.)

COSENS.   Ha ! Normal ! Thank you, Effie.
(EFFIE *exits*.)
You want to say something, Miss White ?

LUCY.   Only this, Doctor, that if you telegraph for Miss Goodwillie to come to London, you will, of course, tell her what is the matter with the Professor, though you won't tell us.

COSENS.   H'm ! Ah—ahem ! I won't send for Miss Goodwillie, Miss White.

LUCY (*who is writing out a telegram*).   Is there any prescription to be made up ?

COSENS.   No, I——

LUCY.   I thought there was always a prescription. And as I am going to the telegraph office I could leave it at the chemist's.

COSENS.   Thank you. Just a moment till I write it out.
(*He sits, and there is a little comedy got out of his not knowing what to write. He looks at her sideways. She is very demure. He writes.*)
Please see that it is made up at once.

LUCY (*earnestly*).   Yes, indeed. I 'll run all the way !
(*She goes.*)
(COSENS *looks after her suspiciously. He rings bell. Enter* EFFIE.)

COSENS.   Effie, what was the expression on Miss White's face when you passed her in the hall just now ?

EFFIE.   She was laughing, sir.

COSENS.   H'm ! I thought so, Effie. Call her back.
(*Exit* EFFIE. COSENS *alone, pulls himself together. Enter* LUCY.)

LUCY.   You want me ?

COSENS.   Miss White, you are a clever girl, and I have been making a fool of myself. Give me back that prescription.
(*She does so ; he tears it in two and throws it into waste-paper basket.*)

LUCY.   Why do you do that ?

COSENS.   In acknowledgment of my defeat. You have guessed rightly, Miss White ; the Professor's case baffles me.

LUCY (*frankly*).   That 's honest. I like you now.

COSENS.   H'm !   I 'm not sure whether I like you.

LUCY.   Oh, dear !   (*Produces handkerchief.*)

COSENS.   None of that.

(*She puts away handkerchief.*)
You have taught me a lesson, Miss White.

LUCY.   My Aunt Emily used to say that if it were not for women, men would never learn anything.

COSENS.   H'm !   I don't know that I like your Aunt Emily either.   Well, I admit I don't know what is the matter with the Professor.   (*Suddenly seizing her wrist.*)   Do you ?

LUCY (*affecting indignation*).   How dare you insult me ! Just because I am the poor secretary !   If I had a brother—— (*She goes off in tears.*)

COSENS (*contrite, calling after her.*)   I beg your pardon, Miss White.   How could you know ?   I am a brute to make you cry.   (*Suddenly suspicious.*)   Was she crying ?

(*Enter* EFFIE *with a glass of water and a box of pills.*)

EFFIE.   Did you call, sir ?

COSENS.   Effie, did Miss White seem much affected when she went out just now ?

EFFIE.   Yes, sir, she was laughing.

COSENS.   Laughing !   Damn !   I am going after her. (*Exit.*)

EFFIE (*going to door after him and calling*).   Is the master to go on taking his pills ?   (*Reads inscription on pill-box.*)   One pill to be taken every four hours.   (*Lays them on small table. She begins to tidy up table, though evidently aware that this is forbidden.*)

(*Enter the* PROFESSOR *in long dressing-gown.   He pauses in deep thought, stands on tiptoe, sighs, sees* EFFIE.)

PROFESSOR.   Effie, what are you doing at that table ?   Go away.   Go away.   Mustn't do that—very wrong.

EFFIE.   I *will* tidy.

PROFESSOR.   You shall not tidy.

EFFIE.   If I remain on here, I tidy.

PROFESSOR.   Then you shall not remain on here.

EFFIE.   What way to talk is that ?   How could you do without me ?

PROFESSOR.   That 's true.   Don't leave me, Effie.   Effie, tidy upstairs, tidy downstairs, tidy all the drawers, tidy the kitchen range—tidy me, if you must—— (*Appealing*) But don't tidy that table !

(*She moves from table to small table and takes box of pills and tumbler, bringing them to table. The* PROFESSOR *goes to back of chair, drums on it with his fingers, stands on tiptoe, sighs, sees* EFFIE *offering him glass of water, takes it, holds it up to light, says :*)

What 's this ?

EFFIE.   The pills the Doctor prescribed.

PROFESSOR.   Oh yes, the pills. (*Stares.*) I don't believe the Doctor knows what is the matter with me. Go away, woman. I must work, work.

(*Exit* EFFIE. *The* PROFESSOR *puts down glass of water, takes a pill and sip of water, puts glass back and pill-box on table. Sits at table, takes up pen—arranges papers— lapses into thought, bites pen, cries ' Come, come '—waits for a moment. Starts and rearranges papers. Is perplexed by the idea that* EFFIE *told him to do something but cannot remember what it is. Is about to call her, remembers the pills, takes one and a sip of water. He tries to work. Absently dips pen in glass of water, finds it won't work, puts pen in mouth, reaches for large ink-bottle, puts ink in water, takes up fresh pen, dips in inkstand, writes. He is bothered by pen in mouth. Removes it, stops, pauses, struck by a thought. Puts pen behind ear, takes pill, takes up inky water, is surprised, sees another goblet, fills it with water, goes on writing without drinking. Leaves off. Rings bell. Takes up fresh pen.* EFFIE *enters.*)

PROFESSOR.   Well, well, what is it ? What *do* you want ?

EFFIE.   You rang, sir ?

PROFESSOR (*absently*). Did I ? What for ? (*Pause.*) Perhaps I rang for my boots, Effie ?

EFFIE.   You have them on.

PROFESSOR.   Have I ? (*Lifting up left foot.*) Bless me, so I have.

EFFIE.   **Was it for Miss White ?**

PROFESSOR (*always unconsciously happy at mention of her name*). Ah, that 's it. Surely she is very late this morning.

EFFIE.   She has been here, but she went to the telegraph office.

PROFESSOR (*gloomily*).   Oh !
> (*Pause.*)

EFFIE.   Is there anything else you want, sir ?

PROFESSOR.   How can I get on with my work, Effie, if you will stand there chattering all day ?   Go away—go away !

> (EFFIE *goes quickly.   The* PROFESSOR *writes.   Clock on mantelpiece begins to strike ten, and the* PROFESSOR, *writing with his right hand, waves it to be silent with his left.*)

Hush !   Silence !   Quiet there !   (*Listens to last stroke.*)   Come in, come in !   (*Calling*) Effie !

> (EFFIE *enters.*)

EFFIE.   What is it now ?

PROFESSOR.   I think I heard Miss White knocking.

EFFIE.   No, sir.   (*Seeing clock.*)   It was just your clock striking.   Miss White 's at the telegraph office.

PROFESSOR.   Still at the telegraph office.

> (EFFIE *goes.   He goes on writing.   Short knock.   He starts to his feet and shakes his fist at the clock, calling :*)

Effie !

> (EFFIE *enters.*)

Stop that clock !

EFFIE.   Eh !   It was a knock this time.

> (*Knock.*)

PROFESSOR.   Ah !   But that 's not Miss White's knock.

EFFIE (*aside*).   I canna remember your ever knowing anybody's knock before.   (*Goes to window.*)   I can just see a gentleman's back.   It looks to me like the back of one of those folks you call literary aspirants.   What come wi' an introduction and read their manuscripts to you.

PROFESSOR (*excitedly*).   Don't let him in.

> (*Knock.*)

EFFIE.   He seems determined to get in.

PROFESSOR.   Keep the door on the chain.   Say I 'm out.

EFFIE.   Tell a lie, na, I couldna.   But I 'll do that if you 'll go out at the side door and stand on the steps.

PROFESSOR.   Very well.

> (*She goes to get his hat, cane and coat and returns immediately with them.*)

PROFESSOR.   It would look rather undignified, but I know what I 'll do.   I 'll go out and do what my sister told me to do, in her last letter. (*Rises and unfastens dressing-gown.*)

EFFIE.   What was that ? (*Having put coat and stick on sofa.*)

PROFESSOR.   Well, now, what was it ? (*Taking hat which* EFFIE *is holding towards him.*)   It was either to complain about the butcher's bill or to order a new suit of clothes. (*Puts on hat and is going.*)

EFFIE (*bringing him back*).   You 've got your gown on.

PROFESSOR (*smiling*).   Oh yes, very wrong, very wrong. Take it off.

(*She puts it on sofa and is getting him into coat, etc.*) Ah, that 's better, that 's better ! (*Patting her on the shoulder.*) Good girl, good girl, how thoughtful of you.

(*Puts on coat, is going towards his armchair.   He is going to write.* EFFIE *stops him and points to his hat.*) Oh yes, of course, going out, going out.

EFFIE.   Well, what was it your sister told you to do ?

PROFESSOR.   Eh ?   Oh, where 's her letter ? (*Searches pockets, hat, etc., to find his watch in trousers' pocket.*)   So there you are !   I have been looking for you. (*Finds letter in pocket.*) Ah, here it is, now we shall see.   ' Always change your flannels on Wednesdays and Sundays.'   Yes, I 've done that.   ' Never carry cheques or bank-notes loose in your trousers' pocket.'

(*The* PROFESSOR *looks at* EFFIE, *puts his right hand into pocket, draws out bank-note, shakes his head at* EFFIE, *muttering.*) Very wrong, I mustn't do that, I mustn't do that.

(*Changes bank-note from right to left hand, goes on reading letter, absent-mindedly putting note into left trousers' pocket.   A knock is heard.*) Ah, here it is, here it is : ' Get your hair cut at once, for if it is not cut by the time I next see you, I 'll put a bowl on your head and cut it myself.'   Effie, I think I 'd better slip out by the side door and get my hair cut.

(*He leaves on tiptoe.* EFFIE *puts gown on chair.* COSENS *enters.*)

COSENS.   I thought they were never going to let me in.

EFFIE.   I didna know it was you, Doctor, and the Professor 's gone out.

COSENS.   It is Miss White I want to see. (*Gives* EFFIE *his umbrella.*)

EFFIE.   She's at the telegraph office. (*Taking umbrella to hatrack in hallway.*)

COSENS.   No, I looked in there for her. I shall wait——

EFFIE (*from hatrack in hall*).   Is it raining, sir ?

COSENS.   A little.

EFFIE.   Then the Professor will get wet. (*Goes to window.*) I see him. Of all the absent-minded men, if he isn't holding up his stick and thinking it is an umbrella ! Well, I never, he's gone past the hairdresser's. Oh !

COSENS.   What ?

EFFIE.   He's gone into the telegraph office.
     (*Light knock.*)

COSENS.   If that is Miss White, send her here.

EFFIE.   It's no Miss White, but it sounds like a lady's knock, and it's no safe to let ladies into this house. (*Going to door.*)

COSENS.   Why ?

EFFIE.   The Professor is so absent-minded.
     (EFFIE *goes.* COSENS, *left alone, puzzles, looks at waste-paper basket, etc.*)

LADY GILDING (*heard off*).   Ah ! But we must see the Doctor.
     (*Enter* LADY GILDING.)

COSENS.   Lady Gilding.

LADY GILDING.   Doctor Cosens. (*Shakes hands.*) I didn't know it was you who was attending the Professor. We only heard of his illness last night.

COSENS.   He is not precisely an invalid. He is able to be out.

LADY GILDING.   But not to work, I understand. Poor man ! (*Calling*) George !
     (*Enter* SIR GEORGE GILDING *and the* DOWAGER LADY GILDING, *who looks about twenty.*)
George, the Professor is suffering from—what did you say it was, Doctor Cosens ?

COSENS.   Heamtontitus.

DOWAGER.   Fancy !

SIR GEORGE.   Ah—ah—a troublesome thing, I believe.

LADY GILDING. You don't know my husband, Doctor Cosens? George, Dr. Cosens; Mamma, Dr. Cosens; Dr. Cosens, Mamma.

(*They bow.*)

COSENS. Mamma! Wonderful!

DOWAGER. You are surprised?

COSENS. I assure you, ladies, that nothing has surprised me so much in the whole course of my professional experience.

SIR GEORGE. It is not so surprising as it seems, Doctor—ah—Cosens—— This lady is my father's widow. He married a second time, late in life, and——

DOWAGER (*humorously*). And they call me mamma to annoy me!

(*She sits. COSENS and SIR GEORGE go up stage talking. LADY GILDING sits on the sofa by DOWAGER.*)

LADY GILDING. Mamma!

DOWAGER. Mildred, how hateful of you to call me by that hideous name.

LADY GILDING. My dear, of what should a woman be prouder than to be called by the sacred name of mother?

SIR GEORGE. Mildred, Miss Goodwillie is not in London.

DOWAGER. Miss Goodwillie away!

COSENS. Yes, she has been in Scotland for a month.

LADY GILDING. Is she at Tullochmains?

COSENS. Yes, yes. You know it?

SIR GEORGE. My dear sir, I may say Tullochmains belongs to me. I am member for it.

LADY GILDING. We are the Professor's dearest friends.

DOWAGER. We so admire him—and we flatter ourselves that he likes us a tiny bit also.

SIR GEORGE. He will be extremely vexed if he misses us.

(*The PROFESSOR is entering, when he sees them and retires hurriedly. EFFIE appears also.*)

DOWAGER. Ah, Effie, we shall remain a little on the chance of the Professor's returning soon.

(*EFFIE looks despairingly towards the PROFESSOR, who is evidently making signs to her to get rid of the visitors.*)

EFFIE. Then, my lady, will you please come to the drawing-room?

COSENS.   Is it worth while, Effie ?
(EFFIE *signs to him, pointing.*)
Yes, let us go to the drawing-room.
(DOWAGER *sitting on sofa apparently crying.*)
LADY GILDING.   We 'll follow you, George.
(*Exeunt* COSENS, SIR GEORGE, *and* EFFIE.)
Why are you looking such a picture of woe ?

DOWAGER.   Miss Goodwillie has been away a month.

LADY GILDING.   Nothing to cry about in that.

DOWAGER.   But the Professor has been alone.   To think what I might have done with that man in a month.

LADY GILDING.   Not much.

DOWAGER.   I am not sure that he is not already rather fond of me.

LADY GILDING.   He runs away from you.

DOWAGER.   Perhaps that is his shy way of showing it.

LADY GILDING.   Do you really think that the man cares twopence about you ?

DOWAGER (*who has a strong comic sense*).   Well, twopence is rather a large sum—still, don't dash my hopes, Mildred.   He has admitted to me that he feels more at ease with me than with other women.   It 's a beginning.   And my extraordinary charm ought to do the rest.

LADY GILDING.   Well, heaven knows George and I would be glad enough to see you comfortably settled again.

DOWAGER.   And well I know why.

LADY GILDING.   It 's because your frivolity is painful to us. We want you to have a sphere of usefulness.   Every woman should have a sphere.

DOWAGER.   Fiddlesticks !   It is because George's father left it in his will that if I married again, my paltry five hundred a year was to go to George.

LADY GILDING.   No, mamma, as if such a worldly thought had ever entered our heads !

DOWAGER.   Mildred, a little less of the ' mamma,' if you please.   Let us rejoin darling George.
(*Exeunt* DOWAGER *and* LADY GILDING.   *The* PROFESSOR *enters cautiously.*)

PROFESSOR.   Are they gone, Effie ?   The side door ?

EFFIE.   They did not take the hint to go, so you 'll need to speak to them in the drawing-room.

C

PROFESSOR.   I won't.

EFFIE.   You must.

PROFESSOR.   I will not.   The side door, Effie !

EFFIE (*takes off his hat*).   Oh, you promised to get your hair cut.

PROFESSOR.   So I have, Effie, so I have.   (*Feeling.*)   Bless my soul, I thought I had.   (*Removes pen from ear suddenly.*)   The man must have forgotten.   Careless, careless !

EFFIE.   Did you remember to take your pill ?

> (*Takes up pill-box—counts pills, is horrified, and exits with pill-box.   The* PROFESSOR *left alone sets to work, rises, sees dressing-gown, puts it on instead of coat, sits.* DOWAGER *peeps in.*)

DOWAGER.   Professor !

PROFESSOR (*without looking up*).   Have you got rid of them, Effie ?

DOWAGER (*giggles, retires, and returns noisily*).   Ah, Professor !

PROFESSOR.   Lady Gilding.   (*Rises and shakes hands.*)

DOWAGER.   I am so sorry to hear you are unwell, and dear Miss Goodwillie away, too.

PROFESSOR.   I don't know what is wrong with me—but I can't work.

DOWAGER.   You work too much—that must be it.   Come over here and talk to me.

PROFESSOR (*who really thinks her nice*).   You are very kind.

> (*She goes to sofa rather afraid of electric machine, sits. The* PROFESSOR *goes towards her.* DOWAGER *turns to him, motions him to be seated.   He sits, the electric machine between them.*)

DOWAGER.   If we had known your sister was away, we would have come often to see you.

PROFESSOR.   Yes, she told me not to tell you.   (*Innocently*)   I suppose she was afraid that you would find me a handful.   I 'm unfortunately very boorish.

DOWAGER.   No, indeed.

PROFESSOR (*who thinks her a dear, kindly woman*).   It 's very kind of you to say that.   I enjoyed myself very much that day you took me to the Zoo.

DOWAGER.   But, dear Professor, I waited for you and you never came.

PROFESSOR (*distressed*). Did I not ? I must have forgotten. Very wrong. Very wrong.

DOWAGER. You did enjoy yourself that night we went to the theatre, didn't you ?

PROFESSOR. That was very delightful. (*Doubtfully*) I went there, didn't I ?

DOWAGER. Yes, yes, I called for you !

PROFESSOR (*proud*). Aha, I didn't forget that ! A most amusing play. I forget what it was called, but you ought to go and see it.

DOWAGER. I will ! Professor, why shouldn't you and I be great friends ? I assure you I would esteem it an honour.

PROFESSOR. The honour would be mine. You 're so young and charming.

DOWAGER. It is dear of you to put it in that way. You must have guessed that my life is a rather lonely one. George and Mildred are the dearest creatures, of course, but not very sympathetic, and what I crave for is sympathy, not so much to get it, I think, as to give it. Don't you think *that* is the true woman's sphere ?

PROFESSOR (*whose mind has evidently been wandering*). But suppose we introduced another galvanometer ?

DOWAGER. What ?

PROFESSOR. And decrease the pressure on piston.

DOWAGER. I don't think you follow me.

PROFESSOR (*turning to her*). Oh, I—I beg your pardon. I was thinking of my last chapter. It 's very unmannerly of me, very !

DOWAGER. On the contrary, it is delightful to me to hear you discussing your work with me. I am so interested in your electrical discoveries. Now how (*Indicating machine between them*) is such a delightful little duck of a thingumbob—but don't you think it is rather in the way ?

PROFESSOR. It always stands there.

DOWAGER. Ah ! A very useful and wonderful little thing it is, I don't doubt. *I* can't be wonderful, but I do wish I could, at least, be useful.

PROFESSOR. I 'm sure you are.

DOWAGER. I don't know. A widow has so few opportunities. Some people press me to marry them. What do you think ?

PROFESSOR.   I wouldn't.

DOWAGER.   That is my inclination also.   But if ever I do marry—mind you, I don't think I ever will—but if I should, it will be someone I can look up to, not a boy, not too young a man, but one whose intellect—for I worship intellect—indeed, I—are you listening ?

PROFESSOR.   I beg your pardon, but would you mind saying that over again ?

> (*Enter* LUCY.   *She takes off her hat.*   DOWAGER *stares at her in amazement.   The* PROFESSOR *follows* DOWAGER'S *glance, sees* LUCY, *rises, shakes hands with her.   He clumsily crosses behind table to place chair for her.   He sits and beams on* LUCY, *who goes on opening letters.*)

DOWAGER.   Professor.

> (*He doesn't notice her.*)

Professor !

> (*He goes to her.*)

Who is this ?

PROFESSOR (*glowing*).   My new secretary.

DOWAGER.   Engaged since Miss Goodwillie left ?

PROFESSOR.   Yes.

DOWAGER (*to* LUCY).   But you are not a man.

LUCY.   I 'm—sorry.

DOWAGER.   Your secretaries used to be men.

PROFESSOR.   Oh, men are no use.

DOWAGER.   Does Miss Goodwillie know that your new secretary is a lady ?

PROFESSOR.   Does she ?   No, I believe I forgot to mention it.

DOWAGER.   Introduce us, Professor.

PROFESSOR.   Miss White, Lady Gilding.

DOWAGER.   How do you do, Miss White ?

LUCY.   Thank you, I am quite well.

DOWAGER.   If you have work—elsewhere—please don't let me detain you.

LUCY.   We do it here, thank you, Lady Gilding.

> (LUCY *bows to* DOWAGER *and resumes her chair, all with great civility.*)

DOWAGER.   Professor, I am dying to see your new laboratory. Will you show it to me ?

PROFESSOR.   I—are you——   Oh, certainly, Lady Gilding, I shall be delighted.   (*Is about to rise and looks woefully at* LUCY.) Miss Lucy !

LUCY.   Let me show it to you, Lady Gilding.   This way.

DOWAGER.   But——

LUCY.   No trouble at all.

> (*The* DOWAGER *with a gesture of despair goes and* LUCY *follows.   There is a pause and the* PROFESSOR *stares after them.*)

SIR GEORGE (*heard off stage*).   Monstrous !   It is monstrous ! There is no other word for it.

> (*The* PROFESSOR *rises and is stealing off but is seen by* LADY GILDING, *who enters followed by* SIR GEORGE *and* COSENS.)

LADY GILDING.   Ah, Professor.

> (*She goes to him, he turns, shakes hands.*)

You 're just in time to catch us ; we were going.

SIR GEORGE.   Sorry you are not well, though.   (*Shakes hands with* PROFESSOR.)

PROFESSOR.   I dare say it is only laziness.   Idle fellow, idle fellow !   What was it you were saying was monstrous as you came in, Sir George ?

SIR GEORGE.   Oh, I was speaking of ladies' dress.   The fact is, Professor, I had not long been married when certain absurdities in connection with ladies' dress were forcibly brought home to me.

COSENS.   And to me.

SIR GEORGE.   For instance : I ask you, Professor, as an unprejudiced outsider, how many yards of material do you think are required to make a dress for Lady Gilding ?

PROFESSOR.   Four yards.

SIR GEORGE.   Nineteen yards.

PROFESSOR.   Impossible !   Why, a large-sized dust cloth is only four yards.

SIR GEORGE.   Ah, you see my point exactly.   But I was determined to show that it could be done with four yards, and I did it.   I myself, Professor, superintended the making of a dress for Lady Gilding out of four yards, and presented it to her on her birthday.   It was a perfect fit, Mildred ?

LADY GILDING. Yes, George.

PROFESSOR. This is it? (*Pointing to dress.*)

SIR GEORGE. Oh no, she never wears it. She looks upon *my* dress as sacred, don't you, Mildred?

LADY GILDING. Yes, George.

(*She crosses to* DOWAGER, *who enters.* COSENS *joins* SIR GEORGE *and the* PROFESSOR.)

Wherever have you been?

DOWAGER. Seeing the horrid smelly laboratory with the Professor's secretary.

LADY GILDING. A red-haired man. I remember him.

DOWAGER. No, a new secretary—a woman.

LADY GILDING. What?

DOWAGER. Yes, I thought so too at first, but it is all right; she's the simplest little thing.

SIR GEORGE. I assure you, it isn't merely frocks. Take a lady's hat, for instance—say, Mildred's hat—excuse me, Mildred. (*Takes off her hat.*) Now, this is a large hat—how, I ask you, should that affect the cost?

PROFESSOR. That should make it more expensive.

SIR GEORGE. It should, but it does not. This is a comparatively cheap hat, because it is large. But—(*Takes scissors from table and cuts at hat, puts scissors back on the table*)—let us take away this ribbon and these feathers.

LADY GILDING (*horrified*). George!

SIR GEORGE. Excuse me, Mildred. The price of the hat is now doubled.

PROFESSOR. Bless my soul!

SIR GEORGE. There is nothing left now but the straw and this bow. (*Takes up scissors and cuts at hat.*) I take away the straw.

LADY GILDING. George!

SIR GEORGE. Excuse me, Mildred. And there being nothing left now except the ribbon, the price of the hat—(*Holding up bow of velvet*)—becomes something appalling. And now, Mildred, we must go.

(LADY GILDING *ruefully arranges hat.*)

DOWAGER. I hope you will excuse us calling at this early hour, Professor, we were so anxious when we heard of your illness. You must dine with us to-night.

LADY GILDING.   Yes, indeed !

PROFESSOR.   It is—ah—very good of you, but——

DOWAGER.   No refusals.   8.30.

LADY GILDING (*holding out her hand to* PROFESSOR).   Good-bye, dear Professor.

PROFESSOR.   Good-bye, so glad you 're going—came, came.
(SIR GEORGE *and* LADY GILDING *and* DOWAGER *go.   The* PROFESSOR *sees them out and returns.*)
Very nice people, extraordinarily kind to me.

COSENS.   They seem very fond of you—especially the little Dowager.

PROFESSOR.   She is a charming woman—very cultured.   It is remarkable how interested she is in electricity.

COSENS (*dryly*).   Is she now !

PROFESSOR.   She is of a very sympathetic nature.

COSENS.   I 'm sure she is, but how do you know ?

PROFESSOR.   She told me—at least, I think she did.

COSENS.   Remember, you 're dining with them to-night.

PROFESSOR (*hotly*).   I 'm doing nothing of the sort.

COSENS.   I heard you promise.

PROFESSOR (*sighing*).   Did you ?   I didn't mean to.   I 'm a muddle-head outside my work, and now I 'm getting muddled even at it.   I know what 's the matter with me, Doctor, my brain 's in a dry rot !

COSENS.   Well, a man can be quite happy without a brain. Sir George, for instance !   But, perhaps, that is because he has a wife.   Why don't you marry ?

PROFESSOR.   Marry !   You vindictive fellow !

COSENS.   Ah, you were not such a woman-hater in our College days.

PROFESSOR.   Yes, I was always the same.

COSENS.   You remember the old lodgings in Edinburgh six flights up ?

PROFESSOR.   And the bed, it was so small that I had to get up when you wanted to lie down.

COSENS.   Do you remember Jack Pettigrew ?   He married his landlady's daughter.

PROFESSOR.   Oh, lots of them married their landlady's daughters.

COSENS.   Fleming didn't.

PROFESSOR.   No, he married his landlady.

COSENS.   Bob Sandeman died.

PROFESSOR.   Ah, but he wasn't true to Agnes.   It made a great difference to her.

COSENS.   But she 's got over it ?

PROFESSOR.   I 'm not quite sure.

COSENS.   There was Crichton, who took so many prizes that we all predicted he would become Lord Chancellor.

PROFESSOR.   Ned Crichton.

COSENS.   Where is he now ?

PROFESSOR.   I think he is driving a cab in New York.

COSENS.   You were a gay dog in those days.

PROFESSOR.   I was nothing of the kind.

COSENS.   Don't you remember that girl you kissed at McAuly's graduation supper ?

PROFESSOR.   I didn't kiss her.

COSENS.   Yes, you did.

PROFESSOR.   No, I did not.

COSENS.   I saw you—I forget her name.

PROFESSOR (*sweetly*).   It was Millie Watson.

(COSENS *points triumphantly at him.   The* PROFESSOR *jumps up in confusion.*)

COSENS.   You confess ?

(PROFESSOR *turns and beams on him.*)

Ah, we were not dull old boys then !

PROFESSOR.   No, and your hair used to curl.   (*Patting* COSENS *on head.*)

COSENS.   We never foresaw a time when we should live in the same city and not see each other once a year—eh, Goodwillie ?

PROFESSOR.   You didn't call me Goodwillie then.

COSENS.   Tom !

PROFESSOR.   Dick, old boy !

(*They hit lightly at each other until body blow, when they sit.*)

Dick, do you really know what 's the matter with me ?

COSENS.   Tom, I don't.

PROFESSOR.   I thought not.   (*Goes to table and sits.*)

COSENS (*following him*).   But I mean to find out before I leave the house.

PROFESSOR. My brain is giving way, that's what it is.

COSENS. Why do you stick so closely to your work ? Why not give yourself a rest ?

PROFESSOR. I can't, Dick. Sticking closely to my work has become my life.

COSENS. And robbed you of your youth and all its pleasures —made an old man of you before your time. Ever since we were boys you have done nothing but work. Tom, how old are you ?

PROFESSOR. I don't know exactly. (*Calling*) Effie ! How old . . . Oh no, she wouldn't know either. I 've given up having birthdays, Dick.

COSENS. You 're younger than I am ; why, you can't be much over forty, and you look fifty or more. Give up your work for a bit.

PROFESSOR. I can't, Dick. I must finish my book—at any rate I must try.

COSENS. Then try to do some work here now. I am going to have a cigar and big think over you.

PROFESSOR. No use. And you mustn't smoke here. Bad for the machines. Go to the drawing-room if you want to smoke.

COSENS. All right ! I have solved some stiff cases with the help of a cigar.

PROFESSOR. It can't possibly tell you why I am unable to work nowadays.

COSENS. It shall ! Here is what I have to place before it. My friend, Goodwillie, is an enthusiastic electrician, whose work has hitherto engrossed him to such an extent that it has become his world. Within the last month, however, he has been unable to give his mind to his work.

PROFESSOR. Can't do it, can't do it.

COSENS. The question therefore is : has he given his mind to something else—something that now engrosses him more than electricity ?

PROFESSOR. Nonsense, you are insulting my work, Dick !

COSENS. The cigar has got to tell me what that something is. Can I help it ? Yes, to an extent. I can tell it that the only change which has come into your life of late is that your sister has not been here as usual to look after you. Now is that sufficient to account for your break-down ?

PROFESSOR. Pooh, Dick, pooh ! She has left me alone before.

COSENS. And you are positive that there has been no other change in your life since she went to Tullochmains ?

PROFESSOR. Absolutely none.

(COSENS *rings bell.*)

Now, why did you do that ?

COSENS. I want Miss White—to ask her some questions.

PROFESSOR. Miss White ? What can Miss White tell you about me ?

COSENS. I don't know—but she puzzles me.

(*Enter* EFFIE.)

Effie, send Miss White here.

(*Exit* EFFIE.)

PROFESSOR. Miss White can have nothing to tell you. She has not been here long enough. Why, it was after Agnes left that she became my secretary.

COSENS (*excitedly*). What ?

PROFESSOR. Miss White never *saw* me until a month ago.

COSENS. A month ago ! (*Great excitement kept up by* COSENS *until his exit.*)

PROFESSOR. Now why are you so excited ?

COSENS. Tom, I won't see Miss White until I 've had my cigar. (*Going.*) Oh, if it should be that ! If it should be that ! (*Exit.*)

PROFESSOR (*calling after him*). If it should be that ! If it should be what ? What are you drivelling about ?

(*Enter* LUCY.)

LUCY. Effie said Dr. Cosens wanted to see me.

PROFESSOR (*rising hurriedly, shakes her hand*). He changed his mind, I think. Miss Lucy, I must get through some work to-day.

(*He holds her hand for a time. He places chair for her and stands looking at her.*)

LUCY. The papers are all ready. (*Sitting.*) I think I found a mistake on sheet B 32.

PROFESSOR. Very likely ! B 32 ?

LUCY (*looks through papers*). Section 104. You say that Steinhall's magneto-electric machine was introduced in 1835. Should it not be galvanometer ?

PROFESSOR.   Did I write magneto ?

LUCY.   Yes.

PROFESSOR.   Criminal—quite criminal !

(*A slight pause ; he prepares to write.*)

LUCY.   Shall I go on with the copy ?

PROFESSOR.   If you please.

(LUCY *looks among papers and he watches her.*)

LUCY.   Have you a pen ?

PROFESSOR.   Yes, take mine.

(*Gives her his own, watches her a moment, places another pen handy for her, moves water-bottle, corrects proof, hands it to her after business with blotting-pad.*)

There is the corrected sheet.

(LUCY *takes it, puts it in its place and goes on writing. He watches her, then leans back in chair reflecting. He sighs.*)

Lucy !

LUCY.   Did you speak ?

PROFESSOR.   No, I don't think so.

(*The writing is resumed.* PROFESSOR *watches her, sighs, then comes to himself.*)

I don't seem to be able to do any work to-day.

LUCY.   I 'll sit over there.   I think my being so near disturbs you.   (*Takes paper and pen and goes to table.*)

PROFESSOR.   I don't see how that can be ; my other secretaries always sat here.

(*She writes.* PROFESSOR, *unable to keep his mind upon his work, finally takes papers and chair and goes over and sits at the table.*)

LUCY.   You were to sit over there.

PROFESSOR.   Bless my soul, what am I doing here ?   (*Returns to table.*)

LUCY.   Did Sommering found his bi-signal alphabet on that of Schilling ?

PROFESSOR.   Sommering ?   Never !

LUCY.   I thought not.

PROFESSOR.   Have I put Schilling before Sommering ?

LUCY.   Yes.

PROFESSOR.   I used to have an intellect.   I really had, Miss White.   All gone, all gone !

LUCY.   There is something that I can't make out.

(PROFESSOR *goes to her.*)

What is it that the small spring Z is joined to ? (*Hands him paper.*)

(COSENS *enters, comes slowly in front of table and listens.*)

PROFESSOR (*reading*). ' A steel spring X is connected by a copper cylinder Y with the terminal BD, and a small spring Z is joined by means of the circular bar EFG to the terminal $LUCY$.'

(PROFESSOR *goes to table and takes diagram.*)

Hullo, Dick. (*Looks at diagram, showing it to* LUCY.) There is no $LUCY$ in the diagram.

LUCY.   No.

PROFESSOR.   Doctor, do you see any $LUCY$?

COSENS.   Yes.

PROFESSOR.   Where ?

COSENS (*pointing to* LUCY).   There.

PROFESSOR.   Eh ? Oh, her name. This is no jesting matter, Dick, I must resign my chair. (*Taps his brow.*) Cotton wool, cotton wool.

(COSENS *lowers on* LUCY, *who quakes beneath his gaze. He opens door for her and she goes as if in disgrace.*)

COSENS.   Tom, I 've found out what 's the matter with you.

PROFESSOR.   What ?

COSENS.   Can you stand a shock ?

PROFESSOR.   Tell me the worst—quick !   Is it grave ?

COSENS.   It is very grave. My poor friend, you are in love. (*Emphatically.*)

PROFESSOR.   What !   In love—I—you—how dare you, Dick ? Playing with me. Very cruel.

COSENS.   Oh, I didn't give it to you. You are in love, and at your age it 's bound to be a bad case. You ought to have had it long ago.

PROFESSOR.   Love ! *Horrible !* (*Dazed.*)

COSENS.   Ah ! you feel that it is true !

PROFESSOR.   Love—me ! (*Suddenly*) Who is the woman ?

COSENS.   You don't know ?

PROFESSOR.   I haven't an idea.

COSENS.   Poor Tom !

PROFESSOR.   But it is impossible—I was all right a month ago.

COSENS.   Do you think it can't happen in a month?

PROFESSOR (*fiercely*).   Then who is the woman?

COSENS.   Why should I know?   I only recognise the symptoms.   I am not acquainted with your lady friends.

PROFESSOR.   Lady friends?   (*Growing pale*) Dick, it can't be the little Dowager, can it?   I haven't been paying attentions to her without knowing it, have I?

COSENS.   Search your heart, Tom!

PROFESSOR.   Dick, when we were sitting there, she and I— I think she was talking about love to me!

COSENS.   Are you sure, Tom, that you didn't talk about it to her?

PROFESSOR.   Dick!   (*He rings bell.*)

COSENS.   Poor old man!

PROFESSOR.   Brain addled!   Might do anything.

(*Enter* EFFIE.)

Effie, have you noticed me paying particular attention to any lady lately?

EFFIE.   Losh preserve us.

PROFESSOR.   To the Dowager, for instance?   Have you?

EFFIE.   No, sir.

PROFESSOR.   On your oath?

EFFIE.   On my oath, sir.

PROFESSOR.   Do you hear that, Dick?   Effie would know. It's all right—right as rain.   (*To* EFFIE) Send Miss White here.

(*Exit* EFFIE.)

COSENS.   Why do you want Miss White?

PROFESSOR.   To ask her the same question.

COSENS.   Good heavens!

PROFESSOR.   Why are you so surprised?   If such a thing has been going on with any other lady than the Dowager she must have noticed it.   She has been with me constantly.

(LUCY *enters, followed by* EFFIE.)

I don't need you any more, Effie.

(EFFIE *goes reluctantly.*)

Miss White, since you have been in this house, have I spoken a dozen sentences to any lady besides yourself?

LUCY.   Not so far as I know.

PROFESSOR.   That won't do.   On your oath.

LUCY.   On my oath.

PROFESSOR.   There, Dick, that settles it.   Confess that you were merely trying to frighten me.

COSENS (*almost whispering*).   I was doing nothing of the kind.   I was telling you the truth.

PROFESSOR.   Snap my fingers !   (*Snaps them at* COSENS.) Snap my fingers !

(PROFESSOR *glares at him and goes.*)

COSENS.   So, Miss White.

LUCY.   Please don't fold your arms in that way.   It frightens me.   I 'll do anything you like.   Shall I say 99 ?

COSENS.   I have found you out !   You know what I mean ! I wonder you have not managed to lure him to a proposal.

LUCY.   Thank you.

COSENS.   But I suppose you have been cautious with your fish lest the first glimpse of the hook should frighten him.

LUCY.   That must be the reason.

COSENS.   Is it ?

LUCY.   Who am I that I should contradict you ?

(*Enter* EFFIE.)

EFFIE.   The Professor wants you, Miss White.

(EFFIE *goes.*)

LUCY.   Very well.   (*Going.*)

COSENS.   What are you going to do now ?

LUCY.   Such a clever man does not need to be told that.

COSENS.   The game is up, Miss White.

LUCY.   Is it ?

COSENS.   Isn't it ?

LUCY.   You know best.

COSENS.   I don't understand you.   But either you leave the Professor's service or I tell him what you have been up to. Which is it to be ?

LUCY.   99.

(*She goes.* COSENS *stamps about not sure what to do, starts to go and changes mind.   Enter* PROFESSOR *with a Gladstone bag.*)

COSENS.   What are you doing, Tom ?

PROFESSOR.   Packing.   (*Puts bag on table, and begins to pack all sorts of things in it.*)   There 's a train to Tullochmains at 11.35 and I have just time to catch it.   Effie will follow with my things to-morrow.

COSENS.   Good !   Very good !   Capital !

(EFFIE *runs in with* PROFESSOR'S *coat, takes off his dressing-gown, and puts coat on him.*)

PROFESSOR.   Not that I believe it is love, but you have agitated me, and I know that under the circumstances Agnes's advice to me would be the same as when I was in Paris.

COSENS.   When was that ?

PROFESSOR.   Years ago.

(*Enter* LUCY *with some papers.*)
Miss Lucy, I cannot find my folio H.

(*She gets it from drawer and packs it in bag.*)

COSENS.   What about Paris ?

PROFESSOR.   I 'd gone out for a walk and forgotten what hotel I was stopping at.   Agnes wasn't with me, but I knew that she knew my address, so I telegraphed to her to telegraph back to me at once where I was staying.

COSENS.   And did she ?

PROFESSOR.   No, she telegraphed me to do best thing. Best thing—' Come home at once.'

(*The* PROFESSOR *goes.* EFFIE *follows with bag.* LUCY *at table is busy arranging papers.*)

COSENS (*triumphantly*).   So, Miss White, fate has been too strong for you.

LUCY.   A woman soon goes to the wall, doesn't she ?

COSENS.   What will *you* do now ?

LUCY.   Does it matter ?

COSENS.   Not to me.   But I feel rather sorry for you.   To lose your place just when everything seemed to be going nicely. Yes, I 'm sorry for you.

LUCY.   Please, no flowers—by request.

COSENS.   I like your pluck.   And as I leave now, Miss White, I bear you no malice.   Indeed, if I can help you to another situation——

(*She brings out her handkerchief and dabs her eyes. He stares.* PROFESSOR *hurries on with a telegraph form.*)

PROFESSOR. Effie—isn't Effie here? I want to send a telegram to Agnes. (*Writing it out.*) Put on your hat, Miss Lucy, we have just time to catch the train.

(LUCY *puts on hat at mirror.*)

COSENS. What, is she going with you?

PROFESSOR. Of course, I always take my secretary with me.

(COSENS *is staggered.* LUCY *looks quaintly at him.*)

COSENS (*firmly*). Tom, I have something to tell you.

PROFESSOR. One moment, Dick. I must have this sent off. Effie!

(*He goes.* LUCY *goes to table, and puts papers together.*)

COSENS (*going*). Very clever of you, Miss White, but as you *will* have it, I shall tell him now who the woman is.

LUCY. Ah!

(*She takes the waste-paper basket to table, lays it on chair, takes out two pieces of paper, lays them on table, and puts them together.*)

COSENS (*anxiously*). What is that?

LUCY. Your prescription for the Professor.

COSENS. Give it to me!

LUCY. Oh no!

COSENS. What are you going to do with it?

LUCY. I oughtn't to keep it to myself, ought I? I think of sending it to the *British Medical Journal*.

COSENS. Eh?

LUCY. With a note from me, saying that it is the eminent Dr. Cosens' cure for love. You will be a specialist after to-day, Doctor.

COSENS (*very much embarrassed*). You—you—if I don't tell him who the woman is, will you give me that prescription?

(LUCY *nods.*)

Come, then.

(LUCY *refuses to give it him yet.*)

PROFESSOR (*returning*). Didn't you say you had something to tell me, Dick?

COSENS. No, Tom, I don't think so.

(*He holds out hand for the prescription.* LUCY *gives it him, and he looks at it.*)

COSENS (*aside*). Quinine.

PROFESSOR.   Try a run north to see us, Dick.

COSENS.   I should like to, Tom, but—— (*Shaking hands.*)

LUCY (*mockingly*).   Do, Doctor.

COSENS (*meekly*).   Thank you, Miss White.

(*Enter* EFFIE.)

EFFIE.   The cab is at the door, sir. (*She has his hat and stick.*)

PROFESSOR.   Mind, Dick, I don't believe in your diagnosis, I don't believe a word of it, for there is no woman, and how could any one love vacuum?—quite absurd, quite absurd— but in case—just in case, there is no harm in taking precaution, and if there is such a woman——

EFFIE (*from door*).   You'll need all your time, sir.

PROFESSOR.   If there is such a woman, there is no harm in running away from her, is there? I have you there! Have you there.   Take my arm, Miss White.

(*The* PROFESSOR *and* LUCY *go.* COSENS *raises his hands helplessly to heaven, but cannot help seeing the humour of the situation.*)

ACT II

A CORNFIELD at harvest time. The corn down is already cut and standing in stooks. Effie is sitting on stook, knitting a stocking. Enter Pete, sheepishly. He is in corduroys, without coat, and strings are tied round the trousers below his knees. He is eating an apple. He comes and gazes at her fondly but cautiously. She knits demurely.

PETE.   Effie !

EFFIE.   Pete !

PETE.   It 's yoursel', Effie ?

EFFIE.   I dinna deny it, Pete.

PETE.   It 's dinner time, lassie.

EFFIE.   It 's dinner time to common folk, but it 's hardly breakfast time to their betters. The likes of you doesna ken what they do in grand society. You should see the Professor's house in London. I may say the walls is papered in bank notes.

PETE.   And yet he doesna work. He just invents electricity machines.

EFFIE.   He is a great man.

PETE.   Maybe, but I dinna approve o' him.

EFFIE.   What for no ?

PETE.   Because, Effie, there 's na electricity machines in the Bible !

EFFIE.   He 's a religious man.

PETE.   I question it. He has put English windows into his cottage, that open outwards. There 's no windows in the Bible that open outwards. All the windows in the Bible slide up and down.

(*Pause.*)

EFFIE.   It may be so.

PETE.   It is so. It 's the Scotch way. Effie !

EFFIE.   Pete !

82

PETE.   I 'm like the Professor in one respect—I 'm a single man.

EFFIE.   Any coward can be a single man.   It 's the only calling that 's open to them.

PETE.   I 'm not a coward—I 'm just cautious.   Effie, I 've had something on the tip o' my tongue to say to you this three years.

EFFIE.   What about ?

PETE.   About—about marriage.

EFFIE (*coyly*).   What about marriage ?
   (*Enter* HENDERS *with sickle.*)

PETE.   It 's—an honourable estate, Effie.

EFFIE.   It is, Pete.

PETE (*fondly*).   But it 's for life—Effie !

EFFIE.   I 'm listening, Pete.

PETE.   I 'm holding mysel' with an awful effort.   I hinna kent you lang enough to say what I want to say.

EFFIE.   Five years.

PETE.   That 's no lang for such a risky thing.

EFFIE.   Be courageous, Pete.

PETE.   I will.   (*Starts to embrace her, but becomes scared. Draws back and walks away.*)   I 'll bide a wee.   It 's so chancey. Good day to you, Effie.

EFFIE.   Good day.

   (PETE *goes.*   HENDERS *comes towards* EFFIE.   *He is very domineering in manner.*)

HENDERS.   What was Pete saying to you, Effie ?

EFFIE (*coquettishly*).   Different things.

HENDERS.   He wasn't asking you to marry him, was he ?

EFFIE.   That might be one of the things.

HENDERS.   Was it ?

EFFIE.   No, Henders.

HENDERS.   Effie, dinna tak' Pete, if he asks you to marry him.

EFFIE.   What for no ?

HENDERS.   Because there 's better than him to be got.   Tell me this first, do you like him or me best, Effie ?

EFFIE.   You, Henders.

HENDERS.   A lot better ?

EFFIE.   Humpha.   No comparison.

HENDERS.   Ay ; well, in that case, there 's no hurry. Good day to you, Effie.

> (*He goes.* EFFIE *watches him and sighs. Enter* DOWAGER *with corn sheaf, dressed in her charming idea of a harvesting dress.*)

DOWAGER.   Oh, Effie ! Do show me how to make the thingumbob that goes round—the waistbelt, you know.

EFFIE.   The band, my lady. It 's this way.

DOWAGER (*kneeling over sheaf*).   Charming ! But I don't want to learn. I want you to find the Professor and give him this letter.

EFFIE (*taking letter*).   Yes, my lady.

DOWAGER.   And, Effie, here comes Miss Goodwillie. She needn't see the letter. It 's only about electricity.

> (EFFIE *goes.* MISS GOODWILLIE *enters. She is outwardly hard.*)

Ah, Miss Goodwillie. Effie has been teaching me to bind. Such fun.

MISS GOODWILLIE.   I feel sure Effie never taught you to bind in that way. That is not binding, that 's strangling.

> (*Enter* LADY GILDING, *coming down stage, dressed in harvesting costume, similar to* DOWAGER, *and carrying sheaf.*)

LADY GILDING.   How do you think our harvesting is progressing, Miss Goodwillie ?

MISS GOODWILLIE.   I think you hold your sheaf, Lady Gilding, as if it were an infant.

DOWAGER.   Ha, ha, so you do, Mildred ! (*Acting three ways*) Good child, naughty child, upside-down child.

> (LADY GILDING *flings down sheaf. Enter* SIR GEORGE.)

SIR GEORGE.   I hope you are admiring our handiwork, Miss Goodwillie ?

MISS GOODWILLIE.   I wonder you don't go and play at something else.

LADY GILDING.   Play !

SIR GEORGE.   Play ! I assure you, Miss Goodwillie, you make a great mistake. (*Sits on stook.*)

LADY GILDING.   So much so, that George has completely exhausted himself, and I mean to consult Dr. Yellowlees about him.

MISS GOODWILLIE.   Do, and get the doctor to stop this tom-foolery, if I may call it so.

SIR GEORGE.   Tomfoolery ! You don't seem to understand, Miss Goodwillie, that I am cutting my own corn by the sweat of my brow, because, as a member of Parliament, I want to know by personal experience just how my constituents live.

LADY GILDING.   And I, as George's wife, assist, so that manual labour may be elevated in the eyes of the wives of the working classes.

DOWAGER.   We are even wearing dresses such as those worn by the common things while harvesting.

MISS GOODWILLIE.   Hum ! Bond Street ?

DOWAGER (*confidentially*).   No, a clever little creature of a maid I have. I get her cheap because she drinks.

   (HENDERS *enters. He draws near listening. He has an old letter-box in his hand.*)

MISS GOODWILLIE.   And you really hold, Sir George, that there is no difference between your harvesting and that of the poor ?

SIR GEORGE.   Absolutely none.

   (*Enter gorgeous* MALE SERVANT *and* PAGE-BOY *carrying lunch-basket and champagne.*)

SERVANT.   Where shall we lay the luncheon, Sir George ?

SIR GEORGE (*pointing*).   Down by the stream.

   (*The* SERVANTS *leave, followed by* SIR GEORGE. MISS GOODWILLIE *and* HENDERS *laugh loudly.*)

MISS GOODWILLIE.   What have you got there, Henders ?

HENDERS.   I found it in the field when I was cutting—it 's your old letter-box.

MISS GOODWILLIE (*agitated*).   The old letter-box !

HENDERS.   Ay, it had blown down in the winter, I suppose.

MISS GOODWILLIE.   The old letter-box ! What are you going to do with it ?

HENDERS.   It hasna been in use this dozen years, except for starlings to build in.

MISS GOODWILLIE.   I know.

HENDERS.   So I meant to nail it up in my garden and see if they would build in it there, but if you want it.—I——

MISS GOODWILLIE.   I want it ? No ! Give it to me.

   (*He starts to hand it to her.*)

Take it away, but don't nail it up anywhere.   Burn it.
> (*She goes agitatedly.*)

DOWAGER.   Why has Miss Goodwillie gone, man ?

HENDERS.   I wonder.   She 's shaking like a leaf.

DOWAGER.   Shaking ?   Why ?

LADY GILDING.   I heard and understand.

HENDERS.   It 's mair than I do.   It 's queer.   (*Exit.*)

DOWAGER (*sitting on stook*).   And it 's more than I do.

LADY GILDING.   Then you don't know that Miss Goodwillie had a love story ?

DOWAGER.   Never !   There *are* audacious men !   Tell me about it.

> (*They sit on fallen sheaf.*)

LADY GILDING.   As I understand, the affair took place more than twenty years ago.   In the Professor's student days, he brought a friend named Bob Sandeman here, one summer, and Miss Goodwillie fell in love with him and he with her, but he was too poor even to get engaged to her.   He went away to Australia, and the understanding was, that as soon as he could make a living there he was to write and ask her to go out to him.   But he never did.

DOWAGER.   He wasn't so audacious as that !   What became of him ?

LADY GILDING.   He got on very well.

DOWAGER.   I can guess.   He married a cornstalk and they call each other ' cooee.'

LADY GILDING.   No, he never married ; he died years ago.

DOWAGER.   But what had the old letter-box to do with this ?

LADY GILDING.   It had been erected at the foot of the hill to save the postman the trouble of climbing to the house, and every day for years Miss Goodwillie used to go and look in the letter-box for her letter.

DOWAGER.   Cooee !

LADY GILDING.   They say she was as white as a ghost in those days.

DOWAGER.   Poor thing.   But still—cooee, cooee !

LADY GILDING.   And she cried herself into a fever.

DOWAGER.   No wonder men have little respect for women.

LADY GILDING.   George says he believes the man ran off to Australia to avoid her.

DOWAGER.   And so ends this strange, eventful history.

LADY GILDING.   And he also says that he fears the Professor is not a marrying man either, sweet.

DOWAGER.   What does that matter, *love*, when I am a marrying woman?

LADY GILDING.   George is afraid that it matters a great deal, *darling*.

DOWAGER.   That is because George never realised how he came to be married himself, *pet*.

LADY GILDING.   Mamma!

(*Enter* DR. COSENS.)

COSENS.   Lady Gilding! (*Goes to* LADIES, *shakes hands*.)

DOWAGER.   Dr. Cosens!

LADY GILDING.   This is an unexpected pleasure.

DOWAGER.   Did the Goodwillies know you are coming?

COSENS.   No, it is a surprise visit. I found I had a week-end to spare and the Professor's case interested me so much that— here I am.

LADY GILDING.   They will be delighted to see you.

COSENS.   I was told in the village that I should find them here.

LADY GILDING.   Yes, everyone is here to-day, seeing my husband cut his corn.

DOWAGER.   His latest fad.

LADY GILDING.   Mamma!

COSENS.   Cut his corn! Ha, ha! But can you tell me how the Professor is now?

DOWAGER.   Yes, Doctor, I admit I think I can.

COSENS.   Ha!

DOWAGER.   Mildred, I'll follow you in a minute. I am sure George is looking for you, precious. He must have cut himself by this time.

LADY GILDING.   You will lunch with us, Doctor, presently.

COSENS.   Delighted!

LADY GILDING.   And afterwards I should love to show baby to you.

COSENS.   I look forward to that.

DOWAGER.   He's such a dear.

LADY GILDING.   He really is, and he is so fond of his grand-mamma.

(*Exit* LADY GILDING.)

DOWAGER. Had a good journey, Dr. Cosens ?

COSENS. Capital ! Carriage to myself all the way. I thought you were still in London, Lady Gilding.

DOWAGER. No, we came north—soon after the Professor.

COSENS. Indeed !

DOWAGER. My candour surprises you, I see, but the fact is, that that simple little Lucy thing has told me all.

COSENS. May I ask what ' that simple little Lucy thing ' has told you ?

DOWAGER. That, in your opinion, our dear Professor is in love without knowing it.

COSENS. Ha, I fancied ' that simple little Lucy thing ' would keep that to herself. (*Suddenly*) Did she tell you who I think the lady is ?

DOWAGER. Yes, of course.

COSENS. Who ?

(DOWAGER *taps herself, complacently kisses* au revoir *to him, and* COSENS, *left alone, laughs boisterously, and sits. He is found in this condition by* DR. YELLOWLEES, *who comes binding but otherwise very professional.* YELLOW-LEES *stares at* COSENS' *amusement.*)

YELLOWLEES. Dr. Cosens, isn't it ?

COSENS (*pulling himself together*). Eh ? I beg pardon——

YELLOWLEES. You don't remember me ! I had the pleasure of meeting you here two years ago—Dr. Yellowlees.

COSENS. Ah, yes ! You are attending the Professor, are you not ?

YELLOWLEES. Yes ; I understand he was in your hands before he left London.

COSENS. He was. But I wager he did not tell you what I thought was the matter with him.

YELLOWLEES. No. He said you 'd been baffled.

COSENS. H'm ! And you have been more successful ?

YELLOWLEES. With all deference—excuse my saying I have.

COSENS. Capital ! And what is the Professor's ailment ?

YELLOWLEES (*casually*). Lumbago !

COSENS (*after staring at him*). Lumbago ! Splendid ! Of course, it is lumbago. Why did I not think of that ?

YELLOWLEES. We all make our little mistakes at times.

COSENS. Thanks. It's very nice of you to put it in that way.

YELLOWLEES. Perhaps we of the younger school——

COSENS. Quite so. You know a thing or two more than we old fogies.

YELLOWLEES. Not at all, not at all. What did you think it was ?

COSENS. I was going to say that I diagnosed the Professor's ailment as a clear case of *cherchez la femme*.

YELLOWLEES (*puzzled and making one word of it*). Chershy-lafam ? Something new ?

COSENS. It's all the rage in the south just now. Quite knocked out appendicitis.

YELLOWLEES. Chershy la fam ! What are the symptoms ?

COSENS. Obviously as in lumbago. Catches you in the back. Doubles you up.

YELLOWLEES. Ha !

(*Enter* LADY GILDING *excitedly. She shrieks outside.* COSENS *rises.*)

LADY GILDING. Oh, oh !

YELLOWLEES. What's the matter ? (*Meets her.*)

LADY GILDING. Oh, that little imp, Lucy White——ugh !

COSENS. Again ! What is she doing now ?

LADY GILDING. She tried to put a mouse down my back.

YELLOWLEES. Most shameful. My dear lady, how could she have so presumed ?

LADY GILDING. She said that I was looking so painfully respectable——that she felt she must make me jump. (*Sits on stook.*)

COSENS (*who has been privately amused*). I must tell her what I think of this. A mouse ! Most offensive. (*Exit.*)

YELLOWLEES (*comforting* LADY GILDING). There, you'll soon be yourself again, Lady Gilding, if you can contrive not to think of the mouse. Get it out of your mind's eye.

LADY GILDING. But I can't——ugh !

YELLOWLEES. Shall I call Sir George ?

LADY GILDING. No, I don't want to bother him, for he has been a little out of sorts for some days.

YELLOWLEES. That's very true. That's very true.

LADY GILDING. You have noticed it ?

YELLOWLEES. Yes, yes! He isn't quite himself. Bad colour. I have been keeping an eye on him.

LADY GILDING. What is wrong with him, Doctor?

YELLOWLEES. Eh—ah—oh, well——

LADY GILDING. He gets angry when I speak of it, which makes me the more anxious.

YELLOWLEES. Naturally. Irritable—a sure indication.

LADY GILDING. Tell me candidly, Doctor.

YELLOWLEES. Lady Gilding, I will. (*Very importantly*) This is a case of—of chershy la fam.

LADY GILDING. What?

YELLOWLEES. Yes, indeed. Quite an epidemic of it in London this year.

LADY GILDING. *Cherchez la femme!*

YELLOWLEES. Precisely.

LADY GILDING. How dare you!

YELLOWLEES. No need for alarm, Lady Gilding. These cases have to *run their course*.

LADY GILDING (*crying*). Who is she?

YELLOWLEES. Eh?

LADY GILDING. You won't tell me? Very well. But I shall go straight home and make inquiries, and I warn you and Sir George that I'll find out before I am a day older.

(*Exit in agitation.* YELLOWLEES *ponders. Enter* COSENS *and* MISS GOODWILLIE.)

COSENS. Yes, a capital journey. Carriage to myself all the way. (*He sees* YELLOWLEES.) Ah, Doctor, did you get the mouse?

YELLOWLEES. You said Chershylafam, didn't you?

COSENS. That's it.

YELLOWLEES. I suppose I'll find it among the S's?

COSENS. Are you going to look it up in the books?

YELLOWLEES. I might as well.

COSENS. Good.

(YELLOWLEES *bows and exits.*)

(*Amused.*) Great! I like this fellow. I'll tell you why presently. You are sure my visit does not put you about?

MISS GOODWILLIE. Quite the contrary. The only thing is, that you must sleep at the Inn.

COSENS. That will suit me famously.

MISS GOODWILLIE.   Our cottage is so small that even Miss White had to get a bedroom in the village.

COSENS.   Speaking of Miss White, I was looking for her just now when I met you.

MISS GOODWILLIE.   Ah !

COSENS.   How is she doing here ?

(MISS GOODWILLIE *makes depreciating gesture.*)

I thought so.

MISS GOODWILLIE.   Why didn't you write and tell me of what was going on in London ?

COSENS.   To begin with, it took me a week to find out.

MISS GOODWILLIE.   It took me ten minutes.

COSENS.   And, besides, to tell you the truth—Miss White was too clever for me.

MISS GOODWILLIE.   Clever, bah ! The stupidest woman is more than a match for the cleverest man.

COSENS.   And she and I are neither one nor the other. Well, what is the situation now ?

(LUCY's *voice is heard calling* ' Peepbo.')

Eh !

MISS GOODWILLIE.   Here they come. So you can judge for yourself.

(COSENS *and* MISS GOODWILLIE *kneel behind stack.* LUCY *again calls* ' Peepbo ' *and hides by stack. She then calls* ' Peepbo.' *Enter* PROFESSOR *gaily, with fishing-rod and creel. He looks over rick and points at her. They don't see* MISS GOODWILLIE *and* COSENS.)

PROFESSOR.   Ah ha, found ! Now, Miss Lucy, I 'll tell you what we 'll do. You shall stay there and I 'll pretend I can't find you.

LUCY (*laughing*).   Don't you think it 's rather childish.

PROFESSOR.   Not at all ! It 's splendid fun.

COSENS (*rising*).   Peepbo ! Hello, Tom ! Do, Miss White !

PROFESSOR.   Hello, Dick !

(LUCY *jumps up.*)

Why, when did you come ?

COSENS.   Just arrived——

PROFESSOR.   Had you a good——

COSENS.   Capital ! Carriage to myself all the way. And how are you, Tom ?

PROFESSOR.   Much better—am I not, Miss Lucy?

LUCY.   Anyone can see you are, isn't it so, Miss Goodwillie?

(MISS GOODWILLIE *shows displeasure*.)

PROFESSOR.   I say, Dick, do you remember what you thought was the matter with me?

COSENS.   I do!

LUCY.   And fancy, it turned out to be lumbago, Doctor. **Is** quinine good for lumbago?

(COSENS *winces*.)

PROFESSOR.   Of course it was lumbago. Do I look as if it was the other thing, Dick? Ha, ha, Agnes, come here. Listen, Miss Lucy. I have such a joke for you, it is something I have not breathed to a soul, because it gave me such a fright at the time. You won't mind my telling them, Dick?

COSENS.   Why should I?

PROFESSOR.   Well, you know, it does turn the laugh against you.

COSENS.   H'm!

PROFESSOR.   It's this, Agnes. Listen, Miss Lucy. Dr. Cosens thought I had lost my power to work because I was in love, ha, ha, ha!

(*Laughs*, COSENS *and* LUCY *laugh*, MISS GOODWILLIE *does not*.)

LUCY.   You're not laughing, Miss Goodwillie.

(MISS GOODWILLIE *goes up stage angrily*. COSENS *laughs heartily*.)

PROFESSOR.   Unless it was one of your jokes, Dick, you are a trump to take it so well.

COSENS.   H'm! It is another joke I am laughing at, Tom. But as you are mending so rapidly, I suppose you are at work on your book again?

(LUCY *rises*.)

PROFESSOR.   Eh—ah—no! I haven't done anything to my book. The fact is, I have been so busy with other things——

COSENS.   Such as 'Peepbo.'

PROFESSOR.   Well, at all events, if I was in love I wouldn't be playing 'peepbo' with Miss White, would I?

COSENS.   What would you be doing?

LUCY.   He would be with his inamorata, of course—wouldn't you, Professor?

PROFESSOR (*rises*).   Naturally.   Surely you see that, Dick.

(COSENS *looks in* PROFESSOR's *creel.*   LUCY *goes.*)

COSENS (*to* PROFESSOR).   And is this all ?   (*Holding up a small trout.*)

PROFESSOR.   All !   I should think it is all.

COSENS.   I thought you put the little ones back.

PROFESSOR (*taking fish*).   Little ones.   It 's a half-pounder.

COSENS.   You don't mind my smoking, do you, Miss Goodwillie ?

MISS GOODWILLIE.   Oh no.   Tom, give the Doctor one of your cigars.

PROFESSOR.   Eh !   Oh yes.

COSENS.   Thank you.

(PROFESSOR *signs him ' No.'*   COSENS *is perplexed.*)

MISS GOODWILLIE.   You have them with you ?

PROFESSOR.   Oh yes, I have them with me.   (*Finds them.*) Ah, here they are.

(*Hands case to* MISS GOODWILLIE *who hands them to* COSENS, *still signing to him.*   COSENS *takes one and puts it in his mouth.*)

MISS GOODWILLIE.   I bought these for Tom.

COSENS (*hurriedly removing cigar from his mouth*).   Oh !

MISS GOODWILLIE.   Yes, he was actually paying fifty shillings a hundred for his cigars, and I got these for twelve and sixpence.   They are quite as large, Tom.   (*Gives case to* PROFESSOR.)

PROFESSOR.   Yes—quite as—large.   (*Moves up and looks off.*)

COSENS.   They are wonderfully large, but I shall keep this one until after dinner, it is so—large.

PROFESSOR (*feeling a vacuum*).   Miss Lucy has gone !   (*Looks for her.*)

(MISS GOODWILLIE *signs hurriedly to* COSENS *to take him away, and goes.*)

COSENS (*crossing to* PROFESSOR *and taking him by arm and dragging him across stage*).   Come along, Tom, and show me the sights.   I 'm burning to revisit them.   The bridge and the kirk—and the kirk and the bridge.   Is the village pump mended yet ?

PROFESSOR.   But Miss White ?

MISS GOODWILLIE.   Oh, I want to talk with her.

PROFESSOR. Good, very good. I am so glad you and she get on so well together, Agnes.

MISS GOODWILLIE. Don't we ?

COSENS. Come, Tom.

PROFESSOR. Dick, could you jump that stook ?

COSENS. Not I.

PROFESSOR. Then look here. Hold my hat. (*Hands hat to* COSENS, *throws rod and creel down, jumps over stook.*) What do you think of that ?

COSENS. For a man with lumbago, capital.

PROFESSOR. Look out ! (*Jumps back.*)

COSENS. Hang it, Tom, you seem to have put off the Professor since you came north, and to have become a boy again.

PROFESSOR. That is so, Dick, and I can't understand it. Very odd—very—it must be something in the air.

(COSENS *looks at* MISS GOODWILLIE, *who signs to him to take* PROFESSOR *away.*)

COSENS. Let us go.

PROFESSOR. Yes.

(*Just as they are going* LUCY's *voice is heard calling 'Peepbo.'*)

PROFESSOR (*going*). You heard that. Where is Miss Lucy ? Where can she be ? I wonder where Miss Lucy is ?

(*Jumps stook and exit.* COSENS *laughs.*)

MISS GOODWILLIE. Now you know the situation—and you seem to enjoy it more than I do.

COSENS. You seem to like it so little that I wonder you have not ended it.

MISS GOODWILLIE. I wish I could, but I can't send the woman away without telling Tom the reason, and then he is just as likely as not to propose to her.

COSENS. Or would it frighten him out of his wits ?

MISS GOODWILLIE. Who can say ?

COSENS. Do you want him always to remain a bachelor ?

MISS GOODWILLIE. Till I can find the right woman for him.

COSENS. Men are independent creatures, you know. Suppose Tom has found the right woman for himself.

MISS GOODWILLIE. Lucy White ?

COSENS.   After all, you know nothing against her.

MISS GOODWILLIE.   I wish I did.

COSENS.   Except that Tom loves her.

MISS GOODWILLIE.   Loves her, bah !

COSENS.   How bitterly you speak of love.

MISS GOODWILLIE.   Your old friend, Bob Sandeman, taught me what a man's love amounts to, and I am not afraid to put an end to Tom's.

COSENS.   Are you doing right ?

MISS GOODWILLIE.   I know what is best for Tom Goodwillie.

COSENS.   And I suppose no one can be expected to think of what might be best for Lucy White ?

(LUCY *runs on in game*.)

MISS GOODWILLIE.   Ah, Miss White, we were talking about you.

LUCY.   That must be why my ear was burning.   And which of you thinks the worst of me ?

MISS GOODWILLIE.   I do.

COSENS.   Miss Goodwillie, come !

MISS GOODWILLIE.   I must speak, whatever happens.   This girl shall be told what I think of her.

LUCY.   I know already.

MISS GOODWILLIE.   We were discussing your plot to marry my brother.

COSENS.   No, no !

LUCY.   Oh yes, I am sure it is true.

MISS GOODWILLIE.   I said that Tom is so simple that you may succeed.   That you are a mere adventuress.   That you obtained your position as his secretary merely with a desire to entrap him, and that you would stop at nothing, absolutely nothing, in order to do so.

COSENS.   Miss Goodwillie, you really go too far.

LUCY (*to* MISS GOODWILLIE).   Have you finished ?

MISS GOODWILLIE.   For the present.

LUCY.   And you won't withdraw those words ?

MISS GOODWILLIE.   No !

LUCY.   I give you one last chance. (*Takes stage*.)   You know that I have never encouraged the Professor.   In your heart you are afraid that had I cared to do so, I could be engaged to him at this moment. You know that since I came here I have been treated as a pariah ; yes, by all of you, from the Dowager, who patronises me, and your Lady Gilding and her husband, who call me by my surname, down to your brother, whose belief that no one could love Lucy White, even while he does it, is the greatest insult of all.

COSENS (*to* MISS GOODWILLIE). Be just to her, my friend.

LUCY. All this you know to be true, and still have you no pity for me nor for the position I am in through no fault of my own ?

MISS GOODWILLIE. None !

LUCY. Very well, then I 'll have none for you. The great desire of your life has been to keep your brother single. To have no one come between his love for you and your selfish love for him, and I—I have respected that desire—but now I will do so no longer.

MISS GOODWILLIE. Hoity-toity, Miss. I am not afraid of you.

COSENS. Miss White, I am not your enemy. If you tell me that you truly love Tom——

LUCY. Would you believe my word ?

COSENS. I may be a fool but—yes, I would. Do you ?

LUCY (*after hesitation*). What has he done to deserve my love ? (*Exit.*)

COSENS. She does care for him. Miss Goodwillie, if you don't mind I will beat a retreat to the cottage.

MISS GOODWILLIE. Why ?

COSENS. For one reason, I see the Dowager coming. By the way, is *she* seeing much of the Professor ?

MISS GOODWILLIE. I fling them as much together as I can— to keep him away from Miss White.

COSENS. Oho ! Is that wise ?

MISS GOODWILLIE. I am not afraid of her.

COSENS. H'm ! Well, Miss White seems to have challenged the field, so I should like to get out of it.

MISS GOODWILLIE. She alarms you ?

COSENS. Mortally. When it comes to Lucy White versus the field, I feel sure that Lucy White will win.

MISS GOODWILLIE. You think so ?

COSENS. I do, and what is more, excuse me, I am inclined to think that it will serve the field jolly well right. (*Exit.*)

> (DOWAGER *enters as he is going. She is humming gaily, waggles hand to him in high spirits, evidently meaning that all is going well. He responds and exits, amused.* MISS GOODWILLIE *is picking up* PROFESSOR'S *rod and creel.*)

MISS GOODWILLIE.   You seem to be in high spirits.

DOWAGER.   I am !   I don't know why.   Perhaps just because it 's such a beautiful world.

MISS GOODWILLIE.   I can't say it is striking me in that light. By the way, I hope you are to take Tom off to lunch.

DOWAGER.   I shall be only too delighted.

> (*Exit* MISS GOODWILLIE.   DOWAGER *kisses hand after her, hums, skips about gaily, looks about her and calls.*)

DOWAGER.   Lucykins !

> (*Enter* LUCY.)

What do you think, Lucy, Miss Goodwillie has asked me to invite Thomas to lunch.   She is evidently on my side.

> (DOWAGER *seizes her and dances with her gaily.*)

Do you know why I am so fond of you to-day, you quaint, simple Whitey ?

LUCY.   Perhaps it 's because you want me to do something for you.

DOWAGER.   Fancy your guessing.   It is this !   I want you to keep every one away from this part of the field for the next half-hour——

LUCY.   Except the Professor ?

DOWAGER.   Right again !

LUCY.   It is so good of you to let me help you.

> (*Enter* PETE *at back gathering out corn.*)

DOWAGER.   Oh, there are heaps of things I mean to let you do for me besides that.

LUCY.   Thank you.

DOWAGER.   I expect the Prof—— (*Sees* PETE) Go away, man.

PETE.   I have Sir George's orders.

DOWAGER.   Most provoking !

LUCY (*to* PETE).   Pete, why haven't you asked Effie to marry you ?

PETE.   Because there 's no hurry.

LUCY.   There is a hurry, unless you want Henders to have her.

PETE.   What's that ?   What do you mean ?

LUCY.   Do you see the pink figure over there ?   (*Pointing.*)

PETE.   Ay, it's Effie.

LUCY.   And a man hurrying towards her—there !

PETE.   No !

LUCY.   You do, Lady Gilding ?

DOWAGER.   Distinctly.

LUCY.   Well, that is Henders, and he's going straight to propose to her.

PETE.   What's to be done ?

LUCY.   I know what I'd do if I were you.

PETE.   What ?

LUCY.   I'd run along the wood on this side and get to Effie before him.

PETE.   I will.   (*He runs off.*)

DOWAGER.   Clever !   Is it true about Henders ?

LUCY.   No, but I want to help Effie to a husband.

DOWAGER.   She would have preferred Henders.

LUCY.   Are you sure of that ?

DOWAGER.   She told me so.

LUCY.   Then I won't let Pete get her.   (*Turns and calls off*) Henders !

DOWAGER.   What does it matter ?   She will be quite satisfied with Pete.

LUCY.   She is a dear girl and she has been kind to me.   (*Calls*) Henders !

        (*Enter* HENDERS *with sickle.*)
Look at Pete !

HENDERS.   What's he up to ?

LUCY.   He's off to propose to Effie.

HENDERS.   Wh—at !

        (*Throws down sickle and runs off.*   DOWAGER *and* LUCY *laugh heartily.*)

LUCY.   Now it is a race for a wife.   (*Sits on stook.*)

DOWAGER.   Yes, and mine is to be a swoon for a husband.

LUCY.   A swoon ?

DOWAGER.   Yes, listen—it's lovely.   A little while ago I sent a letter to the Professor by Effie asking him to meet me here at two o'clock, as I had something very particular to say to him.

LUCY. Meaning, of course, that you hope to get him to say something very particular to you.

DOWAGER. Exactly !

LUCY (*curiously*). Tell me, do you really care for him ?

DOWAGER. I shouldn't wonder. And I assure you I mean to make him very happy. Somebody once said to me that I was the one woman in the world for the Professor ; I forget who it was—perhaps it was myself—but that doesn't matter, and obviously Miss Goodwillie is quite favourable.

LUCY. You don't really think him in love with you, do you ?

DOWAGER. Not with my hand on my heart, Lucy. Still, what else can be making him so gay and sportive ?

LUCY. Don't you think it just possible that there might be some other woman ?

DOWAGER. You naughty ! He never sees any other woman.

LUCY. After all, there 's me.

DOWAGER. You ? You droll thing. Naturally he sees you and Effie. But I mean a lady.

LUCY. Ah, yes.

DOWAGER. Of course, you are a lady in a sense.

LUCY. No, no ! (*Sits on stook.*)

DOWAGER. Yes, in a sense. I am a faithful radical. Now listen and learn. The great difficulty with men is not to make them fall in love with you, but to get them to propose. So I have devised such a simple little scheme for helping the Professor out of his difficulty.

LUCY. How thoughtful of you. . . .

DOWAGER. It is this. When he arrives here, he will find me in a swoon. This is where I intend to faint. Do you see the result ?

LUCY. Not quite.

DOWAGER. Ah, you are obtuse. The Professor sees that I 've fainted. His first impulse is to rush to the river for water —but he has nothing to carry it in.

LUCY. His hat !

DOWAGER. Oh, he is too stupid to think of that.

LUCY. This tin pan. (*Pointing to one.*)

DOWAGER. Ah ! (*Hides it in rick.*) That settles the tin pan ! In a moment he sees that he must carry me to the river ; he lifts me up gently, he hurries off with his lovely burden and— but there is no more to be said, for the woman who is in a man's arms and can't draw a proposal out of him, is—well, she 's no true helpmate.

LUCY. What a sweetly simple scheme.

DOWAGER. Isn't it ? And quite justifiable. I feel as if I were a lovely little cupid, standing on one toe and firing an arrow into the dense one's breast. (*She realises the picture.*) Whitey, you may almost congratulate me already.

LUCY. I do.

DOWAGER. Do you think I should lie this way—or this way ? (*Tries.*) Ugh ! (*Starting up.*)

LUCY. What is it ?

DOWAGER. Spiders !

LUCY. You should have a rug to faint on.

DOWAGER. A capital idea. There are some near the gate. I 'll get one. Lucy, if the Professor comes before his time, keep him away from this spot till I return.

LUCY. Very well.

DOWAGER (*going*). How cleverly you managed Henders and Pete. It is simply the best joke I know of.

LUCY. Oh, I could show you a much better joke than that.

DOWAGER. You clever little thing. You shall !
(*The* DOWAGER *goes.*)

LUCY (*looking after her*). I will.
(PROFESSOR *is heard calling* 'LADY GILDING.')
I will !

(LUCY *faints, as* DOWAGER *has shown her, on stook.* PROFESSOR *comes on looking for* DOWAGER. *He finds* LUCY *lying there and is anguished.*)

PROFESSOR. Miss Lucy ! Fainted ! Hie, hie, help ! Oh, Miss Lucy ! Water ! The river ! Look up, Miss Lucy. Dear Miss Lucy !
(*He carries her off.* EFFIE *enters moodily knitting.* PETE *rushes on breathlessly.*)

PETE. Effie !

EFFIE. Pete—you 're out of breath.

PETE.   Effie, quick—will you ?

EFFIE.   Will I what ?

PETE (*jumps, looking for* HENDERS).   Will you take me, Effie ?

EFFIE.   Do you mean, will I marry you ?

PETE.   Ay ! Will you ?

EFFIE.   Where 's Henders ?

PETE.   I 've no idea. Will you ?

EFFIE.   Ay, I will.

PETE.   I 've won ! (*Mops brow.*)

EFFIE (*perhaps expecting endearments*).   Is that all, Pete ?

PETE (*heavy-witted*).   All ?   What more could there be ?

EFFIE.   That 's no for a lassie to say. (*Pointedly*) You 've crumpled me terrible.

PETE.   Me ?   I never touched you !

EFFIE.   So you didna. I 'll always mind that about you, Pete. (*She is going.*)

PETE.   Where are you going, Effie ?

EFFIE.   To tell everybody I 'm promised to you.

PETE.   Is that necessary ? (*Following her.*)

EFFIE.   Ay, it 'll make me feel surer o' you. Good day to you, Pete.

(*Exit* EFFIE. *He stares after her and mops his brow. Enter* HENDERS *hurriedly.*)

HENDERS.   Whaur 's Effie ?

PETE.   You 're ower late, my man.

HENDERS.   She 's yours ?

PETE.   She 's mine.

HENDERS.   Dagont ! (*Sits on sheaf.*)

PETE.   You 're michty jelly-ous o' me, Henders !

HENDERS.   Jelly-ous !   Not me.

PETE.   What ?   Think shame to pretend.

HENDERS.   Poor Pete.

PETE.   Marriage is an honourable estate.

HENDERS.   It 's michty risky.

PETE.   It is risky. Once they have you, they have you. There 's no way out, no, man, no ! But—but Effie 's a jewel.

HENDERS.   It 's a good thing you think so. William Todd thought that about Christy Lunan, but whaur is Willium now ?

PETE.   They say she makes him wander about the house in his stocking soles in case his boots messes the floor.

HENDERS.   Poor Willium, I liked him fine.

PETE.   You speak as if he was dead.

HENDERS.   He 's married.

PETE.   Effie 's a beauty, Henders.

HENDERS.   It doesna wear.

PETE.   I ken her weel.

HENDERS.   I hope you 'll never ken her better.

PETE.   Henders, you terrify me.   Ah, you wanted her yoursel'.

HENDERS.   Not me !

PETE.   But you did.   It was hearing you were off to put it to her that made me do 't.

HENDERS.   You 've made an awful mistake, Pete.   I wasna after Effie.   I was after you to warn you against being in a hurry.   You 're so fearful rash when your blood 's up.

PETE.   I am, woe 's me, I 'm lost.   Henders, I 'm away to ask Effie to let me off.

HENDERS.   Pete, did you kiss her ?

PETE.   No !

HENDERS.   What for no ?

PETE.   I never thoucht o 't.

(*Exit* PETE, *while* HENDERS *looks contemptuously after him and shakes his fist and repeatedly grins, as if he saw a good scheme. Enter* DOWAGER, *carrying rug. She is in high spirits.*)

DOWAGER.   What are you grinning at, man ?   Go away and grin somewhere else.

HENDERS.   The very thing I was thinking of doing, your ladyship.   He never thought of it !

DOWAGER.   What ?

HENDERS.   That 's what he said.   He never thought of it.

(*When* HENDERS *has gone,* DOWAGER *arranges rug cosily, in high spirits—looks about and evidently sees* PROFESSOR *coming—lies down on rug in affected swoon. Enter* PROFESSOR *excitedly and* MISS GOODWILLIE *simultaneously, and not seeing* DOWAGER, *who is hidden by stook.*)

PROFESSOR.   Agnes !

MISS GOODWILLIE.   Tom, I 've been looking for you every——

PROFESSOR.   Agnes, Agnes, Dick was right.

MISS GOODWILLIE.   In what ?

PROFESSOR.   I am in love.

MISS GOODWILLIE.   Tom !

PROFESSOR.   With Miss Lucy.

(DOWAGER *listens horrified.*)

MISS GOODWILLIE.   Oh, Tom !

PROFESSOR.   I found her lying over there a few moments ago. She had fainted.

(*Horror of* DOWAGER.)

I called for help—no one heard me. I thought of water—I had nothing to bring it in, so I lifted her in my arms and carried her to the riverside. Agnes, I no sooner had her in my arms than I realised that I loved her.

(DOWAGER *crawls out of sight in stook.*)

MISS GOODWILLIE.   Where is she now ?

PROFESSOR.   When she came to herself she ran away from me.

MISS GOODWILLIE.   Tom, have you asked her to marry you ?

PROFESSOR.   I had no time. Where are you going, Agnes ?

MISS GOODWILLIE.   After her !

PROFESSOR.   To plead for me. Agnes, you dear sister, you are going to plead for me.

(MISS GOODWILLIE *goes.* PROFESSOR *excitedly follows her and* DOWAGER *peeps out from stook a picture of comic woe.*)

ACT III

EXTERIOR of Professor's cottage. Moonlight. The time is
eight o'clock p.m. When the curtain rises the windows
are opened but the room is not lit up. Piano is being
played in an amateur way inside. Effie comes out of
gate carrying two empty water-pails. She disappears. Pete
enters stealthily and sees her.

PETE.   Effie !
     (*She does not look round. He follows her. Enter* DR.
     YELLOWLEES. *He knocks at door and the music ceases.*
     YELLOWLEES *enters house. Enter* SIR GEORGE, LADY
     GILDING, *and* DOWAGER. *They are in evening dress
     with wraps.*)
SIR GEORGE.   Then what I have to tell the Professor and
Miss Goodwillie is this : that Miss White's swoon was a
deliberate sham.
LADY GILDING.   As mamma can testify, for she saw it.
DOWAGER.   I happened to be passing at the time.
SIR GEORGE.   I feel a little nervous about intruding.
DOWAGER.   What is there to be afraid of ?
LADY GILDING.   You insisted on our hurrying over dinner
so that we might expose the creature before it was too
late.
DOWAGER.   Don't forget that if the Professor—succeeds in
winning me—you get five hundred pounds a year.
     (*Music recommences.*)
SIR GEORGE.   Please don't talk so sordidly.
     (*They are about to enter gate, when* YELLOWLEES *comes
     out of it.*)
LADY GILDING.   Ah, Doctor, have you been paying a pro-
fessional visit ?
YELLOWLEES.   I intended to, but the Professor is out.
104

SIR GEORGE.   Miss Goodwillie ?

YELLOWLEES.   Out also.

(*A bang is heard on piano.*)

DOWAGER.   Then who is that sitting on the piano ?

YELLOWLEES.   Dr. Cosens.

(*Piano ceases.*)

SIR GEORGE.   Then we need not go in ?

DOWAGER.   Let us stroll along the lane—we may meet them.

SIR GEORGE.   Very well.

LADY GILDING.   I 'll follow you—I have something to say to Dr. Yellowlees.

(SIR GEORGE *and* DOWAGER *go.*)

Now, Doctor.

YELLOWLEES (*thinking he is going to be scolded*).   If it is about my saying that Sir George was suffering from chershyla-fam——

LADY GILDING.   It is.

YELLOWLEES.   I wish to ask your pardon.   The fact is, I don't know what chershylafam is.   It 's not in the medical dictionary.

LADY GILDING (*archly*).   It ought to be—and you know what it is very well, Doctor.   Indeed, it was most good of you to put the little matter to me in such a delicate way. I thank you.

YELLOWLEES (*more puzzled than ever*).   I—really——

LADY GILDING.   You will be pleased to know that it is not so serious as you probably feared.   Of course, I inquired into the matter at once.

YELLOWLEES.   Ah—ah—quite so !

LADY GILDING.   But without telling Sir George.   You see, had he known I was interfering, he might—don't you think——

YELLOWLEES.   He might—he might !

LADY GILDING.   Of course, I have dismissed her.

YELLOWLEES.   Of course !   Oh, certainly.

LADY GILDING.   I thought it right to let you know this, as you are so fully acquainted with the circumstances.

YELLOWLEES.   So fully acquainted—ha, just so !

LADY GILDING.   Not a word of it to Sir George.

YELLOWLEÉS.   Not a word.

(LADY GILDING *goes.* YELLOWLEES *stares in perplexity, then hears someone coming out of house and exits swaggering. The newcomer is* DR. COSENS, *without his hat, who comes and leans over gate, smoking a pipe. An unseen bird in tree whistles and he whistles back to it. They keep this up until* PROFESSOR *enters excitedly.*)

PROFESSOR.   Dick !

COSENS.   At last, Tom.   I haven't seen you since I met you in the field.   I was beginning to think that the mysterious woman had run away with you, and married you against your will.

PROFESSOR.   None of that, Dick.   I won't listen to a word against marriage.   Most unmanly—very.

COSENS.   Hullo !

PROFESSOR.   I hold that it is the duty of every man to marry.

COSENS.   Hullo !   And how long have you been of that opinion ?

PROFESSOR.   Always.

COSENS.   Tom !

PROFESSOR (*joining him*).   Dick, I 'm in love !

COSENS.   At last !   And do you know who the lady is ?

PROFESSOR.   Do I know ?   What a question to ask !   Who could it be but Lucy White ?   Dick, how blind you are.

COSENS (*lolling on seat*).   Stand still and talk rationally.

PROFESSOR.   I can't stand still.   I have walked fifteen miles since I made the great discovery.   I feel as if I should never be able to stand still again.

COSENS.   Oh yes, you will.

PROFESSOR.   Ah, Dick, I think you are laughing at me ! Am I only an old fool ?   I think you are, Dick, she couldn't possibly.   Between ourselves, I am a little short-sighted and rather hard of hearing, and I sometimes give in one knee.   I shouldn't wonder, though, I had to get spectacles and an ear-trumpet and a crutch all at the same time.

COSENS.   The greater need of a wife.   No, I am not laughing at you, Tom.   Have you asked her to marry you ?

PROFESSOR.   I had begun to—in the field—it was all coming out in a rush, when she ran away.   Dick, no one could love me, eh ?

COSENS (*chaffing*).   Oh, I don't know.   For one thing, you are fairly wealthy.

PROFESSOR.   Ah, girls don't marry for money, Dick.

COSENS.   Simple old boy.

PROFESSOR.   Yes, that is it—I am an old boy, already.

COSENS.   You look twenty years younger than you did a week ago.

PROFESSOR.   I feel it, Dick.   I feel it, but it is impossible she can care for me.

COSENS.   Does your sister know about it, Tom ?

PROFESSOR.   Yes ; as soon as I told her she went off to look for Lucy.

COSENS.   Ha ! I can guess why she did that.

PROFESSOR.   So can I, Dick.   She has gone to plead for me. So like Agnes !   (*Sitting in seat under window.*)

     (COSENS *smiles.*)

But I am afraid it will be of no use.   Old fossil—the dustbin. That 's the place.

COSENS.   Tom, my opinion is, that the girl is in love with you.

PROFESSOR.   Dick !   Don't buoy me up with false hopes, Dick.   (*Jumping up from seat.*)

COSENS.   And my advice to you is——

PROFESSOR.   Yes ?

COSENS.   First, put on a decent hat——

PROFESSOR.   Yes ; I have one.   I certainly used to have one.

COSENS.   And your most elegant coat.

PROFESSOR.   Yes ?   The one I was fitted for.   That 's the one.

COSENS.   Assume a martial air, twirl a cane in one hand and march straight to her lodgings and propose to her.

PROFESSOR.   I will.

COSENS.   Cut a dash, Tom.

PROFESSOR.   Precisely.   That 's the thing.   (*Coming back.*) How do you cut it, Dick ?

COSENS.   In with you.

    (*The* PROFESSOR *goes into house leaving* COSENS *chuckling and re-lighting his pipe.*)

PROFESSOR (*opening window*).   Dick, you must have noticed that she is utterly unlike any other woman you ever saw ?

COSENS (*who has risen and gone to window*).   Oh, of course.

PROFESSOR.   Her laugh, Dick !

COSENS.   Ah !

PROFESSOR.   Once I saw her cry !

COSENS.   Never !

PROFESSOR.   It was in London.

COSENS.   You don't say so !

PROFESSOR.   She was twenty last birthday.

COSENS.   Wonderful !

(PROFESSOR *disappears for a second and then returns.*)

PROFESSOR.   Dick, I am even uglier than I thought.

COSENS.   Oh, go and tidy yourself up. Stop, I 'll come in and help you.

(COSENS *enters house.* PROFESSOR *disappears from window.* EFFIE *is heard off stage singing a snatch of* 'When the Kye comes Hame.' *She comes in from field with water,* PETE *following her.*)

PETE.   Oh, Effie !

EFFIE.   Tell me blunt, man, what is it you want if you ken yoursel' ?

PETE.   Fine I ken what I want. I want you to give me up, Effie.

EFFIE.   What for should I give you up ?

PETE.   I 've changed my mind, Effie.

EFFIE.   Is there some other woman ?

PETE.   There 's no other woman. Far frae it ! It 's just that on consideration I think the thing 's too venture-some.

EFFIE.   You 've been ill to come by, Pete, and I refuse to give you up. The whole countryside is already ringing with the news of my victory.

PETE.   It 's true, it 's true, I 'm a marked man. (*Appealing*) What is it you see in me, Effie, that 's so terrible adorable ?

EFFIE.   I see nothing partikler. *You 're* not my choice, but I 'm yours—and we 'll get on fine.

PETE.   You 're ower young to marry.

EFFIE.   Havers ! Many a woman is a widow at my age.

PETE.   My blood was up. I spoke in haste.

EFFIE.   Then you can repent at your leisure.

PETE.   Effie, I 'm a terrible bad character.

EFFIE. I 'll reform you.

PETE. I drink !

EFFIE. Ay !

PETE. I swear !

EFFIE. Ay !

PETE. In fact, I 'm just a regular devil.

EFFIE. Deevil or no deevil, Pete, you 're the man for me.

PETE (*to her back*). Effie woman ! Effie !

(*He goes very despondently. Enter* PROFESSOR *in tall hat, frock-coat, flower in it, and cane in hand.* COSENS *looks out at window at him.*)

COSENS. Good luck to you, Tom.

PROFESSOR (*referring to cane*). Dick, how do you twirl it ? (*Tries.*)

COSENS. Capital !

PROFESSOR. How do you think I look, Dick ? (*Referring to hat*) You know I never wear this except at funerals. I don't think she 'll know it 's me, Dick ?

COSENS (*chaffing*). Perhaps that will increase your chances !

PROFESSOR (*almost going—returning*). You know, I don't feel so old.

COSENS. You 're not.

PROFESSOR. Dick, I remember I was rather good at games. I had an off-break.

COSENS. Tell her that.

PROFESSOR. I once bled a boy's nose at school.

COSENS. Good.

PROFESSOR. What extraordinary things are coming back to me ! I used to draw caricatures of my schoolmasters !

COSENS. You did !

PROFESSOR. It is my solemn opinion, Dick—that I had quite a sense of fun !

COSENS. You 'll simply bowl her over, Tom.

PROFESSOR. You know I never believed I had a chance with her, and now I feel almost hopeful.

COSENS. That 's the way to win them. Be off, before it goes.

PROFESSOR (*going and returning*). Dick, I 've lost hope. What can she see in me ?

COSENS. My dear Tom, when women love us we should

never ask why.   All we can be sure of is that they see something
in us which isn't there.

> (*The* PROFESSOR *goes.* COSENS *leans out of window as if
> watching him.* COSENS *evidently indicates to him to wear
> hat more jauntily.   Signs to waggle cane.   Shows ap-
> proval and claps hands.   While he is doing so,* MISS GOOD-
> WILLIE *enters, and observes his antics.*)

MISS GOODWILLIE.   Whatever are you doing, Doctor ?

COSENS.   Observe the hat—and the cane.

MISS GOODWILLIE.   Where has he gone ?

COSENS.   Prepare to receive cavalry, my friend ; Tom is off
to the cottage where Miss White is living to propose to her.

MISS GOODWILLIE.   Ah !   I think I can stop that.   The
Gildings have just told me something that will show Tom
what she is, when I tell it to him.

COSENS.   Whatever it is, I don't believe it.

MISS GOODWILLIE.   *I* do.

COSENS.   You are so cynical, Miss Goodwillie, you believe
in no one.

MISS GOODWILLIE.   I believe in everything—except women
—and men.

COSENS.   Where are you going now ?

MISS GOODWILLIE.   To tax her with it before Tom.

> (COSENS *flings up his arms and disappears from window.*
> MISS GOODWILLIE *is going, but evidently sees someone else
> coming and turns and sits on seat.   Enter* LUCY.)

I have been looking for you for some hours, Miss White.

LUCY.   I was out when you called.   So I have come to see
you.

MISS GOODWILLIE.   To triumph over me ?

LUCY.   No, to let you triumph over me.

MISS GOODWILLIE.   What ?   Don't you know that your
scheme has succeeded.   He wants to marry you.

LUCY.   It is your scheme that has succeeded—your scheme
to make me unworthy of him.   Yes, I am an adventuress now.
But don't forget that it is you who have made me one.

MISS GOODWILLIE.   How ?

LUCY.   I have known for quite a long time that a word from
me would open his eyes to what you were so anxious he should
never see, but I would not speak it.   It is true that he knows

he loves me now, but only as the result of a shameless trick I played on him.

MISS GOODWILLIE. I have heard all about that, but I admit I don't quite see why you should tell me. (*Suspicious*) I suppose it is because you guessed I knew already.

LUCY. Go on thinking the worst of me. It doesn't matter now. I have degraded myself, and I am going away.

MISS GOODWILLIE (*on her guard*). Is this true?

LUCY. My box is packed and I leave for London to-night.

MISS GOODWILLIE. Without seeing my brother?

LUCY. I should prefer that.

MISS GOODWILLIE. With no explanations? He would follow you by the next train.

LUCY. You can tell him what I did. That will cure him.

MISS GOODWILLIE (*who secretly does not believe that it would cure him*). How do I know that he will not follow you still?

LUCY (*eagerly*). You think he might forgive me?

MISS GOODWILLIE (*dissembling*). Never!

LUCY. No, no! He has such a scorn of guile. He has said to me that guile is the one thing in a woman that he would never overlook.

MISS GOODWILLIE. And it is true. He is coming.

LUCY. Let me go.

MISS GOODWILLIE (*cunningly*). Stop! There is a better way. He need not despise you.

LUCY (*eagerly*). Oh!

MISS GOODWILLIE. I need tell him nothing. It will be sufficient if you simply say to him that you don't love him.

LUCY. Don't love him! How could he look at me and believe the words?

MISS GOODWILLIE. It would be best for him, Miss White.

LUCY. Very well.

(*Enter* PROFESSOR.)

PROFESSOR. Agnes, you have not seen Miss Lucy?

MISS GOODWILLIE. Yes. (*Indicating her.*)

PROFESSOR. Miss Lucy? I see Agnes has been speaking to you about me. There is no hope for me, Agnes?

MISS GOODWILLIE. It is for her to say, Tom. Is there any hope for him, Miss White?

LUCY. No!

PROFESSOR.   You could not—perhaps—in time——

MISS GOODWILLIE.   Could you, Miss White?

LUCY.   No!

(AGNES *goes to* TOM *to console him.*)

PROFESSOR.   Not now, dear. (*To* LUCY) I—I—how could I have been so presumptuous? Forgive me, Miss Lucy.

(PROFESSOR *goes into house.*)

MISS GOODWILLIE.   You have done well. (*Rather hard still*) And now there is nothing further to keep you here.

LUCY (*looking round sadly*).   No, it's all over—— (*Pathetically*) I did not tell him I was going away.

MISS GOODWILLIE.   It is not necessary now. I will tell him and he will understand.   Good-bye.

(LUCY *hesitates.*)

LUCY.   I have hurt him so. Why shouldn't I tell him what I did and let him decide. Perhaps he—— (*She makes a movement after him and hesitates.*)

MISS GOODWILLIE (*coldly, though knowing this may ruin her plans*).   Very well, go in and tell him—but I should have thought it was best to leave him thinking well of you.

LUCY.   I will go.   You are very hard.

MISS GOODWILLIE.   Yes, I am hard.   Good-bye, Miss White. I wish you well.

(MISS GOODWILLIE *goes into house.* LUCY *meets* HENDERS, *who enters with a letter, a lantern, and a wheelbarrow.*)

LUCY.   Henders, I am going to London by to-night's mail. Will you take my box to the station?

HENDERS.   I will—I'll take it on my barrow. Are you leaving for good, Miss?

LUCY.   Yes—for good.

HENDERS.   Miss Lucy, bide a wee—here's a queer sort of a letter. I wonder if you could make head or tail of it?

LUCY.   You want me to read it?

HENDERS.   Ay.

(LUCY *sits down at gate and reads letter, puzzled.*)

LUCY.   I don't understand.   Whose letter is this?

HENDERS.   That's the query.   I found it.

LUCY.   In this envelope?

HENDERS.   No! That's a clean envelope I put it in; the real envelope was all tattered.

LUCY.   But there was an address on it ?

HENDERS.   No, the writing was faded off it.

LUCY.   I can't guess who it is for.   Have you read it ?

HENDERS.   Just the little words.

LUCY.   It begins : ' My beloved one,' and ends ' Yours till death, Bob.'

HENDERS.   Ay, ay—that sounds like swearing.

LUCY.   Listen !   (*Reads*) 'My Beloved One !   At last, at last I am able to ask you the question I had no right to ask while I was a penniless man.   But you always knew that you were all the world to me, and that I came out here to try to make a home that you could share.   It has been a long struggle, but I have conquered, and so I can ask you : will you be my wife ? '

HENDERS.   Can it be somebody after Effie ?

LUCY.   There is a good deal more, and then it ends: ' It may be that I am too late.   If so, dear Agnes, do not answer this and I will understand.   But God grant that I am in time. Yours till death, Bob.'

HENDERS.   Agnes—Bob !   (*Heavily*) It sounds to me as if it was some man, name of Bob, writing to a woman, name of Agnes.

LUCY.   ' P.S.—Address me to 41 Fourth Street, Melbourne.'

HENDERS.   That's Australia.

LUCY.   I can't make out the date.

HENDERS.   But it maun be many years old, for the letter-box hasna been used for ages.

LUCY.   What letter-box ?

HENDERS.   The Professor's old letter-box, whaur I found it.

LUCY.   You found it in——   Ah, it must be *her* letter !

HENDERS.   You ken wha it's to ?

LUCY.   I believe I do.   But how could it have lain unseen in the letter-box all these years ?

HENDERS.   The letter-box was lined wi' zinc, and the letter had slipped between the zinc and the wood.   It never would have been found but for my cleverness in breaking the box. Wha is she, Miss ?

LUCY.   I have no right to tell you.

HENDERS.   But I give you the right.

LUCY.   No, no, Henders !

HENDERS. What are you to do with it?

LUCY. I am to hand it on to its rightful owner. There shall be one woman happy to-night, at any rate. She has waited a very long time for it. No, that seems a harsh way of doing it. I'll give it to the Professor and then he can break the dear news to her.

HENDERS. To her? Is it someone he kens?

LUCY. Henders, you'll need all your time to take my box to the station.

(*Exit* HENDERS. LUCY *writes something on letter. At same time* MISS GOODWILLIE *appears in the room, lighting lamp.* LUCY *goes to side and calls '*EFFIE*' two or three times.* MISS GOODWILLIE *hears and comes to window suspiciously.* EFFIE *comes out.*)

EFFIE. It's you, Miss White?

LUCY. Give this letter to the Professor.

EFFIE (*eagerly*). A secret letter.

LUCY. It is very important.

EFFIE. Oh, Miss White, I've been guessing that you and him is fond o' one another. Is it a love-letter?

LUCY. Yes—it is—a love-letter.

(MISS GOODWILLIE *nods significantly, retires from window.*)

EFFIE. Then I'll no let her see it, for she would just tear it up.

LUCY. Tear it up! If she did that she would deprive herself of the dearest pleasure life now holds for her.

EFFIE. How could that be?

LUCY. It isn't our affair, Effie.

EFFIE (*taking letter*). A love-letter. I've often heard o' them, but this is the first I've ever seen. Love's a fine thing, Miss White.

LUCY. Yes, Effie, and I hope you will have abundance of it.

EFFIE (*sadly*). I'm doubtin' it's not for common folk like me, Miss. We have our wistful hopes, but in the end we maun just tak' what we can get.

LUCY. You mustn't talk of Henders in that way, you know.

EFFIE. I would never talk of Henders in that way, Miss White. He was the wistful hope, I was speaking of Pete. I'll give the Professor your letter.

LUCY.   Thank you, Effie.

(LUCY *goes and* EFFIE *stands gazing at letter*.)

MISS GOODWILLIE (*appearing at window*).   Effie, give me that letter.

EFFIE (*concealing it*).   What letter, ma'am?

MISS GOODWILLIE.   Miss White's letter to the Professor.

EFFIE.   But it's a—it's a——

MISS GOODWILLIE.   A love-letter.   Yes, I heard her.   Give it me at once.

(EFFIE *hands up letter and re-enters house.* MISS GOOD-WILLIE *is tempted to read letter, then tears it in two and is about to do so again when* PROFESSOR *enters room. He is now in his old coat, etc.*)

PROFESSOR.   What are you doing, Agnes?

MISS GOODWILLIE (*slipping letter into her pocket*).   Nothing. (*He sits at window sighing.   She watches him.*) Is it as bad as that, Tom?   (*Goes to him, hand on shoulder.*)

PROFESSOR.   Pretty bad, Agnes.

MISS GOODWILLIE.   Tom, you and I used to be all in all to each other.

PROFESSOR.   We must be so again, Agnes.

MISS GOODWILLIE.   I have always tried to make you happy.

PROFESSOR.   You have been my guardian angel all my life.

MISS GOODWILLIE.   I am so proud of you, Tom.

PROFESSOR.   In the dark days, Agnes, I should have lost heart but for you.   Three times I made an advance—and three times I had to begin the world over again.   But at last, I triumphed by the grace of God and the faith of one woman!

MISS GOODWILLIE.   Ah, Tom!

PROFESSOR.   Help me to be brave again, Agnes.

MISS GOODWILLIE.   There is your book to finish.   (*Gets his MSS.*)

PROFESSOR.   Ah, work, work, there is nothing like it. Work is the only woman for me!   The sparkling face of her, Agnes, when she opens your eyes of a morning and cries, ' Up, up, we have a glorious day's toil before us.'   I have run back to her from dinners and marriages and funerals.   How often she and I have sat up through the night on tiptoe, so as not to wake the dawn!

MISS GOODWILLIE (*getting his papers*). And I will be your amanuensis again, Tom.

PROFESSOR. For to-night. We must not ask Miss Lucy to come to-night. (*Sweetly*) Don't you think it is a very pretty name——Miss Lucy ?

(MISS GOODWILLIE *goes to tobacco jar and fills his pipe.*)

Look for page 141 B, Agnes.

MISS GOODWILLIE. There, Tom. (*Handing him pipe and lighting it.*) Just as I used to do.

PROFESSOR. Ah, Agnes !

MISS GOODWILLIE. I shall sit here.

PROFESSOR. Just as you used to do.

MISS GOODWILLIE. Did you say 141 B ?

PROFESSOR. Yes, read out, and I 'll correct **as we** go along.

MISS GOODWILLIE. ' The machine consists of two glass discs, *A* and *D*, carefully covered with a fine varnish—a fine varnish. The plate *D* is somewhat larger than the plate *A*.' Are you listening, Tom ?

PROFESSOR. I forgot for a moment. This is in—in Miss Lucy's handwriting. Her writing is very like herself, don't you think ?

MISS GOODWILLIE. ' The plate *D* is stationary and is kept in its place by four circular grooved rings of vulcanite placed in horizontal——' Tom, do you feel as if you couldn't live without her ?

PROFESSOR. Who am I, Agnes, that I should ask so much of God ? I must not be a selfish man. Agnes, do you remember James Spens who used to be my great friend when we were boys ?

MISS GOODWILLIE. Of course. He is a smith now. His smithy is only a few miles from here.

PROFESSOR. I passed it to-day. I had a talk with him about auld lang syne.

MISS GOODWILLIE. He is tremendously proud of your success, Tom.

PROFESSOR (*simply*). Is he ? Yes, I think he said that. I saw his wife, also, and a pair of such splendid children. I knew which of us two had been a success, Agnes.

MISS GOODWILLIE (*moved, but going on*). 'Horizontal glass rods which—which——'

  (PROFESSOR'S *head sinks on table. She is affected but tries to go on.*)

'are connected by——' (*She gives way, rises, produces letter, looks sadly at it, hands it to him.*) Tom! I haven't been fair to you.

PROFESSOR. What is this? (*Eagerly*) From Lucy?

MISS GOODWILLIE. Yes.

  (*Her back is now towards him. He reads letter to himself, and you see from his face how it affects him.*)

MISS GOODWILLIE (*still with back to him*). Is it—a dear letter, Tom?

PROFESSOR. It is, indeed.

MISS GOODWILLIE. I'll try to be glad.

PROFESSOR. Agnes, do you know what is in this letter?

MISS GOODWILLIE. I can guess.

PROFESSOR. You could never guess, dear sister. Look, do you see what Miss Lucy has written on it: 'Found in the old letter-box between the lining and the wood-work.'

  (*He hands it to her and she reads.*)

MISS GOODWILLIE. Tom, do you think—it can be——?

PROFESSOR. It is Bob Sandeman's letter at last!

MISS GOODWILLIE. Henders must have found it. (*She reads.*) Tom, he was true to me!

PROFESSOR. To think of it lying in that box all these years, and now Bob is dead.

MISS GOODWILLIE. But he was true to me!

PROFESSOR. And does that make such a difference, Agnes?

MISS GOODWILLIE. Difference! Oh, Tom!

PROFESSOR. Dear sister!

  (*They embrace.*)

If only Bob's letter hadn't come too late.

MISS GOODWILLIE. Too late for me, Tom, but not too late for you.

PROFESSOR. How can it affect me? (*Softly*) Agnes, you thought it was from Miss Lucy to me.

MISS GOODWILLIE. She knew it was my letter and she let me have it. How good of her.

PROFESSOR. Of course she did, Agnes. She is as fond of you as you are of her.

MISS GOODWILLIE. Courage, Tom, I am going to see her now.

PROFESSOR. But what difference can it make to me, Agnes ?

MISS GOODWILLIE. You shall see, you shall see. Oh, Tom, I nearly tore it up. (*Exit into house.*)

PROFESSOR. But why ?

(PROFESSOR *shakes head hopelessly.* HENDERS *comes, wheeling barrow containing luggage. He whistles cautiously for* EFFIE. PROFESSOR *looks out of window and sees him.*)

Whose luggage is that, Henders ?

HENDERS. Miss White's.

PROFESSOR. What ! Where are you taking it ?

HENDERS. To the station.

PROFESSOR. Miss White is going away ?

HENDERS. Did you no ken ?

PROFESSOR. Wait a moment. I am coming out.

(*As he goes* EFFIE *comes out.*)

HENDERS. Effie, the Professor didna ken Miss Lucy was going away.

EFFIE. Going away ? I didna ken myself.

HENDERS. What can be her meaning ? Dagont ! Men are reasonable beings, but women——

EFFIE. What are women ?

HENDERS. Well, the most I can say for them is that they are beings capable of reason.

(PROFESSOR *comes out.*)

PROFESSOR. Where is Miss White going ?

HENDERS. To London, she said.

PROFESSOR. Impossible !

HENDERS. You can ask hersel', for she 's coming ahint me.

PROFESSOR. Ha ! (*Exit.*)

EFFIE. I 'll tell you a pretty thing. He 's in love wi' her.

HENDERS. As I am wi' you.

EFFIE. Away wi' you. I 'm Pete's property.

HENDERS. But you would rather be mine.

EFFIE. That may be.

HENDERS. It must be ! It 's human natur'. There are some men born wi' a power over women that no lassie can resist. They are what may be called dead shots. Now, Effie, I am far frae vain, but you canna deny that I am one o' these men !

EFFIE. I canna deny it.

HENDERS. Exactly ! But when the like o' me wants a thing, he has to get it. Now you are the thing I want.

EFFIE. I like the sound of you fine, but I 'm promised to Pete.

HENDERS. I have been working on Pete, and, as you ken, he wants to cry off.

EFFIE. You 've been slow in coming to me.

HENDERS. Just because I want to make Pete pay for his impudence. And pay in cash—I 'm a practical man.

EFFIE. Henders, if you and me—it would be fine !

HENDERS. And it 's to be. You 're my darlin', Effie, what am I to you ?

EFFIE. Nothing so long as I 'm promised to Pete. Here 's the Professor coming with Miss Lucy.

HENDERS. Quick, give me a kiss.

EFFIE. Na, I 'm Pete's as yet. You have no rights.

HENDERS. I 'll have the rights before the nine o'clock bell rings, but I would like to kiss you once without the rights.

EFFIE. Ay, weel, I 'll be true to Pete till nine o'clock. (*Softly*) But I 'll keep what you 're wanting ready for you, Henders.

> (EFFIE *goes into house. As* HENDERS *goes,* PROFESSOR *and* LUCY *enter.*)

PROFESSOR. Of course, if you are determined to leave us—we must let you go, Miss Lucy.

LUCY. It is better so.

PROFESSOR. I have driven you away.

LUCY. No—I—I want to go.

PROFESSOR. If I had only kept my presumption to myself.

LUCY. You are everything that is good and noble.

PROFESSOR. Good and noble ! If you only knew what I think of myself.

LUCY. I know so well. You think you are quite old, don't you ? and entirely without personal attraction ?

PROFESSOR. Of course I know I am getting old—and I was always very plain. It doesn't matter now, but it used to depress me when I suddenly saw my face in a looking-glass. I would have had quite a different youth if there had been no looking-glasses.

LUCY. And you are very dull, aren't you?

PROFESSOR. I have been a dull man all my life. My students laugh at my absent-mindedness. Children in the street mimic my ungainly ways. Pity when children don't like you. Pity! Can't be helped!

LUCY. You are quite sure that in the eyes of my discerning sex you could never compete with pretty young gentlemen in tall, stiff collars?

PROFESSOR (sadly). I can't wear tall collars, Miss Lucy, can't wear them. (Anxiously) If you think you could like me better in a tall collar——

LUCY. No, indeed, I wouldn't.

PROFESSOR. Missed his chance, missed his chance. I never knew what to say to any woman but you, Lucy. I liked to see them if they were pretty and they didn't know that I knew whether they were pretty or not, but I always knew. Miss Lucy, you won't believe it, but I once had a smile—quite a nice smile.

LUCY. A smile!

PROFESSOR. It was when I was at school. It was a mixed school, girls as well as boys, you know. And the girls had a plebiscite about which boy had the sweetest smile—and I won! Queer! Made me self-conscious, and I have never smiled since.

LUCY. You would win for the sweetest smile to-day.

PROFESSOR. Kind, Miss Lucy, but no good. Curmudgeon now.

LUCY. Don't.

PROFESSOR. I had nothing to offer you worth having. Only this bent form for your youthful one, only this crabbed face for yours so beautiful; such a face without guile you have, Miss Lucy.

(She quivers.)

It was no bargain for an honourable man.

LUCY. Without guile. Ah, if only—— (She turns away.)

PROFESSOR. I see everything clearly now, why I was so light-hearted in the field to-day, why I jumped those corn-stooks. It was my youth come to me at last. I had no youth at the age when I should have had it. I passed it by in my eagerness for science; I was engrossed in science when I should have been jumping the stooks. The things we have missed come not back to man nor woman. Very sad. Now I see that every man must love once, for it is his birthright, but if we do not seize it at the right age, we can only love, we cannot make others love us——we have forgotten the way.

LUCY. You hurt my heart.

PROFESSOR. I must not do that. I have been presumptuous, but I am not going to whine because I cannot pluck the stars. And when the great glory that I have missed comes into your life there is no one who will rejoice more heartily than the old Professor. It has not come yet?

(*She can't answer.*)

Ah! I believe it has! Has it, Miss Lucy?

LUCY. Yes.

PROFESSOR. And he loves you? How could he help it.

LUCY. He loves me because he does not know me as I am.

PROFESSOR. Because he does know, you mean. Am I not to be told his name?

LUCY. No!

PROFESSOR. Ah, but I can picture him, and he is not ungainly and absent-minded, and he does not wear a faded velvet coat. Miss Lucy, do not weep for me; see how glad your news has made me, and when the wedding-bells are ringing I shall be there to give you away, and with a face so happy in your happiness that I——that I——

LUCY. Good-bye.

PROFESSOR (*taking her hand*). You see, I am not—not breaking down. Good-bye, Miss Lucy! Miss Lucy!

(*He tries to smile.* LUCY *goes. He waves to her, then sits on seat sadly.* MISS GOODWILLIE *comes out, wearing bonnet.*)

MISS GOODWILLIE. I thought you were in the house, Tom.

PROFESSOR. You are not going to see Miss Lucy, Agnes?

MISS GOODWILLIE. Yes, I am.

PROFESSOR.   Then you are going the wrong way.
(*She turns.*)
She is leaving us, Agnes.

MISS GOODWILLIE.   No, she is not.

PROFESSOR.   She has gone.

MISS GOODWILLIE.   Passed !

PROFESSOR.   She is going to London.
(COSENS *enters room.*)

MISS GOODWILLIE (*looking at watch*).   I have just time.

PROFESSOR.   You are going to the station to say good-bye to her ?

MISS GOODWILLIE.   I am going—to the station.

COSENS (*appearing at window*).   Are you coming in, Tom ?

PROFESSOR.   Yes. (*Enters house.*)

MISS GOODWILLIE.   Doctor Cosens, tell him what I have been telling you—about my treatment of Lucy.

COSENS.   Good ! (*Closes window and pulls down blind and moves lamp.*)
(HENDERS *comes on, wheeling empty barrow.*)

MISS GOODWILLIE.   You have been to the station with Miss White's luggage ?

HENDERS.   Ay !

MISS GOODWILLIE.   Then go to the station again and bring it back.
(*She goes.   Enter* PETE.)

HENDERS.   Did you hear that, Pete—first take the luggage to the station.   Second, bring it back.   Dagont, women is a mysterious sex.   They are the most mysterious sex I ken.

PETE.   They 're terrible dangerous.   They have no pity.

HENDERS.   There 's one has had pity on you.   It 's queer to think you 'll soon be Pete Maclean, the married man.

PETE.   Woe is me, Henders.
(PETE *offers his snuff-mill.*)

HENDERS.   Have you been singing love songs to Effie at her window, Pete ?

PETE.   Far frae it.

HENDERS.   You are looking the very picture of a proud and happy lover.

PETE.   I dinna feel like that.   Henders, I have come to offer her my eight-day clock to let me off.

HENDERS. Marriage scares you?

PETE. The thought o't puts me in a sweat o' terror.

HENDERS. And no wonder. But she 'll no let you off, Pete—unless.

PETE. Unless? If you could see any way out?

HENDERS. Unless you can get another man to take your place.

PETE. Oh, Henders, if *you* would only—will you, Henders?

HENDERS. Me tak' her?

PETE. Henders, I always thought she was made for you.

HENDERS. Did you now?

PETE. She 's a noble critter, Henders—what a neat waist she has. There 's scarcely her equal at baking or washing, and she 's a wonder wi' her needles. To have a canty bit stocky o' a wifey at your own fireside, man—to see her smiling at the door—to hear her singing about the hoose! Take her, Henders! Take her, man!

HENDERS. Pete, rather than see you suffer, I am willing to make this sacrifice.

PETE. Henders! I 'll be your best man!

HENDERS. But, of course, this arrangement will cost you something.

PETE. My eight-day clock for a marriage present.

HENDERS. Ay, to Effie. But what will your marriage present to me be?

PETE. To you?

HENDERS. That butter dish o' yours is a bonny thing—I 'll take the butter dish. Also your picture o' Bobby Burns sitting on a tree playing the concertina, also six knives and forks, also a spade, also three sackfuls o' potatoes.

PETE. Onything else?

HENDERS. Ay, that new china spittoon o' yours takes my fancy. Now, as a single man, you have no need for a spittoon, so I 'll take it.

PETE. I 'll rather marry her mysel'.

HENDERS. Very well, good night to you, Pete. (*Murmurs*) Pete Maclean, the married man.

PETE. Henders!

HENDERS. What!

PETE. I—I—oh, Henders man, you can have them.

HENDERS.   That's richt.   It's a bargain, then?

PETE.   It's a bargain.

(*They snuff*, HENDERS *giving his snuff-box this time.*)

HENDERS.   Good nicht to ye, Pete.

PETE.   Good nicht to you, Henders.

(*Exit* HENDERS.   PETE *looks after him, then calls to* EFFIE, *who comes out.*)

PETE.   Effie !

EFFIE.   Quick, Pete, tell me, am I yours or his?

PETE.   His.

(EFFIE'S *face beams*.   HENDERS *is heard whistling.*)

Listen to the boldness of him !

(EFFIE *is going.*)

Whaur are you going, Effie ?

EFFIE.   I have just time to give Henders something before the nine o'clock bell rings ;   (*Meaning the kiss*) something that he would rather have than all the eight-day clocks in the county.

PETE.   What can that be ?

EFFIE.   You'll never know—you poor, spiritless critter. (*She goes.*)

PETE (*bewildered and rather fond of her*).   Have I made an awful mistake ?   Effie, Effie woman !

(*The nine o'clock bell begins to strike in distance.   He goes heavily.   When the bell has ceased*, MISS GOODWILLIE *and* LUCY *enter.*)

LUCY (*looking at cottage*).   I never expected to see it again. Miss Goodwillie, if you had not told me I could not have believed that he would forgive me for deceiving him so shamelessly in the field.

MISS GOODWILLIE.   Lucy, I have a confession to make to you. He does not know of that.

LUCY.   Oh !   You said you had told him !

MISS GOODWILLIE.   It was my only way to get you back.

LUCY.   You have deceived me !

MISS GOODWILLIE.   He is so unhappy, Lucy, and my letter is a voice from the dead, telling me not to part true lovers.   Lucy dear, it rests with you to say that Bob's last letter to me was not written in vain.   Go inside to him.

LUCY.   If I do, I must tell him all.

MISS GOODWILLIE.   It's not necessary.

LUCY. It is necessary for me. I could never look him in the face again, if I didn't first tell him all.

MISS GOODWILLIE. Then tell him ' all,' and be thankful it is so little you have to tell him.

LUCY. Little !

MISS GOODWILLIE. You have only brought him to his senses by a naughty trick. The Humane Society should give you a medal.

LUCY. ' I would never overlook guile in a woman,' those were his words.

MISS GOODWILLIE. It is your part to make him eat them.

LUCY. You said yourself, he would never forgive me.

MISS GOODWILLIE. Pooh ! I was just taking advantage of your being an emotional goose. You are a sensible woman in other matters, but a goose is what you have been about this. You wouldn't be half-way to London before you saw that all you have done is the merest trifle.

LUCY. He will be so—amazed.

MISS GOODWILLIE. He will, indeed ! And then how he will chuckle ! If he is the good fellow I think him.

LUCY. No, no !

MISS GOODWILLIE. And then he will shout for me to come and hear what a clever Miss Lucy it is ! Go !

LUCY. I 'm so frightened. You don't think it would be better if I just went and drowned myself !

MISS GOODWILLIE. Here is something for luck. (*Kisses her.*) He thinks Lucy White is the loveliest name in the world. Tell him you are getting tired of it.

> (*Enter* LUCY *into house.* MISS GOODWILLIE *produces her torn letter to read. She hears voices, glances at window, full of curiosity. Enter* SIR GEORGE, LADY GILDING, *and* DOWAGER.)

DOWAGER. Miss Goodwillie, let us congratulate you.

LADY GILDING. On your merciful escape from the woman White.

MISS GOODWILLIE. Thank you. Won't you sit down ? It is so pleasant out of doors.

> (*They sit. She stands, with glances at window.*)

SIR GEORGE. We met the man, Henders, a quarter of an hour ago wheeling her luggage to the station.

LADY GILDING.   And we climbed the little hill and watched her train go off.

MISS GOODWILLIE.   Oh, indeed !

SIR GEORGE.   Is the Professor at home ?

MISS GOODWILLIE (*who is taking eager peeps at window*). Yes.   But he is——very busy just now.

LADY GILDING.   He has reached an important point in his labours, has he not ?

MISS GOODWILLIE.   A very important point.

DOWAGER.   And how is he getting on ?

MISS GOODWILLIE.   I 'm not sure ; I wish I knew.

(COSENS *comes to gate.*)

COSENS.   Good evening, all.

SIR GEORGE.   Perhaps the Doctor can tell us.

LADY GILDING.   We are asking, Doctor, how the Professor is getting on ?

COSENS.   He sent me out this moment to tell Miss Goodwillie that he is getting on famously.

MISS GOODWILLIE.   You really mean that, Doctor ?

COSENS.   I mean it.

MISS GOODWILLIE.   Then it is all right.

DOWAGER.   I am so glad.

SIR GEORGE.   We have been congratulating Miss Goodwillie on sending Miss White back to London.

COSENS.   Ah ! (*Looks at* MISS GOODWILLIE.)

(*The figures of* PROFESSOR *and* LUCY *are seen in shadow on blind.* COSENS, *from where he is standing, sees them.* MISS GOODWILLIE *sees also.   The others, being seated beneath window, do not see.*)

LADY GILDING.   I hope he is not missing her.

COSENS.   Not in the least.

(PROFESSOR *is seen, in shadow, putting fingers through* LUCY's *hair.*)

DOWAGER.   She is in her right place, at last !

(LUCY *is seen with head on* PROFESSOR's *chest.*)

COSENS.   She is !

MISS GOODWILLIE.   She is.   And now I have something to tell you all.   I want Tom to marry.

DOWAGER.   Mildred !

LADY GILDING.   Mamma !

MISS GOODWILLIE. What is more, the woman I should like to see him married to, is—very near him at this moment.

DOWAGER. George!

MISS GOODWILLIE. I believe she loves him.

DOWAGER. She does! Oh! You make me so happy.

(COSENS, *who is leaning over the gate, chuckles.*) Dear Miss Goodwillie, come and sit beside me.

MISS GOODWILLIE. With pleasure.

(PROFESSOR'S *hand is seen opening window a little.*)

LADY GILDING. What was that?

MISS GOODWILLIE. It must be Tom opening his window.

DOWAGER. That is where he works, isn't it? The last time I was in that room he gave me an electric shock.

COSENS. You don't need to be in the room for that. He could give you an electric shock, though you were sitting here and he upstairs.

LADY GILDING. How clever!

DOWAGER. I wish he would.

PROFESSOR. Dearest!

(DOWAGER *rises.*)

MISS GOODWILLIE (*as if she had heard nothing*). What is it?

DOWAGER. I thought—I must have been mistaken.

SIR GEORGE. Miss Goodwillie, the match to which you refer will give me complete satisfaction.

LADY GILDING. It has our warm approval.

MISS GOODWILLIE. Thank you.

PROFESSOR. Darling!

SIR GEORGE. Do you hear anything?

DOWAGER. Not just now—but a moment ago——

LADY GILDING. I heard nothing.

MISS GOODWILLIE. Nor I.

SIR GEORGE. Strange.

LADY GILDING. I am sure she will make him a good wife, Miss Goodwillie.

MISS GOODWILLIE. I am certain of it.

DOWAGER. How kind you are, dear.

MISS GOODWILLIE. I only say what I think, Lady Gilding.

DOWAGER. Call me 'Emily.'

MISS GOODWILLIE. Certainly, if you wish it, Emily.

PROFESSOR.   For I know now that the greatest glory in a man's life is to have his arms round the girl he loves——
    (LUCY *is seen in shadow whispering to him.*)
SIR GEORGE.   Mildred !
    (SIR GEORGE, DOWAGER, *and* LADY GILDING *stare at each other.* COSENS *and* MISS GOODWILLIE *pretend to have heard nothing.*)
MISS GOODWILLIE.   I suppose you will have all your harvest in by the end of the week, Sir George ?
SIR GEORGE.   Eh—ah—oh !   Yes !   Mildred, did you ?
LADY GILDING.   Distinctly.
DOWAGER.   So did I.
MISS GOODWILLIE.   What is it ?
SIR GEORGE.   Nothing !
COSENS.   It will be a pity if the weather breaks down.
PROFESSOR.   Say it again.
LUCY.   I love you.   You are sure you forgive me ?
PROFESSOR.   Quite !
DOWAGER and LADY GILDING.   White !
PROFESSOR.   Did you hear an echo just now ?
COSENS.   The corn becomes so draggled in wet weather, but I believe the glass says ' set fair.'
PROFESSOR.   Forgive your pretending to faint ?   Of course I do !   It showed that you loved me so much that you couldn't wait till I discovered for myself that I loved you.   Ha, ha, ha !
SIR GEORGE.   Fudge !
MISS GOODWILLIE.   What ?
LUCY.   It was the Dowager who gave me the idea.
LADY GILDING.   Mamma !
LUCY.   And so we may say that we owe our happiness to the Dowager.
PROFESSOR.   We must thank her, dear.
SIR GEORGE.   Oh, Emily.
PROFESSOR.   If the Dowager had not written me that letter, you would not be in my arms now, Lucy.
DOWAGER.   I feel sick.
LADY GILDING.   Let us go home, George !   Good evening !
MISS GOODWILLIE.   Going already ?
PROFESSOR.   There is one thing in her letter that I could not make out ?

DOWAGER (*alarmed*). Come away.

PROFESSOR. It is this—after her signature, there are three crosses. What can they mean ?

LUCY. Three crosses ! Oh !

LADY GILDING. Mamma !

(SIR GEORGE *and* LADY GILDING *go.*)

MISS GOODWILLIE. Any message to Lucy—Emily ?

DOWAGER (*after seeing the humour of it and bursting into laughter*). Tell her, with my love, that I should like to slap her. (*Exit.*)

(COSENS *laughs.* MISS GOODWILLIE *goes to seat and sits.*)

COSENS. And the beauty of it is that those two upstairs have not an idea that they have put a whole family to flight ! Hullo, Tom !

(*Enter* PROFESSOR *and* LUCY.)

PROFESSOR (*in garden*). Doctor, this is my wife.

(LUCY *whispers to him.*)

Ah—ah—not yet.

COSENS. I congratulate you both heartily.

LUCY. But how about his illness, Doctor ? Hadn't you better prescribe something for him ? Quinine, for instance ?

MISS GOODWILLIE. She had you there.

COSENS. She always has me.

(PROFESSOR *and* LUCY *come out of gate.*)

Where are you going, Tom ?

PROFESSOR. We think—I thought—I thought—that is——

LUCY. He means—I mean—we—we mean——

MISS GOODWILLIE. They are going out for a walk.

COSENS (*slyly*). Good—I 'll come with you.

PROFESSOR. But—but—we—ah——

LUCY. I—he—we thought——

COSENS. Oh, I am not tired.

PROFESSOR. Dick, I won't let you come.

MISS GOODWILLIE. Off you go.

COSENS. You must put on your frock-coat, Tom.

LUCY. I like him best in the old coat.

COSENS. Put up her parasol to keep the sun off her, Tom.

(PROFESSOR *is doing so when he remembers there is no sun.*)

MISS GOODWILLIE. Take him away, Lucy.

E

COSENS.   Hie !   Hadn't you better both come back and
have an hour at the book ?

PROFESSOR.   What book ?

COSENS.   Your great book.

(PROFESSOR *snaps his fingers.* COSENS *laughs.* LUCY
and PROFESSOR *go off.* EFFIE *and* HENDERS *pass in
solemn ecstasy, he with his arm round her waist. They
don't see* COSENS *and* MISS GOODWILLIE *who have gone
in at gate.* COSENS *looks up to trees and whistles like a
bird to its mate. An unseen bird replies.* COSENS *and*
MISS GOODWILLIE *smile to each other, but the bird goes
on.)*

THE LITTLE MINISTER

Produced at the Haymarket Theatre on November 6, 1897, with the following cast :

EARL OF RINTOUL . . .	*W. G. Elliot*
REV. GAVIN DISHART . . .	*Cyril Maude*
CAPTAIN HALLIWELL . . .	*C. M. Hallard*
THOMAS WHAMOND . . .	*Brandon Thomas*
SNECKY HOBART	*Mark Kinghorne*
SILVA TOSH	*F. H. Tyler*
ANDREW MEALMAKER . . .	*E. Holman Clark*
ROB DOW	*Sydney Valentine*
MICHA DOW	*Sydney Fairbrother*
JOE CRUICKSHANKS . . .	*Eardley Turner*
SERGEANT DAVIDSON . . .	*Clarence Blakiston*
THWAITES	*H. H. Welch*
NANNY WEBSTER	*Mrs. E. H. Brooke*
FELICE	*Nina Cadiz*
JEAN	*Mary Mackenzie*
LADY BABBIE	*Winifred Emery*

———

The play ran for 320 performances. Revivals : Duke of York's, September 3, 1914 (131 performances) ; Queen's, November 7, 1923 (133 performances).

ACT I

SCENE: Caddam Wood on a moonlight evening in May. Time: about 1830. A wood fire is burning on the ground. At the fire sits Tammas Whamond and Snecky Hobart asleep. Bob Dow patrols, carrying a pike, on rocks. They wear corduroy and weavers' night-caps, etc. At back is seen the further part of the town of Thrums. The wood rises at back to suggest that the nearer part of the town lies in hollow below. All the lights of the town are out except in five windows. As Dow patrols he shivers with cold. Joe Cruickshanks, another weaver, descends tree. When near the ground he jumps. Dow, startled, runs at him with raised pike.

DOW. Wha is that?

CRUICKSHANKS (*drawing back*). Lay down your pike. It's only me.

DOW. As sure as death, Joe Cruickshanks, I thought it was the red-coats. (*Grounds pike.*) Is all quiet?

CRUICKSHANKS (*going to fire*). The whole countryside lies as still as salt. And not a red-coat to be seen for miles around. Rob, if I had been a red-coat, what would you have done?

DOW (*fiercely*). Brained you!

CRUICKSHANKS. My certie, Rob Dow, for a religious man, you 're a fierce character.

DOW (*threateningly*). Do you say I 'm no a *religious man*?
(CRUICKSHANKS *draws back in fear, then moves a step.* DOW's *expression changes.*)
Genesis, Exodus, Leviticus, Numbers, Deuteronomy, Joshua, Judges, Ruth——

CRUICKSHANKS (*following him, puzzled*). What 's that?

DOW (*turning slowly to* CRUICKSHANKS). I promised him if I was in a fury to repeat these names and then he said my passion would have passed away. (*Humbly*) Joe, I 'm ashamed o' mysel'. (*Gazes at town.*)

133

CRUICKSHANKS (*looking after him, amazed at his sincerity*). This beats cock-fighting.

(*The unseen town clock begins to strike ten.*)

(*At third strike*) Ten o'clock, my watching is ended. (*Heaps sticks on fire.*)

(*While the clock strikes,* SERGEANT DAVIDSON *and another Soldier enter stealthily on rocks. At sight of watchers,* DAVIDSON *signs to Soldier to retire. Soldier and* DAVIDSON *retire. Clock stops.*)

CRUICKSHANKS. Wake up, Snecky—Tammas, wake up ! (*Shaking them.*)

WHAMOND (*a very stern tall man*). Is all quiet ?

CRUICKSHANKS. All 's quiet. We need have no fear o' the red-coats coming *this* night.

WHAMOND. Whaur is Rob Dow ?

CRUICKSHANKS. There he stands, watching the lights o' the town go out. Rob Dow, the bonny swearer that was, and now not so much as one lonely damn on him !

WHAMOND (*sternly*). Joe Cruickshanks, swear not at all.

DOW (*who had taken his cap off while clock was striking and has it now in his hand*). I wasna watching the lights o' the toon go out ; I was watching one light that winna go out for hours.

WHAMOND (*seated at fire and not looking round*). Ay, the red light—that 's Mr. Dishart's window. There he sits studying far into the night—a beacon, yes, a shining light to us all.

SNECKY (*who is an echo of* WHAMOND). A beacon, ay, it 's well said.

CRUICKSHANKS. It fair amazes me ! The Little Minister— that insignificant man—hasna been in Thrums a month—and yet see what he has made o' Rob Dow—roaring, drunken, cussin' Rob Dow ! How did he manage it, Rob ?

DOW. I 'll tell you. It was the very first day he preached here. I was in the kirk making sport of him, when all at once he flung out his arm at me like this, and says he sternly, ' Come forward.' And when I wouldna budge, the little critter loupit out o' the pulpit and grippit me by the neck : ' Thou hulking man of sin,' he roared, as if it were the Day of Judgment, ' sit down on the stair and listen to me or I 'll run you out of the house of God !' Then he shook me like a rat ! *It was grand.*

WHAMOND.   And ever since that day Rob Dow has been as one born again.

SNECKY.   He has—oh ay.   Drink is a terrible snare, except maybe on solemn occasions.

WHAMOND.   I say unto you, drink not at all.   But if I did touch this thing, it would need a mighty skite of drink to move me, something far beyond the possibilities of the likes of you.

SNECKY.   Oh yes, it would, oh yes.

DOW.   But I have a hard tussle wi' mysel' yet, when the craving for drink is on me.   ' Send your laddie, send little Micah for me at any hour of the day or night,' he said, ' and I 'll come to you straight and sit wi' you the long night through '—and by God, he has kept his word.   So now you see what that red light is to me.

WHAMOND.   And to all of us.   For it means that no temptation that is of the earth earthly, will draw Gavin Dishart from his heavenly studies.

(*Red light suddenly goes out.*)

CRUICKSHANKS.   The light 's out !

(*All are taken aback.*)

SNECKY (*rising*).   Losh, Tammas, what think you does this mean ?

WHAMOND (*pulling* SNECKY *down again*).   It only means that he has been called away on some errand of mercy.

CRUICKSHANKS (*coming down from rocks*).   Dinna be so sure ; what would you say if it meant he had gone out to meet the temptation that is of the earth earthly ?   Does that mean a woman, Tammas ?

WHAMOND.   Peace, thou blasphemer !

DOW (*looking at his pike, considering whether he shall strike* CRUICKSHANKS *with it or not, then flinging it down he comes down to* CRUICKSHANKS *and takes him by the throat*).   You leering mole-catcher——   (*Hurling him to ground and threatening.*)

CRUICKSHANKS (*dragging himself away, warningly*).   Genesis, Exodus, Joshua——

DOW.   Eh ?   (*Succumbs.*)

WHAMOND.   I say to thee also, Rob Dow, peace—make not an idol of any man.

DOW (*going towards* WHAMOND).   You mak' an idol o' him yoursel'.

WHAMOND (*to* SNECKY, *ashamed*). It 's true !

SNECKY (*ashamed*). *I* canna help it.

CRUICKSHANKS. Ay, ay, lads, you have a terrible faith in him, but it doesna keep you frae deceiving him——

OMNES. Eh ?

CRUICKSHANKS. Yes, deceiving him, every one o' you.

   (*All are angry.*)

OMNES. Eh ?

CRUICKSHANKS. What would he say, think you, if he was to find out that night after night when his window is a beacon —(*Mimicking* WHAMOND)—yea, a shining light to you all, you are up here, *breaking the law* ?

   (*All are shamefaced.*)

WHAMOND. Man's law !

DOW and SNECKY. Ay, man's law !

   (DOW *sits by fire.*)

CRUICKSHANKS. Ay, and ready to break men's heads. This is a simple-looking horn, but what would he say if he kent that three blasts on it is to be the signal to the town that the red-coats are coming ? Some night when all is as still as the grave he 'll hear this horn blow three times, and then he 'll see that sleeping town waken into life and his holy congregation gathering to defy *the sojers of the King*.

OMNES. Ay, to defy them !

CRUICKSHANKS. What will he say to that—you religious critturs ?

   (*By this time all the lights in the town are out.*)

DOW (*starting up*). Whisht ! (*Moves on to rocks.*)

WHAMOND. Did you hear anything ?

   (WHAMOND *and* SNECKY *rise.*)

CRUICKSHANKS. Quick ! Quick !

   (*All seize weapons.* MICAH DOW, *a boy, runs on excitedly up rocks.*)

MICAH (*running to* DOW). Father !

DOW. Is it the red-coats ? Joe, the horn !

   (CRUICKSHANKS *picks up horn and is about to blow.*)

MICAH. No, it 's Mr. Dishart.

WHAMOND. The Minister !

MICAH. Now you 'll catch it, Tammas.

WHAMOND (*picks up his pike and helps with fire*).   Down wi'
the horn !

(CRUICKSHANKS *throws horn down again.*)

Hide your pikes !

(MICAH *climbs tree.* CRUICKSHANKS *hides horn in
mound of leaves, crosses to fire, helps to trample it out,
then gets up on rocks.* WHAMOND *takes pike.* SNECKY
does likewise. DOW *assists with putting out of fire.*)

SNECKY.   If he prays, we 're done for.

(*Enter* GAVIN *sternly.*)

GAVIN (*on rocks*).   Tammas Whamond, all of you—what do
you here at this hour ?

WHAMOND (*slyly*).   We just dandered up, Mr. Dishart, to
have a look at—at——   (*To* SNECKY) What is it strangers
come up here to gape at ?

SNECKY.   The view.

WHAMOND.   Ay, at the view.   We saw your light go out,
sir.   Have you come here to look at—at——

GAVIN.   No, I have not come here to look at the view.   My light
went out when the news reached me that members of my congregation were in this wood—armed—and for an illegal purpose.

SNECKY (*slyly*).   Keep 's a' !   I wonder if it can be Jeems
Mealmaker and Ekky Curr ?   You mind we saw them in the
wood, Rob ?

DOW.   Ay, we did !

GAVIN (*reproachfully*).   Even you, Rob Dow—even Dow !

(DOW *is in anguish.*)

(*Speaks sternly*) Liars all !   Stand forward !

(WHAMOND, SNECKY, *and* DOW *do so sullenly but obedient.*)

Now, the truth !

WHAMOND (*moving forward a step*).   This, then, is the
truth.   You must have heard o' the riot that took place afore
you came to Thrums.   The manufacturers suddenly lowered
the price o' the web, and what did that mean to a town o'
weavers ?   It meant starvation.

GAVIN (*sadly*).   I know.   I have had sad proof of it.

WHAMOND.   Was it likely we were to sit dumb under it ?
We rose against them——

DOW (*exulting*).   We made a bonfire o' their doors and
windows !   (*Sees* GAVIN *looking at him and becomes abject.*)

WHAMOND.   The constables frae Glamis came crawling
into the town.   Lord Rintoul was wi' them.   You ken wha I
mean ?

GAVIN.   I know he has a great house a few miles from here.
That is all I know.   Is he Scotch ?

WHAMOND.   No, he just English.   The man is hardly ever
here.   His hame is in England, but happening to be here the
now, he maun mix himsel' up in our affairs, and he cam' into
the town to read the Riot Act because he is our Baron Bailie ;
but he had got no farther than ' George, by the grace of God,
King of England,' when a clod of earth drove the Riot Act
down his throat.   You 're a good shot, Rob !

(DOW *is chuckling when he again sees* GAVIN *looking at
him.*)
As for what happened after that we 'd better no tell.

MICAH.   I 'll tell !   (*Sees* DOW *signing to him.*)   No, I
winna.

WHAMOND.   I will.   They had brought a cart wi' them to
carry the ring-leaders back to Glamis tied hand and foot.   But
we filled it wi' constables tied hand and foot instead, and we
carted them back to within a mile of Glamis whaur we tumbled
them into a field.

CRUICKSHANKS (*pointing to* DOW).   And there 's the religious
man that drove the cart !   (*Laughs.*)

(GAVIN *sits by fire.*)

WHAMOND (*moving over to* GAVIN).   Is it likely, Mr.
Dishart, they will let that go unpunished ?   No !   Rintoul, we
ken, is greedy for revenge.   And, what's waur, Captain Halliwell
at the Glamis Barracks is hand and glove wi' him, because he
wants to marry Rintoul's daughter—the Lady Barbara.

SNECKY.   Ay, that 's the reason !

WHAMOND.   We have sure word that when next the
constables come, Halliwell and his red-coats will come wi'
them, and that 's what we 're watching for here, night after
night.

GAVIN (*rising*).   Madmen, would you resist trained soldiers ?

OMNES.   Ay, ay !

WHAMOND.   No, no.

SNECKY.   No, no.

WHAMOND.   We would just rouse the town so that the men

wanted may slip quietly out of it. That would prevent resistance, you see—so we are really here in the cause of law and order.

SNECKY.   So we are !   (*Surprised.*)

GAVIN.   You children.   And for every one wanted now, there will be a score brought to justice presently. (*With a gesture*) Home, every one of you !

(*They are sullen.*)

Thomas Whamond, you are my chief elder—lead the way !

WHAMOND.   No !

(GAVIN *signs for him to go.* WHAMOND *hesitates a little, then gets up followed by* SNECKY.)

GAVIN.   Rob Dow, are you the man I was so proud of ?

(DOW *in passion of remorse goes up on to rocks.* GAVIN *again signs to them to go. They move a step back.*)

WHAMOND (*comes down a step—with emphasis*).   Mr. Dishart, it 's much you expect, and we do it—but dinna forget this, the more you expect of us, the more shall we expect of you.   Mind that !

(*Exit* WHAMOND *followed by* SNECKY. CRUICKSHANKS *follows, threatened by* DOW. GAVIN *sits down moodily on tree trunk.* DOW *stands by tree on rocks.*)

MICAH (*gets off tree and goes timidly*).   Are you angry wi' my father ?

GAVIN (*gently*).   No, Micah—but he must not fight, you know.

MICAH (*proudly*).   He hasna been drunk for three weeks. (*Very boastfully*) That 's a father.

GAVIN (*putting arm round him*).   Poor boy !

DOW.   You 're pitying him—no wonder.

GAVIN (*sighing*).   No, Rob, I was not pitying Micah.   I was half wishing, Micah, that I could be a boy again like you.   *I* used to play marbles.

MICAH (*amazed*).   You !

GAVIN.   There is a devil in all of us.   Only yesterday, Micah, I caught myself going up the Manse stairs two steps at a time.

MICAH.   You did !

GAVIN.   Once, Rob, when I was a boy I went fishing—on the Sabbath day !

DOW.   The trout aye bite better on the Sabbath.   It 's queer. God's critters tempting decent men.

GAVIN. I used to draw comic pictures in my school-books. I am afraid I liked to be thought funny. (*Sighing.*) But it has all gone, Rob. The cares of a congregation soon take the nonsense out of one.

(MICAH *lies down on rock.*)

I suppose it is as well.

DOW (*sorry for him*). No, it 's a shame. We 're a hard, dour set for a man of twenty-one to be put in charge o'.

GAVIN. Hard, dour, perhaps. But so needy, you are hanging on to existence by the teeth. When I see you all on the Sabbath in your poor worn blacks, that to the grand world might be an object of mirth, but that I know to be possible to you only because of your struggle to enter God's house respectably, then I—I love my congregation, Rob. The men's battered old lum hats, so hard to come by, take on a radiance to me and are about the best thing I know.

DOW. I wish I saw you married, Mr. Dishart.

GAVIN. Who would have me, Rob ?

DOW (*grandly*). There 's not a lady in the land that wouldna be proud to be Mistress Gavin Dishart. (*Fiercely*) Did any woman ever refuse you ?

(GAVIN *shakes his head.*)

I would like to see her try it !

MICAH. So would I !

GAVIN (*smiling*). I must take you both with me when I go a-wooing !

DOW. Every member of the congregation would like to go wi' you ! Ay, that 's another shame. We canna leave you to yourself, and here am I as bad as the rest. Come away, Micah. Good night, Mr. Dishart.

GAVIN. Good night, Rob.

(*Exit* DOW. MICAH, *following him a few steps, comes back.*)

MICAH (*sitting on ground by him*). Mr. Dishart, how did you play at bools ?

GAVIN. I remember we made a ring on the ground in this way (*Turns round on his heel*), and then we went down like this. (*Kneels.*) Micah, swear you 'll never tell my elders that you saw me playing marbles.

(*They play in dumb show, without marbles.*)

MICAH. I swear !

GAVIN. Well, you take the marble so, and flick it——
(*A woman is heard singing in the distance. They are so busy over their game that it goes on for some little time before they hear it.*)
What is that ? (*Rising, takes up his hat and puts it on.*)

MICAH. It 's some woman singing in the wood.

GAVIN (*sternly*). At this hour !
(ROB *calls* MICAH *in distance.*)
That is your father calling you, Micah—run !
(MICAH *runs up on rocks, looks off down cut.*)

MICAH. I see her—she 's dancing !

GAVIN. The wanton !

MICAH. She 's an Egyptian !

GAVIN. A gipsy ! Go !
(*Exit* MICAH *scared.* GAVIN *stands down awaiting the gipsy. The singing grows louder and* BABBIE *enters singing and dancing in wild joyousness. She is dressed as a gipsy with bare feet, etc. He stands, transfixed with indignation, as she enters without seeing him. He extends his arm and cries :* 'Woman !' *She stops abruptly. He cries :* 'Woman, stand forward !' *She flings him a kiss and dances off as she had come on. She turns before she disappears to beckon to him mockingly. He cries :* 'Woman !' *furiously, and exits in pursuit of her.* CRUICKSHANKS *comes stealing on and has begun to ascend tree, when* BABBIE *runs on.*)

BABBIE (*to* CRUICKSHANKS *by tree*). Are you a Thrums man ?—quick, before the Minister comes back.

CRUICKSHANKS. You—you—— (*Comes down, staring at her in amazement.*) Behears ! It 's her little leddyship !

BABBIE (*distressed*). No, no—I am a gipsy.

CRUICKSHANKS (*triumphant*). It winna do—I ken you. You 're Lord Rintoul's daughter, the Lady Barbara—and in an Egyptian's clothes ! (*Reprovingly*) Your leddyship, does your father ken o' this ?

BABBIE. How did you know me ? I was never in Thrums before.

CRUICKSHANKS. I 'm the only man here that ever saw you. I was mole-catching at Rintoul at the time.

BABBIE. Don't tell anyone !

CRUICKSHANKS (*heavily*).   It may be my solemn duty.

BABBIE.   When I have done it to save you !   To let Thrums know that the soldiers are coming to-night !

CRUICKSHANKS (*aghast*).   The night !   (*Steps back and looks off.*)

BABBIE.   I heard Captain Halliwell and my father discussing it.

CRUICKSHANKS.   You came here to warn us ?

BABBIE.   I don't quite know what it was that brought me here.   Just the fun of outwitting them—or to save the poor weavers—or merely the call of the moon.   Did the moon never tap on your window and cry, ' Come out, Mr. Mole-catcher ? '

CRUICKSHANKS.   Never !

BABBIE.   ' Come out and be mad.'   It does on mine.   So I slipped into these and came.   Stole away !   We have danced together through the woods.

CRUICKSHANKS.   Together !   There was someone wi' you ?

BABBIE.   The moon and I.   Did I tell you we were mad ?   We danced, danced, danced.   (*She dances across stage.*)

    (CRUICKSHANKS *follows her.   Four Soldiers cross at back.*)

CRUICKSHANKS (*going down to her—aghast*).   The sojers !

    (*They crouch down behind bush.   At exit of Soldiers,* BABBIE *rises.* CRUICKSHANKS *cautiously comes from behind bush.*)

BABBIE.   We can't get into the town now—they are between us and it.   This is what they are to do.   They are to surround the town quietly before the constables march into it.   How far is it from here to the nearest houses of the town ?

CRUICKSHANKS.   Not a minute.

BABBIE.   A minute !   And yet we can't reach them.   Quick, is there no way of alarming the people ?

CRUICKSHANKS.   The horn !   (*Lifts it.*)   We were to blow three blasts on this horn if we saw the red-coats.

BABBIE.   Then blow—blow !

CRUICKSHANKS.   Canny, your leddyship, canny.   If I were to blow, it might gie the town a chance, but the sojers would come back and nab *me*.   No, no, I 'm off !   (*Flings down horn.*)

BABBIE.   Where to ?

CRUICKSHANKS.   Out o' this countryside.   I 'm a single

man, and wherever there's moles to catch, that's hame to me.

BABBIE.   You would run away !

CRUICKSHANKS.   Ay, and quick.   But I 'll keep your secret —for you 've done a glorious thing this night—you 've saved Joe Cruickshanks !   (*Exits quickly.*)

BABBIE.   Coward, coward !

> (*Lifts horn and tries to blow it—calls after him : ' I can't blow it.   Coward ! '   She utters ejaculation of despair.   GAVIN's voice is heard calling 'Woman ! ')*

He will do !   (*Without looking round she sinks to the ground concealing horn, and covering her face with her hands pretends to cry.*)   Oh ! Oh ! Oh !

GAVIN (*entering*).   Woman ! Woman !   (*Crosses down to her.   He is rather breathless.*)   How dared you mock me !

BABBIE.   Oh ! Oh ! Oh !

GAVIN (*a little less sternly*).   What is your name ?

BABBIE (*as if terrified*).   Babbie.

> (*She speaks Scotch for the remainder of this scene with GAVIN, though she had spoken English to CRUICKSHANKS.*)

GAVIN.   Babbie ?   Babbie what ?

BABBIE.   Just Babbie.   I 'm no mairried yet !

GAVIN.   Take care.   Stand up.

> (*She jumps up hurriedly, affecting terror, but still with hands over face.   The horn is left at her feet.*)

Uncover your face.

BABBIE.   I daurna.   It 's so ugly.

GAVIN.   What difference, think you, does that make to a minister ?

> (BABBIE *suddenly drops her hands and pushes out her head so that her face is close to his.   Pause, in which he stares at her in admiration.*)

BABBIE (*demurely*).   I 'm glad you like it.   (*Turns away.*)

GAVIN (*recoiling*).   I never said——

BABBIE.   But what difference does that make to a minister ?

GAVIN (*sternly*).   Oh !

BABBIE (*sinks down again in distress*).   Oh ! Oh ! Oh !

> (GAVIN *looks at her in doubt as to whether her grief is genuine.   He seems to be melting when she peeps at him roguishly through her fingers.*)

GAVIN. I have sworn to drive all gipsies from these parts. This town is hot against them and with reason. Begone to your associates, and tell them that from me.

BABBIE (*weeping*). I wish I could but I 've lost them. I 've been out telling fortunes—— (*Rises and turns to him.*) Tell your fortune, pretty gentleman?

GAVIN (*stamping*). Certainly not!

BABBIE. Oh! (*Crosses to tree trunk and sits.*) He 's angry again! Oh! Oh! Oh!

GAVIN (*after pause—more gently*). Come, come, you *are* an odd girl—don't cry. Are you crying?

BABBIE (*tearfully*). When you speak to me—(*Sniff*)—so kindly—(*Smiling*)—I could near kiss you.

GAVIN (*in a low voice, after looking hurriedly about him*). What did you say?

BABBIE. I said—Oh, if I could only blow on the horn!

GAVIN. What horn?

BABBIE. This horn. (*Picking it up.*) I so often lose my way, they gave me this horn to blaw on, so that they could hear and come for me. But I canna blaw it. (*Crying.*)

GAVIN. Do you think your friends are in the wood?

BABBIE. I ken my father 's in the wood and my—my sweetheart! (*Makes face aside.*) But they little think I am here!

GAVIN. Then I shall blow it for you.

BABBIE (*doubtfully*). But could you?

GAVIN (*indignantly*). Could I! Give it me.
(*She does so, and he blows loudly on the horn. Then turns proudly to her.*)
There!

BABBIE. It was grandly done.

GAVIN. I wonder if they heard?

BABBIE (*taking a side glance at the town*). I wonder! I dinna suppose you could blaw louder. It needs a strong man to blaw a lusty blast.

GAVIN (*indignantly*). I *am* a strong man.
(*Blows a long blast and, to the concealed delight of* BABBIE, *lights appear.*)
They must have heard that.

BABBIE. Again!

GAVIN. That must suffice.

BABBIE. I see the blowing tires you.

GAVIN. Tires me !

(*He blows again. One or two other lights go in. Moving lights are seen. A drum is heard.* GAVIN *listens in surprise, but does not look round.*)

The town drum—

(*Distant shouts from town commence.*)

at this hour—very odd !

(BABBIE *taps him demurely on shoulder and points to the town where about eight lights altogether are now visible. He looks and is astounded.*)

I can't understand it. Did you hear that ? (*Looks down at the town—and is astounded.*) Crowds of people are gathering in the square. (*He comes down a step.*) What can it mean ?

BABBIE (*following him a step*). It means that the town is rising agin' the sojers.

GAVIN. Soldiers ? There are no soldiers.

(*Bugle sounds the 'Double.'*)

BABBIE. The wood is full o' them ! You hear !

(*Drum stops.*)

There's a chance for them yet. The alarm has been sounded.

GAVIN. What? After I forbade it ! (*Sternly*) Who sounded the alarm ?

BABBIE (*looking through bush*). You did.

GAVIN. I ?

BABBIE (*pointing*). On the horn !

(*Bugle and military drum starts off.* GAVIN *is paralysed with consternation. The horn drops from his hand. The town is now dimly lit. The roaring of the mob increases in volume.* GAVIN *goes threateningly after* BABBIE *as if he could throttle her.* CAPTAIN HALLIWELL *is heard giving orders.*)

HALLIWELL (*off*). Extend to the right !—open out through the whin bushes until you're in touch with the flank company.

BABBIE. Oh !

(*She flies off.* GAVIN *turns and rushes out. Drum stops. Enter eight Soldiers followed by* CAPTAIN HALLIWELL *and* LORD RINTOUL.)

LORD RINTOUL (*troubled*).   Halliwell, who blew that horn and alarmed the town ?

HALLIWELL (*self-confident*).   We shall soon know, Rintoul. Be calm, I shall get your pretty weavers.

LORD RINTOUL.   You said your men saw that minister fellow order the watchers to their homes ?

HALLIWELL.   Yes—and then I delayed the advance to give them time to get to bed.

LORD RINTOUL.   A blunder !

HALLIWELL.   It was the wish of the constables, who said that if they could get into the town unseen, they knew where to lay hands on every man they want.   So we were lying in the wood waiting quietly, when suddenly a horn sounded three times—

(*An old villager enters.*)

—and in a moment the town was in an uproar.

LORD RINTOUL.   Oh !

HALLIWELL.   Don't be flurried, we shall have some fun now.

LORD RINTOUL.   If we should fail again !

HALLIWELL (*to villager, as to a child*).   Shoo !

(*Villager bolts and* HALLIWELL *laughs.*)

Fail again !   My dear Rintoul !   *I* am with you this time, and my men are already a hoop of steel round the town.   We have your weavers so.   (*Making a hoop of his arms.*)   Just as I told Lady Barbara we should have them.   I only wish she were here, now, to see how neatly I am doing it.   It 's too easy, you know—like shooting rabbits.

(*Enter female villager over rocks.*)

Shoo !

(*Shouts from town recommence.   She rushes away. Noise of crowd.* HALLIWELL *saunters up to back and surveys town through glasses.*)

(*To* LORD RINTOUL) Aha !   Someone is addressing them from the top of an outside stair !   I believe—yes, it is that minister. Ho, ho !   He prevails upon them—they fling down their weapons.   There 's to be no fun after all !—Hallo—Oh, by Jove !—splendid !   Rintoul, a woman is addressing them from another stair.

LORD RINTOUL.   A woman !

HALLIWELL. I think—yes—she is exhorting them to fight ! Oh, bravo ! The minister shakes his fist at her—and she—oh, the little rebel—she blows him a kiss ! They turn from him to her—splendid ! I am really enjoying it now ! She is leading them—they are gone ! (*Comes down.*)

LORD RINTOUL. Gone—where ? (*Rather anxiously.*)

HALLIWELL. Into the arms of my loving soldiers, of course. (*Complacently making the circle again with his arms. Enter* MICAH, *who runs to* HALLIWELL.)

MICAH. Oh, sir, dinna tak' my father. It wasna him that drove the cart—it was me. I 'm little but I 'm terrible bad.

HALLIWELL. Who blew that horn, boy ?
(*A bugle is heard.*)

LORD RINTOUL. Quick ! Tell us.
(*Military drums off.*)

MICAH. I think it was a woman—an Egyptian.

HALLIWELL. A woman again ! (*Throws him down by fire.*) What a town of Amazons !

LORD RINTOUL. Can it be the same woman ?

HALLIWELL. I hope so. I shall introduce you to her presently. (*To* MICAH) Her name ?

MICAH. I dinna ken. Naebody in Thrums ever saw her afore.

LORD RINTOUL. Odd !

HALLIWELL. Joan of Arc, I expect.

MICAH. Mr Dishart—that 's the minister—tried to chase her out of the wood. But she had come back.

HALLIWELL. Very sociable of her.
(*Enter* NANNY *followed by a crowd of women, distracted and partially dressed. After the women are on, a child also runs in and clings to one of them. Cries of* ' This is him—This is the Captain—Here 's RINTOUL,' *etc.*)
They can't resist the red coat, Rintoul !

LORD RINTOUL. I grow uneasy.

HALLIWELL. You can't think how uneasy she is to be presently !
(*Drum and shouts stop.*)

NANNY (*on rock*). For mercy's sake, Captain, pity, have pity !

VILLAGERS. Pity, sir—have mercy, sir (*Etc.*).

HALLIWELL (*going to foot of bank*). You are all charming people, I am sure, but I can do nothing for you.

(MICAH *joins crowd.*)

VILLAGERS. Oh, sir, mercy ! (*Etc., etc.*)

(*Some run off.* MICAH *sneaks off after them.*)

NANNY. Our men folk will be killed——

VILLAGERS. Ay, ay.

NANNY. That woman 's egging them on to fight.

VILLAGERS. Ay, she 's making them fight.

HALLIWELL. What 's that ? A woman ?

NANNY. An Egyptian.

VILLAGERS. Ay, ay, an Egyptian.

NANNY. She cried to them, if they would defy the minister and follow her she would save them.

LORD RINTOUL. Who can this woman be ?

VILLAGERS. I wonder—I never saw her (*Etc.*).

HALLIWELL. What is she like ?

NANNY. She has red hair.

HALLIWELL. A red-headed gipsy !

LORD RINTOUL. There are lots of them.

HALLIWELL. What is her appearance ?

NANNY. She 's snod but no unco snod.

HALLIWELL. Eh ?

NANNY. I mean she 's a couthie tawpie but no sair in order.

HALLIWELL. What on earth is that ?

NANNY. A tasty stocky but no happit up to the nines.

HALLIWELL. Oh, help ! Can you understand that, Rintoul ?

LORD RINTOUL. It is quite simple. You, woman, was this gipsy tall or short, fat or thin ?

JEAN. She was a ga'en about hizzie an' giy an' custie.

LORD RINTOUL. Oh, was she ! Would you know her if you saw her again ?

JEAN. Brawly.

LORD RINTOUL. They would know her or not know her, brawly, Halliwell, that is something to the good. Can you describe her clothes with the same lucidity ?

JEAN. A well-faured custie, perjink, and fell orra. (Ay.)

LORD RINTOUL. My God, it 's a great country.

HALLIWELL. Whatever she is like, I promise you, Rintoul, she shall be in the local jail before the night is out.

LORD RINTOUL. Yes, jail for the hussy.

(*Enter* GAVIN *dejectedly.*)

NANNY. Mr. Dishart, this is the Captain—that 's Rintoul—plead wi' them. (*Gives way for him to come forward.*)

GAVIN (*eagerly—going to them*). Lord Rintoul——

LORD RINTOUL (*holding his hand up*). It is impossible——

(*Groans from crowd.*)

But we thank you, Mr. Dishart, for the services you have rendered us to-night, first in ordering the men who were watching here to their homes, for we saw you, and again, as we have just learned, for trying to drive away this gipsy wench. (*Shakes hands.*)

(*Exit* NANNY *with the villagers.* GAVIN *is startled.*)

HALLIWELL. At least it was not your fault that the warning horn was sounded. I thank you, sir.

(*Drum and bugle sound assembly. Enter* SERGEANT DAVIDSON.)

Well, have the constables got their prisoners, Davidson? You can speak freely before Mr. Dishart. He is our friend. (*Anxious*) Speak, man.

(*Drum stops.*)

DAVIDSON. I am afraid it is all up, Captain, for to-night.

HALLIWELL. Eh?

DAVIDSON. The men the constables are after broke our ranks and have made for the country, where it would be impossible to find them to-night.

(LORD RINTOUL *is speechless with rage* ; GAVIN *is secretly pleased.*)

HALLIWELL (*furious*). They broke through a line of fixed bayonets !

DAVIDSON. We had orders to threaten with our bayonets, but to use the butt end of our muskets only if they came to close quarters.

HALLIWELL (*to* DAVIDSON). They could not know that.

DAVIDSON. They did know it. A woman told them.

LORD RINTOUL. A woman !

GAVIN. A gipsy ?

DAVIDSON. Yes.

HALLIWELL. Damnation !

LORD RINTOUL (*going to him, bitterly*). Oh, Halliwell, Halliwell !

(*Shouts of triumph from town.*)

They have heard the news down there, you see. (*Jeering*) You have the weavers, so ! (*Making a hoop of his arms*) You will be the laughing-stock of the country by to-morrow.

HALLIWELL (*following him, testily*). You failed yourself before.

LORD RINTOUL. At least I was not fooled by a woman !

(*Exit* LORD RINTOUL. CAPTAIN HALLIWELL *is beside himself.*)

HALLIWELL. Davidson—this gipsy——

DAVIDSON. She is in this part of the wood. (*Pointing*) We chased her into it.

HALLIWELL. Then she at least shall not escape us. Bring up every man on this side. They are no longer needed there—and we shall hem her in.

DAVIDSON. The wood is full of women looking for their men folk. What are we to do with them ?

HALLIWELL. Let not one pass until we have caught the gipsy.

DAVIDSON. Yes, sir.

(*Exeunt* HALLIWELL *and* DAVIDSON. GAVIN *is now alone.* DOW *creeps on from back.*)

GAVIN. Rob, why did you not escape with the others ?

DOW. That Egyptian—she 's a terrible woman.

GAVIN (*with conviction*). Rob, I think she is the—— (*Pauses.*)

DOW. I think she is, sir. But there 's one she didna draw away frae you.

GAVIN. Not one.

DOW. I 'm here to prove it—by offering mysel' to the red-coats.

GAVIN. Come back.

DOW. You dinna want it !

DAVIDSON (*off*). Open out, there, open out, extend in skirmishing order through the wood !

GAVIN. Hide, Rob !

(*Soldiers enter with* SERGEANT DAVIDSON.)

DAVIDSON. Search those clumps of whin. Into them—into them. (*Runs up on to bank and exits.*) Who goes there? (*Off*) Up the bank; beat the bushes on both sides. See that she doesn't break over. After her, after her!

> (GAVIN *is self-conscious and looking pleased at* DOW'S *escape. He moves; as he does so his foot strikes against something. He lifts it up; it is the horn. He flings it from him, then picks it up again, puts it on ground.* BABBIE *runs on. She is now wearing an old-fashioned poke-bonnet and a cloak which reaches to her feet. She is evidently pursued and desperate.*)

DAVIDSON (*still off*). There she goes! There! There! Hem her in!

GAVIN. You! (*Recoils from her as she goes towards him.*)

BABBIE. Help me! (*Taking his right arm.*)

GAVIN. Avaunt, woman!

DAVIDSON (*off*). This way—follow me—we have her now.

> (*He enters with two Soldiers, and they are rushing off when he sees* GAVIN *and* BABBIE.)

Halt! It is you, Mr. Dishart—and——?

BABBIE (*speaking in English voice*). Introduce me, dear.

> (GAVIN *gasps*.)

Ah, Sergeant, you may chide me for venturing here, but where should a woman be on such a night save by her husband's side? (*Gives* GAVIN'S *arm a tender squeeze.*)

DAVIDSON. It is Mrs. Dishart?

> (BABBIE *bows*.)

My service to you, ma'am.

GAVIN (*coming to himself*). Sergeant, I must inform you——

BABBIE. Yes, yes, love, about the woman in a gipsy dress.

DAVIDSON. You saw her? Which way?

BABBIE. She came stealing out here, and then ran back that way. (*Pointing*) A wild, dishevelled creature.

DAVIDSON. That's her! (*To Soldiers*) She has doubled! After her!

> (*Exeunt Soldiers.*)

I must follow them. You and your good lady will excuse me, sir.

GAVIN. Sergeant, I must——

BABBIE. Darling, let us go home.

GAVIN (*stung*). Darling!

BABBIE (*as if he were addressing her*). Yes, love ?

GAVIN. Sergeant——

DAVIDSON (*turning*). Had you anything to say, sir ?

BABBIE (*challenging*). Have you ?

GAVIN (*after critical pause*). No.

DAVIDSON. Then good night, Mrs. Dishart—your servant, sir.

> (*Exit* DAVIDSON.)

(*Off*) No, no. Back this way ! Down that bank, as hard as you can ! Follow me !

> (BABBIE *looks quaintly at* GAVIN *and curtseys. Noise of the Soldiers dies away.*)

GAVIN (*in horror—like one waking from a dream*). You said you were my wife !

BABBIE. You didn't contradict me !

GAVIN. No, I didn't ! Why ?

BABBIE. How can I tell ? (*Jumps on tree stump.*) I wish now I had said I was your mother. (*Jumps off stump. With feeling*) Ah, forgive me. You have saved me after the way I—— (*Goes up on rocks and climbs tree. Impulsively*) I think you really are a very nice man.

GAVIN. No, no, I had nothing to do with it ! Yes, I had— and I am a minister !

BABBIE. You can't help that.

GAVIN (*almost fiercely*). How did you know that the bayonets would not be used ? Ah, I see ! That sweetheart you spoke of, I thought he was a gipsy. He is a soldier ! It was he who told you !

BABBIE. Yes, he is a soldier, and it was he who told me ! Boo ! (*Gets down from tree.*)

GAVIN. But this dress—the way you talk——

> (BABBIE *jumps down, steps off rocks one by one.*)

Just now you spoke as broadly as any woman in my congregation, and now a bonnet and a cloak suddenly convert you into a fine lady. Who are you ?

BABBIE. Perhaps it is the cloak that has bewitched me. (*Slips out of it and speaks Scotch.*) Ay, ay, ou losh, it was juist the cloak that did it. My certie, what a differ a bonny cloak makes to a woman ! (*Puts cloak on again.*)

GAVIN. Where did you get those things ?

BABBIE.　In a cottage at the edge of the wood.

GAVIN.　Nanny Webster's cottage ! You stole them ?

BABBIE.　She lent them to me in her absence. I shall take them back to her—— (*Sits on stump.*)

GAVIN (*moving to her—eagerly*). When ?

BABBIE.　Some day next week.

GAVIN.　Some day next week. (*Coming to himself.*) How can you presume to tell *me* that !

BABBIE (*indignantly*).　You asked !

(*Bugle sounds* 'Retire.' GAVIN *looks off, then returns to her.*)

GAVIN (*nonplussed*).　Have you no respect for law and order ?

BABBIE.　I am afraid I haven't. Poor ill-used minister, don't be afraid of yourself. If your awful conduct this night is discovered, I promise to give myself up, and then no blame can attach to you.

GAVIN (*anxiously*).　No, no, it would mean prison for you. You must promise me not to do that.

BABBIE.　And let you bear the brunt ! Never !

GAVIN.　Do as you are ordered, woman !

(*She backs away from him, pretends fear of him, but really admires this. She curtseys and sits on stump.*)

This must end. There are no soldiers now in this part of the wood. So your way is open. Go !

BABBIE (*putting her face close to his*). Won't you say good-bye ? (*Looking over his shoulder.*)

GAVIN.　Go. I hope never to see your face again.

BABBIE.　I can't help your not liking my face. (*Moving a few steps from him, then returns again.*) Don't you like me ?

GAVIN (*in hollow tones and speaking to himself rather than to her*). Can a man like a woman against his will ?

BABBIE.　Of course he can. That is the very nicest way of being liked.

(*Enter* WHAMOND *and* DOW *up at back.*)

GAVIN (*suddenly*).　That soldier—your sweetheart—I don't like him ! (*Kicks leaves about, hands in pockets.*)

BABBIE (*like a child*). Does oo not ? Poo, poo soldier !

GAVIN.　Go ! (*Anxiously*) Are you to be married to that man ?

BABBIE.   Unless I find someone I like better !

(*He starts, she hesitates, then looks at him. He turns his back on her. She then takes flower from her waist, puts it into his hand, and runs off. He looks at it lovingly, then holds the flower at arm's length as if afraid of it.* WHAMOND *and* DOW *are concealed by the trees.* DOW *tries to hold* WHAMOND *in check, but* WHAMOND *now breaks forward, seizes the flower and dashes it to the ground.*)

WHAMOND (*sternly*).   Lift it if you dare !

(*After a slight pause* GAVIN *lifts flower, and with a fine gesture puts it in his button-hole. He goes off at back, almost strutting, leaving* WHAMOND *looking fierce and* DOW *anxious.*)

ACT II

Scene I

NANNY'S COTTAGE. An old-fashioned Scotch kitchen, bedroom and workshop combined. It should be a very small room, so full that there is little space to move about in.

> (*Curtain rises on* NANNY *sitting at work at a hand-loom which clacks busily. Enter* BABBIE *at back looking about her curiously. She shuts door and comes forward. She is in gipsy dress, and carries cloak and bonnet. She enters softly, looking about curiously and laughing to herself as if it were a joke. She peeps at* NANNY, *who continues working, not seeing her, owing to web being a screen.*)

NANNY. Was that onybody ?

BABBIE. Only me.

NANNY (*coming from loom*). Wha are you ?

BABBIE. Nanny, I am your cloak and bonnet come back.

NANNY (*coming to her—fervently*). The Lord be thankit !

BABBIE (*giving cloak to* NANNY). You thought I meant to keep them ?

NANNY. I had my doubts o' you. It was a terrible temptation to an Egyptian lassie.

> (*In agony because* BABBIE *is taking off bonnet carelessly.*)
Be kindlier to the strings ! (*Takes bonnet reverently.*) I 'm thinking you dinna wear a bonnet like that every day !

BABBIE. Nanny, it was splendid to feel that I was in the fashion for once in my life.

NANNY (*putting on bonnet*). I believe you ! (*Looking at herself in glass between the bed and door with delight.*) Ay, it 's fine to be in the fashion ! The most blessed thing I can think of is to be sitting reverent in the kirk, and to be in the fashion at the same time.

155

BABBIE (*impulsively*). Nanny, you are an old dear, and you look sweet in it. (*Kisses her.*)

NANNY. Nae ! Nae ! Wha wouldna look sweet in that bonnet ? (*Goes to glass again.*) Yes, it sets me pretty ! It does ! Umpha ! (*Takes it off and puts it on table.*) Lassie, I tell you what I 'll do. (*Magnificently, her face shining with delight and importance.*) I 'll let you see my new merino ! (*With great importance gets merino dress out of bed.*) What think you ?—what do you say to this ?

BABBIE (*to please her*). Oh ! How beautiful ! How lovely to wake up in the morning and remember you have a dress like that !

NANNY. Yes, I sometimes lie snoozing and thinking of it ! (*Affecting humility.*) Ah, no !—it 's nothing—it 's common. (*In agony because* BABBIE *is fingering it.*) For mercy's sake, lassie, take tent of yoursel'—are your hands clean ?

(BABBIE *shows her hands.*)

Ay, they are—well done—haud out your arms.

(BABBIE *holds out her arms and* NANNY *puts dress in them as if it were a child.*)

There ! He ! He ! He !

BABBIE. The precious ! You dear, there must be a joy in owning this that even religion can't give. (*As in a transport of delight.*) Nanny, if you leave it here another moment I am sure I shall run off with it ! (*Makes a step for door.*) I can't help myself. (*Moving up to door.*) My feet are hurrying me to the door.

NANNY (*running up to her*). What 's that ? Stop ! You limmer, you. (*Takes merino and hurriedly returns it and bonnet to bed.*) It was ill done of me to put such temptation before you.

(BABBIE *sits on stool and spins wheel. As* NANNY *comes down to table again for cloak, she feels there is something in pocket, draws it out ; it is a package.*)

What 's this ? (*Smells it.*) It 's tea ! (*Delighted*) Did you bring this to me ?

(BABBIE *nods.*)

You good crittur ! (*With sudden fear, crossing over to her.*) But—was it honestly come by ?

BABBIE. Oh, Nanny ! Of course it was.

NANNY.   Turn round three times, haud up your hand, and then say, ' I swear.'

(BABBIE *does so.*)

It 's grand of you.

> (*There is a knock on the door. Much excited and signing caution she puts tea on table and goes to door and sees the* MINISTER'S *foot through the crevice at bottom of it—whispering:* ' It 's him ! It 's the Minister ! There 's his noble foot.' *She is on tiptoe and waggling fist for caution—her face aglow with triumph.*)

BABBIE (*eagerly*).   Mr. Dishart ! Oh ! Oh ! Oh ! What 's to be done ?   Will he wipe his feet on me ?

NANNY (*waggling fist excitedly*).   Keep still ! (*In whisper*) Work the loom and then he 'll think we dinna hear him.

> (BABBIE *goes on tiptoe to the loom and works it, and with incredible quickness* NANNY *puts the cloak into the bed. Another knock. She moves about on tiptoe, tidies herself up, letting down gown and sleeves, doing hair, putting on fresh white mutch. Another knock. While the loom is clacking,* NANNY *with same swiftness tidies up room, flinging ungenteel articles into the bed. Goes to bookshelf, comes to table and puts four books primly round table with large Bible in centre, hanging merino conspicuously on nail—all the work of a minute. Another knock.* NANNY *signs to* BABBIE *to stop working and then speaks in a loud, surprised, genteel voice.*)

Deary me, was that a knock at the door ? (*Nods knowingly and shakes fist to* BABBIE, *then goes and opens door. Enter* GAVIN.)

GAVIN.   May I come in ?

NANNY.   It 's Mr. Dishart ! This *is* a surprise ! (*Bows him forward.*)

GAVIN (*coming in and shutting door*).   Busy as usual, Mrs. Webster ?

NANNY (*in a transport, appealing to Heaven*).   Mrs. Webster he calls me, as if I was a lady with a brass knocker on her door. I like it fine.   And ' May I come in ? ' he says, as if onybody would keep him out ! He ! He ! (*Takes his hat and puts it on loom.*)

GAVIN.   You are alone.   I thought I heard talking.

> (BABBIE *suddenly works loom.*)

NANNY.   Lassie !

(BABBIE *mischievously works loom.*)

You brat ! Lassie, come forward and make your lowliest to the Minister.

(GAVIN *starts at sight of her. She laughs and mischievously bows several times, to his annoyance.* NANNY *meantime has gone for an armchair and wheels it to him.*)

A chair, Mr. Dishart ! (*Puts him proudly into it ; in a sort of whisper*) It 's the Egyptian. She has brought me back my things.

GAVIN.   I am glad she has had that honesty.

BABBIE.   Oh, thank you, sir. (*Bows profusely.*)

GAVIN (*starting up*). Woman, if you bow to me again I shall run you out at that door.

(BABBIE *collapses on stool by wheel, as if in terror.*)

NANNY (*behind table*). Have a care, lassie. (*Exulting*) Every day this week has Mr. Dishart come here to see if you have brought back my things.

(BABBIE *looks at* GAVIN, *who winces.*)

BABBIE.   What an interest you must have in Nanny, Mr. Dishart.

NANNY.   It makes me a proud woman. They call me the peacock nowadays.

BABBIE.   No wonder ! (*Sentimentally, to* NANNY) To be *his* peacock !

(GAVIN *glares at her.*)

Nanny, I have offended him again. What *is* the right thing to say to a minister ? Shall we ask him to drink a dish of tea with us ?

NANNY.   We couldna presume.

GAVIN (*genially*). I should like it, Mrs. Webster.

BABBIE.   There !

NANNY.   You 'll sit doun to your tea in this house ! Eh, the honour—lassie, the cloth 's in that drawer—eh, the jealousy this 'll cause in Thrums ! Mysy Grossurs 'll take to her bed ! (*Rushes across to fire and busies herself with kettle.*)

(BABBIE *goes to drawer.*)

GAVIN (*gaily—rising*). I want to help.

NANNY.   Na ! na ! Lord preserve 's, no !

BABBIE (*cavalierly*). Yes, you help ! (*Coming to table with cloth ; to* GAVIN) Lift these books.

> (*To* NANNY'S *surprise he does as he is bid, then doesn't know what to do with them.* BABBIE *bustles about getting things ready. She spreads cloth and returns to cupboard, leaving* GAVIN *unable to put books down anywhere. She returns with butter and scone, and sees him in difficulty.*)

(*Wearily*) Put them down ! (*Puts her things on table, then sees he is still in difficulty, takes them from him, and puts books back on shelf, sighing over his stupidity.*) Get the tea-pot. Now the tea ! (*She sees that he is helpless again.*) There it is, staring you in the face.

> (*He brings it to her.*)

Give it to Nanny.

> (*He does so. She goes and gets three plates from dresser, then stands looking at him.*)

Now get the bannocks, and butter some scones.

> (*The bannocks are stacked round fire.* NANNY *turns round and sees. She puts tea in tea-pot and packet of tea on mantelpiece.*)

NANNY. Heaven help her, she 's ordering about the Minister !

> (GAVIN *lets knife fall.*)

BABBIE. Stupid ! Sit down there—and don't rise till I give you permission !

> (*He sits contrite in armchair, hands in pockets.*)

Nanny, if men would keep their hands in their pockets all day, the world's affairs would be more easily managed. (*Goes up to table for milk jug, sugar basin, spoons, cups and saucers, ready on tray.*)

NANNY. You limmer ! (*Anxiously*) Dinna heed her, Mr. Dishart ; she 's an English gipsy as you can tell by her tongue —and they ken no better.

> (BABBIE *brings tray with cups.*)

Do you think the Minister is to drink out o' my second best cups ? (*Takes away one cup and saucer from her.*) They do fine for you and me, but *I 'll* let you see what he is to drink out o'.

> (*Exit* NANNY, *proudly.* BABBIE *goes to table and puts tray down. They look at each other, very self-conscious.* BABBIE *sits at wheel and sets it spinning.* GAVIN *rises and is about to speak when* BABBIE *starts up.*)

BABBIE (*anticipating him*). Woman, stand forward ! (*She is contrite.*) Ah, don't be angry. After all, I *have* saved your weavers—(*Skips round him*)—for no further action is to be taken against them, if they are good boys and girls in future. Do you know that ?

GAVIN. It has been officially announced. (*Anxiously*) But you are not included. (*Tragically*) Have you not heard that Lord Rintoul has issued a warrant for your apprehension ?

BABBIE. I know. Isn't it a darling of a warrant !

GAVIN. A what ! Have you absolutely *no*——

BABBIE. No—absolutely.

GAVIN (*sighing*). Babbie, why do you always make fun of me ?

BABBIE (*standing by wheel*). Because—because you are such a boy.

GAVIN. My congregation don't think me a boy.

BABBIE. They don't know you so well as I do.

GAVIN (*shyly*). Do you think you know me well ?
     (*She nods.*)
I wish I understood you. (*Scratching head.*)

BABBIE. Don't you ?

GAVIN. Sometimes I think I do—and then I don't. (*Sighs.*) The strange thing is that when you annoy me——

BABBIE. Then you get so angry. Wow-wow !

GAVIN. I pretend to be angry, but—yes, let the truth be told, I believe I like it all the time. (*Turns away as if this were a terrible revelation.*)
     (BABBIE *looks at him unseen, rather fondly.*)
You say you know me, but you see you did not know that ! (*Wheeling round with sudden suspicion.*) Or did you know it ?

BABBIE (*sits again, faltering*). I—I am not quite sure.
     (*They hear* NANNY *coming.* BABBIE *works the wheel. Enter* NANNY, *carefully carrying a cup and saucer.*)

NANNY (*coming to table*). This is what Mr. Dishart is to drink out o'. (*Puts it on table, puts armchair by table for* GAVIN. *She is very excited.*) This is *your* chair, Mr. Dishart.
     (GAVIN *sits.*)

BABBIE. Shall I sit here ?

NANNY.   Keep us a' !   The lassie thinks her and me is to
sit down wi' the Minister !

(BABBIE *jumps up.*)

You ignorant crittur, we 're just to stand and serve him, and
when he has risen, we 'll sit down.

BABBIE.   Delightful !   Nanny, you pour out his tea, and I
shall hold his plate.   (*Takes a plate in left hand and kneels.*)

GAVIN (*rises, thundering*).   Sit down both—I command you !

(*They sit.* NANNY, *above the table, pours out tea.* BABBIE,
*affecting fear, nervously holds out plate for him to take a
piece of scone.   He smiles and is about to take a piece, but*
BABBIE *draws back the plate.   He frowns at her, then
she gives it.*)

GAVIN (*very severely*).   Thank you.

(*While this is going on,* NANNY *pours out the tea.   She
hands* GAVIN *his cup and saucer ; he takes it.*)

Thank you, Mrs. Webster.   (*Then he eats a piece of scone.*)
Your scones are delicious, Mrs. Webster.

NANNY (*off her head with delight*).   Eh—eh—you hear what
he says !   They are my own baking !   He said 'delicious.'   It
was his very word !

GAVIN.   I am enjoying my tea immensely.

NANNY.   Oh, the glory !

BABBY.   He is here, Nanny !   He is drinking tea with you
and me !

NANNY.   Ay, and he might be drinking it in Rintoul Castle
wi' her little leddyship hersel'.

BABBIE.   No !

NANNY.   Umpha !   (*Importantly*) Him and Lord Rintoul is
friends now.

(BABBIE *looks at* GAVIN.)

BABBIE.   Friends ?

GAVIN (*awkwardly*).   The fact is—I have had a letter from
Lord Rintoul, thanking me—for the help—I gave the soldiers,
the other night !

BABBIE.   The help ?   Oh !   I see !

(*He cannot face her.*)

NANNY (*impressively*).   *And* inviting him to call at the castle !

BABBIE.   How kind !

NANNY.   The whole town is ringing with it.

F

GAVIN (*drawing a long face*). He—he is most cordial. I am visiting almost daily on the estate just now, because two of my congregation, who are tenants there, are ill. And Lord Rintoul has requested his daughter to meet me at these houses and to assist me in my work in whatever way I think best.

BABBIE. This is in return for your—help on the night of the riot ?

GAVIN. Y—y—yes. (*Stirs his tea very quickly.*)

BABBIE. What is—what is her little leddyship like ?

NANNY. Ay, what is she like, sir ?

GAVIN. I don't know—she has never come near me. (*Drinks his tea.*)

BABBIE. Disobeying her father. The naughty !

GAVIN. She visits these poor people and, to do her justice, is very kind to them, but she seems to avoid going near them when I am there.

NANNY. The impidence !

GAVIN (*smiling like an old cackling wife*). She has more important people to be nice to, Mrs. Webster. I have heard that she and Captain Halliwell—— (*He nods his head in a gossipy way.*)

NANNY (*nodding also and drinking in the gossip*). Oh, ho ! ho ! Oh, ho ! ho !

BABBIE. Oh, ho ! ho ! (*Nodding.*)

(*They are putting heads over table as they cackle.*)

GAVIN. But she lives chiefly in England and has never even been in Thrums ; so how can we expect her to have an interest in its minister ? (*Leans back in chair.*)

BABBIE. Oh, no !

NANNY. I have heard a droll thing about her.

(*They become gossipy over table again.*)

They say she has a French servant woman that has nothing to do except wait on *her* alone !

BABBIE (*incredulous*). No !

GAVIN (*with a man-of-the-world air*). It is quite possible. They are called lady's-maids.

BABBIE. What a lot you know, sir !

NANNY (*gurgling with laughter*). It's said—that she dresses her leddyship—and undresses her—like an infant—and brushes her hair ! I've even heard she washes her ! (*Big laugh.*)

(BABBIE *joins in* NANNY'S *laughter.*)

BABBIE. Excuse me, sir. It sounds so queer !

GAVIN. I can't help laughing myself !

(*They laugh together.*)

Small chance, you see, of the like of her drinking tea with the like of me. (*Hands cup for more tea.*)

BABBIE. How much those English ladies miss ! (*An idea.*) Maybe she 's kept busy drinking tea with the Captain.

GAVIN. Very likely.

NANNY. There 's a song his sojers sing about him nowadays.

GAVIN (*shocked*). That offensive Johnny Cope song. Even my congregation sing it.

NANNY. I 've heard it maddens him.

BABBIE. It will need a lot of tea, Nanny, to wash that song out of him ! I know it.

(*She sings a verse without accompaniment, but with gay gestures and waving tea-cup.*)

> Our Halliwell to Caddam came
> To catch the wicked weaver men,
> But deil a weaver had he when
> He counted them in the morning !

(*Chorus sung by* BABBIE *and* NANNY.)

> Hey, gallant captain, have you catched her yet ?
> Or has the gipsy beat ye yet ?
> She led you a dance till you were gyte
> And your sojers laughed in the morning.

GAVIN. Enough ! Enough !

NANNY. The Lord forgie me, but fine would I like to join in the second verse myself !

BABBIE. Do, Nanny, do.

(BABBIE *signs encouragement and she and* NANNY *sing.*)

> For days the English captain proud
> Kept glowering watch on Caddam Wood,
> For her that didna as she should,
> By nicht, nor yet by morning !

(*They both sing chorus, and* GAVIN *himself, like one bewitched, joins in it.* BABBIE *artfully stops, so that* GAVIN *sings the last two lines alone.* NANNY *also stops, astonished at hearing him, rises and stands with arms round* BABBIE. *When finished he realises with horror what he has done.*)

NANNY.   Lassie, we forget that he is the Captain's friend now.   (*Sits again.*)

(GAVIN *takes up tea-cup.*)

BABBIE.   He almost forgot himself, didn't he?   (*With sudden thought*) Nanny, I can guess why the little ladyship has no interest in Mr. Dishart.   It is because he is a married man!

(GAVIN's *cup rattles in saucer.*)

NANNY (*laughing*).   A——married man!   Mr. Dishart, she takes you for a married man!   (*Big laugh.*)

(GAVIN *tries to carry it off with awkward laugh.*)

BABBIE.   Is he not?   I thought the lady you introduced to the soldiers that night——

(*He tries to stop her by shaking a spoon at her.*)

(*Taking the spoon.*)   Thank you.   I hope I have said nothing unpleasant.

NANNY.   Him married!   But every single leddy in this countryside would jump at him like a bird at a berry.   (*Chuckling*) Ay, and it 's the talk o' the town that one o' them has got him at last.

BABBIE (*sharply*).   Oh?

NANNY.   We dinna ken who she is yet, but we 're doing our best to find out.

GAVIN (*turning away, with a groan*).   I am sure of that.

(BABBIE *doesn't like it.*)

NANNY.   What 's the matter wi' the lassie?

BABBIE.   Nothing!   (*To* GAVIN) Is this true?

GAVIN (*stoutly*).   It is the first I have heard of it.   So you have permission to tell the tale, Mrs. Webster.

NANNY (*eagerly*).   You 'll no be angry?   (*With enjoyment of the gossip.*)   It was about a week since—he came home wi' a flower in his coat, a thing he was *never* known to do till that night.   It was a red rose!

BABBIE (*understanding*).   A red rose!

GAVIN (*wanting to stop* NANNY).   Mrs. Webster, I 'd rather you didn't——

BABBIE (*turning round again*).   You gave her permission. (*Her manner has changed to geniality.*)

NANNY. You said I could tell ! For days he kept it in a glass of water on his study table—and there he would sit looking fond like at it.

GAVIN (*half turning away in his chair*). Nonsense ! Not at all.

NANNY. Jean saw you—that 's the Manse servant. She chanced to be near the door.

GAVIN (*hugging his knee*). Hoots ! I remember I flung the thing out of the window.

BABBIE. You did ?

NANNY. Ay ! he did, as if it maddened him. Andrew Soutar was sitting on the Manse dyke.

GAVIN (*to* BABBIE). There ! You see !

NANNY. And then you ran out and picked it up again.

GAVIN (*turning to her*). How could you———— ?

NANNY. Jemima Tosh was peeping through the gate.

GAVIN. Oh ! It was she, was it ! Mrs. Webster, I swear to you I took so little care of that rose that I don't even know what became of it.

NANNY. But I ken.

GAVIN (*with a half-groan*). Oh !

BABBIE. Tell me !

NANNY. Well, when the Minister was out, Jean used to take favoured parties into the study to see the rose, and they gossiped about wha the lady could be, till Tibbie Birse and Bell Dundas got so curious that they stole the rose—it being of an uncommon kind—and now they 're going the round o' all the gentry's gardens trying to match it—so as to find out wha she is !

(GAVIN *rises* ; BABBIE *looking at him demurely.*)
You 've no finished, sir ? You 've eaten nothing.

GAVIN. Yes, I have made a very good tea, Mrs. Webster. Thank you. (*Plays with spinning-wheel.*)

NANNY (*whispering*). Rise up, lassie, he 's finished. (*Abruptly takes the cup out of* BABBIE's *hand.*) You winna tell me her name, Mr. Dishart ?

GAVIN (*looking at her, then at his feet, then at her again, sharply*). No ! (*Sends spinning-wheel going quickly.*)

(*Exit* NANNY *sighing, with tray.* BABBIE *looks approvingly at him. He turns quickly, they catch each other's eye. He sighs and folds his arms.*)

BABBIE (*faintly*).   I think I had better go !
      (*No answer.   GAVIN turns wheel.*)
Good-bye.
      GAVIN (*hoarsely*).   You should never have come.
      BABBIE (*indignantly*).   Oh !   Good-bye for ever. (*Goes to door.*)   Unless you apologise I will never speak to you again.
            (*She waits expectant ; rattles door latch.   He says nothing.*)
Did you apologise ?
      GAVIN.   I did not. (*Fiercely turns wheel round.*)
      BABBIE (*nonplussed*).   Yes, you did—I heard you. (*Comes down to him quaintly.*)   I forgive you, Mr. Gavin Dishart !
      GAVIN (*meaning first to be angry and then endearingly*). Babbie.
      BABBIE.   What ?
            (*His arms go out lovingly.   In alarm he checks himself and breathes heavily like one who has had a narrow escape.*)
      GAVIN.   You are everything a woman ought not to be.
            (*BABBIE hangs more and more limp with each charge he brings against her.*)
As a minister I despise you for your want of seriousness ; you are no respecter of the proprieties.   That humility in the presence of your superiors, which so well becomes a maiden, is totally and lamentably lacking in you.   Everything about you is wrong——
            (*She looks up.*)
Your very hair infuriates me——
            (*She holds her hair.*)
As a wife—a wife !   Can any sane man conceive you as a wife !
(*Goes down a step.*)
      BABBIE (*looking up suddenly*).   You are not proposing to me, are you ?
      GAVIN.   Heaven forbid !   Then why is it——
      BABBIE.   Why is what ?
      GAVIN.   I don't know.   But you—you—your hair—your eyes—— (*His arm rises admonishingly.*)
            (*Enter NANNY.*)
      NANNY (*gleefully*).   Eh, but she 's catching it now.
      GAVIN.   Go away !   Go away !
      NANNY.   Lassie, you 're to catch it now !
            (*NANNY goes off rubbing her hands gleefully.*)
      GAVIN (*intensely*).   Babbie, I never kissed a woman before.

BABBIE.   Before what ?

   (*He is startled.   He goes for his hat on loom, then turns to her.*)

GAVIN.   Are you never serious ?

BABBIE.   Yes.

GAVIN.   When ?

BABBIE (*lugubriously, and in a sort of solemn burlesque*).   When I—when I think of how I am going to end.   I have read my future, Mr. Dishart, and it is not to be a glorious one.   (*Sits in armchair.*)   This flibberty-gibbet of a Babbie is to get her licks in the end.   (*Reading her hand*)   I see him—I see my husband !

   GAVIN (*going to her, eagerly*).   You won't care for him ?

   BABBIE (*examining her hand*).   Will I—or won't I ?   This line—but that line—no, I don't believe I will.

GAVIN.   Then why ?

   BABBIE (*half serious for the first time*).   I suppose just for the fun of the thing.   Haven't you seen that I do everything for fun ?   It tosses me in the air ; I am just a bubble.   Some day, foof !—(*making the action of blowing*)—and I shall be blown out.

   GAVIN (*ardently*).   A soldier is not the right man for you.

BABBIE.   The right man for me !   I see him !

GAVIN.   Tell me, woman !

BABBIE.   He is everything I am not, and nothing that I am.

   GAVIN (*seeing himself in this*).   Yes, yes.

BABBIE.   He must be a *man*—not a *bubble*——

GAVIN.   No !

BABBIE.   One who takes the world by the throat——

GAVIN.   All ministers do.

   (*They are not looking at each other.*)

   BABBIE.   A man who has a mind of his own, and having once made it up, stands to it in defiance of everyone.

   GAVIN.   Thomas Whamond.

   BABBIE.   If I love him it must be because he has shown me what love is.   If I have a soul, he has got to find it for me.   He must compel me somehow to think—he must be my master——

   GAVIN (*carried away*).   Your master !   (*Going close to her*) Babbie, I am that man !

   (*The awfulness of what he has said strikes them both ; they stare at each other aghast.   GAVIN seizes his hat and rushes in horror from the room.*)

SCENE II

THE Manse Garden : It is early evening, some days later.

(*As curtain rises* JEAN *is taking down towels from line. She exits with basket in one arm, apron in other, and pin in mouth.*

Nothing is now left of the washing except rope. While this is going on, GAVIN *is seen passing and re-passing window (whose blind is not drawn). He is walking up and down room composing, muttering to himself, etc. Once he stands looking out at window composing, then walks about again.* BABBIE, *in gipsy dress and carrying a lighted lantern and a shawl, passes along behind wall and enters at gate. Her movements and glances behind her show that she fears someone is pursuing her. She sees* GAVIN *at window, is delighted, but hides beneath it so that he may not see her. She mischievously flashes lantern three times. Once he is about to look out ; she hides ; he withdraws. Again she flashes light on window. Suddenly she starts away, hears someone, looks over wall, is alarmed, and runs off hastily.* DOW *passes behind wall, looking about him in wrath, and enters at gate. At that moment* JEAN, *the woman servant, opens door to come out.* DOW *pounces on her in front of Manse door.*)

JEAN (*screaming*).   Let go !

DOW (*releasing her and backing*).   It 's you, Jean ?

JEAN.   Wha would it be ?   You widow man !   Wha did you think it was ?

DOW (*conciliatory*).   Nobody.   (*Eagerly*) I 'm looking for nobody.   I 've seen nobody.

JEAN.   You 're drunk again.

DOW (*eagerly*).   Ay, that 's it.   I 'm just drunk.   (*Looking at window*) Is he there ?   He hasna left the house ?   (*Fiercely*) Tell me !

(JEAN *shrinks from him.* GAVIN *opens window.*)

GAVIN.   Jean, was that lightning a moment ago ?

JEAN.   I saw no lightning, sir. (*Continues winding up clothes-line*).

(DOW *starts*.)

GAVIN.   I could have sworn I saw several flashes on the window.   Has Thomas Whamond come for the key of the church?

JEAN.   No, he hasna come yet.

GAVIN.   You are coming to the prayer meeting, I hope, Rob?

DOW.   Ay, of course.

(GAVIN *shuts window, pulls down blind and disappears.*
JEAN goes on rolling up the rope, which she leaves hanging
on hook on Manse wall.)

JEAN.   Would you shame the kirk by coming to the prayer meeting in corduroys?   Away hame and put on your blacks!

DOW.   I'm no coming to the meeting.   I have other work to do. (*Darkly*) If she—if she——

JEAN.   Wha?   Wha are you raving about?   A woman?

DOW (*going to her*).   No, no, there's no woman, I tell you —I'm drunk.

WHAMOND (*off*).   Jean!

DOW.   That's Tammas Whamond!   If you tell him I saw a woman here I'll throttle you! (*Grips her arm.*)

(*She releases herself.   Enter* WHAMOND *in his blacks,*
aged silk hat, etc.)

WHAMOND.   I've come for the key of the kirk, Jean.

JEAN (*producing key from her pocket*).   There it is. (*Gives him the key.*)   And it's time I was putting on my blacks. (*Looks admiringly at* GAVIN's *window.*) Tammas, he's sitting there, studying to the last moment.   At times I'm near terrified that some day he'll walk straight out of that window in a fit of sublime thought.

(*Exit into Manse.* WHAMOND *looks inquiringly at*
DOW.)

WHAMOND (*harshly*).   What are you prowling about here for?

DOW.   Nothing.   I've no reason.

WHAMOND.   You have a reason, and the reason is an Egyptian trollop.   *I* ken what makes ye haunt this garden.

DOW (*startled*).   You dinna mean——

WHAMOND (*going to him*).   I mean that I 've been watching as well as you.   I mean I ken about a lovers' meeting in Nanny Webster's house.   Ay, and about another since then, at the Kaims o' Erly.

DOW (*relieved*).   Is that all ?

WHAMOND.   All !   Is there mair ?

DOW (*eagerly*).   No, no, may I be struck dead if there is.

    (WHAMOND *fiercely grips* DOW's *arm*.)

WHAMOND.   You 're all in a trem'le.   What is 't ?

DOW.   Nothing — I swear.   I was going when you cam.

WHAMOND (*grimly*).   Let 's see you go.

    (DOW *hesitates*.)

Let 's see you go.

    (*After hesitation*, DOW *exits through gate*.   DOW *returns stealthily and steals through gate to see if* WHAMOND *has gone.   He turns and* WHAMOND *confronts him.   They look at each other.*   MICAH *enters*.)

WHAMOND.   Laddie, what 's the matter wi' your father ?

DOW (*warningly*).   Naething.

MICAH.   Naething.

    (WHAMOND *goes off sternly*.)

MICAH (*coming to* DOW—*entreating*).   Father, come awa' hame.

DOW.   Not me.   Micah, did you see a woman wi' a lantern ?

MICAH.   Is it her that has bewitched the Minister ?

DOW.   Speak low.

MICAH.   What is she like ?

DOW.   She 's bonny—but she 's the devil.

MICAH.   You mak' me shiver !   I saw no woman wi' a lantern, but I saw lightning.

DOW.   Lightning !   Quick—whaur did you see it ?

MICAH.   In the back-end o' the wood.

DOW.   It 's her again !   Out o' my way.   (*He seizes* MICAH *by the shoulders*.)

MICAH.   Father, come hame !   Come hame !

DOW (*flinging* MICAH *from him*).   I 've other work to do ! (*Exit*.)

MICAH. Enerty ! Feenity ! Fickerty Feg !
El ! Del ! Dolmans egg.
Irky ! Birky ! Ravens croak,
Into Hell and let her smoke.

(While he recites these lines MICAH *goes twice round well looking into it. Enter* BABBIE. *She is flashing light on* GAVIN'S *window when she hears* MICAH. *She goes to him, puts down lantern and shawl above the well.)*

BABBIE. Hallo, hallo, little barelegs, whatever are you doing ?

MICAH *(looking up at her quickly)*. I was wishing. This is a wishing-well. I was wishing the woman was in Hell.

BABBIE. You *are* a dear boy ! What woman is it ?

MICAH. The woman who has sent my father to the drink again. He says she should be burned for a witch.

BABBIE. No doubt it would be a lovely end for her ! But if he dislikes her so much how can she have such power over him ?

MICAH. It 's no my father she has bewitched.

BABBIE. Who is it, then ?

MICAH. It 's Mr. Dishart.

(BABBIE gets a shock. Throughout remainder of scene she is quite unemotional, merely quiet, like one a little dazed who needs time to think it all out.)

BABBIE *(after pause)*. Why should that send your father to the drink ?

MICAH. Because my father 's terrible fond o' him, and when the congregation ken about the woman they 'll turn agin the Minister, and they 'll stone him out o' Thrums.

BABBIE. Stone *him*—oh, but this is nonsense.

MICAH. It 's truth.

(MICAH goes to BABBIE, touches her, and retreats from her in fear.)

BABBIE. Why do you stare at me ?

(Lights in church windows appear.)

MICAH. You 're—you 're the woman !

BABBIE. What makes you think that ?

MICAH. You 're so bonny. *(Going to her.)* Are you the woman ?

BABBIE.   I suppose I am the woman.

MICAH.   Oh, woman, will you no gang awa' ! When my father 's wild wi' the drink I have to sleep in the field, and it 's terrible cauld. (*Appealingly.*)

BABBIE.   I expect it is.

MICAH (*pleadingly*).   I 'll gie you my rabbit if you 'll gang awa'.

(*She turns from him.   He thinks she is refusing.*)
I 'll gie you them both.

BABBIE.   Keep your rabbits, boy, and dry your eyes—I am going away. (*She is thinking of* GAVIN *rather than of* MICAH.) It 's really true—that they could be such savages to *him* ?

MICAH.   I swear til 't. You 'll leave the Minister alone now for ever and ever ?

BABBIE (*still subdued*).   High time ! Yes, for ever and ever.
(*The church bell begins to ring.*)

MICAH.   That 's the prayer-meeting bell. He 'll be coming out.

BABBIE (*eagerly*).   Will he ?
(*She runs off quickly.* MICAH *follows and gets between her and the Manse door.*)

MICAH.   You said you would gang awa' !

BABBIE.   Yes, much better. I am going. (*She looks up at window, turns away from it.   She has suddenly a fit of shivering —every bit of her shivers.*)

MICAH (*after some time*).   What makes you shiver so terrible ?

BABBIE.   Was I shivering ?

MICAH (*touched*).   Maybe you 're fond o' him ?

BABBIE.   Maybe. I wonder. I hadn't thought of it. That 's the worst of me, little boy. (*She stops and addresses* GAVIN'S *window in a mixture of comedy, recklessness and feeling.*) Good-bye ! Did you call me ? No ? Doesn't matter. It was just a bubble that floated this way to ask you kindly to blow her out. Best for you. Blow, little—master ! Thank you. (*She curtseys as if* GAVIN *had obeyed, then she addresses* MICAH) *I* 'm blown out, boy ! The Egyptian is done for. Hurray !

(*She exits, half laughing, dancing and singing, much as she first appeared in Act I.   The only words being heard —'Hurray !   Hurray !'—are obviously done to defy her emotions.   A devil-may-care exit.   After pause*

MICAH *follows her off. There is a pause in which men and women, all in Sunday clothes, pass behind wall. They move along in old-fashioned Scotch manner and only upper part of them is visible. The bell continues ringing slowly. Enter* SNECKY HOBART. *As he is passing behind wall* BABBIE *screams in distance. He stops and listens, then comes through gate.* BABBIE *screams again.* JEAN, *in Sunday clothes, comes out at Manse door going to church.*)

JEAN. It 's you, Snecky.

SNECKY. Jean, did you hear onything ? It sounded like a woman screaming.

JEAN (*loftily*). I can neither hear nor see. I 'm wearing my black alpaca.

(JEAN *passes out at gate and exits. When* JEAN *is at gate more churchgoers come on.* SNECKY *sits on seat and dusts his boots with his handkerchief.* ANDREW, *passing, comes to rest at gate.*)

ANDREW (*over wall*). A grand night for the meeting, Snecky.

SNECKY. It is, Andrew. Ah, oh ! man, it is. Andrew, did you hear a woman scream ?

ANDREW. No—I was thinking o' higher things.

(*He passes on.*)

SNECKY. It 's queer.

(*He goes through gate and exits. More churchgoers come on. Lights in Manse go out.* GAVIN *comes out at Manse door, shutting it, and meets* NANNY.)

NANNY (*in agitation*). Mr. Dishart——

GAVIN. Good evening, Mrs. Webster.

NANNY. Mr. Dishart—the Egyptian !

GAVIN (*startled*). Has anything happened ?

NANNY. Yes. In the wood. Rob Dow has got grip o' her. He 's struck her.

GAVIN. Struck her ?

NANNY. He 's taking her to Rintoul.

GAVIN. To Rintoul ! Nanny, they will fling her into jail !

NANNY. That 's what he wants—so as to keep her frae coming near you.

GAVIN. In the wood, you say ! (*Is rushing off.*)

NANNY. Come back ! Your prayer meeting !

(BABBIE *screams again.* GAVIN *hesitates, then rushes off. The bell rings violently as if to recall him to his duties.* NANNY *is in despair.*)

What will they say to this ?

(*Is going towards gate, turns and hastily exits. The bell rings a little longer, then stops.* WHAMOND *and* SNECKY *enter at gate.*)

WHAMOND (*looking at window*). His light 's out. He canna be in the Manse. (*Crosses to Manse door and rings bell furiously.*)

SNECKY. It 's extraordinary—ay, it 's strange.

(*Enter* ANDREW *and* SILVA *through gate.*)

ANDREW. What can have become o' the Minister ?

WHAMOND. He 's no in the Manse.

SILVA. I never kent the like occur afore.

WHAMOND (*savagely*). And you 'll never ken it occur again !

(*Exit into Manse.*)

ANDREW. Tammas is looking awful black and dour.

SNECKY. He is, ay, he is.

(*Light in Manse goes up.*)

ANDREW. He needna be, for the one thing we 're sure o' is that nothing but duty o' the highest kind would keep Mr. Dishart frae the prayer meeting.

(*Light in Manse goes out.*)

SNECKY. Oh, losh, ay, oh yes, we have the completest confidence in him—but it 's suspicious.

ANDREW. You may say so.

(*They are waggling their heads solemnly when* WHAMOND *returns with a sheet of paper in his hand.*)

WHAMOND. He 's gone.

SNECKY. Tal, sal, dal, it cows ! What 's that in your hand, Tammas ?

WHAMOND. It 's what he was writing up to the last minute, I 'm thinking, for the ink 's jimply dry.

ANDREW. It 'll be his Sabbath sermon. What 's his text, Tammas ?

WHAMOND. I canna see.

SILVA. Here 's a lantern. (*Holds up* BABBIE's *lantern to let* WHAMOND *read.*)

SNECKY.   What's the text, Tammas?
(*All listen greedily.*)

WHAMOND (*surprised*).   It's headed, 'Her Boy Am I.'

SNECKY.   'Her Boy Am I'!   I canna mind o' that text.

ANDREW.   I think it's in Ephesians.

SNECKY.   How does he treat it, Tammas?

WHAMOND (*solemnly reading*)—

> 'I would I were the favoured wind
> That fans her cheek so fair,
> Oh, let me be a thread to bind
> The glories of her hair.'

(*He stops grimly.   He understands, but the others look puzzled.*)

SILVA (*to* SNECKY).   Snecky, what think you?

SNECKY (*puzzled*).   Oh, man, man, it's really—ay, it's nobly said, oh, ay, ay!   (*Solemnly.*)

ANDREW.   But what does it mean?

SNECKY.   He doesna ken what it means, Tammas!

WHAMOND.   Do you?

SNECKY.   I didna exactly see the meaning o't myself, but, oh, ay, ay!   Ooo!   Oo!

WHAMOND.   Maybe this is plainer—

> 'Oh, ask me not to count the cost,
> My Babbie's arms to fly.
> The man who hesitates is lost,
> And so, Her Boy Am I.'

SNECKY (*heavily, after a pause*).   Oh, lads, lads, that's the true religion.

ANDREW.   Tammas, does every line begin with a capital letter?

WHAMOND.   It does.

ANDREW.   Then in my opinion it has nothing to do wi' sermons.   It's poetry.

SNECKY.   Dinna say that, Andrew.

ANDREW.   *Also*, in my opinion, it's about a woman!

SNECKY.   Keeps a'!

ANDREW.   I' maun be the lady that gae him the rose!

SILVA.   So it will.   She maun be a terrible fine woman that

would make a minister use sic language. Tammas, you 're
looking dour.

WHAMOND (*sternly and sadly*).   And well I may, for I have
a woeful duty to perform.

(*All grow serious.*)

Friends, Mr. Dishart is not the noble youth we thought him.

SILVA (*fiercely*).   Have a care what you 're saying.

WHAMOND.   The fine lady you 're all so curious about, I
ken wha she is.   I saw her gie him the rose, I saw him philander-
ing wi' her in the wood, I ken o' secret meetings they 've had
since then.   I ken wha has bewitched him, and I 've warned
him, but he 's hers, body and soul—she 's the Egyptian !

(*Sensation.*)

SNECKY.   ⌈None of that.
ANDREW.   ⟨Ca' canny.
SILVA.   ⌊Can you prove this ?   (*Fiercely shakes lantern in*
WHAMOND'S *face.*)

WHAMOND.   I wish I couldna.   (*Pointing at lantern*)
Whaur did you get this ?   It 's no the Manse lantern.

SILVA.   I found it here.   That shawl was round it.   (*Points
to shawl on ground.*)

WHAMOND (*picking up shawl from above well*).   A gipsy
shawl !   (*Drops it again.*)

SNECKY.   You dinna say——

WHAMOND.   Yes, I say it.   We ken now wha the Minister
is awa' wi'.

(*Their heads are bowed in grief.* WHAMOND *speaks quietly.*)
Silva, go back to the kirk.

SILVA.   Tammas, it 's your duty to tell them—you 're chief
elder.   I was fond of the young man—and I canna.

WHAMOND (*with quiet force*).   God give me strength to do
my duty, for I love the lad even as my own son.   Go back to
the kirk, Will'um, and you maun keep the prayer meeting in his
place.   Tell them nothing till I come, and then if they have to
be told—I 'll tell them.

(SILVA *goes slowly, puts lantern down above well, and
goes through gate.*)

You away and look for him.   Take the Prosen Road.   When
you find him, bring him here to me.

(ANDREW *exits.*)

WHAMOND (*to* SNECKY).   Lock that door.

     (SNECKY, *wondering, locks Manse door.*)

Bring the key to me.

     (SNECKY *gives him the key and sits on seat.*)

Gavin Dishart, if you canna account for this night's work, never again shall you preach in that kirk, never again shall you enter that Manse door !

     SNECKY (*heavily*).   It 's hard on him—and it 's hard on us all—but ' Her Boy Am I ' !   That settles him.

     (WHAMOND *stands implacable.*)

ACT III

RINTOUL CASTLE. An ancient hall in an old Scottish baronial house. Except for softer chairs, etc., this chamber is much as it was in the days when Jacobites lived at Rintoul. Many of the old adornments still left, the whole suggesting poverty as well as pride of ancestry. An austere room with the colour mostly gone out of it. The time is an hour after that of Act II, Scene II.

> (THWAITES, *an elderly butler (English), is discovered lighting a lamp ; lifts lamp on table. He places it on table above fireplace. To him comes down the stair the French maid,* FELICE. *She speaks broken English.*)

FELICE (*on staircase, excited, but cautious*). Mr. Thwaites ! Mr. Thwaites ! What shall I do ? (*At foot of stairs.*) His lordship, he say to me, where is Lady Barbara ? I say, she is in her room. (*Looking at door.*) He say, let her know that Captain Halliwell is here. I say I go, and I come, but all the time I know that Lady Barbara is nowhere.

THWAITES (*a stolid man*). Is she *not* in her room ?

FELICE. *Non !* Nor is she anywhere in the house. She have gone—vanished away—for hours——

THWAITES. It 's queer.

FELICE. It is the deuce.

THWAITES. I have heard talk of some secret passage out of the castle that was used, they say, in Jacobite days. But I never found it.

FELICE. Perhaps *she*—found it ?

THWAITES. The door is handier.

FELICE. Ah, you think so ! But I say to myself there may be ways ! It all depend if she have a lover—then there is always ways ?

> (*From some distance, song begins to be played on the bagpipes* THWAITES *and* FELICE *chuckle and smile to each other.*)

178

That song—again !
> (*She catches* THWAITES' *right arm and they dance round once.*)

THWAITES.   Halliwell's own men play it to badger him ! Well, unlucky in war, it's said, lucky in love.
> (*Music dies away.*)

FELICE.   Love ! No, no. She does not love Dick Halliwell. She never jumps at mention of his name.

THWAITES.   Jumps ?

FELICE. *Mais oui.* It is the proof. You say to me 'William' —I do not jump. You say to me—what is your name ?

THWAITES.   Samuel.

FELICE.   You say to me 'Samuel'—I do not jump. But there is the name *François.* (*Clasps her hands.*) It is long ago—he is in France—France ! And I am here among savages—he is married with much children and he is grown very fat—but still at his name I jump—not very much now—but a little jump to the sweet memory of love. (*She says 'François' sweetly to herself and gives a little jump.*) *Voilà !*

> (*She goes off. Bagpipes off commence again.* THWAITES *exits smiling. Presently the panel picture is cautiously slid back and we see* BABBIE *peering out of the blackness behind, a lighted candle in her hand. The picture is not a big one. She can just get through. She is in the gipsy dress and is pale and very frightened. After closing panel she steals down and blows out light and puts candlestick on table. Seeing that there is no one about she goes to door, when she realises that there is someone in the room. In desperation she quickly lies down on couch, pulls rugs over her to conceal costume, and pretends to be asleep. At that point music has died away.* FELICE *comes out, suddenly sees her and gives a little squeal of surprise, then stands looking at* BABBIE *with an expressive face.* BABBIE, *affecting sleep, yawns and moves on couch, which unfortunately exposes some of gipsy dress, at which* FELICE *stares.* BABBIE *sees dress and hurriedly conceals it, but this exposes her bare foot. She takes a peep at* FELICE *and pretends to sleep again, not knowing what else to do.* FELICE *goes up stage and takes chair above writing-table and sits at head of couch.*)

BABBIE (*assuming surprise*).   Is that you, Felice ?

FELICE.   Not if my lady does not wish it.

BABBIE.   What are you doing ?   (*Looking away from her.*)

FELICE.   I thought, my lady, you might wish to dress—unless you are already dressed.

BABBIE (*flinging up the sponge*).   I think I shall raise your wages, Felice.

FELICE.   You are very good, my lady.   (*Curious*) I did not see you enter.

BABBIE.   Didn't you ?   (*Shuddering*) Felice, I have had such a dreadful adventure.   A man——

FELICE (*delighted and with interest*).   A man, my lady ?

BABBIE.   I have just escaped from the clutches of a wild, ferocious man who was dragging me here——   (*Holding rug up to neck.*)

FELICE.   Here !   To your own home ?

BABBIE (*very seriously frightened*).   He did not know that !   He has nearly broken my arm.   (*In trouble about* GAVIN.)   But there is worse than that—thoughtless fool that I have been.

THWAITES (*off*).   What name, sir ?

GAVIN (*off*).   Mr. Dishart.

> (BABBIE, *hearing this, hurries off.*   FELICE *moves chair back to table.   Enter* THWAITES, *followed by* GAVIN.)

THWAITES.   I will tell his lordship you are here, sir.

> (THWAITES *goes up the stairs.*   GAVIN *puts hat on chair in entrance and coming forward sees* FELICE, *who is pretending to be occupied and is wondering whether this newcomer is connected with the escapade.*)

GAVIN (*as soon as* THWAITES *has disappeared*).   Girl—quick, tell me—the gipsy—is she here ?

FELICE (*in a quiver*).   But what gipsy, sir ?

GAVIN.   She is not !   (*Relieved, he sits on couch.*)

FELICE.   Some of the gipsies around here I know.   There is Black Annie.

> (*He turns away.*)

Mysy, Babbie——   (*Sympathetic*) Oh, sir——

> (*She hesitates.   Then gleefully points at door, and* GAVIN *is going excited to it when* THWAITES *reappears on stair.*)

THWAITES (*at foot of stairs*).   His lordship will see you, sir, in a few minutes.   (*He goes off.*)

GAVIN. She is there ? (FELICE *nods sympathetically. He hesitates.*) Please go away. (*She reluctantly goes toward entrance. Turns to her*) Why did you tell me ?

FELICE. You jump ! (*Clasps hands, sighs, and—disappears by entrance.*)

(GAVIN *boldly opens door.*)

GAVIN. Babbie ! (*Backs from door.*)

(BABBIE *comes out in trouble to foot of couch.*)

BABBIE (*miserably ashamed of herself*). Oh, why did you come here ?

GAVIN (*manfully*). To save you, Babbie, have no fear. I heard what Rob Dow had done, and I followed. Courage, I am by your side. I will compel them to set you free.

BABBIE (*who can't help being amused, but touched*). Oh, the dear man you are.

GAVIN (*quickly*). Am I, Babbie, am I—to you ?

BABBIE. Perhaps. But you are a minister—and I—— (*She is in abject distress.*) The very birds on the moors would laugh at it. If you could only laugh at it, too, my dear ! (*Imploringly.*)

GAVIN. All I know is that you said ' my dear.'

BABBIE. I shouldn't have said it—I don't even know that I meant it. Naughty things leap out of me, Mr. Dishart— and I can't overtake them. I wish I could. (*Turns to him.*)

GAVIN (*going to her*). I will overtake them for you.

BABBIE (*smiling sweetly*). I should keep you running about all your life.

GAVIN (*laughing*). It is what I have been doing this last week and more.

BABBIE (*laughing, impulsively*). It was fun, wasn't it ? (*Stops laughing, remorseful*) There ! That is another one ! I am bitterly ashamed. I never thought until that boy—and then the man ! I never dreamt that I was placing you in danger. If you could say that you forgive me—the gipsy girl. I wasn't a woman on that mad moonlight night when I came dancing into your life. I was just a wild thing too full of glee. You don't blame the birds when they are made giddy by their own song. Please, please, let it be so with me. (*Clasps her hands.*)

GAVIN. Forgive you ! What have I to forgive you—for bringing me the great glory of my life ? Your song ! Babbie, your song has come to me for evermore !

BABBIE (*weakly*). Has it ? No, it hasn't, it mustn't ! (*Tremulous*) It is only a fancy of the moment, dear Gavin Dishart, it will quickly pass away.

GAVIN. Never while life endures. Babbie, if you could care for me——

BABBIE. I do—for the moment.

(GAVIN *steps back.*)

(*With self-abnegation*) I have never done anything all my days except for the moment. How can I tell that I would be different in this ?

GAVIN. Leave all to me.

BABBIE (*reflecting*). How lightly men ask women to leave all to them !

GAVIN. As my wife——

BABBIE (*sitting in armchair above fire, weakly*). It is a nice word.

GAVIN. Babbie—— (*Moves close to chair.*)

BABBIE. Let me look at you. (*Takes his arm.*) You dear foolish little minister ! Would you really dare to marry a gipsy girl ?

GAVIN (*grandly*). Dare !

BABBIE. Your congregation—those fierce men !

GAVIN. When I marry it will be to please myself. If they object I—I will knock them about as with a flail, even Thomas Whamond.

BABBIE. I love to listen to you.

GAVIN. And when they know you better they will see you with my eyes.

BABBIE. Or you would see me with theirs !

GAVIN. Cast aside fear, dear heart. Strange though it might be to you at first to be a minister's wife——

BABBIE. So much stranger than you think ! (*Looking at fire : she can't prevent her shoulders heaving with laughter, then sobers, looking at him*) Can you really think of me as mistress of a manse ?

GAVIN. I can think of you as nothing else. (*Gleefully bending over her*) Why should you be afraid, with me to love you and sustain you ?

BABBIE. It sounds so pretty till one begins to think ! (*Quaintly longing, looking straight in front*) Tell me how you would love me and sustain me.

GAVIN (*eagerly*).   No doubt, after what you have been accustomed to, the Manse will seem a very large house to you at first, but you will soon get used to it.

BABBIE (*faintly*).   Shall I ?

GAVIN.   Your life must often have been hard—oh, the joy to me in making it sumptuous !

BABBIE (*murmuring*).   Sumptuous !

GAVIN.   Babbie—(*Turns to her*)—there is a drawing-room !

BABBIE.   No !

GAVIN.   I have been using it as a study, but out goes the table, out go the books.   It's a large room, sixteen feet by twelve.

BABBIE (*jumping up in glee*).   Sixteen feet by twelve !   Let me see.

          (*Both laugh.*)
(*She measures on floor with her feet.*)   Oh !

GAVIN.   As far as from here to that wall, and nearly as wide. Babbie, that shall be your room !

BABBIE.   Let me shut my eyes and see it.   I love it when I shut my eyes—but when I open them—oh, wow, wow, wow ! Minister dear !

GAVIN.   I ought to tell you that I am a man of considerable means.

BABBIE.   Are you ?

GAVIN.   My congregation make the sum up to a hundred and forty pounds a year !

BABBIE.   So much !

GAVIN.   I told them they were going too fast, but they *would* do it. (*With sudden transport, shyly taking her hands*) Babbie, I shall buy you a silk dress—(*Backs away a little*)—yes, black, with beads on it !

BABBIE.   Oh, let me shut my eyes again !

GAVIN (*apologetic*).   Of course, you would have to wear shoes.

BABBIE.   What, every day ?

GAVIN (*stepping back*).   As *my* wife——

BABBIE.   And stockings, too ?

GAVIN.   My position, you know. (*Goes to a little above her—a glorious secret.*)   But sometimes—in the evening—not often, but sometimes—when we are alone together, you and I——

BABBIE (*fascinated*).   You and I !   (*She puts her head on his shoulder.*)

GAVIN (*over her shoulder*).   My wife and I !—I mean when we are really alone—that is, when the blinds are down and the shutters are on, and the servant has gone to bed—— (*A sudden thought*) Babbie, you will have a servant !

BABBIE.   Oh, it is too much !

GAVIN.   Not at all.   And when on such a night as I spoke of Mrs. Dishart——

BABBIE.   Mrs. Dishart ?

GAVIN.   She will slip out of her drawing-room, and her husband——

BABBIE.   Her husband !

GAVIN.   That is me.

BABBIE (*breathless*).   Is that you ?

GAVIN.   It must be me when you are the wife.

BABBIE (*wistfully*).   Must it ?

GAVIN (*gloriously*).   Yes.   He will pretend not to notice. And presently there will come popping into the drawing-room a barefooted girl in a gipsy frock, with rowan berries in her hair, and he will pretend to be shocked, and he will exclaim——

BABBIE (*coming quickly forward with left hand raised and still carried away*).   ' Woman, stand forward ! '

GAVIN (*glorious*).   Yes !   And then when he sees her face— oh, her face—he will say, ' My beloved,' and take her in his arms—(*Laughs*)—you know how !

> (*She is expecting him to do it, and is disappointed when he doesn't.*)

BABBIE (*plaintively*).   No, I don't know how !

> (*He embraces her rapturously and she loves it.   Then she breaks away.*)

GAVIN.   My own, my own.   (*Goes up stage dancing with joy.*)   Shouldn't I have done it ?

BABBIE (*crushed*).   I wanted you to do it.   I suppose I made you do it.

GAVIN.   Darling, darling, darling—oh, what a word !   I would have done it at any rate.

BABBIE (*slightly appeased*).   Would you ?   (*Going to him and taking hold of the lapels of his coat*) You won't want to do it in another moment. Little man, big man, I can't go on with this. This horrible woman does not have the courage. You and I—we are of different worlds, my lovely loving dear. I couldn't face yours. I must tell you why. It is not because I am a gipsy. . . . My father . . .

GAVIN (*stoutly*). I care not what *he* may have done—not though he were a criminal—I love you and that is enough.

BABBIE. A criminal! My poor father! (*She can't help laughing rather hysterically.*)

GAVIN. You laugh.

BABBIE (*putting hands on his shoulders*). Don't grudge me laughing, dear solemn, twisty mouth, darling little necktie. (*Fingers necktie.*) I am going to tell you the truth now. (*Faltering*) Oh, dear! I am going to hurt my pretty *darling* Gavin.

GAVIN. You can't hurt me. I love you! I love you! (*Starts back*) Oh!

BABBIE. What is it? Speak.

GAVIN. I 've just remembered! My prayer meeting!
    (*A door shuts upstairs. In despair she hurries back into her room and shuts the door.* LORD RINTOUL *comes down the stair followed by* CAPTAIN HALLIWELL.)

LORD RINTOUL (*on staircase : genially*). Ah, Mr. Dishart —(*Coming down to* GAVIN *at fire*)—my humblest apologies for keeping you waiting so long. (*Shakes hands.*) You and Captain Halliwell already know each other.

    (HALLIWELL *acknowledges* GAVIN.)
Let me thank you again for the good services you rendered us on that—not very fortunate occasion.

HALLIWELL. I thank you also, Mr. Dishart—though nothing came of it.

LORD RINTOUL (*signing to* GAVIN *to be seated*). One thing at all events has come of it—that I welcome you heartily, Mr. Dishart, to Rintoul.

    (HALLIWELL *sits on couch.*)

GAVIN (*awkwardly*). You are very good. (*The door is much on his mind.*)

HALLIWELL (*indifferently*). I hope Mrs. Dishart is well. She was very agitated that night, Sergeant Davidson told me. You may remember you introduced him to her in the wood.

GAVIN. I remember! (*He looks at fire.*)

LORD RINTOUL.   Which reminds me——that we have not yet called on her   I must ask my daughter to do so.

GAVIN (*hurriedly*).   There is no necessity to——

LORD RINTOUL (*genially*).   It will be a pleasure to her.   You have been seeing a good deal of her lately——so she tells me.

(GAVIN *wonders*.)

I hope she has been of real service to you while you were visiting my tenants.   I instructed her to give you every help in her power, and I may say that if she has made as favourable an impression upon you as she assures me you have made upon her, I shall be vastly pleased.

GAVIN (*puzzled, but not wishing to expose his lordship's daughter*).   Thank you——I quite——thank you.   (*He feels that he is weak, and rises manfully to be bold*) Lord Rintoul——

(*Here the music of song on pipes begins again off but is nearer now.* CAPTAIN HALLIWELL *winces and is obviously very angry.   He paces to and fro.* LORD RINTOUL *thoroughly enjoys the situation and looks at* GAVIN *with a twinkle.   He rings bell.   After a pause* THWAITES *comes to him.* LORD RINTOUL *says something to* THWAITES *in low voice.* THWAITES *goes.   The music continues,* CAPTAIN HALLIWELL *is more and more angry.* GAVIN *can't help exchanging a smile with* LORD RINTOUL, *which* CAPTAIN HALLIWELL *sees.   Suddenly the music stops.*)

LORD RINTOUL (*explanatory to* HALLIWELL).   They are not *my* men, you know.

(HALLIWELL *frowns.* LORD RINTOUL *addresses* GAVIN.)

Captain Halliwell is not musical.

GAVIN (*rising again to his task*).   Lord Rintoul, the kindness of your reception makes it the more desirable that I should acquaint you at once with my object in coming here.   It was not, I need hardly say, to talk of your daughter——however accomplished——but to plead with you——and with you, too, sir, for another and less happy woman.

LORD RINTOUL.   I confess I don't follow you.

GAVIN.   I mean the gipsy girl.

(HALLIWELL *swings round at this.*)

It is admitted that no further action is to be taken against the misguided weavers——why, then, not show a similar clemency to her ?

LORD RINTOUL (*surprised*). Well-a-day, Mr. Dishart ! I have not been so taken aback since one of your weavers plugged my mouth with a divot.

GAVIN.   Her intentions were the most generous——

LORD RINTOUL.   So was the divot !

GAVIN.   You, Captain Halliwell——

HALLIWELL.   I tell you, Mr. Dishart, decisively, that this matter does not end until I have that accursed jade in jail.

GAVIN.   You are pitiless !

HALLIWELL.   Quite ! So no more of this.

LORD RINTOUL (*slyly*).   You forget the song, Mr. Dishart !

GAVIN (*hesitating, and then breaking out passionately*).   There shall be more of it, sir. When I heard that a madman had seized her and was dragging her here for a reason you little understand, I ran after him to tear her from him. I was too late, but I am not too late to beg of you—and if that is useless, to insist—that you set her free.

LORD RINTOUL (*astounded.*)   The gipsy—here ?

GAVIN.   Is it not poor fooling to pretend to me that she is not here ?

LORD RINTOUL.   But, my dear man——

HALLIWELL.   Excuse me, Rintoul, this seems to have become my affair. (*Signing caution to* LORD RINTOUL) Well, Mr. Dishart, suppose she is here—what then ?

GAVIN (*scornfully*).   Suppose !

HALLIWELL (*exchanging a look with* LORD RINTOUL).   I admit that she is here.

(LORD RINTOUL *perceives the scheme.*)

What has that to do with you ? And what gives you the right to insist on her being released ?

GAVIN.   This. She is innocent of the charges brought against her. It was not she who prevented your arresting the rioters.

HALLIWELL (*scoffing*).   Indeed !

GAVIN.   It was I !

LORD RINTOUL.   What 's that ? Come, come, Mr. Dishart, we know better. You forget that you were overheard denouncing the watchers as law-breakers and ordering them to their homes.

HALLIWELL.   We know also that you were seen trying to

chase the gipsy from the wood immediately before she blew that infernal horn.

GAVIN. She did not blow the horn—I blew it ! It was I who alarmed the town !

LORD RINTOUL (*kindly*). Be careful. Come, come, you must not say a thing like that.

GAVIN. It is the truth.

HALLIWELL. On your oath, sir.

GAVIN. On my oath.

HALLIWELL. Rintoul, you heard him !

LORD RINTOUL (*to give* GAVIN *another chance*). I am not sure that I did.

GAVIN (*stoutly*). I am prepared to repeat every word of it if necessary—I alone did it.

LORD RINTOUL. Well, we must accept that and it is certainly bad enough—but why tell us ?

HALLIWELL. You were playing with us !

GAVIN. As you will.

HALLIWELL. There is a heavy punishment, sir.

GAVIN. I am prepared to meet it.

LORD RINTOUL. May I ask you why you admit this to us ?

GAVIN. That the innocent may be set at liberty. Do as you choose with me.

LORD RINTOUL (*quizzically*). This is rather awkward, Halliwell.

HALLIWELL. I don't see it in that light. It means simply the issue of another warrant—for him.

LORD RINTOUL. Perhaps that means simply the issue of more divots—for me.

HALLIWELL. I must say, Rintoul, I think I have done this pretty neatly.

LORD RINTOUL. A Machiavelli ! Mr. Dishart, I am sorry for you.

HALLIWELL. More than I am. Gad, sir, before you came here to make such a confession, you might have thought of Mrs. Dishart.

(GAVIN *gulps.*)

GAVIN. There is no Mrs. Dishart.

HALLIWELL (*wheeling round*). What do you mean now ? There is your wife.

GAVIN (*with a salt taste in his mouth*). I have no wife.

LORD RINTOUL (*bewildered*). No wife? Then who was——?
(*He suddenly smells a rat.*)

HALLIWELL (*stepping forward, suddenly suspicious*). It was not——

GAVIN. Yes, it was the gipsy.

(*They are bereft of speech.* RINTOUL *and* HALLIWELL *exchange glances.*)

HALLIWELL. So that explains how she slipped through our fingers !

GAVIN. That explains it.

HALLIWELL (*calling for action*). Rintoul !

GAVIN. You have *me*. Let the gipsy go.

LORD RINTOUL (*to* HALLIWELL, *slyly*). Are you to let the gipsy go—(*Laughs*)—Halliwell ?

(*He and* HALLIWELL *look at each other and are merry over the situation. Their laughter increases.*)
You don't join with us, Mr. Dishart, in our homely mirth ?

HALLIWELL. It can't be expected of him till he knows the reason of it. As you justly say, sir, we have you, but the cream of the situation is that you have put yourself into our hands for nothing. You have surprised us, Mr. Dishart, but we have also a surprise for you. (*Bowing ironically*) Allow me to tell you that the gipsy is not here ; she has not been arrested, and we know where she is no more than yourself. (*Laughs and rejoins* RINTOUL.)

GAVIN. This is idle, sir. She is in that room.

LORD RINTOUL. In that room ?

(*Neither of them credits him.*)

GAVIN. I know it.

(FELICE *has come in with lighted candle and is about to go upstairs, listening eagerly.*)

LORD RINTOUL (*puzzled*). Felice !

(*She comes forward in concealed trepidation.*)
You told me her ladyship was in her room ?

FELICE. Yes, my lord.

GAVIN. It was this girl who——

(*He stops, seeing* FELICE *sign to him imploringly.* LORD RINTOUL *sees it also ; he looks sternly from one to the other.* FELICE *would get between him and the door, but by a gesture he stops her. He opens door.*)

LORD RINTOUL.   Babbie, I want you.

(BABBIE, *after pause, comes out, now dressed as befits her rank—not a full evening dress, but in striking contrast to the gipsy.* GAVIN *gets a great shock. She controls her emotion.* FELICE *is relieved.*)

You know this gentleman ?   He insists that there was a gipsy girl in your room.

BABBIE (*self-controlled*).   I was quite alone, father.

LORD RINTOUL.   You heard what Lady Barbara said, Mr. Dishart ?

GAVIN (*manfully*).   I heard.   I made—a strange mistake.

HALLIWELL.   We should all like to know how, sir ?

(GAVIN *looks at* FELICE.)

FELICE.   I think I can explain, my lord.   This gentleman, he was shown in here, and he ask me if a gipsy girl here.   He seem very excited—I think good jest to say, ' Yes.'   He say, ' Where, where ? '   I point to her ladyship's room and run away laughing.

GAVIN.   Yes, it was she who told me.

(LORD RINTOUL *signs sternly to her to go.* BABBIE *and* FELICE *exchange glances as* FELICE *exits.* GAVIN *pulls himself together.*)

HALLIWELL.   Not so fast, sir.   Rintoul, I must ask you to make out the warrant for this man's arrest.

BABBIE.   What ?

LORD RINTOUL.   I wonder.

BABBIE.   What has he done ?

HALLIWELL (*expecting approval of himself*).   Listen to this, Lady Barbara.   It was he who prevented my seizing those weavers.   It was he who blew the horn and roused the town.   The woman he passed off as his wife was the gipsy, and he did it so that she might escape us.   He has confessed it all !

BABBIE (*to* GAVIN).   Why ?

HALLIWELL.   I drew it out of him.   I pretended that we had caught the gipsy, and he offered himself in her place.   It was all done to save her.

BABBIE.   I see.

LORD RINTOUL.   In a way it was a chivalrous thing to do, Halliwell.

HALLIWELL. Our duty is quite clear. (*Folds arms, looks at* GAVIN.) The warrant !

LORD RINTOUL. If you insist. (*He sits at table, but reluctantly.*)

BABBIE. No !

GAVIN. Don't be so sorry for me—Lady Barbara. This seems a very little matter to me—now.

HALLIWELL. Rintoul ! (*Indicating that he wants the warrant.*)

BABBIE. No, father, you shall not.

LORD RINTOUL (*growing stern*). Why not ?

BABBIE. Because this is the man I love.

(*This has its startling effect on all three.*)
And he loves me, and I will not give him up. At first it appalled me, it appals me still. I may be mad, I know I am mad, but Mr. Dishart is the one man on earth to me, father, and I will never marry any other.

HALLIWELL (*at last finding his tongue and crossing to* RINTOUL). It was you who invited him about the place, Rintoul—it was you who flung them together !

LORD RINTOUL. Is what Lady Barbara says true ?

(LORD RINTOUL's *good nature is all gone now.*)

GAVIN (*to* RINTOUL). She was all the world to me.

BABBIE. Was ?

GAVIN. Is. I cannot wonder at your anger—it must seem monstrous to you that I should have raised my eyes to her.

HALLIWELL. Oh no ! a minister is always looking upwards, is he not ?

GAVIN. You speak scornfully, sir, but I believe you have found the reason why I love her.

LORD RINTOUL. Damnation—the warrant ! (*Goes to writing-table.*)

BABBIE. If you sign that, father, won't it mean getting into the song yourself ?

LORD RINTOUL (*on consideration, throwing down pen and picking up warrant*). I give you one last chance, sir. This shall not be issued if I have your word that you never approach my daughter again. (*Turns and looks at* BABBIE.)

GAVIN. I make no bargains—I decline. But I am a man

of honour, I hope, and I would marry no man's daughter without his consent—you may be sure of that.

(BABBIE'S *head jerks up at this.*)

Nor would she, I am certain, marry anyone against your wish.

(*This is not precisely how* BABBIE *is looking.*)

LORD RINTOUL. So she has repeatedly said. (*Looking up at* BABBIE.)

(*She hangs her head. He considers warrant.*)

I shall think it over. (*Puts warrant in pocket.*)

HALLIWELL. Quite a family affair. And now, my reverend gentleman, as it seems no immediate action is to be taken, I think you expressed a desire to go. (*Holds out* GAVIN'S *hat*) Allow me.

GAVIN (*taking hat*). As for you, sir, you are naturally perturbed ; but your breeks fit you beautifully.

(RINTOUL *laughs.* GAVIN *looks at him, then goes to* BABBIE, *kisses her and exits after glancing at* RINTOUL *and* HALLIWELL. HALLIWELL *runs off after him.*)

LORD RINTOUL (*to* BABBIE). By all that's infernal—he kissed you !

BABBIE (*large-eyed*). I thought he did, father ! (*Runs to armchair by fire and sits.*)

LORD RINTOUL (*following her down*). You shall suffer for this !

(*Re-enter* HALLIWELL.)

HALLIWELL. But the man—the man—is he to get off scot-free ?

LORD RINTOUL. I'll see to *him*—I tell you I'll make short shrift of *him*. (*With idea*) Halliwell, suppose—we *do* arrest him, then—but no, that would drag me into it. (*He has produced warrant again—again pockets it.*)

HALLIWELL. Here's an idea. If I—but they would get wind of that !

(BABBIE *gets up quickly and kneels in chair, looking at them.*)

LORD RINTOUL (*producing warrant*). I could compel him—but could I ? (*Pockets it.*)

HALLIWELL. The one course open——

LORD RINTOUL. Yes ?

HALLIWELL. No, it isn't open now ! (*To* BABBIE, *sarcastically*) Lady Barbara, I congratulate you.

(BABBIE *sits in chair and puts fingers in her ears, looking at fire.* RINTOUL *paces up and down.*)

His first choice was a somewhat different woman. The gipsy he wanders woods with ! The vagrant he passes off as his wife—a pretty trollop, they tell me. (*She remains listless and unhappy.*)

LORD RINTOUL. That woman—I wish to God she *was* his wife.

HALLIWELL. Yes, because then—— (*He is suddenly made speechless by a magnificent idea.*) Ye powers ! Why did I not think of it before ? (*Gloriously*) Rintoul, what if she *were* his wife—and *is* !

(BABBIE *becomes suddenly alert.*)

LORD RINTOUL. Eh ?

HALLIWELL. Something better—a thousand times better—than the warrant ! Don't you see—he acknowledged this gipsy as his wife before witnesses—Sergeant Davidson and two of my men. Does not that constitute a marriage by the laws of Scotland ?

(BABBIE *jumps out of chair.*)

BABBIE. What ! (*Sits.*)

LORD RINTOUL. Halliwell ! There have been many such cases. If the witnesses will swear to it, those two are man and wife as much as though they had been married in St. Paul's Cathedral by the Archbishop of Canterbury.

BABBIE. Oh ! (*Scared.*)

HALLIWELL. And they will swear to it ! We have him now !

LORD RINTOUL. We have him now !

BABBIE. Father ! (*Really meaning that this must be stopped.*)

LORD RINTOUL (*sternly*). Not a word.

(BABBIE *sits again.*)

HALLIWELL (*gloating*). They have been married, Lady Barbara, for—let me see—for eleven days !

BABBIE (*in a gasp that may be ecstasy or trepidation*). Eleven days !

LORD RINTOUL. After him, Halliwell—we mustn't keep the poor devil in ignorance.

G

HALLIWELL.   This is what I shall do.   With your permission I propose to send one of your servants on horseback to the barracks with orders to Davidson and the two other witnesses to meet me at Dishart's house.

LORD RINTOUL.   Agreed, agreed !

BABBIE (*scared*).   No—no—you can't !

LORD RINTOUL.   Silence !

(BABBIE *skips back to chair and sits again.*)

HALLIWELL.   I shall drive in from here and meet them there.

LORD RINTOUL.   Off you go.

HALLIWELL.   Dishart should be there as soon as I, as he can cross the river by the stepping-stones.   And then I will have news for both him and his weavers !

LORD RINTOUL.   News, news !   I 'll come with you, Halli-well.   Oh, much better than this warrant !   (*He tears it up and flings it on table.*)

HALLIWELL.   Bravo !   Good evening, Barbara.

(*She turns to him, kneeling on chair ; he holds out his hand.*) Won't you ?

BABBIE (*without taking it, and with a meaning he does not understand*).   Good luck, Dick !   (*Sweetly*) He will be very broken, remember.   You will be gentle with him, won't you ? (*She kneels on hearth-rug and takes up poker.*)

HALLIWELL.   Oh, certainly.   (*Turns to go.*)

BABBIE.   He was *rather* nice to you, you know—(*Turns to him with left hand on floor*)—about your breeks.

(CAPTAIN HALLIWELL *goes quickly off frowning, and observing a smile pass between father and daughter.* BABBIE *takes advantage of the smile.*)

His breeks !   (*Coaxingly*) Dear father !   (*Arm round his neck.*)

LORD RINTOUL (*promptly assuming the stern parent*).   None of your trying to get round me.   (*Putting her arm down.*)

BABBIE (*nearly crying over the difficulty of the situation*).   I don't know what to do !

LORD RINTOUL.   There is nothing for you to do.   You shall leave it all to us.

BABBIE.   You are sure that is the best plan ?

LORD RINTOUL.   Quite sure.

BABBIE (*as if to herself*).   Leave it all to father—he knows best.

LORD RINTOUL.   Besides, the law must take its course.

BABBIE (*clinging to the word*).   Yes, the law.   We can't go against the law, can we, father ?

LORD RINTOUL.   He is married, and he must face it.

BABBIE.   You 've got to face it, Mr. Dishart.   And she——— (*Sits by him.*)   She has got to face it too, hasn't she ?

LORD RINTOUL.   Must I pack you off to England, Babbie, or are you to come to your senses and confront this situation like a girl of spirit ?

BABBIE.   My senses !   Where are they ?   It is as if you had taken them away between you.

LORD RINTOUL.   Surely a daughter of mine can't go on caring for a man who has been playing with her.

BABBIE (*nicely*).   He hasn't, daddy, he loves me dearly.   He only called—that woman—his wife to save her.   Mere kindness.   Why shouldn't I love him still ?

LORD RINTOUL.   Kindness !   If you knew all I know !

BABBIE (*sharply*).   Oh !   (*Pointedly*)   How much do you know, father ?

LORD RINTOUL (*palpably lying*).   Babbie, he kissed her that night in the wood !

BABBIE.   No, he didn't.

LORD RINTOUL.   My dear, I was there, and you weren't. . . .

BABBIE.   You mean ?

LORD RINTOUL.   I mean I saw him do it.

BABBIE.   Take care, father, this is very important.   If *you* say *you* saw that———

LORD RINTOUL.   I do say it.

BABBIE.   Then I don't see why I shouldn't let things take their course.

LORD RINTOUL.   You give him up ?

BABBIE.   Father, if he is really married to this gipsy, *I* won't interfere to save him.

LORD RINTOUL.   That 's my true daughter.

BABBIE (*growing nervous again*).   At least, I don't think I will.   I am not sure.

LORD RINTOUL.   No weakening.

BABBIE (*facing him*).   Father, he must have been running after this girl at the very time he was making love to me.

LORD RINTOUL (*who is still sitting*).   I know he was.

BABBIE (*as if enraged*).   Oo !   (*Sits again, changing.*)   You won't do anything else to him, will you ?   (*Head on his shoulder.*)

LORD RINTOUL (*chuckling*).   To find himself married to that wench will be punishment enough for anyone.   (*Laughs.*)

BABBIE (*laughing*).   I dare say.

LORD RINTOUL.   A man must take the consequences of his rash acts.

BABBIE.   And so must the woman !   (*Big laugh.*)

LORD RINTOUL.   Exactly.   If ever man brought his doom upon himself he has done it.

BABBIE.   His doom !   Make way, Mr. Dishart, for your doom.   (*Suddenly afraid.*)   It is so irrevocable !   Irrevocable is an awful word, father.   (*Sits.*)   Shouldn't we let him off ?

LORD RINTOUL (*sternly*).   Now, now.   None of that.   Be brave.

BABBIE.   Perhaps it 's being rather hard on *her* ?

LORD RINTOUL.   You would have pity for her !   I expect she 's hungering for him.

BABBIE.   I dare say she is.   (*Changing*) I 'm frightened, father.

LORD RINTOUL.   All this pother !

BABBIE.   Father, you are *sure* you saw him kiss her in the wood ?

LORD RINTOUL.   Twice !

BABBIE.   Oh, that decides it !   Father, I shall have no mercy on him now.

LORD RINTOUL.   That 's my girl.

BABBIE.   Father, do your duty.

LORD RINTOUL.   I will.

(*He rises and crosses to fire.   She goes to him wheedlingly, yet half panic-stricken.*)

BABBIE.   There is just one other little thing—a very little thing—so tiny, just about that size.   (*Holding up her finger.*)

LORD RINTOUL (*at once suspicious*).   Well ?

BABBIE (*faltering*).   It would be easier to say if you would sit down, daddy——   (*She rather forces him back into armchair by fire.*)   You see, I—I——   (*Kneels by him.*)   I want to come with you, father.

LORD RINTOUL.   That would be vindictive.   No, no, I can't have that.   Besides, it would be too painful to you.

BABBIE.   I feel—I feel I could stand it.   Do let me come.

LORD RINTOUL.   You will stay at home.

BABBIE.   Father, I so want to see his face—when he hears *his doom.*   (*Head on his arm.*)

LORD RINTOUL.   It will certainly be worth observing !

BABBIE.   Then I may come !

LORD RINTOUL.   No, you may not.   I 'll tell you all about it when I get back.

BABBIE.   That won't be quite the same thing.   Father, I am a regrettably odd sort of girl, am I not ?

LORD RINTOUL.   You are indeed.

BABBIE.   And I am in a very excited state.   If you leave me behind I may do something monstrous.   Don't you think that for the next few hours it would be wise not to let me out of your sight.

LORD RINTOUL.   Gad, there 's more in that than you know ! After all, there is no particular reason against your coming. (*Looks at her.*)

BABBIE.   Oo !   (*Picks up cushion off couch and throws it up.*)

LORD RINTOUL.   But remember, this is my affair and Halliwell's.   I will have no interference.

BABBIE.   I promise not to say a word.   I shall leave it all to you.   (*Puts cushion back on sofa.*)

LORD RINTOUL.   Then on with a cloak and bonnet.   I shall be down in a moment.   (*Going to stair—he turns*) If I thought you might make a scene——

BABBIE.   *I* won't.   But I dare say somebody else will ! (*Both laughing.*)

LORD RINTOUL (*going upstairs, amused*).   I guarantee somebody else will !   A certain gentleman !   A certain gentleman !

> (*Leaves chuckling.* BABBIE, *left alone, pauses half-way to door with sinking courage.   From this point onwards she is more or less hysterical.*)

BABBIE.   Of course, I can't do it—never meant to do it. Oh, father, why did you tell that fib about the kiss ?   Think, Babbie, think, and draw back.

> (*Door opens and* FELICE *comes out, carrying a bonnet and cloak.   She is a correct maid, though secretly thrilled.*)

Remember, *irrevocable* !   Why—what, you have been listening, Felice !

FELICE.   My lady—eleven days.   (*She jumps.*)

BABBIE.   I don't want them, you know—I am not going. (*But she meekly lets cloak be put on her. Then with sudden thought*) Felice, I hope father will not think afterwards that I have deceived him ! (*Partly to herself—part vaguely to* FELICE) A minister ! I am very fond of him and he is sixteen feet by twelve, but there are sure to be mothers' meetings and I can't do it. (*Hands back the garments.*)   And now I must be a spinster all my life—I must either be a spinster all my life or have been married for eleven days ! (*At this thought she rushes into garments again, then has another fear.*)   Perhaps he would rather not !   Irrevocable !   I daren't do it—I can't.   I hear father coming ! (*Takes bonnet from* FELICE.)   I will tell him the truth.

FELICE (*disappointedly*).   My lady !

BABBIE.   Go away, Felice. (*Putting on bonnet.*)

FELICE (*reluctantly*).   But my lady !

BABBIE.   Please.

> (FELICE *goes off to room under compulsion.* BABBIE *is alone again.*)

'Father,' I will say, 'I am the gipsy ;   do you like me in this bonnet ? ' (*Speaking hysterically as if it were all one sentence.*) I couldn't possibly do it perhaps the other goes better with the cloak poor father but blue is my colour. (*Picks up torn warrant from table, then crosses down to couch and sits.*)   Gavin, Gavin, I love you so much in a silk dress black with beads on it and my father has been married to a gipsy for eleven days ! (*She has the pieces of torn warrant, lifts, kisses and puts in her bosom with little cries.*)

> (LORD RINTOUL, *coated for driving, reappears, and speaks as he comes down the stairs.*)

LORD RINTOUL.   I see Halliwell has got the dog-cart out. We mustn't keep him waiting.

BABBIE.   Father, I have something to say to you. (*She is genuinely loving as she pushes him excitedly into a chair and hugs him excitingly.*)

LORD RINTOUL (*struggling in her embrace*).   What is it ?   Quick ! (*She dabs frenzied little kisses on odd parts of him, his head, nose, chin, hat, and knees, all the while uttering hysterical sounds.*)

BABBIE (*retreating a little*).   I have something to say to you.

LORD RINTOUL.   What is it ?   What is it ?   Well—well !
(*Instead of saying it she rushes at him again on the other side and dabs more kisses on him—then standing to make confession.*)

BABBIE.   It 's this—it 's this—father, I am quite ready !
(*She puts her hand on his arm and they commence to go off.*)

ACT IV

The Manse Garden. It is now moonlight. The church is still lit up, and singing is going on in it in old-fashioned style, *i.e.* a man's voice in distance is indistinctly heard reading a line of a psalm, then the congregation sing it, and so on.

PRECENTOR.

'Snares, fire and brimstone, furious storms on sinners He shall rain.'

(*Congregation intones above line.*)

PRECENTOR.

'This as the portion of their cup doth unto them pertain.'

(*Congregation intones above line.* SNECKY, WHAMOND, *and* ANDREW *are sitting on wall of gate. They all have their hats in their hands.* DOW *is sitting miserably on wall.* MICAH *sits on wall with feet up.*)

SNECKY (*when the singing ceases*). That's the psalm finished.

(*They put on hats simultaneously.*)

Tammas, they have been in the kirk an hour and a half, and we canna keep them ony longer. You said you would tell them as soon as the psalm was finished.

WHAMOND. Will'um will be offering up a prayer now. I'll tell them when the prayer is finished.

SNECKY. It's the fourth time you've said that. Tammas, you're as loth to tell them as we are oursel's.

WHAMOND. It must be done. (*Gets off wall.*)

DOW. Your face is hard—your mind's made up. Afore this night is out he'll be without a hame and without a kirk—and it's me that has brought it on him. If he hadna run off wi' her, he would be at the prayer meeting this minute. (*Rises.*) It's me as has done this—me!

(*His grief affects them all, but they keep firm. Sentiment must be kept out of it.*)

200

WHAMOND (*affected, but compelling himself to be fierce*). Dinna break down ! Bear no ill-will, Rob, to an auld man that has a hard duty to do this night.

(WHAMOND *takes snuff and then offers snuff-box to* DOW. DOW *tries to take snuff, but cannot.*)

DOW.   I call you all to witness, I've done with religion—I 'd rather be playing cards in Hell than singing psalms in Heaven.

(DOW *exits through gate and* MICAH *follows him.*)

SNECKY.   Poor Rob !

ANDREW.   This is the end o't, and Mr. Dishart so highly edicated. That's the extraordinar' thing. He goes daft about a woman, and him so highly edicated.

SNECKY.   'Her Boy Am I.' What a sermon could be preached frae that text.

WHAMOND.   There never was a man that kent more about women, judged by his sermons.

SNECKY (*with a long groan*). Oh ! How he exposed them !

WHAMOND.   Mary, Martha, Sarah, Ruth, Hagar—he made the very teeth of them rattle in their mouths. It fair made me ashamed of being a married man.

ANDREW.   How he warned the young men about being careful in their choice. 'A religious woman is the only pearl of price,' says he, 'and see to it she belongs to your own denomination,' says he, 'and be no too hasty and watch her first in her home,' says he, 'for it is the good daughter that makes the good wife.'

WHAMOND.   You would have said he kent all about the women as plain as though he had wandered through them with a lighted candle.

SNECKY.   And yet it has come to this, as it comes to every son of Adam. For a while he thinks women is the poor miserable critturs we all ken them to be, till on a woeful day he sees one, very like the others, and something inside him goes crack, whether he be highly edicated or highly ignorant.

(*Enter* SILVA *at gate.*)

SILVA.   Tammas ! Tammas, there 's a queer piece o' gossip being handed frae mouth to mouth in the kirk.

WHAMOND (*sternly*). Gossip in the kirk !

SNECKY.   Oh, shame, shame ! (*Eagerly*) What is 't ?

SILVA. It's about him. Thae twa women, Bell Dundas and Tibbie Birse, that has been searching far and near to match the rose he was so fond o'——

ANDREW. They 're no at the meeting.

SILVA. They came creeping in a quarter of an hour since, near daft wi' triumph, for they 've found out that the rose only grows in the green-house o' Rintoul.

SNECKY. Keep 's all ! She had stolen it frae there !

SILVA. Ay ; undoubtedly, but that 's no what they think in the kirk, where the news ran round as soft as if a mouse was carrying it. At the back pews it was only that the rose had been pluckit at Rintoul ; half a dozen pews down they were whispering had he got it frae Lady Barbara ; and as I came out, Bell McQuhathy grips my hand and implores me to tell her for the love o' Heaven if it 's true that the minister is away buying the ring.

SNECKY. Oh, midgins, midgins !

ANDREW. Mr. Dishart married on a ladyship ! What a glory to our kirk !

(WHAMOND nods.)

SNECKY. And what a cause of jealousy—to other kirks !

SILVA. Tammas, this will only mak' them the more merciless when you tell them the truth.

WHAMOND. That 's so. He 's doomed.

ANDREW. H'st !

(WHAMOND, SILVA, and ANDREW look off. All listen intently. ANDREW nods to them excitedly. They look significantly to each other. WHAMOND looks straight before him. All follow his example. Enter GAVIN through gate. He stops, nervous, and taken aback at sight of them. They ignore him.)

GAVIN (trying to brazen it out). It is a beautiful night—quite like an evening in June.

(WHAMOND snorts. GAVIN takes SNECKY by arm.)
(Fiercely) Hobart—it—is—quite—like—an evening—in—June !

SNECKY (slowly). ' Her Boy Am I.'

GAVIN. Thomas Whamond !

(WHAMOND points slowly over his shoulder to the kirk.)

WHAMOND. Your prayer meeting. I see you 've been

running, Mr. Dishart ! That's no state for a minister's
hat.

> (GAVIN *takes off hat.*)

And your hair !

> (GAVIN *puts hat on again. All look at each other again.*
> GAVIN *goes to Manse door, rattles it, trying vainly to open*
> *it, then looks at* WHAMOND. WHAMOND *folds his arms*
> *again.* DOW *and* MICAH *re-enter anxiously at gate.*)

GAVIN.   Thomas Whamond, the key of the Manse,—quick !

WHAMOND (*fiercely*).   No ! Whaur have you been, Mr.
Dishart ?

GAVIN.   Don't attempt to hector me, sir. The key !

WHAMOND (*sadly*).   We have no desire to hector you, Mr.
Dishart. Our hearts are ower heavy for that. But what kept
you frae the meeting ?

GAVIN (*more softly*).   You have a right to ask me, but I cannot
tell you.

ANDREW.   Mr. Dishart, we ken all.

SNECKY.   Ay, we ken all—and the rest we can guess.

WHAMOND.   Say it wasna the Egyptian woman, and we'll
believe you. But say it was—and you shall never again cross
the threshold o' that Manse.

MICAH.   Oh, Mr. Dishart, say it. Look at my father and
say it !

> (WHAMOND *takes out key.*)

GAVIN.   I cannot say it.

> (*Elders become adamant.* WHAMOND *puts key of Manse*
> *into his pocket.*)

ANDREW (*hard, turning to* WHAMOND).   Tammas, the congregation is waiting—are you coming ?

WHAMOND (*sternly*).   I'm coming.

> (SNECKY *goes with him, and* SILVA *and* ANDREW *also turn*
> *to go.*)

DOW (*suddenly guarding the way*).   You pass me first !

GAVIN.   Rob, there must be no brawling here. Fall
back !

DOW (*breaking out*).   No, I winna fall back—and there shall
be brawling here ! Mr. Dishart, let me break their heads for
once, and I promise you I'll be a religious man for evermore.

GAVIN.   I forbid you.

WHAMOND.   Follow me.

   (*Some sound is heard.   They all look off.*)

ANDREW.   Wha are they?   Tak' tent o' yoursel's, lads!

MICAH.   The red-coats!   The red-coats!

WHAMOND.   Coming here!

GAVIN.   So soon!

   (*They fall back in consternation as* SERGEANT DAVIDSON
   and two Soldiers enter.)

Don't be alarmed!   These men have not come for you.

DAVIDSON.   I don't know what we have come for, Mr.
Dishart.   A servant from Rintoul came galloping into the
barracks with orders from the Captain to meet him here.   I
know no more.

SNECKY.   He 's no here.

DAVIDSON.   He will be here directly.   His dog-cart is on the
brae.

GAVIN (*to* DOW).   They have come for me.

   (DOW *turns up and threatens Soldiers.*)

No violence, Rob.

DAVIDSON.   I hope I see you well, sir.   My compliments to
Mrs. Dishart.

WHAMOND.   To wha?   (*Looks amazed at* GAVIN, *who turns
away.*)   Wha did he say?

MICAH.   I see the carriage!

DOW (*on wall*).   They 're getting out o't.   That 's Halliwell!

SNECKY.   And that 's Rintoul himself!

DOW.   There 's a woman wi' them.

GAVIN.   A woman?

DOW.
WHAMOND.   }Ay, it is—it 's a woman.   Wha can she be?
SILVA.

ANDREW.   She 's a younger kimmer.

DAVIDSON.   I see her face, Mr. Dishart; it 's your good
lady.

   (GAVIN *has no answer.*)

DOW.   Behears!   This beats all!   It 's the Egyptian!

SNECKY.   Oh! keep 's a' tod!   Dod!   Ay, faags, is that
her?   But she 's unca grand dressed for an Egyptian!

ANDREW.   Here they come!

WHAMOND. She's dressed up to the nines—but it's her !

OMNES. Ay, ay, they've catched her.

WHAMOND. Ay, they've got her.

(*Enter* LORD RINTOUL *with* BABBIE, *followed by* CAPTAIN HALLIWELL, *swaggering.* BABBIE *is very demure and trembling.*)

HALLIWELL. You are here, Davidson—that is well ! (*Gloating*) Good evening, Mr. Dishart—you scarcely thought you would see us so soon again—eh ?

GAVIN. You have lost no time, sir ; but I know what you have come for, and I am ready.

HALLIWELL. He knows what we have come for, Rintoul !

LORD RINTOUL (*grimly*). I think not, Mr. Dishart !

GAVIN. You are here to arrest me.

WHAMOND. Arrest him ?

HALLIWELL. Not at all.

(GAVIN *is surprised.*)

BABBIE (*faltering*). It is something much worse than that !

WHAMOND. Worse, eh ! (*Defending* GAVIN) Let's see you lay hand on our minister !

DOW. It'll be a bloody hand. Micah, bring my pike with the thick handle.

(MICAH *runs off.* LORD RINTOUL *stops him with a gesture.*)

LORD RINTOUL. Stop ! You men—my dispute with you is ended, let that be understood—but allow me to put a question to you. If a man and woman resident in Scotland—declare themselves married before witnesses, does that constitute a marriage ?

WHAMOND. What are you after ? You ken it does—everybody kens that !

SNECKY. We had a case o' the kind here—ay, and the man tried to get out o't. He said it was just done for fun. But he couldna—she *had* him ! They were tied for life.

LORD RINTOUL (*to* GAVIN). You hear, Mr. Dishart.

WHAMOND (*suddenly guessing*). You dinna mean that he——

SNECKY. Him !

ANDREW. Mr. Dishart !

HALLIWELL (*who, with* LORD RINTOUL, *has been enjoying* GAVIN'S *surprise and horror of Elders*). Davidson, come forward !

GAVIN (*excitedly*).   Stop ! Lord Rintoul ! (*To* HALLIWELL) I see what you are here for now—but I warn you—desist ! You don't know what you are doing.

HALLIWELL.   You will permit us to be the best judges of that.   Davidson, what are your grounds for thinking that Mr. Dishart is a married man ?

GAVIN.   Stop ! (*To* BABBIE) Do you not see what the object of all this is ?

BABBIE (*faltering*).   People must take the consequences of their rash acts !

HALLIWELL.   Does that satisfy you, sir ?   Answer me, Davidson.

(GAVIN *continues to stare at* BABBIE, *who sometimes peeps at him half-frightened.*)

DAVIDSON.   On the night we came after the rioters, I met Mr. Dishart in the wood.   The woman was wi' him.   They passed themselves off to me as man and wife.   I 'm sorry, Mr. Dishart, but I have two witnesses.   (*Signing to Soldiers.*)

HALLIWELL.   You corroborate the sergeant's evidence ?

SOLDIERS.   Yes, Captain.

LORD RINTOUL (*to* WHAMOND).   Is that sufficient, sir ?

WHAMOND.   It was the Egyptian ?

HALLIWELL.   Yes, he admitted it to me this evening.

LORD RINTOUL (*stepping forward and producing a document*). This is a paper in which his confession, as made to both of us, is set forth and signed by myself and Captain Halliwell.   We wrote it out in the dog-cart ;   shall I read it to you all ?

WHAMOND (*sorrowfully, after looking at* GAVIN).   It 's no necessary.

DOW.   All is over.

LORD RINTOUL.   It is far from my intention, Mr. Dishart, to crow over you—though you have tried me sore.

HALLIWELL.   We feel deeply for you.   (*Chuckling.*)

LORD RINTOUL.   But I am a magistrate, and there is no getting past this document—it is your marriage lines.

HALLIWELL.   Your marriage lines, sir.

BABBIE.   Your—marriage—lines—sir !

(GAVIN *goes towards her.   She retreats from him in fear and sits on seat.*)

GAVIN.   Sergeant——

DAVIDSON.   I must stick to my words, Mr. Dishart—you called that woman there your wife.

(LORD RINTOUL *and* CAPTAIN HALLIWELL, *who have been complacent, start.*)

HALLIWELL.   What 's that ?

DAVIDSON.   I am only saying, Captain, that is the woman. (*Seeing something is wrong.*)   Is that not what you wanted me to say ?

LORD RINTOUL.   You are a fool, man.   It was the gipsy that he married.

DAVIDSON.   Begging your lordship's pardon, but that *is* the gipsy.

WHAMOND.   Do you think we dinna ken her because she 's grand dressed ?

LORD RINTOUL.   That—that is my daughter !

(*This causes a stir.*)

SNECKY.   ?   (*Licks his lips.*)

WHAMOND.   His daughter ?

(*Pause.*)

DAVIDSON.   Heaven help me, what have I done ?

HALLIWELL.   I tell you—that is Lady Barbara Yuill.

LORD RINTOUL (*wildly*).   Mr. Dishart—Babbie, tell them who you are.

BABBIE (*quaking*).   But I—I—I am not quite sure, father !

WHAMOND (*grandly*).   I think I can tell you who she is—that 's Lady Barbara *Dishart* !

LORD RINTOUL (*choking and going to* BABBIE).   Was—was it you ?

(BABBIE *rises, retreats quaking, then nods.*)

How ?

(*Elders all gather, with their heads together.*)

BABBIE.   By the secret staircase !   You remember I told you—you ought to have that panel nailed up !   I wanted to save the weavers.   You always said I took my sense of humour from you, father !   And then he—(*Looking at* GAVIN)— he thought I was a gipsy.   It was so stupid of him, just because I was wearing a gipsy dress—and he made love to me——

WHAMOND.   The Minister !   (*Looks at* GAVIN.)

BABBIE.   Yes, you did !   I was very angry——

GAVIN. Oh !

BABBIE. I *was*—so I went out to meet him again, just to show him that—just to *show* him—and he thought I was a gipsy all the time, and—(*Desperate*)—and—so stupid of him—and so—father—

(HALLIWELL *stamps his foot.*)

—it is all Dick's fault !

HALLIWELL. My fault !

WHAMOND. The Captain's fault !

(*Soldiers chuckle.* HALLIWELL *glares at them.*)

BABBIE. Well, if it isn't your fault, it is this man's. (*Looks reprovingly at* GAVIN.) I won't have father blamed !

LORD RINTOUL (*stepping back*). You—you—— (*Frantic.*)

(BABBIE *retreats and sits on doorstep of Manse.* HALLIWELL *is about to seize the paper which is on seat, but* MICAH *seizes it, gives it to* DOW.)

HALLIWELL. Mr. Dishart, it cannot be that you are willing to take advantage of Lord Rintoul's infernal blunder ?

RINTOUL. *My* blunder ! Yours from beginning to end.

WHAMOND. It matters little whether he is willing to take advantage of it or no, but I think I ken four simple auld men that mean to do.

SNECKY. Four simple auld men—it 's nobly said.

(*Elders are gathered complacently round* WHAMOND *to great delight of* DOW.)

WHAMOND. Rob Dow, that paper. (*To* MICAH) Micah, send the congregation here.

(*Exit* MICAH *triumphantly.*)

HALLIWELL (*desperately*). Rintoul, I have been laughed at sufficiently about this gipsy, but when this is known—— !

LORD RINTOUL (*pettishly*). Always thinking of yourself !

WHAMOND (*facing the Elders*). My best plan, I think, will be to read this document to the congregation—the marriage lines, as it has been truly called !

(*He eyes* LORD RINTOUL *and* CAPTAIN HALLIWELL, *who groan.*)

Unless—— ?

HALLIWELL (*eagerly*). Unless ?

WHAMOND. Unless your lordship was just to tell them that

your daughter is—what 's the word ?—engaged to be married to Mr. Dishart. Then we could have a second marriage at Rintoul, and none but oursel's standing solemnly here need ever ken about the first.

HALLIWELL. Rintoul, you must do it.

RINTOUL (*rebelliously*). *Must*, sir !

HALLIWELL. If you don't—I shall order my men to arrest the gipsy.

GAVIN (*fiercely*). Sir !

HALLIWELL. I swear it !

BABBIE. Father !

(*A hum of people is heard.*)

WHAMOND. Which is it to be ?

LORD RINTOUL. It will all leak out in any case.

WHAMOND. Which is it to be ?

LORD RINTOUL. Fold up that paper. (*Groans.*)

(BABBIE *takes the document from* WHAMOND. *The Congregation come crowding in excitedly, led by* NANNY, *some through gate, some get on walls. They are chattering— cries of '* It 's her, it 's her ladyship———' 'That 's RINTOUL—eh, the red-coats, lads, lads, losh,' *etc., etc.* WHAMOND *signs silence. Those in front are pushed forward.*)

MAN (*in front*). Tell them to stop shoving, Tammas.

WHAMOND. Stand back there !

(*The two Soldiers shove Crowd back.*)

Now, my lord. (*To* LORD RINTOUL.)

LORD RINTOUL (*reluctantly*). My—my friends———

(*Excited murmurs from Crowd.*)

My daughter here and your minister—they have—you know what young people are—they———

VOICES (*from the crowd*). Are they to be married ?

LORD RINTOUL (*sulkily*). Yes, that is it.

NANNY. And you are willing ?

(LORD RINTOUL *looks furiously at* CAPTAIN HALLIWELL.)

HALLIWELL (*maliciously*). Lord Rintoul is *delighted*.

(*Joyous shouts from Crowd.* LORD RINTOUL *is scowling at* HALLIWELL, *who smiles at him maliciously.*)

JEAN (*bursting forward*). A ladyship ! I 'm to be a ladyship's servant ! (*Turns to back, calls grandiloquently*) Sanders McCormick, are you there ?

VOICE (*inside gate from unseen man in Crowd*). Ay, I am, Jean !

JEAN. Then here 's my answer now, Sanders. (*With a grand wave of her arms*) It 's hopeless. (*Curtseys to* BABBIE.)
(*Laughter from Crowd.*)

LORD RINTOUL. My daughter asks me to tell you that it was Captain Halliwell who brought this match about. So three cheers for Captain Halliwell !

(HALLIWELL *is furious. The Crowd cheer.* HALLIWELL *exits furiously at gate, followed by Soldiers and* DAVIDSON. *The Crowd leaves, cheering and laughing.* NANNY *goes down to* BABBIE, *shakes hands.*)

GAVIN. Rob ! (*He grasps* DOW's *hand.*)

DOW. I 'm glad. I 'm glad.
(DOW *exits through gate.*)

NANNY. I see the whole thing clear now ! (*To* GAVIN) *You* kent she was a leddyship all the time !

(SILVA *and* ANDREW *shake hands with* GAVIN.)

SNECKY (*gleaming—to* GAVIN). Mr. Dishart, ' Her Boy Am I.'

WHAMOND. Mr. Dishart. I want to give you your first marriage present, the key of the Manse. (*Hands key, shakes hands, and goes to* BABBIE.) I 'm Chief Elder.

(BABBIE *kisses him. He stands amazed and then exits through gate, followed by Elders. Exeunt all Weavers.* GAVIN *crosses and unlocks Manse door. He puts hat on seat and he and* BABBIE *look at* LORD RINTOUL *and then at each other.* BABBIE *signs to him to leave it to her. She takes courage by kissing marriage lines and makes* GAVIN *kiss them. She goes half-way to* LORD RINTOUL *and stops.*)

BABBIE. Father—— (*Kneels and puts arms round his neck.*) Father, I am so sorry this has occurred. I love him so much, father, I really do—but—but—but I love my dear sweet darling father best. What did you say, father ?

LORD RINTOUL (*who has so far submitted without gesture*). Mr. Dishart, may I go inside—out of this girl's sight ?

(*As* LORD RINTOUL *is taking a step toward Manse door, cheering is heard in distance. He grins.*)

Listen to them cheering Halliwell ! (*Laughing.*)

> (*The cheering turns into a snatch of the hated song, which dies away.*)

BABBIE (*quickly*).   You had the best of it with Dick, at all events, father ! (*Laughing.*)

LORD RINTOUL (*chuckling*).   Hadn't I ! (*Sternly*) You minx ! (*He has started to go to the door when he turns and looks at her curiously.*)   Do you understand the seriousness of it ?

> (*She is serious and can only nod in reply. He is moved and speaks kindly.*)

If you are afraid, child, and he is generous—you can perhaps leave him still.

BABBIE (*going to him and putting hand in his, sweetly*).   Daddy dear, I am afraid—but I am not so afraid as that.

LORD RINTOUL (*wondering*).   Not afraid for yourself, Mr. Dishart ?

GAVIN.   No, sir.

LORD RINTOUL.   She is—an odd one, you know.

GAVIN.   Yes, I know.

BABBIE.   You do !

LORD RINTOUL.   Both so confident. (*He is thinking of their future.*) I wonder. (*More lightly*) Mr. Dishart, if you would just let me bring this about her shoulders for once. I think I might forgive her in time.

> (GAVIN *smiles.* LORD RINTOUL *goes into Manse.* GAVIN *and* BABBIE, *who are some distance apart, are arrested in their desire to rush into each other's arms by a boy-and-girl shyness.*)

GAVIN.   Babbie, my wife.

BABBIE (*after a pause*).   Eleven days.

> (*They embrace.*)

GAVIN.   I do like being married.

BABBIE.   So do I—to you, I mean.

GAVIN.   That's what I mean, too.

BABBIE (*a little tremulously as she looks at the church*).   Is that it ?

GAVIN.   Yes, my dear church.

> (*Lights in Manse appear.*)

BABBIE.   I can't think what father meant when he said, ' I wonder.'

GAVIN.   Babbie, that is the window of your drawing-room.
(*She blows it a kiss.*)
Just come a little nearer this way.

BABBIE.   Was it from there you threw the rose ?

GAVIN.   Yes, it fell there ;   no, a little farther to the left,
there.

BABBIE.   I shall plant a rose-tree there.   (*Places her hand on
his breast.*)

GAVIN.   My dear wife, it is a beautiful May evening and
before we go indoors I should so like to walk you once round
the premises as if I owned you, you know, to let the stars see us.
(*He shyly crooks his arm and she puts her hand in it.
They make a brief turn of the garden and he is now
strutting while she is shy.   They get to Manse door.*)
Babbie !
(SNECKY, ANDREW, WHAMOND, SILVA, *and* DOW *kneel
behind wall, with arms on wall.*   GAVIN *and* BABBIE *run
into the Manse.*)

THE WEDDING GUEST

Produced at the Garrick Theatre on September 27, 1900, with the following cast :

MR. FAIRBAIRN . . .	*Brandon Thomas*
PAUL DIGBY . . .	*H. B. Irving*
THE REV. MR. GIBSON .	*Henry Vibart*
PROVOST CROSBIE . . .	*Charles Daly*
BAILIE BLAIR . . .	*Fewlass Llewellyn*
MEIKLE	*A. E. George*
MARGARET FAIRBAIRN .	*Dorothea Baird*
LADY JANET DUNWOODIE .	*Kate Sergeantson*
BLANCHE RIPLEY . . .	*Ethelwyn Arthur-Jones*
MRS. TEVIOT . . .	*Augusta Dewsnap*
JENNY GEDDES . . .	*Joan Burnett*
MAID	*Blanche Wilmot*
KATE OMMANEY . . .	*Violet Vanbrugh*
COL. FARQUHAR . . .	*J. Corny Kavanagh*
ALEXANDER RIACH . .	*Mr. Bridges*
THE SHIRRAH . . .	*Ernest Martin*
SIR HENRY DUNN, BART.	*L. Pollock*
MR. MENZIES . . .	*Langhorne Burton*
THE FISCAL . . .	*Mr. Stanley*
GORDON OF THE WHAUPS .	*Mr. Flood*
FOOTMEN	*Messrs. Herbert and Vincent*

The play ran for 100 performances.

ACT I

DRAWING-ROOM at the Old Keep. At back a large open window from which steps lead down into garden. Against the walls are narrow tables covered with wedding presents. The room is gaily decorated with flowers, and the time is noon on a summer's day.

> (*The curtain rises on* MARGARET *in wedding dress, and* BLANCHE *in bridesmaid's dress.* MARGARET *is practising moving about in long train which* BLANCHE *solemnly holds up at end. They go round and round the room, winding in and out among the furniture. Enter* PAUL DIGBY, *the bridegroom.*)

PAUL. Margaret, how lovely——

BLANCHE. H'sh! Don't speak. She is rehearsing how to carry her train.

PAUL. It is like learning to bicycle. Margaret, try if you can go alone now.

MARGARET (*bravely*). Let go, Blanche.

> (MARGARET *nervously winds in and out by herself.*)

PAUL. Splendid! (*Her train catches in a chair.*) Back pedal! (*He has to jump train.*)

BLANCHE. Now stop at the spot where you are to stand during the ceremony.

MARGARET (*triumphant and breathless*). There!

BLANCHE. But is that where the bride and bridegroom stand? I thought you stood over here.

MARGARET (*sitting down, almost in tears*). Oh, Blanche! Oh! Oh! Oh! and we are to be married in half an hour!

> (*Enter* MEIKLE, *the butler, with flowers.*)

Meikle, my chief bridesmaid does not know where we are to stand yet!

> (MEIKLE *looks sadly at* BLANCHE.)

BLANCHE (*in despair*).   I can't help it.   The idea of your being married in a room seems so odd to me.

MEIKLE (*who is most Scotch when he is trying to be very English*). Beg pardon, miss, but where might the English be married?

BLANCHE.   In church, of course.

(MEIKLE *smiles tolerantly*.)

PAUL.   We English give Meikle a good deal of amusement, Miss Ripley.

MEIKLE.   Beg pardon, sir, I do my best to keep it in.   (*Tries not to laugh at the quaint ways of the English*.)

MARGARET.   Let us go through the ceremony again.   Meikle, don't go—come here.   Stand there—you are the bridegroom.

PAUL.   No, no, I am the bridegroom.

MARGARET.   That would be unlucky.   Let me see, I am the minister, and Blanche can be the bride, and you are the father giving her away.   Now then, stupid, go out and bring her in on your arm.

(PAUL *and* BLANCHE *go out gaily*.   MEIKLE *becomes entangled in train*.)

MARGARET.   Oh!   Don't move, Meikle!   I must take it off —it will be soiled.   Do you see the hook?   Lift it up—gently— don't breathe.

MEIKLE.   Beg pardon, miss, but——

MARGARET.   Don't speak—your words might fall on it. (*Between them they take off train and she spreads it out lovingly on chair at back*.)

PAUL (*putting his head in at door*).   Are you ready?

MARGARET.   Wait a moment till I feel more like a man. Come in when I say ' Pop.'

(PAUL *withdraws his head*.   MARGARET *tries to look mannish—after pause :*)

Pop !

(*Enter* PAUL, *very fatherly, with* BLANCHE *on his arm. He puts her by* MEIKLE'S *side and stands behind*.)

(*Solemnly*) I need not tell you, my young friends, that you are about to take an important step.   James Meikle, do you take this——

MEIKLE.   Excuse me, miss, but the certificate is read first.

MARGARET.   Oh yes.   (*Indifferently*) I hereby certify that it is certified, etc.   (*With unction*) James Meikle, do you——

MEIKLE.   Then comes the prayer, then the exhortation——

BLANCHE.   Do we kneel at the prayer ?

MARGARET.   No, we shut our eyes only.   Well, consider that finished.   James Meikle, do——

MEIKLE.   Join hands, miss.

MARGARET (*effusively*).   Ah !   Join hands.

(MEIKLE *and* BLANCHE *join hands.*)

James Meikle, do you take this woman, Blanche Ripley, to be your lawful wedded wife ?

(MEIKLE *hesitates.*)

BLANCHE.   You are not very complimentary, Meikle.

MEIKLE (*in distress*).   The fact is, miss, I am a married man and, according to Scotch law, if I was to say ' I do ' before witnesses——

BLANCHE (*startled*).   You—you don't mean—— !

MEIKLE.   It would be bigamy, miss.

(*Horror of* BLANCHE.)

PAUL (*affecting seriousness*).   Shall we go on with the ceremony ?

(BLANCHE *rushes out.*)

MEIKLE.   Begging everybody's pardon.   (*Exit apologetically*).

(PAUL *and* MARGARET *have been laughing, but now that they are alone they stand apart looking at each other self-consciously and love-sick.*   PAUL *goes nearer her and gazes with arms folded.   She gazes, then modestly lets her eyes fall as if overpowered by the splendour of him.   He puts his hands on her shoulders and they gaze with adoration.*)

PAUL.   How beautiful you look—my bride !

(*They sigh, then wake up.*)

Any more wedding gifts ?

MARGARET (*sadly*).   Another salad bowl !

PAUL.   That makes—nine—salad bowls !   But let us look on the bright side, as your father would say.   Margaret, I have good news—two offers for my ' Birth of Sorrow ' picture.

(*He draws her on to couch.*)

MARGARET (*impulsively*).   Oh, tell me !   Quick !

PAUL.   I want you to decide which I should accept.   The one is from a dealer who offers five hundred pounds.

MARGARET.   The dear man !

PAUL.   The other is from the French Government—two thousand francs.

MARGARET.   How splendid !   How much is that ?

PAUL.   About eighty pounds.

MARGARET.   The impertinence !

PAUL.   But, dear, it is the eighty pounds I should like you to let me take.

MARGARET.   Paul !

PAUL.   Think of the honour.   My picture chosen by the Government of France to hang in the Luxembourg.

MARGARET.   But five hundred pounds !

PAUL.   Shall we accept it ?

MARGARET.   No, no.   I am an ignorant girl, dear ; but I begin to see what it is to be an artist's wife.   Paul, the picture shall go to Paris.

PAUL (*delighted*).   My noble girl !   Time enough to paint for money, dear, when I am an Academician with half a dozen chins.

MARGARET.   It is you who are noble.   I have heard people say, again and again, that no one could conceive such subjects as yours, much less paint them, who was not a noble character himself.   So there !

PAUL (*sadly*).   Ah, they don't understand.   It is only the best of us, Margaret, that goes into our pictures.   A man may rise above himself for an hour, and yet be a poor thing enough for the rest of the day.   And it has been so with me.

MARGARET.   Paul, it is when you say such things that I love you most.

PAUL.   Because you don't believe them.

MARGARET.   No !   (*He sighs and she has a sudden thought.*) Paul, have you ever kept anything from me ?

PAUL (*after hesitating*).   How could I ?

MARGARET.   Do you know, I almost wish you had. (*Shuddering*) Because I have kept something from you.

PAUL.   Impossible !

MARGARET.   Yes, I have, about a man !   I have wanted to tell you, but it was so awful.   Oh, let me tell you now. (*With a rush*) Paul, when I was seventeen, it was in the conservatory—his name was Jack—he kissed me !

PAUL.   Is that all, dear ?

MARGARET. All? Is it not enough? Could there be worse?

PAUL (*fondly*). You child!

MARGARET. And now we know everything about each other.

(*He turns away with a pained face.*)

And we are as much in love as ever!

PAUL (*passionately*). Margaret, if you were to love me one tittle less——

MARGARET. As if I could!

(*Enter up steps and through window* CAPTAIN ARMITAGE, *a gay young man.*)

ARMITAGE (*with the privileged importance of a best man*). Aha, young man! Come with me at once and have your hair curled.

PAUL. Armitage, begone!

ARMITAGE. Come, sir, I insist. I am your best man, and don't give me the slip again. Why, the guests are beginning to arrive.

MARGARET. Already! (*Jumping up.*)

ARMITAGE. I heard Mr. Fairbairn say that Lady Janet Dunwoodie's carriage is in the avenue.

MARGARET. Aunt Janet!

(*Runs out gleefully.*)

ARMITAGE (*surveying* PAUL). A bit nervous?

PAUL (*boldly*). Not in the least.

ARMITAGE. You look like a ghost.

PAUL (*nervously*). Stop it!

ARMITAGE (*observing train*). Hallo, what's this?

PAUL (*not paying much attention and thinking about other things*). Margaret's train. She took it off.

ARMITAGE. And leaves it lying about in this careless way! Hasn't even rolled it up! Upon my soul, I think you have both gone crazy, and if I wasn't here to take charge of you I believe the marriage would never come off. Disgraceful! (*Folds up train and puts it in ingle-nook.*) There now, that's what I call tidy.

PAUL (*who has been communing with himself*). Armitage, this Aunt Janet—I don't know her, though she lives near here, and Margaret is very anxious that she should like me. (*Anxiously*) Do you think she will like me?

ARMITAGE. I shouldn't think so. You are not the sort of man I would fancy if I were a woman. Shouldn't wonder if she were to dote on me, though.

PAUL. She is said to be very formidable. A *grande dame*.

ARMITAGE. I thought there were no Scotch *grandes dames*.

PAUL. My young friend, there are only Scotch ones.

ARMITAGE. You alarm me. Married ?

PAUL. No. Fairbairn told me she was once engaged, but broke off the marriage on discovering that the man—well, she discovered something about a woman.

(He speaks in a pained voice. ARMITAGE looks at him cynically. PAUL turns away, unable to face him. MARGARET enters with LADY JANET. She is an aristocratic, haughty old lady, with a sense of humour and a suspicion of young gentlemen.)

MARGARET. Paul, here is Aunt Janet !

LADY JANET. Is this Mr. Digby ? *(Looking at ARMITAGE.)*

ARMITAGE *(with a complacency that ruffles all her feathers).* Only his best man, Lady Janet.

LADY JANET *(with excessive politeness).* I 'm glad of that.

(It dawns slowly on ARMITAGE that she is not paying him a compliment.)

MARGARET. This is Paul, auntie.

(PAUL comes forward and bows. LADY JANET shakes hands.)

LADY JANET. I seem to know your face, Mr. Digby. Ever been in this part of the world before ?

PAUL. Only once—before I knew Margaret—I was sketching, eighteen months ago.

LADY JANET. Ah, indeed.

MARGARET. That was how it began, auntie, though I didn't meet him then. But father met him and that led to his asking father to go and see his pictures when we were next in London. And that led to *my* going to the studio—and that led to—to—— *(She blushes.)*

ARMITAGE *(willing to give her ladyship another chance).* To my wanting to lead him off now, to curl his hair.

(LADY JANET surveys him, and ARMITAGE'S complacency again deserts him.)

LADY JANET *(to MARGARET).* Then I knew him before you

did. (*To* PAUL) I was sure I remembered your face. I saw you—it must have been on that occasion you speak of—you were making a sketch—let me see—of some fishing-boats.

PAUL (*smiling*). I remember—and you asked to see the sketch—you didn't think much of it !

LADY JANET. I liked the boats, but the figure was wrong. You should have had a boatman or a fisher-girl—instead of an elegantly dressed lady. Who was she, by-the-bye ?

PAUL (*with an effort*). She was—a lady who happened to be there—so I put her in.

LADY JANET. I see. (*Turns to look at presents.*)

MARGARET (*brightly*). There, Captain Armitage, you can take him away and curl his hair now.

ARMITAGE. Come along, young man ! (*He makes a last attempt to impress* LADY JANET.) I am a great hand at hair-curling, Lady Janet.

(*He reflects, then exits hastily after* PAUL.)

LADY JANET. What a lot of ugly presents you have got, Margaret !

MARGARET. They are sweet ! But never mind the presents, auntie. Do you like my wedding gown ?

LADY JANET. Delicious.

MARGARET. This is the train. (*Looks for it.*) Why—what—ah, I can see, my maid has been in and carried it off. (*Effusively*) Auntie, what do you think of *him* ? Isn't he heavenly ?

LADY JANET (*tantalisingly*). Hum !

MARGARET. Auntie !

LADY JANET. There, there, you goose—I like him.

(MARGARET *kisses her hand.*)

Ah, you baby, you are only ten years old.

MARGARET. Eighteen.

LADY JANET. Ten. You were ten when your mother died, and your father has kept you at that—like a stopped clock.

MARGARET. Well, Paul likes me at ten.

LADY JANET. We all like you at ten, but——

MARGARET. And if I am more ignorant than most girls, Aunt Janet, it was father who brought me up so. It is his theory.

LADY JANET. Or is it only his laziness ? Easy-going Fairbairn, we used to call him, and Look-on-the-bright-side Fairbairn and

Hope-for-the-best Fairbairn. They were phrases always in his mouth.

MARGARET. Father is very clever ; he is an optimist.

LADY JANET. All lazy men are.

(MARGARET *is offended.* LADY JANET *rises and pets her.*) Well, good-bye, dear little Margaret Fairbairn. In a few minutes there will be no Margaret Fairbairn in the world—a Mrs. Paul Digby will have taken her place.

MARGARET (*timidly*). But she will be the same person. It is only a new label.

LADY JANET (*with feeling*). My child, it is much more than that.

MARGARET (*almost in a whisper*). Aunt Janet, last night I was so full of glee and I brought out my wedding gown and blew kisses to it, and I said, ' O God, make me a good wife to Paul,' and suddenly, while I was so happy, a cold chill fell upon my heart and I was afraid. (*Clinging to her*) Aunt Janet, I was afraid.

LADY JANET. I know, my lamb, I know—every woman knows, and not a man among them, not a man. But I cannot help you—I can pray for you, pray that you are being united to a good man, but I cannot guide you. (*Rather bitterly*) I am only an old maid.

MARGARET (*kissing her*). Dear !

LADY JANET (*brightly*). Upon my soul, Margaret, I believe I have been jealous of you, filling your head with presentiments on your wedding day.

(*Enter* MEIKLE.)

MEIKLE. Begging your pardon, my lady, but the young woman you brought with you——

LADY JANET. Bless me, I had forgotten her——

MARGARET. Your maid ?

LADY JANET. No, only a woman—a lady—— Is she a lady, Meikle ?

MEIKLE. I couldn't quite make up my mind, my lady.

LADY JANET. Nor could I. But she is English, she told me, and is lodging at one of the villages near here—I don't know which. I found her by the side of the road, seemingly very faint, and I thought odd—as if she were almost off her head. She kept muttering to herself.

MARGARET. Oh, poor thing !

LADY JANET. We soon brought her to, and she has recovered her wits, if she ever lost them—but as this was the nearest house I thought the best thing I could do was to bring her here, and ask Meikle to give her a glass of wine.

MARGARET. Yes.

MEIKLE. I have done so, miss, and now she says she is able to walk home.

MARGARET. Meikle, the poor thing must not walk. Get someone to drive her home. Do you know her ?

MEIKLE. Never set eyes on her before.

LADY JANET. She told me she was a Mrs. Ommaney.

MARGARET ? A stranger and ill. Have I time to see her, Meikle ?

MEIKLE (*seeking to dissuade her*). Only ten minutes, miss.

MARGARET. Then show her in here.

(*Exit* MEIKLE *protesting*.)

LADY JANET. Why should you take this trouble, Margaret —on your wedding day, too ?

MARGARET. On my wedding day, auntie, I should so love to be kind to everyone.

LADY JANET. Well, I hope she will be more grateful to you than she was to me. She said I was quizzing her—and so I was !

(*Enter* MEIKLE.)

MEIKLE. Mrs. Ommaney.

(MEIKLE *retires when* MRS. OMMANEY *enters. She is well dressed, rather too gaily, but seems a lady. Her face is pale. She enters quietly and with a lack of interest, but on seeing* LADY JANET *she bridles*.)

MARGARET (*to her*). Mrs. Ommaney, my aunt has told me that you are ill. Do sit down.

MRS. OMMANEY (*sitting and speaking quietly*). I am all right now, thank you. I took no food to-day. That is all.

LADY JANET. Why ?

MRS. OMMANEY (*listlessly*). Oh, I forgot—I had other things to think of.

LADY JANET. What other things ?

(MRS. OMMANEY *bridles again*.)

MARGARET. Aunt Janet !

LADY JANET. You were very strange in your manner when I found you.

MRS. OMMANEY (*in distress*). Was I ?

LADY JANET. You were muttering to yourself.

MRS. OMMANEY (*defiantly*). No, I wasn't. (*Anxiously*) What was I saying ?

LADY JANET. That 's what I want to know.

(MRS. OMMANEY *turns on her angrily.*)

MARGARET (*to* LADY JANET). Don't.

MRS. OMMANEY (*looking* LADY JANET *over*). You are ' my lady,' I understand.

LADY JANET. Yes, but don't let that terrify you.

MRS. OMMANEY. It doesn't. It is what people used to call me.

LADY JANET. Why ?

MARGARET (*to* MRS. OMMANEY). Don't answer her.

MRS. OMMANEY. Oh, she won't sleep until she knows. Because my father, who is a Cornish fisherman, educated me beyond my station, with the result that I must needs fly to London. I got into a dressmaker's shop there. My figure was admired, so I was the woman on whom the gowns were tried, to show them off to customers who were fools enough to think they would look as I looked in them. (*Looking at* LADY JANET'S *cloak.*) Yes, I have tried on that cloak. (*Examining it with deliberate impertinence.*) Yes.

LADY JANET (*amused as well as indignant*). The minx !

MARGARET. Auntie, it serves you right. Mrs. Ommaney, I have ordered a carriage to take you back to your lodgings.

MRS. OMMANEY. I need no one's charity.

LADY JANET. There ! I told you !

MARGARET. To please me.

MRS. OMMANEY (*indifferently*). Oh, very well.

MARGARET. You see, auntie, no one can resist a bride.

MRS. OMMANEY. A bride ! Are you a bride ? (*With first show of interest.*)

MARGARET. I am to be married——here——in a few minutes.

MRS. OMMANEY. Here ?

MARGARET. Yes. But you are English, are you not ? So you had been married in a church.

MRS. OMMANEY (*suspiciously*). You are prying !

LADY JANET.   Of course we are.

MARGARET.   No, no !

LADY JANET.   Well, I am.   That 's where the fun of being an old woman comes in.   Why have you come to this part of the world, Mrs. Ommaney ?

MARGARET (*in despair*).   Oh !   (*In coaxing voice*) Auntie, you have just time to go and take off your bonnet.

> (LADY JANET *affects indignation but* MARGARET *gets rid of her.*)

MRS. OMMANEY (*in mental distress*).   I wasn't strange in my manner——I wasn't——I wasn't !

MARGARET.   No, of course not, Mrs. Ommaney, and do forgive me.   Indeed I did not mean to pry.

MRS. OMMANEY (*without much interest*).   I believe you——you have a good face——I wish you luck.   But I don't care who knows why I am here——(*Bitterly*)——I came for a fool's reason—— because I had been here before——an eternity ago.

MARGARET.   Alone ?

MRS. OMMANEY (*sharply*).   No——not alone.   I had been happy here once and so I wanted to see the place again.   The footpath by the cliffs, the boats in the bay, the cows munching on their way home down green lanes, the little arbour in the wood——

MARGARET.   I know——they call it the Lover's Seat.

MRS. OMMANEY.   We called it that, too.   It seemed so beautiful then !

MARGARET.   And now ?

MRS. OMMANEY.   Now the path by the cliff is but a muddy cattle track, and I turned shuddering from the boats and the green lanes and I went to the Lover's Seat and spat on it.

MARGARET.   Ah, I begin to see.   He was with you the first time, but when you came back——

MRS. OMMANEY.   I came back alone.   Yes, that 's it.   Oh, it 's a common enough story.   Turn me out now, revile me.

MARGARET.   Revile you !   My dear, my dear, I am so sorry for you.

MRS. OMMANEY (*surprised*).   You mean it ?   You sweet girl.   I thought you would——

MARGARET.   Upbraid you for speaking so bitterly of your loss ?   No——no !

H

MRS. OMMANEY (*suddenly*).   But do you understand ?

MARGARET.   Indeed I do.   It flashed upon me when you said those words, ' I came back alone.'   Your husband is dead now.   Mrs. Ommaney, I believe it was your wedding trip. Was it ?   It was !   And I have been speaking of my happiness to you.   Can you ever forgive me ?

MRS. OMMANEY (*grimly*).   I forgive you !

(MR. FAIRBAIRN'S *voice is heard shouting from garden.*)

MR. FAIRBAIRN (*outside*).   Come along—we must be there to receive the guests.

MRS. OMMANEY.   Time I was off.   Good luck !   (*Exit wearily.*)

MARGARET.   Oh, don't go !

(*Enter* MR. FAIRBAIRN *and* PAUL *from verandah.*)

MR. FAIRBAIRN (*affectionately*).   Whom were you speaking to, Margaret ?

MARGARET.   A poor lady with such a sad history, father. She is a widow.

MR. FAIRBAIRN (*whose optimism is entirely sincere*).   Dear, dear !   But perhaps it was all for the best.   Always look on the bright side, Margaret.

PAUL.   Is she coming to the wedding ?

MARGARET.   Oh, no——   (*Suddenly*) Paul, shall I ask her ?

PAUL.   By all means, if you want to.

MARGARET.   How good of you !   I shall.   (*Exit.*)

MR. FAIRBAIRN.   Ah me, to think that I am losing my dear daughter.

PAUL.   I should like to think, Mr. Fairbairn, that you could find a bright side even to that, but I fear it is impossible.

MR. FAIRBAIRN (*reflecting*).   Difficult, but not impossible.   I shall smoke in the drawing-room now.   And the minister has promised to drop in of an evening.   We play draughts together. (*Chuckling*) He gets so angry when I beat him !   I usually beat him !

(*Enter* ARMITAGE *excitedly.*)

ARMITAGE.   Digby, have you got the ring ?

PAUL.   Yes.   (*Feels pockets.*)   It 's gone !   (*Is rushing off wildly.*)

ARMITAGE (*laughing*).   I 've got it !   (*Gives it to* PAUL.)

(*Enter* MEIKLE *importantly.*)

MEIKLE.   Are you all ready, sir ?   They are coming.

ARMITAGE.   One moment, Meikle.

(*Exit* MEIKLE.)

Young man, your hour has come. You are about to be turned off. (*Offering hand*) Friend of my youth, farewell !

(PAUL *is wildly putting on gloves.*)

PAUL.   Stop it, Armitage !

(BLANCHE *enters with flowers in basket.*)

BLANCHE.   Button-holes for you, pretty gentlemen. Oh, Mr. Digby, how you are shaking.

MR. FAIRBAIRN.   Be calm. Take it easy. Think of something else.

PAUL.   I 've split my glove !

MR. FAIRBAIRN.   Don't look at it and you will forget it 's split.

MEIKLE (*at door*).   The Honourable Mrs. Teviot and the Misses Teviot.

(MRS. TEVIOT *and the* MISSES TEVIOT *enter and shake hands, moving towards centre with* PAUL *and* ARMITAGE *while* MR. FAIRBAIRN *remains near door.* BLANCHE *goes about giving button-holes to guests.* PAUL *has got rid of his nervousness.*)

ARMITAGE.   How do you think my man is looking, Mrs. Teviot ?

MRS. TEVIOT (*looking at* PAUL).   I think you deserve great credit, Captain Armitage. I don't see a grey hair in his head.

MEIKLE.   Provost Crosbie and Mrs. Crosbie—Colonel and Lady Farquhar—Mr. Alexander Riach.

(*These guests enter, shake hands, etc.* FAIRBAIRN *remains at door greeting guests.*)

PROVOST (*to* PAUL).   Great admirer of your paintings, sir ; have not seen them yet. But they will come some day to the Pans.

PAUL.   Very good of you to say so.

PROVOST.   Oh yes, they will. Everything good finds its way to the Pans.

MEIKLE.   Bailie Blair—the Shirrah and Miss Bella Innes—Sir Henry and Lady Dunn.

(*A slight pause after each announcement, during which guests exchange greetings, look at presents, etc. The* BAILIE *is an inquisitive little man who thinks artists deeply interesting but not quite respectable.*)

BAILIE.   Proud to shake hands with you, Mr. Digby.

(*He is about to do it but is pushed aside by the* SHIRRAH, *who shakes hands.   He tries it again and* SIR HENRY *pushes him aside.   He then succeeds.*)

MEIKLE.   Mr. and Mrs. Menzies—the Misses Cranston—the Fiscal.

(*These enter.*)

BAILIE (*who has been gazing at* PAUL *as at the outside of a circus*).   I am far from wishing to seem inquisitive, sir, but may I ask you what your income is ?

ARMITAGE.   Do you think my man looks fit, Miss Innes ?

MISS INNES.   Ah, one can never tell.

PROVOST.   And that is true, Miss Innes.   There was Mr. Carmichael, our grocer, a bold man at a bargain, and yet on his marriage day when he should have been standing by his bride's side he—where was it they found him hiding, Sarah ?   (*To his wife*) Was it in the cellar, or beneath the counter ?

PAUL.   Thank you, Provost ; very encouraging.

MEIKLE.   Lady Janet Dunwoodie.

(*Enter* LADY JANET.)

MRS. TEVIOT.   I remember one wedding I was at.   The bridegroom was a soldier, but when he should have said ' I do,' he burst into tears.

PAUL.   Oh, I promise you I shall say it fast enough.

MEIKLE.   Lady Fenton, Lady Alice Fenton—Gordon of the Whaups—Mrs. Grieg and the Misses Grieg.

(*They enter ;* FAIRBAIRN *goes out.*)

ARMITAGE (*to* LADY JANET).   I say, Lady Janet, they are trying to frighten my man.

LADY JANET.   And he is quite sufficiently frightened as it is. Have you heard, Mrs. Teviot, that he and Margaret are not to remain for the wedding breakfast ?   They are to run away immediately after the ceremony.

SEVERAL.   Oh, shame !

PAUL.   Margaret's wish, I assure you, ladies—not mine.

MRS. TEVIOT.   And where do you go ?

PAUL.   Only to the Dower House for the first fortnight.

LADY JANET.   Margaret will not even wait to change her dress.

MRS. TEVIOT.   Oh ! But as the Dower House is so near—we can all call on them !   (*There is some laughter at this.*)

MEIKLE (*coming into centre of room, impressively*). H'sh !
The minister !

(*The talking suddenly ceases. Enter* REV. MR. GIBSON,
*a sweet old gentleman. He is dressed in ordinary outdoor
dress of a clergyman.*)

MR. GIBSON (*whispering to* MEIKLE). Which is the bridegroom ?

MEIKLE. This, sir. (*To* PAUL) Mr. Gibson, sir !

MR. GIBSON (*shaking hands with* PAUL). Ah ! Mr. Digby,
what shall we do without our Margaret ?

PAUL. I am thankful to say, Mr. Gibson, that her father
has already found a bright side. You are to drop in frequently
and play draughts with him.

MR. GIBSON (*smiling*). The worst of it is, Fairbairn gets so
angry when I win—and I usually win !

(*Solemn music as of organ begins.* BLANCHE *runs off. All
look expectant.* MR. GIBSON *and* MEIKLE *whisper—*MR.
GIBSON *points out in dumb show how he wants guests
to stand and then reads certificates to himself while* MEIKLE
puts guests in their places. MARGARET'S *maid hurries in
excitedly, looks about for train and exits despairing.* MR.
GIBSON *and* MEIKLE *stare after her.* BLANCHE *rushes in
and looks for train. She whispers to* MEIKLE *and* MR.
GIBSON. *The three whisper with their heads close together.* PAUL *joins them—whispering. He signs to*
ARMITAGE *who joins them—whispering.* ARMITAGE
nods and complacently produces bundle and gives it to
BLANCHE. *To his surprise she is in agony. She weeps,
then with withering disdain exits with bundle.* PAUL,
MR. GIBSON, *and* MEIKLE *signify their contempt for*
ARMITAGE—*he is crushed.* MR. GIBSON *paces floor,
measuring off the exact distance from bride and bridegroom at which he is to stand. He signs to* MEIKLE. MEIKLE
then beckons and the servants come in. He places them.
MEIKLE *and* MR. GIBSON *take last look round ; they nod
to each other.* MEIKLE *signs to guests that the moment has
arrived. Then he goes out. Enter* MR. FAIRBAIRN *with*
MARGARET *on his arm, followed by* BLANCHE *and other
bridesmaids (two of them children). They take up position
beside* PAUL. *Music ceases.* MEIKLE *brings* MRS.

OMMANEY *in and she stands listlessly behind servants, not looking at what is going on.   All look at* PAUL *and* MARGARET, *smiling and interested except the minister is examining papers in his hand.*)

MR. GIBSON (*referring to paper*).   It is here certified that Paul Digby, bachelor, of the parish of Chelsea, London, and Margaret Fairbairn, of this parish, have been duly proclaimed according to the laws of their respective churches and we are now met together to solemnise the marriage.

(*All bow and there is a slight pause to indicate prayer by the minister.   At the words* ' Paul Digby,' MRS. OMMANEY *has started and gazes transfixed at* PAUL. *All others looking at the couple, she is not observed.* PAUL *and* MARGARET *are looking down.   During the silent prayer, while all the heads are bowed,* PAUL *looks up and his eyes fall on* MRS. OMMANEY. *Horror, entreaty and other feelings have been sweeping over her face, but as he sees her and is astounded, relentless purpose is in his eyes.   His look begs for mercy but she looks implacable, her meaning being to expose him.   As the prayer ends, the line of servants comes nearer, concealing* MRS. OMMANEY *from* PAUL *and the guests but not from the audience, who see that she is nearly fainting from excitement.*)

MR. GIBSON.   Paul Digby and Margaret Fairbairn, it cannot be that you have come here lightly to assume the sacred obligations of husband and wife.   Nevertheless I do call upon you even now, if any impediment there be, to speak out and stay my hand.

(*Pause in which* MRS. OMMANEY'S *arms are outstretched as if in appeal to* PAUL.)

You will now join hands.

(*They do so.*)

MR. GIBSON.   Paul Digby, do you take this woman, Margaret Fairbairn, to be your married wife, and do you promise and covenant before these witnesses to be a loving and faithful husband to her until you shall be separated by death ?

PAUL (*after a pause in which all eyes turn upon him in surprise*). I do.

(MRS. OMMANEY, *still hidden by the servants, is trying to speak, but cannot.*)

MR. GIBSON. Margaret Fairbairn, do you take this man, Paul Digby, to be your married husband, and do you promise and covenant before these witnesses to be a loving and faithful wife to him until you shall be separated by death?

MARGARET (*tremulously*). I do.

(*Pause.* PAUL *seems bewildered.*)

ARMITAGE (*in whisper*). The ring.

(PAUL *puts ring on* MARGARET'S *finger.* MRS. OMMANEY *faints and is caught by a servant. The slight disturbance turns all eyes in that direction, but as* MRS. OMMANEY *is behind line of servants it is only seen that someone is being helped out.* MR. GIBSON *stops and looks round.*)

MRS. TEVIOT. One of the servants fainted, I think.

SEVERAL GUESTS. A servant——one of the servants fainted—— a servant.

MR. GIBSON. I do now declare you to be husband and wife, and may all blessings fall upon you and may you look for strength to meet sorrow when it comes, as come it must, and may you be long-suffering and forbearing, each one with the shortcomings of the other. And may grace abide with us always.

(*There is a pause, then a hubbub of voices as the guests gather round the couple, congratulating, shaking hands, kissing, etc. The stage is full of animation owing to this ;* PAUL *is like one dazed, but controls his agitation.* MR. GIBSON, *who has gone to table where there is ink and pen, signs to him to come.* PAUL *goes and* MR. GIBSON *puts pen into his hand.* PAUL *signs like one in a dream——the air is full of congratulations, etc.*)

LADY JANET (*kissing* MARGARET). God bless you, Mrs. Digby.

MR. GIBSON. Not so fast! She is not Mrs. Digby until she has signed this paper. Sign, Margaret Fairbairn.

(MARGARET *does so.*)

There is no Margaret Fairbairn now!

(*More laughing and kissing and hand-shaking.*)

MARGARET (*as the butler is passing*). Meikle, which of the servants was it that fainted?

MEIKLE. It was that lady, Mrs. Ommaney.

MARGARET. Poor thing. Is she still here?

MEIKLE. No, ma'am, she recovered and went away on foot.

PAUL (*in agitation*).   Where has she gone ?

MEIKLE.   I don't know, sir.

(*Hurrahing is heard outside.*)

MR. FAIRBAIRN (*kissing* MARGARET).   Margaret, the carriage is at the door.   Remember, always look on the bright side.

MARGARET (*looking at* PAUL).   It will be so easy !

MR. GIBSON.   For better, for worse, Margaret, **for richer, for poorer !**

MR. FAIRBAIRN.   And not a cloud in the sky !

(PAUL *and* MARGARET *are going toward door, the guests making a lane for them.* ARMITAGE *and* MEIKLE *bring rice and slippers.   Exeunt the pair amid showers of rice and slippers.*)

ACT II

SCENE : Mrs. Ommaney's lodgings at the Pans. The interior is humble, but there is a picturesque view through the window of sea and rocks. There is a bedroom door, and when this is open, part of the bedroom is disclosed.

> (*Curtain rises on* JENNY GEDDES, *aged* 14, *who is nursing a baby.*)

JENNY (*moving about*). Hush-a-bye ! Oh, you English baby, will you never sleep ? It 's your time, I tell you. Look at the clock if you dinna believe me.

> (*The clock shows the time to be about* 5 *p.m.*)

N'yum, n'yum ! N'yum, n'yum ! (*Puts her on sofa.*) I believe you understand every word I say to you. This is a chair, and that there 's the window and the beautiful thing outside the window is the world. And this is the beautifullest lodgings in the Pans and I 'm your beautiful nurse.

> Baby Ommaney is your name,
> England is your nation,
> And you 're lodging this week with my mama
> In her beautiful habitation.

Baby, I just hates you for no sleeping. (*Kissing her*) I hates you, I hates you ! You bonny, will you sleep if I put you in your bed ?

> (*Knock is heard.   She runs to window.*)

Oh, baby !   A carriage and pair !

> (*Exit into bedroom with child whom she is seen placing in a cradle.   Enter* MARGARET *trying to look as if she had been married for years.*)

MARGARET (*calling*).   Mrs. Geddes ! Jenny !

> (*Enter* JENNY.)

JENNY.   Miss Margaret !

MARGARET.   Not Miss Margaret any longer, Jenny !

JENNY. I forgot. Oh, miss, let me see it. (*Looking at* MARGARET'S *left hand*.)

MARGARET (*consciously*). See what, Jenny ?

JENNY. Oh, miss, when there's just one thing in the world !

(MARGARET *shows her wedding ring gleefully*.)

JENNY (*to ring*). Oh, the bonny, oh, the crittur, oh, the pet ! (*Kisses her hand to it*.) Miss Margaret, when you woke up this morning and saw that on your finger did you scream out ' Hurray ! ' ?

MARGARET. But how is Mrs. Ommaney ? I have come to see her.

JENNY. She's out, miss ; she's been out for hours. Are you acquaint with her ?

MARGARET. A little—but I heard by accident a few minutes ago only, that she was lodging with you. I have been visiting my old nurse, Goody Lindsay, Jenny, and she told me. When does Mrs. Ommaney come back ?

JENNY. I canna say. She just said she was going out to see a friend.

MARGARET. I did not know she had friends here.

JENNY. Nor I. (*Proudly*) And it's no just a woman, it's a man.

MARGARET. But I am glad. Well, Jenny, you must put up with my company until Mr. Digby comes for me.

JENNY. Is *he* coming ?

MARGARET. I dropped him at the station and the arrangement was that he should pick me up at Goody's ; but he was sure to know her house by the carriage at the door, so when he sees it at your door——

JENNY. He'll think this is Goody's. That grand man coming here ! (*Going hurriedly*.)

MARGARET. Where are you going, Jenny ?

JENNY. To put on my diamond necklace !

MARGARET. Come back. He will prefer you as you are.

JENNY. Not him, ma'am. I ken men better than that.

MARGARET. Come, I want to talk to you. How is your mother ?

JENNY (*very old-fashioned*). She's just about the same, ma'am, there about it, off and on, nothing to boast of, ma'am, and nothing to complain of. She 's helping at the post-office. The post-mistress has the neuralgy again so mother 's there helping.

MARGARET. And you are left in charge ?

(JENNY *nods.*)

You like your lodger ?

JENNY (*carelessly*). Yes. (*Ecstatically*) But the baby ! Oh, oh !

MARGARET. Baby ? Has Mrs. Ommaney a baby ?

JENNY. Oh, ma'am, of all the babies ! (*Runs to bedroom door and calls in*) Eat you, I 'll eat you ! She 's sound, miss— I mean, ma'am. Sometimes she sleeps and sometimes she wakes up—I never see such a baby !

MARGARET. Poor fatherless child. Was Mrs. Ommaney unwell when she came home yesterday ?

JENNY. She was terrible excited, but she locked herself up in her room and I never saw her. But I heard her—even after I was in my bed I heard her walking up and down, up and down, and I was feared in case in the morning she would be like— like she was that other time. (*Shudders.*)

MARGARET. What other time ?

JENNY (*still quaking*). Dinna ask, ma'am ! And she was quiet this morning and telled me she was going out to call on a friend, a gentleman. Oh, ma'am, when she comes back I hope she winna be like—like she was that once. (*Quakes.*)

MARGARET. Jenny, what *was* that other time ? You are shaking.

JENNY. So did she ! Oh, if you had seen how she shook !

MARGARET. Tell me—I insist.

JENNY. You winna tell my mother ? I promised Mrs. Ommaney no to tell her.

MARGARET. But why ?

JENNY. Because mother would be feared and send her away, and then I should lose baby.

MARGARET. Very well.

JENNY. It was a week ago, ma'am—the third night after she came here. She had been out wandering all day on the cliffs and round by the Lover's Seat.

MARGARET. Ah, I know why she goes there.

JENNY. And she came in at dusk terrible excited. Then about an hour after——ah !

MARGARET. Go on.

JENNY. She was sitting in the bedroom before her looking-glass and I was brushing out her hair. But by-and-by I noticed she was shaking and I said, 'What makes you shake ?' But she never spoke and I looked up——and saw her face in the looking-glass. Oh, ma'am, it wasna the face of a sane woman !

MARGARET. Jenny !

JENNY. She spoke to hersel', ma'am, first wi' a wild, suspicious face and then so sweet and pretty, and she said kind things to me——but she didna ken me nor where she was.

MARGARET. How did it end ?

JENNY. She lay doun on the bed saying words like ' Love ' and ' Darling.'

MARGARET. Ah, her husband !

JENNY. And then she fell asleep for an hour and when she woke she was just as sane as you or me. She said, ' Why did I lie down, Jenny ? '

MARGARET. You told her ?

JENNY. Yes, and it made her cry and wring her hands. She said she had just twice in her life been like that before and it never lasted above an hour.

MARGARET. Poor woman.

JENNY. If she should be like that again !

MARGARET (soothing her). No, no, we must look on the bright side. We must hope for the best. Don't tremble—— what can I do to make you happy again ?

JENNY. Maybe, if I was to put on my diamond necklace ?

MARGARET (shaking head at her). Well, off you go.

JENNY. And if baby cries, will you call me ? (Looks in at bedroom door.) Well, I never, if she hasna woke up again. Oh, the wonder !

MARGARET. You little mother ! Jenny, the best I can wish you is that when you are married you may have as many children as the little old woman who lived in a shoe.

JENNY (in a transport of delight). Oh, ma'am !

(Exit JENNY. MARGARET, left alone, is very conscious of her wedding ring. She kisses it gleefully. Then stretches out arm and gazes at ring, then tries to avert her head ;

*then peeps at ring over her shoulder, then determinedly
covers left hand with right, then can't resist another peep,
then kisses ring again and runs to bedroom door.)*

MARGARET (*peeping in at bedroom*). Bo! baby! I am
coming in to see you. Mrs. Paul Digby presents her compliments to Miss Ommaney and may she come in and hug her?

(She enters bedroom, leaving door partly open. JENNY
*reappears wearing necklace of glass of which she is very
proud, and listens.)*

Poor little spinster. There, I was a spinster once myself, baby;
but it is so long, long ago, that I have quite forgotten what it
was like.

JENNY. And it was only yesterday!

MARGARET (*calling*). Jenny, you are listening! Go away!
(Exit JENNY *hurriedly.)*

(To baby) She was listening, the naughty Jenny! My watch?
Oh, yes, you can eat my watch. No, let me put it to your ear.
Now listen. Tick, tick, tick, tick, tick, tick.

(Enter MRS. OMMANEY *in cloak and bonnet; she looks
sullen and disappointed; lets cloak drop on table, hangs
bonnet up in cupboard; coming back to table, sees her
cloak on it and flings it to back of stage, sits down by fire
wearily.)*

I hear Jennie again. I shall shut the door, baby, and then she
can't hear.

*(*MARGARET *shuts door without looking out;* MRS. OM-
MANEY *has started to her feet. Enter* JENNY.)*

MRS. OMMANEY. Oh, Jenny, who is in there?

JENNY (*gleefully*). Oh, ma'am, it's Miss Margaret—Mrs.
Digby, I mean.

MRS. OMMANEY (*fiercely*). She—with my child! (*Strides
towards door, stops—laughs grimly.*) How did she know I was
lodging here?

JENNY. A woman told her.

MRS. OMMANEY. It is fate! Has she been talking of—(*With
quiet sarcasm*)—her dear husband?

JENNY (*sharply*). You dinna ken her. Mr. Digby doesna
ken she has come to see you.

MRS. OMMANEY (*grimly*). No, I'll swear he doesn't. (*Suddenly*) But I thought they had gone out together.

JENNY. Who telled ye?

MRS. OMMANEY. Never mind. (*Laughs—kisses her hand to bedroom door.*)

JENNY. Did you see your friend, ma'am?

MRS. OMMANEY (*listless*). No, he was out.

JENNY (*inquisitively*). I suppose you winna tell me what your business with him was?

MRS. OMMANEY. Yes, Jenny, I will tell you. He has broken his promise to me and my business is to expose him. Unless——

JENNY. Unless what, ma'am?

MRS. OMMANEY. Unless he is willing to buy my silence.

(JENNY *looks puzzled.*)

Oh, he knows the value of it, Jenny. (*Doggedly*) But it is not to be bought with money. He shan't buy it with money.

JENNY. With what, then?

MRS. OMMANEY. Jenny, do you think me pretty?

JENNY. Oh, ma'am, what can that have to do with it?

MRS. OMMANEY (*passionately*). It has everything to do with it. It is life or death to me now. Quick, I was pretty once.

(JENNY *makes no answer and* MRS. OMMANEY *sinks back in distress into chair.*)

All gone, all gone! (*Pitifully*) Never mind, pity may do as well.

JENNY. I dinna understand, ma'am.

MRS. OMMANEY. You will understand soon—unless he agrees. Everyone will understand. It will be the talk of the place, I promise you. (*Pointing towards bedroom*) Get rid of her.

JENNY. But she is waiting for Mr. Digby.

MRS. OMMANEY (*starting up*). What! You said he did not know she was coming here. He can't have known.

JENNY. She didna ken hersel'. But she told him to come for her to the door where her carriage was standing. She meant it would be Goody Lindsay's door.

MRS. OMMANEY. He will come here—here! (*Quickly*) I want to see him alone. Get rid of her and——

(MARGARET *opens door and addresses* JENNY. MRS. OMMANEY *being up stage is invisible to* MARGARET.)

MARGARET. Jenny!

(JENNY *goes to door.*)

Don't you see Mr. Digby coming yet?

JENNY. No, ma'am, but——

> (MRS. OMMANEY *signs to silence* JENNY. MARGARET *goes back to child, leaving door partly open.*)

MARGARET (*in fun*). Baby, I am a grass widow !

> (MRS. OMMANEY *signs imperiously to* JENNY *to go. Exit* JENNY.)

Are you laughing, baby ? When your mother's tears fall on your face do you laugh on only ? Oh, I see now why God gives the merriest babies to mothers who are the most sorrowful. It is because, when baby laughs, mother forgets to weep.

> (*The hardness goes out of* MRS. OMMANEY'S *face—she is moved.*)

This is my wedding ring, baby, kiss it !

> (MRS. OMMANEY *starts up, forming the word* ' No ' *with her lips.*)

Did you ever kiss your mother's wedding ring, baby ?

> (MRS. OMMANEY *looks bitterly at her left hand on which there is no ring.*)

If she doesn't come soon, dear, I won't be able to see her, for my Paul has taken a sudden dislike to this place, and we are going away to-morrow to a beautiful country called Switzerland.

MRS. OMMANEY (*excitedly*). What !

MARGARET. Jenny, you 're horrid. (*Rises and shuts door.*)

MRS. OMMANEY (*in a white heat, her voice intent but low*). Running away from me, are you, Paul Digby ? No, no. And from your child that you don't know of yet. You shall know of her now. (*Calling*) Jenny !

> (*Enter* JENNY. MRS. OMMANEY *conceals her fury.*)

Jenny, you thought I disliked your Miss Margaret. Listen to this. As soon as her husband comes in I mean to give them a marriage present.

JENNY (*delighted*). Oh !

MRS. OMMANEY (*with cruel glee and so intense that her voice drops almost to a whisper*). Such an *uncommon* marriage present, Jenny, and in a way it belongs to Mr. Digby already, as much as to me. But he has never seen it ; he does not even know of its existence. Is not that a curious present ?

JENNY. Terrible curious. And you will give it to them as soon as he comes in ?

MRS. OMMANEY. As soon as he comes in. See if he is coming.

JENNY. Oh, what fun ! (*Exit* JENNY.)

MRS. OMMANEY. What fun, what fun ! Run away from me. No, no ! (*Waves hand as if beckoning* PAUL *forwards.*) Looking for your wife, are you ? Ha, ha ! In here, Mr. Digby—(*Pointing to the bedroom door*)—with your child. Where else should she be ? Wife and child, wife and child. (*Her voice is low, so that* MARGARET *shan't hear her, but vehement.*)

(JENNY *runs in.* MRS. OMMANEY'S *face is from her.*)

JENNY (*excitedly*). I see him coming.

MRS. OMMANEY. Ah !

JENNY (*opening bedroom door and entering*). He's coming, Miss Margaret.

(*She goes out of sight.* MRS. OMMANEY *stares at entrance, waving to him to come quickly. She is gloating. The door has been left open and* MARGARET *can be heard again.*)

MARGARET. He is coming, baby ! Paul is coming ; I am so happy, I could dance. Look, look !

(*She is heard and seen dancing and humming a nursery song.* MRS. OMMANEY *gloats over this, rubbing her hands together with glee, stopping now and again to wave to* PAUL *to come in, and then pointing at bedroom. Presently* MARGARET *ceases.* MRS. OMMANEY *is now staring at bedroom door. A vacant look comes into her face ; she looks about her as if uncertain where she is ; her eyes identify nothing as they roam about the room. She is frightened. She sees door of bedroom, and a gleam of intelligence comes back. She moves arms again as if conducting dancing and hums* MARGARET'S *song, then sinks into chair and now stares straight before her, muttering, as if in fear, to herself. She begins to shake ; the shaking becomes more violent, until her arms are striking the sides of the chair and her feet are rattling on the floor. When it lessens and stops, her face is now foolish but sweet ; she simpers to herself amiably. Enter* JENNY. MRS. OMMANEY *looks at her sweetly but without recognition.*)

JENNY. Oh, ma'am ! (*Shrinks.*)

MRS. OMMANEY (*puzzled*). Who are you ?

JENNY (*calling*).   Miss Margaret.

> (*Enter* MARGARET.   *She sees* MRS. OMMANEY'S *condition and shrinks.*)

Oh, Miss Margaret, she *is*—the same as that other time.

MRS. OMMANEY (*to* MARGARET).   Miss Margaret ! Is that your name ?

MARGARET.   Poor woman !

MRS. OMMANEY (*sweetly*).   Poor woman ? I remember. (*Looks softly at* MARGARET.)   It was my wedding day and you were there ; I was so happy, but you, poor woman.

MARGARET.   Jenny, she is confusing me with herself.

JENNY (*to* MRS. OMMANEY).   Come and lie down.

MRS. OMMANEY.   I was in my wedding gown but you—— (*Proudly*) He preferred me, you know.

> (MARGARET *sits tearfully.*)

Don't cry, pretty dear.   (*Going pityingly to her*) Shall I let you see my love's portrait ?   It is on this locket—(*On her neck*)— I can't open it.

JENNY.   Come and see baby.

MRS. OMANNEY (*vacantly*).   Baby ? (*Looking at bedroom*) So that 's your baby ! And you look such a good one ! (*Giggling*) Miss Margaret ! (*Becoming sweet again as she sees* MARGARET *is distressed*) I won't tell.   But you mustn't call yourself Miss Margaret.   Call yourself Mrs. Margaret—then no one will know.   (*Nods as if this were a clever idea.*)

> (*A knock at door.*)

MARGARET (*starting*).   Paul !

MRS. OMMANEY.   We are to be married and I am not dressed yet.

> (*Exit into bedroom hurriedly with* JENNY.   MARGARET *meets* PAUL *as he enters.*)

PAUL (*in high spirits*).   Margaret, it is all arranged.

MARGARET (*clinging to him*).   I thought you were never coming.

PAUL.   Lady Janet detained me.   She stayed last night at Old Keep but is on her way home now.

MARGARET.   You have seen auntie ?

PAUL.   I left her in the post-office but I had to tell her you were visiting your old nurse.   (*Dolefully*) And, of course, she said she must see you.

MARGARET. But, Paul, this is not nurse's house. Mrs. Ommaney is here——

PAUL. What ! (*He is like one turned to stone.*)

MARGARET. And, poor lady, she——

JENNY (*calling excitedly*). Miss Margaret !

MARGARET. Oh !

(*Enter* MRS. OMMANEY ; *she has flung a gay shawl over her shoulders and enters simpering over her appearance. She takes* PAUL'S *presence as a matter of course.* JENNY *stands at bedroom door.*)

MRS. OMMANEY. Naughty man, where are the flowers ? (*Displaying herself in shawl*) How do you like it ? It is my wedding gown. Is the cab at the door ? (*Trips to window.*)

PAUL. My God !

MARGARET. It is heart-rending.

PAUL. What does it mean ?

MARGARET. She has been like this, it seems, more than once before. She has been ill, Paul, and that and the great sorrow that has come into her life have affected her brain at times.

JENNY. Oh, sir, she was quite sensible just a minute since.

PAUL. But I can't——

MARGARET. Humour her, Paul—I will explain afterwards.

JENNY. Come and rest, ma'am—come. (*Trying to take* MRS. OMMANEY *to sofa.*)

MRS. OMMANEY. Rest—when I am going to be married ?

MARGARET (*going to her*). You *are* married now. The cab has brought you back.

MRS. OMMANEY (*to* PAUL). Am I ?

(MARGARET *signs to him to agree.*)

PAUL. Yes.

MRS. OMMANEY (*gleefully as a child*). I am married ! (*With grand dignity to* JENNY) Do you know who I am ? I am Mrs. Margaret.

(JENNY *tries to take her to sofa.*)

MARGARET (*to* PAUL). Don't you see, Paul, she has confused me with herself.

MRS. OMMANEY (*holding out her arms to* PAUL). You—I want you.

MARGARET (*to* PAUL). Yes, humour her. She thinks you are her husband.

PAUL. You will lie down, won't you ?

(PAUL *helps* MRS. OMMANEY *to sofa, where she sits. Exit* JENNY *into bedroom.*)

MRS. OMMANEY (*with childish wonder*). Those skinny arms, are they mine ? How tiny the wrist has grown, how thin the fingers. (*To* PAUL, *plaintively*) You will never weary of me again ? When I bore you, you won't say it, will you ? You will say instead, ' Poor little thin fingers, poor little pretty ways, all gone, all gone ! '

MARGARET (*putting hand on* PAUL'S *shoulder*). Paul, I begin to think he is not dead. I believe he deserted her !

PAUL. No—not that !

MRS. OMMANEY (*striking* MARGARET'S *arm off* PAUL). Hands off !

MARGARET. Did he desert you ?

MRS. OMMANEY (*looking up*). Where is it—the letter ? I left it on the mantelpiece—long, long ago.

PAUL (*eagerly*). Yes, tell her what was in the letter !

MRS. OMMANEY (*confidentially*). I said in it that I was leaving him because I had ceased to care for him. (*Giggles.*)

MARGARET. You left him !

(MRS. OMMANEY *nods as if she had done a clever thing.*)

PAUL (*eagerly*). You see, Margaret, he was not so bad as you thought.

MARGARET. But why did you leave him ?

MRS. OMMANEY (*wailing*). Because I loved him so !

(PAUL *at back of sofa is much startled.*)

He ! he ! he ! He hated the life, I bored him, he hungered to be free——

MARGARET. Did he say that ?

(PAUL *is more and more startled.*)

MRS. OMMANEY. No, he kept it to himself—honour, you know—he ! he ! he ! but she knew—who was she—she was Miss Margaret—so she pitied him and pretended she was glad to go away. What a joke !

MARGARET. You did this for his sake ? Paul, do you see ?

PAUL (*huskily*). I see !

MRS. OMMANEY. I want to look at my face. (*Simpering*) So much admired.

(MARGARET *gives her hand mirror.*)

MRS. OMMANEY (*looking at herself in it*). What a fright! Who is she? (*Addressing herself to reflection*) Oh, my dear, you are on your last legs—it is all UP with you.
> (*Pulls* PAUL'S *arm lovingly beneath her head and lies down.*)

I am so tired, I want to sleep.
> (PAUL *kneels by the side of her and presently signs to* MARGARET *that she is falling asleep.* MARGARET *goes on tiptoe to window and looks out.*)

MRS. OMMANEY (*muttering*). That is Miss Margaret—and she looks such a good one. (*Sitting up excitedly*) Marriage present—what was it?
> (PAUL *induces her to lie down again.* MARGARET *comes softly to sofa.*)

Pretty ways, all gone, all gone; he hated the life; he didn't let on but she knew—so sad—(*Hums* MARGARET'S *song*)—you are on your last legs, it is all UP with you; poor lady, poor soul!

MARGARET (*after a pause*). She is asleep.
> (PAUL *gently disengages his arm and rises.*)

Paul, do you think he is alive and was cruel to her?

PAUL (*huskily*). I don't think he meant to be cruel.
> (*A knock is heard.*)

LADY JANET (*calling, unseen*). Are you here, Margaret?
> (MARGARET *cries* 'H'sh!' *and runs towards door, meeting* LADY JANET.)

LADY JANET (*embracing her*). I went to Goody Lindsay's and she told me you were here. I fear——

PAUL. H'sh! (*Looking only at* MRS. OMMANEY.)

LADY JANET (*seeing sleeping figure*). Mrs. Ommaney! (*Growing hard.*) Which reminds me——

MARGARET. You will waken her.

LADY JANET. That won't distress me. Margaret——
> (PAUL *raises his arm to enforce silence.* MARGARET *whispers to* LADY JANET.)

LADY JANET (*surprised*). Really!
> (MARGARET *whispers again.*)

Bless me! (*Goes and looks at* MRS. OMMANEY.) Well, I have no desire to waken her, but what I have to say must be said. Margaret, this woman has deceived us——

PAUL (*sternly*). Not so loud. (*He continues looking at* MRS. OMMANEY.)

LADY JANET (*lowering her voice*). The woman of this house —she is working at the post-office——

MARGARET. I know.

LADY JANET. She has just told me all about our Mrs. Ommaney. She is not a widow.

MARGARET. But, auntie, we have begun to suspect that ourselves. Her husband and she——

LADY JANET. Husband ! He was not her husband.

(PAUL *turns and looks at* LADY JANET. MARGARET *is bewildered.*)

MARGARET. They are not married ? It can't be true.

LADY JANET. She admitted it herself to Mrs. Geddes.

MARGARET. Some things she said just now—so strange— Paul ! (*Looking at bedroom door*) It can't be true.

LADY JANET. She does not even make the pretence of wearing a wedding ring.

(MARGARET *looks at* MRS. OMMANEY's *left hand—then shrinks back.*)

MARGARET. Paul, let us go.

PAUL. Have you no pity for her now, Margaret ?

MARGARET. No.

LADY JANET. She has been here before. Can he be a man of these parts ? I should like to know.

PAUL. It is no business of ours.

MARGARET. Yes, we might compel him to marry her. And, auntie, you can find out. She told me that the locket she is wearing contains his portrait.

LADY JANET. Aha ! (*Going towards* MRS. OMMANEY.)

PAUL. You would not——

LADY JANET. Oh, yes, I would.

PAUL. Margaret—a sleeping woman !

LADY JANET (*unfastens locket*). Now we shall see.

(PAUL *and* LADY JANET *are on opposite sides of the sleeping figure.* MARGARET's *head is bowed and she does not look up.* PAUL *is staring at* LADY JANET *who opens locket leisurely. She sees who it is and gazes with horror.*)

MARGARET (*without raising head*). Do you know him ?

LADY JANET (*after looking fiercely at* PAUL, *slips locket into her pocket*).   No, I never saw him before.

MARGARET.   Auntie, she can't stay here.   Think of simple Jenny.

LADY JANET (*harshly*).   I shall see to that.

PAUL (*looking at her*).   I shall see to that.

LADY JANET.   No.

PAUL (*determinedly*).   Yes.

LADY JANET (*significantly*).   Your part is with your wife. Good-bye, Margaret.

MARGARET.   Paul, take me home.

> (*She is now looking with repugnance at* MRS. OMMANEY. LADY JANET *signs to* PAUL *to go.   He shakes his head determinedly.   Their voices and actions are very subdued as there is greater reason than ever that they should not waken the sleeper.*)

LADY JANET (*yielding*).   He will see you into the carriage, dear, and then perhaps you won't mind going home alone. I—I want his advice about what should be done.

MARGARET (*in a low voice*).   Very well.

> (*Exeunt* MARGARET *and* PAUL.)

LADY JANET (*in burst of emotion*).   Margaret !   My innocent little Margaret !   Oh, woman, woman !

> (*Enter* JENNY *from bedroom.*)

JENNY.   Miss Marga—— (*Curtseying*) My lady !

LADY JANET.   Mrs. Digby has gone.   Had you anything to say to her ?

JENNY.   Just that baby was sleeping.

LADY JANET.   Ah, I had forgotten.   Your mother told me about her.   Is she in there ?

JENNY.   Yes, my lady ! (*Going towards entrance.*)

LADY JANET.   Stop !   Does Mr. Digby know there is a child ?

JENNY.   I'm no sure. (*Exit* JENNY.)

LADY JANET (*to herself*).   Does he know ?

> (*Enter* PAUL.)

PAUL (*after they have looked in silence at each other*).   I did not desert her.   I am not seeking to defend myself.   I had promised her never to marry, but I did *not* desert her.

> (LADY JANET *is immovable.*)

She will probably be herself again when she wakes, so the girl told Margaret. When she wakes, she will find me here—alone. We must have it out together, what she means to do. And I must do my duty by her—first by Margaret, but also by her.

LADY JANET (*continuing to look fixedly at him*). Only by those two? Then you do not know!

PAUL. Know what? You must trust me and leave me alone with her. Take Jenny away also. We must have the house to ourselves.

LADY JANET. I trust you and I will go—and take Jenny—but there will still be a third person in the house.

(PAUL *is puzzled*.)

Your child.

(PAUL *stands rigid.* LADY JANET *points to bedroom. He goes into bedroom. She remains motionless leaning on her staff. After a pause* PAUL *comes out.*)

PAUL (*very sorrowful*). I did not know—I never thought——

LADY JANET. Men never do.

(*She goes out slowly at entrance and is seen taking* JENNY *with her. Outer door is heard shutting. There is a great stillness.* PAUL *is stricken but quiet. He goes to side of sofa. His overcoat is on chair. He places it carefully over* MRS. OMMANEY, *then sits down on chair near fire by her side.*)

ACT III

THE curtain is lowered only for a moment between Acts II and III to indicate the passing of time. When it rises Mrs. Ommaney is still asleep on sofa and Paul still sitting by her side. Dusk has come on and their figures are only dimly discernible. The fire has burned low. In the stillness the waves are heard breaking on the beach. Paul rises and strikes a match. By its light he looks first at Mrs. Ommaney's face and then at the clock which shows that two hours have elapsed. He shuts window and pulls curtains, then gropes his way out by the light of the match.

(*The pulling of the curtains has made* MRS. OMMANEY *stir and open her eyes, unnoticed by him. When he has gone she speaks languidly without getting up.*)

MRS. OMMANEY. Is that you, Jenny ? Have I been asleep ? (*Sitting up and yawning.*) Are you there ? How dark—— (*Rising bewildered*) Why—what—— (*Disturbed*) Something has happened ! (*A match is heard being struck ; she goes towards entrance.*) Jenny !

(*A light comes along passage and she retreats backwards as it approaches. Enter* PAUL *carrying a lamp.*)

You !

(PAUL *looks anxiously at her.*)

Why do you look at me so ?

PAUL. Thank God ! (*Puts down lamp and sinks into chair.*)

MRS. OMMANEY. When did you come here ? Let me think. (*Presses her hands to her temples.*) Ah ! (*Flings open bed-room door.*) Come out ! (*Seizes lamp and enters bedroom, returns.*) Where is she ? Your wife !

PAUL. She is gone. We are alone in the house, you and I—and our child.

MRS. OMMANEY. So you know about *her* ! Where is your Margaret ? She was there a moment ago.

PAUL.   Nearly two hours ago.   You have been—asleep.

MRS. OMMANEY.   Sleeping ?   While she—— I don't remember your coming in.

PAUL.   You were—excited.

MRS. OMMANEY (*pressing her temples again and beginning to understand*).   Excited ?   Not—not that !   (*Entreatingly.*)

PAUL (*painfully*).   The girl Jenny says it happened before.

MRS. OMMANEY.   Again, again !   (*Covers her face with her hands.*)

PAUL (*goes to her pityingly*).   Kate !

MRS. OMMANEY (*defiantly*).   Don't try to get round me.   You promised me never to marry.   You have broken your promise. (*In a hard voice, without looking up*) Tell me what happened.

> (PAUL *sits down beside her, and the whole act is played
> very quietly.*)

PAUL.   I came for my wife.   I did not know that you were in the house.

MRS. OMMANEY.   I remember.   I was waiting to give you a wedding gift !   (*She looks grimly at bedroom.*)

PAUL.   What wedding gift ?   You don't mean——

MRS. OMMANEY.   Yes, I do !   You broke your promise.   Go on.

PAUL.   You had got into that excited state before I came, but we persuaded you to sleep, and then my wife went away.

MRS. OMMANEY.   Does she know ?

PAUL.   Not everything.   Her aunt came in.   Jenny's mother had told her all she knew of you, and she repeated it to Margaret

MRS. OMMANEY.   But you—do they know that you were the man ?

PAUL.   You had told my wife that your locket contained his portrait——

MRS. OMMANEY (*feeling for locket*).   Ah, it is gone.   Well ?

PAUL.   Lady Janet opened it—and saw.

MRS. OMMANEY.   And your wife—your wife ?

PAUL.   My wife does not know.   Lady Janet kept it from her.

MRS. OMMANEY.   Then why are you here alone ?

PAUL.   Margaret would not remain after——

MRS. OMMANEY.   After she knew what sort of woman I was ! Recoiled from me, did she ?   Hid her pretty eyes in horror, eh ?

That is what her ' sympathy ' is worth, and it nearly took me in. There was a moment when I hesitated, and almost—— (*Laughs shrilly*) But I am glad she was pitiless.

PAUL. She is so innocent—if you knew how a man worships innocence in a woman.

MRS. OMMANEY. In one woman, but not in others !

PAUL (*bows his head*). Kate, I believe your letter, I never questioned it. I have learned only to-day why you left me, and the generosity of it crushes me in the dust.

MRS. OMMANEY. How did you learn ?

PAUL. You told me yourself, before you fell asleep. At least believe this, that had I understood I would not have let you go.

MRS. OMMANEY. I know. But oh, you were glad to be free ! Can you deny it ?

　　　　(PAUL *cannot answer.*)

Your heart leapt within you, did it not ?

PAUL. I was distraught with grief and shame.

MRS. OMMANEY. But joy came in the morning !

PAUL. You said you were going home—I thought of following you.

MRS. OMMANEY (*bitingly*). Did you go ?

PAUL. You asked me in the letter not to do so.

MRS. OMMANEY. How obedient a man can be sometimes ! But you would not have found me at my father's. I remained in London. I went back to the dressmaking that I should never have left.

PAUL. Kate, I make no pretence. I was too willing to believe you. But for you I had no feeling save pity. It was myself I loathed and the life I was leading.

MRS. OMMANEY. The life and I were one. And yet until we met I had been a good woman. I had sat to other painters before I knew you ; I had been a popular enough model. I was a harum-scarum, I suppose, but no harm had come of it.

PAUL. You were a good woman—till we met. That is my condemnation.

MRS. OMMANEY. And you had been a good man. That is mine. Funny, isn't it ?

　　　　(PAUL *makes a movement of dissent.*)

Yes, you had. They called you the hermit ; your Spartan virtue was the talk of the studios.

PAUL.　I lived too much in my art, and my solitary thoughts. I shrank from men's free talk of women, and yet when I left them it was to brood of the things they spoke of ; theirs was a healthier life than mine. ' It is not good for man that he be alone.' And then you came into my life, and you rang through it like a peal of bells in a lonely house. At first I only meant to be your friend. Ah, Kate, those Bohemian days, when **you** and I were only comrades.

MRS. OMMANEY.　The dear old studio **fire** !

PAUL.　How poor I was.

MRS. OMMANEY.　How happy we were !

PAUL.　Ah, but Kate !

MRS. OMMANEY.　Yes, it was soon over.

PAUL.　The end came. Our friends **were** looking on and smiling, Kate. They called me a lucky dog. At first I could have struck them, for they did not disguise their meaning ; but they had put the idea into my head, and it flourished there and grew apace.

MRS. OMMANEY (*passionately*).　It was not only that ? Speak, you loved me !

PAUL.　You took possession of every chamber of my mind. There was no one in the world to me but you.

MRS. OMMANEY.　That was enough for me. I was willing to let all else go. I was up to date. Up to date !

PAUL.　We thought it such a fine thing to defy the conventions.

MRS. OMMANEY.　I gloried in the risk. When a woman loves, the more she must venture the better pleased she is. And, Paul, we were happy at first, you loved me——

PAUL.　I was deliriously happy at first, but soon——

MRS. OMMANEY.　You awakened—and it was all over ! Did you know her in those days ?

PAUL.　Not till after you left me. What I felt was a sense of shame—I hated myself—I could not work—I saw I had given away my manhood.

MRS. OMMANEY.　I gave it you back again—a little tarnished.

PAUL.　I have tried to cleanse it.

MRS. OMMANEY.　And in the meantime I have borne a child !

PAUL (*bowed*).　Kate, when you left me, did you know of her ?

MRS. OMMANEY.　I knew ! Now do you understand why

I could not go back to my father ?   At least I have hidden it
from him.

PAUL.   Why did you not tell me ?   If I had known——— !

MRS. OMMANEY.   Why did you not ask ? (*He has no answer.*)
Yes, I took away that secret with me also.   I was not to be
generous by halves.

(PAUL *opens bedroom door and stands looking in.* MRS.
OMMANEY *is bitterly sarcastic.*)

Pity she didn't die, isn't it ?   But she is very healthy ; hard on
you that, isn't it ?   But they are often carried off in the measles ;
she might get run over in the street, too ;   there's always a
chance !

(PAUL *looks at her and then exits into bedroom.* MRS.
OMMANEY *remains in parlour.*)

This is a gentleman come to see you, baby ; don't be frightened,
he won't touch you.   Don't stretch out your little hand to him,
he won't take it.   Don't offer your mouth to him, he won't
kiss it.   He may kiss other babies yet, but not you.

(*Suddenly a gratified look comes into her face, and she
sinks in chair.* PAUL *comes out.*)

You kissed her !

(*He is very remorseful—door is heard opening—and they
both rise.* PAUL *goes to window.*)

PAUL.   It is Lady Janet come back.

(*Enter* LADY JANET.)

LADY JANET (*to* PAUL, *after looking from one to other*).   Well ?

(PAUL *has no answer.*)

MRS. OMMANEY.   You have something of mine, I understand ?

(LADY JANET *hands her the locket.*)

MRS. OMMANEY (*opens it*).   Where is the portrait ?

LADY JANET.   I destroyed it. (*To* PAUL) Is it arranged ?

MRS. OMMANEY.   We were coming to that.

LADY JANET.   How much ?

PAUL (*sternly*).   Lady Janet, for shame !

MRS. OMMANEY.   Pooh, I don't mind her ! (*With shrinking
disdain*) What can she know about women !   What can the
virtuous spinster know ?   I have borne a child ; I am a woman.
What are you who dare interfere with a woman—you childless
thing !

PAUL. Kate !

LADY JANET (*with emotion*). It is true, it is true.

(*Exit* LADY JANET, *sorrowfully*.)

MRS. OMMANEY. She said, ' Is it arranged ? ' Paul, you broke your promise—what are you to do ?

PAUL. Anything, anything ! Kate, you and our child shall be well provided for.

(MRS. OMMANEY *turns away*.)

You must take it. Oh, it is so pitifully little I can do.

MRS. OMMANEY (*eagerly, but half afraid*). It need not be pitifully little, Paul, if—(*Hesitates*)—I shall do whatever you ask of me, live where you please, go into the country far from her, be so patient. Paul, I need never again be as you have seen me to-day. Only my wild craving for you brought it on. It turned my brain. There shall be no more of that. I will be so contented ; so happy ; you will say I am my old self again—when you come to see me.

PAUL (*startled*). But I can't do that ! Everything else.

MRS. OMMANEY. Only now and again—she will never know.

PAUL. Kate, do you know what you are proposing to me ?

MRS. OMMANEY. You will do it—speak !

PAUL. No !

MRS. OMMANEY (*changing from entreaty to passion*). But you shall ! It is the price of my silence !

PAUL. You say this—you who have done so much for me.

MRS. OMMANEY. The conditions have changed. I would never have troubled you again had you not married, I swore it. But you have broken your promise.

PAUL. I have broken it, but—surely that is a little thing to you now.

MRS. OMMANEY. A little thing ! It was everything to me, it gave me a kind of self-respect as I sat dressmaking once more, it was an excuse to my conscience for calling myself a married woman. I could exult in your growing fame, because of it ; it made me a part of that fame, for in leaving you I had done something to make you ambitious again. Often I have stood outside your studio with my child in my arms and I have whispered to her proudly, ' But he never took up with another woman.' She was to be your only child. Was there nothing to me in that ?

PAUL. I deserve no mercy—but Margaret ?

MRS. OMMANEY. How much pity had she for me ? (*Lovingly*) Paul, it is not much to ask. Give me something to live for.

PAUL. It can't be.

(*She rises, looking determined. Enter* LADY JANET.)

LADY JANET. Mr. Digby, Margaret is coming back ! I saw her carriage in the bend of the road.

MRS. OMMANEY (*exultingly*). Coming back ! She is coming back to be told all. Innocent little Margaret ! Thinks her spotless husband is staying too long ! Sisterly little Margaret, who was so anxious to be my friend ; merciless little Margaret ! (*Turning to* PAUL) Do you still refuse ?

PAUL. Yes.

LADY JANET. Mr. Digby, you can refuse nothing ! What did she ask ?

PAUL. That I should—it amounts to this, that I should have two homes.

LADY JANET. Woman ! She was good to you—kind——

MRS. OMMANEY. Till she knew what I was, till she knew I needed kindness, and then she ran from me—did she not ?

PAUL. She was appalled ; it seemed too awful to her ; she could say nothing, do nothing.

MRS. OMMANEY. She has found the words now, and is coming back to cast them at me.

LADY JANET. There must be some other way. Mrs. Ommaney, I am wealthier than he. I will give you thousands ; I will beggar myself.

MRS. OMMANEY. No, no, no.

PAUL. Kate !

MRS. OMMANEY. Choose !

LADY JANET. She is here !

MRS. OMMANEY. Which is it to be. (*To* PAUL.)

PAUL (*passionately*). Leave it to me to tell her.

MRS. OMMANEY. No.

LADY JANET (*broken*). She is here !

MRS. OMMANEY. She has come back for my wedding gift. It is at hand, and ready ! (*Exit* MRS. OMMANEY *into bedroom, which is in darkness.*)

PAUL (*to* LADY JANET, *whose face asks question*). She means the child.

(There is a knock at the door.)

LADY JANET.   God forgive me, but——can you not temporise ? In time she——

PAUL.   No.

LADY JANET.   For Margaret's sake——yes !

PAUL.   For Margaret's honour——no !

(Enter MARGARET.*)*

MARGARET *(speaking eagerly as she enters)*.   Is she better ?

PAUL.   Yes.

MARGARET *(looking about her)*.   Auntie, she has not gone ?

LADY JANET.   No.

MARGARET.   I am so glad I am in time.

LADY JANET.   Margaret, come away ! This is no place for you.

MARGARET.   Auntie, she is a woman, and so am I.   She is in distress and I can help her.   This is the place for me.

PAUL.   Why did you come back ?

MARGARET.   Because of that ; because I saw how cruel, how unwomanly I had been.   How sweet she was when she sat on the sofa telling us her pitiful story, what a baby I was to run from her !   Aunt Janet, if I had been in her place——if I had loved a villain, oh, I don't know what I might have fallen to.   If she had been in mine, if she had loved a man like Paul——

LADY JANET.   There are only good women and bad.

MARGARET.   I had always thought so, but her story has lifted a veil from the eyes of an ignorant girl.   Good women and bad ! I became a woman when I saw how much they have in common. Where is she ?

*(*MRS. OMMANEY *comes out ; her face is unfathomable.)*

MRS. OMMANEY.   I am here.

MARGARET.   Mrs. Ommaney, can you forgive me ?

MRS. OMMANEY.   I have heard every word you said.

MARGARET.   Were they driving you away ?——they shan't. Auntie, how dare you ! Paul, Mrs. Ommaney is my friend. *(She puts her arm round* MRS. OMMANEY, *and stands like one defending her.)*

LADY JANET.   Margaret, you must not——

MARGARET.   Auntie, you are on the side of the men ; so was I.   I am on the side of my sisters now.

LADY JANET (*appealingly*).   Mr. Digby !

(PAUL *takes a step forward.*)

MARGARET.   Not my husband himself shall take my arm from her.

PAUL (*to* MRS. OMMANEY).   Speak—and quickly.

MRS. OMMANEY (*quietly to* MARGARET, *after looking at* PAUL).   I have a wedding present—I should like to give you.

LADY JANET.   Woman !

MRS. OMMANEY.   It is this—my locket.

(PAUL *and* LADY JANET *start.*)

It was something else I meant to give you, but you will like this better.   As you know, his face was in it, but it has been taken out.   So perhaps you will not object.   I hope your husband will not object to your having it from me.   You sweet girl, you and I shall never meet again, but I should like to think that you had put your husband's face in it instead of the face that used to be there and wore it sometimes in memory of a good woman's victory over a bad one.

(MARGARET *kisses locket.*)

It will remind you, Mr. Digby, of what was the great event in the life of a woman—and a little episode in the life of a man.

MARGARET.   We shall meet again and often.

MRS. OMMANEY.   Never !   I want you all to go away now. (*To* PAUL) May I kiss her ?

(PAUL *is too affected to speak.*   MARGARET *kisses her.*)

Take her away.

PAUL.   What are you to do ?

MRS. OMMANEY.   Work and forget—if I can.   Go !

(She sits down a forlorn figure.   LADY JANET *signs to* MARGARET *and they go towards door;* PAUL *follows a step, and stops, looking in agitation at* MRS. OMMANEY.)

LADY JANET.   Come !

(PAUL *stands looking and* LADY JANET *grows anxious.*)

Come, I command you.

PAUL (*huskily*).   I can't come.

MARGARET.   Paul, why ?

PAUL.   Because I believe in God, and I hear Him calling to me to speak.   Margaret, it was I who did this thing.   I am the man !

(MRS. OMMANEY *starts up.*   MARGARET *looks from one to the other, dazed.*)

MARGARET (*after a pause*).   Paul, did you say anything ?

PAUL.   I am the man.

MARGARET (*after pause, with growing enlightenment*).   Mrs. Ommaney, Aunt Janet, he did not say it ?   (*Imploringly*) Speak !

LADY JANET.   My dear, my dear !

(MARGARET *turns from her to* PAUL ; *she points to bedroom door.*)

PAUL.   It is my child.

(MARGARET *reels, but* LADY JANET *catches her.*)

LADY JANET.   You are still his wife.

MARGARET.   His wife !   Oh, dear God, what have I done that you let me marry this man !

PAUL (*with a cry of agony*).   Margaret !

MARGARET.   A betrayer of women, he is my husband ! Oh, sir, must I thank you for that ?   I loved you, and yet you married me.   You might have dealt with me as you have dealt with her.   I thank you.

MRS. OMMANEY.   Hear me !

MARGARET (*vehemently*).   You, you !   It is such women as you.   No, I beg your pardon.   This man, I took him from you ;   I did not understand ;   he is yours, yours and your child's.

(*Slowly takes off ring, and hands it to* MRS. OMMANEY. PAUL *takes a step towards her—she recoils.*)

Aunt Janet, I am going back to my father.

(*She goes away quietly.*   LADY JANET *slowly follows her; the outer door is heard opening and shutting.*)

MRS. OMMANEY.   Why did you tell ?

PAUL (*huskily*).   I am glad I told.

MRS. OMMANEY (*in a whisper—a wild hope springing into her face*).   Paul !

(*He shudders and avoids her, her head droops ; she hands him the ring, it remains in his fingers a moment, then he lets it drop.   It is heard striking the floor.*)

I

ACT IV

THE scene is the same as Act I. It is evening and the lamps are lit. The curtain rises on Mr. Fairbairn in evening dress and Mr. Gibson in clerical dress playing at draughts at a small table. Meikle is packing up presents and putting them into a hamper. The players are absorbed in their game. Mr. Gibson's eyes are almost shut as he peers at the board. He is as anxious as if he were preaching his trial sermon. Mr. Fairbairn is cool and deliberate. Mr. Fairbairn moves emphatically and sits back. Mr. Gibson moves cunningly and slowly, then sits expectantly. Mr. Fairbairn moves and then Mr. Gibson moves quickly and triumphantly. He tries politely to conceal his glory but his face is wreathed in smiles. He sits back, with legs over arm of chair, and casts triumphant side looks at Mr. Fairbairn. Mr. Fairbairn realises that he is in difficulties and ponders, frowning, half moves, when Mr. Gibson whips round to play. Mr. Fairbairn glares at him. Mr. Gibson sits back abashed. Meikle comes to back of table and looks on. Mr. Gibson does not see him. Meikle signs the best move to Mr. Fairbairn, who plays it. Meikle goes back. Mr. Gibson is to play triumphantly, when he finds that he has been checked. The triumph goes from his face. He does not know what to do ; he puffs up his cheeks with wind while Mr. Fairbairn lolls back elated. Mr. Gibson lifts his opponent's King to play.

MR. FAIRBAIRN. Excuse me, that 's my King you are lifting.

MR. GIBSON. I beg your pardon. (*Pauses—he sees a good move—lifts same King.*)

MR. FAIRBAIRN. That 's my King again.

MR. GIBSON. Dear me ! Dear me !

(MR. GIBSON *moves doubtfully.* MR. FAIRBAIRN *replies boldly.* MR. GIBSON *moves again anxiously, evidently digging a pit for his opponent.* MR. FAIRBAIRN *replies emphatically, evidently thinking that it is he who is digging the pit.* MR. GIBSON *makes a sly move.* MR. FAIRBAIRN *jumps a man, and looks jubilant.* MR. GIBSON *gloriously jumps three men, and sits back with delight.* MR. FAIR-BAIRN *is aghast, and loses his temper.*)

MR. FAIRBAIRN. I decline to play it out.

MR. GIBSON. Too bad ! too bad ! Every time I beat you we have this scene.

MR. FAIRBAIRN. *You* beat me !

MR. GIBSON. Fairbairn, I will never play with you again.

MR. FAIRBAIRN. Who wants you to ? Do you think I 'm afraid you would beat me ?

MR. GIBSON. If you are not afraid, why don't you play it out ?

MR. FAIRBAIRN. Who 's afraid to play it out ?

MR. GIBSON. *You* are afraid to play it out.

MR. FAIRBAIRN. I *will* play it out.

MR. GIBSON. Then why don't you play it out ?

MR. FAIRBAIRN. I tell you what, Gibson——

(MEIKLE, *who has been looking at them, now comes down and lifts draught-board, and exit with it.*)

MR. FAIRBAIRN. Meikle, how dare you !

MR. GIBSON. Meikle, bring back that board !
(*They sit cowed and sullen.*)

MR. GIBSON (*rising, shortly*). Good night, Fairbairn.

MR. FAIRBAIRN (*without looking round*). Good night.

(MR. GIBSON *is going, when he is arrested by the entrance of* MEIKLE, *carrying a tray, with wine.* MEIKLE *puts it on table and busies himself at another table, opening cigar-box.* MR. GIBSON *stands looking at tray like one in a dream.* MR. FAIRBAIRN *turns pettishly and sees tray. Their passions die away as they look at it.*)

MR. FAIRBAIRN. A glass of port, Gibson, to drink the health of the happy couple.

MR. GIBSON. Thank you, Fairbairn. (*Sits.*) Half a glass.

MR. FAIRBAIRN. Say ' when.'
(*He half fills glass, looks up, pours in more, looks up, but* MR. GIBSON *is so busy wiping his spectacles that he does not notice.*)

MR. GIBSON (*hurriedly, when glass is full*). Stop !
(*They are about to drink.*)

Before we drink their health, Fairbairn, I want to apologise for my unseemly warmth just now. It was all my fault. I behaved like a donkey.

MR. FAIRBAIRN (*genially*).   Not at all ! The blame is mine ; it was I who behaved like a donkey.

MR. GIBSON.   Excuse me, Fairbairn, I was the donkey.

MR. FAIRBAIRN.   Come, come, I insist on taking the blame.

MR. GIBSON (*a little irritably*).   Surely, Fairbairn, when I say it was I——

MR. FAIRBAIRN.   I tell you, you behaved splendidly.

MR. GIBSON.   Now, we must have this matter cleared up. I was the donkey.

MR. FAIRBAIRN.   I tell you I was.

MR. GIBSON.   You were not.

MR. FAIRBAIRN.   I *was*.

MR. GIBSON.   Fairbairn, I will never drink a glass of wine with you again.

(MEIKLE *offers cigar-box ; he takes cigar, still fuming, and bites off end.*)

MR. FAIRBAIRN.   As you please, for I venture to say——

(MEIKLE *offers box.*   MR. FAIRBAIRN *takes cigar and bites off end.*   MEIKLE *offers light.*)

MR. GIBSON.   Of all the obstinate——

MR. FAIRBAIRN.   Of all the thick-headed——

(MEIKLE *gives him light.   They smoke contentedly and their passions vanish, while* MEIKLE *returns to hamper.*)

Gibson, your health. (*He drinks.*)

MR. GIBSON.   Thank you, Fairbairn, your health ! (*He drinks.*) God bless you, Fairbairn.

MR. FAIRBAIRN.   God bless you, Gibson.

(*They shake hands across table.*   MEIKLE, *who has lifted hamper to carry it out, smiles tolerantly on them.   They turn and look at him.   Exit* MEIKLE, *sedately, with hamper.*)

An impudent fellow !

MR. GIBSON.   A very impudent fellow !

MR. FAIRBAIRN.   I brought Margaret up wisely, Gibson— eh ? Janet thought I kept her a child too long, but see how splendidly it has turned out. Don't look for troubles and you won't find them. If they are in front of you, walk round.

MR. GIBSON (*holding up glass*).   Mr. and Mrs. Digby !

MR. FAIRBAIRN.   May they always be as happy as they are at this moment.

MR. GIBSON.   Billing and cooing, sir, billing and cooing.

MR. FAIRBAIRN.   That's it !

(*Enter* MEIKLE.)

MEIKLE.   Lady Janet Dunwoodie.

(*They start up in surprise. Enter* LADY JANET, *and* MEIKLE *withdraws after looking uneasily at her.*)

MR. FAIRBAIRN.   You, Janet, come back !

LADY JANET.   I changed my mind, you see. Took pity on your loneliness.

MR. GIBSON (*not quite believing her*).   Bravo ! When you came in, Lady Janet, we were just on the point of——

LADY JANET.   Saying good night ? So sorry, Mr. Gibson, but it is getting late, so I won't press you to stay. (*Rings*) Give my love to Nellie. I hope she likes this hot weather.

MR. GIBSON.   She likes it very much, but it does not like her. And, I fear——

LADY JANET.   There, there, what a hurry you are in to be off. But good night, if you must go.

MR. GIBSON (*meekly*).   Good night, Fairbairn.

MR. FAIRBAIRN.   Good night.

(*Exit* MR. GIBSON *perturbed and fearing that something is wrong.*)

MR. FAIRBAIRN (*uneasily, but persuading himself that everything is well*).   We have been drinking their health, you know— the happy couple.

LADY JANET.   Alec, the happy couple have separated, Margaret has come back to you.

MR. FAIRBAIRN (*bewildered*).   Here, Margaret ! Separated ! What do you mean ?

LADY JANET.   You had better ask her. You will find her in her old room. She went up the back staircase to avoid Mr. Gibson.

MR. FAIRBAIRN (*still bewildered, but in great anxiety*).   But— but—where is her husband ?

(*Enter* MEIKLE, *who comes to table to remove wine, etc.* MR. FAIRBAIRN *signs to* LADY JANET *to conceal what has happened from* MEIKLE *and exits.* LADY JANET *stands watching* MEIKLE, *who takes anxious side-glances at her.*)

LADY JANET (*suspiciously*).   Well, why don't you go, Meikle?

MEIKLE (*suddenly facing her with emotion*).   My lady, I am an auld servant, I have served in this house faithfully since Miss Margaret was that high ; and her ways, they were so bonny—she 's so innocent like—she has said things to me so innocent that, being a grey-haired man, acquainted full sore with wickedness of the world, I have just hurried out of the room and said ' God bless her,' behind the door.

LADY JANET (*gravely*).   A loyal servant has his privileges, Meikle.   What is it you want to know?

MEIKLE.   My young mistress that was married yesterday has come back here without her man.   (*Clenching his fist and speaking with strong feeling*) I am but an auld servant, but I want to know where Mr. Digby is?

(*After slight pause enter* PAUL.   LADY JANET *conceals her surprise at seeing him.*   MEIKLE'S *expression changes to joy.*)

Oh, sir, but I am glad to see you!   My lady, you will pardon me, I was a doited old fool!

(*Lifts tray, but leaves cigar-box, and exit, looking very happy.*   PAUL *looks at* LADY JANET *inquiringly.*)

LADY JANET.   He was afraid until you came, that something was wrong.   Why have you followed us?

PAUL (*drearily*).   What else was there for me to do?   (*Pause.*) She came with me.

LADY JANET.   Mrs. Ommaney?   Where is she?

PAUL.   We were told Margaret had gone to her room.   She has followed her to tell how it all happened—and to give her back the ring.

LADY JANET (*shaking her head*).   It will not be done so easily as that.

PAUL.   But how, Lady Janet?   Is there any way?   I am prepared to do anything.

LADY JANET (*suddenly*).   Mr. Digby, are you sorry you confessed?

PAUL.   No—no.

LADY JANET.   Nor am I—for I need despise you no more. (*Standing looking at him wistfully*) I believe he was just such a man as you—some one I used to know, and thought the world of thirty weary years ago.   Oh, you men, you men!   Why does not God speak and make the way clear for women. (PAUL *bows his head.*) If you had told Margaret before !

PAUL. I wanted to do it ; the more I loved her, the more I hungered to have her know me as I am ; but the words would not come—she was so innocent.

LADY JANET. You did not even tell her father. (*No answer.*) Did you ? (*No answer.*) Are you keeping something from me ? (*No answer.*) Oh, how you men stick by each other !

> (*Enter* MR. FAIRBAIRN *looking very broken and in great distress about* MARGARET. *He is entirely sincere in the views to which he gives expression.*)

MR. FAIRBAIRN (*looking at* PAUL *fiercely*). You—villain ! My poor child ! Oh, the horror of it ! Oh, the awfulness ! (*Anxiously*) Do the servants know ?

LADY JANET. Not yet.

MR. FAIRBAIRN (*weakly*). That 's something.

LADY JANET (*sharply*). Alec, how much of this did you know before the wedding ?

MR. FAIRBAIRN. Not a word.

LADY JANET (*to* PAUL). What have you to say to that ?

PAUL. Nothing. (*He looks a little scornfully at* MR. FAIRBAIRN, *who winces.*)

LADY JANET (*noting this by-play*). He is shielding you, Alec, and you don't deserve it. What was it ? (*Suddenly*) I can guess—he offered to tell you, and you would not listen !

MR. FAIRBAIRN. I knew there had been something ; but he gave me his word of honour that it was all past and done with —so I declined to hear more.

LADY JANET. Oh, Alec ! (*She rises and moves about sadly— he walks by her side speaking.*)

MR. FAIRBAIRN. My rule, Janet—look on the bright side, you know. Let sleeping dogs lie. I dislike painful subjects— my sensitive nature—I——

LADY JANET. Poor Alec !

MR. FAIRBAIRN (*leaving* LADY JANET). Why is the woman with Margaret ?

> (*Enter* MRS. OMMANEY, *she stops unseen by* PAUL *and* MR. FAIRBAIRN.)

PAUL. ' The woman ' is my one hope now. If Margaret

ever looks at me again it will be by the help of ' the woman.'
You don't know her, Mr. Fairbairn, nor of what generosity
she is capable.

MR. FAIRBAIRN. No, Mr. Digby, I don't know that kind
of woman. I never knew them. I have always avoided them
like the plague. And I wonder, sir, which of us will face his
Maker the less fearfully for that ?

MRS. OMMANEY (*taking a step forward and surprising them*).
He who has brought one of them to this pass, or you who have
avoided them all like the plague—I wonder !

PAUL (*eagerly—going to her*). Have you anything to tell me ?

MRS. OMMANEY. She flung the ring upon the floor.

(*He is overcome.*)

LADY JANET. Oh ! (*She goes out.*)

MRS. OMMANEY. But she is coming down.

MR. FAIRBAIRN (*snatching at this straw*). That 's something!

PAUL. Is there any hope for me ?

MRS. OMMANEY. I believe she has something to propose. I
don't know what it is.

(*Enter* MARGARET. PAUL *goes to her, but she draws
back in repugnance.*)

MARGARET (*lifting a handful of rice which is in a bowl on centre
table and letting it run through her fingers back into bowl*). Rice !

MR. FAIRBAIRN. We gathered it off the floor and put it in
that bowl for luck.

MARGARET. Luck !

PAUL. Margaret, whatever you ask me to do, I will do it.

MARGARET. What am I to do, father ? I have longed for
your advice, there is no one so wise as you. Do you see any
bright side now ?

MR. FAIRBAIRN (*going to her*). Margaret—the servants
don't know.

MARGARET (*surprised and pained*). Oh, father !

MR. FAIRBAIRN. But it is a great thing, my child. And
though Mr. Digby was led astray——

PAUL (*sternly*). No.

MR. FAIRBAIRN (*frowning at him*). He is very repentant,
and a wife's duty, Margaret, her privilege—to forgive. Forgiveness ! What a beautiful word it is, and woman is so
forgiving that—that——

MARGARET.   That men may count on it !

(MR. FAIRBAIRN *is silenced for a moment.*)

MR. FAIRBAIRN.   And of course we must not forget this lady—a competence—quite a large sum——

(PAUL *stamps his foot.*)

Oh, I insist on facing the situation unflinchingly.   Now I happen to know a farmer—a widower—who is in need of a housekeeper——

PAUL.   Mr. Fairbairn !   (*Lifts his arm to beg* MR. FAIRBAIRN *to stop.*)

MRS. OMMANEY.   Let him go on.   Leave me, please, with this gentleman.

(*Exit* PAUL.)

I think I know what is coming, Mr. Fairbairn.   Your farmer lives in Australia, doesn't he ?

MR. FAIRBAIRN.   How did you know ?

MRS. OMMANEY.   Oh, I have read them also.

MR. FAIRBAIRN (*puzzled*).   Read them ?   Read what ?   I know the man—a splendid climate.

MRS. OMMANEY.   Where I should be out of your way.

MR. FAIRBAIRN.   Exac—— (*Stops sharply.*)

MRS. OMMANEY.   And I could begin a new life there.

MR. FAIRBAIRN (*enthusiastically*).   A new life in a new country !

MRS. OMMANEY.   With a baby !

MR. FAIRBAIRN.   We would not take your child from you. (*Nobly*) No.

MARGARET.   Father !   Father !   (*Buries her head in her hands.*)

MRS. OMMANEY.   Let him go on.   You were to say, I think, that I could write to them once a year ?

MR. FAIRBAIRN.   At Christmas time.

MRS. OMMANEY.   Saying what a beautiful peace had come into my life, and baby is such a comfort, and that sweet-smelling flowers are growing up the porch of my rustic home !

MR. FAIRBAIRN (*delighted*).   Yes, yes !

MRS. OMMANEY.   Honeysuckle ?

MR. FAIRBAIRN.   Anything you like.

MRS. OMMANEY.   I should prefer honeysuckle.   It is usually honeysuckle.   Do let it be honeysuckle.

MR. FAIRBAIRN. A strange woman, but she will do it. (*Affectionately*) So you see I have found the bright side, and soon, Margaret, this painful episode will be as if it had never been. (*He is elated and honestly believes that he has found the way out.*)

MARGARET. But it has been.

MR. FAIRBAIRN (*puzzled*). Yes. (*Brightening*) We must have the courage to turn our backs on it.

MARGARET (*rising*). Father, don't say another word, lest I learn to despise you.

MR. FAIRBAIRN (*astounded*). Margaret—you forget yourself.

MARGARET. Father—it is a thing you never do.

MR. FAIRBAIRN. This from my child ! Whom I brought up so innocently.

MARGARET. So innocently ! But you don't deserve even the credit for that, father. It was easier to keep me a child than to make a woman of me. That is all you did. What I thought your fine philosophy, it was only an avoidance of disagreeable truths. Do you think—but you don't think, you have shirked the trouble of thinking for so long that now, when you must, you can't. And I am in the same plight. I am your true daughter, father ! (*Sits sobbing.*)

MR. FAIRBAIRN (*with sympathy, but feebly*). Don't cry, dear —don't—it pains me—I am so sensitive—Margaret, bear up— the darkest clouds have a silver—try to put a bright face—— (*He does not complete these phrases, having an uncomfortable feeling that there is something wrong with them to-day.*) For my sake, Margaret—my heart—the doctor said—my heart, you know—weak ! (*Pettishly—sitting*) Very well, don't think of me—blame me—go on—blame me.

MARGARET (*going to him*). Father, if we could help one another !

MR. FAIRBAIRN (*brightening*). We shall—we shall ! I may have been to blame—I was—yes, I insist on saying it, I was— but henceforth—(*Grandly*)—Margaret—you will see a change.

(*She presses his hand gratefully.*)

MRS. OMMANEY. I forgot one thing. Do I marry the farmer ?

MR. FAIRBAIRN (*very pleased with himself*). Ah, madam, you jest, but you see before you a changed man. Margaret, if you know of any way out, let me hear it.

MRS. OMMANEY. Yes, let us hear it. (*Sits indifferently.*)

MARGARET (*ringing bell*). I have something to propose, father. The world will scoff, but—I am trying to do what is right.

MR. FAIRBAIRN (*contemptuously*). The world ! My child, you shall never hear me use a worldly argument again.

(*Enter* MEIKLE. MR. FAIRBAIRN'S *manner changes suddenly and he tries to look as if all was well with the world.* MARGARET *looks at him pained, but he does not see her.*)

MARGARET. Meikle, see if you can find Mr. Digby.

MR. FAIRBAIRN (*jovially*). These young married people, Meikle ! Can't do without each other for a moment, ha ! ha ! ha !

(*Exit* MEIKLE *also smiling.* MR. FAIRBAIRN *sees* MARGARET'S *reproachful look and winces.*)

It was to deceive the servants.

MARGARET (*sadly*). And you promised——

MR. FAIRBAIRN (*dejectedly*). I forgot !

(*Enter* PAUL.)

PAUL. You sent for me.

MARGARET. To hear the only condition on which I will consent to return to you.

(*He bows.*)

It is that we—you and I—take the child.

MRS. OMMANEY (*starting up*). What ! (*She now listens quietly but sharply.*)

MR. FAIRBAIRN. Eh—ah—adopt it ?

MARGARET. Does a man adopt his own child, Mr. Digby ?

MR. FAIRBAIRN. No, no—course—why say adopt ? Why use the word ? The only difficulty—and it can be got round —yes, yes—is whose child shall we say it is ?

MARGARET (*to* PAUL). Whose ?

PAUL. You mean—we are to tell the truth ?

(*She inclines her head.*)

MR. FAIRBAIRN. Tell the truth ! Shamed, shamed !

MARGARET. Father, your promise ! The truth must be right.

MR. FAIRBAIRN (*feebly*). The truth—I suppose so.

(*Vehemently*) Margaret, why can't you let sleeping dogs——
(*Hopeless, going downcast.*) I am not a man—you were right—
I am only a thing swaddled in comfortable phrases.

 (*Some real horror of himself has awakened in him and his
is a pitiful figure.*)

MARGARET. Father, there is a man beneath them still.

MR. FAIRBAIRN. Is there ? Is there ?

MRS. OMMANEY. I give up.

 (*He seeks to escape from this new world in which he, who
has always been so pleased with himself, cuts so poor a
figure.*)

MR. FAIRBAIRN (*with dignity*). You have killed me between
you. (*Is going off with dignity, turns, hesitates, toddles back to
table, and lifts cigar-box—feebly*) My heart, you know—weak.
(*Exit with cigar-box apologetically.*)

MARGARET (*to* PAUL). Do you share his views ?

PAUL (*passionately*). Margaret, it is yourself you are
punishing.

MARGARET. I will face facts.

PAUL. I have no option—I agree—if you are willing.
(*To* MRS. OMMANEY.)

MRS. OMMANEY. Oh, don't think of me !

MARGARET. But it is for you that we do it. So that you
may be able to go back to your father. You said he did not
know of the child, he need never know now.

PAUL. Ah, Margaret, you see there must be deception
somewhere.

MARGARET. Then let him be the one to profit by it. In
making her father happy she will become happy herself, and
the bright side of things will—— (*Shuddering*) Ah, that
phrase !

MRS. OMMANEY. It is a fairy tale !

MARGARET. Your father——

MRS. OMMANEY (*indifferently*). My father ! (*Rapturously*)
My child !

MARGARET. But the shame——

MRS. OMMANEY. The glory ! She is mine.

MARGARET. I would teach her to love your memory as——

MRS. OMMANEY. I want her to love myself ! Such as she
may love one of her parents, she must scorn the other. If one

of them is to be scorned, let it be her father ; if one of them is to be loved, it shall be her mother !

(MARGARET *sits sadly.* MRS. OMMANEY *goes nearer her.*) Oh, you baby, trying to do what is right ! Your father is a selfish old man, you are a generous girl, but you tell the same fairy tale. You have brought the honeysuckle from Australia and planted it at my father's door. That is all the difference !

MARGARET (*in distress*). I am my father's daughter !

(*Enter* LADY JANET.)

LADY JANET. Well ?

MRS. OMMANEY. They thought they could have my child.

MARGARET. Auntie, what are we to do ?

MRS. OMMANEY (*speaking as if this was her ultimatum*). Do as you will. I have done enough for you—you boy and girl making so much ado about your love ! I, too, was heroic, but the mood has passed. I am going back to my father, but my child goes with me.

(*Stroll up and out on balcony, where she stands with her back to them.*)

MARGARET (*going after her—passionately*). Mrs. Ommaney——

LADY JANET (*checking her*). Would you rob her of her last chance ?

MARGARET (*sitting, bitterly*). I suppose that is what I have been trying to do—looking for a bright side for myself !

PAUL (*going to her*). No, Margaret, you have only been a woman trying to do what was beyond her strength—perhaps overlooking to do what is within her. I have no right to say that, but——

LADY JANET. Yes, Margaret Digby, there is something for you to do. You can do your duty by your stricken husband. See how beautiful the world is. (*Pointing to sky which is now serene with stars*) You can go out hand in hand, and thank God for it.

MARGARET (*bitterly*). Forget and forgive !

LADY JANET (*solemnly*). And be forgiven. My child, he has done a cruel and shameful wrong to her, and to you, and to another woman—the woman who bore him ; but his remorse will be long, and two of these women ask the third one to help him to bear it. (*Speaking with still more emotion*)

Margaret, another woman also asks that of you—a woman who has grown old without being a wife or a mother—a woman who thinks that her poor tragedy is a heavier one to bear than yours.

MARGARET (*surprised*).   You ask it—you who——

LADY JANET (*trembling*).   There have been times when I have envied even such women as she.

MARGARET.   But, auntie, you refused to marry the man you loved because——

LADY JANET.   Because he had done this thing.

MARGARET.   And I honoured you for it—we all honoured you for it !

LADY JANET.   And I pretended to plume myself on it.   I kept a bold face before the world.   I deceived you all, rarely —but in my heart I regretted it bitterly—I have regretted it all my life.

MARGARET.   I don't know what to do.   The world has slipped from under my feet, and I can catch hold of nothing.   I am only a girl, and I don't know what to do.

PAUL.   You loved me once, Margaret.

MARGARET.   The man I loved—he was not the real Paul.

PAUL.   The real Paul needs you so much more than the other.

(*Enter* MEIKLE.)

MEIKLE.   Your coachman, Mr. Digby.   He would like to know, sir, whether he is to put up the horses ?

(PAUL *and* LADY JANET *look at* MARGARET.)

MARGARET (*after pause*).   No—we are going back now.

(*Exit* MEIKLE.   LADY JANET *lifts* MARGARET'S *cloak, hands it to* PAUL *and joins* MRS. OMMANEY *on verandah.* PAUL *looks from the cloak to* MARGARET.   *She lets him put it on her.*)

PAUL.   Margaret, I make no vows—but—trust me !   You will wear my ring again ?

(*She inclines her head.*)

I will get it.   (*Going.*)

MARGARET (*in low voice*).   You will not find it there.

PAUL.   She said you flung it——

MARGARET.   I picked it up—when she had gone.

(*She slowly takes a thin gold chain from her neck.   At the end of it is the ring which has been concealed in her bosom. She hands it to him. He takes ring off chain and puts it on her finger. Her face is averted, but she turns round and her arms go out to him.)*

MARGARET. Paul !

PAUL. Margaret, what can I do to atone ?

MARGARET. Help unhappy women.

(They are going out hand in hand, when they meet MRS. OMMANEY *and* LADY JANET. PAUL *takes a step forward to* MRS. OMMANEY. MARGARET *holds out her hand. She turns her back on them determinedly.* LADY JANET *signs to them to go. Exeunt* PAUL *and* MARGARET.)

LADY JANET. Come—to say good-bye—to wish them——

MRS. OMMANEY (*fiercely*). No ! I have done enough. I will not wish them luck !

*(*LADY JANET *goes on to verandah.* MRS. OMMANEY *stands still, looking bitter and vindictive. Then, half cynically, yet with a generous impulse, she takes up two handfuls of rice and flings it after them. She is left, a defiant, sorrowful figure.* LADY JANET, *who has seen her fling the rice, steals back to her and holds out her hand, and* MRS. OMMANEY *rests her weary head upon the shoulder of the woman who may become her friend.)*

QUALITY STREET

Produced at the Vaudeville Theatre on September 17, 1902, with the following cast :

VALENTINE BROWN . . .	*Seymour Hicks*
ENSIGN BLADES	*A. Vane Tempest*
LIEUT. SPICER	*Stanley Brett*
RECRUITING SERGEANT . .	*George Shelton*
A WATERLOO VETERAN .	*Charles Daly*
MASTER ARTHUR WELLESLEY TOMSON	*Master George Hersee*
MISS SUSAN THROSSEL . .	*Marion Terry*
MISS WILLOUGHBY . .	*Henrietta Watson*
MISS FANNY WILLOUGHBY .	*Irene Rooke*
MISS HENRIETTA TURNBULL .	*Constance Hyem*
MISS CHARLOTTE PARRATT .	*May Taverner*
PATTY	*Rosina Filippi*
ISABELLA	*Winifred Hall*
HARRIET	*Edith Heslewood*
MISS PHOEBE THROSSEL .	*Ellaline Terriss*

The play ran for 459 performances. Revived at the Haymarket on August 11, 1921, it ran for 344 performances.

ACT I

THE BLUE AND WHITE ROOM

The scene is the blue and white room in the house of the Misses Susan and Phoebe Throssel in Quality Street ; and in this little country town there is a satisfaction about living in Quality Street which even religion cannot give. Through the bowed window at the back we have a glimpse of the street. It is pleasantly broad and grass-grown, and is linked to the outer world by one demure shop, whose door rings a bell every time it opens and shuts. Thus by merely peeping, every one in Quality Street can know at once who has been buying a Whimsy cake, and usually why. This bell is the most familiar sound of Quality Street. Now and again ladies pass in their pattens, a maid perhaps protecting them with an umbrella, for flakes of snow are falling discreetly. Gentlemen in the street are an event ; but, see, just as we raise the curtain, there goes the recruiting sergeant to remind us that we are in the period of the Napoleonic wars. If he were to look in at the window of the blue and white room all the ladies there assembled would draw themselves up ; they know him for a rude fellow who smiles at the approach of maiden ladies and continues to smile after they have passed. However, he lowers his head to-day so that they shall not see him, his present design being converse with the Misses Throssel's maid.

The room is one seldom profaned by the foot of man, and everything in it is white or blue. Miss Phoebe is not present, but here are Miss Susan, Miss Willoughby and her sister Miss Fanny, and Miss Henrietta Turnbull. Miss Susan and Miss Willoughby, alas, already wear caps ; but all the four are dear ladies, so refined that we ought not to be discussing them without a more formal introduction. There seems no sufficient reason why we should choose Miss Phoebe as our heroine rather than any one of the others, except, perhaps, that we like her name

best.   But we gave her the name, so we must support our choice
and say that she is slightly the nicest, unless, indeed, Miss Susan
is nicer.

Miss Fanny is reading aloud from a library book while the
others sew or knit.   They are making garments for our brave
soldiers now far away fighting the Corsican Ogre.

MISS FANNY.   '. . . And so the day passed and evening
came, black, mysterious, and ghost-like.   The wind moaned
unceasingly like a shivering spirit, and the vegetation rustled
uneasily as if something weird and terrifying were about to
happen.   Suddenly out of the darkness there emerged a *Man*.
(*She says the last word tremulously but without looking up.
The listeners knit more quickly.*)
The unhappy Camilla was standing lost in reverie when,
without pausing to advertise her of his intentions, he took both
her hands in his.
(*By this time the knitting has stopped, and all are listening
as if mesmerised.*)
Slowly he gathered her in his arms——
(MISS SUSAN *gives an excited little cry.*)
MISS FANNY.   And rained hot, burning——'
MISS WILLOUGHBY.   Sister !
MISS FANNY (*greedily*).   ' On eyes, mouth——'
MISS WILLOUGHBY (*sternly*).   Stop.   Miss Susan, I am
indeed surprised you should bring such an amazing, indelicate
tale from the library.
MISS SUSAN (*with a slight shudder*).   I deeply regret, Miss
Willoughby——   (*Sees* MISS FANNY *reading quickly to herself.*)
Oh, Fanny !   If you please, my dear.
(*Takes the book gently from her.*)
MISS WILLOUGHBY.   I thank you.
(*She knits severely.*)
MISS FANNY (*a little rebel*).   Miss Susan is looking at the end.
(MISS SUSAN *closes the book guiltily.*)
MISS SUSAN (*apologetically*).   Forgive my partiality for
romance, Mary.   I fear 'tis the mark of an old maid.
MISS WILLOUGHBY.   Susan, that word !
MISS SUSAN (*sweetly*).   'Tis what I am.   And you also,
Mary, my dear.

MISS FANNY (*defending her sister*).   Miss Susan, I protest.

MISS WILLOUGHBY (*sternly truthful*).   Nay, sister, 'tis true. We are known everywhere now, Susan, you and I, as the old maids of Quality Street.   (*General discomfort.*)

MISS SUSAN.   I am happy Phoebe will not be an old maid.

MISS HENRIETTA (*wistfully*).   Do you refer, Miss Susan, to V. B. ?

(MISS SUSAN *smiles happily to herself.*)

MISS SUSAN.   Miss Phoebe of the ringlets as he has called her.

MISS FANNY.   Other females besides Miss Phoebe have ringlets.

MISS SUSAN.   But you and Miss Henrietta have to employ papers, my dear.   (*Proudly*) Phoebe, never.

MISS WILLOUGHBY (*in defence of Fanny*).   I do not approve of Miss Phoebe at all.

MISS SUSAN (*flushing*).   Mary, had Phoebe been dying you would have called her an angel, but that is ever the way. 'Tis all jealousy to the bride and good wishes to the corpse.   (*Her guests rise, hurt.*)   My love, I beg your pardon.

MISS WILLOUGHBY.   With your permission, Miss Susan, I shall put on my pattens.

(MISS SUSAN *gives permission almost haughtily, and the ladies retire to the bedroom,* MISS FANNY *remaining behind a moment to ask a question.*)

MISS FANNY.   A bride ?   Miss Susan, do you mean that V. B. has declared ?

MISS SUSAN.   Fanny, I expect it hourly.

(MISS SUSAN, *left alone, is agitated by the terrible scene with* MISS WILLOUGHBY.

Enter PHOEBE *in her bonnet, and we see at once that she really is the nicest.   She is so flushed with delightful news that she almost forgets to take off her pattens before crossing the blue and white room.*)

MISS SUSAN.   You seem strangely excited, Phoebe.

PHOEBE.   Susan, I have met a certain individual.

MISS SUSAN.   V. B. ?   (PHOEBE *nods several times, and her gleaming eyes tell* MISS SUSAN *as much as if they were a romance from the library.*)   My dear, you are trembling.

PHOEBE (*bravely*).   No—oh no.

MISS SUSAN.   You put your hand to your heart.

PHOEBE.   Did I ?

MISS SUSAN (*in a whisper*).   My love, has he offered ?

PHOEBE (*appalled*).   Oh, Susan.

(*Enter* MISS WILLOUGHBY, *partly cloaked.*)

MISS WILLOUGHBY.   How do you do, Miss Phoebe.   (*Portentously*) Susan, I have no wish to alarm you, but I am of opinion that there is a man in the house.   I suddenly felt it while putting on my pattens.

MISS SUSAN.   You mean—a follower—in the kitchen ? (*She courageously rings the bell, but her voice falters.*)   I am just a little afraid of Patty.

(*Enter* PATTY, *a buxom young woman, who loves her mistresses and smiles at them, and knows how to terrorise them.*)

Patty, I hope we may not hurt your feelings, but——

PATTY (*sternly*).   Are you implicating, ma'am, that I have a follower ?

MISS SUSAN.   Oh no, Patty.

PATTY.   So be it.

MISS SUSAN (*ashamed*).   Patty, come back.   (*Humbly*) I told a falsehood just now ; I am ashamed of myself.

PATTY (*severely*).   As well you might be, ma'am.

PHOEBE (*so roused that she would look heroic if she did not spoil the effect by wagging her finger at* PATTY).   How dare you.   There is a man in the kitchen.   To the door with him.

PATTY.   A glorious soldier to be so treated !

PHOEBE   The door.

PATTY.   And if he refuses ?

(*They look perplexed.*)

MISS SUSAN.   Oh dear !

PHOEBE.   If he refuses send him here to me.

(*Exit* PATTY.)

MISS SUSAN.   Lion-hearted Phoebe.

MISS WILLOUGHBY.   A soldier ?   (*Nervously*) I wish it may not be that impertinent recruiting sergeant.   I passed him in the street to-day.   He closed one of his eyes at me and then quickly opened it.   I knew what he meant.

PHOEBE.   He does not come.

MISS SUSAN.   I think I hear their voices in dispute.

(*She is listening through the floor. They all stoop or go on their knees to listen, and when they are in this position the* RECRUITING SERGEANT *enters unobserved. He chuckles aloud. In a moment* PHOEBE *is alone with him.*)

SERGEANT (*with an Irish accent*).   Your servant, ma'am

PHOEBE (*advancing sternly on him*).   Sir—— (*She is perplexed, as he seems undismayed.*)   Sergeant—— (*She sees mud from his boots on the carpet.*)   Oh! oh! (*Brushes carpet.*) Sergeant, I am wishful to scold you, but would you be so obliging as to stand on this paper while I do it?

SERGEANT.   With all the pleasure in life, ma'am.

PHOEBE (*forgetting to be angry*).   Sergeant, have you killed people?

SERGEANT.   Dozens, ma'am, dozens.

PHOEBE.   How terrible.   Oh, sir, I pray every night that the Lord in His loving-kindness will root the enemy up.   Is it true that the Corsican Ogre eats babies?

SERGEANT.   I have spoken with them as have seen him do it, ma'am.

PHOEBE.   The Man of Sin.   Have you ever seen a vivandiere, sir?   (*Wistfully*) I have sometimes wished there were vivandieres in the British Army.   (*For a moment she sees herself as one.*)   Oh, Sergeant, a shudder goes through me when I see you in the streets enticing those poor young men.

SERGEANT.   If you were one of them, ma'am, and death or glory was the call, you would take the shilling, ma'am.

PHOEBE.   Oh, not for that.

SERGEANT.   For King and Country, ma'am?

PHOEBE (*grandly*).   Yes, yes, for that.

SERGEANT (*candidly*).   Not that it is all fighting.   The sack of captured towns—the loot.

PHOEBE (*proudly*).   An English soldier never sacks nor loots.

SERGEANT.   No, ma'am.   And then—the girls.

PHOEBE.   What girls?

SERGEANT.   In the towns that—that we don't sack

PHOEBE.   How they must hate the haughty conqueror.

SERGEANT.   We are not so haughty as all that.

PHOEBE (*sadly*).   I think I understand.   I am afraid,

Sergeant, you do not tell those poor young men the noble things I thought you told them.

SERGEANT.　Ma'am, I must e'en tell them what they are wishful to hear.　There ha' been five, ma'am, all this week, listening to me and then showing me their heels, but by a grand stroke of luck I have them at last.

PHOEBE.　Luck?

(MISS SUSAN *opens door slightly and listens.*)

SERGEANT.　The luck, ma'am, is that a gentleman of the town has enlisted.　That gave them the push forward.

(MISS SUSAN *is excited.*)

PHOEBE.　A gentleman of this town enlisted?　(*Eagerly*) Sergeant, who?

SERGEANT.　Nay, ma'am, I think it be a secret as yet.

PHOEBE.　But a gentleman!　'Tis the most amazing, exciting thing.　Sergeant, be so obliging.

SERGEANT.　Nay, ma'am, I can't.

MISS SUSAN (*at door, carried away by excitement*).　But you must, you must!

SERGEANT (*turning to the door*).　You see, ma'am——

(*The door is hurriedly closed.*)

PHOEBE (*ashamed*).　Sergeant, I have not been saying the things I meant to say to you.　Will you please excuse my turning you out of the house somewhat violently.

SERGEANT.　I am used to it, ma'am.

PHOEBE.　I won't really hurt you.

SERGEANT.　Thank you kindly, ma'am.

PHOEBE (*observing the bedroom door opening a little, and speaking in a loud voice*).　I protest, sir; we shall permit no followers in this house.　Should I discover you in my kitchen again I shall pitch you out—neck and crop.　Begone, sir.

(*The* SERGEANT *retires affably.　All the ladies except* MISS HENRIETTA *come out, admiring* PHOEBE.　*The* WILLOUGHBYS *are attired for their journey across the street.*)

MISS WILLOUGHBY.　Miss Phoebe, we could not but admire you.

(PHOEBE, *alas, knows that she is not admirable.*)

PHOEBE.　But the gentleman recruit?

MISS SUSAN.　Perhaps they will know who he is at the woollen-draper's.

MISS FANNY.   Let us inquire.

(*But before they go* MISS WILLOUGHBY *has a duty to perform.*)

MISS WILLOUGHBY.   I wish to apologise.   Miss Phoebe, you are a dear, good girl.   If I have made remarks about her ringlets, Susan, it was jealousy.   (PHOEBE *and* MISS SUSAN *wish to embrace her, but she is not in the mood for it.*)   Come, sister.

MISS FANNY (*the dear woman that she is*).   Phoebe, dear, I wish you very happy.

(PHOEBE *presses her hand.*)

MISS HENRIETTA (*entering, and not to be outdone*).   Miss Phoebe, I give you joy.

(*The three ladies go, the two younger ones a little tearfully, and we see them pass the window.*)

PHOEBE (*pained*).   Susan, you have been talking to them about V. B.

MISS SUSAN.   I could not help it.   (*Eagerly*) Now, Phoebe, what is it you have to tell me ?

PHOEBE (*in a low voice*).   Dear, I think it is too holy to speak of.

MISS SUSAN.   To your sister ?

PHOEBE.   Susan, as you know, I was sitting with an unhappy woman whose husband has fallen in the war.   When I came out of the cottage *he* was passing.

MISS SUSAN.   Yes ?

PHOEBE.   He offered me his escort.   At first he was very silent—as he has often been of late.

MISS SUSAN.   *We* know why.

PHOEBE.   Please not to say that I know why.   Suddenly he stopped and swung his cane.   You know how gallantly he swings his cane.

MISS SUSAN.   Yes, indeed.

PHOEBE.   He said : ' I have something I am wishful to tell you, Miss Phoebe ; perhaps you can guess what it is.'

MISS SUSAN.   Go on !

PHOEBE.   To say I could guess, sister, would have been un-ladylike.   I said : ' Please not to tell me in the public thorough-fare ' ; to which he instantly replied : ' Then I shall call and tell you this afternoon.'

MISS SUSAN.   Phoebe !

(*They are interrupted by the entrance of* PATTY *with tea.*

They see that she has brought three cups, and know that this is her impertinent way of implying that mistresses, as well as maids, may have a ' follower.'   When she has gone they smile at the daring of the woman, and sit down to tea.)

PHOEBE.   Susan, to think that it has all happened in a single year.

MISS SUSAN.   Such a genteel competency as he can offer ; such a desirable establishment.

PHOEBE.   I had no thought of that, dear.   I was recalling our first meeting at Mrs. Fotheringay's quadrille party.

MISS SUSAN.   We had quite forgotten that our respected local physician was growing elderly.

PHOEBE.   Until he said : ' Allow me to present my new partner, Mr. Valentine Brown.'

MISS SUSAN.   Phoebe, do you remember how at the tea-table he facetiously passed the cake-basket with nothing in it !

PHOEBE.   He was so amusing from the first.   I am thankful, Susan, that I too have a sense of humour.   I am exceedingly funny at times ; am I not, Susan ?

MISS SUSAN.   Yes, indeed.   But he sees humour in the most unexpected things.   I say something so ordinary about loving, for instance, to have everything either blue or white in this room, and I know not why he laughs, but it makes me feel quite witty.

PHOEBE (*a little anxiously*).   I hope he sees nothing odd or quaint about us.

MISS SUSAN.   My dear, I am sure he cannot.

PHOEBE.   Susan, the picnics !

MISS SUSAN.   Phoebe, the day when he first drank tea in this house !

PHOEBE.   He invited himself.

MISS SUSAN.   He merely laughed when I said it would cause such talk.

PHOEBE.   He is absolutely fearless.   Susan, he has smoked his pipe in this room.

(*They are both a little scared.*)

MISS SUSAN.   Smoking is indeed a dreadful habit.

PHOEBE.   But there is something so dashing about it.

MISS SUSAN (*with melancholy*).   And now I am to be left alone.

PHOEBE. No.

MISS SUSAN. My dear, I could not leave this room. My lovely blue and white room. It is my husband.

PHOEBE (*who has become agitated.*) Susan, you must make my house your home. I have something distressing to tell you.

MISS SUSAN. You alarm me.

PHOEBE. You know Mr. Brown advised us how to invest half of our money.

MISS SUSAN. I know it gives us eight per cent., though why it should do so I cannot understand, but very obliging, I am sure.

PHOEBE. Susan, all that money is lost ; I had the letter several days ago.

MISS SUSAN. Lost ?

PHOEBE. Something burst, dear, and then they absconded.

MISS SUSAN. But Mr. Brown——

PHOEBE. I have not advertised him of it yet, for he will think it was his fault. But I shall tell him to-day.

MISS SUSAN. Phoebe, how much have we left ?

PHOEBE. Only sixty pounds a year, so you see you must live with us, dearest.

MISS SUSAN. But Mr. Brown—he——

PHOEBE (*grandly*). He is a man of means, and if he is not proud to have my Susan I shall say at once : ‘ Mr. Brown—the door.’

(*She presses her cheek to* MISS SUSAN's.)

MISS SUSAN (*softly*). Phoebe, I have a wedding gift for you.

PHOEBE. Not yet ?

MISS SUSAN. It has been ready for a long time. I began it when you were not ten years old and I was a young woman. I meant it for myself, Phoebe. I had hoped that he—his name was William—but I think I must have been too unattractive, my love.

PHOEBE. Sweetest—dearest——

MISS SUSAN. I always associate it with a sprigged poplin I was wearing that summer, with a breadth of coloured silk in it, being a naval officer ; but something happened, a Miss Cicely Pemberton, and they are quite big boys now. So long ago, Phoebe—he was very tall, with brown hair—it was most foolish of me, but I was always so fond of sewing—with long straight legs and such a pleasant expression.

PHOEBE.   Susan, what was it ?

MISS SUSAN.   It was a wedding-gown, my dear.   Even plain women, Phoebe, we can't help it ; when we are young we have romantic ideas just as if we were pretty.   And so the wedding-gown was never used.   Long before it was finished I knew he would not offer, but I finished it, and then I put it away.   I have always hidden it from you, Phoebe, but of late I have brought it out again, and altered it.

(She goes to ottoman and unlocks it.)

PHOEBE.   Susan, I could not wear it.   (MISS SUSAN *brings the wedding-gown.)*   Oh ! how sweet, how beautiful !

MISS SUSAN.   You will wear it, my love, won't you ?   And the tears it was sewn with long ago will all turn into smiles on my Phoebe's wedding-day.

(They are tearfully happy when a knock is heard on the street door.)

PHOEBE.   That knock.

MISS SUSAN.   So dashing.

PHOEBE.   So imperious.   *(She is suddenly panic-stricken.)* Susan, I think he kissed me once.

MISS SUSAN *(startled).*   You *think* ?

PHOEBE.   I know he did.   That evening—a week ago, when he was squiring me home from the concert.   It was raining, and my face was wet ; he said that was why he did it.

MISS SUSAN.   Because your face was wet ?

PHOEBE.   It does not seem a sufficient excuse now.

MISS SUSAN *(appalled).*   Oh, Phoebe, before he had offered ?

PHOEBE *(in distress).*   I fear me it was most unladylike.

(VALENTINE BROWN is shown in.   He is a frank, genial young man of twenty-five who honestly admires the ladies, though he is amused by their quaintness.   He is modestly aware that it is in the blue and white room alone that he is esteemed a wit.)

BROWN.   Miss Susan, how do you do, ma'am ?   Nay, Miss Phoebe, though we have met to-day already I insist on shaking hands with you again.

MISS SUSAN.   Always so dashing.

(VALENTINE laughs and the ladies exchange delighted smiles.)

VALENTINE *(to MISS SUSAN).*   And my other friends, I hope I find them in health ?   The spinet, ma'am, seems quite herself to-day; I trust the ottoman passed a good night?

MISS SUSAN (*beaming*). We are all quite well, sir.

VALENTINE. May I sit on this chair, Miss Phoebe? I know Miss Susan likes me to break her chairs.

MISS SUSAN. Indeed, sir, I do not. Phoebe, how strange that he should think so.

PHOEBE (*instantly*). The remark was humorous, was it not?

VALENTINE. How you see through me, Miss Phoebe.

(*The sisters again exchange delighted smiles.* VALENTINE *is about to take a seat.*)

MISS SUSAN (*thinking aloud*). Oh dear, I feel sure he is going to roll the coverlet into a ball and then sit on it.

(VALENTINE, *who has been on the point of doing so, abstains and sits guiltily.*)

VALENTINE. So I am dashing, Miss Susan? Am I dashing, Miss Phoebe?

PHOEBE. A—little, I think.

VALENTINE. Well, but I have something to tell you to-day which I really think is rather dashing. (MISS SUSAN *gathers her knitting, looks at* PHOEBE, *and is preparing to go.*) You are not going, ma'am, before you know what it is?

MISS SUSAN. I—I—indeed—to be sure—I—I know, Mr. Brown.

PHOEBE. Susan!

MISS SUSAN. I mean I do not know. I mean I can guess— I mean —— Phoebe, my love, explain. (*She goes out.*)

VALENTINE (*rather disappointed*). The explanation being, I suppose, that you both know, and I had flattered myself 'twas such a secret. Am I then to understand that you had foreseen it all, Miss Phoebe?

PHOEBE. Nay, sir, you must not ask that.

VALENTINE. I believe in any case 'twas you who first put it into my head.

PHOEBE (*aghast*). Oh, I hope not.

VALENTINE. Your demure eyes flashed so every time the war was mentioned; the little Quaker suddenly looked like a gallant boy in ringlets.

(*A dread comes over* PHOEBE, *but it is in her heart alone; it shows neither in face nor voice.*)

PHOEBE.   Mr. Brown, what is it you have to tell us ?

VALENTINE.   That I have enlisted, Miss Phoebe.   Did you surmise it was something else ?

PHOEBE.   You are going to the wars ?   Mr. Brown, is it a jest ?

VALENTINE.   It would be a sorry jest, ma'am.   I thought you knew.   I concluded that the recruiting sergeant had talked.

PHOEBE.   The recruiting sergeant ?   I see.

VALENTINE.   These stirring times, Miss Phoebe—he is but half a man who stays at home.   I have chafed for months.   I want to see whether I have any courage, and as to be an army surgeon does not appeal to me, it was enlist or remain behind. To-day I found that there were five waverers.   I asked them would they take the shilling if I took it, and they assented.   Miss Phoebe, it is not one man I give to the King, but six.

PHOEBE (*brightly*).   I think you have done bravely.

VALENTINE.   We leave shortly for the Petersburgh barracks, and I go to London to-morrow ; so this is good-bye.

PHOEBE.   I shall pray that you may be preserved in battle, Mr. Brown.

VALENTINE.   And you and Miss Susan will write to me when occasion offers ?

PHOEBE.   If you wish it.

VALENTINE (*smiling*).   With all the stirring news of Quality Street.

PHOEBE.   It seems stirring to us ; it must have been merely laughable to you, who came here from a great city.

VALENTINE.   Dear Quality Street—that thought me dashing !   But I made friends in it, Miss Phoebe, of two very sweet ladies.

PHOEBE (*timidly*).   Mr. Brown, I wonder why you have been so kind to my sister and me ?

VALENTINE.   The kindness was yours.   If at first Miss Susan amused me—— (*Chuckling*) To see her on her knees decorating the little legs of the couch with frills as if it were a child !   But it was her sterling qualities that impressed me presently.

PHOEBE.   And did—did I amuse you also ?

VALENTINE.   Prodigiously, Miss Phoebe.   Those other

ladies, they were always scolding you, your youthfulness shocked them.   I believe they thought you dashing.

PHOEBE (*nervously*).   I have sometimes feared that I was perhaps too dashing.

VALENTINE (*laughing at this*).   You delicious Miss Phoebe. You were too quiet.   I felt sorry that one so sweet and young should live so grey a life.   I wondered whether I could put any little pleasures into it.

PHOEBE.   The picnics ?   It was very good of you.

VALENTINE.   That was only how it began, for soon I knew that it was I who got the pleasures and you who gave them. You have been to me, Miss Phoebe, like a quiet, old-fashioned garden full of the flowers that Englishmen love best because they have known them longest : the daisy, that stands for innocence, and the hyacinth for constancy, and the modest violet and the rose.   When I am far away, ma'am, I shall often think of Miss Phoebe's pretty soul, which is her garden, and shut my eyes and walk in it.

> (*She is smiling gallantly through her pain when* MISS SUSAN *returns.*)

MISS SUSAN.   Have you—is it—you seem so calm, Phoebe.

PHOEBE (*pressing her sister's hand warningly and imploringly*). Susan, what Mr. Brown is so obliging as to inform us of is not what we expected—not that at all.   My dear, he is the gentle-man who has enlisted, and he came to tell us that and to say good-bye.

MISS SUSAN.   Going away ?

PHOEBE.   Yes, dear.

VALENTINE.   Am I not the ideal recruit, ma'am : a man without a wife or a mother or a sweetheart ?

MISS SUSAN.   No sweetheart ?

VALENTINE.   Have you one for me, Miss Susan ?

PHOEBE (*hastily, lest her sister's face should betray the truth*). Susan, we shall have to tell him now.   You dreadful man, you will laugh and say it is just like Quality Street.   But indeed since I met you to-day and you told me you had something to communicate we have been puzzling what it could be, and we concluded that you were going to be married.

VALENTINE.   Ha ! ha ! ha !   Was that it !

PHOEBE.   So like women, you know.   We thought we

perhaps knew her. (*Glancing at the wedding-gown.*) We were even discussing what we should wear at the wedding.

VALENTINE. Ha! ha! I shall often think of this. I wonder who would have me, Miss Susan? (*Rising.*) But I must be off ; and God bless you both.

MISS SUSAN (*forlorn*). You are going!

VALENTINE. No more mud on your carpet, Miss Susan ; no more coverlets rolled into balls. A good riddance. Miss Phoebe, a last look at the garden.

(*Taking her hand and looking into her face.*)

PHOEBE. We shall miss you very much, Mr. Brown.

VALENTINE. There is one little matter. That investment I advised you to make, I am happy it has turned out so well.

PHOEBE (*checking* MISS SUSAN, *who is about to tell of the loss of the money*). It was good of you to take all that trouble, sir. Accept our grateful thanks.

VALENTINE. Indeed I am glad that you are so comfortably left ; I am your big brother. Good-bye again. (*Looks round.*) This little blue and white room and its dear inmates, may they be unchanged when I come back. Good-bye.

(*He goes.* MISS SUSAN *looks forlornly at* PHOEBE, *who smiles pitifully.*)

PHOEBE. A misunderstanding ; just a mistake. (*She shudders, lifts the wedding-gown and puts it back in the ottoman.* MISS SUSAN *sinks sobbing into a chair.*) Don't, dear, don't—we can live it down.

MISS SUSAN (*fiercely*). He is a fiend in human form.

PHOEBE. Nay, you hurt me, sister. He is a brave gentleman.

MISS SUSAN. The money ; why did you not let me tell him ?

PHOEBE (*flushing*). So that he might offer to me out of pity, Susan ?

MISS SUSAN. Phoebe, how are we to live, with the quartern loaf at one and tenpence ?

PHOEBE. Brother James——

MISS SUSAN. You know very well that brother James will do nothing for us.

PHOEBE. I think, Susan, we could keep a little school— for genteel children only, of course. I would do most of the teaching.

MISS SUSAN.   You a schoolmistress—Phoebe of the ringlets ; every one would laugh.

PHOEBE.   I shall hide the ringlets away in a cap like yours, Susan, and people will soon forget them.   And I shall try to look staid and to grow old quickly.   It will not be so hard to me as you think, dear.

MISS SUSAN.   There were other gentlemen who were attracted by you, Phoebe, and you turned from them.

PHOEBE.   I did not want them.

MISS SUSAN.   They will come again, and others.

PHOEBE.   No, dear ; never speak of that to me any more. (*In woe*) I let him kiss me.

MISS SUSAN.   You could not prevent him.

PHOEBE.   Yes, I could.   I know I could now.   I wanted him to do it.   Oh, never speak to me of others after that. Perhaps he saw I wanted it and did it to please me.   But I meant—indeed I did—that I gave it to him with all my love. Sister, I could bear all the rest ; but I have been unladylike.

(*The curtain falls, and we do not see the sisters again for ten years.*)

ACT II

THE SCHOOL

Ten years later. It is the blue and white room still, but many of Miss Susan's beautiful things have gone, some of them never to return ; others are stored upstairs. Their place is taken by grim scholastic furniture : forms, a desk, a globe, a blackboard, heartless maps. It is here that Miss Phoebe keeps school. Miss Susan teaches in the room opening off it, once the spare bedroom, where there is a smaller blackboard (for easier sums) but no globe, as Miss Susan is easily alarmed. Here are the younger pupils unless they have grown defiant, when they are promoted to the blue and white room to be under Miss Phoebe's braver rule. They really frighten Miss Phoebe also, but she does not let her sister know this.

It is noon on a day in August, and through the window we can see that Quality Street is decorated with flags. We also hear at times martial music from another street. Miss Phoebe is giving a dancing lesson to half a dozen pupils, and is doing her very best ; now she is at the spinet while they dance, and again she is showing them the new step. We know it is Miss Phoebe because some of her pretty airs and graces still cling to her in a forlorn way, but she is much changed. Her curls are out of sight under a cap, her manner is prim, the light has gone from her eyes and buoyancy from her figure ; she looks not ten years older but twenty, and not an easy twenty. When the children are not looking at her we know that she has the headache.

PHOEBE (*who is sometimes at the spinet and sometimes dancing*). Toes out. So. Chest out, Georgy. Point your toes, Miss Beveridge—so. So—keep in line ; and young ladies, remember your toes. (GEORGY *in his desire to please has protruded the wrong part of his person. She writes a C on his chest with chalk.*) C stands for chest, Georgy. This is S.

(MISS SUSAN *darts out of the other room. She is less worn than* MISS PHOEBE.)

MISS SUSAN (*whispering so that the pupils may not hear*). Phoebe, how many are fourteen and seventeen?

PHOEBE (*almost instantly*). Thirty-one.

MISS SUSAN. I thank you. (*She darts off.*)

PHOEBE. That will do, ladies and gentlemen. You may go. (*They bow or curtsey, and retire to* MISS SUSAN'S *room, with the exception of* ARTHUR WELLESLEY TOMSON, *who is standing in disgrace in a corner with the cap of shame on his head, and* ISABELLA, *a forbidding-looking, learned little girl.* ISABELLA *holds up her hand for permission to speak.*)

ISABELLA. Please, ma'am, father wishes me to acquire algebra.

PHOEBE (*with a sinking*). Algebra! It—it is not a very ladylike study, Isabella.

ISABELLA. Father says, will you or won't you?

PHOEBE. And you are thin. It will make you thinner, my dear.

ISABELLA. Father says I am thin but wiry.

PHOEBE. Yes, you are. (*With feeling*) You are very wiry, Isabella.

ISABELLA. Father says, either I acquire algebra or I go to Miss Prothero's establishment.

PHOEBE. Very well, I—I will do my best. You may go. (ISABELLA *goes and* PHOEBE *sits wearily.*)

ARTHUR (*fingering his cap*). Please, ma'am, may I take it off now?

PHOEBE. Certainly not. Unhappy boy—— (ARTHUR *grins.*) Come here. Are you ashamed of yourself?

ARTHUR (*blithely*). No, ma'am.

PHOEBE (*in a terrible voice*). Arthur Wellesley Tomson, fetch me the implement. (ARTHUR *goes briskly for the cane, and she hits the desk with it.*) Arthur, surely that terrifies you?

ARTHUR. No, ma'am.

PHOEBE. Arthur, why did you fight with that street boy?

ARTHUR. 'Cos he said that when you caned you did not draw blood.

PHOEBE. But I don't, do I?

ARTHUR. No, ma'am.

PHOEBE. Then why fight him ?   (*Remembering how strange boys are*) Was it for the honour of the school ?

ARTHUR. Yes, ma'am.

PHOEBE. Say you are sorry, Arthur, and I won't punish you. (*He bursts into tears.*)

ARTHUR. You promised to cane me, and now you are not going to do it.

PHOEBE (*incredulous*). Do you *wish* to be caned ?

ARTHUR (*holding out his hand eagerly*). If you please, Miss Phoebe.

PHOEBE. Unnatural boy. (*She canes him in a very unprofessional manner.*)   Poor dear boy.
(*She kisses the hand.*)

ARTHUR (*gloomily*). Oh, ma'am, you will never be able to cane if you hold it like that.   You should hold it like this, Miss Phoebe, and give it a wriggle like that.
(*She is too soft-hearted to follow his instructions.*)

PHOEBE (*almost in tears*). Go away.

ARTHUR (*remembering that women are strange*). Don't cry, ma'am ; I love you, Miss Phoebe.
(*She seats him on her knee, and he thinks of a way to please her.*)
If any boy says you can't cane I will blood him, Miss Phoebe.
(PHOEBE *shudders, and* MISS SUSAN *again darts in. She signs to* PHOEBE *to send* ARTHUR *away.*)

MISS SUSAN (*as soon as* ARTHUR *has gone*). Phoebe, if a herring and a half cost three ha'pence, how many for elevenpence ?

PHOEBE (*instantly*). Eleven.

MISS SUSAN. William Smith says it is fifteen ; and he is such a big boy, do you think I ought to contradict him ?   May I say there are differences of opinion about it ?   No one can be really sure, Phoebe.

PHOEBE. It is eleven.   I once worked it out with real herrings.   (*Stoutly*) Susan, we must never let the big boys know that we are afraid of them.   To awe them, stamp with the foot, speak in a ferocious voice, and look them unflinchingly in the face. (*Then she pales.*)   Oh, Susan, Isabella's father insists on her acquiring algebra.

MISS SUSAN. What is algebra exactly ; is it those three-cornered things ?

PHOEBE. It is *x* minus *y* equals *z* plus *y* and things like that. And all the time you are saying they are equal, you feel in your heart, why should they be.

(*The music of the band swells here, and both ladies put their hands to their ears.*)

It is the band for to-night's ball. We must not grudge their rejoicings, Susan. It is not every year that there is a Waterloo to celebrate.

MISS SUSAN. I was not thinking of that. I was thinking that *he* is to be at the ball to-night ; and we have not seen him for ten years.

PHOEBE (*calmly*). Yes, ten years. We shall be glad to welcome our old friend back, Susan. I am going into your room now to take the Latin class.

(*A soldier with a girl passes—a yokel follows angrily.*)

MISS SUSAN. Oh, that weary Latin, I wish I had the whipping of the man who invented it.

(*She returns to her room, and the sound of the music dies away.* MISS PHOEBE, *who is not a very accomplished classical scholar, is taking a final peep at the declensions when* MISS SUSAN *reappears excitedly.*)

PHOEBE. What is it ?

MISS SUSAN (*tragically*). William Smith ! Phoebe, I tried to look ferocious, indeed I did, but he saw I was afraid, and before the whole school he put out his tongue at me.

PHOEBE. Susan !

(*She is lion-hearted ; she remembers* ARTHUR'S *instructions, and practises with the cane.*)

MISS SUSAN (*frightened*). Phoebe, he is much too big. Let it pass.

PHOEBE. If I let it pass I am a stumbling-block in the way of true education.

MISS SUSAN. Sister !

PHOEBE (*grandly*). Susan, stand aside.

(*Giving the cane* ARTHUR'S *most telling flick, she marches into the other room. Then, while* MISS SUSAN *is listening nervously,* CAPTAIN VALENTINE BROWN *is ushered in by* PATTY. *He is bronzed and soldierly. He wears the whiskers of the period, and is in uniform. He has lost his left hand, but this is not at first noticeable.*)

PATTY. Miss Susan, 'tis Captain Brown !

MISS SUSAN. Captain Brown !

VALENTINE (*greeting her warmly*). Reports himself at home again.

MISS SUSAN (*gratified*). You call this home ?

VALENTINE. When the other men talked of their homes, Miss Susan, I thought of this room. (*Looking about him*) Maps—desks—heigho ! But still it is the same dear room. I have often dreamt, Miss Susan, that I came back to it in muddy shoes. (*Seeing her alarm*) I have not, you know ! Miss Susan, I rejoice to find no change in you ; and Miss Phoebe—Miss Phoebe of the ringlets—I hope there be as little change in her ?

MISS SUSAN (*painfully*). Phoebe of the ringlets ! Ah, Captain Brown, you need not expect to see her.

VALENTINE. She is not here ? I vow it spoils all my home-coming.

(*At this moment the door of the other room is flung open and* PHOEBE *rushes out, followed by* WILLIAM SMITH, *who is brandishing the cane.* VALENTINE *takes in the situation, and without looking at* PHOEBE *seizes* WILLIAM *by the collar and marches him out of the school.*)

MISS SUSAN. Phoebe, did you see who it is ?

PHOEBE. I saw. (*In a sudden tremor*) Susan, I have lost all my looks.

(*The pupils are crowding in from* MISS SUSAN'S *room, and she orders them back and goes with them.* VALENTINE *returns, and speaks as he enters, not recognising* PHOEBE, *whose back is to him.*)

VALENTINE. A young reprobate, madam, but I have deposited him on the causeway. I fear——

(*He stops, puzzled because the lady has covered her face with her hands.*)

PHOEBE. Captain Brown.

VALENTINE. Miss Phoebe, it is you ?

(*He goes to her, but he cannot help showing that her appearance is a shock to him.*)

PHOEBE (*without bitterness*). Yes, I have changed very much, I have not worn well, Captain Brown.

VALENTINE (*awkwardly*). We—we are both older, Miss Phoebe.

(He holds out his hand warmly, with affected high spirits.)

PHOEBE *(smiling reproachfully)*. It was both hands when you went away. *(He has to show that his left hand is gone ; she is overcome.)* I did not know. *(She presses the empty sleeve in remorse.)* You never mentioned it in your letters.

VALENTINE *(now grown rather stern)*. Miss Phoebe, what did *you* omit from your letters ? that you had such young blackguards as that to terrify you.

PHOEBE. He is the only one. Most of them are dear children ; and this is the last day of the term.

VALENTINE. Ah, ma'am, if only you had invested all your money as you laid out part by my advice. What a monstrous pity you did not.

PHOEBE. We never thought of it.

VALENTINE. You look so tired.

PHOEBE. I have the headache to-day.

VALENTINE. You did not use to have the headache. Curse those dear children.

PHOEBE *(bravely)*. Nay, do not distress yourself about me. Tell me of yourself. We are so proud of the way in which you won your commission. Will you leave the army now ?

VALENTINE. Yes ; and I have some intention of pursuing again the old life in Quality Street. *(He is not a man who has reflected much. He has come back thinking that all the adventures have been his, and that the old life in Quality Street has waited, as in a sleep, to be resumed on the day of his return.)* I came here in such high spirits, Miss Phoebe.

PHOEBE *(with a wry smile)*. The change in me depresses you.

VALENTINE. I was in hopes that you and Miss Susan would be going to the ball. I had brought cards for you with me to make sure.

(She is pleased and means to accept. He sighs, and she understands that he thinks her too old.)

PHOEBE. But now you see that my dancing days are done.

VALENTINE *(uncomfortably)*. Ah, no.

PHOEBE *(taking care he shall not see that he has hurt her)*. But you will find many charming partners. Some of them have been my pupils. There was even a pupil of mine who fought at Waterloo.

VALENTINE. Young Blades ; I have heard him on it. *(She*

puts her hand wearily to her head.)   Miss Phoebe—what a dull grey world it is !

(*She turns away to hide her emotion, and* MISS SUSAN *comes in.*)

MISS SUSAN.   Phoebe, I have said that you will not take the Latin class to-day, and I am dismissing them.

VALENTINE.   Latin ?

PHOEBE (*rather defiantly*).   I am proud to teach it.   (*Breaking down*) Susan—his arm—have you seen ?

(MISS SUSAN *also is overcome, but recovers as the children crowd in.*)

MISS SUSAN.   Hats off, gentlemen salute, ladies curtsey—to the brave Captain Brown.

(CAPTAIN BROWN *salutes them awkwardly, and they cheer him, to his great discomfort, as they pass out.*)

VALENTINE (*when they have gone*).   A terrible ordeal, ma'am.

(*The old friends look at each other, and there is a silence.* VALENTINE *feels that all the fine tales and merry jests he has brought back for the ladies have turned into dead things. He wants to go away and think.*)

PHOEBE.   I wish you very happy at the ball.

VALENTINE (*sighing*).   Miss Susan, cannot we turn all these maps and horrors out till the vacation is over ?

MISS SUSAN.   Indeed, sir, we always do.   By to-morrow this will be my dear blue and white room again, and that my sweet spare bedroom.

PHOEBE.   For five weeks !

VALENTINE (*making vain belief*).   And then—the—the dashing Mr. Brown will drop in as of old, and, behold, Miss Susan on her knees once more putting tucks into my little friend the ottoman, and Miss Phoebe—Miss Phoebe——

PHOEBE.   Phoebe of the ringlets !

(*She goes out quietly.*)

VALENTINE (*miserably*).   Miss Susan, what a shame it is.

MISS SUSAN (*hotly*).   Yes, it is a shame.

VALENTINE (*suddenly become more of a man*).   The brave Captain Brown !   Good God, ma'am, how much more brave are the ladies who keep a school.

(PATTY *shows in two visitors,* MISS CHARLOTTE PARRATT *and* ENSIGN BLADES.   CHARLOTTE *is a pretty minx who*

we are glad to say does not reside in Quality Street, and
BLADES *is a callow youth, inviting admiration.*)

CHARLOTTE (*as they salute*).　But I did not know you had
company, Miss Susan.

MISS SUSAN.　'Tis Captain Brown—Miss Charlotte Parratt.

CHARLOTTE (*gushing*).　The heroic Brown ?

VALENTINE.　Alas, no, ma'am, the other one.

CHARLOTTE.　Miss Susan, do you see who accompanies
me ?

MISS SUSAN.　I cannot quite recall——

BLADES.　A few years ago, ma'am, there sat in this room a
scrubby, inky little boy—I was that boy.

MISS SUSAN.　Can it be our old pupil—Ensign Blades ?

(*She thinks him very fine, and he bows, well pleased.*)

BLADES.　Once a little boy and now your most obedient,
ma'am.

MISS SUSAN.　You have come to recall old memories ?

BLADES.　Not precisely ; I—Charlotte, explain.

CHARLOTTE.　Ensign Blades wishes me to say that it must
seem highly romantic to you to have had a pupil who has fought
at Waterloo.

MISS SUSAN.　Not exactly *romantic*.　I trust, sir, that when
you speak of having been our pupil you are also so obliging as to
mention that it was during our first year.　Otherwise it makes
us seem so elderly.

(*He bows again, in what he believes to be a quizzical
manner.*)

CHARLOTTE.　Ensign Blades would be pleased to hear, Miss
Susan, what you think of him as a whole.

MISS SUSAN.　Indeed, sir, I think you are monstrous fine.
(*Innocently*) It quite awes me to remember that we used to whip
him.

VALENTINE (*delighted*).　Whipped him, Miss Susan !　(*In
solemn burlesque of* CHARLOTTE) Ensign Blades wishes to indicate
that it was more than Buonaparte could do.　We shall meet
again, bright boy.

(*He makes his adieux and goes.*)

BLADES.　Do you think he was quizzing me ?

MISS SUSAN (*simply*).　I cannot think so.

BLADES.　He said ' bright boy,' ma'am.

MISS SUSAN.   I am sure, sir, he did not mean it.

(PHOEBE *returns.*)

PHOEBE.   Charlotte, I am happy to see you.   You look delicious, my dear—so young and fresh.

CHARLOTTE.   La !   Do you think so, Miss Phoebe ?

BLADES.   Miss Phoebe, your obedient.

PHOEBE.   It is Ensign Blades !   But how kind of you, sir, to revisit the old school.   Please to sit down.

CHARLOTTE.   Ensign Blades has a favour to ask of you, Miss Phoebe.

BLADES.   I learn, ma'am, that Captain Brown has obtained a card for you for the ball, and I am here to solicit for the honour of standing up with you.

(*For the moment* PHOEBE *is flattered.   Here, she believes, is some one who does not think her too old for the dance. Then she perceives a meaning smile pass between* CHARLOTTE *and the* ENSIGN.)

PHOEBE (*paling*).   Is it that you desire to make sport of me ?

BLADES (*honestly distressed*).   Oh no, ma'am, I vow—but I —I am such a quiz, ma'am.

MISS SUSAN.   Sister !

PHOEBE.   I am sorry, sir, to have to deprive you of some entertainment, but I am not going to the ball.

MISS SUSAN (*haughtily*).   Ensign Blades, I bid you my adieux.

BLADES (*ashamed*).   If I have hurt Miss Phoebe's feelings I beg to apologise.

MISS SUSAN.   *If* you have hurt them.   Oh, sir, how is it possible for any one to be as silly as you seem to be.

BLADES (*who cannot find the answer*).   Charlotte—explain.

(*But* CHARLOTTE *considers that their visit has not been sufficiently esteemed and departs with a cold curtsey, taking him with her.*

MISS SUSAN *turns sympathetically to* PHOEBE, *but* PHOEBE, *fighting with her pain, sits down at the spinet and plays at first excitedly a gay tune, then slowly, then comes to a stop with her head bowed.   Soon she jumps up courageously, brushes away her distress, gets an algebra book from the desk and sits down to study it.* MISS SUSAN *is at the window, where ladies and gentlemen are now seen passing in ball attire.*)

MISS SUSAN.   What book is it, Phoebe?

PHOEBE.   It is an algebra.

MISS SUSAN.   They are going by to the ball.   *(In anger)* My Phoebe should be going to the ball, too.

PHOEBE.   You jest, Susan.   (MISS SUSAN *watches her read.* PHOEBE *has to wipe away a tear; soon she rises and gives way to the emotion she has been suppressing ever since the entrance of* VALENTINE.) Susan, I hate him.   Oh, Susan, I could hate him if it were not for his poor hand.

MISS SUSAN.   My dear.

PHOEBE.   He thought I was old, because I am weary, and he should not have forgotten.   I am only thirty.   Susan, why does thirty seem so much more than twenty-nine?   *(As if* VALENTINE *were present)* Oh, sir, how dare you look so pityingly at me?   Because I have had to work so hard,—is it a crime when a woman works?   Because I have tried to be courageous— have I been courageous, Susan?

MISS SUSAN.   God knows you have.

PHOEBE.   But it has given me the headache, it has tired my eyes.   Alas, Miss Phoebe, all your charm has gone, for you have the headache, and your eyes are tired.   He is dancing with Charlotte Parratt now, Susan.   'I vow, Miss Charlotte, you are selfish and silly, but you are sweet eighteen.'   'Oh la, Captain Brown, what a quiz you are.'   That delights him, Susan; see how he waggles his silly head.

MISS SUSAN.   Charlotte Parratt is a goose.

PHOEBE.   'Tis what gentlemen prefer.   If there were a sufficient number of geese to go round, Susan, no woman of sense would ever get a husband.   'Charming Miss Charlotte, you are like a garden; Miss Phoebe was like a garden once, but 'tis a faded garden now.'

MISS SUSAN.   If to be ladylike——

PHOEBE.   Susan, I am tired of being ladylike.   I am a young woman still, and to be ladylike is not enough.   I wish to be bright and thoughtless and merry.   It is every woman's birthright to be petted and admired; I wish to be petted and admired.   Was I born to be confined within these four walls?   Are they the world, Susan, or is there anything beyond them?   I want to know.   My eyes are tired because for ten years they have seen nothing but maps

and desks.   Ten years !   Ten years ago I went to bed a
young girl and I woke with this cap on my head.   It is not
fair.   This is not me, Susan, this is some other person, I want
to be myself.

MISS SUSAN.   Phoebe, Phoebe, you who have always been so
patient !

PHOEBE.   Oh no, not always.   If you only knew how I
have rebelled at times, you would turn from me in horror.
Susan, I have a picture of myself as I used to be ; I sometimes
look at it.   I sometimes kiss it, and say, ' Poor girl, they have
all forgotten you.   But I remember.'

MISS SUSAN.   I cannot recall it.

PHOEBE.   I keep it locked away in my room.   Would you
like to see it ?   I shall bring it down.   My room !   Oh,
Susan, it is there that the Phoebe you think so patient has the
hardest fight with herself, for there I have seemed to hear and
see the Phoebe of whom this (*looking at herself*) is but an image
in a distorted glass.   I have heard her singing as if she thought
she was still a girl.   I have heard her weeping ; perhaps it was
only I who was weeping ; but she seemed to cry to me, ' Let
me out of this prison, give me back the years you have taken
from me.   Oh, where are my pretty curls ? ' she cried.   ' Where
is my youth, my youth ! '

(*She goes out, leaving* MISS SUSAN *woeful.   Presently* SUSAN
takes up the algebra book and reads.)

MISS SUSAN.   ' A stroke B multiplied by B stroke C equal
AB stroke a little 2 ; stroke AC add BC.'   Poor Phoebe !
' Multiply by C stroke A and we get '—Poor Phoebe !   ' C a B
stroke a little 2 stroke AC little 2 add BC.'   Oh, I cannot
believe it !   ' Stroke a little 2 again, add AB little 2 add a little
2 C stroke a BC.' . . .

(PATTY *comes in with the lamp.*)

PATTY.   Hurting your poor eyes reading without a lamp.
Think shame, Miss Susan.

MISS SUSAN (*with spirit*).   Patty, I will not be dictated to.
(PATTY *looks out at window.*)   Draw the curtains at once.   I
cannot allow you to stand gazing at the foolish creatures who
crowd to a ball.

PATTY (*closing curtains*).   I am not gazing at them, ma'am ;
I am gazing at my sweetheart.

MISS SUSAN. Your sweetheart ? (*Softly*) I did not know you had one.

PATTY. Nor have I, ma'am, as yet. But I looks out, and thinks I to myself, at any moment he may turn the corner. I ha' been looking out at windows waiting for him to oblige by turning the corner this fifteen years.

MISS SUSAN. Fifteen years, and still you are hopeful ?

PATTY. There is not a more hopeful woman in all the king's dominions.

MISS SUSAN. You who are so much older than Miss Phoebe.

PATTY. Yes, ma'am, I ha' the advantage of her by ten years.

MISS SUSAN. It would be idle to pretend that you are specially comely.

PATTY. That may be, but my face is my own, and the more I see it in the glass the more it pleases me. I never look at it but I say to myself, ' Who is to be the lucky man ? '

MISS SUSAN. 'Tis wonderful.

PATTY. This will be a great year for females, ma'am. Think how many of the men that marched away strutting to the wars have come back limping. Who is to take off their wooden legs of an evening, Miss Susan ? You, ma'am, or me ?

MISS SUSAN. Patty !

PATTY (*doggedly*). Or Miss Phoebe ? (*With feeling*) The pretty thing that she was, Miss Susan.

MISS SUSAN. Do you remember, Patty ? I think there is no other person who remembers unless it be the Misses Willoughby and Miss Henrietta.

PATTY (*eagerly*). Give her a chance, ma'am, and take her to the balls. There be three of them this week, and the last ball will be the best, for 'tis to be at the barracks, and you will need a carriage to take you there, and there will be the packing of you into it by gallant squires and the unpacking of you out, and other devilries.

MISS SUSAN. Patty !

PATTY. If Miss Phoebe were to dress young again and put candles in her eyes that used to be so bright, and coax back her curls——

(PHOEBE *returns, and a great change has come over her. She is young and pretty again.   She is wearing the wedding-*

gown of ACT I., *her ringlets are glorious, her figure youthful, her face flushed and animated.*   PATTY *is the first to see her, and is astounded.*   PHOEBE *signs to her to go.*)

PHOEBE (*when* PATTY *has gone*).   Susan.   (MISS SUSAN *sees and is speechless.*)   Susan, this is the picture of my old self that I keep locked away in my room, and sometimes take out of its box to look at.   This is the girl who kisses herself in the glass and sings and dances with glee until I put her away frightened lest you should hear her.

MISS SUSAN.   How marvellous !   Oh, Phoebe !

PHOEBE.   Perhaps I should not do it, but it is so easy.   I have but to put on the old wedding-gown and tumble my curls out of the cap.   (*Passionately*) Sister, am I as changed as he says I am ?

MISS SUSAN.   You almost frighten me.
(*The band is heard.*)

PHOEBE.   The music is calling to us.   Susan, I will celebrate Waterloo in a little ball of my own.   See, my curls have begun to dance, they are so anxious to dance.   One dance, Susan, to Phoebe of the ringlets, and then I will put her away in her box and never look at her again.   Ma'am, may I have the honour ?   Nay, then I shall dance alone.   (*She dances.*)   Oh, Susan, I almost wish I were a goose.

(*Presently* PATTY *returns.   She gazes at* MISS PHOEBE *dancing.*)

PATTY.   Miss Phoebe !

PHOEBE (*still dancing*).   Not Miss Phoebe, Patty.   I am not myself to-night, I am—let me see, I am my niece.

PATTY (*in a whisper to* SUSAN).   But Miss Susan, 'tis Captain Brown.

MISS SUSAN.   Oh, stop, Phoebe, stop !

PATTY.   Nay, let him see her !

(MISS SUSAN *hurries scandalised into the other room as* VALENTINE *enters.*)

VALENTINE.   I ventured to come back because——   (PHOEBE *turns to him—he stops abruptly, bewildered.*)   I beg your pardon, madam, I thought it was Miss Susan or Miss Phoebe.

(*His mistake surprises her, but she is in a wild mood and curtseys, then turns away and smiles.   He stares as if half-convinced.*)

PATTY (*with an inspiration*).   'Tis my mistresses' niece, sir ;
she is on a visit here.

(*He is deceived.   He bows gallantly, then remembers the
object of his visit.   He produces a bottle of medicine.*)

VALENTINE.   Patty, I obtained this at the apothecary's for
Miss Phoebe's headache.   It should be taken at once.

PATTY.   Miss Phoebe is lying down, sir.

VALENTINE.   Is she asleep ?

PATTY (*demurely*).   No, sir, I think she be wide awake.

VALENTINE.   It may soothe her.

PHOEBE.   Patty, take it to Aunt Phoebe at once.

(PATTY *goes out sedately with the medicine.*)

VALENTINE (*after a little awkwardness, which* PHOEBE *enjoys*).
Perhaps I may venture to present myself, Miss——Miss—— ?

PHOEBE.   Miss——Livvy, sir.

VALENTINE.   I am Captain Brown, Miss Livvy, an old friend
of both your aunts.

PHOEBE (*curtseying*).   I have heard them speak of a dashing
Mr. Brown.   But I think it cannot be the same.

VALENTINE (*a little chagrined*).   Why not, ma'am ?

PHOEBE.   I ask your pardon, sir.

VALENTINE.   I was sure you must be related.   Indeed, for
a moment the likeness——even the voice——

PHOEBE (*pouting*).   La, sir, you mean I am like Aunt Phoebe.
Every one says so——and indeed 'tis no compliment.

VALENTINE.   'Twould have been a compliment once.   You
must be a daughter of the excellent Mr. James Throssel who
used to reside at Great Buckland.

PHOEBE.   He is still there.

VALENTINE.   A tedious twenty miles from here, as I remember.

PHOEBE.   La !   I have found the journey a monstrous quick
one, sir.

(*The band is again heard.   She runs to the window to peep
between the curtains, and his eyes follow her admiringly.*)

VALENTINE (*eagerly*).   Miss Livvy, you go to the ball ?

PHOEBE.   Alas, sir, I have no card.

VALENTINE.   I have two cards for your aunts.   As Miss
Phoebe has the headache, your Aunt Susan must take you to the
ball.

PHOEBE   Oh, oh ! (*Her feet move to the music.*)   Sir, I cannot control my feet.

VALENTINE.   They are already at the ball, ma'am ; you must follow them.

PHOEBE (*with all the pent-up mischief of ten years*).   Oh, sir, do you think some pretty gentleman might be partial to me at the ball ?

VALENTINE.   If that is your wish——

PHOEBE.   I should love, sir, to inspire frenzy in the breast of the male. (*With sudden collapse*) I dare not go—I dare not.

VALENTINE.   Miss Livvy, I vow——

(*He turns eagerly to* MISS SUSAN, *who enters.*)

I have ventured, Miss Susan, to introduce myself to your charming niece.

(MISS SUSAN *would like to run away again, but the wicked* MISS PHOEBE *is determined to have her help.*)

PHOEBE.   Aunt Susan, do not be angry with your Livvy— your Livvy, Aunt Susan.   This gentleman says he is the dashing Mr. Brown, he has cards for us for the ball, Auntie.   Of course we cannot go—we dare not go.   Oh, Auntie, hasten into your bombazine.

MISS SUSAN (*staggered*).   Phoebe——

PHOEBE.   Aunt Phoebe wants me to go.   If I say she does you know she does !

MISS SUSAN.   But my dear, my dear.

PHOEBE.   Oh, Auntie, why do you talk so much.   Come, come.

VALENTINE.   I shall see to it, Miss Susan, that your niece has a charming ball.

PHOEBE.   He means he will find me sweet partners.

VALENTINE.   Nay, ma'am, I mean *I* shall be your partner.

PHOEBE (*who is not an angel*).   Aunt Susan, he still dances !

VALENTINE.   *Still*, ma'am ?

PHOEBE.   Oh, sir, you are indeed dashing.   Nay, sir, please not to scowl, I could not avoid noticing them.

VALENTINE.   Noticing what, Miss Livvy ?

PHOEBE.   The grey hairs, sir.

VALENTINE.   I vow, ma'am, there is not one in my head.

PHOEBE.   He is such a quiz.   I so love a quiz.

VALENTINE.   Then, ma'am, I shall do nothing but quiz you at the ball.   Miss Susan, I beg you——

MISS SUSAN.   Oh, sir, dissuade her.

VALENTINE.   Nay, I entreat.

PHOEBE.   Auntie !

MISS SUSAN.   Think, my dear, think, we dare not.

PHOEBE (*shuddering*).   No, we dare not, I cannot go.

VALENTINE.   Indeed, ma'am——

PHOEBE.   'Tis impossible.

(*She really means it, and had not the music here taken an unfair advantage of her it is certain that* MISS PHOEBE *would never have gone to the ball.   In after years she and* MISS SUSAN *would have talked together of the monstrous evening when she nearly lost her head, but regained it before it could fall off.   But suddenly the music swells so alluringly that it is a thousand fingers beckoning her to all the balls she has missed, and in a transport she whirls* MISS SUSAN *from the blue and white room to the bed-chamber where is the bombazine.* VALENTINE *awaits their return like a conqueror, until* MISS LIVVY'S *words about his hair return to trouble him.   He is stooping, gazing intently into a small mirror, extracting the grey hairs one by one, when* PATTY *ushers in the sisters* WILLOUGHBY *and* MISS HENRIETTA. MISS HENRIETTA *is wearing the new veil, which opens or closes like curtains when she pulls a string.   She opens it now to see what he is doing, and the slight sound brings him to his feet.*)

MISS HENRIETTA.   'Tis but the new veil, sir ; there is no cause for alarm.

(*They have already learned from* PATTY, *we may be sure, that he is in the house, but they express genteel surprise.*)

MISS FANNY.   Mary, surely we are addressing the gallant Captain Brown !

VALENTINE.   It is the Misses Willoughby and Miss Henrietta.   'Tis indeed a gratification to renew acquaintance with such elegant and respectable females.

(*The greetings are elaborate.*)

MISS WILLOUGHBY.   You have seen Miss Phoebe, sir ?

VALENTINE.   I have had the honour.   Miss Phoebe, I regret to say, is now lying down with the headache.   (*The ladies*

*are too delicately minded to exchange glances before a man, but they
are privately of opinion that this meeting after ten years with the
dazzling* BROWN *has laid* MISS PHOEBE *low. They are in a twitter
of sympathy with her, and yearning to see* MISS SUSAN *alone, so that
they may draw from her an account of the exciting meeting.)* You
do not favour the ball to-night ?

MISS FANNY.   I confess balls are distasteful to me.

MISS HENRIETTA.   'Twill be a mixed assembly.   I am
credibly informed that the woollen-draper's daughter has
obtained a card.

VALENTINE (*gravely*).   Good God, ma'am, is it possible ?

MISS WILLOUGHBY.   We shall probably spend the evening
here with Miss Susan at the card table.

VALENTINE.   But Miss Susan goes with me to the ball,
ma'am.

(*This is scarcely less exciting to them than the overthrow of
the Corsican.*)

VALENTINE.   Nay, I hope there be no impropriety.   Miss
Livvy will accompany her.

MISS WILLOUGHBY (*bewildered*).   Miss Livvy ?

VALENTINE.   Their charming niece.

(*The ladies repeat the word in a daze.*)

MISS FANNY.   They had not apprised us that they have a
visitor.

(*They think this reticence unfriendly, and are wondering
whether they ought not to retire hurt, when* MISS SUSAN
*enters in her bombazine, wraps, and bonnet. She starts at
sight of them, and has the bearing of a guilty person.*)

MISS WILLOUGHBY (*stiffly*).   We have but now been advertised of your intention for this evening, Susan.

MISS HENRIETTA.   We deeply regret our intrusion.

MISS SUSAN (*wistfully*).   Please not to be piqued, Mary.
'Twas so—sudden.

MISS WILLOUGHBY.   I cannot remember, Susan, that your
estimable brother had a daughter.   I thought all the three
were sons.

MISS SUSAN (*with deplorable readiness*).   Three sons and a
daughter.   Surely you remember little Livvy, Mary ?

MISS WILLOUGHBY (*bluntly*).   No, Susan, I do not.

MISS SUSAN.   I—I must go.   I hear Livvy calling.

MISS FANNY (*tartly*).   I hear nothing but the band.   We are not to see your niece ?

MISS SUSAN.   Another time—to-morrow.   Pray rest a little before you depart, Mary.   I—I—Phoebe Livvy—the headache——

(*But before she can go another lady enters gaily.*)

VALENTINE.   Ah, here is Miss Livvy.

(*The true culprit is more cunning than* MISS SUSAN, *and before they can see her she quickly pulls the strings of her bonnet, which is like* MISS HENRIETTA'S, *and it obscures her face.*)

MISS SUSAN.   This—this is my niece, Livvy—Miss Willoughby, Miss Henrietta, Miss Fanny Willoughby.

VALENTINE.   Ladies, excuse my impatience, but——

MISS WILLOUGHBY.   One moment, sir.   May I ask, Miss Livvy, how many brothers you have ?

PHOEBE.   Two.

MISS WILLOUGHBY.   I thank you.

(*She looks strangely at* MISS SUSAN, *and* MISS PHOEBE *knows that she has blundered.*)

PHOEBE (*at a venture*).   Excluding the unhappy Thomas.

MISS SUSAN (*clever for the only moment in her life*).   We never mention him.

(*They are swept away on the arms of the impatient* CAPTAIN.)

MISS WILLOUGHBY, MISS HENRIETTA, AND MISS FANNY.   What has Thomas done ?

(*They have no suspicion as yet of what* MISS PHOEBE *has done ; but they believe there is a scandal in the Throssel family, and they will not sleep happily until they know what it is.*)

ACT III

THE BALL

A BALL, but not the one to which we have seen Miss Susan and Miss Phoebe rush forth upon their career of crime. This is the third of the series, the one of which Patty has foretold with horrid relish that it promises to be specially given over to devil-ries. The scene is a canvas pavilion, used as a retiring room and for card play, and through an opening in the back we have glimpses of gay uniforms and fair ladies intermingled in the bravery of the dance. There is coming and going through this opening, and also through slits in the canvas. The pavilion is fantastically decorated in various tastes, and is lit with lanterns. A good-natured moon, nevertheless, shines into it benignly. Some of the card tables are neglected, but at one a game of quadrille is in progress. There is much movement and hilarity, but none from one side of the tent, where sit several young ladies, all pretty, all appealing and all woeful, for no gallant comes to ask them if he may have the felicity. The nervous woman chaperoning them, and afraid to meet their gaze lest they scowl or weep in reply, is no other than Miss Susan, the most unhappy Miss Susan we have yet seen ; she sits there gripping her com-posure in both hands. Far less susceptible to shame is the brazen Phoebe, who may be seen passing the opening on the arm of a cavalier, and flinging her trembling sister a mischievous kiss. The younger ladies note the incident ; alas, they are probably meant to notice it, and they cower, as under a blow.

HARRIET (*a sad-eyed, large girl, who we hope found a romance at her next ball*). Are we so disagreeable that no one will dance with us ? Miss Susan, 'tis infamous ; they have eyes for no one but your niece.

CHARLOTTE. Miss Livvy has taken Ensign Blades from me.

308

HARRIET. If Miss Phoebe were here, I am sure she would not allow her old pupils to be so neglected.

(*The only possible reply for* MISS SUSAN *is to make herself look as small as possible. A lieutenant comes to them, once a scorner of woman, but now* SPICER *the bewitched.* HARRIET *has a moment's hope.*)

How do you do, sir?

SPICER (*with dreadful indifference, though she is his dear cousin*). Nay, ma'am, how do *you* do? (*Wistfully*) May I stand beside you, Miss Susan?

(*He is a most melancholic young man, and he fidgets her.*)

MISS SUSAN (*with spirit*). You have been standing beside me, sir, nearly all the evening.

SPICER (*humbly. It is strange to think that he had been favourably mentioned in despatches*). Indeed, I cannot but be cognisant of the sufferings I cause by attaching myself to you in this unseemly manner. Accept my assurances, ma'am, that you have my deepest sympathy.

MISS SUSAN. Then why do you do it?

SPICER. Because you are her aunt, ma'am. It is a scheme of mine by which I am in hopes to soften her heart. Her affection for you, ma'am, is beautiful to observe, and if she could be persuaded that I seek her hand from a passionate desire to have you for my Aunt Susan—do you perceive anything hopeful in my scheme, ma'am?

MISS SUSAN. No, sir, I do not.

(SPICER *wanders away gloomily, takes too much to drink, and ultimately becomes a general.* ENSIGN BLADES *appears, frowning, and* CHARLOTTE *ventures to touch his sleeve.*)

CHARLOTTE. Ensign Blades, I have not danced with you once this evening.

BLADES (*with the cold brutality of a lover to another she*). Nor I with you, Charlotte. (*To* SUSAN) May I solicit of you, Miss Susan, is Captain Brown Miss Livvy's guardian; is he affianced to her?

MISS SUSAN. No, sir.

BLADES. Then by what right, ma'am, does he interfere? Your elegant niece had consented to accompany me to the shrubbery—to look at the moon. And now Captain Brown forbids it. 'Tis unendurable.

CHARLOTTE.   But you may see the moon from here, sir.

BLADES (*glancing at it contemptuously*).   I believe not, ma'am. (*The moon still shines on.*)

MISS SUSAN (*primly*).   I am happy Captain Brown forbade her.

BLADES.   Miss Susan, 'twas but because he is to conduct her to the shrubbery himself.

(*He flings out pettishly, and* MISS SUSAN *looks pityingly at the wall-flowers.*)

MISS SUSAN.   My poor Charlotte !   May I take you to some very agreeable ladies ?

CHARLOTTE (*tartly*).   No, you may not.   I am going to the shrubbery to watch Miss Livvy.

MISS SUSAN.   Please not to do that.

CHARLOTTE (*implying that* MISS SUSAN *will be responsible for her early death*).   My chest is weak.   I shall sit among the dew.

MISS SUSAN.   Charlotte, you terrify me.   At least, please to put this cloak about your shoulders.   Nay, my dear, allow me.

(*She puts a cloak around* CHARLOTTE, *who departs vindictively for the shrubbery.   She will not find* LIVVY *there, however, for next moment* MISS PHOEBE *darts in from the back.*)

PHOEBE (*in a gay whisper*).   Susan, another offer—Major Linkwater—rotund man, black whiskers, fierce expression ; he has rushed away to destroy himself.

(*We have been unable to find any record of the Major's tragic end.*)

AN OLD SOLDIER (*looking up from a card table, whence he has heard the raging of* BLADES).   Miss Livvy, ma'am, what is this about the moon ?

(PHOEBE *smiles roguishly.*)

PHOEBE (*looking about her*).   I want my cloak, Aunt Susan.

MISS SUSAN.   I have just lent it to poor Charlotte Parratt.

PHOEBE.   Oh, Auntie !

OLD SOLDIER.   And now Miss Livvy cannot go into the shrubbery to see the moon ;   and she is so fond of the moon !

(MISS PHOEBE *screws her nose at him merrily, and darts back to the dance, but she has left a defender behind her.*)

A GALLANT (*whose name we have not succeeded in discovering*). Am I to understand, sir, that you are intimating disparagement

of the moon ?   If a certain female has been graciously pleased
to signify approval of that orb, any slight cast upon the moon,
sir, I shall regard as a personal affront.

OLD SOLDIER.   Hoity-toity.

(But he rises, and they face each other, as MISS SUSAN *feels,
for battle.   She is about to rush between their undrawn
swords when there is a commotion outside ; a crowd gathers
and opens to allow some officers to assist a fainting woman
into the tent.   It is* MISS PHOEBE, *and* MISS SUSAN *with a
cry goes on her knees beside her.   The tent has filled with
the sympathetic and inquisitive, but* CAPTAIN BROWN, *as a
physician, takes command, and by his order they retire.   He
finds difficulty in bringing the sufferer to, and gets little help
from* MISS SUSAN, *who can only call upon* MISS PHOEBE *by
name.)*

VALENTINE.   Nay, Miss Susan, 'tis useless calling for Miss
Phoebe.   'Tis my fault ; I should not have permitted Miss
Livvy to dance so immoderately.   Why do they delay with the
cordial ?

*(He goes to the back to close the opening, and while he is doing
so the incomprehensible* MISS PHOEBE *seizes the opportunity
to sit up on her couch of chairs, waggle her finger at* MISS
SUSAN, *and sign darkly that she is about to make a genteel
recovery.)*

PHOEBE.   Where am I ?   Is that you, Aunt Susan ?   What
has happened ?

VALENTINE *(returning).*   Nay, you must recline, Miss Livvy.
You fainted.   You have over-fatigued yourself.

PHOEBE.   I remember.

(BLADES enters with the cordial.)

VALENTINE.   You will sip this cordial.

BLADES.   By your leave, sir.

(He hands it to PHOEBE himself.)

VALENTINE.   She is in restored looks already, Miss Susan.

PHOEBE.   I am quite recovered.   Perhaps if you were to
leave me now with my excellent aunt——

VALENTINE.   Be off with you, apple cheeks.

BLADES.   Sir, I will suffer no reference to my complexion ;
and, if I mistake not, this charming lady was addressing you.

PHOEBE.   If you please, both of you.   *(They retire together, and no sooner have they gone than* MISS PHOEBE *leaps from the couch, her eyes sparkling. She presses the cordial on* MISS SUSAN.) Nay, drink it, Susan. I left it for you on purpose. I have such awful information to impart. Drink (MISS SUSAN *drinks tremblingly and then the bolt is fired.*) Susan, Miss Henrietta and Miss Fanny are here !

MISS SUSAN. Phoebe !

PHOEBE. Suddenly my eyes lighted on them. At once I slipped to the ground.

MISS SUSAN. You think they did not see you ?

PHOEBE. I am sure of it. They talked for a moment to Ensign Blades, and then turned and seemed to be going towards the shrubbery.

MISS SUSAN. He had heard that you were there with Captain Brown. He must have told them.

PHOEBE. I was not. But oh, sister, I am sure they suspect, else why should they be here ? They never frequent balls.

MISS SUSAN. They have suspected for a week, ever since they saw you in your veil, Phoebe, on the night of the first dance. How could they but suspect, when they have visited us every day since then and we have always pretended that Livvy was gone out ?

PHOEBE. Should they see my face it will be idle to attempt to deceive them.

MISS SUSAN. Idle indeed ; Phoebe, the scandal ! You— a schoolmistress !

PHOEBE. That is it, sister. A little happiness has gone to my head like strong waters.

(*She is very restless and troubled.*)

MISS SUSAN. My dear, stand still, and think.

PHOEBE. I dare not, I cannot. Oh, Susan, if they see me we need not open school again.

MISS SUSAN. We shall starve.

PHOEBE (*passionately*). This horrid, forward, flirting, heartless, hateful little toad of a Livvy.

MISS SUSAN. Brother James's daughter, as we call her !

PHOEBE. 'Tis all James's fault.

MISS SUSAN. Sister, when you know that James has no daughter !

PHOEBE. If he had really had one, think you I could have

been so wicked as to personate her ?   Susan, I know not what I am saying, but you know who it is that has turned me into this wild creature.

MISS SUSAN.   Oh, Valentine Brown, how could you ?

PHOEBE.   To weary of Phoebe—patient, ladylike Phoebe—the Phoebe whom I have lost—to turn from her with a ' Bah, you make me old,' and become enamoured in a night of a thing like this !

MISS SUSAN.   Yes, yes, indeed ; yet he has been kind to us also.   He has been to visit us several times.

PHOEBE.   In the hope to see her.   Was he not most silent and gloomy when we said she was gone out ?

MISS SUSAN.   He is infatuate—— (*She hesitates*) Sister, you are not partial to him still ?

PHOEBE.   No, Susan, no.   I did love him all those years, though I never spoke of it to you.   I put hope aside at once, I folded it up and kissed it and put it away like a pretty garment I could never wear again, I but loved to think of him as a noble man.   But he is not a noble man, and Livvy found it out in an hour.   The gallant !   I flirted that I might enjoy his fury. Susan, there has been a declaration in his eyes all to-night, and when he cries ' Adorable Miss Livvy, be mine,' I mean to answer with an ' Oh, la, how ridiculous you are.   You are much too old—I have been but quizzing you, sir.'

MISS SUSAN.   Phoebe, how can you be so cruel ?

PHOEBE.   Because he has taken from me the one great glory that is in a woman's life.   Not a man's love—she can do without that—but her own dear sweet love for him. He is unworthy of my love ; that is why I can be so cruel.

MISS SUSAN.   Oh, dear.

PHOEBE.   And now my triumph is to be denied me, for we must steal away home before Henrietta and Fanny see us.

MISS SUSAN.   Yes, yes.

PHOEBE (*dispirited*).   And to-morrow we must say that Livvy has gone back to her father, for I dare keep up this deception no longer.   Susan, let us go.

(*They are going dejectedly, but are arrested by the apparition of* MISS HENRIETTA *and* MISS FANNY *peeping into the tent.* PHOEBE *has just time to signify to her sister that she will confess all and beg for mercy, when the intruders speak.*)

MISS HENRIETTA (*not triumphant but astounded*).   You, Miss Phoebe ?

PHOEBE (*with bowed head*).   Yes.

MISS FANNY.   How amazing !   You do not deny, ma'am, that you are Miss Phoebe ?

PHOEBE (*making confession*).   Yes, Fanny, I am Miss Phoebe. (*To her bewilderment* HENRIETTA *and* FANNY *exchange ashamed glances.*)

MISS HENRIETTA.   Miss Phoebe, we have done you a cruel wrong.

MISS FANNY.   Phoebe, we apologise.

MISS HENRIETTA.   To think how excitedly we have been following her about in the shrubbery.

MISS FANNY.   She is wearing your cloak.

MISS HENRIETTA.   Ensign Blades told us she was gone to the shrubbery.

MISS FANNY.   And we were convinced there was no such person.

MISS HENRIETTA.   So of course we thought it must be you.

MISS FANNY (*who has looked out*).   I can discern her in the shrubbery still.   She is decidedly taller than Phoebe.

MISS HENRIETTA.   I thought she looked taller.   I meant to say so.   Phoebe, 'twas the cloak deceived us.   We could not see her face.

PHOEBE (*beginning to understand*).   Cloak ?   You mean, Henrietta—you mean, Fanny——

MISS FANNY.   'Twas wicked of us, my dear, but we—we thought that you and Miss Livvy were the same person.   (*They have evidently been stalking* CHARLOTTE *in* MISS PHOEBE'S *cloak.* MISS SUSAN *shudders, but* MISS PHOEBE *utters a cry of reproach, and it is some time before they can persuade her to forgive them.   It is of course also some time before we can forgive* MISS PHOEBE.*) Phoebe, you look so pretty.   Are they paying you no attentions, my dear ?

(PHOEBE *is unable to resist these delightful openings.   The imploring looks* MISS SUSAN *gives her but add to her enjoyment.   It is as if the sense of fun she had caged a moment ago were broke loose again.*)

PHOEBE.   Alas, they think of none but Livvy.   They come to me merely to say that they adore her.

MISS HENRIETTA.   Surely not Captain Brown?

PHOEBE.   He is infatuate about her.

MISS FANNY.   Poor Phoebe!

(*They make much of her, and she purrs naughtily to their stroking, with lightning peeps at* MISS SUSAN. *Affronted Providence seeks to pay her out by sending* ENSIGN BLADES *into the tent. Then the close observer may see* MISS PHOEBE'S *heart sink like a bucket in a well.* MISS SUSAN *steals from the tent.*)

MISS HENRIETTA.   Mr. Blades, I have been saying that if I were a gentleman I would pay my addresses to Miss Phoebe much rather than to her niece.

BLADES.   Ma'am, excuse me.

MISS HENRIETTA (*indignant that* MISS PHOEBE *should be slighted so publicly*).   Sir, you are a most ungallant and deficient young man.

BLADES.   Really, ma'am, I assure you——

MISS HENRIETTA.   Not another word, sir.

PHOEBE (*in her most old-maidish manner*).   Miss Fanny, Miss Henrietta, it is time I spoke plainly to this gentleman.   Please leave him to me.   Surely 'twill come best from me.

MISS HENRIETTA.   Indeed, yes, if it be not too painful to you.

PHOEBE.   I must do my duty.

MISS FANNY (*wistfully*).   If we could remain——

PHOEBE.   Would it be seemly, Miss Fanny?

MISS HENRIETTA.   Come, Fanny.   (*To* BLADES) Sir, you bring your punishment upon yourself.

(*They press* PHOEBE'S *hand, and go.   Her heart returns to its usual abode.*)

BLADES (*bewildered*).   Are you angry with me, Miss Livvy?

PHOEBE.   Oh, no.

BLADES.   Miss Livvy, I have something to say to you of supreme importance to me.   With regard to my complexion, I am aware, Miss Livvy, that it has retained a too youthful bloom.   My brother officers comment on it with a certain lack of generosity.   (*Anxiously*) Might I inquire, ma'am, whether you regard my complexion as a subject for light talk?

PHOEBE.   No indeed, sir, I only wish I had it.

BLADES (*who has had no intention of offering, but is suddenly carried off his feet by the excellence of the opportunity, which is no doubt responsible for many proposals).*   Miss Livvy, ma'am, you may have it.

> *(She has a great and humorous longing that she could turn before his affrighted eyes into the schoolmistress she really is. She would endure much to be able at this moment to say, ' I have listened to you,* ENSIGN BLADES, *with attention, but I am really* MISS PHOEBE, *and I must now request you to fetch me the implement.'   Under the shock, would he have surrendered his palm for punishment ?   It can never be known, for as she looks at him longingly,* LIEUTENANT SPICER *enters, and he mistakes the meaning of that longing look)*

SPICER.   'Tis my dance, ma'am—'tis not his

BLADES.   Leave us, sir.   We have matter of moment to discuss.

SPICER *(fearing the worst).*   His affection, Miss Livvy, is not so deep as mine.   He is a light and shallow nature.

PHOEBE.   Pooh !   You are both light and shallow natures.

BLADES.   Both, ma'am ?   *(But he is not sure that he has not had a miraculous escape.)*

PHOEBE *(severely).*   'Tis such as you, with your foolish flirting ways, that confuse the minds of women and make us try to be as silly as yourselves.

SPICER *(crushed).*   Ma'am.

PHOEBE.   I did not mean to hurt you.   *(She takes a hand of each and tries to advise them as if her curls were once more hidden under a cap.)*   You are so like little boys in a school.   Do be good.   Sit here beside me.   I know you are very brave——

BLADES.   Ha !

PHOEBE.   And when you come back from the wars it must be so delightful to you to flirt with the ladies again.

SPICER.   Oh, ma'am.

PHOEBE.   As soon as you see a lady with a pretty nose you cannot help saying that you adore her.

BLADES *(in an ecstasy).*   Nay, I swear.

PHOEBE.   And you offer to her, not from love, but because you are so deficient in conversation.

SPICER.   Charming, Miss Livvy.

PHOEBE *(with sudden irritation).*   Oh, sir, go away ; go away, both of you, and read improving books.

> *(They are cast down.   She has not been quite fair to these*

gallants, for it is not really of them she has grown weary so much as of the lady they temporarily adore.   If MISS PHOEBE *were to analyse her feelings she would find that her remark is addressed to* LIVVY, *and that it means, ' I have enjoyed for a little pretending to be you, but I am not you and I do not wish to be you.   Your glitter and the airs of you and the racket of you tire me, I want to be done with you, and to be back in quiet Quality Street, of which I am a part ; it is really pleasant to me to know that I shall wake up to-morrow slightly middle-aged.'   With the entrance of* CAPTAIN BROWN, *however, she is at once a frivol again.   He frowns at sight of her cavaliers.*)

VALENTINE.   Gentlemen, I instructed this lady to rest, and I am surprised to find you in attendance.   Miss Livvy, you must be weary of their fatuities, and I have taken the liberty to order your chaise.

PHOEBE.   It is indeed a liberty.

BLADES.   An outrage.

PHOEBE.   I prefer to remain.

VALENTINE.   Nay.

PHOEBE.   I promised this dance to Ensign Blades.

SPICER.   To me, ma'am.

PHOEBE.   And the following one to Lieutenant Spicer. Mr. Blades, your arm.

VALENTINE.   I forbid any further dancing.

PHOEBE.   Forbid.   La !

BLADES.   Sir, by what right——

VALENTINE.   By a right which I hope to make clear to Miss Livvy as soon as you gentlemen have retired.

(PHOEBE *sees that the declaration is coming.   She steels herself.*)

PHOEBE.   I am curious to know what Captain Brown can have to say to me.   In a few minutes, Mr. Blades, Lieutenant Spicer, I shall be at your service.

VALENTINE.   I trust not.

PHOEBE.   I give them my word.

(*The young gentlemen retire, treading air once more.* BROWN *surveys her rather grimly.*)

VALENTINE.   You are an amazing pretty girl, ma'am, but you are a shocking flirt.

PHOEBE. La !

VALENTINE. It has somewhat diverted me to watch them go down before you. But I know you have a kind heart, and that if there be a rapier in your one hand there is a handkerchief in the other ready to staunch their wounds.

PHOEBE. I have not observed that they bled much.

VALENTINE. The Blades and the like, no. But one may, perhaps.

PHOEBE (*obviously the reference is to himself*). Perhaps I may wish to see him bleed.

VALENTINE (*grown stern*). For shame, Miss Livvy. (*Anger rises in her, but she wishes him to proceed.*) I speak, ma'am, in the interests of the man to whom I hope to see you affianced.

(*No, she does not wish him to proceed. She had esteemed him for so long, she cannot have him debase himself before her now.*)

PHOEBE. Shall we—I have changed my mind, I consent to go home. Please to say nothing.

VALENTINE. Nay——

PHOEBE. I beg you.

VALENTINE. No. We must have it out.

PHOEBE. Then if you must go on, do so. But remember I begged you to desist. Who is this happy man ?

(*His next words are a great shock to her.*)

VALENTINE. As to who he is, ma'am, of course I have no notion. Nor, I am sure, have you, else you would be more guarded in your conduct. But some day, Miss Livvy, the right man will come. Not to be able to tell him all, would it not be hard ? And how could you acquaint him with this poor sport ? His face would change, ma'am, as you told him of it, and yours would be a false face until it was told. This is what I have been so desirous to say to you—by the right of a friend.

PHOEBE (*in a low voice but bravely*). I see.

VALENTINE (*afraid that he has hurt her*). It has been hard to say and I have done it bunglingly. Ah, but believe me, Miss Livvy, it is not the flaunting flower men love ; it is the modest violet.

PHOEBE. The modest violet ! *You* dare to say that.

VALENTINE. Yes, indeed, and when you are acquaint with what love really is——

PHOEBE. Love !   What do you know of love ?

VALENTINE (*a little complacently*).   Why, ma'am, I know all about it.   I am in love, Miss Livvy.

PHOEBE (*with a disdainful inclination of the head*).   I wish you happy.

VALENTINE.   With a lady who was once very like you, ma'am.
> (*At first* PHOEBE *does not understand, then a suspicion of his meaning comes to her.*)

PHOEBE.   Not—not—oh no.

VALENTINE.   I had not meant to speak of it, but why should not I ?   It will be a fine lesson to you, Miss Livvy.   Ma'am, it is your Aunt Phoebe whom I love.

PHOEBE (*rigid*).   You do not mean that.

VALENTINE.   Most ardently.

PHOEBE.   It is not true ; how dare you make sport of her.

VALENTINE.   Is it sport to wish she may be my wife ?

PHOEBE.   Your wife !

VALENTINE.   If I could win her.

PHOEBE (*bewildered*).   May I solicit, sir, for how long you have been attached to Miss Phoebe ?

VALENTINE.   For nine years, I think.

PHOEBE.   You think !

VALENTINE.   I want to be honest.   Never in all that time had I thought myself in love.   Your aunts were my dear friends, and while I was at the wars we sometimes wrote to each other, but they were only friendly letters.   I presume the affection was too placid to be love.

PHOEBE.   I think that would be Aunt Phoebe's opinion.

VALENTINE.   Yet I remember, before we went into action for the first time—I suppose the fear of death was upon me— some of them were making their wills—I have no near relative —I left everything to these two ladies.

PHOEBE (*softly*).   Did you ?
> (*What is it that* MISS PHOEBE *begins to see as she sits there so quietly, with her hands pressed together as if upon some treasure ?   It is* PHOEBE *of the ringlets with the stain taken out of her.*)

VALENTINE.   And when I returned a week ago and saw Miss Phoebe, grown so tired-looking and so poor——

PHOEBE.   The shock made you feel old, I know.

VALENTINE.   No, Miss Livvy, but it filled me with a sudden passionate regret that I had not gone down in that first engagement.   They would have been very comfortably left.

PHOEBE.   Oh, sir !

VALENTINE.   I am not calling it love.

PHOEBE.   It was sweet and kind, but it was not love.

VALENTINE.   It is love now.

PHOEBE.   No, it is only pity.

VALENTINE.   It is love.

PHOEBE (*she smiles tremulously*).   You really mean Phoebe— tired, unattractive Phoebe, that woman whose girlhood is gone. Nay, impossible.

VALENTINE (*stoutly*).   Phoebe of the fascinating playful ways, whose ringlets were once as pretty as yours, ma'am.   I have visited her in her home several times this week—you were always out—I thank you for that !   I was alone with her, and with fragrant memories of her.

PHOEBE.   Memories !   Yes, that is the Phoebe you love, the bright girl of the past—not the schoolmistress in her old-maid's cap.

VALENTINE.   There you wrong me, for I have discovered for myself that the schoolmistress in her old-maid's cap is the noblest Miss Phoebe of them all.   (*If only he would go away, and let* MISS PHOEBE *cry.*)   When I enlisted, I remember I compared her to a garden.   I have often thought of that.

PHOEBE.   'Tis an old garden now.

VALENTINE.   The paths, ma'am, are better shaded.

PHOEBE.   The flowers have grown old-fashioned.

VALENTINE.   They smell the sweeter.   Miss Livvy, do you think there is any hope for me ?

PHOEBE.   There was a man whom Miss Phoebe loved—long ago.   He did not love her.

VALENTINE.   Now here was a fool !

PHOEBE.   He kissed her once.

VALENTINE.   If Miss Phoebe suffered him to do that she thought he loved her.

PHOEBE.   Yes, yes.   (*She has to ask him the ten years old question.*)   Do you opinion that this makes her action in allowing it less reprehensible ?   It has been such a pain to her ever since.

VALENTINE. How like Miss Phoebe ! (*Sternly*) But that man was a knave.

PHOEBE. No, he was a good man—only a little—inconsiderate. She knows now that he has even forgotten that he did it. I suppose men are like that ?

VALENTINE. No, Miss Livvy, men are not like that. I am a very average man, but I thank God I am not like that.

PHOEBE. It was you.

VALENTINE (*after a pause*). Did Miss Phoebe say that ?

PHOEBE. Yes.

VALENTINE. Then it is true.

(*He is very grave and quiet.*)

PHOEBE. It was raining and her face was wet. You said you did it because her face was wet.

VALENTINE. I had quite forgotten.

PHOEBE. But she remembers, and how often do you think the shameful memory has made her face wet since ? The face you love, Captain Brown, you were the first to give it pain. The tired eyes—how much less tired they might be if they had never known you. You who are torturing me with every word, what have you done to Miss Phoebe ? You who think you can bring back the bloom to that faded garden, and all the pretty airs and graces that fluttered round it once like little birds before the nest is torn down—bring them back to her if you can, sir ; it was you who took them away.

VALENTINE. I vow I shall do my best to bring them back. (MISS PHOEBE *shakes her head.*) Miss Livvy, with your help——

PHOEBE. My help ! I have not helped. I tried to spoil it all.

VALENTINE (*smiling*). To spoil it ? You mean that you sought to flirt even with me. Ah, I knew you did. But that is nothing.

PHOEBE. Oh, sir, if you could overlook it.

VALENTINE. I do.

PHOEBE. And forget these hateful balls.

VALENTINE. Hateful ! Nay, I shall never call them that. They have done me too great a service. It was at the balls that I fell in love with Miss Phoebe.

PHOEBE. What can you mean ?

VALENTINE. She who was never at a ball ! (*Checking himself humorously.*) But I must not tell you, it might hurt you.

L

PHOEBE. Tell me.

VALENTINE (*gaily*).   Then on your own head be the blame. It is you who have made me love her, Miss Livvy.

PHOEBE. Sir ?

VALENTINE.   Yes, it is odd, and yet very simple.   You who so resembled her as she was ! for an hour, ma'am, you bewitched me ; yes, I confess it, but 'twas only for an hour.   How like, I cried at first, but soon it was, how unlike.   There was almost nothing she would have said that you said ; you did so much that she would have scorned to do.   But I must not say these things to you !

PHOEBE.   I ask it of you, Captain Brown

VALENTINE.   Well ! Miss Phoebe's 'ladylikeness,' on which she set such store that I used to make merry of the word—I gradually perceived that it is a woman's most beautiful garment, and the casket which contains all the adorable qualities that go to the making of a perfect female.   When Miss Livvy rolled her eyes—ah !

(*He stops apologetically.*)

PHOEBE.   Proceed, sir.

VALENTINE.   It but made me the more complacent that never in her life had Miss Phoebe been guilty of the slightest deviation from the strictest propriety. (*She shudders.*)   I was always conceiving her in your place.   Oh, it was monstrous unfair to you.   I stood looking at you, Miss Livvy, and seeing in my mind her and the pretty things she did, and you did not do ; why, ma'am, that is how I fell in love with Miss Phoebe at the balls.

PHOEBE.   I thank you.

VALENTINE.   Ma'am, tell me, do you think there is any hope for me ?

PHOEBE.   Hope !

VALENTINE.   I shall go to her.   ' Miss Phoebe,' I will say —oh, ma'am, so reverently—' Miss Phoebe, my beautiful, most estimable of women, let me take care of you for ever more.'

(MISS PHOEBE *presses the words to her heart and then drops them.*)

PHOEBE.   Beautiful.   La, Aunt Phoebe !

VALENTINE.   Ah, ma'am, you may laugh at a rough soldier so much enamoured, but 'tis true.   ' Marry me, Miss Phoebe,'

I will say, 'and I will take you back through those years of hardships that have made your sweet eyes too patient. Instead of growing older you shall grow younger. We will travel back together to pick up the many little joys and pleasures you had to pass by when you trod that thorny path alone.'

PHOEBE. Can't be—can't be.

VALENTINE. Nay, Miss Phoebe has loved me. 'Tis you have said it.

PHOEBE. I did not mean to tell you.

VALENTINE. She will be my wife yet.

PHOEBE. Never.

VALENTINE. You are severe, Miss Livvy. But it is because you are partial to her, and I am happy of that.

PHOEBE (*in growing horror of herself*). I partial to her? I am laughing at both of you. Miss Phoebe! La, that old thing!

VALENTINE (*sternly*). Silence!

PHOEBE. I hate her and despise her. If you knew what she is——

(*He stops her with a gesture.*)

VALENTINE. I know what you are.

PHOEBE. That paragon who has never been guilty of the slightest deviation from the strictest propriety.

VALENTINE. Never.

PHOEBE. That garden——

VALENTINE. Miss Livvy, for shame.

PHOEBE. Your garden has been destroyed, sir; the weeds have entered it, and all the flowers are choked.

VALENTINE. You false woman, what do you mean?

PHOEBE. I will tell you. (*But his confidence awes her.*) What faith you have in her.

VALENTINE. As in my God. Speak.

PHOEBE. I cannot tell you.

VALENTINE. No, you cannot.

PHOEBE. It is too horrible.

VALENTINE. You are too horrible. Is not that it?

PHOEBE. Yes, that is it.

(MISS SUSAN *has entered and caught the last words.*)

MISS SUSAN (*shrinking as from a coming blow*). What is too horrible?

VALENTINE. Ma'am, I leave the telling of it to her, if she

dare.   And I devoutly hope those are the last words I shall ever address to this lady.

    (*He bows and goes out in dudgeon.*   MISS SUSAN *believes all is discovered and that* MISS PHOEBE *is for ever shamed.*)

    MISS SUSAN (*taking* PHOEBE *in her arms*).   My love, my dear, what terrible thing has he said to you ?

    PHOEBE (*forgetting everything but that she is loved*).   Not terrible—glorious !   Susan, 'tis Phoebe he loves, 'tis me, not Livvy !   He loves me, he loves me !   Me—Phoebe !

    (MISS SUSAN's *bosom swells.   It is her great hour as much as* PHOEBE's.)

ACT IV

THE BLUE AND WHITE ROOM

IF we could shut our eyes to the two sisters sitting here in woe, this would be, to the male eye at least, the identical blue and white room of ten years ago ; the same sun shining into it and playing familiarly with Miss Susan's treasures. But the ladies are changed. It is not merely that Miss Phoebe has again donned her schoolmistress's gown and hidden her curls under the cap. To see her thus once more, her real self, after the escapade of the ball, is not unpleasant, and the cap and gown do not ill become the quiet room. But she now turns guiltily from the sun that used to be her intimate, her face is drawn, her form condensed into the smallest space, and her hands lie trembling in her lap. It is disquieting to note that any life there is in the room comes not from her but from Miss Susan. If the house were to go on fire now it would be she who would have to carry out Miss Phoebe.

Whatever of import has happened since the ball, Patty knows it, and is enjoying it. We see this as she ushers in Miss Willoughby. Note also, with concern, that at mention of the visitor's name the eyes of the sisters turn affrightedly, not to the door by which their old friend enters, but to the closed door of the spare bed-chamber. Patty also gives it a meaning glance ; then the three look at each other, and two of them blanch.

MISS WILLOUGHBY (*the fourth to look at the door*). I am just run across, Susan, to inquire how Miss Livvy does now.

MISS SUSAN. She is still very poorly, Mary.

MISS WILLOUGHBY. I am so unhappy of that. I conceive it to be a nervous disorder ?

MISS SUSAN (*almost too glibly*). Accompanied by trembling, flutterings, and spasms.

MISS WILLOUGHBY. The excitements of the ball. You have summoned the apothecary at last, I trust, Phoebe ?

(MISS PHOEBE, *once so ready of defence, can say nothing.*)

325

MISS SUSAN (*to the rescue*).   It is Livvy's own wish that he should not be consulted.

MISS WILLOUGHBY (*looking longingly at the door*).   May I go in to see her ?

MISS SUSAN.   I fear not, Mary.   She is almost asleep, and it is best not to disturb her.   (*Peeping into the bedroom*) Lie quite still, Livvy, my love, quite still.

(*Somehow this makes* PATTY *smile so broadly that she finds it advisable to retire.*   MISS WILLOUGHBY *sighs, and produces a small bowl from the folds of her cloak.*)

MISS WILLOUGHBY.   This is a little arrowroot, of which I hope Miss Livvy will be so obliging as to partake.

MISS SUSAN (*taking the bowl*).   I thank you, Mary.

PHOEBE (*ashamed*).   Susan, we ought not——

MISS SUSAN (*shameless*).   I will take it to her while it is still warm.

(*She goes into the bedroom.*   MISS WILLOUGHBY *gazes at* MISS PHOEBE, *who certainly shrinks.   It has not escaped the notice of the visitor that* MISS PHOEBE *has become the more timid of the sisters, and she has evolved an explanation.*)

MISS WILLOUGHBY.   Phoebe, has Captain Brown been apprised of Miss Livvy's illness ?

PHOEBE (*uncomfortably*).   I think not, Miss Willoughby.

MISS WILLOUGHBY (*sorry for* PHOEBE, *and speaking very kindly*).   Is this right, Phoebe ?   You informed Fanny and Henrietta at the ball of his partiality for Livvy.   My dear, it is hard for you, but have you any right to keep them apart ?

PHOEBE (*discovering only now what are the suspicions of her friends*).   Is that what you think I am doing, Miss Willoughby ?

MISS WILLOUGHBY.   Such a mysterious illness.   (*Sweetly*) Long ago, Phoebe, I once caused much unhappiness through foolish jealousy.   That is why I venture to hope that you will not be as I was, my dear.

PHOEBE.   I jealous of Livvy !

MISS WILLOUGHBY (*with a sigh*).   I thought as little of the lady I refer to, but he thought otherwise.

PHOEBE.   Indeed, Miss Willoughby, you wrong me.

(*But* MISS WILLOUGHBY *does not entirely believe her, and there is a pause, so long a pause that unfortunately* MISS SUSAN *thinks she has left the house.*)

MISS SUSAN (*peeping in*).　Is she gone ?

MISS WILLOUGHBY (*hurt*).　No, Susan, but I am going.

MISS SUSAN (*distressed*).　Mary !

(*She follows her out, but* MISS WILLOUGHBY *will not be comforted, and there is a coldness between them for the rest of the day.* MISS SUSAN *is not so abashed as she ought to be. She returns, and partakes with avidity of the arrowroot.*)

MISS SUSAN.　Phoebe, I am well aware that this is wrong of me, but Mary's arrowroot is so delicious.　The ladies'-fingers and petticoat-tails those officers sent to Livvy, I ate them also ! (*Once on a time this would have amused* MISS PHOEBE, *but her sense of humour has gone.　She is crying.*)　Phoebe, if you have such remorse you will weep yourself to death.

PHOEBE.　Oh, sister, were it not for you, how gladly would I go into a decline.

MISS SUSAN (*after she has soothed* PHOEBE *a little*).　My dear, what is to be done about her ?　We cannot have her supposed to be here for ever.

PHOEBE.　We had to pretend that she was ill to keep her out of sight ; and now we cannot say she has gone away, for the Misses Willoughby's windows command our door, and they are always watching.

MISS SUSAN (*peeping from the window*).　I see Fanny watching now.　I feel, Phoebe, as if Livvy really existed.

PHOEBE (*mournfully*).　We shall never be able to esteem ourselves again.

MISS SUSAN (*who has in her the makings of a desperate criminal*). Phoebe, why not marry him ?　If only we could make him think that Livvy had gone home.　Then he need never know.

PHOEBE.　Susan, you pain me.　She who marries without telling all—hers must ever be a false face.　They are his own words.

(PATTY *enters importantly*.)

PATTY.　Captain Brown.

PHOEBE (*starting up*).　I wrote to him, begging him not to come.

MISS SUSAN (*quickly*).　Patty, I am sorry we are out.

(*But* VALENTINE *has entered in time to hear her words.*)

VALENTINE (*not unmindful that this is the room in which he is esteemed a wit*).　I regret that they are out, Patty, but I will await their return. (*The astonishing man sists on the ottoman beside* MISS SUSAN, *but politely ignores her presence.*) It is not my wish to detain you, Patty.

> (PATTY *goes reluctantly, and the sisters think how like him, and how delightful it would be if they were still the patterns of propriety he considers them.*)

PHOEBE (*bravely*). Captain Brown.

VALENTINE (*rising*). You, Miss Phoebe. I hear Miss Livvy is indisposed ?

PHOEBE. She is—very poorly.

VALENTINE. But it is not that unpleasant girl I have come to see, it is you.

MISS SUSAN (*meekly*). How do you do ?

VALENTINE (*ignoring her*). And I am happy, Miss Phoebe, to find you alone.

MISS SUSAN (*appealingly*). How do you do, sir ?

PHOEBE. You know quite well, sir, that Susan is here.

VALENTINE. Nay, ma'am, excuse me. I heard Miss Susan say she was gone out. Miss Susan is incapable of prevarication.

MISS SUSAN (*rising—helpless*). What am I to do ?

PHOEBE. Don't go, Susan—'tis what he wants.

VALENTINE. I have her word that she is not present.

MISS SUSAN. Oh dear.

VALENTINE. My faith in Miss Susan is absolute. (*At this she retires into the bedroom, and immediately his manner changes. He takes* MISS PHOEBE'S *hands into his own kind ones.*) You coward, Miss Phoebe, to be afraid of Valentine Brown.

PHOEBE. I wrote and begged you not to come.

VALENTINE. You implied as a lover, Miss Phoebe, but surely always as a friend.

PHOEBE. Oh yes, yes.

VALENTINE. You told Miss Livvy that you loved me once. How carefully you hid it from me !

PHOEBE (*more firmly*). A woman must never tell. You went away to the great battles. I was left to fight in a little one. Women have a flag to fly, Mr. Brown, as well as men, and old maids have a flag as well as women. I tried to keep mine flying.

VALENTINE. But you ceased to care for me. (*Tenderly*) I dare ask your love no more, but I still ask you to put yourself into my keeping. Miss Phoebe, let me take care of you.

PHOEBE.   It cannot be.

VALENTINE.   This weary teaching ! Let me close your school.

PHOEBE.   Please, sir.

VALENTINE.   If not for your own sake, I ask you, Miss Phoebe, to do it for mine. In memory of the thoughtless recruit who went off laughing to the wars. They say ladies cannot quite forget the man who has used them ill ; Miss Phoebe, do it for me because I used you ill.

PHOEBE.   I beg you—no more.

VALENTINE (*manfully*).   There, it is all ended. Miss Phoebe, here is my hand on it.

PHOEBE.   What will you do now ?

VALENTINE.   I also must work. I will become a physician again, with some drab old housekeeper to neglect me and the house. Do you foresee the cobwebs gathering and gathering, Miss Phoebe ?

PHOEBE.   Oh, sir !

VALENTINE.   You shall yet see me in Quality Street, wearing my stock all awry.

PHOEBE.   Oh, oh !

VALENTINE.   And with snuff upon my sleeve.

PHOEBE.   Sir, sir !

VALENTINE.   No skulker, ma'am, I hope, but gradually turning into a grumpy, crusty, bottle-nosed old bachelor.

PHOEBE.   Oh, Mr. Brown !

VALENTINE.   And all because you will not walk across the street with me.

PHOEBE.   Indeed, sir, you must marry—and I hope it may be some one who is really like a garden.

VALENTINE.   I know but one. That reminds me, Miss Phoebe, of something I had forgot. (*He produces a paper from his pocket.*) 'Tis a trifle I have wrote about you. But I fear to trouble you.

(PHOEBE'S *hands go out longingly for it.*)

PHOEBE (*reading*).   'Lines to a Certain Lady, who is Modestly unaware of her Resemblance to a Garden. Wrote by her servant, V. B.'

(*The beauty of this makes her falter.   She looks up.*)

VALENTINE (*with a poet's pride*).   There is more of it, ma'am.

PHOEBE (*reading*).

> The lilies are her pretty thoughts,
> Her shoulders are the may,
> Her smiles are all forget-me-nots,
> The path 's her gracious way,
> The roses that do line it are
> Her fancies walking round,
> 'Tis sweetly smelling lavender
> In which my lady 's gowned.

(MISS PHOEBE *has thought herself strong, but she is not able to read such exquisite lines without betraying herself to a lover's gaze.*)

VALENTINE (*excitedly*).   Miss Phoebe, when did you cease to care for me ?

PHOEBE (*retreating from him but clinging to her poem*).   You promised not to ask.

VALENTINE.   I know not why you should, Miss Phoebe, but I believe you love me still !

(MISS PHOEBE *has the terrified appearance of a detected felon.*)

(MISS SUSAN *returns.*)

MISS SUSAN.   You are talking so loudly.

VALENTINE.   Miss Susan, does she care for me still ?

MISS SUSAN (*forgetting her pride of sex*).   Oh, sir, how could she help it !

VALENTINE.   Then by Gad, Miss Phoebe, you shall marry me though I have to carry you in my arms to the church.

PHOEBE.   Sir, how can you !

(*But* MISS SUSAN *gives her a look which means that it must be done if only to avoid such a scandal.   It is at this inopportune moment that* MISS HENRIETTA *and* MISS FANNY *are announced.*)

MISS HENRIETTA.   I think Miss Willoughby has already popped in.

PHOEBE (*with a little spirit*).   Yes, indeed.

MISS SUSAN (*a mistress of sarcasm*).   How is Mary, Fanny ? She has not been to see us for several minutes.

MISS FANNY (*somewhat daunted*).   Mary is so partial to you, Susan.

VALENTINE. Your servant, Miss Henrietta, Miss Fanny.

MISS FANNY. How do you do, sir ?

MISS HENRIETTA (*wistfully*). And how do you find Miss Livvy, sir ?

VALENTINE. I have not seen her, Miss Henrietta.

MISS HENRIETTA. Indeed !

MISS FANNY. Not even you ?

VALENTINE. You seem surprised ?

MISS FANNY. Nay, sir, you must not say so ; but really, Phoebe !

PHOEBE. Fanny, you presume !

VALENTINE (*puzzled*). If one of you ladies would deign to enlighten me. To begin with, what is Miss Livvy's malady ?

MISS HENRIETTA. He does not know ? Oh, Phoebe.

VALENTINE. Ladies, have pity on a dull man, and explain.

MISS FANNY (*timidly*). Please not to ask us to explain. I fear we have already said more than was proper. Phoebe, forgive.

(*To* CAPTAIN BROWN *this but adds to the mystery, and he looks to* PHOEBE *for enlightenment.*)

PHOEBE (*desperate*). I understand, sir, there is a belief that I keep Livvy in confinement because of your passion for her.

VALENTINE. My passion for Miss Livvy ? Why, Miss Fanny, I cannot abide her—nor she me. (*Looking manfully at* MISS PHOEBE) Furthermore, I am proud to tell you that this is the lady whom I adore.

MISS FANNY. Phoebe ?

VALENTINE. Yes, ma'am.

(*The ladies are for a moment bereft of speech, and the uplifted* PHOEBE *cannot refrain from a movement which, if completed, would be a curtsey. Her punishment follows promptly.*)

MISS HENRIETTA (*from her heart*). Phoebe, I am so happy 'tis you.

MISS FANNY. Dear Phoebe, I give you joy. And you also, sir. (MISS PHOEBE *sends her sister a glance of unutterable woe, and escapes from the room. It is most ill-bred of her.*) Miss Susan, I do not understand !

MISS HENRIETTA. Is it that Miss Livvy is an obstacle ?

MISS SUSAN (*who knows that there is no hope for her but in flight*). I think I hear Phoebe calling me—a sudden indisposition. Pray excuse me, Henrietta. (*She goes.*)

MISS HENRIETTA. We know not, sir, whether to offer you our felicitations?

VALENTINE (*cogitating*). May I ask, ma'am, what you mean by an obstacle? Is there some mystery about Miss Livvy?

MISS HENRIETTA. So much so, sir, that we at one time thought she and Miss Phoebe were the same person.

VALENTINE. Pshaw!

MISS FANNY. Why will they admit no physician into her presence?

MISS HENRIETTA. The blinds of her room are kept most artfully drawn.

MISS FANNY (*plaintively*). We have never seen her, sir. Neither Miss Susan nor Miss Phoebe will present her to us.

VALENTINE (*impressed*). Indeed.

(MISS HENRIETTA and MISS FANNY, *encouraged by his sympathy, draw nearer the door of the interesting bed-chamber. They falter. Any one who thinks, however, that they would so far forget themselves as to open the door and peep in, has no understanding of the ladies of Quality Street. They are, nevertheless, not perfect, for* MISS HENRIETTA *knocks on the door.*)

MISS HENRIETTA. How do you find yourself, dear Miss Livvy?

(*There is no answer. It is our pride to record that they come away without even touching the handle. They look appealingly at* CAPTAIN BROWN, *whose face has grown grave.*)

VALENTINE. I think, ladies, as a physician——

(*He walks into the bedroom. They feel an ignoble drawing to follow him, but do not yield to it. When he returns his face is inscrutable.*)

MISS HENRIETTA. Is she very poorly, sir?

VALENTINE. Ha.

MISS FANNY. We did not hear you address her.

VALENTINE. She is not awake, ma'am.

MISS HENRIETTA. It is provoking.

MISS FANNY (*sternly just*). They informed Mary that she was nigh asleep.

VALENTINE. It is not a serious illness I think, ma'am.

With the permission of Miss Phoebe and Miss Susan I will make myself more acquaint with her disorder presently. (*He is desirous to be alone.*) But we must not talk lest we disturb her.

MISS FANNY.   You suggest our retiring, sir ?

VALENTINE.   Nay, Miss Fanny——

MISS FANNY.   You are very obliging ; but I think, Henrietta——

MISS HENRIETTA (*rising*).   Yes, Fanny.

(*No doubt they are the more ready to depart that they wish to inform* MISS WILLOUGHBY *at once of these strange doings. As they go,* MISS SUSAN *and* MISS PHOEBE *return, and the adieux are less elaborate than usual. Neither visitors nor hostesses quite know what to say.* MISS SUSAN *is merely relieved to see them leave, but* MISS PHOEBE *has read something in their manner that makes her uneasy.*)

PHOEBE.   Why have they departed so hurriedly, sir ?   They —they did not go in to see Livvy ?

VALENTINE.   No.

(*She reads danger in his face.*)

PHOEBE.   Why do you look at me so strangely ?

VALENTINE (*somewhat stern*).   Miss Phoebe, I desire to see Miss Livvy.

PHOEBE.   Impossible.

VALENTINE.   Why impossible ?   They tell me strange stories about no one's seeing her.   Miss Phoebe, I will not leave this house until I have seen her.

PHOEBE.   You cannot. (*But he is very determined, and she is afraid of him.*) Will you excuse me, sir, while I talk with Susan behind the door ?

(*The sisters go guiltily into the bedroom, and* CAPTAIN BROWN *after some hesitation rings for* PATTY.)

VALENTINE.   Patty, come here.   Why is this trick being played upon me ?

PATTY (*with all her wits about her*).   Trick, sir !   Who would dare ?

VALENTINE.   I know, Patty, that Miss Phoebe has been Miss Livvy all the time.

PATTY.   I give in !

VALENTINE.   Why has she done this ?

PATTY (*beseechingly*).   Are you laughing, sir ?

VALENTINE.   I am very far from laughing.

PATTY (*turning on him*).   'Twas you that began it, all by not knowing her in the white gown.

VALENTINE.   Why has this deception been kept up so long ?

PATTY.   Because you would not see through it.   Oh, the wicked denseness.   She thought you were infatuate with Miss Livvy because she was young and silly.

VALENTINE.   It is infamous.

PATTY.   I will not have you call her names.   'Twas all playful innocence at first, and now she is so feared of you she is weeping her soul to death, and all I do I cannot rouse her.   ' I ha' a follower in the kitchen, ma'am,' says I, to infuriate her. ' Give him a glass of cowslip wine,' says she, like a gentle lamb.   And ill she can afford it, you having lost their money for them.

VALENTINE.   What is that ?   On the contrary, all the money they have, Patty, they owe to my having invested it for them.

PATTY.   That is the money they lost.

VALENTINE.   You are sure of that ?

PATTY.   I can swear to it.

VALENTINE.   Deceived me about that also.   Good God ; but why ?

PATTY.   I think she was feared you would offer to her out of pity.   She said something to Miss Susan about keeping a flag flying.   What she meant I know not.   (*But he knows, and he turns away his face.*)   Are you laughing, sir ?

VALENTINE.   No, Patty, I am not laughing.   Why do they not say Miss Livvy has gone home ?   It would save them a world of trouble.

PATTY.   The Misses Willoughby and Miss Henrietta— they watch the house all day.   They would say she cannot be gone, for we did not see her go.

VALENTINE (*enlightened at last*).   I see !

PATTY.   And Miss Phoebe and Miss Susan wring their hands, for they are feared Miss Livvy is bedridden here for all time.   (*Now his sense of humour asserts itself.*)   Thank the Lord, you 're laughing !

(*At this he laughs the more, and it is a gay* CAPTAIN BROWN *on whom* MISS SUSAN *opens the bedroom door.   This desperate woman is too full of plot to note the change in him.*)

MISS SUSAN.   I am happy to inform you, sir, that Livvy finds herself much improved.

VALENTINE (*bowing*).   It is joy to me to hear it.

MISS SUSAN.   She is coming in to see you.

PATTY (*aghast*).   Oh, ma'am !

VALENTINE (*frowning on* PATTY).   I shall be happy to see the poor invalid.

PATTY.   Ma'am—— !

(*But* MISS SUSAN, *believing that so far all is well, has returned to the bed-chamber.* CAPTAIN BROWN *bestows a quizzical glance upon the maid.*)

VALENTINE.   Go away, Patty.   Anon I may claim a service of you, but for the present, go.

PATTY.   But—but——

VALENTINE.   Retire, woman.

(*She has to go, and he prepares his face for the reception of the invalid.* PHOEBE *comes in without her cap, the ringlets showing again.   She wears a dressing jacket and is supported by* MISS SUSAN.)

VALENTINE (*gravely*).   Your servant, Miss Livvy.

PHOEBE (*weakly*).   How do you do ?

VALENTINE.   Allow me, Miss Susan.

(*He takes* MISS SUSAN's *place ; but after an exquisite moment* MISS PHOEBE *breaks away from him, feeling that she is not worthy of such bliss.*)

PHOEBE.   No, no, I—I can walk alone—see.

(*She reclines upon the couch.*)

MISS SUSAN.   How do you think she is looking ?

(*He makes a professional examination of the patient, and they are very ashamed to deceive him, but not so ashamed that they must confess.*)

What do you think ?

VALENTINE (*solemnly*).   She will recover.   May I say, ma'am, it surprises me that any one should see much resemblance between you and your Aunt Phoebe.   Miss Phoebe is decidedly shorter and more thick-set.

PHOEBE (*sitting up*).   No, I am not.

VALENTINE.   I said Miss Phoebe, ma'am.   (*She reclines.*) But tell me, is not Miss Phoebe to join us ?

PHOEBE.   She hopes you will excuse her, sir.

MISS SUSAN (*vaguely*).   Taking the opportunity of airing the room.

VALENTINE.   Ah, of course.

MISS SUSAN (*opening bedroom door and calling mendaciously*). Captain Brown will excuse you, Phoebe.

VALENTINE.   Certainly, Miss Susan.   Well, ma'am, I think I could cure Miss Livvy if she is put unreservedly into my hands.

MISS SUSAN (*with a sigh*).   I am sure you could.

VALENTINE.   Then you are my patient, Miss Livvy.

PHOEBE (*nervously*).   'Twas but a passing indisposition, I am almost quite recovered.

VALENTINE.   Nay, you still require attention.   Do you propose making a long stay in Quality Street, ma'am ?

PHOEBE.   I—I—I hope not.   It—it depends.

MISS SUSAN (*forgetting herself*).   Mary is the worst.

VALENTINE.   I ask your pardon ?

PHOEBE.   Aunt Susan, you are excited.

VALENTINE.   But you are quite right, Miss Livvy ; home is the place for you.

PHOEBE.   Would that I could go !

VALENTINE.   You are going.

PHOEBE.   Yes—soon.

VALENTINE.   Indeed, I have a delightful surprise for you, Miss Livvy, you are going to-day.

PHOEBE.   To-day ?

VALENTINE.   Not merely to-day, but now.   As it happens, my carriage is standing idle at your door, and I am to take you in it to your home—some twenty miles if I remember.

PHOEBE.   You are to take me ?

VALENTINE.   Nay, 'tis no trouble at all, and as your physician my mind is made up.   Some wraps for her, Miss Susan.

MISS SUSAN.   But—but——

PHOEBE (*in a panic*).   Sir, I decline to go.

VALENTINE.   Come, Miss Livvy, you are in my hands.

PHOEBE.   I decline.   I am most determined.

VALENTINE.   You admit yourself that you are recovered.

PHOEBE.   I do not feel so well now.   Aunt Susan !

MISS SUSAN.   Sir——

VALENTINE.   If you wish to consult Miss Phoebe——

MISS SUSAN.   Oh, no.

VALENTINE.   Then the wraps, Miss Susan.

PHOEBE.   Auntie, don't leave me.

VALENTINE.   What a refractory patient it is.   But reason with her, Miss Susan, and I shall ask Miss Phoebe for some wraps.

PHOEBE.   Sir !

(*To their consternation he goes cheerily into the bedroom.* MISS PHOEBE *saves herself by instant flight, and nothing but mesmeric influence keeps* MISS SUSAN *rooted to the blue and white room.   When he returns he is loaded with wraps, and still cheerfully animated, as if he had found nothing untoward in* LIVVY's *bed-chamber.*)

VALENTINE.   I think these will do admirably, Miss Susan.

MISS SUSAN.   But Phoebe——

VALENTINE.   If I swathe Miss Livvy in these——

MISS SUSAN.   Phoebe——

VALENTINE.   She is still busy airing the room.   (*The extraordinary man goes to the couch as if unable to perceive that its late occupant has gone, and* MISS SUSAN *watches him, fascinated.*) Come, Miss Livvy, put these over you.   Allow me—this one over your shoulders, so.   Be so obliging as to lean on me.   Be brave, ma'am, you cannot fall—my arm is round you ; gently, gently, Miss Livvy ; ah, that is better ; we are doing famously ; come, come.   Good-bye, Miss Susan, I will take every care of her.

(*He has gone, with the bundle on his arm, but* MISS SUSAN *does not wake up.   Even the banging of the outer door is unable to rouse her.   It is heard, however, by* MISS PHOEBE, *who steals back into the room, her cap upon her head to give her courage.*)

PHOEBE.   He is gone !   (MISS SUSAN's *rapt face alarms her.*) Oh, Susan, was he as dreadful as that ?

MISS SUSAN (*in tones unnatural to her*).   Phoebe, he knows all.

PHOEBE.   Yes, of course he knows all now.   Sister, did his face change ?   Oh, Susan, what did he say ?

MISS SUSAN.   He said 'Good-bye, Miss Susan.'   That was almost all he said

PHOEBE.   Did his eyes flash fire ?

MISS SUSAN.   Phoebe, it was what he did.   He—he took Livvy with him.

PHOEBE. Susan, dear, don't say that. You are not distraught, are you?

MISS SUSAN (*clinging to facts*) He did; he wrapped her up in a shawl.

PHOEBE. Susan? You are Susan Throssel, my love. You remember me, don't you? Phoebe, your sister. I was Livvy also, you know, Livvy.

MISS SUSAN. He took Livvy with him.

PHOEBE (*in woe*) Oh, oh! sister, who am I?

MISS SUSAN. You are Phoebe.

PHOEBE. And who was Livvy?

MISS SUSAN. You were.

PHOEBE. Thank heaven.

MISS SUSAN. But he took her away in the carriage.

PHOEBE. Oh dear! (*She has quite forgotten her own troubles now.*) Susan, you will soon be well again. Dear, let us occupy our minds. Shall we draw up the advertisement for the reopening of the school?

MISS SUSAN. I do so hate the school.

PHOEBE. Come, dear, come, sit down. Write, Susan. (*Dictating*) 'The Misses Throssel have the pleasure to announce——'

MISS SUSAN. Pleasure! Oh, Phoebe.

PHOEBE. 'That they will resume school on the 5th of next month. Music, embroidery, the backboard, and all the elegancies of the mind. Latin—shall we say algebra?'

MISS SUSAN. I refuse to write algebra.

PHOEBE. —for beginners.

MISS SUSAN. I refuse. There is only one thing I can write; it writes itself in my head all day. 'Miss Susan Throssel presents her compliments to the Misses Willoughby and Miss Henrietta Turnbull, and requests the honour of their presence at the nuptials of her sister Phoebe and Captain Valentine Brown.'

PHOEBE. Susan!

MISS SUSAN. Phoebe! (*A door is heard banging.*) He has returned!

PHOEBE. Oh cruel, cruel. Susan, I am so alarmed.

MISS SUSAN. I will face him.

PHOEBE. Nay, if it must be, I will.

(*But when he enters he is not very terrible.*)

VALENTINE.   Miss Phoebe, it is not raining, but your face is wet.   I wish always to kiss you when your face is wet.

PHOEBE.   Susan !

VALENTINE.   Miss Livvy will never trouble you any more, Miss Susan.   I have sent her home.

MISS SUSAN.   Oh, sir, how can you invent such a story for us.

VALENTINE.   I did not.   I invented it for the Misses Willoughby and Miss Henrietta, who from their windows watched me put her into my carriage.   Patty accompanies her, and in a few hours Patty will return alone.

MISS SUSAN.   Phoebe, he has got rid of Livvy !

PHOEBE.   Susan, his face hasn't changed !

VALENTINE.   Dear Phoebe Throssel, will you be Phoebe Brown ?

PHOEBE (*quivering*).   You know everything ?   And that I am not a garden ?

VALENTINE.   I know everything, ma'am—except that.

PHOEBE (*so very glad to be prim at the end*).   Sir, the dictates of my heart enjoin me to accept your too flattering offer.   (*He puts her cap in his pocket.   He kisses her.   MISS SUSAN is about to steal away.*)   Oh, sir, Susan also.   (*He kisses MISS SUSAN also ; and here we bid them good-bye.*)

THE ADMIRABLE CRICHTON

Produced at the Duke of York's Theatre on November 4, 1902, with the following cast:

THE EARL OF LOAM . . .	*Henry Kemble*
HON. ERNEST WOOLLEY . .	*Gerald du Maurier*
REV. JOHN TREHERNE . . .	*Clarence Blakiston*
LORD BROCKLEHURST . . .	*Carter Pickford*
A NAVAL OFFICER . . .	*J. C. Buckstone*
MR. CRICHTON	*H. B. Irving*
TOMPSETT	*Compton Coutts*
LADY MARY LASENBY . .	*Irene Vanbrugh*
LADY CATHERINE LASENBY . .	*Sybil Carlisle*
LADY AGATHA LASENBY . .	*Muriel Beaumont*
COUNTESS OF BROCKLEHURST . .	*Fanny Coleman*
FISHER	*Margaret Fraser*
TWEENY	*Pattie Browne*

The play ran for 328 performances. Revivals: Duke of York's, March 2, 1908 (118 performances); Royalty, January 31, 1920 (134 performances).

ACT I

AT LOAM HOUSE, MAYFAIR

A MOMENT before the curtain rises, the Hon. Ernest Woolley drives up to the door of Loam House in Mayfair. There is a happy smile on his pleasant, insignificant face, and this presumably means that he is thinking of himself. He is too busy over nothing, this man about town, to be always thinking of himself, but, on the other hand, he almost never thinks of any other person. Probably Ernest's great moment is when he wakes of a morning and realises that he really is Ernest, for we must all wish to be that which is our ideal. We can conceive him springing out of bed light-heartedly and waiting for his man to do the rest. He is dressed in excellent taste, with just the little bit more which shows that he is not without a sense of humour : the dandiacal are often saved by carrying a smile at the whole thing in their spats, let us say. Ernest left Cambridge the other day, a member of the Athenæum (which he would be sorry to have you confound with a club in London of the same name). He is a bachelor, but not of arts, no mean epigrammatist (as you shall see), and a favourite of the ladies. He is almost a celebrity in restaurants, where he dines frequently, returning to sup ; and during this last year he has probably paid as much in them for the privilege of handing his hat to an attendant as the rent of a working-man's flat. He complains brightly that he is hard up, and that if somebody or other at Westminster does not look out the country will go to the dogs. He is no fool. He has the shrewdness to float with the current because it is a labour-saving process, but he has sufficient pluck to fight, if fight he must (a brief contest, for he would soon be toppled over). He has a light nature, which would enable him to bob up cheerily in new conditions and return unaltered to the old ones. His selfishness is his most endearing quality. If he has his way he will spend his life like a cat in pushing his betters out of the soft places, and until he is old he will be fondled in the process.

He gives his hat to one footman and his cane to another, and mounts the great staircase unassisted and undirected. As a nephew of the house he need show no credentials even to Crichton, who is guarding a door above.

It would not be good taste to describe Crichton, who is only a servant ; if to the scandal of all good houses he is to stand out as a figure in the play, he must do it on his own, as they say in the pantry and the boudoir. We are not going to help him. We have had misgivings ever since we found his name in the title, and we shall keep him out of his rights as long as we can. Even though we softened to him he would not be a hero in these clothes of servitude ; and he loves his clothes. How to get him out of them ? It would require a cataclysm. To be an indoor servant at all is to Crichton a badge of honour ; to be a butler at thirty is the realisation of his proudest ambitions. He is devotedly attached to his master, who, in his opinion, has but one fault, he is not sufficiently contemptuous of his inferiors. We are immediately to be introduced to this solitary failing of a great English peer.

This perfect butler, then, opens a door, and ushers Ernest into a certain room. At the same moment the curtain rises on this room, and the play begins.

It is one of several reception-rooms in Loam House, not the most magnificent but quite the softest ; and of a warm afternoon all that those who are anybody crave for is the softest. The larger rooms are magnificent and bare, carpetless, so that it is an accomplishment to keep one's feet on them ; they are sometimes lent for charitable purposes ; they are also all in use on the night of a dinner-party, when you may find yourself alone in one, having taken a wrong turning ; or alone, save for two others who are within hailing distance. This room, however, is comparatively small and very soft. There are so many cushions in it that you wonder why, if you are an outsider and don't know that it needs six cushions to make one fair head comfy. The couches themselves are cushions as large as beds, and there is an art of sinking into them and of waiting to be helped out of them. There are several famous paintings on the walls, of which you may say ' Jolly thing that,' without losing caste as knowing too much ; and in cases there are glorious miniatures, but the daughters of the house cannot tell you of whom ; ' there is a catalogue somewhere.'   There are a thousand or so of roses in basins, several library novels, and a row of weekly illustrated newspapers lying against each other like fallen soldiers.   If any one disturbs this row Crichton seems to know of it from afar and appears noiselessly and replaces the wanderer.   One thing unexpected in such a room is a great array of tea-things.   Ernest spots them with a twinkle, and has his epigram at once unsheathed.   He dallies, however, before delivering the thrust.

ERNEST.   I perceive, from the tea-cups, Crichton, that the great function is to take place here.

CRICHTON (*with a respectful sigh*).   Yes, sir.

ERNEST (*chuckling heartlessly*).   The servants' hall coming up to have tea in the drawing-room !   (*With terrible sarcasm*) No wonder you look happy, Crichton.

CRICHTON (*under the knife*).   No, sir.

ERNEST.   Do you know, Crichton, I think that with an effort you might look even happier.   (CRICHTON *smiles wanly.*) You don't approve of his lordship's compelling his servants to be his equals—once a month ?

CRICHTON.   It is not for me, sir, to disapprove of his lordship's Radical views.

ERNEST.   Certainly not.   And, after all, it is only once a month that he is affable to you.

CRICHTON.   On all other days of the month, sir, his lordship's treatment of us is everything that could be desired.

ERNEST.   (*This is the epigram.*)   Tea-cups !   Life, Crichton, is like a cup of tea ; the more heartily we drink, the sooner we reach the dregs.

CRICHTON (*obediently*).   Thank you, sir.

ERNEST (*becoming confidential, as we do when we have need of an ally*).   Crichton, in case I should be asked to say a few words to the servants, I have strung together a little speech.   (*His hand strays to his pocket.*)   I was wondering where I should stand.

(*He tries various places and postures, and comes to rest leaning over a high chair, whence, in dumb show, he addresses a gathering.*   CRICHTON, *with the best intentions, gives him a footstool to stand on, and departs, happily unconscious that*

ERNEST *in some dudgeon has kicked the footstool across the room.*)

ERNEST (*addressing an imaginary audience, and desirous of startling them at once*).   Suppose you were all little fishes at the bottom of the sea——

(*He is not quite satisfied with his position, though sure that the fault must lie with the chair for being too high, not with him for being too short.* CRICHTON'S *suggestion was not perhaps a bad one after all.   He lifts the stool, but hastily conceals it behind him on the entrance of the* LADIES CATHERINE *and* AGATHA, *two daughters of the house.* CATHERINE *is twenty, and* AGATHA *two years younger.   They are very fashionable young women indeed, who might wake up for a dance, but they are very lazy,* CATHERINE *being two years lazier than* AGATHA.)

ERNEST (*uneasily jocular, because he is concealing the footstool*). And how are my little friends to-day ?

AGATHA (*contriving to reach a settee*).   Don't be silly, Ernest. If you want to know how we are, we are dead.   Even to think of entertaining the servants is so exhausting.

CATHERINE (*subsiding nearer the door*).   Besides which, we have had to decide what frocks to take with us on the yacht, and that is such a mental strain.

ERNEST.   You poor overworked things.   (*Evidently* AGATHA *is his favourite, for he helps her to put her feet on the settee, while* CATHERINE *has to dispose of her own feet.*)   Rest your weary limbs.

CATHERINE (*perhaps in revenge*).   But why have you a footstool in your hand ?

AGATHA.   Yes ?

ERNEST.   Why ?   (*Brilliantly ; but to be sure he has had time to think it out.*)   You see, as the servants are to be the guests I must be butler.   I was practising.   This is a tray, observe.

(*Holding the footstool as a tray, he minces across the room like an accomplished footman.   The gods favour him, for just here* LADY MARY *enters, and he holds out the footstool to her.*)
Tea, my lady ?

(LADY MARY *is a beautiful creature of twenty-two, and is of a natural hauteur which is at once the fury and the envy of her sisters.   If she chooses she can make you seem so insignificant that you feel you might be swept away with the crumb-brush.   She seldom chooses, because of the trouble of preening herself as she does it ; she is usually content to show that you merely tire her eyes.   She often seems to be about to go to sleep in the middle of a remark : there is quite a long and anxious pause, and then she continues, like a clock that hesitates, bored in the middle of its strike.*)

LADY MARY (*arching her brows*).   It is only you, Ernest ; I thought there was some one here (*and she also bestows herself on cushions*).

ERNEST (*a little piqued, and deserting the footstool*).   Had a very tiring day also, Mary ?

LADY MARY (*yawning*).   Dreadfully.   Been trying on engagement-rings all the morning.

ERNEST (*who is as fond of gossip as the oldest club member*). What 's that ?   (*To* AGATHA) Is it Brocklehurst ?

(*The energetic* AGATHA *nods.*)

You have given your warm young heart to Brocky ?

(LADY MARY *is impervious to his humour, but he continues bravely.*)

I don't wish to fatigue you, Mary, by insisting on a verbal answer, but if, without straining yourself, you can signify Yes or No, won't you make the effort ?

(*She indolently flashes a ring on her most important finger, and he starts back melodramatically.*)

The ring !   Then I am too late, too late !   (*Fixing* LADY MARY *sternly, like a prosecuting counsel.*)   May I ask, Mary, does Brocky know ?   Of course, it was that terrible mother of his who pulled this through.   Mother does everything for Brocky.   Still, in the eyes of the law you will be, not her wife, but his, and, therefore, I hold that Brocky ought to be informed. Now——

(*He discovers that their languorous eyes have closed.*)

If you girls are shamming sleep in the expectation that I shall awaken you in the manner beloved of ladies, abandon all such hopes.

(CATHERINE *and* AGATHA *look up without speaking.*)

LADY MARY (*speaking without looking up*).   You impertinent boy.

ERNEST (*eagerly plucking another epigram from his quiver*).   I knew that was it, though I don't know everything.   Agatha, I 'm not young enough to know everything.

(*He looks hopefully from one to another, but though they try to grasp this, his brilliance baffles them.*)

AGATHA (*his secret admirer*).   *Young* enough ?

ERNEST (*encouragingly*).   Don't you see ?   I 'm not young enough to know everything.

AGATHA.   I 'm sure it 's awfully clever, but it 's so puzzling.

(*Here* CRICHTON *ushers in an athletic, pleasant-faced young clergyman,* MR. TREHERNE, *who greets the company.*)

CATHERINE.   Ernest, say it to Mr. Treherne.

ERNEST.   Look here, Treherne, I 'm not young enough to know everything.

TREHERNE.   How do you mean, Ernest ?

ERNEST (*a little nettled*).   I mean what I say.

LADY MARY.   Say it again ; say it more slowly.

ERNEST.   I 'm—not—young—enough—to—know—everything.

TREHERNE.   *I* see.   What you really mean, my boy, is that you are not old enough to know everything.

ERNEST.   No, I don't.

TREHERNE.   I assure you that 's it.

LADY MARY.   Of course it is.

CATHERINE.   Yes, Ernest, that 's it.

(ERNEST, *in desperation, appeals to* CRICHTON.)

ERNEST.   I am not young enough, Crichton, to know everything.

(*It is an anxious moment, but a smile is at length extorted from* CRICHTON *as with a corkscrew.*)

CRICHTON.   Thank you, sir.   (*He goes.*)

ERNEST (*relieved*).   Ah, if you had that fellow's head, Treherne, you would find something better to do with it than play cricket.   I hear you bowl with your head.

TREHERNE (*with proper humility*).   I 'm afraid cricket is all I 'm good for, Ernest.

CATHERINE (*who thinks he has a heavenly nose*).   Indeed, it isn't.   You are sure to get on, Mr. Treherne.

TREHERNE.   Thank you, Lady Catherine.

CATHERINE.   But it was the bishop who told me so.   He

said a clergyman who breaks both ways is sure to get on in England.

TREHERNE.　I 'm jolly glad.

(*The master of the house comes in, accompanied by* LORD BROCKLEHURST. *The* EARL OF LOAM *is a widower, a philanthropist, and a peer of advanced ideas. As a widower he is at least able to interfere in the domestic concerns of his house—to rummage in the drawers, so to speak, for which he has felt an itching all his blameless life ; his philanthropy has opened quite a number of other drawers to him ; and his advanced ideas have blown out his figure. He takes in all the weightiest monthly reviews, and prefers those that are uncut, because he perhaps never looks better than when cutting them ; but he does not read them, and save for the cutting it would suit him as well merely to take in the covers. He writes letters to the papers, which are printed in a type to scale with himself, and he is very jealous of those other correspondents who get his type. Let laws and learning, art and commerce die, but leave the big type to an intellectual aristocracy. He is really the reformed House of Lords which will come some day.*

Young LORD BROCKLEHURST *is nothing save for his rank. You could pick him up by the handful any day in Piccadilly or Holborn, buying socks—or selling them.*)

LORD LOAM (*expansively*).　You are here, Ernest.　Feeling fit for the voyage, Treherne ?

TREHERNE.　Looking forward to it enormously.

LORD LOAM.　That 's right.　(*He chases his children about as if they were chickens.*)　Now then, Mary, up and doing, up and doing.　Time we had the servants in.　They enjoy it so much.

LADY MARY.　They hate it.

LORD LOAM.　Mary, to your duties.　(*And he points severely to the tea-table.*)

ERNEST (*twinkling*).　Congratulations, Brocky.

LORD BROCKLEHURST (*who detests humour*).　Thanks.

ERNEST.　Mother pleased ?

LORD BROCKLEHURST (*with dignity*).　Mother is very pleased.

ERNEST.　That 's good.　Do you go on the yacht with us ?

LORD BROCKLEHURST.　Sorry I can't.　And look here, Ernest, I will *not* be called Brocky.

ERNEST.   Mother don't like it ?

LORD BROCKLEHURST.   She does not.   (*He leaves* ERNEST, *who forgives him and begins to think about his speech.*   CRICHTON *enters.*)

LORD LOAM (*speaking as one man to another*)   We are quite ready, Crichton.   (CRICHTON *is distressed.*)

LADY MARY (*sarcastically*).   How Crichton enjoys it !

LORD LOAM (*frowning*).   He is the only one who doesn't ; pitiful creature.

CRICHTON (*shuddering under his lord's displeasure*).   I can't help being a Conservative, my lord.

LORD LOAM.   Be a man, Crichton.   You are the same flesh and blood as myself.

CRICHTON (*in pain*).   Oh, my lord !

LORD LOAM (*sharply*).   Show them in ; and, by the way, they were not all here last time.

CRICHTON.   All, my lord, except the merest trifles.

LORD LOAM.   It must be every one.   (*Lowering*) And remember this, Crichton, for the time being you are my equal. (*Testily*) I shall soon show you whether you are not my equal. Do as you are told.

(CRICHTON *departs to obey, and his lordship is now a general.   He has no pity for his daughters, and uses a terrible threat.*) And girls, remember, no condescension.   The first who condescends recites.   (*This sends them scurrying to their labours.*) By the way, Brocklehurst, can you do anything ?

LORD BROCKLEHURST.   How do you mean ?

LORD LOAM.   Can you do anything—with a penny or a handkerchief, make them disappear, for instance ?

LORD BROCKLEHURST.   Good heavens, no.

LORD LOAM.   It 's a pity.   Every one in our position ought to be able to do something.   Ernest, I shall probably ask you to say a few words ; something bright and sparkling.

ERNEST.   But, my dear uncle, I have prepared nothing.

LORD LOAM.   Anything impromptu will do.

ERNEST.   Oh—well—if anything strikes me.

(*He unostentatiously gets the footstool into position behind the chair.*   CRICHTON *reappears to announce the guests, of whom the first is the housekeeper.   They should be well-mannered.   Nothing farcical, please.*)

CRICHTON (*reluctantly*). Mrs. Perkins.

LORD LOAM (*shaking hands*). Very delighted, Mrs. Perkins. Mary, our friend, Mrs. Perkins.

LADY MARY. How do you do, Mrs. Perkins ? Won't you sit here ?

LORD LOAM (*threateningly*). Agatha !

AGATHA (*hastily*). How do you do ? Won't you sit down ?

LORD LOAM (*introducing*). Lord Brocklehurst—my valued friend, Mrs. Perkins.

(LORD BROCKLEHURST *bows and escapes. He has to fall back on* ERNEST.)

LORD BROCKLEHURST. For heaven's sake, Ernest, don't leave me for a moment ; this sort of thing is utterly opposed to all my principles.

ERNEST (*airily*). You stick to me, Brocky, and I 'll pull you through.

CRICHTON. Monsieur Fleury.

ERNEST. The chef.

LORD LOAM (*shaking hands with the chef*). Very charmed to see you, Monsieur Fleury.

FLEURY. Thank you very much.

(FLEURY *bows to* AGATHA, *who is not effusive*.)

LORD LOAM (*warningly*). Agatha—recitation !

(*She tosses her head, but immediately finds a seat and tea for* M. FLEURY. TREHERNE *and* ERNEST *move about, making themselves amiable*. LADY MARY *is presiding at the tea-tray*.)

CRICHTON. Mr. Rolleston.

LORD LOAM (*shaking hands with his valet*). How do you do, Rolleston ?

(CATHERINE *looks after the wants of* ROLLESTON.)

CRICHTON. Mr. Tompsett.

(TOMPSETT, *the coachman, is received with honours, from which he shrinks, but with quiet dignity*.)

CRICHTON. Miss Fisher.

(*This superb creature is no less than* LADY MARY'S *maid, and even* LORD LOAM *is a little nervous*.)

LORD LOAM. This is a pleasure, Miss Fisher.

ERNEST (*unabashed*). If I might venture, Miss Fisher— (*and he takes her unto himself*).

CRICHTON.   Miss Simmons.

LORD LOAM (*to* CATHERINE'S *maid*).   You are always welcome, Miss Simmons.

ERNEST (*perhaps to kindle jealousy in* MISS FISHER).   At last we meet.   Won't you sit down?

CRICHTON.   Mademoiselle Jeanne.

LORD LOAM.   Charmed to see you, Mademoiselle Jeanne.

(*A place is found for* AGATHA'S *maid, and the scene is now an animated one; but still our host thinks his girls are not sufficiently sociable.   He frowns on* LADY MARY.)

LADY MARY (*in alarm*).   Mr. Treherne, this is Fisher, my maid.

LORD LOAM (*sharply*).   Your what, Mary?

LADY MARY.   My friend.

CRICHTON.   Thomas.

LORD LOAM.   How do you do, Thomas?

(*The first footman gives him a reluctant hand.*)

CRICHTON.   John.

LORD LOAM.   How do you do, John?

(ERNEST *signs to* LORD BROCKLEHURST, *who hastens to him.*)

ERNEST (*introducing*).   Brocklehurst, this is John.   I think you have already met on the door-step.

CRICHTON.   Jane.

(*She comes, wrapping her hands miserably in her apron.*)

LORD LOAM (*doggedly*).   Give me your hand, Jane.

CRICHTON.   Gladys.

ERNEST.   How do you do, Gladys?   You know my uncle?

LORD LOAM.   Your hand, Gladys.

(*He bestows her on* AGATHA.)

CRICHTON.   Tweeny.

(*She is a very humble and frightened kitchen-maid, of whom we are to see more.*)

LORD LOAM.   So happy to see you.

FISHER.   John, I saw you talking to Lord Brocklehurst just now; introduce me.

LORD BROCKLEHURST (*who is really a second-rate* JOHN).   That is an uncommon pretty girl; if I must feed one of them, Ernest, that is the one.

(*But* ERNEST *tries to part him and* FISHER *as they are about to shake hands.*)

ERNEST. No you don't, it won't do, Brocky. (*To* MISS FISHER) You are too pretty, my dear. Mother wouldn't like it. (*Discovering* TWEENY) Here is something safer. Charming girl, Brocky, dying to know you ; let me introduce you. Tweeny, Lord Brocklehurst—Lord Brocklehurst, Tweeny.

> (BROCKLEHURST *accepts his fate ; but he still has an eye for* FISHER, *and something may come of this.*)

LORD LOAM (*severely*). They are not all here, Crichton.

CRICHTON (*with a sigh*). Odds and ends.

> (*A* STABLE-BOY *and a* PAGE *are shown in, and for a moment no daughter of the house advances to them.*)

LORD LOAM (*with a roving eye on his children*). Which is to recite ?

> (*The last of the company are, so to say, embraced.*)

LORD LOAM (*to* TOMPSETT, *as they partake of tea together*). And how are all at home ?

TOMPSETT. Fairish, my lord, if 'tis the horses you are inquiring for ?

LORD LOAM. No, no, the family. How 's the baby ?

TOMPSETT. Blooming, your lordship.

LORD LOAM. A very fine boy. I remember saying so when I saw him ; nice little fellow.

TOMPSETT (*not quite knowing whether to let it pass*). Beg pardon, my lord, it 's a girl.

LORD LOAM. A girl ? Aha ! ha ! ha ! exactly what I said. I distinctly remember saying, If it 's spared it will be a girl.

> (CRICHTON *now comes down.*)

LORD LOAM. Very delighted to see you, Crichton.

> (CRICHTON *has to shake hands.*)

Mary, you know Mr. Crichton ?

> (*He wanders off in search of other prey.*)

LADY MARY. Milk and sugar, Crichton ?

CRICHTON. I 'm ashamed to be seen talking to you, my lady.

LADY MARY. To such a perfect servant as you all this must be most distasteful. (CRICHTON *is too respectful to answer.*) Oh, please to speak, or I shall have to recite. You do hate it, don't you ?

CRICHTON. It pains me, your ladyship. It disturbs the etiquette of the servants' hall. After last month's meeting the

M

page-boy, in a burst of equality, called me Crichton.   He was dismissed.

LADY MARY.   I wonder—I really do—how you can remain with us.

CRICHTON.   I should have felt compelled to give notice, my lady, if the master had not had a seat in the Upper House.   I cling to that.

LADY MARY.   Do go on speaking.   Tell me, what did Mr. Ernest mean by saying he was not young enough to know everything?

CRICHTON.   I have no idea, my lady.

LADY MARY.   But you laughed.

CRICHTON.   My lady, he is the second son of a peer.

LADY MARY.   Very proper sentiments.   You are a good soul, Crichton.

LORD BROCKLEHURST (*desperately to* TWEENY).   And now tell me, have you been to the Opera?   What sort of weather have you been having in the kitchen?   (TWEENY *gurgles*.) For Heaven's sake, woman, be articulate.

CRICHTON (*still talking to* LADY MARY).   No, my lady; his lordship may compel us to be equal upstairs, but there will never be equality in the servants' hall.

LORD LOAM (*overhearing this*).   What's that?   No equality?   Can't you see, Crichton, that our divisions into classes are artificial, that if we were to return to Nature, which is the aspiration of my life, all would be equal?

CRICHTON.   If I may make so bold as to contradict your lordship——

LORD LOAM (*with an effort*).   Go on.

CRICHTON.   The divisions into classes, my lord, are not artificial.   They are the natural outcome of a civilised society.   (*To* LADY MARY) There must always be a master and servants in all civilised communities, my lady, for it is natural, and whatever is natural is right.

LORD LOAM (*wincing*).   It is very unnatural for me to stand here and allow you to talk such nonsense.

CRICHTON (*eagerly*).   Yes, my lord, it is.   That is what I have been striving to point out to your lordship.

AGATHA (*to* CATHERINE).   What is the matter with Fisher? She is looking daggers.

CATHERINE.   The tedious creature; some question of etiquette, I suppose.

(*She sails across to* FISHER.

How are you, Fisher?

FISHER (*with a toss of her head*).   I am nothing, my lady, I am nothing at all.

AGATHA.   Oh dear, who says so?

FISHER (*affronted*).   His lordship has asked that kitchen wench to have a second cup of tea.

CATHERINE.   But why not?

FISHER.   If it pleases his lordship to offer it to *her* before offering it to *me*——

AGATHA.   So that is it.   Do you want another cup of tea, Fisher?

FISHER.   No, my lady—but my position—I should have been asked first.

AGATHA.   Oh dear.

(*All this has taken some time, and by now the feeble appetites of the uncomfortable guests have been satiated. But they know there is still another ordeal to face—his lordship's monthly speech. Every one awaits it with misgiving—the servants lest they should applaud, as last time, in the wrong place, and the daughters because he may be personal about them, as the time before.* ERNEST *is annoyed that there should be this speech at all when there is such a much better one coming, and* BROCKLEHURST *foresees the degradation of the peerage. All are thinking of themselves alone save* CRICHTON, *who knows his master's weakness, and fears he may stick in the middle.* LORD LOAM, *however, advances cheerfully to his doom. He sees* ERNEST'S *stool, and artfully stands on it, to his nephew's natural indignation. The three ladies knit their lips, the servants look down their noses, and the address begins.*)

LORD LOAM.   My friends, I am glad to see you all looking so happy.   It used to be predicted by the scoffer that these meetings would prove distasteful to you.   Are they distasteful?   I hear you laughing at the question.

(*He has not heard them, but he hears them now, the watchful* CRICHTON *giving them a lead.*)

No harm in saying that among us to-day is one who was formerly hostile to the movement, but who to-day has been won over. I refer to Lord Brocklehurst, who, I am sure, will presently say to me that if the charming lady now by his side has derived as much pleasure from his company as he has derived from hers, he will be more than satisfied.

(*All look at* TWEENY, *who trembles.*)

For the time being the artificial and unnatural—I say unnatural (*glaring at* CRICHTON, *who bows slightly*)—barriers of society are swept away. Would that they could be swept away for ever.

(*The* PAGE-BOY *cheers, and has the one moment of prominence in his life. He grows up, marries and has children, but is never really heard of again.*)

But that is entirely and utterly out of the question. And now for a few months we are to be separated. As you know, my daughters and Mr. Ernest and Mr. Treherne are to accompany me on my yacht, on a voyage to distant parts of the earth. In less than forty-eight hours we shall be under weigh.

(*But for* CRICHTON's *eye the reckless* PAGE-BOY *would repeat his success.*)

Do not think our life on the yacht is to be one long idle holiday. My views on the excessive luxury of the day are well known, and what I preach I am resolved to practise. I have therefore decided that my daughters, instead of having one maid each as at present, shall on this voyage have but one maid between them.

(*Three maids rise ; also three mistresses.*)

CRICHTON. My lord !

LORD LOAM. My mind is made up.

ERNEST. I cordially agree.

LORD LOAM. And now, my friends, I should like to think that there is some piece of advice I might give you, some thought, some noble saying over which you might ponder in my absence. In this connection I remember a proverb, which has had a great effect on my own life. I first heard it many years ago. I have never forgotten it. It constantly cheers and guides me. That proverb is—that proverb was—the proverb I speak of——

(*He grows pale and taps his forehead.*)

LADY MARY. Oh dear, I believe he has forgotten it.

LORD LOAM (*desperately*). The proverb—that proverb to which I refer——

> (*Alas, it has gone. The distress is general. He has not even the sense to sit down. He gropes for the proverb in the air. They try applause, but it is no help.*)

I have it now—(*not he*).

LADY MARY (*with confidence*). Crichton.

> (*He does not fail her. As quietly as if he were in goloshes, mind as well as feet, he dismisses the domestics; they go according to precedence but without servility, and there must be no attempt at 'comic effect.' Then he signs to* MR. TREHERNE, *and they conduct* LORD LOAM *with dignity from the room. His hands are still catching flies; he still mutters, 'The proverb—'; but he continues, owing to* CRICHTON'S *treatment, to look every inch a peer. The ladies have now an opportunity to air their indignation.*)

LADY MARY. One maid among three grown women!

LORD BROCKLEHURST. Mary, I think I had better go. That dreadful kitchen-maid——

LADY MARY. I can't blame you, George.

> (*He salutes her.*)

LORD BROCKLEHURST. Your father's views are shocking to me, and I am glad I am not to be one of the party on the yacht. My respect for myself, Mary, my natural anxiety as to what mother will say. I shall see you, darling, before you sail.

> (*He bows to the others and goes.*)

ERNEST. Selfish brute, only thinking of himself. What about my speech?

LADY MARY. One maid among three of us. What's to be done?

ERNEST. Pooh! You must do for yourselves, that's all.

LADY MARY. Do for ourselves. How can we know where our things are kept?

AGATHA. Are you aware that dresses button up the back?

CATHERINE. How are we to get into our shoes and be prepared for the carriage?

LADY MARY. Who is to put us to bed, and who is to get us up, and how shall we ever know it 's morning if there is no one to pull up the blinds?

> (CRICHTON *crosses on his way out.*)

ERNEST.   How is his lordship now ?

CRICHTON.   A little easier, sir.

LADY MARY.   Crichton, send Fisher to me.   (*He goes.*)

ERNEST.   I have no pity for you girls, I——

LADY MARY.   Ernest, go away, and don't insult the broken-hearted.

ERNEST.   And uncommon glad I am to go.   Ta-ta, all of you.   He asked me to say a few words.   I came here to say a few words, and I 'm not at all sure that I couldn't bring an action against him.

(*He departs, feeling that he has left a dart behind him. The girls are alone with their tragic thoughts.*)

LADY MARY (*become a mother to the younger ones at last*).   My poor sisters, come here.   (*They go to her doubtfully.*)   We must make this draw us closer together.   I shall do my best to help you in every way.   Just now I cannot think of myself at all.

AGATHA.   But how unlike you, Mary.

LADY MARY.   It is my duty to protect my sisters.

CATHERINE.   I never knew her so sweet before, Agatha. (*Cautiously*) What do you propose to do, Mary ?

LADY MARY.   I propose when we are on the yacht to lend Fisher to you when I don't need her myself.

AGATHA.   Fisher ?

LADY MARY (*who has the most character of the three*).   Of course, as the eldest, I have decided that it is *my* maid we shall take with us.

CATHERINE (*speaking also for* AGATHA.)   Mary, you toad.

AGATHA.   Nothing on earth would induce Fisher to lift her hand for either me or Catherine.

LADY MARY.   I was afraid of it, Agatha.   That is why I am so sorry for you.

(*The further exchange of pleasantries is interrupted by the arrival of* FISHER.)

LADY MARY.   Fisher, you heard what his lordship said ?

FISHER.   Yes, my lady.

LADY MARY (*coldly, though the others would have tried blandishment.*)   You have given me some satisfaction of late, Fisher, and to mark my approval I have decided that you shall be the maid who accompanies us.

FISHER (*acidly*).   I thank you, my lady.

LADY MARY. That is all ; you may go.

FISHER (*rapping it out*). If you please, my lady, I wish to give notice.

(CATHERINE *and* AGATHA *gleam, but* LADY MARY *is of sterner stuff.*)

LADY MARY (*taking up a book*). Oh, certainly—you may go.

CATHERINE. But why, Fisher ?

FISHER. I could not undertake, my lady, to wait upon three. *We* don't do it. (*In an indignant outburst to* LADY MARY.) Oh, my lady, to think that this affront——

LADY MARY (*looking up*). I thought I told you to go, Fisher.

(FISHER *stands for a moment irresolute ; then goes. As soon as she has gone* LADY MARY *puts down her book and weeps. She is a pretty woman, but this is the only pretty thing we have seen her do yet.*)

AGATHA (*succinctly*). Serves you right.

(CRICHTON *comes.*)

CATHERINE. It will be Simmons after all. Send Simmons to me.

CRICHTON (*after hesitating*). My lady, might I venture to speak ?

CATHERINE. What is it ?

CRICHTON. I happen to know, your ladyship, that Simmons desires to give notice for the same reason as Fisher.

CATHERINE. Oh !

AGATHA (*triumphant*). Then, Catherine, we take Jeanne.

CRICHTON. And Jeanne also, my lady.

(LADY MARY *is reading, indifferent though the heavens fall, but her sisters are not ashamed to show their despair to* CRICHTON.)

AGATHA. We can't blame them. Could any maid who respected herself be got to wait upon three ?

LADY MARY (*with languid interest*). I suppose there are such persons, Crichton ?

CRICHTON (*guardedly*). I have heard, my lady, that there are such.

LADY MARY (*a little desperate*). Crichton, what 's to be done ? We sail in two days ; could one be discovered in the time ?

AGATHA (*frankly a supplicant*). Surely you can think of some one ?

CRICHTON (*after hesitating*).   There is in this establishment, your ladyship, a young woman——

LADY MARY.   Yes ?

CRICHTON.   A young woman, on whom I have for some time cast an eye.

CATHERINE (*eagerly*).   Do you mean as a possible lady's-maid ?

CRICHTON.   I had thought of her, my lady, in another connection.

LADY MARY.   Ah !

CRICHTON.   But I believe she is quite the young person you require.   Perhaps if you could see her, my lady——

LADY MARY.   I shall certainly see her.   Bring her to me. (*He goes.*)   You two needn't wait.

CATHERINE.   Needn't we ?   We see your little game, Mary.

AGATHA.   We shall certainly remain and have our two-thirds of her.

(*They sit there doggedly until* CRICHTON *returns with* TWEENY, *who looks scared.*)

CRICHTON.   This, my lady, is the young person.

CATHERINE (*frankly*).   Oh dear !

(*It is evident that all three consider her quite unsuitable.*)

LADY MARY.   Come here, girl.   Don't be afraid.

(TWEENY *looks imploringly at her idol.*)

CRICHTON.   Her appearance, my lady, is homely, and her manners, as you may have observed, deplorable, but she has a heart of gold.

LADY MARY.   What is your position downstairs ?

TWEENY (*bobbing*).   I 'm a tweeny, your ladyship.

CATHERINE.   A what ?

CRICHTON.   A tweeny ; that is to say, my lady, she is not at present, strictly speaking, anything ; a *between* maid ; she helps the vegetable maid.   It is she, my lady, who conveys the dishes from the one end of the kitchen table, where they are placed by the cook, to the other end, where they enter into the charge of Thomas and John.

LADY MARY.   I see.   And you and Crichton are—ah—keeping company ?

(CRICHTON *draws himself up.*)

TWEENY (*aghast*).   A butler don't keep company, my lady.

LADY MARY (*indifferently*). Does he not ?

CRICHTON. No, your ladyship, we butlers may—(*he makes a gesture with his arms*)—but we do not keep company.

AGATHA. I know what it is ; you are engaged ?

(TWEENY *looks longingly at* CRICHTON.)

CRICHTON. Certainly not, my lady. The utmost I can say at present is that I have cast a favourable eye.

(*Even this is much to* TWEENY.)

LADY MARY. As you choose. But I am afraid, Crichton, she will not suit us.

CRICHTON. My lady, beneath this simple exterior are concealed a very sweet nature and rare womanly gifts.

AGATHA. Unfortunately, that is not what we want.

CRICHTON. And it is she, my lady, who dresses the hair of the ladies'-maids for our evening meals.

(*The ladies are interested at last.*)

LADY MARY. She dresses Fisher's hair ?

TWEENY. Yes, my lady, and I does them up when they goes to parties.

CRICHTON (*pained, but not scolding*). Does *!*

TWEENY. Doos. And it 's me what alters your gowns to fit them.

CRICHTON. *What* alters !

TWEENY. Which alters.

AGATHA. Mary ?

LADY MARY. I shall certainly have her.

CATHERINE. *We* shall certainly have her. Tweeny, we have decided to make a lady's-maid of you.

TWEENY. Oh lawks !

AGATHA. We are doing this for you so that your position socially may be more nearly akin to that of Crichton.

CRICHTON (*gravely*). It will undoubtedly increase the young person's chances.

LADY MARY. Then if I get a good character for you from Mrs. Perkins, she will make the necessary arrangements.

(*She resumes reading.*)

TWEENY (*elated*). My lady !

LADY MARY. By the way, I hope you are a good sailor.

TWEENY (*startled*). You don't mean, my lady, I 'm to go on the ship ?

LADY MARY.   Certainly.

TWEENY.   But—— (*To* CRICHTON) You ain't going, sir ?

CRICHTON.   No.

TWEENY (*firm at last*).   Then neither ain't I.

AGATHA.   You must.

TWEENY.   Leave him !   Not me.

LADY MARY.   Girl, don't be silly.   Crichton will be—considered in your wages.

TWEENY.   I ain't going.

CRICHTON.   I feared this, my lady.

TWEENY.   Nothing 'll budge me.

LADY MARY.   Leave the room.

(CRICHTON *shows* TWEENY *out with marked politeness.*)

AGATHA.   Crichton, I think you might have shown more displeasure with her.

CRICHTON (*contrite*).   I was touched, my lady.   I see, my lady, that to part from her would be a wrench to me, though I could not well say so in her presence, not having yet decided how far I shall go with her.

(*He is about to go when* LORD LOAM *returns, fuming.*)

LORD LOAM.   The ingrate !   The smug !   The fop !

CATHERINE.   What is it now, father ?

LORD LOAM.   That man of mine, Rolleston, refuses to accompany us because you are to have but one maid.

AGATHA.   Hurrah !

LADY MARY (*in better taste*).   Darling father, rather than you should lose Rolleston, we will consent to take all the three of them.

LORD LOAM.   Pooh, nonsense !   Crichton, find me a valet who can do without three maids.

CRICHTON.   Yes, my lord.   (*Troubled*) In the time—the more suitable the party, my lord, the less willing will he be to come without the—the usual perquisites.

LORD LOAM.   Any one will do.

CRICHTON (*shocked*).   My lord !

LORD LOAM.   The ingrate !   the puppy !

(AGATHA *has an idea, and whispers to* LADY MARY.)

LADY MARY.   I ask a favour of a servant ?—never !

AGATHA.   Then I will.   Crichton, would it not be very distressing to you to let his lordship go, attended by a valet who

might prove unworthy ?   It is only for three months ; don't
you think that you—you yourself—you——

> (*As* CRICHTON *sees what she wants he pulls himself up with
> noble, offended dignity, and she is appalled.*)

I beg your pardon.

> (*He bows stiffly.*)

CATHERINE (*to* CRICHTON).   But think of the joy to Tweeny.

> (CRICHTON *is moved, but he shakes his head.*)

LADY MARY (*so much the cleverest*).   Crichton, do you think
it safe to let the master you love go so far away without you
while he has these dangerous views about equality ?

> (CRICHTON *is profoundly stirred.   After a struggle he goes
> to his master, who has been pacing the room.*)

CRICHTON.   My lord, I have found a man.

LORD LOAM.   Already ?   Who is he ?

> (CRICHTON *presents himself with a gesture.*)

Yourself ?

CATHERINE.   Father, how good of him.

LORD LOAM (*pleased, but thinking it a small thing*).   Uncommon good.   Thank you, Crichton.   This helps me nicely
out of a hole ; and how it will annoy Rolleston !   Come with
me, and we shall tell him.   Not that I think you have lowered
yourself in any way.   Come along.

> (*He goes, and* CRICHTON *is to follow him, but is stopped by*
> AGATHA *impulsively offering him her hand.*)

CRICHTON (*who is much shaken*).   My lady—a valet's hand !

AGATHA.   I had no idea you would feel it so deeply ; why
did you do it ?

> (CRICHTON *is too respectful to reply.*)

LADY MARY (*regarding him*).   Crichton, I am curious.   I
insist upon an answer.

CRICHTON.   My lady, I am the son of a butler and a lady's-
maid—perhaps the happiest of all combinations ; and to me the
most beautiful thing in the world is a haughty, aristocratic
English house, with every one kept in his place.   Though I
were equal to your ladyship, where would be the pleasure to me ?
It would be counterbalanced by the pain of feeling that Thomas
and John were equal to me.

CATHERINE.   But father says if we were to return to
Nature——

CRICHTON.   If we did, my lady, the first thing we should do would be to elect a head.   Circumstances might alter cases ; the same person might not be master ; the same persons might not be servants.   I can't say as to that, nor should we have the deciding of it.   Nature would decide for us.

LADY MARY.   You seem to have thought it all out carefully, Crichton.

CRICHTON.   Yes, my lady.

CATHERINE.   And you have done this for us, Crichton, because you thought that—that father needed to be kept in his place ?

CRICHTON.   I should prefer you to say, my lady, that I have done it for the house.

AGATHA.   Thank you, Crichton.   Mary, be nicer to him. (*But* LADY MARY *has begun to read again.*)   If there was any way in which we could show our gratitude ?

CRICHTON.   If I might venture, my lady, would you kindly show it by becoming more like Lady Mary ?   That disdain is what we like from our superiors.   Even so do we, the upper servants, disdain the lower servants, while they take it out of the odds and ends.

(*He goes, and they bury themselves in cushions.*)

AGATHA.   Oh dear, what a tiring day.

CATHERINE.   I feel dead.   Tuck in your feet, you selfish thing.

(LADY MARY *is lying reading on another couch.*)

LADY MARY.   I wonder what he meant by circumstances might alter cases.

AGATHA (*yawning*).   Don't talk, Mary, I was nearly asleep.

LADY MARY.   I wonder what he meant by the same person might not be master, and the same persons might not be servants.

CATHERINE.   Do be quiet, Mary, and leave it to Nature ; he said Nature would decide.

LADY MARY.   I wonder——

(*But she does not wonder very much.   She would wonder more if she knew what was coming.   Her book slips unregarded to the floor.   The ladies are at rest until it is time to dress.*)

ACT II

THE ISLAND

Two months have elapsed, and the scene is a desert island in the Pacific, on which our adventurers have been wrecked.

The curtain rises on a sea of bamboo, which shuts out all view save the foliage of palm trees and some gaunt rocks. Occasionally Crichton and Treherne come momentarily into sight, hacking and hewing the bamboo, through which they are making a clearing between the ladies and the shore ; and by and by, owing to their efforts, we shall have an unrestricted outlook on to a sullen sea that is at present hidden. Then we shall also be able to note a mast standing out of the water—all that is left, saving floating wreckage, of the ill-fated yacht the *Bluebell*. The beginnings of a hut will also be seen, with Crichton driving its walls into the ground or astride its roof of saplings, for at present he is doing more than one thing at a time. In a red shirt, with the ends of his sailor's breeches thrust into wading-boots, he looks a man for the moment ; we suddenly remember some one's saying—perhaps it was ourselves—that a cataclysm would be needed to get him out of his servant's clothes, and apparently it has been forthcoming. It is no longer beneath our dignity to cast an inquiring eye on his appearance. His features are not distinguished, but he has a strong jaw and green eyes, in which a yellow light burns that we have not seen before. His dark hair, hitherto so decorously sleek, has been ruffled this way and that by wind and weather, as if they were part of the cataclysm and wanted to help his chance. His muscles must be soft and flabby still, but though they shriek aloud to him to desist, he rains lusty blows with his axe, like one who has come upon the open for the first time in his life, and likes it. He is as yet far from being an expert woodsman—mark the blood on his hands at places where he has hit them instead of the tree ; but note also that he does not waste time in bandaging them—he

365

rubs them in the earth and goes on. His face is still of the discreet pallor that befits a butler, and he carries the smaller logs as if they were a salver ; not in a day or a month will he shake off the badge of servitude, but without knowing it he has begun.

But for the hatchets at work, and an occasional something horrible falling from a tree into the ladies' laps, they hear nothing save the mournful surf breaking on a coral shore.

They sit or recline huddled together against a rock, and they are farther from home, in every sense of the word, than ever before. Thirty-six hours ago, they were given three minutes in which to dress, without a maid, and reach the boats, and they have not made the best of that valuable time. None of them has boots, and had they known this prickly island they would have thought first of boots. They have a sufficiency of garments, but some of them were gifts dropped into the boat—Lady Mary's tarpaulin coat and hat, for instance, and Catherine's blue jersey and red cap, which certify that the two ladies were lately before the mast. Agatha is too gay in Ernest's dressing-gown, and clutches it to her person with both hands as if afraid that it may be claimed by its rightful owner. There are two pairs of bath slippers between the three of them, and their hair cries aloud and in vain for hairpins.

By their side, on an inverted bucket, sits Ernest, clothed neatly in the garments of day and night, but, alas, bare-footed. He is the only cheerful member of this company of four, but his brightness is due less to a manly desire to succour the helpless than to his having been lately in the throes of composition, and to his modest satisfaction with the result. He reads to the ladies, and they listen, each with one scared eye to the things that fall from trees.

ERNEST (*who has written on the fly-leaf of the only book saved from the wreck*). This is what I have written. 'Wrecked, wrecked, wrecked ! on an island in the Tropics, the following : the Hon. Ernest Woolley, the Rev. John Treherne, the Ladies, Mary, Catherine, and Agatha Lasenby, with two servants. We are the sole survivors of Lord Loam's steam yacht *Bluebell*, which encountered a fearful gale in these seas, and soon became a total wreck. The crew behaved gallantly, putting us all into the first boat. What became of them I cannot tell, but we,

after dreadful sufferings, and insufficiently clad, in whatever
garments we could lay hold of in the dark '—

LADY MARY. Please don't describe our garments.

ERNEST. —' succeeded in reaching this island, with the
loss of only one of our party, namely, Lord Loam, who flung
away his life in a gallant attempt to save a servant who had
fallen overboard.'

(*The ladies have wept long and sore for their father, but
there is something in this last utterance that makes them
look up.*)

AGATHA. But, Ernest, it was Crichton who jumped overboard trying to save father.

ERNEST (*with the candour that is one of his most engaging
qualities*). Well, you know, it was rather silly of uncle to fling
away his life by trying to get into the boat first ; and as this
document may be printed in the English papers, it struck me,
an English peer, you know——

LADY MARY (*every inch an English peer's daughter*). Ernest,
that is very thoughtful of you.

ERNEST (*continuing, well pleased*). —' By night the cries of
wild cats and the hissing of snakes terrify us extremely '—(*This
does not satisfy him so well, and he makes a correction*)—' terrify
the ladies extremely. Against these we have no weapons except
one cutlass and a hatchet. A bucket washed ashore is at present
our only comfortable seat '—

LADY MARY (*with some spirit*). And Ernest is sitting on it.

ERNEST. H'sh ! Oh, do be quiet. —' To add to our
horrors, night falls suddenly in these parts, and it is then that
savage animals begin to prowl and roar.'

LADY MARY. Have you said that vampire bats suck the
blood from our toes as we sleep ?

ERNEST. No, that's all. I end up, ' Rescue us or we
perish. Rich reward. Signed Ernest Woolley, in command
of our little party.' This is written on a leaf taken out of a book
of poems that Crichton found in his pocket. Fancy Crichton
being a reader of poetry ! Now I shall put it into the bottle
and fling it into the sea.

(*He pushes the precious document into a soda-water bottle,
and rams the cork home. At the same moment, and without
effort, he gives birth to one of his most characteristic epigrams.*)

The tide is going out, we mustn't miss the post.

(*They are so unhappy that they fail to grasp it, and a little petulantly he calls for* CRICHTON, *ever his stand-by in the hour of epigram.* CRICHTON *breaks through the undergrowth quickly, thinking the ladies are in danger.*)

CRICHTON.   Anything wrong, sir ?

ERNEST (*with fine confidence*).   The tide, Crichton, is a postman who calls at our island twice a day for letters.

CRICHTON (*after a pause*).   Thank you, sir.

(*He returns to his labours, however, without giving the smile which is the epigrammatist's right, and* ERNEST *is a little disappointed in him.*)

ERNEST.   Poor Crichton ! I sometimes think he is losing his sense of humour.   Come along, Agatha.

(*He helps his favourite up the rocks, and they disappear gingerly from view.*)

CATHERINE.   How horribly still it is.

LADY MARY (*remembering some recent sounds*).   It is best when it is still.

CATHERINE (*drawing closer to her*).   Mary, I have heard that they are always very still just before they jump.

LADY MARY.   Don't. (*A distinct chopping is heard, and they are startled.*)

LADY MARY (*controlling herself*).   It is only Crichton knocking down trees.

CATHERINE (*almost imploringly*).   Mary, let us go and stand beside him.

LADY MARY (*coldly*).   Let a servant see that I am afraid !

CATHERINE.   Don't, then ; but remember this, dear, they often drop on one from above.

(*She moves away, nearer to the friendly sound of the axe, and* LADY MARY *is left alone. She is the most courageous of them as well as the haughtiest, but when something she had thought to be a stick glides toward her, she forgets her dignity and screams.*)

LADY MARY (*calling*).   Crichton, Crichton !

(*It must have been* TREHERNE *who was tree-felling, for* CRICHTON *comes to her from the hut, drawing his cutlass.*)

CRICHTON (*anxious*).   Did you call, my lady ?

LADY MARY (*herself again, now that he is there*). I ! Why should I ?

CRICHTON. I made a mistake, your ladyship. (*Hesitating*) If you are afraid of being alone, my lady——

LADY MARY. Afraid ! Certainly not. (*Doggedly*) You may go.

(*But she does not complain when he remains within eyesight cutting the bamboo. It is heavy work, and she watches him silently.*)

LADY MARY. I wish, Crichton, you could work without getting so hot.

CRICHTON (*mopping his face*). I wish I could, my lady.

(*He continues his labours.*)

LADY MARY (*taking off her oilskins*). It makes me hot to look at you.

CRICHTON. It almost makes me cool to look at your ladyship.

LADY MARY (*who perhaps thinks he is presuming*). Anything I can do for you in that way, Crichton, I shall do with pleasure.

CRICHTON (*quite humbly*). Thank you, my lady.

(*By this time most of the bamboo has been cut, and the shore and sea are visible, except where they are hidden by the half completed hut. The mast rising solitary from the water adds to the desolation of the scene, and at last tears run down LADY MARY's face.*)

CRICHTON. Don't give way, my lady, things might be worse.

LADY MARY. My poor father !

CRICHTON. If I could have given my life for his——

LADY MARY. You did all a man could do. Indeed I thank you, Crichton. (*With some admiration and more wonder*) You are a man.

CRICHTON. Thank you, my lady.

LADY MARY. But it is all so awful. Crichton, is there any hope of a ship coming ?

CRICHTON (*after hesitation*). Of course there is, my lady.

LADY MARY (*facing him bravely*). Don't treat me as a child. I have got to know the worst, and to face it. Crichton, the truth.

CRICHTON (*reluctantly*). We were driven out of our course, my lady ; I fear far from the track of commerce.

LADY MARY.   Thank you ; I understand.
(*For a moment, however, she breaks down.   Then she clenches her hands and stands erect.*)
CRICHTON (*watching her, and forgetting perhaps for the moment that they are not just a man and woman*).   You 're a good pluckt 'un, my lady.
LADY MARY (*falling into the same error*).   I shall try to be. (*Extricating herself.*)   Crichton, you presume !
CRICHTON.   I beg your ladyship's pardon ; but you are.
(*She smiles, as if it were a comfort to be told this even by* CRICHTON.)
And until a ship comes we are three men who are going to do our best for you ladies.
LADY MARY (*with a curl of the lip*).   Mr. Ernest does no work.
CRICHTON (*cheerily*).   But he will, my lady.
LADY MARY.   I doubt it.
CRICHTON (*confidently, but perhaps thoughtlessly*).   No work —no dinner—will make a great change in Mr. Ernest.
LADY MARY.   No work—no dinner.   When did you invent that rule, Crichton ?
CRICHTON (*loaded with bamboo*).   I didn't invent it, my lady. I seem to see it growing all over the island.
LADY MARY (*disquieted*).   Crichton, your manner strikes me as curious.
CRICHTON (*pained*).   I hope not, your ladyship.
LADY MARY (*determined to have it out with him*).   You are not implying anything so unnatural, I hope, as that if I and my sisters don't work there will be no dinner for *us* ?
CRICHTON (*brightly*).   If it is unnatural, my lady, that is the end of it.
LADY MARY.   If ?   Now I understand.   The perfect servant at home holds that we are all equal now.   I see.
CRICHTON (*wounded to the quick*).   My lady, can you think me so inconsistent ?
LADY MARY.   That is it.
CRICHTON (*earnestly*).   My lady, I disbelieved in equality at home because it was against nature, and for that same reason I as utterly disbelieve in it on an island.
LADY MARY (*relieved by his obvious sincerity*).   I apologise.

CRICHTON (*continuing unfortunately*). There must always, my lady, be one to command and others to obey.

LADY MARY (*satisfied*). One to command, others to obey. Yes. (*Then suddenly she realises that there may be a dire meaning in his confident words.*) Crichton !

CRICHTON (*who has intended no dire meaning*). What is it, my lady ?

(*But she only stares into his face and then hurries from him. Left alone he is puzzled, but being a practical man he busies himself gathering firewood, until* TWEENY *appears excitedly carrying cocoa-nuts in her skirt. She has made better use than the ladies of her three minutes' grace for dressing.*)

TWEENY (*who can be happy even on an island if* CRICHTON *is with her*). Look what I found !

CRICHTON. Cocoa-nuts. Bravo !

TWEENY. They grows on trees with this round them.

CRICHTON. Where did you think they grew ?

TWEENY. I thought as how they grew in rows on top of little sticks.

CRICHTON (*wrinkling his brows*). Oh, Tweeny, Tweeny !

TWEENY (*anxiously*). Have I offended of your feelings again, sir ?

CRICHTON. A little.

TWEENY (*in a despairing outburst*). I 'm full o' vulgar words and ways ; and though I may keep them in their holes when you are by, as soon as I 'm by myself out they comes in a rush like beetles when the house is dark. I says them gloating-like, in my head—' Blooming,' I says, and ' All my eye,' and ' Ginger,' and ' Nothink ' ; and all the time we was being wrecked I was praying to myself, ' Please the Lord it may be an island as it 's natural to be vulgar on.'

(*A shudder passes through* CRICHTON, *and she is abject.*) That 's the kind I am, sir. I 'm 'opeless. You 'd better give me up.

(*She is a pathetic, forlorn creature, and his manhood is stirred.*)

CRICHTON (*wondering a little at himself for saying it*). I won't give you up. It is strange that one so common should attract one so fastidious ; but so it is. (*Thoughtfully*) There is something about you, Tweeny, there is a *je ne sais quoi* about you.

TWEENY (*knowing only that he has found something in her to commend*). Is there, is there ? Oh, I am glad.

CRICHTON (*putting his hand on her shoulder like a protector*). We shall fight your vulgarity together. (*All this time he has been arranging sticks for his fire.*) Now get some dry grass.

(*She brings him grass, and he puts it under the sticks. He produces an odd lens from his pocket, and tries to focus the sun's rays.*)

TWEENY. Why, what 's that ?

CRICHTON (*the ingenious creature*). That 's the glass from my watch and one from Mr. Treherne's, with a little water between them. I 'm hoping to kindle a fire with it.

TWEENY (*properly impressed*). Oh, sir !

(*After one failure the grass takes fire, and they are blowing on it when excited cries near by bring them sharply to their feet.* AGATHA *runs to them, white of face, followed by* ERNEST.)

ERNEST. Danger ! Crichton, a tiger-cat !

CRICHTON (*getting his cutlass*). Where ?

AGATHA. It is at our heels.

ERNEST. Look out, Crichton.

CRICHTON. H'sh !

(TREHERNE *comes to his assistance, while* LADY MARY *and* CATHERINE *join* AGATHA *in the hut.*)

ERNEST. It will be on us in a moment.

(*He seizes the hatchet and guards the hut. It is pleasing to see that* ERNEST *is no coward.*)

TREHERNE. Listen !

ERNEST. The grass is moving. It 's coming.

(*It comes. But it is no tiger-cat ; it is* LORD LOAM *crawling on his hands and knees, a very exhausted and dishevelled peer, wondrously attired in rags. The girls see him, and with glad cries rush into his arms.*)

LADY MARY. Father !

LORD LOAM. Mary—Catherine—Agatha ! Oh dear, my dears, my dears, oh dear !

LADY MARY. Darling.

AGATHA. Sweetest.

CATHERINE. Love.

TREHERNE. Glad to see you, sir.

ERNEST.   Uncle, uncle, dear old uncle.

(*For a time such happy cries fill the air, but presently* TREHERNE *is thoughtless.*)

TREHERNE.   Ernest thought you were a tiger-cat.

LORD LOAM (*stung somehow to the quick*).   Oh, did you ?   I knew you at once, Ernest ; I knew you by the way you ran.

(ERNEST *smiles forgivingly.*)

CRICHTON (*venturing forward at last*).   My lord, I am glad.

ERNEST (*with upraised finger*).   But you are also idling, Crichton.   (*Making himself comfortable on the ground.*)   We mustn't waste time.   To work, to work.

CRICHTON (*after contemplating him without rancour*).   Yes, sir.

(*He gets a pot from the hut and hangs it on a tripod over the fire, which is now burning brightly.*)

TREHERNE.   Ernest, you be a little more civil.   Crichton, let me help.

(*He is soon busy helping* CRICHTON *to add to the strength of the hut.*)

LORD LOAM (*gazing at the pot as ladies are said to gaze on precious stones*).   Is that—but I suppose I 'm dreaming again. (*Timidly*) It isn't by any chance a pot on top of a fire, is it ?

LADY MARY.   Indeed, it is, dearest.   It is our supper.

LORD LOAM.   I have been dreaming of a pot on a fire for two days.   (*Quivering*) There 's nothing in it, is there ?

ERNEST.   Sniff, uncle.   (LORD LOAM *sniffs.*)

LORD LOAM (*reverently*).   It smells of onions !

(*There is a sudden diversion.*)

CATHERINE.   Father, you have boots !

LADY MARY.   So he has.

LORD LOAM.   Of course I have.

ERNEST (*with greedy cunning*).   You are actually wearing boots, uncle.   It 's very unsafe, you know, in this climate.

LORD LOAM.   Is it ?

ERNEST.   We have all abandoned them, you observe.   The blood, the arteries, you know.

LORD LOAM.   I hadn't a notion.

(*He holds out his feet, and* ERNEST *kneels.*)

ERNEST.   Oh Lord, yes.

(*In another moment those boots will be his.*)

LADY MARY (*quickly*).   Father, he is trying to get your boots from you.   There is nothing in the world we wouldn't give for boots.

ERNEST (*rising haughtily, a proud spirit misunderstood*).   I only wanted the loan of them.

AGATHA (*running her fingers along them lovingly*).   If you lend them to any one, it will be to us, won't it, father?

LORD LOAM.   Certainly, my child.

ERNEST.   Oh, very well.   (*He is leaving these selfish ones.*) I don't want your old boots.   (*He gives his uncle a last chance.*) You don't think you could spare me *one* boot?

LORD LOAM (*tartly*).   I do not.

ERNEST.   Quite so.   Well, all I can say is I 'm sorry for you. (*He departs to recline elsewhere.*)

LADY MARY.   Father, we thought we should never see you again.

LORD LOAM.   I was washed ashore, my dear, clinging to a hencoop.   How awful that first night was.

LADY MARY.   Poor father.

LORD LOAM.   When I woke, I wept.   Then I began to feel extremely hungry.   There was a large turtle on the beach.   I remembered from the *Swiss Family Robinson* that if you turn a turtle over he is helpless.   My dears, I crawled towards him, I flung myself upon him—(*here he pauses to rub his leg*)—the nasty, spiteful brute.

LADY MARY.   You didn't turn him over?

LORD LOAM (*vindictively, though he is a kindly man*).   Mary, the senseless thing wouldn't wait; I found that none of them would wait.

CATHERINE.   We should have been as badly off if Crichton hadn't——

LADY MARY (*quickly*).   Don't praise Crichton.

LORD LOAM.   And then those beastly monkeys.   I always understood that if you flung stones at them they would retaliate by flinging cocoa-nuts at you.   Would you believe it, I flung a hundred stones, and not one monkey had sufficient intelligence to grasp my meaning.   How I longed for Crichton.

LADY MARY (*wincing*).   For us also, father?

LORD LOAM.   For you also.   I tried for hours to make a fire. The authors say that when wrecked on an island you can obtain a light by rubbing two pieces of stick together. (*With feeling*) The liars !

LADY MARY.   And all this time you thought there was no one on the island but yourself ?

LORD LOAM.   I thought so until this morning.   I was searching the pools for little fishes, which I caught in my hat, when suddenly I saw before me—on the sand——

CATHERINE.   What ?

LORD LOAM.   A hairpin.

LADY MARY.   A hairpin !   It must be one of ours. (*Greedily*) Give it me, father.

AGATHA.   No, it 's mine.

LORD LOAM.   I didn't keep it.

LADY MARY (*speaking for all three*).   Didn't keep it ?   Found a hairpin on an island, and didn't keep it ?

LORD LOAM (*humbly*).   My dears.

AGATHA (*scarcely to be placated*).   Oh, father, we have returned to Nature more than you bargained for.

LADY MARY.   For shame, Agatha. (*She has something on her mind.*) Father, there is something I want you to do at once—I mean to assert your position as the chief person on the island.

(*They are all surprised.*)

LORD LOAM.   But who would presume to question it ?

CATHERINE.   She must mean Ernest.

LADY MARY.   Must I ?

AGATHA.   It is cruel to say anything against Ernest.

LORD LOAM (*firmly*).   If any one presumes to challenge my position, I shall make short work of him.

AGATHA.   Here comes Ernest ; now see if you can say these horrid things to his face.

LORD LOAM.   I shall teach him his place at once.

LADY MARY (*anxiously*).   But how ?

LORD LOAM (*chuckling*).   I have just thought of an extremely amusing way of doing it. (*As* ERNEST *approaches*) Ernest.

ERNEST (*loftily*).   Excuse me, uncle, I 'm thinking.   I 'm planning out the building of this hut.

LORD LOAM.   I also have been thinking.

ERNEST.   That don't matter.

LORD LOAM.   Eh ?

ERNEST.   Please, please, this is important.

LORD LOAM.   I have been thinking that I ought to give you my boots.

ERNEST.   What !

LADY MARY.   Father.

LORD LOAM (*genially*).   Take them, my boy. (*With a rapidity we had not thought him capable of,* ERNEST *becomes the wearer of the boots.*)   And now I dare say you want to know why I give them to you, Ernest ?

ERNEST (*moving up and down in them deliciously*).   Not at all. The great thing is, ' I 've got 'em, I 've got 'em.'

LORD LOAM (*majestically, but with a knowing look at his daughters*).   My reason is that, as head of our little party, you, Ernest, shall be our hunter, you shall clear the forests of these savage beasts that make them so dangerous. (*Pleasantly*) And now you know, my dear nephew, why I have given you my boots.

ERNEST.   This is my answer.

    (*He kicks off the boots.*)

LADY MARY (*still anxious*).   Father, assert yourself.

LORD LOAM.   I shall now assert myself. (*But how to do it ? He has a happy thought.*)   Call Crichton.

LADY MARY.   Oh, father !

    (CRICHTON *comes in answer to a summons, and is followed by* TREHERNE.)

ERNEST (*wondering a little at* LADY MARY'S *grave face*). Crichton, look here.

LORD LOAM (*sturdily*).   Silence ! Crichton, I want your advice as to what I ought to do with Mr. Ernest. He has defied me.

ERNEST.   Pooh !

CRICHTON (*after considering*).   May I speak openly, my lord ?

LADY MARY (*keeping her eyes fixed on him*).   That is what we desire.

CRICHTON (*quite humbly*).   Then I may say, your lordship, that I have been considering Mr. Ernest's case at odd moments ever since we were wrecked.

ERNEST.   My case ?

LORD LOAM (*sternly*).   Hush.

CRICHTON.   Since we landed on the island, my lord, it seems to me that Mr. Ernest's epigrams have been particularly brilliant.

ERNEST (*gratified*). Thank you, Crichton.

CRICHTON. But I find—I seem to find it growing wild, my lord, in the woods, that sayings which would be justly admired in England are not much use on an island. I would therefore most respectfully propose that henceforth every time Mr. Ernest favours us with an epigram his head should be immersed in a bucket of cold spring water.

(*There is a terrible silence.*)

LORD LOAM (*uneasily*). Serve him right.

ERNEST. I should like to see you try to do it, uncle.

CRICHTON (*ever ready to come to the succour of his lordship*). My feeling, my lord, is that at the next offence I should convey him to a retired spot, where I shall carry out the undertaking in as respectful a manner as is consistent with a thorough immersion.

(*Though his manner is most respectful, he is resolute ; he evidently means what he says.*)

LADY MARY (*a ramrod*). Father, you must not permit this ; Ernest is your nephew.

LORD LOAM (*with his hand to his brow*). After all, he is my nephew, Crichton ; and, as I am sure, he now sees that I am a strong man——

ERNEST (*foolishly in the circumstances*). A strong man. You mean a stout man. You are one of mind to two of matter.

(*He looks round in the old way for approval. No one has smiled, and to his consternation he sees that* CRICHTON *is quietly turning up his sleeves.* ERNEST *makes an appealing gesture to his uncle ; then he turns defiantly to* CRICHTON.)

CRICHTON. Is it to be before the ladies, Mr. Ernest, or in the privacy of the wood ? (*He fixes* ERNEST *with his eye.* ERNEST *is cowed.*) Come.

ERNEST (*after a long time*). Oh, all right.

CRICHTON (*succinctly*). Bring the bucket.

(ERNEST *hesitates. He then lifts the bucket and follows* CRICHTON *to the nearest spring.*)

LORD LOAM (*rather white*). I 'm sorry for him, but I had to be firm.

LADY MARY.   Oh, father, it wasn't you who was firm. Crichton did it himself.

LORD LOAM.   Bless me, so he did.

LADY MARY.   Father, be strong.

LORD LOAM (*bewildered*).   You can't mean that my faithful Crichton——

LADY MARY.   Yes, I do.

TREHERNE.   Lady Mary, I stake my word that Crichton is incapable of acting dishonourably.

LADY MARY.   I know that; I know it as well as you. Don't you see, that is what makes him so dangerous?

TREHERNE.   By Jove, I—I believe I catch your meaning.

CATHERINE.   He is coming back.

LORD LOAM (*who has always known himself to be a man of ideas*).   Let us all go into the hut, just to show him at once that it is *our* hut.

LADY MARY (*as they go*).   Father, I implore you, assert yourself now and for ever.

LORD LOAM.   I will.

LADY MARY.   And, please, don't ask him how you are to do it.

(CRICHTON *returns with sticks to mend the fire.*)

LORD LOAM (*loftily, from the door of the hut*).   Have you carried out my instructions, Crichton?

CRICHTON (*deferentially*).   Yes, my lord.

(ERNEST *appears, mopping his hair, which has become very wet since we last saw him.   He is not bearing malice, he is too busy drying, but* AGATHA *is specially his champion.*)

AGATHA.   It's infamous, infamous.

LORD LOAM (*strongly*).   *My* orders, Agatha.

LADY MARY.   Now, father, please.

LORD LOAM (*striking an attitude*).   Before I give you any further orders, Crichton——

CRICHTON.   Yes, my lord.

LORD LOAM (*delighted*).   Pooh!   It's all right.

LADY MARY.   No.   Please go on.

LORD LOAM.   Well, well.   This question of the leadership; what do you think now, Crichton?

CRICHTON.   My lord, I feel it is a matter with which *I* have nothing to do.

LORD LOAM. Excellent. Ha, Mary? That settles it, I think.

LADY MARY. It seems to, but—I 'm not sure.

CRICHTON. It will settle itself naturally, my lord, without any interference from us.

(The reference to Nature gives general dissatisfaction.)

LADY MARY. Father.

LORD LOAM (*a little severely*). It settled itself long ago, Crichton, when I was born a peer, and you, for instance, were born a servant.

CRICHTON (*acquiescing*). Yes, my lord, that was how it all came about quite naturally in England. We had nothing to do with it there, and we shall have as little to do with it here.

TREHERNE (*relieved*). That 's all right.

LADY MARY (*determined to clinch the matter*). One moment. In short, Crichton, his lordship will continue to be our natural head.

CRICHTON. I dare say, my lady, I dare say.

CATHERINE. But you must *know*.

CRICHTON. Asking your pardon, my lady, one can't be sure —on an island.

(They look at each other uneasily.)

LORD LOAM (*warningly*). Crichton, I don't like this.

CRICHTON (*harassed*). The more I think of it, your lordship, the more uneasy I become myself. When I heard, my lord, that you had left that hairpin behind——

(He is pained.)

LORD LOAM (*feebly*). One hairpin among so many would only have caused dissension.

CRICHTON (*very sorry to have to contradict him*). Not so, my lord. From that hairpin we could have made a needle; with that needle we could, out of skins, have sewn trousers—of which your lordship is in need; indeed, we are all in need of them.

LADY MARY (*suddenly self-conscious*). All?

CRICHTON. On an island, my lady.

LADY MARY. Father.

CRICHTON (*really more distressed by the prospect than she*). My lady, if Nature does not think them necessary, you may be sure she will not ask you to wear them. (*Shaking his head*) But among all this undergrowth——

LADY MARY.   Now you see this man in his true colours.

LORD LOAM (*violently*).   Crichton, you will either this moment say, ' Down with Nature,' or——

CRICHTON (*scandalised*).   My lord !

LORD LOAM (*loftily*).   Then this is my last word to you ; take a month's notice.

(*If the hut had a door he would now shut it to indicate that the interview is closed.*)

CRICHTON (*in great distress*).   Your lordship, the disgrace——

LORD LOAM (*swelling*).   Not another word : you may go.

LADY MARY (*adamant*).   And don't come to me, Crichton, for a character.

ERNEST (*whose immersion has cleared his brain*).   Aren't you all forgetting that this is an island ?

(*This brings them to earth with a bump.*   LORD LOAM *looks to his eldest daughter for the fitting response.*)

LADY MARY (*equal to the occasion*).   It makes only this difference—that you may go at once, Crichton, to some other part of the island.

(*The faithful servant has been true to his superiors ever since he was created, and never more true than at this moment ; but his fidelity is founded on trust in Nature, and to be untrue to it would be to be untrue to them.   He lets the wood he has been gathering slip to the ground, and bows his sorrowful head.   He turns to obey.   Then affection for these great ones wells up in him.*)

CRICHTON.   My lady, let me work for you.

LADY MARY.   Go.

CRICHTON.   You need me so sorely ; I can't desert you ; I won't.

LADY MARY (*in alarm, lest the others may yield*).   Then, father, there is but one alternative, *we* must leave him.

(LORD LOAM *is looking yearningly at* CRICHTON.)

TREHERNE.   It seems a pity.

CATHERINE (*forlornly*).   *You* will work for us ?

TREHERNE.   Most willingly.   But I must warn you all that, so far, Crichton has done nine-tenths of the scoring.

LADY MARY.   The question is, are we to leave this man ?

LORD LOAM (*wrapping himself in his dignity*).   Come, my dears.

CRICHTON.   My lord !

LORD LOAM.   Treherne—Ernest—get our things.

ERNEST.   We don't have any, uncle.   They all belong to Crichton.

TREHERNE.   Everything we have he brought from the wreck —he went back to it before it sank.   He risked his life.

CRICHTON.   My lord, anything you would care to take is yours.

LADY MARY (*quickly*).   Nothing.

ERNEST.   Rot !   If I could have your socks, Crichton——

LADY MARY.   Come, father ;   we are ready.

(*Followed by the others, she and* LORD LOAM *pick their way up the rocks.   In their indignation they scarcely notice that daylight is coming to a sudden end.*)

CRICHTON.   My lord, I implore you—*I* am not desirous of being head.   Do you have a try at it, my lord.

LORD LOAM (*outraged*).   A try at it !

CRICHTON (*eagerly*).   It may be that you will prove to be the best man.

LORD LOAM.   *May* be !   My children, come.

(*They disappear proudly but gingerly up those splintered rocks.*)

TREHERNE.   Crichton, I 'm sorry ;   but of course I must go with them.

CRICHTON.   Certainly, sir.

(*He calls to* TWEENY, *and she comes from behind the hut, where she has been watching breathlessly.*) Will you be so kind, sir, as to take her to the others.

TREHERNE.   Assuredly.

TWEENY.   But what do it all mean ?

CRICHTON.   Does, Tweeny, does.   (*He passes her up the rocks to* TREHERNE.)   We shall meet again soon, Tweeny. Good-night, sir.

TREHERNE.   Good-night.   I dare say they are not far away.

CRICHTON (*thoughtfully*).   They went westward, sir, and the wind is blowing in that direction.   That may mean, sir, that Nature is already taking the matter into her own hands.   They are all hungry, sir, and the pot has come a-boil.   (*He takes off the lid.*)   The smell will be borne westward.   That pot is full of Nature, Mr. Treherne.   Good-night, sir.

TREHERNE. Good-night.

(*He mounts the rocks with* TWEENY, *and they are heard for a little time after their figures are swallowed up in the fast growing darkness.* CRICHTON *stands motionless, the lid in his hand, though he has forgotten it and his reason for taking it off the pot. He is deeply stirred, but presently is ashamed of his dejection, for it is as if he doubted his principles. Bravely true to his faith that Nature will decide now as ever before, he proceeds manfully with his preparations for the night. He lights a ship's lantern, one of several treasures he has brought ashore, and is filling his pipe with crumbs of tobacco from various pockets, when the stealthy movements of some animal in the grass startles him. With the lantern in one hand and his cutlass in the other, he searches the ground around the hut. He returns, lights his pipe, and sits down by the fire, which casts weird moving shadows. There is a red gleam on his face ; in the darkness he is a strong and perhaps rather sinister figure. In the great stillness that has fallen over the land, the wash of the surf seems to have increased in volume. The sound is indescribably mournful. Except where the fire is, desolation has fallen on the island like a pall.*

Once or twice, as Nature dictates, CRICHTON *leans forward to stir the pot, and the smell is borne westward. He then resumes his silent vigil.*

Shadows other than those cast by the fire begin to descend the rocks. They are the adventurers returning. One by one they steal nearer to the pot until they are squatted round it, with their hands out to the blaze. LADY MARY *only is absent. Presently she comes within sight of the others, then stands against a tree with her teeth clenched. One wonders, perhaps, what Nature is to make of her.*)

ACT III

THE HAPPY HOME

THE scene is the hall of their island home two years later. This sturdy log-house is no mere extension of the hut we have seen in process of erection, but has been built a mile or less to the west of it, on higher ground and near a stream. When the master chose this site, the others thought that all he expected from the stream was a sufficiency of drinking water. They know better now every time they go down to the mill or turn on the electric light.

This hall is the living-room of the house, and walls and roof are of stout logs. Across the joists supporting the roof are laid many home-made implements, such as spades, saws, fishing-rods, and from hooks in the joists are suspended cured foods, of which hams are specially in evidence. Deep recesses half-way up the walls contain various provender in barrels and sacks. There are some skins, trophies of the chase, on the floor, which is otherwise bare. The chairs and tables are in some cases hewn out of the solid wood, and in others the result of rough but efficient carpentering. Various pieces of wreckage from the yacht have been turned to novel uses : thus the steering-wheel now hangs from the centre of the roof, with electric lights attached to it encased in bladders. A lifebuoy has become the back of a chair. Two barrels have been halved and turn coyly from each other as a settee.

The farther end of the room is more strictly the kitchen, and is a great recess, which can be shut off from the hall by folding-doors. There is a large open fire on it. The chimney is half of one of the boats of the yacht. On the walls of the kitchen proper are many plate-racks, containing shells ; there are rows of these of one size and shape, which mark them off as dinner plates or bowls ; others are as obviously tureens. They are arranged primly as in a well-conducted kitchen ; indeed, neat-ness and cleanliness are the note struck everywhere, yet the effect of the whole is romantic and barbaric.

The outer door into this hall is a little peculiar on an island. It is covered with skins and is in four leaves, like the swing-doors of fashionable restaurants, which allow you to enter without allowing the hot air to escape. During the winter season our castaways have found this contrivance useful, but Crichton's brain was perhaps a little lordly when he conceived it. Another door leads by a passage to the sleeping-rooms of the house, which are all on the ground-floor, and to Crichton's work-room, where he is at this moment, and whither we should like to follow him, but in a play we may not, as it is out of sight. There is a large window space without a window, which, however, can be shuttered, and through this we have a view of cattle-sheds, fowl-pens, and a field of grain. It is a fine summer evening.

Tweeny is sitting there, very busy plucking the feathers off a bird and dropping them on a sheet placed for that purpose on the floor. She is trilling to herself in the lightness of her heart. We may remember that Tweeny, alone among the women, had dressed wisely for an island when they fled the yacht, and her going-away gown still adheres to her, though in fragments. A score of pieces have been added here and there as necessity compelled, and these have been patched and repatched in incongruous colours ; but, when all is said and done, it can still be maintained that Tweeny wears a skirt. She is deservedly proud of her skirt, and sometimes lends it on important occasions when approached in the proper spirit.

Some one outside has been whistling to Tweeny ; the guarded whistle which, on a less savage island, is sometimes assumed to be an indication to cook that the constable is willing, if the coast be clear. Tweeny, however, is engrossed, or perhaps she is not in the mood for a follower, so he climbs in at the window undaunted, to take her willy-nilly. He is a jolly-looking labouring man, who answers to the name of Daddy, and —— But though that may be his island name, we recognise him at once. He is Lord Loam, settled down to the new conditions, and enjoying life heartily as handy-man about the happy home. He is comfortably attired in skins. He is still stout, but all the flabbiness has dropped from him ; gone too is his pomposity ; his eye is clear, brown his skin ; he could leap a gate.

In his hands he carries an island-made concertina, and such is the exuberance of his spirits that, as he alights on the floor, he bursts into music and song, something about his being a chickety chickety chick chick, and will Tweeny please to tell him whose chickety chick is she. Retribution follows sharp. We hear a whir, as if from insufficiently oiled machinery, and over the passage door appears a placard showing the one word 'Silence.' His lordship stops, and steals to Tweeny on his tiptoes.

LORD LOAM. I thought the Gov. was out.

TWEENY. Well, you see he ain't. And if he were to catch you here idling——

> (LORD LOAM *pales. He lays aside his musical instrument and hurriedly dons an apron.* TWEENY *gives him the bird to pluck, and busies herself laying the table for dinner.*)

LORD LOAM (*softly*). What is he doing now ?

TWEENY. I think he is working out that plan for laying on hot and cold.

LORD LOAM (*proud of his master*). And he 'll manage it too. The man who could build a blacksmith's forge without tools——

TWEENY (*not less proud*). He made the tools.

LORD LOAM. Out of half a dozen rusty nails. The saw-mill, Tweeny ; the speaking-tube ; the electric lighting ; and look at the use he has made of the bits of the yacht that were washed ashore. And all in two years. He is a master I 'm proud to pluck for.

> (*He chirps happily at his work, and she regards him curiously.*)

TWEENY. Daddy, you 're of little use, but you 're a bright, cheerful creature to have about the house. (*He beams at this commendation.*) Do you ever think of old times now ? We was a bit different.

LORD LOAM (*pausing*). Circumstances alter cases.

> (*He resumes his plucking contentedly.*)

TWEENY. But, Daddy, if the chance was to come of getting back ?

LORD LOAM. I have given up bothering about it.

TWEENY. You bothered that day long ago when we saw a

N

ship passing the island.   How we all ran like crazy folk into the water, Daddy, and screamed and held out our arms.   (*They are both a little agitated.*)   But it sailed away, and we 've never seen another.

LORD LOAM.   If the electrical contrivance had been made then that we have now we could have attracted that ship's notice.   (*Their eyes rest on a mysterious apparatus that fills a corner of the hall.*)   A touch on that lever, Tweeny, and in a few moments bonfires would be blazing all round the shore.

TWEENY (*backing from the lever as if it might spring at her*). It 's the most wonderful thing he has done.

LORD LOAM (*in a reverie*).   And then—England—home !

TWEENY (*also seeing visions*).   London of a Saturday night !

LORD LOAM.   My lords, in rising once more to address this historic chamber——

TWEENY.   There was a little ham and beef shop off the Edgware Road——

(*The visions fade ; they return to the practical.*)

LORD LOAM.   Tweeny, do you think I could have an egg to my tea ?

(*At this moment a wiry, athletic figure in skins darkens the window.   He is carrying two pails, which are suspended from a pole on his shoulder, and he is ERNEST.   We should say that he is ERNEST completely changed if we were of those who hold that people change.   As he enters by the window he has heard LORD LOAM's appeal, and is perhaps justifiably indignant.*)

ERNEST.   What is that about an egg ?   Why should you have an egg ?

LORD LOAM (*with hauteur*).   That is my affair, sir.   (*With a Parthian shot as he withdraws stiffly from the room.*)   The Gov. has never put *my* head in a bucket.

ERNEST (*coming to rest on one of his buckets, and speaking with excusable pride*).   Nor mine for nearly three months.   It was only last week, Tweeny, that he said to me, ' Ernest, the water cure has worked marvels in you, and I question whether I shall require to dip you any more.' (*Complacently*) Of course that sort of thing encourages a fellow.

TWEENY (*who has now arranged the dinner-table to her satis-*

faction). I will say, Erny, I never seen a young chap more improved.

ERNEST (*gratified*). Thank you, Tweeny ; that 's very precious to me.

(*She retires to the fire to work the great bellows with her foot, and* ERNEST *turns to* TREHERNE, *who has come in looking more like a cow-boy than a clergyman. He has a small box in his hand which he tries to conceal.*)

What have you got there, John ?

TREHERNE. Don't tell anybody. It is a little present for the Gov. ; a set of razors. One for each day in the week.

ERNEST (*opening the box and examining its contents*). Shells ! He 'll like that. He likes sets of things.

TREHERNE (*in a guarded voice*). Have you noticed that ?

ERNEST. Rather.

TREHERNE. He is becoming a bit magnificent in his ideas.

ERNEST (*huskily*). John, it sometimes gives me the creeps.

TREHERNE (*making sure that* TWEENY *is out of hearing*). What do you think of that brilliant robe he got the girls to make for him ?

ERNEST (*uncomfortably*). I think he looks too regal in it.

TREHERNE. Regal ! I sometimes fancy that is why he is so fond of wearing it. (*Practically*) Well, I must take these down to the grindstone and put an edge on them.

ERNEST (*button-holing him*). I say, John, I want a word with you.

TREHERNE. Well ?

ERNEST (*become suddenly diffident*). Dash it all, you know, you 're a clergyman.

TREHERNE. One of the best things the Gov. has done is to insist that none of you forget it.

ERNEST (*taking his courage in his hands*). Then—would you, John ?

TREHERNE. What ?

ERNEST (*wistfully*). Officiate at a marriage ceremony, John ?

TREHERNE (*slowly*). Now, that is really odd.

ERNEST. Odd ? Seems to me it 's natural. And whatever is natural, John, is right.

TREHERNE. I mean that same question has been put to me to-day already.

ERNEST (*eagerly*).   By one of the women ?

TREHERNE.   Oh no ; they all put it to me long ago.   This was by the Gov. himself.

ERNEST.   By Jove !   (*Admiringly*) I say, John, what an observant beggar he is.

TREHERNE.   Ah !   You fancy he was thinking of you ?

ERNEST.   I do not hesitate to affirm, John, that he has seen the love-light in my eyes.   You answered——

TREHERNE.   I said Yes, I thought it would be my duty to officiate if called upon.

ERNEST.   You 're a brick.

TREHERNE (*still pondering*).   But I wonder whether he *was* thinking of you ?

ERNEST.   Make your mind easy about that.

TREHERNE.   Well, my best wishes.   Agatha is a very fine girl.

ERNEST.   Agatha ?   What made you think it was Agatha ?

TREHERNE.   Man alive, you told me all about it soon after we were wrecked.

ERNEST.   Pooh !   Agatha is all very well in her way, John, but I am flying at bigger game.

TREHERNE.   Ernest, which is it ?

ERNEST.   Tweeny, of course.

TREHERNE.   Tweeny ?   (*Reprovingly*) Ernest, I hope her cooking has nothing to do with this.

ERNEST (*with dignity*).   Her cooking has very little to do with it.

TREHERNE.   But does she return your affection ?

ERNEST (*simply*).   Yes, John, I believe I may say so.   I am unworthy of her, but I think I have touched her heart.

TREHERNE (*with a sigh*).   Some people seem to have all the luck.   As you know, Catherine won't look at me.

ERNEST.   I 'm sorry, John.

TREHERNE.   It 's my deserts ; I 'm a second eleven sort of chap.   Well, my heartiest good wishes, Ernest.

ERNEST.   Thank you, John.   How is the little black pig to-day ?

TREHERNE (*departing*).   He has begun to eat again.

(*After a moment's reflection* ERNEST *calls to* TWEENY.)

ERNEST.   Are you very busy, Tweeny ?

TWEENY (*coming to him good-naturedly*).   There is always work to do ; but if you want me, Ernest——

ERNEST.   There is something I should like to say to you if you could spare me a moment.

TWEENY.   Willingly.   What is it ?

ERNEST.   What an ass I used to be, Tweeny.

TWEENY (*tolerantly*).   Oh, let bygones be bygones.

ERNEST (*sincerely, and at his very best*).   I 'm no great shakes even now.   But listen to this, Tweeny ; I have known many women, but until I knew you I never knew any woman.

TWEENY (*to whose uneducated ears this sounds dangerously like an epigram*).   Take care—the bucket.

ERNEST (*hurriedly*).   I didn't mean it in that way.   (*He goes chivalrously on his knees.*)   Ah, Tweeny, I don't undervalue the bucket, but what I want to say now is that the sweet refinement of a dear girl has done more for me than any bucket could do.

TWEENY (*with large eyes*).   Are you offering to walk out with me, Erny ?

ERNEST (*passionately*).   More than that.   I want to build a little house for you—in the sunny glade down by Porcupine Creek.   I want to make chairs for you and tables ; and knives and forks, and a sideboard for you.

TWEENY (*who is fond of language*).   I like to hear you. (*Eyeing him*) Would there be any one in the house except myself, Ernest ?

ERNEST (*humbly*).   Not often ; but just occasionally there would be your adoring husband.

TWEENY (*decisively*).   It won't do, Ernest.

ERNEST (*pleading*).   It isn't as if I should be much there.

TWEENY.   I know, I know ; but I don't love you, Ernest, I 'm that sorry.

ERNEST (*putting his case cleverly*).   Twice a week I should be away altogether—at the dam.   On the other days you would never see me from breakfast time to supper.

(*With the self-abnegation of the true lover.*) If you like I 'll even go fishing on Sundays.

TWEENY.   It 's no use, Erny.

ERNEST (*rising manfully*).   Thank you, Tweeny ; it can't be helped.   (*Then he remembers.*)   Tweeny, we shall be disappointing the Gov.

TWEENY (*quaking*).   What 's that ?

ERNEST.   He wanted us to marry.

TWEENY (*blankly*).   You and me ? the Gov. !   (*Her head droops woefully.   From without is heard the whistling of a happier spirit, and* TWEENY *draws herself up fiercely*.)   That 's her ; that 's the thing what has stole his heart from me.

> (*A stalwart youth appears at the window, so handsome and tingling with vitality that, glad to depose* CRICHTON, *we cry thankfully, ' The hero at last.'   But it is not the hero ; it is the heroine.   This splendid boy, clad in skins, is what Nature has done for* LADY MARY.   *She carries bow and arrows and a blow-pipe, and over her shoulder is a fat buck, which she drops with a cry of triumph.   Forgetting to enter demurely, she leaps through the window.*)

(*Sourly*) Drat you, Polly, why don't you wipe your feet ?

LADY MARY (*good-naturedly*).   Come, Tweeny, be nice to me.   It 's a splendid buck.

> (*But* TWEENY *shakes her off, and retires to the kitchen fire.*)

ERNEST.   Where did you get it ?

LADY MARY (*gaily*).   I sighted a herd near Penguin's Creek, but had to creep round Silver Lake to get to windward of them. However, they spotted me and then the fun began.   There was nothing for it but to try and run them down, so I singled out a fat buck and away we went down the shore of the lake, up the valley of rolling stones ;   he doubled into Brawling River and took to the water, but I swam after him ;   the river is only half a mile broad there, but it runs strong.   He went spinning down the rapids, down I went in pursuit ;   he clambered ashore, I clambered ashore ;   away we tore helter-skelter up the hill and down again. I lost him in the marshes, got on his track again near Bread Fruit Wood, and brought him down with an arrow in Firefly Grove.

TWEENY (*staring at her*).   Aren't you tired ?

LADY MARY.   Tired !   It was gorgeous.

> (*She runs up a ladder and deposits her weapons on the joists. She is whistling again.*)

TWEENY (*snapping*).   I can't abide a woman whistling.

LADY MARY (*indifferently*).   I like it.

TWEENY (*stamping her foot*).   Drop it, Polly, I tell you.

LADY MARY.   I won't.   I 'm as good as you are.

> (*They are facing each other defiantly.*)

ERNEST (*shocked*). Is this necessary ? Think how it would pain *him*.

(LADY MARY'S *eyes take a new expression. We see them soft for the first time.*)

LADY MARY (*contritely*). Tweeny, I beg your pardon. If my whistling annoys you, I shall try to cure myself of it.

(*Instead of calming* TWEENY, *this floods her face in tears.*) Why, how can that hurt you, Tweeny dear ?

TWEENY. Because I can't make you lose your temper.

LADY MARY (*divinely*). Indeed, I often do. Would that I were nicer to everybody.

TWEENY. There you are again. (*Large-eyed*) What makes you want to be so nice, Polly ?

LADY MARY (*with fervour*). Only thankfulness, Tweeny. (*She exults.*) It is such fun to be alive.

(*So also seem to think* CATHERINE *and* AGATHA, *who bounce in with fishing-rods and creel. They, too, are in manly attire.*)

CATHERINE. We've got some ripping fish for the Gov.'s dinner. Are we in time ? We ran all the way.

TWEENY (*tartly*). You'll please to cook them yourself, Kitty, and look sharp about it.

(*She retires to her hearth, where* AGATHA *follows her.*)

AGATHA (*yearning*). Has the Gov. decided who is to wait upon him to-day ?

CATHERINE (*who is cleaning her fish*). It's my turn.

AGATHA (*hotly*). I don't see that.

TWEENY (*with bitterness*). It's to be neither of you, Aggy ; he wants Polly again.

(LADY MARY *is unable to resist a joyous whistle.*)

AGATHA (*jealously*). Polly, you toad.

(*But they cannot make* LADY MARY *angry.*)

TWEENY (*storming*). How dare you look so happy ?

LADY MARY (*willing to embrace her*). I wish, Tweeny, there was anything I could do to make you happy also.

TWEENY. Me ! Oh, I'm happy. (*She remembers* ERNEST, *whom it is easy to forget on an island.*) I've just had a proposal, I tell you.

(LADY MARY *is shaken at last, and her sisters with her.*)

AGATHA. A proposal ?

CATHERINE (*going white*). Not—not——
(*She dare not say his name.*)

ERNEST (*with singular modesty*). You needn't be alarmed : it was only me.

LADY MARY (*relieved*). Oh, you !

AGATHA (*happy again*). Ernest, you dear, I got such a shock.

CATHERINE. It was only Ernest (*showing him her fish in thankfulness*). They are beautifully fresh ; come and help me to cook them.

ERNEST (*with simple dignity*). Do you mind if I don't cook fish to-night ? (*She does not mind in the least. They have all forgotten him. A lark is singing in three hearts.*) I think you might all be a little sorry for a chap. (*But they are not even sorry, and he addresses* AGATHA *in these winged words*) I 'm particularly disappointed in you, Aggy ; seeing that I was half engaged to you, I think you might have had the good feeling to be a little more hurt.

AGATHA. Oh, bother.

ERNEST (*summing up the situation in so far as it affects himself*). I shall now go and lie down for a bit.

(*He retires coldly but unregretted.* LADY MARY *approaches* TWEENY *with her most insinuating smile.*)

LADY MARY. Tweeny, as the Gov. has chosen me to wait on him, please may I have the loan of *it* again ?
(*The reference made with such charming delicacy is evidently to* TWEENY'S *skirt.*)

TWEENY (*doggedly*). No, you mayn't.

AGATHA (*supporting* TWEENY). Don't you give it to her.

LADY MARY (*still trying sweet persuasion*). You know quite well that he prefers to be waited on in a skirt.

TWEENY. I don't care. Get one for yourself.

LADY MARY. It is the only one on the island.

TWEENY. And it 's mine.

LADY MARY (*an aristocrat after all*). Tweeny, give me that skirt directly.

CATHERINE. Don't.

TWEENY. I won't.

LADY MARY (*clearing for action*). I shall make you.

TWEENY. I should like to see you try.

(*An unseemly fracas appears to be inevitable, but something*

*happens.   The whir is again heard, and the notice is dis-
played ' Dogs delight to bark and bite.'   Its effect is in-
stantaneous and cheering.   The ladies look at each other
guiltily and immediately proceed on tiptoe to their duties.
These are all concerned with the master's dinner.   CATH-
ERINE attends to his fish.   AGATHA fills a quaint toast-rack
and brings the menu, which is written on a shell.   LADY
MARY twists a wreath of green leaves around her head, and
places a flower beside the master's plate.   TWEENY signs
that all is ready, and she and the younger sisters retire into
the kitchen, closing the screen that separates it from the
rest of the room.   LADY MARY beats a tom-tom, which is
the dinner-bell.   She then gently works a punkah, which we
have not hitherto observed, and stands at attention.   No
doubt she is in hopes that the Gov. will enter into conversation with her, but she is too good a parlour-maid to let her
hopes appear in her face.   We may watch her manner with
complete approval.   There is not one of us who would not
give her £26 a year.*

*The master comes in quietly, a book in his hand, still the only
book on the island, for he has not thought it worth while to
build a printing-press.   His dress is not noticeably different
from that of the others, the skins are similar, but perhaps
these are a trifle more carefully cut or he carries them better.
One sees somehow that he has changed for his evening meal.
There is an odd suggestion of a dinner jacket about his doe-
skin coat.   It is, perhaps, too grave a face for a man of
thirty-two, as if he were overmuch immersed in affairs, yet
there is a sunny smile left to lighten it at times and bring back
its youth ; perhaps too intellectual a face to pass as strictly
handsome, not sufficiently suggestive of oats.   His tall figure
is very straight, slight rather than thick-set, but nobly
muscular.   His big hands, firm and hard with labour
though they be, are finely shaped—note the fingers so much
more tapered, the nails better tended than those of his
domestics ; they are one of many indications that he is of a
superior breed.   Such signs, as has often been pointed out,
are infallible.   A romantic figure, too.   One can easily see
why the women-folks of this strong man's house both adore
and fear him.*

He does not seem to notice who is waiting on him to-night, but inclines his head slightly to whoever it is, as she takes her place at the back of his chair. LADY MARY *respectfully places the menu-shell before him, and he glances at it.*)

CRICHTON.   Clear, please.

(LADY MARY *knocks on the screen, and a serving hutch in it opens, through which* TWEENY *offers two soup plates.* LADY MARY *selects the clear, and the aperture is closed. She works the punkah while the master partakes of the soup.*)

CRICHTON (*who always gives praise where it is due*).   An excellent soup, Polly, but still a trifle too rich.

LADY MARY.   Thank *you*.

(*The next course is the fish, and while it is being passed through the hutch we have a glimpse of three jealous women.* LADY MARY'S *movements are so deft and noiseless that any observant spectator can see that she was born to wait at table.*)

CRICHTON (*unbending as he eats*).   Polly, you are a very smart girl.

LADY MARY (*bridling, but naturally gratified*).   La !

CRICHTON (*smiling*).   And I 'm not the first you 've heard it from, I 'll swear.

LADY MARY (*wriggling*).   Oh Gov. !

CRICHTON.   Got any followers on the island, Polly ?

LADY MARY (*tossing her head*).   Certainly not.

CRICHTON.   I thought that perhaps John or Ernest——

LADY MARY (*tilting her nose*).   I don't say that it 's for want of asking.

CRICHTON (*emphatically*).   I 'm sure it isn't.

(*Perhaps he thinks he has gone too far.*)
You may clear.

(*Flushed with pleasure, she puts before him a bird and vegetables, sees that his beaker is filled with wine, and returns to the punkah. She would love to continue their conversation, but it is for him to decide. For a time he seems to have forgotten her.*)

CRICHTON (*presently*).   Did you lose any arrows to-day ?

LADY MARY.   Only one in Firefly Grove.

CRICHTON.   You were as far as that ?   How did you get across the Black Gorge ?

LADY MARY.   I went across on the rope.

CRICHTON.   Hand over hand ?

LADY MARY (*swelling at the implied praise*).   I wasn't in the least dizzy.

CRICHTON (*moved*).   You brave girl !   (*He sits back in his chair a little agitated.*)   But never do that again.

LADY MARY (*pouting*).   It is such fun, Gov.

CRICHTON (*decisively*).   I forbid it.

LADY MARY (*the little rebel*).   I shall.

CRICHTON (*surprised*).   Polly !

(*He signs to her sharply to step forward, but for a moment she holds back petulantly, and even when she does come it is less obediently than like a naughty, sulky child.   Nevertheless, with the forbearance that is characteristic of the man, he addresses her with grave gentleness rather than severely.*)

You must do as I tell you, you know.

LADY MARY (*strangely passionate*).   I won't.

CRICHTON (*smiling at her fury*).   We shall see.   Frown at me, Polly ; there, you do it at once.   Clench your little fists, stamp your feet, bite your ribbons——

(*A student of women, or at least of this woman, he knows that she is about to do those things, and thus she seems to do them to order.   LADY MARY screws up her face like a baby and cries.   He is immediately kind.*)

You child of Nature ; was it cruel of me to wish to save you from harm ?

LADY MARY (*drying her eyes*).   I 'm an ungracious wretch. Oh Gov., I don't try half hard enough to please you.   I 'm even wearing—(*she looks down sadly*)—when I know you prefer *it*.

CRICHTON (*thoughtfully*).   I admit I do prefer *it*.   Perhaps I am a little old-fashioned in these matters.

(*Her tears again threaten.*)

Ah, don't, Polly ; that 's nothing.

LADY MARY.   If I could only please you, Gov.

CRICHTON (*slowly*).   You do please me, child, very much— (*he half rises*)—very much indeed.   (*If he meant to say more he checks himself.   He looks at his plate.*)   No more, thank you.

(The simple island meal is soon ended, save for the walnuts and the wine, and CRICHTON *is too busy a man to linger long over them. But he is a stickler for etiquette, and the table is cleared charmingly, though with dispatch, before they are placed before him.* LADY MARY *is an artist with the crumb-brush, and there are few arts more delightful to watch. Dusk has come sharply, and she turns on the electric light. It awakens* CRICHTON *from a reverie in which he has been regarding her.)*

CRICHTON.   Polly, there is only one thing about you that I don't quite like.

(She looks up, making a moue, *if that can be said of one who so well knows her place. He explains.)*
That action of the hands.

LADY MARY.   What do I do ?

CRICHTON.   This—like one washing them.   I have noticed that the others tend to do it also.   It seems odd.

LADY MARY *(archly).*   Oh Gov., have you forgotten ?

CRICHTON.   What ?

LADY MARY.   That once upon a time a certain other person did that ?

CRICHTON *(groping).*   You mean myself ?   *(She nods, and he shudders.)*   Horrible !

LADY MARY *(afraid she has hurt him).*   You haven't for a very long time.   Perhaps it is natural to servants.

CRICHTON.   That must be it.   *(He rises.)*   Polly !   *(She looks up expectantly, but he only sighs and turns away.)*

LADY MARY *(gently).*   You sighed, Gov.

CRICHTON.   Did I ?   I was thinking.   *(He paces the room and then turns to her agitatedly, yet with control over his agitation. There is some mournfulness in his voice.)*   I have always tried to do the right thing on this island.   Above all, Polly, I want to do the right thing by you.

LADY MARY *(with shining eyes).*   How we all trust you.   That is your reward, Gov.

CRICHTON *(who is having a fight with himself).*   And now I want a greater reward.   Is it fair to you ?   Am I playing the game ?   Bill Crichton would like always to play the game.   If we were in England——

(He pauses so long that she breaks in softly.)

LADY MARY.   We know now that we shall never see England again.

CRICHTON.   I am thinking of two people whom neither of us has seen for a long time—Lady Mary Lasenby, and one Crichton, a butler.

(He says the last word bravely, a word he once loved, though it is the most horrible of all words to him now.)

LADY MARY.   That cold, haughty, insolent girl.   Gov., look around you and forget them both.

CRICHTON.   I had nigh forgotten them.   He has had a chance, Polly—that butler—in these two years of becoming a man, and he has tried to take it.   There have been many failures, but there has been some success, and with it I have let the past drop off me, and turned my back on it.   That butler seems a far-away figure to me now, and not myself.   I hail him, but we scarce know each other.   If I am to bring him back it can only be done by force, for in my soul he is now abhorrent to me. But if I thought it best for you I 'd haul him back ; I swear as an honest man, I would bring him back with all his obsequious ways and deferential airs, and let you see the man you call your Gov. melt for ever into him who was your servant.

LADY MARY *(shivering)*.   You hurt me.   You say these things, but you say them like a king.   To me it is the past that was not real.

CRICHTON *(too grandly)*.   A king !   I sometimes feel——

(For a moment the yellow light gleams in his green eyes. We remember suddenly what TREHERNE and ERNEST said about his regal look.   He checks himself.)

I say it harshly, it is so hard to say, and all the time there is another voice within me crying——   *(He stops.)*

LADY MARY *(trembling but not afraid)*.   If it is the voice of Nature——

CRICHTON *(strongly)*.   I know it to be the voice of Nature.

LADY MARY *(in a whisper)*.   Then, if you want to say it very much, Gov., please say it to Polly Lasenby.

CRICHTON *(again in the grip of an idea)*.   A king !   Polly, some people hold that the soul but leaves one human tenement for another, and so lives on through all the ages.   I have occasionally thought of late that, in some past existence, I may have been a king. It has all come to me so naturally, not as if I had to work it out, but—as—if—I—remembered.

> 'Or ever the knightly years were gone,
> With the old world to the grave,
> I was a *king* in Babylon,
> And you were a Christian slave.'

It may have been ; you hear me, it may have been.

LADY MARY (*who is as one fascinated*). It may have been.

CRICHTON. I am lord over all. They are but hewers of wood and drawers of water for me. These shores are mine. Why should I hesitate ; I have no longer any doubt. I do believe I am doing the right thing. Dear Polly, I have grown to love you ; are you afraid to mate with me ? (*She rocks her arms ; no words will come from her.*)

> 'I was a king in Babylon,
> And you were a Christian slave.'

LADY MARY (*bewitched*). You are the most wonderful man I have ever known, and I am not afraid.

(*He takes her to him with mastership. Presently he is seated, and she is at his feet looking up adoringly in his face. As the tension relaxes she speaks with a smile.*)

I want you to tell me—every woman likes to know—when was the first time you thought me nicer than the others ?

CRICHTON (*stroking her hair*). I think a year ago. We were chasing goats on the Big Slopes, and you out-distanced us all ; you were the first of our party to run a goat down ; I was proud of you that day.

LADY MARY (*blushing with pleasure*). Oh Gov., I only did it to please you. Everything I have done has been out of the desire to please you. (*Suddenly anxious*) If I thought that in taking a wife from among us you were imperilling your dignity——

CRICHTON (*decisively*). Have no fear of that, dear. I have thought it all out. The wife, Polly, always takes the same position as the husband.

LADY MARY. But I am so unworthy. It was sufficient to me that I should be allowed to wait on you at that table.

CRICHTON. You shall wait on me no longer. At whatever

table I sit, Polly, you shall soon sit there also. (*Boyishly*) Come, let us try what it will be like.

LADY MARY. As your servant at your feet.

CRICHTON. No, as my consort by my side.

(*They are sitting thus when the hatch is again opened and coffee offered. But* LADY MARY *is no longer there to receive it. Her sisters peep through in consternation. In vain they rattle the cup and saucer.* AGATHA *brings the coffee to* CRICHTON.)

CRICHTON (*forgetting for the moment that it is not a month hence*). Help your mistress first, girl. (*Three women are bereft of speech, but he does not notice it. He addresses* CATHERINE *vaguely.*) Are you a good girl, Kitty?

CATHERINE (*when she finds her tongue*). I try to be, Gov.

CRICHTON (*still more vaguely*). That's right.

(*He takes command of himself again, and signs to them to sit down.* ERNEST *comes in cheerily, but finding* CRICHTON *here is suddenly weak. He subsides on a chair, wondering what has happened.*)

CRICHTON (*surveying him*). Ernest. (ERNEST *rises.*) You are becoming a little slovenly in your dress, Ernest; I don't like it.

ERNEST (*respectfully*). Thank you. (ERNEST *sits again.* DADDY *and* TREHERNE *arrive.*)

CRICHTON. Daddy, I want you.

LORD LOAM (*gloomily*). Is it because I forgot to clean out the dam?

CRICHTON (*encouragingly*). No, no. (*He pours some wine into a goblet.*) A glass of wine with you, Daddy.

LORD LOAM (*hastily*). Your health, Gov.

(*He is about to drink, but the master checks him.*)

CRICHTON. And hers. Daddy, this lady has done me the honour to promise to be my wife.

LORD LOAM (*astounded*). Polly!

CRICHTON (*a little perturbed*). I ought first to have asked your consent. I deeply regret—but Nature; may I hope I have your approval?

LORD LOAM. May you, Gov.? (*Delighted*) Rather! Polly!

(*He puts his proud arms round her.*)

TREHERNE.   We all congratulate you, Gov., most heartily.

ERNEST.   Long life to you both, sir.

(There is much shaking of hands, all of which is sincere.)

TREHERNE.   When will it be, Gov. ?

CRICHTON *(after turning to* LADY MARY, *who whispers to him).* As soon as the bridal skirt can be prepared. *(His manner has been most indulgent, and without the slightest suggestion of patronage.   But he knows it is best for all that he should keep his place, and that his presence hampers them.)*   My friends, I thank you for your good wishes, I thank you all.   And now, perhaps you would like me to leave you to yourselves.   Be joyous.   Let there be song and dance to-night.   Polly, I shall take my coffee in the parlour—you understand.

(He retires with pleasant dignity.   Immediately there is a rush of two girls at LADY MARY.)

LADY MARY.   Oh, oh ! Father, they are pinching me.

LORD LOAM *(taking her under his protection).*   Agatha, Catherine, never presume to pinch your sister again.   On the other hand, she may pinch you henceforth as much as ever she chooses.

(In the meantime TWEENY *is weeping softly, and the two are not above using her as a weapon.)*

CATHERINE.   Poor Tweeny, it 's a shame.

AGATHA.   After he had almost promised *you.*

TWEENY *(loyally turning on them).*   No, he never did.   He was always honourable as could be.   'Twas me as was too vulgar. Don't you dare say a word agin that man.

ERNEST *(to* LORD LOAM).   You 'll get a lot of tit-bits out of this, Daddy.

LORD LOAM.   That 's what I was thinking.

ERNEST *(plunged in thought).*   I dare say *I* shall have to clean out the dam now.

LORD LOAM *(heartlessly).*   I dare say.

(His gay old heart makes him again proclaim that he is a chickety chick.   He seizes the concertina.)

TREHERNE *(eagerly).*   That 's the proper spirit.

(He puts his arm round CATHERINE, *and in another moment they are all dancing to Daddy's music.   Never were people happier on an island.   A moment's pause is presently created by the return of* CRICHTON, *wearing the wonderful robe of*

which we have already had dark mention.   Never has he looked more regal, never perhaps felt so regal.   We need not grudge him the one foible of his rule, for it is all coming to an end.)

CRICHTON (*graciously, seeing them hesitate*).   No, no ; I am delighted to see you all so happy.   Go on.

TREHERNE.   We don't like to before you, Gov.

CRICHTON (*his last order*).   It is my wish.

(*The merrymaking is resumed, and soon* CRICHTON *himself joins in the dance.   It is when the fun is at its fastest and most furious that all stop abruptly as if turned to stone. They have heard the boom of a gun.   Presently they are alive again.* ERNEST *leaps to the window.*)

TREHERNE (*huskily*).   It was a ship's gun ! (*They turn to* CRICHTON *for confirmation ; even in that hour they turn to* CRICHTON.)   Gov. ?

CRICHTON.   Yes.

(*In another moment* LADY MARY *and* LORD LOAM *are alone.*)

LADY MARY (*seeing that her father is unconcerned*).   Father, you heard.

LORD LOAM (*placidly*).   Yes, my child.

LADY MARY (*alarmed by his unnatural calmness*).   But it was a gun, father.

LORD LOAM (*looking an old man now, and shuddering a little*). Yes—a gun—I have often heard it.   It's only a dream, you know ;   why don't we go on dancing ?

(*She takes his hands, which have gone cold.*)

LADY MARY.   Father.   Don't you see, they have all rushed down to the beach ?   Come.

LORD LOAM.   Rushed down to the beach ;   yes, always that —I often dream it.

LADY MARY.   Come, father, come.

LORD LOAM.   Only a dream, my poor girl.

(CRICHTON *presently returns.   He is pale but firm.*)

CRICHTON.   We can see lights within a mile of the shore— a great ship.

LORD LOAM.   A ship—always a ship.

LADY MARY.   Father, this is no dream.

LORD LOAM (*looking timidly at* CRICHTON).   It's a dream, isn't it ?   There's no ship ?

CRICHTON (*soothing him with a touch*).   You are awake, Daddy, and there is a ship.

LORD LOAM (*clutching him*).   You are not deceiving me ?

CRICHTON.   It is the truth.

LORD LOAM (*reeling*).   True ?—a ship—at iast !
(*He goes after the others pitifully.*)

CRICHTON (*quietly*).   There is a small boat between it and the island ; they must have sent it ashore for water.

LADY MARY.   Coming in ?

CRICHTON.   No.   That gun must have been a signal to recall it.   It is going back.   They can't hear our cries.

LADY MARY (*pressing her temples*).   Going away !   So near— so near.   (*Almost to herself*) I think I 'm glad.

CRICHTON (*cheerily*).   Have no fear.   I shall bring them back.
(*He goes towards the table on which is the electrical apparatus.*)

LADY MARY (*standing on guard as it were between him and the table*).   What are you going to do ?

CRICHTON.   To fire the beacons.

LADY MARY.   Stop !   (*She faces him.*)   Don't you see what it means ?

CRICHTON (*firmly*).   It means that our life on the island has come to a natural end.

LADY MARY (*huskily*).   Gov., let the ship go.

CRICHTON.   The old man—you saw what it means to him.

LADY MARY.   But I am afraid.

CRICHTON (*adoringly*).   Dear Polly.

LADY MARY.   Gov., let the ship go.   (*She clings to him, but though it is his death sentence he loosens her hold*).

CRICHTON.   Bill Crichton has got to play the game.
(*He pulls the levers.   Soon through the window one of the beacons is seen flaring red.   There is a long pause.   Alarms and excursions outside.   ERNEST is the first to reappear.*)

ERNEST.   Polly, Gov., the boat has turned back.   (*He is gone.   There is more disturbance.   He returns.*)   They are English sailors ; they have landed !   We are rescued, I tell you, rescued !

LADY MARY (*wanly*).   Is it anything to make so great a to-do about ?

ERNEST (*staring*).   Eh ?

LADY MARY.　Have we not been happy here ?

ERNEST.　Happy ? lord, yes.

LADY MARY (*catching hold of his sleeve*).　Ernest, we must never forget all that the Gov. has done for us.

ERNEST (*stoutly*).　Forget it ?　The man who could forget it would be a selfish wretch and a—— But I say, this makes a difference !

LADY MARY (*quickly*).　No, it doesn't.

ERNEST (*his mind tottering*).　A mighty difference !

(*The others come running in, some weeping with joy, others boisterous. For some time dementia rules. Soon we see bluejackets gazing through the window at the curious scene.* LORD LOAM *comes accompanied by a naval officer, whom he is continually shaking by the hand.*)

LORD LOAM.　And here, sir, is our little home.　Let me thank you in the name of us all, again and again and again.

OFFICER.　Very proud, my lord.　It is indeed an honour to have been able to assist so distinguished a gentleman as Lord Loam.

LORD LOAM.　A glorious, glorious day.　I shall show you our other rooms.　Come, my pets.　Come, Crichton.

(*He has not meant to be cruel. He does not know he has said it. It is the old life that has come back to him. They all go. All leave* CRICHTON *except* LADY MARY.)

LADY MARY (*stretching out her arms to him*).　Dear Gov., I will never give you up.

(*There is a salt smile on his face as he shakes his head to her. He lets the cloak slip to the ground. She will not take this for an answer ; again her arms go out to him. Then comes the great renunciation. By an effort of will he ceases to be an erect figure ; he has the humble bearing of a servant. His hands come together as if he were washing them.*)

CRICHTON (*it is the speech of his life*).　My lady.

(*She goes away. There is none to salute him now, unless we do it.*)

ACT IV

THE OTHER ISLAND

SOME months have elapsed, and we have again the honour of waiting upon Lord Loam in his London home. It is the room of the first act, but with a new scheme of decoration, for on the walls are exhibited many interesting trophies from the island, such as skins, stuffed birds, and weapons of the chase, labelled 'Shot by Lord Loam,' 'Hon. Ernest Woolley's Blowpipe,' etc. There are also two large glass cases containing other odds and ends, including, curiously enough, the bucket in which Ernest was first dipped, but there is no label calling attention to the incident.

It is not yet time to dress for dinner, and his lordship is on a couch, hastily yet furtively cutting the pages of a new book. With him are his two younger daughters and his nephew, and they also are engaged in literary pursuits ; that is to say, the ladies are eagerly but furtively reading the evening papers, on copies of which Ernest is sitting complacently but furtively, doling them out as called for. Note the frequent use of the word 'furtive.' It implies that they are very reluctant to be discovered by their butler, say, at their otherwise delightful task.

AGATHA (*reading aloud, with emphasis on the wrong words*). 'In conclusion, we most heartily congratulate the Hon. Ernest Woolley. This book of his, regarding the adventures of himself and his brave companions on a desert isle, stirs the heart like a trumpet.'

(*Evidently the book referred to is the one in* LORD LOAM'S *hands.*)

ERNEST. Here is another.

CATHERINE (*reading*). 'From the first to the last of Mr. Woolley's engrossing pages it is evident that he was an ideal man to be wrecked with, and a true hero.' (*Half-admiringly*) Ernest !

404

ERNEST (*calmly*). That's how it strikes *them*, you know. Here's another one.

AGATHA (*reading*). 'There are many kindly references to the two servants who were wrecked with the family, and Mr. Woolley pays the butler a glowing tribute in a footnote.'

(*Some one coughs uncomfortably.*)

LORD LOAM (*who has been searching the index for the letter L*). Excellent, excellent. At the same time I must say, Ernest, that the whole book is about yourself.

ERNEST (*genially*). As the author——

LORD LOAM. Certainly, certainly. Still, you know, as a peer of the realm—(*with dignity*)—I think, Ernest, you might have given me one of your adventures.

ERNEST. I say it was you who taught us how to obtain a fire by rubbing two pieces of stick together.

LORD LOAM (*beaming*). Do you, do you? I call that very handsome. What page?

(*Here the door opens, and the well-bred CRICHTON enters with the evening papers as subscribed for by the house. Those we have already seen have perhaps been introduced by ERNEST 'furtively.' Every one except the intruder is immediately self-conscious, and when he withdraws there is a general sigh of relief. They pounce on the new papers. ERNEST evidently gets a shock from one, which he casts contemptuously on the floor.*)

AGATHA (*more fortunate*). Father, see page 81. 'It was a tiger-cat,' says Mr. Woolley, 'of the largest size. Death stared Lord Loam in the face, but he never flinched.'

LORD LOAM (*searching his book eagerly*). Page 81.

AGATHA. 'With presence of mind only equalled by his courage, he fixed an arrow in his bow.'

LORD LOAM. Thank you, Ernest ; thank you, my boy.

AGATHA. 'Unfortunately he missed.'

LORD LOAM. Eh ?

AGATHA. 'But by great good luck I heard his cries '——

LORD LOAM. My cries ?

AGATHA. —'and rushing forward with drawn knife, I stabbed the monster to the heart.'

(LORD LOAM *shuts his book with a pettish slam. There might be a scene here were it not that* CRICHTON *reappears*

*and goes to one of the glass cases.   All are at once on the
alert, and his lordship is particularly sly.*)

LORD LOAM.   Anything in the papers, Catherine ?

CATHERINE.   No, father, nothing—nothing at all.

ERNEST (*it pops out as of yore*).   The papers !   The papers
are guides that tell us what we ought to do, and then we don't
do it.

> (CRICHTON *having opened the glass case has taken out the
> bucket, and* ERNEST, *looking round for applause, sees him
> carrying it off, and is undone.   For a moment of time he
> forgets that he is no longer on the island, and with a sigh he
> is about to follow* CRICHTON *and the bucket to a retired spot.
> The door closes, and* ERNEST *comes to himself.*)

LORD LOAM (*uncomfortably*).   I told him to take it away.

ERNEST.   I thought—(*he wipes his brow*)—I shall go and
dress.

(*He goes.*)

CATHERINE.   Father, it 's awful having Crichton here.
It 's like living on tiptoe.

LORD LOAM (*gloomily*).   While he is here we are sitting on a
volcano.

AGATHA.   How mean of you !   I am sure he has only
stayed on with us to—to help us through.   It would have
looked so suspicious if he had gone at once.

CATHERINE (*revelling in the worst*).   But suppose Lady
Brocklehurst were to get at him and pump him.   She is the
most terrifying, suspicious old creature in England ;   and
Crichton simply can't tell a lie.

LORD LOAM.   My dear, that is the volcano to which I was
referring.   (*He has evidently something to communicate.*)   It is
all Mary's fault.   She said to me yesterday that she would
break her engagement with Brocklehurst unless I told him
about—you know what.

(*All conjure up the vision of* CRICHTON.)

AGATHA.   Is she mad ?

LORD LOAM.   She calls it common honesty.

CATHERINE.   Father, have you told him ?

LORD LOAM (*heavily*).   She thinks I have, but I couldn't.
She is sure to find out to-night.

(*Unconsciously he leans on the island concertina, which he has perhaps been lately showing to an interviewer as something made for* TWEENY.   *It squeaks, and they all jump.*)

CATHERINE.   It is like a bird of ill-omen.

LORD LOAM (*vindictively*).   I must have it taken away ; it has done that twice.

(LADY MARY *comes in.   She is in evening dress.   Undoubtedly she meant to sail in, but she forgets, and despite her garments it is a manly entrance.   She is properly ashamed of herself.   She tries again, and has an encouraging success.   She indicates to her sisters that she wishes to be alone with papa.*)

AGATHA.   All right, but we know what it 's about.   Come along, Kit.

(*They go.*   LADY MARY *thoughtlessly sits like a boy, and again corrects herself.   She addresses her father, but he is in a brown study, and she seeks to draw his attention by whistling.   This troubles them both.*)

LADY MARY.   How horrid of me !

LORD LOAM (*depressed*).   If you would try to remember——

LADY MARY (*sighing*).   I do ; but there are so many things to remember.

LORD LOAM (*sympathetically*).   There are—— (*In a whisper*) Do you know, Mary, I constantly find myself secreting hairpins.

LADY MARY.   I find it so difficult to go up steps one at a time.

LORD LOAM.   I was dining with half a dozen members of our party last Thursday, Mary, and they were so eloquent that I couldn't help wondering all the time how many of their heads *he* would have put in the bucket.

LADY MARY.   I use so many of his phrases.   And my appetite is so scandalous.   Father, I usually have a chop before we sit down to dinner.

LORD LOAM.   As for my clothes—— (*wriggling*).   My dear, you can't think how irksome collars are to me nowadays

LADY MARY.   They can't be half such an annoyance, father, as——

(*She looks dolefully at her skirt.*)

LORD LOAM (*hurriedly*).   Quite so—quite so.   You have dressed early to-night, Mary.

LADY MARY.   That reminds me ; I had a note from Brocklehurst saying that he would come a few minutes before his mother as——as he wanted to have a talk with me. He didn't say what about, but of course we know.

(*His lordship fidgets.*)

(*With feeling*) It was good of you to tell him, father. Oh, it is horrible to me—— (*covering her face*). It seemed so natural at the time.

LORD LOAM (*petulantly*). Never again make use of that word in this house, Mary.

LADY MARY (*with an effort*). Father, Brocklehurst has been so loyal to me for these two years that I should despise myself were I to keep my—my extraordinary lapse from him. Had Brocklehurst been a little less good, then you need not have told him my strange little secret.

LORD LOAM (*weakly*). Polly—I mean Mary—it was all Crichton's fault, he——

LADY MARY (*with decision*). No, father, no ; not a word against him, though I haven't the pluck to go on with it ; I can't even understand how it ever was. Father, do you not still hear the surf ? Do you see the curve of the beach ?

LORD LOAM. I have begun to forget—— (*In a low voice*) But they were happy days ; there was something magical about them.

LADY MARY. It was glamour. Father, I have lived Arabian nights. I have sat out a dance with the evening star. But it was all in a past existence, in the days of Babylon, and I am myself again. But he has been chivalrous always. If the slothful, indolent creature I used to be has improved in any way, I owe it all to him. I am slipping back in many ways, but I am determined not to slip back altogether—in memory of him and his island. That is why I insisted on your telling Brocklehurst. He can break our engagement if he chooses. (*Proudly*) Mary Lasenby is going to play the game.

LORD LOAM. But my dear——

(LORD BROCKLEHURST *is announced.*)

LADY MARY (*meaningly*). Father, dear, oughtn't you to be dressing ?

LORD LOAM (*very unhappy*). The fact is—before I go—I want to say——

LORD BROCKLEHURST. Loam, if you don't mind, I wish very specially to have a word with Mary before dinner.

LORD LOAM.   But——
LADY MARY.   Yes, father.

(*She induces him to go, and thus courageously faces* LORD BROCKLEHURST *to hear her fate.*)

I am ready, George.

LORD BROCKLEHURST (*who is so agitated that she ought to see he is thinking not of her but of himself.*)   It is a painful matter— I wish I could have spared you this, Mary.

LADY MARY.   Please go on.

LORD BROCKLEHURST.   In common fairness, of course, this should be remembered, that two years had elapsed.   You and I had no reason to believe that we should ever meet again.

(*This is more considerate than she had expected.*)

LADY MARY (*softening*).   I was so lost to the world, George.

LORD BROCKLEHURST (*with a groan*).   At the same time, the thing is utterly and absolutely inexcusable——

LADY MARY (*recovering her hauteur*).   Oh !

LORD BROCKLEHURST.   And so I have already said to mother.

LADY MARY (*disdaining him*).   You have told her ?

LORD BROCKLEHURST.   Certainly, Mary, certainly ; I tell mother everything.

LADY MARY (*curling her lip*).   And what did she say ?

LORD BROCKLEHURST.   To tell the truth, mother rather pooh-poohed the whole affair.

LADY MARY (*incredulous*).   Lady Brocklehurst pooh-poohed the whole affair !

LORD BROCKLEHURST.   She said, ' Mary and I will have a good laugh over this.'

LADY MARY (*outraged*).   George, your mother is a hateful, depraved old woman.

LORD BROCKLEHURST.   Mary !

LADY MARY (*turning away*).   Laugh indeed, when it will always be such a pain to me.

LORD BROCKLEHURST (*with strange humility*).   If only you would let me bear all the pain, Mary.

LADY MARY (*who is taken aback*).   George, I think you are the noblest man——

(*She is touched, and gives him both her hands. Unfortunately he simpers.*)

LORD BROCKLEHURST.   She was a pretty little thing.

(*She stares, but he marches to his doom.*)

Ah, not beautiful like you.   I assure you it was the merest folly ; there were a few letters, but we have got them back. It was all owing to the boat being so late at Calais.   You see she had such large, helpless eyes.

LADY MARY (*fixing him*).   George, when you lunched with father to-day at the club——

LORD BROCKLEHURST.   I didn't.   He wired me that he couldn't come.

LADY MARY (*with a tremor*).   But he wrote you ?

LORD BROCKLEHURST.   No.

LADY MARY (*a bird singing in her breast*).   You haven't seen him since ?

LORD BROCKLEHURST.   No.

(*She is saved.   Is he to be let off also ?   Not at all.   She bears down on him like a ship of war.*)

LADY MARY.   George, who and what is this woman ?

LORD BROCKLEHURST (*cowering*).   She was—she is—the shame of it—a lady's-maid.

LADY MARY (*properly horrified*).   A what ?

LORD BROCKLEHURST.   A lady's-maid.   A mere servant, Mary.   (LADY MARY *whirls round so that he shall not see her face.*) I first met her at this house when you were entertaining the servants ; so you see it was largely your father's fault.

LADY MARY (*looking him up and down*).   A lady's-maid ?

LORD BROCKLEHURST (*degraded*).   Her name was Fisher.

LADY MARY.   My maid !

LORD BROCKLEHURST (*with open hands*).   Can you forgive me, Mary ?

LADY MARY.   Oh George, George !

LORD BROCKLEHURST.   Mother urged me not to tell you anything about it ; but——

LADY MARY (*from her heart*).   I am so glad you told me.

LORD BROCKLEHURST.   You see there was nothing catastrophic in it.

LADY MARY (*thinking perhaps of another incident*).   No, indeed.

LORD BROCKLEHURST (*inclined to simper again*).   And she behaved awfully well.   She quite saw that it was because the boat was late. I suppose the glamour to a girl in service of a man in high position——

LADY MARY. Glamour !—yes, yes, that was it.

LORD BROCKLEHURST. Mother says that a girl in such circumstances is to be excused if she loses her head.

LADY MARY (*impulsively*). George, I am so sorry if I said anything against your mother. I am sure she is the dearest old thing.

LORD BROCKLEHURST (*in calm waters at last*). Of course for women of our class she has a very different standard.

LADY MARY (*grown tiny*). Of course.

LORD BROCKLEHURST. You see, knowing how good a woman she is herself, she was naturally anxious that I should marry some one like her. That is what has made her watch your conduct so jealously, Mary.

LADY MARY (*hurriedly thinking things out*). I know. I—I think, George, that before your mother comes I should like to say a word to father.

LORD BROCKLEHURST (*nervously*). About this ?

LADY MARY. Oh no ; I shan't tell him of this. About something else.

LORD BROCKLEHURST. And you do forgive me, Mary ?

LADY MARY (*smiling on him*). Yes, yes. I—I am sure the boat was *very* late, George.

LORD BROCKLEHURST (*earnestly*). It really was.

LADY MARY. I am even relieved to know that you are not quite perfect, dear. (*She rests her hands on his shoulders. She has a moment of contrition.*) George, when we are married, we shall try to be not an entirely frivolous couple, won't we ? We must endeavour to be of some little use, dear.

LORD BROCKLEHURST (*the ass*). *Noblesse oblige.*

LADY MARY (*haunted by the phrases of a better man*). Mary Lasenby is determined to play the game, George.

(*Perhaps she adds to herself, ' Except just this once.' A kiss closes this episode of the two lovers ; and soon after the departure of* LADY MARY *the* COUNTESS OF BROCKLEHURST *is announced. She is a very formidable old lady.*)

LADY BROCKLEHURST. Alone, George ?

LORD BROCKLEHURST. Mother, I told her all ; she has behaved magnificently.

LADY BROCKLEHURST (*who has not shared his fears*). Silly boy. (*She casts a supercilious eye on the island trophies.*) So these are the wonders they brought back with them. Gone away to dry her eyes, I suppose?

LORD BROCKLEHURST (*proud of his mate*). She didn't cry, mother.

LADY BROCKLEHURST. No? (*She reflects.*) You're quite right. I wouldn't have cried. Cold, icy. Yes, that was it.

LORD BROCKLEHURST (*who has not often contradicted her*). I assure you, mother, that wasn't it at all. She forgave me at once.

LADY BROCKLEHURST (*opening her eyes sharply to the full*). Oh!

LORD BROCKLEHURST. She was awfully nice about the boat being late; she even said she was relieved to find that I wasn't quite perfect.

LADY BROCKLEHURST (*pouncing*). She said that?

LORD BROCKLEHURST. She really did.

LADY BROCKLEHURST. I mean *I* wouldn't. Now if *I* had said that, what would have made me say it? (*Suspiciously*) George, is Mary all we think her?

LORD BROCKLEHURST (*with unexpected spirit*). If she wasn't, mother, you would know it.

LADY BROCKLEHURST. Hold your tongue, boy. We don't really know what happened on that island.

LORD BROCKLEHURST. You were reading the book all the morning.

LADY BROCKLEHURST. How can I be sure that the book is true?

LORD BROCKLEHURST. They all talk of it as true.

LADY BROCKLEHURST. How do I know that they are not lying?

LORD BROCKLEHURST. Why should they lie?

LADY BROCKLEHURST. Why shouldn't they? (*She reflects again.*) If I had been wrecked on an island, I think it highly probable that I should have lied when I came back. Weren't some servants with them?

LORD BROCKLEHURST. Crichton, the butler.

(*He is surprised to see her ring the bell.*)
Why, mother, you are not going to——

LADY BROCKLEHURST.   Yes, I am.   (*Pointedly*) George, watch whether Crichton begins any of his answers to my questions with ' The fact is.'

LORD BROCKLEHURST.   Why ?

LADY BROCKLEHURST.   Because that is usually the beginning of a lie.

LORD BROCKLEHURST (*as* CRICHTON *opens the door*).   Mother, you can't do these things in other people's houses.

LADY BROCKLEHURST (*coolly, to* CRICHTON).   It was I who rang.   (*Surveying him through her eyeglass.*)   So you were one of the castaways, Crichton ?

CRICHTON.   Yes, my lady.

LADY BROCKLEHURST.   Delightful book Mr. Woolley has written about your adventures.   (CRICHTON *bows.*)   Don't you think so ?

CRICHTON.   I have not read it, my lady.

LADY BROCKLEHURST.   Odd that they should not have presented you with a copy.

LORD BROCKLEHURST.   Presumably Crichton is no reader.

LADY BROCKLEHURST.   By the way, Crichton, were there any books on the island ?

CRICHTON.   I had one, my lady—Henley's poems.

LORD BROCKLEHURST.   Never heard of him.

(CRICHTON *again bows.*)

LADY BROCKLEHURST (*who has not heard of him either*).   I think you were not the only servant wrecked ?

CRICHTON.   There was a young woman, my lady.

LADY BROCKLEHURST.   I want to see her.   (CRICHTON *bows, but remains.*)   Fetch her up.

(*He goes.*)

LORD BROCKLEHURST (*almost standing up to his mother*). This is scandalous.

LADY BROCKLEHURST (*defining her position*).   I am a mother. (CATHERINE *and* AGATHA *enter in dazzling confections, and quake in secret to find themselves practically alone with* LADY BROCKLEHURST.)

(*Even as she greets them*) How d'you do, Catherine— Agatha ?   You didn't dress like this on the island, I expect ! By the way, how did you dress ?

(*They have thought themselves prepared, but——*)

AGATHA. Not—not so well, of course, but quite the same idea.

> (*They are relieved by the arrival of* TREHERNE, *who is in clerical dress.*)

LADY BROCKLEHURST. How do you do, Mr. Treherne ? There is not so much of you in the book as I had hoped.

TREHERNE (*modestly*). There wasn't very much of me on the island, Lady Brocklehurst.

LADY BROCKLEHURST. How d' ye mean ?

> (*He shrugs his honest shoulders.*)

LORD BROCKLEHURST. I hear you have got a living, Treherne. Congratulations

TREHERNE. Thanks.

LORD BROCKLEHURST. Is it a good one ?

TREHERNE. So-so. They are rather weak in bowling, but it 's a good bit of turf.

> (*Confidence is restored by the entrance of* ERNEST, *who takes in the situation promptly, and, of course, knows he is a match for any old lady.*)

ERNEST (*with ease*). How do you do, Lady Brocklehurst.

LADY BROCKLEHURST. Our brilliant author !

ERNEST (*impervious to satire*). Oh, I don't know.

LADY BROCKLEHURST. It is as engrossing, Mr. Woolley, as if it were a work of fiction.

ERNEST (*suddenly uncomfortable*). Thanks, awfully. (*Recovering*) The fact is——

> (*He is puzzled by seeing the Brocklehurst family exchange meaning looks.*)

CATHERINE (*to the rescue*). Lady Brocklehurst, Mr. Treherne and I—we are engaged.

AGATHA. And Ernest and I.

LADY BROCKLEHURST (*grimly*). I see, my dears ; thought it wise to keep the island in the family.

> (*An awkward moment this for the entrance of* LORD LOAM *and* LADY MARY, *who, after a private talk upstairs, are feeling happy and secure.*)

LORD LOAM (*with two hands for his distinguished guest*). Aha ! ha, ha ! younger than any of them, Emily.

LADY BROCKLEHURST. Flatterer. (*To* LADY MARY) You seem in high spirits, Mary.

LADY MARY (*gaily*). I am.

LADY BROCKLEHURST (*with a significant glance at* LORD BROCKLEHURST). After——

LADY MARY. I—I mean. The fact is——
(*Again that disconcerting glance between the Countess and her son.*)

LORD LOAM (*humorously*). She hears wedding bells, Emily, ha, ha !

LADY BROCKLEHURST (*coldly*). Do you, Mary ? Can't say I do ; but I 'm hard of hearing.

LADY MARY (*instantly her match*). If you don't, Lady Brocklehurst, I 'm sure I don't.

LORD LOAM (*nervously*). Tut, tut. Seen our curios from the island, Emily ? I should like you to examine them.

LADY BROCKLEHURST. Thank you, Henry. I am glad you say that, for I have just taken the liberty of asking two of them to step upstairs.

(*There is an uncomfortable silence, which the entrance of* CRICHTON *with* TWEENY *does not seem to dissipate.* CRICHTON *is impenetrable, but* TWEENY *hangs back in fear.*)

LORD BROCKLEHURST (*stoutly*). Loam, I have no hand in this.

LADY BROCKLEHURST (*undisturbed*). Pooh, what have I done ? You always begged me to speak to the servants, Henry, and I merely wanted to discover whether the views you used to hold about equality were adopted on the island ; it seemed a splendid opportunity, but Mr. Woolley has not a word on the subject.

(*All eyes turn to* ERNEST.)

ERNEST (*with confidence*). The fact is——
(*The fatal words again.*)

LORD LOAM (*not quite certain what he is to assure her of*). I assure you, Emily——

LADY MARY (*as cold as steel*). Father, nothing whatever happened on the island of which I, for one, am ashamed, and I hope Crichton will be allowed to answer Lady Brocklehurst's questions.

LADY BROCKLEHURST. To be sure. There 's nothing to make a fuss about, and we 're a family party. (*To* CRICHTON) Now, truthfully, my man.

CRICHTON (*calmly*).   I promise that, my lady.

(*Some hearts sink, the hearts that could never understand
a Crichton.*)

LADY BROCKLEHURST (*sharply*).   Well, were you all equal
on the island ?

CRICHTON.   No, my lady.   I think I may say there was as
little equality there as elsewhere.

LADY BROCKLEHURST.   All the social distinctions were
preserved ?

CRICHTON.   As at home, my lady.

LADY BROCKLEHURST.   The servants ?

CRICHTON.   They had to keep their place.

LADY BROCKLEHURST.   Wonderful.   How was it managed ?
(*With an inspiration*) You, girl, tell me that.

(*Can there be a more critical moment ?*)

TWEENY (*in agony*).   If you please, my lady, it was all the
Gov.'s doing.

(*They give themselves up for lost.*   LORD LOAM *tries to sink
out of sight.*)

CRICHTON.   In the regrettable slang of the servants'
hall, my lady, the master is usually referred to as the
Gov.

LADY BROCKLEHURST.   I see.   (*She turns to* LORD LOAM.)
You——

LORD LOAM (*reappearing*).   Yes, I understand that is what
they called me.

LADY BROCKLEHURST (*to* CRICHTON).   You didn't even take
your meals with the family ?

CRICHTON.   No, my lady, I dined apart.

(*Is all safe ?*)

LADY BROCKLEHURST (*alas*).   You, girl, also ?   Did you
dine with Crichton ?

TWEENY (*scared*).   No, your ladyship.

LADY BROCKLEHURST (*fastening on her*).   With whom ?

TWEENY.   I took my bit of supper with—with Daddy and
Polly and the rest.

(*Væ victis.*)

ERNEST (*leaping into the breach*).   Dear old Daddy—he was
our monkey.   You remember our monkey, Agatha ?

AGATHA.   Rather !   What a funny old darling he was.

CATHERINE (*thus encouraged*). And don't you think Polly was the sweetest little parrot, Mary ?

LADY BROCKLEHURST. Ah ! I understand ; animals you had domesticated ?

LORD LOAM (*heavily*). Quite so—quite so.

LADY BROCKLEHURST. The servants' teas that used to take place here once a month——

CRICHTON. They did not seem natural on the island, my lady, and were discontinued by the Gov.'s orders.

LORD BROCKLEHURST. A clear proof, Loam, that they were a mistake here.

LORD LOAM (*seeing the opportunity for a diversion*). I admit it frankly. I abandon them. Emily, as the result of our experiences on the island, I think of going over to the Tories.

LADY BROCKLEHURST. I am delighted to hear it.

LORD LOAM (*expanding*). Thank you, Crichton, thank you ; that is all.

(*He motions to them to go, but the time is not yet.*)

LADY BROCKLEHURST. One moment. (*There is a universal but stifled groan.*) Young people, Crichton, will be young people, even on an island ; now, I suppose there was a certain amount of—shall we say sentimentalising, going on ?

CRICHTON. Yes, my lady, there was.

LORD BROCKLEHURST (*ashamed*). Mother !

LADY BROCKLEHURST (*disregarding him*). Which gentleman ? (*To* TWEENY) You, girl, tell me.

TWEENY (*confused*). If you please, my lady——

ERNEST (*hurriedly*). The fact is——

(*He is checked as before, and probably says ' D—n ' to himself, but he has saved the situation.*)

TWEENY (*gasping*). It was him—Mr. Ernest, your ladyship.

LADY BROCKLEHURST (*counsel for the prosecution*). With which lady ?

AGATHA. I have already told you, Lady Brocklehurst, that Ernest and I——

LADY BROCKLEHURST. Yes, *now* ; but you were two years on the island. (*Looking at* LADY MARY) Was it this lady ?

TWEENY. No, your ladyship.

LADY BROCKLEHURST. Then I don't care which of the others it was. (TWEENY *gurgles*.) Well, I suppose that will do.

o

LORD BROCKLEHURST.   Do ! I hope you are ashamed of yourself, mother. (*To* CRICHTON, *who is going*) You are an excellent fellow, Crichton ; and if, after we are married, you ever wish to change your place, come to us.

LADY MARY (*losing her head for the only time*). Oh no, impossible.

LADY BROCKLEHURST (*at once suspicious*). Why impossible ? (LADY MARY *cannot answer, or perhaps she is too proud.*) Do you see why it should be impossible, my man ?

(*He can make or mar his unworthy Mary now. Have you any doubt of him ?*)

CRICHTON.   Yes, my lady.   I had not told you, my lord, but as soon as your lordship is suited I wish to leave service.

(*They are all immensely relieved, except poor* TWEENY.)

TREHERNE (*the only curious one*). What will you do, Crichton ?

(CRICHTON *shrugs his shoulders.*)

CRICHTON.   Shall I withdraw, my lord ?

(*He withdraws with* TWEENY; *the thunderstorm is over.*)

LADY BROCKLEHURST (*thankful to have made herself unpleasant*). Horrid of me, wasn't it ? But if one wasn't disagreeable now and again, it would be horribly tedious to be an old woman. He will soon be yours, Mary, and then—think of the opportunities you will have of being disagreeable to me. On that understanding, my dear, don't you think we might——?

(*Their cold lips meet.*)

LORD LOAM (*vaguely*). Quite so—quite so.

(CRICHTON *announces dinner, and they file out.* LADY MARY *stays behind a moment and impulsively holds out her hand.*)

LADY MARY.   To wish you every dear happiness.

CRICHTON (*an enigma to the last*). The same to you, my lady.

LADY MARY.   Do you despise me, Crichton ? (*The man who could never tell a lie makes no answer.*) I am ashamed of myself, but I am the sort of woman on whom shame sits lightly. (*He does not contradict her.*) You are the best man among us.

CRICHTON.   On an island, my lady, perhaps ; but in England, no.

LADY MARY (*not inexcusably*).   Then there is something wrong with England.

CRICHTON.   My lady, not even from you can I listen to a word against England.

LADY MARY.   Tell me one thing : you have not lost your courage ?

CRICHTON.   No, my lady.

(*She goes.   He turns out the lights.*)

LITTLE MARY

Produced at Wyndham's Theatre on September 24, 1903, with the following cast :

THE EARL OF CARLTON . .	*John Hare*
LORD ROLFE (his Son) . .	*Gerald du Maurier*
TERENCE REILLY	*Henry Vibart*
SIR JENNINGS PYKE . . .	*Eric Lewis*
DR. TOPPING	*Clarence Blakiston*
EARL OF PLUMLEIGH (a Schoolboy)	*A. E. Matthews*
MR. DEIGHTON	*Compton Coutts*
COUNTESS OF PLUMLEIGH . .	*Enid Spencer-Brunton*
LADY MILLY	*Fyfe Alexander*
ELEANOR GRAY	*Margaret Fraser*
MOIRA LONEY	*Nina Boucicault*

The play ran for 208 performances.

ACT I

THE scene is the parlour of a chemist's shop in London. It is in darkness. There is, however, a glass door at back leading into the shop, which is seen brightly lighted. At the back of the shop is the street door which leads into a dull, second-class street. A street organ is grinding out a popular tune. The street door opens, ringing a bell as it does so, and a quietly dressed lady enters. Nothing they say is heard, but she is seen asking for and buying something. He hands her package and she leaves the shop. After her exit the door-bell again rings and Lord Carlton enters. He hands Mr. Reilly a prescription about which they talk. A policeman is here seen passing the shop and the organ stops abruptly, the policeman having motioned with his hand that the organ is to move on. Then Mr. Reilly comes into the parlour carrying a lamp. He has taken off the shop counter. He puts lamp down on counter. Lord Carlton follows him in.

There is still a light in the shop, but the room is also now seen. It is comfortable but plebeian, and has some unusual features. The corner of the room is fitted up as a sort of home-made laboratory, and there are chemist's bottles, retorts, etc., standing on it. Elsewhere are advertisements, etc., as if the shop had overflowed into the parlour. There is an easy, high-backed chair by the fire, a round table, two horse-hair chairs, and a chest of drawers. Standing on a round tray on the chest of drawers is a water-bottle and glass. On the door are three pegs, and on the centre peg is hanging an old dressing-gown of Mr. Reilly's ; hanging from a shelf by the counter is a towel. Fitted into this counter or home-made laboratory is an enamelled basin, which stands under a water-tap. There is a dentist's chair with a low Chesterfield armchair containing small cushion. The round table is covered by a red table-cloth ; on it is a work-basket, crackers (bonbons) which have been opened, chocolates, paper cap out of bonbon, large size ; on top of chest of drawers is a hand mirror. By chair is a small wooden horse and two children's picture-books are lying on the floor. Fixed in the wall is a formidable safe.

Against back of parlour are what seem to be three boxes about 3 feet long, fastened to the wall. They are fixed one underneath the other, the top box being about 8 feet from the floor, and to this box is a ladder fastened to the side, leading from it to the floor. There is a similar box 8 feet from the floor on the other wall.

The parlour being lit, Mr. Reilly and Lord Carlton are now more clearly seen. Mr. Reilly is dignified, patriarchal, about eighty years old, and there should be something fine and striking in his appearance, such as goes with our conception of an alchemist of mediaeval days. He speaks good English, but with a refined Irish accent. He wears a black skull-cap but otherwise is in ordinary careless attire. His face is intellectual and worn with study ; he has a long greyish beard. His manner is dignified and courteous ; he has the eyes of the idealist which lack lustre when he is speaking of ordinary affairs, from which his mind tends to wander, but they are capable of intense concentration and fire. He is absolutely sincere. Lord Carlton is a smart, well-groomed man of fashion ; kind, cynic with some boyishness of spirit still left in him. He has a quizzical manner which enables him to be humorous without smiling.

LORD CARLTON. Really, I must not inconvenience you in this way, I can wait quite well in the shop.

MR. REILLY. It is no inconvenience, and the shop is chilly. There is a fire here.

LORD CARLTON. Well—you are uncommon good—and to a perfect stranger, too.

MR. REILLY. Not quite a stranger, my lord.

LORD CARLTON. You know me ?

MR. REILLY. Your lordship's name is on the prescription ! That is why I invited you into the parlour.

LORD CARLTON (*cynically*). I see.

MR. REILLY (*with simple dignity*). Might I look at you, my lord, for a moment. I am an old man, and I have seen few of the sights. (*He looks at* LORD CARLTON *and then speaks with dignity*) Thank you, my lord !

(LORD CARLTON *bows.*)

If you will take a chair I shall have the prescription made up in ten minutes.

(LORD CARLTON *sits in chair.* MR. REILLY *has the prescription in his hand.*)

I understand you wish this prescription to be made up ?

LORD CARLTON. Yes. They are powders I frequently take for nervous headache.

MR. REILLY (*the words evidently having some meaning of his own to him*). Nervous headache. He said nervous headache—why not ?

LORD CARLTON. You don't believe in them ?

MR. REILLY (*coming to himself quickly*). I am a chemist and druggist, my lord—not a doctor. (*Looking at prescription.*) He often takes them.

LORD CARLTON (*stoutly in their defence*). Often, and they do me good.

MR. REILLY (*slowly*). He wishes me to make up these powders —because he thinks he is subject to nervous headaches—and he believes they do him good. Certainly, my lord.

(*Exit into the shop, oblivious of the fact that* LORD CARLTON *is wondering at him.* LORD CARLTON *rises.*)

LORD CARLTON. Queer old fish !

(LORD CARLTON *left to himself evidently thinks* MR. REILLY *a queer old fish, looks about and evidently thinks it an odd room, puts his hat down on the chest, picks up hand mirror which is lying on it.*)

(*Testily to his reflection*) Ugly beast !

(*Puts mirror down again.*)

Ah, old friend ! (*Crosses to fire and is stirring it, rattles fire-irons.*)

CHILD (*unseen*). Is that you, mother ?

(LORD CARLTON *looks round and is surprised to see no one —he turns and looks this way and that.*)

LORD CARLTON (*at a venture*). Yes, my darling, it is I, your mother.

(*There is no answer—the boxes strike him as curious, goes up the ladder, and looks into box. This evidently solves the mystery for him. He descends ladder amused and self-conscious, and goes on tiptoes to easy-chair by fire. A little boy in a night-gown peeps up from box, which is now seen to be a novel kind of cot, and is evidently looking for him excitedly.*)

BOY (*to another box*).   Rosy !

GIRL (*a little girl looks up*).   Yes !

(LORD CARLTON *peeps at them behind chair.* BOY *signs caution to* GIRL.   LORD CARLTON *pulls up his legs on to the chair and cowers not to be seen by them.*

Enter MOIRA, *singing and carrying a baby. She is an old-fashioned little girl of twelve, very earnest and practical and quaint, and with all the airs of an experienced mother. She carries the baby with extraordinary rapture and her face shines with the glory of holding such a treasure.*

LORD CARLTON *is not seen by her owing to his position in the chair, and he listens entertained, without disclosing himself—the child speaks excitedly.*)

CHILD.   Mother !

MOIRA (*who, like* MR. REILLY, *speaks English, but with pretty aroma of Irish in it, sternly*).   Billy, you naughty boy—lie down !

CHILD.   But, mother——

MOIRA (*sternly*).   You are asleep, Billy, and don't you forget it.

(*He lies down—she addresses the* GIRL *in the other box.*)

(*To* GIRL) Lie down, you wicked toodlums. (*Then addressing the baby in her arms, whom she hugs adoringly*) No wonder you scorn them, Baby—I never had such a family—really I don't know what we poor mothers are coming to—we shall have to give up having babies. (*Kissing it each time*) We shall— we shall—we shall. (*She goes to the chest of drawers, gets out bed-clothes—speaking the while*) Baby, do you know why I love you the best of them all ? It 's because you 're my littlest. (*Bending over the child*) Littlest—littlest. (*Hurries with bed-clothes to cot and arranges them, making cooing noises at baby all the time—coming to baby in jumps, speaks severely.*)

> To bed, to bed, you sleepy head,
> Oh, tarry a while, says slow,
> Put on the pan, said greedy Nan,
> We 'll sup before we go.

(*Lifts baby*) Golden curls, the day I have to cut them off, that day, Baby, I shall die.

(*Puts baby in cot and hangs over it worshipping it. While putting baby in,* MOIRA *sings.* LORD CARLTON *feels that he ought to disclose himself, he stands up by chair, and clears his throat.* MOIRA *is startled, sees him, and rushing back to cot, stands defending it with outstretched arms like a wild animal protecting her cubs.*)

LORD CARLTON. Don't be alarmed, madam, I have no desire to deprive you of your Benjamin.

MOIRA (*cautious*). Who are you?

LORD CARLTON. The nice old gentleman asked me to wait here while my prescription was being made up.

MOIRA (*appeased and timid*). Oh, very well. I thought that—— (*She comes nearer and can't help looking at him with wistful admiration.*) Oh! How well your coat sets you!

(*He bows, and suddenly a new thought clouds her.*)

LORD CARLTON (*with feeling*). My dear little girl, if my presence here disturbs you——

MOIRA. It's not that—but what will you think of me! (*Pleading, excusing herself*) You see, it is my birthday and so I let them play a little longer than usual—meaning to tidy up when they were in bed. (*Eager*) I swear that's why the room is in such disorder. (*Bitterly*) But now, of course, you'll go and tell all your friends that I am a bad housewife.

LORD CARLTON. On the contrary, everything seems to me to be in apple-pie order.

MOIRA (*refusing to be comforted*). You say that to please me. I dare say you have been counting the crumbs on the carpet.

LORD CARLTON. No. I have been too busy occupied in counting these. (*Indicating boxes.*)

MOIRA (*unable to resist this—with shy pleasure*). There are four. (*She makes a little chuckle of delight over having four.*)

LORD CARLTON. Four—and your age?

MOIRA. I am twelve to-day.

LORD CARLTON (*grandly*). Would you mind shaking hands with me?

MOIRA (*gives him her hand*). Thank you, sir.

(*She beckons him to come over to her.* LORD CARLTON *crosses to her, she lowers her voice so as not to be heard by the boxes.*)

MOIRA. They are not really mine.

LORD CARLTON (*affecting surprise*). No?

MOIRA (*wistfully*). Did you think they were?

LORD CARLTON. They called you by that sweetest of names, you know.

MOIRA (*sighing*). Yes.

LORD CARLTON. Do you wish they were yours?

MOIRA (*hysterical with ecstasy*). Ah! Ah! (*Signing caution.*) They think I'm their mother.

 (BILLY *looks out; she speaks with a pointed look at* LORD CARLTON.)

Good night, my boy.

CHILD. Good night, mother.

 (*He lies down—she nods triumphantly at* LORD CARLTON, *who signs that he will keep her secret. She flies about putting room to rights, picking up small wooden horse and picture-books which she places on the top of chest of drawers.*)

LORD CARLTON. I say, little Irish girl——

MOIRA (*turns to him, anxiously*). I didn't tell you I was Irish.

LORD CARLTON. Why shouldn't you?

MOIRA (*primly*). Because it is sinful to boast. (*Kneels in front of fire.*)

LORD CARLTON (*emphatically—like a schoolboy*). I like you!

MOIRA. Do you? But you should see me in my muslin with the pink spots.

LORD CARLTON. I should like to—but you are not very polite, you know. You should be entertaining me.

MOIRA (*anxious*). I doubt my manners are bad.

LORD CARLTON. It is so easy for a lady to entertain a gentleman.

MOIRA (*eager*). It is?

LORD CARLTON. She simply sits beside him and smiles pleasantly.

 (MOIRA *sits at opposite side of table and tries to smile pleasantly.*)

MOIRA (*with itching hands*). Doesn't she do anything with her hands?

LORD CARLTON (*considerately*). Well, if she has a family she is permitted to sew.

MOIRA. Oh, thank you, sir. (*Seizing sewing and sews.*)

LORD CARLTON (*leaning across table like a boy*).   I say, you tell me all about you, and I 'll tell you all about me.

MOIRA (*gleefully—entering into the joke*).   Yes !

LORD CARLTON.   What is your name ?

MOIRA.   Moira.

LORD CARLTON.   I like it.   (*Confidentially*) And the old gentleman—I gather he 's not your husband ?

MOIRA (*gravely*).   No, I 'm not old enough to have a husband—he 's my Grandpa.

LORD CARLTON.   And your parents are dead, Moira ?

MOIRA.   Yes, sir, but how did you know ?

LORD CARLTON.   From the way you look after your little brothers and sisters.

MOIRA.   H'sh !   (*Guardedly*) They are no relation.   I just take them in to mother them.   They are widowers' children from near by.

LORD CARLTON.   Good heavens !   Sort of *crèche* !

MOIRA.   What ?   (*Quickly on the defence.*)   Grandpa does not make me do it, though the money 's useful.   You see, I have a lot of time on my hands for we have just the one floor.

LORD CARLTON.   Surely there is a servant ?

MOIRA (*excitedly*).   Servant !   No servants for me.   *I* know them—idle hussies.

CHILD (*popping up*).   Mother, could I have just one more chocolate ?

MOIRA (*severely—rising*).   Certainly not.

LORD CARLTON (*rises*).   Oh, yes, let him have one.   Here, Billy, catch !   Catch !

(*Goes and flings up chocolate, which* BILLY *immediately puts in his mouth.*)

MOIRA.   You will be sick to-morrow, Billy.

CHILD (*with conviction*).   I shall be sick to-night.

(MOIRA *sits by the table.*   BOY *lies down.*   LORD CARLTON *returning, sees that* MOIRA *is offended with him.*)

LORD CARLTON (*appealing*).   Moira !   (*She turns away.*)   It was only one !

(*She is still cold.   He tries another way of getting round her.*) Moira, I am a widower.   (*Sits.*)

MOIRA (*turning to him*).   Oh dear, dear, dear.   (*Sudden thought*) Have you any . . . ?   (*Looks at boxes.*)

LORD CARLTON. Boxes. One. Boy.

MOIRA (*ecstatic*). Ah ! Aha ! (*Old-fashioned*) They 're such a trouble—really they 're such a nuisance ! Has the precious had his measles ?

LORD CARLTON. Yes.

MOIRA. English ?

LORD CARLTON (*patriotically*). I hope so.

MOIRA. Of course, it 's an anxious time, but better get them over while they 're young—that 's what *I* say.

LORD CARLTON. My very words ! (*Rises.*)

MOIRA (*suddenly*). You weren't thinking of asking me to take him ? No, you 're too grand.

LORD CARLTON. You are full up, you know.

MOIRA. However many there are, I have always room for one more.

LORD CARLTON. Ah, but he is quite a big boy now. Why, he is four years older than you.

MOIRA. That 's the worst of them—they grow up so quick. Is he doing for himself ?

LORD CARLTON (*leaning over back of chair*). He will never do for himself. (*With some feeling*) You have a house and grandfather to look after, my child, and four boxes to fill up the time, while he is still at school playing marbles, or the like, and presently he will go to Oxford to play more marbles, or I may send him into the Army to play marbles there.

MOIRA (*amazed*). But won't he tire of marbles ?

LORD CARLTON. Oh yes, we tire of them, but we go on playing.

MOIRA. But when he gets married ?

LORD CARLTON. They will both play. (*Sits in chair at table.*)

MOIRA. If I married him I should soon put a stop to his marbles.

LORD CARLTON. And why shouldn't you marry him ?

MOIRA (*quickly*). I can't promise. (*Politely*) You see, I don't know him.

LORD CARLTON. No—he 's rather like me.

MOIRA. Oh, if he 's like you and loved me *very very* dearly perhaps I might have him.

LORD CARLTON (*pleased*). Do you like me, Moira ?

MOIRA (*earnestly*). Very, very much indeed.

LORD CARLTON (*after pluming himself*).   I am trying to picture you, my dear, in my set.

MOIRA.   Are you very rich ?

LORD CARLTON.   So rich that sometimes I think I shall be ruined in income-tax.

MOIRA.   Perhaps—perhaps you are a lord.

LORD CARLTON (*sorry*).   Now you are going to spoil everything.   Yes, Moira, I am a lord.   (*Rises and crosses to fireplace.*)

MOIRA (*rises*).   Oh, lord—please be a better man for Grandpa's sake !

LORD CARLTON (*turning to her*).   Hullo !

MOIRA.   Grandpa knows all about you.

LORD CARLTON.   I hope not everything.

MOIRA.   Everything.   (*As something Grandpa has told her.*) Your blood is not *really* blue, you know.

LORD CARLTON.   Alas, no.

MOIRA (*puzzled*).   Then what 's the difference between you and the likes of us ?   Have you black roofs to your mouths ?

LORD CARLTON.   I mustn't betray the secrets of my class. So Grandpa doesn't think much of us, Moira ?

MOIRA.   Oh yes, he does—he loves you !   And he says that anything you do that 's wrong is not really your fault, it is because you are so ill.

LORD CARLTON.   Oho !   That 's it, is it ?

MOIRA.   You are so very unwell all of you.   That prescription won't do you much good.

LORD CARLTON.   Well, I thought Grandpa seemed rather sceptical.

MOIRA.   That 's not what 's the matter with you.

LORD CARLTON.   What isn't ?

MOIRA.   Why, what the doctor says it is.

LORD CARLTON.   Gad, I 've suspected that.   What *is* the matter with us, Moira ?

MOIRA.   Oh, I don't know.   Nobody knows except Grandpa. I think it is all in the book.   (*Impressively*) Grandpa is writing a book about you.

LORD CARLTON.   Is he ?

MOIRA.   Yes, it 's in the safe.

LORD CARLTON (*going to safe*).   Ha !

MOIRA.   It is locked.

LORD CARLTON. I feel terrified—you are sure it is about us ? (*Sits in armchair.*)

MOIRA. I think it is not so much *about* you as how to cure you.

LORD CARLTON. Grandpa is sure he can cure us ?

MOIRA (*confident*). Oh yes, it 's quite simple.

LORD CARLTON. Is it, by Jove !

MOIRA. You see, there is a spring in you all that is not working—and Grandpa is going to touch the spring and set you all going again.

LORD CARLTON. That will be ripping ! And why is Grandpa going to do this, Moira ?

MOIRA. Because he is an Irishman with a passionate love for the English people.

LORD CARLTON. Ah !

MOIRA. And I 'm to help him—I don't know how—but I am to help ! (*Sits in chair.*)

LORD CARLTON. So ! He is a deuce of a fellow this Grandpa ! (*Sorry for him—goes to her.*) Grandpa isn't a little odd, is he, Moira ?

MOIRA. Odd ? Grandpa is a wonderful man, lord. (*Proudly*) And as he walks down the street thinking great thoughts and saying them to himself, the neighbours go like this. (*Taps her forehead.*)

LORD CARLTON. And what do they mean by that ?

MOIRA. They mean what an intellect Grandpa has.

LORD CARLTON. Poor little girl !

(*Is very sorry for her and is patting her when enter* MR. REILLY *with the powders.*)

MR. REILLY. I fear I have exceeded my time.

LORD CARLTON. I think not ; you see I have been pleasantly occupied in making a new friend.

MR. REILLY. She is a good girl. Those are the powders, my lord—one and three.

LORD CARLTON. I am much obliged. (*Pays with two-shilling piece.*)

MR. REILLY. Do you mind coppers ?

LORD CARLTON. Not at all.

(MR. REILLY *counts out and gives* LORD CARLTON *ninepence in coppers.*)

MR. REILLY. Nine. Thank you, my lord.

(*They both have superfine manners here.*)
I hope the powders will do you good.

LORD CARLTON (*getting hat off chest of drawers*). Thanks,
and in the same spirit may I wish you success in—any little
affair you may have in hand.

  (MR. REILLY *bows and goes into shop.* LORD CARLTON
  goes up to MOIRA *and shakes hands with her.*)

LORD CARLTON. Good-bye, Moira.

MOIRA. Good-bye, lord.

LORD CARLTON. *Dear* Moira !

MOIRA. *Dear* lord !

  (LORD CARLTON *exits.* MOIRA *turns to her basket, takes
  up work.* LORD CARLTON *again appears at door, having
  returned ; he calls to* MOIRA.)

LORD CARLTON. Mother !

  (*She turns round inquiringly.* *He signs that he has said
  it to deceive the children.* *She signs with pleased smile
  that she understands, they nod their heads at one another.
  Exit* LORD CARLTON *through shop.* MR. REILLY *sees him
  out, lowers gas in shop till the shop is vaguely seen and
  returns to* MOIRA, *who has been seeing that the children
  are all right, and looking through window into shop.*)

MOIRA (*by door leading from shop, dragging him down*).
Grandpa, he is one of them—he is a lord.

MR. REILLY (*stirred*). I know. My child, are they not
splendid—these English !

MOIRA. Oh, Grandpa—they are beautiful.

MR. REILLY. They have not their equals in the world.
(*Pauses—stops looking in front of him.*) But they are very ill.

  (*Unties his apron, puts it on arm of chair, and then he sits
  in chair by fire thinking deeply.*)

MOIRA (*sitting on table*). Have you closed for the night,
Grandpa ?

  (*He is thinking too profoundly to hear her ; almost without
  his knowing it, she takes off his coat, puts his dressing-gown
  on him and slippers on his feet—makes him comfortable
  like a mother a child.* MOIRA *kneels by chair.*)

MR. REILLY (*to himself*). Strange, but a fair omen.

MOIRA. What, Grandpa ?

MR. REILLY.   That one of them should come here on this night of nights !

MOIRA.   Because it is my birthday !

MR. REILLY.   Oh, your birthday, my child.

MOIRA.   Yes.   Don't you remember ?   I am twelve to-day. (*Rises off her knees.*)   We have been having such fun.   Look ! (*She takes from table a paper cap that has come out of a cracker and puts it on her head, where it remains.*)   Don't you want to kiss me on my birthday, Grandpa ?

MR. REILLY.   Yes, my child.

(*She is pleased and runs to him gaily and holds up her face, but he has already forgotten her in deep thoughts. She is so disappointed that she cries a little, then bravely conquers her feelings.*)

MOIRA (*sits sewing—brightly*).   Are you going to write to-night, Grandpa ?

MR. REILLY.   No, Moira—I am never to write any more.

MOIRA.   Never to write any more !   Why, I can't remember a night when you were not writing the book.

MR. REILLY.   Your mother used to say that to me also, my dear—often, often.   I remember another young woman who sat by that fire watching the book grow—she was your grandmother, Moira.   Wife, child, grandchild !   (*Rises*) Moira ! (*Gets key off chain which is round his neck.*)   Bring me the book.

(MOIRA *takes key, goes to safe which she unlocks.*   MR. REILLY *crosses to writing-table to receive books, puts spectacles on.   He moves the work-basket to the top end of the table to make room for it.   The book is in three formidable volumes.   She brings first Volumes* 1 *and* 2, *which are so heavy that she carries them with difficulty in her arms.   As* MR. REILLY *takes books, she lifts work-basket off the table and places it under the table.   He takes the two volumes, placing them side by side.   Sits and gloats over them, opens Vol.* 2, *is looking at it when* MOIRA *brings Vol.* 3 *which contains a piece of blotting-paper.   He closes Vol.* 2 *placing Vol.* 3 *on it, finally leaving it open at blank page where the blotting-paper is.*)

MOIRA (*pathetically*).   How you love them, Grandpa, you wouldn't forget to kiss them.

MR. REILLY.   My book !   Moira, here am I—not this weary

frame that is almost worn quite away, but this—this is what I
have grown into—in this I shall pass young and hale down the
ages. (*Leans head on book—rises—points to where pen is on
chest of drawers.*) Moira, the pen !

MOIRA.   But I thought you were to write no more.
   (*Gets ink-stand with pen in it from chest of drawers and
   puts them on table by books.*)

MR. REILLY (*puts* MOIRA *in his seat*).   There are but two words
to write.   I thought once my wife should write them and then
I thought your mother, but you shall write them, my child.
   (*Puts* MOIRA *in his chair, then takes pen, dips it into the
   ink-stand, gives it to* MOIRA, *points to book.*)
Write here—'*The End.*'

MOIRA.   The End, Grandpa ?

MR. REILLY.   The book is finished.   Write—'*The End.*'
   (*She writes.   He stands over her watching.*)
The end !   The end !
   (*Blots book, takes it, looks at it, shuts it, puts it down on
   Vol. 2, takes off spectacles, puts them on Vol. 3, leaves top
   of table and sits in chair.*)

MR. REILLY.   My end !

MOIRA (*going to him*).   Dearest !   Dearest !

MR. REILLY.   I am a little agitated, Lucy.

MOIRA.   I am Moira, dear ; mother was Lucy.

MR. REILLY (*pats her hand*).   I sometimes forget you are
the little Moira who has never said a word against the book.
They tired of it—they hated the book.   It was because I
experimented on them.   They didn't like that.   Women are
strange.

MOIRA (*goes to him*).   But you said I should read the book
when the time came.

MR. REILLY.   The time has come !   (*Taking Vol.* 1 *off table
and holding it*) You *shall* read it, Moira, and I shall sit and watch
you read it, and after I am gone you shall still sit reading it.   I
have saved money for you, my child, for six years, and all that
time until you are eighteen you shall do nothing but read the
book.

MOIRA.   Oh, Grandpa, how I shall love it.

MR. REILLY.   And then you shall go out among the great
ones and make converts.

MOIRA. I shall ? (*Backs a little.*)

MR. REILLY. You, Moira !

MOIRA (*afraid*). But you will come with me ?

MR. REILLY. I shall always be with you, for the book is I. You must carry me about with you everywhere—but no eyes but yours must see me. Not even those you are curing must know the nature of the cure. It would startle them too much. These noble ones must be saved by stealth.

MOIRA. But won't that be deceiving, Grandpa ?

MR. REILLY. It is for their great good.

MOIRA. And am I not to be truthful any more ? I can't do it, I can't do it.

MR. REILLY (*fiercely*). You refuse ? (*Rises.*) Then all my life work is for naught, and into the fire I go. (*Crosses to fireplace. Threatens to burn the book.*)

MOIRA (*crosses to him, appalled*). No, no, Grandpa ! I will do it, I will do it.

(*Restrains him by putting hand on his arm.*)

MR. REILLY (*with feeling*). My child—I am a little sorry for you, for I cannot but see in what career—(*Looks at cots*)—your greatest happiness would have lain. But we are doing it for the good of the dear Saxons. For England, Moira, from the grateful Irish.

MOIRA. I don't love them as much as I did.

MR. REILLY. To save him who was here just now.

MOIRA. Oh, I should love to save him.

MR. REILLY. Self must be sacrificed and all your aspirations turned into the path of duty.

MOIRA (*feverishly*). Yes, yes.

MR. REILLY (*indicating cots*). All these must go.

MOIRA (*alarmed*). The children ! Grandpa ! Oh, that would kill me.

MR. REILLY. Nothing must interfere with the book.

MOIRA. And am I to have nothing to mother ?

MR. REILLY. What an ordinary woman your desire craves to make you—and what an extraordinary woman you are to be ! Sit down, Moira.

(MOIRA *sits.*)

Sit down here by the fire, and begin your studies. (*Goes up for lamp.*) My old eyes are hungering to see you as you will be for the next six years. (*Has lamp and holds it in front for* MOIRA *to read by.*)

> (*She is sitting dubiously by the fire with Vol.* I. *He stands looking at her with lamp in hand. Gloating.*)

What is it called, my child—read the title.

MOIRA. 'The Medium, or how to cure our best people,' a pamphlet by Terence Reilly.

MR. REILLY. When I began it I meant it to be a pamphlet.

MOIRA. What is the Medium, Grandpa ?

MR. REILLY (*uneasy*). H'sh, the book will tell you. Begin, Moira, begin.

> (*She begins reading, and after watching her he exits into the shop with lamp. At his exit, finding the light gone, she looks round, then goes on her knees nearer the fire and reads by its light. He watches her through the window from the shop, still holding lamp.*)

ACT II

LADY GEORGY's country cottage. The scene is in the courtyard.
This courtyard is enclosed on all three sides, at back and on right
by the house, and on the left by a fine yew hedge. The walls
of the house are white and solid, in centre of back wall is a
quaintly narrow door, the upper half of which is in glass panes.
This door is practical and opens into a morning-room. On each
side of the door is a pretty window, and though the room cannot
be seen through the windows, you can see through them and
through windows on other side of the house, a pretty piece of
garden bathed in sunlight. The right side of the house has
french windows opening on to courtyard. The suggestion is
that the house is large and irregular and straggling in the cottage
style. Against the wall are cherry trees with ripe fruit. The
yew hedge is clipped artificially to represent a peacock, etc. On
top and in centre of it is an opening leading into garden. Tri-
folium in its red berry is clinging to the hedge in patches and
also growing against the back' wall. At foot of wall and hedge
a border of flowers, mostly purple, grow around. Clematis
especially is in evidence. There are no roses. In the courtyard
is a pedestal with sundial painted on it. The courtyard is paved
with flag-stones broken into irregular pieces. Part of it has
gone green with age and damp. There is one comfortable
boudoir chair with cushion. There is one stone seat with
cushion. There are no canvas chairs of the kind common in
gardens. On the other side of the hedge grows a cherry tree,
the top of which is conspicuously laden with fruit.

> (LADY GEORGY *is seated on seat, book in hand. She is a
> handsome, fashionable woman ; from the way she fidgets
> she is evidently restless. She is looking at a window as if
> expecting something to happen. She rises, she sighs, goes
> aimlessly and looks through opening in hedge, then turns
> and goes quickly towards window and stamps foot in*

438

irritation because nothing happens. Enter CECIL *from door at back which is just wide enough to admit one person. He is quite a nice boy of twenty-one. He is preoccupied and comes down stage and addresses audience. Busy with pipe.*)

CECIL. Ladies and gentlemen—may I say friends ?

LADY GEORGY. What ! Oh ! I hope you slept well, Cecil.

CECIL. Thanks, Aunt Georgy, only so-so. (*Puzzled*) I sleep all right in the day-time but somehow I can't sleep at night. I suppose it 's something in the air. (*Seeing she is not attending to him, returns to audience*) Ladies and gentlemen, may I say friends ?

LADY GEORGY (*irritated*). Oh, do say friends.

CECIL (*good-naturedly contrite*). I say, am I a worry ?

LADY GEORGY. Oh, no, but really, Cecil, as you have only been engaged a fortnight, I think it is rather unnecessary that you should be making up your speech for the wedding breakfast already.

CECIL (*impressed*). You think so ?

LADY GEORGY. Especially as your father says he won't allow the marriage to take place at all.

CECIL. Allow ! I like that ! (*By sundial—stretching himself grandly.*) Who 's twenty-one ? Is anything wrong, Aunt Georgy ?

LADY GEORGY (*hesitates by stone seat, then makes confession*). Cecil, something awful is to take place in this house within the next ten minutes. You know whom I am expecting to-day ? (*Sits.*)

CECIL. The Stormy Petrel. Rather !

LADY GEORGY. I wish they didn't call her that.

CECIL (*crosses to* LADY GEORGY *and sits on arm of seat*). Miss Loney seems such an inadequate name for a woman who has set society in a blaze.

LADY GEORGY (*eagerly*). She has, Cecil, hasn't she ? They say she and her medium have some wonderful cures, and so was it very dreadful of me to invite them down here to see whether they could do anything for poor Millicent. It 's quite *possible* they are not frauds.

CECIL. There 's always the off chance.

LADY GEORGY. Of course I never saw her—and it does seem suspicious her having a medium.

CECIL. Suspicious but exciting ! I hope the medium's pretty.

LADY GEORGY. I know nothing about her except that her name is Little Mary.

CECIL. I have a feeling that Little Mary will turn out to be a duck.

LADY GEORGY (*despairingly*). Cecil, I meant to have them here without the doctors knowing anything about it.

CECIL. They would be furious if they did know.

LADY GEORGY. Well, look in at that window.

CECIL. Who are they ?

LADY GEORGY. The one is our local doctor.

CECIL. Oho !

LADY GEORGY. The other is much worse. He is a specialist from London, Sir Jennings Pyke, come to consult about Millicent.

(CECIL *goes back to seat, sits.*)

I didn't understand he was coming, and now every moment I am expecting Miss Loney and her medium, and if these four should meet ? (*Rises and turns facing* CECIL.) Oh, my goodness gracious !

CECIL. Jehoshaphat !

(*Enter* LORD PLUMLEIGH *lazily from door at back. He is a boy of fourteen, and is munching an apple.*)

LORD PLUMLEIGH. Morning, mater. (*Up by door—lazily leaning against door.*)

LADY GEORGY (*severely*). It is past eleven and you have just finished breakfast, Digby.

LORD PLUMLEIGH (*munching*). Not quite finished.

(CECIL *rises, goes up slowly to* DIGBY.)

Have the hanky-pankies come yet ?

LADY GEORGY (*shuddering*). No.

CECIL. Lazy little beast !

LORD PLUMLEIGH. Morning, Cecil—may I say friend ?

(CECIL *sits down.*)

LADY GEORGY. Digby, I've a letter from Dr. Pym saying you are the idlest boy in the whole school.

LORD PLUMLEIGH (*genially*). I can tell you how he knows that. We had a plebiscite about which was the idlest and I won. Not sure that I deserved it though. I think some of the fellows voted for me because I am a lord. (*Sees that* LADY GEORGY *is fidgeting.*)

(LADY GEORGY *looks in entrance of hedge and back again to seat.*)

(*To* CECIL) Anything the matter? (*Crosses to* CECIL *behind sundial.*)

(CECIL *tells him the state of affairs in a low voice.* LORD PLUMLEIGH *is mischievously delighted and grins at his mother.* CECIL *coughs warningly and exits through window as enter* SIR JENNINGS *and* DR. TOPPING. SIR JENNINGS *is elderly, polished, genial when he pleases.* DR. TOPPING *is younger, proud of being in a great house, and full of the etiquette proper between an ordinary practitioner and a consulting physician. Thus he opens window for* SIR JENNINGS *and remains standing till* SIR JENNINGS *is seated, etc.* LORD PLUMLEIGH *is by centre door.*)

SIR JENNINGS.   Well, dear lady, we have seen your daughter, and we have had our little consultation. Your son?

LADY GEORGY.   Lord Plumleigh—Sir Jennings Pyke.

LORD PLUMLEIGH (*takes off his cap and shakes hands with* SIR JENNINGS).   I hope you 're decent.

SIR JENNINGS (*pleasantly*).   Thank you—and you?

LORD PLUMLEIGH.   I 'm decent. Much illness about just now, Topping?

DR. TOPPING.   A great deal, my lord—a very trying summer.

SIR JENNINGS.   I don't remember a more trying summer.

DR. TOPPING (*impressed*).   Don't you, Sir Jennings?

LADY GEORGY.   But Millicent?

SIR JENNINGS.   I find her, dear lady, in safe hands. In very safe hands indeed. (*He bows to* TOPPING, *sits by* LADY GEORGY.)

(DR. TOPPING *bows.*)

SIR JENNINGS.   After carefully considering the case I have come to the conclusion that the same treatment should be continued. (*Turns to* DR. TOPPING) Perhaps a slight change in the phosphates, Dr. Topping—a little less iron.

DR. TOPPING.   Certainly, Sir Jennings.

SIR JENNINGS.   *I* think so. (*Turns to* DR. TOPPING) Do you think so?

DR. TOPPING.   Yes.

SIR JENNINGS.   Yes, I think so.   Otherwise as before. (*Turning to* LADY GEORGY) In such a case as this, dear lady, we cannot over-estimate the importance of *building-up*. Two years ago, as I understand, Lady Millicent received a great shock ?

LADY GEORGY.   You remember the circumstances ?   She was engaged to be married to Sir Frank Cosham, and his sudden death was the blow from which she has never rallied.   She recovered so far from the fever that followed, but she regains no strength—no spirit.   It is nearly two years since she has been able to move about except in an invalid chair.

DR. TOPPING.   And how angelically she bears it.   I never go near her without feeling that I am in the presence of a cathedral.

SIR JENNING.   Yes.   A broken lily.

DR. TOPPING.   Or, better still, of a broken lily.

SIR JENNINGS.   Ah, dear, dear—well ! well ! well ! We must build her up.

(LORD PLUMLEIGH *after arranging cushion sits in chair.*) Now, dear lady, there are two physicians greater in this matter than either Dr. Topping—

(DR. TOPPING *bows to him.*) —or myself.

DR. TOPPING.   Oh ! Sir Jennings !

SIR JENNINGS.   Myself !   Namely Dr. Food and Dr. Sleep. It is not too much to say that for the present when Lady Millicent is not sleeping she should be eating, when not eating she should be sleeping.

LORD PLUMLEIGH.   That 's just what I do !   (*Lying on chair.*)

LADY GEORGY.   We have tried that for so long—we have tried everything.

SIR JENNINGS.   Has she been to Homburg ?

LADY GEORGY.   Oh yes.

SIR JENNINGS.   The mud baths at Swalbach ?

LADY GEORGY.   We have tried them also.

SIR JENNINGS.   The Engadine ?

LADY GEORGY.   Yes.

SIR JENNINGS.   The Canary Islands ?

LADY GEORGY.   No ;   we haven't tried them.

SIR JENNINGS. Oh! I strongly recommend the Canary Islands.

DR. TOPPING (*impressed*). Do you, Sir Jennings?

SIR JENNINGS. Yes, I happen to know a medical man there.

DR. TOPPING. Most fortunate.

SIR JENNINGS. I shall give you a note to him.

DR. TOPPING. Thank you, Sir Jennings.

LADY GEORGY. It all seems so hopeless. (*Rises.*)

(TOPPING *goes to* LORD PLUMLEIGH.)

SIR JENNINGS (*rising genially*). Oh, no, no, no, with time, dear lady—give us time. (*To* TOPPING) Well, well, Dr. Topping, I think—— (*Meaning that he has finished, goes to sundial, examining it.*)

DR. TOPPING. The cheque, Lady Plumleigh.

LADY GEORGY. Yes. (*Gives him an envelope.*)

SIR JENNINGS. *Tempus fugit.* Ah, how true, how true. (*Looking at sundial.*)

DR. TOPPING. Thank you. (*Calls to* SIR JENNINGS) Eh—Sir Jennings, eh—— (*Offers envelope.*)

SIR JENNINGS (*coming to* TOPPING). What's that? Oh yes!

(*Puts it carelessly into waistcoat pocket, hums.*)

Ta ra, ra, ra, la ra la ra ra. (*Turns looking at house.*) Charming place you have here, Lady Plumleigh. Charming!

LORD PLUMLEIGH. I say, Sir Jennings—

(SIR JENNINGS *turns to him.*)

—have you heard of this lady who has been making such a sensation lately? They call her the Stormy Petrel.

(SIR JENNINGS' *manner changes to hardness.* DR. TOPPING *has not heard of the lady, but is prepared to look whatever is expected of him.*)

Have you met her?

SIR JENNINGS. There is nothing I should like better.

(LORD PLUMLEIGH *gloats over his mother's uneasiness.*)

LADY GEORGY (*faintly*). I suppose—quite a fraudulent person?

SIR JENNINGS. Entirely so, dear lady. A worker of miracles, Topping.

DR. TOPPING. Very sad.

SIR JENNINGS. And with the help of a medium. Oh, I

assure you there are people who *think* she has saved their lives.

DR. TOPPING.   And this is the twentieth century.

LADY GEORGY (*sits in seat*).   Of course they do tell marvellous stories about her.   There was Lord Mauleverer, for instance, who used to be so swathed in gout that he was a bundle rather than a man.   What was it his son told you, Digby, about Miss Loney?

LORD PLUMLEIGH.   He said she had his pa hopping about in no time.   But how does she do it?   (*This to* SIR JENNINGS.)

SIR JENNINGS.   Ah, there you have me?   (*He says it as if it were a witty and pregnant remark.*)

DR. TOPPING (*in same spirit*).   Precisely.

LADY GEORGY.   I have heard that her patients are sworn to secrecy.   At all events they will tell nothing.

DR. TOPPING.   Tricky—very tricky.

SIR JENNINGS.   But clever !

DR. TOPPING.   Oh, clever !

LORD PLUMLEIGH.   Mother says that to invite such hanky-pankies to one's house is an insult to the medical profession.

(*Sound of wheels.*   LADY GEORGY *starts up.*)

SIR JENNINGS.   I quite agree, dear lady.

LORD PLUMLEIGH.   What 's the matter, mother—did you hear anything?

LADY GEORGY.   No—I—no !

DR. TOPPING.   I think I hear the sound of wheels.

LORD PLUMLEIGH.   It must be those ladies you are expecting, mother.   (*Rises*) Oh, here they come.

(LADY GEORGY *is desperate.*   DEIGHTON, *the butler, shows in* LORD CARLTON, *not greatly altered by the six years that have elapsed.*   LORD CARLTON *crosses to* LORD PLUMLEIGH.)

LORD PLUMLEIGH (*comes back to chair*).   It 's only you, uncle ?

LORD CARLTON (*shakes hands with* LORD PLUMLEIGH).   Plum, my boy, are you decent ?

(LORD PLUMLEIGH *turns from him.*)

He seems disappointed, Georgy.   (*Turns to* LADY GEORGY.)

LADY GEORGY (*relieved*).   But I am delighted.

LORD PLUMLEIGH.   We were expecting two ladies, you see.

LORD CARLTON. Ah well, I don't think they came by my train.

> (LADY GEORGY *crosses to* LORD PLUMLEIGH. LORD CARLTON *crosses to* SIR JENNINGS.)

Ah, Sir Jennings ! (*Shakes hands.*) I hope this doesn't mean that our dear little Millicent is worse ?

SIR JENNINGS. No, no, a little consultation—that is all.

LORD CARLTON. If I am in the way——

SIR JENNINGS. On the contrary, I fear we are in your way.

LORD CARLTON. Well, I must return to town to-day, and I should like a few words with Lady Plumleigh—if you have quite finished.

SIR JENNINGS. Quite.

> (SIR JENNINGS *going a step towards* LADY GEORGY.)

May we—dear lady, have a look at the gardens ?

LADY GEORGY. Oh yes. Digby will show them to you. Digby, come and show the garden.

LORD PLUMLEIGH. Bother ! We were talking of the Stormy Petrel, uncle—what do *you* think of her ?

> (SIR JENNINGS *and* DR. TOPPING *listen.*)

LORD CARLTON. Well, from all I hear, my Plum, I should say she would be none the worse for six months' hard.

SIR JENNINGS and DR. TOPPING. Very good.

LADY GEORGY (*shudders—calls* LORD PLUMLEIGH). Digby !

> (*Exeunt* SIR JENNINGS *and* DR. TOPPING *and* LORD PLUMLEIGH.)

Of course you 've come about Cecil ?

LORD CARLTON. What else ? Where is he ?

LADY GEORGY. In the gardens. Shall I send for him ?

LORD CARLTON. No, no ! Georgy, I 'm at my wits' end about him—an actress—— !

LADY GEORGY. Oh, it 's awful ! (*Reproving*) You didn't take my advice, David.

LORD CARLTON. Well, I sent my lawyer to her with a handsome offer, but she showed him the door. (*Chuckling*) I should have liked to have seen her showing old pomposity the door !

LADY GEORGY. David, your fatal sense of humour !

LORD CARLTON. Yes. (*Gravely*) I 'm serious enough about this.

LADY GEORGY. But you didn't take my advice about the private inquiry.

LORD CARLTON. Georgy, I couldn't. Your detective fellow came to me for instructions—but who am I to send a spy nosing into a woman's history ? I sent him away. It was as much as I could do to avoid kicking him downstairs.

LADY GEORGY. That 's all the thanks I get !

LORD CARLTON (*sits*). No, no, my dear. I 'm devoutly thankful to you for contriving to keep Cecil here and preventing him gallivanting after her. I call it uncommon clever of you.

LADY GEORGY (*defiantly*). It *is* clever—but you won't say so when I tell you how I contrived it.

LORD CARLTON (*strongly*). Have you been up to anything ?

LADY GEORGY. Well, I may as well tell you at once. Eleanor is here.

LORD CARLTON. Here !

LADY GEORGY. She has been here as long as Cecil. (*Quaking*) That 's my cleverness, David.

LORD CARLTON (*rises—furious*). Oh, is it ?

LADY GEORGY. You might have pity on me. I wander about with my arm round her waist and call you the most horrid names.

LORD CARLTON. Thanks——

LADY GEORGY. I look on at her dying till I 'm sick of it. She is good at dying, and she dies all over the house. (*Plaintively*) I can see by these cushions that she 's been dying here this morning.

LORD CARLTON. Why is she here ?

LADY GEORGY. Don't you see, by pretending to be her friend, I gain her confidence—and all the time *I* have been quietly employing that detective. Oh, she doted on me !

LORD CARLTON. Georgy, it isn't pretty.

LADY GEORGY. There 's a proverb, isn't there, about setting a woman to catch a woman ?

LORD CARLTON. Something like that ! Yes, yes, and the result ?

LADY GEORGY. I know the worst.

LORD CARLTON. Then there is a worst ? (*Kindly*) Poor girl !

LADY GEORGY.　Oh, my dear, you don't understand.　Surely in a case of this kind there can be but one worse.　(*Tragically*) David—there is nothing whatever against her—she is a perfectly nice girl.

(LORD CARLTON *can't help chuckling.*)

It seems there are quite a number of nice actresses nowadays. I don't know what the stage is coming to.

(*Goes to him—sees him chuckling—in dudgeon.*)

Laugh on, but will you laugh when you read in the play-bills ' Princess Prettytoes—Lady Rolfe ' ?

LORD CARLTON.　Stop it !　(*Wincing.*)

LADY GEORGY.　Oh, she is to continue to follow her art— they both say so.

LORD CARLTON.　Stop it, I say !　Ah, here is Cecil !

(*Enter* CECIL.　*He is in deadly earnest and looks sternly at* LORD CARLTON.)

CECIL.　So, father !

LORD CARLTON.　So, my boy !

LADY GEORGY (*shocked*).　Cecil, won't you shake hands with your father ?

CECIL.　My dear aunt, your kindness to me and Eleanor I can never forget, but I ask you to be so good as to leave me alone with this gentleman.

(LORD CARLTON *coughs, controls his sense of humour. Exit* LADY GEORGY.　CECIL *folds his arms in Napoleonic manner, and speaks with biting severity.　When* CECIL *folds his arms* LORD CARLTON *retreats a little in mock terror.*)

Father, you gave me birth.

LORD CARLTON (*bows*).　Oh, not at all.

CECIL.　I never thanked you for that—I do so now.　(*He is pleased with this and assumes another Napoleonic pose.*)

LORD CARLTON.　Do you know, Cecil, I think I shall have to have you painted as Napoleon.

(CECIL *drops his Napoleon in annoyance.*)

Come, Cecil, old man, we mustn't quarrel.

CECIL.　I have no wish to quarrel, but you must own, father, that you are a little trying.

LORD CARLTON.　Well, perhaps I am, but you see it 's rather trying to have such a strapping son.

CECIL.   Well, I can't help you being a little chap.

LORD CARLTON (*wincing*).   Well, I suppose you can't.   I don't think you and I have ever had a square talk together. Why shouldn't we?   (*Gets him to sit.*)   Have you ever wondered, Cecil, what sort of a fellow I am?

CECIL (*wistfully*).   Often!

LORD CARLTON.   I have often wondered what sort of a fellow you are.   I suppose that is what makes a father and son so uncomfortable in each other's presence.

CECIL.   Do you ever get the creeps when you 're left alone with me?

LORD CARLTON.   Mortally!   My first instinct is to steal away.

CECIL.   So is mine.

LORD CARLTON.   And the worst of it is that I know that you know how I am feeling and that you know that I know how you are feeling.

CECIL (*gloomy*).   Yes.

LORD CARLTON.   They tell me you are quite bright and witty in the society of others.

CECIL.   I have heard the same of you.

LORD CARLTON.   It 's an awkward relationship, Cecil. (*Looking at one another.*)

CECIL (*leaning forward*).   Oh well, we 've got to go through with it.

LORD CARLTON.   And yet I suppose we are fond of each other.

CECIL (*like a true Englishman is uneasy at the introduction of sentiment*).   That 's not a thing to speak about, surely.

LORD CARLTON (*determinedly*).   I tell you bluntly, my boy, I 'm fond of you.

CECIL (*raising himself up—looking round*).   Good lord, father, if anyone were to hear you.

LORD CARLTON.   Well, have you got anything civil to say to me?

CECIL (*cautious tone*).   Oh, I don't know—I sometimes bragged about you at Eton.

LORD CARLTON (*quite moved*).   Did you?   What sort of things?

CECIL (*almost sulky through having to talk about it*).   I don't

know.　I told them about that time when you saved the street
boy from the fire and got so burned.

LORD CARLTON.　Did you tell them how you sat up with me
for three nights running ?

CECIL.　No.　Did I ?　I had forgotten.

LORD CARLTON.　I haven't.　You held my hand, Cecil.

CECIL (*raising himself*).　Is it fair, father, to cast these things
up against a fellow ?

LORD CARLTON.　I only want to hear you say for once that
you like me.　Come on, Cecil, and we 'll never allude to this
unpleasant subject again.　If you feel a shyness about saying it
put your hand on my knee, and I 'll take that in lieu of speech.

　　　(CECIL *ultimately puts hand on knee and quickly with-
　　　draws it.*)

Come, that 's over.

CECIL (*becoming haughty—rising*).　It 's Eleanor I want to
speak of.

LORD CARLTON.　Oh yes !　(*Pulls him down.*)　We are coming
to her, we are coming to her.　How like me you are, Cecil !
(*With a sigh*) Yet I don't want you to be too like me.　I have
been a lazy dog all my life, my boy, and I want to see you a
better man than your father.

CECIL.　Oh well, I don't complain of your wanting me to work.

LORD CARLTON.　But you don't do it.

CECIL.　That 's another question.

LORD CARLTON.　I want to see you shine, Cecil.

CECIL.　Oh, yes—father !　It 's all very well to say that, but
when it comes to the point who is it that prevents me shining !
You !

LORD CARLTON (*ashamed—yet half gleeful*).　Do I ?

CECIL.　Yes.　At the critical moment you go and shine
yourself.

　　　(LORD CARLTON *laughs.*)

It has been so as far back as I can remember.　Whatever your
intention may be the result is that you always *score* off me.
When we *practised* at cricket I could hit you out of the field,
but when it came to a match, who was it that bowled me in the
first over ?　*My own father !*

LORD CARLTON (*properly ashamed*).　I couldn't resist it, Cecil,
I couldn't resist it.

P

CECIL. There 's a good deal of the old Adam in you yet. At my coming-of-age ball, who was it went off dancing with all the prettiest girls ?

LORD CARLTON. Ah ! I meant to leave them to you, Cecil, but—you see it seemed such a short time since my own coming-of-age ball, and then you young chappies always seem to expect to keep all the pretty girls to yourselves. There 's nothing upsets an old boy like that. But never again, my boy, never again.

CECIL (*turns to* LORD CARLTON). No, for I am a boy no longer. At last we meet as man to man.

LORD CARLTON. That 's what I desire. I wish you to know, Cecil, how anxious I am to be your friend to-day—in this affair between you and Eleanor.

CECIL. Is friendship possible between father and son ?

LORD CARLTON. Let us prove that it is.

(*Holds out hand*—CECIL *takes it doubtfully,* LORD CARLTON *pulls* CECIL *to him.*) You know you 've been in love before, Cecil.

CECIL (*sternly—dropping his father's hand and stepping back*). Father !—if you really want my friendship not one word about those trumpery affairs.

LORD CARLTON. Oh, very good, sir, very good.

CECIL. All I ask is common-sense. Eleanor and I have been talking you over.

LORD CARLTON. Oh, have you !

CECIL. She asked me to give you another chance.

LORD CARLTON. That was sweet of her.

CECIL. She says—you don't mean to be cruel but that you have forgotten that you once had a love story yourself. The trouble is that as the son grows up the father grows old—I don't know if you have noticed it, father, but you 're not the man you were.

LORD CARLTON (*stung*). Poof ! I 'm only forty-five.

CECIL. Well, it is now acknowledged that after forty a man's only blocking the way.

LORD CARLTON. A little more of this, Cecil, and I shall block the way by walking off with Eleanor myself. I can play Napoleon too. (*He copies* CECIL's *pose à la Napoleon.*)

(CECIL *is genuinely alarmed.*)

CECIL.   I only said so because Eleanor was so nice about your age.

LORD CARLTON. Was she ?

CECIL. Oh yes. (*Thinking he is making a good impression*) She said an awfully pretty thing, father.

LORD CARLTON. Yes !

CECIL. About wanting to be a staff on which you might lean as you went downhill.

LORD CARLTON. What !

CECIL (*his manner changing to boyish appeal*). I say, dad !
> (LORD CARLTON *is really touched, but moves away signifying that he is not to be got round.* CECIL *goes to him wistfully.*)

I 'm awfully fond of her, dad, and she 's awfully fond of me—and she 's waiting behind that hedge.

LORD CARLTON (*amused and touched*). Oh, is she, Cecil ?

CECIL. Come, dad, if you like me as you say you do you 'll understand, you must have been in love with an actress yourself once.

> (LORD CARLTON *smiles to himself and in a reverie remembers a pleasant time he once had, then frowns as if they had quarrelled, smiles as if he had forgiven, shakes head as if remembering that it ended sadly—then sighs.* CECIL *has been watching him.*)

CECIL. What was her name, dad ?

LORD CARLTON (*wakening up*). Whose name ?

CECIL. The actress you were thinking of.

LORD CARLTON (*severely*). How dare you ?

CECIL (*laughing*). Come, dad——

LORD CARLTON. It 's no good, Cecil—but you may bring her to me.

> (CECIL *exits and returns—brings in* ELEANOR, *a pretty, timid girl ; she is a lady.*)

CECIL (*a little grandly*). Dad—this—this is Eleanor.

LORD CARLTON (*to* ELEANOR *who is afraid*). Please don't look on me as an ogre, Eleanor. (*Taking her hand*) I could say some pretty things to you—if Cecil were some other man's son.

ELEANOR (*faintly, but courageously*). The stage is the noblest profession in the world.

LORD CARLTON. I know—I know.

ELEANOR (*timidly*).   Did you see our show ?
(LORD CARLTON *winces*.)

CECIL.   If you had seen her in the ' Bayswater Girl,' father !

LORD CARLTON.   Ah, I missed that.

ELEANOR.   It was beautifully put on.   Five thousand pounds if a penny.

LORD CARLTON.   The ancient Greeks spent less on their plays, Eleanor.

ELEANOR.   Yes.   They were easily pleased.   (*Proudly*.)

CECIL.   It *was* a success, but it was you who made it the hit, dearest.

ELEANOR.   And it wasn't a fat part either, Cecil.

CECIL.   It was what she did with it, dad.

LORD CARLTON.   That this young lady has genius I have no doubt.

CECIL.   The *D.T.* said ' This charming little lady.'

LORD CARLTON.   The *Pink One* said, ' What ho ! Eleanor ' !

ELEANOR (*modestly*).   Every one has been very kind.

CECIL (*going to him*).   Dad, if you could see her die.

LORD CARLTON (*hastily*).   Oh yes, some other time, my boy. Some other time.

CECIL.   You see she has never had her chance yet.   But if one of those brutes of dramatists were to write a human play *round* her, I don't mean a sort of play that makes you think— thank goodness ours is a healthy-minded public, and declines to think.

ELEANOR.   Cecil, a tragedy with a happy ending !

CECIL.   Colossal—that 's what she would be, sir—simply colossal.

LORD CARLTON (*craftily*).   But why shouldn't we have it done, my boy ?

CECIL.   You mean it ?

LORD CARLTON.   Why not ? A play something like ' Much Ado about Nothing.'

ELEANOR.   Yes, that 's a pretty little play.

LORD CARLTON.   Yes.

CECIL.   Dad ! As soon as we are married !

LORD CARLTON.   Instead of being married—it would be a much bigger thing, Eleanor.

ELEANOR.   Oh, Cecil !

CECIL.   How dare you !

LORD CARLTON.   Ah, well, well ! Miss Gray, I have no wish to appear ungallant, but you must have known for some weeks my feeling with regard to this engagement. I have other views for my son. If it were in my power I should lock Cecil up, but he is of age and can disregard my wishes. I have no wish to play the heavy father, I shall not curtail his allowance nor order him out of my sight, but there would be neither pleasure nor benefit to either of us in our seeing much of each other in future. He will doubtless get on quite well without me—better, Cecil, than I shall get on without you.

CECIL.   That is your ultimatum ?

LORD CARLTON.   Yes.

CECIL (takes ELEANOR's hand).   Then this is mine. I shall not only marry this lady, but I shall go on the stage myself.

LORD CARLTON.   Good heavens !

CECIL.   What more splendid career than to hold as ' 'twere the mirror up to nature ' ?   Come, Eleanor.

LORD CARLTON.   Cecil, you are joking !

CECIL (turns, coming back again, still holding ELEANOR's hand). It is you who are miserably narrow. Do you think that Eleanor will be the first actress to marry a lord ?

ELEANOR.   It is almost expected of us nowadays.

(CECIL shakes her hand approvingly and lets it go, steps towards LORD CARLTON.)

LORD CARLTON (in disgust). Ah !

CECIL.   It is the very calling for our set, sir—mark my words, in ten years' time we shall all be on the stage—all the brainy ones. Your sneers do not excite me, sir, it is a well-known saying that no man is a hero to his father.

(Exit haughtily with ELEANOR.)

LORD CARLTON (after a moment of exasperation).   Idiot !

(Exit through french windows. DEIGHTON the butler comes carrying bag, shows in MOIRA. She is now eighteen, but has the old serious face and ways ; she is quietly dressed.)

DEIGHTON.   I thought her ladyship was here, but I shall find her, madam. (Turns as though to go through window with bag.)

MOIRA (quickly).   My bag, please.

DEIGHTON.   It will be quite safe, I assure you.

MOIRA. *Please* give me my bag.

(*He gives it and she puts it on sundial.*)

DEIGHTON. Her ladyship instructed me that you would be accompanied by another lady.

MOIRA (*sitting primly*). I came alone.

DEIGHTON (*follows her to seat*). May I inquire if your friend is to follow, madam ? I ask, that a carriage may meet her.

MOIRA. Oh, she will not require a carriage.

DEIGHTON. The luggage.

MOIRA. She has no luggage.

DEIGHTON. I beg your pardon—I—I understood you were both here for some weeks.

MOIRA. Yes, probably.

DEIGHTON. The lady—her ladyship called her—Miss Mary——

MOIRA. Did she not say Little Mary ?

DEIGHTON. Yes, madam, she did. Her ladyship instructed the housekeeper to give Miss—Little Mary—the room next to yours.

MOIRA. She will not require a room.

DEIGHTON (*thinking he has solved it*). She will share your room.

MOIRA. Oh no.

(*Exit* DEIGHTON *correctly, but puzzled and scandalised.* MOIRA *rises and goes to bag, is nervous and ill at ease— speaks to bag.*)

Oh, Grandpa, I 'm so frightened.

(*She looks and is enraptured by what she sees ; she controls herself as enters the object of her joy,* LORD CARLTON. *He is still fuming after* CECIL, *but stops abruptly on seeing a lady.*)

LORD CARLTON. I beg your pardon, madam—my sister Lady Plumleigh—may I introduce myself, Lord Carlton, her brother ?

(*She bows timidly—he has a vague recollection of her.*)

Do you know, I think we have met before, haven't we ?

MOIRA (*pained*). You don't remember ?

LORD CARLTON. Yes, yes, of course. Delighted. And how is everybody ?

MOIRA.   You have forgotten me ?

LORD CARLTON.   My dear young lady, how can you say such a thing ! My sister said she was expecting friends, but didn't say whom. Well, are they all—pretty fit ?

MOIRA.   Who ?

LORD CARLTON.   Our friends, of course !

MOIRA.   Where ?

LORD CARLTON.   At—the old place. (*He can't face her reproachful eyes.*) I give it up.

MOIRA (*sighing*).   Yes, it is best to be honest !

LORD CARLTON.   And yet I seem to know your face !

MOIRA.   It was long ago.   I was only——

LORD CARLTON (*excited*).   Stop ! (*He is beginning to remember ; she waits eagerly.*) A little room—somewhere—a bookseller's shop !

MOIRA (*disappointed*).   No.

LORD CARLTON.   A shop !

MOIRA.   Yes.

LORD CARLTON.   Your name——

MOIRA.   We didn't know each other's names, we——

LORD CARLTON.   I called you—— (*Can't get it.*)

MOIRA (*carried away by excitement*).   Lord !

LORD CARLTON (*triumphantly*).   Mother !

(*He takes her hands delighted, she is joyous, then suddenly weeps, sits.*)

MOIRA.   Please forgive me, it is because you remembered. I haven't been called by that name for six years.

LORD CARLTON.   Not even by the occupants of the boxes ?

MOIRA.   No, they were taken away.

LORD CARLTON.   And the old gentleman ?

MOIRA.   Grandpa.   He died three years ago.

LORD CARLTON (*quite touched*).   And that little girl—had to do without boxes.

MOIRA.   Yes. (*Tragically*) And now I am afraid to go near children for fear I have lost my way with them.

LORD CARLTON (*sits by her incredulous*).   *You* lose your way with them.

MOIRA.   Perhaps I have.

LORD CARLTON.   And what a way you had with them !

MOIRA (*beaming*).   Hadn't I ? (*Seeing them in her mind's eye and clasping them—with wistful gravity*) Lord, do you ever wish you had been Eve ?

LORD CARLTON (*solemnly, and feeling his old delight in her*). Eve ? Do you know, I don't believe I ever had.

MOIRA (*ecstatic*). To have been Eve, and to have had the first one ! Not to have had a notion what they were like and then to have one. Oh, the sweet !

LORD CARLTON. Dear little Cain—— I say, Mother !

MOIRA. Yes !

LORD CARLTON. Let me give you a tip. You get my sister to put you into the purple room. It is next the nurseries.

MOIRA. Are there children ?

LORD CARLTON. Two. And from that room you can hear them playing, falling into the fire-irons, dancing, screaming, having their bath, getting up at five o'clock in the morning.

MOIRA. Do you ?

LORD CARLTON. Yes, I had the room once—for one night.

MOIRA. Ah, you 're too kind. Everyone will be wanting it.

LORD CARLTON. Well, of course, the demand for it is enormous—but I shall insist.

MOIRA (*changing*). Perhaps I 'd better not have it, it might tempt me away from my work.

LORD CARLTON. You have come here to work.

MOIRA (*uneasily*). Yes.

LORD CARLTON. For Lady Plumleigh ?

MOIRA. Yes.

LORD CARLTON. I see—I understand—I was wondering——— (*Seeing she is not happy*) Well, I am quite sure the little girl of the boxes is not afraid of work.

MOIRA. Oh, but that wasn't work. That was doing all the dear things I love to do. Work is doing what you don't like to do.

LORD CARLTON. And that is the kind of work you 've come to do now ?

MOIRA. Yes.

LORD CARLTON. I 'm sorry—I 'm very sorry. You make me feel ashamed. Gad, I remember you had just the same effect before.

MOIRA (*wistfully*). Do you do anything ?

LORD CARLTON. Not a blessed thing.

MOIRA. That's because you are so ill !

LORD CARLTON. No, I 'm very well. (*Remembers*) Now who was it who used to say that ? That we were splendid people, but very ill ?

MOIRA (*half afraid*). Grandpa.

LORD CARLTON. Of course ! Grandpa ! (*Chuckles.*)

MOIRA (*anxious*). He was to touch a spring and set you all going again.

LORD CARLTON. The very words. What a pity that he died —for we need him more than ever.

MOIRA (*trying to subdue excitement*). Don't you remember that I was trying to help him ?

LORD CARLTON. Well, now is your chance. (*Wryly*) If you would only begin on my boy.

MOIRA. But I thought you said he was always playing marbles.

LORD CARLTON. He is still at them. Now if you would only touch a spring and set him going.

MOIRA. I had rather it was you.

LORD CARLTON (*with humorous alarm, falling back a little*). None of that, Mother—no meddling with me—I 've been lazy too long—I 'm a lifer. (*He plays with her bag and its weight amazes him.*) Oh, lord, how surprisingly heavy !

MOIRA (*goes to bag—because she can say nothing else*). Yes.

(*Enter* LADY GEORGY ; MOIRA *turns to her ;* LADY GEORGY *flattered at seeing these two together.*)

MOIRA. Lady Plumleigh ?

LADY GEORGY. I have only just heard of your arrival—— David, you haven't been saying horrid things to her ?

LORD CARLTON. Horrid things ? On the contrary, I am delighted to see this lady.

LADY GEORGY (*astonished*). Already ? (*To* MOIRA) You clever thing !

(LORD PLUMLEIGH *wheels* LADY MILLICENT *to front of seat in bath-chair. She is a sweet, pale invalid of nineteen with no spirit.*)

LORD CARLTON (*comes to her*). Ah, Milly ! My dear child, are you better ?

LADY MILLICENT. I must be thankful I am no worse, uncle. (*Seeing* MOIRA) Mother—— Is it ?

LADY GEORGY.   Yes, and she has made a convert already—
your uncle.

LORD PLUMLEIGH.   I say !

LADY MILLICENT (*to* LORD CARLTON).   I am so glad !

LORD CARLTON.   A convert ?

MOIRA (*in anguish—but trying to be calm*).   Lady Plumleigh,
Lord Carlton does not know who I am.   Won't you please tell
him ?

LADY GEORGY (*crushed*).   You don't know ?

LORD CARLTON (*beginning to wonder*).   Not by name.   Will
you introduce me ?   (*Goes to* MOIRA.)

LADY GEORGY (*flattering*).   Lord Carlton—Miss Loney.
    (*They are all prepared for a scene, but the name is nothing
    to him.*)

LORD CARLTON (*shaking her hand*).   Delighted to meet Miss
Loney—but I know a better name for her than that.

LADY MILLICENT (*thinking like the others that he means the
Stormy Petrel*).   And you don't mind.   Mother, he doesn't mind.

LADY GEORGY (*relieved*).   Dear David, you knew all the
time !

MOIRA.   He does not know yet—please tell him.

LADY GEORGY.   I—I——   (*Hesitates.*)
    (LORD CARLTON *wonders.*)

LORD PLUMLEIGH.   Mater——   (*Gloating*) See who are
coming !
    (*Enter* SIR JENNINGS *and* DR. TOPPING.)

SIR JENNINGS.   A dream of a garden, dear lady, a dream !
    (LORD CARLTON *goes up to* LORD PLUMLEIGH.)

LADY GEORGY.   Yes, I—Sir Jennings, it seems inhospitable,
but the coachman says you have just time to catch your train.
    (LORD CARLTON *looks at his watch.*)

SIR JENNINGS.   Oh, then we must be off.   Thank you so
much.   (*Shakes hands with* LADY GEORGY) Good-bye.   (*A
step down to* LADY MILLICENT) Good-bye, Lady Millicent.
(*Bows to* MOIRA.)

LORD CARLTON.   Sir Jennings, you have lots of time—I
am going by the same train.   Before you go I should like to
present a lady to you.

SIR JENNINGS.   Ah !   (*Comes back ; is attracted by* MOIRA'S
face.)   I shall be delighted indeed.

LORD CARLTON (*watching for effect on* SIR JENNINGS).   Sir Jennings Pyke—Miss Loney.

(SIR JENNINGS *in the act of bowing pulls himself up sharply.*)

SIR JENNINGS.   Not—not *the* Miss Loney ?

MOIRA.   I am the Miss Loney you mean, Sir Jennings.

SIR JENNINGS.   Was this insult prepared, my lord ?

LORD CARLTON.   I am aware of no insult.

SIR JENNINGS.   We are all entitled to our opinion.   I am content to know this lady by her more picturesque name.

LORD CARLTON.   What is that ?

DR. TOPPING.   Don't you know, my lord ?   The Stormy Petrel.

LORD CARLTON.   This lady !   Impossible.

MOIRA.   That is who I am.   (*There is a timid dignity about her.*)

LORD CARLTON (*after a pause*).   Sir Jennings, I beg your pardon.

(MOIRA *shivers but stands quietly.*)

SIR JENNINGS (*turning to* LADY PLUMLEIGH *severely*).   Am I to understand that this lady has been introduced into the house to effect one of her marvellous cures on Lady Millicent ?

LADY GEORGY.   Oh no, oh dear no, I—I should never dream of such a thing; I never meant to trust her—not absolutely, you know !

SIR JENNINGS.   Lady Plumleigh—I *warn* you *solemnly* against putting your daughter's *life* in the hands of this lady. You know something of what happened when she was at Frisby Court.

LADY GEORGY.   I know that she cured Colonel Frisby.

SIR JENNINGS.   And that as soon as he was cured he tried to blow his brains out.

LORD CARLTON.   Surely she was not responsible for that, Sir Jennings ?

MOIRA.   Yes, I think I was.

(*A look between* SIR JENNINGS *and* DR. TOPPING ; *they are uncomfortable.*)

SIR JENNINGS.   It is but one of the several scandals that have procured for her the name of which she is doubtless proud.

DR. TOPPING.   A lady who makes use of a medium !

LORD PLUMLEIGH.   Miss Loney, where *is* Little Mary ?

MOIRA.   She is here.

LADY GEORGY.   Deighton told me she hadn't come with you.

MOIRA.   I found her here when I arrived.

LADY GEORGY.   Here !

LORD CARLTON.   An invisible medium !   Georgy, surely you are not going on with this.

SIR JENNINGS.   Are we to withdraw from the case, or is she ?

LADY GEORGY (*desperately*).   Milly must decide.

LADY MILLICENT.   Please let there be no unpleasantness on my account.

DR. TOPPING (*coming to* LADY PLUMLEIGH).   In time——

LADY GEORGY.   Time !   Miss Loney—can you make her well ?

MOIRA.   I think so.

LADY GEORGY.   In—time ?

MOIRA.   In a month.

SIR JENNINGS (*turns to* DR. TOPPING).   A month exactly, Topping.

DR. TOPPING.   Yet she knows nothing about the case.

MOIRA.   I have made inquiries about the case.

SIR JENNINGS.   Which leaves you confident ?

MOIRA.   Yes.

SIR JENNINGS.   Lady Millicent—have you decided ?

LADY MILLICENT.   Dear Sir Jennings, I am not worth all this unpleasantness.   I don't think I even wish to get well again.   Let us leave it to her.

SIR JENNINGS (*hesitates, he crosses to* MOIRA).   Madam.

MOIRA (*soft but firm*).   I was invited here.   I felt it was just the sort of house that needed me, and I shall remain unless I am turned out.

LADY GEORGY.   I can't turn her out.

SIR JENNINGS.   Then we withdraw.   (*Goes to door—turns and listens.*)

MOIRA (*with an effect—crosses to* LADY GEORGY).   Lady Plumleigh, I think it is only right to warn you that the effect of my presence here may not be limited to Lady Millicent. It is probable that I may have a strange effect on everyone in the house.   What this effect may be I know as little as themselves, but those who prefer to remain as they are will be wise to leave.

LORD PLUMLEIGH.   That sounds jolly exciting.

SIR JENNINGS.   Lady Plumleigh, Lady Millicent. (*Bowing to them.*) Lord Carlton. (*Gives supercilious look at* MOIRA *and then goes up to door, turns to* DR. TOPPING) We had better go, Topping, before *we* are changed.

> (SIR JENNINGS *bows stiffly and exits with* DR. TOPPING, LADY GEORGY *follows them off.*)

LORD CARLTON.   Georgy, I wish to speak to Miss Loney.

> (LADY GEORGY *exits in distress after doctors.*)

Digby. (*Motions to* LORD PLUMLEIGH *to take* LADY MILLICENT *off.*)

> (LORD PLUMLEIGH *wheels* LADY MILLICENT *off.*)

MOIRA (*who has remained very still*).   Say all the cruel hard things you want to say.

LORD CARLTON (*compassionately*).   I want to say nothing cruel or hard.   I suppose I ought to take it with a laugh.   But that little girl of the boxes.   I don't know what sort of a struggle she went through before she sank to this, but it must have been grim.

> (*She beats her hands together, meaning that it was grim.*)

In memory of her, won't you give this up?

> (*She has an internal struggle.*)

Come, let me help you.

> (*Her manner indicates there can be no turning back.*)

There is still time. (*In a last appeal—puts his hand on her shoulder*) So that you may look little children in the face.

MOIRA (*after a painful struggle*).   I don't undertake to do anything that I can't perform.

LORD CARLTON (*takes his hand off her.   In pain but scornful*).   Why say this to me?

MOIRA (*beseeching*).   Remain and test me!

LORD CARLTON (*giving her up*).   Not I.   Good-bye, Miss Loney!   I despise you!   You are a common cheat!

MOIRA (*stabbed by these words—pause*).   You hurt my heart!

LORD CARLTON (*turns, comes to her—changing his mind*).   Very well, then.   I shall stay.

MOIRA (*to whom this is the great thing—silently*).   Oh! Oh! (*Presses her hands in delight.*)

LORD CARLTON. But I shall watch, and if I detect you at any roguery, why, madam, in the interests of society in general I shall expose you publicly. I shall not stop short of putting you in jail.

MOIRA (*fervently*). Oh, thank you, thank you. But it is right that I should remind you of one thing.

LORD CARLTON (*suspicious*). Ah !

MOIRA. That while the others are changing, you may change too.

LORD CARLTON (*drily*). I think not. You see, I have no faith.

MOIRA. Faith does not matter. You will be changed just the same. It may be a very startling change.

LORD CARLTON. I shall risk it.

(*Exit through french window.*)

MOIRA (*in exultation to her bag*). Grandpa ! I shall save them !

ACT III

THE scene is the room into which the door at the back in Act II led, and the time is morning—a month having elapsed between the Acts. It is a pretty room on the cottage model, but luxurious. It is used as both hall and library. At back the glass door and windows of Act II are seen now from inside. View through them is of the courtyard. There is a large bulging cottage window looking on to rose garden. The wall and the back of the room has book-cases fitted into recesses. Fireplace fitted as book-case. Near window a Sandow apparatus is fixed in wall. Bell-pull. A staircase. Against stair, a writing-desk with revolving cover over it. Curtains, chair covers, etc., are of chintz which has a good deal of purple in it. The morning sun brings out the colour of this purple. At back is door with wide passage.

(DEIGHTON, *the butler, shows in* LORD CARLTON. LORD CARLTON *is in travelling garb and* DEIGHTON *helps him to disrobe.* LORD CARLTON *looks at watch—holds it to his ear ; butler takes his hat and coat.*)

LORD CARLTON. What time do you make it, Deighton ? (*Looking at his watch.*)

DEIGHTON. Eight thirty-five, my lord. (*Looks at his.*)

LORD CARLTON (*winding up his watch*). I always forget to wind up my watch when I travel by the night train. Anything happened since I left, Deighton ?

DEIGHTON. No, my lord—everything going on just as usual.

LORD CARLTON (*disappointed—though he had expected nothing better*). H'm, well, don't let me disturb the house. I shall have a smoke and in an hour or so I expect some of them will be toddling down. Breakfast anything after ten, isn't it ?

DEIGHTON (*heavily*). Breakfast is at eight sharp, my lord.

LORD CARLTON (*taken aback*). In *this* house ? (*Amazed*) Here ? When did this happen ?

DEIGHTON (*considering*). Your lordship has been gone a fortnight?

LORD CARLTON. Yes, and I was here a fortnight.

DEIGHTON. I think breakfast had begun to be earlier before your lordship left, and it has been getting earlier and earlier— (*Dazed*)—until now it is at eight.

LORD CARLTON. And you said nothing had happened.

DEIGHTON. I thought your lordship was referring to—Miss Loney.

LORD CARLTON (*with a sigh*). Ah well, I suppose I was. (*Returning to inquiries.*) Everybody in the house breakfasts at eight?

DEIGHTON. All except Lord Plumleigh—he breakfasts alone, my lord.

LORD CARLTON. I bet he does at about eleven.

DEIGHTON. No, my lord—at seven-thirty.

LORD CARLTON. What?

(LORD PLUMLEIGH *enters. His indolent manner has gone; he moves briskly, like one who knows the value of time.*)

LORD PLUMLEIGH. Got back, uncle! (*Shakes hands.*) Hope you're decent—seen mother? (*Goes up to Sandow exerciser.*)

LORD CARLTON (*surprised*). Not yet.

(*Exit* DEIGHTON.)

LORD PLUMLEIGH (*seizing the Sandow apparatus*). You will excuse me going on with things, won't you? I can talk just the same. (*Goes vigorously to work at exercises.*)

LORD CARLTON (*sits—staring*). Are you always as busy as this, Plum?

LORD PLUMLEIGH (*counting at exercise*). Eight—nine—ten. Here's my time-table. (*Gets card from desk and immediately plunges into another exercise.*)

LORD CARLTON. What's this? (*Taking card and reading*) 6.30—leap out of bed; 7—run a mile, walk a mile; 7.30—breakfast; 8—Botany; 8.45—Herodotus; 11—run a mile, walk a mile; 12—Latin verse; 2—dinner. Dinner?

LORD PLUMLEIGH. We dine in the middle of the day now.

LORD CARLTON (*astounded*). What!

LORD PLUMLEIGH. We have no late dinner. Ever so much better. But we dress for tea at six. Nine—ten—— (*Finishes exercise, and goes to desk without losing a moment.*) This is my new desk—the top slides back, you see, so that I can begin at once. (*He suits the action to words, so that as he finishes speaking he has sat down and is intent on his studies.*)

LORD CARLTON. When did this ambition seize you?

LORD PLUMLEIGH. I don't know. It's just as if I had suddenly wakened up.

LORD CARLTON (*with sudden idea—rises and goes across to* LORD PLUMLEIGH). Plum, have you been seeing much of Miss Loney lately?

LORD PLUMLEIGH (*without looking up*). No—very little. Do you remember she pretended she was going to change us all! Jolly rot!

(*Enter* LADY GEORGY *with book.*)

LADY GEORGY. David!

LORD CARLTON. I have turned up again, Georgy.

(LADY MILLICENT *is carried in in bath-chair.*)

LADY GEORGY. You must be famished?

LORD CARLTON. No, I breakfasted in the train. (*He crosses to* LADY MILLICENT; *with feeling he says*) Milly! (*Gets centre.*) Why, Georgy! I declare she's got quite a colour in her cheeks.

LADY GEORGY (*bitterly*). Yes, that is all the grand cure amounts to. (*She sighs.*) David—— (*She is about to storm.*)

LORD PLUMLEIGH (*holding up his hand in indignation with them for disturbing him*). Mater, if you please.

(*All are properly humbled and speak in lower tones.*)

LORD CARLTON. You've taken to rising early nowadays, Georgy?

LADY GEORGY. Yes, it is such a help to the servants.

LORD CARLTON. Oh, since when have you taken to considering the servants?

LADY GEORGY (*carelessly*). Only lately, I think.

LORD CARLTON. I think so, too. And what is this about dining in the middle of the day?

LADY GEORGY. *You* can have something later if you like.

LORD CARLTON. Thanks. Don't you?

LADY GEORGY. Oh no—we feel so much better without it.

LORD CARLTON (*sharply*). Who put you up to this?

LADY GEORGY (*indignantly*). No one. It is entirely my own idea.

LORD CARLTON. H'm !

LORD PLUMLEIGH (*again annoyed by their talking*). I say—
how can I study, etc.

> (*Closes his book with a bang, and full of reproachful
> glances makes a pile of books and papers and with a hand
> clock on top of them exits upstairs carrying them in-
> dignantly. LADY GEORGY has followed PLUMLEIGH to
> foot of staircase to pacify him.*)

LADY GEORGY (*turns to* LORD CARLTON). David, what a
mistake it has all been ! The woman has never tried to do
anything.

LORD CARLTON (*who is sorry and troubled about* MOIRA).
Well, she has done no harm, Georgy. Her time is up—let
her go away quietly.

LADY GEORGY. She doesn't deserve it—and she is not to
get it.

LORD CARLTON. Um !

LADY MILLICENT. It is a secret, mother.

LADY GEORGY. Not from your uncle. You see, David,
he is in the neighbourhood, so I seized the opportunity of
begging him to come over.

LORD CARLTON. Who ?

LADY GEORGY. Sir Jennings. *Oh*, I had to humble myself
before he would consent.

LORD CARLTON. Well, you must let her get away before
his arrival.

LADY GEORGY. She doesn't know he is coming. Milly
wouldn't let me tell her.

LORD CARLTON (*annoyed*). Milly !

LADY GEORGY (*surprised at his displeasure*). Surely *you* are
the last person to complain—you who were against her from
the first.

LORD CARLTON. No, I wasn't.

LADY GEORGY. Why, you talked of the police.

LORD CARLTON. No, I didn't.

LADY GEORGY (*indignant*). David.

> (*He can't look her in the face. Exit* LADY GEORGY
> *upstairs, disdainfully.*)

LADY MILLICENT (*in a little voice*). Are you angry with me,
uncle ?

LORD CARLTON (*keeping away from her*).   I am disgusted with you.

LADY MILLICENT.   For bringing Sir Jennings back ?

LORD CARLTON.   No, I suppose that had to be done.   But you might have let her slip away quietly first.   It is like hitting a woman when she 's down.   (*Sits.*)

LADY MILLICENT (*curiously*).   If you are so interested in her, why did you go away ?

LORD CARLTON (*sighing*).   Perhaps that was the reason.

LADY MILLICENT.   Then why have you come back ?

LORD CARLTON (*miserably*).   I don't know.   Milly, somehow it is terrible to me to have to disbelieve in Moira Loney.

(*She is pleased and blows him a kiss unseen by him.*) That dear, honest little girl—(*With sudden change*)—that lying little jade.

LADY MILLICENT.   Uncle, Moira Loney is a dear.   (*Sitting up excitedly.*)

LORD CARLTON (*goes to her—brightening—sadly*).   No, she isn't.

LADY MILLICENT.   Uncle, if you knew what I know !

LORD CARLTON.   Eh ?   What ?

LADY MILLICENT.   Listen——   (*Is about to confide when enter* DEIGHTON *and first footman.*)

DEIGHTON.   Are we to take you upstairs, my lady ?

LADY MILLICENT.   Please, Deighton.   (*She lies back, an invalid again, and they lift her chair and carry her off upstairs.*)

LORD CARLTON.   Milly, what were you going to say ?

LADY MILLICENT (*in a die-away voice*).   I am so tired, uncle. (LORD CARLTON *is going off after* MILLY *is carried upstairs, when he sees* CECIL *coming.   He gets newspaper and sits on sofa.   Enter* CECIL—*he has got away down to sofa before he sees his father, then turns and is going off, tiptoes up to door.   By door he hesitates, shuts door— he pulls himself together and comes pleasantly to table.*)

CECIL.   How are you, father ?

LORD CARLTON.   Is that you, Cecil ?   I 'm all right, how are you ?

CECIL.   All right.   (*Starts humming, is stopped by a look from* LORD CARLTON.)

(LORD CARLTON *crosses to fireplace, reaches for book. They are self-conscious in each other's presence, but* CECIL

is trying to be genial while LORD CARLTON *is brusque.*
CECIL *follows* LORD CARLTON *to fireplace.*)

CECIL (*thinks he sees a chance to please*). Is the book out of your reach, father——shall I get it down for you ?

LORD CARLTON (*fiercely*). No ! (*Looking up into* CECIL'S *face*) I 'm as tall as you are.

CECIL. I dare say you are, dad.

(LORD CARLTON *sits on sofa again.*)

LORD CARLTON (*tartly*). When is the wedding going to take place ?

CECIL (*pleasantly*). We thought the last week in October. You see——

LORD CARLTON. I don't want to hear about it.

CECIL (*mildly remonstrating*). You asked.

LORD CARLTON. No, I didn't ! (*Takes up paper.*)

CECIL. Sorry. (*Controlling himself.*) I thought you did.

(LORD CARLTON *behind paper is surprised at his forbearance.*)

Have a cigarette, father ? (*Producing case.*)

LORD CARLTON (*ungraciously*). No, thanks. (*Gets his own cigarette case out and takes out cigarette.*) I prefer my own.

CECIL (*unconquerably*). I don't wonder. You get the best cigarettes I know.

LORD CARLTON (*a little mollified*). I spent years in searching for them though. (*Lights cigarette.*)

CECIL. They were worth it. The odd thing is I know men who get them from the same place, but they are not the same cigarettes. (*Sits.*)

LORD CARLTON (*pleased*). No, they are not——they are not. Have one, Cecil ?

CECIL. Thanks awfully. (*Abandons his own cigarette case, which he puts in his pocket, and takes one of his father's, who gives him a light.*) Ah ! That 's the real thing.

LORD CARLTON. *They are good.* So those chappies get them from the same place but they are not the same cigarettes. That 's the best thing I 've heard for a long time. (*Chuckles immoderately.*)

(CECIL *enjoys the joke with him.*)

(*Suddenly he stops suspiciously.*) Cecil, you 're trying to get round me ! What 's your game ?

CECIL (*humble and sincere*). If I have tried to please you there's no harm in that, is there? I have been a poor sort of a son to you, father—wish I were a better one. That's all it means.

LORD CARLTON (*struck by his sincerity—yet feeling there can be but one explanation*). You must be wanting something.

CECIL. I—no—nothing. (*Returns to chair—looks at him*) I am only twenty-one, father—scarcely more than a boy, do you think?

LORD CARLTON. On the contrary, a man is at his ripest at twenty-one.

    (CECIL *sighs.*)

Are you in a hole, Cecil?

CECIL. I? Oh no. (*Wistfully*) Were you ever in a hole, father, when you were my age?

LORD CARLTON (*after seeing in his mind's eye a hole of long ago, sits smiling over it*). I think we're going to have a change in the weather, Cecil.

CECIL (*accepting this as ending the subject—rises, bravely*). All right——

LORD CARLTON. No offence, my boy. (*Pushes* CECIL *on sofa, and then sits himself on chair.*)

CECIL (*doggedly*). How did you get out of it?

LORD CARLTON. Well, when things became desperate—I went to my mother.

CECIL. Yes—I wish I—— (*Is going to say he wishes he had a mother—tries to be plucky.*) You get them direct from Egypt, don't you? (*Looking at cigarettes.*)

LORD CARLTON. Cairo.

CECIL. I don't see how your mother could have done anything if it was really a hole. (*He is leaning on table with hand on edge of it.*)

LORD CARLTON. You don't know much about mothers.

CECIL. No.

    (LORD CARLTON *lays his hand on* CECIL'S *for a minute— after slight pause, during which* CECIL *has looked at his hand—he takes hand off table.*)

CECIL. The duty on them must come pretty heavy.

LORD CARLTON. About 30s. on the thousand. But then I get them fresh, and even although—— (*Gives up pretence*) What is it, Cecil?

CECIL. Father, I 'm in an awful hole.

LORD CARLTON. Yes.

CECIL. I, it—— (*Finds explanation difficult.*) You must have noticed that I am not like other young men. (*Sits marvelling at himself.*) I am strangely different, father, from any other young man I have ever known.

LORD CARLTON. Are you? By Jove, Cecil, I haven't an idea what it is.

CECIL (*woefully*). It 's this—I am somehow not so keen to get married as I was, dad.

LORD CARLTON. I thought that was it.

CECIL (*surprised*). Did you ?

LORD CARLTON (*drily*). Yes.

CECIL (*changing to indignation*). I should like to know, sir, how the devil—— (*Sits miserably, looks up—bitterly*) Splendid triumph for you, father—your only son broken-hearted— chuckle away—go on sneering—keep it up, dad.

LORD CARLTON (*who has been doing none of these things*). Poor old Cecil.

CECIL (*pathetic and deadly sincere*). I don't know how it has come about, I really don't. Eleanor is more adorable than ever —she really is—but somehow it doesn't have the effect upon me that it used to have. Her nut-brown hair which used to entrance me as much as if I had never noticed that woman and her hair before—now, when it escapes from its coils I merely think it looks untidy. And then this always talking about show, and if either of us says anything smart she expects us to exchange seats just as they do on the stage—and I wish she wouldn't die quite so much. Oh no, it 's all my fault ! Take me out and drown me like a dog.

LORD CARLTON. By Jove !

CECIL. She loves me so much she can't even look at me without her eyes becoming wet with adoration.

LORD CARLTON. It is a hole, Cecil.

CECIL (*slowly*). Was there ever a man of twenty-one so strangely placed before?

LORD CARLTON. Never, my boy, since the world began.

CECIL (*indignantly, as if demanding an answer*). What has come over me ?

LORD CARLTON. You have fallen out of love.

CECIL. But how ? I am like a different man.

LORD CARLTON. I can't explain that. (*Suddenly*) Cecil, has it come suddenly—as if you have wakened up ?

CECIL. No, I think it came gradually.

LORD CARLTON. Ah !

CECIL. What do you mean ?

LORD CARLTON. Nothing. And so she looks at you with tears of adoration, my boy ?

CECIL. Yes ! We were out riding this morning and you should have seen her. (*Abjectly*) There 's no way out, father.

LORD CARLTON (*watching him, sharply*). Oh yes, there is.

CECIL (*with sudden hope*). How ?

LORD CARLTON. You have only got to behave like a cad, and the thing 's done.

CECIL (*hotly*). I 'm not going to behave like a cad.

LORD CARLTON (*rapping it out*). Oh yes, you are. We give it another name in our set—we say the boy was got at, but the lady has been squared. We call it eternal human comedy, but if she is a good girl—as she very often is—it has taken away her self-respect, which is a low, dirty thing to do, Cecil—and it 's what you are going to do to Eleanor.

CECIL (*rising manfully*). That 's where you are wrong, dad. I am going to marry Eleanor and I am going to be such a husband to her—(*Strikes table*)—that she will never know, dad.

LORD CARLTON (*quietly—watching him*). Then why did you come to me ?

CECIL. I had no other body to go to and I thought there might be some honourable way out. Have no fear, dad—I 'm going to do the fair thing by Eleanor.

LORD CARLTON. You 're not a bad boy, Cecil. If you hadn't felt bitterly sorry for the girl I should never have cared to take your hand again ; I was waiting to find out. (*Shakes hands.*)

CECIL. I 'll get on all right.

(*Both are a little ashamed of their emotion.*) I suppose it 's not worth their while to send less than a thousand at a time ?

LORD CARLTON. They send a hundred ; I get a hundred weekly myself—it 's a standing order. (*He fidgets.*) Well, that 's settled, Cecil.

CECIL (*getting up*). Yes.

LORD CARLTON (*really uneasy but speaking in a matter-of-fact way*). You leave the rest to me.

CECIL. Um !

LORD CARLTON (*cheerfully*). Suppose you—go and have some fishing in Norway.

CECIL (*suspicious and sharp*). Why should I ?

LORD CARLTON (*testily*). You don't suppose I 'm to let this affair go on ?

CECIL. It *is* to go on. (*Indignantly*) After all you 've said, too.

LORD CARLTON. My dear boy, that was only to try you. We 've got ourselves to think of now.

CECIL. No, we haven't.

LORD CARLTON (*annoyed*). Cecil ! (*Tries to get round him.*) It 's nothing to make a fuss about—often happens in the best families.

CECIL. Go on, *father*—I am waiting to see if I shall ever care to take your hand again.

LORD CARLTON. Oh, lord ! Oh, lord ! (*Contains himself.*) My dear boy, I 'm not thinking of ourselves, I 'm thinking only of *her*.

CECIL. It is only natural that she should think me rather splendid. I don't mean for myself, I 'm a poor bargain—but our name, father—the house—our ancient lineage.

LORD CARLTON. Good heavens, yes—I 'm not blaming her. What must *we* seem in the eye of a girl who never had a grandfather. Poor soul—but something must be done. (*Rings bell.*)

CECIL. I won't have it, father. Everything I have said to you is in the strictest confidence.

LORD CARLTON. Leave the rest to me, leave the rest to me.
(*Enter* DEIGHTON.)
Deighton, if Miss Gray is in the house, say I wish to speak to her.

(*Exit* DEIGHTON.)

CECIL. Father ! (*Pleading*) Deighton ! (*Returns to* LORD CARLTON.) I warn you, father. Nothing of this to her—I shall deny everything.

LORD CARLTON (*fiercely*). Go away !
(*Enter* ELEANOR, *rather shrinkingly.*)

LORD CARLTON.   How do you do, Eleanor ?

ELEANOR.   I hope you had a good journey.

(CECIL *puts his cigarette down on ash-tray on desk.*)

LORD CARLTON.   Thanks—yes—I—— (*His natural kindness makes it difficult for him to proceed.*)   Eleanor—I——

CECIL (*manfully*).   Father ! Eleanor, dearest, I am overjoyed to be able to tell you that father has at last consented to our marriage. (*He looks proudly at his father, who scowls at him.*)

ELEANOR (*sits on sofa*).   It is so sweet of you both. (*Suddenly she bursts into tears.*)

(LORD CARLTON *and* CECIL *look at each other.* CECIL *points to* ELEANOR *and motions* LORD CARLTON *to go to her.* LORD CARLTON *shakes his head and in turn motions* CECIL *to go to her.*)

CECIL (*kneels to* ELEANOR).   What is it, dearest ?

ELEANOR.   Cecil, I—I have wanted to say it for days, and now that Lord Carlton is so kind I must. Oh, Cecil, I want you to let me off.

(*Sensation.* LORD CARLTON *crosses between* CECIL *and* ELEANOR, *prevents* CECIL *speaking.*)

LORD CARLTON.   What did you say, Eleanor ?

ELEANOR (*rising—ashamed*).   I want him to let me off.

LORD CARLTON (*again preventing* CECIL *from speaking*). Any reason, Eleanor ?

ELEANOR.   I don't love him—I thought I did, but I don't.

LORD CARLTON.   I see.

ELEANOR.   There can be no true love that is not founded on respect, and—(*Goes to him*)—Oh, Cecil, I don't respect you.

(*Though* CECIL *has been positively delighted by the unexpected turn affairs have taken, this rather staggers him.*)

CECIL.   Don't you, Eleanor ?

LORD CARLTON (*enjoying it—goes to her*).   Speak out, my dear—don't be frightened.

ELEANOR.   I have been asking myself of late what there is in you to win a woman's love, and I can find no answer.

CECIL.   No !

ELEANOR.   Your title—your wealth—they are mere accidents of your birth. I said to myself, he deserves no credit for them. The amount of sense that has come to me quite suddenly positively bewilders me, Cecil.

LORD CARLTON (*going right up to her and turning to her so that she faces him*). What else did you say to yourself, Eleanor ?

ELEANOR. I said—he will simply be his father over again.

LORD CARLTON. What ? (*Pulled up*) Eh ?

ELEANOR. And then your family history is so fishy.

LORD CARLTON. What 's that ? What 's that ?

ELEANOR. I have been reading it—such bad, worthless people. Of course I don't blame you for your ancestors—but I am so proud of my parentage—— (*Turns to him*) Oh, Cecil, let me off !

(LORD CARLTON *is furious*.)

CECIL. Of course, Eleanor, if it is your wish there is no more to be said.

ELEANOR. I 'm so awfully sorry. I was blind to all this before, but now I seem to see it with extraordinary clearness. I had hoped you might have guessed, Cecil—you must have seen me crying?

CECIL (*blankly*). Was that what your tears meant ?

ELEANOR. Yes.

(*A look between* CECIL *and* LORD CARLTON. LORD CARLTON *is entertained by this. Goes round sofa to table.* ELEANOR *gives* CECIL *back his ring.*)

Dear Cecil—you have borne it bravely.

(CECIL *looks away.*)

LORD CARLTON. Don't you think we should bring this painful interview to a close ?

ELEANOR. Cecil, for the last time.

(*She holds up her face and he kisses her reverently on the forehead—crosses to* LORD CARLTON.)

If you would forgive me also.

LORD CARLTON. My dear Eleanor, if it is your wish, of course we must submit.

(*Exit* ELEANOR *overcome with sorrow for them.* LORD CARLTON *and* CECIL *survey each other quizzically, then chuckle.*)

LORD CARLTON. We 've done it, Cecil.

CECIL. We 've done it. And we thought it would be so difficult.

LORD CARLTON (*taking the credit for it*). It was perfectly easy.

CECIL. She gave us some nasty ones though.

LORD CARLTON (*a little staggered*). Yes ! (*Gaily*) But they were cheap at the price. (*Taking* CECIL's *arm elatedly*) Cecil, my boy, there never was such a family as ours for falling on its feet.

(*They walk up and down, arm in arm, excitedly.*)

CECIL. We have a genius for it.

LORD CARLTON. The scrapes we all get into—the way we get out of them.

(*They stop walking and* LORD CARLTON *pulls* CECIL *round.*)

Think of your great-grandfather, Cecil, just think of him— and yet he died in his bed after all.

CECIL. Dad, the more I think of it, the more convinced I am that I must have been born for some great end.

LORD CARLTON. There 's a sweet little Cherub who sits up aloft to look after the life of poor Cecil.

CECIL. And if I knew his name I would—— (*Is arrested by seeing* LORD CARLTON *in sudden excitement.*) What is it ?

LORD CARLTON (*like one who has solved a mystery*). Moira Loney !

CECIL. Where ?

LORD CARLTON. Everywhere.

CECIL. I don't see——

LORD CARLTON. Mark my words—Moira Loney. (*Goes up to inner room.*)

CECIL (*follows* LORD CARLTON, *first startled as he understands* LORD CARLTON's *meaning*). You don't mean—— (*Puts idea aside as ridiculous.*) Poof !

(LORD CARLTON *draws him into inner room, points to door where doctors are coming in. Exit* CECIL. *Enter* DEIGHTON, *showing in* SIR JENNINGS *and* DR. TOPPING. LORD CARLTON *watches them unseen.*)

DEIGHTON. Her ladyship's instructions, sir, are that I should show you at once to Lady Millicent's room.

SIR JENNINGS. Quite so—yes, yes. Ah ! Then I think, Dr. Topping, we had better not wait.

(*They are about to ascend the stairs when* MOIRA *appears coming down. The sight of them is a shock to her—she stops on the stair, timid, and bows, but they still stand and ignore her.*)

MOIRA.   I didn't know you were coming—they never told me.

SIR JENNINGS (*they still ignore her*).   I think, Dr. Topping——
(DR. TOPPING *passes* SIR JENNINGS *who follows him up-stairs. She stands aside to let them pass, they wait, she comes down, then without looking at her they go up; she is hurt and addresses them appealingly from below.*)

MOIRA.   Sir Jennings!
(*Still taking no notice they exit with* DEIGHTON. *She stands, weeps at desk.* LORD CARLTON, *who has looked sternly at the doctors, comes down and regards her quizzically.*)

LORD CARLTON.   Miss Loney.

MOIRA (*rising, glad to see him but frightened*).   You have come back! You—don't seem to be angry with me.

LORD CARLTON.   No.

MOIRA.   You will be soon.

LORD CARLTON.   I dare say. But for the moment, won't you shake hands?

MOIRA.   Sir Jennings is here.

LORD CARLTON.   I saw him, and I saw the way he treated you. On my soul, Moira, I am sorry he should have this triumph over you, for I do believe you have made some changes in this house. Moira, don't you think you would be happier if you were to tell me how you do it?

MOIRA.   Oh, I can't. I daren't. Grandpa warned me. (*Sits on sofa, weeping.*)

LORD CARLTON (*to* MOIRA).   Don't cry, little girl. Moira, why are you crying?

MOIRA.   Because I am so lonely. Nobody loves me, and I do so want to be loved.

LORD CARLTON.   Do you? Whom do you want to love you?

MOIRA.   Everybody. I can't do without everybody loving me.

LORD CARLTON.   You want to mother the lot of us, isn't that it? You are the oddest little soul and the dearest. (*Looking up to top of staircase*) But here comes our Waterloo.

(SIR JENNINGS *and* DR. TOPPING *appear at top of staircase. They come downstairs with* LADY GEORGY *followed by* LORD PLUMLEIGH.)

Ah ! Ah ! We meet again, Sir Jennings. (*Shakes hands with*
SIR JENNINGS.)

(*The Doctor bows to the others ;* LORD PLUMLEIGH *comes
downstairs softly, listening.*)

And how is the invalid ?

SIR JENNINGS. I have no wish to alarm the family——

MOIRA. Oh dear—— (*Goes towards door.*)

SIR JENNINGS. If the lady who has been attending Lady
Millicent is present, may I ask that she remain ?

LADY GEORGY. Miss Loney.

LORD CARLTON (*sorry for* MOIRA, *whose distress he misunder-
stands*). Is it necessary, Sir Jennings ? This lady admits she
has failed. Why rub it in ?

(LADY GEORGY *sits by desk.*)

SIR JENNINGS (*sitting*). I merely wish to do my duty.

(CECIL *enters and remains in inner room.* ELEANOR
enters.)

DR. TOPPING. We have no desire to rub it in. (*Rubs it in
with his hands.*)

MOIRA. Very well, I shall remain. But on one point
Lord Carlton is in error—I do not admit that I have failed.

LORD CARLTON (*disappointed in her*). Miss Loney !

SIR JENNINGS. Dear lady, we are grieved to find your sweet
daughter decidedly worse.

(ELEANOR *sits on oak chest by fireplace.*)

MOIRA (*goes to him*). Oh no, indeed.

(*Her manner throughout is that of a dear girl pained to
see* SIR JENNINGS *humiliated and wanting to save him.*)

SIR JENNINGS (*gives her a look and turns to* DR. TOPPING).
Her pulse, Topping ?

DR. TOPPING. We don't like it.

SIR JENNINGS. Her colour ?

DR. TOPPING. Hectic.

MOIRA. Oh, why didn't you make a more careful
examination ?

SIR JENNINGS (*indignant at her audacity in daring to address
him*). Madam ! Lady Plumleigh, all my advice has been set at
naught—the nourishing food every two hours——

MOIRA. I disbelieved in it.

SIR JENNINGS. The rest and sleep throughout the day.

MOIRA.   I discontinued it.

DR. TOPPING (*solemnly*).   Out of her own mouth.

MOIRA.   Oh dear !   Sir Jennings, I am so sorry.

SIR JENNINGS.   It is too late for that.   I must make this matter known.

DR. TOPPING.   *Pro bono publico.*

LORD CARLTON (*who has been watching* MOIRA).   I confess I am puzzled ; but it seems to me, Sir Jennings, that this lady is sorry, not for herself, but for you.

SIR JENNINGS (*scandalised*).   For me !

MOIRA.   Yes, yes—yes indeed, Sir Jennings, and now you have said everything you want to say, haven't you ?   Oh please go away before she has time to do anything that might hurt your feelings.

SIR JENNINGS.   This is unpardonable.

MOIRA (*with anxious look upstairs*).   She is such a very naughty girl.   At any moment she—— (*To* LORD CARLTON) Oh ! please advise them to go.

LORD CARLTON (*crossing to* SIR JENNINGS. *He has been greatly puzzled*).   Sir Jennings, it seems crazy to me—I am amazed at myself but I can't help it.   I believe in this girl ; I believe she is trying honestly to save you from some bitter mortification, and against all rhyme and reason my advice to you is—to hook it.

SIR JENNINGS.   And I decline.

MOIRA.   Oh dear !

(*From upstairs a voice is heard singing gaily ; it draws nearer.*)

LORD PLUMLEIGH (*rises—on stairs*).   That 's Milly's voice. (*All rise as* LADY MILLICENT *appears at top of stairs, where she has walked alone.* ELEANOR *stands with back to fireplace.*)

LADY MILLICENT (*at top of stairs—kissing hand*).   Good morning, everybody.   Mother, I 'm well again, I 'm well, I 'm well.   (*She comes downstairs in little jumps crying ' I 'm well ' at each jump, and finally falls into her mother's arms.*)

LADY GEORGY.   But how ?

LADY MILLICENT.   Mother, she hadn't been here many days when I felt new life coming back to me.   At first I feared to raise your hopes, but when each day I got stronger a desire seized me not to tell you the great news till I was wholly well.

(LADY MILLICENT *turns to the doctors.*)

And I made her keep the news also. You have always seen me in the chair, but secretly I was walking again—practising—look, uncle. (*Dances and hums tune.*) And yesterday there came into my head—(*Speaking quickly*)—a curiosity to see what the real doctors would say about me if I didn't tell them I was cured.

LORD CARLTON. Did you speak, Sir Jennings ?

(SIR JENNINGS *has kept well control of himself.*)

MOIRA (*distressed*). Indeed, I knew nothing of this.

LADY MILLICENT (*crossing to* MOIRA). No, she didn't ! (*Both sit on settee.*) She 's so soft-hearted she wouldn't have permitted it. And I had drawn a solemn promise from her not to tell anyone I was better until *I* told mother.

LORD CARLTON. She tried hard to warn you, Sir Jennings. Have you nothing to say to her ?

SIR JENNINGS. If Miss Loney will be so good as to explain her treatment I shall be pleased to listen.

MOIRA (*alarmed and rising*). I can't do that—not yet.

SIR JENNINGS. Quite so, quite so. (*Pulls himself together, goes to* LADY GEORGY.) Dear lady, yes. It is a great pleasure to me to say that I find your daughter much improved—most gratifying—yes, gratifying. It makes my eyes young again, Lady Millicent, to see you able to jump so vigorously—jump, yes. I think, Topping——

DR. TOPPING (*who has been staring at* MOIRA). Certainly, Sir Jennings.

MOIRA (*to* SIR JENNINGS). Ah, Sir Jennings, don't be angry with me. I couldn't help curing her—indeed I couldn't. It was so easy. You are much, much cleverer than I am.

LORD CARLTON. She is trying to mother Sir Jennings. (*Goes and talks to* CECIL, *who is by plate rack.*)

SIR JENNINGS (*bowing to him and preserving his dignity*). Topping, if you are quite ready—— (*Goes in inner room.*)

DR. TOPPING. Quite—ah—ah——

(*He is wondering whether reference is to cheque. He whispers to* LADY GEORGY *who is sitting down at desk. She has cheque in envelope and hands it to* DR. TOPPING, *who then calls* SIR JENNINGS *and puts it in nis hand.*)

SIR JENNINGS (*surprised to find cheque*). What, what ? Ah, ah ! (*Twiddles it.*) Well, do you know I hardly like—— (*Doesn't quite like to take it after business, puts cheque in pocket.*) Oh, but still—accept my heartiest congratulations again, dear lady. (*Shaking hands.*) If you are quite ready, Topping. *Good-bye.* Goody-bye, good-bye, everybody. Ah, Carlton——

> (*Catches* LORD CARLTON'S *eye, realises the situation, pulls himself up short and exits after* DR. TOPPING, *carrying the situation. The others turn and stare at* MOIRA, *who is quite unassuming—except* LORD CARLTON, *who stands apart watching her.*)

LADY MILLICENT. ⎫ Oh, my sweetest !
LADY GEORGY.   ⎬ Dear, darling girl !
ELEANOR.   ⎭ You clever little thing.

CECIL. Miss Loney, was it you—that—me, you know ?

> (MOIRA *nods ; all are impressed.*)

ELEANOR. Miss Loney, I—I think *I* am different—was it you ?

> (MOIRA *nods.*)

LORD PLUMLEIGH. How about me ?

> (LADY GEORGY *puts her hand on* LORD PLUMLEIGH'S *shoulder.*)

MOIRA. You also.

CECIL. I say, is Little Mary in it ?

MOIRA. Oh yes.

LADY MILLICENT. Wonderful.

CECIL. Miss Loney, is there anything you can't do ?

MOIRA (*woefully*). I can do—almost anything. I suppose I am the most remarkable woman alive. (*Smiling*) But—I don't want to be. (*Passionately*) I should so love to be an ordinary woman.

LORD CARLTON. You 'll never be that.

MOIRA (*crushed*). Oh ! Oh ! (*Weeps.*)

LADY GEORGY. David—— (*To* MOIRA) My dear, how can you cry in the moment of your triumph ?

MOIRA. I don't want to triumph, I want to be loved. I can't do without everybody loving me.

ELEANOR. We do love you, dear, sweet ! (*Embracing* MOIRA.)

LADY GEORGY. Child, we adore you. (*Goes on knees.*)

LADY MILLICENT. Moira, I 'm yours until death us do part. (*Kneels down in front of her.*)

MOIRA. Dear. (*Embraces* LADY MILLICENT.) Sweet ! (*Embraces* LADY GEORGY.)

LADY MILLICENT. And now, darling, tell us how you 've done it.

MOIRA. Oh, I can't—I dare not—Grandpa warned me. I so *long* to tell you but I dare not.

LORD CARLTON. Why do you long to tell, Moira ?

MOIRA. So that I might have someone to help me.

CECIL. Miss Loney, I am that person.

LADY MILLICENT. No, Cecil, I am. I claim that right.

LADY GEORGY (*rises from her knees*). We all are. Moira, tell us and we shall carry on your noble labours. It is a solemn promise.

MOIRA. Oh, I can't—I am afraid.

ELEANOR. Courage.

LADY GEORGY. Come, dear. (*Goes to* MOIRA.)

LADY MILLICENT. Do tell us, darling. Do, dear.

(LADY MILLICENT *goes to* MOIRA *also*.)

MOIRA. I can't. I can't. (*Sees* LORD CARLTON, *goes to him.*) Do *you* ask me to tell ? I shall tell if you wish it.

(*All take a step towards* LORD CARLTON.)

LORD CARLTON. I wish it, Moira.

MOIRA. Then I shall tell.

(*All give an exclamation of relief and pleasure.*)

Ah—(*Turning to* LADY PLUMLEIGH)—Lady Plumleigh, may I have Grandpa here while I am telling ? He would love to be here ?

(ELEANOR *and* CECIL *give one another a look.*)

LADY GEORGY (*staggered, takes* LADY MILLICENT'S *hand for support*). Grandpa ? (*Looks at* LADY MILLICENT ; *turns and looks at* MOIRA *again.*) But where is he ?

MOIRA. He is upstairs.

(*They feel eerie.*)

LADY GEORGY. Upstairs ? (*Looks at* LADY MILLICENT.)

LADY MILLICENT (*grandly*). Mother, we must not doubt her —consent.

LADY GEORGY (*uneasily*). Oh certainly, my dear.

MOIRA (*alarmed again*). Might I have Deighton to help me ?

LADY GEORGY (*weakly*). If you wish it, Moira. (*Goes up and rings bell.*)

MOIRA (*at foot of staircase*). Oh, I do hope I am doing the right thing.

LADY MILLICENT (*calling*). Deighton !

(*Enter* DEIGHTON.)

Ask him, mother.

LADY GEORGY (*gasping*). Deighton, will you go upstairs with Miss Loney, and help her to—bring down her grandpapa. (*Takes hold of* LORD PLUMLEIGH'S *hand for a second.*)

(MOIRA *goes upstairs.* DEIGHTON *is startled, but like a well-bred servant follows* MOIRA *upstairs.*)

ELEANOR. It feels quite eerie.

LADY MILLICENT. Yes.

LORD CARLTON (*motions* LADY GEORGY *to come round. They sit*). Don't you think now she's gone we might have a guess at what Little Mary is ?

CECIL (*severely, noticing something frivolous in* LORD CARLTON). We at least know, father, that it is something noble and beautiful.

LORD CARLTON. Good boy—— You, Milly ?

LADY MILLICENT. I should say it is an inner conscience. But perhaps I ought not to speak, for Moira has already told me that it is something inside us.

LORD CARLTON. Something inside us !

ELEANOR. I am convinced there is Christian Science in it.

LADY GEORGY. I know this—that ever since Moira entered this house I have felt the phenomena of active spiritual life stirred within me.

LADY MILLICENT. I feel that also—to me, uncle, Little Mary is a religion.

LORD CARLTON. Quite so. Something inside us. All I can say, ladies and gentlemen, is that I feel profoundly uneasy.

(MOIRA *enters carrying one of the volumes, No.* 3, *downstairs, followed by* DEIGHTON *with the other two. She puts hers on table, he puts his on top of them.*)

MOIRA. Thank you, Deighton.

(*Exit* DEIGHTON *uneasily.*)

This is Grandpa.

(LADY GEORGY *and all except* LORD CARLTON *rise perturbed.*)

LADY MILLICENT. Why not, mother ? Now, Moira.

(LADY GEORGY, ELEANOR, *and* LADY MILLICENT *sit.* LADY GEORGY *subsides.*)

MOIRA (*faintly*). You will go on loving me, won't you ?

LADY MILLICENT. My angel, we swear.

ELEANOR. You are making us so nervous.

MOIRA (*to* LADY MILLICENT). I have done you good, haven't I ?—you can't deny that.

LADY GEORGY. Moira, whatever it is how could we deny that ?

LORD CARLTON. And so, in the name of Beelzebub, out with it.

MOIRA (*to books*). Grandpa ! (*Opens Vol.* I *and addresses company*) Grandpa had a profound conviction that the dear, darling English people suffer from eating too much.

CECIL. I shouldn't wonder. I 'm told the way the poor gorge on Sundays is perfectly sickening.

MOIRA. It isn't the poor Grandpa means. He says here that what the poor do on Sundays the best people do every day of the week. They have *three solid meals a day, lunch, dinner, supper*, and that 's why they have to go to Homburg and such like places once a year, to be washed out and scraped down.

LADY GEORGY. *I* was never ordered to Homburg.

LORD CARLTON. I was.

MOIRA. Grandpa knew it would never do to tell you what was really the matter with you. You are so delicately minded. He said to me, ' Either you must invent some milder name for their—their medium, or they will all fly from the cure.' And so, after thinking about it for a long time, I invented the name of ' Little Mary.'

LADY GEORGY. Moira, what is this thing ?

MOIRA (*who has been calm but is now agitated*). I hate the name as much as you do, but I must say it once—it 's the only way, oh dear—stomach.

(*All rise.* CECIL *steps back from settee with his hand on his brow.*)

LADY GEORGY. You don't dare to insinuate.

ELEANOR.   Really, I never heard of such a thing.

LADY MILLICENT.   Disgusting ! Preposterous !

MOIRA (*wheedling*).   Please, please, and now we need never mention it again. Let us call it the organ. Oh, let us all look our organ firmly in the face, and dear England will once again be invincible as in the great Shakespearean days.

LADY GEORGY.   This, this organ ?

MOIRA.   We all have them.

LADY GEORGY.   Speak for yourself.

LADY MILLICENT.   Moira—what have you been doing with *mine* ?

MOIRA.   Dearest Milly, I know that what made you ill was the death of him you loved.

LADY MILLICENT.   You do me *that* justice !

MOIRA.   But you didn't rally.

LADY MILLICENT.   I thought it wicked to want to rally.

MOIRA.   That was the food.

ELEANOR.   Monstrous !   (*Sits on settee.*)

MOIRA.   The moment the weight was taken off the organ you began to think healthily again. You made the effort and were cured ; the desire to be up and doing came to you.

(*All except* LORD CARLTON *say* 'Oh !'   CECIL *indignantly turns his back to her and looks out of window.*)

Grandpa discovered the amazing truth that what we are depends chiefly on what we eat.

CECIL.   Never, never !

MOIRA.   That we are good or bad, stupid or enterprising, cynics or in love, mainly as the result of diet. Whatever you want to be, this book contains the recipes.

(*All turn round to her.*)

It 's all here, what our finest feelings are composed of.

(LADY MILLICENT *and* ELEANOR *rise and step towards her.* MOIRA *turns over leaves of Vol.* I *and looks at them.*)

CECIL.   Not love !

MOIRA.   Love is mostly phosphate of lime.

CECIL.   Faugh !   (*Turns from her and leans on mantel-piece.*)

(LADY MILLICENT *and* ELEANOR *collapse on settee and cry* 'Oh !')

MOIRA.   Lady Plumleigh, you wish Digby to be fonder of you than he is ; the book tells you precisely what to give him.

LADY GEORGY. Horrible !

(LADY MILLICENT *and* ELEANOR *rise.*)

MOIRA. Don't go. (*Rushing to* LADY GEORGY, *who is going.*) Don't go. Be patriots. Think of the fate of England if the working classes were to become as stupid as the best people. I want you to form a league with ' one day one dinner ' for its motto. Grandpa calls it Home Rule for England. He foresees the time coming when all the best people will greet each other with the words ' Good morning ! How is Little Mary ? '

(CECIL, *who is standing with back to fireplace, here embraces* LADY MILLICENT *and* ELEANOR, *who collapse in his arms.*)

LADY GEORGY. This is too much. (*Rings bell.*) You will leave by the night train.

LORD CARLTON (*rises and crosses to* LADY GEORGY, *thinking she is going to order* MOIRA *from the house*). Georgy, what are you going to do ?

LADY GEORGY (*by foot of stairs*). I have been hurt in the most sensitive place.

LORD CARLTON. Admitted ! We have all been so, but only by the truth. The bitter, unpalatable truth. (*Puts hand on book.*) Grandpa, you old scoundrel ! Georgy, this old Irish-man, out of his passionate love for the English people, has put his finger on the spot. (*Touching his ' organ.'*)

LADY GEORGY. I don't care. I won't stand it. I 'm going to assert myself.

(*Enter* DEIGHTON.)

Deighton, we shall dine to-night at eight. (*Looks at* MOIRA.) Come, Digby, Milly, Eleanor, Cecil. (*A triumphant look at* MOIRA.) A long dinner.

(*Exeunt in order,* LORD PLUMLEIGH, LADY MILLICENT, ELEANOR, CECIL, LADY GEORGY, *also* DEIGHTON *much gratified.*)

MOIRA (*in agony*). Grandpa was right. He warned me against telling. Oh, must I begin again, all alone, all alone ! (*Falls on knees by table.*) I have been imprisoned in the books all these years ! Oh, Grandpa, let me out. (*Lifts books bravely and is going off upstairs with them.*)

LORD CARLTON (*has been watching her, and as she reaches the stairs*). Mother ! (*She gives a little glad cry, the books slip to the steps.*) You pathetic little girl, you have done something for everybody except for me.

MOIRA. Is there anything you want?

LORD CARLTON. There is indeed. I have set my heart, Moira, on being five-and-twenty again.

MOIRA (*tragically*). Oh, I can't do it.

LORD CARLTON. What, such a little thing as that?

MOIRA. I am so sorry. Is there nothing else?

LORD CARLTON. You see, mother, if you could have done that I could have done all the rest myself. (*Moves away, comes back—after smiling at her.*) Moira, if you marry, you will never let that husband idle again!

MOIRA. Never.

LORD CARLTON. No more clubs for Miss Loney's husband.

MOIRA. Oh no!

LORD CARLTON. No eternal cigarette smoking.

MOIRA. No.

LORD CARLTON. No suppers in restaurants, or breakfasts in bed.

MOIRA. Work, noble work, for every moment of the day!

LORD CARLTON. Yes. That's if he were a young man, but if he was an old one, Moira.

MOIRA. You mean yourself?

LORD CARLTON. I mean myself. Am I too old?

MOIRA. I have so longed to mother you, lord, ever since I saw you in the shop; I can't do without mothering you.

LORD CARLTON. Then stay with me, mother, and try and make a man of me. The grateful will never let the Irish go.

PETER PAN

OR

THE BOY WHO WOULD NOT GROW UP

Produced at the Duke of York's Theatre on December 27, 1904, with the following cast:

PETER PAN	*Nina Boucicault*
MR. DARLING	*Gerald du Maurier*
MRS. DARLING	*Dorothea Baird*
WENDY MOIRA ANGELA DARLING	*Hilda Trevelyan*
JOHN NAPOLEON DARLING	*Master George Hersee*
MICHAEL NICHOLAS DARLING	*Winifred Geoghegan*
NANA	*Arthur Lupino*
TINKER BELL	*Jane Wren*
TOOTLES	*Joan Burnett*
NIBS	*Christine Silver*
SLIGHTLY	*A. W. Baskcomb*
CURLY	*Alice Dubarry*
FIRST TWIN	*Pauline Chase*
SECOND TWIN	*Phyllis Beadon*
CAPTAIN JAS HOOK	*Gerald du Maurier*
SMEE	*George Shelton*
GENTLEMAN STARKEY	*Sydney Harcourt*
COOKSON	*Charles Trevor*
CECCO	*Frederick Annerley*
MULLINS	*Hubert Willis*
JUKES	*James English*
NOODLER	*John Kelt*
GREAT BIG LITTLE PANTHER	*Philip Darwin*
TIGER LILY	*Miriam Nesbitt*
LIZA	*Ela Q. May*

The play ran for 145 performances. There have been 34 Christmas-tide revivals.

TO THE FIVE

A DEDICATION

SOME disquieting confessions must be made in printing at last the play of *Peter Pan* ; among them this, that I have no recollection of having written it. Of that, however, anon. What I want to do first is to give Peter to the Five without whom he never would have existed. I hope, my dear sirs, that in memory of what we have been to each other you will accept this dedication with your friend's love. The play of Peter is streaky with you still, though none may see this save ourselves. A score of Acts had to be left out, and you were in them all. We first brought Peter down, didn't we, with a blunt-headed arrow in Kensington Gardens ? I seem to remember that we believed we had killed him, though he was only winded, and that after a spasm of exultation in our prowess the more soft-hearted among us wept and all of us thought of the police. There was not one of you who would not have sworn as an eye-witness to this occurrence ; no doubt I was abetting, but you used to provide corroboration that was never given to you by me. As for myself, I suppose I always knew that I made Peter by rubbing the five of you violently together, as savages with two sticks produce a flame. That is all he is, the spark I got from you.

We had good sport of him before we clipped him small to make him fit the boards. Some of you were not born when the story began and yet were hefty figures before we saw that the game was up. Do you remember a garden at Burpham and the initiation there of No. 4 when he was six weeks old, and three of you grudged letting him in so young ? Have you, No. 3, forgotten the white violets at the Cistercian abbey in which we cassocked our first fairies (all little friends of St. Benedict), or your cry to the Gods, ' Do I just kill one pirate all the time ? ' Do you remember Marooners' Hut in the

haunted groves of Waverley, and the St. Bernard dog in a
tiger's mask who so frequently attacked you, and the literary
record of that summer, *The Boy Castaways*, which is so much
the best and the rarest of this author's works? What was it
that made us eventually give to the public in the thin form of
a play that which had been woven for ourselves alone? Alas,
I know what it was, I was losing my grip. One by one as you
swung monkey-wise from branch to branch in the wood of
make-believe you reached the tree of knowledge. Sometimes
you swung back into the wood, as the unthinking may at a
cross-road take a familiar path that no longer leads to home ;
or you perched ostentatiously on its boughs to please me,
pretending that you still belonged ; soon you knew it only as
the vanished wood, for it vanishes if one needs to look for it.
A time came when I saw that No. 1, the most gallant of you
all, ceased to believe that he was ploughing woods incarnadine,
and with an apologetic eye for me derided the lingering faith of
No. 2 ; when even No. 3 questioned gloomily whether he did
not really spend his nights in bed. There were still two who
knew no better, but their day was dawning. In these circumstances, I suppose, was begun the writing of the play of Peter.
That was a quarter of a century ago, and I clutch my brows in
vain to remember whether it was a last desperate throw to
retain the five of you for a little longer, or merely a cold decision
to turn you into bread and butter.

This brings us back to my uncomfortable admission that I
have no recollection of writing the play of *Peter Pan*, now being
published for the first time so long after he made his bow upon
the stage. You had played it until you tired of it, and tossed
it in the air and gored it and left it derelict in the mud and went
on your way singing other songs ; and then I stole back and
sewed some of the gory fragments together with a pen-nib.
That is what must have happened, but I cannot remember
doing it. I remember writing the story of *Peter and Wendy*
many years after the production of the play, but I might have
cribbed that from some typed copy. I can haul back to mind
the writing of almost every other assay of mine, however
forgotten by the pretty public ; but this play of Peter, no.
Even my beginning as an amateur playwright, that noble
mouthful, *Bandelero the Bandit*, I remember every detail of

its composition in my school days at Dumfries. Not less vivid
is my first little piece, produced by Mr. Toole. It was called
Ibsen's Ghost, and was a parody of the mightiest craftsman that
ever wrote for our kind friends in front. To save the manage-
ment the cost of typing I wrote out the ' parts,' after being told
what parts were, and I can still recall my first words, spoken so
plaintively by a now famous actress,—' To run away from my
second husband just as I ran away from my first, it feels quite
like old times.' On the first night a man in the pit found
Ibsen's Ghost so diverting that he had to be removed in hysterics.
After that no one seems to have thought of it at all. But what
a man to carry about with one ! How odd, too, that these
trifles should adhere to the mind that cannot remember the long
job of writing Peter. It does seem almost suspicious, especially
as I have not the original MS. of *Peter Pan* (except a few stray
pages) with which to support my claim. I have indeed another
MS., lately made, but that ' proves nothing.' I know not
whether I lost that original MS. or destroyed it or happily gave
it away. I talk of dedicating the play to you, but how can I
prove it is mine ? How ought I to act if some other hand,
who could also have made a copy, thinks it worth while to
contest the cold rights ? Cold they are to me now as that
laughter of yours in which Peter came into being long before
he was caught and written down. There is Peter still, but to
me he lies sunk in the gay Black Lake.

Any one of you five brothers has a better claim to the author-
ship than most, and I would not fight you for it, but you should
have launched your case long ago in the days when you most
admired me, which were in the first year of the play, owing to
a rumour's reaching you that my spoils were one-and-sixpence
a night. This was untrue, but it did give me a standing among
you. You watched for my next play with peeled eyes, not for
entertainment but lest it contained some chance witticism of
yours that could be challenged as collaboration ; indeed I
believe there still exists a legal document, full of the Aforesaid
and Henceforward to be called Part-Author, in which for some
such snatching I was tied down to pay No. 2 one halfpenny
daily throughout the run of the piece.

During the rehearsals of Peter (and it is evidence in my
favour that I was admitted to them) a depressed man in overalls,

carrying a mug of tea or a paint-pot, used often to appear by my side in the shadowy stalls and say to me, 'The gallery boys won't stand it.' He then mysteriously faded away as if he were the theatre ghost. This hopelessness of his is what all dramatists are said to feel at such times, so perhaps he was the author. Again, a large number of children whom I have seen playing Peter in their homes with careless mastership, constantly putting in better words, could have thrown it off with ease. It was for such as they that after the first production I had to add something to the play at the request of parents (who thus showed that they thought me the responsible person) about no one being able to fly until the fairy dust had been blown on him; so many children having gone home and tried it from their beds and needed surgical attention.

Notwithstanding other possibilities, I think I wrote Peter, and if so it must have been in the usual inky way. Some of it, I like to think, was done in that native place which is the dearest spot on earth to me, though my last heart-beats shall be with my beloved solitary London that was so hard to reach. I must have sat at a table with that great dog waiting for me to stop, not complaining, for he knew it was thus we made our living, but giving me a look when he found he was to be in the play, with his sex changed. In after years when the actor who was Nana had to go to the wars he first taught his wife how to take his place as the dog till he came back, and I am glad that I see nothing funny in this; it seems to me to belong to the play. I offer this obtuseness on my part as my first proof that I am the author.

Some say that we are different people at different periods of our lives, changing not through effort of will, which is a brave affair, but in the easy course of nature every ten years or so. I suppose this theory might explain my present trouble, but I don't hold with it; I think one remains the same person throughout, merely passing, as it were, in these lapses of time from one room to another, but all in the same house. If we unlock the rooms of the far past we can peer in and see ourselves, busily occupied in beginning to become you and me. Thus, if I am the author in question the way he is to go should already be showing in the occupant of my first compartment, at whom I now take the liberty to peep. Here he is at the age of seven or so with his fellow-conspirator Robb, both in glengarry bonnets. They are giving an entertainment in a tiny old washing-house that still stands. The charge for admission is preens, a bool, or a peerie (I taught you a good deal of Scotch, so possibly you can follow that), and apparently the culminating Act consists in our trying to put each other into the boiler, though some say that I also addressed the spell-bound audience. This washing-house is not only the theatre of my first play, but has a still closer connection with Peter. It is the original of the little house the Lost Boys built in theNever Land for Wendy, the chief difference being that it never wore John's tall hat as a chimney. If Robb had owned a lum hat I have no doubt that it would have been placed on the washing-house.

Here is that boy again some four years older, and the reading he is munching feverishly is about desert islands ; he calls them wrecked islands. He buys his sanguinary tales surreptitiously in penny numbers. I see a change coming over him ; he is blanching as he reads in the high-class magazine, *Chatterbox*, a fulmination against such literature, and sees that unless his greed for islands is quenched he is for ever lost. With gloaming he steals out of the house, his library bulging beneath his palpitating waistcoat. I follow like his shadow, as indeed I am, and watch him dig a hole in a field at Pathhead farm and bury his islands in it ; it was ages ago, but I could walk straight to that hole in the field now and delve for the remains. I peep into the next compartment. There he is again, ten years older, an undergraduate now and craving to be a real explorer, one of those who do things instead of prating of them, but otherwise unaltered ; he might be painted at twenty on top of a mast, in his hand a spy-glass through which he rakes the horizon for an elusive strand. I go from room to room, and he is now a man, real exploration abandoned (though only because no one would have him). Soon he is even concocting other plays, and quaking a little lest some low person counts how many islands there are in them. I note that with the years the islands grow more sinister, but it is only because he has now to write with the left hand, the right having given out ; evidently one thinks more darkly down the left arm. Go to the keyhole of the compartment where he and I join up, and you may see us wondering whether they would stand one more island. This journey through the house may not convince any one that I wrote Peter, but it does suggest me as a likely person. I pause to ask myself whether I read *Chatterbox* again, suffered the old agony, and buried that MS. of the play in a hole in a field.

Of course this is over-charged. Perhaps we do change ; except a little something in us which is no larger than a mote in the eye, and that, like it, dances in front of us beguiling us all our days. I cannot cut the hair by which it hangs.

The strongest evidence that I am the author is to be found, I think, in a now melancholy volume, the aforementioned *The Boy Castaways* ; so you must excuse me for parading that work here. Officer of the Court, call *The Boy Castaways*. The witness steps forward and proves to be a book you remember well though you have not glanced at it these many years. I pulled it out of a bookcase just now not without difficulty, for its recent occupation has been to support the shelf above. I suppose, though I am uncertain, that it was I and not you who hammered it into that place of utility. It is a little battered and bent after the manner of those who shoulder burdens, and ought (to our shame) to remind us of the witnesses who sometimes get an hour off from the cells to give evidence before his Lordship. I have said that it is the rarest of my printed works, as it must be, for the only edition was limited to two copies, of which one (there was always some devilry in any matter connected with Peter) instantly lost itself in a railway carriage. This is the survivor. The idlers in court may have assumed that it is a handwritten screed, and are impressed by its bulk. It is printed by Constable's (how handsomely you did us, dear Blaikie), it contains thirty-five illustrations and is bound in cloth with a picture stamped on the cover of the three eldest of you ' setting out to be wrecked.' This record is supposed to be edited by the youngest of the three, and I must have granted him that honour to make up for his being so often lifted bodily out of our adventures by his nurse, who kept breaking into them for the fell purpose of giving him a midday rest. No. 4 rested so much at this period that he was merely an honorary member of the band, waving his foot to you for luck when you set off with bow and arrow to shoot his dinner for him ; and one may rummage the book in vain for any trace of No. 5. Here is the title-page, except that you are numbered instead of named—

THE BOY
CASTAWAYS
OF BLACK LAKE ISLAND

Being a record of the Terrible
Adventures of Three Brothers
in the summer of 1901
faithfully set forth
by No. 3.

LONDON
Published by J. M. Barrie
in the Gloucester Road
1901

There is a long preface by No. 3 in which we gather your ages at this first flight. 'No. 1 was eight and a month, No. 2 was approaching his seventh lustrum, and I was a good bit past four.' Of his two elders, while commending their fearless dispositions, the editor complains that they wanted to do all the shooting and carried the whole equipment of arrows inside their shirts. He is attractively modest about himself, 'Of No. 3 I prefer to say nothing, hoping that the tale as it is unwound will show that he was a boy of deeds rather than of words,' a quality which he hints did not unduly protrude upon the brows of Nos. 1 and 2. His preface ends on a high note, 'I should say that the work was in the first instance compiled as a record simply at which we could whet our memories, and that it is now published for No. 4's benefit. If it teaches him by example lessons in fortitude and manly endurance we shall consider that we were not wrecked in vain.'

Published to whet your memories. Does it whet them? Do you hear once more, like some long-forgotten whistle beneath your window (Robb at dawn calling me to the fishing !) the not quite mortal blows that still echo in some of the chapter headings ?—' Chapter II, No. 1 teaches Wilkinson (his master) a Stern Lesson—We Run away to Sea. Chapter III, A Fearful Hurricane—Wreck of the " Anna Pink "—We go crazy from Want of Food—Proposal to eat No. 3—Land Ahoy.' Such are two chapters out of sixteen. Are these again your javelins cutting tunes in the blue haze of the pines ; do you sweat as you scale the dreadful Valley of Rolling Stones, and cleanse your hands of pirate blood by scouring them carelessly in Mother Earth ? Can you still make a fire (you could do it once, Mr. Seton-Thompson taught us in, surely an odd place, the Reform Club) by rubbing those sticks together ? Was it the travail of hut-building that subsequently advised Peter to find a ' home under the ground ' ? The bottle and mugs in that lurid picture, ' Last night on the Island,' seem to suggest that you had changed from Lost Boys into pirates, which was probably also a tendency of Peter's. Listen again to our stolen saw-mill, man's proudest invention ; when he made the saw-mill he beat the birds for music in a wood.

The illustrations (full-paged) in *The Boy Castaways* are all photographs taken by myself ; some of them indeed of phenomena that had to be invented afterwards, for you were always off doing the wrong things when I pressed the button. I see that we combined instruction with amusement ; perhaps we had given our kingly word to that effect. How otherwise account for such wording to the pictures as these : ' It is undoubtedly,' says No. 1 in a fir tree that is bearing unwonted fruit, recently tied to it, ' the *Cocos nucifera*, for observe the slender columns supporting the crown of leaves which fall with a grace that no art can imitate.' ' Truly,' continues No. 1 under the same tree in another forest as he leans upon his trusty gun, ' though the perils of these happenings are great, yet would I rejoice to endure still greater privations to be thus rewarded by such wondrous studies of Nature.' He is soon back to the practical, however, ' recognising the Mango (*Magnifera indica*) by its lancet-shaped leaves and the cucumber-shaped fruit.' No. 1 was certainly the right sort of voyager to be wrecked with, though if my memory fails me not, No. 2, to whom these strutting observations were addressed, sometimes protested because none of them was given to him. No. 3 being the author is in surprisingly few of the pictures, but this, you may remember, was because the lady already darkly referred to used to pluck him from our midst for his siesta at 12 o'clock, which was the hour that best suited the camera. With a skill on which he has never been complimented the photographer sometimes got No. 3 nominally included in a wild-life picture when he was really in a humdrum house kicking on the sofa. Thus in a scene representing Nos. 1 and 2 sitting scowling outside the hut it is untruly written that they scowled because ' their brother was within singing and playing on a barbaric instrument. The music,' the unseen No. 3 is represented as saying (obviously forestalling No. 1), ' is rude and to a cultured ear discordant, but the songs like those of the Arabs are full of poetic imagery.' He was perhaps allowed to say this sulkily on the sofa.

Though *The Boy Castaways* has sixteen chapter-headings, there is no other letterpress ; an absence which possible purchasers might complain of, though there are surely worse ways of writing a book than this. These headings anticipate much of the play of *Peter Pan*, but there were many incidents of our Kensington Gardens days that never got into the book, such as our Antarctic exploits when we reached the Pole in advance of our friend Captain Scott and cut our initials on it for him to find, a strange foreshadowing of what was really to happen. In *The Boy Castaways* Captain Hook has arrived but is called Captain Swarthy, and he seems from the pictures to have been a black man. This character, as you do not need to be told, is held by those in the know to be autobiographical. You had many tussles with him (though you never, I think, got his right arm) before you reached the terrible chapter (which might be taken from the play) entitled ' We Board the Pirate Ship at Dawn—A Rakish Craft—No. 1 Hew-them-Down and No. 2 of the Red Hatchet—A Holocaust of Pirates—Rescue of Peter.' (Hullo, Peter rescued instead of rescuing others ? I know what that means and so do you, but we are not going to give away all our secrets.) The scene of the Holocaust is the Black Lake (afterwards, when we let women in, the Mermaids' Lagoon). The pirate captain's end was not in the mouth of a crocodile though we had crocodiles on the spot (' while No. 2 was removing the crocodiles from the stream No. 1 shot a few parrots, *Psittacidae*, for our evening meal '). I think our captain had divers deaths owing to unseemly competition among you, each wanting to slay him single-handed. On a special occasion, such as when No. 3 pulled out the tooth himself, you gave the deed to him, but took it from him while he rested. The only pictorial representation in the book of Swarthy's fate is in two parts. In one, called briefly 'We string him up,' Nos. 1 and 2, stern as Athos, are hauling him up a tree by a rope, his face snarling as if it were a grinning mask (which indeed it was), and his garments very like some of my own stuffed with bracken. The other, the same scene next day, is called 'The Vultures had Picked him Clean,' and tells its own tale.

The dog in *The Boy Castaways* seems never to have been called Nana but was evidently in training for that post. He originally belonged to Swarthy (or to Captain Marryat?), and the first picture of him, lean, skulking, and hunched (how did I get that effect?), 'patrolling the island' in that monster's interests, gives little indication of the domestic paragon he was to become. We lured him away to the better life, and there is, later, a touching picture, a clear forecast of the Darling nursery, entitled 'We trained the dog to watch over us while we slept.' In this he also is sleeping, in a position that is a careful copy of his charges; indeed any trouble we had with him was because, once he knew he was in a story, he thought his safest course was to imitate you in everything you did. How anxious he was to show that he understood the game, and more generous than you, he never pretended that he was the one who killed Captain Swarthy. I must not imply that he was entirely without initiative, for it was his own idea to bark warningly a minute or two before twelve o'clock as a signal to No. 3 that his keeper was probably on her way for him (Disappearance of No. 3); and he became so used to living in the world of Pretend that when we reached the hut of a morning he was often there waiting for us, looking, it is true, rather idiotic, but with a new bark he had invented which puzzled us until we decided that he was demanding the password. He was always willing to do any extra jobs, such as becoming the tiger in mask, and when after a fierce engagement you carried home that mask in triumph, he joined in the procession proudly and never let on that the trophy had ever been part of him. Long afterwards he saw the play from a box in the theatre, and as familiar scenes were

unrolled before his eyes I have never seen a dog so bothered.
At one matinee we even let him for a moment take the place
of the actor who played Nana, and I don't know that any
members of the audience ever noticed the change, though he
introduced some ' business ' that was new to them but old to
you and me. Heigh-ho, I suspect that in this reminiscence I
am mixing him up with his successor, for such a one there had
to be, the loyal Newfoundland who, perhaps in the following
year, applied, so to say, for the part by bringing hedgehogs
to the hut in his mouth as offerings for our evening repasts.
The head and coat of him were copied for the Nana of
the play.

They do seem to be emerging out of our island, don't they,
the little people of the play, all except that sly one, the chief
figure, who draws farther and farther into the wood as we
advance upon him? He so dislikes being tracked, as if
there were something odd about him, that when he dies he
means to get up and blow away the particle that will be
his ashes.

Wendy has not yet appeared, but she has been trying to come
ever since that loyal nurse cast the humorous shadow of woman
upon the scene and made us feel that it might be fun to let in
a disturbing element. Perhaps she would have bored her way
in at last whether we wanted her or not. It may be that even
Peter did not really bring her to the Never Land of his free will,
but merely pretended to do so because she would not stay away.
Even Tinker Bell had reached our island before we left it. It
was one evening when we climbed the wood carrying No. 4 to
show him what the trail was like by twilight. As our lanterns
twinkled among the leaves No. 4 saw a twinkle stand still for a
moment and he waved his foot gaily to it, thus creating Tink.
It must not be thought, however, that there were any other
sentimental passages between No. 4 and Tink ; indeed, as he
got to know her better he suspected her of frequenting the hut
to see what we had been having for supper, and to partake of the
same, and he pursued her with malignancy.

A safe but sometimes chilly way of recalling the past is to
force open a crammed drawer. If you are searching for anything in particular you don't find it, but something falls out at
the back that is often more interesting. It is in this way that I

get my desultory reading, which includes the few stray leaves of
the original MS. of Peter that I have said I do possess, though
even they, when returned to the drawer, are gone again, as if
that touch of devilry lurked in them still.　They show that in
early days I hacked at and added to the play.　In the drawer I
find some scraps of Mr. Crook's delightful music, and other
incomplete matter relating to Peter.　Here is the reply of a boy
whom I favoured with a seat in my box and injudiciously asked
at the end what he had liked best.　'What I think I liked best,'
he said, ' was tearing up the programme and dropping the bits on
people's heads.'　Thus am I often laid low.　A copy of my
favourite programme of the play is still in the drawer.　In the
first or second year of Peter No. 4 could not attend through illness, so we took the play to his nursery, far away in the country,
an array of vehicles almost as glorious as a travelling circus ; the
leading parts were played by the youngest children in the London
company, and No. 4, aged five, looked on solemnly at the performance from his bed and never smiled once.　That was my
first and only appearance on the real stage, and this copy
of the programme shows I was thought so meanly of as an
actor that they printed my name in smaller letters than the
others.

　　I have said little here of Nos. 4 and 5, and it is high time I had
finished.　They had a long summer day, and I turn round twice
and now they are off to school.　On Monday, as it seems, I was
escorting No. 5 to a children's party and brushing his hair in the
ante-room ; and by Thursday he is placing me against the wall
of an underground station and saying, ' Now I am going to get
the tickets ; don't move till I come back for you or you 'll lose
yourself.'　No. 4 jumps from being astride my shoulders fishing, I knee-deep in the stream, to becoming, while still a schoolboy, the sternest of my literary critics.　Anything he shook his
head over I abandoned, and conceivably the world has thus been
deprived of masterpieces.　There was for instance an unfortunate little tragedy which I liked until I foolishly told No. 4
its subject, when he frowned and said he had better have a look
at it　He read it, and then, patting me on the back, as only he
and No. 1 could touch me, said, ' You know you can't do this
sort of thing.'　End of a tragedian.　Sometimes, however,
No. 4 liked my efforts, and I walked in the azure that day when

he returned *Dear Brutus* to me with the comment ' Not so bad.' In earlier days, when he was ten, I offered him the MS. of my book *Margaret Ogilvy*. ' Oh, thanks,' he said almost immediately, and added, ' Of course my desk is awfully full.' I reminded him that he could take out some of its more ridiculous contents. He said, ' I have read it already in the book.' This I had not known, and I was secretly elated, but I said that people sometimes liked to preserve this kind of thing as a curiosity. He said ' Oh ' again. I said tartly that he was not compelled to take it if he didn't want it. He said, ' Of course I want it, but my desk——' Then he wriggled out of the room and came back in a few minutes dragging in No. 5 and announcing triumphantly, ' No. 5 will have it.'

The rebuffs I have got from all of you ! They were especially crushing in those early days when one by one you came out of your belief in fairies and lowered on me as the deceiver. My grandest triumph, the best thing in the play of *Peter Pan* (though it is not in it), is that long after No. 4 had ceased to believe, I brought him back to the faith for at least two minutes. We were on our way in a boat to fish the Outer Hebrides (where we caught *Mary Rose*), and though it was a journey of days he wore his fishing basket on his back all the time, so as to be able to begin at once. His one pain was the absence of Johnny Mackay, for Johnny was the loved gillie of the previous summer who had taught him everything that is worth knowing (which is a matter of flies) but could not be with us this time as he would have had to cross and re-cross Scotland to reach us. As the boat drew near the Kyle of Lochalsh pier I told Nos. 4 and 5 it was such a famous wishing pier that they had now but to wish and they should have. No. 5 believed at once and expressed a wish to meet himself (I afterwards found him on the pier searching faces confidently), but No. 4 thought it more of my untimely nonsense and doggedly declined to humour me. ' Whom do you want to see most, No. 4 ? ' ' Of course I would like most to see Johnny Mackay.' ' Well, then, wish for him.' ' Oh, rot.' ' It can't do any harm to wish.' Contemptuously he wished, and as the ropes were thrown on the pier he saw Johnny waiting for him, loaded with angling paraphernalia. I know no one less like a fairy than Johnny Mackay, but for two minutes No. 4 was quivering in another world than ours. When he came to he gave me a smile which meant that we understood each other, and thereafter neglected me for a month, being always with Johnny. As I have said, this episode is not in the play ; so though I dedicate *Peter Pan* to you I keep the smile, with the few other broken fragments of immortality that have come my way.

ACT I

THE NURSERY

The night nursery of the Darling family, which is the scene of our opening Act, is at the top of a rather depressed street in Bloomsbury. We have a right to place it where we will, and the reason Bloomsbury is chosen is that Mr. Roget once lived there. So did we in days when his *Thesaurus* was our only companion in London ; and we whom he has helped to wend our way through life have always wanted to pay him a little compliment. The Darlings therefore lived in Bloomsbury.

It is a corner house whose top window, the important one, looks upon a leafy square from which Peter used to fly up to it, to the delight of three children and no doubt the irritation of passers-by. The street is still there, though the steaming sausage shop has gone ; and apparently the same cards perch now as then over the doors, inviting homeless ones to come and stay with the hospitable inhabitants. Since the days of the Darlings, however, a lick of paint has been applied ; and our corner house in particular, which has swallowed its neighbour, blooms with awful freshness as if the colours had been discharged upon it through a hose. Its card now says 'No children,' meaning maybe that the goings-on of Wendy and her brothers have given the house a bad name. As for ourselves, we have not been in it since we went back to reclaim our old *Thesaurus*.

That is what we call the Darling house, but you may dump it down anywhere you like, and if you think it was your house you are very probably right. It wanders about London looking for anybody in need of it, like the little house in the Never Land.

The blind (which is what Peter would have called the theatre curtain if he had ever seen one) rises on that top room, a shabby little room if Mrs. Darling had not made it the hub of creation by her certainty that such it was, and adorned it to match with a loving heart and all the scrapings of her purse. The door on the right leads into the day nursery, which she has no right to have, but she made it herself with nails in her mouth and a paste-pot in her hand. This is the door the children will come in by. There are three beds and (rather oddly) a large dog-kennel ; two of these beds, with the kennel, being on the left and the other on the right. The coverlets of the beds (if visitors are expected) are made out of Mrs. Darling's wedding-gown, which was such a grand affair that it still keeps them pinched. Over each bed is a china house, the size of a linnet's nest, containing a night-light. The fire, which is on our right, is burning as dis-creetly as if it were in custody, which in a sense it is, for support-ing the mantelshelf are two wooden soldiers, home-made, begun by Mr. Darling, finished by Mrs. Darling, repainted (un-fortunately) by John Darling. On the fire-guard hang incom-plete parts of children's night attire. The door the parents will come in by is on the left. At the back is the bathroom door, with a cuckoo clock over it ; and in the centre is the window, which is at present ever so staid and respectable, but half an hour hence (namely at 6.30 p.m.) will be able to tell a very strange tale to the police.

The only occupant of the room at present is Nana the nurse, reclining, not as you might expect on the one soft chair, but on the floor. She is a Newfoundland dog, and though this may shock the grandiose, the not exactly affluent will make allow-ances. The Darlings could not afford to have a nurse, they could not afford indeed to have children ; and now you are beginning to understand how they did it. Of course Nana has been trained by Mrs. Darling, but like all treasures she was born to it. In this play we shall see her chiefly inside the house, but she was just as exemplary outside, escorting the two elders to school with an umbrella in her mouth, for instance, and butting them back into line if they strayed.

The cuckoo clock strikes six, and Nana springs into life. This first moment in the play is tremendously important, for if the actor playing Nana does not spring properly we are undone. She will probably be played by a boy, if one clever enough can be found, and must never be on two legs except on those rare occasions when an ordinary nurse would be on four. This Nana must go about all her duties in a most ordinary manner, so that you know in your bones that she performs them just so every evening at six ; naturalness must be her passion ; indeed, it should be the aim of every one in the play, for which she is now setting the pace. All the characters, whether grown-ups or babes, must wear a child's outlook on life as their only important adornment. If they cannot help being funny they are begged to go away. A good motto for all would be ' The little less, and how much it is.'

Nana, making much use of her mouth, ' turns down ' the beds, and carries the various articles on the fire-guard across to them. Then pushing the bathroom door open, she is seen at work on the taps preparing Michael's bath ; after which she enters from the day nursery with the youngest of the family on her back.

MICHAEL (*obstreperous*). I won't go to bed, I won't, I won't. Nana, it isn't six o'clock yet. Two minutes more, please, one minute more ? Nana, I won't be bathed, I tell you I will not be bathed.

> (*Here the bathroom door closes on them, and* MRS. DARLING, *who has perhaps heard his cry, enters the nursery. She is the loveliest lady in Bloomsbury, with a sweet mocking mouth, and as she is going out to dinner to-night she is already wearing her evening gown because she knows her children like to see her in it. It is a delicious confection made by herself out of nothing and other people's mistakes. She does not often go out to dinner, preferring when the children are in bed to sit beside them tidying up their minds, just as if they were drawers. If* WENDY *and the boys could keep awake they might see her repacking into their proper places the many articles of the mind that have strayed during the day, lingering humorously over some of their contents, wondering where on earth they picked this thing up, making discoveries sweet and not so sweet, pressing this to her cheek and hurriedly stowing that out of sight. When they wake in the morning the naughtinesses with which they went to bed are not, alas, blown away, but they are placed at the bottom of the drawer ; and on the top, beautifully aired, are their prettier thoughts ready for the new day.*
>
> *As she enters the room she is startled to see a strange little face outside the window and a hand groping as if it wanted to come in.*)

MRS. DARLING.   Who are you ?   (*The unknown disappears ;
she hurries to the window.*)   No one there.   And yet I feel sure
I saw a face.   My children !   (*She throws open the bathroom
door and* MICHAEL'S *head appears gaily over the bath.   He
splashes ; she throws kisses to him and closes the door.* ' *Wendy,
John,*' *she cries, and gets reassuring answers from the day nursery.
She sits down, relieved, on* WENDY'S *bed ; and* WENDY *and* JOHN
*come in, looking their smallest size, as children tend to do to a mother
suddenly in fear for them.*)

JOHN (*histrionically*).   We are doing an act ; we are playing
at being you and father.   (*He imitates the only father who has
come under his special notice.*)   A little less noise there.

WENDY.   Now let us pretend we have a baby.

JOHN (*good-naturedly*).   I am happy to inform you, Mrs.
Darling, that you are now a mother.   (WENDY *gives way to
ecstasy.*)   You have missed the chief thing ; you haven't asked,
' boy or girl ? '

WENDY.   I am so glad to have one at all, I don't care which
it is.

JOHN (*crushingly*).   That is just the difference between
gentlemen and ladies.   Now you tell me.

WENDY.   I am happy to acquaint you, Mr. Darling, you
are now a father.

JOHN.   Boy or girl ?

WENDY (*presenting herself*).   Girl.

JOHN.   Tuts.

WENDY.   You horrid.

JOHN.   Go on.

WENDY.   I am happy to acquaint you, Mr. Darling, you
are again a father.

JOHN.   Boy or girl ?

WENDY.   Boy. (JOHN *beams.*)   Mummy, it 's hateful of him.
     (MICHAEL *emerges from the bathroom in* JOHN'S *old pyjamas
     and giving his face a last wipe with the towel.*)

MICHAEL (*expanding*).   Now, John, have me.

JOHN.   We don't want any more.

MICHAEL (*contracting*).   Am I not to be born at all ?

JOHN.   Two is enough.

MICHAEL (*wheedling*).   Come, John ; boy, John.   (*Appalled*) Nobody wants me !

MRS. DARLING.   I do.

MICHAEL (*with a glimmer of hope*).   Boy or girl ?

MRS. DARLING (*with one of those happy thoughts of hers*).   Boy.
(*Triumph of* MICHAEL ; *discomfiture of* JOHN.   MR. DAR-
LING arrives, in no mood unfortunately to gloat over this
domestic scene.   He is really a good man as breadwinners go,
and it is hard luck for him to be propelled into the room now,
when if we had brought him in a few minutes earlier or later
he might have made a fairer impression.   In the city where
he sits on a stool all day, as fixed as a postage stamp, he is so
like all the others on stools that you recognise him not by his
face but by his stool, but at home the way to gratify him is to
say that he has a distinct personality.   He is very con-
scientious, and in the days when* MRS. DARLING *gave up
keeping the house books correctly and drew pictures instead
(which he called her guesses), he did all the totting up for her,
holding her hand while he calculated whether they could have
Wendy or not, and coming down on the right side.   It is
with regret, therefore, that we introduce him as a tornado,
rushing into the nursery in evening dress, but without his
coat, and brandishing in his hand a recalcitrant white tie.*)

MR. DARLING (*implying that he has searched for her everywhere
and that the nursery is a strange place in which to find her*).   Oh,
here you are, Mary.

MRS. DARLING (*knowing at once what is the matter*).   What is
the matter, George dear ?

MR. DARLING (*as if the word were monstrous*).   Matter !   This
tie, it will not tie.   (*He waxes sarcastic.*)   Not round my neck.
Round the bed-post, oh yes ; twenty times have I made it up round
the bed-post, but round my neck, oh dear no ; begs to be excused.

MICHAEL (*in a joyous transport*).   Say it again, father, say it
again !

MR. DARLING (*witheringly*).   Thank you.   (*Goaded by a
suspiciously crooked smile on* MRS. DARLING's *face*) I warn you,
Mary, that unless this tie is round my neck we don't go out to
dinner to-night, and if I don't go out to dinner to-night I never
go to the office again, and if I don't go to the office again you and
I starve, and our children will be thrown into the streets.

(*The children blanch as they grasp the gravity of the
situation.*)

MRS. DARLING. Let me try, dear.

(*In a terrible silence their progeny cluster round them. Will she succeed ? Their fate depends on it. She fails— no, she succeeds. In another moment they are wildly gay, romping round the room on each other's shoulders. Father is even a better horse than mother.* MICHAEL *is dropped upon his bed,* WENDY *retires to prepare for hers,* JOHN *runs from* NANA, *who has reappeared with the bath towel.*)

JOHN (*rebellious*). I won't be bathed. You needn't think it.

MR. DARLING (*in the grand manner*). Go and be bathed at once, sir.

(*With bent head* JOHN *follows* NANA *into the bathroom.* MR. DARLING *swells.*)

MICHAEL (*as he is put between the sheets*). Mother, how did you get to know me ?

MR. DARLING. A little less noise there.

MICHAEL (*growing solemn*). At what time was I born, mother ?

MRS. DARLING. At two o'clock in the night-time, dearest.

MICHAEL. Oh, mother, I hope I didn't wake you.

MRS. DARLING. They are rather sweet, don't you think, George ?

MR. DARLING (*doting*). There is not their equal on earth, and they are ours, ours !

(*Unfortunately* NANA *has come from the bathroom for a sponge and she collides with his trousers, the first pair he has ever had with braid on them.*)

MR. DARLING. Mary, it is too bad ; just look at this ; covered with hairs. Clumsy, clumsy !

(NANA *goes, a drooping figure.*)

MRS. DARLING. Let me brush you, dear.

(*Once more she is successful. They are now by the fire, and* MICHAEL *is in bed doing idiotic things with a teddy bear.*)

MR. DARLING (*depressed*). I sometimes think, Mary, that it is a mistake to have a dog for a nurse.

MRS. DARLING. George, Nana is a treasure.

MR. DARLING. No doubt ; but I have an uneasy feeling at times that she looks upon the children as puppies.

MRS. DARLING (*rather faintly*). Oh no, dear one, I am sure she knows they have souls.

MR. DARLING (*profoundly*). I wonder, I wonder.

(*The opportunity has come for her to tell him of something that is on her mind.*)

MRS. DARLING. George, we must keep Nana, I will tell you why. (*Her seriousness impresses him.*) My dear, when I came into this room to-night I saw a face at the window.

MR. DARLING (*incredulous*). A face at the window, three floors up ? Pooh !

MRS. DARLING. It was the face of a little boy ; he was trying to get in. George, this is not the first time I have seen that boy.

MR. DARLING (*beginning to think that this may be a man's job*). Oho !

MRS. DARLING (*making sure that* MICHAEL *does not hear*). The first time was a week ago. It was Nana's night out, and I had been drowsing here by the fire when suddenly I felt a draught, as if the window were open. I looked round and I saw that boy—in the room.

MR. DARLING. In the room ?

MRS. DARLING. I screamed. Just then Nana came back and she at once sprang at him. The boy leapt for the window. She pulled down the sash quickly, but was too late to catch him.

MR. DARLING (*who knows he would not have been too late*). I thought so !

MRS. DARLING. Wait. The boy escaped, but his shadow had not time to get out ; down came the window and cut it clean off.

MR. DARLING (*heavily*). Mary, Mary, why didn't you keep that shadow ?

MRS. DARLING (*scoring*). I did. I rolled it up, George ; and here it is.

(*She produces it from a drawer. They unroll and examine the flimsy thing, which is not more material than a puff of smoke, and if let go would probably float into the ceiling without discolouring it. Yet it has human shape. As they nod their heads over it they present the most satisfying picture on earth, two happy parents conspiring cosily by the fire for the good of their children.*)

MR DARLING. It is nobody I know, but he does look a scoundrel.

MRS. DARLING. I think he comes back to get his shadow, George.

MR. DARLING (*meaning that the miscreant has now a father to deal with*). I dare say. (*He sees himself telling the story to the other stools at the office.*) There is money in this, my love. I shall take it to the British Museum to-morrow and have it priced.

(*The shadow is rolled up and replaced in the drawer.*)

MRS. DARLING (*like a guilty person*). George, I have not told you all ; I am afraid to.

MR. DARLING (*who knows exactly the right moment to treat a woman as a beloved child*). Cowardy, cowardy custard.

MRS. DARLING (*pouting*). No, I 'm not.

MR. DARLING. Oh yes, you are.

MRS. DARLING. George, I 'm not.

MR. DARLING. Then why not tell ? (*Thus cleverly soothed she goes on.*)

MRS. DARLING. The boy was not alone that first time. He was accompanied by—I don't know how to describe it ; by a ball of light, not as big as my fist, but it darted about the room like a living thing.

MR. DARLING (*though open-minded*). That is very unusual. It escaped with the boy ?

MRS. DARLING. Yes. (*Sliding her hand into his.*) George, what can all this mean ?

MR. DARLING (*ever ready*). What indeed !

(*This intimate scene is broken by the return of* NANA *with a bottle in her mouth.*)

MRS. DARLING (*at once dissembling*). What is that, Nana ? Ah, of course ; Michael, it is your medicine.

MICHAEL (*promptly*). Won't take it.

MR. DARLING (*recalling his youth*). Be a man, Michael.

MICHAEL. Won't.

MRS. DARLING (*weakly*). I 'll get you a lovely chocky to take after it. (*She leaves the room, though her husband calls after her.*)

MR. DARLING. Mary, don't pamper him. When I was your age, Michael, I took medicine without a murmur. I said ' Thank you, kind parents, for giving me bottles to make me well.'

(WENDY, *who has appeared in her night-gown, hears this and believes.*)

WENDY. That medicine you sometimes take is much nastier, isn't it, father ?

MR. DARLING (*valuing her support*). Ever so much nastier. And as an example to you, Michael, I would take it now (*thankfully*) if I hadn't lost the bottle.

WENDY (*always glad to be of service*). I know where it is, father. I 'll fetch it.

(*She is gone before he can stop her He turns for help to* JOHN, *who has come from the bathroom attired for bed.*)

MR. DARLING. John, it is the most beastly stuff. It is that sticky sweet kind.

JOHN (*who is perhaps still playing at parents*). Never mind, father, it will soon be over.

(*A spasm of ill-will to* JOHN *cuts through* MR. DARLING, *and is gone.* WENDY *returns panting.*)

WENDY. Here it is, father ; I have been as quick as I could.

MR. DARLING (*with a sarcasm that is completely thrown away on her*). You have been wonderfully quick, precious quick !

(*He is now at the foot of* MICHAEL'S *bed*, NANA *is by its side, holding the medicine spoon insinuatingly in her mouth.*)

WENDY (*proudly, as she pours out* MR. DARLING'S *medicine*). Michael, now you will see how father takes it.

MR. DARLING (*hedging*). Michael first.

MICHAEL (*full of unworthy suspicions*). Father first.

MR. DARLING. It will make me sick, you know.

JOHN (*lightly*). Come on, father.

MR. DARLING. Hold your tongue, sir.

WENDY (*disturbed*). I thought you took it quite easily, father, saying ' Thank you, kind parents, for———— '

MR. DARLING. That is not the point ; the point is that there is more in my glass than in Michael's spoon. It isn't fair, I swear though it were with my last breath, it is not fair.

MICHAEL (*coldly*). Father, I 'm waiting.

MR. DARLING. It 's all very well to say you are waiting ; so am I waiting.

MICHAEL. Father 's a cowardy custard.

MR. DARLING. So are you a cowardy custard.

(*They are now glaring at each other.*)

MICHAEL. I am not frightened.

MR. DARLING. Neither am I frightened.

MICHAEL. Well, then, take it.

MR. DARLING. Well, then, you take it.

WENDY (*butting in again*). Why not take it at the same time ?

MR. DARLING (*haughtily*). Certainly. Are you ready, Michael ?

WENDY (*as nothing has happened*). One—two—three.

(MICHAEL *partakes, but* MR. DARLING *resorts to hanky-panky.*)

JOHN. Father hasn't taken his !

(MICHAEL *howls.*)

WENDY (*inexpressibly pained*). Oh father !

MR. DARLING (*who has been hiding the glass behind him*). What do you mean by ' oh father ' ? Stop that row, Michael. I meant to take mine but I—missed it. (NANA *shakes her head sadly over him, and goes into the bathroom. They are all looking as if they did not admire him, and nothing so dashes a temperamental man.*) I say, I have just thought of a splendid joke. (*They brighten.*) I shall pour my medicine into Nana's bowl, and she will drink it thinking it is milk ! (*The pleasantry does not appeal, but he prepares the joke, listening for appreciation.*)

WENDY. Poor darling Nana !

MR. DARLING. You silly little things ; to your beds every one of you ; I am ashamed of you.

(*They steal to their beds as* MRS. DARLING *returns with the chocolate.*)

MRS. DARLING. Well, is it all over ?

MICHAEL. Father didn't—— (*Father glares.*)

MR. DARLING. All over, dear, quite satisfactorily. (NANA *comes back.*) Nana, good dog, good girl ; I have put a little milk into your bowl. (*The bowl is by the kennel, and* NANA *begins to lap, only begins. She retreats into the kennel.*)

MRS. DARLING. What is the matter, Nana ?

MR. DARLING (*uneasily*). Nothing, nothing.

MRS. DARLING (*smelling the bowl*). George, it is your medicine !

(*The children break into lamentation. He gives his wife an imploring look ; he is begging for one smile, but does not get it. In consequence he goes from bad to worse.*)

MR. DARLING. It was only a joke. Much good my wearing myself to the bone trying to be funny in this house.

WENDY (*on her knees by the kennel*).   Father, Nana is crying.

MR. DARLING.   Coddle her ; nobody coddles me.   Oh dear no.   I am only the bread-winner, why should I be coddled ? Why, why, why ?

MRS. DARLING.   George, not so loud ; the servants will hear you.

(*There is only one maid, absurdly small too, but they have got into the way of calling her the servants.*)

MR. DARLING (*defiant*).   Let them hear me ; bring in the whole world.   (*The desperate man, who has not been in fresh air for days, has now lost all self-control.*)   I refuse to allow that dog to lord it in my nursery for one hour longer.   (NANA *supplicates him.*)   In vain, in vain, the proper place for you is the yard, and there you go to be tied up this instant.

(NANA *again retreats into the kennel, and the children add their prayers to hers.*)

MRS. DARLING (*who knows how contrite he will be for this presently*).   George, George, remember what I told you about that boy.

MR. DARLING.   Am I master in this house or is she ?   (*To* NANA *fiercely*) Come along.   (*He thunders at her, but she indicates that she has reasons not worth troubling him with for remaining where she is.   He resorts to a false bonhomie.*)   There, there, did she think he was angry with her, poor Nana ?   (*She wriggles a response in the affirmative.*)   Good Nana, pretty Nana.   (*She has seldom been called pretty, and it has the old effect.   She plays rub-a-dub with her paws, which is how a dog blushes.*)   She will come to her kind master, won't she ? won't she ?   (*She advances, retreats, waggles her head, her tail, and eventually goes to him.   He seizes her collar in an iron grip and amid the cries of his progeny drags her from the room.   They listen, for her remonstrances are not inaudible.*)

MRS. DARLING.   Be brave, my dears.

WENDY.   He is chaining Nana up !

(*This unfortunately is what he is doing, though we cannot see him.   Let us hope that he then retires to his study, looks up the word ' temper ' in his Thesaurus, and under the influence of those benign pages becomes a better man.   In the meantime the children have been put to bed in unwonted*

R

silence, and MRS. DARLING *lights the night-lights over the beds.)*

JOHN (*as the barking below goes on*). She is awfully unhappy.

WENDY. That is not Nana's unhappy bark. That is her bark when she smells danger.

MRS. DARLING (*remembering that boy*). Danger ! Are you sure, Wendy ?

WENDY (*the one of the family, for there is one in every family, who can be trusted to know or not to know*). Oh yes

(*Her mother looks this way and that from the window.*)

JOHN. Is anything there ?

MRS. DARLING. All quite quiet and still. Oh, how I wish I was not going out to dinner to-night.

MICHAEL. Can anything harm us, mother, after the night-lights are lit ?

MRS. DARLING. Nothing, precious. They are the eyes a mother leaves behind her to guard her children.

(*Nevertheless we may be sure she means to tell* LIZA, *the little maid, to look in on them frequently till she comes home. She goes from bed to bed, after her custom, tucking them in and crooning a lullaby.*)

MICHAEL (*drowsily*). Mother, I 'm glad of you.

MRS. DARLING (*with a last look round, her hand on the switch*). Dear night-lights that protect my sleeping babes, burn clear and steadfast to-night.

(*The nursery darkens and she is gone, intentionally leaving the door ajar. Something uncanny is going to happen, we expect, for a quiver has passed through the room, just sufficient to touch the night-lights. They blink three times one after the other and go out, precisely as children (whom familiarity has made them resemble) fall asleep. There is another light in the room now, no larger than* MRS. DAR-LING'S *fist, and in the time we have taken to say this it has been into the drawers and wardrobe and searched pockets, as it darts about looking for a certain shadow. Then the window is blown open, probably by the smallest and therefore most mischievous star, and* PETER PAN *flies into the room. In so far as he is dressed at all it is in autumn leaves and cobwebs.*)

PETER (*in a whisper*). Tinker Bell, Tink, are you there ?
(*A jug lights up.*) Oh, do come out of that jug. (TINK *flashes*

hither and thither.)   Do you know where they put it ?   (*The answer comes as of a tinkle of bells ; it is the fairy language.* PETER *can speak it, but it bores him.*)   Which big box ?   This one ?   But which drawer ?   Yes, do show me.   (TINK *pops into the drawer where the shadow is, but before* PETER *can reach it,* WENDY *moves in her sleep.   He flies on to the mantelshelf as a hiding-place.   Then, as she has not waked, he flutters over the beds as an easy way to observe the occupants, closes the window softly, wafts himself to the drawer and scatters its contents to the floor, as kings on their wedding day toss ha'pence to the crowd.   In his joy at finding his shadow he forgets that he has shut up* TINK *in the drawer.   He sits on the floor with the shadow, confident that he and it will join like drops of water.   Then he tries to stick it on with soap from the bathroom, and this failing also, he subsides dejectedly on the floor.   This wakens* WENDY, *who sits up, and is pleasantly interested to see a stranger.*)

WENDY (*courteously*).   Boy, why are you crying ?

(*He jumps up, and crossing to the foot of the bed bows to her in the fairy way.* WENDY, *impressed, bows to him from the bed.*)

PETER.   What is your name ?

WENDY (*well satisfied*).   Wendy Moira Angela Darling. What is yours ?

PETER (*finding it lamentably brief.*)   Peter Pan.

WENDY.   Is that all ?

PETER (*biting his lip*).   Yes.

WENDY (*politely*).   I am so sorry.

PETER.   It doesn't matter.

WENDY.   Where do you live ?

PETER.   Second to the right and then straight on till morning.

WENDY.   What a funny address !

PETER.   No, it isn't.

WENDY.   I mean, is that what they put on the letters ?

PETER.   Don't get any letters.

WENDY.   But your mother gets letters ?

PETER.   Don't have a mother.

WENDY.   Peter !

(*She leaps out of bed to put her arms round him, but he draws back ; he does not know why, but he knows he must draw back*)

PETER.   You mustn't touch me.

WENDY.   Why ?

PETER.   No one must ever touch me.

WENDY.   Why ?

PETER.   I don't know.

(*He is never touched by any one in the play.*)

WENDY.   No wonder you were crying.

PETER.   I wasn't crying.   But I can't get my shadow to stick on.

WENDY.   It has come off !   How awful.   (*Looking at the spot where he had lain.*)   Peter, you have been trying to stick it on with soap !

PETER (*snappily*).   Well then ?

WENDY.   It must be sewn on.

PETER.   What is ' sewn ' ?

WENDY.   You are dreadfully ignorant.

PETER.   No, I 'm not.

WENDY.   I will sew it on for you, my little man.   But we must have more light.   (*She touches something, and to his astonishment the room is illuminated.*)   Sit here.   I dare say it will hurt a little.

PETER (*a recent remark of hers rankling*).   I never cry.   (*She seems to attach the shadow.   He tests the combination.*)   It isn't quite itself yet.

WENDY.   Perhaps I should have ironed it   (*It awakes and is as glad to be back with him as he to have it.   He and his shadow dance together.   He is showing off now.   He crows like a cock. He would fly in order to impress Wendy further if he knew that there is anything unusual in that.*)

PETER.   Wendy, look, look ; oh the cleverness of me !

WENDY.   You conceit ; of course I did nothing !

PETER.   You did a little.

WENDY (*wounded*).   A little !   If I am no use I can at least withdraw.

(*With one haughty leap she is again in bed with the sheet over her face.   Popping on to the end of the bed the artful one appeals.*)

PETER.   Wendy, don't withdraw.   I can't help crowing, Wendy, when I 'm pleased with myself.   Wendy, one girl is worth more than twenty boys.

WENDY (*peeping over the sheet*).   You really think so, Peter ?

PETER.   Yes, I do.

WENDY.   I think it's perfectly sweet of you, and I shall get up again.   (*They sit together on the side of the bed.*)   I shall give you a kiss if you like.

PETER.   Thank you.   (*He holds out his hand.*)

WENDY (*aghast*).   Don't you know what a kiss is ?

PETER.   I shall know when you give it me.   (*Not to hurt his feelings she gives him her thimble.*)   Now shall I give you a kiss ?

WENDY (*primly*).   If you please.   (*He pulls an acorn button off his person and bestows it on her.   She is shocked but considerate.*)   I will wear it on this chain round my neck.   Peter, how old are you ?

PETER (*blithely*).   I don't know, but quite young, Wendy. I ran away the day I was born.

WENDY.   Ran away, why ?

PETER.   Because I heard father and mother talking of what I was to be when I became a man.   I want always to be a little boy and to have fun ; so I ran away to Kensington Gardens and lived a long time among the fairies.

WENDY (*with great eyes*).   You know fairies, Peter !

PETER (*surprised that this should be a recommendation*).   Yes, but they are nearly all dead now.   (*Baldly*) You see, Wendy, when the first baby laughed for the first time, the laugh broke into a thousand pieces and they all went skipping about, and that was the beginning of fairies.   And now when every new baby is born its first laugh becomes a fairy.   So there ought to be one fairy for every boy or girl.

WENDY (*breathlessly*).   Ought to be ?   Isn't there ?

PETER.   Oh no.   Children know such a lot now   Soon they don't believe in fairies, and every time a child says ' I don't believe in fairies ' there is a fairy somewhere that falls down dead.   (*He skips about heartlessly.*)

WENDY.   Poor things !

PETER (*to whom this statement recalls a forgotten friend*).   I can't think where she has gone.   Tinker Bell, Tink, where are you ?

WENDY (*thrilling*).   Peter, you don't mean to tell me that there is a fairy in this room !

PETER (*flitting about in search*).   She came with me.   You don't hear anything, do you ?

WENDY.   I hear—the only sound I hear is like a tinkle of bells.

PETER.   That is the fairy language.   I hear it too.

WENDY.   It seems to come from over there.

PETER (*with shameless glee*).   Wendy, I believe I shut her up in that drawer !

> (*He releases* TINK, *who darts about in a fury using language it is perhaps as well we don't understand.*)

You needn't say that ;   I 'm very sorry, but how could I know you were in the drawer ?

WENDY (*her eyes dancing in pursuit of the delicious creature*). Oh, Peter, if only she would stand still and let me see her !

PETER (*indifferently*).   They hardly ever stand still.

> (*To show that she can do even this* TINK *pauses between two ticks of the cuckoo clock.*)

WENDY.   I see her, the lovely !   where is she now ?

PETER.   She is behind the clock.   Tink, this lady wishes you were her fairy.   (*The answer comes immediately.*)

WENDY.   What does she say ?

PETER.   She is not very polite.   She says you are a great ugly girl, and that she is my fairy.   You know, Tink, you can't be my fairy because I am a gentleman and you are a lady.

> (TINK *replies.*)

WENDY.   What did she say ?

PETER.   She said ' You silly ass.'   She is quite a common girl, you know.   She is called Tinker Bell because she mends the fairy pots and kettles.

> (*They have reached a chair,* WENDY *in the ordinary way and* PETER *through a hole in the back.*)

WENDY.   Where do you live now ?

PETER.   With the lost boys.

WENDY.   Who are they ?

PETER.   They are the children who fall out of their prams when the nurse is looking the other way.   If they are not claimed in seven days they are sent far away to the Never Land. I 'm captain.

WENDY.   What fun it must be.

PETER (*craftily*).   Yes, but we are rather lonely.   You see, Wendy, we have no female companionship.

WENDY.   Are none of the other children girls ?

PETER.   Oh no ; girls, you know, are much too clever to fall out of their prams.

WENDY.   Peter, it is perfectly lovely the way you talk about girls.   John there just despises us.

(PETER, *for the first time, has a good look at* JOHN.   *He then neatly tumbles him out of bed.*)

You wicked ! you are not captain here.   (*She bends over her brother who is prone on the floor.*)   After all he hasn't wakened, and you meant to be kind.   (*Having now done her duty she forgets* JOHN, *who blissfully sleeps on.*)   Peter, you may give me a kiss.

PETER (*cynically*).   I thought you would want it back.
(*He offers her the thimble.*)

WENDY (*artfully*).   Oh dear, I didn't mean a kiss, Peter.   I meant a thimble.

PETER (*only half placated*).   What is that ?

WENDY.   It is like this.   (*She leans forward to give a demonstration, but something prevents the meeting of their faces.*)

PETER (*satisfied*).   Now shall I give you a thimble ?

WENDY.   If you please.   (*Before he can even draw near she screams.*)

PETER.   What is it ?

WENDY.   It was exactly as if some one were pulling my hair !

PETER.   That must have been Tink.   I never knew her so naughty before.

(TINK *speaks.   She is in the jug again.*)

WENDY.   What does she say ?

PETER.   She says she will do that every time I give you a thimble.

WENDY.   But why ?

PETER (*equally nonplussed*).   Why, Tink ?   (*He has to translate the answer.*)   She said ' You silly ass ' again.

WENDY.   She is very impertinent.   (*They are sitting on the floor now.*)   Peter, why did you come to our nursery window ?

PETER.   To try to hear stories.   None of us knows any stories.

WENDY.   How perfectly awful !

PETER.   Do you know why swallows build in the eaves of houses ?   It is to listen to the stories.   Wendy, your mother was telling you such a lovely story.

WENDY.   Which story was it ?

PETER.   About the prince, and he couldn't find the lady who wore the glass slipper.

WENDY.   That was Cinderella. Peter, he found her and they were happy ever after.

PETER.   I am glad. (*They have worked their way along the floor close to each other, but he now jumps up.*)

WENDY.   Where are you going ?

PETER (*already on his way to the window*).   To tell the other boys.

WENDY.   Don't go, Peter. I know lots of stories. The stories I could tell to the boys !

PETER (*gleaming*).   Come on ! We'll fly.

WENDY.   Fly ? You can fly !

(*How he would like to rip those stories out of her ; he is dangerous now.*)

PETER.   Wendy, come with me.

WENDY.   Oh dear, I mustn't. Think of mother. Besides, I can't fly.

PETER.   I'll teach you.

WENDY.   How lovely to fly !

PETER.   I'll teach you how to jump on the wind's back and then away we go. Wendy, when you are sleeping in your silly bed you might be flying about with me, saying funny things to the stars. There are mermaids, Wendy, with long tails. (*She just succeeds in remaining on the nursery floor.*) Wendy, how we should all respect you.

(*At this she strikes her colours.*)

WENDY.   Of course it's awfully fas-cin-a-ting ! Would you teach John and Michael to fly too ?

PETER (*indifferently*).   If you like.

WENDY (*playing rum-tum on* JOHN).   John, wake up ; there is a boy here who is to teach us to fly.

JOHN.   Is there ? Then I shall get up. (*He raises his head from the floor.*) Hullo, I am up !

WENDY.   Michael, open your eyes. This boy is to teach us to fly.

(*The sleepers are at once as awake as their father's razor ; but before a question can be asked* NANA'S *bark is heard.*)

JOHN. Out with the light, quick, hide !

(*When the maid* LIZA, *who is so small that when she says she will never see ten again one can scarcely believe her, enters with a firm hand on the troubled* NANA's *chain the room is in comparative darkness.*)

LIZA. There, you suspicious brute, they are perfectly safe, aren't they ? Every one of the little angels sound asleep in bed. Listen to their gentle breathing. (NANA's *sense of smell here helps to her undoing instead of hindering it. She knows that they are in the room.* MICHAEL, *who is behind the curtain window, is so encouraged by* LIZA's *last remark that he breathes too loudly,* NANA *knows that kind of breathing and tries to break from her keeper's control.*) No more of it, Nana. (*Wagging a finger at her*) I warn you if you bark again I shall go straight for master and missus and bring them home from the party, and then won't master whip you just ! Come along, you naughty dog.

(*The unhappy* NANA *is led away. The children emerge exulting from their various hiding-places. In their brief absence from the scene strange things have been done to them ; but it is not for us to reveal a mysterious secret of the stage. They look just the same.*)

JOHN. I say, can you really fly ?

PETER. Look ! (*He is now over their heads.*)

WENDY. Oh, how sweet !

PETER. I 'm sweet, oh, I am sweet !

(*It looks so easy that they try it first from the floor and then from their beds, without encouraging results.*)

JOHN (*rubbing his knees*). How do you do it ?

PETER (*descending*). You just think lovely wonderful thoughts and they lift you up in the air. (*He is off again.*)

JOHN. You are so nippy at it ; couldn't you do it very slowly once ? (PETER *does it slowly.*) I 've got it now, Wendy. (*He tries ; no, he has not got it, poor stay-at-home, though he knows the names of all the counties in England and* PETER *does not know one.*)

PETER. I must blow the fairy dust on you first. (*Fortunately his garments are smeared with it and he blows some dust on each.*) Now, try ; try from the bed. Just wriggle your shoulders this way, and then let go.

(*The gallant* MICHAEL *is the first to let go, and is borne across the room.*)

MICHAEL (*with a yell that should have disturbed* LIZA). I flewed !

(JOHN *lets go, and meets* WENDY *near the bathroom door though they had both aimed in an opposite direction.*)

WENDY.   Oh, lovely !

JOHN (*tending to be upside down*).   How ripping !

MICHAEL (*playing whack on a chair*).   I do like it !

THE THREE.   Look at me, look at me, look at me !

(*They are not nearly so elegant in the air as* PETER, *but their heads have bumped the ceiling, and there is nothing more delicious than that.*)

JOHN (*who can even go backwards*).   I say, why shouldn't we go out ?

PETER.   There are pirates.

JOHN.   Pirates ! (*He grabs his tall Sunday hat.*)   Let us go at once !

(TINK *does not like it. She darts at their hair. From down below in the street the lighted window must present an unwonted spectacle ; the shadows of children revolving in the room like a merry-go-round. This is perhaps what* MR. *and* MRS. DARLING *see as they come hurrying home from the party, brought by* NANA *who, you may be sure, has broken her chain.* PETER'S *accomplice, the little star, has seen them coming, and again the window blows open.*)

PETER (*as if he had heard the star whisper 'Cave'*).   Now come !

(*Breaking the circle he flies out of the window over the trees of the square and over the house-tops, and the others follow like a flight of birds. The broken-hearted father and mother arrive just in time to get a nip from* TINK *as she too sets out for the Never Land.*)

ACT II

THE NEVER LAND

WHEN the blind goes up all is so dark that you scarcely know it has gone up. This is because if you were to see the island bang (as Peter would say) the wonders of it might hurt your eyes. If you all came in spectacles perhaps you could see it bang, but to make a rule of that kind would be a pity. The first thing seen is merely some whitish dots trudging along the sward, and you can guess from their tinkling that they are probably fairies of the commoner sort going home afoot from some party and having a cheery tiff by the way. Then Peter's star wakes up, and in the blink of it, which is much stronger than in our stars, you can make out masses of trees, and you think you see wild beasts steal-ing past to drink, though what you see is not the beasts them-selves but only the shadows of them. They are really out pictorially to greet Peter in the way they think he would like them to greet him ; and for the same reason the mermaids basking in the lagoon beyond the trees are carefully combing their hair ; and for the same reason the pirates are landing in-visibly from the longboat, invisibly to you but not to the redskins, whom none can see or hear because they are on the war-path. The whole island, in short, which has been having a slack time in Peter's absence, is now in a ferment because the tidings has leaked out that he is on his way back ; and everybody and every-thing know that they will catch it from him if they don't give satisfaction. While you have been told this the sun (another of his servants) has been bestirring himself. Those of you who may have thought it wiser after all to begin this Act in spectacles may now take them off.

What you see is the Never Land. You have often half seen it before, or even three-quarters, after the night-lights were lit, and you might then have beached your coracle on it if you had not always at the great moment fallen asleep. I dare say you have chucked things on to it, the things you can't find in the morning.   In the daytime you think the Never Land is only make-believe, and so it is to the likes of you, but this is the Never Land come true.   It is an open-air scene, a forest, with a beautiful lagoon beyond but not really far away, for the Never Land is very compact, not large and sprawly with tedious distances between one adventure and another, but nicely crammed.   It is summer time on the trees and on the lagoon but winter on the river, which is not remarkable on Peter's island where all the four seasons may pass while you are filling a jug at the well. Peter's home is at this very spot, but you could not point out the way into it even if you were told which is the entrance, not even if you were told that there are seven of them.   You know now because you have just seen one of the lost boys emerge.   The holes in these seven great hollow trees are the ' doors ' down to Peter's home, and he made seven because, despite his cleverness, he thought seven boys must need seven doors.

    The boy who has emerged from his tree is Slightly, who has perhaps been driven from the abode below by companions less musical than himself   Quite possibly a genius, Slightly has with him his home-made whistle to which he capers entrancingly, with no audience save a Never ostrich which is also musically inclined.   Unable to imitate Slightly's graces the bird falls so low as to burlesque them and is driven from the entertainment. Other lost boys climb up the trunks or drop from branches, and now we see the six of them, all in the skins of animals they think they have shot, and so round and furry in them that if they fall they roll.   Tootles is not the least brave though the most unfortunate of this gallant band.   He has been in fewer adventures than any of them because the big things constantly happen while he has stepped round the corner ; he will go off, for instance, in some quiet hour to gather firewood, and then when he returns the others will be sweeping up the blood.   Instead of souring his nature this has sweetened it and he is the humblest of the band. Nibs is more gay and debonair, Slightly more conceited. Slightly thinks he remembers the days before he was lost, with their manners and customs.   Curly is a pickle, and so often has he had to deliver up his person when Peter said sternly, ' Stand forth the one who did this thing,' that now he stands forth whether he has done it or not.   The other two are First Twin and Second Twin, who cannot be described because we should probably be describing the wrong one. Hunkering on the ground or peeping out of their holes, the six are not unlike village gossips gathered round the pump.

TOOTLES.   Has Peter come back yet, Slightly ?

SLIGHTLY (*with a solemnity that he thinks suits the occasion*). No, Tootles, no.

(*They are like dogs waiting for the master to tell them that the day has begun.*)

CURLY (*as if Peter might be listening*).   I do wish he would come back.

TOOTLES.   I am always afraid of the pirates when Peter is not here to protect us.

SLIGHTLY.   I am not afraid of pirates.   Nothing frightens me.   But I do wish Peter would come back and tell us whether he has heard anything more about Cinderella.

SECOND TWIN (*with diffidence*).   Slightly, I dreamt last night that the prince found Cinderella.

FIRST TWIN (*who is intellectually the superior of the two*). Twin, I think you should not have dreamt that, for I didn't, and Peter may say we oughtn't to dream differently, being twins, you know.

TOOTLES.   I am awfully anxious about Cinderella.   You see, not knowing anything about my own mother I am fond of thinking that she was rather like Cinderella.

(*This is received with derision.*)

NIBS.   All I remember about my mother is that she often said to father, ' Oh, how I wish I had a cheque book of my own.'   I don't know what a cheque book is, but I should just love to give my mother one.

SLIGHTLY (*as usual*).   My mother was fonder of me than your mothers were of you.   (*Uproar.*)   Oh yes, she was. Peter had to make up names for you, but my mother had wrote my name on the pinafore I was lost in.   ' Slightly Soiled ' ; that 's my name.

(*They fall upon him pugnaciously ; not that they are really worrying about their mothers, who are now as important to them as a piece of string, but because any excuse is good enough for a shindy.   Not for long is he belaboured, for a*

*sound is heard that sends them scurrying down their holes ;
in a second of time the scene is bereft of human life. What
they have heard from near-by is a verse of the dreadful song
with which on the Never Land the pirates stealthily trumpet
their approach—*

> Yo ho, yo ho, the pirate life,
> The flag of skull and bones,
> A merry hour, a hempen rope,
> And hey for Davy Jones !

*The pirates appear upon the frozen river dragging a raft,
on which reclines among cushions that dark and fearful man,*
CAPTAIN JAS HOOK. *A more villainous-looking brother-
hood of men never hung in a row on Execution dock. Here,
his great arms bare, pieces of eight in his ears as ornaments,
is the handsome* CECCO, *who cut his name on the back of the
governor of the prison at Gao. Heavier in the pull is the
gigantic black who has had many names since the first one
terrified dusky children on the banks of the Guidjo-mo.*
BILL JUKES *comes next, every inch of him tattooed, the same*
JUKES *who got six dozen on the* Walrus *from Flint. Following these are* COOKSON, *said to be* BLACK MURPHY'S
brother (but this was never proved) ; and GENTLEMAN
STARKEY, *once an usher in a school ; and* SKYLIGHTS
(*Morgan's Skylights*) ; *and* NOODLER, *whose hands are
fixed on backwards ; and the spectacled boatswain,* SMEE,
the only Nonconformist in HOOK'S *crew ; and other ruffians
long known and feared on the Spanish main.*
   Cruelest jewel in that dark setting is HOOK *himself,
cadaverous and blackavised, his hair dressed in long curls
which look like black candles about to melt, his eyes blue as the
forget-me-not and of a profound insensibility, save when he
claws, at which time a red spot appears in them. He has an
iron hook instead of a right hand, and it is with this he claws.
He is never more sinister than when he is most polite, and the
elegance of his diction, the distinction of his demeanour,
show him one of a different class from his crew, a solitary
among uncultured companions. This courtliness impresses
even his victims on the high seas, who note that he always
says ' Sorry ' when prodding them along the plank. A man*

of indomitable courage, the only thing at which he flinches is the sight of his own blood, which is thick and of an unusual colour. At his public school they said of him that he ' bled yellow.' In dress he apes the dandiacal associated with Charles II., having heard it said in an earlier period of his career that he bore a strange resemblance to the ill-fated Stuarts. A holder of his own contrivance is in his mouth enabling him to smoke two cigars at once. Those, however, who have seen him in the flesh, which is an inadequate term for his earthly tenement, agree that the grimmest part of him is his iron claw.

　　They continue their distasteful singing as they disembark—

> Avast, belay, yo ho, heave to,
> A-pirating we go,
> And if we 're parted by a shot
> We 're sure to meet below !

　　NIBS, *the only one of the boys who has not sought safety in his tree, is seen for a moment near the lagoon, and* STARKEY'S *pistol is at once upraised. The captain twists his hook in him.*)

STARKEY (*abject*).　Captain, let go !

HOOK.　Put back that pistol, first.

STARKEY.　'Twas one of those boys you hate ; I could have shot him dead.

HOOK.　Ay, and the sound would have brought Tiger Lily's redskins on us.　Do you want to lose your scalp ?

SMEE (*wriggling his cutlass pleasantly*).　That is true.　Shall I after him, Captain, and tickle him with Johnny Corkscrew ? Johnny is a silent fellow.

HOOK.　Not now.　He is only one, and I want to mischief all the seven.　Scatter and look for them.　(*The boatswain whistles his instructions, and the men disperse on their frightful errand. With none to hear save* SMEE, HOOK *becomes confidential.*) Most of all I want their captain, Peter Pan.　'Twas he cut off my arm.　I have waited long to shake his hand with this. (*Luxuriating*) Oh, I 'll tear him !

SMEE (*always ready for a chat*).　Yet I have oft heard you say your hook was worth a score of hands, for combing the hair and other homely uses.

HOOK.   If I was a mother I would pray to have my children
born with this instead of that (*his left arm creeps nervously
behind him.   He has a galling remembrance*).   Smee, Pan flung
my arm to a crocodile that happened to be passing by.

SMEE.   I have often noticed your strange dread of crocodiles.

HOOK (*pettishly*).   Not of crocodiles but of that one crocodile.
(*He lays bare a lacerated heart.*)   The brute liked my arm so
much, Smee, that he has followed me ever since, from sea to sea,
and from land to land, licking his lips for the rest of me.

SMEE (*looking for the bright side*).   In a way it is a sort of
compliment.

HOOK (*with dignity*).   I want no such compliments ; I want
Peter Pan, who first gave the brute his taste for me.   Smee, that
crocodile would have had me before now, but by a lucky chance
he swallowed a clock, and it goes tick, tick, tick, tick inside him ;
and so before he can reach me I hear the tick and bolt.   (*He
emits a hollow rumble.*)   Once I heard it strike six within
him.

SMEE (*sombrely*).   Some day the clock will run down, and
then he 'll get you.

HOOK (*a broken man*).   Ay, that is the fear that haunts me.
(*He rises.*)   Smee, this seat is hot ; odds, bobs, hammer and
tongs, I am burning.

> (*He has been sitting, he thinks, on one of the island mush-
> rooms, which are of enormous size.   But this is a hand-
> painted one placed here in times of danger to conceal a
> chimney.   They remove it, and tell-tale smoke issues ;
> also, alas, the sound of children's voices.*)

SMEE.   A chimney !

HOOK (*avidly*).   Listen !   Smee, 'tis plain they live here,
beneath the ground.   (*He replaces the mushroom.   His brain
works tortuously.*)

SMEE (*hopefully*).   Unrip your plan, Captain.

HOOK.   To return to the boat and cook a large rich cake of
jolly thickness with sugar on it, green sugar.   There can be but
one room below, for there is but one chimney.   The silly moles
had not the sense to see that they did not need a door apiece.
We must leave the cake on the shore of the mermaids' lagoon.
These boys are always swimming about there, trying to catch
the mermaids.   They will find the cake and gobble it up,

because, having no mother, they don't know how dangerous 'tis to eat rich damp cake.   They will die !

SMEE (*fascinated*).   It is the wickedest, prettiest policy ever I heard of.

HOOK (*meaning well*).   Shake hands on 't.

SMEE.   No, Captain, no.

(*He has to link with the hook, but he does not join in the song.*)

HOOK.   Yo ho, yo ho, when I say ' paw,'
             By fear they 're overtook,
             Naught 's left upon your bones when you
             Have shaken hands with Hook !

(*Frightened by a tug at his hand,* SMEE *is joining in the chorus when another sound stills them both.   It is a tick, tick as of a clock, whose significance* HOOK *is, naturally, the first to recognise.   ' The crocodile !' he cries, and totters from the scene.* SMEE *follows.   A huge crocodile, of one thought compact, passes across, ticking, and oozes after them. The wood is now so silent that you may be sure it is full of redskins.* TIGER LILY *comes first.   She is the belle of the Piccaninny tribe, whose braves would all have her to wife, but she wards them off with a hatchet.   She puts her ear to the ground and listens, then beckons, and* GREAT BIG LITTLE PANTHER *and the tribe are around her, carpeting the ground.   Far away some one treads on a dry leaf.*)

TIGER LILY.   Pirates !   (*They do not draw their knives ; the knives slip into their hands.*)   Have um scalps ?   What you say ?

PANTHER.   Scalp um, oho, velly quick.

THE BRAVES (*in corroboration*).   Ugh, ugh, wah.

(*A fire is lit and they dance round and over it till they seem part of the leaping flames.* TIGER LILY *invokes Manitou ; the pipe of peace is broken ; and they crawl off like a long snake that has not fed for many moons.* TOOTLES *peers after the tail and summons the other boys, who issue from their holes.*)

TOOTLES.   They are gone.

SLIGHTLY (*almost losing confidence in himself*).   I do wish Peter was here.

FIRST TWIN.   H'sh !   What is that ?   (*He is gazing at the*

lagoon and shrinks back.) It is wolves, and they are chasing
Nibs !

> (*The baying wolves are upon them quicker than any boy can
> scuttle down his tree.*)

NIBS (*falling among his comrades*).   Save me, save me !

TOOTLES.   What should we do ?

SECOND TWIN.   What would Peter do ?

SLIGHTLY.   Peter would look at them through his legs ; let
us do what Peter would do.

> (*The boys advance backwards, looking between their legs at
> the snarling red-eyed enemy, who trot away foiled.*)

FIRST TWIN (*swaggering*).   We have saved you, Nibs.   Did
you see the pirates ?

NIBS (*sitting up, and agreeably aware that the centre of interest
is now to pass to him*).   No, but I saw a wonderfuller thing,
Twin.   (*All mouths open for the information to be dropped into
them.*)   High over the lagoon I saw the loveliest great white
bird.   It is flying this way.   (*They search the firmament.*)

TOOTLES.   What kind of a bird, do you think ?

NIBS (*awed*).   I don't know ; but it looked so weary, and as
it flies it moans ' Poor Wendy.'

SLIGHTLY (*instantly*).   I remember now there are birds called
Wendies.

FIRST TWIN (*who has flown to a high branch*).   See, it comes,
the Wendy !   (*They all see it now.*)   How white it is !   (*A
dot of light is pursuing the bird malignantly.*)

TOOTLES.   That is Tinker Bell.   Tink is trying to hurt the
Wendy.   (*He makes a cup of his hands and calls*) Hullo, Tink !
(*A response comes down in the fairy language.*)   She says Peter
wants us to shoot the Wendy.

NIBS   Let us do what Peter wishes.

SLIGHTLY.   Ay, shoot it ; quick, bows and arrows.

TOOTLES (*first with his bow*).   Out of the way, Tink ; I 'll
shoot it.   (*His bolt goes home, and* WENDY, *who has been fluttering
among the tree-tops in her white nightgown, falls straight to earth.
No one could be more proud than* TOOTLES.)   I have shot the
Wendy ; Peter will be so pleased.   (*From some tree on which*
TINK *is roosting comes the tinkle we can now translate, ' You silly
ass.'*   TOOTLES *falters.*)   Why do you say that ?   (*The others
feel that he may have blundered, and draw away from* TOOTLES.)

SLIGHTLY (*examining the fallen one more minutely*). This is no bird ; I think it must be a lady.

NIBS (*who would have preferred it to be a bird*). And Tootles has killed her.

CURLY. Now I see, Peter was bringing her to us. (*They wonder for what object.*)

SECOND TWIN. To take care of us ? (*Undoubtedly for some diverting purpose.*)

OMNES (*though every one of them had wanted to have a shot at her*). Oh, Tootles !

TOOTLES (*gulping*). I did it. When ladies used to come to me in dreams I said ' Pretty mother,' but when she really came I shot her ! (*He perceives the necessity of a solitary life for him.*) Friends, good-bye.

SEVERAL (*not very enthusiastic*). Don't go.

TOOTLES. I must ; I am so afraid of Peter.

  (*He has gone but a step toward oblivion when he is stopped by a crowing as of some victorious cock.*)

OMNES. Peter !

  (*They make a paling of themselves in front of* WENDY *as* PETER *skims round the tree-tops and reaches earth.*)

PETER. Greeting, boys ! (*Their silence chafes him.*) I am back ; why do you not cheer ? Great news, boys, I have brought at last a mother for us all.

SLIGHTLY (*vaguely*). Ay, ay.

PETER. She flew this way ; have you not seen her ?

SECOND TWIN (*as* PETER *evidently thinks her important*). Oh mournful day !

TOOTLES (*making a break in the paling*). Peter, I will show her to you.

THE OTHERS (*closing the gap*). No, no.

TOOTLES (*majestically*). Stand back all, and let Peter see.

  (*The paling dissolves, and* PETER *sees* WENDY *prone on the ground.*)

PETER. Wendy, with an arrow in her heart ! (*He plucks it out.*) Wendy is dead. (*He is not so much pained as puzzled.*)

CURLY. I thought it was only flowers that die.

PETER. Perhaps she is frightened at being dead ? (*None of them can say as to that.*) Whose arrow ? (*Not one of them looks at* TOOTLES.)

TOOTLES.   Mine, Peter.

PETER (*raising it as a dagger*).   Oh dastard hand !

TOOTLES (*kneeling and baring his breast*).   Strike, Peter ; strike true.

PETER (*undergoing a singular experience*).   I cannot strike ; there is something stays my hand.

(*In fact* WENDY's *arm has risen.*)

NIBS.   'Tis she, the Wendy lady.   See, her arm.   (*To help a friend*) I think she said ' Poor Tootles.'

PETER (*investigating*).   She lives !

SLIGHTLY (*authoritatively*).   The Wendy lady lives.

(*The delightful feeling that they have been cleverer than they thought comes over them and they applaud themselves.*)

PETER (*holding up a button that is attached to her chain*).   See, the arrow struck against this.   It is a kiss I gave her ; it has saved her life.

SLIGHTLY.   I remember kisses ; let me see it.   (*He takes it in his hand.*)   Ay, that is a kiss.

PETER.   Wendy, get better quickly and I 'll take you to see the mermaids.   She is awfully anxious to see a mermaid.

(TINKER BELL, *who may have been off visiting her relations, returns to the wood and, under the impression that* WENDY *has been got rid of, is whistling as gaily as a canary.   She is not wholly heartless, but is so small that she has only room for one feeling at a time.*)

CURLY.   Listen to Tink rejoicing because she thinks the Wendy is dead !   (*Regardless of spoiling another's pleasure*) Tink, the Wendy lives.

(TINK *gives expression to fury.*)

SECOND TWIN (*tell-tale*).   It was she who said that you wanted us to shoot the Wendy.

PETER.   She said that ?   Then listen, Tink, I am your friend no more.   (*There is a note of acerbity in* TINK's *reply ; it may mean ' Who wants you ? '*)   Begone from me for ever.   (*Now it is a very wet tinkle.*)

CURLY.   She is crying.

TOOTLES.   She says she is your fairy.

PETER (*who knows they are not worth worrying about*).   Oh well, not for ever, but for a whole week.

(TINK *goes off sulking, no doubt with the intention of giving*

all her friends an entirely false impression of WENDY's
   appearance.)
Now what shall we do with Wendy ?

CURLY.   Let us carry her down into the house.

SLIGHTLY.   Ay, that is what one does with ladies.

PETER.   No, you must not touch her ; it wouldn't be
sufficiently respectful.

SLIGHTLY.   That is what I was thinking.

TOOTLES.   But if she lies there she will die.

SLIGHTLY.   Ay, she will die.   It is a pity, but there is no
way out.

PETER.   Yes, there is.   Let us build a house around her !
(*Cheers again, meaning that no difficulty baffles* PETER.)   Leave
all to me.   Bring the best of what we have.   Gut our house.
Be sharp.   (*They race down their trees.*)

   (*While* PETER *is engrossed in measuring* WENDY *so that the
   house may fit her,* JOHN *and* MICHAEL, *who have probably
   landed on the island with a bump, wander forward, so
   draggled and tired that if you were to ask* MICHAEL *whether
   he is awake or asleep he would probably answer* ' *I haven't
   tried yet.*')

MICHAEL (*bewildered*).   John, John, wake up.   Where is
Nana, John ?

JOHN (*with the help of one eye but not always the same eye*).   It
is true, we did fly !   (*Thankfully*) And here is Peter.   Peter, is
this the place ?

   (PETER, *alas, has already forgotten them, as soon maybe he
   will forget* WENDY.   *The first thing she should do now that
   she is here is to sew a handkerchief for him, and knot it as a
   jog to his memory.*)

PETER (*curtly*).   Yes.

MICHAEL.   Where is Wendy ?   (PETER *points.*)

JOHN (*who still wears his hat*).   She is asleep.

MICHAEL.   John, let us wake her and get her to make supper
for us.

   (*Some of the boys emerge, and he pinches one.*)
John, look at them !

PETER (*still house-building*).   Curly, see that these boys help
in the building of the house.

JOHN.   Build a house ?

CURLY.   For the Wendy.

JOHN (*feeling that there must be some mistake here*).   For Wendy ?   Why, she is only a girl.

CURLY.   That is why we are her servants.

JOHN (*dazed*).   Are you Wendy's servants ?

PETER.   Yes, and you also.   Away with them.   (*In another moment they are woodsmen hacking at trees, with* CURLY *as overseer.*)   Slightly, fetch a doctor.   (SLIGHTLY *reels and goes.   He returns professionally in* JOHN'S *hat.*)   Please, sir, are you a doctor ?

SLIGHTLY (*trembling in his desire to give satisfaction*).   Yes, my little man.

PETER.   Please, sir, a lady lies very ill.

SLIGHTLY (*taking care not to fall over her*).   Tut, tut, where does she lie ?

PETER.   In yonder glade.   (*It is a variation of a game they play.*)

SLIGHTLY.   I will put a glass thing in her mouth.   (*He inserts an imaginary thermometer in* WENDY'S *mouth and gives it a moment to record its verdict.   He shakes it and then consults it.*)

PETER (*anxiously*).   How is she ?

SLIGHTLY.   Tut, tut, this has cured her.

PETER (*leaping joyously*).   I am glad.

SLIGHTLY.   I will call again in the evening.   Give her beef tea out of a cup with a spout to it, tut, tut.

(*The boys are running up with odd articles of furniture.*)

PETER (*with an already fading recollection of the Darling nursery*).   These are not good enough for Wendy.   How I wish I knew the kind of house she would prefer !

FIRST TWIN.   Peter, she is moving in her sleep.

TOOTLES (*opening* WENDY'S *mouth and gazing down into the depths*).   Lovely !

PETER.   Oh, Wendy, if you could sing the kind of house you would like to have.

(*It is as if she had heard him.*)

WENDY (*without opening her eyes*).

> I wish I had a woodland house,
> The littlest ever seen,
> With funny little red walls
> And roof of mossy green.

(*In the time she sings this and two other verses, such is the urgency of* PETER'S *silent orders that they have knocked down trees, laid a foundation and put up the walls and roof, so that she is now hidden from view. 'Windows,' cries* PETER, *and* CURLY *rushes them in, 'Roses,' and* TOOTLES *arrives breathless with a festoon for the door. Thus springs into existence the most delicious little house for beginners.*)

FIRST TWIN. I think it is finished.

PETER. There is no knocker on the door. (TOOTLES *hangs up the sole of his shoe.*) There is no chimney ; we must have a chimney. (*They await his deliberations anxiously.*)

JOHN (*unwisely critical*). It certainly does need a chimney.

(*He is again wearing his hat, which* PETER *seizes, knocks the top off it and places on the roof. In the friendliest way smoke begins to come out of the hat.*)

PETER (*with his hand on the knocker*). All look your best ; the first impression is awfully important. (*He knocks, and after a dreadful moment of suspense, in which they cannot help wondering if any one is inside, the door opens and who should come out but* WENDY ! *She has evidently been tidying a little. She is quite surprised to find that she has nine children.*)

WENDY (*genteelly*). Where am I ?

SLIGHTLY. Wendy lady, for you we built this house.

NIBS and TOOTLES. Oh, say you are pleased.

WENDY (*stroking the pretty thing*). Lovely, darling house !

FIRST TWIN. And we are your children.

WENDY (*affecting surprise*). Oh ?

OMNES (*kneeling, with outstretched arms*). Wendy lady, be our mother ! (*Now that they know it is pretend they acclaim her greedily.*)

WENDY (*not to make herself too cheap*). Ought I ? Of course it is frightfully fascinating ; but you see I am only a little girl ; I have no real experience.

OMNES. That doesn't matter. What we need is just a nice motherly person.

WENDY. Oh dear, I feel that is just exactly what I am.

OMNES. It is, it is, we saw it at once.

WENDY. Very well then, I will do my best. (*In their glee they go dancing obstreperously round the little house, and she sees she*

must be firm with them as well as kind.)   Come inside at once,
you naughty children, I am sure your feet are damp.   And
before I put you to bed I have just time to finish the story of
Cinderella.

(*They all troop into the enchanting house, whose not least
remarkable feature is that it holds them.   A vision of* LIZA
*passes, not perhaps because she has any right to be there ;
but she has so few pleasures and is so young that we just let
her have a peep at the little house.   By and by* PETER *comes
out and marches up and down with drawn sword, for the
pirates can be heard carousing far away on the lagoon, and
the wolves are on the prowl.   The little house, its walls so
red and its roof so mossy, looks very cosy and safe, with a
bright light showing through the blind, the chimney smoking
beautifully, and* PETER *on guard.   On our last sight of him
it is so dark that we just guess he is the little figure who has
fallen asleep by the door.   Dots of light come and go.   They
are inquisitive fairies having a look at the house.   Any other
child in their way they would mischief, but they just tweak*
PETER'S *nose and pass on.   Fairies, you see, can touch him.*)

ACT III

THE MERMAIDS' LAGOON

IT is the end of a long playful day on the lagoon. The sun's rays have persuaded him to give them another five minutes, for one more race over the waters before he gathers them up and lets in the moon. There are many mermaids here, going plop-plop, and one might attempt to count the tails did they not flash and disappear so quickly. At times a lovely girl leaps in the air seeking to get rid of her excess of scales, which fall in a silver shower as she shakes them off. From the coral grottoes beneath the lagoon, where are the mermaids' bed-chambers, comes fitful music.

One of the most bewitching of these blue-eyed creatures is lying lazily on Marooners' Rock, combing her long tresses and noting effects in a transparent shell. Peter and his band are in the water unseen behind the rock, whither they have tracked her as if she were a trout, and at a signal ten pairs of arms come whack upon the mermaid to enclose her. Alas, this is only what was meant to happen, for she hears the signal (which is the crow of a cock) and slips through their arms into the water. It has been such a near thing that there are scales on some of their hands. They climb on to the rock crestfallen.

WENDY (*preserving her scales as carefully as if they were rare postage stamps*). I did so want to catch a mermaid.

PETER (*getting rid of his*). It is awfully difficult to catch a mermaid.

> (*The mermaids at times find it just as difficult to catch him, though he sometimes joins them in their one game, which consists in lazily blowing their bubbles into the air and seeing who can catch them. The number of bubbles PETER has flown away with! When the weather grows cold mer-*

maids migrate to the other side of the world, and he once went with a great shoal of them half the way.)

They are such cruel creatures, Wendy, that they try to pull boys and girls like you into the water and drown them.

WENDY (*too guarded by this time to ask what he means precisely by ' like you,' though she is very desirous of knowing*). How hateful !

(*She is slightly different in appearance now, rather rounder, while* JOHN *and* MICHAEL *are not quite so round. The reason is that when new lost children arrive at his underground home* PETER *finds new trees for them to go up and down by, and instead of fitting the tree to them he makes them fit the tree. Sometimes it can be done by adding or removing garments, but if you are bumpy, or the tree is an odd shape, he has things done to you with a roller, and after that you fit.*

The other boys are now playing King of the Castle, throwing each other into the water, taking headers and so on ; but these two continue to talk.)

PETER. Wendy, this is a fearfully important rock. It is called Marooners' Rock. Sailors are marooned, you know, when their captain leaves them on a rock and sails away.

WENDY. Leaves them on this little rock to drown ?

PETER (*lightly*). Oh, they don't live long. Their hands are tied, so that they can't swim. When the tide is full this rock is covered with water, and then the sailor drowns.

(WENDY *is uneasy as she surveys the rock, which is the only one in the lagoon and no larger than a table. Since she last looked around a threatening change has come over the scene. The sun has gone, but the moon has not come. What has come is a cold shiver across the waters which has sent all the wiser mermaids to their coral recesses. They know that evil is creeping over the lagoon. Of the boys* PETER *is of course the first to scent it, and he has leapt to his feet before the words strike the rock—*

' And if we 're parted by a shot
We 're sure to meet below.'

The games on the rock and around it end so abruptly that several divers are checked in the air. There they hang waiting for the word of command from PETER. *When they get it they strike the water simultaneously, and the rock is at once as bare as if suddenly they had been blown off it. Thus the pirates find it deserted when their dinghy strikes the rock and is nearly stove in by the concussion.)*

SMEE. Luff, you spalpeen, luff ! (*They are* SMEE *and* STARKEY, *with* TIGER LILY, *their captive, bound hand and foot.*) What we have got to do is to hoist the redskin on to the rock and leave her there to drown.

(*To one of her race this is an end darker than death by fire or torture, for it is written in the laws of the Piccaninnies that there is no path through water to the happy hunting ground. Yet her face is impassive ; she is the daughter of a chief and must die as a chief's daughter ; it is enough.*)

STARKEY (*chagrined because she does not mewl*). No mewling. This is your reward for prowling round the ship with a knife in your mouth.

TIGER LILY (*stoically*). Enough said.

SMEE (*who would have preferred a farewell palaver*). So that's it ! On to the rock with her, mate.

STARKEY (*experiencing for perhaps the last time the stirrings of a man*). Not so rough, Smee ; roughish, but not so rough.

SMEE (*dragging her on to the rock*). It is the captain's orders.

(*A stave has in some past time been driven into the rock, probably to mark the burial place of hidden treasure, and to this they moor the dinghy.*)

WENDY (*in the water*). Poor Tiger Lily !

STARKEY. What was that ? (*The children bob.*)

PETER (*who can imitate the captain's voice so perfectly that even the author has a dizzy feeling that at times he was really* HOOK). Ahoy there, you lubbers !

STARKEY. It is the captain ; he must be swimming out to us.

SMEE (*calling*). We have put the redskin on the rock, Captain.

PETER. Set her free.

SMEE. But, Captain——

PETER. Cut her bonds, or I 'll plunge my hook in you.

SMEE. This is queer !

STARKEY (*unmanned*). Let us follow the captain's orders.

(*They undo the thongs and* TIGER LILY *slides between their legs into the lagoon, forgetting in her haste to utter her war-*

cry, but PETER *utters it for her, so naturally that even the
lost boys are deceived.   It is at this moment that the voice
of the true* HOOK *is heard.*)

HOOK.   Boat ahoy !

SMEE (*relieved*).   It is the captain.

(HOOK *is swimming, and they help him to scale the rock.   He
is in gloomy mood.*)

STARKEY.   Captain, is all well ?

SMEE.   He sighs.

STARKEY.   He sighs again.

SMEE (*counting*).   And yet a third time he sighs.   (*With
foreboding*) What 's up, Captain ?

HOOK (*who has perhaps found the large run damp cake untouched*).   The game is up.   Those boys have found a
mother !

STARKEY.   Oh evil day !

SMEE.   What is a mother ?

WENDY (*horrified*).   He doesn't know !

HOOK (*sharply*).   What was that ?

(PETER *makes the splash of a mermaid's tail.*)

STARKEY.   One of them mermaids.

HOOK.   Dost not know, Smee ?   A mother is——   (*He finds
it more difficult to explain than he had expected, and looks about him
for an illustration.   He finds one in a great bird which drifts past
in a nest as large as the roomiest basin.*)   There is a lesson in
mothers for you !   The nest must have fallen into the water,
but would the bird desert her eggs ?   (PETER, *who is now more or
less off his head, makes the sound of a bird answering in the negative.
The nest is borne out of sight.*)

STARKEY.   Maybe she is hanging about here to protect
Peter ?

(HOOK's *face clouds still further and* PETER *just manages not
to call out that he needs no protection.*)

SMEE (*not usually a man of ideas*).   Captain, could we not
kidnap these boys' mother and make her our mother ?

HOOK.   Obesity and bunions, 'tis a princely scheme.   We
will seize the children, make them walk the plank, and Wendy
shall be our mother !

WENDY.   Never !   (*Another splash from* PETER.)

HOOK.   What say you, bullies ?

SMEE.   There is my hand on't.

STARKEY.   And mine.

HOOK.   And there is my hook.   Swear.   (*All swear.*)   But I had forgot ; where is the redskin ?

SMEE (*shaken*).   That is all right, Captain ; we let her go.

HOOK (*terrible*).   Let her go ?

SMEE.   'Twas your own orders, Captain.

STARKEY (*whimpering*).   You called over the water to us to let her go.

HOOK.   Brimstone and gall, what cozening is here ?   (*Disturbed by their faithful faces*) Lads, I gave no such order.

SMEE.   'Tis passing queer.

HOOK (*addressing the immensities*).   Spirit that haunts this dark lagoon to-night, dost hear me ?

PETER (*in the same voice*).   Odds, bobs, hammer and tongs, I hear you.

HOOK (*gripping the stave for support*).   Who are you, stranger, speak.

PETER (*who is only too ready to speak*).   I am Jas Hook, Captain of the *Jolly Roger*.

HOOK (*now white to the gills*).   No, no, you are not.

PETER.   Brimstone and gall, say that again and I 'll cast anchor in you.

HOOK.   If you are Hook, come tell me, who am I ?

PETER.   A codfish, only a codfish.

HOOK (*aghast*).   A codfish ?

SMEE (*drawing back from him*).   Have we been captained all this time by a codfish ?

STARKEY.   It 's lowering to our pride.

HOOK (*feeling that his ego is slipping from him*).   Don't desert me, bullies.

PETER (*top-heavy*).   Paw, fish, paw !

(*There is a touch of the feminine in* HOOK, *as in all the greatest pirates, and it prompts him to try the guessing game.*)

HOOK.   Have you another name ?

PETER (*falling to the lure*).   Ay, ay.

HOOK (*thirstily*).   Vegetable ?

PETER.   No.

HOOK.   Mineral ?

PETER.   No.

HOOK.   Animal ?

PETER (*after a hurried consultation with* TOOTLES).   Yes.

HOOK.   Man ?

PETER (*with scorn*).   No.

HOOK.   Boy ?

PETER.   Yes.

HOOK.   Ordinary boy ?

PETER.   No !

HOOK.   Wonderful boy ?

PETER (*to* WENDY'S *distress*).   Yes !

HOOK.   Are you in England ?

PETER.   No.

HOOK.   Are you here ?

PETER.   Yes.

HOOK (*beaten, though he feels he has very nearly got it*).   Smee, you ask him some questions.

SMEE (*rummaging his brains*).   I can't think of a thing.

PETER.   Can't guess, can't guess !   (*Foundering in his cockiness*) Do you give it up ?

HOOK (*eagerly*).   Yes.

PETER.   All of you ?

SMEE and STARKEY.   Yes.

PETER (*crowing*).   Well, then, I am Peter Pan !

(*Now they have him.*)

HOOK.   Pan !   Into the water, Smee.   Starkey, mind the boat.   Take him dead or alive !

PETER (*who still has all his baby teeth*).   Boys, lam into the pirates !

(*For a moment the only two we can see are in the dinghy, where* JOHN *throws himself on* STARKEY. STARKEY *wriggles into the lagoon and* JOHN *leaps so quickly after him that he reaches it first.   The impression left on* STARKEY *is that he is being attacked by the* TWINS.   *The water becomes stained.   The dinghy drifts away.   Here and there a head shows in the water, and once it is the head of the crocodile. In the growing gloom some strike at their friends,* SLIGHTLY *getting* TOOTLES *in the fourth rib while he himself is pinked by* CURLY.   *It looks as if the boys were getting the worse of it, which is perhaps just as well at this point, because* PETER, *who will be the determining factor in the end, has a perplex-*

ing way of changing sides if he is winning too easily. HOOK'S *iron claw makes a circle of black water round him from which opponents flee like fishes. There is only one prepared to enter that dreadful circle. His name is* PAN. *Strangely, it is not in the water that they meet.* HOOK *has risen to the rock to breathe, and at the same moment* PETER *scales it on the opposite side. The rock is now wet and as slippery as a ball, and they have to crawl rather than climb. Suddenly they are face to face.* PETER *gnashes his pretty teeth with joy, and is gathering himself for the spring when he sees he is higher up the rock than his foe. Courteously he waits ;* HOOK *sees his intention, and taking advantage of it claws twice.* PETER *is untouched, but unfairness is what he never can get used to, and in his bewilderment he rolls off the rock. The crocodile, whose tick has been drowned in the strife, rears its jaws, and* HOOK, *who has almost stepped into them, is pursued by it to land. All is quiet on the lagoon now, not a sound save little waves nibbling at the rock, which is smaller than when we last looked at it. Two boys appear with the dinghy, and the others despite their wounds climb into it. They send the cry ' Peter—Wendy ' across the waters, but no answer comes.)*

NIBS. They must be swimming home.

JOHN. Or flying.

FIRST TWIN. Yes, that is it. Let us be off and call to them as we go.

(The dinghy disappears with its load, whose hearts would sink it if they knew of the peril of WENDY *and her captain. From near and far away come the cries ' Peter—Wendy ' till we no longer hear them.*

Two small figures are now on the rock, but they have fainted. A mermaid who has dared to come back in the stillness stretches up her arms and is slowly pulling WENDY *into the water to drown her.* WENDY *starts up just in time.)*

WENDY. Peter !

(He rouses himself and looks around him.)

Where are we, Peter ?

PETER. We are on the rock, but it is getting smaller. Soon the water will be over it. Listen !

(They can hear the wash of the relentless little waves.)

WENDY.   We must go.

PETER.   Yes.

WENDY.   Shall we swim or fly ?

PETER.   Wendy, do you think you could swim or fly to the island without me ?

WENDY.   You know I couldn't, Peter ; I am just a beginner.

PETER.   Hook wounded me twice.   (*He believes it ; he is so good at pretend that he feels the pain, his arms hang limp.*)   I can neither swim nor fly.

WENDY.   Do you mean we shall both be drowned ?

PETER.   Look how the water is rising !

(*They cover their faces with their hands. Something touches* WENDY *as lightly as a kiss.*)

PETER (*with little interest*).   It must be the tail of the kite we made for Michael ; you remember it tore itself out of his hands and floated away.   (*He looks up and sees the kite sailing overhead.*) The kite ! Why shouldn't it carry you ? (*He grips the tail and pulls, and the kite responds.*)

WENDY.   Both of us !

PETER.   It can't lift two.   Michael and Curly tried.

(*She knows very well that if it can lift her it can lift him also, for she has been told by the boys as a deadly secret that one of the queer things about him is that he is no weight at all. But it is a forbidden subject.*)

WENDY.   I won't go without you.   Let us draw lots which is to stay behind.

PETER.   And you a lady, never ! (*The tail is in her hands, and the kite is tugging hard. She holds out her mouth to* PETER, *but he knows they cannot do that.*)   Ready, Wendy!

(*The kite draws her out of sight across the lagoon.*

The waters are lapping over the rock now, and PETER *knows that it will soon be submerged. Pale rays of light mingle with the moving clouds, and from the coral grottoes is to be heard a sound, at once the most musical and the most melancholy in the Never Land, the mermaids calling to the moon to rise.* PETER *is afraid at last, and a tremor runs through him, like a shudder passing over the lagoon ; but on the lagoon one shudder follows another till there are hundreds of them, and he feels just the one.*)

PETER (*with a drum beating in his breast as if he were a real boy at last*). To die will be an awfully big adventure.

(*The blind rises again, and the lagoon is now suffused with moonlight. He is on the rock still, but the water is over his feet. The nest is borne nearer, and the bird, after cooing a message to him, leaves it and wings her way upwards. PETER, who knows the bird language, slips into the nest, first removing the two eggs and placing them in STARKEY'S hat, which has been left on the stave. The hat drifts away from the rock, but he uses the stave as a mast. The wind is driving him toward the open sea. He takes off his shirt, which he had forgotten to remove while bathing, and unfurls it as a sail. His vessel tacks, and he passes from sight, naked and victorious. The bird returns and sits on the hat.*)

ACT IV

THE HOME UNDER THE GROUND

WE see simultaneously the home under the ground with the children in it and the wood above ground with the redskins on it. Below, the children are gobbling their evening meal ; above, the redskins are squatting in their blankets near the little house guarding the children from the pirates. The only way of communicating between these two parties is by means of the hollow trees.

The home has an earthen floor, which is handy for digging in if you want to go fishing ; and owing to there being so many entrances there is not much wall space. The table at which the lost ones are sitting is a board on top of a live tree trunk, which has been cut flat but has such growing pains that the board rises as they eat, and they have sometimes to pause in their meals to cut a bit more off the trunk. Their seats are pumpkins or the large gay mushrooms of which we have seen an imitation one concealing the chimney. There is an enormous fireplace which is in almost any part of the room where you care to light it, and across this Wendy has stretched strings, made of fibre, from which she hangs her washing. There are also various tomfool things in the room of no use whatever.

Michael's basket bed is nailed high up on the wall as if to protect him from the cat, but there is no indication at present of where the others sleep. At the back between two of the tree trunks is a grindstone, and near it is a lovely hole, the size of a band-box, with a gay curtain drawn across so that you cannot see what is inside. This is Tink's withdrawing-room and bed-chamber, and it is just as well that you cannot see inside, for it is so exquisite in its decoration and in the personal apparel spread out on the bed that you could scarcely resist making off with something. Tink is within at present, as one can guess from a glow showing through the chinks. It is her own glow, for though she has a chandelier for the look of the thing, of course she lights her residence herself.　She is probably wasting valuable time just now wondering whether to put on the smoky blue or the apple-blossom.

All the boys except Peter are here, and Wendy has the head of the table, smiling complacently at their captivating ways, but doing her best at the same time to see that they keep the rules about hands-off-the-table, no-two-to-speak-at-once, and so on. She is wearing romantic woodland garments, sewn by herself, with red berries in her hair which go charmingly with her complexion, as she knows ; indeed she searched for red berries the morning after she reached the island.　The boys are in picturesque attire of her contrivance, and if these don't always fit well the fault is not hers but the wearers', for they constantly put on each other's things when they put on anything at all.　Michael is in his cradle on the wall.　First Twin is apart on a high stool and wears a dunce's cap, another invention of Wendy's, but not wholly successful because everybody wants to be dunce.

It is a pretend meal this evening, with nothing whatever on the table, not a mug, nor a crust, nor a spoon.　They often have these suppers and like them on occasions as well as the other kind, which consist chiefly of bread-fruit, tappa rolls, yams, mammee apples and banana splash, washed down with calabashes of poepoe.　The pretend meals are not Wendy's idea ; indeed she was rather startled to find, on arriving, that Peter knew of no other kind, and she is not absolutely certain even now that he does eat the other kind, though no one appears to do it more heartily.　He insists that the pretend meals should be partaken of with gusto, and we see his band doing their best to obey orders.

WENDY (*her fingers to her ears, for their chatter and clatter are deafening*).　Si-lence !　Is your mug empty, Slightly ?

SLIGHTLY (*who would not say this if he had a mug*).　Not quite empty, thank you.

NIBS.　Mummy, he has not even begun to drink his poe-poe.

SLIGHTLY (*seizing his chance, for this is tale-bearing*).　I complain of Nibs !

(JOHN *holds up his hand.*)

WENDY.　Well, John ?

JOHN.　May I sit in Peter's chair as he is not here ?

WENDY. In your father's chair ?   Certainly not.

JOHN. He is not really our father.   He did not even know
how to be a father till I showed him.

(*This is insubordination.*)

SECOND TWIN.   I complain of John !

(*The gentle* TOOTLES *raises his hand.*)

TOOTLES (*who has the poorest opinion of himself*).   I don't
suppose Michael would let me be baby ?

MICHAEL.   No, I won't.

TOOTLES.   May I be dunce ?

FIRST TWIN (*from his perch*).   No.   It's awfully difficult to
be dunce.

TOOTLES.   As I can't be anything important would any of
you like to see me do a trick ?

OMNES.   No.

TOOTLES (*subsiding*).   I hadn't really any hope.

(*The tale-telling breaks out again.*)

NIBS.   Slightly is coughing on the table.

CURLY.   The twins began with tappa rolls.

SLIGHTLY.   I complain of Nibs !

NIBS.   I complain of Slightly !

WENDY.   Oh dear, I am sure I sometimes think that spinsters
are to be envied.

MICHAEL.   Wendy, I am too big for a cradle.

WENDY.   You are the littlest, and a cradle is such a nice
homely thing to have about a house.   You others can clear
away now.   (*She sits down on a pumpkin near the fire to her
usual evening occupation, darning.*)   Every heel with a hole in it !

(*The boys clear away with dispatch, washing dishes they
don't have in a non-existent sink and stowing them in a cupboard that isn't there.   Instead of sawing the table-leg to-
night they crush it into the ground like a concertina, and are
now ready for play, in which they indulge hilariously.*

*A movement of the Indians draws our attention to the
scene above.   Hitherto, with the exception of* PANTHER,
*who sits on guard on top of the little house, they have been
hunkering in their blankets, mute but picturesque ; now all
rise and prostrate themselves before the majestic figure of*
PETER, *who approaches through the forest carrying a gun
and game bag.   It is not exactly a gun.   He often wanders*

*away alone with this weapon, and when he comes back you
are never absolutely certain whether he has had an adventure or not.　He may have forgotten it so completely that
he says nothing about it ; and then when you go out you find
the body.　On the other hand he may say a great deal about
it, and yet you never find the body.　Sometimes he comes
home with his face scratched, and tells* WENDY, *as a thing of
no importance, that he got these marks from the little people
for cheeking them at a fairy wedding, and she listens politely,
but she is never quite sure, you know ; indeed the only one
who is sure about anything on the island is* PETER.)

PETER.　The Great White Father is glad to see the Piccaninny braves protecting his wigwam from the pirates.

TIGER LILY.　The Great White Father save me from pirates.
Me his velly nice friend now ; no let pirates hurt him.

BRAVES.　Ugh, ugh, wah !

TIGER LILY.　Tiger Lily has spoken.

PANTHER.　Loola, loola !　Great Big Little Panther has spoken.

PETER.　It is well.　The Great White Father has spoken.

(*This has a note of finality about it, with the implied ' And
now shut up,' which is never far from the courteous recep-
tions of well-meaning inferiors by born leaders of men.　He
descends his tree, not unheard by* WENDY.)

WENDY.　Children, I hear your father's step.　He likes you
to meet him at the door.　(PETER *scatters pretend nuts among
them and watches sharply to see that they crunch with relish.*)
Peter, you just spoil them, you know !

JOHN (*who would be incredulous if he dare*).　Any sport, Peter?

PETER.　Two tigers and a pirate.

JOHN (*boldly*).　Where are their heads ?

PETER (*contracting his little brows*).　In the bag.

JOHN.　(*No, he doesn't say it.　He backs away.*)

WENDY (*peeping into the bag*).　They are beauties !　(*She
has learned her lesson.*)

FIRST TWIN.　Mummy, we all want to dance.

WENDY.　The mother of such an armful dance !

SLIGHTLY.　As it is Saturday night ?

(*They have long lost count of the days, but always if they
want to do anything special they say this is Saturday night,
and then they do it.*)

WENDY.   Of course it is Saturday night, Peter ?   (*He shrugs
an indifferent assent.*)   On with your nighties first.

(*They disappear into various recesses, and* PETER *and*
WENDY *with her darning are left by the fire to dodder
parentally.   She emphasises it by humming a verse of* ' *John
Anderson my Jo,*' *which has not the desired effect on* PETER.
*She is too loving to be ignorant that he is not loving enough,
and she hesitates like one who knows the answer to her
question.*)
What is wrong, Peter ?

PETER (*scared*).   It is only pretend, isn't it, that I am their
father ?

WENDY (*drooping*).   Oh yes.

(*His sigh of relief is without consideration for her feelings.*)
But they are ours, Peter, yours and mine.

PETER (*determined to get at facts, the only things that puzzle
him*).   But not really ?

WENDY.   Not if you don't wish it.

PETER.   I don't.

WENDY (*knowing she ought not to probe but driven to it by
something within*).   What are your exact feelings for me, Peter ?

PETER (*in the class-room*).   Those of a devoted son, Wendy.

WENDY (*turning away*).   I thought so.

PETER.   You are so puzzling.   Tiger Lily is just the same ;
there is something or other she wants to be to me, but she says
it is not my mother.

WENDY (*with spirit*).   No, indeed it isn't.

PETER.   Then what is it ?

WENDY.   It isn't for a lady to tell.

(*The curtain of the fairy chamber opens slightly, and* TINK,
*who has doubtless been eavesdropping, tinkles a laugh of
scorn.*)

PETER (*badgered*).   I suppose she means that she wants to be
my mother.

(TINK'S *comment is* ' *You silly ass.*')

WENDY (*who has picked up some of the fairy words*).   I almost
agree with her !

(*The arrival of the boys in their nightgowns turns* WENDY'S
*mind to practical matters, for the children have to be
arranged in line and passed or not passed for cleanliness.*

SLIGHTLY *is the worst.　At last we see how they sleep, for in a babel the great bed which stands on end by day against the wall is unloosed from custody and lowered to the floor. Though large, it is a tight fit for so many boys, and* WENDY *has made a rule that there is to be no turning round until one gives the signal, when all turn at once.*

　　FIRST TWIN *is the best dancer and performs mightily on the bed and in it and out of it and over it to an accompaniment of pillow fights by the less agile ; and then there is a rush at* WENDY.)

NIBS.　Now the story you promised to tell us as soon as we were in bed !

WENDY (*severely*).　As far as I can see you are not in bed yet. (*They scramble into the bed, and the effect is as of a boxful of sardines.*)

WENDY (*drawing up her stool*).　Well, there was once a gentleman——

CURLY.　I wish he had been a lady.

NIBS.　I wish he had been a white rat.

WENDY.　Quiet !　There was a lady also.　The gentleman's name was Mr. Darling and the lady's name was Mrs. Darling——

JOHN.　I knew them !

MICHAEL (*who has been allowed to join the circle*).　I think I knew them.

WENDY.　They were married, you know ; and what do you think they had ?

NIBS.　White rats ?

WENDY.　No, they had three descendants.　White rats are descendants also.　Almost everything is a descendant.　Now these three children had a faithful nurse called Nana.

MICHAEL (*alas*).　What a funny name !

WENDY.　But Mr. Darling——(*faltering*) or was it Mrs. Darling ?—was angry with her and chained her up in the yard ; so all the children flew away.　They flew away to the Never Land, where the lost boys are.

CURLY.　I just thought they did ; I don't know how it is, but I just thought they did.

TOOTLES.　Oh, Wendy, was one of the lost boys called Tootles ?

WENDY. Yes, he was.

TOOTLES (*dazzled*). Am I in a story? Nibs, I am in a story!

PETER (*who is by the fire making Pan's pipes with his knife, and is determined that* WENDY *shall have fair play, however beastly a story he may think it*). A little less noise there.

WENDY (*melting over the beauty of her present performance, but without any real qualms*). Now I want you to consider the feelings of the unhappy parents with all their children flown away. Think, oh think, of the empty beds. (*The heartless ones think of them with glee.*)

FIRST TWIN (*cheerfully*). It's awfully sad.

WENDY. But our heroine knew that her mother would always leave the window open for her progeny to fly back by; so they stayed away for years and had a lovely time.

(PETER *is interested at last.*)

FIRST TWIN. Did they ever go back?

WENDY (*comfortably*). Let us now take a peep into the future. Years have rolled by, and who is this elegant lady of uncertain age alighting at London station?

(*The tension is unbearable.*)

NIBS. Oh, Wendy, who is she?

WENDY (*swelling*). Can it be—yes—no—yes, it is the fair Wendy!

TOOTLES. I am glad.

WENDY. Who are the two noble portly figures accompanying her? Can they be John and Michael? They are. (*Pride of* MICHAEL.) 'See, dear brothers,' says Wendy, pointing upward, 'there is the window standing open.' So up they flew to their loving parents, and pen cannot inscribe the happy scene over which we draw a veil. (*Her triumph is spoilt by a groan from* PETER *and she hurries to him.*) Peter, what is it? (*Thinking he is ill, and looking lower than his chest*) Where is it?

PETER. It isn't that kind of pain. Wendy, you are wrong about mothers. I thought like you about the window, so I stayed away for moons and moons, and then I flew back, but the window was barred, for my mother had forgotten all about me and there was another little boy sleeping in my bed.

(*This is a general damper.*)

JOHN. Wendy, let us go back !

WENDY. Are you sure mothers are like that ?

PETER. Yes.

WENDY. John, Michael ! (*She clasps them to her.*)

FIRST TWIN (*alarmed*). You are not to leave us, Wendy ?

WENDY. I must.

NIBS. Not to-night ?

WENDY. At once. Perhaps mother is in half-mourning by this time ! Peter, will you make the necessary arrangements ?

(*She asks it in the steely tones women adopt when they are prepared secretly for opposition.*)

PETER (*coolly*). If you wish it.

(*He ascends his tree to give the redskins their instructions. The lost boys gather threateningly round* WENDY.)

CURLY. We won't let you go !

WENDY (*with one of those inspirations women have, in an emergency, to make use of some male who need otherwise have no hope*). Tootles, I appeal to you.

TOOTLES (*leaping to his death if necessary*). I am just Tootles and nobody minds me, but the first who does not behave to Wendy I will blood him severely. (PETER *returns.*)

PETER (*with awful serenity*). Wendy, I told the braves to guide you through the wood as flying tires you so. Then Tinker Bell will take you across the sea. (*A shrill tinkle from the boudoir probably means ' and drop her into it.'*)

NIBS (*fingering the curtain which he is not allowed to open*). Tink, you are to get up and take Wendy on a journey. (*Stareyed*) She says she won't !

PETER (*taking a step toward that chamber*). If you don't get up, Tink, and dress at once—— She is getting up !

WENDY (*quivering now that the time to depart has come*). Dear ones, if you will all come with me I feel almost sure I can get my father and mother to adopt you.

(*There is joy at this, not that they want parents, but novelty is their religion.*)

NIBS. But won't they think us rather a handful ?

WENDY (*a swift reckoner*). Oh no, it will only mean having a few beds in the drawing-room ; they can be hidden behind screens on first Thursdays.

(*Everything depends on* PETER.)

OMNES.   Peter, may we go ?

PETER (*carelessly through the pipes to which he is giving a finishing touch*).   All right.

(*They scurry off to dress for the adventure.*)

WENDY (*insinuatingly*).   Get your clothes, Peter.

PETER (*skipping about and playing fairy music on his pipes, the only music he knows*).   I am not going with you, Wendy.

WENDY.   Yes, Peter !

PETER.   No.

(*The lost ones run back gaily, each carrying a stick with a bundle on the end of it.*)

WENDY.   Peter isn't coming !

(*All the faces go blank.*)

JOHN (*even JOHN*).   Peter not coming !

TOOTLES (*overthrown*)   Why, Peter ?

PETER (*his pipes more riotous than ever*).   I just want always to be a little boy and to have fun.

(*There is a general fear that they are perhaps making the mistake of their lives.*)

Now then, no fuss, no blubbering.   (*With dreadful cynicism*) I hope you will like your mothers !   Are you ready, Tink !   Then lead the way.

(TINK *darts up any tree, but she is the only one.   The air above is suddenly rent with shrieks and the clash of steel.   Though they cannot see, the boys know that* HOOK *and his crew are upon the Indians.   Mouths open and remain open, all in mute appeal to* PETER.   *He is the only boy on his feet now, a sword in his hand, the same he slew Barbicue with ; and in his eye is the lust of battle.*

We can watch the carnage that is invisible to the children. HOOK *has basely broken the two laws of Indian warfare, which are that the redskins should attack first, and that it should be at dawn.   They have known the pirate whereabouts since, early in the night, one of* SMEE'S *fingers crackled.   The brushwood has closed behind their scouts as silently as the sand on the mole ; for hours they have imitated the lonely call of the coyote ; no stratagem has been overlooked, but alas, they have trusted to the pale-face's honour to await an attack at dawn, when his courage is known to be at the lowest ebb.* HOOK *falls upon them pell-mell, and one cannot withhold a reluctant admiration for the wit that conceived so subtle a scheme and the fell genius with which it is carried out. If the braves would rise quickly they might still have time to scalp, but this they are forbidden to do by the traditions of their race, for it is written that they must never express surprise in the presence of the pale-face. For a brief space they remain recumbent, not a muscle moving, as if the foe were here by invitation. Thus perish the flower of the Piccaninnies, though not unavenged, for with* LEAN WOLF *fall* ALF MASON *and* CANARY ROBB, *while other pirates to bite dust are* BLACK GILMOUR *and* ALAN HERB, *that same* HERB *who is still remembered at Manaos for playing skittles with the mate of the* Switch *for each other's heads.* CHAY TURLEY, *who laughed with the wrong side of his mouth (having no other), is tomahawked by* PANTHER, *who eventually cuts a way through the shambles with* TIGER LILY *and a remnant of the tribe.*

This onslaught passes and is gone like a fierce wind. The victors wipe their cutlasses, and squint, ferret-eyed, at their leader. He remains, as ever, aloof in spirit and in substance. He signs to them to descend the trees, for he is convinced that PAN *is down there, and though he has smoked the bees it is the honey he wants. There is something in* PETER *that at all times goads this extraordinary man to frenzy; it is the boy's cockiness, which disturbs* HOOK *like an insect. If you have seen a lion in a cage futilely pursuing a sparrow you will know what is meant. The pirates try to do their captain's bidding, but the apertures prove to be not wide enough for them; he cannot even ram them down with a pole. He steals to the mouth of a tree and listens.)*

PETER (*prematurely*).   All is over !

WENDY.   But who has won ?

PETER.   Hst !   If the Indians have won they will beat the tom-tom ; it is always their signal of victory.

(HOOK *licks his lips at this and signs to* SMEE, *who is sitting on it, to hold up the tom-tom. He beats upon it with his claw, and listens for results.*)

TOOTLES.   The tom-tom !

PETER (*sheathing his sword*).   An Indian victory !

(*The cheers from below are music to the black hearts above.*)

You are quite safe now, Wendy. Boys, good-bye. (*He resumes his pipes.*)

WENDY.   Peter, you will remember about changing your flannels, won't you ?

PETER.   Oh, all right !

WENDY.   And this is your medicine.

(*She puts something into a shell and leaves it on a ledge between two of the trees.   It is only water, but she measures it out in drops.*)

PETER.   I won't forget.

WENDY.   Peter, what are you to me ?

PETER (*through the pipes*).   Your son, Wendy.

WENDY.   Oh, good-bye !

(*The travellers start upon their journey, little witting that* HOOK *has issued his silent orders : a man to the mouth of each tree, and a row of men between the trees and the little house.   As the children squeeze up they are plucked from their trees, trussed, thrown like bales of cotton from one pirate to another, and so piled up in the little house.   The only one treated differently is* WENDY, *whom* HOOK *escorts to the house on his arm with hateful politeness.   He signs to his dogs to be gone, and they depart through the wood, carrying the little house with its strange merchandise and singing their ribald song.   The chimney of the little house emits a jet of smoke fitfully, as if not sure what it ought to do just now.*

HOOK *and* PETER *are now, as it were, alone on the island.   Below,* PETER *is on the bed, asleep, no weapon near him ; above,* HOOK, *armed to the teeth, is searching noiselessly for some tree down which the nastiness of him can descend.   Don't be too much alarmed by this ; it is precisely the situation* PETER *would have chosen ; indeed if the whole thing were pretend——.   One of his arms droops over the edge of the bed, a leg is arched, and the mouth is not so tightly closed that we cannot see the little pearls.   He is dreaming, and in his dreams he is always in pursuit of a boy who was never here, nor anywhere : the only boy who could beat him.*

HOOK *finds the tree.   It is the one set apart for* SLIGHTLY *who being addicted when hot to the drinking of water has swelled in consequence and surreptitiously scooped his tree*

*for easier descent and egress.   Down this the pirate wriggles
a passage.   In the aperture below his face emerges and goes
green as he glares at the sleeping child.   Does no feeling of
compassion disturb his sombre breast ?   The man is not
wholly evil : he has a* Thesaurus *in his cabin, and is no
mean performer on the flute.   What really warps him is a
presentiment that he is about to fail.   This is not unconnected
with a beatific smile on the face of the sleeper, whom he
cannot reach owing to being stuck at the foot of the tree.   He,
however, sees the medicine shell within easy reach, and to*
WENDY'S *draught he adds from a bottle five drops of poison
distilled when he was weeping from the red in his eye.   The
expression on* PETER'S *face merely implies that something
heavenly is going on.*   HOOK *worms his way upwards, and
winding his cloak around him, as if to conceal his person from
the night of which he is the blackest part, he stalks moodily
toward the lagoon.*

*A dot of light flashes past him and darts down the nearest
tree, looking for* PETER, *only for* PETER, *quite indifferent
about the others when she finds him safe.)*

PETER *(stirring).*   Who is that ?   (TINK *has to tell her tale,
in one long ungrammatical sentence.)*   The redskins were de-
feated ?   Wendy and the boys captured by the pirates !   I 'll
rescue her, I 'll rescue her !   *(He leaps first at his dagger, and
then at his grindstone, to sharpen it.*   TINK *alights near the shell,
and rings out a warning cry.)*   Oh, that is just my medicine.
Poisoned ?   Who could have poisoned it ?   I promised Wendy
to take it, and I will as soon as I have sharpened my dagger.
(TINK, *who sees its red colour and remembers the red in the pirate's
eye, nobly swallows the draught as* PETER'S *hand is reaching for it.)*
Why, Tink, you have drunk my medicine !   *(She flutters
strangely about the room, answering him now in a very thin tinkle.)*
It was poisoned and you drank it to save my life !   Tink, dear
Tink, are you dying ?   *(He has never called her dear Tink
before, and for a moment she is gay ; she alights on his shoulder,
gives his chin a loving bite, whispers ' You silly ass,' and falls on
her tiny bed.   The boudoir, which is lit by her, flickers ominously.
He is on his knees by the opening.)*

Her light is growing faint, and if it goes out, that means she is
dead !   Her voice is so low I can scarcely tell what she is saying.

She says—she says she thinks she could get well again if children believed in fairies ! (*He rises and throws out his arms he knows not to whom, perhaps to the boys and girls of whom he is not one.*) Do you believe in fairies ? Say quick that you believe ! If you believe, clap your hands ! (*Many clap, some don't, a few hiss. Then perhaps there is a rush of Nanas to the nurseries to see what on earth is happening. But* tink *is saved.*) Oh, thank you, thank you, thank you ! And now to rescue Wendy !

(tink *is already as merry and impudent as a grig, with not a thought for those who have saved her.* peter *ascends his tree as if he were shot up it. What he is feeling is ' Hook or me this time ! ' He is frightfully happy. He soon hits the trail, for the smoke from the little house has lingered here and there to guide him. He takes wing.*)

ACT V

SCENE I

THE PIRATE SHIP

THE stage directions for the opening of this scene are as follows :
—1 Circuit Amber checked to 80. Battens, all Amber
checked, 3 ship's lanterns alight, Arcs : prompt perch 1. Open
dark Amber flooding back, O.P. perch open dark Amber flooding
upper deck. Arc on tall steps at back of cabin to flood back
cloth. Open dark Amber. Warning for slide. Plank ready.
Call Hook.

In the strange light thus described we see what is happening
on the deck of the *Jolly Roger*, which is flying the skull and
crossbones and lies low in the water. There is no need to call
Hook, for he is here already, and indeed there is not a pirate
aboard who would dare to call him. Most of them are at
present carousing in the bowels of the vessel, but on the poop
Mullins is visible, in the only great-coat on the ship, raking with
his glass the monstrous rocks within which the lagoon is cooped.
Such a look-out is supererogatory, for the pirate craft floats
immune in the horror of her name.

From Hook's cabin at the back Starkey appears and leans
over the bulwark, silently surveying the sullen waters. He is
bare-headed and is perhaps thinking with bitterness of his hat,
which he sometimes sees still drifting past him with the Never
bird sitting on it. The black pirate is asleep on deck, yet even
in his dreams rolling mechanically out of the way when Hook
draws near. The only sound to be heard is made by Smee at his
sewing-machine, which lends a touch of domesticity to the night.

Hook is now leaning against the mast, now prowling the
deck, the double cigar in his mouth. With Peter surely at last
removed from his path we, who know how vain a tabernacle is
man, would not be surprised to find him bellied out by the winds

of his success, but it is not so ; he is still uneasy, looking long and
meaninglessly at familiar objects, such as the ship's bell or the
Long Tom, like one who may shortly be a stranger to them.
It is as if Pan's terrible oath ' Hook or me this time ! ' had
already boarded the ship.

HOOK (*communing with his ego*).   How still the night is ;
nothing sounds alive.   Now is the hour when children in their
homes are a-bed ; their lips bright-browned with the good-
night chocolate, and their tongues drowsily searching for belated
crumbs housed insecurely on their shining cheeks.   Compare
with them the children on this boat about to walk the plank.
Split my infinitives, but 'tis my hour of triumph !   (*Clinging to
this fair prospect he dances a few jubilant steps, but they fall below
his usual form.*)   And yet some disky spirit compels me now to
make my dying speech, lest when dying there may be no time
for it.   All mortals envy me, yet better perhaps for Hook to have
had less ambition !   O fame, fame, thou glittering bauble, what
if the very——   (SMEE, *engrossed in his labours at the sewing-
machine, tears a piece of calico with a rending sound which makes
the Solitary think for a moment that the untoward has happened to
his garments.*)   No little children love me.   I am told they
play at Peter Pan, and that the strongest always chooses to be
Peter.   They would rather be a Twin than Hook ; they force
the baby to be Hook.   The baby ! that is where the canker
gnaws.   (*He contemplates his industrious boatswain.*)   'Tis said
they find Smee lovable.   But an hour agone I found him letting
the youngest of them try on his spectacles.   Pathetic Smee, the
Nonconformist pirate, a happy smile upon his face because he
thinks they fear him !   How can I break it to him that they
think him lovable ?   No, bi-carbonate of Soda, no, not even——
(*Another rending of the calico disturbs him, and he has a private
consultation with* STARKEY, *who turns him round and evidently
assures him that all is well.   The peroration of his speech is nevertheless for ever lost, as eight bells strikes and his crew pour forth
in bacchanalian orgy.   From the poop he watches their dance till
it frets him beyond bearing.*)   Quiet, you dogs, or I 'll cast
anchor in you !   (*He descends to a barrel on which there are
playing-cards, and his crew stand waiting, as ever, like whipped
curs.*)   Are all the prisoners chained, so that they can't fly away ?

JUKES.　Ay, ay, Captain.

HOOK.　Then hoist them up.

STARKEY (*raising the door of the hold*).　Tumble up, you ungentlemanly lubbers.

(*The terrified boys are prodded up and tossed about the deck. HOOK seems to have forgotten them; he is sitting by the barrel with his cards.*)

HOOK (*suddenly*).　So ! Now then, you bullies, six of you walk the plank to-night, but I have room for two cabin-boys. Which of you is it to be ? (*He returns to his cards.*)

TOOTLES (*hoping to soothe him by putting the blame on the only person, vaguely remembered, who is always willing to act as a buffer*).　You see, sir, I don't think my mother would like me to be a pirate. Would your mother like you to be a pirate, Slightly ?

SLIGHTLY (*implying that otherwise it would be a pleasure to him to oblige*).　I don't think so. Twin, would your mother like——

HOOK.　Stow this gab. (*To* JOHN) You boy, you look as if you had a little pluck in you. Didst never want to be a pirate, my hearty ?

JOHN (*dazzled by being singled out*).　When I was at school I——what do you think, Michael ?

MICHAEL (*stepping into prominence*).　What would you call me if I joined ?

HOOK.　Blackbeard Joe.

MICHAEL.　John, what do you think ?

JOHN.　Stop, should we still be respectful subjects of King George ?

HOOK.　You would have to swear 'Down with King George.'

JOHN (*grandly*).　Then I refuse !

MICHAEL.　And I refuse.

HOOK.　That seals your doom. Bring up their mother.

(WENDY *is driven up from the hold and thrown to him. She sees at the first glance that the deck has not been scrubbed for years.*)

So, my beauty, you are to see your children walk the plank.

WENDY (*with noble calmness*).　Are they to die ?

HOOK.　They are. Silence all, for a mother's last words to her children.

WENDY.   These are my last words.   Dear boys, I feel that I have a message to you from your real mothers, and it is this, ' We hope our sons will die like English gentlemen.'

(*The boys go on fire.*)

TOOTLES.   I am going to do what my mother hopes.   What are you to do, Twin ?

FIRST TWIN.   What my mother hopes.   John, what are——

HOOK.   Tie her up !   Get the plank ready.

(WENDY *is roped to the mast ; but no one regards her, for all eyes are fixed upon the plank now protruding from the poop over the ship's side.   A great change, however, occurs in the time* HOOK *takes to raise his claw and point to this deadly engine.   No one is now looking at the plank : for the tick, tick of the crocodile is heard.   Yet it is not to bear on the crocodile that all eyes slew round, it is that they may bear on* HOOK.   *Otherwise prisoners and captors are equally inert, like actors in some play who have found themselves ' on ' in a scene in which they are not personally concerned.   Even the iron claw hangs inactive, as if aware that the crocodile is not coming for it.   Affection for their captain, now cowering from view, is not what has given* HOOK *his dominance over the crew, but as the menacing sound draws nearer they close their eyes respectfully.*

There is no crocodile.   It is PETER, *who has been circling the pirate ship, ticking as he flies far more superbly than any clock.   He drops into the water and climbs aboard, warning the captives with upraised finger (but still ticking) not for the moment to give audible expression to their natural admiration.   Only one pirate sees him,* WHIBBLES *of the eye patch, who comes up from below.* JOHN *claps a hand on* WHIBBLES'S *mouth to stifle the groan ; four boys hold him to prevent the thud ;* PETER *delivers the blow, and the carrion is thrown overboard.   ' One ! ' says* SLIGHTLY, *beginning to count.*

STARKEY *is the first pirate to open his eyes.   The ship seems to him to be precisely as when he closed them.   He cannot interpret the sparkle that has come into the faces of the captives, who are cleverly pretending to be as afraid as ever. He little knows that the door of the dark cabin has just closed on one more boy.   Indeed it is for* HOOK *alone he looks, and he is a little surprised to see him.)*

STARKEY (*hoarsely*).   It is gone, Captain !   There is not a sound.

(*The tenement that is* HOOK *heaves tumultuously and he is himself again.*)

HOOK (*now convinced that some fair spirit watches over him*). Then here is to Johnny Plank——

> Avast, belay, the English brig
> We took and quickly sank,
> And for a warning to the crew
> We made them walk the plank !

(*As he sings he capers detestably along an imaginary plank and his copy-cats do likewise, joining in the chorus.*)

> Yo ho, yo ho, the frisky cat,
> You walks along it so,
> Till it goes down and you goes down
> To tooral looral lo !

(*The brave children try to stem this monstrous torrent by breaking into the National Anthem.*)

STARKEY (*paling*).   I don't like it, messmates !

HOOK.   Stow that, Starkey.   Do you boys want a touch of the cat before you walk the plank ?   (*He is more pitiless than ever now that he believes he has a charmed life.*)   Fetch the cat, Jukes ; it is in the cabin.

JUKES.   Ay, ay, sir.   (*It is one of his commonest remarks, and it is only recorded now because he never makes another.   The stage direction ' Exit* JUKES ' *has in this case a special significance. But only the children know that some one is awaiting this unfortunate in the cabin, and* HOOK *tramples them down as he resumes his ditty :*)

> Yo ho, yo ho, the scratching cat
> Its tails are nine you know,
> And when they 're writ upon your back,
> You 're fit to——

(*The last words will ever remain a matter of conjecture, for from the dark cabin comes a curdling screech which wails through the ship and dies away.   It is followed by a sound, almost more eerie in the circumstances, that can only be likened to the crowing of a cock.*)

HOOK.   What was that ?

SLIGHTLY (*solemnly*).   Two !

(CECCO *swings into the cabin, and in a moment returns, livid.*)

HOOK (*with an effort*).   What is the matter with Bill Jukes, you dog ?

CECCO.   The matter with him is he is dead—stabbed.

PIRATES.   Bill Jukes dead !

CECCO.   The cabin is as black as a pit, but there is something terrible in there : the thing you heard a-crowing.

HOOK (*slowly*).   Cecco, go back and fetch me out that doodle-doo.

CECCO (*unstrung*).   No, Captain, no.   (*He supplicates on his knees, but his master advances on him implacably.*)

HOOK (*in his most syrupy voice*).   Did you say you would go, Cecco ?

(CECCO *goes.   All listen.   There is one screech, one crow.*)

SLIGHTLY (*as if he were a bell tolling*).   Three !

HOOK.   'Sdeath and oddsfish, who is to bring me out that doodle-doo ?

(*No one steps forward.*)

STARKEY (*injudiciously*).   Wait till Cecco comes out.

(*The black looks of some others encourage him.*)

HOOK.   I think I heard you volunteer, Starkey.

STARKEY (*emphatically*).   No, by thunder !

HOOK (*in that syrupy voice which might be more engaging when accompanied by his flute*).   My hook thinks you did.   I wonder if it would not be advisable, Starkey, to humour the hook ?

STARKEY.   I 'll swing before I go in there.

HOOK (*gleaming*).   Is it mutiny ?   Starkey is ringleader. Shake hands, Starkey.

(STARKEY *recoils from the claw.   It follows him till he leaps overboard.*)

Did any other gentleman say mutiny ?

(*They indicate that they did not even know the late* STARKEY.)

SLIGHTLY.   Four !

HOOK.   I will bring out that doodle-doo myself.

(*He raises a blunderbuss but casts it from him with a menacing gesture which means that he has more faith in the claw. With a lighted lantern in his hand he enters the cabin.   Not a sound is to be heard now on the ship, unless it be* SLIGHTLY *wetting his lips to say ' Five.'* HOOK *staggers out.*)

HOOK (*unsteadily*).   Something blew out the light.

MULLINS (*with dark meaning*).   Some—thing ?

NOODLER.   What of Cecco ?

HOOK.   He is as dead as Jukes.

(*They are superstitious like all sailors, and* MULLINS *has planted a dire conception in their minds.*)

COOKSON.   They do say as the surest sign a ship 's accurst is when there is one aboard more than can be accounted for.

NOODLER.   I 've heard he allus boards the pirate craft at last. (*With dreadful significance*) Has he a tail, Captain ?

MULLINS.   They say that when he comes it is in the likeness of the wickedest man aboard.

COOKSON (*clinching it*).   Has he a hook, Captain ?

(*Knives and pistols come to hand, and there is a general cry ' The ship is doomed!' But it is not his dogs that can frighten* JAS HOOK. *Hearing something like a cheer from the boys he wheels round, and his face brings them to their knees.*)

HOOK.   So you like it, do you ! By Caius and Balbus, bullies, here is a notion : open the cabin door and drive them in. Let them fight the doodle-doo for their lives. If they kill him we are so much the better ; if he kills them we are none the worse.

(*This masterly stroke restores their confidence ; and the boys, affecting fear, are driven into the cabin. Desperadoes though the pirates are, some of them have been boys themselves, and all turn their backs to the cabin and listen, with arms outstretched to it as if to ward off the horrors that are being enacted there.*

Relieved by Peter of their manacles, and armed with such weapons as they can lay their hands on, the boys steal out softly as snowflakes, and under their captain's hushed order find hiding-places on the poop. He releases WENDY ; *and now it would be easy for them all to fly away, but it is to be* HOOK *or him this time. He signs to her to join the others, and with awful grimness folding her cloak around him, the hood over his head, he takes her place by the mast, and crows.*)

MULLINS.   The doodle-doo has killed them all !

SEVERAL. The ship 's bewitched.

(*They are snapping at* HOOK *again.*)

HOOK. I 've thought it out, lads ; there is a Jonah aboard.

SEVERAL (*advancing upon him*). Ay, a man with a hook.

(*If he were to withdraw one step their knives would be in him, but he does not flinch.*)

HOOK (*temporising*). No, lads, no, it is the girl. Never was luck on a pirate ship wi' a woman aboard. We 'll right the ship when she has gone.

MULLINS (*lowering his cutlass*). It 's worth trying.

HOOK. Throw the girl overboard.

MULLINS (*jeering*). There is none can save you now, missy

PETER. There is one.

MULLINS. Who is that ?

PETER (*casting off the cloak*). Peter Pan, the avenger !

(*He continues standing there to let the effect sink in.*)

HOOK (*throwing out a suggestion*). Cleave him to the brisket.

(*But he has a sinking that this boy has no brisket.*)

NOODLER. The ship 's accurst !

PETER. Down, boys, and at them !

(*The boys leap from their concealment and the clash of arms resounds through the vessel. Man to man the pirates are the stronger, but they are unnerved by the suddenness of the onslaught and they scatter, thus enabling their opponents to hunt in couples and choose their quarry. Some are hurled into the lagoon ; others are dragged from dark recesses. There is no boy whose weapon is not reeking save* SLIGHTLY, *who runs about with a lantern, counting, ever counting.*)

WENDY (*meeting* MICHAEL *in a moment's lull*). Oh, Michael, stay with me, protect me !

MICHAEL (*reeling*). Wendy, I 've killed a pirate !

WENDY. It 's awful, awful.

MICHAEL. No, it isn't, I like it, I like it.

(*He casts himself into the group of boys who are encircling* HOOK. *Again and again they close upon him and again and again he hews a clear space.*)

HOOK. Back, back, you mice. It 's Hook ; do you like him ? (*He lifts up* MICHAEL *with his claw and uses him as a buckler. A terrible voice breaks in.*)

PETER. Put up your swords, boys. This man is mine.

(HOOK *shakes* MICHAEL *off his claw as if he were a drop of water, and these two antagonists face each other for their final bout.   They measure swords at arms' length, make a sweeping motion with them, and bringing the points to the deck rest their hands upon the hilts.*)

HOOK (*with curling lip*).   So, Pan, this is all your doing !

PETER.   Ay, Jas Hook, it is all my doing.

HOOK.   Proud and insolent youth, prepare to meet thy doom.

PETER.   Dark and sinister man, have at thee.

(*Some say that he had to ask* TOOTLES *whether the word was sinister or canister.*

HOOK *or* PETER *this time !   They fall to without another word.*   PETER *is a rare swordsman, and parries with dazzling rapidity, sometimes before the other can make his stroke.*   HOOK, *if not quite so nimble in wrist play, has the advantage of a yard or two in reach, but though they close he cannot give the quietus with his claw, which seems to find nothing to tear at.   He does not, especially in the most heated moments, quite see* PETER, *who to his eyes, now blurred or opened clearly for the first time, is less like a boy than a mote of dust dancing in the sun.   By some impalpable stroke* HOOK'S *sword is whipped from his grasp, and when he stoops to raise it a little foot is on its blade.   There is no deep gash on* HOOK, *but he is suffering torment as from innumerable jags.*)

BOYS (*exulting*).   Now, Peter, now !

(PETER *raises the sword by its blade, and with an inclination of the head that is perhaps slightly overdone, presents the hilt to his enemy.*)

HOOK.   'Tis some fiend fighting me !   Pan, who and what art thou ?

(*The children listen eagerly for the answer, none quite so eagerly as* WENDY.)

PETER (*at a venture*).   I 'm youth, I 'm joy, I 'm a little bird that has broken out of the egg.

HOOK.   To 't again !

(*He has now a damp feeling that this boy is the weapon which is to strike him from the lists of man ; but the grandeur of his mind still holds and, true to the traditions of his flag, he fights on like a human flail.*   PETER *flutters round and*

*through and over these gyrations as if the wind of them blew
him out of the danger zone, and again and again he darts
in and jags.*)

HOOK (*stung to madness*). I 'll fire the powder magazine.
(*He disappears they know not where.*)

CHILDREN. Peter, save us !

(PETER, *alas, goes the wrong way and* HOOK *returns.*)

HOOK (*sitting on the hold with gloomy satisfaction*). In two
minutes the ship will be blown to pieces.

(*They cast themselves before him in entreaty.*)

CHILDREN. Mercy, mercy !

HOOK. Back, you pewling spawn. I 'll show you now the
road to dusty death. A holocaust of children, there is something grand in the idea !

(PETER *appears with a smoking bomb in his hand and tosses
it overboard.* HOOK *has not really had much hope, and he
rushes at his other persecutors with his head down like some
exasperated bull in the ring ; but with bantering cries they
easily elude him by flying among the rigging.*

Where is PETER ? *The incredible boy has apparently
forgotten the recent doings, and is sitting on a barrel playing
upon his pipes. This may surprise others but does not surprise* HOOK. *Lifting a blunderbuss he strikes forlornly not
at the boy but at the barrel, which is hurled across the deck.*
PETER *remains sitting in the air still playing upon his pipes.
At this sight the great heart of* HOOK *breaks. That not
wholly unheroic figure climbs the bulwarks murmuring
' Floreat Etona,' and prostrates himself into the water,
where the crocodile is waiting for him open-mouthed.* HOOK
*knows the purpose of this yawning cavity, but after what he
has gone through he enters it like one greeting a friend.*

The curtain rises to show PETER *a very Napoleon on his
ship. It must not rise again lest we see him on the poop in*
HOOK'S *hat and cigars, and with a small iron claw.*)

SCENE 2

THE NURSERY AND THE TREE-TOPS

THE old nursery appears again with everything just as it was at the beginning of the play, except that the kennel has gone and that the window is standing open. So Peter was wrong about mothers ; indeed there is no subject on which he is so likely to be wrong.

Mrs. Darling is asleep on a chair near the window, her eyes tired with searching the heavens. Nana is stretched out listless on the floor. She is the cynical one, and though custom has made her hang the children's night things on the fire-guard for an airing, she surveys them not hopefully but with some self-contempt.

MRS. DARLING (*starting up as if we had whispered to her that her brats are coming back*). Wendy, John, Michael ! (NANA *lifts a sympathetic paw to the poor soul's lap.*) I see you have put their night things out again, Nana ! It touches my heart to watch you do that night after night. But they will never come back.

(*In trouble the difference of station can be completely ignored, and it is not strange to see these two using the same handkerchief. Enter* LIZA, *who in the gentleness with which the house has been run of late is perhaps a little more masterful than of yore.*)

LIZA (*feeling herself degraded by the announcement*). Nana's dinner is served.

(NANA, *who quite understands what are* LIZA'S *feelings, departs for the dining-room with our exasperating leisureliness, instead of running, as we would all do if we followed our instincts.*)

LIZA. To think I have a master as have changed places with his dog !

MRS. DARLING (*gently*). Out of remorse, Liza.

LIZA (*surely exaggerating*). I am a married woman myself. I don't think it 's respectable to go to his office in a kennel, with the street boys running alongside cheering. (*Even this does not*

rouse her mistress, which may have been the honourable intention.)
There, that is the cab fetching him back ! (*Amid interested cheers from the street the kennel is conveyed to its old place by a cabby and friend, and* MR. DARLING *scrambles out of it in his office clothes.*)

MR. DARLING (*giving her his hat loftily*).   If you will be so good, Liza.   (*The cheering is resumed.*)   It is very gratifying !

LIZA (*contemptuous*).   Lot of little boys.

MR. DARLING (*with the new sweetness of one who has sworn never to lose his temper again*).   There were several adults to-day.
(*She goes off scornfully with the hat and the two men, but he has not a word of reproach for her.   It ought to melt us when we see how humbly grateful he is for a kiss from his wife, so much more than he feels he deserves.   One may think he is wrong to exchange into the kennel, but sorrow has taught him that he is the kind of man who whatever he does contritely he must do to excess ; otherwise he soon abandons doing it.*)

MRS. DARLING (*who has known this for quite a long time*).
What sort of a day have you had, George ?
(*He is sitting on the floor by the kennel.*)

MR. DARLING.   There were never less than a hundred running round the cab cheering, and when we passed the Stock Exchange the members came out and waved.
(*He is exultant but uncertain of himself, and with a word she could dispirit him utterly.*)

MRS. DARLING (*bravely*).   I am so proud, George.

MR. DARLING (*commendation from the dearest quarter ever going to his head*).   I have been put on a picture postcard, dear.

MRS. DARLING (*nobly*).   Never !

MR. DARLING (*thoughtlessly*).   Ah, Mary, we should not be such celebrities if the children hadn't flown away.

MRS. DARLING (*startled*).   George, you are sure you are not enjoying it ?

MR. DARLING (*anxiously*).   Enjoying it !   See my punishment : living in a kennel.

MRS. DARLING.   Forgive me, dear one.

MR. DARLING.   It is I who need forgiveness, always I, never you.   And now I feel drowsy.   (*He retires into the kennel.*)
Won't you play me to sleep on the nursery piano ?   And shut that window, Mary dearest ; I feel a draught.

MRS. DARLING. Oh, George, never ask me to do that. The window must always be left open for them, always, always.

(*She goes into the day nursery, from which we presently hear her playing the sad song of Margaret. She little knows that her last remark has been overheard by a boy crouching at the window. He steals into the room accompanied by a ball of light.*)

PETER. Tink, where are you ? Quick, close the window. (*It closes.*) Bar it. (*The bar slams down.*) Now when Wendy comes she will think her mother has barred her out, and she will have to come back to me ! (TINKER BELL *sulks.*) Now, Tink, you and I must go out by the door. (*Doors, however, are confusing things to those who are used to windows, and he is puzzled when he finds that this one does not open on to the firmament. He tries the other, and sees the piano player.*) It is Wendy's mother ! (TINK *pops on to his shoulder and they peep together.*) She is a pretty lady, but not so pretty as my mother. (*This is a pure guess.*) She is making the box say ' Come home, Wendy.' You will never see Wendy again, lady, for the window is barred ! (*He flutters about the room joyously like a bird, but has to return to that door.*) She has laid her head down on the box. There are two wet things sitting on her eyes. As soon as they go away another two come and sit on her eyes. (*She is heard moaning ' Wendy, Wendy, Wendy.'*) She wants me to unbar the window. I won't ! She is awfully fond of Wendy. I am fond of her too. We can't both have her, lady ! (*A funny feeling comes over him.*) Come on, Tink ; we don't want any silly mothers. (*He opens the window and they fly out.*

It is thus that the truants find entrance easy when they alight on the sill, JOHN *to his credit having the tired* MICHAEL *on his shoulders. They have nothing else to their credit ; no compunction for what they have done, not the tiniest fear that any just person may be awaiting them with a stick. The youngest is in a daze, but the two others are shining virtuously like holy people who are about to give two other people a treat.*)

MICHAEL (*looking about him*). I think I have been here before.

JOHN. It 's your home, you stupid.

WENDY. There is your old bed, Michael.

MICHAEL.   I had nearly forgotten.

JOHN.   I say, the kennel !

WENDY.   Perhaps Nana is in it.

JOHN (*peering*).   There is a man asleep in it.

WENDY (*remembering him by the bald patch*).   It 's father !

JOHN.   So it is !

MICHAEL.   Let me see father.   (*Disappointed*) He is not as big as the pirate I killed.

JOHN (*perplexed*).   Wendy, surely father didn't use to sleep in the kennel ?

WENDY (*with misgivings*).   Perhaps we don't remember the old life as well as we thought we did.

JOHN (*chilled*).   It is very careless of mother not to be here when we come back.

(*The piano is heard again.*)

WENDY.   H'sh !   (*She goes to the door and peeps.*)   That is her playing !   (*They all have a peep.*)

MICHAEL.   Who is that lady ?

JOHN.   H'sh !   It 's mother.

MICHAEL.   Then are you not really our mother, Wendy ?

WENDY (*with conviction*).   Oh dear, it is quite time to be back !

JOHN.   Let us creep in and put our hands over her eyes.

WENDY (*more considerate*).   No, let us break it to her gently.

(*She slips between the sheets of her bed; and the others, seeing the idea at once, get into their beds.   Then when the music stops they cover their heads.   There are now three distinct bumps in the beds.   MRS. DARLING sees the bumps as soon as she comes in, but she does not believe she sees them.*)

MRS. DARLING.   I see them in their beds so often in my dreams that I seem still to see them when I am awake !   I 'll not look again.   (*She sits down and turns away her face from the bumps, though of course they are still reflected in her mind.*)   So often their silver voices call me, my little children whom I 'll see no more.

(*Silver voices is a good one, especially about* JOHN ; *but the heads pop up.*)

WENDY (*perhaps rather silvery*).   Mother !

MRS. DARLING (*without moving*).   That is Wendy.

JOHN (*quite gruff*).   Mother !

MRS. DARLING.   Now it is John.

MICHAEL (*no better than a squeak*).   Mother !

MRS. DARLING.   Now Michael.   And when they call I stretch out my arms to them, but they never come, they never come !

(*This time, however, they come, and there is joy once more in the Darling household. The little boy who is crouching at the window sees the joke of the bumps in the beds, but cannot understand what all the rest of the fuss is about.*

The scene changes from the inside of the house to the outside, and we see MR. DARLING *romping in at the door, with the lost boys hanging gaily to his coat-tails. So we may conclude that* WENDY *has told them to wait outside until she explains the situation to her mother, who has then sent* MR. DARLING *down to tell them that they are adopted. Of course they could have flown in by the window like a covey of birds, but they think it better fun to enter by a door. There is a moment's trouble about* SLIGHTLY, *who somehow gets shut out. Fortunately* LIZA *finds him.*)

LIZA.   What is the matter, boy ?

SLIGHTLY.   They have all got a mother except me.

LIZA (*starting back*).   Is your name Slightly ?

SLIGHTLY.   Yes'm.

LIZA.   Then I am your mother.

SLIGHTLY.   How do you know ?

LIZA (*the good-natured creature*).   I feel it in my bones.

(*They go into the house and there is none happier now than* SLIGHTLY, *unless it be* NANA *as she passes with the importance of a nurse who will never have another day off.* WENDY *looks out at the nursery window and sees a friend below, who is hovering in the air knocking off tall hats with his feet. The wearers don't see him. They are too old. You can't see* PETER *if you are old. They think he is a draught at the corner.*)

WENDY.   Peter !

PETER (*looking up casually*).   Hullo, Wendy.

(*She flies down to him, to the horror of her mother, who rushes to the window.*)

WENDY (*making a last attempt*).   You don't feel you would

like to say anything to my parents, Peter, about a very sweet subject ?

PETER.   No, Wendy.

WENDY.   About me, Peter ?

PETER.   No. (*He gets out his pipes, which she knows is a very bad sign.   She appeals with her arms to* MRS. DARLING, *who is probably thinking that these children will all need to be tied to their beds at night.*)

MRS. DARLING (*from the window*).   Peter, where are you ? Let me adopt you too.

(*She is the loveliest age for a woman, but too old to see* PETER *clearly.*)

PETER.   Would you send me to school ?

MRS. DARLING (*obligingly*).   Yes.

PETER.   And then to an office ?

MRS. DARLING.   I suppose so.

PETER.   Soon I should be a man ?

MRS. DARLING.   Very soon.

PETER (*passionately*).   I don't want to go to school and learn solemn things.   No one is going to catch me, lady, and make me a man.   I want always to be a little boy and to have fun.

(*So perhaps he thinks, but it is only his greatest pretend.*)

MRS. DARLING (*shivering every time* WENDY *pursues him in the air*).   Where are you to live, Peter ?

PETER.   In the house we built for Wendy.   The fairies are to put it high up among the tree-tops where they sleep at night.

WENDY (*rapturously*).   To think of it !

MRS. DARLING.   I thought all the fairies were dead.

WENDY (*almost reprovingly*).   No indeed !   Their mothers drop the babies into the Never birds' nests, all mixed up with the eggs, and the mauve fairies are boys and the white ones are girls, and there are some colours who don't know what they are. The row the children and the birds make at bath time is positively deafening.

PETER.   I throw things at them.

WENDY.   You will be rather lonely in the evenings, Peter.

PETER.   I shall have Tink.

WENDY (*flying up to the window*).   Mother, may I go ?

MRS. DARLING (*gripping her for ever*).   Certainly not.   I have got you home again, and I mean to keep you.

WENDY.   But he does so need a mother.

MRS. DARLING.   So do you, my love.

PETER.   Oh, all right.

MRS. DARLING (*magnanimously*).   But, Peter, I shall let her go to you once a year for a week to do your spring cleaning.

(WENDY *revels in this, but* PETER, *who has no notion what a spring cleaning is, waves a rather careless thanks.*)

MRS. DARLING.   Say good-night, Wendy.

WENDY.   I couldn't go down just for a minute ?

MRS. DARLING.   No.

WENDY.   Good-night, Peter !

PETER.   Good-night, Wendy !

WENDY.   Peter, you won't forget me, will you, before spring-cleaning time comes ?

(*There is no answer, for he is already soaring high. For a moment after he is gone we still hear the pipes.* MRS. DARLING *closes and bars the window.*)

We are dreaming now of the Never Land a year later. It is bed-time on the island, and the blind goes up to the whispers of the lovely Never music. The blue haze that makes the wood below magical by day comes up to the tree-tops to sleep, and through it we see numberless nests all lit up, fairies and birds quarrelling for possession, others flying around just for the fun of the thing and perhaps making bets about where the little house will appear to-night. It always comes and snuggles on some tree-top, but you can never be sure which ; here it is again, you see John's hat first as up comes the house so softly that it knocks some gossips off their perch. When it has settled comfortably it lights up, and out come Peter and Wendy.

Wendy looks a little older, but Peter is just the same. She is cloaked for a journey, and a sad confession must be made about her ; she flies so badly now that she has to use a broomstick.

WENDY (*who knows better this time than to be demonstrative at partings*).   Well, good-bye, Peter ; and remember not to bite your nails.

PETER.   Good-bye, Wendy.

WENDY   I 'll tell mother all about the spring cleaning and the house.

PETER (*who sometimes forgets that she has been here before*). You do like the house ?

WENDY.   Of course it is small.   But most people of our size wouldn't have a house at all.   (*She should not have mentioned size, for he has already expressed displeasure at her growth. Another thing, one he has scarcely noticed, though it disturbs her, is that she does not see him quite so clearly now as she used to do.*) When you come for me next year, Peter—you will come, won't you ?

PETER.   Yes.   (*Gloating*) To hear stories about me !

WENDY.   It is so queer that the stories you like best should be the ones about yourself.

PETER (*touchy*).   Well, then ?

WENDY.   Fancy your forgetting the lost boys, and even Captain Hook !

PETER.   Well, then ?

WENDY.   I haven't seen Tink this time.

PETER.   Who ?

WENDY.   Oh dear !   I suppose it is because you have so many adventures.

PETER (*relieved*).   'Course it is.

WENDY.   If another little girl — if one younger than I am—— (*She can't go on.*)   Oh, Peter, how I wish I could take you up and squdge you !   (*He draws back.*)   Yes, I know. (*She gets astride her broomstick.*)   Home !   (*It carries her from him over the tree-tops.*

In a sort of way he understands what she means by ' Yes, I know,' but in most sorts of ways he doesn't.   It has something to do with the riddle of his being.   If he could get the hang of the thing his cry might become ' To live would be an awfully big adventure ! ' but he can never quite get the hang of it, and so no one is as gay as he.   With rapturous face he produces his pipes, and the Never birds and the fairies gather closer, till the roof of the little house is so thick with his admirers that some of them fall down the chimney. He plays on and on till we wake up.)

PANTALOON
A PLEA FOR AN ANCIENT FAMILY

Produced at the Duke of York's Theatre on April 5, 1905, with the following cast:

CLOWN	A. W. Baskcomb
PANTALOON	Gerald du Maurier
HARLEQUIN	Willie Warde
THE CHILD	Ela Q. May
COLUMBINE	Pauline Chase

PANTALOON

THE scene makes believe to be the private home of Pantaloon and Columbine, though whether they ever did have a private home is uncertain.

In the English version (and with that alone are we concerning ourselves) these two were figures in the harlequinade, which in Victorian days gave a finish to pantomime as vital as a tail to a dog. Now they are vanished from the boards ; or at best they wander through the canvas streets, in everybody's way, at heart afraid of their own policeman, really dead, and waiting, like the faithful old horse, for some one to push them over. Here at the theatre is perhaps a scrap of Columbine's skirt, torn off as she squeezed through the wings for the last time, or even placed there intentionally by her as a souvenir : Columbine to her public, a kiss hanging on a nail.

They are very illusive. One has to toss to find out what was their relation to each other : whether Pantaloon, for instance, was Columbine's father. He was an old, old urchin of the streets over whom some fairy wand had been waved, rather carelessly, and this makes him a child of art ; now we must all be nice to children of art, and the nicest thing we can do for Pantaloon is to bring the penny down heads and give him a delightful daughter. So Columbine was Pantaloon's daughter.

It would be cruel to her to make her his wife, because then she could not have a love-affair.

The mother is dead, to give the little home a touch of pathos. We have now proved that Pantaloon and his daughter did have a home, and as soon as we know that, we know more. We know, for instance, that as half a crown seemed almost a competency to them, their home must have been in a poor locality and conveniently small. We know also that the sitting-room and kitchen combined must have been on the ground floor. We know it, because in the harlequinade they were always flying from the policeman or bashing his helmet, and Pantaloon would have taken ill with a chamber that was not easily commanded by the policeman on his beat.   Even Columbine, we may be sure, refined as she was and incapable of the pettiest larceny, liked the homely feeling of dodging the policeman's eye as she sat at meals.   Lastly, we know that directly opposite the little home was a sausage-shop, the pleasantest of all sights to Pantaloon, who, next to his daughter, loved a sausage.   It is being almost too intimate to tell that Columbine hated sausages ; she hated them as a literary hand's daughter might hate manuscripts.   But like a loving child she never told her hate, and spent great part of her time toasting sausages to a turn before the fire, and eating her own one bravely when she must, but concealing it in the oddest places when she could.

We should now be able to reconstitute Pantaloon's parlour. It is agreeably stuffy, with two windows and a recess between them, from which one may peep both ways for the policeman. The furniture is in horse-hair, no rents showing, because careful Columbine has covered them with antimacassars.   All the chairs (but not the sofa) are as sound of limb as they look except one, and Columbine, who is as light as an air balloon, can sit on this one even with her feet off the floor.   Though the time is summer there is a fire burning, so that Pantaloon need never eat his sausages raw, which he might do inadvertently if Columbine did not take them gently from his hand.   There is a cosy round table with a waxcloth cover adhering to it like a sticking-plaster, and this table is set for tea.   Histrionic dignity is given to the room by a large wicker trunk in which Pantaloon's treasures are packed when he travels by rail, and on it is a printed intimation that he is one of the brightest wits on earth.   Columbine could be crushed, concertina-like, into half of this trunk, and it may be that she sometimes travels thus to save her ticket.   Between the windows hangs a glass case, such as those at inns wherein Piscator preserves his stuffed pike, but this one contains a poker. It is interesting to note that Pantaloon is sufficiently catholic in his tastes to spare a favourable eye for other arts than his own. There are various paintings on the walls, all of himself, with the exception of a small one of his wife.   These represent him not in humorous act but for all time, as, for instance, leaning on a bracket and reading a book, with one finger laid lightly against his nose.

So far our work of reconstitution has been easy, but we now come to the teaser. In all these pictures save one (to be referred to in its proper place) Pantaloon is presented not on the stage but in private life, yet he is garbed and powdered as we know him in the harlequinade. If they are genuine portraits, there-fore, they tell us something profoundly odd about the home life of Pantaloon ; nothing less than this, that as he was on the stage, so he was off it, clothes, powder, and all ; he was not acting a part in the harlequinade, he was merely being himself. It was undoubtedly this strange discovery that set us writing a play about him.

Of course, bitter controversy may come of this, for not every one will agree that we are right. It is well known among the *cognoscenti* that actors in general are not the same off the stage as on ; that they dress for their parts, speak words written for them which they do not necessarily believe, and afterwards wash the whole thing off and then go to clubs and coolly cross their legs. I accept this to be so (though I think it a pity), but Pantaloon was never an actor in their sense ; he would have scorned to speak words written for him by any whippersnapper ; what he said and did before the footlights were the result of mature conviction and represented his philosophy of life. It is the more easy to believe this of him because we are so anxious to believe it of Columbine. Otherwise she could not wear her pretty skirts in our play, and that would be unbearable.

If this noble and simple consistency was the mark of Pantaloon and Columbine (as we have now proved up to the hilt), it must have distinguished no less the other members of the harlequinade. There were two others, the Harlequin and the Clown.

In far-back days, when the world was so young that pieces of the original egg-shell still adhered to it, one boy was so desperately poor that he alone of children could not don fancy dress on fair-days. Presently the other children were sorry for this drab one, so each of them clipped a little bit off his own clothing and gave it to him. These were sewn together and made into a costume for him, by the jolly little tailors who in our days have quite gone out, and that is why Harlequin has come down to us in patchwork. He was a lovely boy with no brains at all (not that this matters), while the Clown was all brain.

It has been our whim to make Pantaloon and Columbine our

chief figures, but we have had to go for them, as it were, to the kitchen ; the true head of the harlequinade was the Clown. You could not become a clown by taking thought, you had to be born one.   It was just a chance.   If the Clown had wished to walk over the others they would have spread themselves on the ground so that he should be able to do it without inconveniencing himself.   Any money they had they got from him, and it was usually pennies.   If they displeased him he caned them.   He had too much power and it brutalised him, as we shall see, but in fairness it should be told that he owed his supremacy entirely to his funniness.   The family worshipped funniness, and he was the funniest.

It is not necessary for our play to reconstitute the homes of Harlequin and Clown, but it could be done.   Harlequin, as a bachelor with no means but with a secret conviction that he was a gentleman, had a sitting-and-bed combined at the top of a house too near Jermyn Street for his purse.   He made up by not eating very much, which was good for his figure.   He always carried his wand, which had curious magical qualities—for instance, it could make him invisible ; but in the street he seldom asked this of it, having indeed a friendly desire to be looked at. He had delightful manners and an honest heart.   The Clown, who, of course, had appearances to keep up, knew the value of a good address, and undoubtedly lived in the Cromwell Road. He smoked cigars with bands round them, and his togs were cut in Savile Row.

Clown and Pantaloon were a garrulous pair, but Columbine and Harlequin never spoke.   I don't know whether they were what we call dumb.   Perhaps if they had tried to talk with their tongues they could have done so, but they never thought of it. They were such exquisite dancers that they did all their talking with their legs.   There is nothing that may be said which they could not express with this leg or that.   It is the loveliest of all languages, and as soft as the fall of snow.

When the curtain rises we see Columbine alone in the little house, very happy and gay, for she has no notion that her tragic hour is about to strike.   She is dressed precisely as we may have seen her on the stage.   It is the pink skirt, the white one being usually kept for Sunday, which is also washing-day ; and we almost wish this had been Sunday, just to show Columbine in white at the tub, washing the pink without letting a single soap-sud pop on to the white. She is toasting bread rhythmically by the fire, and hides the toasting-fork as the policeman passes suspiciously outside. Presently she is in a whirl of emotion because she has heard Harlequin's knock. She rushes to the window and hides (they were always hiding), she blows kisses, and in her excitement she is everywhere and nowhere at once, like a kitten that leaps at nothing and stops half-way. She has the short quick steps of a bird on a lawn. Long before we have time to describe her movements she has bobbed out of sight beneath the table to await Harlequin funnily, for we must never forget that they are a funny family. With a whirl of his wand that is itself a dance, Harlequin makes the door fly open. He enters, says the stage direction, but what it means is that somehow he is now in the room. He probably knows that Columbine is beneath the table, as she hides so often and there are so few places in the room to hide in, but he searches for her elsewhere, even in a jug, to her extreme mirth, for of course she is peeping at him. He taps the wicker basket with his wand and the lid flies open. Still no Columbine! He sits dejectedly on a chair by the table, with one foot toward the spot where we last saw her head. This is irresistible. She kisses the foot. She is out from beneath the table now, and he is pursuing her round the room. They are as wayward as leaves in a gale. The cunning fellow pretends he does not want her, and now it is she who is pursuing him. There is something entrancing in his hand. It is a ring. It is the engagement-ring at last! She falters, she blushes, but she snatches at the ring. He tantalises her, holding it beyond her reach, but soon she has pulled down his hand and the ring is on her finger. They are dancing ecstatically when Pantaloon comes in and has to drop his stick because she leaps into his arms. If she were not so flurried she would see that the aged man has brought excitement with him also.

PANTALOON. Ah, Fairy! Fond of her dad, is she? Sweetest little daughter ever an old 'un had. (*He sees* HARLE-QUIN *and is genial to him, while* HARLEQUIN *pirouettes a How-d' ye-do.*) You here, Boy; welcome, Boy. (*He is about to remove his hat in the ordinary way, but* HARLEQUIN, *to save his prospective father-in-law any little trouble, waves his wand and the hat goes to rest on a door-peg. The little service so humbly tendered pleases* PANTALOON, *and he surveys* HARLEQUIN *with kindly condescension.*) Thank you, Boy. You are a good fellow, Boy, and an artist too, in your limited way, not here (*tapping his head*), not in a brainy way, but lower down (*thoughtfully, and including* COLUMBINE *in his downward survey*). That's where your personality lies—lower down. (*At the noble word personality* COLUMBINE *thankfully crosses herself, and then indicates that tea is ready.*) Tea, Fairy? I have such glorious news; but I will have a dish of tea first. You will join us, Boy? Sit down. (*They sit down to tea, the lovers exchanging shy, happy glances, but soon* PANTALOON *rises petulantly.*) Fairy, there are no sausages! Tea without a sausage. I am bitterly disappointed. And on a day, too, when I have great news. It's almost more than I can bear. No sausages! (*He is old and is near weeping, but* COLUMBINE *indicates with her personality that if he does not forgive her she must droop and die, and soon again he is a magnanimous father.*) Yes, yes, my pet, I forgive you. You can't abide sausages; nor can you, Boy. (*They hide their shamed heads.*) It's not your fault. Some are born with the instinct for a sausage. and some have it not. (*More brightly*) Would you like me to be funny now, my dear, or shall we have tea first? (*They prefer to have tea first, and the courteous old man sits down with them.*) But you do think me funny, don't you, Fairy? Neither of you can look at me without laughing, can you? Try, Boy; try, Fairy. (*They try, but fail. He is moved.*) Thank you both, thank you kindly. If the public only knew how anxiously we listen for the laugh they would be less grudging of it. (*Hastily*) Not that I have any cause of complaint. Every night I get the laugh from my generous patrons, the public, and always by legitimate means. When I think what a favourite I am I cannot keep my seat. (*He rises proudly.*) I am acknowledged by all in the know to be a funny old man. (*He moves about exultantly, looking at the portraits that are to hand him down to posterity.*) That picture of me, Boy, was painted to commemorate my being the second funniest man on earth. Of course Joey is the funniest, but I am the second funniest. (*They have scarcely listened; they have been exchanging delicious glances with face and foot. But at mention of the* CLOWN *they shudder a little, and their hands seek each other for protection.*) This portrait I had took—done— in honour of your birth, my love. I call it ' The Old 'Un on First Hearing that He is a Father.' (*He chuckles long before another picture which represents him in the dress of ordinary people.*) This is me in fancy dress ; it is how I went to a fancy-dress ball. Your mother, Fairy, was with me, in a long skirt ! Very droll we must have looked, and very droll we felt. I call to mind we walked about in this way ; the way the public walks, you know. (*In his gaiety he imitates the walk of the public, and roguish* COLUMBINE *imitates them also, but she loses her balance.*) Yes, try it. Don't flutter so much. Ah, it won't do, Fairy. Your natural way of walking 's like a bird bobbing about on a lawn after worms. Your mother was the same, and when she got low in spirits I just blew her about the room till she was lively again. Blow Fairy about, Boy. (HARLEQUIN *blows her divinely about the room, against the wall, on to seats and off them, and for some sad happy moments* PANTA- LOON *gazes at her, feeling that his wife is alive again. They think it is the auspicious time to tell him of their love, but bashfulness falls upon them. He only sees that their faces shine.*) Ah, she is happy, my Fairy, but I have news that will make her happier ! (*Curiously*) Fairy, you look as if you had something you wanted to tell me. Have you news too ? (*Tremblingly she extends her hand and shows him the ring on it. For a moment he misunder- stands.*) A ring ! Did *he* give you that ? (*She nods raptur- ously.*) Oho, oho, this makes me so happy. I 'll be funnier than ever, if possible. (*At this they dance gleefully, but his next words strike them cold.*) But, the rogue ! He said he wanted me to speak to you about it first. That was my news. Oh, the rogue ! (*They are scared, and sudden fear grips him.*) There 's nothing wrong, is there ? It was Joey gave you that ring, wasn't it, Fairy ? (*She shakes her head, and the movement shakes tears from her eyes.*) If it wasn't Joey, who was it ? (HARLEQUIN *steps forward.*) You ! You are not fond of Boy, are you, Fairy ? (*She is clinging to her lover now, and* PANTALOON *is a little dazed.*) But, my girl, Joey wants you. A clown wants you. When a clown wants you, you are not going to fling yourself away on a harlequin, are you ? (*They go on their knees to him, and he is touched, but also frightened.*)

Don't try to get round me ; now don't.   Joey would be angry
with me.   He can be hard when he likes, Joey can.   (*In a
whisper*) Perhaps he would cane me !   You wouldn't like to
see your dad caned, Fairy.   (COLUMBINE's *head sinks to the floor
in woe, and* HARLEQUIN *eagerly waves his wand.*)   Ah, Boy,
you couldn't defy him.   He is our head.   You can do wonderful things with that wand, but you can't fight Joey with it.
(*Sadly enough the wand is lowered.*)   You see, children, it won't
do.   You have no money, Boy, except the coppers Joey sometimes gives you in an envelope of a Friday night, and we can't
marry without money (*with an attempt at joviality*), can't
marry without money, Boy.   (HARLEQUIN *with a rising chest
produces money.*)   Seven shillings and tenpence !   You have
been saving up, Boy.   Well done !   But it 's not enough.
(COLUMBINE *darts to the mantelshelf for her money-box and rattles
it triumphantly.*   PANTALOON *looks inside it.*)   A half-crown
and two sixpences !   It won't do, children.   I had a pound
and a piano-case when I married, and yet I was pinched.   (*They
sit on the floor with their fingers to their eyes, and with difficulty
he restrains an impulse to sit beside them.*)   Poor souls !   poor
true love !   (*The thought of Joey's power and greatness over-
whelms him.*)   Think of Joey's individuality, Fairy.   He
banks his money, my love.   If you saw the boldness of Joey
in the bank when he hands the slip across the counter and
counts his money, my pet, instead of being thankful for whatever
they give him.   And then he puts out his tongue at them !   The
artist in him makes him put out his tongue at them.   For he is a
great artist, Joey.   He is a greater artist than I am.   I know it
and I admit it.   He has a touch that is beyond me.   (*Imploringly*)
Did you say you would marry him, my love ?   (*She does not
raise her head, and he continues with a new break in his voice.*)
It is not his caning me I am so afraid of, but—but I 'm oldish
now, Fairy, even for an old 'un, and there is something I must
tell you.   I have tried to keep it from myself, but I know.   It
is this :   I am afraid, my sweet, I am not so funny as I used to
be.   (*She encircles his knees in dissent.*)   Yes, it 's true, and
Joey knows it.   On Monday I had to fall into the barrel three
times before I got the laugh.   Joey saw !   If Joey were to
dismiss me I could never get another shop.   I would be like a
dog without a master.   He has been my master so long.   I

have put by nearly enough to keep me, but oh, Fairy, the awfulness of not being famous any longer. Living on without seeing my kind friends in front. To think of my just being one of the public, of my being pointed at in the streets as the old 'un that was fired out of the company because he missed his laughs. And that's what Joey will bring to pass if you don't marry him, my girl. (*It is an appeal for mercy, and* COLUMBINE *is his loving daughter. Her face is wan, but she tries to smile. She hugs the ring to her breast, and then gives it back to* HARLE-QUIN. *They try to dance a last embrace, but their legs are leaden. He kisses her cheeks and her foot and goes away broken-hearted. The brave girl puts her arm round her father's neck and hides her wet face. He could not look at it though it were exposed, for he has more to tell.*) I haven't told you the worst yet, my love. I didn't dare tell you the worst till Boy had gone. Fairy, the marriage is to be to-day ! Joey has arranged it all. It's his humour, and we dare not thwart him. He is coming here to take you to the wedding. (*In a tremble she draws away from him.*) I haven't been a bad father to you, have I, my girl ? When we were waiting for you before you were born, your mother and I, we used to wonder what you would be like, and I— it was natural, for I was always an ambitious man—I hoped you would be a clown. But that wasn't to be, and when the doctor came to me—I was walking up and down this room in a tremble, for my darling was always delicate—when the doctor came to me and said, ' I congratulate you, sir, on being the father of a fine little columbine,' I never uttered one word of reproach to him or to you or to her. (*There is a certain grandeur about the old man as he calls attention to the nobility of his conduct, but it falls from him on the approach of the* CLOWN. *We hear Joey before we see him : he is singing a snatch of one of his triumphant ditties, less for his own pleasure perhaps than to warn the policeman to be on the alert. He has probably driven to the end of the street, and then walked. A tremor runs through* COLUMBINE *at sound of him, but* PANTALOON *smiles, a foolish ecstatic smile. Joey has always been his hero.*) Be ready to laugh, my girl. Joey will be angry if he doesn't get the laugh.

(*The* CLOWN *struts in, as confident of welcome as if he were the announcement of dinner. He wears his motley like an order. A silk hat and an eyeglass indicate his superior social position. A sausage protruding from a pocket shows that he can unbend at times. A masterful man when you don't applaud enough, he is at present in uproarious spirits, as if he had just looked in a mirror. At first he affects not to see his host, to PANTALOON's great entertainment.*)

CLOWN.   Miaw, miaw !

PANTALOON (*bent with merriment*).   He is at his funniest, quite at his funniest.

(CLOWN *kicks him hard but good-naturedly, and* PANTALOON *falls to the ground.*)

CLOWN.   Miaw !

PANTALOON (*reverently*).   What an artist !

CLOWN (*pretends to see* COLUMBINE *for the first time in his life. In a masterpiece of funniness he starts back, like one dazzled by a naked light*).   Oh, Jiminy Crinkles !   Oh, I say, what a beauty !

PANTALOON.   There 's nobody like him.

CLOWN.   It 's Fairy.   It 's my little Fairy.

(*Strange, but all her admiration for this man has gone. He represents nothing to her now but wealth and social rank. He ogles her, and she shrinks from him as if he were something nauseous.*)

PANTALOON (*warningly*).   Fairy !

CLOWN (*showing sharp teeth*).   Hey, what 's this, old 'un ? Don't she admire me ?

PANTALOON.   Not admire you, Joey ?   That 's a good 'un. Joey 's at his best to-day.

CLOWN.   Ain't she ready to come to her wedding ?

PANTALOON.   She 's ready, Joey.

CLOWN (*producing a cane, and lowering*).   Have you told her what will happen to you if she ain't ready ?

PANTALOON (*backing*).   I 've told her, Joey.   (*Supplicating*) Get your hat, Fairy.

CLOWN.   Why ain't she dancing wi' joy and pride ?

PANTALOON.   She is, Joey, she is.

(COLUMBINE *attempts to dance with joy and pride, and the* CLOWN *has been so long used to adulation that he is deceived.*)

CLOWN (*amiable again*).   Parson 's waiting.   Oh, what a lark !

PANTALOON (*with a feeling that lark is not perhaps the happiest word for the occasion*). Get your things, Fairy.

CLOWN (*riding on a chair*). Give me something first, my lovey-dovey. I shuts my eyes and opens my mouth, and waits for what 's my doo. (*She knows what he means, and it is sacrilege to her. But her father's arms are extended beseechingly. She gives the now abhorred countenance a kiss, and runs from the room. The* CLOWN *plays with the kiss as if it were a sausage, a sight abhorrent to* HARLEQUIN, *who has stolen in by the window. Fain would he strike, but though he is wearing his mask, which is a sign that he is invisible, he fears to do so. As if conscious of the unseen presence, the* CLOWN'S *brow darkens.*) Joey, when I came in I saw Boy hanging around outside.

PANTALOON (*ill at ease*). Boy? What can he be wanting?

CLOWN. I know what he is wanting, and I know what he will get. (*He brandishes the cane threateningly. At the same moment the wedding bells begin to peal.*)

PANTALOON. Hark!

CLOWN (*with grotesque accompaniment*). My wedding bells. Fairy's wedding bells. There they go again, here we are again, there they go again, here we are again. (COLUMBINE *returns. She has tried to hide the tears on her cheeks behind a muslin veil. There is a melancholy bouquet in her hand. She passionately desires to be like the respectable public on her marriage day.* HARLEQUIN *raises his mask for a moment that she may see him, and they look long at each other, those two, who are never to have anything lovely to look at again. 'Won't he save her yet?' says her face, but 'I am afraid' says his. Still the bells are jangling.*)

PANTALOON. My girl.

CLOWN. Mine. (*He kisses her, but it is the sausage look that is in his eyes.* PANTALOON, *bleeding for his girl, raises his staff to strike him, but* COLUMBINE *will not have the sacrifice. She gives her arm to the* CLOWN.) To the wedding. To the wedding. Old 'un, lead on, and we will follow thee! Oh, what a lark!

(*They are going toward the door, but in this supreme moment love turns timid Boy into a man. He waves his mysterious wand over them, so that all three are suddenly bereft of movement. They are like frozen figures. He*

*removes his mask and smiles at them with a terrible face.
Fondly and leisurely he gathers* COLUMBINE *in his arms and
carries her out by the window. The* CLOWN *and* PANTA-
LOON *remain there, as if struck in the act of taking a step
forward. The wedding bells are still pealing.*

*The curtain falls for a moment only. It rises on the same
room several years later.*

*The same room ; as one may say of a suit of clothes, out
of which the whilom tenant has long departed, that they are
the same man. A room cold to the touch, dilapidated, fragments of the ceiling fallen and left where they fell, wall-paper
peeling damply, portraits of* PANTALOON *taken down to sell,
unsaleable, and never rehung. Once such a clean room that
its ghost to-day might be* COLUMBINE *chasing a speck of dust,
it is now untended. Even the windows are grimy, which
tells a tale of* PANTALOON's *final capitulation ; while any
heart was left him we may be sure he kept the windows clean
so that the policeman might spy upon him. Perhaps the policeman has gone from the street, bored, nothing doing there now.*

*It is evening and winter time, and the ancient man is
moving listlessly about his room, mechanically blowing life
into his hands as if he had forgotten that there is no real
reason why there should be life in them. The clothes*
COLUMBINE *used to brush with such care are slovenly, the
hair she so often smoothed with all her love is unkempt. He
is smaller, a man who has shrunk into himself in shame, not
so much shame that he is uncared for as that he is forgotten.*

*He is sitting forlorn by the fire when the door opens to
admit his first visitor for years. It is the* CLOWN, *just
sufficiently stouter to look more resplendent. The drum, so
to say, is larger. He gloats over the bowed* PANTALOON
like a spiteful boy.)

CLOWN (*poking* PANTALOON *with his cane*). Who can this
miserable ancient man be ?

(*Visited at last by some one who knows him,* PANTALOON
rises in a surge of joy.)

PANTALOON. You have come back, Joey, after all these years !

CLOWN. Hands off. I came here, my good fellow, to
inquire for a Mr. Joseph.

PANTALOON (*shuddering*). Yes, that 's me ; that 's all that 's left of me ; Mr. Joseph ! Me that used to be Joey.

CLOWN. I think I knew you once, Mr. Joseph ?

PANTALOON. Joey, you 're hard on me. It wasn't my fault that Boy tricked us and ran off wi' her.

CLOWN. May I ask, Mr. Joseph, were you ever on the boards ?

PANTALOON. This to me as was your right hand !

CLOWN. I seem to call to mind something like you as used to play the swell.

PANTALOON (*fiercely*). It 's a lie ! I was born a Pantaloon, and a Pantaloon I 'll die.

CLOWN. Yes, I heard you was dead, Mr. Joseph. Everybody knows it except yourself. (*He gnaws a sausage*).

PANTALOON (*greedily*). Gie me a bite, Joey.

CLOWN (*relentless*). I only bites with the profession. I never bites with the public.

PANTALOON. What brought you here ? Just to rub it in ?

CLOWN. Let 's say I came to make inquiries after the happy pair.

PANTALOON. It 's years and years, Joey, since they ran away, and I 've never seen them since.

CLOWN. Heard of them ?

PANTALOON. Yes, I 've heard. They 're in distant parts.

CLOWN. Answer their letters ?

PANTALOON (*darkening*). No.

CLOWN. They will be doing well, Mr. Joseph, without me ?

PANTALOON (*boastfully*). At first they did badly, but when the managers heard Fairy was my daughter they said the daughter o' such a famous old 'un was sure to draw by reason of her father's name. And they print the name of her father in big letters.

CLOWN (*rapping it out*). It 's you that lie now. I know about them. They go starving like vagabonds from town to town.

PANTALOON. Ay, it 's true. They write that they 're starving.

CLOWN. And they 've got a kid to add to their misery. All vagabonds, father, mother, and kid.

PANTALOON. Rub it in, Joey.

CLOWN. You looks as if you would soon be starving too.

PANTALOON (*not without dignity*). I 'm pinched.

CLOWN. Well, well, I 'm a kindly soul, and what brought me here was to make you an offer.

PANTALOON (*glistening*). A shop ?

CLOWN. For old times' sake.

PANTALOON (*with indecent eagerness*). To be old 'un again ?

CLOWN. No, you crock, but to carry a sandwich-board in the street wi' my new old 'un's name on it.

(PANTALOON *raises his withered arm, but he lets it fall*.)

PANTALOON. May you be forgiven for that, Joey.

CLOWN. Miaw !

PANTALOON (*who is near his end*). Joey, there stands humbled before you an old artist.

CLOWN. Never an artist ?

PANTALOON (*firmly*). An artist—at present disengaged.

CLOWN. Forgotten—clean forgotten.

PANTALOON (*bowing his head*). Yes, that 's it—forgotten. Once famous—now forgotten. Joey, they don't know me even at the sausage-shop. I am just one of the public. My worst time is when we should be going on the stage, and I think I hear the gallery boys calling for the old 'un—' Bravo, old 'un ! ' Then I sort of break up. I sleep bad o' nights. I think sleep would come to me if I could rub my back on the scenery again. (*He shudders*.) But the days are longer than the nights. I allus see how I am to get through to-day, but I sit thinking and thinking how I am to get through to-morrow.

CLOWN. Poor old crock ! Well, so long.

PANTALOON (*offering him the poker*). Joey, gie me one rub before you go—for old times' sake.

CLOWN. You 'll never be rubbed by a clown again, Mr. Joseph.

PANTALOON. Call me Joey once—say ' Good-bye, old 'un ' —for old times' sake.

CLOWN. You will never be called Joey or old un' by a clown again, Mr. Joseph.

(*With a noble gesture* PANTALOON *bids him begone and the* CLOWN *miaws and goes, twisting a sausage in his mouth as if it were a cigar. So he passes from our sight, funny to the last, or never funny, an equally tragic figure.*)

PANTALOON *rummages in the wicker basket among his gods and strokes them lovingly, a painted goose, his famous staff, a bladder on a stick. He does not know that he is hugging the bladder to his cold breast as he again crouches by the fire.*

The door opens, and COLUMBINE *and* HARLEQUIN *peep in, prepared to receive a blow for welcome. Their faces are hollow and their clothes in rags, and, saddest of all, they cannot dance in. They walk in like the weary public.* COLUMBINE *looks as if she could walk as far as her father's feet, but never any farther. With them is the child. This is the great surprise :* HE IS A CLOWN. *They sign to the child to intercede for them, but though only a baby, he is a clown, and he must do it in his own way. He pats his nose, grins deliciously with the wrong parts of his face, and dives beneath the table.* PANTALOON *looks round and sees his daughter on her knees before him.*)

PANTALOON. You ! Fairy ! Come back ! (*For a moment he is to draw her to him, then he remembers.*) No, I 'll have none of you. It was you as brought me to this. Begone, I say begone. (*They are backing meekly to the door.*) Stop a minute. Little Fairy, is it true—is it true my Fairy has a kid ? (*She nods, with glistening eyes that say ' Can you put me out now ? ' The baby peers from under the table, and rubs* PANTALOON'S *legs with the poker. Poor little baby, he is the last of the clowns, and knows not what is in store for him.* PANTALOON *trembles, it is so long since he has been rubbed. He dare not look down.*) Fairy, is it the kid ? (*She nods again ; the moment has come.*) My Fairy's kid ! (*Somehow he has always taken for granted that his grandchild is merely a columbine. If the child had been something greater they would all have got a shop again and served under him.*) Oh, Fairy, if only he had been a clown !

(*Now you see how it is going. The babe emerges, and he is a clown.*

Just for a moment PANTALOON *cries. Then the babe is tantalising him with a sausage.* PANTALOON *revolves round him like a happy teetotum. Who so gay now as* COLUMBINE *and* HARLEQUIN, *dancing merrily as if it were again the morning ? Oh, what a lark is life ! Ring down the curtain quickly, Mr. Prompter, before we see them all swept into the dust-heap.*)

ALICE SIT-BY-THE-FIRE

ALICE SIT-BY-THE-FIRE

Produced at the Duke of York's Theatre on April 5, 1905, with the following cast :

COL. GREY	.	.	.	. Aubrey Smith
MRS. GREY	.	.	.	. Ellen Terry
AMY GREY	.	.	.	. Irene Vanbrugh
COSMO GREY	.	.	.	. A. E. Matthews
STEPHEN ROLLO	.	.	.	. Kenneth Douglas
GINEVRA DUNBAR		.	.	. Lettice Fairfax
NURSE	.	.	.	. Dora Hole
FANNY	.	.	.	. Edith Craig
RICHARDSON	.	.	.	. Hilda Trevelyan

The play ran for 115 performances.

ACT I

ONE would like to peep covertly into Amy's diary (octavo, with the word ' Amy ' in gold letters wandering across the soft brown leather covers, as if it was a long word and, in Amy's opinion, rather a dear). To take such a liberty, and allow the reader to look over our shoulders, as they often invite you to do in novels (which, however, are much more coquettish things than plays), would be very helpful to us ; we should learn at once what sort of girl Amy is, and why to-day finds her washing her hair. We should also get proof or otherwise, that we are interpreting her aright ; for it is our desire not to record our feelings about Amy, but merely Amy's feelings about herself ; not to tell what we think happened, but what Amy thought happened. The book, to be sure, is padlocked, but we happen to know where it is kept. (In the lower drawer of that hand-painted escritoire.) Sometimes in the night Amy, waking up, wonders whether she did lock her diary, and steals downstairs in white to make sure. On these occasions she undoubtedly lingers among the pages, re-reading the peculiarly delightful bit she wrote yesterday ; so we could peep over her shoulder, while the reader peeps over ours. Then why don't we do it ? Is it because this would be a form of eavesdropping, and that we cannot be sure our hands are clean enough to turn the pages of a young girl's thoughts ? It cannot be that, because the novelists do it. It is because in a play we must tell little that is not revealed by the spoken words ; you must ferret out all you want to know from them, although of course now and then we may whisper a conjecture in brackets ; there is no weather even in plays except in melodrama ; the novelist can have sixteen chapters about the hero's grandparents, but there can be very little rummaging in the past for us ; we are expected merely to present our characters as they toe the mark ; then the handkerchief falls, and off they go.

So now we know why we must not spy into Amy's diary. Perhaps we have not always been such sticklers for the etiquette of the thing ; but we are always sticklers on Thursdays, and this is a Thursday.

As you are to be shown Amy's room, we are permitted to describe it, though not to tell (which would be much more interesting) why a girl of seventeen has, as her very own, the chief room of a house. The moment you open the door of this room (and please, you are not to look consciously at the escritoire as if you knew the diary was in it) you are aware, though Amy may not be visible, that there is an uncommonly clever girl in the house. The door does not always open easily, because attached thereto is a curtain which frequently catches in it, and this curtain is hand-sewn (extinct animals) ; indeed a gifted woman's touch is everywhere ; if you are not hand-sewn you are almost certainly hand-painted, but incompletely, for Amy in her pursuit of the arts has often to drop one in order to keep pace with another. Some of the chairs have escaped as yet, but their time will come. The table-cover and the curtains are of a lovely pink, perforated ingeniously with many tiny holes, which when you consider them against a dark background, gradually assume the appearance of something pictorial, such as a basket of odd flowers. The fender-stool is in brown velvet, and there are words on it that invite you to sit down. Some of the letters of this message have been burned away. There are artistic white bookshelves hanging lopsidedly here and there, and they also have pink curtains, no larger than a doll's garments. These little curtains are for covering the parts where there are no books as yet. The pictures on the walls are mostly studies done at school, and include the well-known windmill, and the equally popular old lady by the shore. Their frames are of fir-cones, glued together, or of straws which have gone limp, and droop like streaks of macaroni. There is a cosy corner ; also a milking-stool, but no cow. The lampshades have had ribbons added to them, and from a distance look like ladies of the ballet. The flower-pot also is in a skirt. Near the door is a large screen, such as people hide behind in the more ordinary sort of play ; it will be interesting to see whether we can resist the temptation to hide some one behind it.

A few common weeds rear their profane heads in this innocent garden ; for instance a cruet-stand, a basket of cutlery, and a triangular dish of the kind in which the correct confine cheese. They have not strayed here, they live here ; indeed this is among other things the dining-room of a modest little house in Brompton made beautiful, or nearly so, by a girl, who has a soul above food and conceals its accessories as far as possible from view, in drawers, even in the waste-paper basket. Not a dish, not a spoon, not a fork, is hand-painted, a sufficient indication of her contempt for them.

Amy is present, but is not seen to the best advantage, for she has been washing her hair, and is now drying it by the fire. Notable among her garments are a dressing-jacket and a towel, and her head is bent so far back over the fire that we see her face nearly upside-down. This is no position in which we can do justice to her undoubted facial charm. Seated near her is her brother Cosmo, a boy of thirteen, in naval uniform. Cosmo is a cadet at Osborne, and properly proud of his station, but just now he looks proud of nothing. He is plunged in gloom. The cause of his woe is a telegram, which he is regarding from all points of the compass, as if in hopes of making it send him better news. At last he gives expression to his feelings.

COSMO. All I can say is that if father tries to kiss me, I shall kick him.

(*If* AMY *makes any reply the words arrive upside-down and are unintelligible. The maid announces* MISS DUNBAR. *Then* AMY *rises, brings her head to the position in which they are usually carried ; and she and* GINEVRA *look into each other's eyes. They always do this when they meet, though they meet several times a day, and it is worth doing, for what they see in those pellucid pools is love eternal. Thus they loved at school* (*in their last two terms*), *and thus they will love till the grave encloses them. These thoughts, and others even more beautiful, are in their minds as they gaze at each other now. No man will ever be able to say ' Amy,' or to say ' Ginevra,' with such a trill as they are saying it.*)

AMY. Ginevra, my beloved.

GINEVRA. My Amy, my better self.

AMY. My other me. (*There is something almost painful in love like this.*) Are you well, Ginevra ?

GINEVRA. Quite well, Amy. (*Heavens, the joy of* AMY *because* GINEVRA *is quite well.*) How did my Amy sleep ?

AMY. I had a good night.

(*How happy is* GINEVRA *because* AMY *has had a good night. All this time they have been slowly approaching each other, drawn by a power stronger than themselves. Their intention is to kiss. They do so.* COSMO *snorts, and betakes himself to some other room, his bedroom probably, where a man may be alone with mannish things. The maidens do not resent his rudeness. They know that poor* COSMO'S *time will come, and they are glad to be alone, for they have much to say that is for no other mortal ears. Some of it is sure to go into the diary ; indeed if we were to put our ear to the drawer where the diary is we could probably hear its little heart ticking in unison with theirs.*

It is GINEVRA *who speaks first. She is indeed the bolder of the two. She grips* AMY'S *hand.*)

GINEVRA. Amy, shall we go to *another* to-night ?

(*This does not puzzle* AMY, *she is prepared for it, her honest grey eyes even tell that she has wanted it, but now that it is come she quails a little.*)

AMY. Another theatre ? Ginevra, that would be five in one week.

GINEVRA (*without blanching*). Yes, but it is also only eight in seventeen years.

AMY (*comforted.*) And they have taught us so much, haven't they ? Until Monday, dear, when we went to our first real play we didn't know what Life is.

GINEVRA. We were two raw, unbleached school-girls, Amy—absolutely unbleached.

(*It is such a phrase as this that gives* GINEVRA *the moral ascendancy in their discussions.*)

AMY (*looking perhaps a little unbleached even now*). Of course I had my diary, dear, and I do think that, even before Monday, there were things in it of a not wholly ordinary kind.

GINEVRA. Nothing that necessitated your keeping it locked.

AMY. No, I suppose not. You are quite right, Ginevra.

But we have made up for lost time.   Every night since Monday, including the matinée, has been a revelation.

(She closes her eyes so that she may see the revelations more clearly.   So does GINEVRA.*)*

GINEVRA.   Amy, that heart-gripping scene when the love-maddened woman visited the *man* in his *chambers*.

AMY.   She wasn't absolutely love-maddened, Ginevra ; she really loved her husband best all the time.

GINEVRA.   Not till the last act, darling.

AMY.   Please don't say it, Ginevra.   She was most foolish, especially in the crêpe de chine, but *we* know that she only went to the man's chambers to get back her letters.   How I trembled for her then.

GINEVRA.   I was strangely calm.

AMY.   Oh, Ginevra, I had such a presentiment that the husband would call at those chambers while she was there. And he did.   Ginevra, you remember his knock upon the door. Surely you trembled then ?

*(*GINEVRA *knits her lips triumphantly.)*

GINEVRA.   Not even then, Amy.   Somehow I felt sure that in the nick of time her lady friend would step out from somewhere and say that the letters were *hers*.

AMY.   Nobly compromising herself, Ginevra.

GINEVRA.   Amy, how I love that bit where she says so unexpectedly, with noble self-renunciation, ' He is my affianced husband.'

AMY.   Isn't it glorious !   Strange, Ginevra, that it happened in each play.

GINEVRA.   That was because we always went to the thinking theatres.   Real plays are always about a lady and two men ; and alas, only one of them is her husband.   That is Life, you know.   It is called the odd, odd triangle.

AMY.   Yes, I know.   *(Appealingly)* Ginevra, I hope it wasn't wrong of me to go.   A month ago I was only a school-girl.

GINEVRA.   We both were.

AMY.   Yes, but you are now an art student, in lodgings, with a latch-key of your own ; you have no one dependent on you, while I have a brother and sister to—to form.

GINEVRA.   You must leave it to the Navy, dear, to form

Cosmo, if it can ; and as the sister is only a baby, time enough to form her when she can exit from her pram.

AMY.   I am in a mother's place for the time being, Ginevra.

GINEVRA.   Even mothers go to thinking theatres.

AMY.   Whether mine does, Ginevra, I don't even know. This is a very strange position I am in, awaiting the return from India of parents I have not seen since I was twelve years old. I don't even know if they will like the house.   The rent is as they told me to give, but perhaps my scheme of decoration won't appeal to them ; they may think my housekeeping has been defective, and may not make allowance for my being so new to it.

GINEVRA.   My ownest Amy, if they are not both on their knees to you for the noble way in which you have striven to prepare this house for them——

AMY.   Darling Ginevra, all I ask is to be allowed to do my duty.

GINEVRA.   Listen, then, Amy : your duty is to be able to help your parents in every way when they return.   Your mother having been so long in India can know little about Life ; how sweet, then, for you to be able to place your knowledge at her feet.

AMY.   I had thought of that, dearest

GINEVRA.   Then, Amy, it would be simply wrong of us not to go to another theatre to-night.   I have three and ninepence, so that if you can scrape together one and threepence——

AMY.   Generous girl, it can't be.

GINEVRA.   Why not ?

(*The return of* COSMO *handling the telegram more pugnaciously than ever provides the answer.*)

AMY.   Cosmo, show Miss Dunbar the telegram.

GINEVRA (*reading*). 'Boat arrived Southampton this morning.'

AMY.   A day earlier than they expected.

COSMO (*darkly*).   It 's the other bit I am worrying about.

GINEVRA (*reading*).   ' Hope to reach our pets this afternoon. Kisses from both to all.   Deliriously excited.   Mummy and Dad.'

COSMO.   Pets, kisses ! What can the telegraph people think ?

AMY.   Surely you want to kiss your mother.

COSMO (*stoutly*).   I 'm going to kiss her.   I mean to do it
It 's father I am worrying about ; with his ' kisses from *both* to
all.'   All I can say is that, if father comes slobbering over me,
I 'll surprise him.

(*Here the outer door slams, and the three start to their feet
as if Philippi had dawned. To* COSMO *the slam sounds
uncommonly like a father's kiss. He immediately begins
to rehearse the greeting which is meant to ward off the fatal
blow. 'How are you, father? I'm glad to see you,
father ; it's a long journey from India ; won't you sit
down?'*

AMY (*the first to recover*).   How silly of us ; it is only nurse
with baby.

(*Presumably what we hear is a perambulator backing into
its stall in the passage. Then nurse is distinctly heard in
the adjoining room, and we may gather that this is for the
nonce the nursery of the house, though to most occupants
it would be the back dining-room. There is a door
between the two rooms, and* COSMO, *peeping through
a chink in it, sounds to his fellow-conspirators the All's
Well.*

AMY.   Poor nurse, I suppose I had better show her the
telegram.   She is sure to cry.   She looks upon mother as a
thief who has come to steal baby from her.

(GINEVRA *wags her head to indicate that this is another slice
of Life ; and* NURSE *being called in is confronted with the
telegram. She runs a gamut of emotion without words,
implies that she is nobody and must submit, nods humbly,
sets her teeth, is both indignant and servile, and finally
bursts into tears.* AMY *tries to comfort her, but gets this
terrible answer :*)

NURSE.   They will be bringing a black woman to nurse her
—a yah-yah, they call them.

(AMY *signs to* GINEVRA, *and* GINEVRA *signs to* AMY. *These
two souls perfectly understand each other, and the telegraphy
means that it will be better for dear* GINEVRA *to retire for
a time to dear* AMY'S *sweet little bedroom.* AMY *slips the
diary into the hand of* GINEVRA, *who pops upstairs with it
to read the latest instalment.* NURSE *rambles on.*)

NURSE.   I have had her for seventeen months.   She was

just two months old, the angel, when they sent her to England, and she has been mine ever since. The most of them has one look for their mammas and one look for their nurse, but she knew no better than to have both looks for me. (*She returns to the nursery, wailing ' My reign is over.'*)

COSMO. Do you think Molly *will* chuck nurse for mother ?

AMY (*experienced*). It is the way of children.

COSMO. Shabby little beasts.

AMY. You mustn't say that, Cosmo ; but still it is hard on nurse. Of course (*with swimming eyes*) in a sense it 's hard on all of us——I mean to be expecting parents in these circumstances. There must be almost the same feeling of strangeness in the house as when it is a baby that is expected.

COSMO (*gloomily*). I suppose it is a bit like that. Great Scott, Amy, it can't be quite so bad as that.

(AMY, *who is of a very affectionate nature, is glad to have the comfort of his hand.*)

AMY. What do we really know about mother, Cosmo ?

(*They are perhaps a touching pair.*)

COSMO. There are her letters.

AMY. Can one know a person by letters ?   Does she know you, Cosmo, by your letters to her, saying that your motto is ' Something attempted, something done to earn a night's repose,' and so on.

COSMO. Well, I thought that would please her.

AMY. Perhaps in her letters she says things just to please us.

(COSMO *wriggles.*)

COSMO. This is pretty low of you, damping a fellow when he was trying to make the best of it.

AMY. All I want you to feel, is that as brother and sister, we are allies, you know——against the unknown.

COSMO. Yes, Amy.

AMY. I want to say, dear, that I 'm very sorry I used to shirk bowling to you.

COSMO. That 's nothing. I know what girls are. Amy, it 's all right, I really am fond of you.

AMY. I have tried to be a sort of mother to you, Cosmo.

COSMO. My socks and things——I know. (*Returning anxiously to the greater question*) Amy, do we know anything of them at all ?

AMY.　We know some cold facts, of course.　We know that father is much older than mother.

COSMO.　I can't understand why such an old chap should be so keen to kiss me.

AMY (*in a low voice*).　Mother is forty.

COSMO (*in a still lower voice*).　I thought she was almost more than forty.

AMY.　Don't be so ungenerous, Cosmo.　Of course we must be prepared to see her look older.

COSMO.　Why ?

AMY.　She will be rather yellow, coming from India, you know.　They will both be a little yellow.

(*They exchange forlorn glances.*)

COSMO (*manfully*).　We shan't be any the less fond of them for that, Amy.

AMY.　No, indeed.

(*He has an inspiration.*)

COSMO.　Do you think we should have these yellow flowers in the room ?　They might feel—eh ?

AMY.　How thoughtful of you, dear.　I shall remove them at once.　After all, Cosmo, we seem to know a good deal about them ; and then we know some other things by heredity.

COSMO.　Heredity ?　That 's drink, isn't it ?

AMY.　No, you boy !　It 's something in a play.　It means that if we know ourselves well, we know our parents also. From thinking of myself, Cosmo, I know mother.　In her youth she was one who did not love easily ; but when she loved once it was for aye.　A nature very difficult to understand, but profoundly interesting.　I can feel her *within me,* as she was when she walked down the aisle on that strong arm, to honour and obey him henceforth for aye.　What cared they that they had to leave their native land, they were together for aye.　And so——

(*Her face is flushed.*　COSMO *interrupts selfishly.*)

COSMO.　What about father ?

AMY.　Very nice, unless you mention rupees to him.　You see the pensions of all Indian officers are paid in rupees, which means that for every 2s. due to them they get only 1s. 4d.　If you mention rupees to any one of them he flares up like a burning paper.

COSMO.   I know.   I shall take care.   But what would you say he was like by heredity ?

AMY.   Quiet, unassuming, yet of an intensely proud nature. One who if he was deceived would never face his fellow-creatures, but would bow his head before the wind and die. A strong man.

COSMO.   Do you mean, Amy, that he takes all that from me ?

AMY.   I mean that is the sort of man *my* mother would love.

COSMO.   Yes, but he is just as likely to kiss me as ever.

(*The return of* GINEVRA *makes him feel that this room is no place for him.*)

COSMO.   I think I 'll go and walk up and down outside, and have a look at them as they 're getting out of the cab.   My plan, you see, is first to kiss mother.   Then I 've made up four things to say to father, and it 's after I 've said them that the awkward time will come.   So then I say, ' I wonder what is in the evening papers ' ;   and out I slip, and when I come back you will all have settled down to ordinary life, same as other people.   That 's my plan.

(*He goes off, not without hope, and* GINEVRA *shrugs her shoulders forgivingly.*)

GINEVRA.   How strange boys are.   Have you any ' plan,' Amy ?

AMY.   Only this, dear Ginevra, to leap into my mother's arms.

(GINEVRA *lifts what can only be called a trouser leg, because that is what it is, though they are very seldom seen alone.*)

GINEVRA.   What is this my busy bee is making ?

AMY.   It 's a gentleman's leg.   You hand-sew them and stretch them over a tin cylinder, and they are then used as umbrella stands.   *Art in the Home* says they are all the rage.

GINEVRA.   Oh, Amy, *Boudoir Gossip* says they have quite gone out.

AMY.   Again !   Every art decoration I try goes out before I have time to finish it.

(*She remembers the diary.*)

Did my Ginevra like my new page ?

GINEVRA.   Dearest, that is what I came down to speak about.   You forgot to give me the key.

AMY.   Ginevra, can you ever forgive me ?   Let us go up and read it together.

(With arms locked they seek the seclusion of AMY'S *bedroom.* COSMO *rushes in to tell them that there is a suspicious-looking cab coming down the street, but finding the room empty he departs again to reconnoitre. A cab draws up, a bell rings, and soon we hear the voice of* COLONEL GREY. *He can talk coherently to* FANNY, *he can lend a hand in dumping down his luggage in the passage, he can select from a handful of silver wherewith to pay his cabman : all impossible deeds to his* ALICE, *who would drop the luggage on your toes and cast all the silver at your face rather than be kept another minute from her darlings. ' Where are they ? ' she has evidently cried just before we see her, and* FANNY *has made a heartless response, for it is a dejected* ALICE *that appears in the doorway of the room.)*

ALICE *(woefully).* All out ! even—even baby ?

FANNY.   Yes, ma'am.

(The poor mother, who had entered the house like a whirlwind, subsides into a chair. Her arms fall empty by her side : a moment ago she had six of them, a pair for each child. She cries a little, and when ALICE *cries, which is not often for she is more given to laughter, her face screws up like* MOLLY'S *rather than like* AMY'S. *She is very unlike the sketch of her lately made by the united fancies of her son and daughter ; and she will dance them round the room many times before they know her better.* AMY *will never be so pretty as her mother,* COSMO *will never be so gay, and it will be years before either of them is as young. But it is quite a minute before we suspect this ; we must look the other way while the* COLONEL *dries her tears. He is quite a grizzled veteran, and is trying hard to pretend that having done without his children for so many years, a few minutes more is no great matter. His adorable* ALICE *is this man's one joke. Some of those furrows in his brow have come from trying to understand her, he owes the agility of his mind to trying to keep up with her, the humorous twist in his mouth is the result of chuckling over her.)*

ALICE *(fluttering across the room).* Robert, I dare say my Amy painted that table !

FANNY.   Yes, ma'am, she did.

ALICE.   Robert, Amy's table !

COLONEL.   Yes, but keep cool, memsahib.

FANNY.   I suppose, ma'am, I 'm to take my orders from you now.

ALICE (*so timidly that* FANNY *is encouraged to be bold*).   I suppose so.

FANNY.   The poor miss ! it will be a bit trying for her just at first.

(ALICE *is taken aback.*)

ALICE.   I hadn't thought of that, Robert.

(ROBERT *thinks it time to take command.*)

COLONEL.   Fiddle-de-dee.   Bring your mistress a cup of tea, my girl.

FANNY.   Yes, sir.   Here is the tea-caddy, ma'am.   I can't take the responsibility ; but this is the key.

ALICE (*falteringly*).   Robert, I daren't break into Amy's caddy.   She mightn't like it.   I can wait.

COLONEL.   Rubbish.   Give me the key.   (*Even* FANNY *cannot but admire the* COLONEL *as he breaks into the caddy.*)   That makes me feel I 'm master of my own house already.   Don't stare at me, girl, as if I was a housebreaker.

(FANNY *goes.*)

ALICE.   I feel that is just what we both are !   (*In another moment rapturous*) It 's home, home !   India done, home begun.

(*He is as glad as she.*)

COLONEL.   Home, memsahib.   And we 've never had a real one before.   Thank God, I 'm able to give it you at last.

(*She darts impulsively from one object in the room to another.*)

ALICE.   Look, these pictures !   I 'm sure they are all Amy's work.   They are splendid.   (*With perhaps a moment's misgiving*) Aren't they ?

COLONEL (*guardedly*).   I couldn't have done them.   (*He considers the hand-painted curtains.*)   She seems to have stopped everything in the middle.   Still, I couldn't have done them.   I expect this is what is called a cosy corner.

(*But* ALICE *has found something more precious.   She utters little cries of rapture.*)

COLONEL.   What is it ?

ALICE.   Oh, Robert, a baby's shoe !   My baby.   (*She presses it to her as if it were a dove.   Then she is appalled.*)   Robert, if I had met my baby coming along the street I shouldn't have known her from other people's babies.

COLONEL.   Yes, you would.   Don't break down *now*.   Just think, Alice, after to-day, you will know your baby anywhere.

ALICE.   Oh joy, joy, joy !

(*Then the expression of her face changes to ' Oh woe, woe, woe.'*)

COLONEL.   What is it now, Alice ?

ALICE.   Perhaps she won't like me.

COLONEL.   Impossible.

ALICE.   Perhaps none of them will like me.

COLONEL.   My dear Alice, children always love their mother, whether they see much of her or not.   It 's an instinct.

ALICE.   Who told you that ?

COLONEL.   You goose.   It was yourself.

ALICE.   I 've lost faith in it.

(*He thinks it wise to sound a warning note.*)

COLONEL.   Of course you must give them a little time.

ALICE.   Robert, Robert !   Not another minute.   That 's not the way people ever love me.   They mustn't think me over first or anything of that sort.   If they do I 'm lost ; they must love me at once.

COLONEL.   A good many have done that.   (*Surveying her quizzically as if she were one of* AMY's *incompleted works.*)

ALICE.   You are not implying, Robert, that I ever——— If I ever did I always told you about it afterwards, didn't I ?   And I *certainly* never did it until I was sure you were comfortable.

COLONEL.   You always wrapped me up first.

ALICE.   They were only boys, Robert—poor lonely boys. What are you looking so solemn about ?

COLONEL.   I was trying to picture you as you will be when you settle down.

ALICE (*properly abashed*).   Not settled down yet—with a girl nearly grown up.   And yet it 's true ; it 's the tragedy of Alice Grey.   (*She pulls his hair.*)   Oh, husband, when shall I settle down ?

COLONEL.   I can tell you exactly—in a year from to-day. Alice, when I took you away to that humdrummy Indian

U

station I was already quite a middle-aged bloke. I chuckled over your gaiety, but it gave me lumbago to try to be gay with you.   Poor old girl, you were like an only child who has to play alone.   When for one month in the twelve we went to— to—where the boys were, it was like turning you loose in a sweet-stuff shop.

ALICE.   Robert, darling, what nonsense you do talk.

COLONEL (*making rather a wry face*).   I didn't always like it, memsahib.   But I knew my dear, and could trust her ; and I often swore to myself when I was shaving, ' I won't ask her to settle down until I have given her a year in England.'   A year from to-day, you harum-scarum.   By that time your daughter will be almost grown up herself ; and it wouldn't do to let her pass you.

ALICE.   Robert, here is an idea ; she and I shall come of age together.   I promise ; or I shall try to keep one day in front of her, like the school-mistresses when they are teaching boys Latin.   Dearest, you haven't been disappointed in me as a whole, have you ?   I haven't paid you for all your dear kindnesses to me—in rupees, have I ?

(*His answer is of no consequence, for at this moment there arrives a direct message from heaven.   It comes by way of the nursery, and is a child's cry.   The heart of* ALICE GREY *stops beating for several seconds.   Then it says, ' My Molly ! '   The* NURSE *appears and is at once on the defensive.*)

NURSE.   Is it—Mrs. Grey ?

ALICE (*hastily*).   Yes.   Is my—child in there ?

NURSE.   Yes, ma'am.

COLONEL (*ready to catch her if she falls*).   Alice, be calm.

ALICE (*falteringly*).   May I go in, nurse ?

NURSE (*cold-heartedly*).   She 's sleeping, ma'am, and I have made it a rule to let her wake up naturally.   But I dare say it 's a bad rule.

ALICE (*her hands on her heart*).   I 'm sure it 's a good rule. I shan't wake her, nurse.

COLONEL (*showing the stuff he is made of*).   Gad, I will.   It 's the least she can do to let herself be wakened.

ALICE (*admiring the effrontery of the man*).   Don't interfere, Robert.

COLONEL.   Sleeping? Why, she cried just now.

NURSE.   That is why I came out—to see who was making so much noise.

(*An implacable woman this, and yet when she is alone with* MOLLY *a very bundle of delight.*)

I 'm vexed when she cries—I dare say it 's old-fashioned of me. Not being a yah-yah I 'm at a disadvantage.

ALICE (*swelling*).   After all, she is *my* child.

COLONEL (*firmly*).   Come along, Alice.

ALICE.   I would prefer to go alone, dear.

COLONEL.   All right.   But break it to her that I 'm kicking my heels outside.

(ALICE *gets as far as the door.   The* NURSE *discharges a last duty.*)

NURSE.   You won't touch her, ma'am ; she doesn't like to be touched by strangers.

ALICE.   Strangers !

COLONEL.   Really, nurse.

ALICE.   It 's quite true.

NURSE.   She 's an angel if you have the right way with her.

ALICE.   Robert, if I shouldn't have the right way with her !

COLONEL.   You !

(*But the woman has scored again.*)

ALICE (*willing to go on her knees*).   Nurse, what sort of a way does she like from strangers ?

NURSE.   She 's not fond of a canoodlin' way.

ALICE (*faintly*).   Is she not ?

(*She departs to face her child, and the natural enemy follows her, after giving* COLONEL GREY *a moment in which to discharge her if he dares, that is if he wishes to see his baby wither and die.   One may as well say here that* NURSE *weathered this and many another gale, and remained in the house for many years to be its comfort and its curse.*

FANNY, *with the tea-tray, comes and goes without the* COLONEL'S *being aware of her presence.   He merely knows that he has waved some one away.   The fact is that the* COLONEL *is engrossed in a rather undignified pursuit.   He is listening avidly at the nursery door, and is thus discovered by another member of his family who has entered cautiously. This is* MASTER COSMO, *who, observing the tea-tray, has*

*the happy notion of interposing it between himself and his
father's possible osculatory intentions. He lifts the tray,
and thus armed introduces himself.)*

COSMO.   Hallo, father !

(His father leaves the door and strides to him.)

COLONEL.   Is it—it 's Cosmo.

COSMO *(with the tray well to the fore)*.   I 'm awfully glad to
see you—it 's a long way from India.

COLONEL.   Put that down, my boy, and let me get hold of
you.

COSMO *(ingratiatingly)*.   Have some tea, father.

COLONEL.   Put it down.

*(COSMO does so, and prepares for the worst. The COLONEL
takes both his hands.)*

Let 's have a look at you.   So this is you.

*(He waggles his head, well pleased, while COSMO backs in
a gentlemanly manner.)*

COSMO *(implying that this first meeting is now an affair of the
past)*.   Has Mother gone to lie down ?

COLONEL.   Lie down ?   She 's in there.

(COSMO steals to the nursery door and softly closes it.)
Why do you do that ?

COSMO.   I don't know.   I thought it would be—best.   *(In
a burst of candour)*   This is not the way I planned it, you see.

COLONEL.   Our meeting ?   So you 've been planning it.
My dear fellow, I was planning it too, and my plan——

(He is certainly coming closer.)

COSMO *(hurriedly)*.   Yes, I know.   Now that 's over—our
first meeting, I mean ;   now we settle down.

COLONEL.   Not yet.   Come here, my boy.

*(He draws him to a chair ; he evidently thinks that a father
and his boy of thirteen can sit in the same chair.   COSMO
is burning to be pleasant, but of course there are limits.)*

COSMO.   Look here, father.   Of course, you see—ways
change.   I dare say they did it, when you were a boy, but it
isn't done now.

COLONEL.   What isn't done, you dear fellow ?

COSMO.   Oh—well !—and then taking both hands and
saying ' Dear fellow '—It 's gone out, you know.

(The COLONEL chuckles and forbears.)

COLONEL. I'm uncommon glad you told me, Cosmo. Not having been a father for so long, you see, I'm rather raw at it.

COSMO (*relieved*). That's all right. You'll soon get the hang of it.

COLONEL. If you could give me any other tips?

COSMO (*becoming confidential*). Well, there's my beastly name. Of course you didn't mean any harm when you christened me Cosmo, but—I always sign myself ' C. Grey '—to make the fellows think I'm Charles.

COLONEL. Do they call you that?

COSMO. Lord, no, they call me Grey.

COLONEL. And do you want me to call you Grey?

COSMO (*magnanimously*). No, I don't expect that. But I thought that before people, you know, you needn't call me anything. If you want to attract my attention you could just say ' Hst ! '—like that.

COLONEL. Right you are. But you won't make your mother call you Hst.

COSMO (*sagaciously*). Oh no—of course women are different.

COLONEL. You'll be very nice to her, Cosmo? She had to pinch and save more than I should have allowed—to be able to send you into the navy. We are poor people, you know.

COSMO. I've been planning how to be nice to her.

COLONEL. Good lad. Good lad.

(COSMO *remembers his conversation with* AMY, *and thoughtfully hides the ' yellow flowers ' behind a photograph. This may be called one of his plans for being nice to mother.*)

COSMO. You don't have your medals here, father?

COLONEL. No, I don't carry them about. But your mother does, the goose. They are not very grand ones, Cosmo.

COSMO (*true blue*). Yes, they are.

(*An awkward silence falls. The* COLONEL *has so much to say that he can only look it. He looks it so eloquently that* COSMO'S *fears return. He summons the plan to his help.*)

I wonder what is in the evening papers. If you don't mind, I'll cut out and get one.

(*Before he can cut out, however,* ALICE *is in the room, the picture of distress. No wonder, for even we can hear the baby howling.*)

ALICE (*tragically*).   My baby.   Robert, listen ; that is how I affect her.

(COSMO *cowers unseen.*)

COLONEL.   No, no, darling, it isn't you who have made her cry.   She—she is teething.   It's her teeth, isn't it ?   (*He barks at the nurse, who emerges looking not altogether woeful.*) Say it's her teeth, woman.

NURSE (*taking this as a reflection on her charge*).   She had her teeth long ago.

ALICE (*the forlorn*).   The better to bite me with.

NURSE (*complacently*).   I don't understand it.   She is usually the best-tempered lamb—as you may see for yourself, sir.

(*It is an invitation that the* COLONEL *is eager to accept, but after one step toward the nursery he is true to* ALICE.)

COLONEL.   I *decline* to see her.   I refuse to have anything to do with her till she comes to a more reasonable frame of mind.

(*The* NURSE *retires, to convey possibly this ultimatum to her charge.*)

ALICE (*in the noblest spirit of self-abnegation*).   Go, Robert. Perhaps she—will like you better.

COLONEL.   She's a contemptible child.

(*But that nursery door does draw him strongly.   He finds himself getting nearer and nearer to it.   ' I'll show her,' with a happy pretence that his object is merely to enforce discipline.   The forgotten* COSMO *pops up again ; the* COLONEL *introduces him with a gesture and darts off to his baby.*)

ALICE (*entranced*).   My son !

COSMO (*forgetting all plans*).   Mother !   She envelops him in her arms, worshipping him, and he likes it.

ALICE.   Oh, Cosmo—how splendid you are !

COSMO (*soothingly*).   That's all right, mother.

ALICE.   Say it again.

COSMO.   That's all right.

ALICE.   No, the other word.

COSMO.   Mother.

ALICE.   Again.

COSMO.   Mother—mother——   (*When she has come to*) Are you better now ?

ALICE.   He is my son, and he is in uniform.

COSMO (*aware that allowances must be made*). Yes, I know.

ALICE. Are you glad to see your mother, Cosmo ?

COSMO. Rather ! Will you have some tea ?

ALICE. No, no, I feel I can do nothing for the rest of my life but hug my glorious boy.

COSMO. Of course, I have my work.

ALICE. His work ! Do the officers love you, Cosmo ?

COSMO (*degraded*). Love me ! I should think not.

ALICE. I should like to ask them all to come and stay with us.

COSMO (*appalled*). Great Scott, mother, you can't do things like that.

ALICE. Can't I ? Are you very studious, Cosmo ?

COSMO (*neatly*). My favourite authors are William Shakespeare and William Milton. They are grand, don't you think ?

ALICE. I 'm only a woman, you see ; and I 'm afraid they sometimes bore me, especially William Milton.

COSMO (*with relief*). Do they ? Me, too.

ALICE (*on the verge of tears again*). But not half so much as I bore my baby.

COSMO (*anxious to help her*). What did you do to her ?

ALICE (*appealingly*). I couldn't help wanting to hold her in my arms, could I, Cosmo ?

COSMO (*full of consideration*). No, of course you couldn't. (*He reflects.*) How did you take hold of her ?

ALICE. I suppose in some clumsy way.

COSMO. Not like this, was it ?

ALICE (*gloomily*). I dare say.

COSMO. You should have done it this way.

(*He very kindly shows her how to carry a baby.*)

ALICE (*with becoming humility*). Thank you, Cosmo.

(*He does not observe the gleam in her eye, and is in the high good-humour that comes to any man when any woman asks him to show her how to do anything.*)

COSMO. If you like I 'll show you with a cushion. You see this (*scoops it up*) is wrong ; but this (*he does a little sleight of hand*) is right. Another way is this, with their head hanging over your shoulder, and you holding on firmly to their legs. You wouldn't think it was comfortable, but they like it.

ALICE (*adoring him*).   I see, Cosmo.   (*She practises diligently with the cushion.*)   First this way—then this.

COSMO.   That's first-class.   It's just a knack.   You'll soon pick it up.

ALICE (*practising on him instead of the cushion*).   You darling boy !

COSMO.   I think I hear a boy calling the evening papers.

ALICE (*clinging to him*).   Don't go.   There can be nothing in the evening papers about what my boy thinks of his mother.

COSMO.   Good lord, no.   (*He thinks quickly.*)   You haven't seen Amy yet.   It isn't fair of Amy.   She should have been here to take some of it off me.

ALICE.   Cosmo, you don't mean that I bore you too !

(*He is pained.   It is now he who boldly encircles her.   But his words, though well meant, are not so happy as his action.*)

COSMO.   I love you, mother ; and *I* don't think you're so yellow.

ALICE (*the belle of many stations*).   Yellow ?   (*Her brain reels.*)   Cosmo, do you think me plain ?

COSMO (*gallantly*).   No, I don't.   I'm not one of the kind who judge people by their looks.   The soul, you know, is what I judge them by.

ALICE.   Plain ?   Me !

COSMO (*the comforter*).   Of course it's all right for girls to bother about being pretty.   (*He lures her away from the subject.*) I can tell you a funny thing about that.   We had theatricals at Osborne one night, and we played a thing called 'The Royal Boots.'

ALICE (*clapping her hands*).   *I* played in that, too, last year.

COSMO.   You ?

ALICE.   Yes.   Why shouldn't I ?

COSMO.   But we did it for fun.

ALICE.   So did we.

COSMO (*his views on the universe crumbling*).   You still like fun ?

ALICE.   Take care, Cosmo.

COSMO.   But you're our mother.

ALICE.   Mustn't mothers have fun ?

COSMO (*heavily*).   Must they ?   I see.   You had played the dowager.

ALICE. No, I didn't. I played the girl in the Wellington boots.

COSMO (*blinking*). Mother, *I* played the girl in the Wellington boots.

ALICE (*happily*). My son——this ought to bring us closer together.

COSMO (*who has not yet learned to leave well alone*). But the reason I did it was that we were all boys. Were there no young ladies where you did it, mother?

ALICE. Cosmo.

(*She is not a tamed mother yet, and in sudden wrath she flips his face with her hand. He accepts it as a smack. The* COLONEL *foolishly chooses this moment to make his return. He is in high good-humour, and does not observe that two of his nearest relatives are glaring at each other.*)

COLONEL (*purring offensively*). It's all right now, Alice; she took to me at once.

ALICE (*tartly*). Oh, did she!

COLONEL. Gurgled at me—pulled my moustache.

ALICE. I hope you got on with our dear son as well.

COLONEL. Isn't he a fine fellow?

ALICE. *I* have just been smacking his face.

(*She sits down and weeps, while her son stands haughtily at attention.*)

COLONEL (*with a groan*). Hst, I think you had better go and get that evening paper.

(COSMO *departs with his flag flying, and the bewildered husband seeks enlightenment.*)

Smacked his face. But why, Alice?

ALICE. He infuriated me.

COLONEL. He seems such a good boy.

ALICE (*the lowly*). No doubt he is. It must be very trying to have me for a mother.

COLONEL. Perhaps you were too demonstrative?

ALICE. I dare say. A woman he doesn't know! No wonder I disgusted him.

COLONEL. I can't make it out.

ALICE (*abjectly*). It's quite simple. He saw through me at once; so did baby.

(*The* COLONEL *flings up his hands. He hears whisperings outside the door. He peeps and returns excitedly.*)

COLONEL. Alice, there 's a girl there with Cosmo.

ALICE (*on her feet, with a cry*). Amy!

COLONEL (*trembling*). I suppose so.

ALICE (*gripping him*). Robert, if *she* doesn't love me I shall die.

COLONEL. She will, she will. (*But he has grown nervous.*) Don't be too demonstrative, dearest.

ALICE. I shall try to be cold. Oh, Amy, love me!

(AMY *comes, her hair up, and is at once in her father's arms. Then she wants to leap into the arms of the mother who craves for her. But* ALICE *is afraid of being too demonstrative, and restrains herself. She presses* AMY's *hands only.*)

ALICE. It is you, Amy. How are you, dear? (*She ventures at last to kiss her.*) It is a great pleasure to your father and me to see you again.

AMY (*damped*). Thank you, mother—— Of course I have been looking forward to this meeting very much also.

ALICE (*shuddering*). It is very sweet of you to say so.

('*Oh, how cold,*' *they are both thinking, while the* COLONEL *regards them uncomfortably.* AMY *turns to him. She knows already that there is safe harbourage there.*)

AMY. Would you have known me, father?

COLONEL. I wonder. She 's not like you, Alice?

ALICE. No. *I* used to be demonstrative, Amy——

AMY (*eagerly*). Were you?

ALICE (*hurriedly*). Oh, I grew out of it long ago.

AMY (*disappointed but sympathetic*). The wear and tear of life.

ALICE (*wincing*). No doubt.

AMY (*making conversation*). You have seen Cosmo?

ALICE. Yes.

AMY (*with pardonable curiosity*). What did you think of him?

ALICE. He—seemed a nice boy——

AMY (*hurt*). And baby?

ALICE. Yes—oh yes.

AMY. Isn't she fat?

ALICE. Is she?

(*The* NURSE's *head intrudes.*)

NURSE. If you please, sir—I think baby wants *you*
again.

(*The* COLONEL'S *face exudes complacency, but he has the
grace to falter.*)

COLONEL. What do you think, Alice?

ALICE (*broken under the blow*). By all means, go.

COLONEL. Won't you come also? Perhaps if I am with
you——

ALICE (*after giving him an annihilating look*). No, I—I had
quite a long time with her.

(*The* COLONEL *tiptoes off to his babe with a countenance of
foolish rapture ; and mother and daughter are alone.*)

AMY (*wishing her father would come back*). You can't have
been very long with baby, mother.

ALICE. Quite long enough.

AMY. Oh. (*Some seconds elapse before she can speak again.*)
You will have some tea, won't you?

ALICE. Thank you, dear. (*They sit down to a chilly meal.*)

AMY (*merely a hostess*). Both milk and sugar?

ALICE (*merely a guest*). No sugar.

AMY. I hope you will like the house, mother.

ALICE. I am sure you have chosen wisely. I see you are
artistic.

AMY. The decoration isn't finished. I haven't quite
decided what this room is to be like yet.

ALICE. One never can tell.

AMY (*making conversation*). Did you notice that there is a
circular drive to the house?

ALICE. No, I didn't notice.

AMY. That would be because the cab filled it ; but you can
see it if you are walking.

ALICE. I shall look out for it. (*Grown desperate*) Amy,
have you nothing more important to say to me?

AMY (*faltering*). You mean—the keys? Here they are ;
all with labels on them. And here are the tradesmen's books.
They are all paid up to Wednesday. (*She sadly lets them go.
They lie disregarded in her mother's lap.*)

ALICE. Is there nothing else?

AMY (*with a flash of pride*). Perhaps you have noticed that
my hair is up?

ALICE.   It so took me aback, Amy, when you came into the room.   How long have you had it up ?

AMY (*with large eyes*).   Not very long.   I—I began only to-day.

ALICE (*imploringly*).   Dear, put it down again.   You are not grown up.

AMY (*almost sternly*).   I feel I am a woman now.

ALICE (*abject*).   A woman—you ?   Am I never to know my daughter as a girl !

AMY.   You were married before you were eighteen.

ALICE.   Ah, but I had no mother.   And even at that age I knew the world.

AMY (*smiling sadly*).   Oh, mother, not so well as I know it.

ALICE (*sharply*).   What can you know of the world ?

AMY (*shuddering*).   More, I hope, mother, than you will ever know.

ALICE (*alarmed*).   My child !   (*Seizing her*) Amy, tell me what you know.

AMY.   Don't ask me, please.   I have sworn not to talk of it.

ALICE.   Sworn ?   To whom ?

AMY.   To another.

(ALICE, *with a sinking, pounces on her daughter's engagement finger ; but it is unadorned.*)

ALICE.   Tell me, Amy, who is that other ?

AMY (*bravely*).   It is our secret.

ALICE.   Amy, I beg you——

AMY (*a heroic figure*).   Dear mother, I am so sorry I must decline.

ALICE.   You defy me !   (*She takes hold of her daughter's shoulders.*)   Amy, you drive me frantic.   If you don't tell me at once I shall insist on your father——   Oh, you——

(*It is not to be denied that she is shaking* AMY *when the* COLONEL *once more intrudes.*)

COLONEL (*aghast*).   Good heavens, Alice, again !   Amy, what does this mean ?

AMY (*as she runs, insulted and in tears, from the room*).   It means, father, that I love *you* very much.

COLONEL (*badgered*).   Won't you explain, Alice ?

ALICE.   Robert, I am in terror about Amy.

COLONEL.   Why ?

ALICE.   Don't ask me, dear——not now——not till I have spoken to her again. (*She clings to her husband.*) Robert, there can't be anything in it ?

COLONEL.   If you mean anything wrong with our girl, there isn't, memsahib.   What great innocent eyes she has !

ALICE (*eagerly*).   Yes, yes, hasn't she, Robert ?

COLONEL.   All 's well with Amy, dear.

ALICE.   Of course it is.   It was silly of me—— My Amy.

COLONEL.   And mine.

ALICE.   But she seems to me hard to understand. (*With her head on his breast*) I begin to feel, Robert, that I should have come back to my children long ago——or I shouldn't have come back at all.

(*The* COLONEL *is endeavouring to soothe her when* STEPHEN ROLLO *is shown in.   He is very young——too young to be a villain, too round-faced ; but he is all the villain we can provide for* AMY.   *His entrance is less ostentatious than it might be if he knew of the rôle that has been assigned to him. He thinks indeed (sometimes with a sigh) that he is a very good young man ; and the* COLONEL *and* ALICE *(without the sigh) think so too.   After warm greetings :)*

STEVE.   Alice, I dare say you wish me at Jericho ; but it 's six months since I saw you, and I couldn't wait till to-morrow.

ALICE (*giving him her cheek*).   I believe there 's some one in this house glad to see me at last ; and you may kiss me for that, Steve.

STEVE (*who has found the cheek wet*).   You are not telling me they don't adore her ?

COLONEL.   I can't understand it.

STEVE.   But by all the little gods of India, you know, every one has always adored Alice.

ALICE (*plaintively*).   That 's why I take it so ill, Steve.

STEVE.   Can I do anything ?   See here, if the house is upside down and you would like to get rid of the Colonel for an hour or two, suppose he dines with me to-night ?   I 'm dying to hear all the news of the Punjaub since I left.

COLONEL (*with an eye on the nursery door*).   No, Steve, I—— the fact is——I have an engagement.

ALICE (*vindictively*).   He means he can't leave the baby.

STEVE.   It has taken to *him* ?

COLONEL (*swaggering*). Enormously.

ALICE (*whimpering*). They all have. He has stolen them from me. He has taken up his permanent residence in the nursery.

COLONEL. Pooh, fiddle-de-dee. I shall probably come round to-night to see you after dinner, Steve, and bring memsahib with me. In the meantime——

ALICE (*whose mind is still misgiving her about* AMY). In the meantime I want to have a word with Steve alone, Robert.

COLONEL. Very good. (*Stealing towards the nursery*) Then I shall pop in here again. How is the tea business prospering in London, Steve? Glad you left India?

STEVE. I don't have half the salary I had in India, but my health is better. How are rupees?

COLONEL. Stop it. (*He is making a doll of his handkerchief for the further subjugation of* MOLLY. *He sees his happy face in a looking-glass and is ashamed of it.*) Alice, I wish it was you they loved.

ALICE (*with withering scorn*). Oh, go back to your baby.

(*As soon as the* COLONEL *has gone she turns anxiously to* STEVE.)

Steve, tell me candidly what you think of my girl.

STEVE. But I have never set eyes on her.

ALICE. Oh, I was hoping you knew her well. She goes sometimes to the Deans and the Rawlings—all our old Indian friends——

STEVE. So do I, but we never happened to be there at the same time. They often speak of her, though.

ALICE. What do they say?

STEVE. They are enthusiastic—an ideal, sweet girl.

ALICE (*relieved*). I'm so glad. Now you can go, Steve.

STEVE. It's odd to think of the belle of the Punjaub as a mother of a big girl.

ALICE. Don't; or I shall begin to think it's absurd myself.

STEVE. Surely the boy felt the spell. (*She shakes her head.*) But the boys always did.

ALICE (*wryly*). They were older boys.

STEVE. I believe I was the only one you never flirted with.

ALICE (*smiling*). No one could flirt with you, Steve.

STEVE (*pondering*). I wonder why. (*The problem has troubled him occasionally for years.*)

ALICE. I wonder.

STEVE. I suppose there 's some sort of want in me.

ALICE. Perhaps that 's it. No, it 's because you were always such a good boy.

STEVE (*wincing*). I don't know. Sometimes when I saw you all flirting I wanted to do it too, but I could never think of how to begin. (*With a sigh*) I feel sure there 's something pleasant about it.

ALICE. You 're a dear old donkey, Steve, but I 'm glad you came, it has made the place seem more like home. All these years I was looking forward to home ; and now I feel that perhaps it is the place I have left behind me.

(*The joyous gurgling of* MOLLY *draws them to the nursery door ; and there they are observed by* AMY *and* GINEVRA *who enter from the hall. The screen is close to the two girls, and they have so often in the last week seen stage figures pop behind screens that, mechanically as it were, they pop behind this one.*)

STEVE (*who little knows that he is now entering on the gay career*). Listen to the infant.

ALICE. Isn't it horrid of Robert to get on with her so well. Steve, say Robert 's a brute.

STEVE (*as he bids her good-afternoon*). Of course he is ; a selfish beast.

ALICE. There 's another kiss to you for saying so. (*The doomed woman presents her cheek again.*)

STEVE. And you 'll come to me after dinner to-night, Alice ? Here, I 'll leave my card, I 'm not half a mile from this street.

ALICE. I mayn't be able to get away. It will depend on whether my silly husband wants to stay with his wretch of a baby. I 'll see you to the door. Steve, you 're *much* nicer than Robert.

(*With these dreadful words she and the libertine go.* AMY *and* GINEVRA *emerge white to the lips ; or, at least, they feel as white as that.*)

AMY (*clinging to the screen for support*). He kissed her.

GINEVRA (*sternly*). He called her Alice.

AMY. She is going to his house to-night. An assignation.

GINEVRA. They will be chambers, Amy—they are always chambers. And *after* dinner, he said—so he's stingy, too. Here is his card : ' Mr. Stephen Rollo.'

AMY. I have heard of him. They said he was a nice man.

GINEVRA. The address is Kensington West. That's the new name for West Kensington.

AMY. My poor father. It would kill him.

GINEVRA (*the master mind*). He must never know.

AMY. Ginevra, what's to be done ?

GINEVRA. Thank heaven, we know exactly what to do. It rests with you to save her.

AMY (*trembling*). You mean I must go—to his chambers ?

GINEVRA (*firmly*). At any cost.

AMY. Evening dress ?

GINEVRA. It is always evening dress. And don't be afraid of his Man, dear ; they always have a Man.

AMY. Oh, Ginevra.

GINEVRA. First try fascination. You remember how they fling back their cloak—like this, dear. If that fails, threaten him. You *must* get back the letters. There are always letters.

AMY. If father should suspect and follow ? They usually do.

GINEVRA. Then you must sacrifice yourself for her. Does my dearest falter ?

AMY (*pressing* GINEVRA's *hand*). I will do my duty. Oh, Ginevra, what things there will be to put in my diary to-night.

ACT II

NIGHT has fallen, and Amy is probably now in her bedroom, fully arrayed for her dreadful mission. She says good-bye to her diary—perhaps for aye. She steals from the house—— But we see none of this. We are transported to a very different scene, which (if one were sufficiently daring) would represent a Man's Chambers at Midnight. There is no really valid excuse for shirking this scene, which is so popular that every theatre has it stowed away in readiness ; it is capable of 'setting' itself should the stage-hands forget to do so.

It should be a handsome, sombre room in oak and dark red, with sinister easy-chairs and couches, great curtains discreetly drawn, a door to enter by, a door to hide by, a carelessly strewn table on which to write a letter reluctantly to dictation, another table exquisitely decorated for supper for two, champagne in an ice-bucket, many rows of books which on close examination will prove to be painted wood (the stage Lotharios not being really reading men). The lamps shed a diffused light, and one of them is slightly odd in construction, because it is for knocking over presently in order to let the lady escape unobserved. Through this room moves occasionally the man's man, sleek, imperturbable, announcing the lady, the lady's husband, the woman friend who is to save them ; he says little, but is responsible for all the arrangements going right ; before the curtain rises he may be conceived trying the lamp and making sure that the lady will not stick in the door.

That is how it ought to be, that is how Amy has seen it several times in the past week ; and now that we come to the grapple we wish we could give you what you want, for you do want it, you have been used to it, and you will feel that you are looking at a strange middle act without it. But Steve cannot have such a room as this, he has only two hundred and fifty pounds a year, including the legacy from his aunt. Besides though he is to be a Lothario (in so far as we can manage it) he is not at present aware of this, and has made none of the necessary arrangements : if one of his lamps is knocked over it will certainly explode ; and there cannot be a secret door without its leading into the adjoining house. (Theatres keep special kinds of architects to design their rooms.) There is indeed a little cupboard where his crockery is kept, and if Amy is careful she might be able to squeeze in there. We cannot even make the hour midnight ; it is eight-thirty, quite late enough for her to be out alone.

Steve has just finished dinner, in his comfortable lodgings. He is not even in evening dress, but he does wear a lounge jacket, which we devoutly hope will give him a rakish air to Amy's eyes. He would undoubtedly have put on evening dress if he had known she was coming. His man, Richardson, is waiting on him. When we wrote that we deliberated a long time. It has an air, and with a little low cunning we could make you think to the very end that Richardson was a male. But if the play is acted and you go to see it, you would be disappointed. Steve, the wretched fellow, never had a Man, and Richardson is only his landlady's slavey, aged about fifteen, and wistful at sight of food. We introduce her gazing at Steve's platter as if it were a fairy tale. Steve has often caught her with this rapt expression on her face, and sometimes, as now, an engaging game ensues.

RICHARDSON (*blinking*). Are you finished, sir ?

(*To those who know the game this means, 'Are you to leave the other chop—the one sitting lonely and lovely beneath the dish-cover ? '*)

STEVE. Yes. (*In the game this is merely a tantaliser.*)

RICHARDSON (*almost sure that he is in the right mood and sending out a feeler.*) Then am I to clear ?

STEVE. No.

(*This is intended to puzzle her, but it is a move he has made so often that she understands its meaning at once.*)

RICHARDSON (*in entranced giggles*). He, he, he !

STEVE (*vacating his seat*). Sit down.

RICHARDSON. Again ?

STEVE. Sit down, and clear the enemy out of that dish.

(*By the enemy he means the other chop : what a name for*

a chop. STEVE *plays the part of butler.   He brings her a plate from the little cupboard.*)
Dinner is served, madam.

RICHARDSON (*who will probably be a great duchess some day*). I don't mind if I does have a snack.   (*She places herself at the table after what she conceives to be the manner of the genteelly gluttonous ; then she quakes a little.*)   If Missis was to catch me. (*She knows that* MISSIS *is probably sitting downstairs with her arms folded, hopeful of the chop for herself.*)

STEVE.   You tuck in and I 'll keep watch.

(*He goes to the door to peer over the banisters ; it is all part of the game.* RICHARDSON *promptly tucks in with horrid relish.*)

RICHARDSON.   What makes you so good to me, sir ?

STEVE.   A gentleman is always good to a lady.

RICHARDSON (*preening*).   A lady ?   Go on.

STEVE.   And when I found that at my dinner hour you were subject to growing pains I remembered my own youth. Potatoes, madam ?

RICHARDSON (*neatly*).   If quite convenient.

(*The kindly young man surveys her for some time in silence while she has various happy adventures.*)

STEVE.   Can I smoke, Richardson ?

RICHARDSON.   Of course you can smoke.   I have often seen you smoking.

STEVE (*little aware of what an evening the sex is to give him*). But have I your permission ?

RICHARDSON.   You 're at your tricks again.

STEVE (*severely*).   Have you forgotten already how I told you a true lady would answer ?

RICHARDSON.   I minds, but it makes me that shy.   (*She has, however, a try at it.*)   Do smoke, Mr. Rollo, I loves the smell of it.

(STEVE *lights his pipe ; no real villain smokes a pipe.*)

STEVE.   Smoking is a blessed companion to a lonely devil like myself.

RICHARDSON.   Yes, sir.   (*Sharply*)   Would you say devil to a real lady, sir ?

(STEVE, *it may be hoped, is properly confused, but here the little idyll of the chop is brought to a close by the tinkle of a bell.* RICHARDSON *springs to attention.*)

That will be the friends you are expecting ?

STEVE.   I was only half expecting them, but I dare say you are right.   Have you finished, Richardson ?

RICHARDSON.   Thereabouts.   Would a real lady lick the bone—in company, I mean ?

STEVE.   You know, I hardly think so.

RICHARDSON.   Then I 'm finished.

STEVE (*disappearing*).   Say I 'll be back in a jiffy.   I need brushing, Richardson.

(RICHARDSON, *no longer in company, is about to hold a last friendly communion with the bone when there is a knock at the door, followed by the entrance of a mysterious lady.   You could never guess who the lady is, so we may admit at once that it is* MISS AMY GREY.   AMY *is in evening dress—her only evening dress—and over it is the cloak, which she is presently to fling back with staggering effect.   Just now her pale face is hiding behind the collar of it, for she is quaking inwardly though strung up to a terrible ordeal.   The room is not as she expected, but she knows that men are cunning.*)

AMY (*frowning*).   Are these Mr. Rollo's chambers ?   The woman told me to knock at this door.

(*She remembers with a certain satisfaction that the woman had looked at her suspiciously.*)

RICHARDSON (*the tray in her hand to give her confidence*). Yes, ma'am.   He will be down in a minute, ma'am.   He is expecting you, ma'am.

(*Expecting her, is he !* AMY *smiles the bitter smile of knowledge.*)

AMY.   We shall see.   (*She looks about her.*)   (*Sharply*) Where is his man ?

RICHARDSON (*with the guilt of the chop on her conscience*). What man ?

AMY (*brushing this subterfuge aside*).   His man.   They always have a man.

RICHARDSON (*with spirit*).   He is a man himself.

AMY.   Come, girl ; who waits on him ?

RICHARDSON.   Me.

AMY (*rather daunted*).   No man ?   Very strange.   (*Fortunately she sees the two plates.*)   Stop.   (*Her eyes glisten.*) Two persons have been dining here !   (RICHARDSON *begins to tremble.*) Why do you look so scared ? Was the other a gentleman ?

RICHARDSON. Oh, ma'am.

AMY (*triumphantly*). It was not ! (*But her triumph gives way to bewilderment, for she knows that when she left the house her mother was still in it. Then who can the visitor have been ?*) Why are you trying to hide that plate ? Was it a lady ? Girl, tell me was it a lady ?

RICHARDSON (*at bay*). He—he calls her a lady.

AMY (*the omniscient*). But you know better !

RICHARDSON. Of course I know she ain't a real lady.

AMY. Another woman. And not even a lady. (*She has no mercy on the witness.*) Tell me, is this the first time she has dined here ?

RICHARDSON (*fixed by* AMY's *eye*). No, ma'am—I meant no harm, ma'am.

AMY. I am not blaming *you.* Can you remember how often she has dined here ?

RICHARDSON. Well can I remember. Three times last week.

AMY. Three times in one week ! Monstrous.

RICHARDSON (*with her gown to her eyes*). Yes, ma'am ; I see it now.

AMY (*considering and pouncing*). Do you think she is an adventuress ?

RICHARDSON. What 's that ?

AMY. Does she smoke cigarettes ?

RICHARDSON (*rather spiritedly*). No, she don't.

AMY (*taken aback*). Not an adventuress.

> (*She wishes* GINEVRA *were here to help her. She draws upon her stock of knowledge.*)

Can she be secretly married to him ? A wife of the past turned up to blackmail him ? That 's very common.

RICHARDSON. Oh, ma'am, you are terrifying me.

AMY. I wasn't talking to you. You may go. Stop. How long had she been here before I came ?

RICHARDSON. She—Her what you are speaking about——

AMY. Come, I must know. (*The terrible admission refuses to pass* RICHARDSON's *lips, and of a sudden* AMY *has a dark suspicion.*) Has she gone ? Is she here now ?

RICHARDSON.   It was just a chop.   What makes you so grudging of a chop ?

AMY.   I don't care what they ate.   Has she gone ?

RICHARDSON.   Oh, ma'am.

(The little maid, bearing the dishes, backs to the door, opens it with her foot, and escapes from this terrible visitor.   The drawn curtains attracts AMY'S *eagle eye, and she looks behind them.   There is no one there.   She pulls open the door of the cupboard and says firmly, ' Come out.'   No one comes.   She peeps into the cupboard and finds it empty.   A cupboard and no one in it.   How strange.   She sits down almost in tears, wishing very much for the counsel of* GINEVRA.   *Thus* STEVE *finds her when he returns.)*

STEVE.   I 'm awfully glad, Alice, that you——

(He stops abruptly at sight of a strange lady.   As for AMY, *the word ' Alice ' brings her to her feet.)*

AMY.   Sir.   *(A short remark but withering.)*

STEVE.   I beg your pardon.   I thought—the fact is that I expected—— You see you are a stranger to me—my name is Rollo—you are not calling on me, are you ?   (AMY *inclines her head in a way that* GINEVRA *and she have practised.   Then she flings back her cloak as suddenly as an expert may open an umbrella.   Having done this she awaits results.* STEVE, *however, has no knowledge of how to play his part ; he probably favours musical comedy.   He says lamely :)*   I still think there must be some mistake.

AMY *(in italics)*.   There is no mistake.

STEVE.   Then is there anything I can do for you ?

AMY *(ardently)*.   You can do so much.

STEVE.   Perhaps if you will sit down——

*(AMY *decides to humour him so far.   She would like to sit in the lovely stage way, when they know so precisely where the chair is that they can sit without a glance at it.   But she dare not, though* GINEVRA *would have risked it.* STEVE *is emboldened to say :)*

By the way, you have not told me *your* name.

AMY *(nervously)*.   If you please, do you mind my not telling it ?

STEVE.   Oh, very well.   *(First he thinks there is something innocent about her request, and then he wonders if ' innocent ' is the right word.*)   Well, your business, please ? (*he demands, like the man of the world he hopes some day to be*).

AMY.   Why are you not in evening dress ?

STEVE (*taken aback*).   Does that matter ?

AMY (*though it still worries her*).   I suppose not.

STEVE (*with growing stiffness*).   Your business, if you will be so good ?

> (AMY *advances upon him.   She has been seated in any case as long as they ever do sit on the stage on the same chair.*)

AMY.   Stephen Rollo, the game is up.

> (*She likes this ; she will be able to go on now.*)

STEVE (*recoiling guiltily, or so she will describe it to* GINEVRA). What on earth——

AMY (*suffering from a determination from the mouth of phrases she has collected in five theatres*).   A chance discovery, Mr. Stephen Rollo, has betrayed your secret to me.

STEVE (*awed*).   My secret ?   What is it ? (*He rushes rapidly through a well-spent youth.*)

AMY (*risking a good deal*).   It is this : that woman is your wife.

STEVE.   What woman ?

AMY.   The woman who dined with you here this evening.

STEVE.   With me ?

AMY (*icily*).   This is useless ; as I have already said, the game is up.

STEVE (*glancing in a mirror to make sure he is still the same person*).   You *look* a nice girl, but dash it all !   Whom can you be taking me for ?   Tell me some more about myself.

AMY.   Please desist.   I know everything, and in a way I am sorry for you.   All these years you have kept the marriage a secret, for she is a horrid sort of woman, and now she has come back to blackmail you.   That, however, is not my affair.

STEVE (*with unexpected power of irony*).   Oh, I wouldn't say that.

AMY.   I do say it, Mr. Stephen Rollo.   I shall keep your secret——

STEVE.   Ought you ?

AMY.   ——on one condition, and on one condition only, that you return me the letters.

STEVE.   The letters ?

AMY.   The letters.

(STEVE *walks the length of his room, regarding her sideways.*)

STEVE.   Look here, honestly I don't know what you are talking about. You know, I could be angry with you, but I feel sure you are sincere.

AMY.   Indeed I am.

STEVE.   Well, then, I assure you on my word of honour that no lady was dining with me this evening, and that I have no wife.

AMY (*blankly*).   No wife ! You are sure ? Oh, think !

STEVE.   I swear it.

AMY.   I am very sorry. (*She sinks dispiritedly into a chair.*)

STEVE.   Sorry I have no wife ? (*She nods through her tears.*) Don't cry. How could my having a wife be a boon to you ?

AMY (*plaintively*).   It would have put you in the hollow of my hands.

STEVE (*idiotically*).   And they are nice hands, too.

AMY (*with a consciousness that he might once upon a time have been saved by a good woman*).   I suppose that is how you got round her.

STEVE (*stamping his foot*).   Haven't I told you that she doesn't exist ?

AMY.   I don't mean her—I mean her——

(*He decides that she is a little crazy.*)

STEVE (*soothingly*).   Come now, we won't go into that again. It was just a mistake ; and now that it is all settled and done with, I 'll tell you what we shall do. You will let me get you a cab—— (*She shakes her head.*)   I promise not to listen to the address ; and after you have had a good night you—you will see things differently.

AMY (*ashamed of her momentary weakness, and deciding not to enter it in the diary*).   You are very clever, Mr. Stephen Rollo, but I don't leave this house without the letters.

STEVE (*groaning*).   Are they your letters ?

AMY.   How dare you ! They are the letters written to you, as you well know, by——

STEVE (*eagerly*).   Yes ?

AMY.   —by a certain lady. Spare me the pain, if you are a gentleman, of having to mention her name.

STEVE (*sulkily*).   Oh, all right.

AMY.   She is to pass out of your life to-night.   To-morrow you go abroad for a long time.

STEVE (*with excusable warmth*).   Oh, do I !   Where am I going ?

AMY.   We thought——

STEVE.   We ?

AMY.   A friend and I who have been talking it over.   We thought of Africa—to shoot big game.

STEVE (*humouring her*).   You must be very fond of this lady.

AMY.   I would die for her.

STEVE (*feeling that he ought really to stick up a little for himself*).   After all, am I so dreadful ?   Why shouldn't she love me ?

AMY.   A married woman !

STEVE (*gratified*).   Married ?

AMY.   How can you play with me so, sir ?   She is my mother.

STEVE.   Your mother ?   Fond of me !

AMY.   How dare you look pleased !

STEVE.   I 'm not—I didn't mean to.   I say, I wish you would tell me who you are.

AMY.   As if you didn't know.

STEVE (*in a dream*).   Fond of me !   I can't believe it. (*Rather wistfully*) How could she be ?

AMY.   It was all your fault.   Such men as you—pitiless men—you made her love you.

STEVE (*still elated*).   Do you think I am that kind of man ?

AMY.   Oh, sir, let her go.   You are strong and she is weak. Think of her poor husband, and give me back the letters.

STEVE.   On my word of honour——   (*Here arrives* RICHARDSON, *so anxious to come that she is propelled into the room like a ball.*)   What is it ?

RICHARDSON.   A gentleman downstairs, sir, wanting to see you.

AMY (*saying the right thing at once*).   He must not find me here.   My reputation——

STEVE.   I can guess who it is.   Let me think.   (*He is really glad of the interruption.*)   See here, I 'll keep him downstairs for a moment.   Richardson, take this lady to the upper landing until I have brought him in.   Then show her out.

RICHARDSON.   Oh, lor' !

AMY (*rooting herself to the floor*).   The letters !

STEVE (*as he goes*).   Write to me, write to me.   I must know more of this.

RICHARDSON.   Come quick, miss.

AMY (*fixing her*).   You are not deceiving me ?   You are sure it isn't a lady ?

RICHARDSON.   Yes, miss—he said his name was Colonel Grey.

> (GINEVRA *would have known that it must be the husband, but for the moment* AMY *is appalled.*)

AMY (*quivering*).   Can he suspect !

RICHARDSON (*who has her own troubles*).   About the chop ?

AMY.   If she should come while he is here !

RICHARDSON.   Come along, miss.   What 's the matter ?

AMY.   I can't go away.   I am not going.

> (*She darts into the cupboard.   It is as if she had heard* GINEVRA *cry, '* Amy, the cupboard.*'*)

RICHARDSON (*tugging at the closed door*).   Come out of that. I promised to put you on the upper landing.   You can't go hiding in there, lady.

AMY (*peeping out*).   I can and I will.   Let go the door.   I came here expecting to have to hide.

> (*She closes the door as her father enters with* STEVE.   *The* COLONEL *is chatting, but his host sees that* RICHARDSON *is in distress.*)

STEVE (*who thinks that the lady has been got rid of*).   What is it ?

RICHARDSON.   Would you speak with me a minute, sir ?

STEVE (*pointedly*).   Go away.   You have some work to do on the stair.   Go and do it.   I 'm sorry, Colonel, that you didn't bring Alice with you.

COLONEL.   She is coming on later.

STEVE.   Good.

COLONEL.   I have come from Pall Mall.   Wanted to look in at the club once more, so I had a chop there.

RICHARDSON (*with the old sinking*).   A chop !

> (*She departs with her worst suspicions confirmed.*)

STEVE (*as they pull their chairs nearer to the fire*).   Is Alice coming on from home ?

COLONEL.   Yes, that 's it.   (*He stretches out his legs.*)

Steve, home is the best club in the world.   Such jolly fellows all the members !

STEVE.   You haven't come here to talk about your confounded baby again, have you ?

COLONEL (*apologetically*).   If you don't mind.

STEVE.   I do mind.

COLONEL.   But if you feel you can stand it.

STEVE.   You are my guest, so go ahead.

COLONEL.   She fell asleep, Steve, holding my finger.

STEVE.   Which finger ?

COLONEL.   This one.   As Alice would say, ' Soldiering done, baby begun.'

STEVE.   Poor old chap.

COLONEL.   I have been through a good deal in my time, Steve, but that is the biggest thing I have ever done.

STEVE.   Have a cigar ?

COLONEL.   Brute !   Thanks.

(*Here* AMY, *who cannot hear when the door is closed, opens it slightly.   The* COLONEL *is presently aware that* STEVE *is silently smiling to himself.   The* COLONEL *makes a happy guess.*)

Thinking of the ladies, Steve ?

STEVE (*blandly*).   To tell the truth, I *was* thinking of one.

COLONEL.   She seems to be a nice girl.

STEVE.   She is not exactly a girl.

COLONEL (*twinkling*).   Very fond of you, Steve ?

STEVE.   I have the best of reasons for knowing that she is. (*We may conceive* AMY'S *feelings though we cannot see her.*)   On my soul, Colonel, I think it is the most romantic affair I ever heard of.   I have waited long for a romance to come into my life, but by Javers, it has come at last.

COLONEL.   Graters, Steve.   Does her family like it ?

STEVE (*cheerily*).   No, they are furious.

COLONEL.   But why ?

STEVE (*judiciously*).   A woman's secret, Colonel.

COLONEL.   Ah, the plot thickens.   Do I know her ?

STEVE.   Not you.

COLONEL.   I mustn't ask her name ?

STEVE (*with presence of mind*).   I have a very good reason for not telling you her name.

COLONEL. So? And she is not exactly young? Twice your age, Steve?

STEVE (*with excusable heat*). Not at all. But she is of the age when a woman knows her own mind—which makes the whole affair extraordinarily flattering. (*With undoubtedly a shudder of disgust* AMY *closes the cupboard door.* STEVE *continues to behave in the most gallant manner.*) You must not quiz me, Colonel, for her circumstances are such that her partiality for me puts her in a dangerous position, and I would go to the stake rather than give her away.

COLONEL. Quite so.

(*He makes obeisance to the beauty of the sentiment, and then proceeds to an examination of the hearthrug.*)

STEVE. What are you doing?

COLONEL. Trying to find out for myself whether she comes here.

STEVE. How can you find that out by crawling about my carpet?

COLONEL. I am looking for hairpins—(*triumphantly holding up a lady's glove*)—and I have found one!

(*They have been too engrossed to hear the bell ring, but now voices are audible.*)

STEVE. There is some one coming up.

COLONEL. Perhaps it is *she*, Steve! No, that is Alice's voice. Catch, you scoundrel (*and he tosses him the glove.* ALICE *is shown in, and is warmly acclaimed. She would not feel so much at ease if she knew who, hand on heart, has recognised her through the pantry keyhole*).

STEVE (*as he makes* ALICE *comfortable by the fire*). How did you leave them at home?

ALICE (*relapsing into gloom*). All hating me.

STEVE. This man says that home is the most delightful club in the world.

ALICE. I am not a member; I have been blackballed by my own baby. Robert, I dined in state with Cosmo, and he was so sulky that he ate his fish without salt rather than ask me to pass it.

COLONEL. Where was Amy?

ALICE. Amy said she had a headache and went to bed. I spoke to her through the door before I came out, but she wouldn't answer.

COLONEL.　Why didn't you go in, memsahib?

ALICE.　I did venture to think of it, but she had locked the door. Robert, I really am worried about Amy. She seems to me to behave oddly. There can't be anything wrong?

COLONEL.　Of course not, Alice—eh, Steve?

STEVE.　Bless you, no.

ALICE (*smiling*).　It's much Steve knows about women.

STEVE.　I'm not so unattractive to women, Alice, as you think.

ALICE.　Listen to him, Robert!

COLONEL.　What he means, my dear, is that you should see him with elderly ladies.

ALICE.　Steve, this to people who know you.

(*Here something happens to* AMY'S *skirt. She has opened the door to hear, then in alarm shut it, leaving a fragment of skirt caught in the door. There, unseen, it bides its time.*)

STEVE (*darkly*).　Don't be so sure you know me, Alice.

COLONEL (*enjoying himself*).　Let us tell her, Steve! I am dying to tell her.

STEVE (*grandly*).　No, no.

COLONEL.　We mustn't tell you, Alice, because it is a woman's secret—a poor little fond elderly woman. Our friend is very proud of his conquest. See how he is ruffling his feathers. I shouldn't wonder, you know, though you and I are in the way to-night.

(*But* ALICE'S *attention is directed in another direction: to a little white object struggling in the clutches of a closed door at the back of the room.* STEVE *turns to see what she is looking at, and at the same moment the door opens sufficiently to allow a pretty hand to obtrude, seize the kitten, or whatever it was, and softly reclose the door. For one second* ALICE *did think it might be a kitten, but she knows now that it is part of a woman's dress. As for* STEVE *thus suddenly acquainted with his recent visitor's whereabouts, his mouth opens wider than the door. He appeals mutely to* ALICE *not to betray his strange secret to the* COLONEL.)

ALICE (*with dancing eyes*).　May I look about me, Steve? I have been neglecting your room shamefully.

STEVE (*alarmed, for he knows the woman*).　Don't get up, Alice; there is really nothing to see.

(But she is already making the journey of the room, and drawing nearer to the door.)

ALICE *(playing with him).*   I like your clock.

STEVE.   It is my landlady's.   Nearly all the things are hers. Do come back to the fire.

ALICE.   Don't mind me.   What does this door lead into ?

STEVE.   Only a cupboard.

ALICE.   What do you keep in it ?

STEVE.   Merely crockery—that sort of thing.

ALICE.   I should like to see your crockery, Steve.   Not one little bit of china ?   May I peep in ?

COLONEL *(who is placidly smoking, with his back to the scene of the drama).*   Don't mind her, Steve ; she never could see a door without itching to open it.

(ALICE opens the door, and sees AMY standing there with her finger to her lips, just as they stood in all the five plays. GINEVRA could not have posed her better.)

Well, have you found anything, memsahib ?

(It has been the great shock of ALICE's life, and she sways. But she shuts the door before answering him.)

ALICE *(with a terrible look at STEVE).*   Just a dark little cupboard.

(STEVE, not aware that it is her daughter who is in there, wonders why the lighter aspect of the incident has ceased so suddenly to strike her.   She returns to the fire, but not to her chair.   She puts her arms round the neck of her husband ; a great grief for him is welling up in her breast.)

COLONEL *(so long used to her dear impulsive ways).*   Hullo ! We mustn't let on that we are fond of each other before company.

STEVE *(meaning well, though he had better have held his tongue).* I don't count ;   I am such an old friend.

ALICE *(slowly).*   Such an old friend !

(Her husband sees that she is struggling with some emotion.)

COLONEL.   Worrying about the children still, Alice ?

ALICE *(glad to break down openly).*   Yes, yes, I can't help it, Robert.

COLONEL *(petting her)*   There, there, you foolish woman.

Joy will come in the morning ; I never was surer of anything. Would you like me to take you home now ?

ALICE.   Home.   But, yes, I—let us go home.

COLONEL.   Can we have a cab, Steve ?

STEVE.   I 'll go down and whistle one.   Alice, I 'm awfully sorry that you—that I——

ALICE.   Please, a cab.

(*But though she is alone with her husband now she does not know what she wants to say to him.   She has a passionate desire that he should not learn who is behind that door.*)

COLONEL (*pulling her toward him*).   I think it is about Amy that you worry most.

ALICE.   Why should I, Robert ?

COLONEL.   Not a jot of reason.

ALICE.   Say again, Robert, that everything is sure to come right just as we planned it would.

COLONEL.   Of course it will.

ALICE.   Robert, there is something I want to tell you. You know how dear my children are to me, but Amy is the dearest of all.   She is dearer to me, Robert, than you yourself.

COLONEL.   Very well, memsahib.

ALICE.   Robert dear, Amy has come to a time in her life when she is neither quite a girl nor quite a woman.   There are dark places before us at that age through which we have to pick our way without much help.   I can conceive dead mothers haunting those places to watch how their child is to fare in them.   Very frightened ghosts, Robert.   I have thought so long of how I was to be within hail of my girl at this time, holding her hand—my Amy, my child.

COLONEL.   That is just how it is all to turn out, my Alice.

ALICE (*shivering*).   Yes, isn't it, isn't it ?

COLONEL.   You dear excitable, of course it is.

ALICE (*like one defying him*).   But even though it were not, though I had come back too late, though my daughter had become a woman without a mother's guidance, though she were a bad woman——

COLONEL.   Alice.

ALICE.   Though some cur of a man—Robert, it wouldn't affect my love for her, I should love her more than ever.   If all

others turned from her, if you turned from her, Robert—how
I should love her then.

COLONEL.   Alice, don't talk of such things.

(*But she continues to talk of them, for she sees that the door
is ajar, and what she says now is really to comfort* AMY.
Every word of it is a kiss for AMY.)

ALICE (*smiling through her fears*).   I was only telling you
that nothing could make any difference in my love for Amy.
That was all ; and, of course, if she has ever been a little foolish,
light-headed—at that age one often is—why, a mother would
soon put all that right ; she would just take her girl in her arms
and they would talk it over, and the poor child's troubles would
vanish.   (*Still for* AMY'S *comfort*) And do you think I should
repeat any of Amy's confidences to you, Robert ?   (*Gaily*) Not
a word, sir !   She might be sure of that.

COLONEL.   A pretty way to treat a father.   But you will
never persuade me that there is any serious flaw in Amy.

ALICE.   I 'll never try, dear.

COLONEL.   As for this little tantrum of locking herself into
her room, however, we must have it out with her.

ALICE.   The first thing to-morrow.

COLONEL.   Not a bit of it.   The first thing the moment we
get home.

ALICE (*now up against a new danger*).   You forget, dear,
that she has gone to bed.

COLONEL.   We 'll soon rout her out of bed.

ALICE.   Robert !   You forget that she has locked the door.

COLONEL.   Sulky little darling.   I dare say she is crying her
eyes out for you already.   But if she doesn't open that door
pretty smartly I 'll force it.

ALICE.   You wouldn't do that ?

COLONEL.   Wouldn't I ?   Oh yes, I would.

(*Thus* ALICE *has another problem to meet when* STEVE
returns from his successful quest for a cab.)

Thank you, Steve, you will excuse us running off, I know.
Alice is all nerves to-night.   Come along, dear.

ALICE (*signing to the puzzled* STEVE *that he must somehow get
the lady out of the house at once*).   There is no such dreadful
hurry, is there ?   (*She is suddenly interested in some photographs
on the wall.*)   Are you in this group, Steve ?

STEVE.   Yes, it is an old school eleven.

ALICE.   Let us see if we can pick Steve out, Robert.

COLONEL.   Here he is, the one with the ball.

ALICE.   Oh no, that can't be Steve, surely.   Isn't this one more like him ?   Come over here under the light.

(STEVE *has his moment at the door, but it is evident from his face that the hidden one scorns his blandishments.   So he signs to* ALICE.)

COLONEL.   This is you, isn't it, Steve ?

STEVE.   Yes, the one with the ball.

COLONEL.   I found you at once.   Now, Alice, your cloak.

ALICE.   I feel so comfy where I am.   One does hate to leave a fire, doesn't one.   (*She hums gaily a snatch of a song.*)

COLONEL.   The woman doesn't know her own mind.

ALICE.   You remember we danced to that once on my birthday at Simla.

(*She shows him how they danced at Simla.*)

COLONEL (*to* STEVE, *who is indeed the more bewildered of the two*).   And a few minutes ago I assure you she was weeping on my shoulder !

ALICE.   You were so nice to me that evening, Robert—I gave you a dance.   (*She whirls him gaily round.*)

COLONEL.   You flibberty-gibbet, you make me dizzy.

ALICE.   Shall we sit out the rest of the dance ?

COLONEL.   Not I.   Come along, you unreasonable thing.

ALICE.   Unreasonable.   Robert, I have a reason.   I want to see whether Amy will come.

COLONEL.   Come ?

STEVE.   Come here ?

ALICE.   I didn't tell you before, Robert, because I had so little hope ; but I called to her through the door that I was coming here to meet you, and I said, ' I don't believe you have a headache, Amy ; I believe you have locked yourself in there because you hate the poor mother who loves you,' and I begged her to come with me.   I said, ' If you won't come now, come after me and make me happy.'

COLONEL.   But what an odd message, Alice ; so unlike you.

ALICE.   Was it ?   I don't know.   I always find it so hard, Robert, to be like myself.

COLONEL.   But, my dear, a young girl.

x

ALICE.   She could have taken a cab ; I gave her the address. Don't be so hard, Robert, I am teaching you to dance.   (*She is off with him again.*)

COLONEL.   Steve, the madcap.

(*He falls into a chair, but sees the room still going round. It is* ALICE'S *chance ; she pounces upon* AMY'S *hand, whirls her out of the hiding-place, and seems to greet her at the other door.*)

ALICE.   Amy !

COLONEL (*jumping up*).   Not really ?   Hullo !   I never for a moment—— It was true, then.   Amy, you are a good little girl to come.

AMY (*to whom this is a not unexpected step in the game*).   Dear father.

STEVE (*to whom it is a very unexpected step indeed*).   Amy ! Is this—your daughter, Alice ?

ALICE (*wondering at the perfidy of the creature*).   I forgot that you don't know her, Steve.

STEVE.   But if—if this is your daughter—you are the mother.

ALICE.   The mother ?

COLONEL (*jovially*).   Well thought out, Steve.   He is a master mind, Alice.

STEVE.   But—but——

(*Mercifully* AMY *has not lost her head.   She is here to save them all.*)

AMY.   Introduce me, father.

COLONEL.   He is astounded at our having such a big girl.

STEVE (*thankfully*).   Yes, that 's it.

COLONEL.   Amy, my old friend, Steve Rollo—Steve, this is our rosebud.

STEVE (*blinking*).   How do you do ?

AMY (*sternly*).   How do you do ?

COLONEL.   But, bless me, Amy, you are a swell.

AMY (*flushing*).   It is only evening dress.

COLONEL.   I bet she didn't dress for us, Alice ; it was all done for Steve.

ALICE.   Yes, for Steve.

COLONEL.   But don't clutch me, chicken, clutch your mother.   Steve, why are you staring at Alice ?

(*We know why he is staring at* ALICE, *but of course he is too gallant a gentleman to tell.   Besides, his astonishment has dazed him.*)

STEVE.   Was I ?

ALICE (*with her arms extended*).   Amy, don't be afraid of me.

AMY (*going into them contemptuously*).   I 'm not.

COLONEL (*badgered*).   Then kiss and make it up.

(AMY *bestows a cold kiss upon her mother.*   ALICE *weeps.*) This is too much.   Just wait till I get you home.   Are you both ready ?

(*It is then that* AMY *makes her first mistake.   The glove that the* COLONEL *has tossed to* STEVE *is lying on a chair, and she innocently begins to put it on.   Her father stares at her ; his wife does not know why.*)

ALICE.   We are ready, Robert.   Why don't you come ? Robert, what is it ?

COLONEL (*darkening*).   Steve knows what it is ; Amy doesn't as yet.   The simple soul has given herself away so innocently that it is almost a shame to take notice of it.   But I must, Steve. Come, man, it can't be difficult to explain.

(*In this* STEVE *evidently differs from him.*)

ALICE.   Robert, you frighten me.

COLONEL.   Still tongue-tied, Steve.   Before you came here, Alice, I found a lady's glove on the floor.

ALICE (*quickly*).   That isn't our affair, Robert.

COLONEL.   Yes ; I 'll tell you why.   Amy has just put on that glove.

ALICE.   It isn't hers, dear.

COLONEL.   Do you deny that it is yours, Amy ?   (AMY *has no answer to this.*)   Is it unreasonable, Steve, to ask you when my daughter, with whom you profess to be unacquainted, gave you that token of her esteem ?

STEVE (*helpless*).   Alice.

COLONEL.   What has Alice to do with it ?

AMY (*to the rescue*).   Nothing, nothing, I swear.

COLONEL.   Has there been something going on that I don't understand ?   Are you in it, Alice, as well as they ?   Why has Steve been staring at you so ?

AMY (*knowing so well that she alone can put this matter right*). Mother, don't answer.

STEVE. If I could see Alice alone for a moment, Colonel——

ALICE. Yes.

COLONEL. No. Good heavens, what are you all concealing? Is Amy—my Amy—your elderly lady, Steve? Was that some tasteful little joke you were playing on your old friend, her father?

STEVE. Colonel, I——

AMY (*preparing for the great sacrifice*). I forbid him to speak.

COLONEL. *You* forbid him.

ALICE. Robert, Robert, let me explain. Steve——

AMY. Mother, you must not, you dare not. (*Grandly*) Let all fall on me. It is not true, father, that Mr. Rollo and I were strangers when you introduced us.

ALICE (*wailing*). Amy, Amy!

AMY (*with a touch of the sublime*). It *is* my glove, but it had a right to be here. He is my affianced husband.

(*Perhaps, but it is an open question,* STEVE *is the one who is most surprised to hear this. He seems to want to say something on the subject, but a look of entreaty from* ALICE *silences him.*)

COLONEL. Alice, did you hear her?

ALICE. Surely you don't mean, Robert, that you are not glad?

COLONEL (*incredulous*). Is that how *you* take it?

ALICE (*heart-broken*). How I take it! I am overjoyed. Don't you see how splendid it is ; our old friend Steve.

COLONEL (*glaring at him*). Our old friend, Steve.

(*As for* AMY, *that pale-faced lily, for the moment she stands disregarded. Never mind ;* GINEVRA *will yet do her justice.*)

ALICE. Oh, happy day ! (*Brazenly she takes* STEVE'S *two hands.*) Robert, he is to be our son.

COLONEL. You are very clever, Alice, but do you really think I believe that this is no shock to you ? Oh, woman, why has this deception not struck you to the ground ?

ALICE. Deception ? Amy, Steve, I do believe he thinks that this is as much a surprise to me as it is to him ! Why, Robert, I have known about it ever since I saw Amy alone this afternoon.   She told me at once.   Then in came Steve, and he——

COLONEL.   Is it as bad as that?

ALICE.   As what, dear?

COLONEL.   That my wife must lie to me?

ALICE.   Oh, Robert.

COLONEL.   I am groping only, but I can see now that you felt there was something wrong from the first.   How did you find out?

ALICE (*imploringly*).   Robert, they are engaged to be married; it was foolish of them not to tell you; but, oh, my dear, leave it at that.

COLONEL.   Why did you ask Amy to follow us here?

ALICE.   So that we could all be together when we broke it to you, dear.

COLONEL.   Another lie!   My shoulders are broad; why shouldn't I have it to bear as well as you?

ALICE.   There is nothing to bear but just a little folly.

COLONEL.   Folly!   And neither of them able to say a word?

(*Indeed they are very cold lovers;* AMY's *lip is curled at* STEVE.   *To make matters worse, the cupboard door, which has so far had the decency to remain quiet, now presumes to have its say.   It opens of itself a few inches, creaking guiltily.   Three people are so startled that a new suspicion is roused in the fourth.*)

ALICE (*who can read his face so well*).   She wasn't there, Robert, she wasn't.

COLONEL.   My God!   I understand now; she didn't follow us; she hid there when I came.

ALICE.   No, Robert, no.

(*He goes into the cupboard and returns with something in his hand, which he gives to* AMY.)

COLONEL.   Your other glove, Amy.

ALICE.   I can't keep it from you any longer, Robert; I have done my best.   (*She goes to* AMY *to protect her.*)   But Amy is still my child.

('*What a deceiver,*' AMY *is thinking.*)

COLONEL.   Well, sir, still waiting for that interview with my wife before you can say anything?

STEVE (*a desperate fellow*).   Yes.

ALICE.   You will have every opportunity of explaining, Steve, many opportunities ; but in the meantime—just now, please go, leave us alone. (*Stamping her foot*) Go, please.

(STEVE *has had such an evening of it that he clings dizzily to the one amazing explanation, that* ALICE *loves him not wisely but too well. Never will he betray her, never.*)

STEVE (*with a meaning that is lost on her but is very evident to the other lady present*).   Anything *you* ask me to do, Alice, anything.   I shall go upstairs only, so that if you want me——

ALICE.   Oh, go. (*He goes, wondering whether he is a villain or a hero, which is perhaps a pleasurable state of mind.*)

COLONEL.   You are wondrous lenient to him ; I shall have more to say.   As for this girl—look at her standing there, she seems rather proud of herself.

ALICE.   It isn't really hardness, Robert.   It is because she thinks that you are hard.   Robert, dear, I want you to go away too, and leave Amy to me.   Go home, Robert ; we shall follow soon.

COLONEL (*after a long pause*).   If you wish it.

ALICE.   Leave her to her mother.

(*When he has gone* AMY *leans across the top of a chair, sobbing her little heart away.* ALICE *tries to take her— the whole of her—in her arms, but is rebuffed with a shudder.*)

AMY.   I wonder you can touch me.

ALICE.   The more you ask of your mother the more she has to give.   It is my love you need, Amy ; and you can draw upon it, and draw upon it.

AMY.   Pray excuse me.

ALICE.   How can you be so hard !   My child, I am not saying one harsh word to you.   I am asking you only to hide your head upon your mother's breast.

AMY.   I decline.

ALICE.   Take care, Amy, or I shall begin to believe that your father was right.   What do you think would happen if I were to leave you to him !

AMY.   Poor father !

ALICE.   Poor indeed with such a daughter.

AMY.   He has gone, mother ; so do you really think you need keep up this pretence before me ?

ALICE.   Amy, what you need is a whipping.

AMY.   You ought to know what I need.

(*The agonised mother again tries to envelop her unnatural child.*)

ALICE.   Amy, Amy, it was all Steve's fault.

AMY (*struggling as with a boa constrictor*).   You needn't expect me to believe that.

ALICE.   No doubt you thought at the beginning that he was a gallant gentleman.

AMY.   Not at all ; I knew he was depraved from the moment I set eyes on him.

ALICE.   My Amy ! Then how—how——

AMY.   Ginevra knew too.

ALICE.   She knew !

AMY.   We planned it together—to treat him in the same way as Sir Harry Paskill and Ralph Devereux.

ALICE.   Amy, you are not in your senses. You don't mean that there were others ?

AMY.   There was Major—Major—I forget his name, but he was another.

ALICE (*shaking her*).   Wretched girl.

AMY.   Leave go.

ALICE.   How did you get to know them ?

AMY.   To know them ? They are characters in plays.

ALICE (*bereft*).   Characters in plays ? Plays !

AMY.   We went to five last week.

(*Wild hopes spring up in* ALICE'S *breast.*)

ALICE.   Amy, tell me quickly, when did you see Steve for the first time ?

AMY.   When you were saying good-bye to him this afternoon.

ALICE.   Can it be true ?

AMY.   Perhaps we shouldn't have listened ; but they always listen when there is a screen.

ALICE.   Listened ? What did you hear ?

AMY.   Everything, mother ! We saw him kiss you and heard you make an assignation to meet him here.

ALICE.   I 'll whip you directly ; but go on, darling.

AMY (*childishly*) You shan't whip me. (*Then once more heroic*) As in a flash Ginevra and I saw that there was only one way to save you. I must go to his chambers, and force him to return the letters.

ALICE (*inspired*). My letters?

AMY. Of course. He behaved at first as they all do—pretended that he did not know what I was talking about. At that moment, a visitor; I knew at once that it must be the husband; it always is, it was; I hid. Again a visitor. I knew it must be you, it was; oh, the agony to me in there. I was wondering when he would begin to suspect, for I knew the time would come, and I stood ready to emerge and sacrifice myself to save you.

ALICE. As you have done, Amy?

AMY. As I have done.

(*Once more the arms go round her.*)

I want none of that.

ALICE. Forgive me. (*A thought comes to* ALICE *that enthralls her.*) Steve! Does he know what you think—about me?

AMY. I had to be open with him.

ALICE. And Steve believes it? He thinks that I—I—Alice Grey—oh, ecstasy!

AMY. You need not pretend.

ALICE. What is to be done?

AMY. Though I abhor him I must marry him for aye. Ginevra is to be my only bridesmaid. We are both to wear black.

ALICE (*sharply*). You are sure you don't rather like him, Amy?

AMY. Mother!

ALICE. Amy, weren't you terrified to come alone to the rooms of a man you didn't even know? Some men——

AMY. I was not afraid. I am a soldier's daughter; and Ginevra gave me this.

(*She produces a tiny dagger. This is altogether too much for* ALICE.)

ALICE. My darling!

(*She does have the babe in her arms at last, and now* AMY *clings to her. This is very sweet to* ALICE; *but she knows*

that if she tells AMY *the truth at once its first effect will be to*
make the dear one feel ridiculous.　How can ALICE *hurt*
her AMY *so,* AMY *who has such pride in having saved her ?)*
You do love me a little, Amy, don't you ?

AMY.　Yes, yes.

ALICE.　You don't think I have been really bad, dear ?

AMY.　Oh, no, only foolish.

ALICE.　Thank you, Amy.

AMY (*nestling still closer*).　What are we to do now, dear
dear mother ?

　　(ALICE *has a happy idea ; but that, as the novelists say,*
　　　deserves a chapter to itself.)

ACT III

We are back in the room of the diary. The diary itself is not visible ; it is tucked away in the drawer, taking a nap while it may, for it has much to chronicle before cockcrow. Cosmo also is asleep, on an ingenious arrangement of chairs. Ginevra is sitting bolt upright, a book on her knee, but she is not reading it. She is seeing visions in which Amy plays a desperate part. The hour is late ; every one ought to be in bed.

Cosmo is perhaps dreaming that he is back at Osborne, for he calls out, as if in answer to a summons, that he is up and nearly dressed. He then raises his head and surveys Ginevra.

COSMO. Hullo, you 've been asleep.

GINEVRA. How like a man.

COSMO. I say, I thought you were the one who had stretched herself out, and that I was sitting here very quiet, so as not to waken you.

GINEVRA. Let us leave it at that.

COSMO. Huffy, aren't you ! Have they not come back yet ?

GINEVRA. Not they. And half-past eleven has struck. I oughtn't to stay any longer ; as it is, I don't know what my landlady will say.

(*She means that she does know.*)

COSMO. I 'll see you to your place whenever you like. My uniform will make it all right for you.

GINEVRA. You child. But I simply can't go till I know what has happened. Where, oh where, can they be ?

COSMO. That 's all right. Father told you he had a message from mother saying that they had gone to the theatre.

GINEVRA. But why ?

COSMO. Yes, it seemed to bother him, too.

GINEVRA. The theatre. That is what she *said*.

(*Here* COSMO *takes up a commanding position on the hearth-*

*rug ; it could not be bettered unless with a cigar in the
mouth.*)

COSMO. Look here, Miss Dunbar, it may be that I have a
little crow to pick with mother when she comes back, but I
cannot allow any one else to say a word against her. *Comprenez ?*

(GINEVRA'S *reply is lost to the world because at this moment
AMY'S sparkling eyes show round the door. How softly she
must have crossed the little hall !*)

GINEVRA. Amy, at last !

AMY. Sh ! (*She speaks to some one unseen*) There are only
Ginevra and Cosmo here.

(*Thus encouraged* ALICE *enters. Despite her demeanour
they would see, if they knew her better, that she has been
having a good time, and is in hopes that it is not ended yet.
She comes in, as it were, under* AMY'S *guidance.* GINEVRA
is introduced, and ALICE *then looks to* AMY *for instructions
what to do next.*

AMY (*encouragingly*). Sit down, mother.

ALICE. Where shall I sit, dear ? (AMY *gives her the nicest
chair in the room.*) Thank you, Amy. (*She is emboldened to
address her son.*) Where is your father, Cosmo ?

(COSMO *remembers his slap, and that he has sworn to converse with her no more. He indicates, however, that his
father is in the room overhead.* ALICE *meekly accepts the
rebuff.*

Shall I go to him, Amy ?

AMY (*considerately*). If you think you feel strong enough,
mother.

ALICE. You have given me strength.

AMY. I am so glad. (*She strokes her mother soothingly.*)
What will you tell him ?

ALICE. All, Amy—all, all.

AMY. Brave mother.

ALICE. Who could not be brave with such a daughter ! (*On
reflection*) And with such a son !

(*Helped by encouraging words from* AMY *she departs on her
perilous enterprise. The two conspirators would now give
a handsome competence to* COSMO *to get him out of the room.
He knows it, and sits down.*)

COSMO.   I say, what is she going to tell father?

AMY (*with a despairing glance at* GINEVRA).   Oh, nothing.

GINEVRA (*with a clever glance at* AMY).   Cosmo, you promised to see me home.

COSMO (*the polite*).   Right-o!

GINEVRA.   But you haven't got your boots on.

COSMO.   I won't be a minute.   (*He pauses at the door.*)   I say, I believe you 're trying to get rid of me.   Look here, I won't budge till you tell me what mother is speaking about to father.

AMY.   It is about the drawing-room curtains.

COSMO.   Good lord!

(*As soon as he has gone they rush at each other; they don't embrace; they stop when their noses are an inch apart, and then talk.   This is the stage way for lovers.   It is difficult to accomplish without rubbing noses, but they have both been practising.*)

GINEVRA.   Quick, Amy, did you get the letters?

AMY.   There are no letters.

(GINEVRA *is so taken aback that her nose bobs.   Otherwise the two are absolutely motionless.   She cleverly recovers herself.*)

GINEVRA.   No letters; how unlike life.   You are quite sure?

AMY.   I have my mother's word for it.

GINEVRA.   Is that enough?

AMY.   And you now have mine.

GINEVRA.   Then it hadn't gone far?

AMY.   No, merely a painful indiscretion.   But if father had known it—you know what husbands are.

GINEVRA.   Yes, indeed.   Did he follow her?   (AMY *nods.*) Did you hide?   (AMY *nods again.*)

AMY.   Worse than that, Ginevra.   To deceive him I had to pretend that I was the woman.   And now—Ginevra, can you guess——?

(*Here they have to leave off doing noses.   On the stage it can be done for ever so much longer, but only by those who are paid accordingly.*)

GINEVRA.   You don't mean——?

AMY.   I think I do, but what do you mean?

GINEVRA.   I mean—the great thing.

AMY.   Then it is, yes.   Ginevra, I am affianced to the man, Steve !

(GINEVRA *could here quickly drink a glass of water if there was one in the room.*)

GINEVRA (*wandering round her old friend*).   You seem the same, Amy, yet somehow different.

AMY (*rather complacently*).   That is just how I feel.   But I must not think of myself.   They are overhead, Ginevra. There is an awful scene taking place—up there.   She is telling father all.

GINEVRA.   Confessing ?

AMY.   Everything—in a noble attempt to save me from a widowed marriage.

GINEVRA.   But I thought she was such a hard woman.

AMY.   Not really.   To the world perhaps ; but I have softened her.   All she needed, Ginevra, to bring out her finer qualities was a strong nature to lean upon ; and she says that she has found it in me.   At the theatre and all the way home——

GINEVRA.   Then you did go to the theatre.   Why ?

AMY (*feeling that* GINEVRA *is very young*).   Need you ask ? Oh, Ginevra, to see if we could find a happy ending.   It was mother's idea.

GINEVRA.   Which theatre ?

AMY.   I don't know, but the erring wife confessed all—in one of those mousselines-de-soie that are so fashionable this year ; and mother and I sat—clasping each other's hands, praying it might end happily, though we didn't see how it could.

GINEVRA.   How awful for you.   What did the husband do ?

AMY.   He was very calm and white.   He went out of the room for a moment, and came back so white.   Then he sat down by the fire, and nodded his head three times.

GINEVRA.   I think I know now which theatre it was.

AMY.   He asked her coldly—but always the perfect gentle-man——

GINEVRA.   Oh, that theatre !

AMY.   He asked her whether *he* was to go or she.

GINEVRA.   They must part ?

AMY.   Yes.   She went on her knees to him, and said, ' Are we never to meet again ? ' and he replied huskily, ' Never.' Then she turned and went slowly towards the door.

GINEVRA (*clutching her*). Amy, was that the end ?

AMY. The audience sat still as death, listening for the awful *click* that brings the curtain down.

GINEVRA (*shivering*). I seem to hear it.

AMY. At that moment——

GINEVRA. Yes, yes ?

AMY. The door opened, and, Ginevra, their little child— came in—in her night-gown.

GINEVRA. Quick.

AMY. She came toddling down the stairs—she was bare- footed—she took in the whole situation at a glance—and, run- ning to her father, she said, ' Daddy, if mother goes away what is to become of me ? ' (AMY *gulps and continues.*) And then she took a hand of each and drew them together till they fell on each other's breasts, and then—oh, Ginevra, then—click ! —and the curtain fell.

GINEVRA (*when they are more composed*). How old was the child ?

AMY. Five. She looked more.

GINEVRA (*her brows knitted*). Molly is under two, isn't she ?

AMY. She is not quite twenty months.

GINEVRA. She couldn't possibly do it.

AMY. No ; I thought of that. But she couldn't, you know, even though she was held up. Mother couldn't help thinking the scene was a good omen, though. (*They both look at the ceiling again.*) How still they are.

GINEVRA. Perhaps she hasn't had the courage to tell.

AMY. If so, I must go on with it.

GINEVRA (*feeling rather small beside* AMY). Marry him ?

AMY. Yes. I must dree my weird. Is it dree your weird, or weird your dree ?

GINEVRA. I think they both do. (*She does not really care ; nobler thoughts are surging within her.*) Amy, why can't I make some sacrifice as well as you ?

(AMY *seems about to make a somewhat grudging reply, but the unexpected arrival of the man who has so strangely won her seals her lips.*)

AMY. You ! (*with a depth of meaning*). Oh, sir !

STEVE (*the most nervous of the company*). I felt I must come.

Miss Grey, I am in the greatest distress, as the unhappy cause of all this trouble.

AMY (*coldly*). You should have thought of that before.

STEVE. It was dense of me not to understand sooner—very dense. (*He looks at her with wistful eyes.*) Must I marry you, Miss Grey ?

AMY (*curling her lip*). Ah, that is what you are sorry for !

STEVE. Yes—horribly sorry. (*Hastily*) Not for myself. To tell you the truth, I 'd be—precious glad to risk it—I think.

AMY (*with a glance at* GINEVRA). You would ?

STEVE. But very sorry for you. It seems such a shame to you—so young and attractive—and the little you know of me so—unfortunate.

AMY. You mean you could never love me ?

STEVE. I don't mean that at all.

AMY. Ginevra !

(*Indeed* GINEVRA *feels that she has been obliterated quite long enough.*)

GINEVRA (*with a touch of testiness in her tone*). Amy—introduce me.

AMY. Mr. Stephen Rollo—Miss Dunbar. Miss Dunbar knows all.

(GINEVRA *makes a movement that the cynical might describe as brushing* AMY *aside.*)

GINEVRA. May I ask, Mr. Rollo, what are your views about woman ?

STEVE. Really I——

GINEVRA. Is she, in your opinion, her husband's equal, or is she his chattel ?

STEVE. Honestly, I am so beside myself——

GINEVRA. You evade the question.

AMY. He means chattel, Ginevra.

GINEVRA. Mr. Rollo, I am the friend till death of Amy Grey. Let that poor child go, sir, and I am prepared to take her place beside you—yes, at the altar's mouth.

AMY. Ginevra.

GINEVRA (*making that movement again*). Understand I can neither love nor honour you—at least at first—but I will obey you.

AMY. Ginevra, you take too much upon yourself.

GINEVRA. I *will* make a sacrifice—I will.

AMY. You shall not.

GINEVRA. I feel that I understand this gentleman as no other woman can. It is my mission, Amy——

(*The return of* ALICE *is what prevents* STEVE'S *seizing his hat and flying. It might not have had this effect had he seen the lady's face just before she opened the door.*)

ALICE (*putting her hand to her poor heart*). You have come here, Steve ? Oh no, it is not possible.

STEVE (*looking things unutterable*). How could I help coming ?

AMY (*to the rescue*). Mother, have you—did you ?

ALICE (*meekly*). I have told him all.

STEVE. The Colonel ?

(ALICE *bows her bruised head.*)

AMY (*conducting her to a seat*). Brave, brave. What has he decided ?

ALICE. He hasn't decided yet. He is thinking out what it will be best to do.

STEVE. He knows ? Then I am no longer—— (*His unfinished sentence seems to refer to Amy.*)

AMY (*proudly*). Yes, sir, as he knows, you are, as far as I am concerned, now free.

GINEVRA (*in a murmur*). It's almost a pity. (*She turns to her* AMY) At least, Amy, this makes you and me friends again.

(*We have never quite been able to understand what this meant, but* AMY *knows, for she puts* GINEVRA'S *hand to her sweet lips.*)

ALICE (*who somehow could do without* GINEVRA *to-night*). Cosmo is waiting for you, Miss Dunbar, to see you home.

GINEVRA (*with a disquieting vision of her landlady*). I must go. (*She gives her hand in the coldest way to* MRS. GREY. *Then, with a curtsey to* STEVE *that he can surely never forget*) Mr. Rollo, I am sure there is much good in you. Darling Amy, I shall be round first thing in the morning.

STEVE. Now that she has gone, can we—have a talk ?

ALICE (*looking down*). Yes, Steve.

AMY (*gently*). Mother, what was that you called him ?

ALICE. Dear Amy, I forgot. Yes, Mr. Rollo.

STEVE. Then, Alice——

AMY.   This lady's name, if I am not greatly mistaken, is Mrs. Grey.   Is it not so, mother ?

ALICE.   Yes, Amy.

STEVE.   As you will ; but it is most important that I say certain things to her at once.

ALICE.   Oh, Mr. Rollo.   What do you think, dear ?

AMY (*reflecting*).   If it be clearly understood that this is good-bye, I consent.   Please be as brief as possible.

(*Somehow they think that she is moving to the door, but she crosses only to the other side of the room and sits down with a book.   One of them likes this very much.*)

STEVE (*who is not the one*).   But I want to see her alone.

AMY (*the dearest of little gaolers*).   That, I am afraid, I cannot permit.   It is not that I have not perfect confidence in you, mother, but you must see I am acting wisely.

ALICE.   Yes, Amy.

STEVE (*to his* ALICE).   What has come over you ?   You don't seem to be the same woman.

AMY.   That is just it ; she is not.

ALICE.   I see now only through Amy's eyes.

AMY.   They will not fail you, mother.   Proceed, sir.

(STEVE *has to make the best of it.*)

STEVE.   You told him, then, about your feelings for me ?

ALICE (*studying the carpet*).   He knows now exactly what are my feelings for you.

STEVE (*huskily*).   How did he take it ?

ALICE.   Need you ask ?

STEVE.   Poor old boy.   I suppose he wishes me to stay away from your house now.

ALICE.   Is it unreasonable ?

STEVE.   No, of course not, but——

ALICE.   Will it be terribly hard to you, St—Mr. Rollo ?

STEVE.   It isn't that.   You see I 'm fond of the Colonel, I really am, and it hurts me to think he thinks that I—— It wasn't my fault, was it ?

AMY.   Ungenerous.

ALICE.   He quite understands that it was I who lost my head.

(STEVE *is much moved by the generosity of this.   He lowers his voice.*)

STEVE.   Of course I blame myself now ; but I assure you

honestly I had no idea of it until to-night.　I had thought you were only my friend.　It dazed me ; but as I ransacked my mind many little things came back to me.　I remembered what I hadn't noticed at the time——

AMY.　Louder, please.

STEVE.　I remembered——

AMY.　Is this necessary ?

ALICE.　Please, Amy, let me know what he remembered.

STEVE.　I remembered that your voice was softer to me than when you were addressing other men.

ALICE.　Let me look long at you, Mr. Rollo.　(*She looks long at him.*)

AMY.　Mother, enough.

ALICE.　What more do you remember ?

STEVE.　It is strange to me now that I didn't understand your true meaning to-day when you said I was the only man you couldn't flirt with ; you meant that I aroused deeper feelings.

ALICE.　How you know me.

AMY.　Not the best of you, mother.

ALICE.　No, not the best, Amy.

STEVE.　I can say that I never thought of myself as possessing dangerous qualities.　I thought I was utterly unattractive to women.

ALICE.　You *must* have known about your eyes.

STEVE (*eagerly*).　My eyes ?　On my soul I didn't.

(AMY *wonders if this can be true.* ALICE *rises.　She feels that she cannot control herself much longer.*)

ALICE.　Steve, if you don't go away at once I shall scream.

STEVE (*really unhappy*).　Is it as bad as that ?

AMY (*rising*).　You heard what Mrs. Grey said.　This is very painful to her.　Will you please say good-bye.

(*In the novel circumstances he does not quite know how this should be carried out.*)

ALICE (*also shy*).　How shall we do it, Amy ?　On the brow ?

AMY.　No, mother—with the hand.

(*They do it with the hand, and it is thus that the* COLONEL *finds them.　He would be unable to keep his countenance were it not for a warning look from* ALICE.)

COLONEL (*one of the men who have a genius for saying the right thing*).　Ha !

STEVE.   I am going, Colonel.   I am very sorry that you——
At the same time I wish you to understand that the fault is
entirely mine.

COLONEL (*guardedly*).   Ha !

AMY (*putting an arm round her mother, who hugs it*).   Father,
he came only to say good-bye.   He is not a bad man, and
mother has behaved magnificently.

COLONEL (*cleverly*).   Ha !

AMY.   You must not, you shall not, be cruel to her.

ALICE.   Darling Amy !

COLONEL (*truculently*).   Oh, mustn't I.   We shall see about
that.

STEVE.   Come, come, Colonel.

COLONEL (*doing better than might have been expected*).   Hold
your tongue, sir.

AMY.   I know mother as no other person can know her.   I
begin to think that you have no proper appreciation of her, father.

ALICE (*basely*).   Dear, dear Amy.

AMY.   I dare say she has often suffered in the past——

ALICE.   Oh, Amy, oh.

AMY.   By your—your callousness—your want of sympathy
—your neglect.

ALICE.   My beloved child.

COLONEL (*uneasily*).   Alice, tell her it isn't so.

ALICE.   You hear what he says, my pet.

AMY.   But you don't deny it.

COLONEL.   Deny it, woman.

ALICE.   Robert, Robert !

AMY.   And please not to call my mother 'woman' in my
presence.

COLONEL.   I—I—I—— (*He looks for help from* ALICE,
but she gives him only a twinkle of triumph.   He barks) Child, go
to your room.

AMY (*her worst fears returning*).   But what are you going
to do ?

COLONEL.   That is not your affair.

STEVE.   I must say I don't see that.

AMY (*gratefully*).   Thank you, Mr. Rollo.

COLONEL.   Go to your room.

(*She has to go, but not till she has given her mother a kiss*

*that is a challenge to the world. Then to the bewilderment
of* STEVE *two human frames are rocked with laughter.)*

ALICE. Oh, Robert, look at him. He thinks I worship him.

COLONEL. Steve, you colossal puppy.

STEVE. Eh——what——why ?

ALICE. Steve, tell Robert about my voice being softer to
you than to other men ; tell him, Steve, about your eyes.

(The unhappy youth gropes mentally and physically.)

STEVE. Good heavens, was there nothing in it ?

COLONEL. My boy, I 'll never let you hear the end of this.

STEVE. But if there 's nothing in it, how could your
daughter have thought——

COLONEL. She saw you kiss Alice here this afternoon, you
scoundrel, and, as she thought, make an *assignation* with you.
There, it all came out of that. She is a sentimental lady, is our
Amy, and she has been too often to the theatre.

STEVE. Let me think.

COLONEL. Here is a chair for the very purpose. Now,
think hard.

STEVE. But——but——then why did you pretend before her,
Alice ?

ALICE. Because she thinks that she has saved me, and it
makes her so happy. Amy has a passionate desire to be of
some use in this world she knows so well, and she already
sees her sphere, Steve : it is to look after me. I am not to be
her chaperone, it is she who is to be mine. I have submitted,
you see.

COLONEL *(fidgeting).* She seems to have quite given me up
for you.

ALICE *(blandly).* Oh yes, Robert, quite.

STEVE *(gloomily).* You will excuse my thinking only of
myself. What an ass I 've been.

ALICE. Is it a blow, Steve ?

STEVE. It 's a come-down. Ass, ass, ass ! But I say,
Alice, I 'm awfully glad it 's I who have been the ass and not
you. I really am, Colonel. You see the tragedy of my life is
I 'm such an extraordinarily ordinary sort of fellow that, though
every man I know says some lady has loved him, there never
in all my unromantic life was a woman who cared a Christmas
card for me. It often makes me lonely ; and so when I

thought such a glorious woman as you, Alice——I lost touch of earth altogether ; but now I 've fallen back on it with a whack. But I 'm glad—yes, I 'm glad. You two kindest people Steve Rollo has ever known.—Oh, I say good-night. I suppose you can't overlook it, Alice.

ALICE.   Oh yes, you goose, I can. We are both fond of you—Mr. Rollo.

COLONEL.   Come in, my boy, and make love to *me* as often as you feel lonely.

STEVE.   I may still come to see you ?   I say, I 'm awfully taken with your Amy.

COLONEL.   None of that, Steve.

ALICE.   *We* can drop in on you on the sly, Steve, to admire your orbs ; but you mustn't come here—until Amy thinks it is safe for me. (*When he has gone she adds*) Until *I* think it is safe for Amy.

COLONEL.   When will that be ?

ALICE.   Not for some time.

COLONEL.   He isn't a bad sort, Steve.

ALICE.   Oh, no—she might even do worse some day. But she is to be my little girl for a long time first.

COLONEL.   This will give him a sort of glamour to her, you know.

ALICE.   You are not really thinking, Robert, that my Amy is to fall asleep to-night before she hears the whole true story. Could I sleep until she knows everything !

COLONEL.   Stupid of me. I am a little like Steve in one way, though ; I don't understand why you have kept it up so long.

ALICE.   It isn't the first time you have thought me a harum-scarum.

COLONEL.   It isn't.

ALICE.   The sheer fun of it, Robert, went to my head, I suppose. And then, you see, the more Amy felt herself to be my protectress the more she seemed to love me. I am afraid I have a weakness for the short-cuts to being loved.

COLONEL.   I 'm afraid you have. The one thing you didn't think of is that the more she loves you the less love she seems to have for me.

ALICE.   How selfish of you, Robert.

COLONEL (*suspiciously*).   Or was that all part of the plan ?

ALICE. There was no plan ; there wasn't time for one. But you were certainly rather horrid, Robert, in the way you gloated over me when you saw them take to you. I have been gloating a little perhaps in taking them from you.

COLONEL. Them ? You are going a little too fast, my dear. I have still got Cosmo and Molly.

ALICE. For the moment.

COLONEL. Woman.

ALICE. Remember, Amy said you must not call me that.

(*He laughs as he takes her by the shoulders.*)
Yes, shake me ; I deserve it.

COLONEL. You do indeed (*and he shakes her with a ferocity that would have startled any sudden visitor. No wonder, then, that it is a shock to* COSMO, *who comes blundering in.* ALICE *is the first to see him, and she turns the advantage to unprincipled account.*)

ALICE. Robert, don't hurt me Oh, if Cosmo were to see you !

COSMO. Cosmo does see him. (*He says it in a terrible voice. Probably* COSMO *has been to a theatre or two himself.*)

ALICE. You here, Cosmo !

(*She starts back from her assailant.*)

COLONEL (*feeling a little foolish*). I didn't hear you come in.

COSMO (*grimly*). No, I 'm sure you didn't.

COLONEL (*testily*). No heroics, my boy.

COSMO. Take care, father. (*He stands between them, which makes his father suddenly grin.*) Laugh on, sir. I don't know what this row 's about, but—(*here his arm encircles an undeserving lady*)—this lady is my mother, and I won't have her bullied. What 's a father compared to a mother !

ALICE. Cosmo, darling Cosmo !

COLONEL (*becoming alarmed*). My boy, it was only a jest. Alice, tell him it was only a jest.

ALICE. He says it was only a jest, Cosmo.

COSMO. You are a trump to shield him, mother. (*He kisses her openly, conscious that he is a bit of a trump himself, in which view* ALICE *most obviously concurs.*)

COLONEL (*to his better half*). You serpent.

COSMO. Sir, this language won't do.

COLONEL (*exasperated*). You go to bed, too.

ALICE.   He has sent Amy to bed already.   Try to love your father, Cosmo (*placing many kisses on the spot where he had been slapped*).   Try for my sake, and try to get Amy and Molly to do it, too.   (*Sweetly to her husband*) They will love you in time, Robert ;   at present they can think only of me.   Darling, I 'll come and see you in bed.

COSMO.   I don't like to leave you with him——

ALICE.   Go, my own ;   I promise to call out if I need you.

(*On these terms* COSMO *departs.   The long-suffering husband, arms folded, surveys his unworthy spouse.*)

COLONEL.   You *are* a hussy.

ALICE (*meekly*).   I suppose I am.

COLONEL.   Mind you, I am not going to stand Cosmo's thinking this of me.

ALICE.   As if I would allow it for another hour !   You won't see much of me to-night, Robert.   If I sleep at all it will be in Amy's room.

COLONEL (*lugubriously*).   You will be taking Molly from me to-morrow.

ALICE.   I feel hopeful that Molly, too, will soon be taking care of me.   (*She goes to him in her cajoling way.*)   With so many chaperones, Robert, I ought to do well.   Oh, my dear, don't think that I have learnt no lesson to-night.

COLONEL (*smiling*).   Going to reform at last ?

ALICE (*the most serious of women*).   Yes, Robert.   The Alice you have known is come to an end.   To-morrow——

COLONEL.   If she is different to-morrow I 'll disown her.

ALICE.   It 's summer done, autumn begun.   Farewell, summer, we don't know you any more.   My girl and I are like the little figures in the weather-house ;   when Amy comes out, Alice goes in.   Alice Sit-by-the-Fire henceforth.   The moon is full to-night, Robert, but it isn't looking for me any more. Taxis farewell—advance four-wheelers.   I had a beautiful husband once, black as the raven was his hair——

COLONEL.   Stop it.

ALICE.   Pretty Robert, farewell.   Farewell, Alice that was ; it 's all over, my dear.   I always had a weakness for you ;   but now you must really go ;   make way there for the old lady.

COLONEL.   Woman, you 'll make me cry.   Go to your Amy.

ALICE. Robert——

COLONEL. Go. Go. Go!

(*As he roars it* AMY *peeps in anxiously. She is in her night-gown, and her hair is down and her feet are bare, and she does not look so very much more than five.* ALICE *is unable to resist the temptation.*)

ALICE (*wailing*). Must I go, Robert?

AMY. Going away? Mother! Father, if mother goes away, what is to become of me?

(*She draws them together until their hands clasp. There is now a beatific smile on her face. The curtain sees that its time has come; it clicks, and falls.*)

WHAT EVERY WOMAN KNOWS

Produced at the Duke of York's Theatre in September 3, 1908, with the following cast :

JOHN SHAND	. . . .	*Gerald du Maurier*
ALICK WYLIE	. . . .	*Henry Vibart*
DAVID WYLIE	. . . .	*Sydney Valentine*
JAMES WYLIE	. . . .	*Edmund Gwenn*
MAGGIE WYLIE	. . . .	*Hilda Trevelyan*
MR. VENABLES	. . .	*Norman Forbes*
COMTESSE DE LA BRIÈRE	. .	*Mrs. Tree*
LADY SYBIL LAZENBY	. . .	*Lillah McCarthy*
MAID	. . . .	*Madge Murray*

The play ran for 384 performances. Revived at the Apollo on May 24, 1923. it ran for 285 performances.

ACT I

JAMES WYLIE is about to make a move on the dambrod, and in the little Scotch room there is an awful silence befitting the occasion. James with his hand poised—for if he touches a piece he has to play it, Alick will see to that—raises his red head suddenly to read Alick's face. His father, who is Alick, is pretending to be in a panic lest James should make this move. James grins heartlessly, and his fingers are about to close on the ' man ' when some instinct of self-preservation makes him peep once more. This time Alick is caught : the unholy ecstasy on his face tells as plain as porridge that he has been luring James to destruction. James glares ; and, too late, his opponent is a simple old father again. James mops his head, sprawls in the manner most conducive to thought in the Wylie family, and, protruding his underlip, settles down to a reconsideration of the board. Alick blows out his cheeks, and a drop of water settles on the point of his nose.

You will find them thus any Saturday night (after family worship, which sends the servant to bed) ; and sometimes the pauses are so long that in the end they forget whose move it is.

It is not the room you would be shown into if you were calling socially on Miss Wylie. The drawing-room for you, and Miss Wylie in a coloured merino to receive you ; very likely she would exclaim, ' This is a pleasant surprise ! ' though she has seen you coming up the avenue and has just had time to whip the dustcloths off the chairs, and to warn Alick, David and James, that they had better not dare come in to see you before they have put on a dickey. Nor is this the room in which you would dine in solemn grandeur if invited to drop in and take pot-luck, which is how the Wylies invite, it being a family weakness to pretend that they sit down in the dining-room daily. It is the real living-room of the house, where Alick, who will never get used to fashionable ways, can take off his collar and sit happily in his stocking-soles, and James at times would do so also ; but catch Maggie letting him.

There is one very fine chair, but, heavens, not for sitting on ; just to give the room a social standing in an emergency. It sneers at the other chairs with an air of insolent superiority, like a haughty bride who has married into the house for money. Otherwise the furniture is homely ; most of it has come from that smaller house where the Wylies began. There is the large and shiny chair which can be turned into a bed if you look the other way for a moment. James cannot sit on this chair without gradually sliding down it till he is lying luxuriously on the small of his back, his legs indicating, like the hands of a clock, that it is ten past twelve ; a position in which Maggie shudders to see him receiving company.

The other chairs are horse-hair, than which nothing is more comfortable if there be a good slit down the seat. The seats are heavily dented, because all the Wylie family sit down with a dump. The draught-board is on the edge of a large centre table, which also displays four books placed at equal distances from each other, one of them a Bible, and another the family album. If these were the only books they would not justify Maggie in calling this chamber the library, her dogged name for it ; while David and James call it the west-room and Alick calls it ' the room,' which is to him the natural name for any apartment without a bed in it. There is a bookcase of pitch pine, which contains six hundred books, with glass doors to prevent your getting at them.

No one does try to get at the books, for the Wylies are not a reading family. They like you to gasp when you see so much literature gathered together in one prison-house, but they gasp themselves at the thought that there are persons, chiefly clergy-men, who, having finished one book, coolly begin another. Nevertheless it was not all vainglory that made David buy this library : it was rather a mighty respect for education, as something that he has missed. This same feeling makes him take in the *Contemporary Review* and stand up to it like a man. Alick, who also has a respect for education, tries to read the *Contemporary*, but becomes dispirited, and may be heard muttering over its pages, ' No, no use, no use, no,' and sometimes even ' Oh hell.' James has no respect for education ; and Maggie is at present of an open mind.

They are Wylie and Sons of the local granite quarry, in

which Alick was throughout his working days a mason. It is David who has raised them to this position ; he climbed up himself step by step (and hewed the steps), and drew the others up after him. 'Wylie Brothers,' Alick would have had the firm called, but David said No, and James said No, and Maggie said No ; first honour must be to their father ; and Alick now likes it on the whole, though he often sighs at having to shave every day ; and on some snell mornings he still creeps from his couch at four and even at two (thinking that his mallet and chisel are calling him), and begins to pull on his trousers, until the grandeur of them reminds him that he can go to bed again. Sometimes he cries a little, because there is no more work for him to do for ever and ever ; and then Maggie gives him a spade (without telling David) or David gives him the logs to saw (without telling Maggie).

We have given James a longer time to make his move than our kind friends in front will give him, but in the meantime something has been happening. David has come in, wearing a black coat and his Sabbath boots, for he has been to a public meeting. David is nigh forty years of age, whiskered like his father and brother (Alick's whiskers being worn as a sort of cravat round the neck), and he has the too brisk manner of one who must arrive anywhere a little before any one else. The painter who did the three of them for fifteen pounds (you may observe the canvases on the walls) has caught this characteristic, perhaps accidentally, for David is almost stepping out of his frame, as if to hurry off somewhere ; while Alick and James look as if they were pinned to the wall for life. All the six of them, men and pictures, however, have a family resemblance, like granite blocks from their own quarry. They are as Scotch as peat for instance, and they might exchange eyes without any neighbour noticing the difference, inquisitive little blue eyes that seem to be always totting up the price of things.

The dambrod players pay no attention to David, nor does he regard them. Dumping down on the sofa he removes his 'lastic sides, as his Sabbath boots are called, by pushing one foot against the other, gets into a pair of hand-sewn slippers, deposits the boots as according to rule in the ottoman, and crosses to the fire. There must be something on David's mind to-night, for he pays no attention to the game, neither gives advice (than which nothing is more maddening) nor exchanges a wink with Alick over the parlous condition of James's crown.   You can hear the wag-at-the-wall clock in the lobby ticking.   Then David lets himself go ; it runs out of him like a hymn :

DAVID.   Oh, let the solid ground
                Not fail beneath my feet,
                Before my life has found
                What some have found so sweet.

(*This is not a soliloquy, but is offered as a definite statement. The players emerge from their game with difficulty.*)

ALICK (*with* JAMES's *crown in his hand*).   What's that you're saying, David ?

DAVID (*like a public speaker explaining the situation in a few well-chosen words*).   The thing I'm speaking about is Love.

JAMES (*keeping control of himself*).   Do you stand there and say you're in love, David Wylie ?

DAVID.   Me ; what would I do with the thing ?

JAMES (*who is by no means without pluck*).   I see no necessity for calling it a thing.

(*They are two bachelors who all their lives have been afraid of nothing but Woman.*   DAVID *in his sportive days— which continue—has done roguish things with his arm when conducting a lady home under an umbrella from a soiree, and has both chuckled and been scared on thinking of it afterwards.*   JAMES, *a commoner fellow altogether, has discussed the sex over a glass, but is too canny to be in the company of less than two young women at a time.*)

DAVID (*derisively*).   Oho, has she got you, James ?

JAMES (*feeling the sting of it*).   Nobody has got me.

DAVID.   They'll catch you yet, lad.

JAMES.   They'll never catch me.   You've been nearer catched yourself.

ALICK.   Yes, Kitty Menzies, David.

DAVID (*feeling himself under the umbrella*).   It was a kind of a shave that.

ALICK (*who knows all that is to be known about women and can speak of them without a tremor*).   It's a curious thing, but a man cannot help winking when he hears that one of his friends has been catched.

DAVID. That 's so.

JAMES (*clinging to his manhood*). And fear of that wink is what has kept the two of us single men. And yet what 's the glory of being single ?

DAVID. There 's no particular glory in it, but it 's safe.

JAMES (*putting away his aspirations*). Yes, it 's lonely, but it 's safe. But who did you mean the poetry for, then ?

DAVID. For Maggie, of course.

(*You don't know* DAVID *and* JAMES *till you know how they love their sister* MAGGIE.)

ALICK. I thought that.

DAVID (*coming to the second point of his statement about Love*). I saw her reading poetry and saying those words over to herself.

JAMES. She has such a poetical mind.

DAVID. Love. There 's no doubt as that 's what Maggie has set her heart on. And not merely love, but one of those grand noble loves ; for though Maggie is undersized she has a passion for romance.

JAMES (*wandering miserably about the room*). It 's terrible not to be able to give Maggie what her heart is set on.

(*The others never pay much attention to* JAMES, *though he is quite a smart figure in less important houses.*)

ALICK (*violently*). Those idiots of men.

DAVID. Father, did you tell her who had got the minister of Galashiels ?

ALICK (*wagging his head sadly.*) I had to tell her. And then I—I—bought her a sealskin muff, and I just slipped it into her hands and came away.

JAMES (*illustrating the sense of justice in the Wylie family*). Of course, to be fair to the man, he never pretended he wanted her.

DAVID. None of them wants her ; that 's what depresses her. I was thinking, father, I would buy her that gold watch and chain in Snibby's window. She hankers after it.

JAMES (*slapping his pocket*). You 're too late, David ; I 've got them for her.

DAVID. It 's ill done of the minister. Many a pound of steak has that man had in this house.

ALICK.   You mind the slippers she worked for him ?

JAMES.   I mind them fine ; she began them for William Cathro.   She 's getting on in years, too, though she looks so young.

ALICK.   I never can make up my mind, David, whether her curls make her look younger or older.

DAVID (*determinedly*).   Younger.   Whisht !   I hear her winding the clock.   Mind, not a word about the minister to her, James.   Don't even mention religion this day.

JAMES.   Would it be like me to do such a thing ?

DAVID.   It would be very like you.   And there 's that other matter : say not a syllable about our having a reason for sitting up late to-night.   When she says it 's bed-time, just all pretend we 're not sleepy.

ALICK.   Exactly, and when——

(*Here* MAGGIE *enters, and all three are suddenly engrossed in the dambrod. We could describe* MAGGIE *at great length. But what is the use ? What you really want to know is whether she was good-looking. No, she was not. Enter* MAGGIE, *who is not good-looking. When this is said, all is said. Enter* MAGGIE, *as it were, with her throat cut from ear to ear. She has a soft Scotch voice and a more resolute manner than is perhaps fitting to her plainness ; and she stops short at sight of* JAMES *sprawling unconsciously in the company chair.*)

MAGGIE.   James, I wouldn't sit on the fine chair.

JAMES.   I forgot again.

(*But he wishes she had spoken more sharply. Even profanation of the fine chair has not roused her. She takes up her knitting, and they all suspect that she knows what they have been talking about.*)

MAGGIE.   You 're late, David, it 's nearly bed-time.

DAVID (*finding the subject a safe one*).   I was kept late at the public meeting.

ALICK (*glad to get so far away from Galashiels*).   Was it a good meeting ?

DAVID.   Fairish.   (*With some heat*) That young John Shand *would* make a speech.

MAGGIE.   John Shand ?   Is that the student Shand ?

DAVID.   The same.   It 's true he 's a student at Glasgow

University in the winter months, but in summer he 's just the railway porter here ; and I think it 's very presumptuous of a young lad like that to make a speech when he hasn't a penny to bless himself with.

ALICK.   The Shands were always an impudent family, and jealous.   I suppose that 's the reason they haven't been on speaking terms with us this six years.   Was it a good speech ?

DAVID (*illustrating the family's generosity*).   It was very fine ; but he needn't have made fun of *me*.

MAGGIE (*losing a stitch*).   He dared ?

DAVID (*depressed*).   You see I can *not* get started on a speech without saying things like ' In rising *for* to make a few remarks.'

JAMES.   What 's wrong with it ?

DAVID.   He mimicked me, and said, ' Will our worthy chairman come for to go for to answer my questions ? ' and so on ; and they roared.

JAMES (*slapping his money pocket*).   The sacket.

DAVID.   I did feel bitterly, father, the want of education. (*Without knowing it, he has a beautiful way of pronouncing this noble word.*)

MAGGIE (*holding out a kind hand to him*).   David.

ALICK.   I 've missed it sore, David.   Even now I feel the want of it in the very marrow of me.   I 'm shamed to think I never gave you your chance.   But when you were young I was so desperate poor, how could I do it, Maggie ?

MAGGIE.   It wasn't possible, father.

ALICK (*gazing at the book-shelves*).   To be able to understand these books !   To up with them one at a time and scrape them as clean as though they were a bowl of brose.   Lads, it 's not to riches, it 's to scholarship that I make my humble bow.

JAMES (*who is good at bathos*).   There 's ten yards of them. And they were selected by the minister of Galashiels.   He said——

DAVID (*quickly*).   James.

JAMES.   I mean—I mean——

MAGGIE (*calmly*).   I suppose you mean what you say, James. I hear, David, that the minister of Galashiels is to be married on that Miss Turnbull.

DAVID (*on guard*).   So they were saying.

ALICK.   All I can say is she has made a poor bargain.

MAGGIE (*the damned*).   I wonder at you, father.   He 's a very nice gentleman.   I 'm sure I hope he has chosen wisely.

JAMES.   Not him.

MAGGIE (*getting near her tragedy*).   How can you say that when you don't know her ?   I expect she is full of charm.

ALICK.   Charm ?   It 's the very word he used.

DAVID.   Havering idiot.

ALICK.   What *is* charm, exactly, Maggie ?

MAGGIE.   Oh, it 's—it 's a sort of bloom on a woman.   If you have it, you don't need to have anything else ; and if you don't have it, it doesn't much matter what else you have. Some women, the few, have charm for all ; and most have charm for one.   But some have charm for none.

(*Somehow she has stopped knitting.   Her men-folk are very depressed.   JAMES brings his fist down on the table with a crash.*)

JAMES (*shouting*).   I have a sister that has charm.

MAGGIE.   No, James, you haven't.

JAMES (*rushing at her with the watch and chain*).   Ha'e, Maggie.

(*She lets them lie in her lap.*)

DAVID.   Maggie, would you like a silk ?

MAGGIE.   What could I do with a silk ?   (*With a gust of passion*) You might as well dress up a little brown hen.

(*They wriggle miserably.*)

JAMES (*stamping*).   Bring him here to me.

MAGGIE.   Bring whom, James ?

JAMES.   David, I would be obliged if you wouldn't kick me beneath the table.

MAGGIE (*rising*).   Let 's be practical ; let 's go to our beds. (*This reminds them that they have a job on hand in which she is not to share.*)

DAVID (*slily*).   I don't feel very sleepy yet.

ALICK.   Nor me either.

JAMES.   You 've just taken the very words out of my mouth.

DAVID (*with unusual politeness*).   Good-night to you, Maggie.

MAGGIE (*fixing the three of them*).   *All* of you unsleepy, when, as is well known, ten o'clock is your regular bed-time ?

JAMES.   Yes, it 's common knowledge that we go to our beds at ten.   (*Chuckling*) That 's what we 're counting on.

MAGGIE. Counting on?

DAVID. You stupid whelp.

JAMES. What have *I* done?

MAGGIE (*folding her arms*). There's something up. You've got to tell me, David.

DAVID (*who knows when he is beaten*). Go out and watch, James.

MAGGIE. Watch?

(JAMES *takes himself off, armed, as* MAGGIE *notices, with a stick.*)

DAVID (*in his alert business way*). Maggie, there are burglars about.

MAGGIE. Burglars? (*She sits rigid, but she is not the kind to scream.*)

DAVID. We hadn't meant for to tell you till we nabbed them ; but they've been in this room twice of late. We sat up last night waiting for them, and we're to sit up again to-night.

MAGGIE. The silver plate.

DAVID. It's all safe as yet. That makes us think that they were either frightened away these other times, or that they are coming back for to make a clean sweep.

MAGGIE. How did you get to know about this?

DAVID. It was on Tuesday that the polissman called at the quarry with a very queer story. He had seen a man climbing out at this window at ten past two.

MAGGIE. Did he chase him?

DAVID. It was so dark he lost sight of him at once.

ALICK. Tell her about the window.

DAVID. We've found out that the catch of the window has been pushed back by slipping the blade of a knife between the woodwork.

MAGGIE. David.

ALICK. The polissman said he was carrying a little carpet bag.

MAGGIE. The silver plate *is* gone.

DAVID. No, no. We were thinking that very likely he has bunches of keys in the bag.

MAGGIE. Or weapons.

DAVID. As for that, we have some pretty stout weapons

ourselves in the umbrella stand.   So, if you 'll go to your bed,
Maggie——

MAGGIE.   Me ? and my brothers in danger.

ALICK.   There 's just one of them.

MAGGIE.   The polissman just saw one.

DAVID (*licking his palms*).   I would be very pleased if there
were three of them.

MAGGIE.   I watch with you.   I would be very pleased if
there were four of them.

DAVID.   And they say she has no charm !

(JAMES *returns on tiptoe as if the burglars were beneath the
table.   He signs to every one to breathe no more, and then
whispers his news.*)

JAMES.   He 's there.   I had no sooner gone out than I saw
him sliding down the garden wall, close to the rhubarbs.

ALICK.   What 's he like ?

JAMES.   He 's an ugly customer.   That 's all I could see.
There was a little carpet bag in his hand.

DAVID.   That 's him.

JAMES.   He slunk into the rhodydendrons, and he 's there
now, watching the window.

DAVID.   We have him.   Out with the light.

(*The room is beautified by a chandelier fitted for three gas
jets, but with the advance of progress one of these has been
removed and the incandescent light put in its place.   This
alone is lit.   ALICK climbs a chair, pulls a little chain, and
the room is now but vaguely lit by the fire.   It plays fitfully
on four sparkling faces.*)

MAGGIE.   Do you think he saw you, James ?

JAMES.   I couldn't say, but in any case I was too clever for
him.   I looked up at the stars, and yawned loud at them as if
I was tremendous sleepy.

(*There is a long pause during which they are lurking in the
shadows.   At last they hear some movement, and they steal
like ghosts from the room.   We see DAVID turning out the
lobby light ; then the door closes and an empty room awaits
the intruder with a shudder of expectancy.   The window
opens and shuts as softly as if this were a mother peering in
to see whether her baby is asleep.   Then the head of a man
shows between the curtains.   The remainder of him follows.*)

*He is carrying a little carpet bag. He stands irresolute ;
what puzzles him evidently is that the Wylies should have
retired to rest without lifting that piece of coal off the fire.
He opens the door and peeps into the lobby, listening to the
wag-at-the-wall clock. All seems serene, and he turns on
the light. We see him clearly now. He is* JOHN SHAND,
*age twenty-one, boots muddy, as an indignant carpet can
testify. He wears a shabby topcoat and a cockerty bonnet ;
otherwise he is in the well-worn corduroys of a railway
porter. His movements, at first stealthy, become almost
homely as he feels that he is secure. He opens the bag and
takes out a bunch of keys, a small paper parcel, and a black
implement that may be a burglar's jemmy. This cool
customer examines the fire and piles on more coals. With the
keys he opens the door of the bookcase, selects two large
volumes, and brings them to the table. He takes off his
topcoat and opens his parcel, which we now see contains
sheets of foolscap paper. His next action shows that the
'jemmy' is really a ruler. He knows where the pen and
ink are kept. He pulls the fine chair nearer to the table,
sits on it, and proceeds to write, occasionally dotting the
carpet with ink as he stabs the air with his pen. He is so
occupied that he does not see the door opening, and the Wylie
family staring at him. They are armed with sticks.)*

ALICK (*at last*). When you 're ready, John Shand.

(JOHN *hints back, and then he has the grace to rise, dogged
and expressionless.*)

JAMES (*like a railway porter*). Ticket, please.

DAVID. You can't think of anything clever for to go for
to say now, John.

MAGGIE. I hope you find that chair comfortable, young man.

JOHN. I have no complaint to make against the chair.

ALICK (*who is really distressed*). A native of the town. The
disgrace to your family ! I feel pity for the Shands this night.

JOHN (*glowering*). I 'll thank you, Mr. Wylie, not to pity
my family.

JAMES. Canny, canny.

MAGGIE (*that sense of justice again*). I think you should let
the young man explain. It mayn't be so bad as we thought.

DAVID. Explain away, my billie.

JOHN.   Only the uneducated would need an explanation. I'm a student, (*with a little passion*) and I'm desperate for want of books.   You have all I want here ; no use to you but for display ; well, I came here to study.   I come twice weekly. (*Amazement of his hosts.*)

DAVID (*who is the first to recover*).   By the window.

JOHN.   Do you think a Shand would so far lower himself as to enter your door ?   Well, is it a case for the police ?

JAMES.   It is.

MAGGIE (*not so much out of the goodness of her heart as to patronise the Shands*).   It seems to me it's a case for us all to go to our beds and leave the young man to study ; but not on that chair.   (*And she wheels the chair away from him.*)

JOHN.   Thank you, Miss Maggie, but I couldn't be beholden to you.

JAMES.   My opinion is that he's nobody, so out with him.

JOHN.   Yes, out with me.   And you'll be cheered to hear I'm likely to be a nobody for a long time to come.

DAVID (*who had been beginning to respect him*).   Are you a poor scholar ?

JOHN.   On the contrary, I'm a brilliant scholar.

DAVID.   It's siller, then ?

JOHN (*glorified by experiences he has shared with many a gallant soul*).   My first year at college I lived on a barrel of potatoes, and we had just a sofa-bed between two of us ; when the one lay down the other had to get up.   Do you think it was hardship ?   It was sublime.   But this year I can't afford it.   I'll have to stay on here, collecting the tickets of the illiterate, such as you, when I might be with Romulus and Remus among the stars.

JAMES (*summing up*).   Havers.

DAVID (*in whose head some design is vaguely taking shape*). Whisht, James.   I must say, young lad, I like your spirit. Now tell me, what's your professors' opinion of your future.

JOHN.   They think me a young man of extraordinary promise.

DAVID.   You have a name here for high moral character.

JOHN.   And justly.

DAVID.   Are you serious-minded ?

JOHN.   I never laughed in my life.

DAVID.   Who do you sit under in Glasgow ?

JOHN.   Mr. Flemister of the Sauchiehall High.

DAVID.   Are you a Sabbath-school teacher ?

JOHN.   I am.

DAVID.   One more question. Are you promised ?

JOHN.   To a lady ?

DAVID.   Yes.

JOHN.   I 've never given one of them a single word of encouragement. I 'm too much occupied thinking about my career.

DAVID.   So. (*He reflects, and finally indicates by a jerk of the head that he wishes to talk with his father behind the door.*)

JAMES (*longingly*).   Do you want me too ?
    (*But they go out without even answering him.*)

MAGGIE.   I don't know what maggot they have in their heads, but sit down, young man, till they come back.

JOHN.   My name 's Mr. Shand, and till I 'm called that I decline to sit down again in this house.

MAGGIE.   Then I 'm thinking, young sir, you 'll have a weary wait.

> (*While he waits you can see how pinched his face is. He is little more than a boy, and he seldom has enough to eat. DAVID and ALICK return presently, looking as sly as if they had been discussing some move on the dambrod, as indeed they have.*)

DAVID (*suddenly become genial*).   Sit down, Mr. Shand, and pull in your chair. You 'll have a thimbleful of something to keep the cold out ? (*Briskly*) Glasses, Maggie.

> (*She wonders, but gets glasses and decanter from the sideboard, which JAMES calls the chiffy. DAVID and ALICK, in the most friendly manner, also draw up to the table.*)
You 're not a totaller, I hope ?

JOHN (*guardedly*).   I 'm practically a totaller.

DAVID.   So are we. How do you take it ? Is there any hot water, Maggie ?

JOHN.   If I take it at all, and I haven't made up my mind yet, I 'll take it cold.

DAVID.   You 'll take it hot, James ?

JAMES (*also sitting at the table but completely befogged*).   No, I——

DAVID (*decisively*).   I think you 'll take it hot, James.

JAMES (*sulking*).   I 'll take it hot.

DAVID.   The kettle, Maggie.

(JAMES *has evidently to take it hot so that they can get at the business now on hand while* MAGGIE *goes kitchenward for the kettle.*)

ALICK.   Now, David, quick, before she comes back.

DAVID.   Mr. Shand, we have an offer to make you.

JOHN (*warningly*).   No patronage.

ALICK.   It 's strictly a business affair.

DAVID.   Leave it to me, father.   It 's this——   (*But to his annoyance the suspicious* MAGGIE *has already returned with the kettle.*)   Maggie, don't you see that you 're not wanted ?

MAGGIE (*sitting down by the fire and resuming her knitting*).   I do, David.

DAVID.   I have a proposition to put before Mr. Shand, and women are out of place in business transactions.

(*The needles continue to click.*)

ALICK (*sighing*).   We 'll have to let her bide, David.

DAVID (*sternly*).   Woman.   (*But even this does not budge her.*)   Very well then, sit there, but don't interfere, mind.   Mr. Shand, we 're willing, the three of us, to lay out £300 on your education if——

JOHN.   Take care.

DAVID (*slowly, which is not his wont*).   On condition that five years from now, Maggie Wylie, if still unmarried, can claim to marry you, should such be her wish ; the thing to be perfectly open on her side, but you to be strictly tied down.

JAMES (*enlightened*).   So, so.

DAVID (*resuming his smart manner*).   Now, what have you to say ?   Decide.

JOHN (*after a pause*).   I regret to say——

MAGGIE.   It doesn't matter what he regrets to say, because I decide against it.   And I think it was very ill-done of you to make any such proposal.

DAVID (*without looking at her*).   Quiet, Maggie.

JOHN (*looking at her*).   I must say, Miss Maggie, I don't see what reasons *you* can have for being so set against it.

MAGGIE.   If you would grow a beard, Mr. Shand, the reasons wouldn't be quite so obvious.

JOHN. I 'll never grow a beard.

MAGGIE. Then you 're done for at the start.

ALICK. Come, come.

MAGGIE. Seeing I have refused the young man——

JOHN. Refused !

DAVID. That 's no reason why we shouldn't have his friendly opinion. Your objections, Mr. Shand ?

JOHN. Simply, it 's a one-sided bargain. I admit I 'm no catch at present ; but what could a man of my abilities not soar to with three hundred pounds ? Something far above what she could aspire to.

MAGGIE. Oh, indeed !

DAVID. The position is that without the three hundred you can't soar.

JOHN. You have me there.

MAGGIE. Yes, but——

ALICK. You see *you 're* safeguarded, Maggie ; you don't need to take him unless you like, but he has to take you.

JOHN. That 's an unfair arrangement also.

MAGGIE. I wouldn't dream of it without that condition.

JOHN. Then you *are* thinking of it ?

MAGGIE. Poof !

DAVID. It 's a good arrangement for you, Mr. Shand. The chances are you 'll never have to go on with it, for in all probability she 'll marry soon.

JAMES. She 's tremendous run after.

JOHN. Even if that 's true, it 's just keeping me in reserve in case she misses doing better.

DAVID (*relieved*). That 's the situation in a nutshell.

JOHN. Another thing. Supposing I was to get fond of her ?

ALICK (*wistfully*). It 's very likely.

JOHN. Yes, and then suppose she was to give me the go-by ?

DAVID. You have to risk that.

JOHN. Or take it the other way. Supposing as I got to know her I *could not* endure her ?

DAVID (*suavely*). You have both to take risks.

JAMES (*less suavely*). What you need, John Shand, is a clout on the head.

JOHN. Three hundred pounds is no great sum.

DAVID.   You can take it or leave it.

ALICK.   No great sum for a student studying for the ministry !

JOHN.   Do you think that with that amount of money I would stop short at being a minister ?

DAVID.   That 's how I like to hear you speak.   A young Scotsman of your ability let loose upon the world with £300, what could he not do ?   It 's almost appalling to think of ; especially if he went among the English.

JOHN.   What do you think, Miss Maggie ?

MAGGIE (*who is knitting*).   I have no thoughts on the subject either way.

JOHN (*after looking her over*).   What 's her age ?   She looks young, but they say it 's the curls that does it.

DAVID (*rather happily*).   She 's one of those women who are eternally young.

JOHN.   I can't take that for an answer.

DAVID.   She 's twenty-five.

JOHN.   I 'm just twenty-one.

JAMES.   I read in a book that about four years' difference in the ages is the ideal thing.   (*As usual he is disregarded.*)

DAVID.   Well, Mr. Shand ?

JOHN (*where is his mother ?*).   I 'm willing if she 's willing ?

DAVID.   Maggie ?

MAGGIE.   There can be no ' if ' about it.   It must be an offer.

JOHN.   A Shand give a Wylie such a chance to humiliate him ?   Never.

MAGGIE.   Then all is off.

DAVID.   Come, come, Mr. Shand, it 's just a form.

JOHN (*reluctantly*).   Miss Maggie, will you ?

MAGGIE (*doggedly*).   Is it an offer ?

JOHN (*dourly*).   Yes.

MAGGIE (*rising*).   Before I answer I want first to give you a chance of drawing back.

DAVID.   Maggie.

MAGGIE (*bravely*).   When they said that I have been run after they were misleading you.   I 'm without charm ; nobody has ever been after me.

JOHN.   Oho !

ALICK.   They will be yet.

JOHN (*the innocent*). It shows at least that you haven't been after them.

(*His hosts exchange a self-conscious glance.*)

MAGGIE. One thing more ; David said I 'm twenty-five, I 'm twenty-six.

JOHN. Aha !

MAGGIE. Now be practical. Do you withdraw from the bargain, or do you not ?

JOHN (*on reflection*). It 's a bargain.

MAGGIE. Then so be it.

DAVID (*hurriedly*). And that 's settled. Did you say you would take it hot, Mr. Shand ?

JOHN. I think I 'll take it neat.

(*The others decide to take it hot, and there is some careful business here with the toddy ladles.*)

ALICK. Here 's to you, and your career.

JOHN. Thank you. To you, Miss Maggie. Had we not better draw up a legal document ? Lawyer Crosbie could do it on the quiet.

DAVID. Should we do that, or should we just trust to one another's honour ?

ALICK (*gallantly*). Let Maggie decide.

MAGGIE. I think we would better have a legal document.

DAVID. We 'll have it drawn up to-morrow. I was thinking the best way would be for to pay the money in five yearly instalments.

JOHN. I was thinking, better bank the whole sum in my name at once.

ALICK. I think David's plan 's the best.

JOHN. I think not. Of course if it 's not convenient to you——

DAVID (*touched to the quick*). It 's perfectly convenient. What do you say, Maggie ?

MAGGIE. I agree with John.

DAVID (*with an odd feeling that Maggie is now on the other side*). Very well.

JOHN. Then as that 's settled I think I 'll be stepping. (*He is putting his papers back in the bag.*)

ALICK (*politely*). If you would like to sit on at your books——

JOHN.   As I can come at any orra time now I think I 'll be stepping.   (MAGGIE *helps him into his topcoat.*)

MAGGIE.   Have you a muffler, John ?

JOHN.   I have.   (*He gets it from his pocket.*)

MAGGIE.   You had better put it twice round.   (*She does this for him.*)

DAVID.   Well, good-night to you, Mr. Shand.

ALICK.   And good luck.

JOHN.   Thank you.   The same to you.   And I 'll cry in at your office in the morning before the 6.20 is due.

DAVID.   I 'll have the document ready for you.   (*There is the awkward pause that sometimes follows great events.*)   I think, Maggie, you might see Mr. Shand to the door.

MAGGIE.   Certainly.   (JOHN *is going by the window.*)   This way, John.

(*She takes him off by the more usual exit.*)

DAVID.   He 's a fine frank fellow ;   and you saw how cleverly he got the better of me about banking the money. (*As the heads of the conspirators come gleefully together*)   I tell you, father, he has a grand business head.

ALICK.   Lads, he 's canny.   He 's cannier than any of us.

JAMES.   Except maybe Maggie.   He has no idea what a remarkable woman Maggie is.

ALICK.   Best he shouldn't know.   Men are nervous of remarkable women.

JAMES.   She 's a long time in coming back.

DAVID (*not quite comfortable*).   It 's a good sign. H'sh. What sort of a night is it, Maggie ?

MAGGIE.   It 's a little blowy.

(*She gets a large dust-cloth which is lying folded on a shelf, and proceeds to spread it over the fine chair.   The men exchange self-conscious glances.*)

DAVID (*stretching himself*).   Yes—well, well, oh yes.   It 's getting late.   What is it with you, father ?

ALICK.   I 'm ten forty-two.

JAMES.   I 'm ten-forty.

DAVID.   Ten forty-two.

(*They wind up their watches.*)

MAGGIE.   It 's high time we were bedded.   (*She puts her hands on their shoulders lovingly, which is the very thing they have been trying to avoid.)*   You 're very kind to me.

DAVID.   Havers.

ALICK.   Havers.

JAMES (*but this does not matter*).   Havers.

MAGGIE (*a little dolefully*).   I 'm a sort of sorry for the young man, David.

DAVID.   Not at all.   You 'll be the making of him.   (*She lifts the two volumes.*)   Are you taking the books to your bed, Maggie ?

MAGGIE.   Yes.   I don't want him to know things I don't know myself.

(*She departs with the books ; and* ALICK *and* DAVID, *the villains, now want to get away from each other.*)

ALICK.   Yes—yes.   Oh yes—ay, man—it is so—umpha. You 'll lift the big coals off, David.

(*He wanders away to his spring mattress.* DAVID *removes the coals.*)

JAMES (*who would like to sit down and have an argy-bargy*). It 's a most romantical affair.   (*But he gets no answer.*)   I wonder how it 'll turn out ?   (*No answer.*)   She 's queer, Maggie.   I wonder how some clever writers has never noticed how queer women are.   It 's my belief you could write a whole book about them.   (DAVID *remains obdurate.*)   It was very noble of her to tell him she 's twenty-six.   (*Muttering as he too wanders away.*)   But I thought she was twenty-seven.

(DAVID *turns out the light.*)

ACT II

Six years have elapsed and John Shand's great hour has come. Perhaps his great hour really lies ahead of him, perhaps he had it six years ago ; it often passes us by in the night with such a faint call that we don't even turn in our beds. But according to the trumpets this is John's great hour ; it is the hour for which he has long been working with his coat off ; and now the coat is on again (broadcloth but ill-fitting), for there is no more to do but await results. He is standing for Parliament, and this is election night.

As the scene discloses itself you get, so to speak, one of John Shand's posters in the face. Vote for Shand. Shand, Shand, Shand. Civil and Religious Liberty, Faith, Hope, Freedom. They are all fly-blown names for Shand. Have a placard about Shand, have a hundred placards about him, it is snowing Shand to-night in Glasgow ; take the paste out of your eye, and you will see that we are in one of Shand's committee rooms. It has been a hairdresser's emporium, but Shand, Shand, Shand has swept through it like a wind, leaving nothing but the fixtures ; why shave, why have your head doused in those basins when you can be brushed and scraped and washed up for ever by simply voting for Shand ?

There are a few hard chairs for yelling Shand from, and then rushing away. There is an iron spiral staircase that once led to the ladies' hairdressing apartments, but now leads to more Shand, Shand, Shand. A glass door at the back opens on to the shop proper, screaming Civil and Religious Liberty, Shand, as it opens, and beyond is the street crammed with still more Shand pro and con. Men in every sort of garb rush in and out, up and down the stair, shouting the magic word. Then there is a lull, and down the stair comes Maggie Wylie, decidedly overdressed in blue velvet and (let us get this over) less good-looking than ever. She raises her hands to heaven, she spins round like a little teetotum. To her from the street, suffering from a

686

determination of the word Shand to the mouth, rush Alick and David.   Alick is thinner (being older), David is stouter (being older), and they are both in tweeds and silk hats.

MAGGIE.   David—have they—is he ? quick, quick !

DAVID.   There 's no news yet, no news.   It 's terrible.
(*The teetotum revolves more quickly.*)

ALICK.   For God's sake, Maggie, sit down.

MAGGIE.   I can't, I can't !

DAVID.   Hold her down.
(*They press her into a chair ; JAMES darts in, stouter also. His necktie has gone ; he will never again be able to attend a funeral in that hat.*)

JAMES (*wildly*).   John Shand 's the man for you.   John Shand 's the man for you.   John Shand 's the man for you.

DAVID (*clutching him*).   Have you heard anything ?

JAMES.   Not a word.

ALICK.   Look at her.

DAVID.   Maggie (*he goes on his knees beside her, pressing her to him in affectionate anxiety*).   It was mad of him to dare.

MAGGIE.   It was grand of him.

ALICK (*moving about distraught*).   Insane ambition.

MAGGIE.   Glorious ambition.

DAVID.   Maggie, Maggie, my lamb, best be prepared for the worst.

MAGGIE (*husky*).   I am prepared.

ALICK.   Six weary years has she waited for this night.

MAGGIE.   Six brave years has John toiled for this night.

JAMES.   And you could have had him, Maggie, at the end of five.   The document says five.

MAGGIE.   Do you think I grudge not being married to him yet ?   Was I to hamper him till the fight was won.

DAVID (*with wrinkled brows*).   But if it 's lost ?
(*She can't answer.*)

ALICK (*starting*).   What 's that ?
(*The three listen at the door ; the shouting dies down.*)

DAVID.   They 're terrible still ; what can make them so still ?
(*JAMES spirits himself away.   ALICK and DAVID blanch to hear MAGGIE speaking softly as if to JOHN.*)

MAGGIE.   Did you say you had lost, John ?   Of course you

would lose the first time, dear John. Six years. Very well, we 'll begin another six to-night. You 'll win yet. (*Fiercely*) Never give in, John, never give in !

(*The roar of the multitude breaks out again and comes rolling nearer.*)

DAVID.   I think he 's coming.

(JAMES *is fired into the room like a squeezed onion.*)

JAMES.   He 's coming !

(*They may go on speaking, but through the clang outside none could hear. The populace seem to be trying to take the committee room by assault. Out of the scrimmage a man emerges dishevelled and bursts into the room, closing the door behind him. It is* JOHN SHAND *in a five guinea suit, including the hat. There are other changes in him also, for he has been delving his way through loamy ground all those years. His right shoulder, which he used to raise to pound a path through the crowd, now remains permanently in that position. His mouth tends to close like a box. His eyes are tired, they need some one to pull the lids over them and send him to sleep for a week. But they are honest eyes still, and faithful, and could even light up his face at times with a smile, if the mouth would give a little help.*)

JOHN (*clinging to a chair that he may not fly straight to heaven*). I 'm in ; I 'm elected. Majority two hundred and forty-four ; I 'm John Shand, *M.P.*

(*The crowd have the news by this time and their roar breaks the door open.* JAMES *is off at once to tell them that he is to be Shand's brother-in-law. A teardrop clings to* ALICK'S *nose ;* DAVID *hits out playfully at* JOHN, *and* JOHN *in an ecstasy returns the blow.*)

DAVID.   Fling yourself at the door, father, and bar them out. Maggie, what keeps you so quiet now ?

MAGGIE (*weak in her limbs*). You 're sure you 're in, John ?

JOHN.   Majority 244.   I 've beaten the baronet.   I 've done it, Maggie, and not a soul to help me ; I 've done it alone. (*His voice breaks ; you could almost pick up the pieces.*)   I 'm as hoarse as a crow, and I have to address the Cowcaddens Club yet ; David, pump some oxygen into me.

DAVID.   Certainly, Mr. Shand. (*While he does it,* MAGGIE *is seeing visions.*)

ALICK. What are you doing, Maggie?

MAGGIE. This is the House of Commons, and I 'm John, catching the Speaker's eye for the first time. Do you see a queer little old wifie sitting away up there in the Ladies' Gallery? That 's me. Mr. Speaker, sir, I rise to make my historic maiden speech. I am no orator, sir; voice from Ladies' Gallery, ' Are you not, John? you 'll soon let them see that '; cries of ' Silence, woman,' and general indignation. Mr. Speaker, sir, I stand here diffidently with my eyes on the Treasury Bench; voice from the Ladies' Gallery, ' And you 'll soon have your coat-tails on it, John '; loud cries of ' Remove that little old wifie,' in which she is forcibly ejected, and the honourable gentleman resumes his seat in a torrent of admiring applause.

(ALICK *and* DAVID *waggle their proud heads.*)

JOHN (*tolerantly*). Maggie, Maggie.

MAGGIE. You 're not angry with me, John?

JOHN. No, no.

MAGGIE. But you glowered.

JOHN. I was thinking of Sir Peregrine. Just because I beat him at the poll he took a shabby revenge; he congratulated me in French, a language I haven't taken the trouble to master.

MAGGIE (*becoming a little taller*). Would it help you, John, if you were to marry a woman that could speak French?

DAVID (*quickly*). Not at all.

MAGGIE (*gloriously*). Mon cher Jean, laissez-moi parler le français, voulez-vous un interprète?

JOHN. Hullo!

MAGGIE. Je suis la sœur française de mes deux frères écossais.

DAVID (*worshipping her*). She 's been learning French.

JOHN (*lightly*). Well done.

MAGGIE (*grandly*). They 're arriving.

ALICK. Who?

MAGGIE. Our guests. This is London, and Mrs. John Shand is giving her first reception. (*Airily*) Have I told you, darling, who are coming to-night? There 's that dear Sir Peregrine. (*To* ALICK) Sir Peregrine, this *is* a pleasure. Avez-vous . . . So sorry we beat you at the poll.

JOHN. I 'm doubting the baronet would sit on you, Maggie.

MAGGIE.   I 've invited a lord to sit on the baronet.   *Voilà !*

DAVID (*delighted*).   You thing !   You 'll find the lords expensive.

MAGGIE.   Just a little cheap lord.   (JAMES *enters importantly.*)   My dear Lord Cheap, this is kind of you.

(JAMES *hopes that* MAGGIE'S *reason is not unbalanced.*)

DAVID (*who really ought to have had education*).   How de doo, Cheap ?

JAMES (*bewildered*).   Maggie——

MAGGIE.   Yes, do call me Maggie.

ALICK (*grinning*).   She 's practising her first party, James. The swells are at the door.

JAMES (*heavily*).   That 's what I came to say.   They *are* at the door.

JOHN.   Who ?

JAMES.   The swells ; in their motor.   (*He gives* JOHN *three cards.*)

JOHN.   ' Mr. Tenterden.'

DAVID.   Him that was speaking for you ?

JOHN.   The same.   He 's a whip and an Honourable. ' Lady Sybil Tenterden.'   (*Frowns.*)   Her !   She 's his sister.

MAGGIE.   A married woman ?

JOHN.   No.   ' The Comtesse de la Brière.'

MAGGIE (*the scholar*).   She must be French.

JOHN.   Yes ; I think she 's some relation.   She 's a widow.

JAMES.   But what am I to say to them ?   ('*Mr. Shand's compliments, and he will be proud to receive them*' *is the very least that the Wylies expect.*)

JOHN (*who was evidently made for great ends*).   Say I 'm very busy, but if they care to wait I hope presently to give them a few minutes.

JAMES (*thunderstruck*).   Good God, Mr. Shand !

(*But it makes him* JOHN'S *more humble servant than ever, and he departs with the message.*)

JOHN (*not unaware of the sensation he has created*).   I 'll go up and let the crowd see me from the window.

MAGGIE.   But——but——what are we to do with these ladies ?

JOHN (*as he tramps upwards*).   It 's your reception, Maggie ; this will prove you.

MAGGIE (*growing smaller*).   Tell me what you know about this Lady Sybil ?

JOHN.   The only thing I know about her is that she thinks me vulgar.

MAGGIE.   You ?

JOHN.   She has attended some of my meetings, and I 'm told she said that.

MAGGIE.   What could the woman mean ?

JOHN.   I wonder.   When I come down I 'll ask her.

(*With his departure* MAGGIE'S *nervousness increases.*)

ALICK (*encouragingly*).   In at them, Maggie, with your French.

MAGGIE.   It 's all slipping from me, father.

DAVID (*gloomily*).   I 'm sure to say ' for to come for to go.'

(*The newcomers glorify the room, and* MAGGIE *feels that they have lifted her up with the tongs and deposited her in one of the basins.   They are far from intending to be rude ; it is not their fault that thus do swans scatter the ducks. They do not know that they are guests of the family, they think merely that they are waiting with other strangers in a public room ; they undulate inquiringly, and if* MAGGIE *could undulate in return she would have no cause for offence. But she suddenly realises that this is an art as yet denied her, and that though* DAVID *might buy her evening-gowns as fine as theirs (and is at this moment probably deciding to do so), she would look better carrying them in her arms than on her person.   She also feels that to emerge from wraps as they are doing is more difficult than to plank your money on the counter for them.   The* COMTESSE *she could forgive, for she is old ; but* LADY SYBIL *is young and beautiful and comes lazily to rest like a stately ship of Tarsus.*)

COMTESSE (*smiling divinely, and speaking with such a pretty accent*).   I hope one is not in the way.   We were told we might wait.

MAGGIE (*bravely climbing out of the basin*).   Certainly—I am sure—if you will be so—it is——

(*She knows that* DAVID *and her father are very sorry for her.*)

(*A high voice is heard orating outside.*)

SYBIL (*screwing her nose deliciously*).   He is at it again, auntie.

COMTESSE. Mon Dieu ! (*Like one begging pardon of the universe*) It is Mr. Tenterden, you understand, making one more of his delightful speeches to the crowd. *Would* you be so charming as to shut the door ?

(*This to* DAVID *in such appeal that she is evidently making the petition of her life.* DAVID *saves her.*)

MAGGIE (*determined not to go under*). J'espère que vous— trouvez—cette—réunion—intéressante ?

COMTESSE. Vous parlez français ? Mais c'est charmant ! Voyons, causons un peu. Racontez-moi tout de ce grand homme, toutes les choses merveilleuses qu'il a faites.

MAGGIE. I—I—Je connais—— (*Alas !*)

COMTESSE (*naughtily*). Forgive me, mademoiselle, I thought you spoke French.

SYBIL (*who knows that* DAVID *admires her shoulders*). How wicked of you, auntie. (*To* MAGGIE) I assure you none of us can understand her when she gallops at that pace.

MAGGIE (*crushed*). It doesn't matter. I will tell Mr. Shand that you are here.

SYBIL (*drawling*). Please don't trouble him. We are really only waiting till my brother recovers and can take us back to our hotel.

MAGGIE. I 'll tell him.

(*She is glad to disappear up the stair.*)

COMTESSE. The lady seems distressed. Is she a relation of Mr. Shand ?

DAVID. Not for to say a relation. She 's my sister. Our name is Wylie.

(*But granite quarries are nothing to them.*)

COMTESSE. How do you do ? You are the committee man of Mr. Shand ?

DAVID. No, just friends.

COMTESSE (*gaily to the basins*). Aha ! I know you. Next, please ! Sybil, do you weigh yourself, or are you asleep ?

(LADY SYBIL *has sunk indolently into a weighing-chair.*)

SYBIL. Not quite, auntie.

COMTESSE (*the mirror of la politesse*). Tell me all about Mr. Shand. Was it here that he—picked up the pin ?

DAVID. The pin ?

COMTESSE. As *I* have read, a self-made man always begins

by picking up a pin.   After that, as the memoirs say, his rise
was rapid.

(DAVID, *however, is once more master of himself, and indeed
has begun to tot up the cost of their garments.*)

DAVID.   It wasn't a pin he picked up, my lady ; it was £300.

ALICK (*who feels that* JOHN'S *greatness has been outside the
conversation quite long enough*).   And his rise wasn't so rapid,
just at first, David !

DAVID.   He had his fight.   His original intention was to
become a minister ; he 's university-educated, you know ; he 's
not a working-man member.

ALICK (*with reverence*).   He 's an M.A.   But while he was
a student he got a place in an iron-cementer's business.

COMTESSE (*now far out of her depths*).   Iron-cementer ?

DAVID.   They scrape boilers.

COMTESSE.   I see.   The fun men have, Sybil !

DAVID (*with some solemnity*).   There have been millions
made in scraping boilers.   They say, father, he went into
business so as to be able to pay off the £300.

ALICK (*slily*).   So I 've heard.

COMTESSE.   Aha—it was a loan ?

(DAVID *and* ALICK *are astride their great subject now.*)

DAVID.   No, a gift—of a sort—from some well-wishers.
But they wouldn't hear of his paying it off, father !

ALICK.   Not them !

COMTESSE (*restraining an impulse to think of other things*).
That was kind, charming.

ALICK (*with a look at* DAVID).   Yes.   Well, my lady, he
developed a perfect genius for the iron-cementing.

DAVID.   But his ambition wasn't satisfied.   Soon he had
public life in his eye.   As a heckler he was something fearsome ;
they had to seat him on the platform for to keep him quiet.
Next they had to let him into the Chair.   After that he did
all the speaking ; he cleared all roads before him like a fire-
engine ; and when this vacancy occurred, you could hardly
say it did occur, so quickly did he step into it.   My lady, there
are few more impressive sights in the world than a Scotsman
on the make.

COMTESSE.   I can well believe it.   And now he has said
farewell to boilers ?

DAVID (*impressively*).   Not at all ; the firm promised if he was elected for to make him their London manager at £800 a year.

COMTESSE.   There is a strong man for you, Sybil ; but I believe you *are* asleep.

SYBIL (*stirring herself*).   Honestly I 'm not.   (*Sweetly to the others*) But *would* you mind finding out whether my brother is drawing to a close ?

(DAVID *goes out, leaving poor* ALICK *marooned.   The* COMTESSE *is kind to him.*)

COMTESSE.   Thank you very much.   (*Which helps* ALICK *out.*)   Don't you love a strong man, sleepy head ?

SYBIL (*preening herself*).   I never met one.

COMTESSE.   Neither have I.   But if you *did* meet one, would he wake you up ?

SYBIL.   I dare say he would find there were two of us.

COMTESSE (*considering her*).   Yes, I think he would.   Ever been in love, you cold thing ?

SYBIL (*yawning*).   I have never shot up in flame, auntie.

COMTESSE.   Think you could manage it ?

SYBIL.   If Mr. Right came along.

COMTESSE.   As a girl of to-day it would be your duty to tame him.

SYBIL.   As a girl of to-day I would try to do my duty.

COMTESSE.   And if it turned out that *he* tamed you instead ?

SYBIL.   He would have to do that if he were *my* Mr. Right.

COMTESSE.   And then ?

SYBIL.   Then, of course, I should adore him.   Auntie, I think if I ever really love it will be like Mary Queen of Scots, who said of her Bothwell that she could follow him round the world in her nighty.

COMTESSE.   My petite !

SYBIL.   I believe I mean it.

COMTESSE.   Oh, it is quite my conception of your character. Do you know, I am rather sorry for this Mr. John Shand.

SYBIL (*opening her fine eyes*).   Why ?   He is quite a boor, is he not ?

COMTESSE.   For that very reason.   Because his great hour is already nearly sped.   That wild bull manner that moves the multitude—they will laugh at it in your House of Commons.

SYBIL (*indifferent*). I suppose so.

COMTESSE. Yet if he had education——

SYBIL. Have we not been hearing how superbly he is educated ?

COMTESSE. It is such as you or me that he needs to educate him now. *You* could do it almost too well.

SYBIL (*with that pretty stretch of neck*). I am not sufficiently interested. I retire in your favour. How would you begin ?

COMTESSE. By asking him to drop in, about five, of course. By the way, I wonder is there a Mrs. Shand ?

SYBIL. I have no idea. But they marry young.

COMTESSE. If there is not, there is probably a lady waiting for him, somewhere in a boiler.

SYBIL. I dare say.

(MAGGIE *descends*.)

MAGGIE. Mr. Shand will be down directly.

COMTESSE. Thank you. Your brother has been giving us such an interesting account of his career. I forget, Sybil, whether he said that he was married.

MAGGIE. No, he 's not married ; but he will be soon.

COMTESSE. Ah ! (*She is merely making conversation*.) A friend of yours ?

MAGGIE (*now a scorner of herself*). I don't think much of her.

COMTESSE. In that case, tell me all about her.

MAGGIE. There 's not much to tell. She 's common, and stupid. One of those who go in for self-culture ; and then when the test comes they break down. (*With sinister enjoyment*) She 'll be the ruin of him.

COMTESSE. But is not that sad ! Figure to yourself how many men with greatness before them have been shipwrecked by marrying in the rank from which they sprang.

MAGGIE. I 've told her that.

COMTESSE. But she will not give him up ?

MAGGIE. No.

SYBIL. Why should she if he cares for her ? What is her name ?

MAGGIE. It 's—Maggie.

COMTESSE (*still uninterested*). Well, I am afraid that Maggie is to do for John. (JOHN *comes down*.) Ah, our hero !

JOHN. Sorry I have kept you waiting. The Comtesse ?

COMTESSE.   And my niece Lady Sybil Tenterden.   (SYBIL's *head inclines on its stem.*)   She is not really all my niece ;   I mean I am only half of her aunt.   What a triumph, Mr. Shand !

JOHN.   Oh, pretty fair, pretty fair.   Your brother has just finished addressing the crowd, Lady Sybil.

SYBIL.   Then we must not detain Mr. Shand, auntie.

COMTESSE (*who unless her heart is touched thinks insincerity charming*).   Only one word.   I heard you speak last night. Sublime !   Just the sort of impassioned eloquence that your House of Commons loves.

JOHN.   It 's very good of you to say so.

COMTESSE.   But we must run.   *Bon soir.*

(SYBIL *bows as to some one far away.*)

JOHN.   Good-night, Lady Sybil.   I hear you think I 'm vulgar.

(*Eyebrows are raised.*)

COMTESSE.   My dear Mr. Shand, what absurd——

JOHN.   I was told she said that after hearing me speak.

COMTESSE.   Quite a mistake, I——

JOHN (*doggedly*).   Is it not true ?

SYBIL (' *waking up* ').   You seem to know, Mr. Shand ; and as you press me so unnecessarily—well, yes, that is how you struck me.

COMTESSE.   My child !

SYBIL (*who is a little agitated*).   He would have it.

JOHN (*perplexed*).   What 's the matter ?   I just wanted to know, because if it 's true I must alter it.

COMTESSE.   There, Sybil, see how he values your good opinion.

SYBIL (*her svelte figure giving like a fishing-rod*).   It is very nice of you to put it in that way, Mr. Shand.   Forgive me.

JOHN.   But I don't quite understand yet.   Of course, it can't matter to me, Lady Sybil, what you think of me ; what I mean is, that I mustn't be vulgar if it would be injurious to my career.

(*The fishing-rod regains its rigidity.*)

SYBIL.   I see.   No, of course, I could not affect your career, Mr. Shand.

JOHN (*who quite understands that he is being challenged*). That 's so, Lady Sybil, meaning no offence.

SYBIL (*who has a naughty little impediment in her voice when she is most alluring*). Of course not. And we are friends again ?

JOHN. Certainly.

SYBIL. Then I hope you will come to see me in London as I present no terrors.

JOHN (*he is a man, is* JOHN). I 'll be very pleased.

SYBIL. Any afternoon about five.

JOHN. Much obliged. And you can teach me the things I don't know yet, if you 'll be so kind.

SYBIL (*the impediment becoming more assertive*). If you wish it, I shall do my best.

JOHN. Thank you, Lady Sybil. And who knows there may be one or two things I can teach you.

SYBIL (*it has now become an angel's hiccough*). Yes, we can help one another. Good-bye till then.

JOHN. Good-bye. Maggie, the ladies are going.

(*During this skirmish* MAGGIE *has stood apart. At the mention of her name they glance at one another.* JOHN *escorts* SYBIL, *but the* COMTESSE *turns back*.)

COMTESSE. Are you, then, *the* Maggie ? (MAGGIE *nods rather defiantly and the* COMTESSE *is distressed*.) But if I had known I would not have said those things. Please forgive an old woman.

MAGGIE. It doesn't matter.

COMTESSE. I—I dare say it will be all right. Mademoiselle, if I were you I would not encourage those *tête-à-têtes* with Lady Sybil. I am the rude one, but she is the dangerous one ; and I am afraid his impudence has attracted her. *Bon voyage*, Miss Maggie.

MAGGIE. Good-bye—but I *can* speak French. Je parle français. Isn't that right ?

COMTESSE. But yes, it is excellent. (*Making things easy for her*) C'est très bien.

MAGGIE. Je me suis embrouillée—la dernière fois.

COMTESSE. Good ! Shall I speak more slowly ?

MAGGIE. No, no. Non, non, faster, faster.

COMTESSE. J'admire votre courage !

MAGGIE. Je comprends chaque mot.

COMTESSE. Parfait ! Bravo !

MAGGIE.   Voilà !

COMTESSE.   Superbe !

(*She goes, applauding ; and* MAGGIE *has a moment of elation, which however has passed before* JOHN *returns for his hat.*)

MAGGIE.   Have you more speaking to do, John ?

(*He is somehow in high good-humour.*)

JOHN.   I must run across and address the Cowcaddens Club. (*He sprays his throat with a hand-spray.*)   I wonder if I *am* vulgar, Maggie ?

MAGGIE.   You are not, but *I* am.

JOHN.   Not that *I* can see.

MAGGIE.   Look how overdressed I am, John !   I knew it was too showy when I ordered it, and yet I could not resist the thing.   But I will tone down, I will.   What did you think of Lady Sybil ?

JOHN.   That young woman had better be careful.   She 's a bit of a besom, Maggie.

MAGGIE.   She 's beautiful, John.

JOHN.   She has a neat way of stretching herself.   For playing with she would do as well as another.

(*She looks at him wistfully.*)

MAGGIE.   You couldn't stay and have a talk for a few minutes ?

JOHN.   If you want me, Maggie.   The longer you keep them waiting, the more they think of you.

MAGGIE.   When are you to announce that we 're to be married, John ?

JOHN.   I won't be long.   You 've waited a year more than you need have done, so I think it 's your due I should hurry things now.

MAGGIE.   I think it 's noble of you.

JOHN.   Not at all, Maggie ; the nobleness has been yours in waiting so patiently.   And your brothers would insist on it at any rate.   They 're watching me like cats with a mouse.

MAGGIE.   It 's so little I 've done to help.

JOHN.   Three hundred pounds.

MAGGIE.   I 'm getting a thousand per cent. for it.

JOHN.   And very pleased I am you should think so, Maggie.

MAGGIE.   Is it terrible hard to you, John ?

JOHN. It 's not hard at all. I can say truthfully, Maggie, that all, or nearly all, I 've seen of you in these six years has gone to increase my respect for you.

MAGGIE. Respect !

JOHN. And a bargain 's a bargain.

MAGGIE. If it wasn't that you 're so glorious to me, John, I would let you off.

(*There is a gleam in his eye, but he puts it out.*)

JOHN. In my opinion, Maggie, we 'll be a very happy pair.

(*She accepts this eagerly.*)

MAGGIE. We know each other so well, John, don't we ?

JOHN. I 'm an extraordinary queer character, and I suppose nobody knows me well except myself ; but I know you, Maggie, to the very roots of you.

(*She magnanimously lets this remark alone.*)

MAGGIE. And it 's not as if there was any other woman you —fancied more, John.

JOHN. There 's none whatever.

MAGGIE. If there ever should be—oh, if there ever should be ! Some woman with charm.

JOHN. Maggie, you forget yourself. There couldn't be another woman once I was a married man.

MAGGIE. One has heard of such things.

JOHN. Not in Scotsmen, Maggie ; not in Scotsmen.

MAGGIE. I 've sometimes thought, John, that the difference between us and the English is that the Scotch are hard in all other respects but soft with women, and the English are hard with women but soft in all other respects.

JOHN. You 've forgotten the grandest moral attribute of a Scotsman, Maggie, that he 'll do nothing which might damage his career.

MAGGIE. Ah, but John, whatever you do, you do it so tremendously ; and if you were to love, what a passion it would be.

JOHN. There 's something in that, I suppose.

MAGGIE. And then, what could I do ? For the desire of my life now, John, is to help you to get everything you want, except just that I want you to have me, too.

JOHN. We 'll get on fine, Maggie.

MAGGIE. You 're just making the best of it. They say that

love is sympathy, and if that's so, mine must be a great love for you, for I see all you are feeling this night and bravely hiding; I feel for you as if I was John Shand myself. (*He sighs.*)

JOHN.   I had best go to the meeting, Maggie.

MAGGIE.   Not yet.   Can you look me in the face, John, and deny that there is surging within you a mighty desire to be free, to begin the new life untrammelled?

JOHN.   Leave such maggots alone, Maggie.

MAGGIE.   It's a shame of me not to give you up.

JOHN.   I would consider you a very foolish woman if you did.

MAGGIE.   If I were John Shand I would no more want to take Maggie Wylie with me through the beautiful door that has opened wide for you than I would want to take an old pair of shoon.   Why don't you bang the door in my face, John? (*A tremor runs through* JOHN.)

JOHN.   A bargain's a bargain, Maggie.

   (MAGGIE *moves about, an eerie figure, breaking into little cries.   She flutters round him, threateningly.*)

MAGGIE.   Say one word about wanting to get out of it, and I'll put the lawyers on you.

JOHN.   Have I hinted at such a thing?

MAGGIE.   The document holds you hard and fast.

JOHN.   It does.

   (*She gloats miserably.*)

MAGGIE.   The woman never rises with the man.   I'll drag you down, John.   I'll drag you down.

JOHN.   Have no fear of that, I won't let you.   I'm too strong.

MAGGIE.   You'll miss the prettiest thing in the world, and all owing to me.

JOHN.   What's that?

MAGGIE.   Romance.

JOHN.   Poof!

MAGGIE.   All's cold and grey without it, John.   They that have had it have slipped in and out of heaven.

JOHN.   You're exaggerating, Maggie.

MAGGIE.   You've worked so hard, you've had none of the fun that comes to most men long before they're your age.

JOHN.   I never was one for fun.   I cannot call to mind, Maggie, ever having laughed in my life.

MAGGIE.   You have no sense of humour.

JOHN.   Not a spark.

MAGGIE.   I 've sometimes thought that if you had, it might make you fonder of me.   I think one needs a sense of humour to be fond of me.

JOHN.   I remember reading of some one that said it needed a surgical operation to get a joke into a Scotsman's head.

MAGGIE.   Yes, that 's been said.

JOHN.   What beats me, Maggie, is how you could insert a joke with an operation.

(*He considers this and gives it up.*)

MAGGIE.   That 's not the kind of fun I was thinking of.   I mean fun with the lasses, John—gay, jolly, harmless fun.   They could be impudent fashionable beauties now, stretching themselves to attract you, like that hiccoughing little devil, and running away from you, and crooking their fingers to you to run after them.

(*He draws a big breath.*)

JOHN.   No, I never had that.

MAGGIE.   It 's every man's birthright, and you would have it now but for me.

JOHN.   I can do without, Maggie.

MAGGIE.   It 's like missing out all the Saturdays.

JOHN.   You feel sure, I suppose, that an older man wouldn't suit you better, Maggie ?

MAGGIE.   I couldn't feel surer of anything.   You 're just my ideal.

JOHN.   Yes, yes.   Well, that 's as it should be.

(*She threatens him again.*)

MAGGIE.   David has the document.   It 's carefully locked away.

JOHN.   He would naturally take good care of it.

(*The pride of the Wylies deserts her.*)

MAGGIE.   John, I make you a solemn promise that, in consideration of the circumstances of our marriage, if you should ever fall in love I 'll act differently from other wives.

JOHN.   There will be no occasion, Maggie.

(*Her voice becomes tremulous.*)

MAGGIE.   John, David doesn't have the document.   He thinks he has, but I have it here.

(*Somewhat heavily* JOHN *surveys the fatal paper.*)

JOHN.   Well do I mind the look of it, Maggie.   Yes, yes, that's it.   Umpha !

MAGGIE.   You don't ask why I 've brought it.

JOHN.   Why did you ?

MAGGIE.   Because I thought I might perhaps have the courage and the womanliness to give it back to you.   (JOHN *has a brief dream.*)   Will you never hold it up against me in the future that I couldn't do that ?

JOHN.   I promise you, Maggie, I never will.

MAGGIE.   To go back to the Pans and take up my old life there, when all these six years my eyes have been centred on this night !   I 've been waiting for this night as long as you have been ;   and now to go back there, and wizen and dry up, when I might be married to John Shand !

JOHN.   And you will be, Maggie.   You have my word.

MAGGIE.   Never—never—never.   (*She tears up the document. He remains seated immovable, but the gleam returns to his eye. She rages first at herself and then at him.*)   I 'm a fool, a fool, to let you go.   I tell you, you 'll rue this day, for you need me, you 'll come to grief without me.   There 's nobody can help you as I could have helped you.   I 'm essential to your career, and you 're blind not to see it.

JOHN.   What 's that, Maggie ?   In no circumstances would I allow any meddling with my career.

MAGGIE.   You would never have known I was meddling with it.   But that 's over.   Don't be in too great a hurry to marry, John.   Have your fling with the beautiful dolls first. Get the whiphand of the haughty ones, John.   Give them their licks.   Every time they hiccough let them have an extra slap in memory of me.   And be sure to remember this, my man, that the one who marries you will find you out.

JOHN.   Find me out ?

MAGGIE.   However careful a man is, his wife always finds out his failings.

JOHN.   I don't know, Maggie, to what failings you refer.

(*The Cowcaddens Club has burst its walls, and is pouring this way to raise the new Member on its crest.   The first wave hurls itself against the barber's shop with cries of ' Shand, Shand, Shand !'   For a moment* JOHN *stems the torrent by planting his back against the door.*)

You are acting under an impulse, Maggie, and I can't take advantage of it. Think the matter over, and we 'll speak about it in the morning.

MAGGIE. No, I can't go through it again. It ends to-night and now. Good luck, John.

(*She is immediately submerged in the sea that surges through the door, bringing much wreckage with it. In a moment the place is so full that another cupful could not find standing room. Some slippery ones are squeezed upwards and remain aloft as warnings.* JOHN *has jumped on to the stair, and harangues the flood vainly like another Canute. It is something about freedom and noble minds, and, though unheard, goes to all heads, including the speaker's. By the time he is audible sentiment has him for her own.*)

JOHN. But, gentlemen, one may have too much even of freedom. (*No, no.*) Yes, Mr. Adamson. One may want to be tied. (*Never, never.*) I say yes, Willie Cameron ; and I have found a young lady who I am proud to say is willing to be tied to me. I 'm to be married ! (*Uproar.*) Her name 's Miss Wylie. (*Transport.*) Quiet ; she 's here now. (*Frenzy.*) She was here ! Where are you, Maggie ? (*A small voice—* 'I 'm here.' *A hundred great voices—*'Where—where—where ? ' *The small voice—*' I 'm so little none of you can see me.'*)

(*Three men, name of Wylie, buffet their way forward.*)

DAVID. James, father, have you grip of her ?

ALICK. We 've got her.

DAVID. Then hoist her up.

(*The queer little elated figure is raised aloft. With her fingers she can just touch the stars. Not unconscious of the nobility of his behaviour, the hero of the evening points an impressive finger at her.*)

JOHN. Gentlemen, the future Mrs. John Shand ! (*Cries of* 'Speech, speech !') No, no, being a lady she can't make a speech, but——

(*The heroine of the evening surprises him.*)

MAGGIE. I can make a speech, and I will make a speech, and it 's in two words, and they 're these—(*holding out her arms to enfold all the members of the Cowcaddens Club*)—My Constituents ! (*Dementia.*)

ACT III

A FEW minutes ago the Comtesse de la Brière, who has not recently been in England, was shown into the London home of the Shands. Though not sufficiently interested to express her surprise in words, she raised her eyebrows on finding herself in a charming room ; she had presumed that the Shand scheme of decoration would be as impossible as themselves.

It is the little room behind the dining-room for which English architects have long been famous ; ' Make something of this, and you will indeed be a clever one,' they seem to say to you as they unveil it. The Comtesse finds that John has undoubtedly made something of it. It is his ' study ' (mon Dieu, the words these English use !) and there is nothing in it that offends ; there is so much not in it too that might so easily have been there. It is not in the least ornate ; there are no colours quarrelling with each other (unseen, unheard by the blissful occupant of the revolving chair) ; the Comtesse has not even the gentle satisfaction of noting a ' suite ' in stained oak. Nature might have taken a share in the decorations, so restful are they to the eyes ; it is the working room of a man of culture, probably lately down from Oxford ; at a first meeting there is nothing in it that pretends to be what it is not. Our visitor is a little disappointed, but being fair-minded blows her absent host a kiss for disappointing her.

He has even, she observes with a twinkle, made something of the most difficult of his possessions, the little wife. For Maggie, who is here receiving her, has been quite creditably toned down. He has put her into a little grey frock that not only deals gently with her personal defects, but is in harmony with the room. Evidently, however, she has not ' risen ' with him, for she is as stupid as ever ; the Comtesse, who remembers having liked her the better of the two, could shake her for being so stupid. For instance, why is she not asserting herself in that other apartment ?

704

The other apartment is really a correctly solemn dining-room, of which we have a glimpse through partly open folding-doors. At this moment it is harbouring Mr. Shand's ladies' committee, who sit with pens and foolscap round the large table, awaiting the advent of their leader.   There are nobly wise ones and some foolish ones among them, for we are back in the strange days when it was considered ' unwomanly ' for women to have minds. The Comtesse peeps at them with curiosity, as they arrange their papers or are ushered into the dining-room through a door which we cannot see. To her frivolous lady-ship they are a species of wild fowl, and she is specially amused to find her niece among them. She demands an explanation as soon as the communicating doors close.

COMTESSE.   Tell me, since when has my dear Sybil become one of these ladies ?   It is not like her.

(MAGGIE *is obviously not clever enough to understand the woman question.   Her eye rests longingly on a half-finished stocking as she innocently but densely replies :*)

MAGGIE.   I think it was about the time that my husband took up their cause.

(*The* COMTESSE *has been hearing tales of* LADY SYBIL *and the barbarian ; and after having the grace to hesitate, she speaks with the directness for which she is famed in Mayfair.*)

COMTESSE.   Mrs. Shand, excuse me for saying that if half of what I hear be true, your husband is seeing that lady a great deal too often.   (MAGGIE *is expressionless ; she reaches for her stocking, whereat her guest loses patience.*)   Oh, mon Dieu, put that down ; you can buy them at two francs the pair.   Mrs. Shand, why do not you compel yourself to take an intelligent interest in your husband's work ?

MAGGIE.   I typewrite his speeches.

COMTESSE.   But do you know what they are about ?

MAGGIE.   They are about various subjects.

COMTESSE.   Oh !

(*Did* MAGGIE *give her an unseen quizzical glance before demurely resuming the knitting ?   One is not certain, as* JOHN *has come in, and this obliterates her. ' A Scotsman on the make,' of whom* DAVID *has spoken reverently, is still*

z

to be read—in a somewhat better bound volume—in JOHN
SHAND'S *person ; but it is as doggedly honest a face as ever ;
and he champions women, not for personal ends, but because
his blessed days of poverty gave him a light upon their needs.
His self-satisfaction, however, has increased, and he has
pleasantly forgotten some things.   For instance, he can now
call out ' Porter ' at railway stations without dropping his
hands for the barrow.*   MAGGIE *introduces the* COMTESSE,
and he is still undaunted.)

JOHN.   I remember you well—at Glasgow.

COMTESSE.   It must be quite two years ago, Mr. Shand.

(JOHN *has no objection to showing that he has had a classical
education.*)

JOHN.   *Tempus fugit,* Comtesse.

COMTESSE.   I have not been much in this country since then,
and I return to find you a coming man.

(*Fortunately his learning is tempered with modesty.*)

JOHN.   Oh, I don't know, I don't know.

COMTESSE.   The Ladies' Champion.

(*His modesty is tempered with a respect for truth.*)

JOHN.   Well, well.

COMTESSE.   And you are about, as I understand, to introduce
a bill to give women an equal right with men to grow beards
(*which is all she knows about it.   He takes the remark literally*).

JOHN.   There 's nothing about beards in it, Comtesse.
(*She gives him time to cogitate, and is pleased to note that there is
no result.*)   Have you typed my speech, Maggie ?

MAGGIE.   Yes ; twenty-six pages.   (*She produces it from a
drawer.*)

(*Perhaps* JOHN *wishes to impress the visitor.*)

JOHN.   I 'm to give the ladies' committee a general idea of
it.   Just see, Maggie, if I know the peroration.   ' In conclusion, Mr. Speaker, these are the reasonable demands of every
intelligent Englishwoman '—I had better say British woman—
' and I am proud to nail them to my flag '—

(*The visitor is properly impressed.*)

COMTESSE.   Oho ! defies his leaders !

JOHN.   —' so long as I can do so without embarrassing the
Government.'

COMTESSE.   Ah, ah, Mr. Shand !

JOHN.   'I call upon the Front Bench, sir, loyally but firmly '—

COMTESSE.   Firm again !

JOHN.   —'either to accept my Bill, or to promise *without delay* to bring in one of their own ; and if they decline to do so I solemnly warn them that though I will not press the matter to a division just now '—

COMTESSE.   Ahem !

JOHN.   —' I will bring it forward again in the near future.' And now, Comtesse, *you* know that I 'm not going to divide— and not another soul knows it.

COMTESSE.   I am indeed flattered by your confidence.

JOHN.   I 've only told you because I don't care who knows now.

COMTESSE.   Oh !

(*Somehow* MAGGIE *seems to be dissatisfied.*)

MAGGIE.   But why is that, John ?

JOHN.   I daren't keep the Government in doubt any longer about what I mean to do.   I 'll show the whips the speech privately to-night.

MAGGIE (*who still wants to know*).   But not to go to a division is hedging, isn't it ?   Is that strong ?

JOHN.   To make the speech at all, Maggie, is stronger than most would dare.   They would *do* for me if I went to a division.

MAGGIE.   Bark but not bite ?

JOHN.   Now, now, Maggie, you 're out of your depth.

MAGGIE.   I suppose that 's it.

(*The* COMTESSE *remains in the shallows.*)

COMTESSE.   But what will the ladies say, Mr. Shand ?

JOHN.   They won't like it, Comtesse, but they 've got to lump it.

(*Here the maid appears with a card for* MAGGIE, *who considers it quietly.*)

JOHN.   Any one of importance ?

MAGGIE.   No.

JOHN.   Then I 'm ready, Maggie.

(*This is evidently an intimation that she is to open the folding-doors, and he makes an effective entrance into the dining-room, his thumb in his waistcoat. There is a delicious clapping of hands from the committee, and the door closes. Not till then does* MAGGIE, *who has grown thoughtful, tell her maid to admit the visitor.*)

COMTESSE. Another lady, Mrs. Shand ?

MAGGIE. The card says ' Mr. Charles Venables.'

(*The* COMTESSE *is really interested at last.*)

COMTESSE. Charles Venables ! Do *you* know him ?

MAGGIE. I think I call to mind meeting one of that name at the Foreign Office party.

COMTESSE. One of that name ! He who is a Minister of your Cabinet. But as you know him so little why should he call on you ?

MAGGIE. I wonder.

(MAGGIE'S *glance wanders to the drawer in which she has replaced* JOHN'S *speech.*)

COMTESSE. Well, well, I shall take care of you, petite.

MAGGIE. Do *you* know him ?

COMTESSE. Do I know him ! The last time I saw him he asked me to—to—hem !—ma chérie, it was thirty years ago.

MAGGIE. Thirty years !

COMTESSE. I was a pretty woman then. I dare say I shall detest him now ; but if I find I do not—let us have a little plot —I shall drop this book ; and then perhaps you will be so charming as—as not to be here for a little while ?

(MR. VENABLES, *who enters, is such a courtly seigneur that he seems to bring the eighteenth century with him ; you feel that his sedan chair is at the door. He stoops over* MAGGIE'S *plebeian hand.*)

VENABLES. I hope you will pardon my calling, Mrs. Shand ; we had such a pleasant talk the other evening.

(MAGGIE, *of course, is at once deceived by his gracious manner.*)

MAGGIE. I think it 's kind of you. Do you know each other ? The Comtesse de la Brière.

(*He repeats the name with some emotion, and the* COMTESSE, *half mischievously, half sadly, holds a hand before her face.*)

VENABLES. Comtesse.

COMTESSE. Thirty years, Mr. Venables.

(*He gallantly removes the hand that screens her face.*)

VENABLES. It does not seem so much.

(*She gives him a similar scrutiny.*)

COMTESSE.   Mon Dieu, it seems all that !
(*They smile rather ruefully.*   MAGGIE *like a kind hostess relieves the tension.*)

MAGGIE.   The Comtesse has taken a cottage in Surrey for the summer.

VENABLES.   I am overjoyed.

COMTESSE.   No, Charles, you are not.   You no longer care. Fickle one !   And it is only thirty years.
(*He sinks into a chair beside her.*)

VENABLES.   Those heavenly evenings, Comtesse, on the Bosphorus.

COMTESSE.   I refuse to talk of them.   I hate you.
(*But she drops the book, and* MAGGIE *fades from the room. It is not a very clever departure, and the old diplomatist smiles.   Then he sighs a beautiful sigh, for he does all things beautifully.*)

VENABLES.   It is moonlight, Comtesse, on the Golden Horn.

COMTESSE.   Who are those two young things in a caïque ?

VENABLES.   Is he the brave Leander, Comtesse, and is she Hero of the Lamp ?

COMTESSE.   No, she is the foolish wife of the French Ambassador, and he is a good-for-nothing British attaché trying to get her husband's secrets out of her.

VENABLES.   Is it possible !   They part at a certain garden gate.

COMTESSE.   Oh, Charles, Charles !

VENABLES.   But you promised to come back ;   I waited there till dawn.   Blanche, if you *had* come back——

COMTESSE.   How is Mrs. Venables ?

VENABLES.   She is rather poorly.   *I* think it 's gout.

COMTESSE   And you ?

VENABLES.   I creak a little in the mornings.

COMTESSE.   So do I.   There is such a good man at Wiesbaden.

VENABLES.   The Homburg fellow is better.   The way he patched me up last summer—Oh, Lord, Lord !

COMTESSE.   Yes, Charles, the game is up ;   we are two old fogies.   (*They groan in unison ;   then she raps him sharply on the knuckles.*)   Tell me, sir, what are you doing here ?

VENABLES.   Merely a friendly call.

COMTESSE.   I do not believe it.

VENABLES.   The same woman ; the old delightful candour.

COMTESSE.   The same man ; the old fibs. (*She sees that the door is asking a question.*) Yes, come, Mrs. Shand, I have had quite enough of him ; I warn you he is here for some crafty purpose.

MAGGIE (*drawing back timidly*).   Surely not ?

VENABLES.   Really, Comtesse, you make conversation difficult. To show that my intentions are innocent, Mrs. Shand, I propose that you choose the subject.

MAGGIE (*relieved*).   There, Comtesse.

VENABLES.   I hope your husband is well ?

MAGGIE.   Yes, thank you. (*With a happy thought*) I decide that we talk about him.

VENABLES.   If you wish it.

COMTESSE.   Be careful ; *he* has chosen the subject.

MAGGIE.   *I* chose it, didn't I ?

VENABLES.   You know you did.

MAGGIE (*appealingly*).   You admire John ?

VENABLES.   Very much. But he puzzles me a little. You Scots, Mrs. Shand, are such a mixture of the practical and the emotional that you escape out of an Englishman's hand like a trout.

MAGGIE (*open-eyed*).   Do we ?

VENABLES.   Well, not you, but your husband. I have known few men make a worse beginning in the House. He had the most atrocious bow-wow public-park manner——

COMTESSE.   I remember that manner !

MAGGIE.   No, he hadn't.

VENABLES (*soothingly*).   At first. But by his second session he had shed all that, and he is now a pleasure to listen to. By the way, Comtesse, have you found any dark intention in that ?

COMTESSE.   You wanted to know whether he talks over these matters with his wife ; and she has told you that he does not.

MAGGIE (*indignantly*).   I haven't said a word about it, have I ?

VENABLES.   Not a word. Then, again, I admire him for his impromptu speeches.

MAGGIE.   What is impromptu ?

VENABLES.   Unprepared.   They have contained some grave blunders, not so much of judgment as of taste——

MAGGIE (*hotly*).   *I* don't think so.

VENABLES.   Pardon me.   But he has righted himself subsequently in the neatest way.   I have always found that the man whose second thoughts are good is worth watching.   Well, Comtesse, I see you have something to say.

COMTESSE.   You are wondering whether she can tell you who gives him his second thoughts.

MAGGIE.   Gives them to John ?   I would like to see anybody try to give thoughts to John

VENABLES.   Quite so.

COMTESSE.   Is there anything more that has roused your admiration, Charles ?

VENABLES (*purring*).   Let me see.   Yes, we are all much edified by his humour.

COMTESSE (*surprised indeed*).   His humour ?   That man !

MAGGIE (*with hauteur*).   Why not ?

VENABLES.   I assure you, Comtesse, some of the neat things in his speeches convulse the House.   A word has even been coined for them—Shandisms.

COMTESSE (*slowly recovering from a blow*).   Humour !

VENABLES.   In conversation, I admit, he strikes one as being—ah—somewhat lacking in humour.

COMTESSE (*pouncing*).   You are wondering who supplies his speeches with the humour.

MAGGIE.   Supplies John ?

VENABLES.   Now that you mention it, some of his Shandisms do have a curiously feminine quality.

COMTESSE.   You have thought it might be a woman.

VENABLES.   Really, Comtesse——

COMTESSE.   I see it all.   Charles, you thought it might be the wife !

VENABLES (*flinging up his hands*).   I own up.

MAGGIE (*bewildered*).   Me ?

VENABLES.   Forgive me, I see I was wrong.

MAGGIE (*alarmed*).   Have I been doing John any harm ?

VENABLES.   On the contrary, I am relieved to know that there are no hairpins in his speeches.   If he is at home, Mrs.

Shand, may I see him ?   I am going to be rather charming to him.

MAGGIE (*drawn in two directions*).   Yes, he is—oh yes—but——

VENABLES.   That is to say, Comtesse, if he proves himself the man I believe him to be.

(*This arrests* MAGGIE *almost as she has reached the dining-room door.*)

MAGGIE (*hesitating*).   He is very busy just now.

VENABLES (*smiling*).   I think he will see me.

MAGGIE.   Is it something about his speech ?

VENABLES (*the smile hardening*).   Well, yes, it is.

MAGGIE.   Then I dare say I could tell you what you want to know without troubling him, as I 've been typing it.

VENABLES (*with a sigh*).   I don't acquire information in that way.

COMTESSE.   I trust not.

MAGGIE.   There 's no secret about it.   He is to show it to the whips to-night.

VENABLES (*sharply*).   You are sure of that ?

COMTESSE.   It is quite true, Charles.   I heard him say so ; and indeed he repeated what he called the ' peroration ' before me.

MAGGIE.   I know it by heart.   (*She plays a bold game.*) ' These are the demands of all intelligent British women, and I am proud to nail them to my flag '——

COMTESSE.   The very words, Mrs. Shand.

MAGGIE (*looking at her imploringly*).   ' And I don't care how they may embarrass the Government.'   (*The* COMTESSE *is bereft of speech, so suddenly has she been introduced to the real* MAGGIE SHAND.)   ' If the right honourable gentleman will give us his pledge to introduce a similar Bill this session I will willingly withdraw mine ; but otherwise I solemnly warn him that I will press the matter now to a division.'

(*She turns her face from the great man ; she has gone white.*)

VENABLES (*after a pause*).   Capital.

(*The blood returns to* MAGGIE'S *heart.*)

COMTESSE (*who is beginning to enjoy herself very much*).   Then you are pleased to know that he means to, as you say, go to a division ?

VENABLES. Delighted. The courage of it will be the making of him.

COMTESSE. I see.

VENABLES. Had he been to hedge we should have known that he was a pasteboard knight and have disregarded him.

COMTESSE. I see.

(*She desires to catch the eye of* MAGGIE, *but it is carefully turned from her.*)

VENABLES. Mrs. Shand, let us have him in at once.

COMTESSE. Yes, yes, indeed.

(MAGGIE'S *anxiety returns, but she has to call* JOHN *in.*)

JOHN (*impressed*). Mr. Venables ! This is an honour.

VENABLES. How are you, Shand ?

JOHN. Sit down, sit down. (*Becoming himself again.*) I can guess what you have come about.

VENABLES. Ah, you Scotsmen.

JOHN. Of course I know I'm harassing the Government a good deal——

VENABLES (*blandly*). Not at all, Shand. The Government are very pleased.

JOHN. You don't expect me to believe that ?

VENABLES. I called here to give you the proof of it. You may know that we are to have a big meeting at Leeds on the 24th, when two Ministers are to speak. There is room for a third speaker, and I am authorised to offer that place to you.

JOHN. To me !

VENABLES. Yes.

JOHN (*swelling*). It would be—the Government taking me up.

VENABLES. Don't make too much of it ; it would be an acknowledgment that they look upon you as one of their likely young men.

MAGGIE. John !

JOHN (*not found wanting in a trying hour*). It's a bribe. You are offering me this on condition that I don't make my speech. How can you think so meanly of me as to believe that I would play the women's cause false for the sake of my own advancement. I refuse your bribe.

VENABLES (*liking him for the first time*). Good. But you are wrong. There are no conditions, and we want you to make your speech. Now do you accept ?

JOHN (*still suspicious*).   If you make me the same offer after you have read it.   I insist on your reading it first.

VENABLES (*sighing*).   By all means.

(MAGGIE *is in an agony as she sees* JOHN *hand the speech to his leader.   On the other hand, the* COMTESSE *thrills.*)

But I assure you we look on the speech as a small matter. The important thing is your intention of going to a division ; and we agree to that also.

JOHN (*losing his head*).   What's that ?

VENABLES.   Yes, we agree.

JOHN.   But—but—why, you have been threatening to ex-communicate me if I dared.

VENABLES.   All done to test you, Shand.

JOHN.   To test me ?

VENABLES.   We know that a division on your Bill can have no serious significance ; we shall see to that.   And so the test was to be whether you had the pluck to divide the House.   Had you been intending to talk big in this speech, and then hedge, through fear of the Government, they would have had no further use for you.

JOHN (*heavily*).   I understand.   (*But there is one thing he cannot understand, which is, why* VENABLES *should be so sure that he is not to hedge.*)

VENABLES (*turning over the pages carelessly*).   Any of your good things in this, Shand ?

JOHN (*whose one desire is to get the pages back*).   No, I—no—it isn't necessary you should read it now.

VENABLES (*from politeness only*).   Merely for my own pleasure.   I shall look through it this evening.   (*He rolls up the speech to put it in his pocket.*   JOHN *turns despairingly to* MAGGIE, *though well aware that no help can come from her.*)

MAGGIE.   That's the only copy there is, John.   (*To* VENABLES) Let me make a fresh one, and send it to you in an hour or two.

VENABLES (*good-naturedly*).   I could not put you to that trouble, Mrs. Shand.   I will take good care of it.

MAGGIE.   If anything were to happen to you on the way home, wouldn't whatever is in your pocket be considered to be the property of your heirs ?

VENABLES (*laughing*).   Now there is forethought !   Shand,

I think that after that——! (*He returns the speech to* JOHN, *whose hand swallows it greedily.*) She is Scotch too, Comtesse.

COMTESSE (*delighted*). Yes, she is Scotch too.

VENABLES. Though the only persons likely to do for me in the street, Shand, are your ladies' committee. Ever since they took the horse out of my brougham, I can scent them a mile away.

COMTESSE. A mile? Charles, peep in there.

(*He softly turns the handle of the dining-room door, and realises that his scent is not so good as he had thought it. He bids his hostess and the* COMTESSE *good-bye in a burlesque whisper and tiptoes off to safer places.* JOHN *having gone out with him,* MAGGIE *can no longer avoid the* COMTESSE'S *reproachful eye. That much injured lady advances upon her with accusing finger.*)

COMTESSE. So, madam !

(MAGGIE *is prepared for her.*)

MAGGIE. I don't know what you mean.

COMTESSE. Yes, you do. I mean that there *is* some one who 'helps' our Mr. Shand.

MAGGIE. There's not.

COMTESSE. And it *is* a woman, and it's you.

MAGGIE. I help in the little things.

COMTESSE. The little things ! You are the Pin he picked up and that is to make his fortune. And now what I want to know is whether your John is aware that you help at all.

(JOHN *returns, and at once provides the answer.*)

JOHN. Maggie, Comtesse, I've done it again !

MAGGIE. I'm so glad, John.

(*The* COMTESSE *is in an ecstasy.*)

COMTESSE. And all because you were not to hedge, Mr. Shand.

(*His appeal to her with the wistfulness of a schoolboy makes him rather attractive.*)

JOHN. You won't tell on me, Comtesse ! (*He thinks it out.*) They had just guessed I would be firm because they know I'm a strong man. You little saw, Maggie, what a good turn you were doing me when you said you wanted to make another copy of the speech.

(*She is dense.*)

MAGGIE.   How, John ?

JOHN.   Because now I can alter the end.

(*She is enlightened.*)

MAGGIE.   So you can !

JOHN.   Here 's another lucky thing, Maggie : I hadn't told the ladies' committee that I was to hedge, and so they need never know.   Comtesse, I tell you there 's a little cherub who sits up aloft and looks after the career of John Shand.

(*The* COMTESSE *looks not aloft but toward the chair at present occupied by* MAGGIE.)

COMTESSE.   Where does she sit, Mr. Shand ?

(*He knows that women are not well read.*)

JOHN.   It 's just a figure of speech.

(*He returns airily to his committee room ; and now again you may hear the click of* MAGGIE'S *needles.   They no longer annoy the* COMTESSE ; *she is setting them to music.*)

COMTESSE.   It is not down here she sits, Mrs. Shand, knitting a stocking.

MAGGIE.   No, it isn't.

COMTESSE.   And when I came in I gave him credit for everything ; even for the prettiness of the room !

MAGGIE.   He has beautiful taste.

COMTESSE.   Good-bye, Scotchy.

MAGGIE.   Good-bye, Comtesse, and thank you for coming.

COMTESSE.   Good-bye—Miss Pin.

(MAGGIE *rings genteelly.*)

MAGGIE.   Good-bye.

(*The* COMTESSE *is now lost in admiration of her.*)

COMTESSE.   You divine little wife.   He can't be worthy of it, no man could be worthy of it.   Why do you do it ?

(MAGGIE *shivers a little.*)

MAGGIE.   He loves to think he does it all himself ; that 's the way of men.   I 'm six years older than he is.   I 'm plain, and I have no charm.   I shouldn't have let him marry me. I 'm trying to make up for it.

(*The* COMTESSE *kisses her and goes away.*   MAGGIE, *somewhat foolishly, resumes her knitting.*

Some days later this same room is listening—with the same inattention—to the outpouring of JOHN SHAND'S *love for the*

*lady of the hiccoughs. We arrive—by arrangement—
rather late ; and thus we miss some of the most delightful
of the pangs.*

*One can see that these two are playing no game, or, if they
are, that they little know it.   The wonders of the world (so
strange are the instruments chosen by Love) have been
revealed to* JOHN *in hiccoughs ; he shakes in* SYBIL'S *presence ; never were more swimming eyes ; he who has been
of a wooden face till now, with ways to match, has gone on
flame like a piece of paper ; emotion is in flood in him.   We
may be almost fond of* JOHN *for being so worshipful of love.
Much has come to him that we had almost despaired of his
acquiring, including nearly all the divine attributes except
that sense of humour.   The beautiful* SYBIL *has always
possessed but little of it also, and what she had has been
struck from her by Cupid's flail.   Naked of the saving
grace, they face each other in awful rapture.)*

JOHN.   In a room, Sybil, I go to you as a cold man to a fire.
You fill me like a peal of bells in an empty house.

*(She is being brutally treated by the dear impediment, for
which hiccough is such an inadequate name that even to spell
it is an abomination though a sign of ability.   How to
describe a sound that is noiseless ?   Let us put it thus, that
when* SYBIL *wants to say something very much there are little
obstacles in her way ; she falters, falls perhaps once, and
then is over, the while her appealing orbs beg you not to be
angry with her.   We may express those sweet pauses in
precious dots, which some clever person can afterwards
string together and make a pearl necklace of them.)*

SYBIL.   I should not . . . let you say it, . . . but . . . you
. . . say it so beautifully.

JOHN.   You must have guessed.

SYBIL.   I dreamed . . . I feared . . . but you were . . .
Scotch, and I didn't know what to think.

JOHN.   Do you know what first attracted me to you, Sybil ?
It was your insolence.   I thought, ' I 'll break her insolence
for her.'

SYBIL.   And I thought . . . ' I 'll break his str . . . ength ! '

JOHN.   And now your cooing voice plays round me ; the
softness of you, Sybil, in your pretty clothes makes me think

of young birds. (*The impediment is now insurmountable ; she has to swim for it, she swims toward him.*)   It is you who inspire my work.

(*He thrills to find that she can be touched without breaking.*)

SYBIL.   I am so glad . . . so proud . . .

JOHN.   And others know it, Sybil, as well as I. Only yesterday the Comtesse said to me, ' No man could get on so fast unaided. *Cherchez la femme*, Mr. Shand.'

SYBIL.   Auntie said that ?

JOHN.   I said ' Find her yourself, Comtesse.'

SYBIL.   And she ?

JOHN.   She said ' I have found her,' and I said in my blunt way, ' You mean Lady Sybil,' and she went away laughing.

SYBIL.   Laughing ?

JOHN.   I seem to amuse the woman.

(SYBIL *grows sad.*)

SYBIL.   If Mrs. Shand—— It is so cruel to her. Whom did you say she had gone to the station to meet ?

JOHN.   Her father and brothers.

SYBIL.   It is so cruel to them. We must think no more of this. It is mad . . . ness.

JOHN.   It 's fate. Sybil, let us declare our love openly.

SYBIL.   You can't ask that, now in the first moment that you tell me of it.

JOHN.   The one thing I won't do even for you is to live a life of underhand.

SYBIL.   The . . . blow to her.

JOHN.   Yes. But at least she has always known that I never loved her.

SYBIL.   It is asking me to give . . . up everything, every one, for you.

JOHN.   It 's too much.

(JOHN *is humble at last.*)

SYBIL.   To a woman who truly loves, even that is not too much. Oh ! it is not I who matter—it is you.

JOHN.   My dear, my dear.

SYBIL.   So gladly would I do it to save you ; but, oh, if it were to bring you down !

JOHN.   Nothing can keep me down if I have you to help me.

SYBIL.   I am dazed, John, I . . .

JOHN.   My love, my love.

SYBIL.   I . . . oh . . . here . . .

JOHN.   Be brave, Sybil, be brave.

SYBIL.   . . . .

(*In this bewilderment of pearls she melts into his arms.* MAGGIE *happens to open the door just then ; but neither fond heart hears her.*)

JOHN.   I can't walk along the streets, Sybil, without looking in all the shop windows for what I think would become you best. (*As awkwardly as though his heart still beat against corduroy, he takes from his pocket a pendant and its chain. He is shy, and she drops pearls over the beauty of the ruby which is its only stone.*)   It is a drop of my blood, Sybil.

(*Her lovely neck is outstretched, and he puts the chain round it.* MAGGIE *withdraws as silently as she had come ; but perhaps the door whispered ' d—n ' as it closed, for* SYBIL *wakes out of Paradise.*)

SYBIL.   I thought—— Did the door shut ?

JOHN.   It was shut already.

(*Perhaps it is only that* SYBIL *is bewildered to find herself once again in a world that has doors.*)

SYBIL.   It seemed to me——

JOHN.   There was nothing. But I think I hear voices ; they may have arrived.

(*Some pretty instinct makes* SYBIL *go farther from him.* MAGGIE *kindly gives her time for this by speaking before opening the door.*)

MAGGIE.   That will do perfectly, David. The maid knows where to put them. (*She comes in.*) They 've come, John ; they *would* help with the luggage. (JOHN *goes out.* MAGGIE *is agreeably surprised to find a visitor.*) How do you do, Lady Sybil ? This is nice of you.

SYBIL.   I was so sorry not to find you in, Mrs. Shand.

(*The impediment has run away. It is only for those who love it.*)

MAGGIE.   Thank you. You 'll sit down ?

SYBIL.   I think not ; your relatives——

MAGGIE.   They will be so proud to see that you are my friend.

(*If* MAGGIE *were less simple her guest would feel more comfortable. She tries to make conversation.*)

SYBIL.   It is their first visit to London ?

(*Instead of relieving her anxiety on this point,* MAGGIE *has a long look at the gorgeous armful.*)

MAGGIE.   I 'm glad you are so beautiful, Lady Sybil.

(*The beautiful one is somehow not flattered.   She pursues her investigations with growing uneasiness.*)

SYBIL.   One of them is married now, isn't he ?   (*Still there is no answer ;* MAGGIE *continues looking at her, and shivers slightly.*)   Have they travelled from Scotland to-day ?   Mrs. Shand, why do you look at me so ?   The door did open ! (MAGGIE *nods.*)   What are you to do ?

MAGGIE.   That would be telling.   Sit down, my pretty.

(*As* SYBIL *subsides into what the Wylies with one glance would call the best chair,* MAGGIE'S *men-folk are brought in by* JOHN, *all carrying silk hats and looking very active after their long rest in the train.   They are gazing about them. They would like this lady, they would like* JOHN, *they would even like* MAGGIE *to go away for a little and leave them to examine the room.   Is that linen on the walls, for instance, or just paper ?   Is the carpet as thick as it feels, or is there brown paper beneath it ?   Had* MAGGIE *got anything off that bookcase on account of the worm-holes ?*   DAVID *even discovers that we were simpletons when we said there was nothing in the room that pretended to be what it was not. He taps the marble mantelpiece, and is favourably impressed by the tinny sound.*)

DAVID.   Very fine imitation.   It 's a capital house, Maggie.

MAGGIE.   I 'm so glad you like it.   Do you know one another ?   This is my father and my brothers, Lady Sybil.

(*The lovely form inclines towards them.* ALICK *and* JOHN *remain firm on their legs, but* JAMES *totters.*)

JAMES.   A ladyship !   Well done, Maggie.

ALICK (*sharply*).   James !   I remember you, my lady.

MAGGIE.   Sit down, father.   This is the study.

(JAMES *wanders round it inquisitively until called to order.*)

SYBIL.   You must be tired after your long journey.

DAVID (*drawing the portraits of himself and partners in one lightning sketch*).   Tired, your ladyship ?   We sat on cushioned seats the whole way.

JAMES (*looking about him for the chair you sit on*). Every seat in this room is cushioned.

MAGGIE. You may say all my life is cushioned now, James, by this dear man of mine.

(*She gives* JOHN'S *shoulder a loving pressure, which* SYBIL *feels is a telegraphic communication to herself in a cypher that she cannot read.* ALICK *and the* BROTHERS *bask in the evidence of* MAGGIE'S *happiness.*)

JOHN (*uncomfortably*). And is Elizabeth hearty, James ?

JAMES (*looking down his nose in the manner proper to young husbands when addressed about their wives.*) She 's very well, I thank you kindly.

MAGGIE. James is a married man now, Lady Sybil.

(SYBIL *murmurs her congratulations.*)

JAMES. I thank you kindly. (*Courageously*) Yes, I 'm married. (*He looks at* DAVID *and* ALICK *to see if they are smiling ; and they are.*) It wasn't a case of being catched ; it was entirely of my own free will. (*He looks again ; and the mean fellows are smiling still.*) Is your ladyship married ?

SYBIL. Alas ! no.

DAVID. James ! (*Politely*) You will be yet, my lady.

(SYBIL *indicates that he is kind indeed.*)

JOHN. Perhaps they would like you to show them their rooms, Maggie ?

DAVID. Fine would we like to see all the house as well as the sleeping accommodation. But first—— (*He gives his father the look with which chairmen call on the next speaker.*)

ALICK. I take you, David. (*He produces a paper parcel from a roomy pocket.*) It wasn't likely, Mr. Shand, that we should forget the day.

JOHN. The day ?

DAVID. The second anniversary of your marriage. We came purposely for the day.

JAMES (*his fingers itching to take the parcel from his father*). It 's a lace shawl, Maggie, from the three of us, a pure Tobermory ; you would never dare wear it if you knew the cost.

(*The shawl in its beauty is revealed, and* MAGGIE *hails it with little cries of joy. She rushes at the donors and kisses each of them just as if she were a pretty woman. They are much pleased and give expression to their pleasure in a not very dissimilar manner.*)

ALICK. Havers.

DAVID. Havers.

JAMES. Havers.

JOHN. It 's a very fine shawl.

(*He should not have spoken, for he has set* JAMES's *volatile mind working.*)

JAMES. You may say so. What did you give her, Mr. Shand ?

JOHN (*suddenly deserted by God and man*). Me ?

ALICK. Yes, yes, let 's see it.

JOHN. Oh—I——

(*He is not deserted by* MAGGIE, *but she can think of no way out.*)

SYBIL (*prompted by the impediment, which is in hiding, quite close*). Did he . . . forget ?

(*There is more than a touch of malice in the question.   It is a challenge, and the Wylies as a family are almost too quick to accept a challenge.*)

MAGGIE (*lifting the gage of battle*). John forget ?   Never ! It 's a pendant, father.

(*The impediment bolts.*   JOHN *rises.*)

ALICK. A pendant ?   One of those things on a chain ?

(*He grins, remembering how once, about sixty years ago, he and a lady and a pendant—but we have no time for this.*)

MAGGIE. Yes.

DAVID (*who has felt the note of antagonism and is troubled*). You were slow in speaking of it, Mr. Shand.

MAGGIE. (*This is her fight.*) He was shy, because he thought you might blame him for extravagance.

DAVID (*relieved*).   Oh, that 's it.

JAMES (*licking his lips*).   Let 's see it.

MAGGIE (*a daughter of the devil*).   Where did you put it, John ?

(JOHN's *mouth opens but has nothing to contribute.*)

SYBIL (*the impediment has stolen back again*).   Perhaps it has been . . . mislaid.

(*The* BROTHERS *echo the word incredulously.*)

MAGGIE. Not it. I can't think where we laid it down, John. It 's not on that table, is it, James ? (*The Wylies turn to look, and* MAGGIE's *hand goes out to* LADY SYBIL : JOHN SHAND, *witness. It is a very determined hand, and presently a pendant is placed in it.*) Here it is ! (ALICK *and the* BROTHERS *cluster round it, weigh it and appraise it.*)

ALICK. Preserve me. Is that stone real, Mr. Shand ?

JOHN (*who has begun to look his grimmest*). Yes.

MAGGIE (*who is now ready, if he wishes it, to take him on too*). John says it 's a drop of his blood.

JOHN (*wishing it*). And so it is.

DAVID. Well said, Mr. Shand.

MAGGIE (*scared*). And now, if you 'll all come with me, I think John has something he wants to talk over with Lady Sybil. (*Recovering and taking him on*) Or would you prefer, John, to say it before us all ?

SYBIL (*gasping*). No !

JOHN (*flinging back his head*). Yes, I prefer to say it before you all.

MAGGIE (*flinging back hers*). Then sit down again. (*The Wylies wonderingly obey.*)

SYBIL. Mr. Shand, Mr. Shand !——

JOHN. Maggie knows, and it was only for her I was troubled. Do you think I 'm afraid of *them* ? (*With mighty relief*) Now we can be open.

DAVID (*lowering*). What is it ? What 's wrong, John Shand ?

JOHN (*facing him squarely*). It was to Lady Sybil I gave the pendant, and all my love with it. (*Perhaps* JAMES *utters a cry, but the silence of* ALICK *and* DAVID *is more terrible.*)

SYBIL (*whose voice is smaller than we had thought*). What are you to do ?

(*It is to* MAGGIE *she is speaking.*)

DAVID. She 'll leave it for us to do.

JOHN. That 's what I want.

(*The lords of creation look at the ladies.*)

MAGGIE (*interpreting*). You and I are expected to retire, Lady Sybil, while the men decide our fate. (SYBIL *is ready to obey the law, but* MAGGIE *remains seated.*) Man 's the oak, woman's the ivy.   Which of us is it that's to cling to you, John ?

(*With three stalwarts glaring at him,* JOHN *rather grandly takes* SYBIL's *hand.   They are two against the world.*)

SYBIL (*a heroine*).   I hesitated, but I am afraid no longer ; whatever he asks of me I will do.

(*Evidently the first thing he asks of her is to await him in the dining-room.*)

It will mean surrendering everything for him.   I am glad it means all that.   (*She passes into the dining-room looking as pretty as a kiss.*)

MAGGIE.   So that settles it.

ALICK.   I'm thinking that doesn't settle it.

DAVID.   No, by God !   (*But his love for* MAGGIE *steadies him.   There is even a note of entreaty in his voice.*)   Have you nothing to say to her, man ?

JOHN.   I have things to say to her, but not before you.

DAVID (*sternly*).   Go away, Maggie.   Leave him to us.

JAMES (*who thinks it is about time that he said something*).   Yes, leave him to us.

MAGGIE.   No, David, I want to hear what is to become of me ; I promise not to take any side.

(*And sitting by the fire she resumes her knitting.   The four regard her as on an evening at The Pans a good many years ago.*)

DAVID (*barking*).   How long has this been going on ?

JOHN.   If you mean how long has that lady been the apple of my eye, I'm not sure ; but I never told her of it until to-day.

MAGGIE (*thoughtfully and without dropping a stitch*).   I think it wasn't till about six months ago, John, that she began to be very dear to you.   At first you liked to bring in her name when talking to me, so that I could tell you of any little things I might have heard she was doing.   But afterwards, as she became more and more to you, you avoided mentioning her name.

JOHN (*surprised*).   Did you notice that ?

MAGGIE (*in her old-fashioned way*).   Yes.

JOHN.   I tried to be done with it for your sake.   I've often had a sore heart for you, Maggie.

JAMES.   You're proving it !

MAGGIE.   Yes, James, he had.   I've often seen him looking

at me very sorrowfully of late because of what was in his mind ; and many a kindly little thing he has done for me that he didn't use to do.

JOHN.   You noticed that too !

MAGGIE.   Yes.

DAVID (*controlling himself*).   Well, we won't go into that ; the thing to be thankful for is that it 's ended.

ALICK (*who is looking very old*).   Yes, yes, that 's the great thing.

JOHN.   All useless, sir, it 's not ended ; it 's to go on.

DAVID.   There 's a devil in you, John Shand.

JOHN (*who is an unhappy man just now*).   I dare say there is. But do you think he had a walk over, Mr. David ?

JAMES.   Man, I could knock you down !

MAGGIE.   There 's not one of you could knock John down.

DAVID (*exasperated*).   Quiet, Maggie.   One would think you were taking his part.

MAGGIE.   Do you expect me to desert him at the very moment that he needs me most ?

DAVID.   It 's him that 's deserting you.

JOHN.   Yes, Maggie, that 's what it is.

ALICK.   Where 's your marriage vow ?   And your church attendances ?

JAMES (*with terrible irony*).   And your prize for moral philosophy ?

JOHN (*recklessly*).   All gone whistling down the wind.

DAVID.   I suppose you understand that you 'll have to resign your seat ?

JOHN (*his underlip much in evidence*).   There are hundreds of seats, but there 's only one John Shand.

MAGGIE (*but we don't hear her*).   That 's how I like to hear him speak.

DAVID (*the ablest person in the room*).   Think, man, I 'm old by you, and for long I 've had a pride in you.   It will be beginning the world again with more against you than there was eight years ago.

JOHN.   I have a better head to begin it with than I had eight years ago.

ALICK (*hoping this will bite*).   She 'll have her own money, David !

JOHN. She 's as poor as a mouse.

JAMES (*thinking possibly of his Elizabeth's mother*). We 'll go to her friends, and tell them all. They 'll stop it.

JOHN. She 's of age.

JAMES. They 'll take her far away.

JOHN. I 'll follow, and tear her from them.

ALICK. Your career——

JOHN (*to his credit*). To hell with my career. Do you think I don't know I 'm on the rocks ? What can you, or you, or you, understand of the passions of a man ! I 've fought, and I 've given in. When a ship founders, as I suppose I 'm foundering, it 's not a thing to yelp at. Peace, all of you. (*He strides into the dining-room, where we see him at times pacing the floor.*)

DAVID (*to JAMES, who gives signs of a desire to take off his coat*). Let him be. We can't budge him. (*With bitter wisdom*) It 's true what he says, true at any rate about me. What do I know of the passions of a man ! I 'm up against something I don't understand.

ALICK. It 's something wicked.

DAVID. I dare say it is, but it 's something big.

JAMES. It 's that damned charm.

MAGGIE (*still by the fire*). That 's it. What was it that made you fancy Elizabeth, James ?

JAMES (*sheepishly*). I can scarcely say.

MAGGIE. It was her charm.

DAVID. *Her* charm !

JAMES (*pugnaciously*). Yes, *her* charm.

MAGGIE. She had charm for James.

(*This somehow breaks them up. MAGGIE goes from one to another with an odd little smile flickering on her face.*)

DAVID. Put on your things, Maggie, and we 'll leave his house.

MAGGIE (*patting his kind head*). Not me, David.

(*This is a MAGGIE they have known but forgotten ; all three brighten.*)

DAVID. You haven't given in !

(*The smile flickers and expires.*)

MAGGIE. I want you all to go upstairs, and let me have my try now.

JAMES. Your try ?

ALICK.   Maggie, you put new life into me.

JAMES.   And into me.

(DAVID *says nothing ; the way he grips her shoulder says it for him.*)

MAGGIE.   I 'll save him, David, if I can.

DAVID.   Does he deserve to be saved after the way he has treated you ?

MAGGIE.   You stupid David.   What has that to do with it ?

(*When they have gone,* JOHN *comes to the door of the dining-room.   There is welling up in him a great pity for* MAGGIE, *but it has to subside a little when he sees that the knitting is still in her hand.   No man likes to be so soon supplanted.* SYBIL *follows, and the two of them gaze at the active needles.*)

MAGGIE (*perceiving that she has visitors*).   Come in, John. Sit down, Lady Sybil, and make yourself comfortable.   I 'm afraid we 've put you about.

(*She is, after all, only a few years older than they and scarcely looks her age ; yet it must have been in some such way as this that the little old woman who lived in a shoe addressed her numerous progeny.*)

JOHN.   I 'm mortal sorry, Maggie.

SYBIL (*who would be more courageous if she could hold his hand*). And I also.

MAGGIE (*soothingly*).   I 'm sure you are.   But as it can't be helped I see no reason why we three shouldn't talk the matter over in a practical way.

(SYBIL *looks doubtful, but* JOHN *hangs on desperately to the word practical.*)

JOHN.   If you could understand, Maggie, what an inspiration she is to me and my work.

SYBIL.   Indeed, Mrs. Shand, I think of nothing else.

MAGGIE.   That 's fine.   That 's as it should be.

SYBIL (*talking too much*).   Mrs. Shand, I think you are very kind to take it so reasonably.

MAGGIE.   That 's the Scotch way.   When were you thinking of leaving me, John ?

(*Perhaps this is the Scotch way also ; but* SYBIL *is English, and from the manner in which she starts you would say that something has fallen on her toes.*)

JOHN (*who has heard nothing fall*).   I think, now that it has come to a breach, the sooner the better.   (*His tone becomes that of* JAMES *when asked after the health of his wife.*)   When it is convenient to you, Maggie.

MAGGIE (*making a rapid calculation*).   It couldn't well be before Wednesday.   That's the day the laundry comes home.

(SYBIL *has to draw in her toes again.*)

JOHN.   And it's the day the House rises.   (*Stifling a groan*) It may be my last appearance in the House.

SYBIL (*her arms yearning for him*).   No, no, please don't say that.

MAGGIE (*surveying them sympathetically*).   You love the House, don't you, John, next to her ?   It's a pity you can't wait till after your speech at Leeds.   Mr. Venables won't let you speak at Leeds, I fear, if you leave me.

JOHN.   What a chance it would have been.   But let it go.

MAGGIE.   The meeting is in less than a month.   Could you not make it such a speech that they would be very loth to lose you ?

JOHN (*swelling*).   That's what was in my mind.

SYBIL (*with noble confidence*).   And he could have done it.

MAGGIE.   Then we've come to something practical.

JOHN (*exercising his imagination with powerful effect*).   No, it wouldn't be fair to you if I was to stay on now.

MAGGIE.   Do you think I'll let myself be considered when your career is at stake ?   A month will soon pass for me ; I'll have a lot of packing to do.

JOHN.   It's noble of you, but I don't deserve it, and I can't take it from you.

MAGGIE.   Now's the time, Lady Sybil, for you to have one of your inspiring ideas.

SYBIL (*ever ready*).   Yes, yes—but what ?

(*It is odd that they should both turn to* MAGGIE *at this moment.*)

MAGGIE (*who has already been saying it to herself*).   What do you think of this : I can stay on here with my father and brothers ; and you, John, can go away somewhere and devote yourself to your speech ?

SYBIL.   Yes.

JOHN.   That might be.   (*Considerately*) Away from both of you ?   Where could I go ?

SYBIL (*ever ready*).   Where ?

MAGGIE.   I know.

(*She has called up a number on the telephone before they have time to check her.*)

JOHN (*on his dignity*).   Don't be in such a hurry, Maggie.

MAGGIE.   Is this Lamb's Hotel ?   Put me on to the Comtesse de la Brière, please.

SYBIL (*with a sinking*).   What do you want with auntie ?

MAGGIE.   Her cottage in the country would be the very place.   She invited John and me.

JOHN.   Yes, but——

MAGGIE (*arguing*).   And Mr. Venables is to be there. Think of the impression you could make on *him*, seeing him daily for three weeks.

JOHN.   There 's something in that.

MAGGIE.   Is it you, Comtesse ?   I 'm Maggie Shand.

SYBIL.   You are not to tell her that——?

MAGGIE.   No.   (*To the* COMTESSE) Oh, I 'm very well, never was better.   Yes, yes ; you see I can't, because my folk have never been in London before, and I must take them about and show them the sights.   But John could come to you alone ; why not ?

JOHN (*with proper pride*).   If she 's not keen to have me, I won't go.

MAGGIE.   She 's very keen.   Comtesse, I could come for a day by and by to see how you are getting on.   Yes——yes—— certainly.   (*To* JOHN) She says she 'll be delighted.

JOHN (*thoughtfully*).   You 're not doing this, Maggie, thinking that my being absent from Sybil for a few weeks can make any difference ?   Of course it 's natural you should want us to keep apart, but——

MAGGIE (*grimly*).   I 'm founding no hope on keeping you apart, John.

JOHN.   It 's what other wives would do.

MAGGIE.   I promised to be different.

JOHN (*his position as a strong man assured*).   Then tell her I accept.   (*He wanders back into the dining-room.*)

SYBIL.   I think—(*she is not sure what she thinks*)—I think you are very wonderful.

MAGGIE.   Was that John calling to you ?

SYBIL.   Was it ?   (*She is glad to join him in the dining-room.*)

MAGGIE.   Comtesse, hold the line a minute.   (*She is alone, and she has nearly reached the end of her self-control. She shakes emotionally and utters painful little cries ; there is something she wants to do, and she is loth to do it. But she does it.*)   Are you there, Comtesse ?   There 's one other thing, dear Comtesse ; I want you to invite Lady Sybil also ; yes, for the whole time that John is there.   No, I 'm not mad ; as a great favour to me ; yes, I have a very particular reason, but I won't tell you what it is ; oh, call me Scotchy as much as you like, but consent ; do, do, do.   Thank you, thank you, good-bye.

(*She has control of herself now, and is determined not to let it slip from her again. When they reappear the stubborn one is writing a letter.*)

JOHN.   I thought I heard the telephone again.

MAGGIE (*looking up from her labours*).   It was the Comtesse ; she says she 's to invite Lady Sybil to the cottage at the same time.

SYBIL.   Me !

JOHN.   To invite Sybil ?   Then of course I won't go, Maggie.

MAGGIE (*wondering seemingly at these niceties*).   What does it matter ?   Is anything to be considered except the speech ?   (*It has been admitted that she was a little devil.*)   And, with Sybil on the spot, John, *to help you and inspire you*, what a speech it will be !

JOHN (*carried away*).   Maggie, you really are a very generous woman.

SYBIL (*convinced at last*).   She is indeed.

JOHN.   And you 're queer too.   How many women in the circumstances would sit down to write a letter !

MAGGIE.   It 's a letter to you, John.

JOHN.   To me ?

MAGGIE.   I 'll give it to you when it 's finished, but I ask you not to open it till your visit to the Comtesse ends.

JOHN.   What is it about ?

MAGGIE.   It 's practical.

SYBIL (*rather faintly*).   Practical ?   (*She has heard the word so frequently to-day that it is beginning to have a Scotch sound. She feels she ought to like* MAGGIE, *but that she would like her better*) *if they were farther apart. She indicates that the doctors are troubled about her heart, and murmuring her adieux she goes.* JOHN, *who is accompanying her, pauses at the door.*)

JOHN (*with a queer sort of admiration for his wife*). Maggie, I wish I was fond of you.

MAGGIE (*heartily*). I wish you were, John.

(*He goes, and she resumes her letter. The stocking is lying at hand, and she pushes it to the floor. She is done for a time with knitting.*)

ACT IV

MAN's most pleasant invention is the lawn-mower. All the birds know this, and that is why, when it is at rest, there is always at least one of them sitting on the handle with his head cocked, wondering how the delicious whirring sound is made. When they find out, they will change their note. As it is, you must sometimes have thought that you heard the mower very early in the morning, and perhaps you peeped in *négligé* from your lattice window to see who was up so early. It was really the birds trying to get the note.

On this broiling morning, however, we are at noon, and whoever looks will see that the whirring is done by Mr. Venables. He is in a linen suit with the coat discarded (the bird is sitting on it), and he comes and goes across the Comtesse's lawns, pleasantly mopping his face. We see him through a crooked bowed window generously open, roses intruding into it as if to prevent its ever being closed at night ; there are other roses in such armfuls on the tables that one could not easily say where the room ends and the garden begins.

In the Comtesse's pretty comic drawing-room (for she likes the comic touch when she is in England) sits John Shand with his hostess, on chairs at a great distance from each other. No linen garments for John, nor flannels, nor even knickerbockers ; he envies the English way of dressing for trees and lawns, but is too Scotch to be able to imitate it ; he wears tweeds, just as he would do in his native country where they would be in kilts. Like many another Scot, the first time he ever saw a kilt was on a Sassenach ; indeed kilts were perhaps invented, like golf, to draw the English north. John is doing nothing, which again is not a Scotch accomplishment, and he looks rather miserable and dour. The Comtesse is already at her Patience cards, and occasionally she smiles on him as if not displeased with his long silence. At last she speaks :

COMTESSE.   I feel it rather a shame to detain you here on such a lovely day, Mr. Shand, entertaining an old woman.

JOHN.   I don't pretend to think I'm entertaining you, Comtesse.

COMTESSE.   But you *are*, you know.

JOHN.   I would be pleased to be told how ?

(*She shrugs her impertinent shoulders, and presently there is another heavy sigh from* JOHN.)

COMTESSE.   Again !   Why do not you go out on the river ?

JOHN.   Yes, I can do that.   (*He rises.*)

COMTESSE.   And take Sybil with you. (*He sits again.*)   No ?

JOHN.   I have been on the river with her twenty times.

COMTESSE.   Then take her for a long walk through the Fairloe woods.

JOHN.   We were there twice last week.

COMTESSE.   There is a romantically damp little arbour at the end of what the villagers call the Lovers' Lane.

JOHN.   One can't go there every day.   I see nothing to laugh at.

COMTESSE.   Did I laugh ?   I must have been translating the situation into French.

(*Perhaps the music of the lawn-mower is not to* JOHN'S *mood, for he betakes himself to another room.* MR. VENABLES *pauses in his labours to greet a lady who has appeared on the lawn, and who is* MAGGIE. *She is as neat as if she were one of the army of typists (who are quite the nicest kind of women), and carries a little bag.* *She comes in through the window, and puts her hands over the* COMTESSE'S *eyes.*)

COMTESSE.   They are a strong pair of hands, at any rate.

MAGGIE.   And not very white, and biggish for my size. Now guess.

(*The* COMTESSE *guesses, and takes both the hands in hers as if she valued them.* *She pulls off* MAGGIE'S *hat as if to prevent her flying away.*)

COMTESSE.   Dear abominable one, not to let me know you were coming.

MAGGIE.   It is just a surprise visit, Comtesse.   I walked up from the station.   (*For a moment* MAGGIE *seems to have borrowed* SYBIL'S *impediment.*)   How is—everybody ?

COMTESSE.   He is quite well.   But, my child, he seems to me to be a most unhappy man.

(*This sad news does not seem to make a most unhappy woman of the child.   The* COMTESSE *is puzzled, as she knows nothing of the situation save what she has discovered for herself.*)

Why should that please you, O heartless one ?

MAGGIE.   I won't tell you.

COMTESSE.   I could take you and shake you, Maggie.   Here have I put my house at your disposal for so many days for some sly Scotch purpose, and you will not tell me what it is.

MAGGIE.   No.

COMTESSE.   Very well, then, but I have what you call a nasty one for you.   (*The* COMTESSE *lures* MR. VENABLES *into the room by holding up what might be a foaming glass of lemon squash.*) Alas, Charles, it is but a flower vase.   I want you to tell Mrs. Shand what you think of her husband's speech.

(MR. VENABLES *gives his hostess a reproachful look.*)

VENABLES.   Eh—ah—Shand will prefer to do that himself. I promised the gardener—I must not disappoint him—excuse me——

COMTESSE.   You must tell her, Charles.

MAGGIE.   Please, Mr. Venables, I should like to know.

(*He sits down with a sigh and obeys.*)

VENABLES.   Your husband has been writing the speech here, and by his own wish he read it to me three days ago.   The occasion is to be an important one ; and, well, there are a dozen young men in the party at present, all capable of filling a certain small ministerial post.   (*He looks longingly at the mower, but it sends no message to his aid.*)   And as he is one of them I was anxious that he should show in this speech of what he is capable.

MAGGIE.   And hasn't he ?

(*Not for the first time* MR. VENABLES *wishes that he was not in politics.*)

VENABLES.   I am afraid he has.

COMTESSE.   What is wrong with the speech, Charles ?

VENABLES.   Nothing—and he can still deliver it.   It is a powerful, well-thought-out piece of work, such as only a very able man could produce.   But it has no *special quality* of its own —none of the little touches that used to make an old stager like myself want to pat Shand on the shoulder. (*The* COMTESSE's *mouth twitches, but* MAGGIE *declines to notice it.*)   He pounds on manfully enough, but, if I may say so, with a wooden leg.   It is as good, I dare say, as the rest of them could have done ; but they start with such inherited advantages, Mrs. Shand, that he had to do better.

MAGGIE.   Yes, I can understand that.

VENABLES.   I am sorry, Mrs. Shand, for he interested me. His career has set me wondering whether if *I* had begun as a railway porter I might not still be calling out, ' By your leave.'

(MAGGIE *thinks it probable but not important.*)

MAGGIE.   Mr. Venables, now that I think of it, surely John wrote to me that you were dissatisfied with his first speech, and that he was writing another.

(*The* COMTESSE's *eyes open very wide indeed.*)

VENABLES.   I have heard nothing of that, Mrs. Shand. (*He shakes his wise head.*)   And in any case, I am afraid—— (*He still hears the wooden leg.*)

MAGGIE.   But you said yourself that his second thoughts were sometimes such an improvement on the first.

(*The* COMTESSE *comes to the help of the baggage.*)

COMTESSE.   I remember your saying that, Charles.

VENABLES.   Yes, that has struck me.   (*Politely*) Well, if he has anything to show me——   In the meantime——

(*He regains the lawn, like one glad to escape attendance at* JOHN's *obsequies.   The* COMTESSE *is brought back to speech by the sound of the mower—nothing wooden in it.*)

COMTESSE.   What are you up to now, Miss Pin ?   You know as well as I do that there is no such speech.

(MAGGIE's *mouth tightens.*)

MAGGIE.   I do not.

COMTESSE.   It is a duel, is it, my friend ?

(*The* COMTESSE *rings the bell and* MAGGIE's *guilty mind is agitated.*)

MAGGIE.   What are you ringing for ?

COMTESSE.   As the challenged one, Miss Pin, I have the choice of weapons.   I am going to send for your husband to ask him if he has written such a speech.   After which, I suppose, *you* will ask me to leave you while you and he write it together.

(MAGGIE *wrings her hands.*)

MAGGIE.   You are wrong, Comtesse ; but please don't
do that.

COMTESSE.   You but make me more curious, and my doctor
says that I must be told everything. (*The* COMTESSE *assumes
the pose of her sex in melodrama.*)   Put your cards on the table,
Maggie Shand, or———   (*She indicates that she always pinks her
man.*   MAGGIE *dolefully produces a roll of paper from her bag.*)
What precisely is that ?

(*The reply is little more than a squeak.*)

MAGGIE.   John's speech.

COMTESSE.   You have written it yourself !

(MAGGIE *is naturally indignant.*)

MAGGIE.   It 's typed.

COMTESSE.   You guessed that the speech he wrote unaided
would not satisfy, and you prepared this to take its place !

MAGGIE.   Not at all, Comtesse.   It is the draft of his speech
that he left at home.   That 's all.

COMTESSE.   With a few trivial alterations by yourself, I
swear.   Can you deny it ?

(*No wonder that* MAGGIE *is outraged.   She replaces* JOHN's
speech in the bag with becoming hauteur.)

MAGGIE.   Comtesse, these insinuations are unworthy of you.
May I ask where is my husband ?

(*The* COMTESSE *drops her a curtsey.*)

COMTESSE.   I believe your Haughtiness may find him in the
Dutch garden.   Oh, I see through you.   You are not to show
him your speech.   But you are to get him to write another one,
and somehow ⸱all your additions will be in it.   Think not,
creature, that you can deceive one so old in iniquity as the
Comtesse de la Brière.

(*There can be but one reply from a good wife to such a charge,
and at once the* COMTESSE *is left alone with her shame.
Anon a footman appears.   You know how they come and go.*)

FOOTMAN.   You rang, my lady ?

COMTESSE.   Did I ?   Ah, yes, but why ? (*He is but lately
from the ploughshare and cannot help her.   In this quandary her
eyes alight upon the bag.   She is unfortunately too abandoned to
feel her shame ; she still thinks that she has the choice of weapons.
She takes the speech from the bag and bestows it on her servitor.*)
Take this to Mr. Venables, please, and say it is from Mr. Shand.

(THOMAS—*but in the end we shall probably call him* JOHN— *departs with the dangerous papers ; and when* MAGGIE *returns she finds that the* COMTESSE *is once more engaged on her interrupted game of Patience.*)   You did not find him ?

(*All the bravery has dropped from* MAGGIE'S *face.*)

MAGGIE.   I didn't see him, but I heard him.   *She* is with him.   I think they are coming here.

(*The* COMTESSE *is suddenly kind again.*)

COMTESSE.   Sybil ?   Shall I get rid of her ?

MAGGIE.   No, I want her to be here, too.   Now I shall know.

(*The* COMTESSE *twists the little thing round.*)

COMTESSE.   Know what ?

MAGGIE.   As soon as I look into his face I shall know.

(*A delicious scent ushers in the fair* SYBIL, *who is as sweet as a milking stool.   She greets* MRS. SHAND *with some alarm.*)

MAGGIE.   How do you do, Lady Sybil ?   How pretty you look in that frock.   (SYBIL *rustles uncomfortably.*)   You are a feast to the eye.

SYBIL.   Please, I wish you would not.

(*Shall we describe* SYBIL'S *frock, in which she looks like a great strawberry that knows it ought to be plucked ; or would it be easier to watch the coming of* JOHN ?   *Let us watch* JOHN.)

JOHN.   You, Maggie !   You never wrote that you were coming.

(*No, let us watch* MAGGIE.   *As soon as she looked into his face she was to know something of importance.*)

MAGGIE (*not dissatisfied with what she sees*).   No, John, it's a surprise visit.   I just ran down to say good-bye.

(*At this his face falls, which does not seem to pain her.*)

SYBIL (*foreseeing another horrible Scotch scene*).   To say good-bye ?

COMTESSE (*thrilling with expectation*).   To whom, Maggie ?

SYBIL (*deserted by the impediment, which is probably playing with rough boys in the Lovers' Lane*).   Auntie, do leave us, won't you ?

COMTESSE.   Not I.   It is becoming far too interesting.

MAGGIE.   I suppose there's no reason the Comtesse shouldn't be told, as she will know so soon at any rate ?

2 A

JOHN. That's so. (SYBIL *sees with discomfort that he is to be practical also.*)

MAGGIE. It's so simple. You see, Comtesse, John and Lady Sybil have fallen in love with one another, and they are to go off as soon as the meeting at Leeds has taken place.

> (*The* COMTESSE'S *breast is too suddenly introduced to Caledonia and its varied charms.*)

COMTESSE. Mon Dieu !

MAGGIE. I think that's putting it correctly, John.

JOHN. In a sense. But I'm not to attend the meeting at Leeds. My speech doesn't find favour. (*With a strange humility*) There's something wrong with it.

COMTESSE. I never expected to hear you say that, Mr. Shand.

JOHN (*wondering also*). I never expected it myself. I meant to make it the speech of my career. But somehow my hand seems to have lost its cunning.

COMTESSE. And you don't know how ?

JOHN. It's inexplicable. My brain was never clearer.

COMTESSE. You might have helped him, Sybil.

SYBIL (*quite sulkily*). I did.

COMTESSE. But I thought she was such an inspiration to you, Mr. Shand.

JOHN (*going bravely to* SYBIL's *side*). She slaved at it with me.

COMTESSE. Strange. (*Wickedly becoming practical also*) So now there is nothing to detain you. Shall I send for a fly, Sybil ?

SYBIL (*with a cry of the heart*). Auntie, do leave us.

COMTESSE. I can understand your impatience to be gone, Mr. Shand.

JOHN (*heavily*). I promised Maggie to wait till the 24th, and I'm a man of my word.

MAGGIE. But I give you back your word, John. You can go now.

> (JOHN *looks at* SYBIL, *and* SYBIL *looks at* JOHN, *and the impediment arrives in time to take a peep at both of them.*)

SYBIL (*groping for the practical, to which we must all come in the end*). He must make satisfactory arrangements about you first. I insist on that.

MAGGIE (*with no more imagination than a hen*). Thank you, Lady Sybil, but I have made all my arrangements.

JOHN (*stung*). Maggie, that was my part.

MAGGIE. You see, my brothers feel they can't be away from their business any longer ; and so, if it would be convenient to you, John, I could travel north with them by the night train on Wednesday.

SYBIL. I—I—— The way you put things—— !

JOHN. This is just the 21st.

MAGGIE. My things are all packed. I think you 'll find the house in good order, Lady Sybil. I have had the vacuum cleaners in. I 'll give you the keys of the linen and the silver plate ; I have them in that bag. The carpet on the upper landing is a good deal frayed, but——

SYBIL. Please, I don't want to hear any more.

MAGGIE. The ceiling of the dining-room would be the better of a new lick of paint——

SYBIL (*stamping her foot, small fours*). Can't you stop her ?

JOHN (*soothingly*). She 's meaning well. Maggie, I know it 's natural to you to value those things, because your outlook on life is bounded by them ; but all this jars on me.

MAGGIE. Does it ?

JOHN. Why should you be so ready to go ?

MAGGIE. I promised not to stand in your way.

JOHN (*stoutly*). You needn't be in such a hurry. There are three days to run yet. (*The French are so different from us that we shall probably never be able to understand why the* COMTESSE *laughed aloud here.*) It 's just a joke to the Comtesse.

COMTESSE. It seems to be no joke to you, Mr. Shand. Sybil, my pet, are you to let him off ?

SYBIL (*flashing*). Let him off ? If he wishes it. Do you ?

JOHN (*manfully*). I want it to go on. (*Something seems to have caught in his throat : perhaps it is the impediment trying a temporary home.*) It 's the one wish of my heart. If you come with me, Sybil, I 'll do all in a man's power to make you never regret it.

(*Triumph of the Vere de Veres.*)

MAGGIE (*bringing them back to earth with a dump*). And I can make my arrangements for Wednesday ?

SYBIL (*seeking the* COMTESSE's *protection*). No, you can't.

Auntie, I am not going on with this.   I 'm very sorry for you, John, but I see now——I couldn't face it——

(*She can't face anything at this moment except the sofa pillows.*)

COMTESSE (*noticing* JOHN's *big sigh of relief*).   So *that* is all right, Mr. Shand !

MAGGIE.   Don't you love her any more, John ?   Be practical.

SYBIL (*to the pillows*).   At any rate I have tired of him.   Oh, best to tell the horrid truth.   I am ashamed of myself.   I have been crying my eyes out over it——I thought I was such a different kind of woman.   But I am weary of him.   I think him——oh, so dull.

JOHN (*his face lighting up*).   Are you sure that is how you have come to think of me ?

SYBIL.   I 'm sorry ;   (*with all her soul*) but yes—yes—yes.

JOHN.   By God, it 's more than I deserve.

COMTESSE.   Congratulations to you both.

(SYBIL *runs away ; and in the fulness of time she married successfully in cloth of silver, which was afterwards turned into a bed-spread.*)

MAGGIE.   You haven't read my letter yet, John, have you ?

JOHN.   No.

COMTESSE (*imploringly*).   May I know to what darling letter you refer ?

MAGGIE.   It 's a letter I wrote to him before he left London. I gave it to him closed, not to be opened until his time here was ended.

JOHN (*as his hand strays to his pocket*).   Am I to read it now ?

MAGGIE.   Not before her.   Please go away, Comtesse.

COMTESSE.   Every word you say makes me more determined to remain.

MAGGIE.   It will hurt you, John.   (*Distressed*) Don't read it ; tear it up.

JOHN.   You make me very curious, Maggie.   And yet I don't see what can be in it.

COMTESSE.   But you feel a little nervous ?   Give *me* the dagger.

MAGGIE (*quickly*).   No.   (*But the* COMTESSE *has already got it.*)

COMTESSE. May I ? (*She must have thought they said Yes,
for she opens the letter. She shares its contents with them.*)
' Dearest John, It is at my request that the Comtesse is having
Lady Sybil at the cottage at the same time as yourself.'

JOHN. What ?

COMTESSE. Yes, she begged me to invite you together.

JOHN. But why ?

MAGGIE. I promised you not to behave as other wives
would do.

JOHN. It 's not understandable.

COMTESSE. ' You may ask why I do this, John, and my
reason is, I think that after a few weeks of Lady Sybil, every
day, and all day, you will become sick to death of her.   I am
also giving her the chance to help you and inspire you with your
work, so that you may both learn what her help and her inspiration amount to.   Of course, if your love is the great strong
passion you think it, then those weeks will make you love her
more than ever and I can only say good-bye.   But if, as I
suspect, you don't even now know what true love is, then by
the next time we meet, dear John, you will have had enough
of her.—Your affectionate wife, Maggie ' Oh, why was not
Sybil present at the reading of the will !   And now, if you two
will kindly excuse me, I think I must go and get that poor
sufferer the eau de Cologne.

JOHN. It 's almost enough to make a man lose faith in
himself.

COMTESSE. Oh, don't say that, Mr. Shand.

MAGGIE (*defending him*). You mustn't hurt him.   If you
haven't loved deep and true, that 's just because you have never
met a woman yet, John, capable of inspiring it.

COMTESSE (*putting her hand on* MAGGIE'S *shoulder*). Have
you not, Mr. Shand ?

JOHN. I see what you mean.   But Maggie wouldn't think
better of me for any false pretences.   She knows my feelings
for her now are neither more nor less than what they have
always been.

MAGGIE (*who sees that he is looking at her as solemnly as a
volume of sermons printed by request*). I think no one could be
fond of me that can't laugh a little at me.

JOHN. How could that help ?

COMTESSE (*exasperated*).   Mr. Shand, I give you up.

MAGGIE.   I admire his honesty.

COMTESSE.   Oh, I give you up also. Arcades ambo. Scotchies both.

JOHN (*when she has gone*).   But this letter, it 's not like you. By Gosh, Maggie, you 're no fool.

(*She beams at this, as any wife would.*)
But how could I have made such a mistake ?   It 's not like a strong man.   (*Evidently he has an inspiration.*)

MAGGIE.   What is it ?

JOHN (*the inspiration*).   *Am* I a strong man ?

MAGGIE.   You ?   Of course you are.   And self-made. Has anybody ever helped you in the smallest way ?

JOHN (*thinking it out again*).   No, nobody.

MAGGIE.   Not even Lady Sybil ?

JOHN.   I 'm beginning to doubt it.   It 's very curious, though, Maggie, that this speech should be disappointing.

MAGGIE.   It 's just that Mr. Venables hasn't the brains to see how good it is.

JOHN.   That must be it.   (*But he is too good a man to rest satisfied with this.*)   No, Maggie, it 's not.   Somehow I seem to have lost my neat way of saying things.

MAGGIE (*almost cooing*).   It will come back to you.

JOHN (*forlorn*).   If you knew how I 've tried.

MAGGIE (*cautiously*).   Maybe if you were to try again ; and I 'll just come and sit beside you, and knit.   I think the click of the needles sometimes put you in the mood.

JOHN.   Hardly that ; and yet many a Shandism have I knocked off while you were sitting beside me knitting.   I suppose it was the quietness.

MAGGIE.   Very likely.

JOHN (*with another inspiration*).   Maggie !

MAGGIE (*again*).   What is it, John ?

JOHN.   What if it was you that put those queer ideas into my head !

MAGGIE.   Me ?

JOHN.   Without your knowing it, I mean.

MAGGIE.   But how ?

JOHN.   We used to talk bits over ; and it may be that you dropped the seed, so to speak.

MAGGIE.   John, could it be this, that I sometimes had the idea in a rough womanish sort of way and then you polished it up till it came out a Shandism ?

JOHN (*slowly slapping his knee*).   I believe you 've hit it, Maggie : to think that you may have been helping me all the time—and neither of us knew it !

(*He has so nearly reached a smile that no one can say what might have happened within the next moment if the* COM- TESSE *had not reappeared.*)

COMTESSE.   Mr. Venables wishes to see you, Mr. Shand.

JOHN (*lost, stolen, or strayed a smile in the making*).   Hum !

COMTESSE.   He is coming now.

JOHN (*grumpy*).   Indeed !

COMTESSE (*sweetly*).   It is about your speech.

JOHN.   He has said all he need say on that subject, and more.

COMTESSE (*quaking a little*).   I think it is about the second speech.

JOHN.   What second speech ?

(MAGGIE *runs to her bag and opens it.*)

MAGGIE (*horrified*).   Comtesse, you have given it to him !

COMTESSE (*impudently*).   Wasn't I meant to ?

JOHN.   What is it ?   What second speech ?

MAGGIE.   Cruel, cruel.   (*Willing to go on her knees.*)   You had left the first draft of your speech at home, John, and I brought it here with—with a few little things I 've added myself.

JOHN (*a seven-footer*).   What 's that ?

MAGGIE (*four foot ten at most*).   Just trifles—things I was to suggest to you—while I was knitting—and then, if you liked any of them you could have polished them—and turned them into something good.   John, John—and now she has shown it to Mr. Venables.

JOHN (*thundering*).   As my work, Comtesse ?

(*But the* COMTESSE *is not of the women who are afraid of thunder.*)

MAGGIE.   It is your work—nine-tenths of it.

JOHN (*in the black cap*).   You presumed, Maggie Shand ! Very well, then, here he comes, and now we 'll see to what extent you 've helped me.

VENABLES.   My dear fellow.   My dear Shand, I congratulate you.   Give me your hand.

JOHN.   The speech ?

VENABLES.   You have improved it out of knowledge.   It is the same speech, but those new touches make all the difference.   (JOHN *sits down heavily*.)   Mrs. Shand, be proud of him.

MAGGIE.   I am.   I am, John.

COMTESSE.   You always said that his second thoughts were best, Charles.

VENABLES (*pleased to be reminded of it*).   Didn't I, didn't I ?   Those delicious little touches !   How good that is, Shand, about the flowing tide.

COMTESSE.   The flowing tide ?

VENABLES.   In the first speech it was something like this— ' Gentlemen, the Opposition are calling to you to vote for them and the flowing tide, but I solemnly warn you to beware lest the flowing tide does not engulf you.'   The second way is much better.

COMTESSE.   What is the second way, Mr. Shand ?

(JOHN *does not tell her*.)

VENABLES.   This is how he puts it now.   (JOHN *cannot help raising his head to listen*.)   ' Gentlemen, the Opposition are calling to you to vote for them and the flowing tide, but I ask you cheerfully to vote for us and *dam* the flowing tide.'

(VENABLES *and his old friend the* COMTESSE *laugh heartily, but for different reasons*.)

COMTESSE.   It *is* better, Mr. Shand.

MAGGIE.   *I* don't think so.

VENABLES.   Yes, yes, it 's so virile.   Excuse me, Comtesse, I 'm off to read the whole thing again.   (*For the first time he notices that* JOHN *is strangely quiet*.)   I think this has rather bowled you over, Shand.

(JOHN's *head sinks lower*.)

Well, well, good news doesn't kill.

MAGGIE (*counsel for the defence*).   Surely the important thing about the speech is its strength and knowledge and eloquence, the things that were in the first speech as well as in the second.

VENABLES.   That of course is largely true.   The wit would

not be enough without them, just as they were not enough without the wit. It is the combination that is irresistible. (JOHN's *head rises a little.*) Shand, you are our man, remember that, it is emphatically the best thing you have ever done. How this will go down at Leeds !

(*He returns gaily to his hammock ; but lower sinks JOHN's head, and even the COMTESSE has the grace to take herself off. MAGGIE's arms flutter near her husband, not daring to alight.*)

MAGGIE. You heard what he said, John. It 's the combination. Is it so terrible to you to find that my love for you had made me able to help you in the little things ?

JOHN. The little things ! It seems strange to me to hear you call me by my name, Maggie. It 's as if I looked on you for the first time.

MAGGIE. Look at me, John, for the first time. What do you see ?

JOHN. I see a woman who has brought her husband low.

MAGGIE. Only that ?

JOHN. I see the tragedy of a man who has found himself out. Eh, I can't live with you again, Maggie.

(*He shivers.*)

MAGGIE. Why did you shiver, John ?

JOHN. It was at myself for saying that I couldn't live with you again, when I should have been wondering how for so long you have lived with me. And I suppose you have forgiven me all the time. (*She nods.*) And forgive me still ? (*She nods again.*) Dear God !

MAGGIE. John, am I to go ? or are you to keep me on ? (*She is now a little bundle near his feet.*) I 'm willing to stay because I 'm useful to you, if it can't be for a better reason. (*His hand feels for her, and the bundle wriggles nearer.*) It 's nothing unusual I 've done, John. Every man who is high up loves to think that he has done it all himself ; and the wife smiles, and lets it go at that. It 's our only joke. Every woman knows that. (*He stares at her in hopeless perplexity.*) Oh, John, if only you could laugh at me.

JOHN. I can't laugh, Maggie.

(*But as he continues to stare at her a strange disorder appears in his face. MAGGIE feels that it is to be now or never.*)

MAGGIE.   Laugh, John, laugh.   Watch me; see how
easy it is.

(*A terrible struggle is taking place within him.   He creaks.
Something that may be mirth forces a passage, at first painfully, no more joy in it than in the discoloured water from a
spring that has long been dry.   Soon, however, he laughs
loud and long.   The spring water is becoming clear.*
MAGGIE *claps her hands.   He is saved.*)

OLD FRIENDS

Produced at the Duke of York's Theatre on March 1, 1910, with the following cast :

STEPHEN BRAND	.	.	.	.	*Sydney Valentine*
MRS. BRAND	.	.	.	.	*Lena Ashwell*
CARRY	.	.	.	.	*Dorothy Minto*
REV. J. CARROLL	.	.	.	.	*Hubert Harben*

OLD FRIENDS

IT is a winter evening, and Mr. and Mrs. Brand and their daughter with one guest are sitting round the fire in their small country house near London. He is a prosperous man of about sixty who goes by car to his work in the city daily, and is generally liked. Mrs. Brand, somewhat younger, is knitting and is as quiet as her husband is cheery ; she has perhaps used up her emotions long ago. They are both devoted to their daughter, Carry, an engaging girl of twenty, who is very animated at present ; she has only been ' engaged ' since five o'clock. The visitor is a gentle, elderly clergyman, Mr. Carroll, much loved by his parishioners because he never looks trouble in the face. They have been dining together in honour of the engagement, and Mr. Carroll is sipping a mild glass of whisky and water.

STEPHEN (*in his best jocular manner*). Well, well, all I can say, Carroll, is, Be thankful that you never had a daughter. Just when one is getting used to them, they give notice.

CARROLL (*in the same spirit*). Ah me !

CARRY (*all impetuosity*). Mother, they are laughing at me.

MRS. BRAND (*all placidity*). I wouldn't torment her, Stephen. An engagement ring is quite enough excitement for one evening; and she isn't strong.

STEPHEN (*immediately solicitous*). There, there, Carry ; but you are strong now, aren't you ?

CARRY (*displaying her muscles, or the want of them*). I am frightfully strong now.

CARROLL. You haven't been bothered by those headaches lately, Carry ?

CARRY. Not for ever so long.

STEPHEN. Ah, we mustn't boast. Less than a month ago, wasn't it, Agnes, that one kept her in bed all day ?

MRS. BRAND.   Yes, less than a month.

(CARRY *puts her hand in her mother's, who presses it softly to her breast.*)

CARRY (*cajoling*).   You are fond of Dick, aren't you, father ?

STEPHEN.   He is great.   (*She fondles his face.*)   Not that he is worthy of my Carry—no man could be quite that—eh, Agnes ?

(MRS. BRAND *does not answer.*)

Agnes ?

MRS. BRAND.   No, of course we think that.   (*She rises.*)   It is past our bed-time, Carry.

CARROLL.   And I must be stepping across to the rectory

STEPHEN.   Stay a bit, Carroll.

MRS. BRAND.   Do, if you will excuse our leaving you. Stephen sits late, you know.

STEPHEN.   I am a bad sleeper, and I use this room now (*indicating a door on the right*), so as not to disturb the house. I 'll be glad of your company, Carroll.   It 's a gloomy house when one is alone.

CARRY.   It is the darlingest house.

STEPHEN.   But it is gloomy.   It isn't well lit.

CARRY (*mischievously*).   Just think, Mr. Carroll, father is afraid of the dark.

CARROLL.   Eh, what ?

STEPHEN.   That is her fun.

MRS. BRAND (*not liking the subject*).   Come, Carry, say good-night.

CARRY (*to* CARROLL).   But he is !   He sleeps with the lamp burning.

STEPHEN.   How do you know that ?

CARRY.   I have seen it.

STEPHEN.   You have been downstairs in the night time ?

(CARRY *looks to her mother.*)

MRS. BRAND (*as quietly as ever*).   Yes, it was once I couldn't sleep, and I sent her down for a book.   (*To* CARROLL) Carry sleeps in my room.

STEPHEN (*hardly aware yet that she is grown up*).   It gives me the creeps to think of Carry wandering about the house in the night.

MRS. BRAND.   It was only the once.

STEPHEN. I should think so.

CARRY (*to* CARROLL). Good-night, my dears.

(*She has a loving moment with her father, kissing him impulsively on different parts of his head, which she carefully selects.*)

STEPHEN. Excuse me, Carroll ; she is my only child. (*Affectionately to his wife*) Good-night, Agnes. (*He kisses her, but she does not respond.*) We shall still have each other, Agnes.

MRS. BRAND. Yes.

(*She and* CARRY *go out by the door at the back,* CARRY *flitting like a butterfly.*)

CARROLL (*looking after them*). A very happy picture—very —very. By the way, what did Carry mean by saying you were afraid of the dark ?

STEPHEN (*looking at him as if about to answer, then turning away from the subject*). Make yourself comfortable, Carroll ; fill up again.

CARROLL (*resuming his seat*). No, thank you—I 've not finished yet, and besides I never exceed the one glass. (*Reminiscent*) Ah, Brand, do you remember when you came to live here how I wouldn't take even the one glass in this house ?

STEPHEN (*genially*). You thought that in keeping it here for my friends I was doing an unwise thing ; putting temptation in my own way.

CARROLL. I didn't know how strong you were.

STEPHEN (*thankfully*). I haven't touched it once in these three years, Carroll. I haven't the smallest desire to do so.

CARROLL (*sipping*). A splendid victory.

STEPHEN (*holding up the decanter*). Luddy me, to look at the thing, and think it had me for the best part of my life ! Ugh ! Well, if you 're sure you won't have any more I 'll lock it away. I always do that in case the servants—I wouldn't like to think I left it in their way.

CARROLL (*finishing his glass*). Quite right. I do the same thing myself.

(STEPHEN *locks up the decanter in a cupboard and returns the key to his pocket.*)

STEPHEN (*grimly*). I can remember a time when, wherever this key had been hidden, I would have found it !

CARROLL (*to avoid unpleasant subjects*). I wouldn't rake up the past, Brand ; it 's all dead and done with long ago.

STEPHEN (*also settling down by the fire*). Yes, yes. Dead and done with. It was a big thing I did, Carroll.

CARROLL. A great self-conquest.

STEPHEN. Not many men have done it.

CARROLL. Very few.

STEPHEN. Wonderful, isn't it, that the thing has left no mark on me ?

CARROLL. Very wonderful.

STEPHEN. It hasn't, you know.

CARROLL. Not that I can see.

STEPHEN (*quite prepared to take offence if it is given*). I 've got off almost too cheaply—eh ?

CARROLL. True repentance——

STEPHEN. That 's it. True repentance. (*Half triumphantly*) Very few of my friends ever knew what a slave I was to it. You see what my home life is. I haven't even suffered in business. Why, even when I was a clerk——

CARROLL. Was it going on even then ? Of course I didn't know you at that time.

STEPHEN (*lowering his voice*). Carroll, it was then that it began. I had no predilection for it. No, none. I ordered my glass because the others did—a piece of swagger—but at first it was nauseous to me, and I remember wondering whether they really liked it.

CARROLL. Evil companions.

STEPHEN. They weren't so bad, and they never exceeded as I did, but as it got grip of me I dropped them, I became secretive. I could keep from it almost easily for stretches of time, and then —then—it was as if something came over me that there was no resisting. That is the best description I can give of it—something came over me. Yet I was forging ahead at the office. It is a strange thing to say, but those bouts seemed to do me no harm—they were like a fillip to me.

CARROLL (*uncomfortable*). I don't like you to say that, Brand.

STEPHEN. I know it 's not according to the preachers, but it is how I felt.

CARROLL (*sonorously*). Your conscience, ' the still small voice of conscience.'

STEPHEN (*somehow confidential to-night*). Do you know, I don't think conscience worried me as much as it disturbs people in the books. Not nearly so much as fear. I have held my breath at the narrowness of some of my escapes. But I got off so often that I grew to have a mighty faith in my luck. I backed it.

CARROLL. Not luck, no, no. (*Happily*) You were being reserved for a great end.

STEPHEN. I see that now. But at the time—— Then when I was in the thirties—I met Agnes.

CARROLL (*beaming*). Ah, that is what I want to hear of, and how your love for her made you a new man.

STEPHEN (*emphatic*). My love was there all right, but, Carroll, I was still the same man.

CARROLL. Not you, Brand. No, no ! And if ever afterwards you yielded—at least you told her ?

STEPHEN. By no means. I gave it up for a time—I tried. But we hadn't been long married before I was as bad as ever. For two years or more I contrived to keep it from her. The cunning of me ! My real reason for taking a house in the country was that I could stay a night in town now and again— a night with *it*, Carroll.

CARROLL. Please, please !

STEPHEN (*considering*). Yet in all other matters I was a truthful man, scrupulously honest in business, and there was a high moral tone about me. That seems strange, but it's true.

CARROLL (*fidgeting*). Don't dwell on that. Tell me of the awakening.

STEPHEN. At last she found out. It was one night—— (*He shudders.*) We won't go into that.

CARROLL (*hastily*). Much better not.

STEPHEN. I told her everything then. And I said I couldn't alter myself.

CARROLL. Come, come ! But she—— ?

STEPHEN. She was fine. She insisted that we should fight it together.

CARROLL (*relieved*). And so it was love that did it after all !

STEPHEN (*rather puzzled*). No, Carroll, it wasn't. I made big efforts, but they failed. It's odd to think that I succeeded long after she had abandoned all attempts to help me. For in the end I did it alone.

CARROLL. Masterful ! What was it that gave you strength? Ah, I know.

STEPHEN. No, you don't. What I feel is that I must just have tried harder than before, and finding myself winning I got fresh courage.

CARROLL. I like to hear that.

STEPHEN. At first I didn't dare to tell Agnes. I couldn't be sure of myself. And when at last I did tell her she doubted me. But time convinced her. I haven't touched it these three years. I haven't wanted to.

CARROLL. She must be proud of you, Brand, as I am.

STEPHEN. Yes, she is.

CARROLL. As you must be of yourself.

STEPHEN. I don't pretend not to know that I have done a big thing. (*Mystified nevertheless*) Yet, you know, it wasn't so difficult as you might think. In the end it was almost easy.

CARROLL. What an encouragement to others !

STEPHEN. Yes, that 's so.

CARROLL. Of course Carry knows nothing about this ?

STEPHEN. Not a breath.

CARROLL. Tell me now, what did she mean by saying you were afraid of the dark ?

STEPHEN. Oh, that ! It was only her fun.

CARROLL. Of course, of course.

(*But there is something on* BRAND'S *mind.*)

STEPHEN. Carroll, do you ever sit up late at the rectory alone ?

CARROLL. Often.

STEPHEN (*not so casual as he affects to be*). Odd the way the shadows go creeping about the walls and floors of old houses, isn't it ?

CARROLL. You mean shadows from the fire ?

STEPHEN. Of course. (*Sharply*) What else could I mean ? (*Losing hold of himself*) There is something devilish about them, Carroll !

CARROLL. In what way ?

STEPHEN. They know me. They have some connection with me I don't know what it is.

CARROLL (*soothingly*). You have been working too hard. What connection could they have with you ?

STEPHEN. I don't know—(*husky*) I don't want to know. But they know. Perhaps I 'll know some night, Carroll !

CARROLL. What do you mean by that ? What is the matter with you, Brand ? (*He wishes he had gone home.*) Have you spoken of this to any one ?

STEPHEN. Only to Agnes.

CARROLL. I mean, to a doctor.

STEPHEN (*irritably*). No, I 'm quite well.

CARROLL. You are not. A long holiday——

STEPHEN. All baby talk. I 'm past that now. In the daytime it doesn't worry me at all. I 'm doing my work as well as ever.

CARROLL. That is good, very good. You 'll soon be all right. Turn your back on the thing, Brand, and it will cease to exist.

STEPHEN (*turning his back on* CARROLL). You are no help to me, my friend.

CARROLL (*weakly*). What do you want me to say ?

STEPHEN. It is no use your saying only what I want you to say ; it has gone beyond that. That is why you are no help to me.

CARROLL. Brand, I—— (*He finds no inspiration.*)

STEPHEN (*roughly*). See here, man, can it have anything to do—with the past ? (*Scared*) They are so familiar with me— as if they were old friends come back.

CARROLL (*clinging to this*). Nerves, merely nerves.

STEPHEN (*eager*). Yes, yes—that is what I wanted you to say, that is just—— Ah, Carroll, you merely say it because it is what I wanted you to say.

CARROLL. Not at all, I—I—— (*He stretches out a weak kindly hand.*)

STEPHEN. I won't keep you any longer. I 'll come with you and lock up.

CARROLL (*at the door, anxious to get into the more salubrious night*). Of course if I could—but it *is* getting late ; I 'll see you to-morrow. It 's nothing, I assure you ; it will pass away, pass away. You look tired and dead sleepy, Brand.

STEPHEN. Yes, I am.

CARROLL. A good night's rest is my prescription. You will laugh at this in the morning, laugh at it.

STEPHEN. Morning is all right.

CARROLL (*cheerily*). The man who won that great fight isn't going to be worried by shadows !

STEPHEN (*eager*). After what I have done, it wouldn't be fair on me, would it ?

CARROLL. Ignore them. Let the dead bury their dead.

STEPHEN. Yes—but do they ? Carroll, in those old days when I so often escaped the consequences, I had sometimes a dread that I was only being saved for some worse punishment : I have never paid, you know ; don't you preach that everything has to be paid for ?

CARROLL (*clutching his hat*). Take the word of a clergyman that you have nothing to fear.

STEPHEN (*less perturbed*). Thank you, Carroll. I think I feel a bit better.

CARROLL. How balmy is the night ! A good omen.

(*After seeing him out* BRAND *returns and stands staring at the fire. He opens a book, and puts it away. He lights a lamp and carries it into the bedroom, shutting the door. The room is now only dimly lit by the fire. He reappears without the lamp, looking like one who has just been beginning to undress and has changed his mind. He leaves the door ajar, and we see a little light coming from the bedroom, which shows that he has left the lamp burning there. He hesitates, then sits in his chair by the fire. He is tired out. Soon he is asleep. A coal in the fire falls, and a flame shoots up. Moving shadows are cast against the walls. They flicker and fall. The door at the back opens covertly, and* CARRY *is seen in her night-gown, carrying a lighted taper. The back of the chair would prevent her seeing* STEPHEN, *but it never strikes her to look for him there. She makes sure that she is not being followed, otherwise her attention is fixed on the bedroom door. She lingers at this door. Then she pushes it open inch by inch and enters noiselessly. In a second she is out again, startled, bewildered, sees* STEPHEN *asleep in the chair and blows out the taper, intent on stealing away. In her hurry she has left the bedroom door half open, and this lights the sitting-room to an extent.*

She hesitates, and beats her hands together, then like one who must go on with what she has to do she comes softly to STEPHEN, *cautiously takes his keys from his pocket—she knows which pocket to find them in—then steals hurriedly to the cupboard in which he had locked the decanter, and she is on her knees opening the door when* STEPHEN *wakes up. He sits staring at her, and as it comes to him what the situation means he rises and cries out.* CARRY *starts to her feet, frightened, and then is immediately cunning in self-defence.)*

CARRY (*brightly*). Oh, father, how you startled me. I thought you were in bed.

STEPHEN. What are you doing, Carry?

CARRY. Mother couldn't sleep. I came down to look for the smelling-salts for her. She left them on the table.

STEPHEN. I'll take them to her.

CARRY (*afraid*). No. (*Cunning again*) I promised not to disturb you.

STEPHEN. Carry!

CARRY (*terrified lest any noise brings down her mother*). Don't! You'll wake her. (*She has exposed herself.*)

STEPHEN. My child!

CARRY (*beating her hands*). Oh!

STEPHEN. What were you doing there?

CARRY (*shrinking*). Father, don't look at me so.

STEPHEN. What did you come down for?

CARRY. I don't know; I couldn't help it.

STEPHEN. What is that in your hand?

CARRY. In my hand? Nothing.

STEPHEN. What is it, Carry?

(*She has to show the keys; he takes them.*)

CARRY. Father!

STEPHEN. I see!

CARRY. I couldn't help it. What are you to do to me?

(*He takes her in his arms.*)

STEPHEN. Carry, you'll tell me the truth, won't you?

CARRY (*a child again*). Yes.

STEPHEN. Has this ever happened before?

CARRY. No.

STEPHEN. That night you—said you came down for a book for your mother?

CARRY. That once—only that once.

STEPHEN. Your headaches—was that what they meant ?

CARRY. No.

STEPHEN (*stroking her hair*). My little Carry, you used to come into my room, didn't you—while I was asleep—and get that key ?

CARRY. Don't—don't !

STEPHEN. No dear, I won't. Your mother—if she were to know !

CARRY (*simply*). Mother knows.

STEPHEN. What ?

CARRY. That is why I sleep in her room. Father, I didn't mean to come to-night. But all at once—it—it came over me.

STEPHEN (*listening to his own phrases*). Came over you !

CARRY. I held my breath till she was asleep, and then—then—I don't know how I can be your daughter.

(*He shudders.*)

Here is mother.

(MRS. BRAND *in a wrapper appears with a candle, which lights the room a little more.*)

STEPHEN. Agnes, Agnes !

MRS. BRAND (*quietly*). So you know now, Stephen.

STEPHEN. I know now.

(*She puts down the candle.*)

Why did you keep it from me ?

CARRY. Mother said it would be so awful to you to know.

STEPHEN. Not more awful than to you, Agnes.

CARRY. She said you have always been so good all your life.

STEPHEN. You said that, Agnes ?

MRS. BRAND. Yes.

STEPHEN (*overcome*). To have kept it from me—and to have given her such a reason—the love of woman !

MRS. BRAND (*still quietly*). ' The love of woman ! ' You think it was my love for you that made me spare you ?

STEPHEN. What else ?

MRS. BRAND. When after I married you I found out what you were, I—yes, the love of woman still made me forgive you, pity you, try to help you. But from the day when I discovered what legacy you had given my child—the love of woman changed into something harsher.

CARRY (*bewildered*). Legacy ?

MRS. BRAND. She doesn't know what I mean. The only reason I haven't told her is that I believed she might be able to fight it better if she thought the blame was hers.

STEPHEN. She must know now. Carry, what your mother means—and it is all true—is that for many years I was as you are, but a hundred times worse.

CARRY (*unable to grasp it*). You, father—not you—oh no.

STEPHEN. Yes. And what your mother means is that you get it from me ; can that be possible !

MRS. BRAND. That is the only way I can reason it out.

CARRY (*clinging to* MRS. BRAND). Mother !

MRS. BRAND. You are not to blame, my own ; he never gave you a chance. I have no pity left for you, Stephen ; it has all gone to her.

STEPHEN. Let her have every drop of it.

CARRY. Father, do you think there is any hope ?

STEPHEN (*cheered*). Hope ? Of course there is. Carry, I fought it long ago, and beat it.

CARRY (*wondering*). Are you sure ?

STEPHEN. Your mother knows. Many times I failed, but at last I won. And listen to this, in the end I found it almost easy.

CARRY (*wondering still more*). Easy ?

MRS. BRAND. So easy that you were sometimes puzzled, Stephen, just as you see it puzzles Carry now.

STEPHEN. Yes ; I suppose it was my doggedness.

MRS. BRAND. Oh, Stephen !

CARRY. I don't see how it can have been easy.

MRS. BRAND. It was easy, Carry, because he didn't do it.

STEPHEN. Agnes !

MRS. BRAND. He thinks he did.

STEPHEN. Haven't I given it up ?

MRS. BRAND. Not as I have thought the thing out, Stephen. I don't think you gave it up—I think it gave up you. I was looking on ; I saw. It wearied of you, and left you. But it has come back now—for her. Easy enough to find a way back to the house—for such an old friend of yours. I may be wrong, but that is what I make of it.

CARRY. There is Dick—there is Dick.

STEPHEN. Dick, yes. Isn't it a shame, Agnes, to keep this from him ?

MRS. BRAND. A shame ? Of course it is a shame. But it is her best chance, and I won't let it go.

CARRY. Mother, I want Dick to know.

MRS. BRAND. If all isn't well, dear, in a year's time he shall be told. That is why I said that the engagement must last a year. As for hope, my own, of course there is hope. It is just an ailment you have caught.

CARRY. Please always watch me. But do you think it will be any use ? I feel I shall be watching you, and sometimes you will tire, but will I ever tire ?

MRS. BRAND. You will tire before I do. Stephen, you will help us, won't you ?

STEPHEN. I'll try.

CARRY (*stroking his arm*). Poor Carry, but poor father too.

THE TWELVE-POUND LOOK

Produced at the Duke of York's Theatre on March 1, 1910, with the following cast :

SIR HARRY SIMS	*Edmund Gwenn*
LADY SIMS	*Mary Barton*
KATE	*Lena Ashwell*
TOMBES	*C. C. Calvert*

IF quite convenient (as they say about cheques) you are to conceive that the scene is laid in your own house, and that Harry Sims is you.   Perhaps the ornamentation of the house is a trifle ostentatious, but if you cavil at that we are willing to re-decorate : you don't get out of being Harry Sims on a mere matter of plush and dados.   It pleases us to make him a city man, but (rather than lose you) he can be turned with a scrape of the pen into a K.C., fashionable doctor, Secretary of State, or what you will. We conceive him of a pleasant rotundity with a thick red neck, but we shall waive that point if you know him to be thin.

It is that day in your career when everything went wrong just when everything seemed to be superlatively right.

In Harry's case it was a woman who did the mischief.   She came to him in his great hour and told him she did not admire him.   Of course he turned her out of the house and was soon himself again, but it spoilt the morning for him.   This is the subject of the play, and quite enough too.

Harry is to receive the honour of knighthood in a few days, and we discover him in the sumptuous ' snuggery ' of his home in Kensington (or is it Westminster ?), rehearsing the ceremony with his wife.   They have been at it all the morning, a pleasing occupation.   Mrs. Sims (as we may call her for the last time, as it were, and strictly as a good-natured joke) is wearing her presentation gown, and personates the august one who is about to dub her Harry knight.   She is seated regally.   Her jewelled shoulders proclaim aloud her husband's generosity.   She must be an extraordinarily proud and happy woman, yet she has a drawn face and shrinking ways as if there were some one near her of whom she is afraid.   She claps her hands, as the signal to Harry.   He enters bowing, and with a graceful swerve of the leg.   He is only partly in costume, the sword and the real stockings not having arrived yet.   With a gliding motion that is only delayed while one leg makes up on the other, he reaches his wife, and, going on one knee, raises her hand superbly to his lips. She taps him on the shoulder with a paper-knife and says huskily, ' Rise, Sir Harry.' He rises, bows, and glides about the room, going on his knees to various articles of furniture, and rising from each a knight. It is a radiant domestic scene, and Harry is as dignified as if he knew that royalty was rehearsing it at the other end.

SIR HARRY (*complacently*). Did that seem all right, eh ?

LADY SIMS (*much relieved*). I think perfect.

SIR HARRY. But was it dignified ?

LADY SIMS. Oh, very. And it will be still more so when you have the sword.

SIR HARRY. The sword will lend it an air. There are really the five moments (*suiting the action to the word*)—the glide— the dip—the kiss—the tap—and you back out a knight. It 's short, but it 's a very beautiful ceremony. (*Kindly*) Anything you can suggest ?

LADY SIMS. No—oh no. (*Nervously, seeing him pause to kiss the tassel of a cushion*) You don't think you have practised till you know what to do almost too well ?

(*He has been in a blissful temper, but such niggling criticism would try any man.*)

SIR HARRY. I do not. Don't talk nonsense. Wait till your opinion is asked for.

LADY SIMS (*abashed*). I 'm sorry, Harry. (*A perfect butler appears and presents a card.*) ' The Flora Type-Writing Agency.'

SIR HARRY. Ah, yes. I telephoned them to send some one. A woman, I suppose, Tombes ?

TOMBES. Yes, Sir Harry.

SIR HARRY. Show her in here. (*He has very lately become a stickler for etiquette.*) And, Tombes, strictly speaking, you know, I am not Sir Harry till Thursday.

TOMBES. Beg pardon, sir, but it is such a satisfaction to us.

SIR HARRY (*good-naturedly*). Ah, they like it downstairs, do they ?

TOMBES (*unbending*). Especially the females, Sir Harry.

SIR HARRY. Exactly. You can show her in, Tombes. (*The butler departs on his mighty task.*) You can tell the woman what she is wanted for, Emmy, while I change. (*He is too modest to boast about himself, and prefers to keep a wife in the house for that purpose.*) You can tell her the sort of things about me that will come better from you. (*Smiling happily*) You heard what Tombes said, ' Especially the females.' And he is right. Success ! The women like it even better than the men. And rightly. For they share. *You* share, *Lady* Sims. Not a woman will see that gown without being sick with envy of it. I know them. Have all our lady friends in to see it. It will make them ill for a week.

(*These sentiments carry him off light-heartedly, and presently the disturbing element is shown in. She is a mere typist, dressed in uncommonly good taste, but at contemptibly small expense, and she is carrying her typewriter in a friendly way rather than as a badge of slavery, as of course it is. Her eye is clear ; and in odd contrast to* LADY SIMS, *she is self-reliant and serene.*)

KATE (*respectfully, but she should have waited to be spoken to*). Good morning, madam.

LADY SIMS (*in her nervous way, and scarcely noticing that the typist is a little too ready with her tongue*). Good morning. (*As a first impression she rather likes the woman, and the woman, though it is scarcely worth mentioning, rather likes her.* LADY SIMS *has a maid for buttoning and unbuttoning her, and probably another for waiting on the maid, and she gazes with a little envy perhaps at a woman who does things for herself.*) Is that the type-writing machine ?

KATE (*who is getting it ready for use*). Yes (*not ' Yes, madam,' as it ought to be*). I suppose if I am to work here I may take this off. I get on better without it. (*She is referring to her hat.*)

LADY SIMS. Certainly. (*But the hat is already off.*) I ought to apologise for my gown. I am to be presented this week, and I was trying it on. (*Her tone is not really apologetic. She is rather clinging to the glory of her gown, wistfully, as if not absolutely certain, you know, that it is a glory.*)

KATE. It is beautiful, if I may presume to say so. (*She frankly admires it. She probably has a best, and a second best of her own : that sort of thing.*)

LADY SIMS (*with a flush of pride in the gown*). Yes, it is very beautiful. (*The beauty of it gives her courage.*)   Sit down, please.

KATE (*the sort of woman who would have sat down in any case*). I suppose it is some copying you want done ?   I got no particulars.   I was told to come to this address, but that was all.

LADY SIMS (*almost with the humility of a servant*).   Oh, it is not work for me, it is for my husband, and what he needs is not exactly copying.   (*Swelling, for she is proud of* HARRY) He wants a number of letters answered—hundreds of them— letters and telegrams of congratulation.

KATE (*as if it were all in the day's work*).   Yes ?

LADY SIMS (*remembering that* HARRY *expects every wife to do her duty*).   My husband is a remarkable man.   He is about to be knighted.   (*Pause, but* KATE *does not fall to the floor.*)   He is to be knighted for his services to—(*on reflection*)—for his services.   (*She is conscious that she is not doing* HARRY *justice.*) He can explain it so much better than I can.

KATE (*in her business-like way*).   And I am to answer the congratulations ?

LADY SIMS (*afraid that it will be a hard task*).   Yes.

KATE (*blithely*).   It is work I have had some experience of. (*She proceeds to type.*)

LADY SIMS.   But you can't begin till you know what he wants to say.

KATE.   Only a specimen letter.   Won't it be the usual thing ?

LADY SIMS (*to whom this is a new idea*).   Is there a usual thing ?

KATE.   Oh yes.

(*She continues to type, and* LADY SIMS, *half-mesmerised, gazes at her nimble fingers.   The useless woman watches the useful one, and she sighs, she could not tell why.*)

LADY SIMS.   How quickly you do it.   It must be delightful to be able to do something, and to do it well.

KATE (*thankfully*).   Yes, it is delightful.

LADY SIMS (*again remembering the source of all her greatness*). But, excuse me, I don't think that will be any use.   My husband wants me to explain to you that his is an exceptional case. He did not try to get this honour in any way.   It was a complete surprise to him——

KATE (*who is a practical Kate and no dealer in sarcasm*).   That is what I have written.

LADY SIMS (*in whom sarcasm would meet a dead wall*).   But how could you know ?

KATE.   I only guessed.

LADY SIMS.   Is that the usual thing ?

KATE.   Oh yes.

LADY SIMS.   They don't try to get it ?

KATE.   I don't know.   That is what we are told to say in the letters.

> (*To her at present the only important thing about the letters is that they are ten shillings the hundred.*)

LADY SIMS (*returning to surer ground*).   I should explain that my husband is not a man who cares for honours.   So long as he does his duty——

KATE.   Yes, I have been putting that in.

LADY SIMS.   Have you ?   But he particularly wants it to be known that he would have declined a title were it not——

KATE.   I have got it here.

LADY SIMS.   What have you got ?

KATE (*reading*).   ' Indeed I would have asked to be allowed to decline had it not been that I want to please my wife.'

LADY SIMS (*heavily*).   But how could you know it was that ?

KATE.   Is it ?

LADY SIMS (*who after all is the one with the right to ask questions*).   Do they all accept it for that reason ?

KATE.   That is what we are told to say in the letters.

LADY SIMS (*thoughtlessly*).   It is quite as if you knew my husband.

KATE.   I assure you, I don't even know his name.

LADY SIMS (*suddenly showing that she knows him*).   Oh, he wouldn't like that.

> (*And it is here that* HARRY *re-enters in his city garments, looking so gay, feeling so jolly that we bleed for him.   However, the annoying* KATHARINE *is to get a shock also.*)

LADY SIMS.   This is the lady, Harry.

SIR HARRY (*shooting his cuffs*).   Yes, yes.   Good morning, my dear.

> (*Then they see each other, and their mouths open, but not for words.   After the first surprise* KATE *seems to find some*

humour in the situation, but HARRY *lowers like a thunder-
cloud.*)

LADY SIMS (*who has seen nothing*). I have been trying to
explain to her——

SIR HARRY. Eh—what? (*He controls himself.*) Leave it
to me, Emmy; I'll attend to her.

(LADY SIMS *goes, with a dread fear that somehow she has
vexed her lord, and then* HARRY *attends to the intruder.*)

SIR HARRY (*with concentrated scorn*). You!

KATE (*as if agreeing with him*). Yes, it's funny.

SIR HARRY. The shamelessness of your daring to come
here!

KATE. Believe me, it is not less a surprise to me than it is to
you. I was sent here in the ordinary way of business. I was
given only the number of the house. I was not told the name.

SIR HARRY (*withering her*). The ordinary way of business!
This is what you have fallen to—a typist!

KATE (*unwithered*). Think of it!

SIR HARRY. After going through worse straits, I'll be
bound.

KATE (*with some grim memories*). Much worse straits.

SIR HARRY (*alas, laughing coarsely*). My congratulations.

KATE. Thank you, Harry.

SIR HARRY (*who is annoyed, as any man would be, not to find her
abject*). Eh? What was that you called me, madam?

KATE. Isn't it Harry? On my soul, I almost forget.

SIR HARRY. It isn't Harry to you. My name is Sims, if
you please.

KATE. Yes, I had not forgotten that. It was my name,
too, you see.

SIR HARRY (*in his best manner*). It was your name till you
forfeited the right to bear it.

KATE. Exactly.

SIR HARRY (*gloating*). I was furious to find you here, but
on second thoughts it pleases me. (*From the depths of his moral
nature*) There is a salt justice in this.

KATE (*sympathetically*). Tell me?

SIR HARRY. Do you know what you were brought here
to do?

KATE. I have just been learning. You have been made a

knight, and I was summoned to answer the messages of congratulation.

SIR HARRY. That's it, that's it. You come on this day as my servant!

KATE. I, who might have been Lady Sims.

SIR HARRY. And you are her typist instead. And she has four men-servants. Oh, I am glad you saw her in her presentation gown.

KATE. I wonder if she would let me do her washing, Sir Harry?

(*Her want of taste disgusts him.*)

SIR HARRY (*with dignity*). You can go. The mere thought that only a few flights of stairs separates such as you from my innocent children——

(*He will never know why a new light has come into her face.*)

KATE (*slowly*). You have children?

SIR HARRY (*inflated*). Two.

(*He wonders why she is so long in answering.*)

KATE (*resorting to impertinence*). Such a nice number.

SIR HARRY (*with an extra turn of the screw*). Both boys.

KATE. Successful in everything. Are they like you, Sir Harry?

SIR HARRY (*expanding*). They are very like me.

KATE. That's nice.

(*Even on such a subject as this she can be ribald.*)

SIR HARRY. Will you please to go.

KATE. Heigho! What shall I say to my employer?

SIR HARRY. That is no affair of mine.

KATE. What will you say to Lady Sims?

SIR HARRY. I flatter myself that whatever I say, Lady Sims will accept without comment.

(*She smiles, heaven knows why, unless her next remark explains it.*)

KATE. Still the same Harry.

SIR HARRY. What do you mean?

KATE. Only that you have the old confidence in your profound knowledge of the sex.

SIR HARRY (*beginning to think as little of her intellect as of her morals*). I suppose I know my wife.

KATE (*hopelessly dense*). I suppose so. I was only remem-

bering that you used to think you knew her in the days when I
was the lady. (*He is merely wasting his time on her, and he
indicates the door. She is not sufficiently the lady to retire worsted*)
Well, good-bye, Sir Harry. Won't you ring, and the four men-
servants will show me out?

 (*But he hesitates.*)

 SIR HARRY (*in spite of himself*). As you are here, there is
something I want to get out of you. (*Wishing he could ask it
less eagerly*) Tell me, who was the man?

  (*The strange woman—it is evident now that she has
  always been strange to him—smiles tolerantly.*)

 KATE. You never found out?

 SIR HARRY. I could never be sure.

 KATE (*reflectively*). I thought that would worry you.

 SIR HARRY (*sneering*). It 's plain that he soon left you.

 KATE. Very soon.

 SIR HARRY. As I could have told you. (*But still she
surveys him with the smile of the free. The badgered man has
to entreat.*) Who was he? It was fourteen years ago, and
cannot matter to any of us now. Kate, tell me who he
was?

  (*It is his first youthful moment, and perhaps because of that
  she does not wish to hurt him.*)

 KATE (*shaking a motherly head*). Better not ask.

 SIR HARRY. I do ask. Tell me.

 KATE. It is kinder not to tell you.

 SIR HARRY (*violently*). Then, by James, it was one of my
own pals. Was it Bernard Roche? (*She shakes her head.*)
It may have been some one who comes to my house still.

 KATE. I think not. (*Reflecting*) Fourteen years! You
found my letter that night when you went home?

 SIR HARRY (*impatient*). Yes.

 KATE. I propped it against the decanters. I thought you
would be sure to see it there. It was a room not unlike this,
and the furniture was arranged in the same attractive way.
How it all comes back to me. Don't you see me, Harry, in hat
and cloak, putting the letter there, taking a last look round, and
then stealing out into the night to meet——

 SIR HARRY. Whom?

 KATE. Him. Hours pass, no sound in the room but the

tick-tack of the clock, and then about midnight you return alone. You take——

SIR HARRY (*gruffly*). I wasn't alone.

KATE (*the picture spoilt*). No? oh. (*Plaintively*) Here have I all these years been conceiving it wrongly. (*She studies his face.*) I believe something interesting happened?

SIR HARRY (*growling*). Something confoundedly annoying.

KATE (*coaxing*). Do tell me.

SIR HARRY. We won't go into that. Who was the man? Surely a husband has a right to know with whom his wife bolted.

KATE (*who is detestably ready with her tongue*). Surely the wife has a right to know how he took it. (*The woman's love of bargaining comes to her aid.*) A fair exchange. You tell me what happened, and I will tell you who he was.

SIR HARRY. You will? Very well. (*It is the first point on which they have agreed, and, forgetting himself, he takes a place beside her on the fire-seat. He is thinking only of what he is to tell her, but she, woman-like, is conscious of their proximity.*)

KATE (*tastelessly*). Quite like old times. (*He moves away from her indignantly.*) Go on, Harry.

SIR HARRY (*who has a manful shrinking from saying anything that is to his disadvantage*). Well, as you know, I was dining at the club that night.

KATE. Yes.

SIR HARRY. Jack Lamb drove me home. Mabbett Green was with us, and I asked them to come in for a few minutes.

KATE. Jack Lamb, Mabbett Green? I think I remember them. Jack was in Parliament.

SIR HARRY. No, that was Mabbett. They came into the house with me and——(*with sudden horror*)—was it him?

KATE (*bewildered*). Who?

SIR HARRY. Mabbett?

KATE. What?

SIR HARRY. The man?

KATE. What man? (*Understanding*) Oh no. I thought you said he came into the house with you.

SIR HARRY. It might have been a blind.

KATE. Well, it wasn't. Go on.

SIR HARRY. They came in to finish a talk we had been having at the club.

KATE.   An interesting talk, evidently.

SIR HARRY.   The papers had been full that evening of the elopement of some countess woman with a fiddler.   What was her name ?

KATE.   Does it matter ?

SIR HARRY.   No.   (*Thus ends the countess.*)   We had been discussing the thing and——(*he pulls a wry face*)—and I had been rather warm——

KATE (*with horrid relish*).   I begin to see.   You had been saying it served the husband right, that the man who could not look after his wife deserved to lose her.   It was one of your favourite subjects.   Oh, Harry, say it was that !

SIR HARRY (*sourly*).   It may have been something like that.

KATE.   And all the time the letter was there, waiting ; and none of you knew except the clock.   Harry, it is sweet of you to tell me.   (*His face is not sweet.   The illiterate woman has used the wrong adjective.*)   I forget what I said precisely in the letter.

SIR HARRY (*pulverising her*).   So do I.   But I have it still.

KATE (*not pulverised*).   Do let me see it again.   (*She has observed his eye wandering to the desk.*)

SIR HARRY.   You are welcome to it as a gift.   (*The fateful letter, a poor little dead thing, is brought to light from a locked drawer.*)

KATE (*taking it*).   Yes, this is it.   Harry, how you did crumple it !   (*She reads, not without curiosity.*)   ' Dear husband —I call you that for the last time—I am off.   I am what you call making a bolt of it.   I won't try to excuse myself nor to explain, for you would not accept the excuses nor understand the explanation.   It will be a little shock to you, but only to your pride ;   what will astound you is that any woman could be such a fool as to leave such a man as you.   I am taking nothing with me that belongs to you.   May you be very happy.—Your ungrateful KATE.   P.S.—You need not try to find out who he is.   You will try, but you won't succeed.'   (*She folds the nasty little thing up.*)   I may really have it for my very own ?

SIR HARRY.   You really may.

KATE (*impudently*).   If you would care for a typed copy——?

SIR HARRY (*in a voice with which he used to frighten his grandmother*).   None of your sauce.   (*Wincing*) I had to let them see it in the end.

KATE. I can picture Jack Lamb eating it.

SIR HARRY. A penniless parson's daughter.

KATE. That is all I was.

SIR HARRY. We searched for the two of you high and low.

KATE. Private detectives?

SIR HARRY. They couldn't get on the track of you.

KATE (*smiling*). No?

SIR HARRY. But at last the courts let me serve the papers by advertisement on a man unknown, and I got my freedom.

KATE. So I saw. It was the last I heard of you.

SIR HARRY (*each word a blow for her*). And I married again just as soon as ever I could.

KATE. They say that is always a compliment to the first wife.

SIR HARRY (*violently*). I showed them.

KATE. You soon let them see that if one woman was a fool, you still had the pick of the basket to choose from.

SIR HARRY. By James, I did.

KATE (*bringing him to earth again*). But still, you wondered who he was.

SIR HARRY. I suspected everybody—even my pals. I felt like jumping at their throats and crying, ' It 's you ! '

KATE. You had been so admirable to me, an instinct told you that I was sure to choose another of the same.

SIR HARRY. I thought, it can't be money, so it must be looks. Some dolly face. (*He stares at her in perplexity.*) He must have had something wonderful about him to make you willing to give up all that you had with me.

KATE (*as if he was the stupid one*). Poor Harry !

SIR HARRY. And it couldn't have been going on for long, for I would have noticed the change in you.

KATE. Would you ?

SIR HARRY. I knew you so well.

KATE. You amazing man.

SIR HARRY. So who was he ? Out with it.

KATE. You are determined to know ?

SIR HARRY. Your promise. You gave your word.

KATE. If I must—— (*She is the villain of the piece, but it must be conceded that in this matter she is reluctant to pain him.*) I am sorry I promised. (*Looking at him steadily*) There was no one, Harry ; no one at all.

SIR HARRY (*rising*). If you think you can play with me——

KATE. I told you that you wouldn't like it.

SIR HARRY (*rasping*). It is unbelievable.

KATE. I suppose it is ; but it is true.

SIR HARRY. Your letter itself gives you the lie.

KATE. That was intentional. I saw that if the truth were known you might have a difficulty in getting your freedom ; and as I was getting mine it seemed fair that you should have yours also. So I wrote my good-bye in words that would be taken to mean what you thought they meant, and I knew the law would back you in your opinion. For the law, like you, Harry, has a profound understanding of women.

SIR HARRY (*trying to straighten himself*). I don't believe you yet.

KATE (*looking not unkindly into the soul of this man*). Perhaps that is the best way to take it. It is less unflattering than the truth. But you were the only one. (*Summing up her life.*) You sufficed.

SIR HARRY. Then what mad impulse——

KATE. It was no impulse, Harry. I had thought it out for a year.

SIR HARRY (*dazed*). A year ? One would think to hear you that I hadn't been a good husband to you.

KATE (*with a sad smile*). You were a good husband according to your lights.

SIR HARRY (*stoutly*). I think so.

KATE. And a moral man, and chatty, and quite the philanthropist.

SIR HARRY (*on sure ground*). All women envied you.

KATE. How you loved me to be envied.

SIR HARRY. I swaddled you in luxury.

KATE (*making her great revelation*). That was it.

SIR HARRY (*blankly*). What ?

KATE (*who can be serene because it is all over*). How you beamed at me when I sat at the head of your fat dinners in my fat jewellery, surrounded by our fat friends.

SIR HARRY (*aggrieved*). They weren't so fat.

KATE (*a side issue*). All except those who were so thin.

Have you ever noticed, Harry, that many jewels make women either incredibly fat or incredibly thin ?

SIR HARRY (*shouting*). I have not. (*Is it worth while to argue with her any longer ?*) We had all the most interesting society of the day. It wasn't only business men. There were politicians, painters, writers——

KATE. Only the glorious, dazzling successes. Oh, the fat talk while we ate too much—about who had made a hit and who was slipping back, and what the noo house cost and the noo motor and the gold soup-plates, and who was to be the noo knight.

SIR HARRY (*who it will be observed is unanswerable from first to last*). Was anybody getting on better than me, and consequently you ?

KATE. Consequently me ! Oh, Harry, you and your sublime religion.

SIR HARRY (*honest heart*). My religion ? I never was one to talk about religion, but——

KATE. Pooh, Harry, you don't even know what your religion was and is and will be till the day of your expensive funeral. (*And here is the lesson that life has taught her.*) One's religion is whatever he is most interested in, and yours is Success.

SIR HARRY (*quoting from his morning paper*). Ambition—it is the last infirmity of noble minds.

KATE. Noble minds !

SIR HARRY (*at last grasping what she is talking about*). You are not saying that you left me because of my success ?

KATE. Yes, that was it. (*And now she stands revealed to him.*) I couldn't endure it. If a failure had come now and then—but your success was suffocating me. (*She is rigid with emotion.*) The passionate craving I had to be done with it, to find myself among people who had not got on.

SIR HARRY (*with proper spirit*). There are plenty of them.

KATE. There were none in our set. When they began to go down-hill they rolled out of our sight.

SIR HARRY (*clinching it*). I tell you I am worth a quarter of a million.

KATE (*unabashed*). That is what you are worth to yourself. I 'll tell you what you are worth to me : exactly twelve pounds. For I made up my mind that I could launch myself on the world alone if I first proved my mettle by earning twelve pounds ; and as soon as I had earned it I left you.

SIR HARRY (*in the scales*).   Twelve pounds !

KATE.   That is your value to a woman.   If she can't make it she has to stick to you.

SIR HARRY (*remembering perhaps a rectory garden*).   You valued me at more than that when you married me.

KATE (*seeing it also*).   Ah, I didn't know you then.   If only you had been a man, Harry.

SIR HARRY.   A man ?   What do you mean by a man ?

KATE (*leaving the garden*).   Haven't you heard of them ? They are something fine ; and every woman is loath to admit to herself that her husband is not one.   When she marries, even though she has been a very trivial person, there is in her some vague stirring toward a worthy life, as well as a fear of her capacity for evil.   She knows her chance lies in him.   If there is something good in him, what is good in her finds it and they join forces against the baser parts.   So I didn't give you up willingly, Harry.   I invented all sorts of theories to explain you.   Your hardness—I said it was a fine want of mawkishness.   Your coarseness—I said it goes with strength. Your contempt for the weak—I called it virility.   Your want of ideals was clear-sightedness.   Your ignoble views of women —I tried to think them funny.   Oh, I clung to you to save myself.   But I had to let go ; you had only the one quality, Harry, success ; you had it so strong that it swallowed all the others.

SIR HARRY (*not to be diverted from the main issue*).   How did you earn that twelve pounds ?

KATE.   It took me nearly six months ; but I earned it fairly.   (*She presses her hand on the typewriter as lovingly as many a woman has pressed a rose.*)   I learned this.   I hired it and taught myself.   I got some work through a friend, and with my first twelve pounds I paid for my machine.   Then I considered that I was free to go, and I went.

SIR HARRY.   All this going on in my house while you were living in the lap of luxury !   (*She nods.*)   By God, you were determined.

KATE (*briefly*).   By God, I was.

SIR HARRY (*staring*).   How you must have hated me.

KATE (*smiling at the childish word*). Not a bit—after I saw that there was a way out. From that hour you amused me, Harry ; I was even sorry for you, for I saw that you couldn't help yourself. Success is just a fatal gift.

SIR HARRY. Oh, thank you.

KATE (*thinking, dear friends in front, of you and me perhaps*). Yes, and some of your most successful friends knew it. One or two of them used to look very sad at times, as if they thought they might have come to something if they hadn't got on.

SIR HARRY (*who has a horror of sacrilege*). The battered crew you live among now—what are they but folk who have tried to succeed and failed ?

KATE. That 's it ; they try, but they fail.

SIR HARRY. And always will fail.

KATE. Always. Poor souls—I say of them. Poor soul—they say of me. It keeps us human. That is why I never tire of them.

SIR HARRY (*comprehensively*). Bah ! Kate, I tell you I 'll be worth half a million yet.

KATE. I 'm sure you will. You 're getting stout, Harry.

SIR HARRY. No, I 'm not.

KATE. What was the name of that fat old fellow who used to fall asleep at our dinner-parties ?

SIR HARRY. If you mean Sir William Crackley——

KATE. That was the man. Sir William was to me a perfect picture of the grand success. He had got on so well that he was very, very stout, and when he sat on a chair it was thus (*her hands meeting in front of her*)—as if he were holding his success together. That is what you are working for, Harry. You will have that and the half million about the same time.

SIR HARRY (*who has surely been very patient*). Will you please to leave my house.

KATE (*putting on her gloves, soiled things*). But don't let us part in anger. How do you think I am looking, Harry, compared to the dull, inert thing that used to roll round in your padded carriages ?

SIR HARRY (*in masterly fashion*). I forget what you were like. I 'm very sure you never could have held a candle to the present Lady Sims.

KATE. That is a picture of her, is it not ?

SIR HARRY (*seizing his chance again*). In her wedding-gown.
Painted by an R.A.

KATE (*wickedly*). A knight ?

SIR HARRY (*deceived*). Yes.

KATE (*who likes* LADY SIMS : *a piece of presumption on her
part*). It is a very pretty face.

SIR HARRY (*with the pride of possession*). Acknowledged to
be a beauty everywhere.

KATE. There is a merry look in the eyes, and character in
the chin.

SIR HARRY (*like an auctioneer*). Noted for her wit.

KATE. All her life before her when that was painted. It
is a *spirituelle* face too. (*Suddenly she turns on him with anger,
for the first and only time in the play.*) Oh, Harry, you brute !

SIR HARRY (*staggered*). Eh ? What ?

KATE. That dear creature capable of becoming a noble
wife and mother—she is the spiritless woman of no account
that I saw here a few minutes ago. I forgive you for myself,
for I escaped, but that poor lost soul, oh, Harry, Harry !

SIR HARRY (*waving her to the door*). I 'll thank you——
If ever there was a woman proud of her husband and happy in
her married life, that woman is Lady Sims.

KATE. I wonder.

SIR HARRY. Then you needn't wonder.

KATE (*slowly*). If I was a husband—it is my advice to all
of them—I would often watch my wife quietly to see whether
the twelve-pound look was not coming into her eyes. Two
boys, did you say, and both like you ?

SIR HARRY. What is that to you ?

KATE (*with glistening eyes*). I was only thinking that somewhere there are two little girls who, when they grow up—the
dear, pretty girls who are all meant for the men that don't get
on ! Well, good-bye, Sir Harry.

SIR HARRY (*showing a little human weakness, it is to be feared*).
Say first that you 're sorry.

KATE. For what ?

SIR HARRY. That you left me. Say you regret it bitterly.
You know you do. (*She smiles and shakes her head. He is
pettish. He makes a terrible announcement.*) You have spoilt
the day for me.

KATE (*to hearten him*). I am sorry for that ; but it is only a pin-prick, Harry. I suppose it is a little jarring in the moment of your triumph to find that there is——one old friend ——who does not think you a success ; but you will soon forget it. Who cares what a typist thinks ?

SIR HARRY (*heartened*). Nobody. A typist at eighteen shillings a week !

KATE (*proudly*). Not a bit of it, Harry. I double that.

SIR HARRY (*neatly*). Magnificent !

(*There is a timid knock at the door.*)

LADY SIMS. May I come in ?

SIR HARRY (*rather appealingly*). It is Lady Sims.

KATE. I won't tell. She is afraid to come into her husband's room without knocking !

SIR HARRY. She is not. (*Uxoriously*) Come in, dearest. (*Dearest enters carrying the sword. She might have had the sense not to bring it in while this annoying person is here.*)

LADY SIMS (*thinking she has brought her welcome with her*). Harry, the sword has come.

SIR HARRY (*who will dote on it presently*). Oh, all right.

LADY SIMS. But I thought you were so eager to practise with it.

(*The person smiles at this. He wishes he had not looked to see if she was smiling.*)

SIR HARRY (*sharply*). Put it down.

(LADY SIMS *flushes a little as she lays the sword aside.*)

KATE (*with her confounded courtesy*). It is a beautiful sword, if I may say so.

LADY SIMS (*helped*). Yes.

(*The person thinks she can put him in the wrong, does she ? He 'll show her.*)

SIR HARRY (*with one eye on* KATE). Emmy, the one thing your neck needs is more jewels.

LADY SIMS (*faltering*). More !

SIR HARRY. Some ropes of pearls. I 'll see to it. It 's a bagatelle to me. (KATE *conceals her chagrin, so she had better be shown the door. He rings.*) I won't detain you any longer, miss.

KATE. Thank you.

LADY SIMS. Going already ? You have been very quick

SIR HARRY. The person doesn't suit, Emmy.

LADY SIMS. I'm sorry.

KATE. So am I, madam, but it can't be helped. Good-bye, your ladyship—good-bye, Sir Harry. (*There is a suspicion of an impertinent curtsey, and she is escorted off the premises by* TOMBES. *The air of the room is purified by her going.* SIR HARRY *notices it at once.*)

LADY SIMS (*whose tendency is to say the wrong thing*). She seemed such a capable woman.

SIR HARRY (*on his hearth*). I don't like her style at all.

LADY SIMS (*meekly*). Of course you know best. (*This is the right kind of woman.*)

SIR HARRY (*rather anxious for corroboration*). Lord, how she winced when I said I was to give you those ropes of pearls.

LADY SIMS. Did she? I didn't notice. I suppose so.

SIR HARRY (*frowning*). Suppose? Surely I know enough about women to know that.

LADY SIMS. Yes, oh yes.

SIR HARRY. (*Odd that so confident a man should ask this.*) Emmy, I know you well, don't I? I can read you like a book, eh?

LADY SIMS (*nervously*). Yes, Harry.

SIR HARRY (*jovially, but with an inquiring eye*). What a different existence yours is from that poor lonely wretch's.

LADY SIMS. Yes, but she has a very contented face.

SIR HARRY (*with a stamp of his foot*). All put on. What?

LADY SIMS (*timidly*). I didn't say anything.

SIR HARRY (*snapping*). One would think you envied her.

LADY SIMS. Envied? Oh no—but I thought she looked so alive. It was while she was working the machine.

SIR HARRY. Alive! That's no life. It is you that are alive. (*Curtly*) I'm busy, Emmy. (*He sits at his writing-table.*)

LADY SIMS (*dutifully*). I'm sorry; I'll go, Harry. (*Inconsequentially*) Are they very expensive?

SIR HARRY. What?

LADY SIMS. Those machines?

(*When she has gone the possible meaning of her question startles him. The curtain hides him from us, but we may be sure that he will soon be bland again. We have a comfortable feeling, you and I, that there is nothing of* HARRY SIMS *in us.*)

ROSALIND

Produced at the Duke of York's Theatre on October 14, 1912, with the following cast:

MRS. PAGE	.	.	.	.	.	*Irene Vanbrugh*
CHARLES	.	.	.	.	.	*Donald Calthrop*
MRS. QUICKLY	.	.	.	.	.	*Helen Haye*

ROSALIND

Two middle-aged ladies are drinking tea in the parlour of a
cottage by the sea. It is far from London, and a hundred yards
from the cry of children, of whom middle-aged ladies have often
had enough. Were the room Mrs. Page's we should make a
journey through it in search of character, but she is only a bird
of passage ; nothing of herself here that has not strayed from
her bedroom except some cushions and rugs : touches of character after all maybe, for they suggest that Mrs. Page likes to
sit soft.

The exterior of the cottage is probably picturesque, with a
thatched roof, but we shall never know for certain, it being
against the rules of the game to-day to step outside and look. The
bowed window of the parlour is of the engaging kind that still
brings some carriage folk to a sudden stop in villages, not necessarily to sample the sweets of yester-year exposed within in
bottles ; its panes are leaded ; but Mrs. Quickly will put something more modern in their place if ever her ship comes home.
They will then be used as the roof of the hencoop, and ultimately
some lovely lady, given, like the chickens, to 'picking up things,'
may survey the world through them from a window in Mayfair.
The parlour is, by accident, like some woman's face that scores
by being out of drawing. At present the window is her smile,
but one cannot fix features to the haphazard floor, nor to the
irregular walls, which nevertheless are part of the invitation to
come and stay here. There are two absurd steps leading up to
Mrs. Page's bedroom, and perhaps they are what give the room
its *retroussée* touch. There is a smell of seaweed ; twice a day
Neptune comes gallantly to the window and hands Mrs. Page
the smell of seaweed. He knows probably that she does not
like to have to go far for her seaweed. Perhaps he also suspects
her to be something of a spark, and looks forward to his evening
visits, of which we know nothing.

This is a mere suggestion that there may be more in Mrs.

Page (when the moon is up, say) than meets the eye, but we see at present only what does meet the eye as she gossips with her landlady at the tea-table. Is she good-looking? is the universal shriek; the one question on the one subject that really thrills humanity. But the question seems beside the point about this particular lady, who has so obviously ceased to have any interest in the answer. To us who have a few moments to sum her up while she is still at the tea-table (just time enough for sharp ones to form a wrong impression), she is an indolent, sloppy thing, this Mrs. Page of London, decidedly too plump, and averse to pulling the strings that might contract her; as Mrs. Quickly may have said, she has let her figure go and snapped her fingers at it as it went. Her hair is braided back at a minimum of labour (and the brush has been left on the parlour mantelpiece). She wears at tea-time a loose and dowdy dressing-gown and large flat slippers. Such a lazy woman (shall we venture?) that if she were a beggar and you offered her alms, she would ask you to put them in her pocket for her.

Yet we notice, as contrary to her type, that she is not only dowdy but self-consciously enamoured of her dowdiness, has a kiss for it so to speak. This is odd, and perhaps we had better have another look at her. The thing waggling gaily beneath the table is one of her feet, from which the sprawling slipper has dropped, to remain where it fell. It is an uncommonly pretty foot, and one instantly wonders what might not the rest of her be like if it also escaped from its moorings.

The foot returns into custody, without its owner having to stoop, and Mrs. Page crosses with cheerful languor to a chair by the fire. She has a drawling walk that fits her gown. There is no footstool within reach, and she pulls another chair to her with her feet and rests them on it contentedly. The slippers almost hide her from our view.

DAME QUICKLY. You Mrs. Cosy Comfort!

MRS. PAGE (*whose voice is as lazy as her walk*). That is what I am. Perhaps a still better name for me would be Mrs. Treacly Contentment. Dame, you like me, don't you? Come here, and tell me why.

DAME. What do I like you for, Mrs. Page? Well, for one thing, it is very kind of you to let me sit here drinking tea and gossiping with you, for all the world as if I were your equal. And for another, you always pay your book the day I bring it to you, and that is enough to make any poor woman like her lodger.

MRS. PAGE. Oh, as a lodger I know I 'm well enough, and I love our gossips over the teapot, but that is not exactly what I meant. Let me put it in this way : If you tell me what you most envy in me, I shall tell you what I most envy in you.

DAME (*with no need to reflect*). Well, most of all, ma'am, I think I envy you your contentment with middle-age.

MRS. PAGE (*purring*). I am middle-aged, so why should I complain of it ?

DAME (*who feels that only yesterday she was driving the youths to desperation*). You even say it as if it were a pretty word.

MRS. PAGE. But isn't it ?

DAME. Not when you are up to the knees in it, as I am.

MRS. PAGE. And as I am. But I dote on it. It is such a comfy, sloppy, pull-the-curtains, carpet-slipper sort of word. When I awake in the morning, Dame, and am about to leap out of bed like the girl I once was, I suddenly remember, and I cry ' Hurrah, I 'm middle-aged.'

DAME. You just dumbfounder me when you tell me things like that. (*Here is something she has long wanted to ask.*) You can't be more than forty, if I may make so bold ?

MRS. PAGE. I am forty and a bittock, as the Scotch say. That means forty, and a good wee bit more.

DAME. There ! And you can say it without blinking.

MRS. PAGE. Why not ? Do you think I should call myself a 30-to-45, like a motor car ? Now what I think I envy you for most is for being a grandmamma.

DAME (*smiling tolerantly at some picture the words have called up*). That 's a cheap honour.

MRS. PAGE (*summing up probably her whole conception of the duties of a grandmother*). I should love to be a grandmamma, and toss little toddlekins in the air.

DAME (*who knows that there is more in it than that*). I dare say you will be some day.

(*The eyes of both turn to a photograph on the mantelpiece. It represents a pretty woman in the dress of Rosalind. The* DAME *fingers it for the hundredth time, and* MRS. PAGE *regards her tranquilly.*)

DAME. No one can deny but your daughter is a pretty piece. How old will she be now?

MRS. PAGE. Dame, I don't know very much about the stage, but I do know that you should never, never ask an actress's age.

DAME. Surely when they are as young and famous as this puss is.

MRS. PAGE. She is getting on, you know. Shall we say twenty-three?

DAME. Well, well, it's true you might be a grandmother by now. I wonder she doesn't marry. Where is she now?

MRS. PAGE. At Monte Carlo, the papers say. It is a place where people gamble.

DAME (*shaking her head*). Gamble? Dear, dear, that's terrible. (*But she knows of a woman who once won a dinner service without anything untoward happening afterwards.*) And yet I would like just once to put on my shilling with the best of them. If I were you I would try a month of that place with her.

MRS. PAGE. Not I, I am just Mrs. Cosy Comfort. At Monte Carlo I should be a fish out of water, Dame, as much as Beatrice would be if she were to try a month down here with me.

DAME (*less in disparagement of local society than of that sullen bore the sea, and blissfully unaware that it intrudes even at Monte Carlo*). Yes, I'm thinking she would find this a dull hole. (*In the spirit of adventure that has carried the English far*) And yet, play-actress though she be, I would like to see her, God forgive me.

(*She is trimming the lamp when there is a knock at the door. She is pleasantly flustered, and indicates with a gesture that something is constantly happening in this go-ahead village.*)

DAME. It has a visitor's sound.

(*The lodger is so impressed that she takes her feet off the chair. Thus may* MRS. QUICKLY'S *ancestors have stared at each other in this very cottage a hundred years ago when they thought they heard Napoleon tapping.*)

MRS. PAGE (*keeping her head*). If it is the doctor's lady, she wants to arrange with me about the cutting out for the mothers' meeting.

DAME (*who has long ceased to benefit from these gatherings*). Drat the mothers' meetings.

MRS. PAGE. Oh no, I dote on them. (*She is splendidly active ; in short, the spirited woman has got up.*) Still, I want my evening snooze now, so just tell her I am lying down.

DAME (*thankful to be in a plot*). I will.

MRS. PAGE. Yes, but let me lie down first, so that it won't be a fib.

DAME. There, there. That's such a middle-aged thing to say.

(*In the most middle-aged way* MRS. PAGE *spreads herself on a couch. They have been speaking in a whisper, and as the* DAME *goes to the door we have just time to take note that* MRS. PAGE *whispered most beautifully : a softer whisper than the* DAME'S, *but so clear that it might be heard across a field. This is the most tell-tale thing we have discovered about her as yet.*

Before MRS. QUICKLY *has reached the door it opens to admit an impatient young man in knickerbockers and a Norfolk jacket, all aglow with raindrops. Public school (and the particular one) is written on his forehead, and almost nothing else ; he has scarcely yet begun to surmise that anything else may be required. He is modest and clear-eyed, and would ring for his tub in Paradise ; reputably athletic also, with an instant smile always in reserve for the antagonist who accidentally shins him. Whatever you, as his host, ask him to do, he says he would like to awfully if you don't mind his being a priceless duffer at it ; his vocabulary is scanty, and in his engaging mouth ' priceless ' sums up all that is to be known of good or ill in our varied existence ; at a pinch it would suffice him for most of his simple wants, just as one may traverse the Continent with* Combien ? *His brain is quite as good as another's, but as yet he has referred scarcely anything to it. He respects learning in the aged, but shrinks uncomfortably from it in contemporaries, as persons who have somehow failed. To him the proper way to look upon ability is as something we must all come to in the end. He has a nice taste in the arts, that has come to him by the way of socks, spats and slips, and of these he has a large and happy collection, which he laughs at jollily in public (for his sense of humour is sufficient), but in the privacy of his chamber he sometimes spreads them out like troutlet on the river's bank and has his quiet thrills of exultation. Having lately left Oxford, he is facing the world confidently with nothing to impress it except these and his Fives Choice (having beaten Hon. Billy Minhorn in the final). He has not yet decided whether to drop into business or diplomacy or the bar. (There will be a lot of fag about this); and all unknown to him, there is a grim piece of waste land waiting for him in Canada, which he will make a hash of, or it will make a man of him. Billy will be there too.)*

CHARLES (*on the threshold*). I beg your pardon awfully, but I knocked three times.

DAME (*liking the manner of him, and indeed it is the nicest manner in the world*). What 's your pleasure ?

CHARLES. You see how jolly wet my things are. (*These boys get on delightful terms of intimacy at once.*) I am on a walking tour—not that I have walked much—(*they never boast ; he has really walked well and far*)—and I got caught in that shower. I thought when I saw a house that you might be kind enough to let me take my jacket off and warm my paws, until I can catch a train.

DAME (*unable to whisper to* MRS. PAGE ' *He is good-looking* '). I 'm sorry, sir, but I have let the kitchen fire out.

CHARLES (*peeping over her shoulder*). This fire——?

DAME. This is my lodger's room.

CHARLES. Ah, I see. Still, I dare say that if he knew—— (*He has edged farther into the room, and becomes aware that there is a lady with eyes closed on the sofa.*) I beg your pardon ; I didn't know there was any one here.

(*But the lady on the sofa replies not, and to the* DAME *this is his dismissal.*)

DAME. The station is just round the corner, and there is a waiting-room there.

CHARLES. A station waiting-room fire ; I know them. Is she asleep ?

DAME. Yes.

CHARLES (*who nearly always gets round them when he pouts*). Then can't I stay ? I won't disturb her.

DAME (*obdurate*). I 'm sorry.

CHARLES (*cheerily—he will probably do well on that fruit-farm*). Heigho ! Well, here is for the station waiting-room.

(And he is about to go when MRS. PAGE *signs to the* DAME *that he may stay. We have given the talk between the* DAME *and* CHARLES *in order to get it over, but our sterner eye is all the time on* MRS. PAGE. *Her eyes remain closed as if in sleep and she is lying on the sofa, yet for the first time since the curtain rose she has come to life. As if she knew we were watching her she is again inert, but there was a twitch of the mouth a moment ago that let a sunbeam loose upon her face. It is gone already, popped out of the box and returned to it with the speed of thought. Noticeable as is* MRS. PAGE'S *mischievous smile, far more noticeable is her control of it. A sudden thought occurs to us that the face we had thought stolid is made of elastic.)*

DAME *(cleverly)*. After all, if you're willing just to sit quietly by the fire and take a book——

CHARLES. Rather. Any book. Thank you immensely. *(And in his delightful way of making himself at home he whips off his knapsack and steps inside the fender. 'He is saucy, thank goodness,' is what the* DAME'S *glance at* MRS. PAGE *conveys. That lady's eyelids flicker as if she had discovered a way of watching* CHARLES *while she slumbers. Anon his eye alights on the photograph that has already been the subject of conversation, and he is instantly exclamatory.)*

DAME *(warningly)*. Now, you promised not to speak.

CHARLES. But that photograph. How funny you should have it!

DAME *(severely)*. Hsh! It's not mine.

CHARLES *(with his first glance of interest at the sleeper)*. Hers? *(The eyelids have ceased to flicker. It is placid* MRS. PAGE *again. Never was such an inelastic face.)*

DAME. Yes; only don't talk.

CHARLES. But this is priceless *(gazing at the photograph)*. I must talk. *(He gives his reason.)* I know her *(a reason that would be complimentary to any young lady)*. It is Miss Beatrice Page.

DAME *(who knows the creature man)*. You mean you've seen her?

CHARLES *(youthfully)*. I know her quite well. I have had lunch with her twice. She is at Monte Carlo just now. *(Swelling)* I was one of those that saw her off.

DAME. Yes, that 's the place. Read what is written across her velvet chest.

CHARLES (*deciphering the writing on the photograph*). 'To darling Mumsy with heaps of kisses.' (*His eyes gleam. Is he in the middle of an astonishing adventure?*) You don't tell me—— Is that—— ?

DAME (*as coolly as though she were passing the butter*). Yes, that 's her mother. And a sore trial it must have been to her when her girl took to such a trade.

CHARLES (*waving aside such nonsense*). But I say, she never spoke to me about a mother.

DAME. The more shame to her.

CHARLES (*deeply versed in the traffic of the stage*). I mean she is famed as being almost the only actress who doesn't have a mother.

DAME (*bewildered*). What?

CHARLES (*seeing the uselessness of laying pearls before this lady*). Let me have a look at her.

DAME. It is not to be thought of. (*But an unexpected nod from the sleeper indicates that it may be permitted.*) Oh, well, I see no harm in it if you go softly.

(*He tiptoes to the sofa, but perhaps* MRS. PAGE *is a light sleeper, for she stirs a little, just sufficiently to become more compact, while the slippers rise into startling prominence. Some humorous dream, as it might be, slightly extends her mouth and turns the oval of her face into a round. Her head has sunk into her neck. Simultaneously, as if her circulation were suddenly held up, a shadow passes over her complexion. This is a bad copy of the* MRS. PAGE *we have seen hitherto, and will give* CHARLES *a poor impression of her.*)

CHARLES (*peering over the slippers*). Yes, yes, yes.

DAME. Is she like the daughter, think you?

CHARLES (*judicially*). In a way, very. Hair 's not so pretty. She is not such a fine colour. Heavier build, and I should say not so tall. None of Miss Page's distinction, nothing *svelte* about her. As for the feet (*he might almost have said the palisade*)—the feet—— (*He shudders a little, and so do the feet.*)

DAME. She is getting on, you see. She is forty and a bittock.

CHARLES. A whattock?

DAME (*who has never studied the Doric*). It may be a whattock.

CHARLES (*gallantly*). But there's something nice about her. I could have told she was her mother anywhere. (*With which handsome compliment he returns to the fire, and* MRS. PAGE, *no doubt much gratified, throws a kiss after him. She also signs to the* DAME *a mischievous desire to be left alone with this blade.*)

DAME (*discreetly*). Well, I'll leave you, but, mind, you are not to disturb her.

(*She goes, with the pleasant feeling that there are two clever women in the house; and with wide-open eyes* MRS. PAGE *watches* CHARLES *dealing amorously with the photograph. Soon he returns to her side, and her eyes are closed, but she does not trouble to repeat the trifling with her appearance. She probably knows the strength of first impressions.*)

CHARLES (*murmuring the word as if it were sweet music*). Mumsy. (*With conviction*) You lucky mother.

MRS. PAGE (*in a dream*). Is that you, Beatrice?

(*This makes him scurry away, but he is soon back again, and the soundness of her slumber annoys him.*)

CHARLES (*in a reproachful whisper*). Woman, wake up and talk to me about your daughter.

(*The selfish thing sleeps on, and somewhat gingerly he pulls away the cushion from beneath her head. Nice treatment for a lady.* MRS. PAGE *starts up, and at first is not quite sure where she is, you know.*)

MRS. PAGE. Why—what——

CHARLES (*contritely*). I am very sorry. I'm afraid I disturbed you.

MRS. PAGE (*blankly*). I don't know you, do I?

CHARLES (*who has his inspirations*). No, madam, but it is my misfortune.

MRS. PAGE (*making sure that she is still in the* DAME'S *cottage*). Who are you? and what are you doing here?

CHARLES (*for truth is best*). My name is Roche. I am nobody in particular. I'm just the usual thing; Eton, Oxford, and so to bed—as Pepys would say. I am on a walking tour, on my way to the station, but there is no train till seven, and your landlady let me in out of the rain on the promise that I wouldn't disturb you.

MRS. PAGE (*taking it all in with a woman's quickness*). I see. (*Suddenly*) But you have disturbed me.

CHARLES. I 'm sorry.

MRS. PAGE (*with a covert eye on him*). It wasn't really your fault. This cushion slipped from under me, and I woke up.

CHARLES (*manfully*). No, I—I pulled it away.

MRS. PAGE (*indignant*). You did ! (*She advances upon him like a stately ship.*) Will you please to tell me why ?

CHARLES (*feebly*). I didn't mean to pull so hard. (*Then he gallantly leaps into the breach.*) Madam, I felt it was impossible for me to leave this house without first waking you to tell you of the feelings of solemn respect with which I regard you.

MRS. PAGE. Really !

CHARLES. I suppose I consider you the cleverest woman in the world.

MRS. PAGE. On so short an acquaintance ?

CHARLES (*lucidly*). I mean, to have had the priceless cleverness to have her——

MRS. PAGE. Have her ? (*A light breaks on her.*) My daughter ?

CHARLES. Yes, I know her. (*As who should say, Isn't it a jolly world ?*)

MRS. PAGE. You know Beatrice personally ?

CHARLES (*not surprised that it takes her a little time to get used to the idea*). I assure you I have that honour. (*In one mouthful*) I think she is the most beautiful and the cleverest woman I have ever known.

MRS. PAGE. I thought I was the cleverest.

CHARLES. Yes, indeed ; for I think it even cleverer to have had her than to be her.

MRS. PAGE. Dear me. I must wait till I get a chair before thinking this out. (*A chair means two chairs to her, as we have seen, but she gives the one on which her feet wish to rest to* CHARLES.) You can have this half, Mr.—ah—Mr.—— ?

CHARLES. Roche.

MRS. PAGE (*resting from her labours of the last minute*). You are so flattering, Mr. Roche, I think you must be an actor yourself.

CHARLES (*succinctly*). No, I'm nothing. My father says I'm just an expense. But when I saw Beatrice's photograph there (*the nice boy pauses a moment because this is the first time he has said the name to her mother ; he is taking off his hat to it*) with the inscription on it——

MRS. PAGE. That foolish inscription.

CHARLES (*arrested*). Do you think so ?

MRS. PAGE. I mean foolish, because she has quite spoilt the picture by writing across the chest. That beautiful gown ruined.

CHARLES (*fondly tolerant*). They all do it, even across their trousers ; the men, I mean.

MRS. PAGE (*interested*). Do they ? I wonder why.

CHARLES (*remembering now that other callings don't do it*). It does seem odd. (*But after all the others are probably missing something.*)

MRS. PAGE (*shaking her wise head*). I know very little about them, but I am afraid they are an odd race.

CHARLES (*who has doted on many of them, though he has not known them*). But very attractive, don't you think ? The ladies, I mean.

MRS. PAGE (*luxuriously*). I mix so little with them. I am not a Bohemian, you see. Did I tell you that I have never even seen Beatrice act ?

CHARLES. You haven't ? How very strange. Not even her Rosalind ?

MRS. PAGE (*stretching herself*). No. Is it cruel to her ?

CHARLES (*giving her one*). Cruel to yourself. (*But this is no policy for an admirer of* MISS PAGE.) She gave me her photograph as Rosalind. (*Hurriedly*) Not a postcard.

MRS. PAGE (*who is very likely sneering*). With writing across the chest, I'll be bound.

CHARLES (*stoutly*). Do you think I value it the less for that ?

MRS. PAGE (*unblushing*). Oh no, the more. You have it framed on your mantelshelf, haven't you, so that when the other young bloods who are just an expense drop in they may read the pretty words and say, 'Roche, old man, you are going it.'

CHARLES. Do you really think that I——

MRS. PAGE. Pooh, that was what Beatrice expected when she gave it you.

CHARLES. Silence ! (*She raises her eyebrows, and he is stricken.*) I beg your pardon, I should have remembered that you are her mother.

MRS. PAGE (*smiling on him*). I beg yours. I should like to know, Mr. Roche, where you do keep that foolish photograph.

CHARLES (*with a swelling*). Why, here. (*He produces it in a case from an honoured pocket.*) Won't you look at it ?

MRS. PAGE (*with proper solemnity*). Yes. It is one I like.

CHARLES (*cocking his head*). It just misses her at her best.

MRS. PAGE. Her best ? You mean her way of screwing her nose ?

CHARLES (*who was never sent up for good for lucidity—or perhaps he was*). That comes into it. I mean—I mean her naïveté.

MRS. PAGE. Ah yes, her naïveté. I have often seen her practising it before a glass.

CHARLES (*with a disarming smile*). Excuse me ; you haven't, you know.

MRS. PAGE (*disarmed*). Haven't I ? Well, well, I dare say she is a wonder, but, mind you, when all is said and done, it is for her nose that she gets her salary. May I read what is written on the chest ? (*She reads.*) The baggage ! (*Shaking her head at him*). But this young lady on the other side, who is she, Lothario ?

CHARLES (*boyish and stumbling*). That is my sister. She died three years ago. We were rather—chums—and she gave me that case to put her picture in. So I did.

(*He jerks it out, glaring at her to see if she is despising him. But* MRS. PAGE, *though she cannot be sentimental for long, can be very good at it while it lasts.*)

MRS. PAGE (*quite moved*). Good brother. And it is a dear face. But you should not have put my Beatrice opposite it, Mr. Roche : your sister would not have liked that. It was thoughtless of you.

CHARLES. My sister would have liked it very much. (*Floundering*) When she gave me the case she said to me—you know what girls are—she said, ' If you get to love a woman, put her picture opposite mine, and then when the case is closed I shall be kissing her.'

(*His face implores her not to think him a silly. She is really more troubled than we might have expected.*)

MRS. PAGE (*rising*).   Mr. Roche, I never dreamt——

CHARLES.   And that is why I keep the two pictures together.

MRS. PAGE.   You shouldn't.

CHARLES.   Why shouldn't I ?   Don't you dare to say anything to me against my Beatrice.

MRS. PAGE (*with the smile of ocean on her face*).   Your Beatrice.   You poor boy.

CHARLES.   Of course I haven't any right to call her that. I haven't spoken of it to her yet.   I 'm such a nobody, you see. (*Very nice and candid of him, but we may remember that his love has not set him trying to make a somebody out of the nobody.   Are you perfectly certain, CHARLES, that to be seen with the celebrated PAGE is not almost more delightful to you than to be with her ?   Her mother at all events gives him the benefit of the doubt, or so we interpret her sudden action.   She tears the photograph in two. He protests indignantly.*)

MRS. PAGE.   Mr. Roche, be merry and gay with Beatrice as you will, but don't take her seriously.   (*She gives him back the case.*)   I think you said you had to catch a train.

CHARLES (*surveying his torn treasure.   He is very near to tears, but decides rather recklessly to be a strong man*).   Not yet ; I must speak of her to you now.

MRS. PAGE (*a strong woman without having to decide*).   I forbid you.

CHARLES (*who, if he knew himself, might see that a good deal of gloomy entertainment could be got by desisting here and stalking London as the persecuted of his lady's mamma*).   I have the right. There is no decent man who hasn't the right to tell a woman that he loves her daughter.

MRS. PAGE (*determined to keep him to earth though she has to hold him down*).   She doesn't love you, my friend.

CHARLES (*though a hopeless passion would be another rather jolly thing*).   How do you know ?   You have already said——

MRS. PAGE (*rather desperate*).   I wish you had never come here.

CHARLES (*manfully*).   Why are you so set against me ?   I think if I was a woman I should like at any rate to take a good straight look into the eyes of a man who said he was fond of her daughter.   You might have to say 'No' to him, but—often you must have had thoughts of the kind of man who would one day take her from you, and though I may not be the kind, I assure you, I—I am just as fond of her as if I were. (*Not bad for* CHARLES. *Sent up for good this time.*)

MRS. PAGE (*beating her hands together in distress*). You are torturing me, Charles.

CHARLES. But why? Did I tell you my name was Charles? (*With a happy thought*) She has spoken of me to you! What did she say?

(*If he were thinking less of himself and a little of the woman before him he would see that she has turned into an exquisite supplicant.*)

MRS. PAGE. Oh, boy—you boy! Don't say anything more. Go away now.

CHARLES. I don't understand.

MRS. PAGE. I never had an idea that you cared in that way I thought we were only jolly friends.

CHARLES. We?

MRS. PAGE (*with a wry lip for the word that has escaped her*). Charles, if you must know, can't you help me out a little? Don't you see at last?

(*She has come to him with undulations as lovely as a swallow's flight, mocking, begging, not at all the woman we have been watching; she has become suddenly a disdainful, melting armful. But* CHARLES *does not see.*)

CHARLES (*the obtuse*). I—I——

MRS. PAGE. Very well. But indeed I am sorry to have to break your pretty toy. (*Drooping still farther on her stem.*) Beatrice, Mr. Roche, has not had a mother this many a year. Do you see now?

CHARLES. No.

MRS. PAGE. Well, well. (*Abjectly*) Beatrice, Mr. Roche, is forty and a bittock.

CHARLES. I—you—but—oh no.

MRS. PAGE (*for better, for worse*). Yes, I am Beatrice. (*He looks to the photograph to rise up and give her the lie.*) The writing on the photograph? A jest. I can explain that.

CHARLES. But—but it isn't only on the stage I have seen her. I know her off too.

MRS. PAGE. A little. I can explain that also. (*He is a very woeful young man.*) I am horribly sorry, Charles.

CHARLES (*with his last kick*). Even now——

MRS. PAGE. Do you remember an incident with a pair of scissors one day last June in a boat near Maidenhead?

CHARLES. When Beatrice—when you—when she—cut her wrist?

MRS. PAGE. And you kissed the place to make it well. It left its mark.

CHARLES. I have seen it since.

MRS. PAGE. You may see it again, Charles. (*She offers him her wrist, but he does not look. He knows the mark is there. For the moment the comic spirit has deserted her, so anxious is she to help this tragic boy. She speaks in the cooing voice that proves her to be* BEATRICE *better than any wrist-mark.*) Am I so terribly unlike her as you knew her?

CHARLES (*Ah, to be stabbed with the voice you have loved*). No, you are very like, only—yes, I know now it 's you.

MRS. PAGE (*pricked keenly*). Only I am looking my age to-day. (*Forlorn*) This is my real self, Charles—if I have one. Why don't you laugh, my friend? I am laughing. (*No, not yet, though she will be presently.*) You won't give me away, will you? (*He shakes his head.*) I know you won't now, but it was my first fear when I saw you. (*With a sigh*) And now, I suppose, I owe you an explanation.

CHARLES (*done with the world*). Not unless you wish to.

MRS. PAGE. Oh yes, I wish to. (*The laughter is bubbling up now.*) Only it will leave you a wiser and a sadder man. You will never be twenty-three again, Charles.

CHARLES (*recalling his distant youth*). No, I know I won't.

MRS. PAGE (*now the laughter is playing round her mouth*). Ah, don't take it so lugubriously. You will only jump to twenty-four, say. (*She sits down beside him to make full confession.*) You must often have heard gossip about actresses' ages?

CHARLES. I didn't join in it.

MRS. PAGE. Then you can't be a member of a club.

CHARLES. If they began it——

MRS. PAGE. You wouldn't listen?

CHARLES. Not about you. I dare say I listened about the others.

MRS. PAGE. You nice boy. And now to make you twenty-four. (*Involuntarily, true to the calling she adorns, she makes the surgeon's action of turning up her sleeves.*) You have seen lots of plays, Charles ?

CHARLES. Yes, tons.

MRS. PAGE. Have you noticed that there are no parts in them for middle-aged ladies ?

CHARLES (*who has had too happy a life to notice this or almost anything else*). Aren't there ?

MRS. PAGE. Oh no, not for ' stars.' There is nothing for them between the ages of twenty-nine and sixty. Occasionally one of the less experienced dramatists may write such a part, but with a little coaxing we can always make him say, ' She needn't be more than twenty-nine.' And so, dear Charles, we have succeeded in keeping middle-age for women off the stage. Why, even Father Time doesn't let on about us. He waits at the wings with a dark cloth for us, just as our dressers wait with dust-sheets to fling over our expensive frocks ; but we have a way with us that makes even Father Time reluctant to cast his cloak ; perhaps it is the coquettish imploring look we give him as we dodge him ; perhaps though he is an old fellow he can't resist the powder on our pretty noses. And so he says, ' The enchanting baggage, I 'll give her another year.' When you come to write my epitaph, Charles, let it be in these delicious words, ' She had a long twenty-nine.'

CHARLES. But off the stage—I knew you off. (*Recalling a gay phantom*) Why, I was one of those who saw you into your train for Monte Carlo.

MRS. PAGE. You thought you did. That made it easier for me to deceive you here. But I got out of that train at the next station.

> (*She makes a movement to get out of the train here. We begin to note how she suits the action to the word in obedience to Shakespeare's lamentable injunction ; she cannot mention the tongs without forking two of her fingers.*)

CHARLES. You came here instead ?

MRS. PAGE. Yes, stole here.

CHARLES (*surveying the broken pieces of her*). Even now I can scarcely—— You who seemed so young and gay.

MRS. PAGE (*who is really very good-natured, else would she clout him on the head*). I was a twenty-nine. Oh, don't look so solemn, Charles. It is not confined to the stage. The stalls are full of twenty-nines. Do you remember what fun it was to help me on with my cloak ? Remember why I had to put more powder on my chin one evening ?

CHARLES (*with a groan*). It was only a few weeks ago.

MRS. PAGE. Yes. Sometimes it was Mr. Time I saw in the mirror, but the wretch only winked at me and went his way.

CHARLES (*ungallantly*). But your whole appearance—so girlish compared to——

MRS. PAGE (*gallantly*). To this. I am coming to ' this,' Charles. (*Confidentially ; no one can be quite so delightfully confidential as* BEATRICE PAGE.) You see, never having been more than twenty-nine, not even in my sleep—for we have to keep it up even in our sleep—I began to wonder what middle-age was like. I wanted to feel the sensation. A woman's curiosity, Charles.

CHARLES. Still, you couldn't——

MRS. PAGE. Couldn't I ! Listen. Two summers ago, instead of going to Biarritz—see pictures of me in the illustrated papers stepping into my motor-car, or going a round of country houses—see photograph of us all on the steps—the names, Charles, read from left to right—instead of doing any of these things I pretended I went there, and in reality I came down here, determined for a whole calendar month to be a middle-aged lady. I had to get some new clothes, real, cosy, sloppy, very middle-aged clothes ; and that is why I invented mamma ; I got them for her, you see. I said she was about my figure, but stouter and shorter, as you see she is.

CHARLES (*his eyes wandering up and down her—and nowhere a familiar place*). I can't make out——

MRS. PAGE. No, you are too nice a boy to make it out. You don't understand the difference that a sober way of doing one's hair, and the letting out of a few strings, and sundry other trifles that are no trifles, make ; but you see I vowed that if the immortal part of me was to get a novel sort of rest, my figure should get it also. *Voilà !* And thus all cosy within and without, I took lodgings in the most out-of-the-world spot I knew of, in the hope that here I might find the lady of whom I was in search.

CHARLES. Meaning ?

MRS. PAGE (*rather grimly*). Meaning myself. Until two years ago she and I had never met.

CHARLES (*the cynic*). And how do you like her ?

MRS. PAGE. Better than you do, young sir. She is really rather nice. I don't suppose I could do with her all the year round, but for a month or so I am just wallowing in her. You remember my entrancing little shoes ? (*she wickedly exposes her flapping slippers*). At local dances I sit out deliciously as a wallflower. Drop a tear, Charles, for me as a wallflower. I play cards, and the engaged ladies give me their confidences as a dear old thing ; and I never, never dream of setting my cap at their swains.

CHARLES. How strange. You who, when you liked——

MRS. PAGE (*plaintively*). Yes, couldn't I, Charles ?

CHARLES (*falling into the snare*). It was just the wild gaiety of you.

MRS. PAGE (*who is in the better position to know*). It was the devilry of me.

CHARLES. Whatever it was, it bewitched us.

MRS. PAGE (*candidly, but forgiving herself*). It oughtn't to.

CHARLES. If you weren't all glee you were the saddest thing on earth.

MRS. PAGE. But I shouldn't have been sad on your shoulders, Charles.

CHARLES (*appealing*). You weren't sad on all our shoulders, were you ?

MRS. PAGE (*reassuring*). No, not on all.

> Oh the gladness of her gladness when she's glad,
> And the sadness of her sadness when she's sad,
> But the gladness of her gladness
> And the sadness of her sadness
> Are as nothing, Charles,
> To the badness of her badness when she's bad.

(*This dagger-to-her-breast business is one of her choicest tricks of fence, and is very dangerous if you can coo like* BEATRICE.)

CHARLES (*pinked*). Not a word against yourself.

MRS. PAGE (*already seeing what she has been up to*). Myself ! I suppose even now I am only playing a part.

CHARLES (*who has become her handkerchief*). No, no, this is your real self.

MRS. PAGE (*warily*). Is it ? I wonder.

CHARLES. I never knew any one who had deeper feelings.

MRS. PAGE. Oh, I am always ready with whatever feeling is called for. I have a wardrobe of them, Charles. Don't blame me, blame the public of whom you are one ; the pitiless public that has made me what I am. I am their slave and their plaything, and when I please them they fling me nuts. (*Her voice breaks ; no voice can break so naturally as* BEATRICE'S.) I would have been a darling of a wife—don't you think so, Charles ?—but they wouldn't let me. I am only a bundle of emotions ; I have two characters for each day of the week. Home became a less thing to me than a new part. Charles, if only I could have been a nobody. Can't you picture me, such a happy, unknown woman, dancing along some sandy shore with half a dozen little boys and girls hanging on to my skirts ? When my son was old enough, wouldn't he and I have made a rather pretty picture for the king the day he joined his ship ? And I think most of all I should have loved to deck out my daughter in her wedding-gown.

When her mother tends her before the laughing mirror,
Tying up her laces, looping up her hair——

But the public wouldn't have it, and I had to pay the price of my success.

CHARLES (*heart-broken for that wet face*). Beatrice !

MRS. PAGE. I became a harum-scarum, Charles ; sometimes very foolish—(*with a queer insight into herself*) chiefly through good-nature, I think. There were moments when there was nothing I wouldn't do, so long as I was all right for the play at night. Nothing else seemed to matter. I have kicked over all the traces, my friend. You remember the Scottish poet who

Keenly felt the friendly glow
And softer flame,
But thoughtless follies laid him low
And stained his name.

(*Sadly enough*) Thoughtless follies laid her low, Charles, and stained her name.

2 C

CHARLES (*ready to fling down his glove in her defence*). I don't believe it. No, no, Beatrice—Mrs. Page——

MRS. PAGE. Ah, it's Mrs. Page now.

CHARLES. You are crying.

MRS. PAGE (*with some satisfaction*). Yes, I am crying.

CHARLES. This is terrible to me. I never dreamt your life was such a tragedy.

MRS. PAGE (*coming to*). Don't be so concerned. I am crying, but all the time I am looking at you through the corner of my eye to see if I am doing it well.

CHARLES (*hurt*). Don't—don't.

MRS. PAGE (*well aware that she will always be her best audience*). Soon I'll be laughing again. When I have cried, Charles, then it is time for me to laugh.

CHARLES. Please, I wish you wouldn't.

MRS. PAGE (*already in the grip of another devil*). And from all this, Charles, you have so nobly offered to save me. You are prepared to take me away from this dreadful life and let me be my real self. (CHARLES *distinctly blanches.*) Charles, it is dear and kind of you, and I accept your offer. (*She gives him a come-and-take-me curtsey and awaits his rapturous response. The referee counts ten, but* CHARLES *has not risen from the floor. Goose that he is ; she trills with merriment, though there is a touch of bitterness in it.*) You see the time for laughing has come already. You really thought I wanted you, you conceited boy. (*Rather grandly*) I am not for the likes of you.

CHARLES (*abject*). Don't mock me. I am very unhappy.

MRS. PAGE (*putting her hand on his shoulder in her dangerous, careless, kindly way*). There, there, it is just a game. All life's a game.

> (*It is here that the telegram comes.* MRS. QUICKLY *brings it in ; and the better to read it, but with a glance at* CHARLES *to observe the effect on him,* MRS. PAGE *puts on her large horn spectacles. He sighs.*)

DAME. Is there any answer ? The girl is waiting.

MRS. PAGE. No answer, thank you.

> (MRS. QUICKLY *goes, wondering what those two have had to say to each other.*)

CHARLES (*glad to be a thousand miles away from recent matters*). Not bad news, I hope ?

MRS. PAGE (*wiping her spectacles*). From my manager. It is in cipher, but what it means is that the summer play isn't drawing, and that they have decided to revive *As You Like It* They want me back to rehearse to-morrow at eleven.

CHARLES (*indignant*). They can't even let you have a few weeks.

MRS. PAGE (*returning from London*). What? Heigho, is it not sad? But I had been warned that this might happen.

CHARLES (*evolving schemes*). Surely if you——

(*But she has summoned* MRS. QUICKLY.)

MRS. PAGE (*plaintively*). Alas, Dame, our pleasant gossips have ended for this year. I am called back to London hurriedly.

DAME. Oh dear, the pity! (*She has already asked herself what might be in the telegram.*) Your girl has come back, and she wants you? Is that it?

MRS. PAGE. That's about it. (*Her quiet, sad manner says that we must all dree our weird.*) I must go. Have I time to catch the express?

CHARLES (*dispirited*). It leaves at seven.

MRS. PAGE (*bravely*). I think I can do it. Is that the train you are to take?

CHARLES. Yes, but only to the next station.

MRS. PAGE (*grown humble in her misfortune*). Even for that moment of your company I shall be grateful. Dame, this gentleman turns out to be a friend of Beatrice.

DAME. So he said, but I suspicioned him.

MRS. PAGE. Well, he is. Mr. Roche, this is my kind Dame. I must put a few things together.

DAME. If I can help——

MRS. PAGE. You can send on my luggage to-morrow; but here is one thing you might do now. Run down to the Rectory and tell them why I can't be there for the cutting-out.

DAME. I will.

MRS. PAGE. I haven't many minutes. Good-bye, you dear, for I shall be gone before you get back. I'll write and settle everything. (*With a last look round*) Cosy room! I have had a lovely time.

(*Her face quivers a little, but she does not break down. She passes, a courageous figure, into the bedroom. The slippers plop as she mounts the steps to it.   Her back looks older than we have seen it ; at least such is its intention.*)

DAME (*who has learned the uselessness of railing against fate*). Dearie dear, what a pity !

CHARLES (*less experienced*).   It 's horrible.

DAME (*wisely turning fate into a gossip*).   Queer to think of a lady like Mrs. Page having a daughter that jumps about for a living.   (*Good God, thinks* CHARLES, *how little this woman knows of life.*)   What I sometimes fear is that the daughter doesn't take much care of her.   I dare say she 's fond of her, but does she do the little kind things for her that a lady come Mrs. Page's age needs ?

CHARLES (*wincing*).   She 's not so old.

DAME (*whose mind is probably running on breakfast in bed and such-like matters*).   No, but at our age we are fond of—of quiet, and I doubt she doesn't get it.

CHARLES.   I know she doesn't.

DAME (*stumbling among fine words which attract her like a display of drapery*).   She says it 's her right to be out of the hurly-burly and into what she calls the delicious twilight of middle-age.

CHARLES (*with dizzying thoughts in his brain*).   If she is so fond of it, isn't it a shame she should have to give it up ?

DAME.   The living here ?

CHARLES.   Not so much that as being middle-aged.

DAME.   Give up being middle-aged !   How could she do that ?

(*He is saved replying by* MRS. PAGE, *who calls from the bedroom.*)

MRS. PAGE.   Dame, I hear you talking, and you promised to go at once.

(*The* DAME *apologises, and is off.   CHARLES is left alone with his great resolve, which is no less than to do one of the fine things of history.   It carries him toward the bedroom door, but not quickly ; one can also see that it has a rival who is urging him to fly the house.*)

CHARLES (*with a drum beating inside him*).   Beatrice, I want to speak to you at once.

MRS. PAGE (*through the closed door*).   As soon as I have packed my bag.

CHARLES (*finely*). Don't pack it.

MRS. PAGE. I must.

CHARLES. I have something to say.

MRS. PAGE. I can hear you.

CHARLES (*who had been honourably mentioned for the school prize poem*). Beatrice, until now I hadn't really known you at all. The girl I was so fond of, there wasn't any such girl.

MRS. PAGE. Oh yes, indeed there was.

CHARLES (*now in full sail for a hero's crown*). There was the dear woman who was Rosalind, but she had tired of it. Rosalind herself grew old and gave up the forest of Arden, but there was one man who never forgot the magic of her being there ; and I shall never forget yours. (*Strange that between the beatings of the drum he should hear a little voice within him calling, ' Ass, Charles, you ass ! ' or words to that effect. But he runs nobly on.*) My dear, I want to be your Orlando to the end. (*Surely nothing could be grander. He is chagrined to get no response beyond what might be the breaking of a string.*) Do you hear me ?

MRS. PAGE. Yes. (*A brief answer, but he is off again.*)

CHARLES. I will take you out of that hurly-burly and accompany you into the delicious twilight of middle-age. I shall be staid in manner so as not to look too young, and I will make life easy for you in your declining years. (*' Ass, Charles, you ass ! '*) Beatrice, do come out.

MRS. PAGE. I am coming now. (*She comes out carrying her bag.*) You naughty Charles, I heard you proposing to mamma. (*The change that has come over her is far too subtle to have grown out of a wish to surprise him, but its effect on CHARLES is as if she had struck him in the face.*

Too subtle also to be only an affair of clothes, though she is now in bravery hot from Mdme. Make-the-woman, tackle by Monsieur, a Rosalind cap jaunty on her head, her shoes so small that one wonders whether she was once a child in China. She is a tall, slim young creature, easily breakable ; elegant is the word that encompasses her as we watch the flow of her figure, her head arching on its long stem, and the erect shoulders that we seem, God bless us, to remember as a little hunched. Her eyes dance with life but are easily startled, because they are looking fresh upon the world, wild notes in them as from the woods. Not a woman this but a maid, or so it seems to CHARLES.

She has been thinking very little about him, but is properly gratified by what she reads in his face.)

Do I surprise you as much as that, Charles ?

(*She puts down her bag,* BEATRICE PAGE'S *famous bag. If you do not know it, you do not, alas, know* BEATRICE. *It is seldom out of her hand, save when cavaliers have been sent in search of it. She is always late for everything except her call, and at the last moment she sweeps all that is most precious to her into the bag, and runs. Jewels ? Oh no, pooh ; letters from nobodies, postal orders for them, a piece of cretonne that must match she forgets what, bits of string she forgets why, a book given her by darling What 's-his-name, a broken miniature, part of a watch-chain, a dog's collar, such a neat parcel tied with ribbon (golden gift or biscuits ? she means to find out some day), a purse, but not the right one, a bottle of frozen gum, and a hundred good-natured, scatter-brained things besides. Her servants (who all adore her) hate the bag as if it were a little dog ; swains hate it because it gets lost and has to be found in the middle of a declaration ; managers hate it because she carries it at rehearsals, when it bursts open suddenly like a too tightly laced lady, and its contents are strewn on the stage ; authors make engaging remarks about it until they discover that it has an artful trick of bursting because she does not know her lines. If you complain, really furious this time, she takes you all in her arms. Well, well, but what we meant to say was that when* BEATRICE *sees* CHARLES'S *surprise she puts down her bag.*)

CHARLES. Good God ! Is there nothing real in life ?

(*She curves toward him in one of those swallow-flights which will haunt the stage long after* BEATRICE PAGE *is but a memory. What they say and how they said it soon passes away ; what lives on is the pretty movements like* BEATRICE'S *swallow-flights. All else may go, but the pretty movements remain and play about the stage for ever. They are the only ghosts of the theatre.*)

MRS. PAGE. Heaps of things. Rosalind is real, and I am

Rosalind ; and the forest of Arden is real, and I am going back to it ; and cakes and ale are real, and I am to eat and drink them again. Everything is real except middle-age.

(*She puts her hand on his shoulder in the old, dangerous, kindly, too friendly way. That impulsive trick of yours, madam, has a deal to answer for.*)

CHARLES. But you said——

(*She flings up her hands in mockery ; they are such subtle hands that she can stand with her back to you, and, putting them behind her, let them play the drama.*)

MRS. PAGE. I said ! (*She is gone from him in another flight.*) I am Rosalind and I am going back. Hold me down, Charles, unless you want me to go mad with glee.

CHARLES (*gripping her*). I feel as if in the room you came out of you have left the woman who went into it five minutes ago.

MRS. PAGE (*slipping from him as she slips from all of us.*) I have, Charles, I have. I left the floppy, sloppy old frump in a trunk to be carted to the nearest place where they store furniture ; and I tell you, my friend (*she might have said friends, for it is a warning to the Charleses of every age*), if I had a husband and children I would cram them on top of the cart if they sought to come between me and Arden.

CHARLES (*with a shiver*). Beatrice !

MRS. PAGE. The stage is waiting, the audience is calling, and up goes the curtain. Oh, my public, my little dears, come and foot it again in the forest, and tuck away your double chins.

CHARLES. You said you hated the public.

MRS. PAGE. It was mamma said that. They are my slaves and my playthings, and I toss them nuts. (*He knows not how she got there, but for a moment of time her head caressingly skims his shoulder, and she is pouting in his face.*) Every one forgives me but you, Charles, every one but you.

CHARLES (*delirious*). Beatrice, you unutterable delight——

MRS. PAGE (*worlds away*). Don't forgive me if you would rather not,

> Here 's a sigh to those who love me,
> And a smile to those who hate.

CHARLES (*pursuing her*). There is no one like you on earth, Beatrice. Marry me, marry me (*as if he could catch her*).

MRS. PAGE (*cruelly*). As a staff for my declining years ?

CHARLES. Forget that rubbish and marry me, you darling girl.

MRS. PAGE. I can't and I won't, but I 'm glad I am your darling girl. (*Very likely she is about to be delightful to him, but suddenly she sees her spoil-sport of a bag.*) I am trusting to you not to let me miss the train.

CHARLES. I am coming with you all the way (*as if she needed to be told*). We had better be off.

MRS. PAGE (*seizing the bag*). Charles, as we run to the station we will stop at every telegraph post and carve something sweet on it—' From the East to Western Ind '——

CHARLES (*inspired*). ' No jewel is like Rosalind '——

MRS. PAGE. ' Middle-age is left behind '——

CHARLES. ' For ever young is Rosalind.' Oh, you dear, Motley 's the only wear.

MRS. PAGE. And all the way up in the train, Charles, you shall woo me exquisitely. Nothing will come of it, but you are twenty-three again, and you will have a lovely time.

CHARLES. I 'll win you, I 'll win you.

MRS. PAGE. And eventually you will marry the buxom daughter of the wealthy tallow-chandler——

CHARLES Never, I swear.

MRS. PAGE (*screwing her nose*). And bring your children to see me playing the Queen in *Hamlet*.

(*Here* CHARLES ROCHE, *bachelor, kisses the famous* BEATRICE PAGE. *Another sound is heard.*)

CHARLES. The whistle of the train.

MRS. PAGE. Away, away ! 'Tis Touchstone calling. Fool, I come, I come. (*To bedroom door*) Ta-ta, mamma ! (*They are gone.*)

THE WILL

Produced at the Duke of York's Theatre on September 4, 1913, with the following cast :

Mr. Devizes, Senr.	O. B. Clarence
Mr. Devizes, Junr.	Frank Denton
Philip Ross	Sydney Valentine
Surtees	Lichfield Owen
Sennet	Charles Trevor
Creed	Helen Kelt
Mrs. Ross	Helen Haye

The play was revived at St. Martin's Theatre on August 15, 1925 and at the Westminster on January 23, 1939.

THE WILL

THE scene is any lawyer's office.

It may be, and no doubt will be, the minute reproduction of some actual office, with all the characteristic appurtenances thereof, every blot of ink in its proper place ; but for the purpose in hand any bare room would do just as well.   The only thing essential to the room, save the two men sitting in it, is a framed engraving on the wall of Queen Victoria, which dates sufficiently the opening scene, and will be changed presently to King Edward ; afterwards to King George, to indicate the passing of time.   No other alteration is called for.   Doubtless different furniture came in, and the tiling of the fireplace was renewed, and at last some one discovered that the flowers in the window-box were dead, but all that is as immaterial to the action as the new blue-bottles ;   the succession of monarchs will convey allegorically the one thing necessary, that time is passing, but that the office of Devizes, Devizes, and Devizes goes on.

The two men are Devizes Senior and Junior.   Senior, who is middle-aged, succeeded to a good thing years ago, and as the curtain rises we see him bent over his table making it a better thing.   It is pleasant to think that before he speaks he adds another thirteen and fourpence, say, to the fortune of the firm.

Junior is quite a gay dog, twenty-three, and we catch him skilfully balancing an office ruler on his nose.   He is recently from Oxford——

> If you show him in Hyde Park, lawk, how they will stare,
> Tho' a very smart figure in Bloomsbury Square.

Perhaps Junior is a smarter figure in the office (among the clerks) than he was at Oxford, but this is one of the few things about him that his shrewd father does not know.

There comes to them by the only door into the room a middle-aged clerk called Surtees, who is perhaps worth looking at, though his manner is that of one who has long ceased to think of himself as of any importance to either God or man.   Look at him again, however (which few would do), and you may guess that he has lately had a shock—touched a living wire—and is a little dazed by it.   He brings a card to Mr. Devizes, Senior, who looks at it and shakes his head.

MR. DEVIZES.   'Mr. Philip Ross.'   Don't know him.

SURTEES (*who has an expressionless voice*).   He says he wrote you two days ago, sir, explaining his business.

MR. DEVIZES.   I have had no letter from a Philip Ross.

ROBERT.   Nor I.

(*He is more interested in his feat with the ruler than in a possible client, but* SURTEES *looks at him oddly.*)

MR. DEVIZES.   Surtees looks as if he thought you had.

(ROBERT *obliges by reflecting in the light of* SURTEES's *countenance.*)

ROBERT.   Ah, you think it may have been that one, Surty?

MR. DEVIZES (*sharply*).   What one?

ROBERT.   It was the day before yesterday.   You were out, father, and Surtees brought me in some letters.   His mouth was wide open.   (*Thoughtfully*) I suppose that was why I did it.

MR. DEVIZES.   What did you do?

ROBERT.   I must have suddenly recalled a game we used to play at Oxford.   You try to fling cards one by one into a hat. It requires great skill.   So I cast one of the letters at Surtees's open mouth, and it missed him and went into the fire.   It may have been Philip Ross's letter.

MR. DEVIZES (*wrinkling his brows*).   Too bad, Robert.

ROBERT (*blandly*).   Yes, you see I am out of practice.

SURTEES.   He seemed a very nervous person, sir, and quite young.   Not a gentleman of much consequence.

ROBERT (*airily*).   Why not tell him to write again?

MR. DEVIZES.   Not fair.

SURTEES.   But she——

ROBERT.   She?   Who?

SURTEES.   There is a young lady with him, sir.   She is crying.

ROBERT.   Pretty?

SURTEES.   I should say she is pretty, sir, in a quite inoffensive way.

ROBERT (*for his own gratification*).   Ha!

MR. DEVIZES. Well, when I ring show them in.

ROBERT (*with roguish finger*). And let this be a lesson to you, Surty, not to go about your business with your mouth open. (SURTEES *tries to smile as requested, but with poor success.*) Nothing the matter, Surty? You seem to have lost your sense of humour.

SURTEES (*humbly enough*). I'm afraid I have, sir. I never had very much, Mr. Robert.

(*He goes quietly. There has been a suppressed emotion about him that makes the incident poignant.*)

ROBERT. Anything wrong with Surtees, father?

MR. DEVIZES. Never mind him. I am very angry with you, Robert.

ROBERT (*like one conceding a point in a debating society*). And justly.

MR. DEVIZES (*frowning*). All we can do is to tell this Mr Ross that we have not read his letter.

ROBERT (*bringing his knowledge of the world to bear*). Is that necessary?

MR. DEVIZES. We must admit that we don't know what he has come about.

ROBERT (*tolerant of his father's limitations*). But don't we?

MR. DEVIZES. Do you?

ROBERT. I rather think I can put two and two together.

MR. DEVIZES. Clever boy! Well, I shall leave them to you.

ROBERT. Right.

MR. DEVIZES. Your first case, Robert.

ROBERT (*undismayed*). It will be as good as a play to you to sit there and watch me discovering before they have been two minutes in the room what is the naughty thing that brings them here.

MR. DEVIZES (*drily*). I am always ready to take a lesson from the new generation. But of course we old fogies could do that also.

ROBERT. How?

MR. DEVIZES. By asking them.

ROBERT. Pooh. What did I go to Oxford for?

MR. DEVIZES. God knows. Are you ready?

ROBERT. Quite.

(MR. DEVIZES *rings.*)

MR. DEVIZES. By the way, we don't know the lady's name.

ROBERT. Observe me finding it out.

MR. DEVIZES. Is she married or single ?

ROBERT. I 'll know at a glance. And mark me, if she is married it is our nervous gentleman who has come between her and her husband ; but if she is single it is little Wet Face who has come between him and his wife.

MR. DEVIZES. A Daniel !

(*A young man and woman are shown in : very devoted to each other, though* ROBERT *does not know it. Yet it is the one thing obvious about them ; more obvious than his cheap suit, which she presses carefully beneath the mattress every night, or than the strength of his boyish face. Thinking of him as he then was by the light of subsequent events one wonders whether if he had come alone his face might have revealed something disquieting which was not there while she was by. Probably not ; it was certainly already there, but had not yet reached the surface. With her, too, though she is to be what is called changed before we see them again, all seems serene ; no warning signals ; nothing in the way of their happiness in each other but this alarming visit to a lawyer's office. The stage direction might be ' Enter two lovers.' He is scarcely the less nervous of the two, but he enters stoutly in front of her as if to receive the first charge. She has probably nodded valiantly to him outside the door, where she let go his hand.*)

ROBERT (*master of the situation*). Come in, Mr. Ross (*and he bows reassuringly to the lady*). My partner—indeed my father. (MR. DEVIZES *bows but remains in the background.*)

PHILIP (*with a gulp*). You got my letter ?

ROBERT. Yes—yes.

PHILIP. I gave you the details in it.

ROBERT. Yes, I have them all in my head. (*Cleverly*) You will sit down, Miss—— I don't think I caught the name.

(*As much as to say, ' You see, father, I spotted that she was single at once.'*)

MR. DEVIZES (*who has also formed his opinion*). You didn't ask for it, Robert.

ROBERT (*airily*). Miss—— ?

PHILIP. This is Mrs. Ross, my wife.

(ROBERT *is a little taken aback, and has a conviction that his father is smiling.*)

ROBERT. Ah yes, of course ; sit down, please, Mrs. Ross. (*She sits as if this made matters rather worse.*)

PHILIP (*standing guard by her side*). My wife is a little agitated.

ROBERT. Naturally. (*He tries a 'feeler.'*) These affairs —very painful at the time—but one gradually forgets.

EMILY (*with large eyes*). That is what Mr. Ross says, but somehow I can't help—— (*The eyes fill*). You see, we have been married only four months.

ROBERT. Ah—that does make it—yes, certainly. (*He becomes the wife's champion, and frowns on* PHILIP.)

PHILIP. I suppose the sum seems very small to you ?

ROBERT (*serenely*). I confess that is the impression it makes on me.

PHILIP. I wish it was more.

ROBERT (*at a venture*). You are sure you can't make it more ?

PHILIP. How can I ?

ROBERT. Ha !

EMILY (*with sudden spirit*). I think it's a great deal.

PHILIP. Mrs. Ross is so nice about it.

ROBERT (*taking a strong line*). I think so. But she must not be taken advantage of. And of course we shall have something to say as to the amount.

PHILIP (*blankly*). In what way ? There it is.

ROBERT (*guardedly*). Hum. Yes, in a sense.

EMILY (*breaking down*). Oh dear !

ROBERT (*more determined than ever to do his best for this wronged woman*). I am very sorry, Mrs. Ross. (*Sternly*) I hope, sir, you realise that the mere publicity to a sensitive woman——

PHILIP. Publicity ?

ROBERT (*feeling that he has got him on the run*). Of course for her sake we shall try to arrange things so that the names do not appear. Still——

PHILIP. The names ?

(*By this time* EMILY *is in tears.*)

EMILY. I can't help it. I love him so.

ROBERT (*still benighted*). Enough to forgive him ? (*Seeing himself suddenly as a mediator*) Mrs. Ross, is it too late to patch things up ?

PHILIP (*now in flame*). What do you mean, sir ?

MR. DEVIZES (*who has been quietly enjoying himself*). Yes, Robert, what do you mean precisely ?

ROBERT. Really I—(*he tries brow-beating*) I must tell you at once, Mr. Ross, that unless a client gives us his fullest confidence we cannot undertake a case of this kind.

PHILIP. A case of what kind, sir ? If you are implying anything against my good name——

ROBERT. On your honour, sir, is there nothing against it ?

PHILIP. I know of nothing, sir.

EMILY. Anything against my husband, Mr. Devizes ! He is an angel.

ROBERT (*suddenly seeing that little Wet Face must be the culprit*) Then it is you !

EMILY. Oh, sir, what is me ?

PHILIP. Answer that, sir.

ROBERT. Yes, Mr. Ross, I will. (*But he finds he cannot.*) On second thoughts I decline. I cannot believe it has been all this lady's fault, and I decline to have anything to do with such a painful case.

MR. DEVIZES (*promptly*). Then I will take it up.

PHILIP (*not to be placated*). I think your son has insulted me.

EMILY. Philip, come away.

MR. DEVIZES. One moment, please. As *I* did not see your letter, may I ask Mr. Ross what is your business with us ?

PHILIP. I called to ask whether you would be so good as to draw up my will.

ROBERT (*blankly*). Your will ! Is that all ?

PHILIP. Certainly.

MR. DEVIZES. Now we know, Robert.

ROBERT. But Mrs. Ross's agitation ?

PHILIP (*taking her hand*). She feels that to make my will brings my death nearer.

ROBERT. So that's it !

PHILIP. It was all in the letter.

MR. DEVIZES (*coyly*). Anything to say, Robert ?

ROBERT. Most—ah—extremely—— (*He has an inspiration.*) But even now I 'm puzzled. You are Edgar Charles Ross ?

PHILIP. No, Philip Ross

ROBERT (*brazenly*). Philip Ross ? We have made an odd mistake, father. (*There is a twinkle in* MR. DEVIZES'S *eye. He watches interestedly to see how his son is to emerge from the mess.*) The fact is, Mrs. Ross, we are expecting to-day a Mr. Edgar Charles Ross on a matter—well—of a kind—— Ah me ! (*With fitting gravity*) His wife, in short.

EMILY (*who has not read the newspapers in vain*). How awful. How sad.

ROBERT. Sad indeed. You will quite understand that professional etiquette prevents my saying one word more.

PHILIP. Yes, of course—we have no desire—— But I did write.

ROBERT. Assuredly. But about a will. That is my father's department. No doubt you recall the letter now, father ?

MR. DEVIZES (*who if he won't hinder won't help*). I can't say I do.

ROBERT (*unabashed*). Odd. You must have overlooked it.

MR. DEVIZES. Ha ! At all events, Mr. Ross, I am quite at your service now.

PHILIP. Thank you.

ROBERT (*still ready to sacrifice himself on the call of duty*). You don't need me any more, father ?

MR. DEVIZES. No, Robert ; many thanks. You run off to your club now and have a bit of lunch. You must be tired. Send Surtees in to me. (*To his clients*) My son had his first case to-day.

PHILIP (*politely*). I hope successfully.

MR. DEVIZES. Not so bad. He rather bungled it at first, but he got out of a hole rather cleverly. I think you 'll make a lawyer yet, Robert.

ROBERT. Thank you, father. (*He goes jauntily, with a flower in his button-hole.*)

MR. DEVIZES. Now, Mr. Ross.

(*The young wife's hand goes out for comfort and finds* PHILIP'S *waiting for it.*)

PHILIP. What I want myself is that the will should all go

into one sentence, ' I leave everything of which I die possessed
to my beloved wife.'

MR. DEVIZES (*thawing to the romance of this young couple*).
Well, there have been many worse wills than that, sir.

(EMILY *is emotional.*)

PHILIP. Don't give way, Emily.

EMILY. It was those words, ' of which I die possessed.'
(*Imploring*) Surely he doesn't need to say that—please, Mr.
Devizes ?

MR. DEVIZES. Certainly not. I am confident I can draw
up the will without mentioning death at all.

EMILY (*huskily*). Oh, thank you.

MR. DEVIZES. At the same time, of course, in a legal
document in which the widow is the sole——

(EMILY *again needs attention.*)

PHILIP (*reproachfully*). What was the need of saying
' widow ' ?

MR. DEVIZES. I beg your pardon, Mrs. Ross. I unreservedly withdraw the word ' widow.' Forgive a stupid old
solicitor. (*She smiles gratefully through her tears.* SURTEES
comes in.) Surtees, just take a few notes, please. (SURTEES *sits
in the background and takes notes.*) The facts of the case as I
understand, Mrs. Ross, are these : Your husband—(*quickly*) who
is in the prime of health—but knows life to be uncertain——

EMILY. Oh !

MR. DEVIZES. —though usually, as we learn from holy
script itself, it lasts seven times ten years—and believing that he
will in all probability live the allotted span, nevertheless, because
of his love of you, thinks it judicious to go through the form—
it is a mere form—of making a will.

EMILY (*fervently*). Oh, thank you.

MR. DEVIZES. Any details, Mr. Ross ?

PHILIP. I am an orphan. I live at Belvedere, 14 Tulphin
Road, Hammersmith.

EMILY (*to whom the address has a seductive sound*). We live
there.

PHILIP. And I am a clerk in the employ of Curar and Gow,
the foreign coaling agents.

MR. DEVIZES. Yes, yes. Any private income ?

(*They cannot help sniggering a little at the quaint question.*)

PHILIP. Oh no !

MR. DEVIZES. I see it will be quite a brief will.

PHILIP (*to whom the remark sounds scarcely worthy of a great occasion*). My income is a biggish one.

MR. DEVIZES. Yes ?

EMILY (*important*). He has £170 a year.

MR. DEVIZES. Ah !

PHILIP. I began at £60. But it is going up, Mr. Devizes, by leaps and bounds. Another £15 this year.

MR. DEVIZES. Good.

PHILIP (*darkly*). I have a certain ambition.

EMILY (*eagerly*). Tell him, Philip.

PHILIP (*with a big breath*). We have made up our minds to come to £365 a year before I—retire.

EMILY. That is a pound a day.

MR. DEVIZES (*smiling sympathetically on them*). So it is. My best wishes.

PHILIP. Thank you. Of course the furnishing took a good deal.

MR. DEVIZES. It would.

EMILY. He insisted on my having the very best. (*She ceases. She is probably thinking of her superb spare bedroom.*)

PHILIP. But we are not a penny in debt ; and I have £200 saved.

MR. DEVIZES. I think you have made a brave beginning.

EMILY. They have the highest opinion of him in the office.

PHILIP. Then I am insured for £500.

MR. DEVIZES. I am glad to hear that.

PHILIP. Of course I would like to leave her a house in Kensington and a carriage and pair.

MR. DEVIZES. Who knows, perhaps you will.

EMILY. Oh !

MR. DEVIZES. Forgive me.

EMILY. What would houses and horses be to me without him ?

MR. DEVIZES (*soothingly*). Quite so. What I take Mr. Ross to mean is that when he dies—if he ever should die—everything is to go to his—his spouse.

PHILIP (*dogged*). Yes.

EMILY (*dogged*). No.

PHILIP (*sighing*). This is the only difference we have ever had. Mrs. Ross insists on certain bequests. You see, I have two cousins, ladies, not well off, whom I have been in the way of helping a little. But in my will, how can I ?

MR. DEVIZES. You must think first of your wife.

PHILIP. But she insists on my leaving £50 to each of them. (*He looks appealingly to his wife.*)

EMILY (*grandly*). £100.

PHILIP. £50.

EMILY. Dear, £100.

MR. DEVIZES. Let us say £75.

PHILIP (*reluctantly*). Very well.

EMILY. No, £100.

PHILIP. She'll have to get her way. Here are their names and addresses.

MR. DEVIZES. Anything else ?

PHILIP (*hurriedly*). No.

EMILY. The convalescent home, dear. He was in it a year ago, and they were so kind.

PHILIP. Yes, but——

EMILY. £10. (*He has to yield, with a reproachful, admiring look.*)

MR. DEVIZES. Then if that is all, I won't detain you. If you look in to-morrow, Mr. Ross, about this time, we shall have everything ready for you.

(*Their faces fall.*)

EMILY. Oh, Mr. Devizes, if only it could all be drawn up now, and done with.

PHILIP. You see, sir, we are screwed up to it to-day.

('*Our fate is in your hands,*' *they might be saying, and the lawyer smiles to find himself such a power.*)

MR. DEVIZES (*looking at his watch*). Well, it certainly need not take long. You go out and have lunch somewhere, and then come back.

EMILY. Oh, don't ask me to eat.

PHILIP. We are too excited.

EMILY. Please may we just walk about the street ?

MR. DEVIZES (*smiling*). Of course you may, you ridiculous young wife.

EMILY. I know it's ridiculous of me, but I am so fond of him.

MR. DEVIZES. Yes, it is ridiculous. (*Kindly, and with almost a warning note*) But don't change ; especially if you get on in the world, Mr. Ross.

PHILIP. No fear !

EMILY (*backing from the will, which may now be said to be in existence*). And please don't give us a copy of it to keep. I would rather not have it in the house.

MR. DEVIZES (*nodding reassuringly*). In an hour's time. (*They go, and the lawyer has his lunch, which is simpler than* ROBERT'S : *a sandwich and a glass of wine. He speaks as he eats.*) You will get that ready, Surtees. Here are the names and addresses he left. (*Cheerily*) A nice couple.

SURTEES (*who is hearing another voice*). Yes, sir.

MR. DEVIZES (*unbending*). Little romance of its kind. Makes one feel quite gay.

SURTEES. Yes, sir.

MR. DEVIZES (*struck perhaps by the deadness of his voice*). You don't look very gay, Surtees.

SURTEES. I'm sorry, sir. We can't all be gay. (*He is going out without looking at his employer.*) I'll see to this, sir.

MR. DEVIZES. Stop a minute. Is there anything wrong ? (SURTEES *has difficulty in answering, and* MR. DEVIZES *goes to him kindly.*) Not worrying over that matter we spoke about ? (SURTEES *inclines his head.*) Is the pain worse ?

SURTEES. It's no great pain, sir.

MR. DEVIZES (*uncomfortably*). I'm sure it's not—what you fear. Any specialist would tell you so.

SURTEES (*without looking up*). I have been to one, sir— yesterday.

MR. DEVIZES. Well ?

SURTEES. It's—that, sir.

MR. DEVIZES. He couldn't be sure.

SURTEES. Yes, sir.

MR. DEVIZES. An operation——

SURTEES. Too late, he said, for that. If I had been operated on long ago there might have been a chance.

MR. DEVIZES. But you didn't have it long ago.

SURTEES. Not to my knowledge, sir ; but he says it was

there all the same, always in me, a black spot, not so big as a pin's head, but waiting to spread and destroy me in the fulness of time. All the rest of me as sound as a bell. (*That is the voice that* SURTEES *has been hearing.*)

MR. DEVIZES (*helpless*). It seems damnably unfair.

SURTEES (*humbly*). I don't know, sir. He says there's a spot of that kind in pretty nigh all of us, and if we don't look out it does for us in the end.

MR. DEVIZES (*hurriedly*). No, no, no.

SURTEES. He called it the accursed thing. I think he meant we should know of it and be on the watch. (*He pulls himself together.*) I'll see to this at once, sir.

(*He goes out.* MR. DEVIZES *continues his lunch.*

The curtain falls here for a moment only, to indicate the passing of a number of years. When it rises we see that the engraving of Queen Victoria has given way to one of King Edward.

ROBERT *is discovered, immersed in affairs. He is now a middle-aged man who has long forgotten how to fling cards into a hat. To him comes* SENNET, *a brisk clerk.*)

SENNET. Mrs. Philip Ross to see you, sir.

ROBERT. Mr. Ross, don't you mean, Sennet?

SENNET. No, sir.

ROBERT. Ha. It was Mr. Ross I was expecting. Show her in. (*Frowning*) And, Sennet, less row in the office, if you please.

SENNET (*glibly*). It was those young clerks, sir——

ROBERT. They mustn't be young here, or they go. Tell them that.

SENNET (*glad to be gone*). Yes, sir.

(*He shows in* MRS. ROSS. *We have not seen her for twenty years and would certainly not recognise her in the street. So shrinking her first entrance into this room, but she sails in now like a galleon. She is not so much dressed as richly upholstered. She is very sure of herself. Yet she is not a different woman from the* EMILY *we remember ; the pity of it is that somehow this is the same woman.*)

ROBERT (*who makes much of his important visitor and is also wondering why she has come*). This is a delightful surprise, Mrs. Ross. Allow me. (*He removes her fine cloak with proper solicitude, and* EMILY *walks out of it in the manner that makes it worth possessing.)* This chair, alas, is the best I can offer you.

EMILY (*who is still a good-natured woman if you attempt no nonsense with her*). It will do quite well.

ROBERT (*gallantly*). Honoured to see you in it.

EMILY (*smartly*). Not you. You were saying to yourself, ' Now, what brings the woman here ? '

ROBERT. Honestly, I——

EMILY. And I 'll tell you. You are expecting Mr. Ross, I think ?

ROBERT (*cautiously*). Well—ah——

EMILY. Pooh ! The cunning of you lawyers. I know he has an appointment with you, and that is why I 've come.

ROBERT. He arranged with you to meet him here ?

EMILY (*preening herself*). I wouldn't say that. I don't know that he will be specially pleased to find me here when he comes.

ROBERT (*guardedly*). Oh ?

EMILY (*who is now a woman that goes straight to her goal*). I know what he is coming about. To make a new will.

ROBERT (*admitting it*). After all, not the first he has made with us, Mrs. Ross.

EMILY (*promptly*). No, the fourth.

ROBERT (*warming his hands at the thought*). Such a wonderful career. He goes from success to success.

EMILY (*complacently*). Yes, we 're big folk.

ROBERT. You are indeed.

EMILY (*sharply*). But the last will covered everything.

ROBERT (*on guard again*). Of course it is a matter I cannot well discuss even with you. And I know nothing of his intentions.

EMILY. Well, I suspect some of them.

ROBERT. Ah !

EMILY. And that 's why I 'm here. Just to see that he does nothing foolish.

(*She settles herself more comfortably as* MR. ROSS *is announced. A city magnate walks in. You know he is that before you see that he is* PHILIP ROSS.)

PHILIP (*speaking as he enters*). How do, Devizes, how do.

Well, let us get at this thing at once. Time is money, you know, time is money. (*Then he sees his wife.*) Hello, Emily.

EMILY (*unperturbed*). You didn't ask me to come, Philip, but I thought I might as well.

PHILIP. That's all right.

(*His brow had lowered at first sight of her, but now he gives her cleverness a grin of respect.*)

EMILY. It is the first will you have made without taking me into your confidence.

PHILIP. No important changes. I just thought to save you the—unpleasantness of the thing.

EMILY. How do you mean?

PHILIP (*fidgeting*). Well, one can't draw up a will without feeling for the moment that he is bringing his end nearer. Is that not so, Devizes?

ROBERT (*who will quite possibly die intestate*). Some do have that feeling.

EMILY. But what nonsense. How can it have any effect of that kind one way or the other?

ROBERT. Quite so.

EMILY (*reprovingly*). Just silly sentiment, Philip. I should have thought it would be a pleasure to you, handling such a big sum.

PHILIP (*wincing*). Not handling it, giving it up.

EMILY. To those you love.

PHILIP (*rather shortly*). I'm not giving it up yet. You talk as if I was on my last legs.

EMILY (*imperturbably*). Not at all. It's you that are doing that.

ROBERT (*to the rescue*). Here is my copy of the last will. I don't know if you would like me to read it out?

PHILIP. It's hardly necessary.

EMILY. We have our own copy at home, and we know it well.

PHILIP (*sitting back in his chair*). What do you think I'm worth to-day, Devizes?

(*Every one smiles. It is as if the sun had peeped in at the window.*)

ROBERT. I daren't guess.

PHILIP. An easy seventy thou.

EMILY. And that's not counting the house and the country cottage. We call it a cottage. You should see it !

ROBERT. I have heard of it.

EMILY (*more sharply, though the sun still shines*). Well, go on, Philip. I suppose you are not thinking of cutting me out of anything ?

PHILIP (*heartily*). Of course not. There will be more to you than ever.

EMILY (*coolly*). There's more to leave.

PHILIP (*hesitating*). At the same time——

EMILY. Well ? It's to be mine absolutely, of course. Not just a life interest.

PHILIP (*doggedly*). That is a change I was thinking of.

EMILY. Just what I have suspected for days. Will you please to say why ?

ROBERT (*whose client after all is the man*). Of course it is quite common.

EMILY. I didn't think my husband was quite common.

ROBERT. I only mean that as there are children——

PHILIP. That's what I mean too.

EMILY. And I can't be trusted to leave my money to my own children ! In what way have I ever failed them before ?

PHILIP (*believing it too*). Never, Emily, never. A more devoted mother—— If you have one failing it is that you spoil them.

EMILY. Then what's your reason ?

PHILIP (*less sincerely*). Just to save you worry when I'm gone.

EMILY. It's no worry to me to look after my money.

PHILIP (*bridling*). After all, it's my money.

EMILY. I knew that was what was at the back of your mind.

PHILIP (*reverently*). It's such a great sum.

EMILY. One would think you were afraid I might marry again.

PHILIP (*snapping*). One would think you looked to my dying next week.

EMILY. Tuts !

(PHILIP *is unable to sit still.*)

PHILIP. My money. If you were to invest it badly and

lose it ! I tell you, Devizes, I couldn't lie quiet in my grave if I thought my money was lost by injudicious investments.

EMILY (*coldly*). You are thinking of yourself, Philip, rather than of the children.

PHILIP. Not at all.

ROBERT (*hastily*). How are the two children ?

EMILY. Though I say it myself, there never were better. Harry is at Eton, you know, the most fashionable school in the country.

ROBERT. Doing well, I hope ?

PHILIP (*chuckling*). We have the most gratifying letters from him. Last Saturday he was caught smoking cigarettes with a lord. (*With pardonable pride*) They were sick together.

ROBERT. And Miss Gwendolen ? She must be almost grown up now.

(*The parents exchange important glances.*)

EMILY. Should we tell him ?

PHILIP. Under the rose, you know, Devizes.

ROBERT. Am I to congratulate her ?

EMILY. No names, Philip.

PHILIP. No, no names—but she won't be a plain Mrs., no, sir.

ROBERT Well done, Miss Gwendolen. (*With fitting jocularity*) Now I see why you want a new will.

PHILIP. Yes, that 's my main reason, Emily.

EMILY. But none of your life interests for me, Philip.

PHILIP (*shying*). We 'll talk that over presently.

ROBERT. Will you keep the legacies as they are ?

PHILIP. Well, there 's that £500 for the hospitals.

EMILY. Yes, with so many claims on us, is that necessary ?

PHILIP (*becoming stouter*). I 'm going to make it £1000.

EMILY. Philip !

PHILIP. My mind is made up. I want to make a splash with the hospitals.

ROBERT (*hurrying to the next item*). There is £50 a year each to two cousins, ladies.

PHILIP. I suppose we 'll keep that as it is, Emily ?

EMILY. It was just gifts to them of £100 each at first.

PHILIP. I was poor at that time myself.

EMILY. Do you think it's wise to load them with so much money? They'll not know what to do with it.

PHILIP. They're old.

EMILY. But they're wiry. £75 a year between them would surely be enough.

PHILIP. It would be if they lived together, but you see they don't. They hate each other like cat and dog.

EMILY. That's not nice between relatives. You could leave it to them on condition that they do live together. That would be a Christian action.

PHILIP. There's something in that.

ROBERT. Then the chief matter is whether Mrs. Ross——

EMILY. Oh, I thought that was settled.

PHILIP (*with a sigh*). I'll have to give in to her, sir.

ROBERT. Very well. I suppose my father will want to draw up the will. I'm sorry he had to be in the country to-day.

EMILY (*affable now that she has gained her point*). I hope he is wearing well?

ROBERT. Wonderfully. He is away playing golf.

PHILIP (*grinning*). Golf. I have no time for games. (*Considerately*) But he must get the drawing up of my will. I couldn't deprive the old man of that.

ROBERT. He will be proud to do it again.

PHILIP (*well satisfied*). Ah! There's many a one would like to look over your father's shoulder when he's drawing up my will. I wonder what I'll cut up for in the end. But I must be going.

EMILY. Can I drop you anywhere? I have the greys out.

PHILIP. Yes, at the club.

(*Now* MRS. ROSS *walks into her cloak.*)

Good-day, Devizes. I won't have time to look in again, so tell the old man to come to me.

ROBERT (*deferentially*). Whatever suits you best. (*Ringing.*) He will be delighted. I remember his saying to me on the day you made your first will——

PHILIP (*chuckling*). A poor little affair that.

ROBERT. He said to me you were a couple whose life looked like being a romance.

PHILIP. And he was right—eh, Emily?—though he little thought what a romance.

EMILY.　No, he little thought what a romance.

(*They make a happy departure, and* ROBERT *is left reflecting.*

> *The curtain again falls, and rises immediately, as the engraving shows, on the same office in the reign of King George.　It is a foggy morning and a fire burns briskly.* MR. DEVIZES, SENIOR, *arrives for the day's work just as he came daily for over half a century.　But he has no right to be here now.　A year or two ago they got him to retire, as he was grown feeble ; and there is an understanding that he does not go out of his house alone.　He has, as it were, escaped to-day, and his feet have carried him to the old office that is the home of his mind.　He was almost portly when we saw him first, but he has become little again and as light as the schoolboy whose deeds are nearer to him than many of the events of later years.　He arrives at the office, thinking it is old times, and a clerk surveys him uncomfortably from the door.*)

CREED (*not quite knowing what to do*).　Mr. Devizes has not come in yet, sir.

MR. DEVIZES (*considering*).　Yes, I have.　Do you mean Mr. Robert ?

CREED.　Yes, sir.

MR. DEVIZES (*querulously*).　Always late.　Can't get that boy to settle down.　(*Leniently*) Well, well, boys will be boys —eh, Surtees ?

CREED (*wishing* MR. ROBERT *would come*).　My name is Creed, sir.

MR. DEVIZES (*sharply*).　Creed ?　Don't know you.　Where is Surtees ?

CREED.　There is no one of that name in the office, sir.

MR. DEVIZES (*growing timid*).　No ?　I remember now. Poor Surtees !　(*But his mind cannot grapple with troubles.*) Tell him I want him when he comes in.

(*He is changing, after his old custom, into an office coat.*)

CREED.　That is Mr. Dev—Mr. Robert's coat, sir.

MR. DEVIZES.　He has no business to hang it there.　That is my nail.

CREED. He has hung it there for years, sir.

MR. DEVIZES. Not at all. I must have it. Why does Surtees let him do it? Help me into my office coat, boy.

(CREED *helps him into the coat he has taken off, and the old man is content.*)

CREED (*seeing him lift up the correspondence*). I don't think Mr. Devizes would like you to open the office letters, sir.

MR. DEVIZES (*pettishly*). What's that? Go away, boy. Send Surtees.

(*To the relief of* CREED, ROBERT *arrives, and, taking in the situation, signs to the clerk to go. He has a more youthful manner than when last we saw him has* ROBERT, *but his hair is iron grey. He is kindly to his father.*)

ROBERT. You here, father?

MR. DEVIZES (*after staring at him*). Yes, you are Robert. (*A little frightened*) You are an old man, Robert.

ROBERT (*without wincing*). Getting on, father. But why did they let you come? You haven't been here for years.

MR. DEVIZES (*puzzled*). Years? I think I just came in the old way, Robert, without thinking.

ROBERT. Yes, yes. I'll get some one to go home with you.

MR. DEVIZES (*rather abject*). Let me stay, Robert. I like being here. I won't disturb you. I like the smell of the office, Robert.

ROBERT. Of course you may stay. Come over to the fire. (*He settles his father by the fire in the one arm-chair.*) There; you can have a doze by the fire.

MR. DEVIZES. A doze by the fire. That is all I'm good for now. Once—but my son hangs his coat there now. (*Then he looks up fearfully*) Robert, tell me something in a whisper: Is Surtees dead?

ROBERT (*who has forgotten the name*). Surtees?

MR. DEVIZES. My clerk, you know.

ROBERT. Oh, why, he has been dead this thirty years, father.

MR. DEVIZES. So long. Seems like yesterday.

ROBERT. It is just far back times that seem clear to you now.

MR. DEVIZES (*meekly*). Is it?

(ROBERT *opens his letters, and his father falls asleep.* CREED *comes.*)

CREED. Sir Philip Ross.

(*The great* SIR PHILIP *enters, nearly sixty now, strong of frame still, but a lost man.   He is in mourning, and carries the broken pieces of his life with an air of braggadocio.   It should be understood that he is not a 'sympathetic' part, and any actor who plays him as such will be rolling the play in the gutter.*)

ROBERT (*on his feet at once to greet such a client*). You, Sir Philip ?

PHILIP (*head erect*). Here I am.

ROBERT (*because it will out*). How are you ?

PHILIP (*as if challenged*). I 'm all right—great. (*With defiant jocularity*) Called on the old business.

ROBERT. To make another will ?

PHILIP. You 've guessed it—the very first time. (*He sees the figure by the fire.*)

ROBERT. Yes, it 's my father. He 's dozing. Shouldn't be here at all. He forgets things. It 's just age.

PHILIP (*grimly*). Forgets things. That must be fine.

ROBERT (*conventionally*). I should like, Sir Philip, to offer you my sincere condolences. In the midst of life we are—— How true that is. I attended the funeral.

PHILIP. I saw you.

ROBERT. A much-esteemed lady. I had a great respect for her.

PHILIP (*almost with relish*). Do you mind, when we used to come here about the will, somehow she—we—always took for granted I should be the first to go ?

ROBERT (*devoutly*). These things are hid from mortal eyes.

PHILIP (*with conviction*). There 's a lot hid. We needn't have worried so much about the will if—well, let us get at it. (*Fiercely*) I haven't given in, you know.

ROBERT. We must bow our heads——

PHILIP. Must we ? Am I bowing mine ?

ROBERT (*uncomfortably*). Such courage in the great hour— yes—and I am sure Lady Ross——

PHILIP (*with the ugly humour that has come to him*). She wasn't that.

ROBERT. The honour came so soon afterwards—I feel she

would like to be thought of as Lady Ross. I shall always remember her as a fine lady richly dressed who used——

PHILIP (*harshly*). Stop it. That 's not how I think of her. There was a time before that—she wasn't richly dressed—(*he stamps upon his memories*). Things went wrong, I don't know how. It 's a beast of a world. I didn't come here to talk about that. Let us get to work.

ROBERT (*turning with relief from the cemetery*). Yes, yes, and after all life has its compensations. You have your son who——

PHILIP (*snapping*). No, I haven't. (*This startles the lawyer.*) I 'm done with him.

ROBERT. If he has been foolish——

PHILIP. Foolish ! (*Some dignity comes into the man.*) Sir, I have come to a pass when foolish as applied to my own son would seem to me a very pretty word.

ROBERT. Is it as bad as that ?

PHILIP. He 's a rotter.

ROBERT. It is very painful to me to hear you say that.

PHILIP. More painful, think you, than for me to say it ? (*Clenching his fists*) But I 've shipped him off. The law had to wink at it, or I couldn't have done it. Why don't you say I pampered him and it serves me right ? It 's what they are all saying behind my back. Why don't you ask me about my girl ? That 's another way to rub it in.

ROBERT. Don't, Sir Philip. I knew about her. My sympathy——

PHILIP. A chauffeur ! that is what he was. The man who drove her own car.

ROBERT. I was deeply concerned——

PHILIP. I want nobody's pity. I 've done with both of them, and if you think I 'm a broken man you 're much mistaken. I 'll show them. Have you your papers there ? Then take down my last will. I have everything in my head. I 'll show them.

ROBERT Would it not be better to wait till a calmer——

PHILIP. Will you do it now, or am I to go across the street ?

ROBERT. If I must.

PHILIP. Then down with it. (*He wets his lips.*) I, Philip Ross, of 77 Bath Street, W., do hereby revoke all former wills and testaments, and I leave everything of which I die possessed——

ROBERT. Yes?

PHILIP. Everything of which I die possessed——

ROBERT. Yes?

PHILIP. I leave it—I leave it—— (*The game is up.*) My God, Devizes, I don't know what to do with it.

ROBERT. I—I—really—come——

PHILIP (*cynically*). Can't you make any suggestions?

ROBERT. Those cousins are dead, I think?

PHILIP. Years ago.

ROBERT (*troubled*). In the case of such a large sum——

PHILIP (*letting all his hoarded gold run through his fingers*). The money I've won with my blood. God in heaven. (*Showing his teeth.*) Would that old man like it to play with? If I bring it to you in sacks, will you fling it out of the window for me?

ROBERT. Sir Philip!

PHILIP (*taking a paper from his pocket*). Here, take this. It has the names and addresses of the half-dozen men I've fought with most for gold; and I 've beaten them. Draw up a will leaving all my money to be divided between them, with my respectful curses, and bring it to my house and I 'll sign it.

ROBERT (*properly shocked*). But really I can't possibly——

PHILIP. Either you or another; is it to be you?

ROBERT. Very well.

PHILIP. Then that 's settled. (*He rises with an ugly laugh. He regards* MR. DEVIZES *quizzically.*) So you weren't in at the last will after all, old Sleep by the Fire.

(*To their surprise the old man stirs.*)

MR. DEVIZES. What 's that about a will?

ROBERT. You are awake, father?

MR. DEVIZES (*whose eyes have opened on* PHILIP's *face*). I don't know you, sir.

ROBERT. Yes, yes, father, you remember Mr. Ross. He is Sir Philip now.

MR. DEVIZES (*courteously*). Sir Philip? I wish you joy, sir, but I don't know you.

ROBERT (*encouragingly*). Ross, father.

MR. DEVIZES. I knew a Mr. Ross long ago.

ROBERT. This is the same.

MR. DEVIZES (*annoyed*). No, no. A bright young fellow he was, with such a dear, pretty wife. They came to make a will. (*He chuckles.*) And bless me, they had only twopence halfpenny. I took a fancy to them ; such a happy pair.

ROBERT (*apologetically*). The past is clearer to him than the present nowadays. That will do, father.

PHILIP (*brusquely*). Let him go on.

MR. DEVIZES. Poor souls, it all ended unhappily, you know.

PHILIP (*who is not brusque to him*). Yes, I know. Why did things go wrong, sir ? I sit and wonder, and I can't find the beginning.

MR. DEVIZES That 's the sad part of it. There was never a beginning. It was always there. He told me all about it.

ROBERT. He is thinking of something else ; I don't know what.

PHILIP. Quiet. What was it that was always there ?

MR. DEVIZES. It was always in them—a spot no bigger than a pin's head, but waiting to spread and destroy them in the fulness of time.

ROBERT. I don't know what he has got hold of.

PHILIP. He knows. Could they have done anything to prevent it, sir ?

MR. DEVIZES. If they had been on the watch. But they didn't know, so they weren't on the watch. Poor souls !

PHILIP. Poor souls !

MR. DEVIZES. It 's called the accursed thing. It gets nearly everybody in the end, if they don't look out.

(*He sinks back into his chair and forgets them.*)

ROBERT. He is just wandering.

PHILIP. The old man knows.

(*He slowly tears up the paper he had given* ROBERT.)

ROBERT (*relieved*). I am glad to see you do that.

PHILIP. A spot no bigger than a pin's head. (*A wish wells up in him, too late perhaps.*) I wish I could help some young things before that spot has time to spread and destroy them as it has destroyed me and mine.

ROBERT (*brightly*). With such a large fortune——

PHILIP (*summing up his life*). It can't be done with money, sir.

(*He goes away ; God knows where.*)

2 D

HALF AN HOUR

HALF AN HOUR

Produced at the London Hippodrome on September 29, 1913, with the following cast :

MR. GARSON	. . . . .	*Edmund Gwenn*
DOCTOR BRODIE	. . . . .	*Sydney Valentine*
HUGH PATON	. . . .	*Frank Esmond*
MR. REDDING	. . . .	*J. Woodall-Birde*
BUTLER	. . . .	*James English*
SUSIE	. . . .	*Gertrude Lang*
MRS. REDDING	. . . .	*Netta Westcott*
LADY LILIAN GARSON	. . .	*Irene Vanbrugh*

HALF AN HOUR

Mr. Garson, who is a financier, and his young wife, the lovely Lady Lilian, are in their mansion near Park Lane, but they are not at home this evening to the public eye ; they are in the midst of a brawl which, it may be hoped, does not show them at their best.   There is such a stirring time before them, and only half an hour for it, that we must not keep them waiting.   Indeed they have so much to do that we challenge them to do it.

LADY LILIAN (*a frozen flower*).   Why don't you strike me, Richard ?   I am a woman, and there is no one within call.

GARSON.   A woman !   You useless thing, that is just what you are not.

(*It is evidently his honest if mistaken opinion, and he pushes her from him so roughly that she lies on the couch as she fell, in a touching but perhaps rather impertinent little heap.*)

LILIAN (*who, though a dear woman to some, has a genius for putting her finger on the raw of those she does not favour*).   How strong you are, husband mine !   No wonder I love you !   Now as I have told you why I love you, won't you tell me why you love me ?

(*He fumes inarticulately while she takes off her hat and coat, perhaps in search of that homey feeling.*)

How you have ruffled me !   (*She considers her frock.*)   You know, I can't make up my mind whether green is really my colour.   What do you think ?   Which colour do you like best to knock me about in, Richard ?

GARSON (*with his fists clenched though they are not upraised*). You take care !

LILIAN (*as he stamps the floor*).   Do you mind telling me what all this scene has been about ?

GARSON.   You have me there.   But how does it matter what it is that sets a pair like you and me saying what we think of each other ?

LILIAN. True. But we knew what we thought of each other before.

GARSON. We did. And I 've said to that father of yours——

LILIAN. By the way, I never heard how much you paid Pops for me ?

GARSON. One way or another, a good twenty thousand.

LILIAN. I can't help feeling proud.

GARSON. If I could have got you for half I wouldn't have had you.

LILIAN. How like you to say that, Richard ! Still, there are other pretties for whom you could have had the satisfaction of paying more. There must have been some—dear reason —why you flung the handkerchief to me ?

GARSON. Your rotten old families, all so poor and so well turned out. The come-on look in the melting eyes of you, and the disdain of you. I suppose they went to my head. You were the worst, so I chose you.

LILIAN (clapping her hands). I won !

GARSON. Oh, you didn't need to come to me unless you liked.

LILIAN (shivering). I admit that. It was your money that brought me.

GARSON. Quite so.

LILIAN (with a sincerity that makes us hopeful of her). I 'm sorry, Richard, for both of us.

GARSON. Pooh !

LILIAN. You must at least allow that I never pretended it was anything but your wealth that drew me.

GARSON. I never wanted it to be anything else.

LILIAN. How like you again ! Perhaps that is even some little excuse—though not very much—for me.

GARSON (sneering). Soft sawder !

LILIAN. I dare say. (Surveying the man with curiosity) Why don't we end it ?

GARSON (bellowing). Do you know whom you are talking to ? With my name in the City——

LILIAN. Of course. But if you won't, Richard, has it never struck you that some day I——

GARSON (grinning). Never !

LILIAN. You have a mighty faith in me.

GARSON. Mighty.

LILIAN. May I ask why?

(*He comes to her and taps her bodice.*)

GARSON. In this expensive little breast you know why. (*In case there should be any misunderstanding he slaps his pocket.*)

LILIAN. I see.

GARSON. Tragic lot yours, isn't it?

LILIAN. More tragic than you understand.

GARSON. Bought when you were too young to know what you were doing!

LILIAN. Not so young but that I should have known.

GARSON. Such a rare exquisite creature, too, as you know yourself to be.

LILIAN (*with abnegation*). As I know I am not. But as I long to be. As I think I could be.

GARSON. As you think you could be, had you married a better man.

LILIAN. Mock me, you have some right, but it may be truer than you think.

GARSON. It is what they tell you, I don't doubt.

LILIAN. Who tell me?

GARSON. The live-on-papa cubs.

LILIAN (*shrugging her shoulders*). If I were to let them tell me what they would like to say——

GARSON (*possibly with some penetration*). You do, my pet, and when they have finished you tell them they mustn't say it; and your lip trembles, and one sad tear sits on your sweet eyes, the same little tear that comes when you have overdrawn your bank account.

LILIAN. How you read me!

GARSON. I think so. I think I know the stuff you are made of. I wouldn't try heroics, Lilian; you can't live up to them.

LILIAN. I haven't the courage, I suppose?

GARSON. You have the pluck that let the French Jack-a-dandies go tripping to the guillotine; and perhaps my breed hasn't. But when it comes to living you got to live on us, my girl.

LILIAN (*rising and facing him*). Oh, if—if——

GARSON.   If—if you were to show me !   I am not nervous. In the end you will always be true to Number One.   I have thought you out.

LILIAN (*on fire*).   If I did ?

GARSON.   If you did—if you tried to play any game on me—
    (*He takes grip of her by the wrist.*)

LILIAN (*in her earlier manner*).   Would it be the knife, Richard, or Desdemona's pillow ?

GARSON.   If you brought any shame on me, before I put you to the door I would—I would break you !

LILIAN.   If I did it I wouldn't be here to break.

GARSON.   By the powers, it would be as well for you.

LILIAN.   Unless you wish to do the breaking now, please let go my wrist.

    (*He throws it from him, and their colloquy ends with these
    terrible words :*)

GARSON.   Dinner at half-past, I suppose ?

LILIAN.   I suppose so.

(*When she is alone we see some great resolution struggling
into life in her and adorning her.   It means among other
things, we may conclude, that she does not purpose joining him
at dinner.   She writes a brief letter, puts her wedding-ring
in the envelope and deposits the explosive in the nearest
drawer of his desk.   On top of it she throws all the jewellery
she is wearing and closes the drawer.   She puts on her hat
and coat, and after a last look in a glass at the face she is
leaving behind her—the only face of her that* GARSON *knows
—she leaves his house.*

    *Two hundred yards away is a mews, where odd brainy
people—afterwards sorry for themselves—have here and
there made romantic homes, all tiny but not all over the
garages that have supplanted stables.   This one where* HUGH
PATON *lodges is a complete house, and we find him in a snug
room, though it is only reached by a brief ladder which he frequently jumps.   At present the room is in disorder, the fire
extinguished by the masses of paper he has dumped on it, and
he himself is tousled and in disarray.   He has not quite
finished an extensive packing, and has reached the point of
wondering whether he should reopen that bulging bag to put*

those old football boots in it, or leave them for the good of the house. He is whistling gaily, with broken intervals in which his pipe is in his mouth, and he has a very honest face.

To him enters with a rush the little daughter of the house, whose heart he has won by lifting his hat to her in the mews. She has walked with more dignity ever since, and she is twelve.)

SUSIE. You will be stamping at me, sir, but there is a lady, and though I told her you were just putting on your muffler to start for Egypt, up she would come.

(Up she does come, and she is LILIAN. *When* SUSIE *sees how these two look at each other she knows all, and indeed more, and out of respect for Love she goes down the ladder on her tiptoes.)*

HUGH *(surprised, but with outstretched arms).* You! Oh, my dear!

(She will not let him embrace her yet.)

LILIAN *(the soft-eyed, the tremulous).* No, Hugh. Please listen to me first. You see I have changed my mind, and come after all. Yes, I am here to go with you, if you will have me still. But oh, my Hugh, let there be no mistake. Don't have me, dear, if you would rather—rather not.

(He clasps her to him, and of course she was sure he would.) It isn't really a shock to you, is it? Hugh, you don't despise me in your heart for coming?

HUGH. Dear, my dear!

LILIAN *(merely playing with the idea).* You are so fond of Egypt—perhaps it would be lovelier for you to go back to it alone.

(We are sorry she says this, for she has put it into our own heads. They are about the same age, but as they sit there on one of his trunks he looks younger.)

HUGH *(who is far from agreeing with us).* Egypt, without you? Horrible!

LILIAN. Was it seeming horrible before I came up the ladder?

HUGH *(abashed).* Inconceivable if it wasn't.

LILIAN. You were able to smoke.

HUGH. Mechanically. *(He remembers guiltily that he was even whistling.)* Lilian, that man packing wasn't me. I only began to be again when you lit up the doorway.   Tell me, what made you change your mind so suddenly ?

LILIAN.   Not suddenly.   I longed to go to you, but I was his wife.   Hugh, did you hear me say I *was* his wife ?   What a lovely way of putting it !

HUGH.   My wife now and always.

LILIAN.   The things he said to-night !

HUGH.   There, there, that is all over.   You wrote the letter ?

LILIAN.   Yes, and left it for him.

HUGH.   You said in it that it was to me you were coming ? I asked that of you because I want it all to be above-board.   I am not afraid of him.

LILIAN.   Yes, I said in it that I was going away with you, and I put his wedding-ring inside it.   I have burned all my boats.   Oh, Hugh, if it had turned out that you would rather not !

HUGH.   A nice sort of gent I 'd be.

LILIAN.   He thinks me a rotten, shallow creature.   No, don't interrupt.   Perhaps I was so with him, dear.   What was bad in each of us seemed to call to the other.

HUGH.   If yours ever calls to me I won't recognise the voice.

LILIAN.   He said that in any test I would always go where my bread was best buttered.

HUGH.   He will see his mistake when he finds you have come to me.   (*He starts up*)   I say !   We mustn't be late.   Not another word if you love me.   Try to make these catches snap, while I sit on the trunk.   What are you smiling at ?

LILIAN.   I have just remembered, Hugh, that there were people coming to dinner to-night !

HUGH (*rising triumphant from his struggle with the trunk*).   I have just remembered something more important.   (*With accusing finger*) Woman, where is your trousseau ?

LILIAN.   I have only what you see, my dear.   Here is all the riches I bring you—four and sixpence.   Please take care of my dowry for me, Hugh !

HUGH.   You poor one !   But what fun to buy you a trousseau at Brindisi—if not before.

(*He rings.*)

LILIAN (*catching his gaiety*).   Are you proposing to send out a servant to get a trousseau for me ?

HUGH. What a capital idea ! (*As the little maid arrives*) Susie, skip across to the nearest draper's and buy me a trousseau.

SUSIE. A what, sir ?

HUGH. I can only give you ten minutes—lots of time—sure to have them in stock—need of the age—all ready in Christmas hampers. (*Looking* LILIAN *over*) Size five and a half by one and a quarter—hurry, old 'un, fly.

SUSIE. Whatever do he mean ?

LILIAN. He only means that he wants a taxi.

SUSIE. Oh, that ! Mother 's gone out, and you know what father is, sir, but I 'll get it myself.

HUGH. No, you don't, Susie, not in the rain. Back in a jiffy, Lilian.

(*He is gone, and they hear his boisterous leap of the ladder.*)

SUSIE. He is just bubbling over, and all because he is going off to make dams.

LILIAN (*asking too much*). Has he been bubbling over for long, Susie ?

SUSIE (*innocently giving it*). For days and days. I used to think of him out in Egypt in a very dirty state till I saw a picture of him, all in laundry white, and riding on a camel.

LILIAN. The camel goes on its knees to him, Susie.

SUSIE (*heartily*). I don't wonder at it. (*She is on her own knees giving those finishing touches to the baggage which she knows can only come from a woman's hands.*) There was a thing about him in the paper, and it said ' The ball is at his feet.'

LILIAN. And it is. A great career.

SUSIE (*looking sometimes six and sometimes sixty*). For him. But I have just to make ready for another lodger. That is all the great career there is for the likes of me. (*Wistfully*) I 'm thinking there is a great career for you.

LILIAN (*smiling*). How, Susie ?

SUSIE. Him. (*She rises.*) I wonder would you let me see it. I have never seen them except in shop windows.

LILIAN. What ?

SUSIE. Fine you know. The thing that is on the third finger of your left hand.

LILIAN (*showing a bare finger*). Nothing, you see.

SUSIE (*sharp*). You haven't landed him yet ?

(*She is so disappointed that* LILIAN *is kind.*)

LILIAN. All is lovely, Susie.

SUSIE (*who must have it plainer than that*). You 've got him ?

LILIAN. I 've got him.

SUSIE. Lucky you !

LILIAN. Yes, lucky me. You mustn't grudge him to me, Susie. I haven't always been lucky with men.

SUSIE. Men——oh, men ! Most men deserves all they gets. (*She screws up her eyes and opens them to explain.*) I was just seeing you and him on your camels.

(*There is a knocking on the outer door.*)

LILIAN. There he is.

SUSIE. I haven't got back his key. (*She knows the familiar sounds of the mews.*) It 's not him. There is something wrong.

LILIAN. Quick, Susie.

(*The child is gone for a moment, and* LILIAN *is conscious of some disturbance in the passage below.*)

SUSIE (*reappearing, terrified*). Oh, miss !

LILIAN. Tell me !

SUSIE. They are carrying him into his bedroom.

LILIAN. Not Mr. Paton ? Speak !

SUSIE. It 's him ! He was run over.

(*She disappears again, but the tramp of feet is heard through the open door. A grave man comes up the ladder. He is wearing an overcoat and muffler and he closes the door.*)

DR. BRODIE. Poor lady ! I suppose you——

LILIAN. Tell me !

DR. BRODIE. He was run over by a motor bus. It is very serious.

LILIAN. Tell me !

DR. BRODIE. I must tell you. He is dead.

LILIAN. No, he isn't.

DR. BRODIE. He died as they picked him up.

LILIAN. It isn't true.

DR. BRODIE. A Mr. Paton, they tell me. I don't know him. I am a doctor and I happened to be passing. He only spoke one word.

LILIAN. My name ?

DR. BRODIE The word was Egypt.

LILIAN. He is going there. He had gone out for a taxi. So you see it can't be true.

DR. BRODIE. It is true, alas. (*He gets her into a chair.*) Mrs. Paton, I want to help you in any way possible. There seems to be no one in the house but a very useless man and a child. If you can give me the address of any male relative——

LILIAN (*starting up*). You mustn't bring any one here.

DR. BRODIE. Just to help you with—I don't quite— Excuse me, are you Mrs. Paton? (*The pitiful look she gives him makes him avert his troubled eyes.*) I am sure you will understand that I have no wish to intrude. But some one must communicate with the relatives. And of course an inquiry——

LILIAN. You mean, I have no right to be here?

DR. BRODIE. I don't know whether you have a right or not. But you must know. (*As she shrinks from him*) Pardon me, I won't disturb you any longer.

LILIAN. Don't go. What am I to do?

DR. BRODIE. If it is well for him to have it publicly known that you were here you will of course remain ; but if it would not be well for him, my advice to you—as you ask for it, un-happy lady, is to go at once.

LILIAN (*throwing out her arms*). Where am I to go?

DR. BRODIE. I know nothing of the circumstances. I am only telling you what I think might be best for him.

LILIAN (*dry-eyed*). Is there to be no thought of what would be best for me?

DR. BRODIE (*gently*). Might it not be best for you also?

LILIAN. I have nowhere to go—nowhere.

(*Perhaps he does not quite believe her, but if his manner hardens it is only to gain his point.*)

DR. BRODIE. Better that I should know nothing.

LILIAN. I am not what you think me.

DR. BRODIE. No one is. But prove it, madam, by going.

LILIAN. What is to become of me? (*He shakes his head.*) I loved him—I risked everything for him—I am lost.

DR. BRODIE. Those who risk all and lose have to face the consequences.

LILIAN. I was going with him.

(*He might say, ' You can go with him still, unfortunate one, if you choose,' but of course he does not. Instead he opens the door respectfully. She bows, gives him a pitiful smile of thanks and goes away.*

Let us return to GARSON'S *house and see how his little dinner is faring.*

As MR. GARSON *enters the room in evening dress, his bad temper removed with his clothes, he meets his butler.)*

GARSON.   Have I time to write a note, Withers?

WITHERS.   It is two minutes short of the half-hour, sir.

GARSON (*going to his desk*).   Her ladyship not down yet?

WITHERS.   I believe not, sir.

GARSON.   She isn't usually late.   I didn't hear her in her room.

WITHERS.   Shall I send up to inquire, sir?

GARSON.   Oh no, she will be down directly, no doubt.

(*He sits at a desk and unlocks a drawer with his keys. It is the fatal drawer. Stretching out his hand for some papers he knows to be there, it encounters something metallic, which he draws out. Without rising he feels for further jewellery, but there is evidently no more. He has recognised his find but has no suspicions, and is sitting there chuckling over it when* WITHERS *announces two guests,* MR. *and* MRS. REDDING, *both exuding opulence.)*

REDDING.   You seem to be having a little joke all to yourself, Garson.

GARSON.   Ah, welcome both.

MRS. REDDING.   But the joke?

(*For reply their host holds up the jewels.)*

REDDING.   My eye!   No joke for the party that footed the bill.

GARSON.   I put my hand into that drawer for some papers, and it found these instead.

REDDING.   All I can say is 'Halves.'

MRS. REDDING.   Silly man, they are Lady Lilian's.   I know them quite well.

GARSON.   The joke, Redding, is that I now see why my wife is late for dinner.

MRS. REDDING.   It is we who are early; but tell us.

GARSON.   She must have shoved them in there—(*with a certain pride*) her set are more careless than ours—and then forgotten where she put them. I bet she is searching high and low for them at this moment.

MRS. REDDING (*who would like to say that her set can be fashionably careless also*). The poor dear! But suppose some servant, the awful man who winds the clocks——

GARSON. Oh, they were safe enough. She had happened to find the drawer unlocked but she had the sense to shut it, and all these drawers lock when they shut. (*He shuts the drawer and it clicks, perhaps an effort to tell its master something.*) I have the only key. (*He puts the jewels into his pocket and greets another guest.*)

WITHERS. Dr. Brodie.

GARSON. Very pleased to see you, Brodie, in my little place.

DR. BRODIE. Thank you, Garson. (*He presumes that* MRS. REDDING *is his hostess*) Lady Lilian, I am——

GARSON. No, no, that isn't Lady Lilian.

MRS. REDDING (*archly*). Would that it were, Dr. Brodie!

REDDING (*equally ready*). Oh, come!

GARSON. Dr. Brodie—Mrs. Redding. You have met at the club, Redding.

REDDING. To be sure.

GARSON. I forgot you don't know my wife, Brodie. She will be down in a moment. I must apologise for her being late.

MRS. REDDING. Don't fuss, Mr. Garson. Dr. Brodie knows what women are.

DR. BRODIE. Not I, Mrs. Redding. But I was afraid I should be late myself.

REDDING. Something professional?

DR. BRODIE. Accident in the street. Man knocked over by a motor bus—killed.

GARSON. Rough luck. I can't think what is keeping Lady Lilian.

REDDING. Some one you knew, doctor?

DR. BRODIE. No, but he seems to have done good work in India. Paton is the name.

GARSON. Paton? There was a Paton we met once at dinner who—no, Egypt was his place.

DR. BRODIE. It was Egypt she said. Probably your man.

MRS. REDDING. Was he married?

DR. BRODIE. No, not married. (*He sighs.*) Poor devil!

REDDING. Surely better in the circumstances that he wasn't married.

DR. BRODIE. Oh, much better.

MRS. REDDING. You said ' poor devil.'

DR. BRODIE. Did I ? I was thinking of something else.

MRS. REDDING. Of the lady ?

DR. BRODIE (*not delighting in her*). Did I say there was a lady ?

MRS. REDDING (*smartly*). You are saying it now.

REDDING. Got you, my friend !

DR. BRODIE. Hm ! (*His desire is to drop the subject.*) Beast of a night, Garson.

GARSON. Wet ?

DR. BRODIE. Drizzle. The most dismal sort of London night.

MRS. REDDING. And the poor devil is out in it ?

DR. BRODIE. She is out in it, right enough.

(LADY LILIAN *is not, however, out in it. She now sweeps in from upstairs in a delicious evening confection. She must have dressed in record time, for no doubt she lost a moment trying to open that drawer. She must even have raced her brain, which may be conceived by the fanciful as descending the stairs in pursuit of her.*)

GARSON. You are terribly late, Lilian.

(*She knows at once that nothing has been discovered as yet, and her wits make up on her.*)

LILIAN. Dear Mrs. Redding, I am so ashamed. Forgive me, kind Mr. Redding.

REDDING (*a courtier when approached infantilely*). All I can say, Lady Lilian, is that you were worth waiting for.

(*Then she sees the doctor, and the recognition is mutual.*)

GARSON. Brodie, my wife at last. I forgot, Lilian, whether I mentioned that Dr. Brodie had kindly promised to take pot-luck with us.

LILIAN. No, but I am so pleased, Dr. Brodie—any friend of my husband.

DR. BRODIE. Thank you, Lady Lilian.

MRS. REDDING. He has been telling us such a shocking story.

REDDING. It will spoil my dinner.

GARSON. Not quite, I hope, Redding.

REDDING. No, not quite.

(They have both a gift for this sort of talk, and have sunny times together.)

MRS. REDDING. A man killed in the street. Tell her, Dr. Brodie.

DR. BRODIE. It wouldn't interest Lady Lilian.

GARSON. Yes, by the way it would. You will remember him, Lil.

LILIAN. Some one I know ?

GARSON. Paton is the name. I think it was at the Rossiters' we met him.

LILIAN. A barrister ?

GARSON. No, an engineer—abroad—in a small way.

LILIAN. A dark man, wasn't he ?

DR. BRODIE. No, fair. Evidently if you ever knew him, Lady Lilian, you have forgotten him.

LILIAN. One meets so many.

DR. BRODIE. Just so.

MRS. REDDING. There was a woman in it, Lady Lilian. Do get him to tell us.

LILIAN (*boldly*). Why not ?

DR. BRODIE. Very well. I assure you I pitied her when I thought she was his wife, and still more when I found she wasn't.

GARSON. That sort of woman !

LILIAN. What sort of woman, Richard ?

GARSON (*with delicacy*). Oh, come !

DR. BRODIE. She kept crying, what could she do.

GARSON. She knew what she could do !

LILIAN. What could she do, Richard ?

GARSON. Pooh ! They don't all get run over by motor buses, my dear.

DR. BRODIE. I thought she might find a job—women do nowadays—and live on, true to the dead. After all, it was the test of her.

LILIAN. I suppose it was.

GARSON. What a sentimental fellow you are, Brodie ! That kind can look after themselves all right. I say, Redding, suppose she is a married woman and has bolted back to unsuspecting No. 1 !

REDDING. Lordy!

DR. BRODIE. When she left the house at my request I couldn't have thought so despicably of her as that.

LILIAN   Is it more abject than my husband's—other end for her?

DR. BRODIE. I should say, yes.

REDDING. It's quite possible, you know, Garson. Makes a pretty chump of the husband, though.

GARSON. No doubt. And yet there is humour in it. You don't see, Brodie, that it has its humorous side?

DR. BRODIE. Oh yes, I do, Garson. But as I walked here I was picturing her in dire desolation.

LILIAN. Don't you think she may be in dire desolation still?

DR. BRODIE. Thinking it over, Lady Lilian, I have come to the conclusion that your husband is right, and that I was a sentimental fellow, wasting my sympathy on that lady.

GARSON (*who is not unsusceptible to praise*). Exactly.

(*Dinner is announced, and he is indicating to* BRODIE *to take in* LADY LILIAN, *when* MRS. REDDING, *the only one who has remembered the jewellery, touches her throat and wrists significantly. He gives her and her husband a private wink.*)

Hullo, Lil, where are those emeralds? Didn't you get 'em out of me specially for that frock?

(*Only one of the company, a new acquaintance, notices his hostess go rigid for a moment. So her husband has found the jewels! Something inside her that is clamouring for utterance is about to betray her, when she sees a glance pass from her husband to the drawer. She is uncertain how much has been found out, but she cannot believe that if this man knows everything he could have had the self-control to play cat to her for so long.*)

LILIAN (*taking a risk*). I took them off down here and left them for safety in one of your drawers.

GARSON. Which drawer?

LILIAN (*crossing to it*). This one.

GARSON (*making a sign with his fingers behind his back to the* Reddings.) Best put them on; I like you in 'em.

(*He tosses her his keys, and as she opens the drawer he has another gleeful moment with his accomplices.* BRODIE, *whose attention is confined to her, understands that somehow a crisis has been reached, and oddly enough he does not want her to be caught.)*

LILIAN (*turning round, aghast*). They are gone !

GARSON (*histrionically*). Gone ?

LILIAN. Richard, what is to be done ? My emeralds !

GARSON. Gone ! The police——

LILIAN. Yes, yes !

MRS. REDDING. Mr. Garson, how can you keep it up ? Don't you see she is nearly fainting, and so should I be. Emeralds !

GARSON (*with the conqueror's good nature*). Come, come, Lil, calm yourself. This should be a lesson to you, though. But it 's all right—just a trick I was playing on you. I found them in the drawer.

REDDING (*admiringly*). Never was such a masterpiece at a trick as Garson !

GARSON (*producing the jewels from his pocket like a wizard*). Here they are !

(He gallantly places them on her person, and even gives her a peck, which brings him very near to something she is holding in her hand beneath her handkerchief. GARSON takes in MRS. REDDING, and REDDING has to go without a lady. Before LILIAN and BRODIE follow them she throws a letter into the fire, and as the little spitfire turns to ashes she puts on her finger a wedding-ring that she has taken out of it. She reels for a moment, then looks to BRODIE for his commentary. He has none, but as a medical man he feels her pulse.)

rather attention is confined to her, understands that somehow
a crisis has been reached, and oddly enough he does not want
her to be caught.)

LILIAN (turning round, aghast). They are gone!

CARSON (harmonically) (Gone?

LILIAN. Richard, what is to be done? My emeralds!

CARSON (Gone ! The police——

LILIAN. Yes, yes!

MRS. REDDING. Mr. Carson, how can you keep it up?
Don't you see she is nearly fainting, and so should I be.
Emeralds!

CARSON (with the conjurer's good nature). Come, come,
I'll calm yourself. This should be a lesson to you, though;
but it's all right—just a trick I was playing on you. I found
them in the drawer.

REDDING (admiringly). Never was such a masterpiece of a
trick as Carson!

CARSON (producing the jewels from his pocket like a wizard).
Here they are!

(He gallantly places them on her person, and even gives her
a peck, which wrings him very near to something she is holding in her hand beneath her handkerchief. CARSON takes in
MRS. REDDING, and REDDING has to go without a lady.
Before LILIAN and BRODIE follow them she throws a letter
into the fire, and as the little spitfire turns to ashes she puts
on her finger a wedding-ring that she has taken out of it.
She reels for a moment, then looks to BRODIE for his commentary. He has none, but as a medical man he feels her
pulse.)

THE NEW WORD

THE NEW WORD

Produced at the Duke of York's Theatre on March 22, 1915, with the following cast :

FATHER	O. B. Clarence
MOTHER	Helen Haye
SON	Geoffrey Wilmer
DAUGHTER	Gertrude Lang

THE NEW WORD

ANY room nowadays must be the scene, for any father and any son are the *dramatis personæ*. We could pick them up in Mayfair, in Tooting, on the Veldt, in rectories or in grocers' back parlours, dump them down on our toy stage and tell them to begin. It is a great gathering to choose from, but our needs are small. Let the company shake hands, and all go away but two. In other words, it is war-time.

The two who have remained (it is discovered on inquiry) are Mr. Torrance and his boy ; so let us make use of them. Torrance did not linger in order to be chosen, he was anxious, like all of them, to be off ; but we recognised him, and sternly signed to him to stay. Not that we knew him personally, but the fact is, we remembered him (we never forget a face) as the legal person who reads out the names of the jury before the court opens, and who brushes aside your reasons for wanting to be let off. It pleases our humour to tell Mr. Torrance that we cannot let him off.

He does not look so formidable as when last we saw him, and this is perhaps owing to our no longer being hunched with others on those unfeeling benches. It is not because he is without a wig, for we saw him, on the occasion to which we are so guardedly referring, both in a wig and out of it ; he passed behind a screen without it, and immediately (as quickly as we write) popped out in it, giving it a finishing touch rather like the butler's wriggle to his coat as he goes to the door. There are the two kinds of learned brothers, those who use the screen, and those who (so far as the jury knows) sleep in their wigs. The latter are the swells, and include the judges ; whom, however, we who write have seen in public thoroughfares without their wigs, a horrible sight that has doubtless led many an onlooker to crime.

Mr. Torrance, then, is no great luminary ; indeed, when we accompany him to his house, as we must, in order to set our scene properly, we find that it is quite a suburban affair, only one servant kept, and her niece engaged twice a week to crawl about the floors. There is no fire in the drawing-room, so the family remain on after dinner in the dining-room, which rather gives them away. There is really no one in the room but Roger. That is the truth of it, though to the unseeing eye all the family are there except Roger. They consist of Mr., Mrs., and Miss Torrance. Mr. Torrance is enjoying his evening paper and a cigar, and every line of him is insisting stubbornly that nothing unusual is happening in the house. In the home circle (and now that we think of it, even in court) he has the reputation of being a somewhat sarcastic gentleman; he must be dogged, too, otherwise he would have ceased long ago to be sarcastic to his wife, on whom wit falls like pellets on sandbags; all the dents they make are dimples.

Mrs. Torrance is at present exquisitely employed; she is listening to Roger's step overhead. You know what a delightful step the boy has. And what is more remarkable is that Emma is listening to it too, Emma who is seventeen, and who has been trying to keep Roger in his place ever since he first compelled her to bowl to him. Things have come to a pass when a sister so openly admits that she is only number two in the house.

Remarks well worthy of being recorded fall from these two ladies as they gaze upward. ' I think—didn't I, Emma ? ' is the mother's contribution, while it is Emma who replies in a whisper, ' No, not yet ! '

Mr. Torrance calmly reads, or seems to read, for it is not possible that there can be anything in the paper as good as this. Indeed he occasionally casts a humorous glance at his women-folk. Perhaps he is trying to steady them. Let us hope he has some such good reason for breaking in from time to time on their entrancing occupation.

MR. TORRANCE. Listen to this, dear. It is very important. The paper says, upon apparently good authority, that love laughs at locksmiths.

(*His wife answers without lowering her eyes.*)

MRS. TORRANCE. Did you speak, John ? I am listening.

MR. TORRANCE. Yes, I was telling you that the Hidden Hand has at last been discovered in a tub in Russell Square.

MRS. TORRANCE. I hear, John. How thoughtful!

MR. TORRANCE. And so they must have been made of margarine, my love.

MRS. TORRANCE. I shouldn't wonder, John.

MR. TORRANCE. Hence the name Petrograd.

MRS. TORRANCE. Oh, was that the reason?

MR. TORRANCE. You will be pleased to hear, Ellen, that the honourable gentleman then resumed his seat.

MRS. TORRANCE. That was nice of him.

MR. TORRANCE. As I (*good-naturedly*) now resume mine, having made my usual impression.

MRS. TORRANCE. Yes, John.

(EMMA *slips upstairs to peep through a keyhole, and it strikes her mother that* JOHN *has been saying something. They are on too good terms to make an apology necessary.*)

MRS. TORRANCE (*blandly*). John, I haven't heard a word you said.

MR. TORRANCE. I 'm sure you haven't, woman.

MRS. TORRANCE. I can't help being like this, John.

MR. TORRANCE. Go on being like yourself, dear.

MRS. TORRANCE. Am I foolish?

MR. TORRANCE. Um.

MRS. TORRANCE. Oh, but, John, how can you be so calm— with him up there?

MR. TORRANCE. He has been up there a good deal, you know, since we presented him to an astounded world nineteen years ago.

MRS. TORRANCE. But he—he is not going to be up there much longer, John. (*She sits on the arm of his chair, so openly to wheedle him that it is not worth his while to smile. Her voice is tremulous; she is a woman who can conceal nothing.*) You will be nice to him—to-night—won't you, John?

MR. TORRANCE (*a little pained*). Do I just begin to-night, Ellen?

MRS. TORRANCE. Oh no, no; but I think he is rather— shy of you at times.

MR. TORRANCE (*wryly*). That is because he is my son, Ellen.

MRS. TORRANCE.   Yes—it 's strange ; but—yes.

MR. TORRANCE (*with a twinkle that is not all humorous*).   Did it ever strike you, Ellen, that I am a bit—shy of him ?

(*She is indeed surprised.*)

MRS. TORRANCE.   Of Rogie !

MR. TORRANCE.   I suppose it is because I am his father.

(*She presumes that this is his sarcasm again, and lets it pass at that. It reminds her of what she wants to say.*)

MRS. TORRANCE.   You are so sarcastic (*she has never quite got the meaning of this word*) to Rogie at times.   Boys don't like that, John.

MR. TORRANCE.   Is that so, Ellen ?

MRS. TORRANCE.   Of course I don't mind your being sarcastic to *me*——

MR. TORRANCE.   Much good (*groaning*) my being sarcastic to you !   You are so seldom aware of it.

MRS. TORRANCE.   I am not asking you to be a mother to him, John.

MR. TORRANCE.   Thank you, my dear.

(*She does not know that he is sarcastic again.*)

MRS. TORRANCE.   I quite understand that a man can't think all the time about his son as a mother does.

MR. TORRANCE.   Can't he, Ellen ?   What makes you so sure of that ?

MRS. TORRANCE.   I mean that a boy naturally goes to his mother with his troubles rather than to his father.   Rogie tells me everything.

MR. TORRANCE (*venturing*).   I dare say he might tell me things he wouldn't tell you.

(*She smiles at this. It is very probably sarcasm.*)

MRS. TORRANCE.   I want you to be serious just now.   Why not show more warmth to him, John ?

MR. TORRANCE (*with an unspoken sigh*).   It would terrify him, Ellen.   Two men show warmth to each other ?   Shame, woman !

MRS. TORRANCE.   Two men ! (*indignantly*).   John, he is only nineteen.

MR. TORRANCE (*patting her hand*).   That 's all.   Ellen, it is the great age to be to-day, nineteen.

(EMMA *darts in.*)

EMMA.   Mother, he has unlocked the door !   He is taking a last look at himself in the mirror before coming down !

(*Having made the great announcement, she is off again.*)

MRS. TORRANCE.   You won't be sarcastic, John ?

MR. TORRANCE.   I give you my word—if you promise not to break down.

MRS. TORRANCE (*rashly*).   I promise.   (*She hurries to the door and back again.*)   John, I 'll contrive to leave you and him alone together for a little.

(MR. TORRANCE *is as alarmed as if the judge had looked over the bench and asked him to step up.*)

MR. TORRANCE.   For God's sake, woman, don't do that. Father and son !   He 'll bolt ; or if he doesn't, I will.

(EMMA TORRANCE *throws open the door grandly, and we learn what all the to-do is about.*)

EMMA.   Allow me to introduce 2nd Lieutenant Torrance of the Royal Sussex.   Father—your son ;   2nd Lieutenant Torrance—your father.   Mother—your little Rogie.

(ROGER, *in uniform, walks in, strung up for the occasion. Or the uniform comes forward with* ROGER *inside it.   He has been a very ordinary nice boy up to now, dull at his ' books ' ;   by an effort* MR. TORRANCE *had sent him to an obscure boarding-school, but at sixteen it was evident that an office was the proper place for* ROGER.   *Before the war broke out he was treasurer of the local lawn tennis club, and his golf handicap was seven ;   he carried his little bag daily to and from the city, and his highest relaxation was giggling with girls or about them.   Socially he had fallen from the standards of the home ;   even now that he is in his uniform the hasty might say something clever about ' temporary gentleman.'   But there are great ideas buzzing in* ROGER'S *head, which would never have been there save for the war. At present he is chiefly conscious of his clothes.   His mother embraces him with cries of rapture, while* MR. TORRANCE *surveys him quizzically over the paper ;   and* EMMA, *rushing to the piano, which is of such an old-fashioned kind that it can also be used as a sideboard, plays ' See the Conquering Hero Comes.'*)

ROGER (*in an agony*).   Mater, do stop that chit making an ass of me.

(He must be excused for his ' mater.' That was the sort of school ; and his mother is rather proud of the phrase, though it sometimes makes his father wince.)

MRS. TORRANCE. Emma, please, don't. But I 'm sure you deserve the words, my darling. Doesn't he, John ?

MR. TORRANCE *(missing his chance)*. Hardly yet, you know. Can't be exactly a conquering hero the first night you put them on, can you, Roger ?

ROGER *(hotly)*. Did I say I was ?

MRS. TORRANCE. Oh, John ! Do turn round, Rogie. I never did—I never did !

EMMA. Isn't he a pet !

ROGER. Shut up, Emma.

MRS. TORRANCE *(challenging the world)*. Though I say it who shouldn't—and yet, why shouldn't I ?

MR. TORRANCE. In any case you will—so go ahead, ' mater.'

MRS. TORRANCE. I knew he would look splendid ; but I— of course I couldn't know that he would look quite so splendid as this.

ROGER. I know I look a bally ass. That is why I was such a time in coming down.

MR. TORRANCE. We thought we heard you upstairs strutting about.

MRS. TORRANCE. John ! Don't mind him, Rogie.

ROGER *(haughtily)*. I don't.

MR. TORRANCE. Oh !

ROGER. But I wasn't strutting.

MRS. TORRANCE. That dreadful sword ! No, I would prefer you not to draw it, dear—not till necessity makes you.

MR. TORRANCE. Come, come, Ellen ; that 's rather hard lines on the boy. If he isn't to draw it here, where is he to draw it ?

EMMA *(with pride)*. At the Front, father.

MR. TORRANCE. I thought they left them at home now-adays, Roger ?

ROGER. Yes, mater ; you see, they are a bit in the way.

MRS. TORRANCE *(foolishly)*. Not when you have got used to them.

MR. TORRANCE. That isn't what Roger means.
(His son glares.)

EMMA (*who, though she has not formerly thought much of* ROGER, *is now proud to trot by his side and will henceforth count the salutes*). I know what he means. If you carry a sword the snipers know you are an officer, and they try to pick you off.

MRS. TORRANCE. It's no wonder they are called Huns. Fancy a British sniper doing that! Roger, you will be very careful, won't you, in the trenches?

ROGER. Honour bright, mater.

MRS. TORRANCE. Above all, don't look up.

MR. TORRANCE. The trenches ought to be so deep that they can't look up.

MRS. TORRANCE. What a good idea, John!

ROGER. He's making game of you, mater.

MRS. TORRANCE (*unruffled*). Is he, my own?—very likely. Now about the question of provisions——

ROGER. Oh, lummy, you talk as if I was going off to-night! I mayn't go for months and months.

MRS. TORRANCE. I know—and, of course, there is a chance that you may not be needed at all.

ROGER (*poor boy*). None of that, mater.

MRS. TORRANCE. There is something I want to ask you, John—How long do you think the war is likely to last? (*Her* JOHN *resumes his paper.*) Rogie, I know you will laugh at me, but there are some things that I could not help getting for you.

ROGER. You know, you have knitted enough things already to fit up my whole platoon.

MRS. TORRANCE (*proud almost to tears*). His platoon!

EMMA. Have you noticed how fine all the words in -oon are? Platoon! Dragoon!

MR. TORRANCE. Spittoon.

EMMA. Colonel is good, but rather papaish; Major is nosey; Admiral of the Fleet is scrumptious, but Maréchal de France —that is the best of all.

MRS. TORRANCE. I think there is no word so nice as 2nd Lieutenant. (*Gulping*) Lot of little boys.

ROGER. Mater!

MRS. TORRANCE. I mean, just think of their cold feet. (*She produces many parcels and displays their strange contents.*) These are for putting inside your socks. Those are for outside your socks. I am told that it is also advisable to have straw in your boots.

MR. TORRANCE. Have you got him some straw ?

MRS. TORRANCE. I thought, John, he could get it there. But if you think——

ROGER. He's making fun of you again, mater.

MRS. TORRANCE. I shouldn't wonder. Here are some overalls. One is leather and one fur, and this one is waterproof. The worst of it is that they are from different shops, and each says that the others keep the damp in, or draw the feet. They have such odd names, too. There are new names for everything nowadays. Vests are called cuirasses. Are you laughing at me, Rogie ?

MR. TORRANCE (*sharply*). If he is laughing, he ought to be ashamed of himself.

ROGER (*barking*). Who was laughing ?

MRS. TORRANCE. John !

(EMMA *cuffs her father playfully.*)

MR. TORRANCE. All very well, Emma, but it's past your bedtime.

EMMA (*indignantly*). You can't expect me to sleep on a night like this.

MR. TORRANCE. You can try.

MRS. TORRANCE. 2nd Lieutenant ! 2nd Lieutenant !

MR. TORRANCE (*alarmed*). Ellen, don't break down. You promised.

MRS. TORRANCE. I am not going to break down ; but—but there is a photograph of Rogie when he was very small——

MR. TORRANCE. Go to bed !

MRS. TORRANCE. I happen—to have it in my pocket——

ROGER. Don't bring it out, mater.

MRS. TORRANCE. If I break down, John, it won't be owing to the picture itself so much as because of what is written on the back.

(*She produces it dolefully.*)

MR. TORRANCE. Then don't look at the back.

(*He takes it from her.*)

MRS. TORRANCE (*not very hopeful of herself*). But I know what is written on the back, ' Roger John Torrance, aged two years four months, and thirty-three pounds.'

MR. TORRANCE. Correct. (*She weeps softly.*) There, there, woman. (*He signs imploringly to* EMMA.)

EMMA (*kissing him*). I'm going to by-by. 'Night, mammy. 'Night, Rog. (*She is about to offer him her cheek, then salutes instead, and rushes off, with* ROGER *in pursuit.*)

MRS. TORRANCE. I shall leave you together, John.

MR. TORRANCE (*half liking it, but nervous*). Do you think it's wise ? (*With a groan*) You know what I am.

MRS. TORRANCE. Do be nice to him, dear. (ROGER's *return finds her very artful indeed.*) I wonder where I put my glasses ?

ROGER. I'll look for them.

MRS. TORRANCE. No, I remember now. They are up-stairs in such a funny place that I must go myself. Do you remember, Rogie, that I hoped they would reject you on account of your eyes ?

ROGER. I suppose you couldn't help it.

MRS. TORRANCE (*beaming on her husband*). Did you believe I really meant it, John ?

MR. TORRANCE (*curious*). Did *you*, Roger ?

ROGER. Of course. Didn't you, father ?

MR. TORRANCE. No ! I knew the old lady better.

(*He takes her hand.*)

MRS. TORRANCE (*sweetly*). I shouldn't have liked it, Rogie dear. I'll tell you something. You know your brother Harry died when he was seven. To you, I suppose, it is as if he had never been. You were barely five.

ROGER. I don't remember him, mater.

MRS. TORRANCE. No—no. But I do, Rogie. He would be twenty-one now ; but though you and Emma grew up I have always gone on seeing him as just seven. Always till the war broke out. And now I see him a man of twenty-one, dressed in khaki, fighting for his country, same as you. I wouldn't have had one of you stay at home, though I had had a dozen. That is, if it is the noble war they all say it is. I'm not clever, Rogie, I have to take it on trust. Surely they wouldn't deceive mothers. I'll get my glasses.

(*She goes away, leaving the father and son somewhat moved. It is* MR. TORRANCE *who speaks first, gruffly.*)

MR. TORRANCE. Like to change your mother, Roger ?

ROGER (*gruffly*).   What do *you* think ?

(*Then silence falls.   These two are very conscious of being together, without so much as the tick of a clock to help them.   The father clings to his cigar, sticks his knife into it, studies the leaf, tries crossing his legs another way.   The son examines the pictures on the walls as if he had never seen them before, and is all the time edging toward the door.* MR. TORRANCE *wets his lips ; it must be now or never.*)

MR. TORRANCE.   Not going, Roger ?

ROGER (*counting the chairs*).   Yes, I thought——

MR. TORRANCE.   Won't you—sit down and—have a chat ?

ROGER (*bowled over*).   A what ?   You and me !

MR. TORRANCE.   Why not ?   (*rather truculently*).

ROGER.   Oh—oh, all right (*sitting uncomfortably*). (*The cigar gets several more stabs.*)

MR. TORRANCE.   I suppose you catch an early train to-morrow ?

ROGER.   The 5.20.   I have flag-signalling at half-past six.

MR. TORRANCE.   Phew !   Hours before I shall be up.

ROGER.   I suppose so.

MR. TORRANCE.   Well, you needn't dwell on it, Roger.

ROGER (*indignantly*).   I didn't.   (*He starts up.*)   Good-night, father.

MR. TORRANCE.   Good-night.   Damn.   Come back.   My fault.   Didn't I say I wanted to have a chat with you ?

ROGER.   I thought we had had it.

MR. TORRANCE (*gloomily*).   No such luck.

(*There is another pause.   A frightened ember in the fire makes an appeal to some one to say something.*   MR. TOR-RANCE *rises.   It is now he who is casting eyes at the door.   He sits again, ashamed of himself.*)

MR. TORRANCE (*pleasantly*).   I like your uniform, Roger.

ROGER (*wriggling*).   Haven't you made fun of me enough ?

MR. TORRANCE (*sharply*).   I'm not making fun of you. Don't you see I'm trying to tell you that I'm proud of you ? (ROGER *is at last aware of it, with dread.*)

ROGER.   Good lord, father, *you* are not going to begin now. (*The father restrains himself.*)

MR. TORRANCE.   Do you remember, Roger, my saying that I didn't want you to smoke till you were twenty ?

ROGER. Oh, it's that, is it? (*Shutting his mouth tight*) I never promised.

MR. TORRANCE (*almost with a shout*). It's not that. (*Kindly*) Have a cigar, my boy?

ROGER. Me?

(*A rather shaky hand passes him a cigar-case.* ROGER *selects from it and lights up nervously. He is now prepared for the worst.*)

MR. TORRANCE. Have you ever wondered, Roger, what sort of a fellow I am?

ROGER (*guardedly*). Often.

(MR. TORRANCE *casts all sense of decency to the winds ; such is one of the effects of war.*)

MR. TORRANCE. I have often wondered what sort of fellow you are, Roger. We have both been at it on the sly. I suppose that is what makes a father and son so uncomfortable in each other's presence.

(ROGER *is not yet prepared to meet him half-way, but he casts a fly.*)

ROGER. Do you feel the creeps when you are left alone with me?

MR. TORRANCE. Mortally. My first instinct is to slip away.

ROGER (*with deep feeling*). So is mine.

MR. TORRANCE. You don't say so ! (*with such surprise that the father undoubtedly goes up a step in the son's estimation*). I always seem to know what you are thinking, Roger.

ROGER. Do you? Same here.

MR. TORRANCE. As a consequence it is better, it is right, it is only decent that you and I should be very chary of confidences with each other.

ROGER (*relieved*). I'm dashed glad you see it in that way.

MR. TORRANCE. Oh, quite. And yet, Roger, if you had to answer this question on oath, ' Whom do you think you are most like in this world ? '—I don't mean superficially, but deep down in your vitals—what would you say ? Your mother, your uncle, one of your friends on the golf links ?

ROGER. No.

MR. TORRANCE. Who ?

ROGER (*darkly*). You.

2 E

MR. TORRANCE. Just how I feel.

(*There is such true sympathy in the manly avowal that* ROGER *cannot but be brought closer to his father.*)

ROGER. It's pretty ghastly, father.

MR. TORRANCE. It is. I don't know for which it is worse.

(*They consider each other without bitterness.*)

MR. TORRANCE. You are a bit of a wag at times, Roger.

ROGER. You soon shut me up.

MR. TORRANCE. I have heard that you sparkle more freely in my absence.

ROGER. They say the same about you.

MR. TORRANCE. And now that you mention it, I believe it is true ; and yet, isn't it a bigger satisfaction to you to catch me relishing your jokes than any other person ?

ROGER (*his eyes opening wide*). How did you know that ?

MR. TORRANCE. Because I am so bucked if I see you relishing mine.

ROGER. *Are* you ? (*His hold on the certain things in life is slipping.*) You don't show it.

MR. TORRANCE. That is because of our awkward relationship.

ROGER (*lapsing into gloom*). We have got to go through with it.

MR. TORRANCE (*kicking the coals*). There's no way out.

ROGER. No.

MR. TORRANCE. We have, as it were, signed a compact, Roger, never to let on that we care for each other. As gentlemen we must stick to it.

ROGER. Yes. What are you getting at, father ?

MR. TORRANCE. There is a war on, Roger.

ROGER. That needn't make any difference.

MR. TORRANCE. Yes, it does. My boy, be ready ; I hate to hit you without warning. I'm going to cast a grenade into the middle of you. It's this, I'm fond of you, my boy.

ROGER (*squirming*). Father, if any one were to hear you !

MR. TORRANCE. They won't. The door is shut, Amy is gone to bed, and all is quiet in our street. Won't you—won't you say something civil to me in return, Roger ?

(ROGER *looks at him and away from him.*)

ROGER. I sometimes—bragged about you at school.

MR. TORRANCE (*absurdly pleased*).   Did you ?   What sort of things, Roger ?

ROGER.   I—I forget.

MR. TORRANCE.   Come on, Roger.

ROGER.   Is this fair, father ?

MR. TORRANCE.   No, I suppose it isn't.   (*He attacks the coals again.*)   You and your mother have lots of confidences, haven't you ?

ROGER.   I tell her a good deal.   Somehow——

MR. TORRANCE.   Yes, somehow one can.   (*With the artfulness that comes of years*) I 'm glad you tell her everything.

ROGER (*looking down his cigar*).   Not everything, father. There are things—about oneself——

MR. TORRANCE.   Aren't there, Roger !

ROGER.   Best not to tell her.

MR. TORRANCE.   Yes—yes.   If there are any of them you would care to tell me instead—just if you want to, mind—just if you are in a hole or anything ?

ROGER (*stiffly*).   No, thanks.

MR. TORRANCE.   Any little debts, for instance ?

ROGER.   That 's all right now.   Mother——

MR. TORRANCE.   She did ?

ROGER (*ready to jump at him*).   I was willing to speak to you about them, but——

MR. TORRANCE.   She said, 'Not worth while bothering father.'

ROGER.   How did you know ?

MR. TORRANCE.   Oh, I have met your mother before, you see.   Nothing else ?

ROGER.   No.

MR. TORRANCE.   Haven't been an ass about a girl or anything of that sort ?

ROGER.   Good lord, father !

MR. TORRANCE.   I shouldn't have said it.   In my young days we sometimes—— It 's all different now.

ROGER.   I don't know.   I could tell you things that would surprise you.

MR. TORRANCE.   No !   Not about yourself ?

ROGER.   No.   At least——

MR. TORRANCE.   Just as you like, Roger.

ROGER.   It blew over long ago.

MR. TORRANCE. Then there's no need?

ROGER. No—oh no. It was just—you know—the old, old story.

(He eyes his father suspiciously, but not a muscle in MR. TORRANCE'S *countenance is out of place.)*

MR. TORRANCE. I see. It hasn't—left you bitter about the sex, Roger, I hope?

ROGER. Not now. She—you know what women are.

MR. TORRANCE. Yes, yes.

ROGER. You needn't mention it to mother.

MR. TORRANCE. I won't. *(He is elated to share a secret with* ROGER *about which mother is not to know.)* Think your mother and I are an aged pair, Roger?

ROGER. I never——of course you are not young.

MR. TORRANCE. How long have you known that? I mean, it's true—but I didn't know it till quite lately.

ROGER. That you're old?

MR. TORRANCE. Hang it, Roger, not so bad as that— elderly. This will stagger you; but I assure you that until the other day I jogged along thinking of myself as on the whole still one of the juveniles. *(He makes a wry face.)* I crossed the bridge, Roger, without knowing it.

ROGER. What made you know?

MR. TORRANCE. What makes us know all the new things? —the war. I'll tell you a secret. When we realised in August of 1914 that myriads of us were to be needed, my first thought wasn't that I had a son, but that I must get fit myself.

ROGER. You!

MR. TORRANCE. Funny, isn't it? But, as I tell you, I didn't know I had ceased to be young. I went into Regent's Park and tried to run a mile.

ROGER. Lummy, you might have killed yourself.

MR. TORRANCE. I nearly did—especially as I had put a weight on my shoulders to represent my kit. I kept at it for a week, but I knew the game was up. The discovery was pretty grim.

ROGER. Don't you bother about that part of it. You are doing your share, taking care of mother and Emma.

(MR. TORRANCE emits a laugh of self-contempt.)

MR. TORRANCE. I am not taking care of them. It is you

who are taking care of them.   My friend, you are the head of
the house now.

ROGER.   Father !

MR. TORRANCE.   Yes, we have come back to hard facts, and
the defender of the house is the head of it.

ROGER.   Me ? Fudge.

MR. TORRANCE.   It 's true.   The thing that makes me
wince most is that some of my contemporaries have managed
to squeeze back : back into youth, Roger, though I guess they
were a pretty tight fit in the turnstile.   There is Coxon ; he
is in khaki now, with his hair dyed, and when he and I meet at
the club we know that we belong to different generations.   I 'm
a decent old fellow, but I don't really count any more, while
Coxon, lucky dog, is being damned daily on parade.

ROGER.   I hate your feeling it in that way, father.

MR. TORRANCE.   I don't say it is a palatable draught, but
when the war is over we shall all shake down to the new conditions.   No fear of my being sarcastic to you then, Roger.   I 'll
have to be jolly respectful.

ROGER.   Shut up, father !

MR. TORRANCE.   You 've begun, you see.   Don't worry,
Roger.   Any rawness I might feel in having missed the chance
of seeing whether I was a man—like Coxon, confound him !
—is swallowed up in the pride of giving the chance to you.
I 'm in a shiver about you, but—— It 's all true, Roger, what
your mother said about 2nd Lieutenants.   Till the other day
we were so little of a military nation that most of us didn't know
there *were* 2nd Lieutenants.   And now, in thousands of homes
we feel that there is nothing else.   2nd Lieutenant !   It is
like a new word to us—one, I dare say, of many that the war
will add to our language.   We have taken to it, Roger.   If a
son of mine were to tarnish it——

ROGER (*growling*).   I 'll try not to.

MR. TORRANCE.   If you did, I should just know that there
had been something wrong about me.

ROGER (*gruffly*).   You 're all right.

MR. TORRANCE.   If I am, you are.   (*It is a winning face
that* MR. TORRANCE *turns on his son.*)   I suppose you have been
asking yourself of late, what if you were to turn out to be
a funk !

ROGER.   How did you know ?

MR. TORRANCE.   I know because you are me. Because
ever since there was talk of this commission I have been thinking
and thinking what were you thinking—so as to help you.

(*This itself is a help.* ROGER'S *hand—but he withdraws
it hurriedly.*)

ROGER (*wistfully*).   They all seem to be so frightfully brave,
father.

MR. TORRANCE.   I expect that the best of them had the
same qualms as you before their first engagement.

ROGER.   I—I kind of think, father, that I won't be a funk.

MR. TORRANCE.   I kind of think so too, Roger. (MR.
TORRANCE *forgets himself.*)   Mind you don't be rash, my boy ;
and for God's sake, keep your head down in the trenches.

(ROGER *has caught him out.   He points a gay finger at his
anxious father.*)

ROGER.   You know you laughed at mother for saying that !

MR. TORRANCE.   Did I ?   Your mother thinks that I have
an unfortunate manner with you.

ROGER (*magnanimously*).   Oh, I don't know.   It 's just the
father-and-son complication.

MR. TORRANCE.   That is really all it is.   But she thinks I
should show my affection for you more openly.

ROGER (*wriggling again*).   I wouldn't do that.   Of course
for this once—but in a general way I wouldn't do that. *We*
know, you and I.

MR. TORRANCE.   As long as we know, it 's no one else's
affair, is it ?

ROGER.   That 's the ticket, father.

(*It is to be feared that* MR. TORRANCE *is now taking
advantage of his superior slyness.*)

MR. TORRANCE.   Still, before your mother—to please her—
eh ?

ROGER (*faltering*).   I suppose it would.

MR. TORRANCE.   Well, what do you say ?

ROGER.   I know she would like it.

MR. TORRANCE.   Of course you and I know that such
display is all bunkum—repellent even to our natures.

ROGER.   Lord, yes !

MR. TORRANCE.   But to gratify her ?

ROGER. I should be so conscious.

MR. TORRANCE. So should I.

ROGER (*considering it*). How far would you go?

MR. TORRANCE. Oh, not far. Suppose I called you 'Old Rogie'? There's not much in that.

ROGER. It all depends on the way one says these things.

MR. TORRANCE. I should be quite casual.

ROGER. Hum. What would you like me to call you?

MR. TORRANCE (*severely*). It isn't what would *I* like. But I dare say your mother would beam if you called me 'dear father.'

ROGER. I don't think so.

MR. TORRANCE. You know quite well that you think so, Roger.

ROGER. It's so effeminate.

MR. TORRANCE. Not if you say it casually.

ROGER (*with something very like a snort*). How does one say a thing like that casually?

MR. TORRANCE. Well, for instance, you could whistle while you said it—or anything of that sort.

ROGER. Hum. Of course you—if we were to—be like that, you wouldn't *do* anything.

MR. TORRANCE. How do you mean?

ROGER. You wouldn't paw me?

MR. TORRANCE (*with some natural indignation*). Roger! you forget yourself. (*But apparently it is for him to continue.*) That reminds me of a story I heard the other day of a French general. He had asked for volunteers from his airmen for some specially dangerous job—and they all stepped forward. Pretty good that. Then three were chosen and got their orders and saluted, and were starting off when he stopped them. 'Since when,' he said, 'have brave boys departing to the post of danger omitted to embrace their father?' They did it then. Good story?

ROGER (*lowering*). They were French.

MR. TORRANCE. Yes, I said so. Don't you think it's good?

ROGER. Why do you tell it to me?

MR. TORRANCE. Because it's a good story.

ROGER (*sternly*). You are sure that there is no other reason?

(MR. TORRANCE *tries to brazen it out, but he looks guilty.*) You know, father, that is barred.

(*Just because he knows that he has been playing it low,* MR. TORRANCE *snaps angrily.*)

MR. TORRANCE.   What is barred ?

ROGER.   You know.

MR. TORRANCE (*shouting*).   I know that you are a young ass.

ROGER.   Really, father——

MR. TORRANCE.   Hold your tongue.

(ROGER *can shout also.*)

ROGER.   I must say, father——

MR. TORRANCE.   Be quiet, I tell you.

(*It is in the middle of this competition that the lady who dotes on them both chooses to come back, still without her spectacles.*)

MRS. TORRANCE.   Oh dear ! And I had hoped—— Oh, John !

(MR. TORRANCE *would like to kick himself.*)

MR. TORRANCE.   My fault.

MRS. TORRANCE.   But whatever is the matter ?

ROGER.   Nothing, mater. (*The war is already making him quite clever.*) Only father wouldn't do as I told him.

MR. TORRANCE.   Why the dickens should I ?

(ROGER *is imperturbable ; this will be useful in France.*)

ROGER.   You see, mater, he said I was the head of the house.

MRS. TORRANCE.   You, Rogie ! (*She goes to her husband's side.*) What nonsense !

ROGER (*grinning*).   Do you like my joke, father ?

(*The father smiles upon him and is at once uproariously happy.   He digs his boy boldly in the ribs.*)

MR. TORRANCE.   Roger, you scoundrel !

MRS. TORRANCE.   That 's better.

ROGER (*feeling that things have perhaps gone far enough*).   I think I 'll go to my room now.   You will come up, mater ?

MRS. TORRANCE.   Yes, dear.   I shan't be five minutes, John.

MR. TORRANCE.   More like half an hour.

MRS. TORRANCE (*hesitating*).   There is nothing wrong, is there ?   I thought I noticed a—a——

MR. TORRANCE. A certain liveliness, my dear. No, we were only having a good talk.

MRS. TORRANCE. What about, John?

ROGER (*hurriedly*). About the war.

MR. TORRANCE. About tactics and strategy, wasn't it, Roger?

ROGER. Yes.

MR. TORRANCE. The fact is, Ellen, I have been helping Roger to take his first trench. (*With a big breath*) And we took it too, together, didn't we, Roger?

ROGER (*valiantly*). You bet.

MR. TORRANCE (*sighing*). Though I suppose it is one of those trenches that the enemy retake during the night.

ROGER. Oh, I—I don't know, father.

MRS. TORRANCE. Whatever are you two talking about?

MR. TORRANCE (*in high feather, patting her, but unable to resist a slight boast*). It is very private. *We* don't tell you everything, you know, Ellen.

(*She beams, though she does not understand.*)

ROGER. Come on, mater, it's only his beastly sarcasm again. 'Night, father; I won't see you in the morning.

MR. TORRANCE. 'Night.

(*But* ROGER *has not gone yet. He seems to be looking for something—a book, perhaps. Then he begins to whistle—casually.*)

ROGER. Good-night, dear father.

(MR. JOHN TORRANCE *is left alone, rubbing his hands.*)

A KISS FOR CINDERELLA

Produced at Wyndham's Theatre on March 16, 1916, with the following cast :

MR. BODIE	*O. B. Clarence*
OUR POLICEMAN	*Gerald du Maurier*
MISS THING	*Hilda Trevelyan*
MAN WITH A COAT . . .	*J. W. Macdonald*
MRS. MALONEY	*Alma Ellerslie*
A PROUD WIFE	*Elspeth Douglas Reid*
A COSTER	*Ernest Graham*
MARIE THÉRÈSE	*Violette Kemplen*
GLADYS	*Babs Farren*
DELPHINE	*Alma Bersey*
GRETCHEN	*Sunday Wilshin*
A GODMOTHER	*Stella Campbell*
LORD MAYOR	*Lyston Lyle*
LORD TIMES	*T. Gideon Warren*
THE CENSOR	*D. E. Jefferies*
A KING	*William Lugg*
A QUEEN	*Edith Johnston*
A PRINCE	*Gerald du Maurier*
A PAGE	*Master Ronald Hammond*
A PENGUIN	*F. Mortimer*
A MAID	*Beatrice Fitzgerald*
DOCTOR BRODIE	*Henrietta Watson*
DANNY	*A. E. George*
A PROBATIONER	*Elizabeth Pollock*

RIVALS : *Joan Challis, Esme Biddle, Helen Hamilton, Molly Kelly, Olive Royston, Archie Alban, Noel Barker, and Nan Wilcox.*

———

The play ran for 156 performances. There have been several Christmas revivals.

ACT I

THE least distinguished person in *Who's Who* has escaped, as it were, from that fashionable crush, and is spending a quiet evening at home.   He is curled up in his studio, which is so dark that he would be invisible, had we not obligingly placed his wicker chair just where the one dim ray from the stove may strike his face. His eyes are closed luxuriously, and we could not learn much about him without first poking our fingers into them.   According to the tome mentioned (to which we must return him before morning), Mr. Bodie is sixty-three, has exhibited in the Royal Academy, and is at present unmarried.   They do not proclaim him comparatively obscure : they left it indeed to him to say the final word on this subject, and he has hedged.   Let us put it in this way, that he occupies more space in his wicker chair than in the book, where nevertheless he looks as if it was rather lonely not to be a genius.   He is a painter for the nicest of reasons, that it is delightful to live and die in a messy studio ; for our part, we too should have become a painter had it not been that we always lost our paint-box.   There is no spirited bidding to acquire Mr. Bodie's canvases : he loves them at first sight himself, and has often got up in the night to see how they are faring ; but ultimately he has turned cold to them, and has even been known to offer them, in lieu of alms, to beggars, who departed cursing.   We have a weakness for persons who don't get on, and so cannot help adding, though it is no business of ours, that Mr. Bodie has private means. Curled up in his wicker chair he is benevolently somnolent. We wish we could warn him clandestinely that the policeman is coming.

The policeman comes : in his hand the weapon that has knocked down more malefactors than all the batons—the bull's-eye.   He strikes with it now, right and left, revealing, as if she had just entered the room, a replica of the Venus of Milo, taller than himself though he is a stalwart.   It is the first

877

meeting of these two, but, though a man who can come to the boil, he is as little moved by her as she by him. After the first glance she continues her reflections. Her smile over his head vaguely displeases him. For two pins he would arrest her.

The lantern finds another object, more worthy of his attention, the artist. Mr. Bodie is more restive under the light than was his goddess, perhaps because he is less accustomed to being stared at. He blinks and sits up.

MR. BODIE (*giving his visitor a lesson in manners*). I beg your pardon, officer.

POLICEMAN (*confounded*). Not that, sir ; not at all.

MR. BODIE (*pressing his advantage*). But I insist on begging your pardon, officer.

POLICEMAN. I don't see what for, sir.

MR. BODIE (*fancying himself*). For walking uninvited into the abode of a law-abiding London citizen, with whom I have not the pleasure of being acquainted.

POLICEMAN (*after thinking this out*). But I 'm the one as has done that, sir.

MR. BODIE (*with neat surprise*). So you are, I beg your pardon, officer.

(*With pardonable pride in himself* MR. BODIE *turns on the light. The studio, as we can now gather from its sloped roof, is at the top of a house ; and its window is heavily screened, otherwise we might see the searchlights through it, showing that we are in the period of the great war. Though no one speaks of* MR. BODIE'S *pictures as Bodies, which is the true test of fame, he is sufficiently eminent not to have works of art painted or scratched on his walls, mercy has been shown even to the panels of his door, and he is handsomely stingy of draperies. The Venus stands so prominent that the studio is evidently hers rather than his. The stove has been brought forward so that he can rest his feet on it, whichever of his easy chairs he is sitting in, and he also falls over it at times when stepping back to consider his latest failure. On a shelf is a large stuffed penguin, which is to be one of the characters in the play, and on each side of this shelf are two or three tattered magazines. We had hankered after giving* MR. BODIE *many rows of books, but were well aware that he would get only blocks of wood so cleverly painted to look like books that they would deceive every one except the audience. Everything may be real on the stage except the books. So there are only a few magazines in the studio (and very likely when the curtain rings up it will be found that they are painted too). But* MR. BODIE *was a reader ; he had books in another room, and the careworn actor who plays him must suggest this by his manner.*

Our POLICEMAN *is no bookman ; we who write happen to have it from himself that he had not bought a book since he squeezed through the sixth standard : very tight was his waist that day, he told us, and he had to let out every button. Nevertheless it was literature of a sort that first brought him into our ken. He was our local constable : and common interests, as in the vagaries of the moon in war-time, made him and us cease to look at each other askance. We fell into the way of chatting with him and giving him the evening papers we had bought to read as we crossed the streets. One of his duties was to herd the vagrant populace under our arches during air-raids, and at such times he could be properly gruff, yet comforting, like one who would at once run in any bomb that fell in his beat. When he had all his flock nicely plastered against the dank walls he would occasionally come to rest beside us, and thaw, and discuss the newspaper article that had interested him most. It was seldom a war-record ; more frequently it was something on the magazine page, such as a symposium by the learned on ' Do you Believe in Love at First Sight ? ' Though reticent in many matters he would face this problem openly ; with the guns cracking all around, he would ask for our views wistfully ; he spoke of love without a blush, as something recognised officially at Scotland Yard. At this time he had been in love, to his own knowledge, for several weeks, but whether the god had struck him at first sight he was not certain ; he was most anxious to know, and it was in the hope of our being able to help him out that he told us his singular story. On his face at such times was often an amazed look, as if he were staring at her rather than at us, and seeing a creature almost beyond belief. Our greatest success was in saying that perhaps she had fallen in love at first sight with him, which on reflection nearly doubled him up. He insisted on knowing what had made us put forward this extraordinary suggestion ; he would indeed scarcely leave our company that night, and discussed the possibility with us very much as if it were a police case.*

Our POLICEMAN's *romance, now to be told, began, as we begin, with his climbing up into* MR. BODIE's *studio.* MR. BODIE *having turned on the light gave him the nasty look that means ' And now, my man, what can I do for you ? ' Our* POLICEMAN, *however, was not one to be worsted without striking a blow. He strode to the door, as he has told us, and pointed to a light in the passage.*)

POLICEMAN (*in his most brow-beating voice, so well known under the arches*). Look here, sir, it 's that.

MR. BODIE. I don't follow.

POLICEMAN. Look at that passage window. (*With natural pride in language*) You are showing too much illumination.

BODIE. Oh ! well, surely——

POLICEMAN (*with professional firmness*). It 's agin the regulations. A party in the neighbouring skylight complains.

BODIE (*putting out the light*). If that will do for to-night, I 'll have the window boarded up.

POLICEMAN. Anything so long as it obscures the illumination.

BODIE (*irritated*). Shuts out the light.

POLICEMAN (*determinedly*). Obscures the illumination.

BODIE (*on reflection*). I remember now, I did have that window boarded up.

POLICEMAN (*who has himself a pretty vein of sarcasm*). I don't see the boards.

BODIE. Nor do I see the boards. (*Pondering*) Can she have boned them ?

POLICEMAN. She ? (*He is at once aware that it has become a more difficult case.*)

BODIE. You are right. She is scrupulously honest, and if she took the boards we may be sure that I said she could have them. But that only adds to the mystery.

POLICEMAN (*obligingly*). Mystery ?

BODIE. Why this passion for collecting boards? Try her with a large board, officer. Extraordinary!

POLICEMAN (*heavily*). I don't know what you are talking about, sir. Are you complaining of some woman?

BODIE. Now that is the question. Am I? As you are here, officer, there is something I want to say to you. But I should dislike getting her into trouble.

POLICEMAN (*stoutly*). No man what is a man wants to get a woman into trouble unnecessary.

BODIE (*much struck*). That's true! That's *absolutely* true, officer.

POLICEMAN (*badgered*). It's true, but there's nothing remarkable about it.

BODIE. Excuse me.

POLICEMAN. See here, sir, I'm just an ordinary policeman.

BODIE. I can't let that pass. If I may say so, you have impressed me most deeply. I wonder if I might ask a favour of you. Would you mind taking off your helmet? As it happens, I have never seen a policeman without his helmet.

(*The perplexed officer puts his helmet on the table.*) Thank you. (*Studying the effect*) Of course I knew they took off. You sit also?

(*The* POLICEMAN *sits.*) Very interesting.

POLICEMAN. About this woman, sir——

BODIE. We are coming to her. Perhaps I ought to tell you my name—Mr. Bodie. (*Indicating the Venus*) This is Mrs. Bodie. No, I am not married. It is merely a name given her because she is my ideal.

POLICEMAN. You gave me a turn.

BODIE. Now that I think of it, I believe the name was given to her by the very woman we are talking about.

POLICEMAN (*producing his note-book*). To begin with, who is the woman we are talking about?

BODIE (*becoming more serious*). On the surface, she is just a little drudge. These studios are looked after by a house-keeper, who employs this girl to do the work.

POLICEMAN. H'm! Sleeps on the premises?

BODIE. No; she is here from eight to six.

POLICEMAN. Place of abode?

BODIE. She won't tell any one that.

POLICEMAN. Aha ! What 's the party's name ?

BODIE. Cinderella.

(*The* POLICEMAN *writes it down unmoved.* MR. BODIE *twinkles.*)
Haven't you heard that name before ?

POLICEMAN. Can't say I have, sir. But I 'll make inquiries at the Yard.

BODIE. It was really I who gave her that name, because she seemed such a poor little neglected waif. After the girl in the story-book, you know.

POLICEMAN. No, sir, I don't know. In the Force we find it impossible to keep up with current fiction.

BODIE. She was a girl with a broom. There must have been more in the story than that, but I forget the rest.

POLICEMAN. The point is, that 's not the name she calls herself by ?

BODIE. Yes, indeed it is. I think she was called something else when she came—Miss Thing, or some such name ; but she took to the name of Cinderella with avidity, and now she absolutely denies that she ever had any other.

POLICEMAN. Parentage ?

BODIE (*now interested in his tale*). That 's another odd thing. I seem to remember vaguely her telling me that her parents when alive were very humble persons indeed. Touch of Scotch about her, I should say—perhaps from some distant ancestor ; but Scotch words and phrases still stick to the Cockney child like bits of egg-shell to a chicken.

POLICEMAN (*writing*). Egg-shell to chicken.

BODIE. I find, however, that she has lately been telling the housekeeper quite a different story.

POLICEMAN (*like a counsel*). Proceed.

BODIE. According to this, her people were of considerable position—a Baron and Baroness, in fact.

POLICEMAN. Proceed.

BODIE. The only other relatives she seems to have mentioned are two sisters of unprepossessing appearance.

POLICEMAN (*cleverly*). If this story is correct, what is she doing here ?

BODIE. I understand there is something about her father

having married again, and her being badly treated. She doesn't expect this to last. It seems that she has reason to believe that some very remarkable change may take place in her circumstances at an early date, at a ball for which her godmother is to get her what she calls an invite. This is evidently to be a very swagger function at which something momentous is to occur, the culminating moment being at midnight.

POLICEMAN (*writing*). Godmother. Invite. Twelve P.M. Fishy ! Tell me about them boards now.

BODIE (*who is evidently fond of the child*). You can't think how wistful she is to get hold of boards. She has them on the brain. Carries them off herself into the unknown.

POLICEMAN. I dare say she breaks them up for firewood.

BODIE. No ; she makes them into large boxes.

POLICEMAN (*sagaciously*). Very likely to keep things in.

BODIE. She has admitted that she keeps things in them. But what things ? Ask her that, and her mouth shuts like a trap.

POLICEMAN. Any suspicions ?

(MR. BODIE *hesitates. It seems absurd to suspect this waif —and yet !*)

BODIE. I 'm sorry to say I have. I don't know what the things are, but I do know they are connected in some way with Germany.

POLICEMAN (*darkly*). Proceed.

BODIE (*really troubled*). Officer, she is too curious about Germany.

POLICEMAN. That 's bad.

BODIE. She plies me with questions about it—not openly—very cunningly.

POLICEMAN. Such as—— ?

BODIE. For instance, what would be the punishment for an English person caught hiding aliens in this country ?

POLICEMAN. If she 's up to games of that kind——

BODIE. Does that shed any light on the boxes, do you think ?

POLICEMAN. She can't keep them shut up in boxes.

BODIE. I don't know. She is extraordinarily dogged. She knows a number of German words.

POLICEMAN. That 's ugly.

BODIE. She asked me lately how one could send a letter to

Germany without Lord Haig knowing. By the way, do you, by any chance, know anything against a firm of dressmakers called *Celeste et Cie* ?

POLICEMAN.   Celest A. C. ? No, but it has a German sound.

BODIE.   It 's French.

POLICEMAN.   Might be a blind.

BODIE.   I think she lives at Celeste's. Now I looked up Celeste et Cie in the telephone book, and I find they are in Bond Street. Immensely fashionable.

POLICEMAN.   She lives in Bond Street ? London 's full of romance, sir, to them as knows where to look for it—namely, the police. Is she on the premises ?

BODIE (*reluctantly*).   Sure to be ; it isn't six yet.

POLICEMAN (*in his most terrible voice*).   Well, leave her to me.

BODIE.   You mustn't frighten her. I can't help liking her. She 's so extraordinarily *homely* that you can't be with her many minutes before you begin thinking of your early days. Where were you born, officer ?

POLICEMAN.   I 'm from Badgery.

BODIE.   She 'll make you think of Badgery.

POLICEMAN (*frowning*).   She had best try no games on me.

BODIE.   She will have difficulty in answering questions ; she is so used to asking them. I never knew a child with such an appetite for information. She doesn't search for it in books ; indeed the only book of mine I can remember ever seeing her read, was a volume of fairy tales.

POLICEMAN (*stupidly*).   Well, that don't help us much. What kind of questions ?

BODIE.   Every kind. What is the Censor ? Who is Lord *Times* ?—she has heard people here talking of that paper and its proprietor, and has mixed them up in the quaintest way ; then again—when a tailor measures a gentleman's legs what does he mean when he says—26, 4—32, 11 ? What are doctors up to when they tell you to say 99 ? In finance she has an almost morbid interest in the penny.

POLICEMAN.   The penny ? It 's plain the first thing to find out is whether she 's the slavey she seems to be, or a swell in disguise.

BODIE. You won't find it so easy.

POLICEMAN. Excuse me, sir ; we have an infall*ay*ble way at Scotland Yard of finding out whether a woman is common or a lady.

BODIE (*irritated*). An infallible way.

POLICEMAN (*firmly*). Infallayble.

BODIE. I should like to know what it is.

POLICEMAN. There is nothing against my telling you. (*He settles down to a masterly cross-examination.*) Where, sir, does a common female keep her valuables when she carries them about on her person ?

BODIE. In her pocket, I suppose.

POLICEMAN. And you suppose correctly. But where does a lady keep them ?

BODIE. In the same place, I suppose.

POLICEMAN. There you suppose wrongly. No, sir, here. (*He taps his own chest, and indicates discreetly how a lady may pop something down out of sight.*)

BODIE (*impressed*). I believe you are right, officer.

POLICEMAN. I am right—it 's infallayble. A lady, what with drink and suchlike misfortunes, may forget all her other refinements, but she never forgets that. At the Yard it 's considered as sure as finger-marks.

BODIE. Strange ! I wonder who was the first woman to do it. It couldn't have been Eve this time, officer.

POLICEMAN (*after reflecting*). I see your point. And now I want just to have a look at the party unbeknownst to her. Where could I conceal myself ?

BODIE. Hide ?

POLICEMAN. Conceal myself.

BODIE. That small door opens on to my pantry, where she washes up.

POLICEMAN (*peeping in*). It will do. Now bring her up.

BODIE. It doesn't seem fair—I really can't——

POLICEMAN. War-time, sir.

(MR. BODIE *decides that it is patriotic to ring. The* POLICEMAN *emerges from the pantry with a slavey's hat and jacket.*)

These belong to the party, sir ?

BODIE. I forgot. She keeps them in there. (*He surveys*

the articles with some emotion.) Gaudy feathers. And yet that hat may have done some gallant things. The brave apparel of the very poor ! Who knows, officer, that you and I are not at this moment on rather holy ground.

POLICEMAN (*stoutly*). I see nothing wrong with the feathers. I must say, sir, I like the feathers.

(*He slips into the pantry with the hat and jacket, but forgets his helmet, over which the artist hastily jams a flower bowl. There were visiting-cards in the bowl and they are scattered on the floor.* MR. BODIE *sees them not : it is his first attempt at the conspirator, and he sits guiltily with a cigarette just in time to deceive* CINDERELLA, *who charges into the room as from a catapult. This is her usual mode of entrance, and is owing to her desire to give satisfaction. Our* POLICEMAN, *as he has told us under the arches, was watching her through the keyhole, but his first impressions have been so coloured by subsequent events that it is questionable whether they would be accepted in any court of law. Is prepared to depose that, to the best of his recollection, they were unfavourable. Does not imply by unfavourable any aspersion on her personal appearance. Would accept the phrase ' far from striking ' as summing up her first appearance. Would no longer accept the phrase. Had put her down as being a grown woman, but not sufficiently grown. Thought her hair looked to be run up her finger. Did not like this way of doing the hair. Could not honestly say that she seemed even then to be an ordinary slavey of the areas. She was dressed as one, but was suspiciously clean. On the other hand, she had the genuine hungry look. Among more disquieting features noticed a sort of refinement in her voice and manner, which was characteristic of the criminal classes. Knew now that this was caused by the reading of fairy tales and the thinking of noble thoughts. Noted speedily that she was a domineering character who talked sixteen to the dozen, and at such times reminded him of funny old ladies. Was much struck by her eyes, which seemed to suggest that she was all burning inside. This impression was strengthened later when he touched her hands. Felt at once the curious ' homeliness ' of her, as commented on by* MR. BODIE, *but could swear on oath that this had not at once made him think of Badgery. Could recall not the slightest symptoms of love at first sight On the contrary, listened carefully to the conversation between her and MR. BODIE and formed a stern conclusion about her. Believed that this was all he could say about his first impression.)*

CINDERELLA (*breathlessly*).   Did you rang, sir ?

BODIE (*ashamed*).   Did I ?   I did—but—I—I don't know why.   If you 're a good servant, you ought to know why.

(*The cigarette, disgusted with him, falls from his mouth ; and his little servant flings up her hands to heaven.*)

CINDERELLA (*taking possession of him*).   There you go again ! Fifty years have you been at it, and you can't hold a seegarette in your mouth yet !   (*She sternly produces the turpentine.*)

BODIE (*in sudden alarm*).   I won't be brushed.   I will not be scraped.

CINDERELLA (*twisting him round*).   Just look at that tobaccy ash !   And I cleaned you up so pretty before luncheon.

BODIE.   I will *not* be cleaned again.

CINDERELLA (*in her element*).   Keep still.

(*She brushes, scrapes, and turpentines him.   In the glory of this she tosses her head at the Venus.*)

I gave Mrs. Bodie a good wipe down this morning with soap and water.

BODIE (*indignant*).   That is a little too much.   You know quite well I allow no one to touch her.

(CINDERELLA *leaves him and gazes in irritation at the statue.*)

CINDERELLA.   What *is* it about the woman ?

BODIE (*in his heat forgetting the* POLICEMAN).   She is the glory of glories.

CINDERELLA (*who would be willowy if she were long enough*). She 's thick.

BODIE.   Her measurements are perfection.   All women long to be like her, but none ever can be.

CINDERELLA (*insisting*).   I suppose that 's the reason she has that snigger on her face.

BODIE.   That is perhaps the smile of motherhood.   Some people think there was once a baby in her arms.

CINDERELLA (*with a new interest in Venus*).   Her own ?

BODIE.   I suppose so.

CINDERELLA.   A married woman then ?

BODIE (*nonplussed*).   Don't ask trivial questions.

CINDERELLA (*generously*).   It was clever of you to make her.

BODIE.   I didn't make her.   I was—forestalled.   Some other artist chappie did it.   (*He likes his little maid again.*)   She was dug up, Cinderella, after lying hidden in the ground for more than a thousand years.

CINDERELLA.   And the baby gone ?

BODIE (*snapping*).   Yes.

CINDERELLA.   If I had lost my baby I wouldn't have been found with that pleased look on my face, not in a thousand years.

BODIE.   Her arms were broken, you see, so she had to drop the baby——

CINDERELLA.   She could have up with her knee and catched it.

BODIE (*excitedly*).   By heavens, that may just be what she is doing.   (*He contemplates a letter to the ' Times.'*)

CINDERELLA (*little aware that she may have solved the question of the ages.*)   Beauty 's a grand thing.

BODIE.   It is.

CINDERELLA.   I warrant *she* led them a pretty dance in her day.

BODIE.   Men ?

CINDERELLA.   Umpha !   (*Wistfully.*)   It must be fine to have men so mad about you that they go off their feed and roar.   (*She turns with a sigh to the dusting of the penguin.*)   What did you say this is ?

BODIE (*ignorant of what he is letting himself in for*).   A bishop.

CINDERELLA (*nearly choking*).   The sort that marries swell couples ?

BODIE.   Yes.

CINDERELLA (*huskily, as if it made all the difference to her*).   I never thought of that.

BODIE (*kindly*).   Why should you, you queer little waif.   Do you know why I call you Cinderella ?

CINDERELLA.   Fine, I know.

BODIE. Why is it?

CINDERELLA (*with shy happiness*). It's because I have such pretty feet.

BODIE. You dear little innocent. (*He thinks shame of his suspicions. He is planning how to get rid of the man in the pantry when she brings him back to hard facts with a bump.*)

CINDERELLA (*in a whisper*). Mr. Bodie, if you wanted to get into Buckingham Palace on the dodge, how would you slip by the policeman? (*She wrings her hands.*) The police is everywhere in war-time.

BODIE (*conscious how near one of them is*). They are—be careful, Cinderella.

CINDERELLA. I am—oh, I am! If you knew the precautions I'm taking——

BODIE (*miserable*). Sh!

CINDERELLA (*now in a quiver*). Mr. Bodie, you haven't by any chance got an invite for to-night, have you?

BODIE. What for?

CINDERELLA (*as still as the Venus*). For—for a ball.

BODIE. There are no balls in war-time.

CINDERELLA (*dogged*). Just the one. Mr. Bodie, did you ever see the King?

BODIE. The King? Several times.

CINDERELLA (*as white as the Venus*). Was the Prince of Wales with him?

BODIE. Once.

CINDERELLA. What's he like?

BODIE. Splendid! Quite young, you know. He's not married.

CINDERELLA (*with awful intensity*). No, not yet.

BODIE. I suppose he is very difficult to satisfy.

CINDERELLA (*knitting her lips*). He has never seen the feet that pleased him.

BODIE. Cinderella, your pulse is galloping. You frighten me. What possesses you?

CINDERELLA (*after hesitating*). There is something I want to tell you. Maybe I'll not be coming back after to-night. She has paid me up to to-night.

BODIE. Is she sending you away?

CINDERELLA. No. I've sort of given notice.

BODIE (*disappointed*).   You 've got another place ?
(*She shuts her mouth like a box.*)
Has it anything to do with the Godmother business ?
(*Her mouth remains closed.   He barks at her.*)
Don't, then.   (*He reconsiders her.*)   I like you, you know.
CINDERELLA (*gleaming*).   It 's fine to be liked.
BODIE.   Have you a lonely life ?
CINDERELLA.   It 's kind of lonely.
BODIE.   You won't tell me about your home ?
(*She shakes her head.*)
Is there any nice person to look after you in the sort of way in which you look after me ?
CINDERELLA.   I 'm all alone.   There 's just me and my feet.
BODIE.   If you go I 'll miss you.   We 've had some good times here, Cinderella, haven't we ?
CINDERELLA (*rapturously*).   We have !   You mind that chop you gave me ?   Hey, hey, hey !   (*Considering it judicially.*) That was the most charming chop I ever saw.   And many is the lick of soup you 've given me when you thought I looked down-like.   Do you mind the chicken that was too high for you ?   You give me the whole chicken.   That was a day.
BODIE.   I never meant you to eat it.
CINDERELLA.   I didn't eat it all myself.   I shared it with them.
BODIE (*inquisitively*).   With them ?   With whom ?
(*Her mouth shuts promptly, and he sulks.   She picks up the visiting-cards that litter the floor.*)
CINDERELLA.   What a spill !   If you 're not messing you 're spilling.   Where 's the bowl ?
(*She lifts the bowl and discovers the helmet.   She is appalled.*)
BODIE (*in an agony of remorse pointing to the door*).   Cinderella, quick !
(*But our POLICEMAN has emerged and barred the way.*)
POLICEMAN (*indicating that it is MR. BODIE who must go*).   If *you* please, sir.
BODIE.   I won't !   Don't you dare to frighten her.
POLICEMAN (*settling the matter with the palm of his hand*). That will do.   If I need you I 'll call you.

BODIE (*flinching*).   Cinderella, it's—it's just a form.   I won't be far away.

> (*He departs reluctantly.*)

POLICEMAN (*sternly*).   Stand up.

CINDERELLA (*a quaking figure, who has not sat down*).   I'm standing up.

POLICEMAN.   Now, no sauce.

> (*He produces his note-book.   He is about to make a powerful beginning when he finds her eyes regarding the middle of his person.*)

Now then, what are you staring at ?

CINDERELLA (*hotly*).   That's a poor way to polish a belt. If I was a officer I would think shame of having my belt in that condition.

POLICEMAN (*undoubtedly affected by her homeliness though unconscious of it*).   It's easy to speak ; it's a miserable polish I admit, but mind you, I'm pretty done when my job's over ; and I have the polishing to do myself.

CINDERELLA.   You have no woman person ?

POLICEMAN.   Not me.

CINDERELLA (*with passionate arms*).   If I had that belt for half an hour !

POLICEMAN.   What would you use ?

CINDERELLA.   Spit.

POLICEMAN.   Spit ?   That's like what my mother would have said.   That was in Badgery, where I was born.   When I was a boy at Badgery——

> (*He stops short.   She has reminded him of Badgery !*)

CINDERELLA.   What's wrong ?

POLICEMAN (*heavily*).   How did you manage that about Badgery ?

CINDERELLA.   What ?

POLICEMAN.   Take care, prisoner.

> (*The word makes her shudder.   He sits, prepared to take notes.*)

Name ?

CINDERELLA.   Cinderella.

POLICEMAN.   Take care, Thing.   Occupation, if any ?

CINDERELLA (*with some pride*).   Tempary help.

POLICEMAN.   Last place ?

CINDERELLA.   3 Robert Street.

POLICEMAN.   Scotch?

(*Her mouth shuts.*)

Ah, they 'll never admit that.   Reason for leaving?

CINDERELLA.   I had to go when the war broke out.

POLICEMAN.   Why dismissed?

CINDERELLA (*forlorn*).   They said I was a luxury.

POLICEMAN (*getting ready to pounce*).   Now be cautious. How do you spend your evenings after you leave this building?

(*Her mouth shuts.*)

Have you another and secret occupation?

(*She blanches.*)

Has it to do with boxes?   What do you keep in those boxes? Where is it that these goings-on is going on?   If you won't tell me, I 'm willing to tell you.   It 's at A. C. Celest's . . . In Bond Street, W.

(*He has levelled his finger at her, but it is a pistol that does not go off.   To his chagrin she looks relieved.   He tries hammer blows.*)

Are you living in guilty splendour?   How do you come to know German words?   How many German words do you think *I* know?   Just one, *espionage*.   What 's the German for ' six months hard '?

(*She is now crumpled, and here he would do well to pause and stride up and down the room.   But he cannot leave well alone.*)

What 's this nonsense about your feet?

CINDERELLA (*plucking up courage*).   It 's not nonsense.

POLICEMAN.   I see nothing particular about your feet.

CINDERELLA.   Then I 'm sorry for you.

POLICEMAN.   What is it?

CINDERELLA (*softly as if it were a line from the Bible*).   Their exquisite smallness and perfect shape.

POLICEMAN (*with a friendly glance at the Venus*).   For my part, I 'm partial to big women with their noses in the air.

CINDERELLA (*stung*).   So is everybody.   (*Pathetically*) I 've tried.   But it 's none so easy, with never no butcher's meat in the house.   You 'll see where the su-perb shoulders and the haughty manners come from if you look in shop windows and see the whole of a cow turned inside out and ' Delicious ' printed on it.

POLICEMAN (*always just*).   There's something in that.

CINDERELLA (*swelling*).   But it doesn't matter how fine the rest of you is if you doesn't have small feet.

POLICEMAN.   I never give feet a thought.

CINDERELLA.   The swells think of nothing else. (*Exploding*) Wait till you are at the ball.   Many a haughty beauty with superb uppers will come sailing in—as sure of the prize as if ' Delicious ' was pinned on her—and then forward steps the Lord Mayor, and, *utterly disregarding her uppers,* he points to the bottom of her skirt, and he says ' Lift ! ' and she *has* to lift, and there's a dead silence, and nothing to be heard except the Prince crying ' Throw her out ! '

POLICEMAN (*somewhat staggered by her knowledge of the high life*).   What's all this about a ball ?

(CINDERELLA *sees she has said too much and her mouth shuts.*)

Was you ever at a ball ?

CINDERELLA (*with dignity*).   At any rate I've been at the Horse Show.

POLICEMAN.   A ball's not like a horse show.

CINDERELLA.   You'll see.

POLICEMAN (*reverting to business*).   It all comes to this, are you genteel, or common clay ?

CINDERELLA (*pertly*).   I leaves that to you.

POLICEMAN.   You couldn't leave it in safer hands.   I want a witness to this.

CINDERELLA (*startled*).   A witness !   What are you to do ?

(*With terrible self-confidence he has already opened the door and beckoned.*   MR. BODIE *comes in anxiously.*)

POLICEMAN.   Take note, sir. (*With the affable manner of an Inspector*) We are now about to try a little experiment, the object being to discover whether this party is genteel or common clay.

CINDERELLA.   Oh, Mr. Bodie, what is it ?

BODIE (*remembering what he has been told of the Scotland Yard test*).   I don't like . . . I won't have it.

POLICEMAN.   It gives her the chance of proving once and for all whether she's of gentle blood.

CINDERELLA (*eagerly*).   Does it ?

BODIE.   I must forbid . . .

CINDERELLA (*with dreadful resolution*). I 'm ready. I wants to know myself.

POLICEMAN. *Ve*—ry well. Now then, I heard you say that the old party downstairs had paid you your wages to-day.

CINDERELLA. I see nothing you can prove by that. It was a half-week's wages—1s. 7d. Of course I could see my way clearer if it had been 1s. 9d.

POLICEMAN. That 's neither here nor there. We 'll proceed. Now, very likely you wrapped the money up in a screw of paper. Did you ?

(*She is afraid of giving herself away.*)
Thinking won't help you.

CINDERELLA. It 's *my* money.

BODIE. Nobody wants your money, Cinderella.

POLICEMAN. Answer me. Did you ?

CINDERELLA. Yes.

POLICEMAN. Say ' I did.'

CINDERELLA. I did.

POLICEMAN. And possibly for the sake of greater security you tied a string round it—did you ?

CINDERELLA. I did.

POLICEMAN (*after a glance at* MR. BODIE *to indicate that the supreme moment has come*). You then deposited the little parcel—where ?

BODIE (*in an agony*). Cinderella, be careful !

(*She is so dreading to do the wrong thing that she can only stare. Finally, alas, she produces the fatal packet from her pocket. Quiet triumph of our* POLICEMAN.)

BODIE. My poor child !

CINDERELLA (*not realising yet that she has given herself away*). What is it ? Go on.

POLICEMAN. That 'll do. You can stand down.

CINDERELLA. You 've found out ?

POLICEMAN. I have.

CINDERELLA (*breathless*). And what am I ?

POLICEMAN (*kindly*). I 'm sorry.

CINDERELLA. Am I—common clay ?

(*They look considerately at the floor ; she bursts into tears and runs into the pantry, shutting the door.*)

POLICEMAN (*with melancholy satisfaction*). It 's infallayble.

BODIE. At any rate it shows that there 's nothing against her.

POLICEMAN (*taking him further from the pantry door, in a low voice*). I dunno. There 's some queer things. Where does she go when she leaves this house ? What about that ball ?— and her German connection ?—and them boards she makes into boxes—and A. C. Celest ? Well, I 'll find out.

BODIE (*miserably*). What are you going to do ?

POLICEMAN. To track her when she leaves here. I may have to adopt a disguise. I 'm a masterpiece at that.

BODIE. Yes, but——

POLICEMAN (*stamping about the floor with the exaggerated tread of the Law*). I 'll tell you the rest outside. I must make her think that my suspicions are—allayed. (*He goes cunningly to the pantry door and speaks in a loud voice.*) Well, sir, that satisfies me that she is not the party I was in search of, and so, with your permission, I 'll bid you good evening. What, you 're going out yourself ? Then I 'll be very happy to walk part of the way with you.

(*Nodding and winking, he goes off with heavy steps, taking with him the reluctant* MR. BODIE, *who like one mesmerised also departs stamping.*

MISS THING *peeps out to make sure that they are gone. She is wearing her hat and jacket, which have restored her self-respect. The tears have been disposed of with a lick of the palm. She is again a valiant soul who has had too many brushes with the police not to be able to face another with a tight lip. She is going, but she is not going without her wooden board ; law or no law she cannot do without wooden boards. She gets it from a corner where it has been artfully concealed. An imprudent glance at the Venus again dispirits her. With a tape she takes the Beauty's measurements and then her own, with depressing results. The Gods at last pity her, and advise an examination of her rival's foot. Excursions, alarms, transport. She compares feet and is glorified. She slips off her shoe and challenges Venus to put it on. Then, with a derisive waggle of her foot at the shamed goddess, the little enigma departs on her suspicious business, little witting that a masterpiece of a constable is on her track.*)

ACT II

It is later in the evening of the same day, and this is such a street as harbours London's poor. The windows are so close to us that we could tap on the only one which shows a light. It is on the ground floor, and makes a gallant attempt to shroud this light with articles of apparel suspended within. Seen as shadows through the blind, these are somehow very like Miss Thing, and almost suggest that she has been hanging herself in several places in one of her bouts of energy. The street is in darkness, save for the meagre glow from a street lamp, whose glass is painted red in obedience to war regulations. It is winter time, and there is a sprinkling of snow on the ground.

Our policeman appears in the street, not perhaps for the first time this evening, and flashes his lantern on the suspect's window, whose signboard (boards again !) we now see bears this odd device,

Celeste et Cie.

The Penny Friend.

Not perhaps for the first time this evening he scratches his head at it. Then he pounds off in pursuit of some client who has just emerged with a pennyworth. We may imagine the two of them in conversation in the next street, the law putting leading questions. Meanwhile the 'fourth' wall of the establishment of Celeste dissolves, but otherwise the street is as it was, and we are now in the position of privileged persons looking in at her window. It is a tiny room in which you could just swing a cat, and here Cinderella swings cats all and every evening. The chief pieces of furniture are a table and a bench, both of which have a suspicious appearance of having been made out of boards by some handy character. There is a penny in the slot fireplace which has evidently been lately fed, there is a piece of carpet that has been beaten into nothingness, but is still a carpet, there is a hearth-rug of brilliant rags that is probably

896

gratified when your toes catch in it and you are hurled against the wall. Two pictures—one of them partly framed—strike a patriotic note, but they may be there purposely to deceive. The room is lit by a lamp, and at first sight presents no sinister aspect unless it comes from four boxes nailed against the walls some five or six feet from the floor. In appearance they are not dissimilar to large grocery boxes, but it is disquieting to note that one of them has been mended with the board we saw lately in Mr. Bodie's studio. When our policeman comes, as come we may be sure he will, the test of his acumen will be his box action.

The persons in the room at present have either no acumen or are familiar with the boxes. There are four of them, besides Cinderella, whom we catch in the act of adding to her means of livelihood. Celeste et Cie, a name that has caught her delicate fancy while she dashed through fashionable quarters, is the Penny Friend because here everything is dispensed for that romantic coin. It is evident that the fame of the emporium has spread. Three would-be customers sit on the bench awaiting their turn listlessly and as genteelly unconscious of each other as society in a dentist's dining-room, while in the centre is Cinderella fitting an elderly gentleman with a new coat. There are pins in her mouth and white threads in the coat, suggesting that this is not her first struggle with it, and one of the difficulties with which she has to contend is that it has already evidently been the coat of a larger man. Cinderella is far too astute a performer to let it be seen that she has difficulties, however. She twists and twirls her patron with careless aptitude, kneads him if need be, and has him in a condition of pulp while she mutters for her own encouragement and his intimidation the cryptic remarks employed by tailors, as to the exact meaning of which she has already probed Mr. Bodie.

CINDERELLA (*wandering over her client with a tape*). 35—14. (*She consults a paper on the table.*) Yes, it's 35—14. (*She pulls him out, contracts him and takes his elbows measure.*)

28—7 ; 41—12 ; 15—19. (*There is something wrong, and she has to justify her handiwork.*) You was longer when you came on Monday.

2 F

GENTLEMAN (*very moved by the importance of the occasion*). Don't be saying that, Missy.

CINDERELLA (*pinning up the tails of his coat*).   Keep still.

GENTLEMAN (*with unexpected spirit*).   I warns you, Missy, I won't have it cut.

CINDERELLA (*an artist*).   I 'll give you the bits.

GENTLEMAN.   I prefers to wear them.

(*She compares the coat with the picture of an elegant dummy.*)

Were you going to make me like that picture?

CINDERELLA.   I had just set my heart on copying this one. It 's the Volupty.

GENTLEMAN (*faint-hearted*).   I 'm thinkin' I couldn't stand like that man.

CINDERELLA (*eagerly*).   Fine you could—with just a little practice.   I 'll let you see the effect.

(*She bends one of his knees, extends an arm and curves the other till he looks like a graceful teapot.   She puts his stick in one hand and his hat in the other, and he is now coquettishly saluting a lady.*)

GENTLEMAN (*carried away as he looks at himself in a glass*). By Gosh!   Cut away, Missy!

CINDERELLA.   I 'll need one more try-on.   (*Suddenly*) That 's to say if I 'm here.

GENTLEMAN (*little understanding the poignancy of the remark*).   If it would be convenient to you to have the penny now——

CINDERELLA.   No, not till I 've earned it.   It 's my rule. Good-night to you, Mr. Jennings.

GENTLEMAN.   Good-night, Missy.

(*We see him go out by the door and disappear up the street.*)

CINDERELLA (*sharply*).   Next.

(*An old woman comes to the table and* CINDERELLA *politely pretends not to have seen her sitting there.*)

It 's Mrs. Maloney!

MRS. M.   Cinders, I have a pain.   It 's like a jag of a needle down my side.

CINDERELLA (*with a sigh, for she is secretly afraid of medical cases*).   Wait till I pop the therm-mo-mometer in.   It 's a real one.   (*She says this with legitimate pride.   She removes the instrument from* MRS. MALONEY'S *mouth after a prudent interval, and is not certain what to do next.*)

Take a deep breath. . . . Again. . . . Say 99. (*Her ear is against the patient's chest.*)

MRS. M. 99.

CINDERELLA (*at a venture*). Oho !

MRS. M. It ain't there the pain is—it 's down my side.

CINDERELLA (*firmly*). We never say 99 down there.

MRS. M. What 's wrong wi' me ?

CINDERELLA (*candidly*). I don't want for to pretend, Mrs. Maloney, that the 99 is any guidance to me. I can *not* find out what it 's for. I would make so bold as to call your complaint muscular rheumatics if the pain came when you coughed. But you have no cough.

MRS. M. (*coming to close quarters*). No, but he has—my old man. It 's him that has the pains, not me.

CINDERELLA (*hurt*). What for did you pretend it was you ?

MRS. M. That was his idea. He was feared you might stop his smoking.

CINDERELLA. And so I will.

MRS. M. What 's the treatment ?

CINDERELLA (*writing after consideration on a piece of paper*). One of them mustard leaves.

MRS. M. (*taking the paper*). Is there no medicine ?

CINDERELLA (*faltering*). I 'm a little feared about medicine, Mrs. Maloney.

MRS. M. He 'll be a kind of low-spirited if there 's not a lick of medicine.

CINDERELLA. Have you any in the house ?

MRS. M. There 's what was left over of the powders my lodger had when the kettle fell on his foot.

CINDERELLA. You could give him one of them when the cough is troublesome. Good-night, Mrs. Maloney.

MRS. M. Thank you kindly. (*She puts a penny on the table.*)

CINDERELLA (*with polite surprise*). What 's that ?

MRS. M. It 's the penny.

CINDERELLA. So it is ! Good-night, Mrs. Maloney.

MRS. M. Good-night, Cinders.

(*She departs. The penny falls into* CINDERELLA'S *box with a pleasant clink.*)

CINDERELLA. Next.

(*A woman of 35 comes forward. She is dejected, thin-lipped, and unlovable.*)

MARION (*tossing her head*). You 're surprised to see *me*, I dare say.

CINDERELLA (*guardedly*). I haven't the pleasure of knowing you.

MARION (*glancing at the remaining occupant of the bench*). Is that man sleeping ? Who is he ? I don't know him.

CINDERELLA. He 's sleeping. What can I do for you ?

MARION (*harshly*). Nothing, I dare say. I 'm at Catullo's Buildings. Now they 're turning me out. They say I 'm not respectable.

CINDERELLA (*enlightened*). You 're—that woman ?

MARION (*defiantly*). That 's me.

CINDERELLA (*shrinking*). I don't think there 's nothing I could do for you.

MARION (*rather appealing*). Maybe there is. I see you 've heard my story. They say there 's a man comes to see me at times though he has a wife in Hoxton.

CINDERELLA. I 've heard.

MARION. So I 'm being turned out.

CINDERELLA. I don't think it 's a case for me.

MARION. Yes, it is.

CINDERELLA. Are you terrible fond of him ?

MARION. Fond of him ! Damn him !

(CINDERELLA *shrinks.* MARION *makes sure that the man is asleep.*)

Cinders, they 've got the story wrong ; it 's me as is his wife ; I was married to him in a church. He met that woman long after and took up with her.

CINDERELLA. What ! Then why do you not tell the truth ?

MARION. It 's my pride keeps me from telling. I would rather be thought to be the wrong 'un he likes than the wife the law makes him help.

CINDERELLA. Is that pride ?

MARION. It 's all the pride that 's left to me.

CINDERELLA. I 'm awful sorry for you, but I can't think of no advice to give you.

MARION. It's not advice I want.

CINDERELLA. What is it then?

MARION. It's pity. I fling back all the gutter words they fling at me, but my heart, Cinders, is wet at times. It's wet for one to pity me.

CINDERELLA. I pity you.

MARION. You'll tell nobody?

CINDERELLA. No.

MARION. Can I come in now and again at a time?

CINDERELLA. I'll be glad to see you—if I'm here.

MARION. I'll be slipping away now; he's waking up. (*She puts down her penny.*)

CINDERELLA. I'm not doing it for no penny.

MARION. You've got to take it. That's my pride But —I wish you well, Cinders.

CINDERELLA. I like you. I wish you would wish me luck. Say 'Good luck to you to-night, Cinderella.'

MARION. Why to-night?

(*The little waif, so practical until now, is afire inside again. She needs a confidant almost as much as* MARION.)

CINDERELLA (*hastily*). You see——

(*The* MAN *sits up.*)

Good evening, Missis.

MARION. Good luck to you to-night, Cinderella.

(*She goes.*)

(*The* MAN *slips forward and lifts the penny.*)

CINDERELLA (*returning to earth sharply*). Put that down.

MAN. I was only looking at the newness of it. I was just admiring the design.

(*The newness and the design both disappear into the box. A bearded person wearing the overalls of a seafaring man lurches down the street and enters the emporium. Have we seen him before? Who can this hairy monster be?*)

POLICEMAN (*in an incredibly gruff voice*). I want a penny-worth.

CINDERELLA (*unsuspecting*). Sit down. (*She surveys the coster.*) It's you that belongs to the shirt, isn't it?

MAN. Yes; is't ready?

CINDERELLA. It's ready.

(*It proves to be not a shirt, but a 'front' of linen, very stiff and starched. The laundress cautiously retains possession of it.*)

The charge is a penny.

MAN.   On delivery.

CINDERELLA.   Before delivery.

MAN.   Surely you can trust me.

CINDERELLA.   You 've tried that on before, my man. **Never** again. All in this street knows my rule,—Trust in the Lord ; every other person, Cash.

(*A penny and a ' shirt ' pass between them and he departs. CINDERELLA turns her attention to the newcomer.*)

What 's your pleasure ?

POLICEMAN.   Shave, please.

CINDERELLA (*retreating from his beard*).   Shave ?   I shaves in an ordinary way, but I don't know as I could tackle that.

POLICEMAN.   I thought you was a barber.

CINDERELLA (*bravely*).   I 'll get the lather.

(*She goes doubtfully into what she calls her bedroom. He seizes this opportunity to survey the room. A remarkable man this, his attention is at once riveted on the boxes, but before he can step on a chair and take a peep the barber returns with the implements of her calling. He reaches his chair in time not to be caught by her. She brings a bowl of soap and water and a towel, in which she encases him in the correct manner.*)

CINDERELLA.   You 're thin on the top.

POLICEMAN (*in his winding sheet*).   I 've all run to beard.

CINDERELLA (*the ever ready*).   I have a ointment for the hair ; it is my own invention.   The price is a penny.

POLICEMAN (*gruffly*).   Beard, please.

CINDERELLA.   I 've got some voice-drops.

POLICEMAN.   Beard, please.

CINDERELLA (*as she prepares the lather*).   Is the streets quiet ?

POLICEMAN (*cunningly*).   Hereabouts they are ; but there 's great doings in the fashionable quarters.   A ball, I 'm told.

CINDERELLA (*gasping*).   You didn't see no peculiar person about in this street ?

POLICEMAN.   How peculiar ?

CINDERELLA.   Like a—a flunkey ?

POLICEMAN.   Did I now—or did I not ?

CINDERELLA (*eagerly*). He would be carrying an invite maybe ; it 's a big card.

POLICEMAN. I can't say I saw him.

(*Here an astonishing thing happens. The head of a child rises from one of the boxes. She is unseen by either of the mortals.*)

CINDERELLA (*considering the beard*). How do I start with the like of this ?

POLICEMAN. First you saws . . .

(*She attempts to saw. The beard comes off in her hand.*)

CINDERELLA (*recognising his face*). You !

POLICEMAN (*stepping triumphantly out of his disguise*). Me !

(*As sometimes happens, however, the one who means to give the surprise gets a greater. At sight of his dreaded uniform the child screams, whereat two other children in other boxes bob up and scream also. It is some time before the policeman can speak.*)

So that 's what the boxes was for !

CINDERELLA (*feebly*). Yes.

POLICEMAN (*portentously*). Who and what are these phenomenons ?

CINDERELLA (*protectingly*). Don't be frightened, children. Down !

(*They disappear obediently.*)

There 's no wrong in it. They 're just me trying to do my bit. It 's said all should do their bit in war-time. It was into a hospital I wanted to go to nurse the wounded soldiers. I offered myself at every hospital door, but none would have me, so this was all I could do.

POLICEMAN. You 're taking care of them ?

(*She nods.*)

Sounds all right. Neighbour's children ?

CINDERELLA. The brown box is. She 's half of an orphan, her father 's a blue-jacket, so, of course, I said I would.

POLICEMAN. You need say no more. I pass little blue-jacket.

CINDERELLA. Those other two is allies. She 's French— and her 's a Belgy. (*Calls*) Marie-Therese !

(*The French child sits up.*)

Speak your language to the gentleman, Marie-Therese.

MARIE.   Bon soir, Monsieur—comment portez-vous ?   Je t'aime.   (*She curtseys charmingly to him from the box.*)

POLICEMAN.   Well, I 'm ——d !

CINDERELLA.   Delphine !

(*The Belgian looks up.*)

Make votre bow.

Gladys.

(*The English child bobs up.*)

A friend, Gladys.

(GLADYS *and the* POLICEMAN *grin to each other.*)

GLADYS.   What cheer !

CINDERELLA.   Monsieur is a Britain's defender.

MARIE.   Oh, la, la !   Parlez-vous français, Monsieur ?   Non !
I blow you two kisses, Monsieur—the one is to you (*kisses hand*)
to keep, the other you will give—(*kisses hand*) to Kitch.

POLICEMAN (*writing*).   Sends kiss to Lord Kitchener.

CINDERELLA.   She 's the one that does most of the talking.

POLICEMAN (*who is getting friendly*).   I suppose that other
box is an empty.

(CINDERELLA'S *mouth closes.*)

Is that box empty ?

CINDERELLA.   It 's not exactly empty.

POLICEMAN.   What 's inside ?

CINDERELLA.   She 's the littlest.

(*The children exchange glances, and she is severe.*)

Couchy.

(*They disappear.*)

POLICEMAN.   An ally ?

CINDERELLA.   She 's—she 's—Swiss.

POLICEMAN (*lowering*).   Now then !

CINDERELLA.   She 's not exactly Swiss.   You can guess now
what she is.

POLICEMAN (*grave*).   This puts me in a very difficult position.

CINDERELLA (*beginning to cry*).   Nobody would take her.
She was left over.   I tried not to take her.   I 'm a patriot, I
am.   But there she was—left over—and her so terrible little—
I couldn't help taking her.

POLICEMAN.   I dunno.   (*Quite unfairly*) If her folk had
been in your place and you in hers, they would have shown
neither mercy nor pity for you.

CINDERELLA (*stoutly*).   That makes no difference.

POLICEMAN (*was this the great moment ?*).   I think there's something uncommon about you.

CINDERELLA (*pleased*).   About *me* ?

POLICEMAN.   I suppose she's sleeping ?

CINDERELLA.   Not her !

POLICEMAN.   What's she doing ?

CINDERELLA.   She's strafing !

POLICEMAN.   Who's she strafing ?

CINDERELLA.   Very likely you.   She misses nobody.   You see I've put some barb-wire round her box.

POLICEMAN.   I see now.

CINDERELLA.   It's not really barb-wire.   It's worsted.   I was feared the wire would hurt her.   But it just makes a difference.

POLICEMAN.   How do the others get on with her ?

CINDERELLA.   I makes them get on with her.   Of course there's tongues out, and little things like that.

POLICEMAN.   Were the foreign children shy of you at first ?

CINDERELLA.   Not as soon as they heard my name.   ' Oh, are you Cinderella ? ' they said, in their various languages— and ' when 's the ball ? ' they said.

POLICEMAN.   Somebody must have telled them about you.

CINDERELLA (*happy*).   Not here.   They had heard about me in their foreign lands.   Everybody knows Cinderella : it's fine.   Even her (*indicating the German box*)—the moment I mentioned my name—' Where's your ugly sisters ? ' says she, looking round.

POLICEMAN.   Sisters ?   It's new to me, your having sisters. (*He produces his note-book.*)

CINDERELLA (*uneasily*).   It's kind of staggering to me, too. I haven't been able to manage them yet, but they'll be at the ball.

POLICEMAN.   It's queer.

CINDERELLA.   It *is* queer.

POLICEMAN (*sitting down with her*).   How do you know this ball's to-night ?

CINDERELLA.   It had to be some night.   You see, after I closes my business I have chats with the children about things, and naturally it's mostly about the ball.   I put it off as long as I could, but it had to be some night—and this is the night.

POLICEMAN.   You mean it 's make-believe ?

CINDERELLA (*almost fiercely*).   None of that !

POLICEMAN (*shaking his head*).   I don't like it.

CINDERELLA (*shining*).   You wouldn't say that if you heard the blasts on the trumpet and loud roars of ' Make way for the Lady Cinderella ! '

(*Three heads pop up again.*)

POLICEMAN.   Lady ?

CINDERELLA (*in a tremble of exultation*).   That 's me. That 's what you 're called at royal balls.   Then loud huzzas is heard outside from the excited popu-lace, for by this time the fame of my beauty has spread like wild-fire through the streets, and folks is hanging out at windows and climbing lamp-posts to catch a sight of me.

(*Delight of the children.*)

POLICEMAN.   My sakes, you see the whole thing clear !

CINDERELLA.   I see it from beginning to end—like as if I could touch it—the gold walls and the throne, and the lamp-posts and the horses.

POLICEMAN.   The horses ?

CINDERELLA.   . . . Well, the competitors.   The speeches —everything.   If only I had my invite !   That wasn't a knock at the door, was it ?

POLICEMAN (*so carried away that he goes to see*).   No.

CINDERELLA (*vindictively*).   I dare say that flunkey 's sitting drinking in some public-house.

(*Here* MARIE-THERESE *and* GLADYS, *who have been communicating across their boxes, politely invite the* POLICEMAN *to go away.*)

MARIE.   Bonne nuit, Monsieur.

GLADYS.   Did you say you was going, Mister ?

POLICEMAN.   They 're wonderful polite.

CINDERELLA.   I doubt that 's not politeness.   The naughties —they 're asking you to go away.

POLICEMAN.   Oh !   (*He rises with hauteur.*)

CINDERELLA.   You see we 're to have a bite of supper before I start—to celebrate the night.

POLICEMAN.   Supper with the kids !   When I was a kid in the country at Badgery—— You 've done it again !

CINDERELLA.   Done what ?

POLICEMAN (*with that strange feeling of being at home*). I suppose I would be in the way ?

CINDERELLA. There 's not very much to eat. There 's just one for each.

POLICEMAN. I 've had my supper.

CINDERELLA (*seeing her way*). Have you ? Then I would be very pleased if you would stay.

POLICEMAN. Thank you kindly.

(*She prepares the table for the feast. Eyes sparkle from the boxes.*)

CINDERELLA (*shining*). This is the first party we 've ever had. Please keep an eye on the door in case there 's a knock.

(*She darts into her bedroom, and her charges are more at their ease.*)

MARIE (*sitting up, the better to display her night-gown*). Monsieur, Monsieur, voilà !

GLADYS. Cinderella made it out of watching a shop window.

POLICEMAN (*like one who has known his hostess from infancy*). Just like her.

MARIE (*holding up a finger that is adorned with a ring*). Monsieur !

GLADYS (*more practical*). The fire 's going out.

POLICEMAN (*recklessly*). In with another penny. (*He feeds the fire with that noble coin.*) Fellow allies, I 'm going to take a peep into the German trench ! Hah !

(*He stealthily mounts a chair and puts his hand into GRETCHEN's box. We must presume that it is bitten by the invisible occupant, for he withdraws it hurriedly to the hearty delight of the spectators. This mirth changes to rapture as CINDERELLA makes a conceited entrance carrying a jug of milk and five hot potatoes in their jackets. Handsomely laden as she is, it is her attire that calls forth the applause. She is now wearing the traditional short brown dress of CINDERELLA, and her hair hangs loose. She tries to look modest.*)

CINDERELLA (*displaying herself*). What do you think ?

POLICEMAN (*again in Badgery*). Great ! Turn round. And I suppose you made it yourself out of a shop window ?

CINDERELLA. No, we didn't need no shop window ; we all know exactly what I wear when the knock comes.

GLADYS. Of course we does.

(*A potato is passed up to each and a cup of milk between two. There is also a delicious saucerful of melted lard into which they dip.* GRETCHEN *is now as much in evidence as the others, and quite as attractive ; the fun becomes fast and furious.*)

CINDERELLA (*to* POLICEMAN). A potato ?

POLICEMAN. No, I thank you.

CINDERELLA. Just a snack ?

POLICEMAN. Thank you.

(*She shares with him.*)

CINDERELLA. A little dip ?

POLICEMAN. No, I thank you.

CINDERELLA. Just to look friendly.

POLICEMAN. I thank you. (*Dipping*) To you, Cinderella.

CINDERELLA. I thank you.

POLICEMAN (*proposing a toast*). The King !

CINDERELLA (*rather consciously*). And the Prince of Wales.

GLADYS. And father.

POLICEMAN. The King, the Prince of Wales, and father.

(*The toast is drunk, dipped and eaten with acclamation.* GLADYS, *uninvited, recites ' The Mariners of England.'* MARIE-THERESE *follows (without waiting for the end) with the ' Marseillaise,' and* GRETCHEN *puts out her tongue at both. Our* POLICEMAN *having intimated that he desires to propose another toast of a more lengthy character, the children are lifted down and placed in their night-gowns at the table.*)

POLICEMAN (*suddenly becoming nervous*). I have now the honour to propose Absent Friends.

GLADYS (*with an inspiration to which* MARIE-THERESE *bows elegantly*). Vive la France !

POLICEMAN. I mean our friends at the Front. And they have their children, too. Your boxes we know about, but I dare say there 's many similar and even queerer places, where the children, the smallest of our allies, are sleeping this night within the sound of shells.

MARIE. La petite Belgique. La pauvre enfant !

DELPHINE (*proudly*). Me !

POLICEMAN. So here 's to Absent Friends——

GLADYS (*with another inspiration*). Absent Boxes !

POLICEMAN. Absent Boxes. And there's a party we know about who would like uncommon to have the charge of the lot of them—(*looking at* CINDERELLA). And I couples the toast with the name of the said party.

CINDERELLA (*giving a pennyworth for nothing*). Kind friends, it would be pretending of me not to let on that I know I am the party spoke of by the last speaker—and very kind he is. When I look about me and see just four boxes I am a kind of shamed, but it wasn't very convenient to me to have more. I will now conclude by saying I wish I was the old woman that lived in a shoe, and it doesn't matter how many I had I would have known fine what to do. The end.

(*After further diversion*). It's a fine party. I hope your potato is mealy?

POLICEMAN. I never had a better tatie.

CINDERELLA. Don't spare the skins.

POLICEMAN. But you're eating nothing yourself.

CINDERELLA. I'm not hungry. And, of course, I'll be expected to take a bite at the ball.

(*This reminder of the ball spoils the* POLICEMAN's *enjoyment.*)

POLICEMAN. I wish—you wasn't so sure of the ball.

GLADYS (*in defence*). Why shouldn't she not be sure of it?

DELPHINE. Pourquoi, Monsieur?

CINDERELLA (*rather hotly*). Don't say things like that here.

MARIE. Has Monsieur by chance seen Godmamma coming?

POLICEMAN. Godmamma?

CINDERELLA. That's my Godmother; she brings my ball dress and a carriage with four ponies.

GLADYS. Then away she goes to the ball—hooray—hooray!

CINDERELLA. It's all perfectly simple once Godmother comes.

POLICEMAN (*with unconscious sarcasm*). I can see she's important.

CINDERELLA (*with the dreadful sinking that comes to her at times*). You think she'll come, don't you?

POLICEMAN. Cinderella, your hand's burning—and in this cold room.

CINDERELLA. Say you think she'll come.

POLICEMAN. I—well, I . . . I . . .

GLADYS (*imploringly*).   Say it, Mister !

DELPHINE (*begging*).   Monsieur !   Monsieur !

MARIE.   If it is that you love me, Monsieur !

POLICEMAN (*in distress*).   I question if there was ever before a member of the Force in such a position. (*Yielding*) I expect she 'll come.

> (*This settles it in the opinion of the children, but their eyes are too bright for such a late hour, and they are ordered to bed. Our* POLICEMAN *replaces them in their boxes.*)

CINDERELLA.   One—two—three . . . couchy !

> (*They disappear.*)

POLICEMAN (*awkwardly and trying to hedge*).   Of course this is an out-of-the-way little street for a Godmother to find.

CINDERELLA.   Yes, I 've thought of that.   I 'd best go and hang about outside ; she would know me by my dress.

POLICEMAN (*hastily*).   I wouldn't do that.   It 's a cold night. (*He wanders about the room eyeing her sideways.*) Balls is always late things.

CINDERELLA.   I 'm none so sure.   In war-time, you see, with the streets so dark and the King so kind, it would be just like him to begin early and close at ten instead of twelve.   I must leave before twelve.   If I don't, there 's terrible disasters happens.

POLICEMAN (*unable to follow this*).   The ball might be put off owing to the Prince of Wales being in France.

CINDERELLA.   He catched the last boat.   I 'll go out and watch.

POLICEMAN (*desperate*).   Stay where you are, and—and I 'll have a look for her.

CINDERELLA.   You 're too kind.

POLICEMAN.   Not at all.   I must be stepping at any rate. If I can lay hands on her I 'll march her here, though I have to put the handcuffs on her.

GLADYS (*looking up*).   I think I heard a knock !

> (*The* POLICEMAN *looks out, shakes his head, and finally departs after a queer sort of handshake with* MISS THING.)

CINDERELLA.   He 's a nice man.

GLADYS.   Have you known him long ?

CINDERELLA (*thinking it out*).   A longish time.   He 's head of the secret police ; him and me used to play together as children down in Badgery. His folks live in a magnificent castle with two doors. (*She becomes a little bewildered.*) I 'm all mixed up.

> (*The children are soon asleep. She wanders aimlessly to the door. The wall closes on the little room, and we now see her standing in the street. Our* POLICEMAN *returns and flashes his lantern on her.*)

CINDERELLA. It 's you !

POLICEMAN. It 's me. But there 's no Godmother. There 's not a soul . . . No. . . . Good-night, Cinderella. Go inside.

CINDERELLA (*doggedly*). Not me ! I don't feel the cold— not much. And one has to take risks to get a Prince. The only thing I 'm feared about is my feet. If they was to swell I mightn't be able to get the slippers on, and he would have naught to do with me.

POLICEMAN. What slippers ? If you won't go back, I 'll stop here with you.

CINDERELLA No, I think there 's more chance of her coming if I 'm alone.

POLICEMAN. I 'm very troubled about you.

CINDERELLA (*wistfully*). Do you think I 'm just a liar ? Maybe I am. You see I 'm all mixed up. I 'm sore in need of somebody to help me out.

POLICEMAN. I would do it if I could.

CINDERELLA. I 'm sure. (*Anxiously*) Are you good at riddles ?

> (*He shakes his head.*)

There 's always a riddle before you can marry into a royal family.

POLICEMAN (*with increased gloom*). The whole thing seems to be most terrible difficult.

CINDERELLA. Yes. . . . Good-night.

POLICEMAN. You won't let me stay with you ?

CINDERELLA. No.

> (*He puts his lantern on the ground beside her.*)

What 's that for ?

POLICEMAN (*humbly*). It 's just a sort of guard for you. (*He takes off his muffler and puts it several times round her neck.*)

CINDERELLA. Nice !

POLICEMAN. Good luck.

(*She finds it easiest just to nod in reply.*)
I wish I was a Prince.

CINDERELLA (*suddenly struck by the idea*). You 're kind of like him.

(*He goes away. She sits down on the step to wait. She shivers. She takes the muffler off her neck and winds it round her more valuable feet. She falls asleep.*

Darkness comes, and snow. From somewhere behind, the shadowy figure of CINDERELLA'S *Godmother, beautiful in a Red Cross nurse's uniform, is seen looking benignantly on the waif.* CINDERELLA *is just a little vague huddled form—there is no movement.*)

GODMOTHER. Cinderella, my little godchild !

CINDERELLA (*with eyes unopening*). Is that you, Godmother ?

GODMOTHER. It is I ; my poor god-daughter is all mixed up, and I have come to help her out.

CINDERELLA. You have been long in coming. I very near gave you up.

GODMOTHER. Sweetheart, I couldn't come sooner, because in these days, you know, even the fairy godmother is with the Red Cross.

CINDERELLA. Was that the reason ? I see now ; I thought perhaps you kept away because I wasn't a good girl.

GODMOTHER. You have been a good brave girl ; I am well pleased with my darling godchild.

CINDERELLA. It is fine to be called darling ; it heats me up. I 've been wearying for it, Godmother. Life 's a kind of hard.

GODMOTHER. It will always be hard to you, Cinderella. I can't promise you anything else.

CINDERELLA. I don't suppose I could have my three wishes, Godmother.

GODMOTHER. I am not very powerful in these days, Cinderella ; but what are your wishes ?

CINDERELLA. I would like fine to have my ball, Godmother.

GODMOTHER. You shall have your ball.

CINDERELLA. I would like to nurse the wounded.

GODMOTHER. You shall nurse the wounded.

CINDERELLA. I would like to be loved by the man of my choice, Godmother.

GODMOTHER. You shall be loved by the man of your choice.

CINDERELLA. Thank you kindly. The ball first, if you please, and could you squeeze in the children so that they may see me in my glory?

GODMOTHER. Now let this be my down-trodden godchild's ball, not as balls are, but as they are conceived to be in a little chamber in Cinderella's head.

(She fades from sight. In the awful stillness we can now hear the tiny clatter of horses infinitely small and infinitely far off. It is the equipage of CINDERELLA. *Then an unearthly trumpet sounds thrice, and the darkness is blown away.*

It is the night of the most celebrated ball in history, and we see it through our heroine's eyes. She has, as it were, made everything with her own hands, from the cloths of gold to the ices.

Nearly everything in the ball-room is of gold; it was only with an effort that she checked herself from dabbing gold on the regal countenances. You can see that she has not passed by gin-palaces without thinking about them. The walls and furniture are so golden that you have but to lean against them to acquire a competency. There is a golden throne with gold cloths on it, and the royal seats are three golden rocking-chairs; there would be a fourth golden rocking-chair if it were not that CINDERELLA *does not want you to guess where she is to sit. These chairs are stuffed to a golden corpulency. The panoply of the throne is about twenty feet high—each foot of pure gold; and nested on the top of it is a golden reproduction of the grandest thing* CINDERELLA *has ever seen—the private box of a theatre. In this box sit, wriggle, and sprawl the four children in their night-gowns, leaning over the golden parapet as if to the manner born and carelessly kicking nuggets out of it. They are shouting, pointing, and otherwise behaving badly, eating oranges out of paper bags, then blowing out the bags and bursting them. The superb scene is lit by four street lamps with red glass. Dancing is going on: the ladies all in white, the gentlemen in black with swords. If you were unused to royal balls*

*you would think every one of these people was worth de-
scribing separately ; but, compared to what is coming, it
may be said that* CINDERELLA *has merely pushed them on
with her lovely foot. They are her idea of courtiers, and
have anxious expressions as if they knew she was watching
them. They have character in the lump, if we may put it
that way, but none individually. Thus one cannot smile or
sigh, for instance, without all the others smiling or sighing.
At night they are probably snuffed out like candles and put
away in boxes from which golden hands rouse them for
the next festivity. As children they were not like this ;
they had genuine personal traits, but these have gradually
been blotted out as they basked in royal favour ; thus, if
the* KING *wipes his glasses they all pretend that their
glasses need wiping, and when the* QUEEN *lets her handkerchief fall they all stoop loyally to pick up their own,
which they carry for that very purpose.*

Down the golden steps at the back comes the LORD
MAYOR, *easily recognisable by his enormous chain.*)

LORD MAYOR.   O yes, O yes, make way every one for the
Lord Mayor—namely myself.

(*They all make way for him. Two black boys fling open
lovely curtains.*)

O yes, O yes, make way every one, and also myself, for Lord
Times.

(*This is a magnificent person created by* CINDERELLA *on
learning from* MR. BODIE *that the press is all-powerful and
that the ' Times ' is the press. He carries one hand behind
his back, as if it might be too risky to show the whole of himself at once, and it is noticeable that as he walks his feet do
not quite touch the ground. He is the only person who is
not a little staggered by the amount of gold : you almost feel
that he thinks there is not quite enough of it. He very
nearly sits down on one of the royal rocking-chairs ; and the*
LORD MAYOR, *looking red and unhappy, and as if he had now
done for himself, has to whisper to him that the seats under
the throne are reserved.*)

O yes, O yes, make way for the Censor.

(CINDERELLA *has had a good deal of trouble over this person,
of whom she has heard a great deal in war-time, without*

meeting any one who can tell her what he is like. She has done her best, and he is long and black and thin, dressed as tightly as a fish, and carries an executioner's axe. All fall back from him in fear, except LORD TIMES, *who takes a step forward, and then the* CENSOR *falls back.*)

O yes, O yes, make way everybody for his Royal Highness the King, and his good lady the Queen.

(*The* KING *and* QUEEN *are attired like their portraits on playing cards, who are the only royalties* CINDERELLA *has seen, and they advance grandly to their rocking-chairs, looking as if they thought the whole public was dirt, but not so much despised dirt as dirt with good points.* LORD TIMES *fixes them with his eye, and the* KING *hastily crosses and shakes hands with him.*)

O yes, O yes, make way every one, except the King, and Queen, and Lord Times, for His Highness Prince Hard-to-Please.

(*The heir apparent comes, preceded by trumpeters. His dress may a little resemble that of the extraordinary youth seen by* CINDERELLA *in her only pantomime, but what quite takes our breath away is his likeness to our* POLICEMAN. *If the ball had taken place a night earlier it may be hazarded that the* PRINCE *would have presented quite a different face. It is as if* CINDERELLA'S *views of his personality had undergone some unaccountable change, confusing even to herself, and for a moment the whole scene rocks, the street lamps wink, and odd shadows stalk among the courtiers, shadows of* MR. BODIE, MARION, *and the party in an unfinished coat, who have surely no right to be here. This is only momentarily ; then the palace steadies itself again.*

The KING *rises, and in stately manner addresses his guests in the words* CINDERELLA *conceives to be proper to his royal mouth. As he stands waiting superbly for the applause to cease, he holds on to a strap hanging conveniently above his head. To* CINDERELLA *strap-hanging on the Underground has been a rare and romantic privilege.*)

KING. My loyal subjects, all 'ail ! I am as proud of you as you are of me. It gives me and my good lady much pleasure to see you 'ere by special invite, feasting at our expense. There is a paper bag for each, containing two sandwiches, buttered on

both sides, a piece of cake, a hard-boiled egg, and an orange or
a banana.

(*The cheers of the delighted courtiers gratify him, but the
vulgar children over his head continue their rub-a-dub on the
parapet until he glares up at them.   Even then they continue.*)
Ladies and Gents all, pleasant though it is to fill up with good
victuals, that is not the chief object of this royal invite.   We are
'ere for a solemn purpose, namely, to find a mate for our noble
son.   All the Beauties are waiting in the lobby : no wonder he
is excited.

(*All look at the* PRINCE, *who is rocking and yawning.*)
He will presently wake up ; but first I want to say—(*here he
becomes conscious of* LORD TIMES).   What is it ?

LORD TIMES.   Less talk.

KING.   Certainly.   (*He sits down.*)

PRINCE (*encouraged to his feet by various royal nudges*).   My
liege King and Queen-Mother, you can have the competitors
brought in, and I will take a look at them ; but I have no hope.
My curse is this, that I am a scoffer about females.   I can play
with them for an idle hour and then cast them from me even
as I cast this banana skin.   I can find none so lovely that I may
love her for aye from the depths of my passionate heart.   I am
so blasted particular.   O yes !   O yes !   (*He sits down and
looks helpless.*)

KING (*undismayed*).   All ready ?

(*The* LORD MAYOR *bows.*)
All is ready, my son.

PRINCE (*bored*).   Then let loose the Beauts.

(*To heavenly music from the royal hurdy-gurdies the
Beauties descend the stairs, one at a time.   There are a
dozen of the fine creatures, in impudent confections such as
CINDERELLA has seen in papers in* MR. BODIE'S *studio ;
some of them with ropes of hair hanging down their proud
backs as she has seen them in a hair-dresser's window.   As
we know, she has once looked on at a horse show, and this
has coloured her conception of a competition for a prince.
The ladies prance round the ball-room like high-stepping
steeds ; it is evident that* CINDERELLA *has had them fed
immediately before releasing them ; her pride is to show
them at their very best, and then to challenge them.*

They paw the floor wantonly until LORD TIMES *steps forward. Peace thus restored,* HIS MAJESTY *proceeds.)*

KING.   The first duty of a royal consort being to be *good,* the test of goodness will now be applied by the Lord Mayor. Every competitor who does not pass in goodness will be made short work of.

(*Several ladies quake, and somewhere or other unseen* CINDERELLA *is chuckling.*)

ONE OF THE STEEDS.   I wasn't told about this. It isn't fair.

LORD MAYOR (*darkly*).   If your Grace wishes to withdraw—
(*She stamps.*)

KING.   The Lord Mayor will now apply the test.

LORD MAYOR (*to a gold* PAGE).   The therm-mo-ometers, boy.

(*A whole boxful of thermometers is presented to him by the* PAGE *on bended knee. The* LORD MAYOR *is now in his element. He has ridden in gold coaches and knows what hussies young women often are. To dainty music he trips up the line of Beauties and pops a tube into each pouting mouth. The competitors circle around, showing their paces while he stands, watch in hand, giving them two minutes. Then airily he withdraws the tubes ; he is openly gleeful when he finds sinners. Twice he is in doubt, it is a very near thing, and he has to consult the* KING *in whispers : the* KING *takes the* QUEEN *aside, to whisper behind the door as it were ; then they both look at* LORD TIMES, *who, without even stepping forward, says ' No '—and the doubtfuls are at once bundled out of the chamber with the certainties. Royalty sighs, and the courtiers sigh and the* LORD MAYOR *sighs in a perfunctory way, but there is a tossing of manes from the Beauties who have scraped through.*)

KING (*stirring up the* PRINCE, *who has fallen asleep*).   Our Royal Bud will now graciously deign to pick out a few possibles.

(*His Royal Highness yawns.*)

LORD MAYOR (*obsequiously*).   If your Highness would like a little assistance——

PRINCE (*you never know how they will take things*).   We shall do this for ourselves, my good fellow.

(*He smacks the* LORD MAYOR'S *face with princely elegance. The* LORD MAYOR *takes this as a favour, and the courtiers gently smack each other's faces, and are very proud to be there. The* PRINCE *moves languidly down the line of Beauties considering their charms, occasionally nodding approval but more often screwing up his nose. The courtiers stand ready with nods or noses. Several ladies think they have been chosen, but he has only brought them into prominence to humiliate them; he suddenly says ' Good-bye,' and they have to go, while he is convulsed with merriment. He looks sharply at the courtiers to see if they are convulsed also, and most of them are; the others are flung out.)*

QUEEN (*hanging on to her strap*). Does our Royal one experience no palpitation at all ?

PRINCE (*sleepily*). Ah me, ah me !

LORD TIMES (*irritated*). You are well called 'Ard-to-Please. You would turn up your nose at a lady though she were shaped like Apollo's bow.

(*The* PRINCE *shrugs his shoulder to indicate that love cannot be forced.*)

LORD MAYOR (*darkly*). And now we come to the severer test.

(*With a neat action, rather like taking a lid off a pot, the* LORD MAYOR *lets it be known to the ladies that they must now lift their skirts to show their feet. When this devastating test is concluded, there are only two competitors left in the room.*)

LORD TIMES (*almost as if he were thinking of himself*). Can't have Two.

(*Cards such as* CINDERELLA *saw at the horse show, with ' 1st,' ' 2nd,' and ' 3rd ' on them, are handed to the* PRINCE. *Like one well used to such proceedings, he pins 2nd and 3rd into the ladies' bodices.*)

QUEEN (*gloomily*). But still no first.

(*The children applaud; they have been interfering repeatedly.*)

KING. Come, come, proud youth, you feel no palps at all ?

PRINCE. Not a palp. Perhaps for a moment this one's nose—that one's cock of the head—— But it has passed.

(*He drearily resumes his rocking-chair. No one seems to know what to do next.*)

MARIE (*to the rescue*). The two Ugly Sisters ! Monsieur le Roi, the two Ugly Sisters ! (*She points derisively at the winners.*)

KING (*badgered*).   How did these children get their invites ?
(*This is another thing that no one knows. Once more the
room rocks, and* MR. BODIE *passes across it as if looking for
some one. Then a growing clamour is heard outside.
Bugles sound. The* LORD MAYOR *goes, and returns with
strange news.*)

LORD MAYOR.   Another competitor, my King.   Make way
for the Lady Cinderella.

KING.   Cinderella ?   I don't know her.

GLADYS (*nearly falling out of the box*).   You 'll soon know
her.   Now you 'll see !   Somebody wake the Prince up !
(*The portals are flung open, and* CINDERELLA *is seen alighting from her lovely equipage, which we will not describe
because some one has described it before. But note the little
waggle of her foot just before she favours the ground. We
have thought a great deal about how our* CINDERELLA
*should be dressed for this occasion : white of course, and she
looked a darling in it, but we boggle at its really being of the
grandest stuff and made in the shop where the Beauties got
theirs. No, the material came from poorer warehouses in
some shabby district not far from the street of the penny shop ;
her eyes had glistened as she gazed at it through the windows,
and she paid for it with her life's blood, and made the frock
herself. Very possibly it is bunchy here and there.*

CINDERELLA, *then, comes sailing down into the ball-room,
not a sound to be heard except the ecstatic shrieks of the four
children. She is modest but calmly confident ; she knows
exactly what to do. She moves once round the room to show
her gown, then curtseys to the royal personages ; then,
turning to the* LORD MAYOR, *opens her mouth and signs to
him to pop in the thermometer. He does it as in a dream.
Presently he is excitedly showing the thermometer to the*
KING.)

KING.   Marvellous !   99 !
(*The cry is repeated from all sides. The* QUEEN *hands the*
KING *a long pin from her coiffure, and the* PRINCE *is again
wakened.*)

PRINCE (*with his hand to his brow*).   What, another ?   Oh,
all right ; but you know this is a dog's life.   (*He goes to* CINDER-
ELLA, *takes one glance at her and resumes his chair.*)

LORD MAYOR (*while the children blub*). That settles it, I think. (*He is a heartless fellow.*) That will do. Stand back, my girl.

CINDERELLA (*calmly*). I don't think.

KING. It's no good, you know.

CINDERELLA (*curtseying*). Noble King, there is two bits of me thy son hath not yet seen. I crave my rights. (*She points to the two bits referred to, which are encased in the loveliest glass slippers.*)

KING. True. Boy, do your duty.

PRINCE. Oh, bother!

(*Those words are the last spoken by him in his present state. When we see him again, which is the moment afterwards, he is translated. He looks the same, but so does a clock into which new works have been put. The change is effected quite simply by* CINDERELLA *delicately raising her skirt and showing him her foot. As the exquisite nature of the sight thus vouchsafed to him penetrates his being a tremor passes through his frame; his vices take flight from him and the virtues enter. It is a heady wakening, and he falls at her feet. The courtiers are awkward, not knowing whether they should fall also.* CINDERELLA *beams to the children, who utter ribald cries of triumph.*)

KING (*rotating on his strap*). Give him air. Fill your lungs, my son.

QUEEN (*on hers*). My boy! My boy!

LORD MAYOR (*quickly taking the royal cue*). Oh, lady fair!

(*The* PRINCE'S *palpitations increase in violence.*)

QUEEN. Oh, happy sight!

KING. Oh, glorious hour!

LORD MAYOR (*not sure that he was heard the first time*). Oh, lady fair!

(*The* PRINCE *springs to his feet. He is looking very queer.*)

LORD TIMES (*probably remembering how he looked once*). The Prince is about to propose.

LORD MAYOR. O yes, O yes, O yes!

KING. Proceed, my son.

PRINCE (*with lover-like contortions and addressing himself largely to the feet*). Dew of the morning, garden of delight, sweet petals of enchanted nights, the heavens have opened and through the chink thou hast fallen at my feet, even as I fall at thine.   Thou art not one but twain, and these the twain—Oh, pretty feet on which my lady walks, are they but feet ?   O no, O no, O no !   They are so small I cannot see them.   Hie ! A candle that I may see my lady's feet !

> (*He kisses one foot, and she holds up the other for similar treatment.*)

O Cinderella, if thou wilt deign to wife with me, I 'll do my best to see that through the years you always walk on kisses.

> (*The courtiers practise walking on kisses.*)

LORD MAYOR.   The Prince has proposed.   The Lady Cinderella will now reply.

KING.   Lovely creature, take pity on my royal son.

QUEEN.   Cinderella, be my daughter.

LORD TIMES (*succinctly*).   Yes, or no ?

CINDERELLA.   There 's just one thing.   Before I answer, I would like that little glass thing to be put in his mouth.

LORD MAYOR (*staggered*).   The ther-mo-mometer ?

KING.   In our *Prince's* mouth !

LORD TIMES.   Why not ?

CINDERELLA.   Just to make sure that he is good.

PRINCE (*dismayed*).   Oh, I say !

QUEEN.   Of course he is good, Cinderella—he is our son.

CINDERELLA (*doggedly*).   I would like it put in his mouth.

KING.   But——

PRINCE (*alarmed*).   Pater !

LORD TIMES.   It must be done.

> (*The test is therefore made.   The royal mouth has to open to the thermometer, which is presently passed to the* KING *for examination.   He looks very grave.   The* PRINCE *seizes the tell-tale thing, and with a happy thought lets it fall.*)

PRINCE.   99 !

> (*The joyous cry is taken up by all, and* CINDERELLA *goes divinely on one knee to her lord and master.*)

CINDERELLA (*simply*).   I accepts.

KING (*when the uproar has ceased*).   All make merry.   The fire is going low.   (*Recklessly*) In with another shilling !

> (*A shilling is dumped into the shilling-in-the-slot stove, which blazes up.   The* PRINCE *puts his arm round his love.*)

LORD TIMES (*again remembering his day of days*).   My Prince, not so fast.   There is still the riddle.

PRINCE.   I had forgotten.

CINDERELLA (*quaking*).   I was feared there would be a riddle.

KING (*prompted by* LORD TIMES).   Know ye all, my subjects, that before blue blood can wed there is a riddle ; and she who cannot guess it—(*darkly*) is taken away and censored.

(*The* CENSOR *with his axe comes into sudden prominence behind* CINDERELLA *and the two other competitors*.)
My Lord Times, the riddle.

LORD TIMES.   I hold in my one hand the riddle, and in the other the answer in a sealed envelope, to prevent any suspicion of hanky-panky.   Third prize, forward.   Now, my child, this is the riddle.   On the night of the Zeppelin raids, what was it that every one rushed to save first ?

3RD PRIZE.   The children.

LORD TIMES.   Children not included.

(*The lady is at a loss.*)

PRINCE.   Time's up !   Hoo-ray !

(*He signs callously to the* CENSOR, *who disappears with his victim through a side door, to reappear presently, alone, wiping his axe and skipping gaily.*)

LORD TIMES.   Second prize, forward.   Now, Duchess, answer.

2ND PRIZE.   Her jewels.

(LORD TIMES *shakes his head.*)

PRINCE (*brightly*).   Off with her head.   Drown her in a bucket.

(*The* CENSOR *again removes the lady and does his fell work.*)

LORD TIMES.   First prize, forward.   Now, Cinderella, answer.

(*The* CENSOR, *a kindly man but used to his calling, puts his hand on her shoulder, to lead her away.   She removes it without looking at him.*)

CINDERELLA.   It's not a catch, is it ?

LORD TIMES (*hotly*).   No, indeed.

CINDERELLA.   There's just one thing all true Britons would be anxious about.

KING (*who has been allowed to break the envelope and read the answer*).   But what, Cinderella—what ?

LORD MAYOR (*hedging again*). What, chit ?

CINDERELLA. Their love-letters.

KING and LORD TIMES (*together, but* LORD TIMES *a little in front*). The fair Cinderella has solved the riddle !

LORD MAYOR (*promptly*). Oh, fair lady !

CINDERELLA (*remembering the Venus*). There's just one thing that makes it not quite a perfect ball. I wanted Mrs. Bodie to be one of the competitors—so as I could beat her.

KING. Send for her at once. Take a taxi.

(*A courtier rushes out whistling, and returns with* VENUS, *now imbued with life. Her arms go out wantonly to the* PRINCE. *He signs to the* CENSOR, *who takes her away and breaks her up.*)

PRINCE. I crave a boon. The wedding at once, my lord.

(LORD TIMES *signifies assent.*)

KING. The marriage ceremony will now take place.

CINDERELLA (*calling to the children*). Bridesmaids !

(*They rush down and become her bridesmaids. At the top of the stair appears a penguin—a penguin or a bishop, they melt into each other on great occasions. The regal couple kneel.*)

PENGUIN. Do you, O Prince, take this lady to be your delightful wife—and to adore her for ever ?

PRINCE. I do, I do ! Oh, I do, I do indeed ! I do— I do—I do !

PENGUIN. Do you, Cinderella, loveliest of your sex, take this Prince for husband, and to love, honour, and obey him ?

CINDERELLA (*primly*). If you please.

PENGUIN. The ring ?

(*It is* MARIE-THERESE'S *great hour ; she passes her ring to* CINDERELLA, *who is married in it. Triumphant music swells out as a crown is put upon our Princess's head, and an extraordinarily long train attached to her person. Her husband and she move dreamily round the ball-room, the children holding up the train.* LORD TIMES *with exquisite taste falls in behind them. Then follow the courtiers, all dreamily ; and completing the noble procession is the* LORD MAYOR, *holding aloft on a pole an enormous penny. It has the face of* CINDERELLA *on one side of it—the penny which to those who know life is the most romantic of coins unless its little brother has done better.*)

*The music, despite better intentions, begins to lose its head.
It obviously wants to dance.   Every one wants to dance.
Even* LORD TIMES *has trouble with his legs.*)

KING (*threatening, supplicating*).   Don't dance yet.   I've
got a surprise for you.   Don't dance.   I haven't told you about
it, so as to keep you on the wonder.

(*In vain do they try to control themselves.*)
It 's ices !

(*All stop dancing.*)
(*Hoarsely*) There's an ice-cream for everybody.

(*Amid applause the royal ice-cream barrow is wheeled on
by haughty menials who fill the paper sieves with dabs of the
luscious condiment.   The paper sieves are of gold, but there
are no spoons.   The children, drunk with expectation, forget
their manners and sit on the throne.   Somehow* CINDER-
ELLA'S *penny clients drift in again, each carrying a sieve.*)
None touches till one royal lick has been taken by us four. . . .
(*He gives them a toast.*)　To the Bridal Pair !

(*At the royal word ' Go !' all attack the ices with their
tongues, greedily but gracefully.   They end in the approved
manner by gobbling up the sieves.   It is especially charming
to see the last of* LORD TIMES'S *sieve.   The music becomes
irresistible.   If you did not dance you would be abandoned
by your legs.   It is as if a golden coin had been dropped into
a golden slot.   Ranks are levelled.   The* KING *asks*
GLADYS *for this one ; the* QUEEN *is whisked away by* MR.
BODIE.   *Perhaps they dance like costers : if you had time
to reflect you might think it a scene in the streets.   It becomes too merry to last ; couples are whirled through the
walls as if the floor itself were rotating : soon* CINDERELLA
and her PRINCE *dance alone.   It is then that the clock
begins to strike twelve.* CINDERELLA *should fly now, or woe
befall her.   Alas, she hears nothing save the whispers of
her lover.   The hour has struck, and her glorious gown
shrinks slowly into the tattered frock of a girl with a broom.
Too late she huddles on the floor to conceal the change.   In
another moment the* PRINCE *must see.   The children gather
round her with little cries, and, spreading out their night-
gowns to conceal her, rush her from the scene.   It is then
that the* PRINCE *discovers his loss.   In a frenzy he calls her*

sweet name. The bewildered girl has even forgotten to drop the slipper, without which he shall never find her. MARIE-THERESE, *the ever-vigilant, steals back with it, and leaves it on the floor.*

The ball-room is growing dark. The lamps have gone out. There is no light save the tiniest glow, which has been showing on the floor all the time, unregarded by us. It seems to come from a policeman's lantern. The gold is all washed out by the odd streaks of white that come down like rain. Soon the PRINCE'S *cry of 'Cinderella, Cinderella!' dies away. It is no longer a ball-room on which the lantern sheds this feeble ray. It is the street outside* CINDERELLA'S *door, a white street now, silent in snow. The child in her rags, the* POLICEMAN'S *scarf still round her precious feet, is asleep on the doorstep, very little life left in her, very little oil left in the lantern.)*

ACT III

THE retreat in which Cinderella is to be found two months later has been described to us by our policeman with becoming awe. It seems to be a very pleasant house near the sea, and possibly in pre-war days people were at ease in it. None of that, says the policeman emphatically, with Dr. Bodie in charge. He could wink discreetly at Dr. Bodie in absence, but was prepared to say on oath that no one ever winked at her when she was present. In the old days he had been more than a passive observer of the suffragette in action, had even been bitten by them in the way of business ; had not then gone into the question of their suitability for the vote, but liked the pluck of them ; had no objection to his feelings on the woman movement being summed up in this way, that he had vaguely disapproved of their object, but had admired their methods. After knowing Dr. Bodie he must admit that his views about their object had undergone a change ; was now a whole-hearted supporter, felt in his bones that Dr. Bodie was born to command : astonishing thing about her that she did it so natural-like. She was not in the least mannish or bullying ; she was a very ladylike sort of person, a bit careful about the doing of her hair, and the set of her hat, and she had a soft voice, though what you might call an arbitrary manner. Very noticeable the way she fixed you with her steely eye. In appearance she was very like her room at the retreat, or the room was very like her ; everything in cruel good order, as you might say ; an extraordinarily decorous writing-table near the centre, the sort of table against which you instinctively stood and waited to make your deposition ; the friendliest thing in the room (to a policeman) was the book-cases with wire doors, because the books looked through the wires at you in a homely way like prisoners. It was a sunny room at times, but this did not take away from its likeness to the doctor, who could also smile on occasion.

Into this room Mr. Bodie is shown on a summer afternoon by a maid with no nonsense about her in working hours.

926

MAID (*who knows that male visitors should be impressed at once*).
This way, sir ; I shall see whether Dr. Bodie is disengaged.

BODIE (*doggedly*). *Miss* Bodie.

MAID (*with firm sweetness*). Dr. Bodie, sir. What name
shall I say ?

BODIE (*wincing*). Mr. Bodie ; her brother.

MAID (*unmoved*). I shall tell Dr. Bodie, sir.

BODIE (*a fighter to the last*). Miss Bodie.

MAID. Dr. Bodie, sir.

(*He is surveying the room with manly disapproval when his
sister appears and greets him. She is all that the* POLICE-
MAN *has said of her, and more ; if we did not have a
heroine already we would choose* DR. BODIE. *At the same
time it cannot be denied that she is enough to make any
brother wince. For instance, immediately she has passed
him the time of day, she seems to be considering his case.
Perhaps this is because she has caught him frowning at her
stethoscope. There is certainly a twinkle somewhere about
her face. Before he can step back indignantly she raises one
of his eyelids and comes to a conclusion.*)

DR. BODIE. Oh dear ! Well, Dick, it 's entirely your own
fault.

(MR. BODIE *has a curious trick of kicking backwards with
one foot when people take liberties with him, and a liberty
has been taken with him now.*)

Kick away, Dick, but you needn't pretend that you have no
faith in me as a medical man ; for when you are really ill you
always take the first train down here. In your heart I am the
only doctor you believe in.

BODIE. Stuff, Nellie.

DR. BODIE. Then why did you put Cinderella under my
care ?

BODIE. I didn't know where else to send her when she was
discharged from the hospital. Had to give her a chance of
picking up. (*Thawing*) It was good of you to give her
board and lodging.

DR. BODIE (*sitting down to her day-book*). Not at all. I 'll
send you in a whacking bill for her presently.

BODIE (*kicking*). Well, I 've come all this way to see her.
How is she getting on, Nellie ?

DR. BODIE. She is in the garden. I dare say you can see her from the window.

BODIE. I see some men only ; I believe they are wounded Tommies.

DR. BODIE. Yes. There is a Convalescent Home down here. That is part of my job. Do the men look as if they were gathering round anything ?

BODIE. They do.

DR. BODIE. Ah ! Then that is Cinderella. She is now bossing the British Army, Dick.

BODIE. I might have guessed it ! (*Chuckling*) Does she charge a penny ?

DR. BODIE. Not to the military.

BODIE. Nellie, I have had some inquiries made lately about her parents.

DR. BODIE. She doesn't know much about them herself.

BODIE. No, and we needn't tell her this. Her mother— ah well, poor soul !—and the father was a very bad egg. And from that soil, Nellie, this flower has sprung. Nobody to tend it. Can't you see little Cinderella with her watering-can carefully bringing up herself. I wish I could paint that picture.

(*Perhaps* DR. BODIE *sees the picture even more clearly than her brother does.*)

I see her now. She is on a bed, Nellie.

DR. BODIE. Yes. That is for convenience, for wheeling her about.

BODIE (*waving*). She sees me. And how is she, Nell ?

DR. BODIE. She is always bright ; perhaps too bright.

BODIE. Can't be too bright.

DR. BODIE (*controlling her feelings*). A girl who is found frozen in the street by a policeman and taken to a London hospital, where she has pneumonia—poor little waif ! You know, she is very frail, Dick.

BODIE. I know ; but she will get better, won't she ?

(*He has said it confidently, but his sister looks at him and turns away. He is startled.*)

Come, Nellie, she is going to get better, isn't she ?

DR. BODIE (*not very encouraging*). There is always a chance, Dick. But her body and soul have had to do too long without the little things they needed.

BODIE. She shall have them now, I promise. What are they ?

DR. BODIE. First of all, just food. She has been half starved all her life. And then human affection. She has been starved of that also ; she who has such a genius for it.

(*She goes to the window and calls.*)

No. 7, bring Cinderella in here.

(CINDERELLA *in her bed is wheeled in through the window by the soldier,* DANNY. *She is wearing a probationer's cap and dressing jacket. The bed is a simple iron one, small and low, of the kind that was so common in war hospitals ; it is on tiny pneumatic wheels with ball bearings for easy propulsion. Though frail,* CINDERELLA *is full of glee.*)

BODIE. Hooray, Cinderella !

CINDERELLA. Hooray ! Isn't it lovely. I 'm glad you 've seen me in my carriage. When I saw there was a visitor I thought at first it might be David.

BODIE. David ? I didn't know you . . . Is he a relative ?

(CINDERELLA *finds this extremely funny—so does* DANNY ; *even the* DOCTOR *is discreetly amused.*)

CINDERELLA (*to* DANNY). Tell the men that ! He 's not exactly a relative. (*She pulls* MR. BODIE *down by the lapels of his coat.*) He 's just that great big ridiculous policeman !

BODIE. Oho ! Our policeman again. Does he come all this way to see you ?

CINDERELLA (*her shoulders rising in pride*). Twice already ; and he 's coming again to-day. Mr. Bodie, get the Doctor to take you over the Convalescent Home. There 's a field with cows in it, a whole litter of them ! And the larder ? There 's barrel upon barrel full of eggs and sawdust, and Danny says— this is Danny——

(DANNY, *who is slightly lame and is in hospital blue, comes to attention.*)

Danny says the hens lay in the barrels so as to save time in packing.

(DANNY *finds the severe eye of the Doctor upon him and is abashed.*)

Mr. Bodie, look ! (*displaying her cap*). The Doctor lets me wear it ; it makes me half a nurse, a kind of nurse's help. I make bandages, and they 're took away in glass bottles and sterilised.   Mr. Bodie, as sure as death I 'm doing something for my country.

DR. BODIE.   Cinderella, you 're talking too much.

CINDERELLA (*subsiding meekly*).   Yes, Doctor.

DR. BODIE.   Dick, I am going over to the hospital presently. If you like to come with me—*really* want to see it—no affected interest——

BODIE.   Thanks, I should like it—Dr. Bodie.

DR. BODIE (*to* DANNY).   You are not required any more, No. 7.

(DANNY *is going thankfully, but she suddenly pulls him forward to examine his face.*)
No. 7, you are wearing that brown eye again.

DANNY (*who has a glass eye*).   Yes, Doctor ; you see it 's like this.   First they sent me a brown eye.   Then some meddlesome person finds out my natural eye is blue.   So then they sends me a blue eye.

DOCTOR.   Yes, where is it ?

DANNY.   It was a beautiful eye, Doctor ; but I had taken a fancy to little browny.   And I have a young lady ; so I took the liberty of having the blue eye made up into a brooch and I sent it to her.

DR. BODIE (*without moving a muscle*).   I shall report you.

BODIE (*when the martinet and* DANNY *have gone*).   Are you afraid of her, Cinderella ?   I am.

CINDERELLA.   No !   She sometimes dashes me, but she is a fearful kind lady.   (*She pulls him down again for further important revelations.*)   She 's very particular about her feet.

BODIE (*staggered*).   Is she !   In a feminine way ?

CINDERELLA.   Yes.

BODIE.   Hooray !   Then I have her.   The Achilles Heel ! (*He is once more jerked down.*)

CINDERELLA.   I have a spring bed.

BODIE.   Ah !

CINDERELLA (*in some awe*).   The first time I woke in hospital, an angel with streamers was standing there holding a tray in her hand, and on the tray was a boiled egg.   Then I thought it was the egg you get the day before you die.

BODIE.   What egg is that ?

CINDERELLA (*who in the course of a troubled life has acquired much miscellaneous information*). In the workhouse you always get an egg to your tea the day before you die. (*She whispers*) I know now I'm not the real Cinderella.

BODIE (*taking her hand*). How did you find out?

CINDERELLA (*gravely*). It's come to me. The more I eat the clearer I see things. I think it was just an idea of mine ; being lonely-like I needed to have something to hang on to.

BODIE. That was it. Are you sorry you are not the other one ?

CINDERELLA. I'm glad to be just myself. It's a pity, though, about the glass slippers. That's a lovely idea

BODIE. Yes.

CINDERELLA. Tell me about *Them*.

BODIE. The children ? They are still with me, of course. I am keeping my promise, and they will be with me till you are able to take care of them again. I have them a great deal in the studio in the day-time.

CINDERELLA (*cogitating*). I wonder if that's wise.

BODIE. Oh, they don't disturb me much.

CINDERELLA. I was meaning perhaps the smell of the paint would be bad for them.

BODIE. I see ! Of course I could give up painting.

CINDERELLA (*innocently*). I think that would be safest.

(MR. BODIE *kicks*.)

Are you kind to Gretchen ?

BODIE. I hope so. I feel it's my duty.

CINDERELLA (*troubled*). It'll not be no use for Gretchen if that's how you do it. I'm sure I should get up. (*She attempts to rise.*)

BODIE. Now, now !

CINDERELLA. Are you fond of her, especially when she's bad ?

BODIE (*hurriedly*). Yes, I am, I am ! But she is never bad ! they are all good, they are like angels.

CINDERELLA (*despairing*). Then they're cheating you. Where's my boots ?

BODIE. Quiet ! That's all right.

(*A pretty and not very competent* PROBATIONER *comes in at the window, carrying fishing-rods, followed by* DANNY *with croquet mallets and balls.*)

PROBATIONER (*laden*).   I want to shake hands with you, Mr. Bodie, but you see how I am placed.

CINDERELLA.   Do your pretty bow at any rate.

(*The attractive girl does her pretty bow to* MR. BODIE. *It is one of the few things she does well, and will probably by and by bring her into some safe matrimonial harbour ; but in her country's great hour she is of less value to it than she ought to be. She is of a nice nature and would like to be of use, but things slip through her hands as through her mind ; she cannot even carry a few lengths of fishing-rods without an appeal to heaven. She is counting the pieces now with puckered brow.*)

DANNY (*one of the few men in the world who can carry four croquet balls in two hands*).   You see, sir, there is a pond in the garden, and we have a fishing competition ; and as there are not enough rods the men hides them so as to be sure of having a rod next day.

PROBATIONER.   It is very unfair to the others, Danny.

DANNY (*warmly*).   That 's what I say, Nurse.

CINDERELLA.   The matron found a rod the other morning hidden beneath one of the men's mattresses !

PROBATIONER.   The odd thing is how he could have got it to the house without being seen.   (*Her counting of the pieces ends in her discomfiture.*)

BODIE.   Anything wrong ?

PROBATIONER.   There are only nine pieces.   A whole rod is missing !

CINDERELLA (*trembling for her*).   Nurse, I 'm so sorry !

BODIE.   After all, it 's a trivial matter, isn't it ?

PROBATIONER (*her beautiful empty eyes filling*).   Trivial ! I am responsible.   Just think what Dr. Bodie will say to me !

BODIE.   Are you afraid of her too ?

PROBATIONER.   Afraid !   I should think I am.

DANNY.   And so am I !

(*Before* MR. BODIE *has time to kick, the terrible one re-appears.*)

DR. BODIE.   I am going over to the Home now, Dick.   You must come at once, if you are coming.

BODIE (*cowed and getting his coat*).   Yes, all right.

DR. BODIE.   A greatcoat on a day like this ?   Absurd !

BODIE (*remembering what* CINDERELLA *has told him, and pointing sternly*). French shoes on roads like these, ridiculous !

(DR. BODIE *kicks this time—it is evidently a family trait. Delight of* DANNY.)

DR. BODIE. No. 7, you needn't grin unless there is a reason. Is there a reason ?

DANNY. No, no, Doctor.

DR. BODIE. Fishing-rods all right this time, Nurse ?

PROBATIONER (*faltering*). I am so ashamed, Dr. Bodie ; there is one missing.

DR. BODIE. Again. I must ask you, Nurse, to report yourself to the Matron.

PROBATIONER (*crushed*). Yes, Dr. Bodie.

DR. BODIE (*observing that* DANNY *is stealing away unobtrusively*). No. 7.

DANNY (*still backing*). Yes, Doctor.

DR. BODIE. Come here. What is the matter with your right leg ; it seems stiff.

DANNY (*with the noble resignation of Tommies, of which he has read in the papers*). It 's a twinge of the old stiffness come back, Doctor. I think there 's a touch of east in the wind. The least touch of east seems to find the hole that bullet made. But I 'm not complaining.

DR. BODIE (*brutally*). No, it is I who am complaining.

(*She feels his leg professionally.*) Give me that fishing-rod.

(*The long-suffering man unbuttons, and to his evident astonishment produces the missing rod.*)

DANNY (*without hope but in character*). Well, I am surprised !

DR. BODIE. You will be more surprised presently. Come along, Dick.

(*She takes her brother away.*)

DANNY (*the magnanimous*). She 's great ! Words couldn't express my admiration for that woman—lady—man—doctor.

PROBATIONER. How mean of you, Danny, to get me into trouble.

DANNY (*in the public school manner*). Sorry. But I 'll have to pay for this. (*Seeing visions.*) She has a way of locking one up in the bathroom.

PROBATIONER (*with spirit*). Let us three conspirators

combine to defy her.   Carried.   Proposed, that No. 7, being a male, conveys our challenge to her.   Carried.

CINDERELLA (*gleefully*).   Danny!

DANNY (*of the bull-dog breed*).   I never could refuse the ladies.   (*He uses the stethoscope as a telephone.*)   Give me the Convalescent Home, please.   Is that you, Doctor?   How are you?   We've just rung up to defy you.   Now, now, not another word, or I'll have you locked up in the bathroom. Wait a mo; there's a nurse here wants to give you a piece of her mind.

PROBATIONER (*with the stethoscope*).   Is that you, Miss Bodie?   What?   No, I have decided not to call you Dr. Bodie any more.

(*Alas,* DR. BODIE *returns by the window unseen and hears her.*)

Please to report yourself as in disgrace at once to the Matron. That will do.   Good-bye.   Run along.   Heavens, if she had caught us!

DANNY.   It would have meant permanent residence in the bathroom for me.

(*It is then that they see her.*)

DR. BODIE (*after an awful pause*).   I have come back for my stethoscope, Nurse.

(*The* PROBATIONER *can think of no suitable reply.*)

DANNY (*searching his person*).   I don't think I have it, Doctor.

DR. BODIE.   Don't be a fool, No. 7.

PROBATIONER (*surrendering it*).   Here it is, Dr. Bodie, I— I——

DR. BODIE (*charmingly*).   Thank you.   And, my dear, don't be always Doctor Bodieing me.   That, of course, at the Home, and on duty, but here in my house you are my guest.   I am Miss Bodie to you here.   Don't let me forget that I am a woman.   I assure you I value that privilege.   (*She lingers over* CINDERELLA'S *pillow*)   Dear, you must invite Nurse and Danny to tea with you, and all be happy together.   Little Cinderella, if I will do as a substitute, you haven't altogether lost your Godmother.

(*She goes, shaking a reproving finger at* DANNY.)

DANNY.   We're done again!

PROBATIONER (*reduced to tears*).　Horrid little toad that I 've been.　Some one take me out and shoot me.

(*The* MAID *comes with tea-things.*)

DANNY.　Allow me, maiden.

ELLEN.　Dr. Bodie says I am to bring two more cups.

DANNY (*whose manner is always that of one who, bathroom or no bathroom, feels he is a general favourite*).　If you please, child.

PROBATIONER (*as soon as* ELLEN *has gone*).　Dr. Bodie is an angel.

DANNY (*quite surprised that he has not thought of this before*). That 's what she is !

CINDERELLA.　Danny, can't you say something comforting to poor Nurse?

DANNY (*manfully*).　I 'm thankful to say I can.　Nurse, I 've often had fits of remorse ; and I can assure you that they soon pass away, leaving not a mark behind.

PROBATIONER.　Dear Dr. Bodie !

DANNY.　Exactly.　You 've taken the words out of my mouth.　The only thing for us to think of henceforth is what to do to please her.　Her last words to us were to draw up to the tea-table.　Are we to disregard the last words of that sublime female ?

PROBATIONER (*recovering*).　No !

(*The extra cups having been brought, the company of three settle down to their war-time tea-party, the tray being on* CINDERELLA'S *lap and a guest on each side of her.*)

DANNY.　Our plain duty is now to attack the victuals so as to become strong in that Wonder's service.　Here 's to dear Dr. Bodie, and may she find plenty to do elsewhere till this party is over.

PROBATIONER (*able to toss her head again*).　After all, she put us in a false position.

DANNY.　That 's true.　Down with her !

PROBATIONER.　I drink to you, Danny.

DANNY (*gallantly*).　And I reply with mine.

CINDERELLA.　It 's queer to think I 'm being—what 's the word ?—hostess.

DANNY.　All things are queer ever since the dull old days before the war ; and not the unqueerest is that Daniel Duggan, once a plumber, is now partaking of currant cake with the Lady Charlotte something !

CINDERELLA (*nearly letting her cup fall*).   What ?

PROBATIONER.   You weren't supposed to know that.

CINDERELLA.   Does he mean you ?   Are you——— ?

PROBATIONER.   It's nothing to make a fuss about, Cinderella.   How did you find out, Danny ?

DANNY.   Excuse me, but your haughty manner of wringing out a dishcloth betrayed you ?   My war-worn eyes, of various hues, have had the honour of seeing the Lady Charlotte washing the ward floor.   O memorable day !   O glorified floor !   O blushing dishcloth !

PROBATIONER.   That was just a beginning.   Some day I hope when I rise in the profession to be allowed to wash you, Danny.

DANNY (*bowing grandly*).   The pleasure, my lady, will be mutual.   (*He hums a tune of the moment.*)
' And when I tell them that some day washed by her I 'll be— they 'll never believe me '———

PROBATIONER (*with abandon*).   ' But when I tell them 'twas a jolly good thing for me—they 'll all believe me ! '

DANNY.   And when I tell them—and I certainly mean to tell them—that one day she 'll walk out with me———
    (*In a spirit of devilry he crooks his arm ; she takes it—she walks out with him for a moment.*)

PROBATIONER (*coming to*).   No. 7, what are we doing !

CINDERELLA.   It 's just the war has mixed things up till we forget how different we are.

PROBATIONER (*with a moment of intuition*).   Or it has straightened things out so that we know how like we are.
    (*From the garden comes the sound of a gramophone.*)

CINDERELLA.   David 's a long time in coming.

DANNY.   The four-twenty 's not in yet.

CINDERELLA.   Yes, it is ; I heard the whistle.

DANNY (*sarcastically*).   Would you like me to see if he hasn't lost his way ?   Those policemen are stupid fellows.

CINDERELLA.   None of that, Danny ; but I would like fine if you take a look.

DANNY.   Anything to oblige you, though it brings our social to a close.   None of these little tea-parties after the war is over, fine lady.

PROBATIONER. Oh dear ! I 'll often enjoy myself less, Danny.

DANNY. Daniel Duggan will sometimes think of this day, when you are in your presentation gown and he is on your roof, looking for that there leakage.

PROBATIONER. Oh, Danny, don't tell me that when I meet you with your bag of tools I 'll be a beast. Surely there will be at least a smile of friendship between us in memory of the old days.

DANNY. I wonder ! That 's up to you, my lady. (*But he will be wiser if he arranges that it is to be up to himself.*)

PROBATIONER (*calling attention to the music*). Listen ! No. 7, to-day is ours.

(*She impulsively offers herself for the waltz ; they dance together.*)

DANNY (*when all is over*). Thank you, my lady.

(*She curtseys and he goes out rather finely. It is not likely that her next partner will be equal to her plumber. The two girls are left alone, both nice girls of about the same age ; but the poor one has already lived so long that the other, though there may be decades before her, will never make up on* CINDERELLA. *She gaily lies on the bed beside the patient, and they are a pretty picture.*)

CINDERELLA. He is a droll character, Danny. (*Examining herself in a hand-mirror*) Nurse, would you say my hair is looking right ? He likes the cap.

PROBATIONER (*who will soon forget her, but is under the spell at present*). Your David ?

CINDERELLA (*on her dignity*). He 's not mine, Nurse.

PROBATIONER. Isn't he ?

CINDERELLA. Hey, hey, hey ! Nurse, when he comes you don't need to stay very long.

PROBATIONER (*in the conspiracy*). I won't.

CINDERELLA (*casually*). He might have things to say to me, you see.

PROBATIONER. Yes, he might.

CINDERELLA (*solemnly*). You and me are both very young, but maybe you understand about men better than I do. You 've seen him, and this is terrible important. Swear by Almighty God you 're to tell me the truth. Would you say that man loves little children ?

PROBATIONER (*touched*). Don't frighten me, Cinderella ; I believe him to be that kind of man. Are you fond of your policeman, dear ?

CINDERELLA (*winking*). That's telling ! (*Importantly*) Nurse, did you ever have a love-letter.

PROBATIONER (*making a face*). Not I ! Don't want to ; horrid little explosives ! But have you—has he—— ?

CINDERELLA (*becoming larger*). In my poor opinion, if it's not a love-letter, it's a very near thing.

PROBATIONER. If I could see the darling little detestable ?

CINDERELLA. Oh no, oh no, no, no, no ! But I'll tell you one thing as is in it. This—'There are thirty-four policemen sitting in this room, but I would rather have you, my dear.' What do you think ? That's a fine bit at the end.

PROBATIONER (*sparkling*). Lovely ! Go on, Cinderella, fling reticence to the winds.

CINDERELLA (*doing so*). Unless I am—very far out—in my judgment of men—that man is infatuate about me !

PROBATIONER (*clapping her hands*). The delicious scoundrel ! Cinderella, be merciless to him ! Knife him, you dear ! Give him beans !

CINDERELLA (*gurgling*). I ill-treats him most terrible.

PROBATIONER. That's the way ! down with lovers ! slit them to ribbons ! stamp on them !

CINDERELLA. Sometimes I—— (*She sits up.*) Listen !

PROBATIONER (*alarmed*). It isn't Dr. Bodie, is it ?

CINDERELLA. No, it's *him*.

PROBATIONER. I don't hear a sound.

CINDERELLA. I can hear him fanning his face with his helmet. He has come in such a hurry. Nurse, you watch me being cruel to him.

PROBATIONER. At him, Cinderella, at him !

DANNY (*throwing open the door*). The Constabulary's carriage stops the way.

(*Our* POLICEMAN *stalks in, wetting his lips as he does so.*)

PROBATIONER (*giving him her hand*). How do you do ? You forget, I dare say, that I met you when you were here last ; but I remember ' our policeman.'

(*He is bashful.*)

There she is.

(*The wicked invalid is looking the other way.*)

POLICEMAN.   A visitor to see you, Jane.

CINDERELLA (*without looking round*).   I thought it had a visitor's sound.   (*She peeps at the* PROBATIONER *gleefully.*)

POLICEMAN (*very wooden*).   You don't ask who it is, Jane ?

CINDERELLA.   I thought it might be that great big ridiculous policeman.

(DANNY *laughs, and our* POLICEMAN *gives him a very stern look.*)

POLICEMAN (*after reflection*).   I'm here again, Jane.

CINDERELLA (*admitting it with a glance*).   Perhaps you didn't ought to come so often ; it puts them about.

POLICEMAN (*cleverly*).   But does it put you about, Jane ?

CINDERELLA.   Hey ! Hey ! (*With a cunning waggle of the hand she intimates to the* NURSE *that she may go.*)

DANNY (*who is not so easily got rid of*).   You had best be going too, Robert.   The lady has answered you in the negative.

POLICEMAN (*lowering*).   You make a move there.

(DANNY, *affecting alarm, departs with the* PROBATIONER.)

CINDERELLA.   I like fine to hear you ordering the public about, David.

POLICEMAN (*humbly*).   I'm very pleased, Jane, if there's any little thing about me that gives you satisfaction.

(*He puts down a small parcel that he has brought in.*)

CINDERELLA (*curious*).   What's in the parcel, David ?

POLICEMAN.   That remains to be seen.   (*He stands staring at his divinity.*)

CINDERELLA (*sneering*).   What are you looking at ?

POLICEMAN.   Just at you.

CINDERELLA (*in high delight*).   Me ? There's little to look at in me.   You should see the larder at the Home.   You'll have a cup of China tea and some of this cake ?

POLICEMAN.   No, Jane, no.   (*In a somewhat melancholy voice*) Things to eat have very little interest to me now.

CINDERELLA.   Oh ?

POLICEMAN.   I've gone completely off my feed.

(CINDERELLA *would have liked the* PROBATIONER *to hear this.*)

CINDERELLA (*artfully*).   I wonder how that can be !

POLICEMAN.   Did you get my letter, Jane?

CINDERELLA (*calmly*).   I got it.

POLICEMAN.   Did you—did you think it was a peculiar sort of a letter?

CINDERELLA (*mercilessly*).   I don't mind nothing peculiar in it.

POLICEMAN.   There was no word in it that took you aback, was there?

CINDERELLA.   Not that I mind of.

POLICEMAN (*worried*).   Maybe you didn't read it very careful?

CINDERELLA.   I may have missed something.   What was the word, David?

POLICEMAN (*in gloom*).   Oh, it was just a small affair.   It was just a beginning.   I thought, if she stands that she 'll stand more.   But if you never noticed it—— (*He sighs profoundly.*)

CINDERELLA.   I 'll take another look.

POLICEMAN (*brightening*).   You 've kept it?

CINDERELLA.   I have it here.

POLICEMAN.   I could let you see the word if it 's convenient to you to get the letter out of your pocket.

CINDERELLA.   It 's not in my pocket.

POLICEMAN.   Is it under the pillow?

CINDERELLA.   No.

POLICEMAN (*puzzled*).   Where, then?

(CINDERELLA, *with charming modesty, takes the letter from her bodice.   Her lover is thunderstruck.*)

What made you think of keeping it there?

CINDERELLA.   I didn't think, David; it just came to me.

POLICEMAN (*elate*).   It 's infallayble!   I 'll let you see the word.

CINDERELLA (*smiling at the ridiculous man*).   You don't need to bother, David.   Fine I know what the word is.

POLICEMAN (*anxious*).   And you like it?

CINDERELLA.   If you like it.

POLICEMAN.   That emboldens me tremendous.

CINDERELLA.   I don't like that so much.   If there 's one thing I like more than any other thing in the world——

POLICEMAN (*eager*).   Yes?

CINDERELLA.   It 's seeing you, David, tremendous bold before all other folk, and just in a quake before me.

POLICEMAN (*astounded*). It 's what I am. And yet there 's something bold I must say to you.

CINDERELLA (*faltering genteelly*). Is there ?

POLICEMAN. It 'll be a staggering surprise to you.

(CINDERELLA *giggles discreetly*.)

I promised the Doctor as I came in not to tire you. (*With some awe*) She 's a powerful woman that.

CINDERELLA. If you tire me I 'll hold up my hand just like you do to stop the traffic. Go on, David. Just wait a moment. (*She takes off his helmet and holds it to her thin breast*.) Here 's a friend of mine. Now ?

POLICEMAN (*despairing of himself*). I wish I was a man in a book. It 's pretty the way they say it ; and if ever there was a woman that deserved to have it said pretty to her it 's you. I 've been reading the books. There was one chap that could speak six languages. Jane, I wish I could say it to you in six languages, one down and another come up, till you had to take me in the end.

CINDERELLA. To take you ?

POLICEMAN (*in woe*). Now I 've gone and said it in the poorest, silliest way. Did you hold up your hand to stop me, Jane ?

CINDERELLA. No.

POLICEMAN (*encouraged*). But I 've said it. Will you, Jane ?

CINDERELLA (*doggedly*). Will I what ?

POLICEMAN. Do you not see what I 'm driving at ?

CINDERELLA. Fine I see what you 're driving at !

POLICEMAN. Then won't you help me out ?

CINDERELLA. No.

POLICEMAN. If you could just give me a shove.

CINDERELLA (*sympathetically*). Try Badgery.

POLICEMAN (*brightening*). Have you forgotten that pool in Badgery Water where the half-pounder used—— No, you never was there ! Jane, the heart of me is crying out to walk with you by Badgery Water.

CINDERELLA. That 's better !

POLICEMAN. I would never think of comparing Mrs. Bodie to you. For my part I think nothing of uppers. Feet for me. (*She gives him her hand to hold*.)

My dear !

CINDERELLA.   You said *that* was only a beginning.

POLICEMAN.   My dearest !

CINDERELLA (*glistening*).   I 'm not feeling none tired, David.

POLICEMAN.   My pretty !

CINDERELLA.   Hey ! Hey ! Hey ! Hey !

POLICEMAN.   I don't set up to be a prince, Jane ; but I love you in a princely way, and if you would marry me, you wonder, I 'll be a true man to you till death us do part.   Come on, Cinders.   (*Pause*) It 's the only chance that belt of mine has.

CINDERELLA.   No, no, I haven't took you yet.   There 's a thing you could do for me, that would gratify me tremendous.

POLICEMAN.   It 's done.

CINDERELLA.   I want you to let me have the satisfaction, David, of having refused you once.

POLICEMAN.   Willingly ; but what for ?

CINDERELLA.   I couldn't say.   Just because I 'm a woman. Mind you, I dare say I 'll cast it up at you in the future.

POLICEMAN.   I 'll risk that.   Will you be my princess, Jane ?

CINDERELLA.   You promise to ask again ?   At once ?

POLICEMAN.   Yes.

CINDERELLA.   Say—I do.

POLICEMAN.   I do.

CINDERELLA (*firmly*).   It 's a honour you do me, policeman, to which I am not distasteful.   But I don't care for you in that way, so let there be no more on the subject.   (*Anxiously*) Quick, David !

POLICEMAN.   For the second time, will you marry me, Jane ?

CINDERELLA (*who has been thinking out the answer for several days*).   David, I love thee, even as the stars shining on the parched earth, even as the flowers opening their petals to the sun ; even as mighty ocean with its billows ; even so do I love thee, David.   (*She nestles her head on his shoulder.*)

POLICEMAN.   If only I could have said it like that !

CINDERELLA (*happily*).   That 's just a bit I was keeping handy.   (*Almost in a whisper*) David, do you think I could have a engagement ring ?

POLICEMAN (*squaring his shoulders*).   As to that, Jane, first tell me frankly, do you think the Police Force is romantical ?

CINDERELLA.   They 're brave and strong, but——

POLICEMAN.   The general verdict is no.   And yet a more romantical body of men do not exist.   I have been brooding over this question of engagement rings, and I consider them unromantical affairs.   (*He walks toward his parcel.*)

CINDERELLA.   David, what 's in that parcel ?

POLICEMAN.   Humbly hoping you would have me, Jane, I have had something special made for you——

CINDERELLA (*thrilling*).   Oh, David, what is it ?

POLICEMAN.   It 's a policeman's idea of an engagement ring—

CINDERELLA.   Quick !   Quick !

POLICEMAN.   —for my amazing romantical mind said to me that, instead of popping a ring on the finger of his dear, a true lover should pop a pair of glass slippers upon her darling feet.

CINDERELLA.   David, you 're a poet !

POLICEMAN (*not denying it*).   It 's what you 've made me— and proud I would be if, for the honour of the Force, I set this new fashion in engagement rings.   (*He reveals the glass slippers.*)

(CINDERELLA *holds out her hands for the little doves.*) They 're not for hands.   (*He uncovers her feet.*)

CINDERELLA.   They 're terrible small !   Maybe they 'll not go on !

(*They go on.*)

CINDERELLLA.   They 're like two kisses.

POLICEMAN.   More like two love-letters.

CINDERELLA.   No, David, no,—kisses.

POLICEMAN.   We won't quarrel about it, Cinders ; but at the same time . . . However !

(*He presses her face to him for a moment so that he may not see its transparency.   DR. BODIE has told him something.*)

CINDERELLA. They're brave and strong, but—

POLICEMAN. The general verdict is no. And yet a more romantical body of men do not exist. I have been brooding over this question of engagement rings, and I consider them unromantical affairs. (*He casts scorn on his parcel.*)

CINDERELLA. David, what's in that parcel?

POLICEMAN. Humbly hoping you would have me, Jane, I have had something special made for you—

CINDERELLA (*thrilling*). Oh, David, what is it?

POLICEMAN. It's a policeman's idea of an engagement ring—

CINDERELLA. Quick! Quick!

POLICEMAN. —for my amazing romantical mind said to me that, instead of popping a ring on the finger of his dear, a true lover should pop a pair of glass-slippers upon her darling feet.

CINDERELLA. David, you're a poet!

POLICEMAN (*ruefully*). It's what you've made me—and proud I would be if, for the honour of the Force, I set this new fashion in engagement rings. (*He reveals the glass slippers.*)

(*CINDERELLA holds out her hands for the little doves.*)

They're not for hands. (*He measures her feet.*)

CINDERELLA. They're terrible small. Maybe they'll not go on.

(*They go on.*)

CINDERELLA. They're like two kisses.

POLICEMAN. More like two love-letters.

CINDERELLA. No, David, no,—kisses.

POLICEMAN. We won't quarrel about it, Cinders; but at the same time . . . However—

(*He presses her face to him for a moment so that he may not see its transparency, or Dr. Bodie has told him something.*)

SEVEN WOMEN

Produced at the New Theatre on April 7, 1917, with the following cast :

CAPTAIN RATTRAY, R.N. . . .	*Gordon Ash*
LEONORA	*Irene Vanbrugh*
MR. TOVEY	*Philip Anthony*
MRS. TOVEY	*Netta Westcott*
MAID	*Gladys Calthrop*

This was the revised version of the first act of ' The Adored One,' originally produced at the Duke of York's Theatre on September 4, 1913.

SEVEN WOMEN

MR. and MRS. TOVEY, a pleasant couple of the agreeable age, are in their Chelsea drawing-room, the envied bit of which is the long low twisted window at the back overlooking the river. They never draw the curtains on this view when (as to-night) visitors are expected, for it is one of the fairest in London, especially by night ; but they often ask you to step on to the leads, from which every moving coal-barge with a light on it is floating magic. The Toveys, knowing themselves to be alone, are discussing to-night's dinner at their ease, when up steals the rogue of a curtain. ' The audience, madam,' we say, and go, as primly as if we were the parlour-maid. Perhaps they have not heard us, for the talk continues as if they were still unobserved.

TOVEY (*approvingly*). A capital little menu.

MRS. TOVEY (*though she thinks so herself*). Of course it is a short dinner, Jack, to offer to such a celebrity. (*With a sigh*) I must say it would have been rather nice of you if you could have remembered whether when Captain Rattray was a boy he liked lamb.

TOVEY. My dear, just because Rattray has had this little flutter in China waters I, who haven't seen him for twenty years, am expected to remember whether when we were inky beasts at school he liked lamb. All I do remember is that he was timid and that I punched the heads of the boys who bullied him.

MRS. TOVEY. Yes, I have noticed that is the one thing all men remember about a school friend.

TOVEY. Any further orders, madam ?

MRS. TOVEY (*with gentle resignation*). Well, it would be rather sweet of you if you didn't try to be funny to-night. I am so anxious to make this dinner a success.

TOVEY (*ever explanatory on this subject*). My own, I don't try to be funny ; I am funny.

MRS. TOVEY.   Yes, I know you can't help it, and I don't mind when we are alone.   But in company some of your jokes —that one about the murderess, for instance——

TOVEY.   Best of women ; but even though you are that, do endeavour to be fair.   She was amused by it herself.

MRS. TOVEY.   Ah, but suppose some one present had believed it !

TOVEY (*nobly*).   Very well.   I 'll try to be dull, dear.   (*She has risen quickly.*)   Whither away ?

MRS. TOVEY.   I thought I heard the bell.

TOVEY.   Can't be anybody yet ; there 's half an hour to dinner time.

MRS. TOVEY.   It is some one.   And neither of us dressed ! (*She rushes off.*

The maid ushers in CAPTAIN RATTRAY, *a naval officer, in levee dress.*)

TOVEY.   How are you, Rattray ?

CAPTAIN R.   How do you do, Tovey ?

(*For a moment only are they stiff and self-conscious.*)

TOVEY.   Bobbin, that was !

CAPTAIN R.   Inky Paws, that used to be !   (*They take candid stock of each other.*)

TOVEY.   A little grey at the roots.

CAPTAIN R.   Chest slipped down a bit.

TOVEY.   To think of old Bobbin blossoming into a nut !

CAPTAIN R.   I warned you I was going on to a levee and would have to come in these.

TOVEY.   We wanted you in these ; in fact it was these we wanted even more than you.   Remember the pillow fights, Bobbin ?

CAPTAIN R. (*warmly*).   Rather !   Do you remember you were a bit puny and how I used to fight the brutes who ill-used you ?

TOVEY (*coldly*).   I don't remember that.

CAPTAIN R.   And now I hear little Inky Paws has had the pluck to take unto him a squaw.

TOVEY.   More than you have had.

CAPTAIN R. (*reproducing the face with which he went to his first dance*).   They scare me as much as ever, Jack.

TOVEY.   That reminds me : do you like lamb ?

CAPTAIN R. I could eat lamb by the solid hour.

TOVEY. Then you'll like my wife. By the way, that explains why you come to a dinner-party half an hour before the time

CAPTAIN R. (*giving himself up for lost*). I was asked for eight.

TOVEY. Sure?

CAPTAIN R. (*on oath*). I have your wife's letter with me.

TOVEY. Then you are forgiven. Her mistake. She is dressing wildly now, and if you will excuse me——

CAPTAIN R. Don't mind me.

(TOVEY *is going*.)

Stop, Jack. Who are the other guests?

TOVEY (*pondering*). Let me see.

CAPTAIN R. (*shaking him*). Never mind the men, tell me about the women ; they are the fearsome ones.

TOVEY. Well, we have all kinds for you, not knowing your taste. For instance, there is one dear lady who has no sense of humour.

CAPTAIN R. (*with certain memories*). I am sure there is.

TOVEY. If you want to know which one she is, try them with a funny story. Then there is one who has almost too much sense of humour. If there is anything ridiculous about you, Bobbin, as I dare say there is, she will spot it at once.

CAPTAIN R. Oh, help ; don't put me beside that one.

TOVEY. You would prefer the politician?

CAPTAIN R. The what?

TOVEY. No platform complete without them nowadays. If she drops her handkerchief and you pick it up for her there will be a riot. By the way, she drops her things all over the place. You will know her by that.

CAPTAIN R. Ancient friend, do dress quickly.

TOVEY. You will be all right. Stick to the Very woman. She is one of the good old-fashioned, obedient clinging kind that our fathers knew.

CAPTAIN R. (*disbelieving*). Did you say obedient, Jack?

TOVEY. Sounds like a dream, doesn't it? Speaking of fathers, there is a mother coming. You know, the sort of woman who is a mother and nothing else.

CAPTAIN R. I like those simple souls.

TOVEY. The coquette isn't what you would call a simple soul.

CAPTAIN R. A coquette, too ?

TOVEY. The most audacious flirt of my acquaintance.

(CAPTAIN RATTRAY *is a little complacent.*)
Why that swagger ?

CAPTAIN R. I wasn't swaggering, but I get on rather well with that kind. Once at an India station—— However.

TOVEY. I think that completes the list. (*Disregarding a recent promise*) Stop, though, there is one more—a murderess.

CAPTAIN R. None of your blarney, Jack.

TOVEY. Don't think I am joking. (*Confidentially*) Fact is, since you were last on leave the order of the day for dinners has become a celebrity at any cost.

CAPTAIN R. Draw the line.

TOVEY. We don't nowadays ; life is too strenuous. You will see what deference we pay her. Why, man alive, if it had not been for you the likes of us couldn't have got her. She had a much more exalted engagement, and broke it to meet you.

CAPTAIN R. Tosh !

TOVEY. But listen ; the bell again ! Here 's another who has been asked too early.

CAPTAIN R. Let us hope it is a man.

TOVEY. I hear the swish of skirts. Bobbin, with perfect confidence, I leave you to do the honours.

CAPTAIN R. As you love me, no !

TOVEY. I must scoot.

CAPTAIN R. (*intercepting him*). You are placing me in a horrible position ! No humour—too much humour—public speaker who spills her things, but I mustn't lift them up for her. A Very woman of the clinging kind—a mother and nothing else—a coquette—and a murderess who broke an engagement to meet me. How am I to know which this one is ?

TOVEY (*as he glides past him*). Be a sportsman, my gallant tar, and find out.

(CAPTAIN RATTRAY *is meditating an escape on to the leads when the maid shows in* LEONORA. LEONORA *is an unspeakable darling ; and this is all the guidance that can be given to the lady playing her. She grasps the situation and bows charmingly.* CAPTAIN RATTRAY'S *awkwardness makes a good impression on her.*)

LEONORA. I suppose Mrs. Tovey hasn't yet——

CAPTAIN R. Perhaps I ought to explain——

(*They have spoken simultaneously.*)

CAPTAIN R. I beg your pardon.

LEONORA. You were saying?

CAPTAIN R. No, you.

LEONORA. Please—if I did not know this room——

CAPTAIN R. The fact is that Mr. Tovey——

(*They are at it again; this nonsense puts them on easier terms.*)

CAPTAIN R. I fancy you must be in the same predicament as myself. I have arrived to dinner half an hour too soon.

LEONORA. I was asked for eight o'clock.

CAPTAIN R. And I. But it was a mistake. Dinner is at eight-thirty.

LEONORA. Oh dear!

CAPTAIN R. Mr. Tovey has just told me. He isn't sure whether the same mistake has been made with the others or not.

LEONORA. I see. How horrid of us (*sitting that he may do so also, one of the most excellent things in woman*).

CAPTAIN R. But it isn't our fault.

LEONORA. That is true. Still, how horrid of us.

(*It strikes him that she must be that inconsequential delight to memory dear, the Very woman.*)

CAPTAIN R. (*enlightened*). Ha!

LEONORA (*arrested*). What?

CAPTAIN R. You know, that is just what my mother would have said in the same circumstances. Perhaps I should say that my name is Rattray.

LEONORA. I was sure of it. If I may say so, we are all proud of Captain Rattray.

CAPTAIN R. (*rushing her off the gangway*). Oh, please don't. I did nothing. (*Smiling*) I flatter myself I know something about you also.

LEONORA (*curious*). You do? About me? What?

CAPTAIN R. (*with the modest self-satisfaction that comes to the discriminating*). I have found it out since you came into the room.

LEONORA. But how uncanny. I 'm listening.

CAPTAIN R. I have found out that you are a Very woman.

LEONORA. What is that ?

CAPTAIN R. (*comprehensively*). Ah !

LEONORA. Do tell me.

CAPTAIN R. (*reflecting*). I suppose it is a man's phrase.

LEONORA. That is why I want to know what it means ?

CAPTAIN R. (*in deep waters*). A Very woman is—is—well, she is a clinging woman. All sailors like clinging women.

LEONORA. Do they ? What do they like them to cling to ?

CAPTAIN R. As to that—(*his snotties would enjoy seeing him now*)—I am afraid I seem very stupid. You see, for more than a year I have scarcely spoken to a woman.

LEONORA (*sympathetic*). Constant practice is everything in speaking. I could always speak fairly fluently in committees and so on. But in the Albert Hall——

CAPTAIN R. (*in consternation*). You don't mean—politics ?

LEONORA. Oh yes, why not ? Is anything wrong ?

CAPTAIN R. (*depressed*). Nothing.

(*Her handkerchief falls. He is about to pick it up when he remembers that politicians don't like this.*)
May I ?

LEONORA. Not if it is too much trouble. (*She picks it up herself.*)

CAPTAIN R. I am awfully sorry. The fact is, you gave me a little shock just now.

LEONORA. I did ? How ? Perhaps I am not the woman you thought me after all ?

CAPTAIN R. No, you are not.

(*He is so lugubrious that she laughs.*)

LEONORA. You had better give me up, Captain Rattray.

CAPTAIN R. Not I.

(*She raises her eyebrows at his audacity.*)

LEONORA (*changing the subject*). Mrs. Tovey has a dear house, don't you think ?

CAPTAIN R. (*looking about him for the first time*). Yes, very. Some pretty things here.

LEONORA. Aren't there ? But the real treasures, of course, are the two lovelies on the top floor of the house.

CAPTAIN R. (*mildly surprised*). Oh ?

LEONORA (*explanatory*).   In the room where the night-lights are.

CAPTAIN R. (*who has forgotten domesticity*).   Night-lights?

LEONORA.   Haven't you been up?

CAPTAIN R.   On the top floor? No.

LEONORA.   I thought you were an old school friend of Mr. Tovey?

CAPTAIN R.   I am.

LEONORA.   And he didn't rush you to the top of the house? To the two rooms where the large fire-guards are?

CAPTAIN R.   No; what are the fire-guards for?

LEONORA.   To prevent them falling into the fire, of course.

CAPTAIN R.   Whom? Jack and his wife?

LEONORA.   Oh, I shall never understand men!

CAPTAIN R.   I can't quite—what is it that Jack Tovey keeps at the top floor of the house?

LEONORA (*reproachfully*).   Oh, Captain Rattray, his pretty things.

CAPTAIN R. (*dense*).   Yes, I see—I didn't even know that he was a collector. But what a rum place to keep them.

(*He sees she is shocked.*)
Excuse me, I have been such a long time at sea.

LEONORA (*shocked*).   Captain Rattray, were you never kept on the top floor?

CAPTAIN R.   Only when I was a chicken. (*Daylight reaches him.*) You don't mean to say that Inky Paws—Jack Tovey— that he——?

LEONORA (*nodding delightedly*).   Yes, two! A boy and a girl.

CAPTAIN R.   A boy and a girl? (*He is in touch with her at last.*) That is the best joke I have heard since I came back.

LEONORA.   Joke?

CAPTAIN R.   Well, isn't it?

LEONORA (*wounded*).   Mrs. Tovey's babies are a joke, are they? I can tell you another joke, Captain Rattray. (*Haughtily*) I also am a—collector.

CAPTAIN R.   You?

LEONORA.   It is funny, isn't it!

CAPTAIN R. (*contritely*).   Do forgive me. Somehow I— didn't think of you as a mother.

LEONORA (*to whom this is still more dreadful*).   You didn't think—Captain Rattray, I could forgive you a good deal, but I will never forgive you that. *(She is about to step out on to the leads.)*

CAPTAIN R. *(desperate).* I could eat my hat.

LEONORA *(freezingly).* Not before me, please.

CAPTAIN R. I say, I wasn't speaking against mothers. I think there is nothing like them.

LEONORA *(perhaps a little unfairly).* You said I didn't deserve to be one.

CAPTAIN R. *(stung).* I did not.

LEONORA. You needn't bark. *(She melts easily.)* Surely you might have guessed.

CAPTAIN R. It was dense of me. I can see it now clearly enough.

LEONORA. Oh?

CAPTAIN R. It is written all over you.

LEONORA *(rather tart).* I don't think it is so obvious as that.

CAPTAIN R. No, indeed—that is, whatever you prefer. I say, do let me down softly.

LEONORA *(smiling divinely).* That was almost like Harry !

CAPTAIN R. *(grumpily).* Was it ?

LEONORA *(softly).* He is my son.

CAPTAIN R. *(relieved).* A gorgeous fellow, I 'll be bound. *(Cunningly)* Tell me about him.

LEONORA *(tremulously).* You wouldn't really care to know

CAPTAIN R. I would indeed. It may seem strange to you——

LEONORA. Oh, no.

CAPTAIN R. How old is he ?

LEONORA. Fourteen and two months.

CAPTAIN R. What a ripper.

LEONORA. He is at school.

CAPTAIN R. Well done.

LEONORA. He is in the O.T.C.

CAPTAIN R. Of course he is.

LEONORA. I had a letter from him to-day—he says—— *(It is evidently in the bodice of her gown.)*

CAPTAIN R. Nothing wrong, I hope ?

LEONORA *(in a flood of emotion).* He—he—he wants me to send him a razor.

CAPTAIN R. (*wildly sympathetic*). The ass—the ungrateful booby—the——

LEONORA (*flaming up*). How can you ! You—— Oh, you *man*.

CAPTAIN R. (*hurriedly*). It is myself I mean, not him. Besides, you were almost crying, as if he had hurt you.

LEONORA. Harry hurt me ! Don't you see how splendid it is ?

CAPTAIN R. Rather ! I say, do let me send Harry his first razor.

LEONORA (*pleased*). Oh, no.

CAPTAIN R. After all, I must know more about razors than you do. Other subjects—but razors ?

LEONORA (*in* HARRY'S *interest*). That must be true, of course.

CAPTAIN R. Leave it to me.

LEONORA. Something suitable. He is five feet five and rather fair.

CAPTAIN R. I 'll get that kind.

LEONORA. And—and please—rather a blunt one.

CAPTAIN R. (*admiring her*). I believe you would try it on yourself if that would be any help to Harry.

LEONORA. Of course I would.

CAPTAIN R. May I ask, how many children have you ?

LEONORA (*nervously, to do her justice*). Would you think six a large number ?

CAPTAIN R. Six ?

(*He is a little shaken and loses favour in her eyes.*)

LEONORA (*with one look putting the dastard in his place*). Oh, you would ?

CAPTAIN R. (*recklessly*). Not at all. (*Suddenly seeing which of the women this is*) Ha !

LEONORA. What is it now ?

CAPTAIN R. (*the solution found*). A mother and nothing else !

LEONORA. I beg your pardon.

CAPTAIN R. It is a—a quotation. Mr. Tovey told me there is a lady dining here to-night who is a mother and nothing else.

LEONORA. What an odd way of putting it. I wonder who she can be ?

CAPTAIN R. I wonder !

LEONORA. I never met a woman of whom that could be said.

CAPTAIN R. I have.

LEONORA. Nice?

CAPTAIN R. Distinctly.

(*She accidentally drops her bag and he picks it up at once.*)

LEONORA. Quicker than last time.

CAPTAIN R. (*who could kick himself for being so long in getting at it*). I didn't know you then. (*He keeps the bag in his hand.*)

LEONORA. Yes, it is a nice bag.

CAPTAIN R. (*thoughtfully*). Ha!

LEONORA. I won it last Christmas.

CAPTAIN R. Won it?

LEONORA. Yes, it was one of the prizes at a fancy-dress dance.

(*He is aghast. Is she the mother and nothing else after all?*)

CAPTAIN R. Were *you* in fancy dress?

LEONORA. Yes. I went as a Bacchante.

CAPTAIN R. You did!

LEONORA. I thought it would suit me. Don't you think so?

CAPTAIN R. I dare say. (*He gives her back the bag and draws his hand across his brow.*)

LEONORA (*feeling that he disapproves*). Don't you like dancing?

CAPTAIN R. Oh yes—but—yes, immensely.

LEONORA. I adore it. But your woman wouldn't dance?

CAPTAIN R. My woman?

LEONORA. The one who is a mother and nothing else.

CAPTAIN R. I had forgotten her. No, not as a Bacchante, she—and for a moment I thought that you—— (*As he looks at her a not entirely welcome idea strikes him.*) Would you mind my telling you a funny story?

LEONORA (*surprised*). I should love it.

CAPTAIN R. (*placing a chair for her in the manner of the conjurer*). I ought to explain first that I am telling it you with a purpose.

LEONORA. How odd, a funny story with a purpose!

CAPTAIN R. (*with foreboding*). The fact is, the way you take it will tell me something about you.

LEONORA (*astounded*). It will?

CAPTAIN R. If you would rather I didn't——

LEONORA. Do go on.

CAPTAIN R. Well, it was at a dinner-party the other night. Perhaps you know the story.

LEONORA. I don't recognise it so far.

CAPTAIN R. A lady dining there had talked mostly to the man who took her in ; she had scarcely looked at the man on her other side who was quite young, but extremely bald. Toward the end of dinner, however, he stooped to pick up his napkin——

LEONORA. The bald man ?

CAPTAIN R. Yes.

LEONORA (*excitedly*). I feel sure we are coming to the thing that is to tell you so much about me.

CAPTAIN R. (*a little excited himself*). Well, we are.

LEONORA. How you are watching me !

CAPTAIN R. I can't help it. She turned as he stooped, and seeing nothing but his bald head—it was rather yellow, too— she thought it was fruit being handed round by a servant, and she said : ' No, no melon, thank you.'

(*He looks anxiously at her.*)

LEONORA. And didn't she ?

CAPTAIN R. Didn't she what ?

LEONORA. Didn't she have any melon ?

CAPTAIN R. (*heavily*). I don't know. I believe not.

LEONORA. Well ?

CAPTAIN R. That 's all.

LEONORA. Oh ! (*Politely*) What a good story. (*Suddenly suspicious*) But it can't tell you anything about me ?

CAPTAIN R. Indeed it does.

LEONORA. Tell me.

CAPTAIN R. Never. But I 'll tell you something else now. Before Mr. Tovey hurried away to dress he told me something about each of the ladies who is coming to dinner, but not their names, and all this time I have been trying to find out which of them you are.

LEONORA. The creature ! And which one am I ?

CAPTAIN R. I have just found out. I went wrong several times.

LEONORA. Do tell me.

CAPTAIN R.   Not I.

LEONORA.   At least tell me who the others are.   I may know them.

CAPTAIN R.   I won't tell you the ones I mistook for you, but I 'll tell you the ones I knew from the first you couldn't be.

LEONORA.   Yes, do.

CAPTAIN R.   One is a lady with too much sense of humour.

LEONORA.   Let me think.

CAPTAIN R.   I 'm glad you 're not that one.

LEONORA.   I wonder if I am ?

CAPTAIN R. (with conviction).   No, I know you are not.

LEONORA.   It is that horrid melon that has put you against me.

CAPTAIN R.   I am not at all against you.   Then there is another lady who is a coquette.

LEONORA (with considerable interest).   Tell me every word the man said about her.

CAPTAIN R.   He said : ' She is the most audacious flirt of my acquaintance.'   Can you place her ?

LEONORA.   No.   Are there any more ?

CAPTAIN R.   That was all.   Ah, well, he mentioned one other, but that was only his fun.

LEONORA.   Still tell me.

CAPTAIN R.   He said there was a murderess coming.

(She remembers a certain story of Master Jack's.)

LEONORA.   Oh ?

CAPTAIN R.   Absurd !

LEONORA.   I don't see why it should be so absurd.

CAPTAIN R.   You don't tell me you would come here if you knew a murderess had been invited ?

LEONORA.   I did know she had been invited.

CAPTAIN R.   Ah, of course there is some explanation.

LEONORA (brightly).   Yes, it is really all right.   I thought at first that you were to be fussy about it.

CAPTAIN R.   Fussy !   Would you mind telling me about this woman ?

LEONORA.   She was in a railway carriage with her little girl. A man came into the carriage, and he put down the window. She was quite polite.   She said, ' Would you mind keeping the window up, because my little girl has a cold ? '   He said, ' I 'm sorry, but I feel stifled unless I have a window open.' (*She looks to see if Captain Rattray is taking in the enormity of this man's behaviour.*)

CAPTAIN R. (*attentively*).   Yes ?

LEONORA   She was splendidly patient.   She said, ' But my little girl has a cold.   Please to shut the window.'   He refused. Then there was nothing else for her to do, was there ?

CAPTAIN R. (*rather breathless*).   What did she do ?

LEONORA.   She opened the door and pushed him out.

CAPTAIN R.   You don't mean he was killed ?

LEONORA.   Yes, he fell on the line and killed himself.

CAPTAIN R.   Before her eyes ?

LEONORA.   The train was going rather fast, but she had just time to see him go bump.

CAPTAIN R.   What a dreadful———   And then ?

LEONORA (*finishing her story*).   Then she put up the window. Nothing so very dreadful, you see.

CAPTAIN R. (*dazed*).   Is this England ?

LEONORA (*huffily*).   Oh, if you are to take it in that way.

CAPTAIN R.   This man———

LEONORA.   Of course you take the man's side.

CAPTAIN R. (*exasperated*).   You talk as if you didn't blame her.

LEONORA (*patiently*).   Haven't I told you that her little girl had a cold.

CAPTAIN R.   Damn her little girl !

LEONORA (*imperious*).   Leave me.   Go and dine somewhere else.   Eat your hat.

CAPTAIN R.   But I—but———

LEONORA (*again making for the leads*).   And I came here specially to meet you.   I broke another engagement to meet you.

CAPTAIN R. (*doddering*).   What ?   I was told she did that. Don't tell me you are this woman !

LEONORA.   Yes, I am the woman—and I wish you had been the man !   (*She sinks down by the window, but whether she is sobbing or laughing it would need a woman to say, such as* MRS. TOVEY, *who now returns in evening dress.*)

MRS. TOVEY (*finding herself plunged in drama.*)   Dearest, whatever is the matter ?

(LEONORA *still hides her countenance.*)

Captain Rattray ? I am so delighted. But I don't understand.

LEONORA (*through her fingers*). He has been calling me the most awful names.

MRS. TOVEY. Do you know each other ?

CAPTAIN R. (*sternly*). I wish we didn't, Mrs. Tovey.

LEONORA (*shrinking*). He wants to mast-head me !

MRS. TOVEY. Really, Captain Rattray. (*But she suspects those heaving shoulders of* LEONORA.)

(MR. TOVEY *comes.*)

TOVEY. So sorry to be late, Leonora. Well, what do you think of the great man, Laura ? Doesn't come up to expectation, does he ? But they never do. Hullo, anything wrong ?

LEONORA (*appealing*). Jack, he says I pushed a man out of a railway carriage.

CAPTAIN R. *I* said it !

LEONORA. There he goes again !

TOVEY. But how did you get to know about that, Rattray ?

CAPTAIN R. You told me of the woman, and she has admitted that it was she.

TOVEY. I 'm lost !

MRS. TOVEY. Jack, you are incorrigible !

LEONORA. Tell him, Jack.

TOVEY. Bobbin, it 's all right. Leonora never actually did it. It is just the sort of thing that we often say of her she would do. So silly about her brats, you know.

(*The Captain is unspeakably relieved.*)

LEONORA (*reproachful*). How could you think such a thing of me ?

CAPTAIN R. (*with equal justice*). Why did you deceive me ?

LEONORA (*sweetly*). To pay you back for the melon.

CAPTAIN R. (*as it becomes clearer*). I 'm glad. But, I say, I am so sorry I made you cry.

MRS. TOVEY (*merciless to the real delinquent*). You didn't make her cry, Captain Rattray.

LEONORA. At any rate my eyes are red—oh, dear, and so many people coming.

MRS. TOVEY. Many people ? Whatever makes you think that ?

LEONORA. Captain Rattray said so.

CAPTAIN R.   You told me of seven ladies, Jack.

(MRS. TOVEY *bestows on her husband the sad look of wives.*)

MRS. TOVEY.   Jack, why doesn't the law let me give you up !

TOVEY.   The fact is, Bobbin—you see, Leonora—I—ah— the fact is——

(*The dinner announcement comes opportunely.*)

LEONORA (*only half enlightened*).   But—but—the others ? Aren't we to wait for them ?

CAPTAIN R. (*still entirely benighted*).   Yes, the other guests— all those ladies ?

TOVEY.   You thick-headed sailor-man, give my wife your arm and come into dinner.   There are no other ladies.   This lady—is all those ladies.

LEONORA (*as she goes into dinner with him*).   You wretch, Jack !

CAPTAIN R. (*who needs a moment longer to grasp it*).   All the seven ?   But how can—I see it, I see it.   Mrs. Tovey, she *is* all the seven !

MRS. TOVEY.   She is indeed—and some more.   (*She takes his arm.*)

CAPTAIN R.   Just one other word ; is she a widow ?

MRS. TOVEY.   Yes.

CAPTAIN R.   Good !

THE OLD LADY SHOWS HER MEDALS

THE OLD LADY SHOWS
HER MEDALS

Produced at the New Theatre on April 7, 1917, with the following cast :

PRIVATE DOWEY	. . . . .	*G. H. Mulcaster*
MR. WILLINGS	. . . . .	*Edgar G. Wood*
MRS. DOWEY	. . . . .	*Jean Cadell*
THE CHORUS {	. . . . .	*Ivy Williams*
	. . . . .	*Pollie Emery*
	. . . . .	*Clare Greet*

THE OLD LADY SHOWS
HER MEDALS

THREE nice old ladies and a criminal, who is even nicer, are discussing the war over a cup of tea. The criminal, who is the hostess, calls it a dish of tea, which shows that she comes from Caledonia ; but that is not her crime.

They are all London charwomen, but three of them, including the hostess, are what are called professionally ' charwomen *and*' or simply ' ands.' An ' and ' is also a caretaker when required ; her name is entered as such in ink in a registry book, financial transactions take place across a counter between her and the registrar, and altogether she is of a very different social status from one who, like Mrs. Haggerty, is a charwoman but nothing else. Mrs. Haggerty, though present, is not at the party by invitation ; having seen Mrs. Dowey buying the winkles, she followed her downstairs, and so has shuffled into the play and sat down in it against our wish. We would remove her by force, or at least print her name in small letters, were it not that she takes offence very readily and says that nobody respects her. So, as you have slipped in, you can sit there, Mrs. Haggerty ; but keep quiet.

There is nothing doing at present in the caretaking way for Mrs. Dowey, our hostess ; but this does not damp her, caretaking being only to such as she an extra financially and a halo socially. If she had the honour of being served with an income-tax paper she would probably fill in one of the nasty little compartments with the words, ' Trade—charring ; Profession (if any)—caretaking.' This home of hers (from which, to look after your house, she makes occasionally temporary departures in great style, escorting a barrow) is in one of those what-care-I streets that you discover only when you have lost your way ; on discovering them, your duty is to report them to the authorities, who immediately add them to the map of London. That is why we are now reporting Friday Street. We shall call it, in the rough sketch drawn for to-morrow's press, ' Street in which the criminal resided ' ; and you will find Mrs. Dowey's home therein marked with a ✗.

Her abode really consists of one room, but she maintains that there are two ; so, rather than argue, let us say that there are two. The other one has no window, and she could not swish her old skirts in it without knocking something over ; its grandest display is of tin pans and crockery on top of a dresser which has a lid to it ; you have but to whip off the utensils and raise the lid, and, behold, a bath with hot and cold. Mrs. Dowey is very proud of this possession, and when she shows it off, as she does perhaps too frequently, she first signs to you with closed fist (funny old thing that she is) to approach softly. She then tiptoes to the dresser and pops off the lid, as if to take the bath unawares. Then she sucks her lips, and is modest if you have the grace to do the exclamations.

In the real room is a bed, though that is putting the matter too briefly. The fair way to begin, if you love Mrs. Dowey, is to say to her that it is a pity she has no bed. If she is in her best form she will chuckle, and agree that the want of a bed tries her sore ; she will keep you on the hooks, so to speak, as long as she can ; and then, with that mouse-like movement again, she will suddenly spring the bed on you. You thought it was a wardrobe, but she brings it down from the wall ; and lo, a bed. There is nothing else in her abode (which we now see to contain four rooms—kitchen, pantry, bedroom, and bath-room) that is absolutely a surprise ; but it is full of ' bits,' every one of which has been paid ready money for, and gloated over and tended until it has become part of its owner. Genuine Doweys, the dealers might call them, though there is probably nothing in the place except the bed that would fetch half-a-crown.

Her home is in the basement, so that the view is restricted to the lower half of persons passing overhead beyond the area stairs. Here at the window Mrs. Dowey sometimes sits of a summer evening gazing, not sentimentally at a flower-pot which contains one poor bulb, nor yearningly at some tiny speck of sky, but with unholy relish at holes in stockings, and the like, which are revealed to her from her point of vantage. You, gentle reader, may flaunt by, thinking that your finery awes the street, but Mrs. Dowey can tell (and does) that your soles are in need of neat repair.

Also, lower parts being as expressive as the face to those whose view is thus limited, she could swear to scores of the passers-by in a court of law.

These four lively old codgers are having a good time at the tea-table, and wit is flowing free. As you can see by their everyday garments, and by their pails and mops (which are having a little tea-party by themselves in the corner), it is not a gathering by invitations stretching away into yesterday, it is a purely informal affair ; so much more attractive, don't you think ? than banquets elaborately prearranged. You know how they come about, especially in war-time. Very likely Mrs. Dowey met Mrs. Twymley and Mrs. Mickleham quite casually in the street, and meant to do no more than pass the time of day ; then, naturally enough, the word camouflage was mentioned, and they got heated, but in the end Mrs. Twymley apologised ; then, in the odd way in which one thing leads to another, the winkle man appeared, and Mrs. Dowey remembered that she had that pot of jam and that Mrs. Mickleham had stood treat last time ; and soon they were all three descending the area stairs, followed cringingly by the Haggerty Woman.

They have been extremely merry, and never were four hard-worked old ladies who deserved it better. All a woman can do in war-time they do daily and cheerfully, just as their men-folk are doing it at the Front ; and now, with the mops and pails laid aside, they sprawl gracefully at ease. There is no intention on their part to consider peace terms until a decisive victory has been gained in the field (Sarah Ann Dowey), until the Kaiser is put to the right-about (Emma Mickleham), and singing very small (Amelia Twymley).

At this tea-party the lady who is to play the part of Mrs. Dowey is sure to want to suggest that our heroine has a secret sorrow, namely, the crime ; but you should see us knocking that idea out of her head ! Mrs. Dowey knows she is a criminal, but, unlike the actress, she does not know that she is about to be found out ; and she is, to put it bluntly in her own Scotch way, the merriest of the whole clanjamfry. She presses more tea on her guests, but they wave her away from them in the pretty manner of ladies who know that they have already had more than enough.

MRS. DOWEY.　Just one more winkle, Mrs. Mickleham?

(*Indeed there is only one more. But* MRS. MICKLEHAM *indicates politely that if she took this one it would have to swim for it.* THE HAGGERTY WOMAN *takes it long afterwards when she thinks, erroneously, that no one is looking.*

MRS. TWYMLEY *is sulking. Evidently some one has contradicted her. Probably* THE HAGGERTY WOMAN.)

MRS. TWYMLEY.　I say it is so.

THE HAGGERTY WOMAN.　I say it may be so.

MRS. TWYMLEY.　I suppose I ought to know : me that has a son a prisoner in Germany.　(*She has so obviously scored that all good feeling seems to call upon her to end here. But she continues rather shabbily.*) Being the only lady present that has that proud misfortune.　(*The others are stung.*)

MRS. DOWEY.　My son is fighting in France.

MRS. MICKLEHAM.　Mine is wounded in two places.

THE HAGGERTY WOMAN.　Mine is at Salonaiky.

(*The absurd pronunciation of this uneducated person moves the others to mirth.*)

MRS. DOWEY.　You'll excuse us, Mrs. Haggerty, but the correct pronounciation is Salonikky.

THE HAGGERTY WOMAN (*to cover her confusion*).　I don't think.　(*She feels that even this does not prove her case.*)　And I speak as one that has War Savings Certificates.

MRS. TWYMLEY.　We all have them.

(THE HAGGERTY WOMAN *whimpers, and the other guests regard her with unfeeling disdain.*)

MRS. DOWEY (*to restore cheerfulness*).　Oh, it's a terrible war.

ALL (*brightening*).　It is.　You may say so.

MRS. DOWEY (*encouraged*).　What I say is, the men is splendid, but I'm none so easy about the staff.　That's your weak point, Mrs. Mickleham.

MRS. MICKLEHAM (*on the defence, but determined to reveal nothing that might be of use to the enemy*).　You may take it from me, the staff's all right.

MRS. DOWEY.   And very relieved I am to hear you say it.

(*It is here that* THE HAGGERTY WOMAN *has the remaining winkle.*)

MRS. MICKLEHAM.   You don't understand properly about trench warfare.   If I had a map——

MRS. DOWEY (*wetting her finger to draw lines on the table*).   That's the river Sommy.   Now, if we had barrages here——

MRS. TWYMLEY.   Very soon you would be enfilded. Where's your supports, my lady ?   (MRS. DOWEY *is damped.*)

MRS. MICKLEHAM.   What none of you grasps is that this is a artillery war——

THE HAGGERTY WOMAN (*strengthened by the winkle*).   I say that the word is Salonaiky.   (*The others purse their lips.*)

MRS. TWYMLEY (*with terrible meaning*).   We'll change the subject.   Have you seen this week's *Fashion Chat* ?   (*She has evidently seen and devoured it herself, and even licked up the crumbs.*)   The gabardine with accordion pleats has quite gone out.

MRS. DOWEY (*her old face sparkling*).   My sakes !   You tell me ?

MRS. TWYMLEY (*with the touch of haughtiness that comes of great topics*).   The plain smock has come in again, with silk lacing, giving that charming chic effect.

MRS. DOWEY.   Oho !

MRS. MICKLEHAM.   I must say I was always partial to the straight line (*thoughtfully regarding the want of line in* MRS. TWYMLEY'S *person*), though trying to them as is of too friendly a figure.

(*It is here that* THE HAGGERTY WOMAN'S *fingers close unostentatiously upon a piece of sugar.*)

MRS. TWYMLEY (*sailing into the Empyrean*).   Lady Dolly Kanister was seen conversing across the railings in a dainty *de jou.*

MRS. DOWEY.   Fine would I have liked to see her.

MRS. TWYMLEY.   She is equally popular as maid, wife, and munition-worker.   Her two children is inset.   Lady Pops Babington was married in a tight tulle.

MRS. MICKLEHAM.   What was her going-away dress ?

MRS. TWYMLEY.   A champagny cream velvet with dreamy

corsage.   She's married to Colonel the Hon. Chingford—
'Snubs,' they called him at Eton.

THE HAGGERTY WOMAN (*having disposed of the sugar*).   Very
likely he'll be sent to Salonaiky.

MRS. MICKLEHAM.   Wherever he is sent, she'll have the
same tremors as the rest of us.   She'll be as keen to get the
letters wrote with pencils as you or me.

MRS. TWYMLEY.   Them pencil letters !

MRS. DOWEY (*in her sweet Scotch voice, timidly, afraid she may
be going too far*).   And women in enemy lands gets those pencil
letters and then stop getting them, the same as ourselves.   Let's
occasionally think of that.

(*She has gone too far.   Chairs are pushed back.*)

THE HAGGERTY WOMAN.   I ask you !

MRS. MICKLEHAM.   That's hardly language, Mrs. Dowey.

MRS. DOWEY (*scared*).   Kindly excuse.   I swear to death
I'm none of your pacifists.

MRS. MICKLEHAM.   Freely granted.

MRS. TWYMLEY.   I've heard of females that have no male
relations, and so they have no man-party at the wars.   I've
heard of them, but I don't mix with them.

MRS. MICKLEHAM.   What can the likes of us have to say to
them ?   It's not their war.

MRS. DOWEY (*wistfully*).   They are to be pitied.

MRS. MICKLEHAM.   But the place for them, Mrs. Dowey, is
within doors with the blinds down.

MRS. DOWEY (*hurriedly*).   That's the place for them.

MRS. MICKLEHAM.   I saw one of them to-day buying a flag.
I thought it was very impudent of her.

MRS. DOWEY (*meekly*).   So it was.

MRS. MICKLEHAM (*trying to look modest with indifferent success*).
I had a letter from my son, Percy, yesterday.

MRS. TWYMLEY.   Alfred sent me his photo.

THE HAGGERTY WOMAN.   Letters from Salonaiky is less
common.

(*Three bosoms heave, but not, alas, MRS. DOWEY'S.   Nevertheless she doggedly knits her lips.*)

MRS. DOWEY (*the criminal*).   Kenneth writes to me every
week.   (*There are exclamations.   The dauntless old thing holds
aloft a packet of letters.*)   Look at this.   All his.

(THE HAGGERTY WOMAN *frowns*.)

MRS. TWYMLEY. Alfred has little time for writing, being a bombardier.

MRS. DOWEY (*relentlessly*). Do your letters begin ' Dear mother ' ?

MRS. TWYMLEY. Generally.

MRS. MICKLEHAM. Invariable.

THE HAGGERTY WOMAN. Every time.

MRS. DOWEY (*delivering the knock-out blow*). Kenneth's begin ' Dearest mother.'

(*No one can think of the right reply*.)

MRS. TWYMLEY (*doing her best*). A short man, I should say, judging by yourself.

(*She ought to have left it alone*.)

MRS. DOWEY. Six feet two—and a half.

(*The gloom deepens*.)

MRS. MICKLEHAM (*against her better judgment*). A kilty, did you tell me ?

MRS. DOWEY. Most certainly. He 's in the famous Black Watch.

THE HAGGERTY WOMAN (*producing her handkerchief*). The Surrey Rifles is the famousest.

MRS. MICKLEHAM. There you and the King disagrees, Mrs. Haggerty. His choice is the Buffs, same as my Percy's.

MRS. TWYMLEY (*magnanimously*). Give me the R.H.A. and you can keep all the rest.

MRS. DOWEY. I 'm sure I have nothing to say against the Surreys and the R.H.A. and the Buffs ; but they are just breeches regiments, I understand.

THE HAGGERTY WOMAN. We can't all be kilties.

MRS. DOWEY (*crushingly*). That 's very true.

MRS. TWYMLEY (*it is foolish of her, but she can't help saying it*). Has your Kenneth great hairy legs ?

MRS. DOWEY. Tremendous.

(*The wicked woman : but let us also say ' Poor Sarah Ann Dowey.' For at this moment, enter Nemesis. In other words, the less important part of a clergyman appears upon the stair*.)

MRS. MICKLEHAM. It 's the reverent gent !

MRS. DOWEY (*little knowing what he is bringing her*). I see he has had his boots heeled.

(*It may be said of* MR. WILLINGS *that his happy smile always walks in front of him. This smile makes music of his life; it means that once again he has been chosen, in his opinion, as the central figure in romance. No one can well have led a more drab existence, but he will never know it; he will always think of himself, humbly though elatedly, as the chosen of the gods. Of him must it have been originally written that adventures are for the adventurous. He meets them at every street corner. For instance, he assists an old lady off a bus, and asks her if he can be of any further help. She tells him that she wants to know the way to Maddox the butcher's. Then comes the kind, triumphant smile; it always comes first, followed by its explanation, 'I was there yesterday!' This is the merest sample of the adventures that keep* MR. WILLINGS *up to the mark.*

Since the war broke out, his zest for life has become almost terrible. He can scarcely lift a newspaper and read of a hero without remembering that he knows some one of the same name. The Soldiers' Rest he is connected with was once a china emporium, and (mark my words) he had bought his tea service at it. Such is life when you are in the thick of it. Sometimes he feels that he is part of a gigantic spy drama. In the course of his extraordinary comings and goings he meets with Great Personages, of course, and is the confidential recipient of secret news. Before imparting the news he does not, as you might expect, first smile expansively; on the contrary, there comes over his face an awful solemnity, which, however, means the same thing. When divulging the names of the personages, he first looks around to make sure that no suspicious character is about, and then, lowering his voice, tells you, 'I had that from Mr. Farthing himself—he is the secretary of the Bethnal Green Branch,—h'sh!'

There is a commotion about finding a worthy chair for the reverent, and there is also some furtive pulling down of sleeves, but he stands surveying the ladies through his triumphant smile. This amazing man knows that he is about to score again.)

THE OLD LADY SHOWS HER MEDALS 973

MR. WILLINGS (*waving aside the chairs*). I thank you. But not at all. Friends, I have news.

MRS. MICKLEHAM. News?

THE HAGGERTY WOMAN. From the Front?

MRS. TWYMLEY. My Alfred, sir?

(*They are all grown suddenly anxious—all except the hostess, who knows that there can never be any news from the Front for her.*)

MR. WILLINGS. I tell you at once that all is well. The news is for Mrs. Dowey.

(*She stares.*)

MRS. DOWEY. News for me?

MR. WILLINGS. Your son, Mrs. Dowey—he has got five days' leave. (*She shakes her head slightly, or perhaps it only trembles a little on its stem.*) Now, now, good news doesn't kill.

MRS. TWYMLEY. We 're glad, Mrs. Dowey.

MRS. DOWEY. You 're sure?

MR. WILLINGS. Quite sure. He has arrived.

MRS. DOWEY. He is in London?

MR. WILLINGS. He is. I have spoken to him.

MRS. MICKLEHAM. You lucky woman.

(*They might see that she is not looking lucky, but experience has told them how differently these things take people.*)

MR. WILLINGS (*marvelling more and more as he unfolds his tale*). Ladies, it is quite a romance. I was in the—(*he looks around cautiously, but he knows that they are all to be trusted*)—in the Church Army quarters in Central Street, trying to get on the track of one or two of our missing men. Suddenly my eyes— I can't account for it—but suddenly my eyes alighted on a Highlander seated rather drearily on a bench, with his kit at his feet.

THE HAGGERTY WOMAN. A big man?

MR. WILLINGS. A great brawny fellow. (THE HAGGERTY WOMAN *groans.*) 'My friend,' I said at once, 'welcome back to Blighty.' I make a point of calling it Blighty. 'I wonder,' I said, 'if there is anything I can do for you?' He shook his head. 'What regiment?' I asked. (*Here he very properly lowers his voice to a whisper.*) 'Black Watch, 5th Battalion,' he said. 'Name?' I asked. 'Dowey,' he said.

MRS. MICKLEHAM. I declare! I do declare!

MR. WILLINGS (*showing how the thing was done, with the help of a chair*). I put my hand on his shoulder as it might be thus. ' Kenneth Dowey,' I said, ' I know your mother.'

MRS. DOWEY (*wetting her lips*). What did he say to that ?

MR. WILLINGS. He was incredulous. Indeed, he seemed to think I was balmy. But I offered to bring him straight to you. I told him how much you had talked to me about him.

MRS. DOWEY. Bring him here !

MRS. MICKLEHAM. I wonder he needed to be brought.

MR. WILLINGS. He had just arrived, and was bewildered by the great city. He listened to me in the taciturn Scotch way, and then he gave a curious laugh.

MRS. TWYMLEY. Laugh ?

MR. WILLINGS (*whose wild life has brought him into contact with the strangest people*). The Scotch, Mrs. Twymley, express their emotions differently from us. With them tears signify a rollicking mood, while merriment denotes that they are plunged in gloom. When I had finished he said at once, ' Let us go and see the old lady.'

MRS. DOWEY (*backing, which is the first movement she has made since he began his tale*). Is he—coming ?

MR. WILLINGS (*gloriously*). He has come. He is up there. I told him I thought I had better break the joyful news to you. (*Three women rush to the window.* MRS. DOWEY *looks at her pantry door, but perhaps she remembers that it does not lock on the inside. She stands rigid, though her face has gone very grey.*)

MRS. DOWEY. Kindly get them to go away.

MR. WILLINGS. Ladies, I think this happy occasion scarcely requires you. (*He is not the man to ask of woman a sacrifice that he is not prepared to make himself.*) I also am going instantly.

(*They all survey* MRS. DOWEY, *and understand—or think they understand.*)

MRS. TWYMLEY (*pail and mop in hand*). I would thank none for their company if my Alfred was at the door.

MRS. MICKLEHAM (*similarly burdened*). The same from me. Shall I send him down, Mrs. Dowey ? (*The old lady does not hear her. She is listening, terrified, for a step on the stair.*) Look at the poor, joyous thing, sir. She has his letters in her hand.

(*The three women go.* MR. WILLINGS *puts a kind hand*

on MRS. DOWEY'S *shoulder. He thinks he so thoroughly understands the situation.*)

MR. WILLINGS.   A good son, Mrs. Dowey, to have written to you so often.

(*Our old criminal quakes, but she grips the letters more tightly.* PRIVATE DOWEY *descends.*)

Dowey, my friend, there she is, waiting for you, with your letters in her hand.

DOWEY (*grimly*).   That's great.

(MR. WILLINGS *ascends the stair without one backward glance, like the good gentleman he is ; and the* DOWEYS *are left together, with nearly the whole room between them. He is a great rough chunk of Scotland, howked out of her not so much neatly as liberally ; and in his Black Watch uniform, all caked with mud, his kit and nearly all his worldly possessions on his back, he is an apparition scarcely less fearsome (but so much less ragged) than those ancestors of his who trotted with Prince Charlie to Derby. He stands silent, scowling at the old lady, daring her to raise her head ; and she would like very much to do it, for she longs to have a first glimpse of her son. When he does speak, it is to jeer at her.*)

Do you recognise your loving son, missis ?   ('*Oh, the fine Scotch tang of him,*' *she thinks.*)

MRS. DOWEY (*trembling*).   I'm pleased I wrote so often. ('*Oh, but he's raised,*' *she thinks.*)

(*He strides toward her, and seizes the letters roughly.*)

DOWEY.   Let's see them.

(*There is a string round the package, and he unties it, and examines the letters at his leisure with much curiosity. The envelopes are in order, all addressed in pencil to* MRS. DOWEY, *with the proud words* '*Opened by Censor*' *on them. But the letter paper inside contains not a word of writing.*)

DOWEY.   Nothing but blank paper !   Is this your writing in pencil on the envelope ?

(*She nods, and he gives the matter further consideration.*)

The covey told me you were a charwoman ; so I suppose you picked the envelopes out of waste-paper baskets, or such like, and then changed the addresses ?

(*She nods again ; still she dare not look up, but she is*

admiring his legs. When, however, he would cast the letters into the fire, she flames up with sudden spirit. She clutches them.)

MRS. DOWEY. Don't you burn them letters, mister.

DOWEY. They 're not real letters.

MRS. DOWEY. They 're all I have.

DOWEY *(returning to irony).* I thought you had a son ?

MRS. DOWEY. I never had a man nor a son nor anything. I just call myself Missis to give me a standing.

DOWEY. Well, it 's past my seeing through.

(He turns to look for some explanation from the walls. She gets a peep at him at last. Oh, what a grandly set-up man ! Oh, the stride of him. Oh, the noble rage of him. Oh, Samson had been like this before that woman took him in hand.)

DOWEY *(whirling round on her).* What made you do it ?

MRS. DOWEY. It was everybody's war, mister, except mine. *(She beats her arms.)* I wanted it to be my war too.

DOWEY. You 'll need to be plainer. And yet I 'm d—d if I care to hear you, you lying old trickster.

(The words are merely what were to be expected, and so are endurable ; but he has moved towards the door.)

MRS. DOWEY. You 're not going already, mister ?

DOWEY. Yes, I just came to give you an ugly piece of my mind.

MRS. DOWEY *(holding out her arms longingly).* You haven't gave it to me yet.

DOWEY. You have a cheek !

MRS. DOWEY *(giving further proof of it).* You wouldn't drink some tea ?

DOWEY. Me ! I tell you I came here for the one purpose of blazing away at you.

(It is such a roaring negative that it blows her into a chair. But she is up again in a moment, is this spirited old lady.)

MRS. DOWEY. You could drink the tea while you was blazing away. There 's winkles.

DOWEY. Is there ?

(He turns interestedly toward the table, but his proud Scots character checks him, which is just as well, for what she should have said was that there had been winkles.)

Not me. You're just a common rogue. (*He seats himself far from the table.*) Now, then, out with it. Sit down ! (*She sits meekly ; there is nothing she would not do for him.*) As you char, I suppose you are on your feet all day.

MRS. DOWEY. I'm more on my knees.

DOWEY. That's where you should be to me.

MRS. DOWEY. Oh, mister, I'm willing.

DOWEY. Stop it. Go on, you accomplished liar.

MRS. DOWEY. It's true that my name is Dowey.

DOWEY. It's enough to make me change mine.

MRS. DOWEY. I've been charring and charring and charring as far back as I mind. I've been in London this twenty years.

DOWEY. We'll skip your early days. I have an appointment.

MRS. DOWEY. And then when I was old the war broke out.

DOWEY. How could it affect you ?

MRS. DOWEY. Oh, mister, that's the thing. It didn't affect me. It affected everybody but me. The neighbours looked down on me. Even the posters, on the walls, of the woman saying, ' Go, my boy,' leered at me. I sometimes cried by myself in the dark. You won't have a cup of tea ?

DOWEY. No.

MRS. DOWEY. Sudden-like the idea came to me to pretend I had a son.

DOWEY. You depraved old limmer ! But what in the name of Old Nick made you choose me out of the whole British Army ?

MRS. DOWEY (*giggling*). Maybe, mister, it was because I liked you best.

DOWEY. Now, now, woman.

MRS. DOWEY. I read one day in the papers, ' In which he was assisted by Private K. Dowey, 5th Battalion, Black Watch.'

DOWEY (*flattered*). Did you, now ! Well, I expect that's the only time I was ever in the papers.

MRS. DOWEY (*trying it on again*). I didn't choose you for that alone. I read a history of the Black Watch first, to make sure it was the best regiment in the world.

DOWEY. Anybody could have told you that.

(*He is moving about now in better humour, and, meeting*

*the loaf in his stride, he cuts a slice from it.   He is hardly
aware of this, but* MRS. DOWEY *knows.*)

I like the Scotch voice of you, woman.   It drummles on like
a hill burn.

MRS. DOWEY.   Prosen Water runs by where I was born.
Maybe it teached me to speak, mister.

DOWEY.   Canny, woman, canny.

MRS. DOWEY.   I read about the Black Watch's ghostly piper
that plays proudly when the men of the Black Watch do well,
and prouder when they fall.

DOWEY.   There's some foolish story of that kind.

(*He has another careless slice off the loaf.*)

But you couldn't have been living here at that time, or they
would have guessed.   I suppose you flitted?

MRS. DOWEY.   Yes, it cost me eleven and sixpence.

DOWEY.   How did you guess the *K* in my name stood for
Kenneth?

MRS. DOWEY.   Does it?

DOWEY.   Umpha!

MRS. DOWEY.   An angel whispered it to me in my sleep.

DOWEY.   Well, that's the only angel in the whole black
business.

(*He chuckles.*)

You little thought I would turn up!   (*Wheeling suddenly on
her*) Or did you?

MRS. DOWEY.   I was beginning to weary for a sight of you,
Kenneth.

DOWEY.   What word was that?

MRS. DOWEY.   Mister.

(*He helps himself to butter, and she holds out the jam pot
to him, but he haughtily rejects it.   Do you think she gives
in now?   Not a bit of it.*)

DOWEY (*sarcastic again*).   I hope you're pleased with me
now you see me.

MRS. DOWEY.   I'm very pleased.   Does your folk live in
Scotland?

DOWEY.   Glasgow.

MRS. DOWEY.   Both living?

DOWEY.   Ay.

MRS. DOWEY.   Is your mother terrible proud of you?

DOWEY. Naturally.

MRS. DOWEY. You 'll be going to them ?

DOWEY. After I 've had a skite in London first.

MRS. DOWEY (*sniffing*). So she is in London !

DOWEY. Who ?

MRS. DOWEY. Your young lady.

DOWEY. Are you jealyous ?

MRS. DOWEY. Not me.

DOWEY. You needna be. She 's a young thing.

MRS. DOWEY. You surprises me. A beauty, no doubt ?

DOWEY. You may be sure. (*He tries the jam.*) She 's a titled person. She is equally popular as maid, wife and munition-worker.

(MRS. DOWEY *remembers Lady Dolly Kanister, so familiar to readers of fashionable gossip, and a very leery expression indeed comes into her face.*)

MRS. DOWEY. Tell me more about her, man.

DOWEY. She has sent me a lot of things, especially cakes, and a worsted waistcoat, with a loving message on the enclosed card.

(*The old lady is now in a quiver of excitement. She loses control of her arms, which jump excitedly this way and that.*)

MRS. DOWEY. You 'll try one of my cakes, mister ?

DOWEY. Not me.

MRS. DOWEY. They 're of my own making.

DOWEY. No, I thank you.

(*But with a funny little run she is in the pantry and back again. She pushes a cake before him, at sight of which he gapes.*)

MRS. DOWEY. What 's the matter ? Tell me, oh, tell me, mister !

DOWEY. That 's exactly the kind of cake that her ladyship sends me.

(MRS. DOWEY *is now a very glorious old character indeed.*)

MRS. DOWEY. Is the waistcoat right, mister ? I hope the Black Watch colours pleased you.

DOWEY. Wha—at ! Was it you ?

MRS. DOWEY. I daredna give my own name, you see, and I was always reading hers in the papers.

(*The badgered man looms over her, terrible for the last time.*)

DOWEY.   Woman, is there no getting rid of you !

MRS. DOWEY.   Are you angry ?

(*He sits down with a groan.*)

DOWEY.   Oh, hell !   Give me some tea.

(*She rushes about preparing a meal for him, every bit of her wanting to cry out to every other bit, ' Oh, glory, glory, glory ! ' For a moment she hovers behind his chair. ' Kenneth ! ' she murmurs. ' What ? ' he asks, no longer aware that she is taking a liberty. ' Nothing,' she says, ' just Kenneth,' and is off gleefully for the tea-caddy. But when his tea is poured out, and he has drunk a saucerful, the instinct of self-preservation returns to him between two bites.*)

DOWEY.   Don't you be thinking, missis, for one minute that you have got me.

MRS. DOWEY.   No, no.

(*On that understanding he unbends.*)

DOWEY.   I have a theatre to-night, followed by a randy-dandy.

MRS. DOWEY.   Oho ! Kenneth, this is a queer first meeting !

DOWEY.   It is, woman, oh, it is.   (*Guardedly*) And it 's also a last meeting.

MRS. DOWEY.   Yes, yes.

DOWEY.   So here 's to you—you old mop and pail.   *Ave atque vale.*

MRS. DOWEY.   What 's that ?

DOWEY.   That means Hail and Farewell.

MRS. DOWEY.   Are you a scholar ?

DOWEY.   Being Scotch, there 's almost nothing I don't know.

MRS. DOWEY.   What was you to trade ?

DOWEY.   Carter, glazier, orraman, any rough jobs.

MRS. DOWEY.   You 're a proper man to look at.

DOWEY.   I 'm generally admired.

MRS. DOWEY.   She 's an enviable woman.

DOWEY.   Who ?

MRS. DOWEY.   Your mother.

DOWEY.   Eh ?   Oh, that was just protecting myself from you.   I have neither father nor mother nor wife nor grand-mama.   (*Bitterly*) This party never even knew who his proud parents were.

MRS. DOWEY. Is that—(*gleaming*)—is that true ?

DOWEY. It 's gospel.

MRS. DOWEY. Heaven be praised !

DOWEY. Eh ? None of that ! I was a fool to tell you. But don't think you can take advantage of it. Pass the cake.

MRS. DOWEY. I dare say it 's true we 'll never meet again, Kenneth, but—but if we do, I wonder where it will be ?

DOWEY. Not in this world.

MRS. DOWEY. There 's no telling. (*Leering ingratiatingly*) It might be at Berlin.

DOWEY. Tod, if I ever get to Berlin, I believe I 'll find you there waiting for me !

MRS. DOWEY. With a cup of tea for you in my hand.

DOWEY. Yes, and (*heartily*) very good tea too.

(*He has partaken heavily, he is now in high good humour.*)

MRS. DOWEY. Kenneth, we could come back by Paris !

DOWEY. All the ladies likes to go to Paris.

MRS. DOWEY. Oh, Kenneth, Kenneth, if just once before I die I could be fitted for a Paris gown with dreamy corsage !

DOWEY. You 're all alike, old covey. We have a song about it. (*He sings :*)

> ' Mrs. Gill is very ill,
>   Nothing can improve her
>   But to see the Tuileries
>   And waddle through the Louvre.'

(*No song ever had a greater success. MRS. DOWEY is doubled up with mirth. When she comes to, when they both come to, for there are a pair of them, she cries :*)

MRS. DOWEY. You must learn me that (*and off she goes in song also :*)

> ' Mrs. Dowey 's very ill,
>   Nothing can improve her.'

DOWEY.

> ' But dressed up in a Paris gown
>   To waddle through the Louvre.'

(*They fling back their heads, she points at him, he points at her.*)

MRS. DOWEY (*ecstatically*). Hairy legs !

(*A mad remark, which brings him to his senses ; he remembers who and what she is.*)

DOWEY.   Mind   your   manners !   (*Rising*)   Well,   thank you for my tea.   I must be stepping.

(*Poor* MRS. DOWEY, *he is putting on his kit.*)

MRS. DOWEY.   Where are you living ?

(*He sighs.*)

DOWEY.   That 's the question.   But there 's a place called The Hut, where some of the 2nd Battalion are.   They 'll take me in.   Beggars (*bitterly*) can't be choosers.

MRS. DOWEY.   Beggars ?

DOWEY.   I 've never been here before.   If you knew (*a shadow comes over him*) what it is to be in such a place without a friend. - I was crazy with glee, when I got my leave, at the thought of seeing London at last, but after wandering its streets for four hours, I would almost have been glad to be back in the trenches.

('*If you knew,' he has said, but indeed the old lady knows.*)

MRS. DOWEY.   That 's my quandorum too, Kenneth.

(*He nods sympathetically.*)

DOWEY.   I 'm sorry for you, you poor old body.   (*Shouldering his kit.*)   But I see no way out for either of us.

MRS. DOWEY (*cooing*).   Do you not ?

DOWEY.   Are you at it again !

(*She knows that it must be now or never.   She has left her biggest guns for the end.   In her excitement she is rising up and down on her toes.*)

MRS. DOWEY.   Kenneth, I 've heard that the thing a man on leave longs for more than anything else is a bed with sheets, and a bath.

DOWEY.   You never heard anything truer.

MRS. DOWEY.   Go into that pantry, Kenneth Dowey, and lift the dresser-top, and tell me what you see.

(*He goes.   There is an awful stillness.   He returns, impressed.*)

DOWEY.   It 's a kind of a bath !

MRS. DOWEY.   You could do yourself there pretty, half at a time.

DOWEY.   Me ?

MRS. DOWEY.   There 's a woman through the wall that would be very willing to give me a shake-down till your leave is up.

(*He snorts.*)

DOWEY. Oh, is there !

(She has not got him yet, but there is still one more gun.)

MRS. DOWEY. Kenneth, look !

(With these simple words she lets down the bed. She says no more ; an effect like this would be spoilt by language. Fortunately he is not made of stone. He thrills.)

DOWEY. Gosh ! That 's the dodge we need in the trenches.

MRS. DOWEY. That 's your bed, Kenneth.

DOWEY. Mine ? *(He grins at her.)* You queer old divert. What can make you so keen to be burdened by a lump like me ?

MRS. DOWEY. He ! he ! he ! he !

DOWEY. I tell you, I 'm the commonest kind of man.

MRS. DOWEY. I 'm just the commonest kind of old wifie myself.

DOWEY. I 've been a kick-about all my life, and I 'm no great shakes at the war.

MRS. DOWEY. Yes, you are. How many Germans have you killed ?

DOWEY. Just two for certain, and there was no glory in it. It was just because they wanted my shirt.

MRS. DOWEY. Your shirt ?

DOWEY. Well, they said it was their shirt.

MRS. DOWEY. Have you took prisoners ?

DOWEY. I once took half a dozen, but that was a poor affair too.

MRS. DOWEY. How could one man take half a dozen ?

DOWEY. Just in the usual way. I surrounded them.

MRS. DOWEY. Kenneth, you 're just my ideal.

DOWEY. You 're easily pleased.

(He turns again to the bed.)

Let 's see how the thing works.

(He kneads the mattress with his fist, and the result is so satisfactory that he puts down his kit.)

Old lady, if you really want me, I 'll bide.

MRS. DOWEY. Oh ! oh ! oh ! oh !

(Her joy is so demonstrative that he has to drop a word of warning.)

DOWEY. But, mind you, I don't accept you as a relation.

For your personal glory, you can go on pretending to the neighbours ; but the best I can say for you is that you 're on your probation.   I 'm a cautious character, and we must see how you 'll turn out.

MRS. DOWEY.   Yes, Kenneth.

DOWEY.   And now, I think, for that bath.   My theatre begins at six-thirty.   A cove I met on a bus is going with me.

(*She is a little alarmed.*)

MRS. DOWEY.   You 're sure you 'll come back ?

DOWEY.   Yes, yes.   (*Handsomely*) I leave my kit in pledge.

MRS. DOWEY.   You won't liquor up too freely, Kenneth ?

DOWEY.   You 're the first (*chuckling*) to care whether I do or not.   (*Nothing she has said has pleased the lonely man so much as this.*)   I promise.   Tod, I 'm beginning to look forward to being wakened in the morning by hearing you cry, ' Get up, you lazy swine.'   I 've kind of envied men that had womenfolk with the right to say that.

(*He is passing to the bathroom when a diverting notion strikes him.*)

MRS. DOWEY.   What is it, Kenneth ?

DOWEY.   The theatre.   It would be showier if I took a lady.

(MRS. DOWEY *feels a thumping at her breast.*)

MRS. DOWEY.   Kenneth, tell me this instant what you mean. Don't keep me on the jumps.

(*He turns her round.*)

DOWEY.   No, it couldn't be done.

MRS. DOWEY.   Was it me you were thinking of ?

DOWEY.   Just for the moment (*regretfully*), but you have no style.

(*She catches hold of him by the sleeve.*)

MRS. DOWEY.   Not in this, of course.   But, oh, Kenneth, if you saw me in my merino !   It 's laced up the back in the very latest.

DOWEY.   Hum (*doubtfully*) ; but let 's see it.

(*It is produced from a drawer, to which the old lady runs with almost indecent haste.   The connoisseur examines it critically.*)

DOWEY.   Looks none so bad.   Have you a bit of chiffon for the neck ?   It 's not bombs nor Kaisers nor Tipperary that men in the trenches think of, it 's chiffon.

MRS. DOWEY.   I swear I have, Kenneth.   And I have a bangle, and a muff, and gloves.

DOWEY.   Ay, ay.   (*He considers.*)   Do you think you could give your face less of a homely look ?

MRS. DOWEY.   I 'm sure I could.

DOWEY.   Then you can have a try.   But, mind you, I promise nothing.   All will depend on the effect.

(*He goes into the pantry, and the old lady is left alone.   Not alone, for she is ringed round by entrancing hopes and dreadful fears.   They beam on her and jeer at her, they pull her this way and that ; with difficulty she breaks through them and rushes to her pail, hot water, soap, and a looking-glass.   Our last glimpse of her for this evening shows her staring (not discontentedly) at her soft old face, licking her palm, and pressing it to her hair.   Her eyes are sparkling.*)

One evening a few days later MRS. TWYMLEY *and* MRS. MICKLEHAM *are in* MRS. DOWEY's *house, awaiting that lady's return from some fashionable dissipation.   They have undoubtedly been discussing the war, for the first words we catch are :)*

MRS. MICKLEHAM.   I tell you flat, Amelia, I bows no knee to junkerdom.

MRS. TWYMLEY.   Sitting here by the fire, you and me, as one to another, what do you think will happen after the war ?   Are we to go back to being as we were ?

MRS. MICKLEHAM.   Speaking for myself, Amelia, not me. The war has wakened me up to a understanding of my own importance that is really astonishing.

MRS. TWYMLEY.   Same here.   Instead of being the poor worms the like of you and me thought we was, we turns out to be visible departments of a great and haughty empire.

(*They are well under weigh, and with a little luck we might now hear their views on various passing problems of the day, such as the neglect of science in our public schools.   But in comes* THE HAGGERTY WOMAN, *and spoils everything.   She is attired, like them, in her best, but the effect of her is that her clothes have gone out for a walk, leaving her at home.*)

MRS. MICKLEHAM (*with deep distaste*).   Here 's that submarine again.

(THE HAGGERTY WOMAN *cringes to them, but gets no encouragement.*)

THE HAGGERTY WOMAN. It's a terrible war.

MRS. TWYMLEY. Is that so?

THE HAGGERTY WOMAN. I wonder what will happen when it ends?

MRS. MICKLEHAM. I have no idea.

(*The intruder produces her handkerchief, but does not use it. After all, she is in her best.*)

THE HAGGERTY WOMAN. Are they not back yet?

(*Perfect ladies must reply to a direct question.*)

MRS. MICKLEHAM. No (*icily*). We have been waiting this half hour. They are at the theatre again.

THE HAGGERTY WOMAN. You tell me! I just popped in with an insignificant present for him, as his leave is up.

MRS. TWYMLEY. The same errand brought us.

THE HAGGERTY WOMAN. My present is cigarettes.

(*They have no intention of telling her what their presents are, but the secret leaps from them.*)

MRS. MICKLEHAM. So is mine.

MRS. TWYMLEY. Mine too.

(*Triumph of* THE HAGGERTY WOMAN. *But it is short-lived.*)

MRS. MICKLEHAM. Mine has gold tips.

MRS. TWYMLEY. So has mine.

(THE HAGGERTY WOMAN *need not say a word. You have only to look at her to know that her cigarettes are not gold-tipped. She tries to brazen it out, which is so often a mistake.*)

THE HAGGERTY WOMAN. What care I? Mine is Exquisytos.

(*No wonder they titter.*)

MRS. MICKLEHAM. Excuse us, Mrs. Haggerty (if that's your name), but the word is Exquiseetos.

THE HAGGERTY WOMAN. Much obliged. (*She weeps.*)

MRS. MICKLEHAM. I think I heard a taxi.

MRS. TWYMLEY. It will be her third this week.

(*They peer through the blind. They are so excited that rank is forgotten.*)

THE HAGGERTY WOMAN. What is she in?

MRS. MICKLEHAM. A new astrakhan jacket he gave her, with Venus sleeves.

THE HAGGERTY WOMAN. Has she sold her gabardine coat?

MRS. MICKLEHAM. Not her! She has them both at the theatre, warm night though it is. She's wearing the astrakhan, and carrying the gabardine, flung careless-like over her arm.

THE HAGGERTY WOMAN. I saw her strutting about with him yesterday, looking as if she thought the two of them made a procession.

MRS. TWYMLEY. H'sh! (*peeping*). Strike me dead, if she's not coming mincing down the stair, hooked on his arm!

(*Indeed it is thus that* MRS. DOWEY *enters. Perhaps she had seen shadows lurking on the blind, and at once hooked on to* KENNETH *to impress the visitors. She is quite capable of it.*

Now we see what KENNETH *saw that afternoon five days ago when he emerged from the bathroom and found the old trembler awaiting his inspection. Here are the muff and the gloves and the chiffon, and such a kind old bonnet that it makes you laugh at once; I don't know how to describe it, but it is trimmed with a kiss, as bonnets should be when the wearer is old and frail. We must take the merino for granted until she steps out of the astrakhan. She is dressed up to the nines, there is no doubt about it. Yes, but is her face less homely? Above all, has she the style? The answer is in a stout affirmative. Ask* KENNETH. *He knows. Many a time he has had to go behind a door to roar hilariously at the old lady. He has thought of her as a lark to tell his mates about by and by; but for some reason that he cannot fathom, he knows now that he will never do that.*)

MRS. DOWEY (*affecting surprise*). Kenneth, we have visitors!

DOWEY. Your servant, ladies.

(*He is no longer mud-caked and dour. A very smart figure is this* PRIVATE DOWEY, *and he winks engagingly at the visitors, like one who knows that for jolly company you cannot easily beat charwomen. The pleasantries that he and they have exchanged this week! The sauce he has given them. The wit of* MRS. MICKLEHAM'S *retorts. The badinage of* MRS. TWYMLEY. *The neat giggles of* THE HAGGERTY woman. *There has been nothing like it since you took the countess in to dinner.*)

mrs. twymley. We should apologise. We 're not meaning to stay.

mrs. dowey. You are very welcome. Just wait (*the ostentation of this !*) till I get out of my astrakhan—and my muff—and my gloves—and (*it is the bonnet's turn now*) my Excelsior.

(*At last we see her in the merino (a triumph).*)

mrs. mickleham. You 've given her a glory time, Mr. Dowey.

dowey. It 's her that has given it to me, missis.

mrs. dowey. Hey ! hey ! hey ! hey ! He just pampers me (*waggling her fists*). The Lord forgive us, but this being the last night, we had a sit-down supper at a restaurant! (*Vehemently*) I swear by God that we had champagny wine. (*There is a dead stillness, and she knows very well what it means, she has even prepared for it.*) And to them as doubts my words —here 's the cork.

(*She places the cork, in its lovely gold drapery, upon the table.*)

mrs. mickleham. I 'm sure !

mrs. twymley. I would thank you, Mrs. Dowey, not to say a word against my Alfred.

mrs. dowey. Me !

dowey. Come, come, ladies (*in the masterful way that is so hard for women to resist*) ; if you say another word, I 'll kiss the lot of you.

(*There is a moment of pleased confusion.*)

mrs. mickleham. Really, them sodgers !

the haggerty woman. The kilties is the worst !

mrs. twymley (*heartily*). I 'm sure we don't grudge you your treats, Mrs. Dowey ; and sorry we are that this is the end.

dowey. Yes, it 's the end (*with a troubled look at his old lady*) ; I must be off in ten minutes.

(*The little soul is too gallant to break down in company. She hurries into the pantry and shuts the door.*)

mrs. mickleham. Poor thing ! But we must run, for you 'll be having some last words to say to her.

DOWEY. I kept her out long on purpose so as to have less time to say them in.

(*He more than half wishes that he could make a bolt to a public-house.*)

MRS. TWYMLEY. It's the best way. (*In the important affairs of life there is not much that any one can teach a charwoman.*) Just a mere nothing, to wish you well, Mr. Dowey.

(*All three present him with the cigarettes.*)

MRS. MICKLEHAM. A scraping, as one might say.

THE HAGGERTY WOMAN (*enigmatically*). The heart is warm though it may not be gold-tipped.

DOWEY. You bricks!

THE LADIES. Good luck, cocky.

DOWEY. The same to you. And if you see a sodger man up there in a kilt, he is one that is going back with me. Tell him not to come down, but—but to give me till the last minute, and then to whistle.

(*It is quite a grave man who is left alone, thinking what to do next. He tries a horse laugh, but that proves of no help. He says 'Hell!' to himself, but it is equally ineffective. Then he opens the pantry door and calls.*)

DOWEY. Old lady.

(*She comes timidly to the door, her hand up as if to ward off a blow.*)

MRS. DOWEY. Is it time?

(*An encouraging voice answers her.*)

DOWEY. No, no, not yet. I've left word for Dixon to whistle when go I must.

MRS. DOWEY. All is ended.

DOWEY. Now, then, you promised to be gay. We were to help one another.

MRS. DOWEY. Yes, Kenneth.

DOWEY. It's bad for me, but it's worse for you.

MRS. DOWEY. The men have medals to win, you see.

DOWEY. The women have their medals too.

(*He knows she likes him to order her about, so he tries it again.*)

DOWEY. Come here. No, I'll come to you. (*He stands gaping at her wonderingly. He has no power of words, nor does he quite know what he would like to say.*) God!

MRS. DOWEY.   What is it, Kenneth ?

DOWEY.   You 're a woman.

MRS. DOWEY.   I had near forgot it.

(*He wishes he was at the station with* DIXON.   DIXON *is sure to have a bottle in his pocket.   They will be roaring a song presently.   But in the meantime—there is that son business.   Blethers, the whole thing, of course—or mostly blethers.   But it 's the way to please her.*)

DOWEY.   Have you noticed you have never called me son ?

MRS. DOWEY.   Have I noticed it !   I was feared, Kenneth. You said I was on probation.

DOWEY.   And so you were.   Well, the probation 's ended. (*He laughs uncomfortably.*)   The like of me !   But if you want me you can have me.

MRS. DOWEY.   Kenneth, will I do ?

DOWEY (*artfully gay*).   Woman, don't be so forward.   Wait till I have proposed.

MRS. DOWEY.   Propose for a mother ?

DOWEY.   What for no ?   (*In the grand style*) Mrs. Dowey, you queer carl, you spunky tiddy, have I your permission to ask you the most important question a neglected orphan can ask of an old lady ?

(*She bubbles with mirth.   Who could help it, the man has such a way with him.*)

MRS. DOWEY.   None of your sauce, Kenneth.

DOWEY.   For a long time, Mrs. Dowey, you cannot have been unaware of my sonnish feelings for you.

MRS. DOWEY.   Wait till I get my mop to you !

DOWEY.   And if you 're not willing to be my mother, I swear I 'll never ask another.

(*The old divert pulls him down to her and strokes his hair.*) Was I a well-behaved infant, mother ?

MRS. DOWEY.   Not you, sonny, you were a rampaging rogue.

DOWEY.   Was I slow in learning to walk ?

MRS. DOWEY.   The quickest in our street.   He ! he ! he ! (*She starts up.*)   Was that the whistle ?

DOWEY.   No, no.   See here.   In taking me over you have, in a manner of speaking, joined the Black Watch.

MRS. DOWEY.   I like to think that, Kenneth.

DOWEY. Then you must behave so that the ghost piper can be proud of you. 'Tion ! (*She stands bravely at attention.*) That's the style. Now listen. I've sent in your name as being my nearest of kin, and your allowance will be coming to you weekly in the usual way.

MRS. DOWEY. Hey ! hey ! hey ! Is it wicked, Kenneth ?

DOWEY. I'll take the responsibility for it in both worlds. You see, I want you to be safeguarded in case anything hap——

MRS. DOWEY. Kenneth !

DOWEY. 'Tion ! Have no fear. I'll come back, covered with mud and medals. Mind you have that cup of tea waiting for me. (*He is listening for the whistle. He pulls her on to his knee.*)

MRS. DOWEY. Hey ! hey ! hey ! hey !

DOWEY. What fun we'll have writing to one another ! Real letters this time.

MRS. DOWEY. Yes.

DOWEY. It would be a good plan if you began the first letter as soon as I've gone.

MRS. DOWEY. I will.

DOWEY. I hope Lady Dolly will go on sending me cakes.

MRS. DOWEY. You may be sure.

(*He ties his scarf round her neck.*)

DOWEY. You must have been a bonny thing when you were young.

MRS. DOWEY. Away with you !

DOWEY. That scarf sets you fine.

MRS. DOWEY. Blue was always my colour.

(*The whistle sounds.*)

DOWEY. Old lady, you are what Blighty means to me now. (*She hides in the pantry again. She is out of sight to us, but she does something that makes* PRIVATE DOWEY *take off his bonnet. Then he shoulders his equipment and departs. That is he laughing coarsely with* DIXON.)

We have one last glimpse of the old lady—a month or two after KENNETH'S *death in action. It would be rosemary to us to see her in her black dress, of which she is very proud ; but let us rather peep at her in the familiar garments that make a third to her mop and pail. It is early morning, and*

*she is having a look at her medals before setting off on the
daily round.   They are in a drawer, with the scarf covering
them, and on the scarf a piece of lavender.   First, the black
frock, which she carries in her arms like a baby.   Then her
War Savings Certificates,* KENNETH'S *bonnet, a thin packet
of real letters, and the famous champagne cork.   She kisses
the letters, but she does not blub over them.   She strokes
the dress, and waggles her head over the certificates and
presses the bonnet to her cheeks, and rubs the tinsel of the
cork carefully with her apron.   She is a tremulous old 'un ;
yet she exults, for she owns all these things, and also the penny
flag on her breast.   She puts them away in the drawer,
the scarf over them, the lavender on the scarf.   Her air of
triumph well becomes her.   She lifts the pail and the mop,
and slouches off gamely to the day's toil.)*

DEAR BRUTUS

Produced at Wyndham's Theatre on October 17, 1917, with the following cast :

MR. DEARTH	*Gerald du Maurier*
MR. PURDIE	*Sam Sothern*
MR. COADE	*Norman Forbes*
MATEY	*Will West*
LOB	*Arthur Hatherton*
MRS. DEARTH	*Hilda Moore*
MRS. PURDIE	*Jessie Bateman*
MRS. COADE	*Maude Millett*
JOANNA TROUT	*Doris Lytton*
LADY CAROLINE LANCY . . .	*Lydia Bilbrooke*
MARGARET	*Faith Celli*

———

The play ran for 365 performances. Revivals : Wyndham's, May 6, 1922 (258 performances) ; Playhouse, September 5, 1929 (108 performances) ; Queen's, January 20, 1941 (111 performances).

ACT I

THE scene is a darkened room, which the curtain reveals so
stealthily that if there was a mouse on the stage it is there still.
Our object is to catch our two chief characters unawares ;
they are Darkness and Light.

The room is so obscure as to be invisible, but at the back of
the obscurity are French windows, through which is seen Lob's
garden bathed in moonshine. The Darkness and Light, which
this room and garden represent, are very still, but we should feel
that it is only the pause in which old enemies regard each
other before they come to the grip. The moonshine stealing
about among the flowers, to give them their last instructions,
has left a smile upon them, but it is a smile with a menace in
it for the dwellers in darkness. What we expect to see next
is the moonshine slowly pushing the windows open, so that it
may whisper to a confederate in the house, whose name is
Lob. But though we may be sure that this was about to
happen it does not happen ; a stir among the dwellers in darkness prevents it.

These unsuspecting ones are in the dining-room, and as a
communicating door opens we hear them at play. Several
tenebrious shades appear in the lighted doorway and hesitate
on the two steps that lead down into the unlit room. The
fanciful among us may conceive a rustle at the same moment
among the flowers. The engagement has begun, though not
in the way we had intended.

VOICES.—
' Go on, Coady : lead the way.'
' Oh dear, I don't see why I should go first.'
' The nicest always goes first.'
' It is a strange house if I am the nicest.'
' It *is* a strange house.'
' Don't close the door ; I can't see where the switch is.'
' Over here.'

They have been groping their way forward, blissfully unaware of how they shall be groping there again more terribly before the night is out. Some one finds a switch, and the room is illumined, with the effect that the garden seems to have drawn back a step as if worsted in the first encounter. But it is only waiting.

The apparently inoffensive chamber thus suddenly revealed is, for a bachelor's home, creditably like a charming country house drawing-room and abounds in the little feminine touches that are so often best applied by the hand of man. There is nothing in the room inimical to the ladies, unless it be the cut flowers which are from the garden and possibly in collusion with it. The fireplace may also be a little dubious. It has been hacked out of a thick wall which may have been there when the other walls were not, and is presumably the cavern where Lob, when alone, sits chatting to himself among the blue smoke. He is as much at home by this fire as any gnome that may be hiding among its shadows ; but he is less familiar with the rest of the room, and when he sees it, as for instance on his lonely way to bed, he often stares long and hard at it before chuckling uncomfortably.

There are five ladies, and one only of them is elderly, the Mrs. Coade whom a voice in the darkness has already proclaimed the nicest. She is the nicest, though the voice was no good judge. Coady, as she is familiarly called and as her husband also is called, each having for many years been able to answer for the other, is a rounded old lady with a beaming smile that has accompanied her from childhood. If she lives to be a hundred she will pretend to the census man that she is only ninety-nine. She has no other vice that has not been smoothed out of existence by her placid life, and she has but one complaint against the male Coady, the rather odd one that he has long forgotten his first wife. Our Mrs. Coady never knew the first wife, but it is she alone who sometimes looks at the portrait of her and preserves in their home certain mementoes of her, such as a lock of brown hair, which the equally gentle male Coady must have treasured once but has now forgotten. The first wife had been slightly lame, and in their brief married life he had carried solicitously a rest for her foot, had got so accustomed to doing this that, after a quarter of a century with our Mrs. Coady, he still finds footstools for her as if she were lame also. She has ceased to pucker her face over this, taking it as a kind little thoughtless attention, and indeed with the years has developed a friendly limp.

Of the other four ladies, all young and physically fair, two are married. Mrs. Dearth is tall, of smouldering eye and fierce desires, murky beasts lie in ambush in the labyrinths of her mind, she is a white-faced gypsy with a husky voice, most beautiful when she is sullen, and therefore frequently at her best. The other ladies when in conclave refer to her as The Dearth. Mrs. Purdie is a safer companion for the toddling kind of man. She is soft and pleading, and would seek what she wants by laying her head on the loved one's shoulder, while The Dearth might attain it with a pistol. A brighter spirit than either is Joanna Trout, who, when her affections are not engaged, has a merry face and figure, but can dismiss them both at the important moment, which is at the word 'love.' Then Joanna quivers, her sense of humour ceases to beat and the dullest man may go ahead. There remains Lady Caroline Laney of the disdainful poise, lately from the enormously select school where they are taught to pronounce their *r*'s as *w*'s; nothing else seems to be taught, but for matrimonial success nothing else is necessary. Every woman who pronounces *r* as *w* will find a mate; it appeals to all that is chivalrous in man.

An old-fashioned gallantry induces us to accept from each of these ladies her own estimate of herself, and fortunately it is favourable in every case. This refers to their estimate of themselves up to the hour of ten on the evening on which we first meet them; the estimate may have changed temporarily by the time we part from them on the following morning. What their mirrors say to each of them is, A dear face, not classically perfect but abounding in that changing charm which is the best type of English womanhood; here is a woman who has seen and felt far more than her reticent nature readily betrays; she sometimes smiles, but behind that concession, controlling it in a manner hardly less than adorable, lurks the sigh called Knowledge; a strangely interesting face, mysterious; a line for her tombstone might be, 'If I had been a man what adventures I could have had with her who lies here.'

Are these ladies then so very alike? They would all deny

it, so we must take our own soundings. At this moment of their appearance in the drawing-room at least they are alike in having a common interest. No sooner has the dining-room door closed than purpose leaps to their eyes ; oddly enough, the men having been got rid of, the drama begins.

ALICE DEARTH (*the darkest spirit, but the bravest*). We must not waste a second. Our minds are made up, I think ?

JOANNA. Now is the time.

MRS. COADE (*at once delighted and appalled*). Yes, now if at all ; but should we ?

ALICE. Certainly ; and before the men come in.

MABEL PURDIE. You don't think we should wait for the men ? They are as much in it as we are.

LADY CAROLINE (*unlucky, as her opening remark is without a single* r). Lob would be with them. If the thing is to be done at all it should be done now.

MRS. COADE. Is it quite fair to Lob ? After all, he is our host.

JOANNA. Of course it isn't fair to him, but let's do it, Coady.

MRS. COADE. Yes, let's do it !

MABEL. Mrs. Dearth *is* doing it.

ALICE (*who is writing out a telegram*). Of course I am. The men are not coming, are they ?

JOANNA (*reconnoitring*). No ; your husband is having another glass of port.

ALICE. I am sure he is. One of you ring, please.

(*The bold* JOANNA *rings*.)

MRS. COADE. Poor Matey !

LADY CAROLINE. He wichly desewves what he is about to get.

JOANNA. He is coming ! Don't all stand huddled together like conspirators.

MRS. COADE. It is what we are !

(*Swiftly they find seats, and are sunk thereon like ladies waiting languidly for their lords, when the doomed butler appears. He is a man of brawn, who could cast any one of them forth for a wager ; but we are about to connive at the triumph of mind over matter.*)

ALICE (*always at her best before ' the bright face of danger '*). Ah, Matey, I wish this telegram sent.

MATEY (*a general favourite*). Very good, ma'am. The village post office closed at eight, but if your message is important——

ALICE. It is ; and you are so clever, Matey, I am sure that you can persuade them to oblige you.

MATEY (*taking the telegram*). I will see to it myself, ma'am ; you can depend on its going.

(*There comes a little gasp from* COADY, *which is the equivalent to dropping a stitch in needle-work.*

ALICE (*who is* THE DEARTH *now*). Thank you. Better read the telegram, Matey, to be sure that you can make it out. (MATEY *reads it to himself, and he has never quite the same faith in woman again.* THE DEARTH *continues in a purring voice.*) Read it aloud, Matey.

MATEY. Oh, ma'am !

ALICE (*without the purr*). Aloud.

(*Thus encouraged, he reads the fatal missive.*)

MATEY. 'To Police Station, Great Cumney. Send officer first thing to-morrow morning to arrest Matey, butler, for theft of rings.'

ALICE. Yes, that is quite right.

MATEY. Ma'am ! (*But seeing that she has taken up a book, he turns to* LADY CAROLINE.) My lady !

LADY CAROLINE (*whose voice strikes colder than* THE DEARTH's). Should we not say how many wings ?

ALICE. Yes, put in the number of rings, Matey.

(MATEY *does not put in the number, but he produces three rings from unostentatious parts of his person and returns them without noticeable dignity to their various owners.*)

MATEY (*hopeful that the incident is now closed*). May I tear up the telegram, ma'am ?

ALICE. Certainly not.

LADY CAROLINE. I always said that this man was the culpwit. I am nevaw mistaken in faces, and I see bwoad awwows all over youws, Matey.

(*He might reply that he sees w's all over hers, but it is no moment for repartee.*)

MATEY.   It is deeply regretted.

ALICE (*darkly*).   I am sure it is.

JOANNA (*who has seldom remained silent for so long*).   We may as well tell him now that it is not our rings we are worrying about.   They have just been a means to an end, Matey.

(*The stir among the ladies shows that they have arrived at the more interesting point.*)

ALICE.   Precisely.   In other words that telegram is sent unless——

(MATEY'S *head rises.*)

JOANNA.   Unless you can tell us instantly what peculiarity it is that all we ladies have in common.

MABEL.   Not only the ladies ; all the guests in this house.

ALICE.   We have been here a week, and we find that when Lob invited us he knew us all so little that we begin to wonder why he asked us.   And now from words he has let drop we know that we were invited because of something he thinks we have in common.

MABEL.   But he won't say what it is.

LADY CAROLINE (*drawing back a little from* JOANNA).   One knows that no people could be more unlike.

JOANNA (*thankfully*).   One does.

MRS. COADE.   And we can't sleep at night, Matey, for wondering what this something is.

JOANNA (*summing up*).   But we are sure you know, and if you don't tell us—quod.

MATEY (*with growing uneasiness*).   I don't know what you mean, ladies.

ALICE.   Oh yes, you do.

MRS. COADE.   You must admit that your master is a very strange person.

MATEY (*wriggling*).   He is a little odd, ma'am.   That is why every one calls him Lob ; not Mr. Lob.

JOANNA.   He is so odd that it has got on my nerves that we have been invited here for some sort of horrid experiment. (MATEY *shivers*) You look as if you thought so too !

MATEY.   Oh no, miss, I—he—— (*The words he would keep back elude him.*)   You shouldn't have come, ladies ; you didn't ought to have come.

(*For the moment he is sorrier for them than for himself.*)

LADY CAROLINE.   Shouldn't have come !   Now, my man, what do you mean by that ?

MATEY.   Nothing, my lady : I—I just mean, why did you come if you are the kind he thinks ?

MABEL.   The kind he thinks ?

ALICE.   What kind does he think ?   Now we are getting at it.

MATEY (*guardedly*).   I haven't a notion, ma'am.

LADY CAROLINE (*whose w's must henceforth be supplied by the judicious reader*).   Then it is not necessarily our virtue that makes Lob interested in us ?

MATEY (*thoughtlessly*).   No, my lady ; oh no, my lady. (*This makes an unfavourable impression.*)

MRS. COADE.   And yet, you know, he is rather lovable.

MATEY (*carried away*).   He is, ma'am.   He is the most lovable old devil—I beg pardon, ma'am.

JOANNA.   You scarcely need to, for in a way it is true.   I have seen him out there among his flowers, petting them, talking to them, coaxing them till they simply *had* to grow.

ALICE (*making use perhaps of the wrong adjective*).   It is certainly a divine garden.

(*They all look at the unblinking enemy.*)

MRS. COADE (*not more deceived than the others*).   How lovely it is in the moonlight.   Roses, roses, all the way.   (*Dreamily*) It is like a hat I once had when I was young.

ALICE.   Lob is such an amazing gardener that I believe he could even grow hats.

LADY CAROLINE (*who will catch it for this*).   He is a wonderful gardener ; but is that quite nice at his age ?   What *is* his age, man ?

MATEY (*shuffling*).   He won't tell, my lady.   I think he is frightened that the police would step in if they knew how old he is.   They do say in the village that they remember him seventy years ago, looking just as he does to-day.

ALICE.   Absurd.

MATEY.   Yes, ma'am ; but there are his razors.

LADY CAROLINE.   Razors ?

MATEY.   *You* won't know about razors, my lady, not being married—as yet—excuse me.   But a married lady can tell a man's age by the number of his razors.   (*A little scared*) If you saw his razors—there is a little world of them, from patents of the present day back to implements so horrible, you can picture him with them in his hand scraping his way through the ages.

LADY CAROLINE. You amuse one to an extent. Was he ever married ?

MATEY (*too lightly*). He has quite forgotten, my lady. (*Reflecting*) How long ago is it since Merry England ?

LADY CAROLINE. Why do you ask ?

MABEL. In Queen Elizabeth's time, wasn't it ?

MATEY. He says he is all that is left of Merry England : that little man.

MABEL (*who has brothers*). Lob ? I think there is a famous cricketer called Lob.

MRS. COADE. Wasn't there a Lob in Shakespeare ? No, of course I am thinking of Robin Goodfellow.

LADY CAROLINE. The names are so alike.

JOANNA. Robin Goodfellow was Puck.

MRS. COADE (*with natural elation*). That is what was in my head. Lob was another name for Puck.

JOANNA. Well, he is certainly rather like what Puck might have grown into if he had forgotten to die. And, by the way, I remember now he does call his flowers by the old Elizabethan names.

MATEY. He always calls the Nightingale Philomel, miss— if that is any help.

ALICE (*who is not omniscient*). None whatever. Tell me this, did he specially ask you all for Midsummer week ?

(*They assent.*)

MATEY (*who might more judiciously have remained silent*). He would !

MRS. COADE. Now what do you mean ?

MATEY. He always likes them to be here on Midsummer night, ma'am.

ALICE. Them ? Whom ?

MATEY. Them who have that in common.

MABEL. What can it be ?

MATEY. I don't know.

LADY CAROLINE (*suddenly introspective*). I hope we are all nice women ? We don't know each other very well. (*Certain *suspicions are reborn in various breasts.)*   Does anything startling happen at those times?

MATEY.   I don't know.

JOANNA.   Why, I believe this is Midsummer Eve!

MATEY.   Yes, miss, it is.   The villagers know it.   They are all inside their houses, to-night—with the doors barred.

LADY CAROLINE.   Because of—of him?

MATEY.   He frightens them.   There are stories.

ALICE.   What alarms them?   Tell us—or——   *(She brandishes the telegram.)*

MATEY.   I know nothing for certain, ma'am.   I have never done it myself.   He has wanted me to, but I wouldn't.

MABEL.   Done what?

MATEY *(with fine appeal).*   Oh, ma'am, don't ask me.   Be merciful to me, ma'am.   I am not bad naturally.   It was just going into domestic service that did for me; the accident of being flung among bad companions.   It's touch and go how the poor turn out in this world; all depends on your taking the right or the wrong turning.

MRS. COADE *(the lenient).*   I dare say that is true.

MATEY *(under this touch of sun).*   When I was young, ma'am, I was offered a clerkship in the City.   If I had taken it there wouldn't be a more honest man alive to-day.   I would give the world to be able to begin over again.

(He means every word of it, though the flowers would here, if they dared, burst into ironical applause.)

MRS. COADE.   It is very sad, Mrs. Dearth.

ALICE.   I am sorry for him; but still——

MATEY *(his eyes turning to LADY CAROLINE).*   What do you say, my lady?

LADY CAROLINE *(briefly).*   As you ask me, I should certainly say jail.

MATEY *(desperately).*   If you will say no more about this, ma'am—I'll give you a tip that is worth it.

ALICE.   Ah, now you are talking.

LADY CAROLINE.   Don't listen to him.

MATEY *(lowering).*   You are the one that is hardest on me.

LADY CAROLINE.   Yes, I flatter myself I am.

MATEY *(forgetting himself).*   You might take a wrong turning yourself, my lady.

LADY CAROLINE.   I ?   How dare you, man !
(*But the flowers rather like him for this ; it is possibly what gave them a certain idea.*)

JOANNA (*near the keyhole of the dining-room door*).   The men are rising.

ALICE (*hurriedly*).   Very well, Matey, we agree—if the ' tip ' is good enough.

LADY CAROLINE.   You will regret this.

MATEY.   I think not, my lady.   It 's this :   I wouldn't go out to-night if he asks you.   Go into the garden, if you like. The garden is all right.   (*He really believes this.*)   I wouldn't go farther—not to-night.

MRS. COADE.   But he never proposes to us to go farther. Why should he to-night ?

MATEY.   I don't know, ma'am, but don't any of you go— (*devilishly*) except you, my lady ; I should like you to go.

LADY CAROLINE.   Fellow !

(*They consider this odd warning.*)

ALICE.   Shall I ?   (*They nod and she tears up the telegram.*)

MATEY (*with a gulp*).   Thank you, ma'am.

LADY CAROLINE.   You should have sent that telegram off.

JOANNA.   You are sure you have told us all you know, Matey ?

MATEY.   Yes, miss.   (*But at the door he is more generous.*) Above all, ladies, I wouldn't go into the wood.

MABEL.   The wood ?   Why, there is no wood within a dozen miles of here.

MATEY.   No, ma'am.   But all the same I wouldn't go into it, ladies—not if I was you.

(*With this cryptic warning he leaves them, and any discussion of it is prevented by the arrival of their host.   LOB is very small, and probably no one has ever looked so old except some newborn child.   To such as watch him narrowly, as the ladies now do for the first time, he has the effect of seeming to be hollow, an attenuated piece of piping insufficiently inflated ; one feels that if he were to strike against a solid object he might rebound feebly from it, which would be less disconcerting if he did not obviously know this and carefully avoid the furniture ; he is so light that the subject must not be mentioned in his presence, but it is possible that, were*) *the ladies to combine, they could blow him out of a chair. He enters portentously, his hands behind his back, as if every bit of him, from his domed head to his little feet, were the physical expression of the deep thoughts within him, then suddenly he whirls round to make his guests jump. This amuses him vastly, and he regains his gravity with difficulty. He addresses* MRS. COADE.)

LOB.　　Standing, dear lady ? pray be seated.

(*He finds a chair for her and pulls it away as she is about to sit, or kindly pretends to be about to do so, for he has had this quaint conceit every evening since she arrived.*)

MRS. COADE (*who loves children*).　You naughty !

LOB (*eagerly*).　It is quite a flirtation, isn't it ?

(*He rolls on a chair, kicking out his legs in an ecstasy of satisfaction. But the ladies are not certain that he is the little innocent they have hitherto thought him. The advent of* MR. COADE *and* MR. PURDIE *presently adds to their misgivings.* MR. COADE *is old, a sweet pippin of a man with a gentle smile for all ; he must have suffered much, you conclude incorrectly, to acquire that tolerant smile. Sometimes, as when he sees other people at work, a wistful look takes the place of the smile, and* MR. COADE *fidgets like one who would be elsewhere. Then there rises before his eyes the room called the study in his house, whose walls are lined with boxes marked A. B. C. to Z. and A^2. B^2. C^2. to K^2. These contain dusty notes for his great work on the Feudal System, the notes many years old, the work, strictly speaking, not yet begun. He still speaks at times of finishing it but never of beginning it. He knows that in more favourable circumstances, for instance if he had been a poor man instead of pleasantly well to do, he could have thrown himself avidly into that noble undertaking ; but he does not allow his secret sorrow to embitter him or darken the house. Quickly the vision passes, and he is again his bright self. Idleness, he says in his game way, has its recompenses. It is charming now to see how he at once crosses to his wife, solicitous for her comfort. He is bearing down on her with a footstool when* MR. PURDIE *comes from the dining-room. He is the most brilliant of our company, recently notable in debate at Oxford, where he was president of the Union, as indeed* *nearly everybody one meets seems to have been. Since then he has gone to the bar on Monday, married on Tuesday, and had a brief on Wednesday. Beneath his brilliance, and making charming company for himself, he is aware of intellectual powers beyond his years. As we are about to see, he has made one mistake in his life which he is bravely facing.)*

ALICE.   Is my husband still sampling the port, Mr. Purdie ?

PURDIE (*with a disarming smile for the absent* DEARTH).   Do you know, I believe he is.   Do the ladies like our proposal, Coade ?

COADE.   I have not told them of it yet.   The fact is, I am afraid that it might tire my wife too much.   Do you feel equal to a little exertion to-night, Coady, or is your foot troubling you ?

MRS. COADE (*the kind creature*).   I have been resting it, Coady.

COADE (*propping it on the footstool*).   There !   Is that more comfortable ?   Presently, dear, if you are agreeable we are all going out for a walk.

MRS. COADE (*quoting* MATEY).   The garden is all right.

PURDIE (*with jocular solemnity*).   Ah, but it is not to be the garden.   We are going farther afield.   We have an adventure for to-night.   Get thick shoes and a wrap, Mrs. Dearth ; all of you.

LADY CAROLINE (*with but languid interest*).   Where do you propose to take us ?

PURDIE.   To find a mysterious wood.

(*With the word ' wood ' the ladies are blown upright. Their eyes turn to* LOB, *who, however, has never looked more innocent.*)

JOANNA.   Are you being funny, Mr. Purdie ?   You know quite well that there are not any trees for miles around.   You have said yourself that it is the one blot on the landscape.

COADE (*almost as great a humorist as* PURDIE).   Ah, on ordinary occasions !   but allow us to point out to you, Miss Joanna, that this is Midsummer Eve.

(LOB *again comes sharply under female observation.*)

PURDIE.   Tell them what you told us, Lob.

LOB (*with a pout for the credulous*).   It is all nonsense, of course ; just foolish talk of the villagers. They say that on Midsummer Eve there is a strange wood in this part of the country.

ALICE (*lowering*). Where ?

PURDIE. Ah, that is one of its most charming features. It is never twice in the same place apparently. It has been seen on different parts of the Downs and on Moore Common ; once it was close to Radley village and another time about a mile from the sea. Oh, a sporting wood !

LADY CAROLINE. And Lob is anxious that we should all go and look for it ?

COADE. Not he ; Lob is the only sceptic in the house. Says it is all rubbish, and that we shall be sillies if we go. But we believe, eh, Purdie ?

PURDIE (*waggishly*). Rather !

LOB (*the artful*). Just wasting the evening. Let us have a round game at cards here instead.

PURDIE (*grandly*). No, sir, I am going to find that wood.

JOANNA. What is the good of it when it is found ?

PURDIE. We shall wander in it deliciously, listening to a new sort of bird called the Philomel.

(LOB *is behaving in the most exemplary manner ; making sweet little clucking sounds.*)

JOANNA (*doubtfully*). Shall we keep together, Mr. Purdie ?

PURDIE. No, we must hunt in pairs.

JOANNA (*converted*). I think it would be rather fun. Come on, Coady, I 'll lace your boots for you. I am sure your poor foot will carry you nicely.

ALICE. Miss Trout, wait a moment. Lob, has this wonderful wood any special properties ?

LOB. Pooh ! There 's no wood.

LADY CAROLINE. You 've never seen it ?

LOB. Not I. I don't believe in it.

ALICE. Have any of the villagers ever been in it ?

LOB (*dreamily*). So it 's said ; so it 's said.

ALICE. What did they say were their experiences ?

LOB. That isn't known. They never came back.

JOANNA (*promptly resuming her seat*). Never came back !

LOB. Absurd, of course. You see in the morning the wood was gone ; and so they were gone, too. (*He clucks again.*)

JOANNA.   I don't think I like this wood.

MRS. COADE.   It certainly is Midsummer Eve.

COADE (*remembering that women are not yet civilised*).   Of course if you ladies are against it we will drop the idea.   It was only a bit of fun.

ALICE (*with a malicious eye on* LOB).   Yes, better give it up—to please Lob.

PURDIE.   Oh, all right, Lob.   What about that round game of cards ?

(*The proposal meets with approval.*)

LOB (*bursting into tears*).   I wanted you to go.   I had set my heart on your going.   It is the thing I wanted, and it isn't good for me not to get the thing I want.

(*He creeps under the table and threatens the hands that would draw him out.*)

MRS. COADE.   Good gracious, he has wanted it all the time. You wicked Lob !

ALICE.   Now, you see there *is* something in it.

COADE.   Nonsense, Mrs. Dearth, it was only a joke.

MABEL (*melting*).   Don't cry, Lobby.

LOB.   Nobody cares for me—nobody loves me.   And I need to be loved.

(*Several of them are on their knees to him.*)

JOANNA   Yes, we do, we all love you.   Nice, nice Lobby.

MABEL.   Dear Lob, I am so fond of you.

JOANNA.   Dry his eyes with my own handkerchief.   (*He holds up his eyes but is otherwise inconsolable.*)

LADY CAROLINE.   Don't pamper him.

LOB (*furiously*).   I need to be pampered.

MRS. COADE.   You funny little man.   Let us go at once and look for his wood.

(*All feel that thus alone can his tears be dried.*)

JOANNA.   Boots and cloaks, hats forward.   Come on, Lady Caroline, just to show you are not afraid of Matey.

(*There is a general exodus, and* LOB *left alone emerges from his temporary retirement.   He clucks victoriously, but presently is on his knees again distressfully regarding some flowers that have fallen from their bowl.*)

LOB.   Poor bruised one, it was I who hurt you.   Lob is so

sorry. Lie there! (*To another*) Pretty, pretty, let me see
where you have a pain? You fell on your head; is this the
place? Now I make it better. Oh, little rascal, you are not
hurt at all; you just pretend. Oh dear, oh dear! Sweetheart, don't cry, you are now prettier than ever. You were too
tall. Oh, how beautifully you smell now that you are small.
(*He replaces the wounded tenderly in their bowl.*) Drink, drink.
Now, you are happy again. The little rascal smiles. All
smile, please—nod heads—aha! aha! You love Lob—Lob
loves you.

(JOANNA *and* MR. PURDIE *stroll in by the window.*)

JOANNA. What were you saying to them, Lob?

LOB. I was saying 'Two's company, three's none.'

(*He departs with a final cluck.*)

JOANNA. That man—he suspects!

(*This is a very different* JOANNA *from the one who has so
far flitted across our scene. It is also a different* PURDIE.
*In company they seldom look at each other, though when the
one does so the eyes of the other magnetically respond. We
have seen them trivial, almost cynical, but now we are
to greet them as they know they really are, the great strong-
hearted man and his natural mate, in the grip of the master
passion. For the moment* LOB'S *words have unnerved*
JOANNA *and it is* JOHN PURDIE'S *dear privilege to soothe
her.*)

PURDIE. No one minds Lob. My dear, oh my dear!

JOANNA (*faltering*). Yes, but he saw you kiss my hand.
Jack, if Mabel were to suspect!

PURDIE (*happily*). There is nothing for her to suspect.

JOANNA (*eagerly*). No, there isn't, is there? (*She is
desirous ever to be without a flaw.*) Jack, I am not doing anything wrong, am I?

PURDIE. You!

(*With an adorable gesture she gives him one of her hands,
and manlike he takes the other also.*)

JOANNA. Mabel is your wife, Jack. I should so hate
myself if I did anything that was disloyal to her.

PURDIE (*pressing her hand to her eyes as if counting them, in the
strange manner of lovers*). Those eyes could never be disloyal
—my lady of the nut-brown eyes. (*He holds her from him,*

surveying her, and is scorched in the flame of her femininity.) Oh, the svelteness of you. (*Almost with reproach*) Joanna, why are you so svelte !

(*For his sake she would be less svelte if she could, but she can't. She admits her failure with eyes grown still larger, and he envelops her so that he may not see her. Thus men seek safety.*)

JOANNA (*while out of sight*). All I want is to help her and you.

PURDIE. I know—how well I know—my dear brave love.

JOANNA. I am very fond of Mabel, Jack. I should like to be the best friend she has in the world.

PURDIE. You are, dearest. No woman ever had a better friend.

JOANNA. And yet I don't think she really likes me. I wonder why ?

PURDIE (*who is the bigger brained of the two*). It is just that Mabel doesn't understand. Nothing could make me say a word against my wife——

JOANNA (*sternly*). I wouldn't listen to you if you did.

PURDIE. I love you all the more, dear, for saying that. But Mabel is a cold nature and she doesn't understand.

JOANNA (*thinking never of herself but only of him*). She doesn't appreciate your finer qualities.

PURDIE (*ruminating*). That's it. But of course I am difficult. I always was a strange, strange creature. I often think, Joanna, that I am rather like a flower that has never had the sun to shine on it nor the rain to water it.

JOANNA. You break my heart.

PURDIE (*with considerable enjoyment*). I suppose there is no more lonely man than I walking the earth to-day.

JOANNA (*beating her wings*). It is so mournful.

PURDIE. It is the thought of you that sustains me, elevates me. You shine high above me like a star.

JOANNA. No, no. I wish I was wonderful, but I am not.

PURDIE. You have made me a better man, Joanna.

JOANNA. I am so proud to think that.

PURDIE. You have made me kinder to Mabel.

JOANNA. I am sure you are always kind to her.

PURDIE. Yes, I hope so. But I think now of special little

ways of giving her pleasure. That never-to-be-forgotten day when we first met, you and I !

JOANNA (*fluttering nearer to him*). That tragic, lovely day by the weir. Oh, Jack !

PURDIE. Do you know how in gratitude I spent the rest of that day ?

JOANNA (*crooning*). Tell me.

PURDIE. I read to Mabel aloud for an hour. I did it out of kindness to her, because I had met you.

JOANNA. It was dear of you.

PURDIE. Do you remember that first time my arms—your waist—you are so fluid, Joanna. (*Passionately*) Why are you so fluid ?

JOANNA (*downcast*). I can't help it, Jack.

PURDIE. I gave her a ruby bracelet for that.

JOANNA. It is a gem. You have given that lucky woman many lovely things.

PURDIE. It is my invariable custom to go straight off and buy Mabel something whenever you have been sympathetic to me. Those new earrings of hers—they are in memory of the first day you called me Jack. Her Paquin gown—the one with the beads—was because you let me kiss you.

JOANNA. I didn't exactly let you.

PURDIE. No, but you have such a dear way of giving in.

JOANNA. Jack, she hasn't worn that gown of late.

PURDIE. No, nor the jewels. I think she has some sort of idea now that when I give her anything nice it means that you have been nice to me. She has rather a suspicious nature, Mabel ; she never used to have it, but it seems to be growing on her. I wonder why, I wonder why ?

(*In this wonder which is shared by* JOANNA *their lips meet, and* MABEL, *who has been about to enter from the garden, quietly retires.*)

JOANNA. Was that any one in the garden ?

PURDIE (*returning from a quest*). There is no one there now.

JOANNA. I am sure I heard some one. If it was Mabel ! (*With a perspicacity that comes of knowledge of her sex*) Jack, if she saw us she will think you were kissing me.

(*These fears are confirmed by the rather odd bearing of* MABEL, *who now joins their select party.*)

MABEL (*apologetically*). I am so sorry to interrupt you, Jack ; but please wait a moment before you kiss her again. Excuse me, Joanna. (*She quietly draws the curtains, thus shutting out the garden and any possible onlooker.*) I did not want the others to see you ; they might not understand how noble you are, Jack. You can go on now.

(*Having thus passed the time of day with them she withdraws by the door, leaving JACK bewildered and JOANNA knowing all about it.*)

JOANNA. How extraordinary ! Of all the——! Oh, but how contemptible ! (*She sweeps to the door and calls to MABEL by name.*)

MABEL (*returning with promptitude*). Did you call me, Joanna ?

JOANNA (*guardedly*). I insist on an explanation. (*With creditable hauteur*) What were you doing in the garden, Mabel ?

MABEL (*who has not been so quiet all day*). I was looking for something I have lost.

PURDIE (*hope springing eternal*). Anything important ?

MABEL. I used to fancy it, Jack. It is my husband's love. You don't happen to have picked it up, Joanna ? If so and you don't set great store by it I should like it back—the pieces, I mean.

(MR. PURDIE *is about to reply to this, when* JOANNA *rather wisely fills the breach.*)

JOANNA. Mabel, I—I will not be talked to in that way. To imply that I—that your husband—oh, shame !

PURDIE (*finely*). I must say, Mabel, that I am a little disappointed in you. I certainly understood that you had gone upstairs to put on your boots.

MABEL. Poor old Jack. (*She muses.*) A woman like that !

JOANNA (*changing her comment in the moment of utterance*). I forgive you, Mabel, you will be sorry for this afterwards.

PURDIE (*warningly, but still reluctant to think less well of his wife*). Not a word against Joanna, Mabel. If you knew how nobly she has spoken of you.

JOANNA (*imprudently*). She does know. She has been listening.

(*There is a moment's danger of the scene degenerating into something mid-Victorian. Fortunately a chivalrous man*

is present to lift it to a higher plane. JOHN PURDIE *is one
to whom subterfuge of any kind is abhorrent ; if he has not
spoken out before it is because of his reluctance to give* MABEL
*pain.   He speaks out now, and seldom probably has he
proved himself more worthy.*)

PURDIE.   This is a man's business.   I must be open with
you now, Mabel : it is the manlier way.   If you wish it I shall
always be true to you in word and deed ; it is your right.   But
I cannot pretend that Joanna is not the one woman in the world
for me.   If I had met her before you—it 's Kismet, I suppose.
(*He swells.*)

JOANNA (*from a chair*).   Too late, too late.

MABEL (*although the woman has seen him swell*).   I suppose
you never knew what true love was till you met her, Jack ?

PURDIE.   You force me to say it.   Joanna and I are as one
person.   We have not a thought at variance.   We are one
rather than two.

MABEL (*looking at* JOANNA).   Yes, and that 's the one !
(*With the cheapest sarcasm*) I am so sorry to have marred your
lives.

PURDIE.   If any blame there is, it is all mine ; she is as
spotless as the driven snow.   The moment I mentioned love
to her she told me to desist.

MABEL.   Not she.

JOANNA.   So you *were* listening !   (*The obtuseness of* MABEL
is very strange to her.)   Mabel, don't you see how splendid he is !

MABEL.   Not quite, Joanna.

(*She goes away.   She is really a better woman than this,
but never capable of scaling that higher plane to which he
has, as it were, offered her a hand.*)

JOANNA.   How lovely of you, Jack, to take it all upon
yourself.

PURDIE (*simply*).   It is the man's privilege.

JOANNA.   Mabel has such a horrid way of seeming to put
people in the wrong.

PURDIE.   Have you noticed that ?   Poor Mabel, it is not
an enviable quality.

JOANNA (*despondently*).   I don't think I care to go out now.
She has spoilt it all.   She has taken the innocence out of it,
Jack.

PURDIE (*a rock*). We must be brave and not mind her. Ah, Joanna, if we had met in time. If only I could begin again. To be battered for ever just because I once took the wrong turning, it isn't fair.

JOANNA (*emerging from his arms*). The wrong turning ! Now, who was saying that a moment ago—about himself ? Why, it was Matey.

(*A footstep is heard.*)

PURDIE (*for the first time losing patience with his wife*). Is that her coming back again ? It 's too bad.

(*But the intruder is* MRS. DEARTH, *and he greets her with relief.*)

Ah, it is you, Mrs. Dearth.

ALICE. Yes, it is ; but thank you for telling me, Mr. Purdie. I don't intrude, do I ?

JOANNA (*descending to the lower plane, on which even goddesses snap*). Why should you ?

PURDIE. Rather not. We were—hoping it would be you. We want to start on the walk. I can't think what has become of the others. We have been looking for them everywhere. (*He glances vaguely round the room, as if they might so far have escaped detection.*)

ALICE (*pleasantly*). Well, do go on looking ; under that flower-pot would be a good place. It is my husband I am in search of.

PURDIE (*who likes her best when they are in different rooms*). Shall I rout him out for you ?

ALICE. How too unutterably kind of you, Mr. Purdie. I hate to trouble you, but it would be the sort of service one never forgets.

PURDIE. You know, I believe you are chaffing me.

ALICE. No, no, I am incapable of that.

PURDIE. I won't be a moment.

ALICE. Miss Trout and I will await your return with ill-concealed impatience.

(*They await it across a table, the newcomer in a reverie and* JOANNA *watching her. Presently* MRS. DEARTH *looks up, and we may notice that she has an attractive screw of the mouth which denotes humour.*)

Yes, I suppose you are right ; I dare say I am.

JOANNA (*puzzled*). I didn't say anything.

ALICE. I thought I heard you say, 'That hateful Dearth woman, coming butting in where she is not wanted.'

(JOANNA *draws up her svelte figure, but a screw of one mouth often calls for a similar demonstration from another, and both ladies smile. They nearly become friends.*)

JOANNA. You certainly have good ears.

ALICE (*drawling*). Yes, they have always been rather admired.

JOANNA (*snapping*). By the painters for whom you sat when you were an artist's model ?

ALICE (*measuring her*). So that has leaked out, has it !

JOANNA (*ashamed*). I shouldn't have said that.

ALICE (*their brief friendship over*). Do you think I care whether you know or not ?

JOANNA (*making an effort to be good*). I'm sure you don't. Still, it was cattish of me.

ALICE. It was.

JOANNA (*in flame*). I don't see it.

(MRS. DEARTH *laughs and forgets her, and with the entrance of a man from the dining-room* JOANNA *drifts elsewhere. Not so much a man, this newcomer, as the relic of what has been a good one ; it is the most he would ever claim for himself. Sometimes, brandy in hand, he has visions of the* WILL DEARTH *he used to be, clear of eye, sees him but a field away, singing at his easel or, fishing-rod in hand, leaping a stile. Our* WILL *stares after the fellow for quite a long time, so long that the two melt into the one who finishes* LOB'S *brandy. He is scarcely intoxicated as he appears before the lady of his choice, but he is shaky and has watery eyes.*

ALICE *has had a rather wild love for this man, or for that other one, and he for her, but somehow it has gone whistling down the wind. We may expect therefore to see them at their worst when in each other's company.*)

DEARTH (*who is not without a humorous outlook on his own degradation*). I am uncommonly flattered, Alice, to hear that you have sent for me. It quite takes me aback.

ALICE (*with cold distaste*). It isn't your company I want, Will.

DEARTH.   You know, I felt that Purdie must have delivered your message wrongly.

ALICE.   I want you to come with us on this mysterious walk and keep an eye on Lob.

DEARTH.   On poor little Lob ?   Oh, surely not.

ALICE.   I can't make the man out.   I want you to tell me something ;   when he invited us here, do you think it was you or me he specially wanted ?

DEARTH.   Oh, you.   He made no bones about it ;   said there was something about you that made him want uncommonly to have you down here.

ALICE.   Will, try to remember this :   did he ask us for any particular time ?

DEARTH.   Yes, he was particular about its being Midsummer week.

ALICE.   Ah !   I thought so.   Did he say what it was about me that made him want to have me here in Midsummer week ?

DEARTH.   No, but I presumed it must be your fascination, Alice.

ALICE.   Just so.   Well, I want you to come out with us to-night to watch him.

DEARTH.   Crack-in-my-eye Tommy, spy on my host ! And such a harmless little chap, too.   Excuse me, Alice. Besides, I have an engagement.

ALICE.   An engagement—with the port decanter, I presume.

DEARTH.   A good guess, but wrong.   The decanter is now but an empty shell.   Still, how you know me !   My engagement is with a quiet cigar in the garden.

ALICE.   Your hand is so unsteady, you won't be able to light the match.

DEARTH.   I shall just manage.   (*He triumphantly proves the exact truth of his statement.*)

ALICE.   A nice hand for an artist !

DEARTH.   One would scarcely call me an artist nowadays.

ALICE.   Not so far as any work is concerned.

DEARTH.   Not so far as having any more pretty dreams to paint is concerned.   (*Grinning at himself.*)   Wonder why I have become such a waster, Alice ?

ALICE.   I suppose it was always in you.

DEARTH (*with perhaps a glimpse of the fishing-rod*). I suppose so ; and yet I was rather a good sort in the days when I went courting you.

ALICE. Yes, I thought so. Unlucky days for me, as it has turned out.

DEARTH (*heartily*). Yes, a bad job for you. (*Puzzling unsteadily over himself*) I didn't know I was a wrong 'un at the time ; thought quite well of myself, thought a vast deal more of you. Crack-in-my-eye Tommy, how I used to leap out of bed at 6 A.M. all agog to be at my easel ; blood ran through my veins in those days. And now I 'm middle-aged and done for. Funny ! Don't know how it has come about, nor what has made the music mute. (*Mildly curious*) When did you begin to despise me, Alice ?

ALICE. When I got to know you really, Will ; a long time ago.

DEARTH (*bleary of eye*). Yes, I think that is true. It was a long time ago, and before I had begun to despise myself. It wasn't till I knew you had no opinion of me that I began to go down hill. You will grant that, won't you ; and that I did try for a bit to fight on ? If you had cared for me I wouldn't have come to this, surely ?

ALICE. Well, I found I didn't care for you, and I wasn't hypocrite enough to pretend I did. That 's blunt, but you used to admire my bluntness.

DEARTH. The bluntness of you, the adorable wildness of you, you untamed thing ! There were never any shades in you ; kiss or kill was your motto, Alice. I felt from the first moment I saw you that you would love me or knife me.

(*Memories of their shooting star flare in both of them for as long as a sheet of paper might take to burn.*)

ALICE. I didn't knife you.

DEARTH. No. I suppose that was where you made the mistake. It is hard on you, old lady. (*Becoming watery*) I suppose it 's too late to try to patch things up ?

ALICE. Let 's be honest ; it is too late, Will.

DEARTH (*whose tears would smell of brandy*). Perhaps if we had had children—Pity !

ALICE. A blessing I should think, seeing what sort of a father they would have had.

DEARTH (*ever reasonable*).   I dare say you 're right.   Well, Alice, I know that somehow it 's my fault.   I 'm sorry for you.

ALICE.   I 'm sorry for myself.   If I hadn't married you what a different woman I should be   What a fool I was.

DEARTH.   Ah !   Three things they say come not back to men nor women—the spoken word, the past life, and the neglected opportunity.   Wonder if we should make any more of them, Alice, if they did come back to us.

ALICE.   You wouldn't.

DEARTH (*avoiding a hiccough*).   I guess you 're right.

ALICE.   But I——

DEARTH (*sincerely*).   Yes, what a boon for you.   But I hope it 's not Freddy Finch-Fallowe you would put in my place ;   I know he is following you about again.   (*He is far from threatening her, he has too beery an opinion of himself for that.*)

ALICE.   He followed me about, as you put it, before I knew you.   I don't know why I quarrelled with him.

DEARTH.   Your heart told you that he was no good, Alice.

ALICE.   My heart told me that you *were*.   So it wasn't of much service to me, my heart !

DEARTH.   The Honourable Freddy Finch-Fallowe is a rotter.

ALICE (*ever inflammable*).   You are certainly an authority on the subject.

DEARTH (*with the sad smile of the disillusioned*).   You have me there.   After which brief, but pleasant, little connubial chat, he pursued his dishonoured way into the garden.

(*He is however prevented doing so for the moment by the return of the others.   They are all still in their dinner clothes though wearing wraps.   They crowd in through the door, chattering.*)

LOB.   Here they are !   Are you ready, dear lady ?

MRS. COADE (*seeing that* DEARTH's *hand is on the window curtains*).   Are you not coming with us to find the wood, Mr. Dearth ?

DEARTH.   Alas, I am unavoidably detained.   You will find me in the garden when you come back.

JOANNA (*whose sense of humour has been restored*).   If we ever do come back !

DEARTH.   Precisely.   (*With a groggy bow*) Should we

never meet again, Alice, fare thee well.   Purdie, if you find the tree of knowledge in the wood bring me back an apple.

PURDIE.   I promise.

LOB.   Come quickly.   Matey mustn't see me.   (*He is turning out the lights.*)

LADY CAROLINE (*pouncing*).   Matey?   What difference would that make, Lob?

LOB.   He would take me off to bed ;   it 's past my time.

COADE (*not the least gay of the company*).   You know, old fellow, you make it very difficult for us to embark upon this adventure in the proper eerie spirit.

DEARTH.   Well, I 'm for the garden.

(*He walks to the window, and the others are going out by the door.   But they do not go.   There is a hitch somewhere— at the window apparently, for* DEARTH *having begun to draw the curtains apart lets them fall, like one who has had a shock.   The others remember long afterwards his grave face as he came quietly back and put his cigar on the table. The room is in darkness save for the light from one lamp.*)

PURDIE (*wondering*).   How now, Dearth?

DEARTH.   What is it we get in that wood, Lob?

ALICE.   Ah, he won't tell us that.

LOB (*shrinking*).   Come on !

ALICE (*impressed by the change that has come over her husband*). Tell us first.

LOB (*forced to the disclosure*).   They say that in the wood you get what nearly everybody here is longing for—a second chance.

(*The ladies are simultaneously enlightened.*)

JOANNA (*speaking for all*).   So that desire is what we have in common !

COADE (*with gentle regret*).   I have often thought, Coady, that if I had a second chance I should be a useful man instead of just a nice lazy one.

ALICE (*morosely*).   A second chance !

LOB.   Come on.

PURDIE (*gaily*).   Yes, to the wood—the wood !

DEARTH (*as they are going out by the door*).   Stop, why not go this way ?

(*He pulls the curtains apart, and there comes a sudden in- drawing of breath from all, for no garden is there now.   In*

*its place is an endless wood of great trees ; the nearest of
them has come close to the window. It is a sombre wood,
with splashes of moonshine and of blackness standing very
still in it.*

*The party in the drawing-room are very still also ; there
is scarcely a cry or a movement. It is perhaps strange that
the most obviously frightened is* LOB *who calls vainly for*
MATEY. *The first articulate voice is* DEARTH'S.)

DEARTH (*very quietly*). Any one ready to risk it ?

PURDIE (*after another silence*). Of course there is nothing
in it—just——

DEARTH (*grimly*). Of course. Going out, Purdie ?

(PURDIE *draws back.*)

MRS. DEARTH (*the only one who is undaunted*). A second
chance ! (*She is looking at her husband. They all look at him
as if he had been a leader once.*)

DEARTH (*with his sweet mournful smile*). I shall be back in
a moment—probably.

(*As he passes into the wood his hands rise to his forehead as
if a hammer had tapped him there. He is soon lost to
view.*)

LADY CAROLINE (*after a long pause*). He does not come
back.

MRS. COADE. It 's horrible.

(*She steals off by the door to her room, calling to her husband
to do likewise. He takes a step after her, and stops in the
grip of the two words that holds them all. The stillness
continues. At last* MRS. PURDIE *goes out into the wood,
her hands raised, and is swallowed up by it.*)

PURDIE. Mabel !

ALICE (*sardonically*). You will have to go now, Mr. Purdie.

(*He looks at* JOANNA, *and they go out together, one tap of
the hammer for each.*)

LOB. That 's enough. (*Warningly*) Don't you go, Mrs.
Dearth. You 'll catch it if you go.

ALICE. A second chance !

(*She goes out unflinching.*)

LADY CAROLINE. One would like to know.

(*She goes out.* MRS. COADE'S *voice is heard from the stair
calling to her husband. He hesitates but follows* LADY

CAROLINE.   *To* LOB *now alone comes* MATEY *with a tray of coffee cups.*)

MATEY (*as he places his tray on the table*).   It is past your bed-time, sir.   Say good-night to the ladies, and come along.

LOB.   Matey, look !

(MATEY *looks.*)

MATEY (*shrinking*).   Great heavens, then it 's true !

LOB.   Yes, but I——I wasn't sure.

(MATEY *approaches the window cautiously to peer out, and his master gives him a sudden push that propels him into the wood.* LOB's *back is toward us as he stands alone staring out upon the unknown.   He is terrified still ; yet quivers of rapture are running up and down his little frame.*)

ACT II

WE are translated to the depths of the wood in the enchantment of a moonlight night. In some other glade a nightingale is singing ; in this one, in proud motoring attire, recline two mortals whom we have known in different conditions ; the second chance has converted them into husband and wife. The man, of gross muddy build, lies luxurious on his back, exuding affluence, a prominent part of him heaving playfully, like some little wave that will not rest in a still sea. A handkerchief over his face conceals from us what Colossus he may be, but his mate is our Lady Caroline. The nightingale trills on, and Lady Caroline takes up its song.

LADY CAROLINE. Is it not a lovely night, Jim ! Listen, my own, to Philomel ; he is saying that he is lately married. So are we, you ducky thing. I feel, Jim, that I am Rosalind and that you are my Orlando.

(*The handkerchief being removed,* MR. MATEY *is revealed ; and the nightingale seeks some farther tree.*)

MATEY. What do you say I am, Caroliny ?

LADY CAROLINE (*clapping her hands*). My own one, don't you think it would be fun if we were to write poems about each other and pin them on the tree trunks ?

MATEY (*tolerantly*). Poems ? I never knew such a lass for high-flown language.

LADY CAROLINE. Your lass, dearest. Jim's lass.

MATEY (*pulling her ear*). And don't you forget it.

LADY CAROLINE (*with the curiosity of woman*). What would you do if I were to forget it, great bear ?

MATEY. Take a stick to you.

LADY CAROLINE (*so proud of him*). I love to hear you talk like that ; it is so virile. I always knew that it was a master I needed.

MATEY. It 's what you all need.

1022

LADY CAROLINE. It is, it is, you knowing wretch.

MATEY. Listen, Caroliny. (*He touches his money pocket, which emits a crinkly sound—the squeak of angels.*) That is what gets the ladies.

LADY CAROLINE. How much have you made this week, you wonderful man ?

MATEY (*blandly*). Another two hundred or so. That 's all, just two hundred or so.

LADY CAROLINE (*caressing her wedding-ring*). My dear golden fetter, listen to him. Kiss my fetter, Jim.

MATEY. Wait till I light this cigar.

LADY CAROLINE. Let me hold the darling match.

MATEY. Tidy-looking Petitey Corona, this. There was a time when one of that sort would have run away with two days of my screw.

LADY CAROLINE. How I should have loved, Jim, to know you when you were poor. Fancy your having once been a clerk.

MATEY (*remembering Napoleon and others*). We all have our beginnings. But it wouldn't have mattered how I began, Caroliny : I should have come to the top just the same. (*Becoming a poet himself*) I am a climber, and there are nails in my boots for the parties beneath me. Boots ! I tell you if I had been a bootmaker, I should have been the first bootmaker in London.

LADY CAROLINE (*a humorist at last*). I am sure you would, Jim ; but should you have made the best boots ?

MATEY (*wishing uxoriously that others could have heard this*). Very good, Caroliny ; that is the neatest thing I have heard you say. But it 's late ; we had best be strolling back to our Rolls-Royce.

LADY CAROLINE (*as they rise*). I do hope the ground wasn't damp.

MATEY. Don't matter if it was ; I was lying on your rug. (*Indeed we notice now that he has had all the rug, and she the bare ground. JOANNA reaches the glade, now an unhappy lady who has got what she wanted. She is in country dress and is unknown to them as they are to her.*)

Who is the mournful party ?

JOANNA (*hesitating*). I wonder, sir, whether you happen to have seen my husband ? I have lost him in the wood.

MATEY. We are strangers in these parts ourselves, missis. Have we passed any one, Caroliny ?

LADY CAROLINE (*coyly*). Should we have noticed, dear ? Might it be that old gent over there ? (*After the delightful manner of those happily wed she has already picked up many of her lover's favourite words and phrases.*)

JOANNA. Oh no, my husband is quite young.

(*The woodlander referred to is* MR. COADE *in gala costume ; at his mouth a whistle he has made him from some friendly twig. To its ravishing music he is seen pirouetting charmingly among the trees, his new occupation.*)

MATEY (*signing to the unknown that he is wanted*). Seems a merry old cock. Evening to you, sir. Do you happen to have seen a young gentleman in the wood lately, all by himself, and looking for his wife ?

COADE (*with a flourish of his legs*). Can't say I have.

JOANNA (*dolefully*). He isn't necessarily by himself ; and I don't know that he is looking for me. There may be a young lady with him.

(*The more happily married lady smiles, and* JOANNA *is quick to take offence.*)

JOANNA. What do you mean by that ?

LADY CAROLINE (*neatly*). Oho—if you like that better.

MATEY. Now, now, now—your manners, Caroliny.

COADE. Would he be singing or dancing ?

JOANNA. Oh no—at least, I hope not.

COADE (*an artist to the tips*). Hope not ? Odd ! If he is doing neither I am not likely to notice him, but if I do, what name shall I say ?

JOANNA (*gloating not*). Purdie ; I am Mrs. Purdie.

COADE. I will try to keep a look-out, and if I see him . . . but I am rather occupied at present. . . . (*The reference is to his legs and a new step they are acquiring. He sways this way and that, and, whistle to lips, minuets off in the direction of Paradise.*)

JOANNA (*looking elsewhere*). I am sorry I troubled you. I see him now.

LADY CAROLINE. Is he alone?

(JOANNA *glares at her.*)

Ah, I see from your face that he isn't.

MATEY (*who has his wench in training*). Caroliny, no awkward questions. Evening, missis, and I hope you will get him to go along with you quietly. (*Looking after* COADE) Watch the old codger dancing.

(*Light-hearted as children they dance after him, while* JOANNA *behind a tree awaits her lord.* PURDIE *in knicker-bockers approaches with misgivings to make sure that his* JOANNA *is not in hiding, and then he gambols joyously with a charming confection whose name is* MABEL. *They chase each other from tree to tree, but fortunately not round* JOANNA'S *tree.*)

MABEL (*as he catches her*). No, and no, and no. I don't know you nearly well enough for that. Besides, what would your wife say! I shall begin to think you are a very dreadful man, Mr. Purdie.

PURDIE (*whose sincerity is not to be questioned*). Surely you might call me Jack by this time.

MABEL (*heaving*). Perhaps, if you are very good, Jack.

PURDIE (*of noble thoughts compact*). If only Joanna were more like you.

MABEL. Like me? You mean her face? It is a—well, if it is not precisely pretty, it is a good face. (*Handsomely*) I don't mind her face at all. I am glad you have got such a dependable little wife, Jack.

PURDIE (*gloomily*). Thanks.

MABEL (*seated with a moonbeam in her lap*). What would Joanna have said if she had seen you just now?

PURDIE. A wife should be incapable of jealousy.

MABEL. Joanna jealous? But has she any reason? Jack, tell me, who is the woman?

PURDIE (*restraining himself by a mighty effort, for he wishes always to be true to* JOANNA). Shall I, Mabel, shall I?

MABEL (*faltering, yet not wholly giving up the chase*). I can't think who she is. Have I ever seen her?

PURDIE. Every time you look in a mirror.

MABEL (*with her head on one side*). How odd. Jack, that can't be; when I look in a mirror I see only myself.

2 K

PURDIE (*gloating*).   How adorably innocent you are, Mabel. Joanna would have guessed at once.

    (*Slowly his meaning comes to her, and she is appalled.*)

MABEL.   Not that !

PURDIE (*aflame*).   Shall I tell you now ?

MABEL (*palpitating exquisitely*).   I don't know, I am not sure.   Jack, try not to say it, but if you feel you must, say it in such a way that it would not hurt the feelings of Joanna if she happened to be passing by, as she nearly always is.

    (*A little moan from* JOANNA'S *tree is unnoticed.*)

PURDIE.   I would rather not say it at all than that way. (*He is touchingly anxious that she should know him as he really is.*) I don't know, Mabel, whether you have noticed that I am not like other men.   (*He goes deeply into the very structure of his being.*)   All my life I have been a soul that has had to walk alone.   Even as a child I had no hope that it would be otherwise.   I distinctly remember when I was six thinking how unlike other children I was.   Before I was twelve I suffered from terrible self-depreciation ; I do so still.   I suppose there never was a man who had a more lowly opinion of himself.

MABEL.   Jack, you who are so universally admired !

PURDIE.   That doesn't help ; I remain my own judge.   I am afraid I am a dark spirit, Mabel.   Yes, yes, my dear, let me leave nothing untold however it may damage me in your eyes.   Your eyes !   I cannot remember a time when I did not think of Love as a great consuming passion ; I visualised it, Mabel, as perhaps few have done, but always as the abounding joy that could come to others but never to me.   I expected too much of women : I suppose I was touched to finer issues than most.   That has been my tragedy.

MABEL.   Then you met Joanna.

PURDIE.   Then I met Joanna.   Yes !   Foolishly, as I now see, I thought she would understand that I was far too deep a nature really to mean the little things I sometimes said to her. I suppose a man was never placed in such a position before. What was I to do ?   Remember, I was always certain that the ideal love could never come to me.   Whatever the circumstances, I was convinced that my soul must walk alone.

MABEL.   Joanna, how could you.

PURDIE (*firmly*). Not a word against her, Mabel ; if blame there is, the blame is mine.

MABEL. And so you married her.

PURDIE. And so I married her.

MABEL. Out of pity.

PURDIE. I felt it was a man's part. I was such a child in worldly matters that it was pleasant to me to have the right to pay a woman's bills ; I enjoyed seeing her garments lying about on my chairs. In time that exultation wore off. But I was not unhappy, I didn't expect much, I was always so sure that no woman could ever plumb the well of my emotions.

MABEL. Then you met me.

PURDIE. Then I met you.

MABEL. Too late—never—forever—forever—never. They are the saddest words in the English tongue.

PURDIE. At the time I thought a still sadder word was Joanna.

MABEL. What was it you saw in me that made you love me ?

PURDIE (*plumbing the well of his emotions*). I think it was the feeling that you are so like myself.

MABEL (*with great eyes*). Have you noticed that, Jack ? Sometimes it has almost terrified me.

PURDIE. We think the same thoughts ; we are not two, Mabel ; we are one. Your hair——

MABEL. Joanna knows you admire it, and for a week she did hers in the same way.

PURDIE. I never noticed.

MABEL. That was why she gave it up. And it didn't really suit her. (*Ruminating*) I can't think of a good way of doing dear Joanna's hair. What is that you are muttering to yourself, Jack ? Don't keep anything from me.

PURDIE. I was repeating a poem I have written : it is in two words, ' Mabel Purdie.' May I teach it to you, sweet ? Say ' Mabel Purdie ' to me.

MABEL (*timidly covering his mouth with her little hand*). If I were to say it, Jack, I should be false to Joanna : never ask me to be that. Let us go on.

PURDIE (*merciless in his passion*). Say it, Mabel, say it. See, I write it on the ground with your sunshade.

MABEL. If it could be ! Jack, I 'll whisper it to you.

(*She is whispering it as they wander, not two but one, farther into the forest, ardently believing in themselves ; they are not hypocrites. The somewhat bedraggled figure of* JOANNA *follows them, and the nightingale resumes his love-song.* ' *That 's all you know, you bird !* ' *thinks* JOANNA *cynically. The nightingale, however, is not singing for them nor for her, but for another pair he has espied below. They are racing, the prize to be for the one who first finds the spot where the easel was put up last night. The hobbledehoy is sure to be the winner, for she is less laden, and the father loses time by singing as he comes. Also she is all legs and she started ahead. Brambles adhere to her, one boot has been in the water, and she has as many freckles as there are stars in heaven. She is as lovely as you think she is, and she is aged the moment when you like your daughter best. A hoot of triumph from her brings her father to the spot.*)

MARGARET. Daddy, Daddy. I have won. Here is the place. Crack-in-my-eye Tommy !

(*He comes. Crack-in-my-eye Tommy, this engaging fellow in tweeds, is* MR. DEARTH, *ablaze in happiness and health and a daughter. He finishes his song, picked up in the Latin Quarter.*)

DEARTH. Yes, that is the tree I stuck my easel under last night, and behold the blessed moon behaving more gorgeously than ever. I am sorry to have kept you waiting, old moon ; but you ought to know by now how time passes. Now, keep still, while I hand you down to posterity.

(*The easel is erected,* MARGARET *helping by getting in the way.*)

MARGARET (*critical, as an artist's daughter should be*). The moon is rather pale to-night, isn't she ?

DEARTH. Comes of keeping late hours.

MARGARET (*showing off*). Daddy, watch me, look at me. Please, sweet moon, a pleasant expression. No, no, not as if you were sitting for it ; that is too professional. That is better ; thank you. Now keep it. That is the sort of thing you say to them, Dad.

DEARTH (*quickly at work*). I oughtn't to have brought

you out so late ; you should be tucked up in your cosy bed at home.

MARGARET (*pursuing a squirrel that isn't there*). With the pillow lying anyhow.

DEARTH. Except in its proper place.

MARGARET (*wetting the other foot*). And the sheet over my face.

DEARTH. Where it oughtn't to be.

MARGARET (*more or less upside down*). And Daddy tiptoeing in to take it off.

DEARTH. Which is more than you deserve.

MARGARET (*in a tree*). Then why does he stand so long at the door ? And before he has gone she bursts out laughing, for she has been awake all the time.

DEARTH. That 's about it. What a life ! But I oughtn't to have brought you here. Best to have the sheet over you when the moon is about ; moonlight is bad for little daughters.

MARGARET (*pelting him with nuts*). I can't sleep when the moon 's at the full ; she keeps calling to me to get up. Perhaps I am *her* daughter too.

DEARTH. Gad, you look it to-night.

MARGARET. Do I ? Then can't you paint me into the picture as well as Mamma ? You could call it ' A Mother and Daughter ' or simply ' Two Ladies,' if the moon thinks that calling me her daughter would make her seem too old.

DEARTH. O matre pulchra filia pulchrior. That means, ' O Moon—more beautiful than any twopenny-halfpenny daughter.'

MARGARET (*emerging in an unexpected place*). Daddy, do you really prefer her ?

DEARTH. 'Sh ! She 's not a patch on you ; it 's the sort of thing we say to our sitters to keep them in good humour. (*He surveys ruefully a great stain on her frock.*) I wish to heaven, Margaret, we were not both so fond of apple-tart. And what 's this ! (*Catching hold of her skirt.*)

MARGARET (*unnecessarily*). It 's a tear.

DEARTH. I should think it is a tear.

MARGARET. That boy at the farm did it. He kept calling Snubs after me, but I got him down and kicked him in the stomach. He is rather a jolly boy.

DEARTH.   He sounds it.   Ye Gods, what a night !

MARGARET (*considering the picture*).   And what a moon ! Dad, she is not quite so fine as that.

DEARTH.   'Sh !   I have touched her up.

MARGARET.   Dad, Dad—what a funny man !

(*She has seen* MR. COADE *with whistle, enlivening the wood. He pirouettes round them and departs to add to the happiness of others.* MARGARET *gives an excellent imitation of him at which her father shakes his head, then reprehensibly joins in the dance.   Her mood changes, she clings to him.*)

MARGARET.   Hold me tight, Daddy, I 'm frightened.   I think they want to take you away from me.

DEARTH.   Who, gosling ?

MARGARET.   I don't know.   It 's too lovely, Daddy ; I won't be able to keep hold of it.

DEARTH.   What is ?

MARGARET.   The world—everything—and you, Daddy, most of all.   Things that are too beautiful can't last.

DEARTH (*who knows it*).   Now, how did you find that out ?

MARGARET (*still in his arms*).   I don't know ; Daddy, am I sometimes stranger than other people's daughters ?

DEARTH.   More of a madcap, perhaps.

MARGARET (*solemnly*).   Do you think I am sometimes too full of gladness ?

DEARTH.   My sweetheart, you do sometimes run over with it.   (*He is at his easel again.*)

MARGARET (*persisting*).   To be very gay, dearest dear, is so near to being very sad.

DEARTH (*who knows it*).   How did you find that out, child ?

MARGARET.   I don't know.   From something in me that 's afraid.   (*Unexpectedly*) Daddy, what is a ' might-have-been ' ?

DEARTH.   A might-have-been ?   They are ghosts, Margaret. I dare say I ' might have been ' a great swell of a painter, instead of just this uncommonly happy nobody.   Or again, I ' might have been ' a worthless idle waster of a fellow.

MARGARET (*laughing*).   You !

DEARTH.   Who knows ?   Some little kink in me might have set me off on the wrong road.   And that poor soul I might so easily have been might have had no Margaret.   My word, I 'm sorry for him.

MARGARET. So am I. (*She conceives a funny picture.*) The poor old Daddy, wandering about the world without me !

DEARTH. And there are other ' might-have-beens '—lovely ones, but intangible. Shades, Margaret, made of sad folk's thoughts.

MARGARET (*jigging about*). I am so glad I am not a shade. How awful it would be, Daddy, to wake up and find one wasn't alive.

DEARTH. It would, dear.

MARGARET. Daddy, wouldn't it be awful ! I think men need daughters.

DEARTH. They do.

MARGARET. Especially artists.

DEARTH. Yes, especially artists.

MARGARET. Especially artists.

DEARTH. Especially artists.

MARGARET (*covering herself with leaves and kicking them off*). Fame is not everything.

DEARTH. Fame is rot ; daughters are the thing.

MARGARET. Daughters are the thing.

DEARTH. Daughters are the thing.

MARGARET. I wonder if sons would be even nicer ?

DEARTH. Not a patch on daughters. The awful thing about a son is that never, never—at least, from the day he goes to school—can you tell him that you rather like him. By the time he is ten you can't even take him on your knee. Sons are not worth having, Margaret. Signed, W. Dearth.

MARGARET. But if you were a mother, Dad, I dare say he would let you do it.

DEARTH. Think so ?

MARGARET. I mean when no one was looking. Sons are not so bad. Signed, M. Dearth. But I 'm glad you prefer daughters. (*She works her way toward him on her knees, making the tear larger.*) At what age are we nicest, Daddy ? (*She has constantly to repeat her questions, he is so engaged with his moon.*) Hie, Daddy, at what age are we nicest ? Daddy, hie, hie, at what age are we nicest ?

DEARTH. Eh ? That 's a poser. I think you were nicest when you were two and knew your alphabet up to G but fell over at H. No, you were best when you were half-past three ;

or just before you struck six ; or in the mumps year, when I asked you in the early morning how you were and you said solemnly ' I haven't tried yet.'

MARGARET (*awestruck*). Did I ?

DEARTH. Such was your answer. (*Struggling with the momentous question*) But I am not sure that chicken-pox doesn't beat mumps. Oh Lord, I 'm all wrong. The nicest time in a father's life is the year before she puts up her hair.

MARGARET (*top-heavy with pride in herself*). I suppose that is a splendid time. But there 's a nicer year coming to you. Daddy, there is a nicer year coming to you.

DEARTH. Is there, darling ?

MARGARET. Daddy, the year she does put up her hair !

DEARTH (*with arrested brush*). Puts it up for ever ? You know, I am afraid that when the day for that comes I shan't be able to stand it. It will be too exciting. My poor heart, Margaret.

MARGARET (*rushing at him*). No, no, it will be lucky you, for it isn't to be a bit like that. I am to be a girl and woman day about for the first year. You will never know which I am till you look at my hair. And even then you won't know, for if it is down I shall put it up, and if it is up I shall put it down. And so my Daddy will gradually get used to the idea.

DEARTH (*wryly*). I see you have been thinking it out.

MARGARET (*gleaming*). I have been doing more than that. Shut your eyes, Dad, and I shall give you a glimpse into the future.

DEARTH. I don't know that I want that · the present is so good.

MARGARET. Shut your eyes, please.

DEARTH. No, Margaret.

MARGARET. Please, Daddy.

DEARTH. Oh, all right. They are shut.

MARGARET. Don't open them till I tell you. What finger is that ?

DEARTH. The dirty one.

MARGARET (*on her knees among the leaves*). Daddy, now I am putting up my hair. I have got such a darling of a mirror. It is such a darling mirror I 've got, Dad. Dad, don't look.

I shall tell you about it. It is a little pool of water. I wish we could take it home and hang it up. Of course the moment my hair is up there will be other changes also ; for instance, I shall talk quite differently.

DEARTH. Pooh ! Where are my matches, dear ?

MARGARET. Top pocket, waistcoat.

DEARTH (*trying to light his pipe without opening his eyes*). You were meaning to frighten me just now.

MARGARET. No. I am just preparing you. You see, darling, I can't call you Dad when my hair is up. I think I shall call you Parent.

(*He growls.*)

Parent dear, do you remember the days when your Margaret was a slip of a girl, and sat on your knee ? How foolish we were, Parent, in those distant days.

DEARTH. Shut up, Margaret.

MARGARET. Now I must be more distant to you ; more like a boy who could not sit on your knee any more.

DEARTH. See here, I want to go on painting. Shall I look now ?

MARGARET. I am not quite sure whether I want you to. It makes such a difference. Perhaps you won't know me. Even the pool is looking a little scared. (*The change in her voice makes him open his eyes quickly. She confronts him shyly.*) What do you think ? Will I do ?

DEARTH. Stand still, dear, and let me look my fill. The Margaret that is to be !

MARGARET (*the change in his voice falling clammy on her*). You 'll see me often enough, Daddy, like this, so you don't need to look your fill. You are looking as long as if this were to be the only time.

DEARTH (*with an odd tremor*). Was I ? Surely it isn't to be that.

MARGARET. Be gay, Dad. (*Bumping into him and round him and over him.*) You will be sick of Margaret with her hair up before you are done with her.

DEARTH. I expect so.

MARGARET. Shut up, Daddy. (*She waggles her head, and down comes her hair.*) Daddy, I know what you are thinking of. You are thinking what a handful she is going to be.

DEARTH. Well, I guess she is.

MARGARET (*surveying him from another angle*). Now you are thinking about—about my being in love some day.

DEARTH (*with unnecessary warmth*). Rot !

MARGARET (*reassuringly*). I won't, you know ; no, never. Oh, I have quite decided, so don't be afraid. (*Disordering his hair.*) Will you hate him at first, Daddy ? Daddy, will you hate him ? Will you hate him, Daddy ?

DEARTH (*at work*). Whom ?

MARGARET. Well, if there was ?

DEARTH. If there was what, darling ?

MARGARET. You know the kind of thing I mean, quite well. Would you hate him at first ?

DEARTH. I hope not. I should want to strangle him, but I wouldn't hate him.

MARGARET. *I* would. That is to say, if I liked him.

DEARTH. If you liked him how could you hate him ?

MARGARET. For daring !

DEARTH. Daring what ?

MARGARET. You know. (*Sighing*) But of course I shall have no say in the matter. You will do it all. You do everything for me.

DEARTH (*with a groan*). I can't help it.

MARGARET. You will even write my love-letters, if I ever have any to write, which I won't.

DEARTH (*ashamed*). Surely to goodness, Margaret, I will leave you alone to do that !

MARGARET. Not you ; you will try to, but you won't be able.

DEARTH (*in a hopeless attempt at self-defence*). I want you, you see, to do everything exquisitely. I do wish I could leave you to do things a little more for yourself. I suppose it 's owing to my having had to be father and mother both. I knew nothing practically about the bringing up of children, and of course I couldn't trust you to a nurse.

MARGARET (*severely*). Not you ; so sure you could do it better yourself. That 's you all over. Daddy, do you remember how you taught me to balance a biscuit on my nose, like a puppy ?

DEARTH (*sadly*). Did I ?

MARGARET. You called me Rover.

DEARTH. I deny that.

MARGARET. And when you said ' snap ' I caught the biscuit in my mouth.

DEARTH. Horrible.

MARGARET (*gleaming*). Daddy, I can do it still ! (*Putting a biscuit on her nose*) Here is the last of my supper. Say ' snap,' Daddy.

DEARTH. Not I.

MARGARET. Say ' snap,' please.

DEARTH. I refuse.

MARGARET. Daddy !

DEARTH. Snap !

(*She catches the biscuit in her mouth.*)

Let that be the last time, Margaret.

MARGARET. Except just once more. I don't mean now, but when my hair is really up. If I should ever have a—a Margaret of my own, come in and see me, Daddy, in my white bed, and say ' snap '—and I 'll have the biscuit ready.

DEARTH (*turning away his head*). Right-o !

MARGARET. Dad, if I ever should marry—not that I will, but if I should—at the marriage ceremony will you let me be the one who says ' I do ' ?

DEARTH. I suppose I deserve this.

MARGARET (*coaxingly*). You think I 'm pretty, don't you, Dad, whatever other people say ?

DEARTH. Not so bad.

MARGARET. I *know* I have nice ears.

DEARTH. They are all right now, but I had to work on them for months.

MARGARET. You don't mean to say that you did my *ears* ?

DEARTH. Rather !

MARGARET (*grown humble*). My dimple is my own.

DEARTH. I am glad you think so. I wore out the point of my little finger over that dimple.

MARGARET. Even my dimple ! Have I anything that is really mine ? A bit of my nose or anything ?

DEARTH. When you were a babe you had a laugh that was all your own.

MARGARET. Haven't I got it now ?

DEARTH.   It's gone.   (*He looks ruefully at her.*)   I'll tell you how it went.   We were fishing in a stream—that is to say, I was wading and you were sitting on my shoulders holding the rod.   We didn't catch anything.   Somehow or another—I can't think how I did it—you irritated me, and I answered you sharply.

MARGARET (*gasping*).   I can't believe that.

DEARTH.   Yes, it sounds extraordinary, but I did.   It gave you a shock, and, for the moment, the world no longer seemed a safe place to you ; your faith in me had always made it safe till then.   You were suddenly not even sure of your bread and butter, and a frightened tear came to your eyes.   I was in a nice state about it, I can tell you.   (*He is in a nice state about it still.*)

MARGARET.   Silly !   (*Bewildered*) But what has that to do with my laugh, Daddy ?

DEARTH.   The laugh that children are born with lasts just so long as they have perfect faith.   To think that it was I who robbed you of yours !

MARGARET.   Don't, dear.   I am sure the laugh just went off with the tear to comfort it, and they have been playing about that stream ever since.   They have quite forgotten us, so why should we remember them.   Cheeky little beasts !   Shall I tell you my farthest-back recollection ?   (*In some awe*) I remember the first time I saw the stars.   I had never seen night, and then I saw it and the stars together.   Crack-in-my-eye Tommy, it isn't every one who can boast of such a lovely, lovely recollection for their earliest, is it ?

DEARTH.   I was determined your earliest should be a good one.

MARGARET (*blankly*).   Do you mean to say you planned it ?

DEARTH.   Rather !   Most people's earliest recollection is of some trivial thing ; how they cut their finger, or lost a piece of string.   I was resolved my Margaret's should be something bigger.   I was poor, but I could give her the stars.

MARGARET (*clutching him round the legs*).   Oh, how you love me, Daddikins !

DEARTH.   Yes, I do, rather.

(*A vagrant woman has wandered in their direction, one whom the shrill winds of life have lashed and bled ; here and there ragged graces still cling to her, and unruly passion smoulders, but she, once a dear fierce rebel with eyes of storm, is now first of all a whimperer. She and they meet as strangers.)*

MARGARET (*nicely, as becomes an artist's daughter*). Good evening!

ALICE. Good evening, Missy; evening, Mister.

DEARTH (*seeing that her eyes search the ground*). Lost anything?

ALICE. Sometimes when the tourists have had their sandwiches there are bits left over, and they squeeze them between the roots to keep the place tidy. I am looking for bits.

DEARTH. You don't tell me you are as hungry as that?

ALICE (*with spirit*). Try me. (*Strange that he should not know that once-loved husky voice.*)

MARGARET (*rushing at her father and feeling all his pockets*). Daddy, that was my last biscuit!

DEARTH. We must think of something else.

MARGARET (*taking her hand*). Yes, wait a bit, we are sure to think of something. Daddy, think of something.

ALICE (*sharply*). Your father doesn't like you to touch the likes of me.

MARGARET. Oh yes, he does. (*Defiantly*) And if he didn't, I'd do it all the same. This is a bit of *myself*, Daddy.

DEARTH. That is all you know.

ALICE (*whining*). You needn't be angry with her, Mister; I'm all right.

DEARTH. I am not angry with her; I am very sorry for you.

ALICE (*flaring*). If I had my rights, I would be as good as you—and better.

DEARTH. I dare say.

ALICE. I have had men-servants and a motor car.

DEARTH. Margaret and I never rose to that.

MARGARET (*stung*). I have been in a taxi several times, and Dad often gets telegrams.

DEARTH. Margaret!

MARGARET. I'm sorry I boasted.

ALICE. That's nothing. I have a town house—at least I had . . . At any rate he said there was a town house.

MARGARET (*interested*).   Fancy his not knowing for certain.

ALICE.   The Honourable Mrs. Finch-Fallowe—that 's who I am.

MARGARET (*cordially*).   It 's a lovely name.

ALICE.   Curse him.

MARGARET.   Don't you like him ?

DEARTH.   We won't go into that.   I have nothing to do with your past, but I wish we had some food to offer you.

ALICE.   You haven't a flask ?

DEARTH.   No, I don't take anything myself.   But let me see. . . .

MARGARET (*sparkling*).   I know !   You said we had five pounds.   (*To the needy one*) Would you like five pounds ?

DEARTH.   Darling, don't be stupid ;   we haven't paid our bill at the inn.

ALICE (*with bravado*).   All right ;   I never asked you for anything.

DEARTH.   Don't take me up in that way :   I have had my ups and downs myself.   Here is ten bob and welcome.

(*He surreptitiously slips a coin into* MARGARET'S *hand.*)

MARGARET.   And I have half a crown.   It is quite easy for us.   Dad will be getting another fiver any day.   You can't think how exciting it is when the fiver comes in ;   we dance and then we run out and buy chops.

DEARTH.   Margaret !

ALICE.   It 's kind of you.   I 'm richer this minute than I have been for many a day.

DEARTH.   It 's nothing ;   I am sure you would do the same for us.

ALICE.   I wish I was as sure.

DEARTH.   Of course you would.   Glad to be of any help. Get some victuals as quickly as you can.   Best of wishes, ma'am, and may your luck change.

ALICE.   Same to you, and may yours go on.

MARGARET.   Good-night.

ALICE.   What is her name, Mister ?

DEARTH (*who has returned to his easel*).   Margaret.

ALICE.   Margaret.   You drew something good out of the lucky-bag when you got her, Mister.

DEARTH.   Yes.

ALICE. Take care of her ; they are easily lost.

(*She shuffles away.*)

DEARTH. Poor soul! I expect she has had a rough time, and that some man is to blame for it—partly, at any rate. (*Restless.*) That woman rather affects me, Margaret ; I don't know why. Didn't you like her husky voice? (*He goes on painting.*) I say, Margaret, we lucky ones, let 's swear always to be kind to people who are down on their luck, and then when we are kind let 's be a little kinder.

MARGARET (*gleefully*). Yes, let 's.

DEARTH. Margaret, always feel sorry for the failures, the ones who are always failures—especially in my sort of calling. Wouldn't it be lovely to turn them on the thirty-ninth year of failure into glittering successes ?

MARGARET. Topping.

DEARTH. Topping.

MARGARET. Oh, topping. How could we do it, Dad ?

DEARTH. By letter. 'To poor old Tom Broken Heart, Top Attic, Garret Chambers, S.E. DEAR SIR,—His Majesty has been graciously pleased to purchase your superb picture of Marlow Ferry.'

MARGARET. '*P.S.*—I am sending the money in a bag so as you can hear it chink.'

DEARTH. What could we do for our friend who passed just now ? I can't get her out of my head.

MARGARET. You have made me forget her. (*Plaintively*) Dad, I didn't like it.

DEARTH. Didn't like what, dear ?

MARGARET (*shuddering*). I didn't like her saying that about your losing me.

DEARTH (*the one thing of which he is sure*). I shan't lose you.

MARGARET (*hugging his arm*). It would be hard for me if you lost me, but it would be worse for you. I don't know how I know that, but I do know it. What would you do without me ?

DEARTH (*almost sharply*). Don't talk like that, dear. It is wicked and stupid, and naughty. Somehow that poor woman —I won't paint any more to-night.

MARGARET. Let 's get out of the wood ; it frightens me.

DEARTH. And you loved it a moment ago. Hallo ! (*He*

has seen a distant blurred light in the wood, apparently from a window.)   I hadn't noticed there was a house there.

MARGARET (*tingling*).   Daddy, I feel sure there wasn't a house there !

DEARTH.   Goose.   It is just that we didn't look.   Our old way of letting the world go hang ; so interested in ourselves. Nice behaviour for people who have been boasting about what they would do for other people.   Now I see what I ought to do.

MARGARET.   Let 's get out of the wood.

DEARTH.   Yes, but my idea first.   It is to rouse these people and get food from them for the husky one.

MARGARET (*clinging to him*).   She is too far away now.

DEARTH.   I can overtake her.

MARGARET (*in a frenzy*).   Don't go into that house, Daddy ! I don't know why it is, but I am afraid of that house !

(*He waggles a reproving finger at her.*)

DEARTH.   There is a kiss for each moment until I come back.

(*She wipes them from her face.*)

Oh, naughty, go and stand in the corner.

(*She stands against a tree but she stamps her foot.*)

Who has got a nasty temper !

(*She tries hard not to smile, but she smiles and he smiles, and they make comic faces at each other, as they have done in similar circumstances since she first opened her eyes.*)

I shall be back before you can count a hundred.

(*He goes off humming his song so that she may still hear him when he is lost to sight ; all just as so often before.   She tries dutifully to count her hundred, but the wood grows dark and soon she is afraid again.   She runs from tree to tree calling to her Daddy.   We begin to lose her among the shadows.*)

MARGARET (*out of the impalpable that is carrying her away*). Daddy, come back ; I don't want to be a might-have-been.

ACT III

LOB's room has gone very dark as it sits up awaiting the possible return of the adventurers. The curtains are closed, so that no light comes from outside. There is a tapping on the window, and anon two intruders are stealing about the floor, with muffled cries when they meet unexpectedly. They find the switch and are revealed as Purdie and his Mabel. Something has happened to them as they emerged from the wood, but it is so superficial that neither notices it : they are again in the evening dress in which they had left the house. But they are still being led by that strange humour of the blood.

MABEL (*looking around her curiously*).   A pretty little room ; I wonder who is the owner ?

PURDIE.   It doesn't matter ; the great thing is that we have escaped Joanna.

MABEL.   Jack, look, a man !

(*The term may not be happily chosen, but the person indicated is* LOB *curled up on his chair by a dead fire. The last look on his face before he fell asleep having been a leery one it is still there.*)

PURDIE.   He is asleep.

MABEL.   Do you know him ?

PURDIE.   Not I. Excuse me, sir. Hi ! (*No shaking, however, wakens the sleeper.*)

MABEL.   Darling, how extraordinary !

PURDIE (*always considerate*).   After all, precious, have we any right to wake up a stranger, just to tell him that we are runaways hiding in his house ?

MABEL (*who comes of a good family*).   I think he would expect it of us.

PURDIE (*after trying again*).   There is no budging him.

MABEL (*appeased*).   At any rate, we have done the civil thing.

(*She has now time to regard the room more attentively,*

1041

including the tray of coffee cups which MATEY *had left on
the table in a not unimportant moment of his history.*)
There have evidently been people here, but they haven't
drunk their coffee.   Ugh ! cold as a deserted egg in a bird's
nest.   Jack, if you were a clever detective you could construct
those people out of their neglected coffee cups.   I wonder who
they are and what has spirited them away ?

PURDIE.   Perhaps they have only gone to bed.   Ought we
to knock them up ?

MABEL (*after considering what her mother would have done*).
I think not, dear.   I suppose we have run away, Jack—
meaning to ?

PURDIE (*with the sturdiness that weaker vessels adore*).
Irrevocably.   Mabel, if the dog-like devotion of a lifetime . . .
(*He becomes conscious that something has happened to* LOB'S *leer.
It has not left his face but it has shifted.*)   He is not shamming,
do you think ?

MABEL.   Shake him again.

PURDIE (*after shaking him*).   It 's all right.   Mabel, if the
dog-like devotion of a lifetime. . . .

MABEL.   Poor little Joanna !   Still, if a woman insists on
being a pendulum round a man's neck. . . .

PURDIE.   Do give me a chance, Mabel.   If the dog-like
devotion of a lifetime . . .

(JOANNA *comes through the curtains so inopportunely that
for the moment he is almost pettish.*)
May I say, this is just a little too much, Joanna !

JOANNA (*unconscious as they of her return to her dinner-gown*).
So, sweet husband, your soul is still walking alone, is it ?

MABEL (*who hates coarseness of any kind*).   How can you
sneak about in this way, Joanna ?   Have you no pride ?

JOANNA (*dashing away a tear*).   Please to address me as
Mrs. Purdie, madam.   (*She sees* LOB.)   Who is this man ?

PURDIE.   We don't know ; and there is no waking him.
You can try, if you like.

(*Failing to rouse him* JOANNA *makes a third at table.   They
are all a little inconsequential, as if there were still some
moonshine in their hair.*)

JOANNA.   You were saying something about the devotion
of a lifetime ; please go on.

PURDIE (*diffidently*). I don't like to before you, Joanna.

JOANNA (*becoming coarse again*). Oh, don't mind me.

PURDIE (*looking like a note of interrogation*). I should certainly like to say it.

MABEL (*loftily*). And I shall be proud to hear it.

PURDIE (*kindly*). I should have liked to spare you this, Joanna ; you wouldn't put your hands over your ears ?

JOANNA (*alas*). No, sir.

MABEL. Fie, Joanna. Surely a wife's natural delicacy . . .

PURDIE (*severely*). As you take it in that spirit, Joanna, I can proceed with a clear conscience. If the dog-like devotion of a lifetime—— (*He reels a little, staring at* LOB, *over whose face the leer has been wandering like an insect.*)

MABEL. Did he move ?

PURDIE. It isn't that. I am feeling—very funny. Did one of you tap me just now on the forehead ?

(*Their hands also have gone to their foreheads.*)

MABEL. I think I have been in this room before.

PURDIE (*flinching*). There is something coming rushing back to me.

MABEL. I seem to know that coffee set. If I do, the lid of the milk jug is chipped. It is !

JOANNA. I can't remember this man's name ; but I am sure it begins with L.

MABEL. Lob.

PURDIE. Lob.

JOANNA. Lob.

PURDIE. Mabel, your dress ?

MABLE (*beholding it*). How on earth . . . ?

JOANNA. My dress ! (*To* PURDIE) You were in knicker-bockers in the wood.

PURDIE. And so I am now. (*He sees he is not.*) Where did I change ? The wood ! Let me think. The wood . . . the wood, certainly. But the wood wasn't the wood.

JOANNA (*revolving like one in pursuit*). My head is going round.

MABEL. Lob's wood ! I remember it all. We were here. We did go.

PURDIE. So we did. But how could . . . ? where was . . . ?

JOANNA. And who was . . . ?

MABEL.   And what was . . . ?

PURDIE (*even in this supreme hour a man*).   Don't let go. Hold on to what we were doing, or we shall lose grip of ourselves.   Devotion.   Something about devotion.   Hold on to devotion.   'If the dog-like devotion of a lifetime . . .'   Which of you was I saying that to ?

MABEL.   To me.

PURDIE.   Are you sure ?

MABEL (*shakily*).   I am not quite sure.

PURDIE (*anxiously*).   Joanna, what do you think ?   (*With a sudden increase of uneasiness*) Which of you is my wife ?

JOANNA (*without enthusiasm*).   I am.   No, I am not.   It is Mabel who is your wife !

MABEL.   Me ?

PURDIE (*with a curious gulp*).   Why, of course you are, Mabel !

MABEL.   I believe I am !

PURDIE.   And yet how can it be ?   I was running away with you.

JOANNA (*solving that problem*).   You don't need to do it now.

PURDIE.   The wood.   Hold on to the wood.   The wood is what explains it.   Yes, I see the whole thing.   (*He gazes at* LOB.)   You infernal old rascal !   Let us try to think it out. Don't any one speak for a moment.   Think first.   Love . . . Hold on to love.   (*He gets another tap.*)   I say, I believe I am not a deeply passionate chap at all ; I believe I am just . . . a philanderer !

MABEL.   It is what you are.

JOANNA (*more magnanimous*).   Mabel, what about ourselves?

PURDIE (*to whom it is truly a nauseous draught*).   I didn't know.   Just a philanderer !   (*The soul of him would like at this instant to creep into another body.*)   And if people don't change, I suppose we shall begin all over again now.

JOANNA (*the practical*).   I dare say ; but not with each other. I may philander again, but not with you.

> (*They look on themselves without approval, always a sorry occupation.   The man feels it most because he has admired himself most, or perhaps partly for some better reason.*)

PURDIE (*saying good-bye to an old friend*).   John Purdie, John Purdie, the fine fellow I used to think you !   (*When he is able to look them in the face again*) The wood has taught me one thing, at any rate.

MABEL (*dismally*).　What, Jack ?

PURDIE.　That it isn't accident that shapes our lives.

JOANNA.　No, it 's Fate.

PURDIE (*the truth running through him, seeking for a permanent home in him, willing to give him still another chance, loth to desert him*).　It 's not Fate, Joanna.　Fate is something outside us. What really plays the dickens with us is something in ourselves. Something that makes us go on doing the same sort of fool things, however many chances we get.

MABEL.　Something in ourselves ?

PURDIE (*shivering*).　Something we are born with.

JOANNA.　Can't we cut out the beastly thing ?

PURDIE.　Depends, I expect, on how long we have pampered him.　We can at least control him if we try hard enough.　But I have for the moment an abominably clear perception that the likes of me never really tries.　Forgive me, Joanna——no, Mabel——both of you.　(*He is a shamed man.*)　It isn't very pleasant to discover that one is a rotter.　I suppose I shall get used to it.

JOANNA.　I could forgive anybody anything to-night. (*Candidly*) It is so lovely not to be married to you, Jack.

PURDIE (*spiritless*).　I can understand that.　I do feel small.

JOANNA (*the true friend*).　You will soon swell up again.

PURDIE (*for whom, alas, we need not weep*).　That is the appalling thing.　But at present, at any rate, I am a rag at your feet, Joanna——no, at yours, Mabel.　Are you going to pick me up ?　I don't advise it.

MABEL.　I don't know whether I want to, Jack.　To begin with, which of us is it your lonely soul is in search of ?

JOANNA.　Which of us is the fluid one, or the fluider one ?

MABEL.　Are you and I one ?　Or are you and Joanna one ? Or are the three of us two ?

JOANNA.　He wants you to whisper in his ear, Mabel, the entrancing poem, ' Mabel Purdie.'　Do it, Jack ; there will be nothing wrong in it now.

PURDIE.　Rub it in.

MABEL.　When I meet Joanna's successor——

PURDIE (*quailing*).　No, no, Mabel, none of that.　At least

credit me with having my eyes open at last.   There will be no more of this.   I swear it by all that is——

JOANNA (*in her excellent imitation of a sheep*).   Baa-a, he is off again.

PURDIE.   Oh Lord, so I am.

MABEL.   Don't, Joanna.

PURDIE (*his mind still illumined*).   She is quite right—I was. In my present state of depression—which won't last—I feel there is something in me that will make me go on being the same ass, however many chances I get.   I haven't the stuff in me to take warning.   My whole being is corroded.   Shakespeare knew what he was talking about—

> 'The fault, dear Brutus, is not in our stars,
>   But in ourselves, that we are underlings.'

JOANNA.   For ' dear Brutus ' we are to read ' dear audience,' I suppose ?

PURDIE.   You have it.

JOANNA.   Meaning that we have the power to shape ourselves ?

PURDIE.   We have the power right enough.

JOANNA.   But isn't that rather splendid ?

PURDIE.   For those who have the grit in them, yes.   (*Still seeing with a strange clearness through the chink the hammer has made.*)   And they are not the dismal chappies ; they are the ones with the thin bright faces.   (*He sits lugubriously by his wife and is sorry for the first time that she has not married a better man.*) I am afraid there is not much fight in me, Mabel, but we shall see.   If you catch me at it again, have the goodness to whisper to me in passing, ' Lob's Wood.'   That may cure me for the time being.

MABEL (*still certain that she loved him once but not so sure why*).   Perhaps I will . . . as long as I care to bother, Jack. It depends on you how long that is to be.

JOANNA (*to break an awkward pause*).   I feel that there is hope in that as well as a warning.   Perhaps the wood may prove to have been useful after all.   (*This brighter view of the situation meets with no immediate response. With her next suggestion she reaches harbour.*)   You know, we are not people worth being sorrowful about—so let us laugh.

(*The ladies succeed in laughing though not prettily, but the man has been too much shaken.*)

JOANNA (*in the middle of her laugh*). We have forgotten the others ! I wonder what is happening to them ?

PURDIE (*reviving*). Yes, what about them ? Have *they* changed ?

MABEL. I didn't see any of them in the wood.

JOANNA. Perhaps we did see them without knowing them ; we didn't know Lob.

PURDIE (*daunted*). That 's true.

JOANNA. Won't it be delicious to be here to watch them when they come back, and see them waking up—or whatever it was we did.

PURDIE. What was it we did ? I think something tapped me on the forehead.

MABEL (*blanching*). How do we know the others *will* come back ?

JOANNA (*infected*). We don't know. How awful !

MABEL. Listen !

PURDIE. I distinctly hear some one on the stairs.

MABEL. It will be Matey.

PURDIE (*the chink beginning to close*). Be cautious, both of you ; don't tell him we have had any . . . odd experiences.

(*It is, however,* MRS. COADE *who comes downstairs in a dressing-gown and carrying a candle and her husband's muffler.*)

MRS. COADE. So you are back at last. A nice house, I must say. Where is Coady ?

PURDIE (*taken aback*). Coady ! Did he go into the wood, too ?

MRS. COADE (*placidly*). I suppose so. I have been down several times to look for him.

MABEL. Coady, too !

JOANNA (*seeing visions*). I wonder . . . Oh, how dreadful !

MRS. COADE. What is dreadful, Joanna ?

JOANNA (*airily*). Nothing. I was just wondering what he is doing.

MRS. COADE. Doing ? What should he be doing ? Did anything odd happen to you in the wood ?

PURDIE (*taking command*). No, no, nothing.

JOANNA. We just strolled about, and came back. (*That subject being exhausted she points to* LOB.) Have you noticed him?

MRS. COADE. Oh yes; he has been like that all the time. A sort of stupor, I think; and sometimes the strangest grin comes over his face.

PURDIE (*wincing*). Grin?

MRS. COADE. Just as if he were seeing amusing things in his sleep.

PURDIE (*guardedly*). I dare say he is. Oughtn't we to get Matey to him?

MRS. COADE. Matey has gone, too.

PURDIE. Wha-at!

MRS. COADE. At all events he is not in the house.

JOANNA (*unguardedly*). Matey! I wonder who is with him.

MRS. COADE. Must somebody be with him?

JOANNA. Oh no, not at all.

(*They are simultaneously aware that some one outside has reached the window.*)

MRS. COADE. I hope it is Coady.

(*The other ladies are too fond of her to share this wish.*)

MABEL. Oh, I hope not.

MRS. COADE. Why, Mrs. Purdie?

JOANNA (*coaxingly*). Dear Mrs. Coade, whoever he is, and whatever he does, I beg you not to be surprised. We feel that though we had no unusual experiences in the wood, others may not have been so fortunate.

MABEL. And be cautious, you dear, what you say to them before they come to.

MRS. COADE. 'Come to'? You puzzle me. And Coady didn't have his muffler.

(*Let it be recorded that in their distress for this old lady they forget their own misadventures.* PURDIE *takes a step toward the curtains in a vague desire to shield her ;—and gets a rich reward ; he has seen the coming addition to their circle.*)

PURDIE (*elated and pitiless*). It is Matey!

(*A butler intrudes who still thinks he is wrapped in fur.*)

JOANNA (*encouragingly*). Do come in.

MATEY. With apologies, ladies and gents. . . . May I ask who is host ?

PURDIE (*splashing in the temperature that suits him best*). A very reasonable request. Third on the left.

MATEY (*advancing upon* LOB). Merely to ask, sir, if you can direct me to my hotel ?

(*The sleeper's only response is a slight quiver in one leg.*) The gentleman seems to be reposing.

MRS. COADE. It is Lob.

MATEY. What is lob, ma'am ?

MRS. COADE (*pleasantly curious*). Surely you haven't forgotten ?

PURDIE (*over-riding her*). Anything we can do for you, sir ? Just give it a name.

JOANNA (*in the same friendly spirit*). I hope you are not alone : do say you have some lady friends with you.

MATEY (*with an emphasis on his leading word*). My wife is with me.

JOANNA. His wife ! . . . (*With commendation*) You *have* been quick !

MRS. COADE. I didn't know you were married.

MATEY. Why should you, madam ? You talk as if you knew me.

MRS. COADE. Good gracious, do you really think I don't ?

PURDIE (*indicating delicately that she is subject to a certain softening*). Sit down, won't you, my dear sir, and make yourself comfy.

MATEY (*accustomed of late to such deferential treatment*). Thank you. But my wife . . .

JOANNA (*hospitably*). Yes, bring her in ; we are simply dying to make her acquaintance.

MATEY. You are very good ; I am much obliged.

MABEL (*as he goes out*). Who can she be ?

JOANNA (*leaping*). Who, who, who !

MRS. COADE. But what an extraordinary wood. He doesn't seem to know who he is at all.

MABEL (*soothingly*). Don't worry about that, Coady darling. He will know soon enough.

JOANNA (*again finding the bright side*). And so will the little wife ! By the way, whoever she is, I hope she is fond of butlers.

MABEL *(who has peeped)*.   It is Lady Caroline !

JOANNA *(leaping again)*.   Oh, joy, joy !   And she was so sure she couldn't take the wrong turning !

(LADY CAROLINE *is evidently still sure of it*.)

MATEY.   May I present my wife—Lady Caroline Matey.

MABEL *(glowing)*.   How do you do.

PURDIE.   Your servant, Lady Caroline.

MRS. COADE.   Lady Caroline Matey !   You ?

LADY CAROLINE *(without an* r *in her)*.   Charmed, I 'm sure.

JOANNA *(neatly)*.   Very pleased to meet any wife of Mr. Matey.

PURDIE *(taking the floor)*.   Allow me.   The Duchess of Candelabra.   The Ladies Helena and Matilda M'Nab.   I am the Lord Chancellor.

MABEL.   I have wanted so long to make your acquaintance.

LADY CAROLINE.   Charmed.

JOANNA *(gracefully)*.   These informal meetings are so delightful, don't you ?

LADY CAROLINE.   Yes, indeed.

MATEY *(the introductions being thus pleasantly concluded)*.   And your friend by the fire ?

PURDIE.   I will introduce you to him when you wake up— I mean when he wakes up.

MATEY.   Perhaps I ought to have said that I am *James* Matey.

LADY CAROLINE *(the happy creature)*.   *The* James Matey.

MATEY.   A name not, perhaps, unknown in the world of finance.

JOANNA.   Finance ?   Oh, so you did take that clerkship in the City !

MATEY *(a little stiffly)*.   I began as a clerk in the City, certainly ; and I am not ashamed to admit it.

MRS. COADE *(still groping)*.   Fancy that, now.   And did it save you ?

MATEY.   Save me, madam ?

JOANNA.   Excuse us—we ask odd questions in this house ; we only mean, did that keep you honest ?   Or are you still a pilferer ?

LADY CAROLINE *(an outraged swan)*.   Husband mine, what does she mean ?

JOANNA. No offence ; I mean a pilferer on a large scale.

MATEY (*remembering certain newspaper jealousy*). If you are referring to that Labrador business—or the Working Women's Bank . . .

PURDIE (*after the manner of one who has caught a fly*). O-ho, got him !

JOANNA (*bowing*). Yes, those are what I meant.

MATEY (*stoutly*). There was nothing proved.

JOANNA (*like one calling a meeting*). Mabel, Jack, here is another of us ! You have gone just the same way again, my friend. (*Ecstatically*) There is more in it, you see, than taking the wrong turning ; you would always take the wrong turning. (*The only fitting comment.*) Tra-la-la !

LADY CAROLINE. If you are casting any aspersions on my husband, allow me to say that a prouder wife than I does not to-day exist.

MRS. COADE (*who finds herself the only clear-headed one*). My dear, do be careful.

MABEL. So long as you are satisfied, dear Lady Caroline. But I thought you shrank from all blood that was not blue.

LADY CAROLINE. You thought ? Why should you think about me ? I beg to assure you that I adore my Jim.

> (*She seeks his arm, but her* JIM *has encountered the tray containing coffee cups and a cake, and his hands close on it with a certain intimacy.*)

Whatever are you doing, Jim ?

MATEY. I don't understand it, Caroliny ; but somehow I feel at home with this in my hands.

MABEL. ' Caroliny ' !

MRS. COADE. Look at me well ; don't you remember me ?

MATEY (*musing*). I don't remember you ; but I seem to associate you with hard-boiled eggs. (*With conviction*) You like your eggs hard-boiled.

PURDIE. Hold on to hard-boiled eggs. She used to tip you especially to see to them.

> (MATEY'S *hand goes to his pocket.*)

Yes, that was the pocket.

LADY CAROLINE (*with distaste*). Tip !

MATEY (*without distaste*). Tip !

PURDIE. Jolly word, isn't it ?

MATEY (*raising the tray*).   It seems to set me thinking.

LADY CAROLINE (*feeling the tap of the hammer*).   Why is my work-basket in this house ?

MRS. COADE.   You are living here, you know.

LADY CAROLINE.   That is what a person feels.   But when did I come ?   It is very odd, but one feels one ought to say when did one go.

PURDIE.   She is coming to with a wush !

MATEY (*under the hammer*).   Mr. . . . Purdie !

LADY CAROLINE.   Mrs. Coade !

MATEY.   The Guv'nor !   My clothes !

LADY CAROLINE.   One is in evening dress !

JOANNA (*charmed to explain*).   You will understand clearly in a minute, Caroliny.   You didn't really take that clerkship, Jim ; you went into domestic service ; but in the essentials you haven't altered.

PURDIE (*pleasantly*).   I 'll have my shaving water at 7.30 sharp, Matey.

MATEY (*mechanically*).   Very good, sir.

LADY CAROLINE.   Sir ?   Midsummer Eve !   The wood !

PURDIE.   Yes, hold on to the wood.

MATEY.   You are . . . you are . . . you are Lady Caroline Laney !

LADY CAROLINE.   It is Matey, the butler !

MABEL.   You seemed quite happy with him, you know, Lady Caroline.

JOANNA (*nicely*).   We won't tell.

LADY CAROLINE (*subsiding*).   Caroline Matey !   And I seemed to like it !   How horrible !

MRS. COADE (*expressing a general sentiment*).   It is rather difficult to see what we should do next.

MATEY (*tentatively*).   Perhaps if I were to go downstairs ?

PURDIE.   It would be conferring a personal favour on us all

> (*Thus encouraged* MATEY *and his tray resume friendly relations with the pantry.*)

LADY CAROLINE (*with itching fingers as she glares at* LOB).   It is all that wretch's doing.

> (*A quiver from* LOB's *right leg acknowledges the compliment. The gay music of a pipe is heard from outside.*)

JOANNA (*peeping*). Coady !

MRS. COADE. Coady ? Why is he so happy ?

JOANNA (*troubled*). Dear, hold my hand.

MRS. COADE (*suddenly trembling*). Won't he know me ?

PURDIE (*abashed by that soft face*). Mrs. Coade, I 'm sorry. It didn't so much matter about the likes of us, but for your sake I wish Coady hadn't gone out.

MRS. COADE. We that have been happily married nearly thirty years.

COADE (*popping in buoyantly*). May I intrude ? My name is Coade. The fact is I was playing about in the wood on a whistle, and I saw your light.

MRS. COADE (*the only one with the nerve to answer*). Playing about in the wood with a whistle ?

COADE (*with mild dignity*). And why not, madam ?

MRS. COADE. Madam ! Don't you know me ?

COADE. I don't know you. . . . (*Studying her*) But I wish I did.

MRS. COADE. Do you ? Why ?

COADE. If I may say so, you have a very soft, lovable face.
  (*Several persons breathe again.*)

MRS. COADE (*inquisitorially*). Who was with you, playing whistles in the wood ? (*The breathing ceases.*)

COADE. No one was with me.

(*And is resumed.*)

MRS. COADE. No . . . lady ?

COADE. Certainly not. (*Then he spoils it.*) I am a bachelor.

MRS. COADE. A bachelor ?

JOANNA. Don't give way, dear ; it might be much worse.

MRS. COADE. A bachelor ! And you are sure you never spoke to me before ? Do think.

COADE. Not to my knowledge. Never . . . except in dreams.

MABEL (*taking a risk*). What did you say to her in dreams ?

COADE. I said, ' My dear.' (*This when uttered surprises him.*) Odd !

JOANNA. The darling man !

MRS. COADE (*wavering*). How could you say such things to an old woman ?

COADE (*thinking it out*).   Old ?   I didn't think of you as old.
No, no, young—with the morning dew on your face—coming
across a lawn—in a black and green dress—and carrying such
a pretty parasol.

MRS. COADE (*thrilling*).   That was how he first met me !
He used to love me in black and green ; and it *was* a pretty
parasol.   Look, I am old. . . . So it can't be the same woman.

COADE (*blinking*).   Old.   Yes, I suppose so.   But it is the
same soft, lovable face, and the same kind, beaming smile that
children could warm their hands at.

MRS. COADE.   He always liked my smile.

PURDIE.   So do we all.

COADE (*to himself*).   Emma.

MRS. COADE.   He hasn't forgotten my name !

COADE.   It is sad that we didn't meet long ago.   I think
I have been waiting for you.   I suppose we have met too
late ?   You couldn't overlook my being an old fellow, could
you, eh ?

JOANNA.   How lovely ; he is going to propose to her again.
Coady, you happy thing, he is wanting the same soft face after
thirty years.

MRS. COADE (*undoubtedly hopeful*).   We mustn't be too sure,
but I think that is it.   (*Primly*) What is it exactly that you want,
Mr. Coade ?

COADE (*under a lucky star*).   I want to have the right to hold
the parasol over you.   Won't you be my wife, my dear, and so
give my long dream of you a happy ending ?

MRS. COADE (*preening*).   Kisses are not called for at our age,
Coady, but here is a muffler for your old neck.

COADE.   My muffler ; I have missed it.   (*It is however to
his forehead that his hand goes.   Immediately thereafter he misses
his sylvan attire.*)   Why . . . why . . . what . . . who
. . . how is this ?

PURDIE (*nervously*).   He is coming to.

COADE (*reeling and righting himself*).   Lob !
    (*The leg indicates that he has got it.*)
Bless me, Coady, I went into that wood !

MRS. COADE.   And without your muffler, you that are so
subject to chills.   What are you feeling for in your pocket ?

COADE.   The whistle.   It is a whistle I——   Gone ! of

course it is. It's rather a pity, but . . . (*Anxious*) Have I been saying awful things to you ?

MABEL. You have been making her so proud. It is a compliment to our whole sex. You had a second chance, and have chosen her, again !

COADE. Of course I have. (*Crestfallen.*) But I see I was just the same nice old lazy Coady as before ; and I had thought that if I had a second chance, I could do things. I have often said to you, Coady, that it was owing to my being cursed with a competency that I didn't write my great book. But I had no competency this time, and I haven't written a word.

PURDIE (*bitterly enough*). That needn't make you feel lonely in this house.

MRS. COADE (*in a small voice*). You seem to have been quite happy as an old bachelor, dear.

COADE. I am surprised at myself, Emma, but I fear I was.

MRS. COADE (*with melancholy perspicacity*). I wonder if what it means is that you don't especially need even me. I wonder if it means that you are just the sort of amiable creature that would be happy anywhere, and anyhow ?

COADE. Oh dear, can it be as bad as that !

JOANNA (*a ministering angel she*). Certainly not. It is a romance, and I won't have it looked upon as anything else.

MRS. COADE. Thank you, Joanna. You will try not to miss that whistle, Coady ?

COADE (*getting the footstool for her*). You are all I need.

MRS. COADE. Yes ; but I am not so sure as I used to be that it is a great compliment.

JOANNA. Coady, behave.

(*There is a knock on the window.*)

PURDIE (*peeping*). Mrs. Dearth ! (*His spirits revive.*) She is alone. Who would have expected that of *her* !

MABEL. She is a wild one, Jack, but I sometimes thought rather a dear ; I do hope she has got off cheaply.

(ALICE *comes to them in her dinner gown.*)

PURDIE (*the irrepressible*). Pleased to see you, stranger.

ALICE (*prepared for ejection*). I was afraid such an un-ceremonious entry might startle you.

PURDIE. Not a bit.

ALICE (*defiant*). I usually enter a house by the front door.

PURDIE. I have heard that such is the swagger way.

ALICE (*simpering*). So stupid of me. I lost myself in the wood . . . and . . .

JOANNA (*genially*). Of course you did. But never mind that ; do tell us your name.

LADY CAROLINE (*emerging again*). Yes, yes, your name.

ALICE. Of course, I am the Honourable Mrs. Finch-Fallowe.

LADY CAROLINE. Of course, of course !

PURDIE. I hope Mr. Finch-Fallowe is very well ? We don't know him personally, but may we have the pleasure of seeing him bob up presently ?

ALICE. No, I am not sure where he is.

LADY CAROLINE (*with point*). I wonder if the dear clever police know ?

ALICE (*imprudently*). No, they don't.

(*It is a very secondary matter to her. This woman of calamitous fires hears and sees her tormentors chiefly as the probable owners of the cake which is standing on that tray.*) So awkward, I gave my sandwiches to a poor girl and her father whom I met in the wood, and now . . . isn't it a nuisance —I am quite hungry. (*So far with a mincing bravado.*) May I ?

(*Without waiting for consent she falls to upon the cake, looking over it like one ready to fight them for it.*)

PURDIE (*sobered again*). Poor soul.

LADY CAROLINE. We are so anxious to know whether you met a friend of ours in the wood—a Mr. Dearth. Perhaps you know him, too ?

ALICE. Dearth ? I don't know any Dearth.

MRS. COADE. Oh dear, what a wood !

LADY CAROLINE. He is quite a front-door sort of man ; knocks and rings, you know.

PURDIE. Don't worry her.

ALICE (*gnawing*). I meet so many ; you see I go out a great deal. I have visiting-cards—printed ones.

LADY CAROLINE. How very distingué. Perhaps Mr. Dearth has painted your portrait ; he is an artist.

ALICE. Very likely ; they all want to paint me. I dare say that is the man to whom I gave my sandwiches.

MRS. COADE.   But I thought you said he had a daughter ?

ALICE.   Such a pretty girl ; I gave her half a crown.

COADE.   A daughter ?   That can't be Dearth.

PURDIE (*darkly*).   Don't be too sure.   Was the man you speak of a rather chop-fallen, gone-to-seed sort of person ?

ALICE.   No, I thought him such a jolly, attractive man.

COADE.   Dearth jolly, attractive !   oh no.   Did he say anything about his wife ?

LADY CAROLINE.   Yes, do try to remember if he mentioned her.

ALICE (*snapping*).   No, he didn't.

PURDIE.   He was far from jolly in her time.

ALICE (*with an archness for which the cake is responsible*). Perhaps that was the lady's fault.

(*The last of the adventurers draws nigh, carolling a French song as he comes.*)

COADE.   Dearth's voice.   He sounds quite merry !

JOANNA (*protecting*).   Alice, you poor thing.

PURDIE.   This is going to be horrible.

(*A clear-eyed man of lusty gait comes in.*)

DEARTH.   I am sorry to bounce in on you in this way, but really I have an excuse.   I am a painter of sorts, and . . .

(*He sees he has brought some strange discomfort here.*)

MRS. COADE.   I must say, Mr. Dearth, I am delighted to see you looking so well.   Like a new man, isn't he ?

(*No one dares to answer.*)

DEARTH.   I am certainly very well, if you care to know. But did I tell you my name ?

JOANNA (*for some one has to speak*).   No, but—but we have an instinct in this house.

DEARTH.   Well, it doesn't matter.   Here is the situation ; my daughter and I have just met in the wood a poor woman famishing for want of food.   We were as happy as grigs ourselves, and the sight of her distress rather cut us up.   Can you give me something for her ?   Why are you looking so startled ? (*Seeing the remains of the cake*) May I have this ?

(*A shrinking movement from one of them draws his attention, and he recognises in her the woman of whom he has been speaking.   He sees her in fine apparel and he grows stern.*)

I feel I can't be mistaken ; it was you I met in the wood ?

2 L

Have you been playing some trick on me ?   *(To the others)* It was for her I wanted the food.

ALICE *(her hand guarding the place where his gift lies).*   Have you come to take back the money you gave me ?

DEARTH.   Your dress !   You were almost in rags when I saw you outside.

ALICE *(frightened as she discovers how she is now attired).*   I don't . . . understand . . .

COADE *(gravely enough).*   For that matter, Dearth, I dare say you were different in the wood, too.

    (DEARTH *sees his own clothing.*)

DEARTH.   What . . . !

ALICE *(frightened).*   Where am I ?   *(To* MRS. COADE*)* I seem to know you . . . do I ?

MRS. COADE *(motherly).*   Yes, you do ; hold my hand, and you will soon remember all about it.

JOANNA.   I am afraid, Mr. Dearth, it is harder for you than for the rest of us.

PURDIE *(looking away).*   I wish I could help you, but I can't ; I am a rotter.

MABEL.   We are awfully sorry.   Don't you remember . . . Midsummer Eve ?

DEARTH *(controlling himself).*   Midsummer Eve ?   This room.   Yes, this room. . . . You . . . was it you ? . . . were going out to look for something. . . . The tree of knowledge, wasn't it ?   Somebody wanted me to go, too. . . . Who was that ?   A lady, I think. . . . Why did she ask me to go ?   What was I doing here ?   I was smoking a cigar. . . . I laid it down, there. . . . *(He finds the cigar.)*   Who was the lady ?

ALICE *(feebly).*   Something about a second chance.

MRS. COADE.   Yes, you poor dear, you thought you could make so much of it.

DEARTH.   A lady who didn't like me—*(With conviction.)* She had good reasons, too—but what were they . . .?

ALICE.   A little old man !   He did it.   What did he do ?
    (The hammer is raised.)

DEARTH.   I am . . . it is coming back—I am not the man I thought myself.

ALICE.   I am not Mrs. Finch-Fallowe.   Who am I ?

DEARTH *(staring at her).*   You were that lady.

ALICE. It is you—my husband !
(*She is overcome.*)

MRS. COADE. My dear, you are much better off, so far as
I can see, than if you were Mrs. Finch-Fallowe.

ALICE (*with passionate knowledge*). Yes, yes indeed !
(*Looking at* DEARTH) But he isn't.

DEARTH. Alice ! . . . I—— (*He tries to smile.*) I didn't
know you when I was in the wood with Margaret. She
. . . she . . . Margaret . . . !
(*The hammer falls.*)
O my God !
(*He buries his face in his hands.*)

ALICE. I wish—I wish——
(*She presses his shoulder fiercely and then stalks out by
the door.*)

PURDIE (*to* LOB, *after a time*). You old ruffian.

DEARTH. No, I am rather fond of him, our lonely, friendly
little host. Lob, I thank thee for that hour.
(*The seedy-looking fellow passes from the scene.*)

COADE. Did you see that his hand is shaking again ?

PURDIE. The watery eye has come back.

JOANNA. And yet they are both quite nice people.

PURDIE (*finding the tragedy of it*). We are all quite nice
people.

MABEL. If she were not such a savage !

PURDIE. I dare say there is nothing the matter with her
except that she would always choose the wrong man, good
man or bad man, but the wrong man for her.

COADE. We can't change.

MABEL. Jack says the brave ones can.

JOANNA. ' The ones with the thin bright faces.'

MABEL. Then there is hope for you and me, Jack.

PURDIE (*ignobly*). I don't expect so.

JOANNA (*wandering about the room, like one renewing acquaintance with it after returning from a journey*). Hadn't we better
go to bed ? it must be getting late.

PURDIE. Hold on to bed. (*They all brighten.*)

MATEY (*entering*). Breakfast is quite ready.
(*They exclaim.*)

LADY CAROLINE. My watch has stopped.

JOANNA.   And mine.   Just as well, perhaps !

MABEL.   There is a smell of coffee.

(*The gloom continues to lift.*)

COADE.   Come along, Coady ; I do hope you have not been tiring your foot.

MRS. COADE.   I shall give it a good rest to-morrow, dear.

MATEY.   I have given your egg six minutes, ma'am.

(*Our friends set forth once more upon the eternal round. The curious* JOANNA *remains behind.*)

JOANNA.   A strange experiment, Matey ; does it ever have any permanent effect ?

MATEY (*on whom it has had none*).   So far as I know, not often, miss ; but, I believe, once in a while.

(*There is hope in this for the brave ones.   If we could wait long enough we might see the* DEARTHS *breasting their way into the light.*)

He could tell you.

(*The elusive person thus referred to kicks responsively, meaning perhaps that none of the others will change till there is a tap from another hammer.   But when* MATEY *goes to rout him from his chair he is no longer there.   His disappearance is no shock to* MATEY, *who shrugs his shoulders and opens the windows to let in the glory of a summer morning. The garden has returned, and our queer little hero is busy at work among his flowers.*)

A WELL-REMEMBERED VOICE

Produced at Wyndham's Theatre on June 23, 1918, with the following cast :

MR. DON	*Sir Johnston Forbes-Robertson*
MR. ROGERS . . .	*H. V. Esmond*
MAJOR ARMITAGE . .	*Dawson Milward*
MRS. DON . . .	*Lilian Braithwaite*
LAURA BELL . . .	*Faith Celli*
ANOTHER	*Gerald du Maurier*

A WELL-REMEMBERED VOICE

OUT of the darkness comes the voice of a woman speaking to her dead son.

' But that was against your wish, was it not? Was that against your wish? Would you prefer me not to ask that question? '

The room is so dark that we cannot see her. All we know is that she is one of four shapes gathered round a small table. Beyond the darkness is a great ingle-nook, in which is seated on a settle a man of fifty. Him we can discern fitfully by the light of the fire. It is not sufficiently bright to enable him to read, but an evening paper lies on his knee. He is paying no attention to the party round the table. When he hears their voices it is only as empty sounds.

The mother continues. ' Perhaps I am putting the question in the wrong way. Are you not able to tell us any more? '

A man's voice breaks in. ' There was a distinct movement that time, but it is so irregular.'

' I thought so, but please don't talk. Do you want to tell us more? Is it that you can't hear me distinctly? He seems to want to tell us more, but something prevents him.'

' In any case, Mrs. Don, it is extraordinary. This is the first séance I have ever taken part in, but I must believe now.'

' Of course, Major, these are the simplest manifestations. They are only the first step. But if we are to go on, the less we talk the better. Shall we go on? It is not agitating you too much, Laura? '

A girl answers. ' There was a moment when I—but I wish I was braver. I think it is partly the darkness. I suppose we can't have a little light? '

' Certainly we can, dear. Darkness is quite unnecessary, but I think it helps one to concentrate.'

The Major lights a lamp, and though it casts shadows we see now that the room is an artist's studio. The silent figure in the

1063

ingle-nook is the artist.   Mrs. Don is his wife ; the two men
are Major Armitage and an older friend, Mr. Rogers.   The girl
is Laura Bell.   These four are sitting round the table, their
hands touching :   they are endeavouring to commune with one
who has ' crossed the gulf.'

The Major and Mr. Rogers are but passing shadows in the
play, and even nice Laura is only to flit across its few pages for
a moment on her way to happier things.   We scarcely notice
those three in the presence of Mrs. Don, the gracious, the
beautiful, the sympathetic, whose magnetic force and charm are
such that we wish to sit at her feet at once.   She is intellectual, but
with a disarming smile ; religious, but so charitable ; masterful,
and yet loved of all.   None is perfect, and there must be a flaw
in her somewhere, but to find it would necessitate such a rummage among her many adornments as there is now no time
for.   Perhaps we may come upon it accidentally in the course
of the play.

She is younger than Mr. Don, who, despite her efforts for
many years to cover his deficiencies, is a man of no great account
in a household where the bigger personality of his wife swallows
him like an Aaron's rod.   Mr. Don's deficiencies !   She used
to try very hard, or fairly hard, to conceal them from Dick ;
but Dick knew.   His mother was his chum.   All the lovely
things which happened in that house in the days when Dick was
alive were between him and her ;   those two shut the door softly
on old Don, always anxious not to hurt his feelings, and then
ran into each other's arms.

In the better light Mr. Don is now able to read his paper if
he chooses.   If he has forgotten the party at the table, they have
equally forgotten him.

MRS. DON.   You have not gone away, have you ?   We
must be patient.   Are you still there ?

ROGERS.   I think I felt a movement.

MRS. DON.   Don't talk, please.   Are you still there ?
      (*The table moves.*)

Yes !   It is your mother who is speaking ;   do you understand
that ?
      (*The table moves.*)

Yes.   What shall I ask him now ?

ROGERS. We leave it to you, Mrs. Don.

MRS. DON. Have you any message you want to send us? Yes. Is it important? Yes. Are we to spell it out in the usual way? Yes. Is the first letter of the first word A? Is it B?

(She continues through the alphabet to L, when the table responds. Similarly she finds that the second letter is O.) Is the word *Love*? Yes. But I don't understand that movement. You are not displeased with us, are you? No. Does the second word begin with A?—with B? Yes.

(The second word is spelt out Bade *and the third* Me.*)* Love Bade Me—— If it is a quotation, I believe I know it! Is the fourth word *Welcome*? Yes.

LAURA. Love Bade Me Welcome.

MRS. DON. That movement again! Don't you want me to go on?

LAURA. Let us stop.

MRS. DON. Not unless he wishes it. Why are those words so important? Does the message end there? Is any one working against you? Some one antagonistic? Yes. Not one of ourselves, surely? No. Is it any one we know? Yes. Can I get the name in the usual way? Yes. Is the first letter of this person's name A?—B?——

(It proves to be F. One begins to notice a quaint peculiarity of MRS. DON'S. *She is so accustomed to homage that she expects a prompt response even from the shades.)* Is the second letter A?

(The table moves.)

FA. Fa——?

(She is suddenly enlightened.) Is the word Father? Yes.

(They all turn and look for the first time at MR. DON. *He has heard, and rises apologetically.)*

MR. DON *(distressed)*. I had no intention—— Should I go away, Grace?

(She answers sweetly without a trace of the annoyance she must surely feel.)

MRS. DON. Perhaps you had better, Robert.

ROGERS. I suppose it is because he is an unbeliever? He is not openly antagonistic, is he?

MRS. DON (*sadly enough*).   I am afraid he is.

(*They tend to discuss the criminal as if he was not present.*)

MAJOR.   But he must admit that we do get messages.

MRS. DON (*reluctantly*).   He says we think we do.   He says they would not want to communicate with us if they had such trivial things to say.

ROGERS.   But we are only on the threshold, Don.   This is just a beginning.

LAURA.   Didn't you hear, Mr. Don—'Love Bade Me Welcome'?

MR. DON.   Does that strike you as important, Laura?

LAURA.   He said it was.

MRS. DON.   It might be very important to him, though we don't understand why.

   (*She speaks gently, but there is an obstinacy in him, despite his meekness.*)

MR. DON.   I didn't mean to be antagonistic, Grace.   I thought—I wasn't thinking of it at all.

MRS. DON.   Not thinking of Dick, Robert?   And it was only five months ago!

MR. DON (*who is somehow, without meaning it, always in the wrong*).   I'll go.

ROGERS.   A boy wouldn't turn his father out.   Ask him.

MR. DON (*forlornly*).   As to that—as to that——

MRS. DON.   I shall ask him if you wish me to, Robert.

MR. DON.   No, don't.

ROGERS.   It can't worry you as you are a disbeliever.

MR. DON.   No, but—I shouldn't like you to think that he sent me away.

ROGERS.   He won't.   Will he, Mrs. Don?

MR. DON (*knowing what her silence implies*).   You see, Dick and I were not very—no quarrel or anything of that sort—but I—I didn't much matter to Dick.   I'm too old, perhaps.

MRS. DON (*gently*).   I won't ask him, Robert, if you would prefer me not to.

MR. DON.   I'll go.

MRS. DON.   I'm afraid it is too late now.   (*She turns away from earthly things.*)   Do you want me to break off?

   (*The table moves.*)

Yes.   Do you send me your love, Dick?   Yes.   And to

Laura ? Yes. (*She raises her eyes to* DON, *and hesitates.*) Shall I ask him———?

MR. DON. No, no, don't.

ROGERS. It would be all right, Don.

MR. DON. I don't know.

(*They leave the table.*)

LAURA (*a little agitated*). May I go to my room, Mrs. Don ? I feel I—should like to be alone.

MRS. DON. Yes, yes, Laura dear. I shall come in and see you.

(LAURA *bids them good-night and goes. She likes* MR. DON, *she strokes his hand when he holds it out to her, but she can't help saying, ' Oh, Mr. Don, how could you ? '*)

ROGERS. I think we must all want to be alone after such an evening. I shall say good-night, Mrs. Don.

MAJOR. Same here. I go your way, Rogers, but you will find me a silent companion. One doesn't want to talk ordinary things to-night. Rather not. Thanks, awfully.

ROGERS. Good-night, Don. It 's a pity, you know ; a bit hard on your wife

MR. DON. Good-night, Rogers. Good-night, Major.

(*The husband and wife, left together, have not much to say to each other. He is depressed because he has spoilt things for her. She is not angry. She knows that he can't help being as he is, and that there are fine spaces in her mind where his thoughts can never walk with hers. But she would forgive him seventy times seven because he is her husband. She is standing looking at a case of fishing-rods against the wall. There is a Jock Scott still sticking in one of them.*)

MR. DON (*as if somehow they were evidence against him*). Dick's fishing-rods.

MRS. DON (*forgivingly*). I hope you don't mind my keeping them in the studio, Robert. They are sacred things to *me*.

MR. DON. That 's all right, Grace.

MRS. DON. I think I shall go to Laura now.

MR. DON (*in his inexpressive way*). Yes.

MRS. DON. Poor child !

MR. DON. I 'm afraid I hurt her.

MRS. DON. Dick wouldn't have liked it—but Dick 's gone.

(*She looks a little wonderingly at him.   After all these years, she can sometimes wonder a little still.*)   I suppose you will resume your evening paper !

> (*He answers quietly, but with the noble doggedness which is the reason why we write this chapter in his life.*)

MR. DON.   Why not, Grace ?

> (*She considers, for she is so sure that she must know the answer better than he.*)

MRS. DON.   I suppose it is just that a son is so much more to a mother than to a father.

MR. DON.   I dare say.

MRS. DON (*a little gust of passion shaking her*).   How you can read about the war nowadays !

MR. DON (*firmly to her—he has had to say it a good many times to himself*).   I 'm not going to give in.   (*Apologetically*) I am so sorry I was in the way, Grace.   I wasn't scouting you, or anything of that sort.   It is just that I can't believe in it.

MRS. DON.   Ah, Robert, you would believe if Dick had been to you what he was to me.

MR. DON.   I don't know.

MRS. DON.   In a sense you may be glad that you don't miss him in the way I do.

MR. DON.   Yes, perhaps.

MRS. DON.   Good-night, Robert.

MR. DON.   Good-night, dear.

> (*He is alone now.   He stands fingering the fishing-rods, then wanders back into the ingle-nook.   In the room we could scarcely see him, for it has gone slowly dark there, a grey darkness, as if the lamp, though still burning, was becoming unable to shed light.   Through the greyness we see him very well beyond it in the glow of the fire.   He sits on the settle and tries to read his paper.   He fails.   He is a very lonely man.*
>
> *In the silence something happens.   A well-remembered voice says, ' Father.'*   MR. DON *looks into the greyness from which this voice comes, and he sees his son.   We see no one, but we are to understand that, to* MR. DON, DICK *is standing there in his habit as he lived.   He goes to his boy.*)

MR. DON.   Dick !

DICK.   I have come to sit with you for a bit, father.

(*It is the gay, young, careless voice.*)

MR. DON.   It 's you, Dick ; it 's you !

DICK.   It 's me all right, father.   I say, don't be startled, or anything of that kind.   We don't like that.

MR. DON.   My boy !

(*Evidently* DICK *is the taller, for* MR. DON *has to look up to him.   He puts his hands on the boy's shoulders.*)

DICK.   How am I looking, father ?

MR. DON.   You haven't altered, Dick.

DICK.   Rather not.   It 's jolly to see the old studio again ! (*In a cajoling voice*) I say, father, don't fuss.   Let us be our ordinary selves, won't you ?

MR. DON.   I 'll try, I 'll try.   You didn't say you had come to sit with *me*, Dick ?   Not with *me* !

DICK.   Rather !

MR. DON.   But your mother——

DICK.   It 's you I want.

MR. DON.   Me ?

DICK.   We can only come to one, you see.

MR. DON.   Then why me ?

DICK.   That 's the reason.   (*He is evidently moving about, looking curiously at old acquaintances.*)   Hullo, here 's your old jacket, greasier than ever !

MR. DON.   Me ?   But, Dick, it is as if you had forgotten. It was your mother who was everything to you.   It can't be you if you have forgotten that.   I used to feel so out of it ; but, of course, you didn't know.

DICK.   I didn't know it till now, father ; but heaps of things that I didn't know once are clear to me now.   I didn't know that you were the one who would miss me most ; but I know now.

(*Though the voice is as boyish as ever, there is a new note in it of which his father is aware.* DICK *may not have grown much wiser, but whatever he does know now he seems to know for certain.*)

MR. DON.   *Me* miss you most ?   Dick, I try to paint just as before.   I go to the club.   Dick, I have been to a dinner-party. I said I wouldn't give in.

DICK.   We like that.

MR. DON.   But, my boy——

(MR. DON's *arms have gone out to him again.* DICK *evidently wriggles away from them. He speaks coaxingly.*)

DICK.   I say, father, let's get away from that sort of thing.

MR. DON.   That is so like you, Dick! I'll do anything you ask.

DICK.   Then keep a bright face.

MR. DON.   I've tried to.

DICK.   Good man! I say, put on your old greasy; you are looking so beastly clean.

(*The old greasy is the jacket, and* MR. DON *obediently gets into it.*)

MR. DON.   Anything you like. No, that's the wrong sleeve. Thanks, Dick.

(*They are in the ingle-nook now, and the mischievous boy catches his father by the shoulders.*)

DICK.   Here, let me shove you into your old seat.

(MR. DON *is propelled on to the settle.*)

How's that, umpire!

MR. DON (*smiling*).   Dick, that's just how you used to butt me into it long ago!

(DICK *is probably standing with his back to the fire, chuckling.*)

DICK.   When I was a kid.

MR. DON.   With the palette in my hand.

DICK.   Or sticking to your trousers.

MR. DON.   The mess we made of ourselves, Dick!

DICK.   I sneaked behind the settle and climbed up it.

MR. DON.   Till you fell off.

DICK.   On top of you and the palette.

(*It is good fun for a father and son; and the crafty boy has succeeded in making the father laugh.*)

MR. DON (*sadly*).   Ah, Dick.

(*The son frowns. He is not going to stand any nonsense.*)

DICK.   Now then, behave! What did I say about that face?

(MR. DON *smiles at once, obediently.*)

That's better. I'll sit here.

(*We see from his father's face, which is smiling with difficulty, that* DICK *has plopped into the big chair on the other side of the ingle-nook. His legs are probably dangling over one of its arms.*)

DICK (*rather sharply*). Got your pipe ?

MR. DON. I don't—I don't seem to care to smoke nowadays, Dick.

DICK. Rot ! Just because I am dead. You that pretend to be plucky ! I won't have it, you know. You get your pipe, and look slippy about it.

MR. DON (*obediently*). Yes, Dick. (*He fills his pipe from a jar on the mantelshelf. We may be sure that* DICK *is watching closely to see that he lights it properly.*)

DICK. Now, then, burn your thumb with the match—you always did, you know. That 's the style. You 've forgotten to cock your head to the side. Not so bad. That 's you. Like it ?

MR. DON. It 's rather nice, Dick. Dick, you and me by the fire !

DICK. Yes, but sit still. How often we might have been like this, father, and weren't.

MR. DON. Ah !

DICK. Face ! How is Fido ?

MR. DON. Never a dog missed her master more.

DICK (*frowning*). She doesn't want to go and sit on my grave, or any of that tosh, does she ? As if I were there !

MR. DON (*hastily*). No, no ; she goes ratting, Dick.

DICK. Good old Fido !

MR. DON. Dick, here 's a good one. We oughtn't to keep a dog at all because we are on rations now ; but what do you think Fido ate yesterday ?

DICK. Let me guess. The joint ?

MR. DON. Almost worse than that. She ate all the cook's meat tickets.

(*They laugh together.*)

DICK. That dog will be the death of me.

(*His father shivers but* DICK *does not notice this ; his eyes have drawn him to the fishing-rods.*)

Hullo !

MR. DON. Yes, those are your old fishing-rods.

DICK. Here 's the little hickory ! Do you remember, father, how I got the seven-pounder on a burn-trout cast ? No, you weren't there. That was a day. It was really only six and three-quarters. I put a stone in its mouth the second time we weighed it !

MR. DON.   You loved fishing, Dick.

DICK.   Didn't I ?   Why weren't you oftener with me ?
I 'll tell you a funny thing.   When I went a-soldiering I used
to pray—just standing up, you know—that I shouldn't lose my
right arm, because it would be so awkward for casting.   (*He
cogitates as he returns to the ingle-nook.*)   Somehow I never
thought I should be killed.   Lots of fellows thought that about
themselves, but I never did.   It was quite a surprise to me.

MR. DON.   Oh, Dick !

DICK.   What 's the matter ?   Oh, I forgot.   Face !   (*He
is apparently looking down at his father wonderingly.*)   Haven't
you got over it yet, father ?   I got over it so long ago.   I wish
you people would understand what a little thing it is.

MR. DON.   Tell me, Dick.

DICK.   All right.   (*He is in the chair again.*)   Mind, I
can't tell you where I was killed ; it 's against the regulations.

MR. DON.   I know where.

DICK (*curiously*).   You got a wire, I suppose ?

MR. DON.   Yes.

DICK.   There 's always a wire for officers, even for 2nd
Lieutenants.   It 's jolly decent of them.

MR. DON.   Tell me, Dick, about the—the veil.   I mean the
veil that is drawn between the living and the——

DICK.   The dead ?   Funny how you jib at that word.

MR. DON.   I suppose the veil is like a mist ?

DICK.   The veil 's a rummy thing, father.   Yes, like a mist.
But when one has been at the Front for a bit, you can't think
how thin the veil seems to get ; just one layer of it.   I suppose
it seems thin to you out there because one step takes you through
it.   We sometimes mix up those who have gone through with
those who haven't.   I dare say if I were to go back to my old
battalion the living chaps would just nod to me.

MR. DON.   My boy !

DICK.   Where 's that pipe !   Death ?   Well, to me, before
my day came, it was like some part of the line I had heard a
lot about but never been in.   I mean, never been in to stay,
because, of course, one often popped in and out.

MR. DON.   Dick, the day that you——

DICK.   My day ?   I don't remember being hit, you know.
I don't remember anything till the quietness came.   When you

have been killed it suddenly becomes very quiet ; quieter even than you have ever known it at home. Sunday used to be a pretty quiet day at my tutor's, when Trotter and I flattened out on the first shady spot up the river ; but it is quieter than that. I am not boring you, am I ?

MR. DON. Oh, Dick !

DICK. When I came to, the veil was so thin that I couldn't see it at all ; and my first thought was, Which side of it have I come out on ? The living ones lying on the ground were asking that about themselves, too. There we were, all sitting up and asking whether we were alive or dead ; and some were one, and some were the other. Sort of fluke, you know.

MR. DON. I—I——

DICK. As soon as each had found out about himself he wondered how it had gone with his chums. I halloo'd to Johnny Randall, and he halloo'd back that he was dead, but that Trotter was living. That 's the way of it. A good deal of chaff, of course. By that time the veil was there, and getting thicker, and we lined up on our right sides. Then I could only see the living ones in shadow and hear their voices from a distance. They sang out to us for a while ; but just at first, father, it was rather lonely when we couldn't hear their tread any longer. What are you fidgeting about ? You needn't worry ; that didn't last long ; we were heaps more interested in ourselves than in them. You should have heard the gabbling! It was all so frightfully novel, you see ; and no one quite knew what to do next, whether all to start off together, or wait for some one to come for us. I say, what a lot I 'm talking !

MR. DON. What happened, Dick ?

DICK (*a proud ring coming into the voice*). Ockley came for us. He used to be alive, you know—the Ockley who was keeper of the fives in my first half. I once pointed him out to mother. I was jolly glad he was the one who came for us. As soon as I saw it was Ockley I knew we should be all right.

MR. DON. I like that Ockley.

DICK. Rather. I wish I could remember something funny to tell you, though. There are lots of jokes, but I am such a one for forgetting them.

(*He laughs boisterously. We may be sure that he flings*

back his head. You remember how DICK *used to fling back his head when he laughed?—No, you didn't know him.*)
Father, do you remember little Wantage who was at my private and came on to Ridley's house in my third half? His mother was the one you called Emily.

MR. DON. Emily Wantage's boy?

DICK. That's the card. We used to call him Jemima, because he and his mother were both caught crying when lock-up struck, and she had to clear out.

MR. DON. She was very fond of him.

DICK. Oh, I expect no end. Tell her he's killed.

MR. DON. She knows.

DICK. She had got a wire. That isn't the joke, though. You see he got into a hopeless muddle about which side of the veil he had come out on; and he went off with the other ones, and they wouldn't have him, and he got lost in the veil, running up and down it, calling to us; and just for the lark we didn't answer. (*He chuckles*) I expect he has become a ghost! (*With sudden consideration*) Best not tell his mother that.

(MR. DON *rises, wincing, and* DICK *also is at once on his feet, full of compunction.*)
Was that shabby of me? Sorry, father. We are all pretty young, you know, and we can't help having our fun still.

MR. DON. I'm glad you still have your fun. Let me look at you again, Dick. There is such a serenity about you now.

DICK. Serenity—that's the word! None of us could remember what the word was. It's a ripping good thing to have. I should be awfully bucked if you would have it, too.

MR. DON. I'll try.

DICK. I say, how my tongue runs on! But, after all, it was my show. Now, you tell me some things.

MR. DON. What about, Dick? The war?

DICK (*almost in a shout*). No. We have a fine for speaking about the war. And you know, those fellows we were fighting —I forget who they were?

MR. DON. The Germans.

DICK. Oh yes. Some of them were on the same side of the veil with us, and they were rather decent; so we chummed up in the end and Ockley took us all away together. They were jolly lucky in getting Ockley. There I go again ! Come on, it 's your turn. Has the bathroom tap been mended yet ?

MR. DON. I 'm afraid it is—just tied up with that string still, Dick. It works all right.

DICK. It only needs two screw-nails, you know.

MR. DON. I 'll see to it.

DICK. Do you know whether any one at my tutor's got his fives choice this half ?

MR. DON. I 'm sorry, but——

DICK. Or who is the captain of the boats ?

MR. DON. No, I——

DICK. Whatever have you been doing ? (*He is moving about the room.*) Hullo, here 's mother's workbox ! Is mother all right ?

MR DON. Very sad about you, Dick.

DICK. Oh, I say, that isn't fair. Why doesn't she cheer up ?

MR. DON. It isn't so easy, my boy.

DICK. It 's pretty hard lines on me, you know.

MR. DON. How is that ?

DICK. If you are sad, I have to be sad. That 's how we have got to work it off. You can't think how we want to be bright.

MR. DON. I 'll always remember that, and I 'll tell your mother. Ah, but she won't believe me, Dick ; you will have to tell her yourself.

DICK. I can't do that, father. I can only come to one.

MR. DON. She should have been the one ; she loved you best, Dick.

DICK. Oh, I don't know Do you ever (*with a slight hesitation*) see Laura now ?

MR. DON. She is staying with us at present.

DICK. Is she ? I think I should like to see her.

MR. DON. If Laura were to see you——

DICK. Oh, she wouldn't see me. She is not dressed in black, is she ?

MR. DON. No, in white.

DICK. Good girl ! I suppose mother is in black ?

MR. DON. Of course, Dick.

DICK. It 's too bad, you know.

MR. DON.   You weren't exactly—engaged to Laura, were you, Dick ?   (*Apologetically*) I never rightly knew.

DICK (*confidentially*).   Father, I sometimes thought of it, but it rather scared me.   I expect that is about how it was with her, too.

MR. DON.   She is very broken about you now.

DICK (*irritated*).   Oh, hang !

MR. DON.   Would you like her to forget you, Dick ?

DICK.   Rather not.   But she might help a fellow a bit. Hullo !

(*What calls forth this exclamation is the little table at which the séance had taken place.   The four chairs are still standing round it, as if they were guarding something.*)

DICK.   Here 's something new, father ; this table.

MR. DON.   Yes, it is usually in the drawing-room.

DICK.   Of course.   I remember.

MR. DON (*setting his teeth*).   Does that table suggest anything to you, Dick ?

DICK.   To me ?   Let me think.   Yes, I used to play backgammon on it.   What is it doing here ?

MR. DON.   Your mother brought it in.

DICK.   To play games on ?   Mother !

MR. DON.   I don't—know that it was a game, Dick.

DICK   But to play anything !   I 'm precious glad she can do that.   Was Laura playing with her ?

MR. DON.   She was helping her.

DICK.   Good for Laura.   (*He is looking at some slips of paper on the table.*)   Are those pieces of paper used in the game ? There is writing on them : ' The first letter is H—the second letter is A—the third letter is R.'   What does it mean ?

MR. DON.   Does it convey no meaning to you, Dick ?

DICK.   To me ?   No ; why should it ?

(MR. DON *is enjoying no triumph.*)

MR. DON.   Let us go back to the fire, my boy.

(DICK *follows him into the ingle-nook.*)

DICK.   But why should it convey a meaning to me ?   I was never much of a hand at indoor games.   (*Brightly*) I bet you Ockley would be good at it.   (*After a joyous rumble*) Ockley's nickname still sticks to him !

MR. DON.   I don't think I know it.

DICK. He was a frightful swell, you know. Keeper of the field, and played at Lord's the same year. I suppose it did go just a little to his head.

(They are back in their old seats, and MR. DON *leans forward in gleeful anticipation. Probably* DICK *is leaning forward in the same way, and this old father is merely copying him.)*

MR. DON. What did you nickname him, Dick?

DICK. It was his fags that did it!

MR. DON. I should like to know it. I say, do tell me, Dick.

DICK. He is pretty touchy about it now, you know.

MR. DON. I won't tell any one. Come on, Dick.

DICK. His fags called him K.C.M.G.

MR. DON. Meaning, Dick?

DICK. Meaning ' Kindly Call Me God ! '

*(*MR. DON *flings back his head; so we know what* DICK *is doing. They are a hilarious pair, perhaps too noisy, for suddenly* MR. DON *looks at the door.)*

MR. DON. I think I heard some one, Dick!

DICK. Perhaps it 's mother!

MR. DON *(nervously)*. She may have heard the row.

*(*DICK'S *eyes must be twinkling.)*

DICK. I say, father, you 'll catch it!

MR. DON. I can't believe, Dick, that she won't see you.

DICK. Only one may see me.

MR. DON. You will speak to her, Dick. Let her hear your voice.

DICK. Only one may hear me. I could make her the one ; but it would mean your losing me.

MR. DON. I can't give you up, Dick.

*(*MRS. DON *comes in, as beautiful as ever, but a little aggrieved.)*

MRS. DON. I called to you, Robert.

MR. DON. Yes, I thought—I was just going to——

(He has come from the ingle-nook to meet her. He looks from her to DICK, *whom he sees so clearly, standing now by the fire. An awe falls upon* MR. DON. *He says her name, meaning, ' See, Grace, who is with us.'*

Her eyes follow his, but she sees nothing, not even two arms outstretched to her.)

MRS. DON.   What is it, Robert ?   What is the matter ?
(*She does not hear a voice say 'Mother.'*)
I heard you laughing, Robert ; what on earth at ?
(*The father cannot speak.*)
DICK (*in a mischievous voice*).   Now you 're in a hole, father !
MRS. DON.   Can I not be told, Robert ?
DICK.   Something in the paper.
(MR. DON *lifts the paper feebly, and his wife understands.*)
MRS. DON.   Oh, a newspaper joke !   Please, I don't want
to hear it.
MR. DON.   Was it my laughing that brought you back,
Grace ?
MRS. DON.   No, that would only have made me shut my
door.   If Dick thought you could laugh !   (*She goes to the little
table.*)   I came back for these slips of paper.   (*She lifts them and
presses them to her breast.*)   These precious slips of paper !
DICK (*forgetting that she cannot hear him*).   How do you mean,
mother ?   Why are they precious ?
(MR. DON *forgets also and looks to her for an answer.*)
MRS. DON.   What is it, Robert ?
MR. DON.   Didn't you hear—anything, Grace ?
MRS. DON.   No.   Perhaps Laura was calling ; I left her
on the stair.
MR. DON.   I wish Laura would come back and say good-
night to me.
MRS. DON.   I dare say she will.
MR. DON.   And, if she could be—rather brighter, Grace.
MRS. DON.   Robert !
MR. DON.   I think Dick would like it.
(*Her fine eyes reproach him mutely.*)
MRS. DON.   Is that how you look at it, Robert ?   Very well,
laugh your fill—if you can.   But if Dick were to appear
before me to-night——
(*In his distress* MR. DON *cries aloud to the figure by the fire.*)
MR. DON.   Dick, if you can appear to your mother, do it.
(*There is a pause in which anything may happen, but nothing
happens.   Yes, something has happened :* DICK *has stuck
to his father.*)
MRS. DON.   Really, Robert !
(*Without a word of reproach, she goes away.   Evidently*

(DICK *comes to his father, who has sunk into a chair, and puts a loving hand on him.* MR. DON *clasps it without looking up.*)

DICK.   Father, that was top-hole of you ! Poor mother, I should have liked to hug her ; but I can't.

MR. DON.   You should have gone to her, Dick ; you shouldn't have minded me.

DICK.   Mother 's a darling, but she doesn't need me as much as you do.

MR. DON.   I don't know.

DICK.   I do. I 'm glad she 's so keen about that game, though.

(*He has returned to the ingle-nook when* LAURA *comes in, eager to make amends to* DICK'S *father if she hurt him when she went out.*)

LAURA (*softly*).   I have come to say good-night, Mr. Don.

MR. DON (*taking both her hands*).   It 's nice of you, Laura.

DICK.   I want her to come nearer to the fire ; I can't see her very well there.

(*For a moment* MR. DON *is caught out again ; but* LAURA *has heard nothing.*)

MR. DON.   Your hands are cold, Laura ; go over to the fire. I want to look at you.

(*She sits on the hearthstone by* DICK'S *feet.*)

LAURA (*shyly*).   Am I all right ?

DICK.   You 're awfully pretty, Laura. You are even prettier than I thought. I remember I used to think, she can't be quite as pretty as I think her ; and then when you came you were just a little prettier.

LAURA (*who has been warming her hands*).   Why don't you say anything ?

MR. DON.   I was thinking of you and Dick, Laura. If Dick had lived, do you think that you and he—— ?

LAURA (*with shining eyes*).   I think—if he had wanted it very much.

MR. DON.   I expect he would, my dear.

(*There is an odd candour about* DICK'S *contribution.*)

DICK.   I think so, too, but I never was quite sure.

LAURA (*who is trembling a little*).   Mr. Don——

MR. DON.   Yes, Laura ?

LAURA. I think there is something wicked about me. I sometimes feel—quite light-hearted—though Dick has gone.

MR. DON. Perhaps, nowadays, the fruit trees have that sort of shame when they blossom, Laura ; but they can't help doing it. I hope you are yet to be a happy woman, a happy wife.

LAURA. It seems so heartless to Dick.

DICK. Not a bit ; it 's what I should like.

MR. DON. It 's what he would like, Laura.

DICK. Do you remember, Laura, I kissed you once. It was under a lilac in the Loudon Woods. I am afraid you were angry.

(*His sweetheart has risen, tasting something bitter-sweet.*)

MR. DON. What is it, Laura ?

LAURA. Somehow—I don't know how—but, for a moment I seemed to smell lilac. Dick was once—nice to me under a lilac. Oh, Mr. Don——

(*She goes to him like a child, and he soothes and pets her. He takes her to the door.*)

MR. DON. Good-night, my dear.

LAURA. Good-night, Mr. Don.

DICK. Good-bye, Laura.

(MR. DON *is looking so glum that the moment they are alone* DICK *has to cry warningly, ' Face ! '*)

Pretty awful things, these partings. Father, don't feel hurt though I dodge the good-bye business when I leave you.

MR. DON. That 's so like you, Dick !

DICK. I 'll have to go soon.

MR. DON. Oh, Dick ! Can't you——

DICK. There 's something I want not to miss, you see.

MR. DON. I 'm glad of that.

DICK. I 'm not going yet ; but I mean that when I do I 'll just slip away.

MR. DON. What I am afraid of is that you won't come back.

DICK. I will—honest Injun—if you keep bright.

MR. DON. But, if I do that, Dick, you might think I wasn't missing you so much.

DICK. We know better than that. You see, if you 're bright, I 'll get a good mark for it.

MR. DON. I 'll be bright.

(DICK *pops him into the settle again.*)

DICK.   Remember your pipe.

MR. DON.   Yes, Dick.

DICK.   Do you still go to that swimming-bath, and do your dumb-bell exercises ?

MR. DON.   No, I——

DICK.   You must.

MR. DON.   All right, Dick, I will.

DICK.   And I want you to be smarter next time.   Your hair 's awful.

MR. DON.   I 'll get it cut.

DICK.   Are you hard at work over your picture of those three Graces ?

MR. DON.   No, I put that away.   I 'm just doing little things nowadays.   I can't——

DICK.   Look here, sonny, you 've got to go on with it. You don't seem to know how interested I am in your future.

MR. DON.   Very well, Dick ; I 'll bring it out again.

(*He hesitates.*)

Dick, there is something I have wanted to ask you all the time.

(*Some fear seems to come into the boy's voice.*)

DICK.   Don't ask it, father.

MR. DON.   I shall go on worrying about it if I don't—but just as you like, Dick.

DICK.   Go ahead ; ask me.

MR. DON.   It is this.   Would you rather be—here—than there ?

DICK.   Not always.

MR. DON.   What is the great difference, Dick ?

DICK.   Well, down here one knows he has risks to run.

MR. DON.   And you miss that ?

DICK.   It must be rather jolly.

MR. DON.   Did you know that was what I was to ask ?

DICK.   Yes.   But, remember, I 'm young at it.

MR. DON.   And your gaiety, Dick ; is it all real, or only put on to help me ?

DICK.   It 's—it 's half and half, father.   Face !

MR. DON.   When will you come again, Dick ?

DICK.   There 's no saying.   One can't always get through.

They keep changing the password. (*His voice grows troubled.*) It 's awfully difficult to get the password.

MR. DON.   What was it to-night?

DICK.   Love Bade Me Welcome.

(MR. DON *rises; he stares at his son.*)

MR. DON.   How did you get it, Dick?

DICK.   I 'm not sure. (*He seems to go closer to his father, as if for protection.*)   There are lots of things I don't understand yet.

DON.   There are things I don't understand either.   Dick, did you ever try to send messages—from there—to us?

DICK.   Me?   No.

MR. DON.   Or get messages from us?

DICK.   No.   How could we?

MR. DON.   Is there anything in it?

(*He is not speaking to his son. He goes to the little table and looks long at it. Has it taken on a sinister aspect? Those chairs, are they guarding a secret?*)

Dick, this table—your mother—how could they——

(*He turns to find that* DICK *has gone.*)

Dick!   My boy!   Dick!

(*The well-remembered voice leaves a message behind it.*)

DICK.   Face!

MARY ROSE

Produced at the Haymarket Theatre on April 22, 1920, with the
following cast :

Mrs. Otery	. . . . .	*Jean Cadell*
Mr. Morland	. . . . .	*Norman Forbes*
Mrs. Morland	. . . . .	*Mary Jerrold*
Mr. Amy .	. . . . .	*Arthur Whitby*
Mary Rose	. . . . .	*Fay Compton*
Harry ⎫ Simon Blake ⎭	. . . . .	*Robert Loraine*
Cameron	. . . . .	*Ernest Thesiger*

The play ran for 399 performances. Revivals: Haymarket,
January 21, 1926, and May 11, 1929.

ACT I

THE scene is a room in a small Sussex manor house that has long been for sale. It is such a silent room that whoever speaks first here is a bold one, unless indeed he merely mutters to himself, which they perhaps allow. All of this room's past which can be taken away has gone. Such light as there is comes from the only window, which is at the back and is incompletely shrouded in sacking. For a moment this is a mellow light, and if a photograph could be taken quickly we might find a disturbing smile on the room's face, perhaps like the Monna Lisa's, which came, surely, of her knowing what only the dead should know. There are two doors, one leading downstairs; the other is at the back, very insignificant, though it is the centre of this disturbing history. The wall-paper, heavy in the adherence of other papers of a still older date, has peeled and leans forward here and there in a grotesque bow, as men have hung in chains; one might predict that the next sound heard here will be in the distant future when another piece of paper loosens. Save for two packing-cases, the only furniture is a worn easy-chair doddering by the unlit fire, like some foolish old man. We might play with the disquieting fancy that this room, once warm with love, is still alive but is shrinking from observation, and that with our departure they cunningly set to again at the apparently never-ending search which goes on in some empty old houses.

Some one is heard clumping up the stair, and the caretaker enters. It is not she, however, who clumps; she has been here for several years, and has become sufficiently a part of the house to move noiselessly in it. The first thing we know about her is that she does not like to be in this room. She is an elderly woman of gaunt frame and with a singular control over herself. There may be some one, somewhere, who can make her laugh still, one never knows, but the effort would hurt her face. Even the war, lately ended, meant very little to her.

She has shown a number of possible purchasers over the house, just as she is showing one over it now, with the true caretaker's indifference whether you buy or not.   The few duties imposed on her here she performs conscientiously, but her greatest capacity is for sitting still in the dark.   Her work over, her mind a blank, she sits thus rather than pay for a candle.   One knows a little more about life when he knows the Mrs. Oterys, but she herself is unaware that she is peculiar, and probably thinks that in some such way do people in general pass the hour before bedtime.   Nevertheless, though saving of her candle in other empty houses, she always lights it on the approach of evening in this one.

The man who has clumped up the stairs in her wake is a young Australian soldier, a private, such as in those days you met by the dozen in any London street, slouching along it forlornly if alone, with sudden stoppages to pass the time (in which you ran against him), or in affable converse with a young lady.   In his voice is the Australian tang that became such a friendly sound to us.   He is a rough fellow, sinewy, with the clear eye of the man with the axe whose chief life-struggle till the war came was to fell trees and see to it that they did not crash down on him.   Mrs. Otery is showing him the house, which he has evidently known in other days, but though interested he is unsentimental and looks about him with a tolerant grin.

MRS. OTERY.   This was the drawing-room.

HARRY.   Not it, no, no, never.   This wasn't the drawing-room, my cabbage ;   at least not in my time.

MRS. OTERY (*indifferently*).   I only came here about three years ago and I never saw the house furnished, but I was told to say this was the drawing-room.   (*With a flicker of spirit*) And I would thank you not to call me your cabbage.

HARRY (*whom this kind of retort helps to put at his ease*).   No offence.   It's a French expression, and many a happy moment have I given to the mademoiselles by calling them cabbages. But the drawing-room !   I was a little shaver when I was here last, but I mind we called the drawing-room the Big Room ; it wasn't a little box like this.

MRS. OTERY.   This is the biggest room in the house.   (*She*

*quotes drearily from some advertisement which is probably
hanging in rags on the gate.)* Specially charming is the
drawing-room with its superb view of the Downs.   This
room is upstairs and is approached by——

HARRY.   By a stair, containing some romantic rat-holes.
Snakes, whether it's the room or not, it strikes cold ; there is
something shiversome about it.

(For the first time she gives him a sharp glance.)
I've shivered in many a shanty in Australy, and thought of the
big room at home and the warmth of it.   The warmth !   And
now this is the best it can do for the prodigal when he returns
to it expecting to see that calf done to a turn.   We live and
learn, missis.

MRS. OTERY.   We live, at any rate.

HARRY.   Well said, my cabbage.

MRS. OTERY.   Thank you, my rhododendron.

HARRY *(cheered)*.   I like your spirit.   You and me would
get on great if I had time to devote to your amusement.   But,
see here, I can make sure whether this was the drawing-room.
If it was, there is an apple-tree outside there, with one of its
branches scraping on the window.   I ought to know, for it
was out at the window down that apple-tree to the ground
that I slided one dark night when I was a twelve-year-old, ran
away from home, the naughty blue-eyed angel that I was, and
set off to make my fortune on the blasted ocean.   The fortune,
my—my lady friend—has still got the start of me, but the
apple-tree should be there to welcome her darling boy.

*(He pulls down the sacking, which lets a little more light
into the room.   We see that the window, which reaches
to the floor, opens outwards.   There were probably long
ago steps from it down into the garden, but they are gone
now, and gone too is the apple-tree.)*
I've won !   No tree : no drawing-room.

MRS. OTERY.   I have heard tell there was once a tree there ;
and you can see the root if you look down.

HARRY.   Yes, yes, I see it in the long grass, and a bit of the
seat that used to be round it.   This is the drawing-room right
enough, Harry, my boy.   There were blue curtains to that
window, and I used to hide behind them and pounce out upon
Robinson Crusoe.   There was a sofa at this end, and I had

my first lessons in swimming on it. You are a fortunate
woman, my petite, to be here drinking in these moving memories.
There used to be a peacock, too. Now, what the hell could a
peacock be doing in this noble apartment?

MRS. OTERY. I have been told a cloth used to hang on the
wall here, tapestries they're called, and that it had pictures of
peacocks on it. I dare say that was your peacock.

HARRY. Gone, even my peacock! And I could have
sworn I used to pull the feathers out of its tail. The clock was
in this corner, and it had a wheezy little figure of a smith that
used to come out and strike the hour on an anvil. My old
man used to wind that clock up every night, and I mind his
rage when he found out it was an eight-day clock. The padre
had to reprove him for swearing. Padre? What's the
English for padre? Damme, I'm forgetting my own
language. Oh yes, parson. Is *he* in the land of the
living still? I can see him clear, a long thin man with a
hard sharp face. He was always quarrelling about pictures
he collected.

MRS. OTERY. The parson here is a very old man, but he is
not tall and thin, he is little and roundish with a soft face and
white whiskers.

HARRY. Whiskers? I can't think he had whiskers.
(*Ruminating*) *Had* he whiskers? Stop a bit, I believe it is his
wife I'm thinking about. I doubt I don't give satisfaction as a
sentimental character. Is there any objection, your ladyship,
to smoking in the drawing-room?

MRS. OTERY (*ungraciously*). Smoke if you want.

(*He hacks into a cake of tobacco with a large clasp knife.*)
That's a fearsome-looking knife.

HARRY. Useful in trench warfare. It's not a knife, it's
a visiting-card. You leave it on favoured parties like this.

(*He casts it at one of the packing-cases, and it sticks quivering in the wood.*)

MRS. OTERY. Were you an officer?

HARRY. For a few minutes now and again.

MRS. OTERY. You're playing with me.

HARRY. You're so *ir*resistible.

MRS. OTERY. Do you want to see the other rooms?

HARRY. I was fondly hoping you would ask me that.

MRS. OTERY. Come along, then. (*She wants to lead him downstairs, but the little door at the back has caught his eye.*)

HARRY. What does that door open on?

MRS. OTERY (*avoiding looking at it*). Nothing, it's just a cupboard door.

HARRY (*considering her*). Who is playing with me now?

MRS. OTERY. I don't know what you mean. Come this way.

HARRY (*not budging*). I'll explain what I mean. That door—it's coming back to me—it leads into a little dark passage.

MRS. OTERY. That's all.

HARRY. That can't be all. Who ever heard of a passage wandering about by itself in a respectable house! It leads— yes—to a single room, and the door of the room faces this way.

(*He opens the door, and a door beyond is disclosed.*)

There's a memory for you! But what the hell made you want to deceive me?

MRS. OTERY. It's of no consequence.

HARRY. I think—yes—the room in there has two stone windows—and wooden rafters.

MRS. OTERY. It's the oldest part of the house.

HARRY. It comes back to me that I used to sleep there.

MRS. OTERY. That may be. If you'll come down with me——

HARRY. I'm curious to see that room first.

(*She bars the way.*)

MRS. OTERY (*thin-lipped and determined*). You can't go in there.

HARRY. Your reasons?

MRS. OTERY. It's—locked. I tell you it's just an empty room.

HARRY. There must be a key.

MRS. OTERY. It's—lost.

HARRY. Queer your anxiety to stop me, when you knew I would find the door locked.

MRS. OTERY. Sometimes it's locked; sometimes not.

HARRY. Is it not you that locks it?

MRS. OTERY (*reluctantly*). It's never locked, it's held.

HARRY. Who holds it?

MRS. OTERY (*in a little outburst*). Quiet, man.

HARRY. You 're all shivering.

MRS. OTERY. I 'm not.

HARRY (*cunningly*). I suppose you are just shivering because the room is so chilly.

MRS. OTERY (*falling into the trap*). That 's it.

HARRY. So you *are* shivering !

(*She makes no answer, and he reflects with the help of his pipe.*)

May I put a light to these bits of sticks ?

MRS. OTERY. If you like. My orders are to have fires once a week.

(*He lights the twigs in the fireplace, and they burn up easily, but will be ashes in a few minutes.*)

You can't have the money to buy a house like this.

HARRY. Not me. It was just my manly curiosity to see the old home that brought me. I 'm for Australy again. (*Suddenly turning on her*) What is wrong with this house ?

MRS. OTERY (*on her guard*). There is nothing wrong with it.

HARRY. Then how is it going so cheap ?

MRS. OTERY. It 's—in bad repair.

HARRY. Why has it stood empty so long ?

MRS. OTERY. It 's—far from a town.

HARRY. What made the last tenant leave in such a hurry ?

MRS. OTERY (*wetting her lips*). You have heard that, have you ? Gossiping in the village, I suppose ?

HARRY. I have heard some other things as well. I have heard they had to get a caretaker from a distance, because no woman hereabout would live alone in this house.

MRS. OTERY. A pack o' cowards.

HARRY. I have heard that that caretaker was bold and buxom when she came, and that now she is a scared woman.

MRS. OTERY. I 'm not.

HARRY. I have heard she 's been known to run out into the fields and stay there trembling half the night.

(*She does not answer, and he resorts to cunning again.*)

Of course, I see they couldn't have meant you. Just foolish stories that gather about an old house.

MRS. OTERY (*relieved*). That 's all.

HARRY (*quickly, as he looks at the little door*). What 's that ?

(MRS. OTERY *screams.*)

I got you that time! What was it you expected to see?
(*No answer.*)
Is it a ghost? They say it's a ghost. What is it gives this
house an ill name?

MRS. OTERY.   Use as brave words as you like when you have
gone, but I advise you, my lad, to keep a civil tongue while you are
here. (*In her everyday voice*) There is no use showing you the rest
of the house. If you want to be stepping, I have my work to do.

HARRY.   We have got on so nicely, I wonder if you would
give me a mug of tea. Not a cup, we drink it by the mugful
where I hail from.

MRS. OTERY (*ungraciously*).   I have no objection.

HARRY.   Since you are so pressing, I accept.

MRS. OTERY.   Come down, then, to the kitchen.

HARRY.   No, no, I'm sure the Prodigal got his tea in the
drawing-room, though what made them make such a fuss about
that man beats me.

MRS. OTERY (*sullenly*).   You are meaning to go into that
room. I wouldn't if I was you.

HARRY.   If you were me you would.

MRS. OTERY (*closing the little door*).   Until I have your
promise——

HARRY (*liking the tenacity of her*).   Very well, I promise—
unless, of course, she comes peeping out at the handsome
gentleman. Your ghost has naught to do wi' me. It's a
woman, isn't it?

(*Her silence is perhaps an assent.*)
See here, I'll sit in this chair till you come back, saying my
prayers. (*Feeling the chair*) You're clammy cold, old dear.
It's not the ghost's chair by any chance, is it?

(*No answer.*)
You needn't look so scared, woman; she doesn't walk till
midnight, does she?

MRS. OTERY (*looking at his knife in the wood*).   I wouldn't
leave that knife lying about.

HARRY.   Oh, come, give the old girl a chance.

MRS. OTERY.   I'll not be more than ten minutes.

HARRY.   She can't do much in ten minutes.

(*At which remark* MRS. OTERY *fixes him with her eyes and
departs.*

HARRY *is now sitting sunk in the chair, staring at the fire. It goes out, but he remains there motionless, and in the increasing dusk he ceases to be an intruder. He is now part of the room, the part long waited for, come back at last. The house is shaken to its foundation by his presence, we may conceive a thousand whispers. Then the crafty work begins. The little door at the back opens slowly to the extent of a foot. Thus might a breath of wind blow it if there were any wind. Presently* HARRY *starts to his feet, convinced that there is some one in the room, very near his knife. He is so sure of the exact spot where she is that for a moment he looks nowhere else.*

In that moment the door slowly closes. He has not seen it close, but he opens it and calls out, ' Who is that? Is any one there ? ' With some distaste he enters the passage and tries the inner door, but whether it be locked or held it will not open. He is about to pocket his knife, then with a shrug of bravado sends it quivering back into the wood— for her if she can get it. He returns to the chair, but not to close his eyes ; to watch and to be watched. The room is in a tremble of desire to get started upon that nightly travail which can never be completed till this man is here to provide the end.

The figure of HARRY *becomes indistinct and fades from sight. When the haze lifts we are looking at the room as it was some thirty years earlier on the serene afternoon that began its troubled story. There are rooms that are always smiling, so that you may see them at it if you peep through the keyhole, and* MRS. MORLAND'S *little drawing-room is one of them. Perhaps these are smiles that she has left lying about. She leaves many things lying about ; for instance, one could deduce the shape of her from studying that corner of the sofa which is her favourite seat, and all her garments grow so like her that her wardrobes are full of herself hanging on nails or folded away in drawers. The pictures on her walls in time take on a resemblance to her or hers though they may be meant to represent a waterfall, every present given to her assumes some characteristic of the donor, and no doubt the necktie she is at present knitting will soon be able to pass as the person for whom it is being knit. It is*

*only delightful ladies at the most agreeable age who have
this personal way with their belongings. Among* MRS.
MORLAND'S *friends in the room are several of whom we
have already heard, such as the blue curtains from which*
HARRY *pounced upon the castaway, the sofa on which he
had his first swimming lessons, the peacock on the wall, the
clock with the smart smith ready to step out and strike his
anvil, and the apple-tree is in full blossom at the open
window, one of its branches has even stepped into the room.*

MR. MORLAND *and the local clergyman are chatting importantly about some matter of no importance, while* MRS.
MORLAND *is on her sofa at the other side of the room, coming
into the conversation occasionally with a cough or a click of
her needles, which is her clandestine way of telling her
husband not to be so assertive to his guest. They are all
middle-aged people who have found life to be on the whole
an easy and happy adventure, and have done their tranquil
best to make it so for their neighbours. The squire is lean,
the clergyman of full habit, but could you enter into them you
would have difficulty in deciding which was clergyman and
which was squire ; both can be peppery, the same pepper.
They are benignant creatures, but could exchange benig-
nancies without altering.* MRS. MORLAND *knows everything
about her husband except that she does nearly all his work
for him. She really does not know this. His work, though
he rises early to be at it, is not much larger than a lady's
handkerchief, and consists of magisterial duties, with now
and then an impressive scene about a tenant's cowshed.
She then makes up his mind for him, and is still unaware
that she is doing it. He has so often heard her say (believing it, too) that he is difficult to move when once he puts his
foot down that he accepts himself modestly as a man of this
character, and never tries to remember when it was that
he last put down his foot. In the odd talks which the
happily married sometimes hold about the future he always
hopes he will be taken first, being the managing one, and she
says little beyond pressing his hand, but privately she has
decided that there must be another arrangement. Probably
life at the vicarage is on not dissimilar lines, but we cannot
tell, as we never meet* MR. AMY'S *wife.* MR. AMY *is even*

more sociable than MR. MORLAND ; *he is reputed to know
every one in the county, and has several times fallen off his
horse because he will salute all passers-by.   On his visits to
London he usually returns depressed because there are so
many people in the streets to whom he may not give a friendly
bow.   He likes to read a book if he knows the residence or a
relative of the author, and at the play it is far more to him
to learn that the actress has three children, one of them down
with measles, than to follow her histrionic genius.   He and
his host have the pleasant habit of print-collecting, and a very
common scene between them is that which now follows.
They are bent over the squire's latest purchase.)*

MR. AMY.   Very interesting.   A nice little lot.   I must say,
James, you have the collector's flair.

MR. MORLAND.   Oh, well, I 'm keen, you know, and when
I run up to London I can't resist going a bust in my small way.
I picked these up quite cheap.

MR. AMY.   The flair.   That is what you have.

MR. MORLAND.   Oh, I don't know.

MR. AMY.   Yes, you have, James.   You got them at
Peterkin's in Dean Street, didn't you ?   Yes, I know you did.
I saw them there.   I wanted them too, but they told me you
had already got the refusal.

MR. MORLAND.   Sorry to have been too quick for you,
George, but it is my way to nip in.   You have some nice prints
yourself.

MR. AMY.   I haven't got your flair, James.

MR. MORLAND.   I admit I don't miss much.

(So far it has been a competition in saintliness.)

MR. AMY   No.   *(The saint leaves him.)*   You missed
something yesterday at Peterkin's, though.

MR. MORLAND.   How do you mean ?

MR. AMY.   You didn't examine the little lot lying beneath
this lot.

MR. MORLAND.   I turned them over ;   just a few odds and
ends of no account.

MR. AMY *(with horrible complacency).*   All except one, James.

MR. MORLAND *(twitching).*   Something good ?

MR. AMY *(at his meekest).*   Just a little trifle of a Gainsborough.

MR. MORLAND (*faintly*). What ! You 've got it ?

MR. AMY. I 've got it. I am a poor man, but I thought ten pounds wasn't too much for a Gainsborough.

(*The devil now has them both.*)

MR. MORLAND. Ten pounds ! Is it signed ?

MR. AMY. No, it isn't signed.

MR. MORLAND (*almost his friend again*). Ah !

MR. AMY. What do you precisely mean by that ' Ah,' James ? If it had been signed, could I have got it for ten pounds ? You are always speaking about your flair ; I suppose I can have a little flair sometimes too.

MR. MORLAND. I am not always speaking about my flair, and I don't believe it is a Gainsborough.

MR. AMY (*with dignity*). Please don't get hot, James. If I had thought you would grudge me my little find—which *you* missed—I wouldn't have brought it to show you.

(*With shocking exultation he produces a roll of paper.*)

MR. MORLAND (*backing from it*). So that 's it.

MR. AMY. This is it. (*The squire has to examine it like a Christian.*) There ! I have the luck this time. I hope you will have it next. (*The exultation passes from the one face into the other.*)

MR. MORLAND. Interesting, George—quite. But definitely not a Gainsborough.

MR. AMY. I say definitely a Gainsborough.

MR. MORLAND. Definitely not a Gainsborough.

(*By this time the needles have entered into the controversy, but they are disregarded.*)

I should say the work of a clever amateur.

MR. AMY. Look at the drawing of the cart and the figure beside it.

MR. MORLAND. Weak and laboured. Look at that horse.

MR. AMY. Gainsborough did some very funny horses.

MR. MORLAND. Granted, but he never placed them badly. That horse destroys the whole balance of the composition.

MR. AMY. James, I had no idea you had such a small nature.

MR. MORLAND. I don't like that remark ; for your sake I don't like it. No one would have been more pleased than myself if you had picked up a Gainsborough. But this ! Besides, look at the paper.

MR. AMY. What is wrong with the paper, Mr. Morland ?

MR. MORLAND. It is machine-made. Gainsborough was in his grave years before that paper was made.

(*After further inspection* MR. AMY *is convinced against his will, and the find is returned to his pocket less carefully than it had been produced.*)

Don't get into a tantrum about it, George.

MR. AMY (*grandly*). I am not in a tantrum, and I should be obliged if you wouldn't George me. Smile on, Mr. Morland, I congratulate you on your triumph ; you have hurt an old friend to the quick. Bravo, bravo. Thank you, Mrs. Morland, for a very pleasant visit. Good-day.

MRS. MORLAND (*prepared*). I shall see you into your coat, George.

MR. AMY. I thank you, Mrs. Morland, but I need no one to see me into my coat. Good-day.

(*He goes, and she blandly follows him. She returns with the culprit.*)

MRS. MORLAND. Now which of you is to say it first ?

MR. AMY. James, I am heartily ashamed of myself.

MR. MORLAND. George, I apologise.

MR. AMY. I quite see that it isn't a Gainsborough.

MR. MORLAND. After all, it 's certainly in the Gainsborough school.

(*They clasp hands sheepishly, but the peacemaker helps the situation by showing a roguish face, and* MR. AMY *departs shaking a humorous fist at her.*)

MRS. MORLAND. I coughed so often, James ; and you must have heard me clicking.

MR. MORLAND. I heard all right. Good old George ! It 's a pity he has no flair. He might as well order his prints by wireless.

MRS. MORLAND. What is that ?

MR. MORLAND. Wireless it 's to be called. There is an article about it in that paper. The fellow says that before many years have passed we shall be able to talk to ships on the ocean.

MRS. MORLAND (*who has resumed her knitting*). Nonsense, James.

MR. MORLAND. Of course it 's nonsense. And yet there is

no denying, as he says, that there are more things in heaven and earth than are dreamt of in our philosophy.

MRS. MORLAND (*becoming grave*).   You and I know that to be true, James.

(*For a moment he does not know to what she is referring.*)

MR. MORLAND (*edging away from trouble*).   Oh, that.   My dear, that is all dead and done with long ago.

MRS. MORLAND (*thankfully*).   Yes.   But sometimes when I look at Mary Rose—so happy——

MR. MORLAND.   She will never know anything about it.

MRS. MORLAND.   No, indeed.   But some day she will fall in love——

MR. MORLAND (*wriggling*).   That infant !   Fanny, is it wise to seek trouble before it comes ?

MRS. MORLAND.   She can't marry, James, without your first telling the man.   We agreed.

MR. MORLAND.   Yes, I supppose I must—though I 'm not certain I ought to.   Sleeping dogs——   Still, I 'll keep my word, I 'll tell him everything.

MRS. MORLAND.   Poor Mary Rose.

MR. MORLAND (*manfully*).   Now then, none of that.   Where is she now ?

MRS. MORLAND.   Down at the boat-house with Simon, I think.

MR. MORLAND.   That is all right.   Let her play about with Simon and the like.   It may make a tomboy of her, but it will keep young men out of her head.

(*She wonders at his obtuseness.*)

MRS. MORLAND.   You still think of Simon as a boy ?

MR. MORLAND.   Bless the woman, he is only a midshipman.

MRS. MORLAND.   A sub-lieutenant now.

MR. MORLAND.   Same thing.   Why, Fanny, I still tip him. At least I did a year ago.   And he liked it : ' Thanks no end, you are a trump,' he said, and then slipped behind the screen to see how much it was.

MRS. MORLAND.   He is a very delightful creature ; but he isn't a boy any more.

MR. MORLAND.   It 's not nice of you to put such ideas into my head.   I 'll go down to the boat-house at once.   If this new invention was in working order, Fanny, I could send him packing without rising from my seat.   I should simply say from this sofa, ' Is my little Mary Rose there ? '

(*To their surprise there is an answer from* MARY ROSE *unseen.*)

MARY ROSE (*in a voice more quaking than is its wont*).   I 'm here, Daddy.

MR. MORLAND (*rising*).   Where are you, Mary Rose ?

MARY ROSE.   I am in the apple-tree.

(MRS. MORLAND *smiles and is going to the window, but her husband checks her with a further exhibition of the marvel of the future.*)

MR. MORLAND.   What are you doing in the apple-tree, hoyden ?

MARY ROSE.   I 'm hiding.

MR. MORLAND.   From Simon ?

MARY ROSE.   No ; I 'm not sure whom I 'm hiding from. From myself, I think.   Daddy, I 'm frightened.

MR. MORLAND.   What has frightened you ?   Simon ?

MARY ROSE.   Yes—partly.

MR. MORLAND.   Who else ?

MARY ROSE.   I am most afraid of my daddy.

MR. MORLAND (*rather flattered*).   Of me ?

(*If there is anything strange about this girl of eighteen who steps from the tree into the room, it is an elusiveness of which she is unaware.   It has remained hidden from her girl friends, though in the after years, in the brief space before they forget her, they will probably say, because of what happened, that there was always something a little odd about* MARY ROSE.   *This oddness might be expressed thus, that the happiness and glee of which she is almost overfull know of another attribute of her that never plays with them.*

There is nothing splendid about MARY ROSE, *never can she become one of those secret women so much less innocent than she, yet perhaps so much sweeter in the kernel, who are the bane or glory, or the bane and glory, of greater lovers than she could ever understand.   She is just a rare and lovely flower, far less fitted than those others for the tragic rôle.*

She butts her head into MRS. MORLAND *with a childish impulsiveness that might overthrow a less accustomed bosom.*)

MARY ROSE (*telling everything*). Mother !

MR. MORLAND. You don't mean that anything has really frightened you, Mary Rose ?

MARY ROSE. I am not sure. Hold me tight, Mother.

MRS. MORLAND. Darling, has Simon been disturbing you ?

MARY ROSE (*liking this way of putting it*). Yes, he has. It is all Simon's fault.

MR. MORLAND. But you said you were afraid even of me.

MARY ROSE. You are the only one.

MR. MORLAND. Is this some game ? Where is Simon ?

MARY ROSE (*in little mouthfuls*). He is at the foot of the tree. He is not coming up by the tree. He wants to come in by the door. That shows how important it is.

MR. MORLAND. What is ?

MARY ROSE. You see, his leave is up to-morrow, and he—wants to see you, Daddy, before he goes.

MR. MORLAND. I am sure he does. And I know why. I told you, Fanny. Mary Rose, do you see my purse lying about ?

MARY ROSE. Your purse, Dad ?

MR. MORLAND. Yes, you gosling. There is a fiver in it, and *that* is what Master Simon wants to see me about.

(MARY ROSE *again seeks her mother's breast.*)

MRS. MORLAND. Oh, James ! Dearest, tell me what Simon has been saying to you ; whisper it, my love.

(MARY ROSE *whispers.*)

Yes, I thought it was that.

MARY ROSE. I am frightened to tell Daddy.

MRS. MORLAND. James, you may as well be told bluntly ; it isn't your fiver that Simon wants, it is your daughter.

(MR. MORLAND *is aghast, and* MARY ROSE *rushes into his arms to help him in this terrible hour.*)

MARY ROSE (*as the injured party*). You will scold him, won't you, Dad ?

MR. MORLAND (*vainly trying to push her from him*). By—by —by the—by all that is horrible I 'll do more than scold him. The puppy, I 'll—I 'll——

MARY ROSE (*entreating*). Not more than scold him, Daddy—not more. Mary Rose couldn't bear it if it was more.

MR. MORLAND (*blankly*). You are not in love with Simon, are you ?

MARY ROSE. Oh-h-h-h !

(*She makes little runnings from the one parent to the other, carrying kisses for the wounds.*)

Daddy, I am so awfully sorry that this has occurred. Mummy, what can we do ? (*She cries.*)

MRS. MORLAND (*soothing her*). My own, my pet. But he is only a boy, Mary Rose, just a very nice boy.

MARY ROSE (*awed*). Mother, that is the wonderful, wonderful thing. He was just a boy——I quite understand that——he was a mere boy till to-day ; and then, Daddy, he suddenly changed ; all at once he became a man. It was while he was ——telling me. You will scarcely know him now, Mother.

MRS. MORLAND. Darling, he breakfasted with us ; I think I shall know him still.

MARY ROSE. He is quite different from breakfast-time. He doesn't laugh any more, he would never think of capsizing the punt intentionally now, he has grown so grave, so manly, so——so *protective*, he thinks of everything now, of freeholds and leaseholds, and gravel soil, and hot and cold, and the hire system.

(*She cries again, but her eyes are sparkling through the rain.*)

MR. MORLAND (*with spirit*). He has got as far as that, has he ! Does he propose that this marriage should take place to-morrow ?

MARY ROSE (*eager to soften the blow*). Oh no, not for quite a long time. At earliest, not till his next leave.

MRS. MORLAND. Mary Rose !

MARY ROSE. He is waiting down there, Mummy. May I bring him in ?

MRS. MORLAND. Of course, dearest.

MR. MORLAND. Don't come with him, though.

MARY ROSE. Oh ! (*She wonders what this means.*) You know how shy Simon is.

MR. MORLAND. I do not.

MRS. MORLAND. Your father and I must have a talk with him alone, you see.

MARY ROSE. I——I suppose so. He so wants to do the right thing, Mother.

MRS. MORLAND.　I am sure he does.

MARY ROSE.　Do you mind my going upstairs into the apple-room and sometimes knocking on the floor ?　I think it would be a help to him to know I am so near by.

MRS. MORLAND.　It would be a help to all of us, my sweet.

MARY ROSE (*plaintively*).　You—you won't try to put him against me, Daddy ?

MR. MORLAND.　I would try my hardest if I thought I had any chance.

(*When she has gone they are a somewhat forlorn pair.*) Poor old mother !

MRS. MORLAND.　Poor old father !　There couldn't be a nicer boy, though.

MR. MORLAND.　No, but—— (*He has a distressing thought.*)

MRS. MORLAND (*quietly*).　Yes, there 's that.

MR. MORLAND.　It got me on the quick when she said, ' You won't try to put him against me, Daddy '—because that is just what I suppose I have got to do.

MRS. MORLAND.　He must be told.

MR. MORLAND (*weakly*).　Fanny, let us keep it to ourselves.

MRS. MORLAND.　It would not be fair to him.

MR. MORLAND.　No, it wouldn't. (*Testily*) He will be an ass if it bothers him.

MRS. MORLAND (*timidly*).　Yes.

(SIMON *comes in, a manly youth of twenty-three in naval uniform. Whether he has changed much since breakfast-time we have no means of determining, but he is sufficiently attractive to make one hope that there will be no further change in the immediate future. He seems younger even than his years, because he is trying to look as if a decade or so had passed since the incident of the boat-house and he were now a married man of approved standing. He has come with honeyed words upon his lips, but suddenly finds that he is in the dock. His judges survey him silently, and he can only reply with an idiotic but perhaps ingratiating laugh.*)

SIMON.　Ha, ha, ha, ha, ha, ha, ha, ha ! (*He ceases uncomfortably, like one who has made his statement.*)

MR. MORLAND.   You will need to say more than that, you know, Simon, to justify your conduct.

MRS. MORLAND.   Oh, Simon, how could you !

SIMON (*with a sinking*).   It seems almost like stealing.

MR. MORLAND.   It is stealing.

SIMON (*prudently*).   Ha, ha, ha, ha, ha, ha !

(*From the ceiling there comes a gentle tapping, as from a senior officer who is indicating that England expects her lieutenant this day to do his duty. SIMON inflates.*)

It is beastly hard on you, of course ; but if you knew what Mary Rose is !

MRS. MORLAND (*pardonably*).   We feel that even we know to some extent what Mary Rose is.

SIMON (*tacking*).   Yes, rather ; and so you can see how it has come about.   (*This effort cheers him.*)   I would let myself be cut into little chips for her ; I should almost like it.   (*With a brief glance at his misspent youth.*)   Perhaps you have thought that I was a rather larky sort in the past ?

MR. MORLAND (*sarcastically*).   We see an extraordinary change in you, Simon.

SIMON (*eagerly*).   Have you noticed that ?   Mary Rose has noticed it too.   That is my inner man coming out.   (*Carefully*) To some young people marriage is a thing to be entered on lightly, but that is not my style.   What I want is to give up larks, and all that, and insure my life, and read the political articles.

(*Further knocking from above reminds him of something else.*)

Yes, and I promise you it won't be like losing a daughter but like gaining a son.

MRS. MORLAND.   Did Mary Rose tell you to say that ?

SIMON (*guiltily*).   Well—— (*Tap, tap.*)   Oh, another thing, I should consider it well worth being married to Mary Rose just to have you, Mrs. Morland, for a mother-in-law.

MR. MORLAND (*pleased*).   Well said, Simon ; I like you the better for that.

MRS. MORLAND (*a demon*).   Did she tell you to say that also ?

SIMON.   Well—— At any rate, never shall I forget the respect and affection I owe to the parents of my beloved wife.

MR. MORLAND.   She is not your wife yet, you know.

SIMON (*handsomely*). No, she isn't. But can she be? Mrs. Morland, can she be?

MRS. MORLAND. That is as may be, Simon. It is only a possible engagement that we are discussing at present.

SIMON. Yes, yes, of course. (*Becoming more difficult to resist as his reason goes.*) I used to be careless about money, but I have thought of a trick of writing the word Economy in the inside of my watch, so that I 'll see it every time I wind up. My people——

MR. MORLAND. We like them, Simon.

(*The tapping is resumed.*)

SIMON. I don't know whether you have noticed a sound from up above?

MR. MORLAND. I did think I heard something.

SIMON. That is Mary Rose in the apple-room.

MRS. MORLAND. No!

SIMON. Yes; she is doing that to help me. I promised to knock back as soon as I thought things were going well. What do you say? May I?

(*He gives them an imploring look, and mounts a chair, part of a fishing-rod in his hand.*)

MR. MORLAND (*an easy road in sight*). I think, Fanny, he might?

MRS. MORLAND (*braver*). No. (*Tremulously*) There is a little thing, Simon, that Mary Rose's father and I feel we ought to tell you about her before—before you knock, my dear. It is not very important, I think, but it is something she doesn't know of herself, and it makes her a little different from other girls.

SIMON (*alighting—sharply*). I won't believe anything against Mary Rose.

MRS. MORLAND. We have nothing to tell you against her.

MR. MORLAND. It is just something that happened, Simon. She couldn't help it. It hasn't troubled us in the least for years, but we always agreed that she mustn't be engaged before we told the man. We must have your promise, before we tell you, that you will keep it to yourself.

SIMON (*frowning*). I promise.

MRS. MORLAND. You must never speak of it even to her.

SIMON.   Not to Mary Rose ?   I wish you would say quickly what it is.

(*They are now sitting round the little table.*)

MR. MORLAND.   It can't be told quite in a word.   It happened seven years ago, when Mary Rose was eleven.   We were in a remote part of Scotland—in the Outer Hebrides.

SIMON.   I once went on shore there from the *Gadfly*, very bleak and barren, rocks and rough grass, I never saw a tree.

MR. MORLAND.   It is mostly like that.   There is a whaling-station.   We went because I was fond of fishing.   I haven't had the heart to fish since.   Quite close to the inn where we put up there is—a little island.

(*He sees that little island so clearly that he forgets to go on.*)

MRS. MORLAND.   It is quite a small island, Simon, uninhabited, no sheep even.   I suppose there are only about six acres of it.   There are trees there, quite a number of them, Scotch firs and a few rowan-trees,—they have red berries, you know.   There seemed to us to be nothing very particular about the island, unless, perhaps, that it is curiously complete in itself.   There is a tiny pool in it that might be called a lake, out of which a stream flows.   It has hillocks and a glade, a sort of miniature land.   That was all we noticed, though it became the most dreaded place in the world to us.

MR. MORLAND (*considerately*).   I can tell him without your being here, Fanny.

MRS. MORLAND.   I prefer to stay, James.

MR. MORLAND.   I fished a great deal in the loch between that island and the larger one.   The sea-trout were wonderful. I often rowed Mary Rose across to the island and left her there to sketch.   She was fond of sketching in those days, we thought them pretty things.   I could see her from the boat most of the time, and we used to wave to each other.   Then I would go back for her when I stopped fishing.

MRS. MORLAND.   I didn't often go with them.   We didn't know at the time that the natives had a superstition against landing on the island, and that it was supposed to resent this. It had a Gaelic name which means ' The Island that Likes to be Visited.'   Mary Rose knew nothing of this, and she was very fond of her island.   She used to talk to it, call it her darling, things like that.

SIMON (*restless*). Tell me what happened.

MR. MORLAND. It was on what was to be our last day. I had landed her on this island as usual, and in the early evening I pulled across to take her off. From the boat I saw her, sitting on a stump of a tree that was her favourite seat, and she waved gaily to me and I to her. Then I rowed over, with, of course, my back to her. I had less than a hundred yards to go, but, Simon, when I got across she wasn't there.

SIMON. You seem so serious about it. She was hiding from you ?

MRS. MORLAND. She wasn't on the island, Simon.

SIMON. But—but—oh, but——

MR. MORLAND. Don't you think I searched and searched ?

MRS. MORLAND. All of us. No one in the village went to bed that night. It was then we learned how they feared the island.

MR. MORLAND. The little pool was dragged. There was nothing we didn't try ; but she was gone.

SIMON (*distressed*). I can't—there couldn't—but never mind that. Tell me how you found her.

MRS. MORLAND. It was the twentieth day after she disappeared. Twenty days !

SIMON. Some boat—— ?

MR. MORLAND. There was no boat but mine.

SIMON. Tell me.

MRS. MORLAND. The search had long been given up, but we couldn't come away.

MR. MORLAND. I was wandering one day along the shore of the loch, you can imagine in what state of mind. I stopped and stood looking across the water at the island, and, Simon, I saw her sitting on the tree-trunk sketching.

MRS. MORLAND. Mary Rose !

MR. MORLAND. She waved to me and went on sketching. I—I waved back to her. I got into the boat and rowed across just in the old way, except that I sat facing her, so that I could see her all the time. When I landed, the first thing she said to me was, 'Why did you row in that funny way, Dad ?' Then I saw at once that she didn't know anything had happened.

SIMON. Mr. Morland ! How could—— ? Where did she say she had been ?

MRS. MORLAND. She didn't know she had been anywhere, Simon.

MR. MORLAND. She thought I had just come for her at the usual time.

SIMON. Twenty days. You mean she had been on the island all that time ?

MR. MORLAND. We don't know.

MRS. MORLAND. James brought her back to me just the same merry unselfconscious girl, with no idea that she had been away from me for more than an hour or two.

SIMON. But when you told her——

MRS. MORLAND. We never told her ; she doesn't know now.

SIMON. Surely you——

MRS. MORLAND. We had her back again, Simon ; that was the great thing. At first we thought to tell her after we got her home ; and then, it was all so inexplicable, we were afraid to alarm her, to take the bloom off her. In the end we decided never to tell her.

SIMON. You told no one ?

MR. MORLAND. Several doctors.

SIMON. How did they explain it ?

MR. MORLAND. They had no explanation for it except that it never took place. You can think that, too, if you like.

SIMON. I don't know what to think. It has had no effect on her, at any rate.

MR. MORLAND. None whatever—and you can guess how we used to watch.

MRS. MORLAND. Simon, I am very anxious to be honest with you. I have sometimes thought that our girl is curiously young for her age—as if—you know how just a touch of frost may stop the growth of a plant and yet leave it blooming—it has sometimes seemed to me as if a cold finger had once touched my Mary Rose.

SIMON. Mrs. Morland !

MRS. MORLAND. There is nothing in it.

SIMON. What you are worrying about is just her innocence —which seems a holy thing to me.

MRS. MORLAND. And indeed it is.

SIMON. If that is all——

MR. MORLAND. We have sometimes thought that she had momentary glimpses back into that time, but before we could question her in a cautious way about them the gates had closed and she remembered nothing. You never saw her talking to —to some person who wasn't there ?

SIMON. No.

MRS. MORLAND. Nor listening, as it were, for some sound that never came ?

SIMON. A sound ? Do you mean a sound from the island ?

MRS. MORLAND. Yes, we think so. But at any rate she has long outgrown those fancies.

(*She fetches a sketch-book from a drawer.*)
Here are the sketches she made. You can take the book away with you and look at them at your leisure.

SIMON. It is a little curious that she has never spoken to me of that holiday. She tells me everything.

MRS. MORLAND. No, that isn't curious, it is just that the island has faded from her memory. I should be troubled if she began to recall it. Well, Simon, we felt we had to tell you. That is all we know, I am sure it is all we shall ever know. What are you going to do ?

SIMON. What do you think !

(*He mounts the chair again, and knocks triumphantly. A happy tapping replies.*)
You heard ? That means it 's all right. You 'll see how she 'll come tearing down to us !

MRS. MORLAND (*kissing him*). You dear boy, you will see how I shall go tearing up to her. (*She goes off.*)

SIMON. I do love Mary Rose, sir.

MR. MORLAND. So do we, Simon. I suppose that made us love her a little more than other daughters are loved. Well, it is dead and done with, and it doesn't disturb me now at all. I hope you won't let it disturb you.

SIMON (*undisturbed*). Rather not. (*Disturbed*) I say, I wonder whether I *have* noticed her listening for a sound ?

MR. MORLAND. Not you. We did wisely, didn't we, in not questioning her ?

SIMON. Oh lord, yes. 'The Island that Likes to be Visited.' It is a queer name. (*Boyishly*) I say, let 's forget all about it. (*He looks at the ceiling.*) I almost wish her mother hadn't gone up to her. It will make Mary Rose longer in coming down.

MR. MORLAND (*humorous*). Fanny will think of nicer things to say to her than you could think of, Simon.

SIMON. Yes, I know. Ah, now you are chaffing me. (*Apologetically*) You see, sir, my leave is up to-morrow.

(MARY ROSE *comes rushing in.*)

Mary Rose !

(*She darts past him into her father's arms.*)

MARY ROSE. It isn't you I am thinking of ; it is father, it is poor father. Oh, Simon, how could you ? Isn't it hateful of him, Daddy !

MR. MORLAND. I should just say it is. Is your mother crying too ?

MARY ROSE (*squeaking*). Yes.

MR. MORLAND. I see I am going to have an abominable day. If you two don't mind very much being left alone, I think I 'll go up and sit in the apple-room and cry with your mother. It is close and dark and musty up there, and when we feel we can't stick it any longer I 'll knock on the floor, Simon, as a sign that we are coming down.

(*He departs on this light note. We see how the minds of these two children match.*)

SIMON. Mary Rose !

MARY ROSE. Oh, Simon—you and me.

SIMON. You and me, that 's it. We are *us*, now. Do you like it ?

MARY ROSE. It is so fearfully solemn.

SIMON. You are not frightened, are you ?

(*She nods.*)

Not at me ?

(*She shakes her head.*)

What at ?

MARY ROSE. At *it*—— Being—married. Simon, after we are married you will sometimes let me play, won't you ?

SIMON. Games ?

(*She nods.*)

Rather. Why, I 'll go on playing rugger myself. Lots of married people play games.

MARY ROSE (*relieved*). I 'm glad ; Simon, do you love me ?

SIMON. Dearest — precious — my life — my sweetheart. Which name do you like best?

MARY ROSE. I'm not sure. They are all very nice. (*She is conscious of the ceiling.*) Oughtn't we to knock to those beloveds to come down?

SIMON. Please don't. I know a lot about old people, darling. I assure you they don't mind very much sitting in dull places.

MARY ROSE. We mustn't be selfish.

SIMON. Honest Injun, it isn't selfishness. You see, I have a ton of things to tell you. About how I put it to them, and how I remembered what you told me to say, and the way I got the soft side of them. They have heard it all already, so it would really be selfish to bring them down.

MARY ROSE. I'm not so sure.

SIMON. I'll tell you what we'll do. Let's go back to the boat-house, and then they can come down and be cosy here.

MARY ROSE (*gleeful*). Let's! We can stay there till tea-time. (*She wants to whirl him away at once.*)

SIMON. It is fresh down there; put on a jacket, my star.

MARY ROSE. Oh, bother!

SIMON (*firmly*). My child, you are in my care now; I am responsible for you, and I order you to put on a jacket.

MARY ROSE. Order! Simon, you do say the loveliest things. I'll put it on at once.

(*She is going towards the little door at the back, but turns to say something important.*)

Simon, I'll tell you a funny thing about me. I may be wrong, but I think I'll sometimes love you to kiss me, and sometimes it will be better not.

SIMON. All right. Tell me, what were you thinking as you sat up there in the apple-room, waiting?

MARY ROSE. Holy things.

SIMON. About love?

(*She nods.*)

MARY ROSE. We'll try to be good, won't we, Simon, please?

SIMON. Rather. Honest Injun, we'll be nailers. Did you think of—our wedding-day?

MARY ROSE. A little.

SIMON. Only a little?

MARY ROSE. But frightfully clearly. (*Suddenly*) Simon, I had such a delicious idea about our honeymoon. There is a place in Scotland—in the Hebrides—I should love to go there.

SIMON (*taken aback*). The Hebrides ?

MARY ROSE. We once went to it when I was little. Isn't it funny, I had almost forgotten about that island, and then suddenly I saw it quite clearly as I was sitting up there. (*Senselessly*) Of course it was the little old woman who pointed it out to me.

(SIMON *is disturbed.*)

SIMON (*gently*). Mary Rose, there are only yourselves and the three maids in the house, aren't there ?

MARY ROSE (*surprised*). You know there are. Whatever makes you ask ?

SIMON (*cautiously*). I thought—I thought I had a glimpse of a little old woman on the stair to-day.

MARY ROSE (*interested*). Who on earth could that be ?

SIMON. It doesn't matter, I had made a mistake. Tell me, what was there particular about that place in the Hebrides ?

MARY ROSE. Oh, the fishing for father. But there was an island where I often—— My little island !

SIMON (*perhaps quite unnecessarily*). What are you listening for, Mary Rose ?

MARY ROSE. Was I ? I don't hear anything. Oh, my dear, my dear, I should love to show you the tree-trunk and the rowan-tree where I used to sketch while father was in the boat. I expect he used to land me on the island because it was such a safe place.

SIMON (*troubled*). That had been the idea. I am not going to spend my honeymoon by the sea, though. And yet I should like to go to the Hebrides—some day—to see that island.

MARY ROSE. Yes, let 's.

(*She darts off through the little door for her jacket.*)

ACT II

An island in the Outer Hebrides. A hundred yards away, across the loch at the back, may be seen the greater island of which this might be but a stone cast into the sea by some giant hand : perhaps an evil stone which the big island had to spew forth but could not sink. It is fair to look upon to-day, all its menace hidden under mosses of various hues that are a bath to the eye ; an island placid as a cow grazing or a sulky lady asleep. The sun which has left the bleak hills beyond is playing hide and seek on it ; one suddenly has the curious fancy to ask, with whom ? A blessed spot it might be thought, rather than sinister, were there not those two trees, a fir and a rowan, their arms outstretched for ever southward, as if they had been struck while in full flight and could no longer pray to their gods to carry them away from this island. A young Highlander, a Cameron, passes in a boat at the back. Mary Rose and Simon come into view on the island. We have already heard them swishing a way through whins and bracken that are unseen. They are dressed as English people dress in Scotland. They have been married for four years and are still the gay young creatures of their engagement day. Their talk is the happy nonsense that leaves no ripple unless the unexpected happens.

MARY ROSE (*thrilled*). I think, I think, I don't think at all, I am quite sure. This is the place. Simon, kiss me, kiss me quick. You promised to kiss me quick when we found the place.

SIMON (*obeying*). I am not the man to break my word. At the same time, Mary Rose, I would point out to you that this is the third spot you have picked out as being the place, and three times have I kissed you quick on that understanding. This can't go on, you know. As for your wonderful island, it turns out to be about the size of the Round Pond.

MARY ROSE. I always said it was little like myself.

1111

SIMON.   It was obviously made to fit you, or you to fit it ;
one of you was measured for the other.   At any rate, we have
now been all round it, and all through it, as my bleeding limbs
testify.   (*The whins have been tearing at him, and he rubs
his legs.*)

MARY ROSE.   They didn't hurt me at all.

SIMON.   Perhaps they like you better than me.   Well, we
have made a good search for the place where you used to sit
and sketch, and you must now take your choice.

MARY ROSE.   It was here.   I told you of the fir and the
rowan-tree.

SIMON.   There were a fir and a rowan at each of the other
places.

MARY ROSE.   Not this fir, not this rowan.

SIMON.   You have me there.

MARY ROSE.   Simon, I know I'm not clever, but I'm
always right.   The rowan-berries !   I used to put them in my
hair.   (*She puts them in her hair again.*)   Darling rowan-tree,
are you glad to see me back ?   You don't look a bit older, how
do you think *I* am wearing ?   I shall tell you a secret.   You
too, firry.   Come closer, both of you.   Put your arms around
me, and listen :   I am married !

(*The branch of which she has been making a scarf disengages itself.*)
It didn't like that, Simon, it is jealous.   After all, it knew me
first.   Dearest trees, if I had known that you felt for me in
that way—but it is too late now.   I have been married for
nearly four years, and this is the man.   His name is Lieutenant
Simon Sobersides.   (*She darts about making discoveries.*)

SIMON (*tranquilly smoking*).   What is it now ?

MARY ROSE.   That moss !   I feel sure there is a tree-trunk
beneath it, the very root on which I used to sit and sketch.

(*He clears away some of the moss.*)

SIMON.   It is a tree-trunk right enough.

MARY ROSE.   I believe—I believe I cut my name on it with
a knife.

SIMON.   This looks like it.   ' M—A—R—' and there it
stops.   That is always where the blade of the knife breaks.

MARY ROSE.   My ownest seat, how I have missed you.

SIMON.   Don't you believe it, old tree-trunk.   She had

forgotten all about you, and you just came vaguely back to her mind because we happened to be in the neighbourhood.

MARY ROSE. Yes, I suppose that is true. You were the one who wanted to come, Simon. I wonder why ?

SIMON (*with his answer ready*). No particular reason. I wanted to see a place you had visited as a child ; that was all. But what a trumpery island it proves to be.

MARY ROSE (*who perhaps agrees with him*). How can you ? Even if it is true, you needn't say it before them all, hurting their feelings. Dear seat, here is one for each year I have been away. (*She kisses the trunk a number of times.*)

SIMON (*counting*). Eleven. Go on, give it all the news. Tell it we don't have a house of our own yet.

MARY ROSE. You see, dear seat, we live with my daddy and mother, because Simon is so often away at sea. You know, the loveliest thing in the world is the navy, and the loveliest thing in the navy is H.M.S. *Valiant*, and the loveliest thing on H.M.S. *Valiant* is Lieutenant Simon Sobersides, and the loveliest thing on Lieutenant Simon Sobersides is the little tuft of hair which will keep standing up at the back of his head.

(SIMON, *who is lolling on the moss, is so used to her prattle that his eyes close.*)

But, listen, you trees, I have a much more wonderful secret than that. You can have three guesses. It is this . . . I—have—got—a baby ! A girl ? No thank you. He is two years and nine months, and he says such beautiful things to me about loving me. Oh, rowan, do you think he means them ?

SIMON. I distinctly heard it say yes.

(*He opens his eyes, to see her gazing entranced across the water.*)

You needn't pretend that you can see him.

MARY ROSE. I do. Can't you ? He is waving his bib to us

SIMON. That is nurse's cap.

MARY ROSE. Then he is waving it. How clever of him. (*She waves her handkerchief.*) Now they are gone. Isn't it funny to think that from this very spot I used to wave to father ? That was a happy time.

SIMON. I should be happier here if I wasn't so hungry. I

wonder where Cameron is. I told him after he landed us to tie up the boat at any good place and make a fire. I suppose I had better try to make it myself.

MARY ROSE. How you can think of food at such a time !

SIMON (*who is collecting sticks*). All very well, but you will presently be eating more than your share.

MARY ROSE. Do you know, Simon, I don't think daddy and mother like this island.

SIMON (*on his guard*). Help me with the fire, you chatterbox. (*He has long ceased to credit the story he heard four years ago, but he is ever watchful for* MARY ROSE.)

MARY ROSE. They never seem to want to speak of it.

SIMON. Forgotten it, I suppose.

MARY ROSE. I shall write to them from the inn this evening. How surprised they will be to know I am there again.

SIMON (*casually*). I wouldn't write from there. Wait till we cross to the mainland.

MARY ROSE. Why not from there ?

SIMON. Oh, no reason. But if they have a distaste for the place, perhaps they wouldn't like our coming. I say, praise me, I have got this fire alight.

MARY ROSE (*who is occasionally pertinacious*). Simon, why did you want to come to my island without me ?

SIMON. Did I ? Oh, I merely suggested your remaining at the inn because I thought you seemed tired. I wonder where Cameron can have got to ?

MARY ROSE. Here he comes. (*Solicitously*) Do be polite to him, dear ; you know how touchy they are.

SIMON. I am learning ! (*The boat, with* CAMERON, *draws in. He is a gawky youth of twenty, in the poor but honourable garb of the ghillie, and is not specially impressive until you question him about the universe.*)

CAMERON (*in the soft voice of the Highlander*). Iss it the wish of Mr. Blake that I should land ?

SIMON. Yes, yes, Cameron, with the luncheon. (CAMERON *steps ashore with a fishing basket.*)

CAMERON. Iss it the wish of Mr. Blake that I open the basket ?

SIMON. We shall tumble out the luncheon if you bring a

trout or two. I want you to show my wife, Cameron, how one cooks fish by the water's edge.

CAMERON. I will do it with pleasure. (*He pauses.*) There iss one little matter ; it iss of small importance. You may haf noticed that I always address you as Mr. Blake. I notice that you always address me as Cameron ; I take no offence.

MARY ROSE. Oh dear, I am sure I always address you as Mr. Cameron.

CAMERON. That iss so, ma'am. You may haf noticed that I always address you as 'ma'am.' It iss my way of indicating that I consider you a ferry genteel young matron, and of all such I am the humble servant. (*He pauses.*) In saying I am your humble servant I do not imply that I am not as good as you are. With this brief explanation, ma'am, I will now fetch the trouts.

SIMON (*taking advantage of his departure*). That is one in the eye for me. But I 'm hanged if I mister him.

MARY ROSE. Simon, do be careful. If you want to say anything to me that is dangerous, say it in French.

(CAMERON *returns with two small sea-trout.*)

CAMERON. The trouts, ma'am, having been cleaned in a thorough and yet easy manner by pulling them up and down in the water, the next procedure iss as follows.

(*He wraps up the trout in a piece of newspaper and soaks them in the water.*)

I now place the soaking little parcels on the fire, and when the paper begins to burn it will be a sure sign that the trouts iss now ready, like myself, ma'am, to be your humble servants. (*He is returning to the boat.*)

MARY ROSE (*who has been preparing the feast*). Don't go away.

CAMERON. If it iss agreeable to Mistress Blake I would wish to go back to the boat.

MARY ROSE. Why ?

(CAMERON *is not comfortable.*)

It would be more agreeable to me if you would stay.

CAMERON (*shuffling*). I will stay.

SIMON. Good man—and look after the trout. It is the most heavenly way of cooking fish, Mary Rose.

CAMERON. It iss a tasty way, Mr. Blake, but I would not use the word heavenly in this connection.

SIMON.   I stand corrected.   (*Tartly*) I must say——

MARY ROSE.   *Prenez garde, mon brave !*

SIMON.   *Mon Dieu !   Qu'il est un drôle !*

MARY ROSE.   *Mais moi, je l'aime ; il est tellement*—— What is the French for an original ?

SIMON.   That stumps me.

CAMERON.   Colloquially *coquin* might be used, though the classic writers would probably say simply *un original*.

SIMON (*with a groan*).   Phew, this is serious.   What was that book you were reading, Cameron, while I was fishing ?

CAMERON.   It iss a small Euripides I carry in the pocket, Mr. Blake.

SIMON.   Latin, Mary Rose !

CAMERON.   It may be Latin, but in these parts we know no better than to call it Greek.

SIMON.   Crushed again !   But I dare say it is good for me. Sit down and have pot-luck with us.

CAMERON.   I thank you, Mr. Blake, but it would not be good manners for a paid man to sit with his employers.

MARY ROSE.   When I ask you, Mr. Cameron ?

CAMERON.   It iss kindly meant, but I haf not been introduced to you.

MARY ROSE.   Oh, but—oh, do let me.   My husband Mr. Blake—Mr. Cameron.

CAMERON.   I hope you are ferry well, sir.

SIMON.   The same to you, Mr. Cameron.   How do you do ? Lovely day, isn't it ?

CAMERON.   It iss a fairly fine day.   (*He is not yet appeased.*)

MARY ROSE (*to the rescue*).   Simon !

SIMON.   Ah !   Do you know my wife ?   Mr. Cameron— Mrs. Blake.

CAMERON.   I am ferry pleased to make Mistress Blake's acquaintance.   Iss Mistress Blake making a long stay in these parts ?

MARY ROSE.   No, alas, we go across to-morrow.

CAMERON.   I hope the weather will be favourable.

MARY ROSE.   Thank you (*passing him the sandwiches*).   And now, you know, you are our guest.

CAMERON.   I am much obliged.   (*He examines the sand-*

wiches with curiosity.) Butcher-meat! This iss ferry excellent.

> (*He bursts into a surprising fit of laughter, and suddenly cuts it off.*)

Please to excuse my behaviour. You haf been laughing at me all this time, but you did not know I haf been laughing at myself also, though keeping a remarkable control over my features. I will now haf my laugh out, and then I will explain. (*He finishes his laugh.*) I will now explain. I am not the solemn prig I haf pretended to you to be, I am really a fairly attractive young man, but I am shy and I haf been guarding against your taking liberties with me, not because of myself, who am nothing, but because of the noble profession it iss my ambition to enter. (*They discover that they like him.*)

MARY ROSE. Do tell us what that is.

CAMERON. It iss the ministry. I am a student of Aberdeen University, and in the vacation I am a boatman, or a ghillie, or anything you please, to help to pay my fees.

SIMON. Well done!

CAMERON. I am obliged to Mr. Blake. And I may say, now that we know one another socially, that there iss much in Mr. Blake which I am trying to copy.

SIMON. Something in me worth copying!

CAMERON. It iss not Mr. Blake's learning; he has not much learning, but I haf always understood that the English manage without it. What I admire in you iss your ferry nice manners and your general deportment, in all which I haf a great deal to learn yet, and I watch these things in Mr. Blake and take memoranda of them in a little note-book.

> (SIMON *expands.*)

MARY ROSE. Mr. Cameron, do tell me that I also am in the little note-book?

CAMERON. You are not, ma'am, it would not be seemly in me. But it iss written in my heart, and also I haf said it to my father, that I will remain a bachelor unless I can marry some lady who iss ferry like Mistress Blake.

MARY ROSE. Simon, you never said anything to me as pretty as that. Is your father a crofter in the village?

CAMERON. Yes, ma'am, when he iss not at the University of Aberdeen.

SIMON.   My stars, does he go there too ?

CAMERON.   He does so.   We share a ferry small room between us.

SIMON.   Father and son.   Is he going into the ministry also ?

CAMERON.   Such iss not his purpose.   When he has taken his degree he will return and be a crofter again.

SIMON.   In that case I don't see what he is getting out of it.

CAMERON.   He iss getting the grandest thing in the world out of it ;   he iss getting education.

(SIMON *feels that he is being gradually rubbed out, and it is a relief to him that* CAMERON *has now to attend to the trout. The paper they are wrapped in has begun to burn.*)

MARY ROSE (*for the first time eating of trout as it should be cooked*).   Delicious !   (*She offers a portion to* CAMERON.)

CAMERON.   No, I thank you.   I haf lived on trouts most of my life.   This butcher-meat iss more of an excellent novelty to me.

(*He has been standing all this time.*)

MARY ROSE.   Do sit down, Mr. Cameron.

CAMERON.   I am doing ferry well here, I thank you.

MARY ROSE.   But, please.

CAMERON (*with decision*).   I will not sit down on this island.

SIMON (*curiously*).   Come, come, are you superstitious, you who are going into the ministry ?

CAMERON.   This island has a bad name.   I haf never landed on it before.

MARY ROSE.   A bad name, Mr. Cameron ?   Oh, but what a shame !   When I was here long ago, I often came to the island.

CAMERON.   Iss that so ?   It was not a chancey thing to do.

MARY ROSE.   But it is a darling island.

CAMERON.   That iss the proper way to speak of it.

MARY ROSE.   I am sure I never heard a word against it. Have you, Simon ?

SIMON (*brazenly*).   Not I.   I have heard that its Gaelic name has an odd meaning—'The Island that Likes to be Visited,' but there is nothing terrifying in that.

MARY ROSE.   The name is new to me, Mr. Cameron.   I think it is sweet.

CAMERON. That iss as it may be, Mistress Blake.

SIMON. What is there against the island?

CAMERON. For one thing, they are saying it has no authority to be here. It was not always here, so they are saying. Then one day it was here.

SIMON. That little incident happened before your time, I should say, Mr. Cameron.

CAMERON. It happened before the time of any one now alive, Mr. Blake.

SIMON. I thought so. And does the island ever go away for a jaunt in the same way?

CAMERON. There are some who say that it does.

SIMON. But you have not seen it on the move yourself?

CAMERON. I am not always watching it, Mr. Blake.

SIMON. Anything else against it?

CAMERON. There iss the birds. Too many birds come here. The birds like this island more than iss seemly.

SIMON. Birds here! What could bring them here?

CAMERON. It iss said they come to listen.

SIMON. To listen to the silence? An island that is as still as an empty church.

CAMERON. I do not know; that iss what they say.

MARY ROSE. I think it is a lovely story about the birds. I expect the kind things come because this island likes to be visited.

CAMERON. That iss another thing; for, mark you, Mistress Blake, an island that had visitors would not need to want to be visited. And why has it not visitors? Because they are afraid to visit it.

MARY ROSE. Whatever are they afraid of?

CAMERON. That iss what I say to them. Whateffer are you afraid of, I say.

MARY ROSE. But what are *you* afraid of, Mr. Cameron?

CAMERON. The same thing that they are afraid of. There are stories, ma'am.

MARY ROSE. Do tell us. Simon, wouldn't it be lovely if he would tell us some misty, eerie Highland stories?

SIMON. I don't know; not unless they are pretty ones.

MARY ROSE. Please, Mr. Cameron! I love to have my blood curdled.

CAMERON.   There iss many stories.   There iss that one of the boy who was brought to this island.   He was no older than your baby.

SIMON.   What happened to him ?

CAMERON.   No one knows, Mr. Blake.   His father and mother and their friends, they were gathering rowans on the island, and when they looked round he was gone.

SIMON.   Lost ?

CAMERON.   He could not be found.   He was never found

MARY ROSE.   Never !   He had fallen into the water ?

CAMERON.   That iss a good thing to say, that he had fallen into the water.   That iss what I say.

SIMON.   But you don't believe it ?

CAMERON.   I do not.

MARY ROSE.   What do the people in the village say ?

CAMERON.   Some say he iss on the island still.

SIMON.   Mr. Cameron !   Oh, Mr. Cameron !   What does your father say ?

CAMERON.   He will be saying that they are not here always, but that they come and go.

SIMON.   They ?   Who are they ?

CAMERON (uncomfortably).   I do not know.

SIMON.   Perhaps he heard what the birds come to listen to !

CAMERON.   That iss what they say.   He had heard the island calling.

SIMON (hesitating).   How does the island call ?

CAMERON.   I do not know.

SIMON.   Do you know any one who has heard the call ?

CAMERON.   I do not.   No one can hear it but those for whom it iss meant.

MARY ROSE.   But if that child heard it, the others must have heard it also, as they were with him.

CAMERON.   They heard nothing.   This iss how it will be. I might be standing close to you, Mistress Blake, as it were here, and I might hear it, ferry loud, terrible, or in soft whispers— no one knows—but I would haf to go, and you will not haf heard a sound.

MARY ROSE.   Simon, isn't it creepy !

SIMON.   But full of holes, I have no doubt.   How long ago is this supposed to have happened, credulous one ?

CAMERON. It was before I was born.

SIMON. I thought so.

MARY ROSE. Simon, don't make fun of my island. Do you know any more ducky stories about it, Mr. Cameron?

CAMERON. I cannot tell them if Mr. Blake will be saying things the island might not like to hear.

SIMON. Not ' chancey,' I suppose.

MARY ROSE. Simon, promise to be good.

SIMON. All right, Cameron.

CAMERON. This one iss about a young English miss, and they say she was about ten years of age.

MARY ROSE. Not so much younger than I was when I came here. How long ago was it?

CAMERON. I think it iss ten years ago this summer.

MARY ROSE. Simon, it must have been the year after I was here!

(SIMON *thinks she has heard enough.*)

SIMON. Very likely. But, I say, we mustn't stay on gossiping. We must be getting back. Did you bail out the boat?

CAMERON. I did not, but I will do it now if such iss your wish.

MARY ROSE. The story first; I won't go without the story.

CAMERON. Well, then, the father of this miss he will be fond of the fishing, and he sometimes landed the little one on the island while he fished round it from the boat.

MARY ROSE. Just as father used to do with me!

SIMON. I dare say lots of bold tourists come over here.

CAMERON. That iss so, if ignorance be boldness, and sometimes——

SIMON. Quite so. But I really think we must be starting.

MARY ROSE. No, dear. Please go on, Mr. Cameron.

CAMERON. One day the father pulled over for his little one as usual. He saw her from the boat, and it iss said she kissed her hand to him. Then in a moment more he reached the island, but she was gone.

MARY ROSE. Gone?

CAMERON. She had heard the call of the island, though no sound came to him.

MARY ROSE. Doesn't it make one shiver!

CAMERON. My father was one of the searchers; for many days they searched.

2 N

MARY ROSE. But it would not take many minutes to search this darling little island.

CAMERON. They searched, ma'am, long after there was no sense in searching.

MARY ROSE. What a curdling story ! Simon dear, it might have been Mary Rose. Is there any more ?

CAMERON. There iss more. It was about a month afterwards. Her father was walking on the shore, over there, and he saw something moving on the island. All in a tremble, ma'am, he came across in the boat, and it was his little miss.

MARY ROSE. Alive ?

CAMERON. Yes, ma'am.

MARY ROSE. I am glad : but it rather spoils the mystery.

SIMON. How, Mary Rose ?

MARY ROSE. Because she could tell them what happened, stupid. Whatever was it ?

CAMERON. It iss not so easy as that. She did not know that anything had happened. She thought she had been parted from her father for but an hour

(MARY ROSE *shivers and takes her husband's hand.*)

SIMON (*speaking more lightly than he is feeling*). You and your bogies and wraiths, you man of the mists.

MARY ROSE (*smiling*). Don't be alarmed, Simon ; I was only pretending.

CAMERON. It iss not good to disbelieve the stories when you are in these parts. I believe them all when I am here, though I turn the cold light of remorseless Reason on them when I am in Aberdeen.

SIMON. Is that ' chancey,' my friend ? An island that has such extraordinary powers could surely send its call to Aberdeen or farther.

CAMERON (*troubled*). I had not thought of that. That may be ferry true.

SIMON. Beware, Mr. Cameron, lest some day when you are preaching far from here the call plucks you out of the very pulpit and brings you back to the island like a trout on a long cast.

CAMERON. I do not like Mr. Blake's way of talking. I will go and bail the boat.

(*He goes back to the boat, which soon drifts out of sight.*)

MARY ROSE (*pleasantly thrilled*). Suppose it were true, Simon !

SIMON (*stoutly*). But it isn't.

MARY ROSE. No, of course not ; but if it had been, how awful for the girl when her father told her that she had been away for weeks.

SIMON. Perhaps she was never told. He may have thought it wiser not to disturb her.

MARY ROSE. Poor girl ! Yes, I suppose that would have been best. And yet—it was taking a risk.

SIMON. How ?

MARY ROSE. Well, not knowing what had happened before, she might come back and—and be caught again. (*She draws closer to him.*) Little island, I don't think I like you to-day.

SIMON. If she ever comes back, let us hope it is with an able-bodied husband to protect her.

MARY ROSE (*comfortably*). Nice people, husbands. You won't let them catch me, will you, Simon ?

SIMON. Let 'em try. (*Gaily*) And now to pack up the remnants of the feast and escape from the scene of the crime. We will never come back again, Mary Rose, I 'm too frightened!

(*She helps him to pack.*)

MARY ROSE. It is a shame to be funny about my island. You poor, lonely isle. I never knew about your liking to be visited, and I dare say I shall never visit you any more. The last time of anything is always sad, don't you think, Simon ?

SIMON (*briskly*). There must always be a last time, dearest dear.

MARY ROSE. Yes—I suppose—for everything. There must be a last time I shall see you, Simon. (*Playing with his hair*) Some day I shall flatten this tuft for the thousandth time, and then never do it again.

SIMON. Some day I shall look for it and it won't be there. That day I shall say ' Good riddance.'

MARY ROSE. I shall cry. (*She is whimsical rather than merry and merry rather than sad.*)

(SIMON *touches her hair with his lips.*)
Some day, Simon, you will kiss me for the last time.

SIMON. That wasn't the last time, at any rate. (*To prove*

it he kisses her again, sportively, little thinking that this may be the last time. She quivers.) What is it ?

MARY ROSE. I don't know ; something seemed to pass over me.

SIMON. You and your last times. Let me tell you, Mistress Blake, there will be a last time of seeing your baby. *(Hurriedly)* I mean only that he can't always be infantile ; but the day after you have seen him for the last time as a baby you will see him for the first time as a little gentleman. Think of that.

MARY ROSE *(clapping her hands)*. The loveliest time of all will be when he is a man and takes me on his knee instead of my putting him on mine. Oh, gorgeous ! *(With one of her sudden changes)* Don't you think the sad thing is that we seldom know when the last time has come ? We could make so much more of it.

SIMON. Don't you believe that. To know would spoil it all. *(The packing is nearly completed.)* I suppose I ought to stamp out the fire ?

MARY ROSE. Let Cameron do that. I want you to come and sit beside me, Simon, and make love to me.

SIMON. What a life. Let me see now, how does one begin ? Which arm is it ? I believe I have forgotten the way.

MARY ROSE. Then I shall make love to you. *(Playing with his hair)* Have I been a nice wife to you, Simon ? I don't mean always and always. There was that awful day when I threw the butter-dish at you. I am so sorry. But have I been a tolerably good wife on the whole, not a wonderful one, but a wife that would pass in a crowd ?

SIMON. Look here, if you are going to butt me with your head in that way, you must take that pin out of your hair.

MARY ROSE. Have I been all right as a mother, Simon ? Have I been the sort of mother a child could both love and respect ?

SIMON. That is a very awkward question. You must ask that of Harry Morland Blake.

MARY ROSE. Have I——— ?

SIMON. Shut up, Mary Rose. I know you ; you will be crying in a moment, and you don't have a handkerchief, for I wrapped it round the trout whose head came off.

MARY ROSE. At any rate, Simon Blake, say you forgive me about the butter-dish.

SIMON.　I am not so sure of that.

MARY ROSE.　And there were some other things—almost worse than the butter-dish.

SIMON.　I should just say there were.

MARY ROSE.　Simon, how can you ?　There was nothing so bad as that.

SIMON (*shaking his head*).　I can smile at it now, but at the time I was a miserable man.　I wonder I didn't take to drink.

MARY ROSE.　Poor old Simon.　But how stupid you were, dear, not to understand.

SIMON.　How could an ignorant young husband understand that it was a good sign when his wife threw the butter-dish at him ?

MARY ROSE.　You should have guessed.

SIMON.　No doubt I was a ninny.　But I had always understood that when a young wife—that then she took the husband aside and went red, or white, and hid her head on his bosom, and whispered the rest.　I admit I was hoping for that ; but all I got was the butter-dish.

MARY ROSE.　I suppose different women have different ways.

SIMON.　I hope so.　(*Severely*) And that was a dastard trick you played me afterwards.

MARY ROSE.　Which ?　Oh, that !　I just wanted you to be out of the way till all was over.

SIMON.　I don't mean your getting me out of the house, sending me to Plymouth.　The dastardliness was in not letting them tell me, when I got back, that—that he had arrived.

MARY ROSE.　It was very naughty of me.　You remember, Simon, when you came in to my room you tried to comfort me by saying it wouldn't be long now—and I let you maunder on, you darling.

SIMON.　Gazing at me with solemn, innocent eyes.　You unutterable brat, Mary Rose !

MARY ROSE.　You should have been able to read in my face how clever I had been.　Oh, Simon, when I said at last, ' Dearest, what is that funny thing in the bassinette ? ' and you went and looked, never shall I forget your face.

SIMON.　I thought at first it was some baby you had borrowed.

MARY ROSE.　I sometimes think so still.　I didn't, did I ?

SIMON. You are a droll one. Always just when I think I know you at last I have to begin at the beginning again.

MARY ROSE (*suddenly*). Simon, if one of us had to—to go—and we could choose which one——

SIMON (*sighing*). She 's off again.

MARY ROSE. Well, but if—I wonder which would be best? I mean for Harry, of course.

SIMON. Oh, I should have to hop it.

MARY ROSE. Dear !

SIMON. Oh, I haven't popped off yet. Steady, you nearly knocked over the pickles. (*He regards her curiously.*) If I did go, I know your first thought would be ' The happiness of Harry must not be interfered with for a moment.' You would blot me out for ever, Mary Rose, rather than he should lose one of his hundred laughs a day.

　　　(*She hides her face.*)

It 's true, isn't it ?

MARY ROSE. It is true, at any rate, that if I was the one to go, that is what I should like you to do.

SIMON. Get off the table-cloth.

　　　(*Her mouth opens.*)

Don't step on the marmalade.

MARY ROSE (*gloriously*). Simon, isn't life lovely ! I am so happy, happy, happy. Aren't you ?

SIMON. Rather.

MARY ROSE. But you can tie up marmalade. Why don't you scream with happiness ? One of us has got to scream.

SIMON. Then I know which one it will be. Scream away, it will give Cameron the jumps.

　　　(CAMERON *draws in.*)

There you are, Cameron. We are still safe, you see. You can count us—two.

CAMERON. I am ferry glad.

SIMON. Here you are (*handing him the luncheon basket*). You needn't tie the boat up. Stay there and I 'll stamp out the fire myself.

CAMERON. As Mr. Blake pleases.

SIMON. Ready, Mary Rose ?

MARY ROSE. I must say good-bye to my island first. Good-bye, old mossy seat, nice rowan. Good-bye, little island that likes too much to be visited. Perhaps I shall come back when I am an old lady with wrinkles, and you won't know your Mary Rose.

SIMON.   I say, dear, do dry up.   I can't help listening to you when I ought to be getting this fire out.

MARY ROSE.   I won't say another word.

SIMON.   Just as it seems to be out, sparks come again.   Do you think if I were to get some stones—— ?

(He looks up and she signs that she has promised not to talk. They laugh to each other. He is then occupied for a little time in dumping wet stones from the loch upon the fire. CAMERON is in the boat with his Euripides. MARY ROSE is sitting demure but gay, holding her tongue with her fingers like a child.

Something else is happening ; the call has come to MARY ROSE. It is at first as soft and furtive as whisperings from holes in the ground, 'Mary Rose, Mary Rose.' Then in a fury as of storm and whistling winds that might be an unholy organ it rushes upon the island, raking every bush for her. These sounds increase rapidly in volume till the mere loudness of them is horrible. They are not without an opponent. Struggling through them, and also calling her name, is to be heard music of an unearthly sweetness that is seeking perhaps to beat them back and put a girdle of safety round her. Once MARY ROSE'S arms go out to her husband for help, but thereafter she is oblivious of his existence. Her face is rapt, but there is neither fear nor joy in it. Thus she passes from view. The island immediately resumes its stillness. The sun has gone down. SIMON by the fire and CAMERON in the boat have heard nothing.)

SIMON *(on his knees)*.   I think the fire is done for at last, and that we can go now.   How cold and grey it has become. *(Smiling, but without looking up)* You needn't grip your tongue any longer, you know. *(He rises.)* Mary Rose, where have you got to? Please don't hide.   Dearest, don't.   Cameron, where is my wife?

(CAMERON rises in the boat, and he is afraid to land. His face alarms SIMON, who runs this way and that and is lost to sight calling her by name again and again. He returns livid.)

Cameron, I can't find her.   Mary Rose !   Mary Rose ! Mary Rose !

ACT III

Twenty-five years have passed, and the scene is again that cosy room in the Morlands' house, not much changed since we last saw it.   If chintzes have faded, others as smiling have taken their place.   The time is a crisp autumn afternoon just before twilight comes.   The apple-tree, not so easy to renew as the chintzes, has become smaller, but there are a few gallant apples on it.   The fire is burning, and round it sit Mr. and Mrs. Morland and Mr. Amy, the Morlands gone smaller like the apple-tree and Mr. Amy bulky, but all three on the whole still bearing their apples.   Inwardly they have changed still less ; hear them at it as of yore.

MR. MORLAND.   What are you laughing over, Fanny ?

MRS. MORLAND.   It is this week's *Punch*, so very amusing.

MR. AMY.   Ah, *Punch*, it isn't what it used to be.

MR. MORLAND.   No, indeed.

MRS. MORLAND.   I disagree.   You two try if you can look at this picture without laughing.

(*They are unable to stand the test.*)

MR. MORLAND.   I think I can say that I enjoy a joke as much as ever.

MRS. MORLAND.   You light-hearted old man !

MR. MORLAND (*humorously*).   Not so old, Fanny.   Please to remember that I am two months younger than you.

MRS. MORLAND.   How can I forget it when you have been casting it up against me all our married life ?

MR. MORLAND (*not without curiosity*).   Fanny and I are seventy-three ; you are a bit younger, George, I think ?

MR. AMY.   Oh yes, oh dear yes.

MR. MORLAND.   You never say precisely what your age is.

MR. AMY.   I am in the late sixties.   I am sure I have told you that before.

MR. MORLAND.   It seems to me you have been in the sixties longer than it is usual to be in them.

1128

MRS. MORLAND (*with her needles*).   James !

MR. MORLAND.   No offence, George.   I was only going to say that at seventy-three I certainly don't feel my age.   How do you feel, George, at—at sixty-six ?   (*More loudly, as if* MR. AMY *were a little deaf.*)   Do you feel your sixty-six years ?

MR. AMY (*testily*).   I am more than sixty-six.   But I certainly don't feel my age.   It was only last winter that I learned to skate.

MR. MORLAND.   I still go out with the hounds.   You forgot to come last time, George.

MR. AMY.   If you are implying anything against my memory, James.

MR. MORLAND (*peering through his glasses*).   What do you say ?

MR. AMY.   I was saying that I have never used glasses in my life.

MR. MORLAND.   If I wear glasses occasionally it certainly isn't because there is anything defective in my eyesight.   But the type used by newspapers nowadays is so vile——

MR. AMY.   There I agree with you.   Especially Bradshaw.

MR. MORLAND (*not hearing him*).   I say the type used by newspapers of to-day is vile.   Don't you think so ?

MR. AMY.   I have just said so.   (*Pleasantly*) You are getting rather dull of hearing, James.

MR. MORLAND.   I am ?   I like that, George !   Why, I have constantly to shout to you nowadays.

MR. AMY.   What annoys me is not that you are a little deaf, you can't help that.   But from the nature of your replies I often see that you are pretending to have heard what I said when you did not.   That is rather vain, James.

MR. MORLAND.   Vain !   Now you brought this on yourself, George.   I have got something here I might well be vain of, and I meant not to show it to you because it will make you squirm.

(MRS. MORLAND *taps warningly.*)

MR. MORLAND.   I didn't mean that, George.   I am sure that you will be delighted.   What do you think of this ?

(*He produces a water-colour which his friend examines at arm's length.*)

Let me hold it out for you, as your arms are so short.

(*The offer is declined.*)

MR. AMY (*with a sinking*).   Very nice.   What do you call it ?

MR. MORLAND.   Have you any doubt ?   I haven't the slightest.   I am sure that it is an early Turner.

MR. AMY (*paling*).   Turner !

MR. MORLAND.   What else can it be ?   Holman suggested a Gurton or even a Dayes.   Absurd !   Why, Dayes was only a glorified drawing-master.   I flatter myself I can't make a mistake about a Turner.   There is something about a Turner difficult to define, but unmistakable, an absolute something. It is a charming view, too ; Kirkstall Abbey obviously.

MR. AMY.   Rivaulx, I am convinced.

MR. MORLAND.   I say Kirkstall.

MRS. MORLAND (*with her needles*).   James !

MR. MORLAND.   Well, you may be right, the place doesn't matter.

MR. AMY.   There is an engraving of Rivaulx in that Copperplate Magazine we were looking at.   (*He turns up the page.*) I have got it, Rivaulx.   (*He brightens.*)   Why, this is funny. It is an engraving of that very picture.   Hello, hello, hello. (*Examining it through his private glass.*)   And it is signed E. Dayes.

(MR. MORLAND *holds the sketch so close to him that it brushes his eyelashes.*)

I wouldn't eat it, James.   So it is by Dayes, the drawing-master, after all.   I am sorry you have had this disappointment.

(MRS. MORLAND *taps warningly, but her husband is now possessed.*)

MR. MORLAND.   You sixty-six, Mr. Amy, you sixty-six !

MR. AMY.   James, this is very painful.   Your chagrin I can well understand, but surely your sense of manhood——I regret that I have outstayed my welcome.   I bid you good afternoon. Thank you, Mrs. Morland, for your unvarying hospitality.

MRS. MORLAND.   I shall see you into your coat, George.

MR. AMY.   It is very kind of you, but I need no one to see me into my coat.

MR. MORLAND.   You will never see your way into it by yourself.

(*This unworthy remark is perhaps not heard, for* MRS. MORLAND *succeeds once more in bringing the guest back.*)

MR. AMY.   James, I cannot leave this friendly house in wrath.

MR. MORLAND.   I am an irascible old beggar, George. What I should do without you——

MR. AMY. Or I without you. Or either of us without that little old dear, to whom we are a never-failing source of mirth.

(*The little old dear curtseys, looking very frail as she does so.*) Tell Simon when he comes that I shall be in to see him to-morrow. Good-bye, Fanny ; I suppose you think of the pair of us as in our second childhood ?

MRS. MORLAND. Not your second, George. I have never known any men who have quite passed their first.

(*He goes smiling.*)

MR. MORLAND (*ruminating by the fire*). He is a good fellow, George, but how touchy he is about his age ! And he has a way of tottering off to sleep while one is talking to him.

MRS. MORLAND. He is not the only one of us who does that.

(*She is standing by the window.*)

MR. MORLAND. What are you thinking about, Fanny ?

MRS. MORLAND. I was thinking about the apple-tree, and that you have given the order for its destruction.

MR. MORLAND. It must come down. It is becoming a danger, might fall on some one down there any day.

MRS. MORLAND. I quite see that it has to go. (*She can speak of* MARY ROSE *without a tremor now.*) But her tree ! How often she made it a ladder from this room to the ground !

(MR. MORLAND *does not ask who, but he very nearly does so.*)

MR. MORLAND. Oh yes, of course. Did she use to climb the apple-tree ? Yes, I think she did.

(*He goes to his wife, as it were for protection.*)

MRS. MORLAND (*not failing him*). Had you forgotten that also, James ?

MR. MORLAND. I am afraid I forget a lot of things.

MRS. MORLAND. Just as well.

MR. MORLAND. It is so long since she—how long is it, Fanny ?

MRS. MORLAND. Twenty-five years, a third of our lifetime. It will soon be dark ; I can see the twilight running across the fields. Draw the curtains, dear.

(*He does so and turns on the lights ; they are electric lights now.*)

Simon's train must be nearly due, is it not ?

MR. MORLAND. In ten minutes or so. Did you forward his telegram ?

MRS. MORLAND. No, I thought he would probably get it sooner if I kept it here.

MR. MORLAND. I dare say. (*He joins her on the sofa, and she sees that he is troubled.*)

MRS. MORLAND. What is it, dear?

MR. MORLAND. I am afraid I was rather thoughtless about the apple-tree, Fanny. I hurt you.

MRS. MORLAND (*brightly*). Such nonsense! Have another pipe, James.

MR. MORLAND (*doggedly*). I will not have another pipe. I hereby undertake to give up smoking for a week as a punishment to myself. (*His breast swells a little.*)

MRS. MORLAND. You will regret this, you know.

MR. MORLAND (*his breast ceasing to swell*). Why is my heart not broken? If I had been a man of real feeling it would have broken twenty-five years ago, just as yours did.

MRS. MORLAND. Mine didn't, dear.

MR. MORLAND. In a way it did. As for me, at the time I thought I could never raise my head again, but there is a deal of the old Adam in me still. I ride and shoot and laugh and give pompous decisions on the bench and wrangle with old George as if nothing much had happened to me. I never think of the island now; I dare say I could go back there and fish. (*He finds that despite his outburst his hand has strayed towards his tobacco-pouch.*) See what I am doing! (*He casts his pouch aside as if it were the culprit.*) I am a man enamoured of myself. Why, I have actually been considering, Fanny, whether I should have another dress suit.

MRS. MORLAND (*picking up the pouch*). And why shouldn't you?

MR. MORLAND. At my age! Fanny, this should be put on my tombstone: 'In spite of some adversity he remained a lively old blade to the end.'

MRS. MORLAND. Perhaps that would be a rather creditable epitaph for any man, James, who has gone through as much as you have. What better encouragement to the young than to be able to tell them that happiness keeps breaking through? (*She puts the pipe, which she has been filling, in his mouth.*)

MR. MORLAND. If I smoke, Fanny, I shall despise myself more than ever.

MRS. MORLAND.　To please me.

MR. MORLAND (*as she holds the light*).　I don't feel easy about it, not at all easy. (*With a happy thought*) At any rate, I won't get the dress suit.

MRS. MORLAND.　Your dress suit is shining like a mirror.

MR. MORLAND.　Isn't it !　I thought of a jacket suit only. The V-shaped waistcoat seems to be what they are all wearing now.

MRS. MORLAND.　Would you have braid on the trousers ?

MR. MORLAND.　I was wondering.　You see——　Oh, Fanny, you are just humouring me.

MRS. MORLAND.　Not at all.　And as for the old Adam in you, dear Adam, there is still something of the old Eve in me. Our trip to Switzerland two years ago, with Simon, I enjoyed every hour of it.　The little card parties here, am I not called the noisy one ? think of the girls I have chaperoned and teased and laughed with, just as if I had never had a girl myself.

MR. MORLAND.　Your brightness hasn't been all pretence ?

MRS. MORLAND.　No, indeed ; I have passed through the valley of the shadow, dear, but I can say thankfully that I have come out again into the sunlight. (*A little tremulously*) I suppose it is all to the good that as the years go by the dead should recede farther from us.

MR. MORLAND.　Some say they don't.

MRS. MORLAND.　You and I know better, James.

MR. MORLAND.　Up there in the misty Hebrides I dare say they think of her as on the island still.　Fanny, how long is it since—since you half thought *that* yourself ?

MRS. MORLAND.　Ever so many years.　Perhaps not the first year.　I did cling for a time——

MR. MORLAND.　The neighbours here didn't like it.

MRS. MORLAND.　She wasn't their Mary Rose, you see.

MR. MORLAND.　And yet her first disappearance——

MRS. MORLAND.　It is all unfathomable.　It is as if Mary Rose was just something beautiful that you and I and Simon had dreamt together.　You have forgotten much, but so have I. Even that room (*she looks towards the little door*) that was hers and her child's during all her short married life—I often go into it now without remembering that it was theirs.

MR. MORLAND.   It is strange.   It is rather terrible.   You are pretty nigh forgotten, Mary Rose.

MRS. MORLAND.   That isn't true, dear.   Mary Rose belongs to the past, and we have to live in the present, for a very little longer.   Just a little longer, and then we shall understand all. Even if we could drag her back to tell us now what these things mean, I think it would be a shame.

MR. MORLAND.   Yes, I suppose so.   Do you think Simon is a philosopher about it also ?

MRS. MORLAND.   Don't be bitter, James, to your old wife. Simon was very fond of her.   He was a true lover.

MR. MORLAND.   Was, was !   Is it all ' was ' about Mary Rose ?

MRS. MORLAND.   It just has to be.   He had all the clever ones of the day advising, suggesting, probing.   He went back to the island every year for a long time.

MR. MORLAND.   Yes, and then he missed a year, and that somehow ended it.

MRS. MORLAND.   He never married again.   Most men would.

MR. MORLAND.   His work took her place.   What a jolly, hearty fellow he is !

MRS. MORLAND.   If you mean he isn't heart-broken, he isn't.   Mercifully the wound has healed.

MR. MORLAND.   I am not criticising, Fanny.   I suppose any one who came back after twenty-five years—however much they had been loved—it might—we—should we know what to say to them, Fanny ?

MRS. MORLAND.   Don't, James. (*She rises.*)   Simon is late, isn't he ?

MR. MORLAND.   Very little.   I heard the train a short time ago, and he might be here—just—if he had the luck to find a cab.   But not if he is walking across the fields.

MRS. MORLAND.   Listen !

MR. MORLAND.   Yes, wheels.   That is probably Simon. He had got a cab.

MRS. MORLAND.   I do hope he won't laugh at me for having lit a fire in his room.

MR. MORLAND (*with masculine humour*).   I hope you put him out some bed-socks

MRS. MORLAND (*eagerly*).　Do you think he would let me ? You wretch !

(*She hurries out, and returns in* SIMON'S *arms.*

He is in a greatcoat and mufti. He looks his years, grizzled with grey hair and not very much of it, and the tuft is gone. He is heavier and more commanding, full of vigour, a rollicking sea-dog for the moment, but it is a face that could be stern to harshness.)

SIMON (*saluting*).　Come aboard, sir.

MRS. MORLAND.　Let me down, you great bear. You know how I hate to be rumpled.

MR. MORLAND.　Not she, loves it. Always did. Get off your greatcoat, Simon. Down with it anywhere.

MRS. MORLAND (*fussing delightedly*).　How cold your hands are. Come nearer to the fire.

MR. MORLAND.　He is looking fit, though.

SIMON.　We need to be fit—these days.

MRS. MORLAND.　So nice to have you again. You do like duck, don't you ? The train was late, wasn't it ?

SIMON.　A few minutes only. I made a selfish bolt for the one cab, and got it.

MR. MORLAND.　We thought you might be walking across the fields.

SIMON.　No, I left the fields to the two other people who got out of the train. One of them was a lady ; I thought something about her walk was familiar to me, but it was darkish, and I didn't make her out.

MRS. MORLAND.　Bertha Colinton, I expect. She was in London to-day.

SIMON.　If I had thought it was Mrs. Colinton I would have offered her a lift. (*For a moment he gleams boyishly like the young husband of other days.*) Mother, I have news ; I have got the *Bellerophon*, honest Injun !

MRS. MORLAND.　The very ship you wanted.

SIMON.　Rather.

MR. MORLAND.　Bravo, Simon.

SIMON.　It is like realising the ambition of one's life. I'm one of the lucky folk, I admit.

(*He says this, and neither of them notices it as a strange remark.*)

MR. MORLAND (*twinkling*).　Beastly life, a sailor's.

SIMON (*cordially*).　Beastly.　I have loathed it ever since I slept in the old *Britannia*, with my feet out at the port-hole to give them air.　We all slept that way ; must have been a pretty sight from the water.　Oh, a beast of a life, but I wouldn't exchange it for any other in the world.　(*Lowering*) And if this war does come——

MR. MORLAND (*characteristically*).　It won't, I 'm sure.

SIMON.　I dare say not.　But they say—however.

MRS. MORLAND.　Simon, I had forgotten.　There is a telegram for you.

SIMON.　Avaunt !　I do trust it is not recalling me.　I had hoped for at least five clear days.

MRS. MORLAND (*giving it to him*).　We didn't open it.

SIMON.　Two to one it is recalling me.

MRS. MORLAND.　It came two days ago.　I don't like them, Simon, never did ; they have broken so many hearts.

SIMON.　They have made many a heart glad too.　It may be from my Harry——at last.　Mother, do you think I was sometimes a bit harsh to him ?

MRS. MORLAND.　I think you sometimes were, my son.

MR. MORLAND.　Open it, Simon.

(SIMON *opens the telegram and many unseen devils steal into the room.*)

MRS. MORLAND (*shrinking from his face*).　It can't be so bad as that.　We are all here, Simon.

(*For a moment he has not been here himself, he has been on an island.　He is a good son to* MRS. MORLAND *now, thinking of her only, placing her on the sofa, going on his knees beside her and stroking her kind face.　Her arms go out to her husband, who has been reading the telegram.*)

MR. MORLAND (*dazed*).　Can't be, can't be !

SIMON (*like some better father than he perhaps has been*).　It is all right, Mother.　Don't you be afraid.　It is good news. You are a brave one, you have come through much, you will be brave for another minute, won't you ?

(*She nods, with a frightened smile.*)
Mother dear, it is Mary Rose.

MR. MORLAND.　It can't be true.　It is too—too glorious to be true.

MRS. MORLAND. Glorious ? Is my Mary Rose alive ?

SIMON. It is all right, all right. I wouldn't say it, surely, if it wasn't true. Mary Rose has come back. The telegram is from Cameron. You remember who he was. He is minister there now. Hold my hand, and I'll read it. 'Your wife has come back. She was found to-day on the island. I am bringing her to you. She is quite well, but you will all have to be very careful.'

MRS. MORLAND. Simon, can it be ?

SIMON. I believe it absolutely. Cameron would not deceive me.

MR. MORLAND. He might be deceived himself ; he was a mere acquaintance.

SIMON. I am sure it is true. He knew her by sight as well as any of us.

MR. MORLAND. But after twenty-five years !

SIMON. Do you think I wouldn't know her after twenty-five years ?

MRS. MORLAND. My—my—she will be—very changed.

SIMON. However changed, Mother, wouldn't I know my Mary Rose at once ! Her hair may be as grey as mine—her face—her little figure—her pretty ways—though they were all gone, don't you think I would know Mary Rose at once ? (*He is suddenly stricken with a painful thought.*) Oh, my God, I saw her, and I didn't know her !

MRS. MORLAND. Simon !

SIMON. It had been Cameron with her. They must have come in my train. Mother, it was she I saw going across the fields—her little walk when she was excited, half a run, I recognised it, but I didn't remember it was hers.

(*Those unseen devils chuckle.*)

MR. MORLAND. It was getting dark.

SIMON (*slowly*). Mary Rose is coming across the fields.

(*He goes out.* MORLAND *peers weakly through the window curtains.* MRS. MORLAND *goes on her knees to pray.*)

MR. MORLAND. It is rather dark. I—I shouldn't wonder though there was a touch of frost to-night. I wish I was more use.

(CAMERON *enters, a bearded clergyman now.*)

MRS. MORLAND. Mr. Cameron ? Tell us quickly, Mr. Cameron, is it true ?

CAMERON. It iss true, ma'am. Mr. Blake met us at the gate and he iss with her now. I hurried on to tell you the things necessary. It iss good for her you should know them at once.

MRS. MORLAND. Please, quick.

CAMERON. You must be prepared to find her—different.

MRS. MORLAND. We are all different. Her age——

CAMERON. I mean, Mrs. Morland, different from what you expect. She iss not different as we are different. They will be saying she iss just as she was on the day she went away.

(MRS. MORLAND *shrinks*.)

These five-and-twenty years, she will be thinking they were just an hour in which Mr. Blake and I had left her in some incomprehensible jest.

MRS. MORLAND. James, just as it was before !

MR. MORLAND. But when you told her the truth ?

CAMERON. She will not have it.

MRS. MORLAND. She must have seen how much older you are.

CAMERON. She does not know me, ma'am, as the boy who was with her that day. When she did not recognise me I thought it best—she was so troubled already—not to tell her.

MR. MORLAND (*appealing*). But now that she has seen Simon. His appearance, his grey hair—when she saw him she would know.

CAMERON (*unhappy*). I am not sure ; it iss dark out there.

MR. MORLAND. She must have known that he would never have left her and come home.

CAMERON. That secretly troubles her, but she will not speak of it. There iss some terrible dread lying on her heart.

MR. MORLAND. A dread ?

MRS. MORLAND. Harry. James, if she should think that Harry is still a child !

CAMERON. I never heard what became of the boy.

MRS. MORLAND. He ran away to sea when he was twelve years old. We had a few letters from Australia, very few ; we don't know where he is now.

MR. MORLAND. How was she found, Mr. Cameron ?

CAMERON. Two men fishing from a boat saw her. She was asleep by the shore at the very spot where Mr. Blake made a fire so long ago. There was a rowan-tree beside it. At first they were afraid to land, but they did.   They said there was such a joy on her face as she slept that it was a shame to waken her.

MR. MORLAND.   Joy?

CAMERON.   That iss so, sir.   I have sometimes thought——

(*There is a gleeful clattering on the stairs of some one to whom they must be familiar ; and if her father and mother have doubted they know now before they see her that* MARY ROSE *has come back.   She enters.   She is just as we saw her last except that we cannot see her quite so clearly.   She is leaping towards her mother in the old impulsive way, and the mother responds in her way, but something steps between them.*)

MARY ROSE (*puzzled*).   What is it ?

(*It is the years.*)

MRS. MORLAND.   My love.

MR. MORLAND.   Mary Rose.

MARY ROSE.   Father.

(*But the obstacle is still there.   She turns timidly to* SIMON, *who has come in with her.*)

What is it, Simon ?

(*She goes confidently to him till she sees what the years have done with him.   She shakes now.*)

SIMON.   My beloved wife.

(*He takes her in his arms and so does her mother, and she is glad to be there, but it is not of them she is thinking, and soon she softly disengages herself.*)

MR. MORLAND.   We are so glad you—had you a comfortable journey, Mary Rose ?   You would like a cup of tea, wouldn't you ?   Is there anything *I* can do ?

(MARY ROSE'S *eyes go from him to the little door at the back.*)

MARY ROSE (*coaxingly to her father*).   Tell me.

MR. MORLAND.   Tell you what, dear ?

MARY ROSE (*appealing to* CAMERON).   You ?

(*He presses her hand and turns away.   She goes to* SIMON *and makes much of him, cajoling him.*)

Simon, my Simon.   Be nice to me, Simon.   Be nice to me, dear Simon, and tell me.

SIMON.   Dearest love, since I lost you—it was a long time ago——

MARY ROSE (*petulant*). It wasn't—please, it wasn't. (*She goes to her mother.*) Tell me, my mother dear.

MR. MORLAND. I don't know what she wants to be told.

MRS. MORLAND. I know.

MARY ROSE (*an unhappy child*). Where is my baby?

(*They cannot face her, and she goes to seek an answer from the room that lies beyond the little door. Her mother and husband follow her.*

MR. MORLAND *and* CAMERON *left alone are very conscious of what may be going on in that inner room.*)

MR. MORLAND. Have you been in this part of the country before, Mr. Cameron?

CAMERON. I haf not, sir. It iss my first visit to England. You cannot hear the sea in this house at all, which iss very strange to me.

MR. MORLAND. If I might show you our Downs——

CAMERON. I thank you, Mr. Morland, but—in such circumstances do not trouble about me at all.

(*They listen.*)

MR. MORLAND. I do not know if you are interested in prints. I have a pencil sketch by Cousins—undoubtedly genuine——

CAMERON. I regret my ignorance on the subject. This matter, so strange—so inexplicable——

MR. MORLAND. Please don't talk of it to me, sir. I am—an old man. I have been so occupied all my life with little things—very pleasant—I cannot cope—cannot cope——

(*A hand is placed on his shoulder so sympathetically that he dares to ask a question.*)

Do you think she should have come back, Mr. Cameron?

(*The stage darkens and they are blotted out. Into this darkness* MRS. OTERY *enters with a candle, and we see that the scene has changed to the dismantled room of the first act.* HARRY *is sunk in the chair as we last saw him.*)

MRS. OTERY (*who in her other hand has a large cup and saucer*). Here is your tea, mister. Are you sitting in the dark? I haven't been more than the ten minutes I promised you. I was——

(*She stops short, struck by his appearance. She holds the candle nearer him. He is staring wide-eyed into the fire, motionless.*)

What is the matter, mister ?   Here is the tea, mister.

(*He looks at her blankly.*)

I have brought you a cup of tea, I have just been the ten minutes.

HARRY (*rising*).   Wait a mo.

(*He looks about him, like one taking his bearings.*)

Gimme the tea.   That 's better.   Thank you, missis.

MRS. OTERY.   Have you seen anything ?

HARRY.   See here, as I sat in that chair—I wasn't sleeping, mind you—it 's no dream—but things of the far past connected with this old house—things I knew naught of—they came crowding out of their holes and gathered round me till I saw— I saw them all so clear that I don't know what to think, woman. (*He is a grave man now.*)   Never mind about that.   Tell me about this—ghost.

MRS. OTERY.   It 's no concern of yours.

HARRY.   Yes, it is some concern of mine.   The folk that used to live here—the Morlands——

MRS. OTERY.   That was the name.   I suppose you heard it in the village ?

HARRY.   I have heard it all my days.   It is one of the names I bear.   I am one of the family.

MRS. OTERY.   I suspicioned that.

HARRY.   I suppose that is what made them come to me as I sat here.   Tell me about them.

MRS. OTERY.   It is little I know.   They were dead and gone before my time, the old man and his wife.

HARRY.   It 's not them I am asking you about.

MRS. OTERY.   They had a son-in-law, a sailor.   The war made a great man of him before it drowned him.

HARRY.   I know that ; he was my father.   Hard I used to think him, but I know better now.   Go on, there 's the other one.

MRS. OTERY (*reluctantly*).   That was all.

HARRY.   There is one more.

MRS. OTERY.   If you must speak of her, she is dead too.   I never saw her in life.

HARRY.   Where is she buried ?

MRS. OTERY.   Down by the church.

HARRY.   Is there a stone ?

MRS. OTERY.   Yes.

HARRY.   Does it say her age ?

MRS. OTERY. No.

HARRY. Is that holy spot well taken care of?

MRS. OTERY. You can see for yourself.

HARRY. I will see for myself. And so it is her ghost that haunts this house?

(*She makes no answer. He struggles with himself.*)

There is no such thing as ghosts. And yet—— Is it true about folk having lived in this house and left in a hurry?

MRS. OTERY. It's true.

HARRY. Because of a ghost—a thing that can't be.

MRS. OTERY. When I came in your eyes were staring; I thought you had seen her.

HARRY. Have you ever seen her yourself?

(*She shivers.*)

Where? In this room?

(*She looks at the little door.*)

In there? Has she ever been seen out of that room?

MRS. OTERY. All over the house, in every room and on the stairs. I tell you I've met her on the stairs, and she drew back to let me pass and said 'Good evening' too, timid-like, and at another time she has gone by me like a rush of wind.

HARRY. What is she like? Is she dressed in white? They are allus dressed in white, aren't they?

MRS. OTERY. She looks just like you or me. But for all that she's as light as air. I've seen—things.

HARRY. You look like it, too. But she is harmless, it seems?

MRS. OTERY. There's some wouldn't say that; them that left in a hurry. If she thought you were keeping it from her she would do you a mischief.

HARRY. Keeping what from her?

MRS. OTERY. Whatever it is she prowls about this cold house searching for, searching, searching. I don't know what it is.

HARRY (*grimly*). Maybe I could tell you. I dare say I could even put her in the way of finding him.

MRS. OTERY. Then I wish to God you would, and let her rest.

HARRY. My old dear, there are worse things than not

finding what you are looking for ; there is finding them so different from what you had hoped. (*He moves about.*) A ghost.   Oh no—and yet, and yet——   See here, I am going into that room.

MRS. OTERY.   As you like ; I care not.

HARRY.   I 'll burst open the door.

MRS. OTERY.   No need ; it 's not locked ; I cheated you about that.

HARRY.   But I tried it and it wouldn't open.

(MRS. OTERY *is very unhappy.*)

You think she is in there ?

MRS. OTERY.   She may be.

HARRY (*taking a deep breath*).   Give me air.

(*He throws open the window and we see that it is a night of stars.*)

Leave me here now.   I have a call to make.

MRS. OTERY (*hesitating*).   I dunno.   You think you 're in no danger, but——

HARRY.   That is how it is to be, missis.   Just ten minutes you were out of the room, did you say ?

MRS. OTERY.   That was all.

HARRY.   God !

(*She leaves him. After a moment's irresolution he sets off upon his quest carrying the candle, which takes with it all the light of the room. He is visible on the other side of the darkness, in the little passage and opening the door beyond. He returns, and now we see the pale ghost of* MARY ROSE *standing in the middle of the room, as if made out of the light he has brought back with him.*)

MARY ROSE (*bowing to him timidly*).   Have you come to buy the house ?

HARRY (*more startled by his own voice than by hers*).   Not me.

MARY ROSE.   It is a very nice house.   (*Doubtfully*) Isn't it ?

HARRY.   It was a nice house once.

MARY ROSE (*pleased*).   Wasn't it !   (*Suspiciously*) Did you know this house ?

HARRY.   When I was a young shaver.

MARY ROSE.   Young ?   Was it you who laughed ?

HARRY.   When was that ?

MARY ROSE (*puzzled*).   There was once some one who

laughed in this house. Don't you think laughter is a very pretty sound?

HARRY (*out of his depths*). Is it? I dare say. I never thought about it.

MARY ROSE. You are quite old.

HARRY. I 'm getting on.

MARY ROSE (*confidentially*). Would you mind telling me why every one is so old? I don't know you, do I?

HARRY. I wonder. Take a look. You might have seen me in the old days—playing about—outside in the garden—or even inside.

MARY ROSE. You—you are not Simon, are you?

HARRY. No. (*Venturing*) My name is Harry.

MARY ROSE (*stiffening*). I don't think so. I strongly object to your saying that.

HARRY. I 'm a queer sort of cove, and I would like to hear you call me Harry.

MARY ROSE (*firmly*). I decline. I regret, but I absolutely decline.

HARRY. No offence.

MARY ROSE. I think you are sorry for me.

HARRY. I am that.

MARY ROSE. I am sorry for me, too.

HARRY (*desperately desirous to help her*). If only there was something I—— I know nothing about ghosts—not a thing; can they sit down? Could you——?

(*He turns the chair toward her.*)

MARY ROSE. That is your chair.

HARRY. What do you mean by that?

MARY ROSE. That is where you were sitting.

HARRY. Were you in this room when I was sitting there?

MARY ROSE. I came in to look at you.

(*A sudden thought makes him cross with the candle to where he had left his knife. It is gone.*)

HARRY. Where is my knife? Were you standing looking at me with my knife in your hand?

(*She is sullenly silent.*)

Give me my knife.

(*She gives it to him.*)

What made you take it?

MARY ROSE.   I thought you were perhaps the one.

HARRY.   The one?

MARY ROSE.   The one who stole him from me.

HARRY.   I see.   Godsake, in a sort of way I suppose I am.
(He sits in the chair.)

MARY ROSE.   Give him back to me.

HARRY.   I wish I could.   But I'm doubting he is gone
beyond recall.

MARY ROSE *(unexpectedly)*.   Who is he?

HARRY.   Do you mean you have forgotten who it is you
are searching for?

MARY ROSE.   I knew once.   It is such a long time ago.   I
am so tired; please can I go away and play now?

HARRY.   Go away?   Where?   You mean back to that
—that place?
(She nods.)
What sort of a place is it?   Is it good to be there?

MARY ROSE.   Lovely, lovely, lovely.

HARRY.   It's not just the island, is it, that's so lovely,
lovely?
(She is perplexed.)
Have you forgotten the island too?

MARY ROSE.   I am sorry.

HARRY.   The island, the place where you heard the call.

MARY ROSE.   What is that?

HARRY.   You have even forgotten the call!   *(With vision)*
As far as I can make out, it was as if, in a way, there were two
kinds of dogs out hunting you—the good and the bad.

MARY ROSE *(who thinks he is chiding her)*.   Please don't be
cross with me.

HARRY.   I am far from cross with you.   I begin to think
it was the good dogs that got you.   Are they ghosts in that
place?

MARY ROSE *(with surprising certainty)*.   No.

HARRY.   You are sure?

MARY ROSE.   Honest Injun!

HARRY.   What fairly does me is, if the place is so lovely,
what made you leave it?

MARY ROSE *(frightened)*.   I don't know.

HARRY.   Do you think you could have fallen out?

MARY ROSE. I don't know. (*She thinks his power is great.*) Please, I don't want to be a ghost any more.

HARRY. As far as I can see, if you wasn't a ghost there you made yourself one by coming back. But it's no use your expecting me to be able to help you. (*She droops at this and he holds out his arms.*) Come to me, ghostie ; I wish you would.

MARY ROSE (*prim again*). Certainly not.

HARRY. If you come, I'll try to help you.

(*She goes at once and sits on his knee.*)

See here, when I was sitting by the fire alone I seemed to hear you as you once were saying that some day when he was a man you would like to sit on your Harry's knee.

MARY ROSE (*vaguely quoting she knows not whom*). The loveliest time of all will be when he is a man and takes me on his knee instead of my taking him on mine.

HARRY. Do you see who I am now ?

MARY ROSE. Nice man.

HARRY. Is that all you know about me ?

MARY ROSE. Yes.

HARRY. There is a name I would like to call you by, but my best course is not to worry you. Poor soul, I wonder if there was ever a man with a ghost on his knee before.

MARY ROSE. I don't know.

HARRY. Seems to me you're feared of being a ghost. I dare say, to a timid thing, being a ghost is worse than seeing them.

MARY ROSE. Yes.

HARRY. Is it lonely being a ghost ?

MARY ROSE. Yes.

HARRY. Do you know any other ghosts ?

MARY ROSE. No.

HARRY. Would you like to know other ghosts ?

MARY ROSE. Yes.

HARRY. I can understand that. And now you would like to go away and play ?

MARY ROSE. Please.

HARRY. In this cold house, when you should be searching, do you sometimes play by yourself instead ?

MARY ROSE (*whispering*). Don't tell.

HARRY.   Not me.   You 're a pretty thing.   What beautiful shoes you have.
(She holds out her feet complacently.)

MARY ROSE.   Nice buckles.

HARRY.   I like your hair.

MARY ROSE.   Pretty hair.

HARRY.   Do you mind the tuft that used to stand up at the back of—of Simon's head ?

MARY ROSE *(merrily)*.   Naughty tuft.

HARRY.   I have one like that.

MARY ROSE *(smoothing it down)*.   Oh dear, oh dear, what a naughty tuft !

HARRY.   My name is Harry.

MARY ROSE *(liking the pretty sound)*.   Harry, Harry, Harry, Harry.

HARRY.   But you don't know what Harry I am.

MARY ROSE.   No.

HARRY.   And this brings us no nearer what 's to be done with you.   I would willingly stay here though I have my clearing in Australy, but you 're just a ghost.   They say there are ways of laying ghosts, but I am so ignorant.

MARY ROSE *(imploringly)*.   Tell me.

HARRY.   I wish I could ; you are even more ignorant than I am.

MARY ROSE.   Tell me.

HARRY.   All I know about them for certain is that they are unhappy because they can't find something, and then once they 've got the thing they want, they go away happy and never come back.

MARY ROSE.   Oh, nic e!

HARRY.   The one thing clear to me is that you have got that thing at last, but you are too dog-tired to know or care. What you need now is to get back to the place you say is lovely, lovely.

MARY ROSE.   Yes, yes.

HARRY.   It sounds as if it might be Heaven, or near thereby.
(She wants him to find out for her.)
Queer, you that know so much can tell nothing, and them that know nothing can tell so much.   If there was any way of getting you to that glory place !

MARY ROSE. Tell me.

HARRY (*desperate*). He would surely send for you, if He wanted you.

MARY ROSE (*crushed*). Yes.

HARRY. It's like as if He had forgotten you.

MARY ROSE. Yes.

HARRY. It's as if nobody wanted you, either there or here.

MARY ROSE. Yes. (*She rises.*) Bad man.

HARRY. It's easy to call me names, but the thing fair beats me. There is nothing I wouldn't do for you, but a mere man is so helpless. How should the likes of me know what to do with a ghost that has lost her way on earth? I wonder if what it means is that you broke some law, just to come back for the sake of—of that Harry? If it was that, it's surely time He overlooked it.

MARY ROSE. Yes.

(*He looks at the open window.*)

HARRY. What a night of stars! Good old glitterers, I dare say they are in the know, but I am thinking you are too small a thing to get a helping hand from them.

MARY ROSE. Yes.

(*The call is again heard, but there is in it now no unholy sound. It is a celestial music that is calling for Mary Rose, Mary Rose, first in whispers and soon so loudly that, for one who can hear, it is the only sound in the world. Mary Rose, Mary Rose. As it wraps her round, the weary little ghost knows that her long day is done. Her face is shining. The smallest star shoots down for her, and with her arms stretched forth to it trustingly she walks out through the window into the empyrean. The music passes with her.* HARRY *hears nothing, but he knows that somehow a prayer has been answered.*)

SHALL WE JOIN THE LADIES?

'First act of an unfinished play' first performed at the opening of the theatre of the Royal Academy of Dramatic Art on May 27, 1921, with the following cast:

SAM SMITH (Host)	. .	*Dion Boucicault*
LADY JANE RAYE	. .	*Fay Compton*
MR. PREEN	. .	*Charles Hawtrey*
LADY WRATHIE	. .	*Sybil Thorndike*
SIR JOSEPH WRATHIE	. .	*Cyril Maude*
MRS. PREEN	. .	*Lady Tree*
CAPTAIN JENNINGS	. .	*Leon Quartermaine*
MRS. CASTRO	. .	*Lillah McCarthy*
MR. VAILE	. .	*Nelson Keys*
MRS. BLAND	. .	*Madge Titheradge*
MR. GOURLAY	. .	*Sir Johnston Forbes-Robertson*
MISS ISIT	. .	*Irene Vanbrugh*
MISS VAILE	. .	*Marie Lohr*
AN OFFICER	. .	*Norman Forbes*
LUCY (Maid)	. .	*Hilda Trevelyan*
DOLPHIN (Butler)	. .	*Gerald du Maurier*

The play was also performed publicly at the Palace Theatre on December 19, 1921, in aid of King George's Pension Fund for Actors and Actresses, with the same cast excepting Sir Joseph Wrathie (*Dennis Eadie*) and Miss Vaile (*Gladys Cooper*). It was produced at the St. Martin's Theatre on August 15, 1923, and ran for 407 performances.

SHALL WE JOIN THE LADIES?

FOR the past week the hospitable Sam Smith has been entertaining a country house party, and we choose to raise the curtain on them towards the end of dinner. They are seated thus, the host facing us :

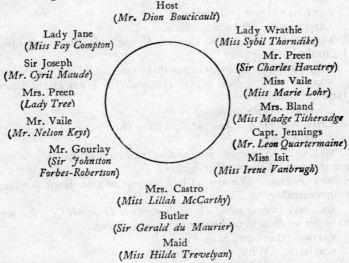

                                 Host
                        (*Mr. Dion Boucicault*)

Lady Jane   Lady Wrathie
(*Miss Fay Compton*)   (*Miss Sybil Thorndike*)

Sir Joseph   Mr. Preen
(*Mr. Cyril Maude*)   (*Sir Charles Hawtrey*)

Mrs. Preen   Miss Vaile
(*Lady Tree*)   (*Miss Marie Lohr*)

Mr. Vaile   Mrs. Bland
(*Mr. Nelson Keys*)   (*Miss Madge Titheradge*)

Mr. Gourlay   Capt. Jennings
(*Sir Johnston*   (*Mr. Leon Quartermaine*)
Forbes-Robertson)   Miss Isit
                                                 (*Miss Irene Vanbrugh*)

                               Mrs. Castro
                        (*Miss Lillah McCarthy*)

                                 Butler
                        (*Sir Gerald du Maurier*)

                                  Maid
                        (*Miss Hilda Trevelyan*)

Smith is a little old bachelor, and sits there beaming on his guests like an elderly cupid. So they think him, but they are to be undeceived. Though many of them have not met until this week, they have at present that genial regard for each other which steals so becomingly over really nice people who have eaten too much.

This is the first act of an unfinished play originally produced at the opening of the Royal Dramatic Academy's Theatre, which accounts for the brilliancy of the cast, and the brilliancy of the cast excuses the proud author for giving it in full.

Dolphin, the butler, is passing round the fruit. The only other attendant is a maid in the background, as for an emergency, and she is as interested in the conversation as he is indifferent to it. If one of the guests were to destroy himself, Dolphin would merely sign to her to remove the debris while he continued to serve the fruit.

In the midst of hilarity over some quip that we are just too late to catch, the youthful Lady Jane counts the company and is appalled.

LADY JANE.   We are thirteen, Lady Wrathie.
    (*Many fingers count.*)
LADY WRATHIE.   Fourteen.
CAPT. JENNINGS.   Twelve.
LADY JANE.   We are thirteen.
HOST.   Oh dear, how careless of me.   Is there anything I can do ?
SIR JOSEPH (*of the city*).   Leave this to me.   All keep your seats.
MRS. PREEN (*perhaps rather thankfully*).   I am afraid Lady Jane has risen.
    (LADY JANE *subsides.*)
LADY WRATHIE.   Joseph, you have risen yourself.
    (SIR JOSEPH *subsides.*)
MRS. CASTRO (*a mysterious widow from Buenos Ayres*).   Were we thirteen all those other nights ?
MRS. PREEN.   We always had a guest or two from outside, you remember.
MISS ISIT (*whose name obviously needs to be queried*).   All we have got to do is to make our number fourteen.
VAILE.   But how, Miss Isit ?
MISS ISIT.   Why, Dolphin, of course.
MRS. PREEN.   It 's too clever of you, Miss Isit. Mr. Smith, Dolphin may sit down with us, mayn't he ?
MRS. CASTRO.   Please, dear Mr. Smith ; just for a moment. That breaks the spell.
SIR JOSEPH.   We won't eat you, Dolphin. (*But he has crunched some similar ones.*)
HOST.   Let me explain to him.   You see, Dolphin, there is a superstition that if thirteen people sit down at table something staggering will happen to one of them before the night is out.   That is it, isn't it ?

MRS. BLAND (*darkly*). Namely, death.

HOST (*brightly*). Yes, namely, death.

LADY JANE. But not before the night is out, you dear ; before the year is out.

HOST. I thought it was before the night is out.

(DOLPHIN *is reluctant.*)

GOURLAY. Sit here, Dolphin.

MISS VAILE. No, I want him.

MISS ISIT. It was my idea, and I insist on having him.

MRS. CASTRO (*moving farther to the left*). Yes, here between us.

(DOLPHIN *obliges.*)

MRS. PREEN (*with childish abandon*). Saved.

HOST. As we are saved, and he does not seem happy, may he resume his duties ?

LADY WRATHIE. Yes, yes ; and now we ladies may withdraw.

PREEN (*the most selfish of the company, and therefore perhaps the favourite*). First, a glass of wine with you, Dolphin.

VAILE (*ever seeking to undermine PREEN's popularity*). Is this wise ?

PREEN (*determined to carry the thing through despite this fellow*). To the health of our friend Dolphin.

(DOLPHIN'S *health having been drunk, he withdraws his chair and returns to the sideboard. As MISS ISIT and MRS. CASTRO had made room for him between them exactly opposite his master, and the space remains empty, we have now a better view of the company. Can this have been the author's object ?*)

SIR JOSEPH (*pleasantly detaining the ladies*). One moment. Another toast. Fellow-guests, to-morrow morning, alas, this party has to break up, and I am sure you will all agree with me that we have had a delightful week. It has not been an eventful week ; it has been too happy for that.

CAPT. JENNINGS. I rise to protest. When I came here a week ago I had never met Lady Jane. Now, as you know, we are engaged. I certainly call it an eventful week.

LADY JANE. Yes, please, Sir Joseph.

SIR JOSEPH. I stand corrected. And now we are in the last evening of it ; we are drawing nigh to the end of a perfect day.

PREEN (*who is also an orator*). In seconding this motion——

VAILE.　Pooh. (*He is the perfect little gentleman, if socks and spats can do it.*)

SIR JOSEPH.　Though I have known you intimately for but a short time, I already find it impossible to call you anything but Sam Smith.

MRS. CASTRO.　In our hearts, Mr. Smith, that is what we ladies call you also.

PREEN.　If I might say a word——

VAILE.　Tuts.

SIR JOSEPH.　Ladies and gentlemen, is he not like a pocket edition of Mr. Pickwick?

GOURLAY (*an artist*).　Exactly. That is how I should like to paint him.

MRS. BLAND.　Mr. Smith, you love, we think that if you were married you could not be quite so nice.

SIR JOSEPH.　At any rate, he could not be quite so simple. For you are a very simple soul, Sam Smith. Well, we esteem you the more for your simplicity. Friends all, I give you the toast of Sam Smith.

(*The toast is drunk with acclamation, and* DOLPHIN, *who has paid no attention to it, again hovers round with wine.*)

HOST (*rising in answer to their appeals and warming them with his Pickwickian smile*).　Ladies and gentlemen, you are very kind, and I don't pretend that it isn't pleasant to me to be praised. Tell me, have you ever wondered why I invited you here?

MISS ISIT.　Because you like us, of course, you muddle-headed darling.

HOST.　Was that the reason?

SIR JOSEPH.　Take care, Sammy, you are not saying what you mean.

HOST.　Am I not? Kindly excuse. I dare say I am as simple as Sir Joseph says. And yet, do you really know me? Does any person ever know another absolutely? Has not the simplest of us a secret drawer inside him with—with a lock to it?

MISS ISIT.　If you have, Mr. Smith, be a dear and open it to us.

MRS. CASTRO.　How delicious. He is going to tell us of his first and only love.

HOST.　Ah, Mrs. Castro, I think I had one once, very nice, but I have forgotten her name. The person I loved best was my brother.

PREEN. I never knew you had a brother.

HOST. I suppose none of you knew. He died two years ago.

SIR JOSEPH. Sorry, Sam Smith.

MRS. PREEN (*drawing the chocolates nearer her*). We should like to hear about him if it isn't too sad.

HOST. Would you? He was many years my junior, and as attractive as I am commonplace. He died in a foreign land. Natural causes were certified. But there were suspicious circumstances, and I went out there determined to probe the matter to the full. I did, too.

PREEN. You didn't say where the place was.

HOST. It was Monte Carlo.

(*He pauses here, as if to give time for something to happen, but nothing does happen except that* MISS ISIT'S *wine-glass slips from her hand to the floor.*)

Dolphin, another glass for Miss Isit.

LADY JANE. Do go on.

HOST. My inquiries were slow, but I became convinced that my brother had been poisoned.

MRS. BLAND. How dreadful. You poor man.

GOURLAY. I hope, Sam Smith, that you got on the track of the criminals?

HOST. Oh yes.

(*A chair creaks.*)

Did you speak, Miss Isit?

MISS ISIT. Did I? I think not. What did you say about the criminals?

HOST. Not criminals; there was only one.

PREEN. Man or woman?

HOST. We are not yet certain. What we do know is that my brother was visited in his rooms that night by some one who must have been the murderer. It was some one who spoke English and who was certainly dressed as a man, but it may have been a woman. There is proof that it was some one who had been to the tables that night. I got in touch with every ' possible,' though I had to follow some of them to distant parts.

LADY WRATHIE. It is extraordinarily interesting.

HOST. Outwardly many of them seemed to be quite respectable people.

SIR JOSEPH. Ah, one can't go by that, Sam Smith.

HOST. I didn't. I made the most exhaustive inquiries into their private lives. I did it so cunningly that not one of them suspected why I was so anxious to make his or her acquaintance ; and then, when I was ready for them, I invited them to my house for a week, and they are all sitting round my table this evening.

(*As the monstrous significance of this sinks into them, there is a hubbub at the table.*)

You wanted to know why I had asked you here, and I am afraid that in consequence I have wandered a little from the toast ; but I thank you, Sir Joseph, I thank you all, for the too kind way in which you have drunk my health.

(*He sits down as modestly as he had risen, but the smile has gone from his face ; and the curious—which includes all the diners—may note that he is licking his lips. In the babel that again breaks forth,* DOLPHIN, *who has remained stationary and vacuous for the speech, goes the round of the table refilling glasses.*)

PREEN (*the first to be wholly articulate*). In the name of every one of us, Mr. Smith, I tell you that this is an outrage.

HOST. I was afraid you wouldn't like it.

SIR JOSEPH. May I ask, sir, whether all this week you have been surreptitiously ferreting into our private affairs, perhaps even rummaging our trunks ?

HOST (*brightening*). That was it. You remember how I pressed you all to show your prowess on the tennis courts and the golf links while I stayed at home ? That was my time for the trunks.

LADY JANE. Was there ever such a man ? Did you—open our letters ?

HOST. Every one of them. And there were some very queer things in them. There was one about a luncheon at the Ritz. ' You will know me,' the man wrote, ' by the gardenia I shall carry in my hand.' Perhaps I shouldn't have mentioned that. But the lady who got that letter need not be frightened. She is married, and her husband is here with her, but I won't tell you any more.

MISS ISIT. I think he should be compelled to tell.

PREEN. Wrathie, there are only two ladies here with their husbands.

SIR JOSEPH. Yours and mine, Preen.

LADY WRATHIE. Joseph, I don't need to tell you it wasn't your wife.

MRS. PREEN. It certainly wasn't yours, Willie.

PREEN. Of that I am well assured.

SIR JOSEPH. Take care what you say, Preen. That is very like a reflection on my wife.

GOURLAY. Let that pass. The other is the serious thing—so serious that it is a nightmare. Whom do you accuse of doing away with your brother, sir? Out with it.

HOST. You are not all turning against me, are you? I assure you I don't accuse any of you yet. I know that one of you did it, but I am not sure which one. I shall know soon.

VAILE. Soon? How soon?

HOST. Soon after the men join the ladies to-night. I ought to tell you that I am to try a little experiment to-night, something I have thought out which I have every confidence will make the guilty person fall into my hands like a ripe plum. (*He indicates rather horribly how he will squeeze it.*)

LADY JANE (*hitting his hand*). Don't do that.

SIR JOSEPH (*voicing the general unrest*). We insist, Smith, on hearing what this experiment is to be.

HOST. That would spoil it. But I can tell you this. My speech had a little pit in it, and all the time I was talking I was watching whether any of you would fall into that pit.

MRS. PREEN (*rising*). I didn't notice any pit.

HOST. You weren't meant to, Mrs. Preen.

PREEN. May I ask, without pressing the personal note, did any one fall into your pit?

HOST. I think so.

CAPT. JENNINGS. Smith, we must have the name of this person.

LADY WRATHIE. Mrs. Preen has fainted.

(PREEN *hurries slowly to his wife's assistance, and there is some commotion.*)

MRS. PREEN. Why—what—who—I am all right now. Willie, go back to your seat. Why are you all staring at me so?

MISS ISIT. Dear Mrs. Preen, we are so glad that you are better. I wonder what upset you?

PREEN (*imprudently*). I never knew her faint before.

MISS ISIT. I expect it was the heat.

PREEN (*nervous*). Say it was the heat, Emily.

MRS. PREEN. No, it wasn't the heat, Miss Isit. It was Mr. Smith's talk of a pit.

PREEN. My dear.

MRS. PREEN. I suddenly remembered how, as soon as that man mentioned that the place of the crime was Monte Carlo, some lady had let her wine-glass fall. That was why I fainted. I can't remember who she was.

LADY WRATHIE. It was Miss Isit.

MRS. PREEN. Really?

MISS ISIT. There is a thing called the law of libel. If Lady Wrathie and Mrs. Preen will kindly formulate their charges——

GOURLAY. Oh, come, let us keep our heads.

HOST. That's what I say.

GOURLAY. What about a motive? Scotland Yard always seeks for that first.

HOST. I see two possible motives. If a woman did it—well, they tended to run after my brother, and you all know of what a woman scorned is capable.

PREEN (*reminiscent*). Rather.

HOST. Then, again, my brother had a large sum of money with him, which disappeared.

SIR JOSEPH. If you could trace that money it might be a help.

HOST. All sorts of things are a help. The way you are all pretending to know nothing about the matter is a help. It might be a help if I could find out which of you has a clammy hand that at this moment wants to creep beneath the table.

(*Not a hand creeps.*)

I'll tell you something more. Murderers' hearts beat differently from other hearts. (*He raises his finger.*) Listen.

(*They listen.*)

Whose was it?

(*A cry from* MISS VAILE *brings her into undesired prominence.*)

MISS VAILE (*explaining*). I thought I heard it. It seemed to come from across the table.

(*This does not give universal satisfaction.*)

Please don't think because this man made me scream that I did it. I never was on a yacht in my life, at Monte Carlo or anywhere else.

(*Nor does even this have the desired effect.*)

VAILE (*sharply*). Bella !

MISS VAILE. Have I said—anything odd ?

GOURLAY. A yacht ? There has been no talk about a yacht.

MISS VAILE (*shrinking*). Hasn't there ?

HOST. Perhaps there should have been. It was on his yacht that my brother died.

MRS. CASTRO. You said in his rooms.

HOST. Yes, that is what I said. I wanted to find out which of you knew better.

LADY JANE. And Miss Vaile——

MISS VAILE. I can explain it all if—if——

MISS ISIT. Yes, give her a little time.

HOST. Perhaps you would all like to take a few minutes.

MISS VAILE. I admit that I was at Monte Carlo—with my brother—when an Englishman died there rather mysteriously on a yacht. When Mr. Smith told us of his brother's death, I concluded that it was probably the same person.

VAILE. I presume that you accept my sister's statement ?

MISS ISIT. Ab-sol-ute-ly.

HOST. She is not the only one of you who knew that yacht. You all admit having been at Monte Carlo two years ago, I suppose ?

CAPT. JENNINGS. One of us wasn't. Lady Jane was never there.

HOST (*with beady eyes*). What do you say to that, Lady Jane ?
    (LADY JANE *falters.*)

CAPT. JENNINGS. Tell him, Jane.

HOST. Yes, tell me.

CAPT. JENNINGS. You never were there ; say so.

LADY JANE. Why shouldn't I have been there ?

CAPT. JENNINGS. No reason. But when I happened to mention Monte Carlo to you the other day I certainly understood—— Jane, I never forget a word you say, and you did say you had never been there.

LADY JANE. So you—you, Jack—you accuse me—you—me——

CAPT. JENNINGS. I haven't, I haven't.

LADY JANE. You have all heard that Captain Jennings and I are engaged. I want you to understand that we are so no longer.

CAPT. JENNINGS. Jane !

(She removes the engagement ring from her finger and hesitates how to transfer it to the donor, who is many seats apart from her. The ever-resourceful DOLPHIN *goes to her with a tray on which she deposits the ring, and it is thus conveyed to the unhappy* JENNINGS. *Next moment* DOLPHIN *has to attend to the maid, who makes an audible gurgle of sympathy with love, which is a breach of etiquette. He opens the door for her, and she makes a shameful exit. He then fills the Captain's glass.)*

HOST *(in one of his nicer moods)*. Take comfort, Captain. If Lady Jane should prove to be the person wanted—mind you, perhaps she isn't—why, then the ring is a matter of small importance, because you would be parted in any case. I mean by the handcuffs. I forgot to say that I have them here. *(He gropes at his feet, where other people merely have a table-napkin.)* Pass them round, Dolphin. Perhaps some of you have never seen them before.

PREEN. A pocket edition of Pickwick we called him ; he is more like a pocket edition of the devil.

HOST. Please, a little courtesy. After all, I am your host.

*(*DOLPHIN *goes the round of the table with the handcuffs on the tray that a moment ago contained a lover's ring. They meet with no success.)*

Do take a look at them, Mrs. Castro ; they are an adjustable pair in case they should be needed for small wrists. Would you like to try them on, Sir Joseph ? They close with a click—a click.

SIR JOSEPH *(pettishly)*. We quite understand.

*(*MRS. BLAND *rises.)*

MRS. BLAND. How stupid of us. We have all forgotten that he said the murderer may have been a woman in man's clothes, and I have just remembered that when we played the charade on Wednesday he wanted the ladies to dress up as men. Was it to see whether one of us looked as if she could have passed for a man that night at Monte Carlo ?

HOST. You 've got it, Mrs. Bland.

SIR JOSEPH. Well, none of you did dress up, at any rate.

MRS. BLAND *(distressed)*. Oh, Sir Joseph. Some of us did dress up, in private, and we all agreed that—of course there 's nothing in it, but we all agreed that the only figure which might have deceived a careless eye was Lady Wrathie's.

PREEN. I say!

LADY WRATHIE. Joseph, do you sit there and permit this?

HOST. Now, now, there is nothing to be touchy about. Have I not been considerate?

SIR JOSEPH. Smith, I hold you to be an impudent scoundrel.

HOST. May not I, who lost a brother in circumstances so painful, appeal for a little kindly consideration from those of you who are innocent—shady characters though you be?

PREEN. I must say that rather touches me. Some of us might have reasons for being reluctant to have our past at Monte inquired into without being the person you are asking for.

HOST. Precisely. I am presuming that to be the position of eleven of you.

LADY WRATHIE. Joseph, I must ask you to come upstairs with me to pack our things.

MISS ISIT. For my part, after poor Mr. Smith's appeal I think it would be rather heartless not to stay and see the thing out. Especially, Mr. Smith, if you would give us just an inkling of what your—little experiment—in the drawing-room—is to be?

HOST. I can't say anything about it except that it isn't to take place in the drawing-room. You ladies are to go this evening to Dolphin's room, where we shall join you presently.

(*Even* DOLPHIN *is taken aback*.)

MRS. PREEN. Why should we go there?

HOST. Because I tell you to, Mrs. Preen.

LADY WRATHIE. I go to no such room. I leave this house at once.

MRS. PREEN. I also.

LADY JANE. All of us. I want to go home.

LADY WRATHIE. Joseph, come.

MRS. PREEN. Willie, I am ready. I wish you a long good-bye, Mr. Smith.

(*Their dignified advance upon the door is spoilt on opening it by their finding a policeman* (*Mr. Norman Forbes*) *standing there. They glare at* MR. SMITH.)

HOST. The ladies will now adjourn to Dolphin's room.

LADY WRATHIE. I say no.

MRS. CASTRO. Let us. Why shouldn't the innocent ones help him?

(*She gives* SMITH *her hand with a disarming smile*.)

HOST. I knew you would be on my side, Mrs. Castro.
Cold hand—warm heart. That is the saying, isn't it ?
    (*She shrinks.*)

LADY WRATHIE. Those who wish to leave this man's
house, follow me.

HOST (*for her special benefit*). My brother's cigarette case
was of faded green leather, and a hole had been burned in the
back of it.
    (*For some reason this takes the fight out of her, and she
    departs for* DOLPHIN'S *room, tossing her head, and followed
    by the other ladies.*)

VAILE (*seeing* SMITH *drop a word to* MISS VAILE *as she goes*).
What did you say to my sister ?

HOST. I only said to her that she isn't your sister. (*The last
lady to go is* MISS ISIT.) So you never met my brother, Miss Isit ?

MISS ISIT. Not that I know of, Mr. Smith.

HOST. I have a photograph of him that I should like to
show you.

MISS ISIT. I don't care to see it.

HOST. You are going to see it. (*It is in his pocket, and he
suddenly puts it before her eyes.*)

MISS ISIT (*surprised*). That is not—— (*She checks herself.*)

HOST. No, that is not my brother. That is some one you
have never seen. But how did you know it wasn't my brother ?
    (*She makes no answer.*)
I rather think you knew Dick, Miss Isit.

MISS ISIT (*dropping him a curtsey*). I rather think I did,
Mr. Sam. What then ?
    (*She goes impudently. Now that the ladies have left the
    room, the men don't quite know what to do except stare at
    their little host. Decanter in one hand and a box of cigar-
    ettes in the other, he toddles down to what would have been
    the hostess's chair had there been a hostess.*)

HOST. Draw up closer, won't you ?
    (*They don't want to, but they do, with the exception of* VAILE,
    who is studying a picture very near the door.)
You are not leaving us, Vaile ?

VAILE. I thought——

HOST (*sharply*). Sit down.

VAILE. Oh, quite.

HOST. You are not drinking anything, Gourlay. Captain, the port is with you.

(*The wine revolves, but no one partakes.*)

PREEN (*heavily*). Smith, there are a few words that I think it my duty to say. This is a very unusual situation.

HOST. Yes. You 'll have a cigarette, Preen?

(*The cigarettes are passed round and share the fate of the wine.*)

GOURLAY. I wonder why Mrs. Bland—she is the only one of them that there seems to be nothing against.

VAILE. A bit fishy, that.

PREEN (*murmuring*). It was rather odd my wife fainting.

CAPT. JENNINGS (*who has been a drooping figure since a recent incident*). I dare say the ladies are saying the same sort of thing about us. (*He lights a cigarette—one of his own.* DOLPHIN *is offering them liqueurs.*)

PREEN (*sulkily*). No, thanks. (*But he takes one.*) Smith, I am sure I speak for all of us when I say we would esteem it a favour if you ask Dolphin to withdraw.

HOST. He has his duties.

GOURLAY (*pettishly, to* DOLPHIN). No, thanks. He gets on my nerves. Can nothing disturb this man?

CAPT. JENNINGS (*also refusing*). No, thanks. Evidently nothing.

SIR JOSEPH (*reverting to a more hopeful subject*). Everything seems to point to its being a woman—wouldn't you say, Smith?

HOST. I wouldn't say everything, Sir Joseph. Dolphin thinks it was a man.

SIR JOSEPH. One of us here?

(SMITH *nods, and they survey their friend* DOLPHIN *with renewed distaste.*)

GOURLAY. Did he know your brother?

HOST. He was my brother's servant out there.

VAILE (*rising*). What? He wasn't the fellow who——?

HOST. Who what, Vaile?

PREEN. I say!

VAILE (*hotly*). What do you say?

PREEN. Nothing (*doggedly*). But I say!

(*Though* DOLPHIN *is now a centre of interest, no one seems able to address him personally.*)

GOURLAY. Are we to understand that you have had Dolphin spying on us here?

HOST. That was the idea. And he helped me by taking your finger-prints.

VAILE. How can that help?

HOST. He sent them to Scotland Yard.

SIR JOSEPH (*vindictively*). Oh, he did, did he?

PREEN. What shows finger-marks best?

HOST. Glass, I believe.

PREEN (*putting down his glass*). Now I see why the Americans went dry.

SIR JOSEPH. Smith, how can you be sure that Dolphin wasn't the man himself?

(MR. SMITH *makes no answer.* DOLPHIN *picks up* SIR JOSEPH'S *napkin and returns it to him.*)

PREEN. Somehow I still cling to the hope that it was a woman.

VAILE. If it is a woman, Smith, what will you do?

HOST. She shall hang by the neck until she is dead. You won't try the benedictine, Vaile?

VAILE. No, thanks.

(*The maid returns with coffee, which she presents under* DOLPHIN'S *superintendence. Most of them accept. The cups are already full.*)

SIR JOSEPH (*in his lighter manner*). Did you notice what the ladies are doing in Dolphin's room, Lucy?

MAID (*in a tremble, and wishing she could fly from this house*). Yes, Sir Joseph, they are wondering, Sir Joseph, which of you it was that did it.

PREEN. How like women!

GOURLAY. By the way, Smith, do you know how the poison was administered?

HOST. Yes, in coffee. (*He is about to help himself.*)

MAID. You are to take the yellow cup, sir.

HOST. Who said so?

MAID. The lady who poured out this evening, sir.

PREEN. Aha, who was she?

MAID. Lady Jane Wraye, sir.

PREEN. I don't like it.

GOURLAY. Smith, don't drink that coffee.

CAPT. JENNINGS (*in wrath*). Why shouldn't he drink it?

GOURLAY. Well, if it was she—a desperate woman—it was given in coffee the other time, remember. But stop, she wouldn't be likely to do it in the same way a second time.

VAILE. I'm not so sure. Perhaps she doesn't suspect that Smith knows how it was given the first time. We didn't know till the ladies had left the room.

PREEN (*admiring him at last*). I say, Vaile, that's good.

CAPT. JENNINGS. I have no doubt she merely meant that she had sugared it to his taste.

VAILE (*smiling*). Sugar!

PREEN (*pinning his faith to* VAILE). Sugar!

GOURLAY. Couldn't we analyse it?

CAPT. JENNINGS (*the one who is at present looking most like a murderer*). Smith, I insist on your drinking that coffee.

VAILE. Lady Jane! Who would have thought it!

PREEN (*become a mere echo of* VAILE). Lady Jane! Who would have thought it!

CAPT. JENNINGS. Give me the yellow cup. (*He drains it to the dregs.*)

SIR JOSEPH. Nobly done, in any case. Look here, Jennings —you are among friends—it hadn't an odd taste, had it?

CAPT. JENNINGS. Not a bit.

VAILE. He wouldn't feel the effects yet.

PREEN. He wouldn't feel them yet.

HOST. Vaile ought to know.

PREEN. Vaile knows.

SIR JOSEPH. Why ought Vaile to know, Smith?

HOST. He used to practise as a doctor.

SIR JOSEPH. You never mentioned that to me, Vaile.

VAILE. Why should I?

HOST. Why should he? He is not allowed to practise now. (*We now see that* VAILE *has unpleasant teeth.*)

PREEN. A doctor—poison—ease of access. (*His passion for* VAILE *is shattered. He gives him back the ring, as* CAPT. JENNINGS *might say, and wanders the room despondently.*)

SIR JOSEPH. We are where we were again.

(DOLPHIN *escorts out the maid, who is not in a condition to go alone.*)

CAPT. JENNINGS. At any rate that fellow has gone.

GOURLAY (*the first to laugh for some time*).   Excuse me.   I suddenly remembered that Wrathie had called this the end of a perfect day.

HOST.   It isn't ended yet.

(MR. PREEN *in his wanderings toward the sideboard encounters a very large glass and a small bottle of brandy.   He introduces them to each other.   He swirls the contents in the glass as if hopeful that it may climb the rim and so escape without his having to drink it.   This is a trick which has become so common with him that when lost in thought he sometimes goes through the motion though there is no glass in his hand.*)

PREEN (*communing with himself*).   I feel I am not my old bright self.   (*Sips.*)   I can't believe for a moment that it was my wife.   (*Sips.*)   And yet—(*sips*)—that fainting, you know.   (*Sips.*)   I should go away for a bit until it blew over.   (*Sips.*)   I don't think I should ever marry again.   (*Sips and sips, and becomes perhaps a little more like his old bright self.*)

GOURLAY.   There is something shocking about sitting here, suspecting each other in this way.   Let us go to that room and have it out.

HOST.   I am quite ready.   Nothing more to drink, anyone ?   Bring your cigarette, Captain.

SIR JOSEPH (*hoarsely*).   Smith—Sam—before we go, can I have a word with you alone ?

HOST.   Sorry, Joseph.   And now, shall we join the ladies ?
(*As they rise, a dreadful scream is heard from the direction of* DOLPHIN'S *room—a woman's scream.   Next moment* DOLPHIN *reappears in the doorway.   He is no longer the imperturbable butler.   He is livid.   He tries to speak, but no words will come out of his mouth.* CAPT. JENNINGS *dashes past him, and the others follow.* DOLPHIN *looks at his master with mingled horror and appeal, and then goes.* SMITH *sits down again to take one glass of brandy.   Where he sits we cannot see his face, but his rigid little back is merciless.   As he rises to follow the others the curtain falls on Act One.*)

BARBARA'S WEDDING

Produced at the Savoy Theatre on August 23, 1927, with the following cast :

THE COLONEL	. . . . .	*Robert Loraine*
DERING	. . . . .	*Henry Oscar*
BARBARA	. . . . .	*Maisie Darrell*
GRANNY	. . . . .	*Mary Jerrold*
KARL	. . . . .	*Osmund Willson*
BILLY	. . . . .	*Frederick Peisley*

BARBARA'S WEDDING

THE Colonel is in the sitting-room of his country cottage, staring through the open windows at his pretty garden. He is a very old man, and is sometimes bewildered nowadays. You must understand that at the beginning of the play he is just seeing visions of the past. No real people come to him, though he thinks they do. He calls to Dering, the gardener, who is on a ladder, pruning. Dering, who comes to him, is a rough, capable young fellow with fingers that are already becoming stumpy because he so often uses his hands instead of a spade. This is a sign that Dering will never get on in the world. His mind is in the same condition as his fingers, working back to clods. He will get a rise of one and sixpence in a year or two, and marry on it and become duller and heavier; and, in short, the clever ones could already write his epitaph.

COLONEL. A beautiful morning, Dering.

DERING. Too much sun, sir. The roses be complaining, and, to make matters worse, Miss Barbara has been watering of them—in the heat of the day.

COLONEL. Has she? She means well. (*But that is not what is troubling him. He approaches the subject diffidently.*) Dering, you heard it, didn't you? (*He is longing to be told that* DERING *heard it.*)

DERING. What was that, sir?

COLONEL. The thunderstorm—early this morning.

DERING. There was no thunderstorm, sir.

COLONEL (*dispirited*). That is what they all say. (*He is too courteous to contradict any one, but he tries again; there is about him the insistence of one who knows that he is right.*) It was at four o'clock. I got up and looked out at the window. The evening primroses were very beautiful.

DERING (*equally dogged*). I don't hold much with evening primroses, sir; but I was out and about at four; there was no thunderstorm.

(*The* COLONEL *still thinks that there was a thunderstorm, but he wants to placate* DERING.)

1169

COLONEL. I suppose I just thought there was one. Perhaps it was some thunderstorm of long ago that I heard. They do come back, you know.

DERING (*heavily*). Do they, sir ?

COLONEL. I am glad to see you moving about in the garden, Dering, with everything just as usual.

(*There is a cautious slyness about this, as if the* COLONEL *was fishing for information; but it is too clever for* DERING, *who is going with a ' Thank you, sir.'*)

No, don't go. (*The old man lowers his voice and makes a confession reluctantly.*) I am—a little troubled, Dering.

(DERING *knows that his master has a wandering mind, and he answers nicely.*)

DERING. Everything be all right, sir.

COLONEL (*with relief*). I'm glad of that. It is pleasant to see that you have come back, Dering. Why did you go away for such a long time ?

DERING. Me, sir ? (*He is a little aggrieved.*) I haven't had a day off since Christmas.

COLONEL. Haven't you ? I thought——

(*The* COLONEL *tries to speak casually, but there is a trembling eagerness in his voice.*)

COLONEL. Is everything just as usual, Dering ?

DERING. Yes, sir. There never were a place as changes less than this.

COLONEL. That's true. Thank you, Dering, for saying that. (*But next moment he has lowered his voice again.*) Dering, there is nothing wrong, is there ? Is anything happening that I am not being told about ?

DERING. Not that I know of, sir.

COLONEL. That is what they all say, but—I don't know. (*He stares at his old sword which is hanging on the wall.*) Where is every one ?

DERING. They're all about, sir. There is a cricket match on at the village green.

COLONEL. Is there ?

DERING. If the wind had a bit of south in it you could hear their voices. You were a bit of a nailer at cricket yourself, sir.

(*The* COLONEL *sees himself standing up to fast ones. He is gleeful over his reminiscences.*)

COLONEL. Ninety-nine against Mallowfield, and then bowled off my pads. Biggest score I ever made. Mallowfield wanted to add one to make it the hundred, but I wouldn't let them. I was pretty good at steering them through the slips, Dering ! Do you remember my late cut ? It didn't matter where point stood, I got past him. You used to stand at point, Dering.

DERING. That was my grandfather, sir. If he was to be believed, he used to snap you regular at point.

(*The* COLONEL *is crestfallen, but he has a disarming smile.*)

COLONEL. Did he ? I dare say he did. I can't play now, but I like to watch it still. (*He becomes troubled again.*) Dering, there 's no cricket on the green to-day. I have been down to look. I don't understand it, Dering. When I got there the green was all dotted with them. But as I watched them they began to go away, one and two at a time ; they weren't given out, you know, they went as if they had been called away. Some of the little shavers stayed on—and then they went off, as if they had been called away too. The stumps were left lying about. Why is it ?

DERING. It 's just fancy, sir. I saw Master Will oiling his bat yesterday.

COLONEL (*avidly*). Did you ? I should have liked to see that. I have often oiled their bats for them. Careless lads, they always forget. Was that nice German boy with him ?

DERING. Mr. Karl ? Not far off, sir. He was sitting by the bank of the stream playing on his flute ; and Miss Barbara, she had climbed one of my apple-trees—she says they are your trees. (*He lowers.*)

COLONEL (*meekly*). They are, you know, Dering.

DERING. Yes, sir, in a sense, but I don't like any of you to meddle with them. And there she sat, pelting the two of them with green apples.

COLONEL. How like her ! (*He shakes his head indulgently.*) I don't know how we are to make a demure young lady of her.

DERING. They say in the village, sir, that Master Will would like to try.

(*To the* COLONEL *this is wit of a high order.*)

COLONEL. Ha ! ha ! he is just a colt himself. (*But the laughter breaks off. He seems to think that he will get the truth if* DERING *comes closer.*) Who are all here now, Dering ; in the house, I mean ?   I sometimes forget.   They grow old so quickly.   They go out at one door in the bloom of youth, and come back by another, tired and grey.   Haven't you noticed it ?

DERING.   No, sir.   The only visitors staying here are Miss Barbara and Mr. Karl.   There's just them and yourselves, sir, you and the mistress and Master Will.   That's all.

COLONEL.   Yes, that's all.   Who is the soldier, Dering ?

DERING.   Soldier, sir ?   There is no soldier here except yourself.

COLONEL.   Isn't there ?   There was a nurse with him. Who is ill ?

DERING.   No one, sir.   There's no nurse.   (*He backs away from the old man.*)   Would you like me to call the mistress, sir ?

COLONEL.   No, she has gone down to the village.   She told me why, but I forget.   Miss Barbara is with her.

DERING.   Miss Barbara is down by the stream, sir.

COLONEL.   Is she ?   I think they said they were going to a wedding.   (*With an old man's curiosity*) Who is being married to-day, Dering ?

DERING.   I have heard of no wedding, sir.   But here is Miss Barbara.

(*It is perhaps the first time that* DERING *has been glad to see* MISS BARBARA, *who romps in, a merry hoyden, running over with animal spirits.*)

COLONEL (*gaily*).   Here's the tomboy !

(BARBARA *looks suspiciously from one to the other.*)

BARBARA.   Dering, I believe you are complaining to the Colonel about my watering the flowers at the wrong time of day.

(*The* COLONEL *thinks she is even wittier than* DERING, *who is properly abashed.*)

DERING.   I did just mention it, miss.

BARBARA.   You horrid !   (*She shakes her mop of hair at the gardener.*)   Dear, don't mind him.   And every time he says they are *his* flowers and *his* apples, you tell me, and I shall say to his face that they are *yours*.

COLONEL.   The courage of those young things !

(DERING's *underlip becomes very pronounced, but he goes off into the garden.* BARBARA *attempts to attend to the* COLONEL's *needs.*)

BARBARA. Let me make you comfy—the way granny does it.

(*She arranges his cushions clumsily.*)

COLONEL. That is not quite the way she does it. Do you call her granny, Barbara?

BARBARA. She asked me to—for practice. Don't you remember why?

(*Of course the* COLONEL *remembers.*)

COLONEL. I know! Billy boy.

BARBARA. You *are* quick to-day. Now, wait till I get your cane.

COLONEL. I don't need my cane while I 'm sitting.

BARBARA. You look so beau'ful, sitting holding your cane. (*She knocks over his cushions.*) Oh dear! I am a clumsy.

COLONEL (*politely*). Not at all, but perhaps if I were to do it for myself. (*He makes himself comfortable.*) That 's better. Thank you, Barbara, very much.

BARBARA. *I* didn't do it. I 'm all thumbs. What a ghastly nurse I should make.

COLONEL. Nurse? (*The* COLONEL'S *troubles return to him.*) Who is she, Barbara?

BARBARA. Who is who, dear?

COLONEL. That nurse?

BARBARA. There 's no nurse here.

COLONEL. Isn't there?

BARBARA (*feeling that she is of less use than ever to-day*). Where is granny?

COLONEL. She has gone down to the village to a wedding.

BARBARA. There 's no wedding. Who could be being married?

COLONEL. I think it 's people I know, but I can't remember who they are. I thought you went too, Barbara.

BARBARA. Not I. Catch me missing it if there had been a wedding!

COLONEL. You and the nurse.

BARBARA. Dear, you have just been imagining things again. Shall I play to you, or sing? (*She knocks over a chair.*) Oh dear, everything catches in me. Would you like me to sing ' Robin Adair,' dear?

COLONEL (*polite, but firm*). No, thank you, Barbara. (*For

a few moments he forgets her ; his mind has gone wandering again.)
Barbara, the house seems so empty.   Where are Billy and Karl ?

BARBARA.   Billy is where Karl is, you may be sure.

COLONEL.   And where is Karl ?

BARBARA.   He is where Billy boy is, you may be sure.

COLONEL.   And where are they both ?

BARBARA.   Not far from where Barbara is, you bet.   (*She
flutters to the window and waves her hand.*)   Do you hear
Karl's flute ?   They have been down all the morning at the
pool where the alder is, trying to catch that bull-trout.

COLONEL.   They didn't get him, I 'll swear !

BARBARA.   You can ask them.

COLONEL.   I spent a lot of my youth trying to get that bull-
trout.   I tumbled in there sixty years ago.

BARBARA.   I tumbled in sixty minutes ago !   It can't be
the same trout, dear.

COLONEL.   Same old rascal !

(BILLY *and* KARL *come in by the window, leaving a fishing-
rod outside.   They are gay, careless, attractive youths.*)

BARBARA (*with her nose in the air*).   You muddy things !

COLONEL (*gaily firing his dart*).   Did you get the bull-trout,
Billy boy ?

BILLY.   He 's a brute that.

COLONEL.   He is, you know.

BILLY.   He came up several times and had a look at my fly.
Didn't flick it, or do anything as complimentary as that.   Just
yawned and went down.

COLONEL.   Yawned, did he ?   Used to wink in my time.
Did you and Billy fish at Heidelberg, Karl ?

KARL.   We were more worthily employed, sir, but we did
unbend at times.   Billy, do you remember——   (*He begins
a gay dance.*)

BILLY.   Not I.   (*Then he joins in.*)

BARBARA.   Young gentlemen, how disgraceful !   (*She joins
in.*)

COLONEL.   Harum-scarums !

KARL.   Does he know about you two ?

BILLY.   He often forgets.   I 'll tell him again.   Grandfather, Barbara and I have something to say to you.   It 's this.
(*He puts his arm round* BARBARA.)

COLONEL (*smiling*). I know—I know. There's nothing like it. I'm very glad, Barbara.

BARBARA. You see, dear, I've loved Billy boy since the days when he tried to catch the bull-trout with a string and a bent pin, and I held on to his pinafore to prevent his tumbling in. We used to play at school at marrying and giving in marriage, and the girl who was my bridegroom had always to take the name of Billy. ' Do you, woman, take this man Billy ——' the clergyman in skirts began, and before I could answer diffidently, some other girl was sure to shout, ' I should rather think she does.'

COLONEL (*in high good humour*). Don't forget the ring, Billy. You know, when I was married I couldn't find the ring !

KARL. Were you married here, sir ?

COLONEL. Yes, at the village church.

BILLY. So were my father and mother.

COLONEL (*as his eyes wander to the garden*). I remember walking back with my wife and bringing her in here through the window. She kissed some of the furniture.

BILLY. I suppose you would like a grander affair, Barbara ?

BARBARA. No, just the same.

BILLY. I hoped you would say that.

BARBARA. But, Billy, I'm to have such a dream of a wedding-gown. Granny is going with me to London to choose it (*laying her head on the* COLONEL's *shoulder*) if you can do without her for a day, dear.

COLONEL (*gallantly*). I shall go with you. I couldn't trust you and granny to choose the gown.

KARL. You must often be pretty lonely, sir, when we are all out and about enjoying ourselves.

COLONEL. They all say that. But that is the time when I'm not lonely, Karl. It's then I see things most clearly— the past, I suppose. It all comes crowding back to me—India, the Crimea, India again—and it's so real, especially the people. They come and talk to me. I seem to see them ; I don't know they haven't been here, Billy, till your granny tells me afterwards.

BILLY. Yes, I know. I wonder where granny is.

BARBARA. It isn't often she leaves you for so long, dear.

COLONEL. She told me she had to go out, but I forget where. Oh, yes, she has gone down to the village to a wedding.

BILLY. A wedding?

BARBARA. It 's curious how he harps on that.

COLONEL. She said to me to listen and I would hear the wedding-bells.

BARBARA. Not to-day, dear.

BILLY. Best not to worry him.

BARBARA. But granny says we should try to make things clear to him.

BILLY. Was any one with granny when she said she was going to a wedding?

COLONEL (*like one begging her to admit it*). You were there, Barbara.

BARBARA. No, dear. He said that to me before. And something about a nurse.

COLONEL (*obstinately*). She was there, too.

BILLY. Any one else?

COLONEL. There was that soldier.

BARBARA. A soldier also!

COLONEL. Just those three.

BILLY. But that makes four. Granny and Barbara and a nurse and a soldier.

COLONEL. They were all there; but there were only three.

BILLY. Odd.

BARBARA (*soothingly*). Never mind, dear. Granny will make it all right. She is the one for you.

COLONEL. She is the one for me.

KARL. If there had been a wedding, wouldn't she have taken the Colonel with her?

BARBARA. Of course she would.

KARL. You are not too old to have a kind eye for a wedding, sir.

COLONEL (*wagging his head*). Aha, aha! You know, if I had gone, very likely I should have kissed the bride. Brides look so pretty on their wedding day. They are often not pretty at other times, but they are all pretty on their wedding day.

KARL. You have an eye for a pretty girl still, sir!

COLONEL. Yes, I have; yes, I have!

BARBARA. I do believe I see it all. Granny has been talking

to you about Billy boy and me, and you haven't been able to wait ; you have hurried on the wedding !

BILLY. Bravo, Barbara, you 've got it.

COLONEL (*doubtfully*). That may be it. Because I am sure you were to be there, Barbara.

BARBARA. Our wedding, Billy !

KARL. It doesn't explain those other people, though.

(*The* COLONEL *moves about in agitation.*)

BARBARA. What is it, dear ?

COLONEL. I can't quite remember, but I think that is why she didn't take me. It is your wedding, Barbara, but I don't think Billy boy is to be there, my love.

BARBARA. Not at my wedding !

BILLY. Grandfather !

COLONEL. There 's something sad about it.

BARBARA. There can't be anything sad about a wedding, dear. Granny didn't say it was a sad wedding, did she ?

COLONEL. She was smiling.

BARBARA. Of course she was.

COLONEL. But I think that was only to please the nurse.

BARBARA. That nurse again ! Dear, don't think any more about it. There 's no wedding.

COLONEL (*gently, though he wonders why they can go on deceiving him*). Is there not ?

(*The village wedding-bells begin to ring. The* COLONEL *is triumphant.*)

I told you ! There is a wedding !

(*The bells ring on gaily.* BILLY *and* BARBARA *take a step nearer to each other, but can go no closer. The bells ring on, and the three young people fade from the scene.*

When they are gone and he is alone, the COLONEL *still addresses them.*

Soon the bells stop. He knows that he is alone now, but he does not understand it. The sun is shining brightly, but he sits very cold in his chair. He shivers. From this point to the end of the play it is the real people he sees as they are now. He is very glad to see his wife coming to him through the open window. She is a dear old lady, and is dressed brightly, as becomes one who has been to a wedding Her face beams to match her gown. She is

*really quite a happy woman again, for it is several years
since any deep sorrow struck her; and that is a long time.
No one, you know, understands the* COLONEL *as she does,
no one can soothe him and bring him out of his imaginings
as she can. He hastens to her. He is no longer cold.
That is her great reward for all she does for him.*)

ELLEN (*tranquilly*). I have come back, John. It hasn't
seemed very long, has it?

COLONEL. No, not long, Ellen. Had you a nice walk?

(*She continues to smile, but she is watching him closely.*)

ELLEN. I haven't been for a walk. Don't you remember
where I told you I was going, John?

COLONEL. Yes, it was to a wedding.

ELLEN (*rather tremulously*). You haven't forgotten whose
wedding, have you?

COLONEL. Tell me, Ellen.

(*He is no longer troubled. He knows that* ELLEN *will tell
him.*)

ELLEN. I have been seeing Barbara married, John.

COLONEL. Yes, it was Barbara's wedding. They wouldn't
—— Ellen, why wasn't I there?

ELLEN (*like one telling him amusing gossip*). I thought you
might be a little troubled if you went, John. Sometimes your
mind—not often, but sometimes if you are agitated—and then
you think you see—people who aren't here any longer. Oh
dear, oh dear, help me with these bonnet strings.

COLONEL. Yes, I know. I'm all right when you are with
me, Ellen. Funny, isn't it?

(*She raises her shoulders in a laugh.*)

ELLEN. It is funny, John. I ran back to you. I was
thinking of you all the time—even more than of Billy boy.

(*The* COLONEL *is very gay.*)

COLONEL. Tell me all about it, Ellen. Did Billy boy lose
the ring? We always said he would lose the ring.

(*She looks straight into his eyes.*)

ELLEN. You have forgotten again, John. Barbara isn't
married to Billy boy.

(*He draws himself up.*)

COLONEL. Not marry Billy? I'll see about that!

(*She presses him into his chair.*)

ELLEN. Sit down, dear, and I'll tell you something again. It is nothing to trouble you, because your soldiering is done, John; and greatly done. My dear, there is war again, and our old land is in it. Such a war as my soldier never knew.

(*He rises. He is a stern old man.*)

COLONEL. A war! That's it, is it? So now I know! Why wasn't I told? I'm not too old yet.

ELLEN. Yes, John, you are too old, and all you can do now is to sit here and—and take care of me. You knew all about it quite clearly this morning. We stood together upstairs by the window listening to the aircraft guns.

COLONEL. I remember! I thought it was a thunderstorm. Dering told me he heard nothing.

ELLEN. Dering?

COLONEL. Our gardener, you know. (*His voice becomes husky.*) Haven't I been talking with him, Ellen?

ELLEN. It is a long time since we had a gardener, John.

COLONEL. Is it? So it is! A war! That is why there is no more cricket on the green.

ELLEN. They have all gone to the war, John.

COLONEL. That's it; even the little shavers. (*He whispers*) Why isn't Billy boy fighting, Ellen?

ELLEN. Oh, John!

COLONEL. Is Billy boy dead? (*She nods.*) Was he killed in action? Tell me, tell me! (*She nods again.*) Good for Billy boy. I knew Billy boy was all right. Don't cry, Ellen. I'll take care of you. All's well with Billy boy.

ELLEN. Yes, I know, John.

(*He hesitates before speaking again.*)

COLONEL. Ellen, who is the soldier? He comes here. He is a captain.

ELLEN. He is a very gallant man, John. It is he who was married to Barbara to-day.

COLONEL (*bitterly*). She has soon forgotten.

ELLEN (*shaking her brave head*). She hasn't forgotten, dear. And it's nearly three years now since Billy died.

COLONEL. So long! We have a medal he got, haven't we?

ELLEN. No, John; he died before he could win any medals.

COLONEL. Karl will be sorry. They were very fond of each other, those two boys, Ellen.

ELLEN. Karl fought against us, dear. He died in the same engagement. They may even have killed each other.

COLONEL. They hadn't known, Ellen.

ELLEN (*with thin lips*). I dare say they knew.

COLONEL. Billy boy and Karl !

(*She tells him some more gossip.*)

ELLEN. John, I had Barbara married from here because she has no people of her own. I think Billy would have liked it.

COLONEL. That was the thing to do, Ellen. Nice of you. I remember everything now. It 's Dering she has married. He was once my gardener !

ELLEN. The world is all being re-made, dear. He is worthy of her.

(*He lets this pass. He has remembered something almost as surprising.*)

COLONEL. Ellen, is Barbara a nurse ?

ELLEN. Yes, John, and one of the staidest and most serene. Who would have thought it of the merry madcap of other days ! They are coming here, John, to say good-bye to you. They have only a few days' leave. She is in France, too, you know. She was married in her nurse's uniform.

COLONEL. Was she ? She told me to-day that—no, it couldn't have been to-day.

ELLEN. You have been fancying you saw them, I suppose. (*She grows tremulous again.*) You will be nice to them, John, won't you, and wish them luck ? They have their trials before them.

COLONEL (*eagerly*). Tell me what to do, Ellen.

ELLEN. Don't say anything about Billy boy, John.

COLONEL. No no, let 's pretend.

ELLEN. And I wouldn't talk about the garden, John ; just in case he is a little touchy about that.

COLONEL (*beginning to fancy himself as a tactician*). Not a word !

ELLEN (*who knows what is the best way to put him on his mettle*). You see, I 'm sure I should make a mess of it, so I 'm trusting to you, John.

COLONEL (*very pleased*). Leave it all to me, Ellen. I 'll be frightfully sly. You just watch me.

(*She goes to the window and calls to the married couple.*

CAPTAIN DERING, *in khaki, is a fine soldierly figure.*
BARBARA, *in her Red Cross uniform, is quiet and resourceful.
An artful old boy greets them.*)

COLONEL. Congratulations, Barbara. No, no, none of
your handshaking ; you don't get past an old soldier in that
way. Excuse me, young man. (*He kisses* BARBARA *and looks
at his wife to make sure that she is admiring him.*) And to you,
Captain Dering—you have won a prize.

DERING (*a gallant gentleman*). I know it ; I 'll try to show
I know it.

COLONEL (*perturbed*). I haven't given Barbara a wedding
present, Ellen. I should like——

BARBARA. Indeed you have, dear, and a lovely one. You
haven't forgotten ?

(*Granny signs to the* COLONEL *and he immediately says,
with remarkable cunning :*)

COLONEL. Oh—that ! I was just quizzing you, Barbara.
I hope you will be as happy, dear, staid Barbara, as if you had
married——

(*He sees that he has nearly given away the situation. He
looks triumphantly at granny as much as to say, ' Observe
me ; I 'm not going to say a word about him.' Granny
comes to his aid.*)

ELLEN. Perhaps Captain Dering has some little things to
do : and you, too, Barbara. They are leaving in an hour, John.

(*For a moment the* COLONEL *is again in danger.*)

COLONEL. If you would like to take Barbara into the
garden, Captain Dering—— (*He recovers himself instantly.*)
No, not the garden, you wouldn't know your way about in the
garden.

DERING (*smiling*). Wouldn't I, Colonel ?

COLONEL. No, certainly not. I 'll show it you some day.
(*He makes gleeful signs to granny.*) But there is a nice meadow
just beyond the shrubbery. Barbara knows the way ; she
often went there with—— (*He checks himself. Granny signs
to them to go, and* BARBARA *kisses both the* COLONEL'S *hands.*)
The Captain will be jealous, you know !

BARBARA. Let me, dear (*arranging his cushions professionally.*)

ELLEN. She is much better at it than I am now, John.

(*The* COLONEL *has one last piece of advice to give.*)

COLONEL. I wouldn't go down by the stream, Barbara— not to the pool where the alder is. There's—there's not a good view there, sir; and a boy—a boy I knew, he often— nobody in particular—just a boy who used to come about the house—he is not here now—he is on duty. I don't think you should go to the alder pool, Barbara.

BARBARA. We won't go there, dear.

(*She and her husband go out, and the* COLONEL *scarcely misses them, he is so eager to hear what his wife thinks of him.*)

COLONEL. Did I do all right, Ellen?

ELLEN. Splendidly. I was proud of you.

COLONEL. I put them completely off the scent! They haven't a notion! I can be very sly, you know, at times. Ellen, I think I should like to have that alder tree cut down. There is no boy now, you see.

ELLEN. I would leave it alone, John. There will be boys again. Shall I read to you; you like that, don't you?

COLONEL. Yes, read to me—something funny, if you please. About Sam Weller! No, I expect Sam has gone to the wars. Read about Mr. Pickwick. He is very amusing. I feel sure that if he had tried to catch the bull-trout he would have fallen in. Just as Barbara did this morning.

ELLEN. Barbara?

COLONEL. She is down at the alder pool. Billy is there with that nice German boy. The noise they make, shouting and laughing!

(*She gets from its shelf the best book for war-time.*)

ELLEN. Which bit shall I read?

COLONEL. About Mr. Pickwick going into the lady's bed- room by mistake.

ELLEN. Yes, dear, though you almost know it by heart. You see, you have begun to laugh already.

COLONEL. You are laughing too, Ellen. I can't help it!

THE BOY DAVID

THE BOY DAVID

Produced at the King's Theatre, Edinburgh, on November 21, 1936, and at His Majesty's Theatre, London, on December 14, 1936, with the following cast :

JESSE	Wilson Coleman
WIFE OF JESSE	Jean Cadell
ELIAB	Basil C. Langton
AMNON	Peter Bull
AMINADAB (Sons of Jesse)	Eric Elliott
SHAMMAH	Robert Eddison
DAVID	Elisabeth Bergner
THE PROPHET SAMUEL	Sir John Martin-Harvey
JONATHAN (Son of Saul)	Bobby Rietti
OPHIR (Captain in the army of Saul)	Leon Quartermaine
SAUL (King of Israel)	Godfrey Tearle
A GUARD	William D'Arcy
NATHAN	Ion Swinley
ABNER (Captain of the Slingers)	John Boxer
ARMOUR-BEARER OF GOLIATH	Ellis Irving
WOMAN OF ENDOR	Margaret Chatwin

The play ran for 55 performances.

ACT I

THE HOUSE OF JESSE IN BETHLEHEM

The Scene is in Bethlehem, and is the dwelling-house of Jesse, a small farmer. The time is about three thousand years ago. The action of the play is almost continuous.

Bethlehem (of which in Act I we see only this room) was a small place in those days, but of a certain importance chiefly for its wool. It was on a hill, protected from enemies by a stout stone wall, and beneath it were the sheep-fields. Jesse's home, like its neighbours, was a one-storey flat-roofed building of stone and bricks which were made of mud. It had an earthen floor in which no doubt his domestic animals scraped for sustenance. This room, which to modern eyes would seem less inviting than the living-room of an agricultural labourer to-day, is strikingly bare of furniture such as to us seem necessities, though there is no real poverty. There are no tables or chairs. There is no carpet, everybody sits on the floor. Here and there are sheep-skins and goat-skins. The ceiling must be as low as possible and the room as small as the exigencies of the stage allow. This is important, as it is to be an intimate scene. The ceiling is raftered and there are some lower rafters on which agricultural implements, sheep-pelts, etc., are obviously stowed away. From the rafters hang a few smoked haunches of mutton and beef. The fire is in the middle of the room. This fire is a large open one of stone and sods sunk into the ground and surrounded by an irregular circle of clay. There is no chimney, and such smoke as there is travels up the walls into a smoky roof and has blackened them. The fire is alight and a big pot stands upon it. There are other culinary utensils near by, mostly of clay blackened by soot. There are two practical doors, namely the entrance up-stage and a door up-stage which leads (though they are not seen) to the store closets, the manger, and other important parts connected with the farmer's occupation. The entrance door is of wood and hard mud and sunk deep into the thick wall. The other door is more slightly made of wood and skins. Both doors are much smaller than those of to-day. They are more like holes in the wall and everyone has to stoop to enter.

There are no pictures on the walls (which are roughly plastered) but here and there again the skins of sheep and goats are hanging, the goat-skins being mostly black. A home-made ladder is against the wall. To reduce the size and height of the room the back part is a loft, stored with sacks and old agricultural gear.

The only window is at the back and is a tiny thing rather high up. It should not seem to be more than two feet square and it has horn in it instead of glass, though there were even in those days glass-blowers in Bethlehem. The walls of this house are very thick, as is evident from various deep recesses in them which are used as cupboards, or for storage. One of them at back, which comes into prominence in the action, has various foods in it in dishes and jars, some of which are made of copper or brass and the common red clay. This red pottery is to be seen to a limited extent in other recesses, but they are not in use.

(The curtain rises on a bright summer afternoon, and there are present ELIAB, AMNON, *and* AMINADAB, *three sons of the house, aged respectively about nineteen, eighteen, and seventeen. They are pleasantly if rather greedily eating their supper in different parts of the room, though with the pot on the fire as the centre of attention.*

All are seated on the floor except ELIAB, *who is lolling against the ladder.* ELIAB *is a soldier, at home on leave from the army of Saul. His soldierly attire, which is of gay skins, gives a martial touch of colour to the scene. He is fair, the others are dark. They are in thin skins of leather and linen drawers, stockings, and sandals, and are labourers such as tanners, millers, or hewers of wood, and their soiled though coloured garments betray their callings. Their sandals are of undressed leather. All the three are tall country striplings and tend to gesticulate and shout when in dispute as if ready to tear each other to*

*pieces, though it passes in a moment. This emotional
exuberance is to be shown at moments by all the characters
in the play. They are supposed to tingle with vitality
and stress far more than in modern plays. Thus their
manners are very unlike the genteel domesticity of our day.
In the opening scene, though they are only gossiping, they
do it with as much excess of word and gesture as if the
house was on fire. All have wooden bowls in their hands
and chunks of home-made bread and they drink from the
bowls, occasionally dipping their bread therein. The food
is the thick soup of many vegetables, still called Minestrone.*

The entrance door opens and SHAMMAH, *another son
of eighteen, enters, balancing two old water-skins on his
shoulders. He is conscious that this is effeminate employ-
ment and scowls at them for implying with mimicry that
the water-skins may fall. He, however, carries them
successfully through door.*

AMNON *slips round to look into the bowl of* ELIAB.
*About a minute should be filled in thus before there is any
talk.* AMNON *points accusingly and dramatically at* ELIAB.)

AMNON. In the name of Israel I call all the world to witness
that there is a piece of flesh in Eliab's bowl ! (*He shouts as if
it were the most dreadful charge.*)

(*There is immediately wild commotion in the Israelite
manner, except from* ELIAB *who remains provokingly calm.*)

ELIAB (*placidly superior and holding up the meat in his fingers*).
I claim it as my due—as a soldier of the king. Observe, Amnon !
(*He devours it.*)

AMINADAB (*passionately*). We husbandmen must suffer **so**
that the soldier be over-fed !

ELIAB (*gnawing*). Ay, it is the law.

AMNON. The other piece of flesh for me ! (*He rushes to the
pot and is stirring it, probing it for the meat.*)

AMINADAB. It is mine !

SHAMMAH. Mine !

AMNON (*pushing him aside violently*). The hewer of wood and
the baker of bread before the tanner !

(*There is about to be a fight for the meat, but all the youths
except* AMNON *withdraw from the pot as their* MOTHER
enters. The name of Jesse's wife I cannot discover, for

there seems to be no record of it. She is a little woman of many cares, somewhat of a drudge, for women were not esteemed of value in Israel ; but this one can nevertheless give blows to her progeny as well as take them from the august Jesse, and is a determined housewife, harsh, and without any sentimentality. She is garbed in her ' working day '—a short gown with her sleeves rolled up, an apron of linen, and in her hand a wooden roller, all to suggest that she has been baking bread. She stops to see what AMNON *is doing.*

He does not see her, but the others do and they await his discomfiture with pleasure. He is stirring the pot with a short wooden rod which stands in the pot for this purpose.)

MOTHER (*like a judge pronouncing sentence*).   Amnon !

(*He leaps, and she looks as if she could leap at him.*)

All of you ravening at your food like wolves in the morning. (*To* AMNON) You have had your share.   (*She takes his bowl from him and signs to him to leave the pot.   They all know that she must be obeyed.*)

AMNON (*with offended dignity*).   I desired merely to lick the stir-pot (*indicating it in his hand*).   It is my workmanship—with my own knife I fashioned it—and I claim this small privilege. (*He licks the stick with as much hauteur as is compatible with the incident and sits again.*)

(*The* MOTHER *sits near fire and partakes of his bowl.* SHAMMAH *returns with an empty bowl and approaches the pot.*)

MOTHER (*stopping him*).   First, Shammah, have you filled the water-skins ?

SHAMMAH.   Ay, and brought them back—to my shame, for all the maidens at the well jeered at me—a man carrying water like a maid.   (*He shouts it like one appealing to the Gods.*)

MOTHER.   Have you tended the kine ?

SHAMMAH.   It is done.   Also I again showed the calf where his legs are, and for what purpose.

MOTHER.   Then make thyself heavy.

(*The* MOTHER *signs to him that he may fill his bowl, and he does so.*)

SHAMMAH (*with another outbreak*).   Even the beasts have to be fed before Shammah approaches the dregs !

ELIAB. But assuredly, brother.

SHAMMAH (*shouting*). It is the part of the youngest to fill water-skins. Why should *I* have to do the tasks of David as well as my own ? I—I—Shammah !

MOTHER (*snapping*). Cease your clatter ! David is keeping the sheep.

AMINADAB (*excitedly*). Shammah, hearken to the things Eliab has been telling us of life in the camp ! He drinks the blood of the grape !

MOTHER (*with spirit*). Your father also drinks wine.

ELIAB (*contemptuous*). From a little gourd !

AMNON (*who considers himself the wit of the household*). While Eliab, the soldier, drinks it like a horse !

ELIAB (*imperturbable*). Even so ! (*He rises and saunters about.*) The old home ! The old pot ! (*He surveys the recess that contains his father's supper.*) Behold, Father's supper awaiteth his return as of yore, kept coyly within our reach ; but which of us would dare to touch ? Behold, even his cake of figs. Figs ! (*Suggestively and wistfully*) Mother ? (*He is craving to eat of his father's repast.*)

MOTHER. Touch not ! You dared once, Eliab, to venture upon your father's supper.

AMNON. Did his staff hurt, Eliab ?

ELIAB. You know better than I, Amnon.

AMINADAB. It is his belt now.

AMNON. Watch him strutting—Eliab the slinger of the king !

ELIAB (*fiercely*). Scoff not, Amnon, at the slingers of Israel. We are now fifteen hundred men, and the sling we know to be the deadliest of all the weapons of war. (*He takes off his sling, which was carried round the waist like a belt, and makes play with it.*)

AMINADAB. As I shall show them when I too am of the army.

AMNON (*displaying his sling*). And I.

ELIAB. You !

AMNON. With this sling can I already bring thine to shame.

ELIAB. Thus says Amnon !

AMNON. Furthermore, some hold that the bow of the Philistines is more deadly than our sling. So it is said.

ELIAB. Never by Saul.

MOTHER (*as loud as they*). No brawling !

(*They subside, but glare at each other.*)

Eliab, even David has now a sling.

ELIAB. It is no weapon for babes.

AMINADAB. He made it himself.

ELIAB. Ah, that kind of sling.

MOTHER. To be fair to the little worthless, he brings back many a straying goat with his pebbles.

AMNON. Fear not that he will do you injury with it, proud soldier, for the pebble ever falls behind him, though he points as if it were speeding toward the horizon.

(*They are all sitting again. Throughout this Act there should be much sitting on the floor.*)

ELIAB. Mother, is David as much a craven as ever ?

MOTHER (*shamed*). Alas, I cannot deny it.

(*They become quieter for a time, and, though they disparage* DAVID, *there is no real ill-will to him. They are really a good-natured family despite their clamour, and we should like, not dislike, them.*)

SHAMMAH. At his age we others could have helped to fence the walls of Bethlehem.

ELIAB. The seven sons of Jesse, as we are called, for none speaks of the eighth. You who began so well with me, mother, why did you not desist before David ?

MOTHER. I know to my shame that the child is timid and backward. (*Contemptuously*) The best that can be said of him is that the sheep like him.

AMNON. Yes, he plays to them, Eliab, on his harp, and they gather round him. They take him for one of their lambs !

(*They laugh over this.*)

AMINADAB. Even our ass is of more account than he.

AMNON. Yea, and David knows it. Hearken, Eliab, when David is from home on it and strangers approach, quickly he dismounts and shows the ass where to hide, for he thinks all covet the ass but that he need not hide himself, for none covets him.

SHAMMAH. I have seen him at such times whisper where it is to hide into the ears of the ass, and lo, that ass does as he directs, so kin are the twain, the one to the other.

MOTHER.　I know not what to make of the miserable.

ELIAB (*patting her with kindly intent*).　Poor soul !　Yet grieve not overmuch.　Is not the laying fowl well content if out of many eggs she sits on but one that is addled ?

MOTHER.　Talk not of him before me.

AMNON (*mockingly*).　Let us rather speak about our soldier brother !　Eliab the Great !

AMINADAB.　Ay, tell us, O mightiness, have you ever spoken with Saul ?

ELIAB (*scandalised*).　I, a foot man, speak to the king !　Are you bereft, Aminadab ?

AMNON.　Bereft !　I have heard that word whispered in the streets of Bethlehem about Saul himself.　A traveller of Hebron has brought tidings hither from the camp of a strangeness that comes upon Saul.

ELIAB (*ablaze*).　Brother, as you live !　Those words !

AMNON (*scared*).　I spoke them not.

(*This is so serious that the turmoil subsides.*)

MOTHER.　Nevertheless, Saul was once but a shepherd.　I remember a time when there was no king in Israel.

SHAMMAH.　In the days of the Judges.　No king in Israel !

MOTHER.　None before Saul—none but the Lord alone and there was no open vision of Him.　The people did demand a king whom they could see, and one Samuel, a mighty prophet of the Lord, did seek out Saul in his fields in Benjamin, and grudgingly anoint him.　(*She says it solemnly.*)

AMINADAB.　Grudgingly ?

MOTHER.　So it is said.

(*Voices get low and cautious.*)

AMNON.　The man of Hebron also says there is now murmuring in the camp of a clashing between these two, Saul and Samuel.

ELIAB.　I say, you spoiler of pelts, there is none in Israel can trouble Saul and live.　Would you learn how to know a king ?

AMNON.　Ay, noble immensity, let us hear and be wise.

ELIAB.　When he comes nigh, though a stranger to you, your knees give way and you prostrate yourself before him.

AMNON (*irrepressible*).　We thank you, good Eliab.　We are now prepared for the coming of a king.

MOTHER (*sternly*).   Impious youth !

(*The entrance door is thrown open and* DAVID *rushes into the room, breathless with excitement.* DAVID *has come down to us from the Old Testament as ' ruddy, and withal of a beautiful countenance, and goodly to look to.' Browning, in his poem ' Saul,' acclaims him as ' God's child, with dew on thy gracious gold hair.' As we see him, he is a child beside his tall brothers. He is bare-legged and should wear little save a sheep-skin crosswise. His mouth opens and shuts in gasps as he tries vainly to give utterance.*)

DAVID.   Mother !

MOTHER (*not lovingly, but irritated with him*).   David, what has befallen you ?

(*He gulps.*)

DAVID (*in a glorious mouthful*).   Mother, I have killed a lion !

(*It is so unexpected that the sons leap to weapons. Next moment the ludicrousness of the statement convulses them and they are again loud and demonstrative. Their mockery of* DAVID *that follows should be fast and without pauses.*)

AMNON.   Our David has killed a lion ! (*He signs to the others to accept the news as grand.*) Mother, behold the conqueror !

(*They gather round* DAVID *in burlesque respect.* DAVID *in his innocence thinks they are extolling him, and he presents a proud and beaming face. He does not notice that the* MOTHER *has sunk down in shame.*)

ELIAB (*grandly declamatory*).   Poor lion that dared to cross the path of David !

DAVID (*ravished with delight over his new popularity*).   There was a bear also !

SHAMMAH (*as if further astounded*).   Mark that ! There was also a bear !

AMINADAB.   There *was* a bear, but there is a bear no longer.

ELIAB.   Did the bear pursue you, brother ?

(DAVID *shakes his head exultantly.*)

AMNON.   Keep us not in anxiety, boy.   Tell us quickly that you also killed the bear, so that fear may go out of us.

DAVID.   I did kill him !

AMNON.   Mother, the bear-killer.

(*They present* DAVID *to her. She turns away her head.*)

ELIAB.   She is in distress, David, lest the lion and the bear mauled you.

DAVID (*hastening to her to relieve her anxiety*). See, mother, I have not a scratch !

AMNON (*examining him*). Not a scratch ! Or did you wash the blood from off you at the well ?

DAVID (*it is a new idea to him*). I had not thought of that.

(*The* MOTHER *covers her face with her apron.*)
Eliab, shall we be called the eight sons of Jesse now ?

ELIAB.   Your tale first.

AMNON.   Ay, let us sit at his feet while he tells us with seemly modesty how he became a man.

(*The brothers sit round him while he stands.*)

DAVID (*gloating*). A man ! Amnon, when I went to the fields this morn, I was a boy. (*This reflection rather scares him.*)

AMNON (*as if it were a wonderful recollection*). I remember you as a boy, brother. But the mighty deed ?

DAVID (*seeing it with terrifying vividness*). I was sitting in my cave under the rock, and lo, the sheep did eat near by.

AMINADAB.   He has now a cave, Eliab, which is almost as big as himself.

DAVID (*jealously*). It is more bigger.

AMNON (*encouragingly*). You were sitting in your cave playing on your harp and—— ?

DAVID (*easily perplexed*). Was I ? I thought I was tending one of the lambs.

AMNON (*politely*). Verily ! Well ?

DAVID.   Suddenly I heard a *roar* !

ELIAB.   I quake ! Was it the lion or the bear ?

DAVID (*trembling horribly*). The lion. It was the biggest lion I have ever seen.

AMNON.   And the only one.

DAVID (*a stickler for accuracy*). It was the biggest if I had ever seen more.

MOTHER (*who has been wringing her hands, isolated*). Wretched boy !

ELIAB.   Fear not, mother, for at that moment David strode out of his cave and killed the lion and then the bear.

DAVID. Didn't I ? But wait till I tell you how I did it !

MOTHER. Cease, you lying child.

DAVID. Lying ? (*He reels.*) Is it all a lie ?

MOTHER. Now is the house of Jesse brought low. I had put milk aside for you. But you shall have neither milk nor the pot.

DAVID. O mother ! (*He is bewildered.*)

AMNON (*signing to him to come away from her*). How did you kill them, heroic one ? (*Confidentially.*)

DAVID (*crushed, and stung by his mother*). I have forgotten. I knew, but I do now forget. Perhaps I just nearly killed them.

SHAMMAH. It was thus, David : you would have killed them if they had been there to kill.

DAVID (*catching at this straw*). Wouldn't I, Shammah ?

ELIAB. I see what happened. It was a bush of the tamarisk you killed.

DAVID (*with a sinking*). Was it only a bush ?

AMINADAB. Courage, it was no bush.

DAVID. No, it wasn't.

AMINADAB. It was one of our father's sheep.

DAVID (*aghast*). One of the sheep ?

ELIAB. Worse than that—it was your pet lamb.

DAVID (*in agony*). My lamb ?

AMNON. It was neither a sheep nor a lamb. It was a lion.

DAVID. Yes !

ELIAB. But you have got the story wrong ; you did not kill the lion, David. It was the lion who killed you.

DAVID. Was that it ? (*Hoarsely*) Am I dead, mother ?

MOTHER (*rising—sternly*). Shammah, to the fields to see to the sheep.

SHAMMAH. Always Shammah—(*Looking at* DAVID)—while *he* escapes punishment.

MOTHER. He shall not escape this time. Hasten.

　　(SHAMMAH *goes out at back.*)

Go from my sight, boy. Your father's belt will deal with you when he returns.

DAVID (*imploringly*). Not father's belt.

　　(*She signs to him to be off.*)

(*He speaks cajolingly from the door*) May I have my milk, mother, after the belt ?

MOTHER. The manger for you.

(DAVID *goes out. The* MOTHER *sits again.*)

Seven sons—and then this one ! (*She is a little broken now.*)

(*They gather round her, grieving for her.*)

ELIAB (*kindly*). Harden not your heart against him, mother, he is but a child and cleaves to folly.

MOTHER (*scorning herself*). There was a time when I thought him wonderful.

ELIAB. So you thought of all of us when we were small.

MOTHER. No, only of him.

(SHAMMAH *returns hastily.*)

SHAMMAH. An old man—a stranger—is in the street asking for the house of Jesse. A hairy man girt in ragged apparel, with a wallet on his shoulder.

ELIAB. I know them, those wanderers who now infest the camp. One of the tribe calling themselves diviners or seers.

SHAMMAH. He looks such a one.

AMINADAB. A mendicant !

AMNON. Maybe a worshipper of gods fashioned by man's hands. Yet I fear them. They have evil spirits. 'Tis said they can turn their faces and walk backwards, and other things as dark. A wizard, Eliab.

MOTHER. May all such be rent from their homes.

ELIAB. They have been. There are no wizards now in the land. Saul has driven them all out of Israel. (*Superstitious*) Yet hold the door against him, Shammah.

MOTHER (*firmly*). Bid him enter.

AMINADAB. See him not. There may be mischief in his wallet.

MOTHER. I fear no one.

(SHAMMAH *ushers in* SAMUEL. *He was probably the greatest of his kind save Moses, and is a striking figure in this scene and can be alarming, though his entrance is quiet and his habiliments of the poorest, mainly a mendicant's long linen cloak of sombre colourless stuff. His feet are bare. In his hand is a long stout staff and on his shoulder a wallet. He is aged and has a beard, grey but not white, and not the long straggling beard usually given to prophets in familiar pictures. He can be straight and arresting on occasion ; he is an aristocrat in the garb of a travelling*

priest and strikes a note of superiority to all around him.
His entrance brings drama into the house. The manners
of all become quieter, restrained. It is a noticeable effect
of SAMUEL'S *entrance.*)

SAMUEL (*unostentatiously*).   Peace be unto this house.

MOTHER (*not much impressed by him, but civil*).   You seek my husband, Jesse the son of Obed ?

SAMUEL.   Even so.

MOTHER.   It is his house, but he is gone to Urusalem to sell his pelts.   (*Thus was Jerusalem then pronounced.*)

SAMUEL.   I will await him.

(*This liberty the brothers resent but they are nervous of*
him. They are all seated on the floor themselves.)

ELIAB.   You intruder !

MOTHER (*sharply*).   Eliab !   (*Courteous but cautious*)   You will break bread in the house of Jesse, for is not this Bethlehem, the house of bread ?

(*He inclines his head, and she puts bread before him.*)

AMNON (*sarcastically*).   And thou wilt drink of our water if it be not forbidden to a holy man ?

(SAMUEL *again inclines his head, and he drinks of a cup*
which AMNON *in mock deference presents on bended*
knee.)

SAMUEL.   A son of thine ?

MOTHER.   They are all sons of mine.

AMNON.   She has seven sons, O prophet.

SAMUEL (*quite politely*).   Thou couldst have spared one of them for a daughter.   This one (*meaning* AMNON, *as he courteously hands back the cup*).

(AMNON *is discomfited, but there should never be any*
straining after comic effect.)

MOTHER.   If it be alms you seek, your handmaid will find a measure of barley.

SAMUEL.   It is not alms.

AMNON.   He speaks in riddles.   Let us look within the wallet.

(SAMUEL *has put it down and they approach it.*)

SAMUEL (*sternly*).   Touch not the sacred wallet.

AMNON.   Why not ?

SAMUEL.   I have hacked a king in pieces for less.

(*They shrink back.*)

MOTHER. What manner of man are you ? For what purpose come you to the house of Jesse ?

SAMUEL. My master sent me.

MOTHER. Who is your master?

SAMUEL. The master of all.

ELIAB (*impressed*). Of all ? Can it be, good man, that you are as I, a servant of the King ?

SAMUEL (*grimly*). I come not here in the service of Saul.

ELIAB. He speaks to the hurt of the King ! Go, blasphemer ! (*He throws open the door and signs for* SAMUEL *to go.*)

SAMUEL. I go not forth until I have discharged my mission. (*He sits and draws his staff across his knees. He is erect and formidable.*)

MOTHER. Your mission ?

SAMUEL. I was sent hither to find one of the brood of Jesse.

MOTHER. There are three others, but they have taken wives and are no longer in Bethlehem.

SAMUEL. Then they concern me not. I was told I should find him in this house.

ELIAB (*hopefully*). And have you found him ? I am the eldest.

SAMUEL. I wait for my master to tell me.

MOTHER. Your master is coming here ?

SAMUEL. He is here.

(*This is unexpected and startling. He rises to his feet and we see him offering up a prayer, though we do not hear the words. At first the sons are scornful. They have mostly been lolling about on the floor so far to show no respect for him ; but they become impressed and gradually, not all together, but one at a time, they rise and stand reverently though bewildered, the* MOTHER *included. We can see that in the prayer he seems to ask questions and to receive answers.*)

ELIAB. Now do you know which of Jesse's brood you seek ?

SAMUEL. Now do I know that it is none of thee. (*To* ELIAB) Fair of countenance and of goodly stature, I had thought for a moment—but He has refused thee, for man looketh on the outward appearance, but He looketh on the heart, and thou art not the man. (*To* AMINADAB *and* SHAMMAH) Also art thou refused—and thou. (*To* AMNON) Nor hath He chosen thee, poor afflicted one.

MOTHER. Then your mission——

SAMUEL. I await the sign.

MOTHER. The sign?

DAVID (*suddenly peering in from the door*). Mother, can I have my milk now?

SAMUEL (*intentionally not looking round*). Who spoke?

MOTHER. Truly I have an eighth son, but he is a child and in a great trespass.

SAMUEL. Let him be brought before me.

ELIAB (*concealing him*). He is in the fields tending his father's flocks.

SAMUEL (*still as if unaware of* DAVID'S *presence*). I came hither through the fields which they said were Jesse's, and there was none tending the flock.

AMNON (*mimicking* SAMUEL). Sawest thou, far-seeing one, aught in the fields but sheep and goats?

SAMUEL (*who is again seated*). Lo, I saw a strange sight. I saw a dead lion.

(*This makes a sensation.*)

ELIAB (*unbelieving*). How now?

(*The brothers look at each other.* AMINADAB *runs out, obviously to make sure for himself, leaving the door open.*)

DAVID (*emerging into full view of* SAMUEL). Was there a bear also?

SAMUEL (*still not looking at him*). Near the lion there lay a dead bear.

DAVID. Eliab! Amnon!

AMNON. They must have killed one another.

DAVID (*hotly*). No, they didn't.

(SHAMMAH *runs out.*)

ELIAB. They were snared or shot.

DAVID. No!

SAMUEL. There was no mark of a weapon upon them. Their necks were broken.

DAVID (*gloriously*). David did it!

(ELIAB *and* AMNON *gape at him and run out after the others, closing the door.* DAVID *goes up to* SAMUEL, *who is not looking at him, pulls his cloak, and speaks shyly.*)

I am David.

> (SAMUEL *at last turns, puts a hand on him, and looks long and seriously at him.*)

Do you think you could get my mother to give me my milk as I am he who killed the lion and the bear ?

SAMUEL (*authoritatively*).   His milk.

> (*She signs reluctantly to* DAVID, *and he runs off gaily to get his milk.*)

Now, wife of Jesse, leave me with thy eighth son.

MOTHER (*perplexed and incredulous*).   Is David the one whom you seek ?

SAMUEL.   I know not yet, but I think he may be that one.

MOTHER.   The sign ?

SAMUEL.   David will give it to me.

MOTHER.   He cannot know.

SAMUEL.   Yet will he give it to me if he is the one.

MOTHER (*impressed*).   I know you not.   What does this presage ?

SAMUEL.   Woman, would you have your son great and terrible ?

MOTHER.   There is no danger to him ?

SAMUEL.   Mother of David, there is much danger.

MOTHER.   Of all my sons, he is the one that most needs help.

SAMUEL.   No longer perhaps from thee.   If he is the one he will be great and terrible, but *you* will have lost him.   In all his mighty history you will have no share.   No record will remain ; even of the *name* of the mother of David.

> (*She shivers.* DAVID *comes back with his cup of milk. The* MOTHER *looks after him as he passes.   She speaks firmly and thrillingly in answer to a look from* SAMUEL.)

MOTHER.   I would have him great and terrible.

> (SAMUEL *bows and points to the door.   She goes off without any faltering and shuts the door behind her.* DAVID *holds up the cup victoriously.   About to drink, he offers it politely to* SAMUEL.)

SAMUEL.   Nay, it is all yours.

DAVID (*finely*).   It is yours and mine.

> (SAMUEL, *pleased with him, just touches it with his lips and hands it back with a bow.* DAVID *bows in acknowledgment of this generosity, and then has a joyous drink that is destitute of manners.*)

SAMUEL. It is good ?

DAVID (*with long-drawn-out ecstasy and his eyes peeping up over the cup*). Oo-o !

SAMUEL. And now tell me how came it to you that you were able to kill a lion and a bear ? (*He is seated and he pulls* DAVID *nearer to him*.)

DAVID (*pondering, but chiefly occupied with his milk*). I think it was my lamb. I was in my cave trying to take a thorn from her foot. Then I heard—a roar ! (*The memory of it is so vivid that he seems to hear it again, and he quakes*.) May I hold your hand ? (*He does so*.)

SAMUEL (*encouragingly*). You put your head out of the cave ?

DAVID (*surprised*). Did I ? (*Cautiously*) No, I pulled it in. It was my lamb that put out her head. She did go out of the cave to see who was making that noise. She did not know about lions. Perhaps she thought it was something to play with. Thus are lambs. (*With increasing drama*) Then I peeped out and I saw my lamb in the mouth of the lion. At that—at that——

(SAMUEL *indicates to him to drink for strength to go on, and* DAVID *does so*.)

SAMUEL (*very eager and also excited*). Now is the moment.

DAVID. Something did come over me.

SAMUEL (*triumphant*). You were exalted !

DAVID. Was I ? (*Proud of himself, yet fearful*) I leapt from the cave like a stone from the sling—thus ! (*He demonstrates*.) I did give one roar like unto the lion's roar. (*He makes the sound of the roar, but all is terribly serious*.) I seized him by his beard and delivered the lamb out of his mouth ; and when he turned against me I did twist the head of him—this way— and that way—hold my cup and I will show you.

(SAMUEL *does so*. DAVID *shows, with eyes bulging from his head*.)

Thus—till he fell dead with a look of wonder on his face. (*He takes back the cup and finishes the drink, and then speaks with more calmness, as of a smaller thing*.) So likewise did I do to the bear.

SAMUEL (*in a tremor*). You were exalted ! (*He raises his hands to heaven and addresses his God for but a moment and in words we do not hear*.)

DAVID. What is exalted ? To what one were you speaking ? (*Putting down his cup.*)

SAMUEL. To Him who killed the lion and the bear for thee.

DAVID (*indignant*). No, He did not. I did it myself. There was no one there.

SAMUEL. To you the glory.

DAVID. Who is He ? (*Stamping his foot.*)

SAMUEL. He is my Master. I am nothing.

DAVID. Where is He ?

SAMUEL. He is here

DAVID. Here ? Up there ?

SAMUEL. He is everywhere—in the seas—on the mountains. He is in that pelt.

(DAVID *is afraid of the pelt.*)

DAVID. I cannot see Him. I cannot hear Him.

SAMUEL. It may not be, with the eyes nor with the ears.

DAVID. How then ? (*He has an idea.*) Now shall I see and hear Him ? (*He covers his ears with his hands and shuts his eyes tight.*) No !

SAMUEL. It will be revealed. You are a simple boy ; but you will become the subtlest of the sons of man.

DAVID. What is subtle ? Is it better than simple ?

SAMUEL (*sadly*). Perhaps some day you will be able to tell me.

DAVID. Then shall we be called the eight sons of Jesse ?

SAMUEL (*as one reading it in a vision*). The other seven sons will bow the knee before you.

DAVID (*enraptured*). They will ? (*Incredulous*) No ? But if I am one of them, then will my cup be full.

SAMUEL. It will be such a cup as no other man has drained.

DAVID. How now ? (*Eager*) Shall I—see Saul ?

SAMUEL (*grimly*). You shall see Saul. (*The vision very clear to him.*) Lo, he will search for *you* in all the caverns and recesses of Judah.

DAVID (*pleased*). Will he find me ?

SAMUEL (*putting the vision from him*). I trust not ! Soon, David, shall your sheep and you be parted, and the well of Bethlehem will know you no more.

DAVID. Never shall I leave my sheep. I do love the fold. (*Wondering a little at himself*) Sometimes when I am sitting

with my harp in the fields and the sheep bells are pleasant—
then do I make thoughts.

SAMUEL (*who is seated*). Stand there, David, and tell me one
of the thoughts you have made while you kept the sheep.

DAVID. Behold. (*He stands in front of* SAMUEL *with his
hands behind his back, like one saying a lesson, and speaks very
simply.*) The Lord is my shepherd ; I shall not want. He
maketh me to lie down in green pastures ; He leadeth me
beside the still waters.

(SAMUEL *rises and looks away, moved. Then he puts a
hand on* DAVID'S *head.*)

SAMUEL (*controlling himself and trying to speak lightly*). You
must finish that thought some day, David.

DAVID (*simply*). Yes.

(SAMUEL *is experiencing the loveliest thrill of a craftsman,
the sudden meeting with another in childhood.*)

SAMUEL. I welcome you among us, brother. I too am one
of those who put things down.

(DAVID *does not understand.* SAMUEL *produces a horn of
oil from his wallet.*)

DAVID. What are you doing ?

SAMUEL. That for which He sent me hither.

DAVID. The Other One ? (*He closes his eyes and ears again,
then opens them, disappointed. He shakes his head.*) No !

SAMUEL. Thus I did, once on a time, to another shepherd.
Kneel, my son.

DAVID. I am afraid.

SAMUEL. Fear not me. When you rise I shall be your
servant.

(*The ceremony of anointing* DAVID *here follows. It is
brief, as is also the silent prayer which follows. The only
words actually heard are those in which* SAMUEL *addresses
his God. They are ' I am that I am,' and he says them
several times. When this is over he speaks.*)

SAMUEL. Rise, Master.

(DAVID *rises, wondering.*)

DAVID. Was He here ?

SAMUEL. He was here.

(*He is looking very gravely at* DAVID *when the* MOTHER
opens the door hesitatingly.)

Nay, come, the servant's part is done.

(*She comes forward, agitated and perplexed.*)

MOTHER.   Will you tell me who you are ?

SAMUEL.   I am called Samuel.

(*She shrinks back.*)

Concerning all you may now hear from the son of Jesse, I warn
you keep your tongue in check till I come again hither.

MOTHER (*with some firmness*).   What you bid me, that will
I do.

DAVID (*excitedly*).   Mother——

MOTHER.   Is the boy safe ?

SAMUEL.   If you be shrewd.   If you have a loose tongue
there is now not a step between him and me—and death.

(*He holds up a hand as blessing her.   Then he prostrates
himself before the shrinking* DAVID *and, rising, takes his
staff and goes out.* DAVID *and his* MOTHER *gaze at each
other.* DAVID *is goggle-eyed.*)

DAVID.   Why did he do that ?

MOTHER (*suspecting much, yet bewildered*).   What else did he ?

DAVID.   He wetted my head from his horn.

MOTHER.   What said he ?   Are you to become a holy man ?

DAVID (*his mind in a whirl*).   I think I am at the beginning
of being holy.

MOTHER.   Eat and be strong.   (*She hastens to the pot.   In a
new respect for him she dares to bring him meat from his father's
store.   There is still no sentimentality about her, but she has awed
feelings that he is perhaps to be great.*)

DAVID (*astounded*).   My father's supper !   (*He eats from
his hands, joyfully.*)   Mother, I think I am to kill more lions.

MOTHER.   If it is that you are to be a holy man, you cannot
go about killing.

DAVID (*who is sitting, eating*).   Yes, I can.   That is what
they do.

(*She is gazing at him, waiting for developments.*)

Mother, I think I killed two lions.

MOTHER.   O son, son, you said yourself that one of them
was a bear.

DAVID (*determinedly*).   There were two bears.   (*Regretfully*)
Of course He helped me—a little.   (*Grudgingly*) He did hold
the bears till I finished with the lions.

MOTHER.   He—Samuel ?   So *he* was there !

DAVID.   Not that one—the Other One.   That one is nothing.   The Other One—He is the One.

MOTHER (*shaking him again*).   There was no other here.

DAVID.   He was here.

MOTHER.   I tell you I watched from the manger.   No other entered this house.

DAVID.   He was also in the manger.   He is everywhere. (*Scared*) Mother, He was in that pelt.

(*She does not know what to make of it.   She brings more food.*)

Father's cake of figs !

(DAVID *hesitates with a piece of cake on the way to his mouth.*)

MOTHER (*firmly*).   Strengthen yourself, my son.

(DAVID *does so.*)

DAVID.   Mother, sometimes I shall be exalted.

MOTHER.   What is that ?

DAVID.   I know not, but when I am exalted, contradict me not, or it will go ill with you, woman.

MOTHER.   What manner is this in which to address me ? (*Becoming more practical*) Poor child, your brothers will soon buffet this vaunting out of you.

DAVID (*cheerfully*).   I shall admonish them, and then they will bow the knee before me.

(*She is proud of him again.   She brings the dates.*)

Father's dates !

MOTHER.   Jesse !   I heard him alight from the ass.

(DAVID *wipes the remnants from his face.   He is apprehensive.   She pushes him down.*)

Do you remain there, still as salt.   He must hear naught save what I see fit to tell him, and that will only be about the lion.

DAVID.   Mother, I think I am now to be exalted.

MOTHER (*wringing her hands*).   Not before your father.

(JESSE *now opens the door, and the ass follows with various loads on it.   The door had been left open when the* MOTHER *came out, and this ass, well knowing its home, goes straight through by itself.* JESSE *shuts the other door and comes in.   He is a rough-bearded man of about fifty, of medium height, of the strong, small farmer type,*

*in skins and leggings and a sheep coat. He mutters a
'Peace to the house' and stretches himself and stamps.
He knows* DAVID *is there by the fire, but* DAVID *is too
insignificant to take special notice of. The* MOTHER, *a
solicitous wife, helps him off with leggings and other things
as they talk. His appearance suggests one who loves sheep,
eats sheep, and dreams sheep, and could almost speak
sheep.*)

MOTHER. Was the road heavy, Jesse ? You are late.

JESSE (*with the good-nature of one who has had a good day's
business*). There is no road for the time being—this most
blessed rain—and I was delayed by the haggling in Urusalem—
but the pelts bartered well. (*He sits.*) Give me to drink.

(*She ascends ladder to the loft.*)

Has anyone sought me ?

MOTHER. Only an old man—one of those wanderers in rags.

JESSE (*with distaste*). Ugh !

MOTHER. But I told him you were in Urusalem, and he
soon passed on his way.

JESSE. So is it always in this little place. Nothing ever
happens in Bethlehem.

(*She has brought down the wine-gourd and he drinks from
it with satisfaction.* DAVID *has been sitting staring,
inconspicuous, and she wants to get him out of the way.*)

MOTHER. See to the ass, David.

JESSE. He tend the ass ! Since when has Jesse returned
from a journey and let any but himself do that ? Ay, even
before I break bread. (*Going*) But I am as hungered as one
lost on Mount Nebo. Do you bring me my supper, and I
will eat as I provender the ass.

MOTHER (*realising that she can defer no longer—afraid*).
O Jesse !

JESSE. What now ? (*He sees something is untoward, and
comes back.*)

(*She shrinks.*)

MOTHER. Your supper, Jesse !

JESSE. Is not all as I enjoined ?

MOTHER. I prepared it for you. But I thought : Jesse
lingers, he is supping at the rest house ; and I ate it—see
the empty shelf.

JESSE. You ate my supper !

(*He advances upon her threateningly. She shrinks. The frenzy of exaltation is now upon* DAVID *and he rises.*)

DAVID. Reprove her not, for I say it was I who did eat thy supper, down to the cake of figs and the dates, and lo, they were good.

JESSE. **Is** this David ? (*He takes off his belt, ominously.*) And you encourage him ! (*He again advances on the* MOTHER.)

DAVID (*protecting her*). Lay not thy hands upon her—I command thee, Jesse son of Obed, put down that belt.

(JESSE *lowers the belt in bewilderment. The* MOTHER *is astounded.*)

MOTHER. Even Jesse obeys him !

JESSE (*furious*). I obey him ? (*He suddenly shrinks back in religious fear.*) Is he possessed ?

MOTHER. He has killed a lion.

JESSE (*shrinking back from him*). Possessed ! And is it so also with you ?

MOTHER (*entreating*). I will tell you of him. Come.

(JESSE, *keeping his distance from* DAVID, *goes out. The* MOTHER *is following ; she turns back for a moment.* DAVID *is quivering from head to foot.*)

MOTHER (*she would fain help him*). Son of Jesse !

DAVID (*who is now about the middle of the room, isolated, while she is near the door*). I know not who or what I am. Something frightens me.

MOTHER. Samuel—he who was here—he may not have passed beyond the walls. Shall I seek him and bring him back to you ?

DAVID. He cannot help me. Not that one.

(*In despair she goes off, without closing the door. After a moment's woe,* DAVID *looks at the pelt, then upwards as* SAMUEL *had done. He has inspiration. He closes his eyes and ears, and calls.*)

Other One, David is in darkness. Will you not tell me what to do ? (*Appealing*) Other One ?

(*When he opens his eyes and takes down his hands, a great change has come over him. He is radiant, all excitement has passed from him. He is normal and serene, an ordinary happy boy. Evidently he has got his answer. He*

*produces his sling, which has been round his waist, un-
observed so far. It is such a sling as boys of to-day often
have—made at home. He sits on the floor, testing the
sling and cleaning out his pouch which was, according to
the Old Testament, a shepherd's bag or scrip. The
MOTHER looks out at doorway. He hears her. He nods
to her three times, meaning that all is lovely. He speaks
happily and briskly, but like an ordinary boy making a
casual statement.*)

DAVID.   Mother, I am to go to the camp of Saul to slay
another lion. I am to go on my father's ass. I am to take my
sling—(*He holds up sling and picks up his harp*)—and my harp.
(*This little programme is far from relieving her. She is
more perplexed than ever. She goes out, closing the door
behind her. DAVID is alone, boyishly engrossed in his sling.*)

ACT II

SCENE I

SAUL AWAITS

IT is an open-air scene, twelve miles distant from Bethlehem, near the camps of Israel and the Philistines. These camps, however, are not visible, though their proximity is suggested by occasional martial sounds from a distance, of trumpets, horns, etc. We are supposed to see a height on the edge of a wood, which wood is continued on the back cloth into mountainous country and should be recognisable as characteristic of Palestine in those days. That is, the trees should be in height little more than what we would call bushes. Palms, oleanders, vines, olives, figs, sycamores were the native trees (except at distant Lebanon, famed for its cedars), and an occasional mighty terebinth (or turpentine) tree. The Israelites are supposed to be massed unseen beyond the wood on left and the Philistines on right. (The time is the morning of the following day, early in autumn.) A trodden path in front from left to right, and here a slight clearing of trees. The only 'practical' properties are a bundle of little tree trunks and a sloped bank. Against the bundle of trunks is a formidable-looking javelin, belonging to Saul.

(The only person on the scene is JONATHAN, *son of Saul. He is a boy of about* DAVID'S *size and age of twelve, and must be played by a real boy. He is cultured, good-looking, and intelligent, but not imaginative, and his chief note is of open honesty. He is attired in armour, mostly of leather, which is ornamental rather than useful, for he is considered too precious to be risked. He is looking dejected, and an occasional horn or trumpet is heard from back, not suggesting activity but merely camp routine. These sounds he*

1208

disregards. He comes and sits on the tree trunks, distressed.

To him there hurriedly enters a real fighting man, OPHIR, *a young captain of Israel.* OPHIR *is brave and devoted to Saul, though presently we see that he can be rather complacent and thick-headed. He salutes* JONATHAN.)

JONATHAN (*remaining seated and glad to welcome a friend*). You, Ophir ! You seek my father ?

OPHIR (*in an excited state*). Ay, Prince Jonathan, I seek the King. I was told I should find him here—far from the camp. My King, far from his camp ! (*It is a cry of anguish, with the Israelite excess of voice and gesture.*)

JONATHAN (*dispirited*). You find Jonathan alone, Ophir, and Jonathan is downcast.

OPHIR (*treating him as a boy and going to him kindly*). I grieve, my lord Jonathan, that you are downcast. (*In a blaze*) But of the downcast is every captain, ay, and every foot man in the army of Israel these forty days.

JONATHAN. None more than Saul himself. Look on him, Ophir.

(OPHIR *looks.*)

OPHIR (*with passionate devotion*). My King !

JONATHAN. See how irresolutely he paces—backwards and forwards.

OPHIR (*in horror of the idea*). Saul grown irresolute !

JONATHAN. Ophir, I think a distress has come upon him. I have seen him with his eyes open, yet he saw me not, and I have touched him and still he knew me not and muttered to himself.

OPHIR (*he speaks low and guardedly*). I have heard of a night when the cry went forth, ' Behold a dark spirit troubleth the King.' And servants were sent out to seek a cunning player on a harp and he played before Saul, and the burden was lifted off him.

JONATHAN. Think of it. He gazes north, south, east and west, for a prophet who never comes.

OPHIR (*grinding his teeth*). This Samuel !

(*A distant horn and trumpets answering, produce an outburst from him.*)

Why falls he not upon the Philistines now drawn up against him?

A King heretofore sweeping his enemies before him, and to-day more like one with clothes rent and with earth upon his face ! (*Begging*) My prince, come to our aid !

JONATHAN. Ah, my friend, he looks upon me as a child, decked in the trappings of war, but shielded from the fray. (*Scorning himself*) That is all we are, my pretty armour and I.

OPHIR. Know you that he even forbids us to take up the challenges to single combat thrown across our lines by insolent Philistines ? There is among them one Goliath who tries us sore, strutting before our outposts daily and crying that Israel cannot find a champion to stand up against him.

JONATHAN (*boyishly*). Goliath ! I have heard of the monster Goliath. Ophir, you must take me to see the sight. Is it true that he is beyond mortal bulk, in a harness of unbeaten brass, and that the staff of his spear is of the thickness of a weaver's beam ?

OPHIR. Truly, the story grows with the telling.

JONATHAN. Ophir, if we are in such a strait, why do the Philistines wait for *us* to strike ?

OPHIR. It is a cunning enemy which knows that our army weakens as the bread becomes spent in our vessels.

JONATHAN. See, my father's javelin. As he moved away he left it here, as a thing of war and therefore of no account.

OPHIR. The javelin of Saul ! (*He treats it with reverence, then kisses it.*)

JONATHAN. Why did you kiss it ?

OPHIR. In forgiveness, my lord Jonathan ; for when I have said my say to Saul I have a sinking that this javelin will enter into me.

JONATHAN (*reproving*). You speak thus of the sweetest master !

OPHIR (*fervently*). He is, he is ! But who has countered Saul and lived ?

JONATHAN (*looking*). He comes back—haste away, Ophir. Leave your words to him unspoken.

OPHIR (*firmly*). What I have to say I must say. (*As one saying good-bye to life*) Israel, farewell.

(SAUL *comes on. He should be presented in the play as a noble figure in Israel's history, though the clouds have begun to gather and he is to be a broken column. He is dark-bearded and at most about forty years of age. For an idea of his appearance a study should be made of Rembrandt's famous picture of David playing before Saul, which, however, is a conception of much later date, and all the garments in the play must be of those Israelite days.*)

SAUL. You bring word from Samuel? (*He is quiet and dignified.*)

OPHIR (*who has saluted him*). There is none, O King.

SAUL (*concealing his feelings*). Then trouble me not further, good Ophir.

OPHIR (*on his knee*). My King, I pray you, hear me. Your captains drew lots who should hazard this, and it fell upon me. Forty days have we lain here, ready but not striking. There is murmuring in the tents ; deserters steal away by night, and the ranks of the Philistines swell as ours diminish. (*Aware of his daring.*) Your captains, O King, beg—they demand—that the battle be engaged.

SAUL. Demand ! (*He becomes dangerous, but retains his kingly quality.*) Take heed to yourself, Ophir. You know the temper of my blood. Now is your head in jeopardy.

OPHIR (*bravely*). As one about to be slain, O King, I speak the words given to me to say. ' The battle now,' they cry, or ' Does a priest rule in Israel ?' (*He bows his head as offering it for the stroke.*)

(SAUL *is very threatening and half draws his sword. For a moment there is silence, and then he controls his passion.* OPHIR *looks up with a brave smile.*)

Am I still alive, O my King ?

SAUL (*with the charm that sits so well on monarchs*). Shake your head, Ophir, and let me see. Ay, it seems not to fall off.

OPHIR. For a moment I thought it to be severed.

SAUL. For a moment perhaps it was. You faithful servant, I return it to you. (*He graciously helps* OPHIR *to rise. He moves away and sits on the tree trunks. There is a smile on his face.*) Now shall we converse more intimately of Saul and his transgressions ? (*He points to the ground.*)

(OPHIR *sits on it near him.* JONATHAN *is on the sloped bank.*)

(SAUL *is still gentle.*) Ophir, who would reign if he could lay down his kingship ? Not Saul, not for another day. (*It is an honestly meant statement, but it is not in accord with* JONATHAN'S *knowledge of him.*)

JONATHAN. *You* say that, father !

SAUL (*smiling like one found out*). You will know it, Jonathan, when you are king after me. (*Fervently*) To be nameless for ever and my tomb unknown—the boon of boons ! What else say my captains ?

OPHIR. They say that a priest's place is not where two armies stand drawn up, the one against the other.

SAUL. Never more, my friend, than then. The charge may not sound till the Blessing comes from on high—(*Lowering*) —and Samuel brings it not.

JONATHAN. Must it come through Samuel ? Have you not told me, father, that the Lord speaks to you direct ?

SAUL (*sternly obedient to his God*). Thus has it been in the past. But now He seeks me out no more, as if His face is turned from me, and He repents that He has made me great. Only through Samuel will He answer me—and Samuel comes not. I must await His bidding, for it is the Lord and not Saul who is King over Israel.

OPHIR (*uncomfortably*). To your captains it looks as if this prophet ruled. Are the days of the Judges come back ? Your captains would know whether you more love Samuel or fear him.

SAUL. I love him as my own soul.

JONATHAN. Oh, father !

SAUL (*defending himself*). There was a time when I loved him even thus, and so has Samuel seemed to love me. (*His fingers suddenly twitch to be at the throat of the prophet.*) Yet now if I could—— (*He controls himself.*) But he is a holy man, and we must all bow before holy men—even kings. I am vowed to this waiting till he comes and I get his bidding to fall to.

(*The venom of it makes them draw back. They hear sound from off.* SAUL *signs to* OPHIR, *who draws his sword and goes. He returns.*)

OPHIR. A messenger from Samuel !

(SAUL *indicates that he is to be brought forward, and from*

*this moment the King is a subtle one, holding himself in
check and concealing his real feelings though his mind is
seething.*

    *A guard, rough-bearded and wearing a loin skin of
leather, brings in the* MESSENGER *who is a young priest
with the fire of asceticism on his face. The* MESSENGER
makes an ungracious obeisance.)

SAUL. Your message, Nathan? Comes the prophet
hither?

MESSENGER. Samuel says thus unto King Saul—' I will
not come to thee nor will I look again upon thee.'

OPHIR (*outraged*). Will not! (*He advances upon the*
MESSENGER.) This fellow——

SAUL. Nay, he seems a friendly soul and finds favour in
mine eyes.

    (*The puzzled* OPHIR, *who is of plodding mind, though
he is not aware of it, signs to* GUARD, *who goes off.*)
Was it not Samuel who, in a day far past, sought me out in
my fields in Benjamin, but I had gone thence to search for my
father's asses?

MESSENGER. Thus I have heard did Samuel.

SAUL. When he found me did he not anoint me King?

    (MESSENGER *makes a grudging assent.*)
Who sent him to Benjamin for that end? And why?

    (MESSENGER *is reluctant to reply, but* SAUL, *quite quiet,
forces it out of him.*)
Come, answer me.

MESSENGER (*reluctant*). It was the Lord — Who even
then was loth to have anyone over Israel save Himself
alone.

SAUL. Yet was I sought out in the smallest of the tribes in
Israel, I who was content in my fields, and thus had my life
disturbed.

MESSENGER. It was done because of this stubborn people,
who clamoured for a visible king.

SAUL (*stoutly*). Ay, a visible king—such as other nations
have.

MESSENGER (*imperiously*). There are no other nations.

SAUL (*humbly*). It is so. For are not the pillars of the earth
the Lord's, and hath not He set the world upon them?

MESSENGER.   Nevertheless I ask how He who is omnipotent did *need* to bow to the wishes of a clamorous people ?

(SAUL *is perhaps being more subtle now than the* MESSENGER *had expected of him*.)

Need ! Have you never asked yourself why you, of little Benjamin, were chosen ?

SAUL (*confidently*).   It was because I had the most kingly qualities.

MESSENGER (*for once smiling at him*).   Ay, you have loved being a King !

SAUL (*with simple dignity*).   I have loved it.

MESSENGER.   And never saw that such a one as you were chosen as a punishment to Israel for its clamour !

SAUL (*to whom this is a shock, but controlling himself*).   Punishment ? Was that just to Saul ?

OPHIR (*in rage*).   Let me speak——

SAUL (*stopping him with a gesture*).   I asked and I have been answered.

MESSENGER.   For long the Lord succoured you, seeing you as one little in your own eyes.

SAUL.   Since then have I not, as He enjoined me, ever gone into the battle in front of my people—striking always the first blow ?

MESSENGER.   Not your people—His people.

SAUL.   Ay, His, yet all who had known me in Benjamin marvelled at the wisdom of my words, crying, ' What is this that has come over the son of Kish ? '

MESSENGER.   And what was it that had come over you ?

SAUL (*sadly*).   I vowed to strip this base tenement of its littleness. To serve the Lord without ceasing till I join those who dwell in dust. Such, when I became King, was the vow of Saul too recent from the plough to know his own wild heart. I had ever meant to go the way I was sent.

MESSENGER.   When you were ordered to destroy the Amalekites, men, women and sucklings, every one and their sheep and their oxen, did you go, Saul, the way you were sent ?

SAUL.   I spared the sheep and the oxen—it was as spoil for my soldiers, for only thus are battles won.

MESSENGER (*scornful*).   Only thus—in Israel ?

SAUL (*humbly*).   I spoke hastily.

MESSENGER. You also sought to spare one of the Amalekites—the man Agag.

SAUL. Because he was, too, a King.

MESSENGER (*contemptuously*). You Kings !

SAUL. In that again I sinned.

MESSENGER. And showed your repentance by building at Carmel a trophy to the glory of the conqueror Saul ! With a crown upon your head. Who said that Saul might wear a crown ?

SAUL. If I had hearkened not to my Master, I sought to atone by making sacrifices—(*Losing his humility*)—with a sufficiency of blood even for Him !

MESSENGER. To obey is better than sacrifices, and to hearken better than the fat of rams. You would be the one-over-all. He who was once little in his own eyes has become too much a King. Thou seest thyself lifted up to the skies like a cedar of Lebanon—*and the Lord wearies of you.*

SAUL (*stung*). Is it that he is jealous of Saul ?

MESSENGER. Now dost thou reveal thyself !

SAUL (*scared*). I meant it not of Him but of Samuel.

MESSENGER. For long Samuel interceded for you, and seeking to placate the wrath, he did himself hew Agag to pieces before your eyes. But at last Samuel removes you from his presence. Take now from me the words I bear from him, and *heed them well.*

JONATHAN. This to my father !

SAUL (*again controlling himself and as one obedient to messengers*). Say on.

MESSENGER. Thus says Samuel unto Saul : ' Get your battle in array, for this day shall the Philistines fall before Israel.'

OPHIR (*exultant*). This day !

SAUL (*with a smile, though undeceived*). You like the prophet better now, Ophir !

OPHIR. I had misjudged him.

SAUL. Be not too sure of that. I think our gentle messenger has more to say.

MESSENGER. I have more. This day, says Samuel, shall the first blow be struck—but not by thee, O King.

OPHIR. What is this ?

SAUL. Let our soft-spoken one proceed.

MESSENGER. When the sun is hot there will come through the tents of Israel one riding on an ass. To him shall be the first blow.

SAUL (*with polite interest*). While the King to whom hitherto has always been the first blow——

MESSENGER. While the King stands aside and waits : *for thus it is decreed.*

OPHIR. This messenger craves for the sublimity of death.

SAUL. Ophir, you are hasty. (*To the* MESSENGER) And if I hearken not to the commands of your master ?

MESSENGER. Then woe unto Saul, for a boy will rule in thy place.

SAUL. Are you in such hurry, Jonathan ?

MESSENGER. Thus ends the message of Samuel, whose prophecies ever come to pass. (*He makes a defiant bow.*)

SAUL (*still in his baffling mood, which is beginning to puzzle even the* MESSENGER). What say you, Ophir, how shall we discharge this messenger ?

JONATHAN. Grant him his craving, father, and let him be quit of life.

SAUL. Thus to a messenger ? (*As if in great good-humour*) Nay, Ophir, fill our friend with honey and the grape and speed him courteously upon his way.

MESSENGER. I am of the holy seed, and I will not eat nor drink of thine.

SAUL (*becoming grim*). If he refuses my bounty, thrust it down the gullet of him till he expands. Saul swears in this, his hour, to be kingly unto all. (*An explosion of cold fury follows.*) Carry this to your prophet, O priest : Greetings from Saul to Samuel, the man of the suspicious eye. Say he has made a King of me again. Inasmuch as he dared not obey my summons hither but sent his croakings by thee from some place of hiding, now I know he fears my wrath when I thought 'twas I feared him—and lo, is his hand lifted off me. I am delivered.

MESSENGER. This is forbidden.

SAUL. Forbidden ! Tell him from me that what is forbidden, that shall I do. I dismiss him from my service. Let him not again call himself prophet, or I will put him to the saw and the lime-kiln.

MESSENGER. The Lord——

SAUL. Him shall I serve as ever when I hear His voice—
(*Defiantly*)—but I will not serve Him through the voice of
Samuel. He must speak to this King direct.

MESSENGER. Now art thou doomed.

SAUL (*sternly*). Go.

(OPHIR *is exultant though startled.* JONATHAN *has been
drinking it in, open-mouthed. At a sign from* OPHIR *the
Guard returns.* SAUL'S *eyes are fixed on the* MESSENGER,
who makes a cowed but not cowardly exit with the Guard.)

OPHIR (*glorious*). Now is Israel redeemed! (*He kisses*
SAUL'S *garment.*)

JONATHAN. You said well, Ophir. There is none can
counter my father and live.

SAUL (*well satisfied with himself*). A boy will rule in my
place! Ay, is it so? Jonathan, are you in such undutiful
haste to reign?

JONATHAN (*embracing him*). Looks it so, thou poor prophet?
(*Horn heard.*)

OPHIR. 'Tis as if Israel already rejoiced with us.

SAUL. Ay, it shall be battle now—and Saul's the first blow!
Thus shall Samuel learn that I—I . . . (*A terrible thought
comes to* SAUL *and stops his utterance.*)

OPHIR. This day is Samuel overthrown. (*Coming towards*
SAUL, *he is startled by the change in his face.*)

JONATHAN. King! King, my father. Ophir, see his
face!

(SAUL *signs with his hand to* OPHIR *to come to him. When*
OPHIR *approaches,* SAUL *speaks to him as one puzzled in a
blank voice.*)

SAUL. Who are you?

(*This should be the first intimation that something has
happened to him. It comes also as a sudden shock to* OPHIR
and JONATHAN, *who look at each other. It should all be
very quiet.*)

JONATHAN (*in apprehension*). Father!

SAUL (*to* OPHIR, *coaxingly*). Come tell me who you are?

OPHIR (*shuddering*). I am Ophir, one of your captains.

SAUL (*politely, but evidently not understanding*). Captains?
(*With some cunning*) And I? Truly I know who I am—but
how am I called?

OPHIR. You are Saul the King.

SAUL (*blankly*). King ? Tell me, soldier, what is this anguish that has come upon me ? Did I hear a voice ? (*He means the voice of the Lord.*)

OPHIR (*as in the presence of the supernatural*). None spoke.

JONATHAN. Oh, father !

SAUL. And this one ? Who is he ?

OPHIR. This is Prince Jonathan, your son.

SAUL. Son ?

JONATHAN. My father !

(*As* SAUL *looks at his son, recognition comes to him, and he speaks lovingly.*)

SAUL. Jonathan ! (*The darkness passes from him slowly and he is the King again. He clasps the boy to him.*) Some voice disturbed the balance of my mind. (*He remembers.*) My son, this Samuel, how do I know what he meant——— ? (*His face becomes dreadful with malignancy—he speaks sternly*) Ophir, as you would live, say to none that you have seen me thus.

OPHIR (*steadily*). I have seen nothing.

(SAUL, *brooding, goes to sloped bank and sits.*)

SAUL. Leave me.

(OPHIR *goes off with a reluctant look at* JONATHAN. JONATHAN *nervously kneels on bank to the right of* SAUL *but close to him.*)

JONATHAN. Do not send me from you. Is it that something in the prophet's words disturbs you ?

SAUL (*who is staring and not looking at him*). It concerns you not. (*Grimly*) Ay, it concerns you ! But go—(*Royally*)— the King would be alone.

(JONATHAN, *disturbed, goes off behind the bank.*)

(*Now in sombre thought with* SAUL'S *words in possession of him*) ' A boy will rule in my place.' How do I know that Samuel means Jonathan ? (*He is sitting staring, immersed in this thought and held by a fixed idea.*)

(DAVID *now enters, riding on his ass, and his small harp is slung on his back. He is not ' exalted ' at present ; he is the cheery shepherd boy, and he and his ass are on the best of terms. He pulls up when he sees the figure on the bank.*)

DAVID. Greeting, friend.

(SAUL *does not hear.* DAVID *dismounts and hesitatingly*

*approaches the stranger, but prevents the ass following
him. Evidently, as told in the first Act, he fears that here
is another one who might covet the ass. He whispers
lovingly into its ears unheard words. He points to some
place where the ass is to keep out of sight. It signifies
understanding with its ears and makes an exit, and he
signs to it to go further and lie down. When he is satisfied
he addresses the stranger again.)*

Greeting, friend. Is it that you can say how I may get me to
the camp of Saul ?

SAUL. Did I not tell you to go ! Yet wait. (*He rises, and
in his present state though he sees* DAVID *plainly he presumes it is
still* JONATHAN. *He leaps as it were at* DAVID, *and putting a
hand on his shoulder walks the astonished boy backward and forward, pouring out his emotion in a torrent.*) Jonathan, know you
of any in high places with sons who may be aiming at the throne ?
You know them better than I. Ahiab, son of Alihab—he will
be great in Judah—what of him ? Or Shetnel—he has a
snarling lip for one so young. It might be Ishbaal the Philistine,
out of my own household.

(DAVID *breaks away from him.*)

DAVID. What is this ? I am David, the son of Jesse.

(SAUL *is now the bewildered one. He looks around for*
JONATHAN *and ' comes to.'*)

SAUL (*roughly*). You seem to be a country boy. Who are
you ? What do you here ?

DAVID (*rather frightened*). I am David, son of Jesse.

SAUL. I know no Jesse.

DAVID. I did but halt to ask you how I may get me to the
camp of Saul. My father is of Bethlehem, and there I do tend
his sheep in the fields.

SAUL. Sheep ? Ay, truly, I see them in your eyes.

DAVID (*disturbed*). Do you ?

SAUL (*who sees that he is being taken literally*). And I hear
the sheep-bells in your voice.

DAVID (*fearing that there must be something wrong with himself*). Can it be so ?

SAUL. Sheep ! I too, boy, have led the sheep home, as many
times as there are stones upon the road to Jericho. I was a
shepherd—once—myself.

DAVID. Were you ? You do not look so now. What is your name ?

SAUL (*introducing them, with a touch of humour*). Son of Jesse, I am——the son of Kish.

(DAVID *bows*.)

DAVID. Was your land fat or lean ?

SAUL. Here and there were fat parcels of ground——but the barren places, David ! (*He begins to be amused by* DAVID.)

DAVID (*sympathetically*). I know ! How I know ! *And* the goats in the barren places——waiting to pounce if one blade springs up. How many sheep had you ?

SAUL. Five hundred, it may be, when I returned from a fray.

DAVID (*astounded*). Five hundred ! No ! And kine ?

SAUL. I forget how many.

DAVID (*scandalised*). *Forget* how many !

SAUL (*seating himself and speaking with apparent gravity*). Listen and direct your ways. I had two camels and an olive press, and my well was bricked.

DAVID (*gasping*). Bricked ! (*Boasting*) Nevertheless there is no water like to the well of Bethlehem which is by the gate.

SAUL. That may be so, but I had a fig-tree that bore twice in the year.

DAVID (*who stands near him with legs wide apart and head thrust forward——impressed*). Truly you were in a big way ! We have a hundred sheep and twenty goats, he's and she's. (*Making the best of his case*) My mother has a flagon shaped like a camel and two painted glasses.

SAUL (*handsomely*). I never had that. But, David, I had——
(SAUL *is falling under the spell of* DAVID, *who takes it all seriously.*)

DAVID. Do not tell me you had a he-goat that danced.

SAUL. Ah me, none of my goats danced.

DAVID (*proudly*). Two of my father's goats dance, as thus. (*He shows.*)

SAUL. Would that I had seen them ! But, David, I had three fields of onions.

DAVID (*overthrown*). Three——fields——of onions ! (*Anxiously*) But had you a vine that grew upside down ?

SAUL. Never.

DAVID (*ashamed of boasting*). Neither had we. But my father travelleth far. Consider of this. He has seen—a bed with four legs !

SAUL. What a man is this Jesse ! Now shall I learn, David, whether thou art worthy of such a father. Behold, a shepherd sits bowed over his staff in woe, the sheep lie on their backs, the kine give no milk, and your two he-goats can dance no more. Then the shepherd smells—what does he smell, David, that causes him to dance with the he-goats and the she-goats and makes the grass to arise and dance with them ?

(DAVID *has been listening anxiously.*)

DAVID (*with a shout and making several syllables of the word*). Rain !

SAUL. A stream ran through my land, David.

DAVID (*incredulous*). With water in it ?

(SAUL *nods.*)

No !

SAUL. Now tell me—(*Unbelieving*)—if you can—what is the tree in which there is ever a whispering as of voices in the highest branches ?

DAVID (*after reflecting*). The mulberry ! There is always a going-on in the tops of the mulberries. (*He is getting wildly excited.*)

SAUL. This one will defeat you. At what time of the year had I and my servants—men and women—at what season of the year had we all purple legs ?

DAVID (*gloriously*). At the treading of the grape ! (*He jumps up and down to show how it is done. Then, in an outburst, he cries*) Shall we be friends, O Shepherd ?

SAUL (*like a boy*). We are.

DAVID. You do look a fine one in that cloak.

SAUL (*amused*). Do I, David ?

DAVID (*who has been leading up to this*). How do you think I look in mine ?

SAUL. Lo, it is good. (*He puts a hand on* DAVID's *shoulder and walks him back and forward.*)

DAVID. My mother made my coat.

SAUL. *My* mother, I do remember, used to make mine !

DAVID (*finding this a remarkable coincidence*). Did she ? We are very like each other, Shepherd.

SAUL. The likeness between us grows every moment ! Did your mother also make your harp ?

> (*They occasionally stop for a moment in their walk and talk and resume walking.* DAVID *is sometimes walking backwards in front of* SAUL.)

DAVID. Oh no. My father did want to belt me for having a harp, but my mother dissuaded him.

SAUL. A good, but perhaps weak mother.

DAVID. She is not weak ! She will let none belt me but herself. (*Standing up for her*) There is in all Bethlehem no woman who can lay on as my mother does.

SAUL. On you ?

DAVID. Verily. (*Gloomily*) It is my appetite. Sometimes she does slip food into my mouth before it is due ; and then she is angered, for behold when I have eaten heartily there is nothing about my person to show for it. Then does she at a time lay on.

SAUL (*laughing*). Son of Jesse, I have a drawing to you.

DAVID (*who is often getting in front of him to look up in his face happily*). Have you, Shepherd ?

SAUL (*jestingly reproving*). But this appetite of yours——

DAVID (*recklessly*). I do also drink ! Hearken ! Coming hither I did see some kine in a field, and I milked one—but my mother has told me never to take without paying, so I did tie half of my bag of provender on to the tail of the cow.

SAUL (*delighted*). Now is this like an hour of my youth in Benjamin come back to me ! David, you should first have bound her hind legs together lest she was with calf, and treacherous. I always did that.

DAVID (*victoriously*). She *was* with calf. And so I did bind her hind legs, even as you did ! Assuredly we are as one.

SAUL. Even so.

> (SAUL *so evidently enjoys this that* DAVID *is prompted to say, after a manner of his own :*)

DAVID. Now you tell *me* why you like *me*, and then will I tell *you* why I like *you*.

SAUL. Let me see. I believe you are close to me because I was such as you when a boy. (*Adopting his manner*) Now do **you** tell me why you like me.

DAVID. I think it must be because I want to be such as you when I am a man.

SAUL (*laughing*). Oh, artful one ! But I had forgotten. Tell me, what brings you to seek your way to the camp of Saul ?

DAVID (*regretfully*). Now do I become subtle.

SAUL (*smiling*). Oho !

DAVID. Do you now ask why I become subtle, and lo, I will tell you.

SAUL. Why have you become subtle, son of Jesse ?

DAVID. I have become subtle because my mother did say : ' Tell naught of why you have set forth to any who may question you on the way, lest they make merry and despoil you of your belongings.'

SAUL (*amusedly*). I am rebuked. (*He sits again.*) David, we are two subtle ones, you and I !

DAVID (*gleeful*). Are you also subtle ?

SAUL. Ay, but it is not subtle of you to come hither. All these paths lead to the camp of Saul, and the neighbourhood of camps is ever dangerous.

(DAVID *nervously goes and sits close to him.*)
Why do you do that ?

DAVID. Because if there is danger to me, I feel safe if I am near you, Shepherd.

SAUL (*grimly*). All have not found safety so close to me, David. But take this token with you and show it to any guard who would bar your way. (*He gives him the token, which is a metal disc about two inches long and one broad.*) It will clear all paths for you.

DAVID. How do you know ? Does Saul say this ?

SAUL. Saul says this.

DAVID. Have you ever seen Saul ?

SAUL. I have seen him.

DAVID (*old-fashioned*). How is it with him ? Is he in good health ? Sleeps he well ? Are kings like men?

SAUL. I sometimes think, David, that Saul is like two men.

DAVID. Are there two of him because he is a king ?

SAUL. Ay, so it must be with kings. There are two within Saul—the one good—the other a roaring lion.

DAVID (*pricking his ears at the word*). A lion ! Why does not the good one in him slay the lion ?

SAUL. I wonder ! Perhaps Saul rather likes his lion !

DAVID. Does he ? Do all the people love Saul ?

SAUL. Nay ! He has his enemies, David, and there is talk of a new unknown one. You have made me forget him. Now we must part. (*He pats the head of* DAVID *and rises.*) Fare you well, son of Jesse, and fortune attend you.

DAVID. So also may it be with you, son of Kish. And may that enemy of Saul be rooted up and cast among the slime !

SAUL (*grimly*). As my soul liveth, he shall be !

(DAVID *goes off, waving a hand. His voice is heard off-stage :* 'Shepherd Man!')

Thou Child of Dew !

(*He communes fiercely with himself.*)

Was it Ahiab Samuel meant—or Shetnel or Ishbaal ? 'A boy will rule in thy place.' It must be one of those three. (*He rises.*) Not this time, Samuel, shall your prophecy come to pass. Saul shall wax greater and greater. (*His hand closes on the javelin.*) There is naught like being a King, and King I will abide.

(*He goes off, muttering :* 'Ahiab, Ishbaal, or Shetnel.')

SCENE II

DAVID AND GOLIATH

THE scene is an outpost of the slingers in advance of the Israelite army. They occupy rocks on stage. The rocks on stage are presently to be occupied by Philistines, but are at present empty. They should be more sloped and grassy. Between the opponents is a glade which covers the centre of the stage. This glade is still pointed out in Palestine to the credulous as the scene of the fight with Goliath, so that it can be reproduced to some extent on the stage. It was called the Vale of Elah, which means 'oak' (so there were probably oaks there in those days). The time is the same day about noon, and the sun is hot.

At back the outlook is partly cut off by rock, but there is an opening and on the back-cloth is a suggestion of Saul's innumerable tents—which were mostly of black goat-skin. They are some distance away and are mere dots in the landscape. We should realise that there is a small plain behind the rocks at back. All the rocks are ' practical.' It is a scene where characters can come and go variously, *i.e.* from the opening at back, up and down the rocks, or down stage on both sides. There should be, wherever it is most convenient scenically, a trickle of water falling into a pool.

(*The curtain rises on a scene of wild tumult between* ISRAELITES *and* PHILISTINES, *though the latter are unseen and are shouting from off-stage, the idea to be suggested being that they are about twenty yards away. No command to attack having as yet been given by either side, those clashes at outposts are no more than brawls. A number of the* ISRAELITES *rush into the glade and up the rock but do not go out of sight.*

The attire of the PHILISTINES *was at once more gay and showy than that of Israel. They varied, as there was no fixed uniform, but shining breastplates, brass helmets, feathered head-dresses were common, and they had better arms and were better disciplined. Their horse-chariots were dreaded by the* ISRAELITES, *who were practically all foot men. At present there are not at the moment more than twenty men visible. They are* SLINGERS *of Israel. The* SLINGERS *carry their slings, but the ban against fighting is still in force and the* SLINGERS *are prohibited from using their weapons. They, however, demonstrate with them as they shout. It is mainly an outburst of cries and vituperations of a deafening kind between the seen* ISRAELITES *and the unseen* PHILISTINES, *so that the actual words are little heard though they will be supplied. They are animals thirsting to be at each other in an eruption of barbaric declamation and big gestures such as are inconceivable nowadays : shouts, taunts, etc., poured forth across the glade like lava, and the wildness of the scene can only be rendered by a producer acquainted with the stage representation of Old Testament turbulent incidents. This turmoil should last, at most, not more than two minutes and be like a bonfire—a leap of flame, then suddenly be burnt out. It ends with the blowing of a horn from the unseen Philistine ranks. An immediate silence follows, and the effect is to make all the* ISRAELITES *drop into hiding, so that they seem to have disappeared.*

The PHILISTINES *appear noisily escorting an important person. They settle on their rocks as he proudly descends into the glade. He is the* ARMOUR-BEARER *of Goliath, finely and picturesquely attired, and with a bugle round his neck. He is a young man and, though self-important, must not be in the least farcical, for nothing may be done to mar the drama of the scene. He stands in the glade and sounds a defiant note on his bugle. Then he addresses the concealed* ISRAELITES.)

ARMOUR-BEARER.   Wake up, you Slingers of this outpost of Saul, and listen to me, the Armour-bearer of Goliath. Find you not that forty days sufficeth you for one sleeping ? Come out from the rocks where you are hiding, and hearken again to the challenge of my master, Goliath of Gath.

ALL.   Come out ! cowards.

ARMOUR-BEARER.   Nay, then, lurk in your hiding holes, you dogs, till he sends servants with whips to lash you out.

FIRST PHILISTINE.   We are the whips !

SECOND PHILISTINE.   The whips of Goliath !

ARMOUR-BEARER.   Thus says Goliath : ' Am I not a Philistine and ye the cravens of Saul ! Go out into your camp and search among all your captains, and let one come there to the Vale of Elah where Goliath awaits him.'

ALL.   Your champion.

ARMOUR-BEARER.   ' Then shall the tent of Goliath become his and the spear of Goliath become his. But if I prevail against him and kill him, then shall ye be our servants and serve us, ye and your Gods.'

ALL.   You shall be our servants.

THIRD PHILISTINE.   The servants of the men of Goliath !

(OPHIR *jumps up fiercely but* JONATHAN *pulls him out of sight.*)

ARMOUR-BEARER.   There is no man among you, no, not one ! Dogs of Israel, the challenge is still open. Get you a champion. Haul him hither by rope. His bugle has but to sound, and Goliath is ready. (*He again blows his challenge.*) Behold !

FOURTH PHILISTINE. Get you a champion.

ALL. Haul him !

ARMOUR-BEARER. His bugle of defiance has but to sound, and lo, the spear of Goliath will be ready in the vale.

(*He returns up the rocks, blows his bugle, and they all exit exultantly. There is now no one left on the Philistine rocks. The Captain of the Slingers,* ABNER, *signals to the* ISRAELITES *to arise, and they do so, raging at the indignity they have had to endure. Some of them leap into the arena, slings in evidence, to pursue the* PHILISTINES, *but he drives them back.*)

A SLINGER. You dogs.

ABNER. We may not fight. The King forbids.

A SLINGER. Skulkers ! It is what we are !

ANOTHER. Ay, it is what we are.

ANOTHER. If we may not let loose our slings, why should we carry them ?

ANOTHER. If we may not fight, why carry our slings ?

ANOTHER. To show no longer are we fighting men ?

A THIRD. Down with our slings, I say—no longer are we fighting men.

ALL. Down with our slings !

(*Several throw down their weapons.* ABNER *draws his sword on them.*)

ABNER. Up with your swords or you shall die by your Captain's hands.

A SLINGER. We have no Captain who could stand up against him.

ALL. We have no Captain.

ANOTHER. Must we wait another forty days till *our* horn answers ?

OTHERS. The horns of Israel are broken.

ALL. Broken, broken, the horns of Israel are broken.

(*An unseen horn, different in tone, is heard as from some distance, low yet clear, and all are stirred.*)

A SLINGER. Did you hear ?

ANOTHER. Someone accepts the challenge !

ANOTHER. Who could he be ?

ABNER. If only I could be he !

ANOTHER. A champion for Israel.

ALL.   A champion for Israel.

OTHERS.   At last !

ANOTHER.   He comes down the hill.

A SLINGER.   Where is he ?

ANOTHER.   Now he is behind a rock.

A SLINGER.   Where ?

ANOTHER.   Over there.

ANOTHER.   Now I see him.

ANOTHER.   He comes this way.

(*Similar cries from* OTHERS.)

ALL.   He comes !   He comes !

A SLINGER.   He comes.

ANOTHER.   A boy.   Lo, it is a boy riding on an ass !

(OTHERS *crowd round up-stage and their excitement changes into mirth.*)

Behold the champion of Israel !

(DAVID *comes riding forward at back on the ass and with a horn in his hand.   He is in his exalted condition, and it should have the effect of keeping the scene serious, which is essential.   He is now a boy of high resolve, with no playfulness about him.*)

DAVID (*with dignity*).   Greetings to this outpost of the Slingers of Israel.   (*All murmur* ' Greetings.')

ABNER (*roughly*).   Whence come you ?

DAVID.   I am David, the son of Jesse, and lo——

ABNER.   I care not whose son you be, nor do I believe you ever had parentage.   What seek you here ?

(OPHIR *and* JONATHAN *enter.*)

DAVID.   I say unto you, speak not thus of my parentage, and I seek here a lion who is called Goliath of Gath.

ABNER.   And when you have found him ?

DAVID (*calm and resolved and simple, and without any boasting*). Then shall I slay him.

ABNER.   With your sling or with your harp ?

DAVID (*with dignity*).   It is to be with my sling.

A SLINGER.   Behold the champion of Israel !

DAVID.   Deride me not because I am a boy.   This day shall I slay Goliath.

A SLINGER.   What say you ?

ANOTHER.   Hast ever heard the like ?

ANOTHER.   This poor Goliath !
(*His quiet assurance impresses the* SLINGERS, *and they are perplexed and ponder.*)
A SLINGER.   What cast of boy is this ?   (*All start murmuring.*)
ABNER (*also puzzled*).   What I would know is, how came it to pass that they let you ride unchecked through the camp of Saul ?
DAVID.   All were kind and sped me on my way, and they did give me this horn on which to blow my challenge, and behold I will blow it again.   (*He is about to do so.*)
ABNER.   Hold him !
SEVERAL.   Hold him !
(SLINGERS *restrain* DAVID.)
A SLINGER.   They sped him on his way !
ANOTHER.   It is unbelievable——
ANOTHER.   Yet the poor soul believes it.
ANOTHER (*with awe*).   Is he bereft ?
DAVID.   I am not bereft.   I am exalted.
A SLINGER.   There are things happening in these days that pass the wit of man.
(OPHIR *and* JONATHAN *have remained in this scene, hardly noticed ; but they have listened intently, and* OPHIR *now comes forward.*)
OPHIR.   Abner !
ABNER (*relieved to see a superior officer*).   Now are you pleasant in my eyes, Ophir, for you are a captain of five hundred and I but of fifty, and there is that to decide which I shall gladly leave to you.   This boy——
OPHIR.   I have heard all.   (*He signs to the* SLINGERS *to stand back.*)
(*They do so, but keeping hand on the ass on which* DAVID *still sits.*)
ABNER.   What to do with him ?   There is something untoward about this boy.
OPHIR.   Ay, more so than you know of.   I have known it since he came here riding on an ass.
ABNER.   He says that all he met in the camp encouraged him on his way.
OPHIR.   Ay, but that I *cannot* believe.   (*He goes to* DAVID.)
Say you, boy, that no guards opposed your coming hither

through the camp to this uttermost outpost of the slingers ?
How could it be so ?

DAVID.   At first they did stay me ribaldly, dragging me from
the ass and otherwise misusing me, but when I showed it to
them they all did speed me on my way.

ABNER.   They were mocking you.

OPHIR.   What showed you to them that did make so great
a man of you ?

DAVID.   This which he gave me. *(He puts the token into the
hands of* OPHIR, *whom it startles.)*

(He shows it to ABNER.*)*

ABNER *(equally taken aback).*   The token of Saul !

OPHIR.   Ay !   *(He calls to* DAVID*)* How came you by this ?

DAVID.   A shepherd did give it to me in a clearing in the
wood.

ABNER.   Shepherd ?

OPHIR.   He was once that.   *(To* DAVID*)* How did he
look ?

DAVID.   He did look noble, and he sat on an open space in
the wood in a purple cloak, and a javelin was near by.

*(*OPHIR *and* ABNER *exchange glances.)*

OPHIR.   He spoke with you ?

DAVID.   He did so.   He is my greatest friend, and I am *his*
greatest friend.

OPHIR *(to* ABNER*).*   Be wary, Abner, the boy knows not who
it was.   A shepherd, he believes ; and so Saul wants him to
believe.   What do you conceive is now in the secret mind of
Saul ?

ABNER.   The token of the King !   No thinking is needed.
All know its meaning : ' Do as the Bearer asks, or incur the
wrath of Saul.'

OPHIR.   Ay, so it means—and what asks this Bearer ?—To
fight Goliath !

ABNER.   That turns it all to folly.

OPHIR *(grimly).*   Does it ?   Let me think.   *(He moves about,
brooding.)*

*(*ABNER *goes to* DAVID.*)*

ABNER.   Now would I make amends.   If you will be pleased
to alight——

DAVID *(with dignity).*   It is my pleasure.   *(He alights and examines his ass solicitously.*) It is a valuable ass (*rubbing his head on it*). Also I do love it.

ABNER. It shall be in my charge, well tended.

DAVID. Peace be yours, O ass. I shall come to see how it is with you when I have slain this Goliath.

(ABNER *gasps at this, but evidently gives orders to a* SLINGER *who mounts the ass and is going with him up-stage.* DAVID *frowns.*)

DAVID. Who is he that doth mount my ass ?

ABNER. His name is Hiram—your ass is safe with him.

(*The ass turns its head and looks oddly at* ABNER.)

DAVID. The ass may be safe with Hiram, but Hiram is not safe with the ass.

(HIRAM *rides the ass off. Immediately they are out of sight a scuffle is heard off.* DAVID *cannot see what has happened, but he explains to* ABNER.)

DAVID. Hiram is no longer on the ass.

(*The* SLINGERS *hasten to see what has happened.* DAVID *and* ABNER *go with them. For a brief space* OPHIR *and* JONATHAN *are alone on the stage.* OPHIR *in his broodings meets* JONATHAN *down-stage, and has shown him the token.*)

JONATHAN. Let the boy go unharmed, Ophir. You can see what hand has touched him—he is afflicted.

OPHIR. My prince, do you forget the words of but an hour ago—' One who shall come riding on an ass ' ?

JONATHAN. Samuel did not say a boy.

OPHIR. He said : ' To that one who comes riding on an ass must be given the first blow, or a boy shall rule in the place of Saul.'

JONATHAN. He meant me.

OPHIR. So we thought, but it has now come to me that this is the boy he meant—and so I believe has it come to the King. (*This is a shock to* JONATHAN.) What asks the boy ? To fight Goliath. What orders this token ? To grant him that boon !

JONATHAN. Of death !

OPHIR. Ay, but in that one stroke he is removed for ever from the path of Saul.

JONATHAN. Poor shepherd boy !

OPHIR (*whose loyalty to his King is still a redeeming feature*).

See you not also that, with the fate of the boy, Samuel falls in the eyes of Israel ?

JONATHAN.   The people know not that this champion is the choice of Samuel.

OPHIR.   Mine the part to let them know.

JONATHAN.   If thus my father wanted he would have made his meaning clear.

OPHIR.   Kings speak not their wishes clear but leave it to their servants to interpret them.

JONATHAN.   Consider your peril, Ophir—what if you interpret him awry ?

OPHIR.   I have considered it.   Yet even if I err the King would still be unharmed.   He would but seem to have followed in the way he was told.   This prophet is a deep one, but he shall find that I am deeper.

JONATHAN.   It is not, I think, the deepness of you that commends you to the King.   If you read him wrongly now——

OPHIR (*finely*).   It would be the end of Ophir, but what matter if I was seeking to serve Saul ?

JONATHAN (*touched by his devotion*).   Truly you love him !

OPHIR (*passionately*).   Ay, do I !

(*Shouts and declamation of the soldiers as they return.* ABNER *pushes forward in front of them.*)

A SLINGER.   Away with the child.   Thus say we all.

ALL.   All.   All.   All.

OPHIR.   How now ?

ABNER (*who has* DAVID'S *horn in his hand*).   His horn.   They took it from him, crying that to let such a one face the man of Gath would be to make sport of us before the Philistines.

(*Cries of corroboration of this rend the air—*' We will not have him—Shall Israel be shamed ?   What means Saul by giving us such a champion ? ')

OPHIR.   First hear me.

(*The turmoil subsides.*)

Israelites, the boy comes not from Saul, he is the choice of Samuel.   Saul scorns this champion, but Samuel proclaims that this boy and no other shall strike the first blow.   For forty days has Saul hungered to fall upon the Philistines, but he cannot because he has been under the weight of a vow to the Prophet.

FIRST SLINGER.   A vow to the Prophet ?

SECOND SLINGER.   Saul is under a vow to Samuel.

THIRD SLINGER.   I have heard of this.

FOURTH SLINGER.   What is this vow?

FIFTH SLINGER.   We know this vow.

SIXTH SLINGER.   It is not to fight.

SEVENTH SLINGER.   Samuel orders it.

EIGHTH SLINGER.   Yes, he orders it.

NINTH SLINGER.   Does Samuel rule in Israel?

TENTH SLINGER.   Ophir, speak. Tell us why Saul obeys him —this Samuel.

OPHIR.   I bring word to you from Saul. Thus says Saul to his people, 'Let Samuel have his wish.' At such a moment what is the life of a boy or the triumph of a braggart? Samuel's be the shame.

ALL.   Yes, Samuel's be the shame.

OPHIR.   For, listen, soldiers. With that first blow Saul is absolved of his vow! Then will he straightway give battle.

ALL.   The battle! The battle!

FIRST SLINGER.   Saul will be absolved of his vow!

SECOND SLINGER.   The forty days are over!

ALL.   The forty days are over!

OPHIR.   See him again this day, Israel, as you have been wont to see him in your front, Saul our King, as he bends backward, astride your enemies, his javelin in his hand. He calls to you once more to smite the Philistines.

ALL.   Smite the Philistines!

OPHIR.   Then shall their cattle be thine, and their wines and their horses and their camels shall be thine, and their chariots shall be thine, and at last there will be workers of iron in this land to forge us swords and spears. Are you ready to be magnified, O Israel? Is it to be the battle?

(*His outburst is gradually received with clamorous cries of* 'The battle, the battle—the forty days are over. Let the boy perish—Hail the King,' *ending with* 'But where is the boy?'

DAVID, *who has been neglected and lost to sight, is now discovered in a parting of the crowd, quite regardless of them, testing pebbles in the water. They regard him wonderingly.*)

ABNER.   What are you doing, boy?

DAVID (*looking up*). I am gathering pebbles for my sling.

A SLINGER. Truly this one is not as others are.

DAVID (*to* JONATHAN). Who are you, boy ?

JONATHAN. My name is Jonathan.

DAVID. My name is David. (*More secretively*) Hearken, Jonathan. They say that he who kills Goliath acquires his tent and his spear.

JONATHAN. It is so, but woe unto you.

DAVID (*very worried*). I fear not to sleep in his tent if there is a lamp. But his spear ! Jonathan, if his spear is like unto a weaver's beam, as they say, how shall I be able to carry it on my shoulder ?

JONATHAN (*astounded*). Is that all that in this dire moment afflicts your mind ?

DAVID. It is chiefly that.

JONATHAN. Thou pitiful !

A SLINGER. Ophir, are we men that we can give him to the spear of the Philistines ?

OPHIR. It is not we who give him. It is Samuel.

A SLINGER. Ay, true, it is not Saul who sends this one to the man of Gath. Samuel's the blame.

ALL. Ay, Samuel's the blame.

OPHIR. The boy's own be the decision.

A SLINGER. Death awaits him.

ANOTHER. Let the boy do as he will.

(OPHIR *takes horn from* ABNER.)

OPHIR (*who sees that he must act quickly before a fickle crowd*). This is his horn. Let him sound it if he dares.

(*He casts the horn on to the glade where* DAVID *is alone.*)

ABNER. Know, boy, there is none in Israel who will face this monster.

A SLINGER. None.

ALL. None of us.

ABNER. For he is as one left over from the giants who were drowned in a deluge and now mourn and groan in Hell beneath the waters. Such is this Goliath, crying mockingly that Israel is without a God.

DAVID. Who is the God of Israel ?

ABNER. Our Maker, the Lord of Hosts, Whom this Goliath defies.

DAVID. Can it be ? (*He looks up, shuts his eyes, then crosses to where the horn lies.*)

JONATHAN (*coming to* DAVID). Touch not the horn, David.

A SLINGER. Touch not the horn.

JONATHAN. Surely now, you are afraid.

(DAVID *shivers, and for the moment his courage is gone.*)

OPHIR (*jeering*). Ah, see how Samuel's champion trembles ! In vain do we await the blast that was to be great in the history of Israel.

A SLINGER. He fears !

DAVID (*though still in a quiver and rather childlike*). Perhaps I am afraid—but thus does David.

> (*He lifts the horn and blows a clear challenging blast. The answer comes from the Philistine camp. All cringe and work around to the left of stage.*)

ARMOUR-BEARER (*off-stage*). Goliath awaits the champion of Israel. Here in the Vale of Elah.

ALL. He is doomed.

(*The scene becomes darker.*)

A SLINGER. A darkness comes upon the land.

ALL. A darkness comes upon the land.

A SLINGER. Who sends it ?

ANOTHER. The Lord deserts us.

ABNER. Or has the boy a friend we know not of ?

OPHIR. He has no friend.

(*The stage is now quite dark.*)

ARMOUR-BEARER (*off*). Goliath awaits.

> (*Challenging trumpets are heard from Philistine camp. All the Israelites creep away, leaving only* DAVID *and* JONATHAN. DAVID *hesitates, then slowly walks up centre and goes toward the Philistine camp. He backs, appalled by what he has seen.* JONATHAN *creeps up to him.*)

JONATHAN (*in whisper*). David ! David, did you see him ?

DAVID. I saw him.

JONATHAN. What think you ?

DAVID. He is of a size even more huge than they said. Jonathan, I am not *quite* sure now that I shall win.

JONATHAN. Fly with me quickly, David. I can save you still.

DAVID. No.

GOLIATH (*off*). Now shall Israel be shamed for mocking me with such a champion. Look, insect, upon Goliath of Gath.

DAVID. Lo, I have looked and you are smaller than they said.

GOLIATH. How many pebbles, little one, are in your wallet?

DAVID. There are five, but I think I shall not need them all.

GOLIATH. I curse thee by my Gods. Come to me and I will give thy flesh to the fowls of the air and to the beasts of the field, thou Israelite who art without a God.

DAVID. Thou comest to me with a sword and with a spear and with a shield, but I come to thee in the Name of Him Whom thou hast defied. This day will He deliver thee into mine hands and I will smite thee, that all the earth will know there is a God in Israel.

(*Poised on the rock,* DAVID *discharges his sling at the unseen* GOLIATH. *The stone whistles through the air. There is a moment of intense silence, followed by the echoing sound of* GOLIATH'S *fall.* DAVID *runs off-stage in the direction from which the sound comes. The darkness gradually lifts, and one by one, very slowly and anxiously, Israelites come on, bewildered and unable to understand what has happened. They do not speak, but stare in the direction of the Philistines.* ABNER *is amongst them. This situation lasts a full minute. Suddenly an Israelite comes on from the side of the Philistines, crying breathlessly and hoarsely:* ' David has slain Goliath! David has slain Goliath! David has slain Goliath!' *Repeating the same words again and again like a madman, he crosses the stage until he disappears from sight. Behind the scene you still hear him repeating this incredible news —spreading the miracle through the tents, his voice growing louder. The few men on the stage are awestruck, whisperingly asking one another,* ' David has slain Goliath?' *as though unable to believe their own words.*

Then there comes a long-drawn cry from the Philistines, ' David has slain Goliath!!!' *With barbaric dancing and wild shouts Israelites pour on to the scene until the stage is quite full. Throughout all the clamour the words* ' David has slain Goliath!' *are continuously heard, taken up by more and more of the thronging Israelites until at last the sentence rises to a jubilant roar.*

Finally DAVID *comes on with* GOLIATH'S *great spear.
Being unable to raise it, he is dragging it along the ground
with both hands.   The Israelites dance wildly around him
until one cries out :* 'The battle ! The battle !' *This
idea is taken up by more and more, until with one accord
they all rush off in the direction of the Philistines, their
voices mingling in one unanimous cry :* 'The battle !
The battle !')*

SCENE III

DAVID PLAYS BEFORE SAUL

IT is the night of the same day, and it is the same scene, except
that the tent of Goliath now occupies a conspicuous place in it ;
and as much of the action is to occur inside this tent, all other
matters must be subservient to a complete view of not all but
most of the inside of the tent to everybody in the house.   This
will require much stage-craft and practical consideration.

The tents of those days were not white, they were indeed
mostly black, made of the skins of black goats, etc., but we can
suppose that Goliath's tent was of a barbaric and bizarre appearance, such as had appealed to his crude imagination, and it is of
skins of various animals sewn together.   It has a centre pole
and, when open, the inside should follow, as far as may be, the
picture already referred to by Rembrandt of David playing before
Saul.   It must be down-stage, not in centre, but nearer to left
than to right, and the opening, which is sometimes closed, must
be to the footlights.   It must be of considerable size, and will
cut off the view of a large part of the scene, but this does not
matter.

A general effect will be got, in glimpses, of the former scene,
with the army tents now lit up here and there and moving
lights, and where there is talk or important business outside the
tent, it is to take place down-stage right where the tent will not
obscure the actors.   The lighting of the scene can vary for
stage effect, but on the whole it is a dark night, and no moon
is visible.

(The effect to be got when the curtain rises is as if it had risen prematurely on stage-hands putting the finishing touches to the erection of the tent, but the workmen are Philistine prisoners, and overseer to them is ABNER, *who is doing it with a whip, which, after the manner of the times, he does not hesitate to use. There is quite a suggestion of savage cruelty. Some of them are in chains, all are sullen and crouching figures and one of them is* GOLIATH'S ARMOUR-BEARER.*

This opening of the scene is to convey its meaning without words, and is to include the carrying to the tent of GOLIATH'S *helmet and armour and rich rugs. When* ABNER *thinks it is finished he relinquishes his whip to an Israelite* GUARD, *who drives the captives away in front of him amid the jeers of the conquerors. The tent has been closed so far, and a light shows through interstices in the covering.* DAVID *and* JONATHAN *are inside but unseen, and the tent is already lit up before rise of curtain.*

Simultaneously there is revelling going on upon the rocks on both sides as well as suggested in the distance. There is music and singing in barbaric joy and leaping over an Israelite victory. The whole thing is of the briefest, as all the appearances of crowds in this play are, but it is furiously wild while it lasts. It is ended abruptly about the same time as the departure of the captives by loud blasts from off-stage, which signify the recall of the revellers to camp. They go quickly but still revelling.

ABNER *is now alone and troubled. He surveys the tent.* OPHIR *comes from back, rather furtively, and they meet down-stage.)*

ABNER.   Ophir !

OPHIR.   Ay, he has let me live but I am no more a captain. Heard you not the recall to camp sounded, Abner ? *(As one dismissing him)* We are no longer needed here.

ABNER *(looking at tent).* Yet would I linger—ay, till the morning light.

OPHIR.   Is the boy within his tent ?

ABNER *(ill at ease).* Yea, and Prince Jonathan with him. Ophir, why has the tent of Goliath that is now David's been pitched in this lonely place ?

OPHIR. Guards have been left him on the rocks. Does he complain ?

ABNER. Nay, he is too ignorant to know fear so long as there is a light within. So was it with me, in the days when I was small. (*Touched*) The two of them are playing with the harness of Goliath. He is now more like a child than a conqueror.

OPHIR (*grimly*). Then all is well.

ABNER. I do not think that in this dark glade all is well. (*Looking round the dark glade*) I think there is danger this night to David.

OPHIR (*lowering*). Who can be the enemy ? Say to me his name, Abner !

(*Obviously* ABNER *could say it but he shrinks, afraid. He listens suspiciously.*)
For what do you listen ?

ABNER. I seem to hear the beating of a heart that is privy to wickedness.

OPHIR. Come, come, thou troubled one, have not the Philistines been consumed ; and their camels, ay, and their horses and even their chariots are now the servants of Israel. All shout this night to the glory of the King whose name you are afraid to speak.

ABNER. Ay, truly, they exult in the King. But they also cry—(*He looks significantly at the tent*)—' There is no boy like this boy ! ' and because of thee, Ophir, they whisper, ' Great is Samuel who sent to us this champion.'

OPHIR (*shuddering*). Speak not of it ! Does David know now who his shepherd is ?

ABNER. I asked Prince Jonathan to say naught of that to him.
(*Bugles are heard again.*)

OPHIR. The second horn. Come, Abner, I shall go with you. All make revel to-night save I !

ABNER (*shivering*). Not all. I was here alone when the first of the darkness came. I was *not* alone. There was evil flitting through this glade.

OPHIR (*similarly moved*). Then let us avoid out of its presence, come. As my soul liveth, never again shall I say of him, whose name we both fear to speak, that he needs aid save from his own javelin.

(*They go off with a last furtive look at the tent. As far as possible their exit should be visible from all parts of the house.* SAUL *comes on and picks up his javelin which is leaning against the tent. A sound from the tent arrests his attention. It is* JONATHAN, *speaking as he emerges. He comes through the slit without opening it and calls in.* SAUL *has moved up-stage.*)

JONATHAN. Truly, David, this time I must go. It was the second horn. (*He comes out.*)

(SAUL, *coming back, meets him down-stage.*)

You, Father ! (*He is afraid of him.*)

SAUL (*lowering*). Again with this boy ! (*Pouring it out*) You son of the perverse rebellious woman, do not I know that you have chosen this son of Jesse to your own confusion ? Jonathan, for as long as this David liveth upon the ground, you shall not be established in this kingdom.

JONATHAN. If so it be, he knows nothing of it.

SAUL. That shall I now learn. (*In another rush*) My son, it is you shall follow after me over Israel—ay, though the Lord Himself say no ! (*Clutching his javelin—secretly*) Jonathan, get you to your tent ; it is not Saul you have seen here to-night ; know *that* when you wake.

JONATHAN (*alarmed*). Father, send me not from you !

(DAVID *puts his head through the slit in the tent.*)

DAVID. Jonathan, did you call ? (*He comes out and is bewildered.*)

JONATHAN. It is the King !

(SAUL *frowns but has to dissemble.*)

DAVID (*enraptured*). No, it is not, Jonathan—it is my Shepherd. (*He bends with his hands on his knees, boy-like, and gazes gloriously at* SAUL.) Son of Kish !

SAUL (*now a crafty man*). Son of Jesse, we meet again.

DAVID. Let me encompass thee. (*He clasps* SAUL *round the legs. In glee he calls out*) Shepherd, know that I am the one who slew Goliath !

SAUL. I have known it for an hour. Hail to the conqueror !

DAVID. Jonathan, it was he gave me the token ! (*To* SAUL) Lo, all the greatness of David has come to me from you.

SAUL (*grimly*). Ay, verily, so I have learned.

JONATHAN. Father——

DAVID. Why do you call him that?

JONATHAN. He is Saul, the King!

(DAVID *gapes and looks at* SAUL *for corroboration.*)

SAUL. Even so.

DAVID. Now if you will swear it to me by my sling, then will I do something.

(SAUL *is for the moment captured by this.*)

SAUL. By your sling, I am the King.

DAVID. Stand away, Jonathan, I know how to do it. (*He makes space for himself, and then prostrates quite prettily before* SAUL.)

(*The third bugle sounds and* SAUL *points imperiously to* JONATHAN. *Exit* JONATHAN *with misgivings.*)

(DAVID *rises and speaks shyly*) Was that right, O King?

SAUL. It was well done.

DAVID. Has Jonathan gone?

SAUL. Ay, it was the third horn. Shall we go into your tent, David, and talk—but on a different matter?

DAVID (*gaily*). Let us. (*He stops* SAUL.) Nay, first wait till I clap my hands. Next, do you pull the opening both ways—wide—and then—lo, you shall see what you shall see.

(SAUL *nods.* DAVID *disappears into the tent.* SAUL *makes sure to his satisfaction that he is alone in the glade—he ponders darkly. The clapping of the hands is heard. He pulls the opening of the tent to its widest and then looks at the picture that has been prepared for him. It is* DAVID *standing majestically, posing as* GOLIATH, *with the helmet on his head and his two hands grasping the hilt of the spear, which is otherwise trailing on the ground.*)

DAVID (*motionless*). What think you?

SAUL (*who finds it difficult not to be enamoured of this boy*). Is this the man of Gath come back to life?

DAVID (*pleased, but reassuring*). Not truly. Saul, it is your David! Behold! (*He struggles to raise the spear vainly, as he strikes a new attitude.*)

SAUL. It is most memorable—though not thus do captains usually carry their spears.

DAVID (*troubled*). I know! (*He has a happy idea—speaks proudly*) This is my way! (*The pride goes from him and he speaks anxiously*) Look—my helmet—if it slips down, then shall I pass from sight !

(SAUL *comes to his aid by taking off the helmet and* DAVID *drags the spear along, leaving it on the ground. He looks at* SAUL *affectionately and speaks in a puzzled confidential way. They are sitting now.*)

King, has it seemed to you that we have something in common, you and I, that we share not with others ?

SAUL (*surprised*). Has that come to *you* also ?

DAVID. A King and a shepherd boy. How can it be, Son of Kish ?

SAUL. Perhaps it is not ordained that you are always to tend sheep.

DAVID (*confident, smiling at him*). Foolish one, things are not ordained about such as David, but only about kings.

(SAUL *turns and comes back to him.*)

SAUL. No thoughts of what may yet come to pass disturb you, David ? I would know this.

DAVID. When I killed Goliath something strange did well up in me. (*Shuddering*) Was it the hereafter, Saul ?

SAUL. That is what I would know.

DAVID (*uneasily*). All I have heard about what is to come to pass is of things done by evil spirits and those who call them up.

SAUL (*strongly*). I, Saul the King, have cut off all such out of this land. (*Huskily*) Nevertheless, one would wish to know. (*Suspiciously*) Said Jonathan anything to you about familiar spirits disquieting me so that a harpist was brought to play before me and drive them away ?

DAVID. No. (*Fearful*) You ! Can one playing on a harp do so ? (*Lighting up*) Saul, I can play on my harp !

SAUL (*agitated—fiercely*). They trouble me not. I tell you I have driven them from my kingdom. (*Secretly*) Yet 'tis said there is still one, called the Woman of Endor. (*Huskily*) There are things that kings should know.

DAVID. Would you foresee that which is to come if you could ?

SAUL. No, no.

DAVID (*breathless*). I would that I could do so. Have you been to the woman ?

SAUL. Nay, not I. But she has come to me, David, in

diverse shapes—even she seemed to be there in this day's battle
—warning me not to approach her and yet crooking her finger
to entice me. (*Suddenly lowering*) What is it that makes me
tell you this? No others have I told. (*He grips him roughly.*)
Now tell me your hidden things. You have them. I know,
you crafty one.

DAVID.　Crafty! (*He rises in alarm.*)

　　　(SAUL *pulls him down and becomes cunningly reassuring.*)

SAUL.　Nay, nay. Tell me, David, how did you know about
prostrating?

DAVID (*comfortable again and in his old friendly fashion*).
Behold, there was an old man I did see do it.

SAUL.　To a king?

DAVID (*merry at the thought*).　No! (*He tells his cause of
merriment.*)　Saul, he did it to me!

SAUL (*gripping him*).　Be still, boy. This old man—how
looked he?

DAVID.　A poor one, but kind. He said he was a prophet.

SAUL.　Did he say his name?

DAVID.　He was called Samuel.

　　　(SAUL *has to take a deep breath before he can speak, but he
　　　remains crafty.*)

SAUL.　Was he?

DAVID.　I do laugh now, but it was not so at the time.

SAUL.　Tell me about that time—so that we may laugh together.

DAVID (*who is boyish and confiding*).　It was in our house at
Bethlehem, and he was secret. He carried a wallet and in it a
horn, and he prayed and wetted my head with wet from the
horn. And when he was going away he did prostrate himself
—before David! (*He laughs at it.*)

　　　(SAUL *controls himself.*)

SAUL.　You said he was secret.

DAVID.　Yes. Saul, there is some one he fears.

SAUL.　There is—and that some one fears him! (*Sharply*)
What makes you think that?

DAVID.　He said to my mother that if she told the thing he
had done there would be but a step between him and me—and
Death. King, protect me. (*In a sudden fear he clings to
SAUL.*)

SAUL (*pushing him away and holding him at arm's length*). David, how did Samuel kill Goliath?

DAVID (*affronted*). Samuel? That one? It was I killed Goliath.

SAUL. Yours the pebble——but think you Saul can be deceived as are the ignorant? How was it?

DAVID (*letting the admission be drawn out of him*). He only helped.

SAUL. Answer me——who was it?

DAVID. I will not tell you. It was not Samuel. It was—— the Other One. Samuel is His servant.

SAUL. At last do I know all. (*He rises and is still kingly, though broken.*) Now am I forsaken.

DAVID (*rising*). You will not tell Jonathan? He thinks I did it all myself. (*Imploring.*)

SAUL (*putting a sorrowful hand on* DAVID'S *head*). Thou doomed boy.

DAVID (*bewildered*). Doomed? Am I doomed, Saul?

SAUL. One of us two friends is doomed.

DAVID (*startled and very childlike*). Do you not like me now?

SAUL (*mournfully*). I like you well. (*He comes to the opening of the tent and, after half-closing it, stands there as if for air.*) David, you should not have told me these things.

(DAVID *has followed him.*)

DAVID (*shrinking*). I know, but I wanted to tell you my things as you have told me yours.

(SAUL *does not answer, but stands rigid, staring.* DAVID *gets his harp from back and comes to opening and, sitting on a stool, though still inside the tent like* SAUL, *begins to play. He occasionally looks up, but is mostly looking at his harp. He has no fear of* SAUL. SAUL *stands much perturbed with one hand on the part of the tent that is still open. The harp music goes on.*)

SAUL (*at last speaking tragically*). There is an enemy in my habitation.

DAVID. An enemy? If it is so, kill him. Saul, kill him! (*He continues to play.*)

SAUL (*after a pause*). I will kill him. David, it is you I am to kill.

DAVID (*looking up and smiling happily*). Oh no, Son of Kish!

(But, seeing SAUL'S *face, he rises and draws back till he is out of sight, but he never stops playing.)*

(For a brief period there is silence except that the harp-playing continues. SAUL *is gazing at him, as has been said of the Rembrandt picture, devilish of one eye and with a tear for* DAVID *in the other. Then he draws close the remaining part of the opening.*

The tent is now shut up. The light continues to show through the interstices; and the harp goes on. SAUL *raises one side of the opening of the tent and throws his javelin. The harp stops abruptly and the light within the tent goes out. After* SAUL *has thrown the javelin at* DAVID *and the harp has stopped and the light gone out in the closed tent, he stands a second listening to the dead silence within the tent. Then with inarticulate cries, laughter and wild gestures he sweeps across the stage triumphant—challenging.*

Suddenly he stands rigid as though hearing a voice call, ' Hast thou slain the Lord's anointed ? ' *Eyes staring wildly, he shakes with fear. Then he turns and in a tremulous voice, as one who calls for help, cries brokenly,* ' David . . . David.'

No sound from within, SAUL, *a doomed figure, with his back to the tent, slowly, unsteadily sinks down on to a tree-trunk and buries his head in his arms. After a few seconds, during which nothing is heard but the heavy breathing of* SAUL, DAVID'S *head peeps out of the tent. He is wide-eyed, bewildered, frightened and very sad.*

At sight of the collapsed SAUL *his first thoughts are only of immediate flight. Noiselessly, swift as a wild animal, with his harp under his arm, he climbs up the rocks in the background, and is almost safely out of reach when he suddenly stops and looks irresolutely at* SAUL. *Something seems to draw him back to the enemy. Stealthily he creeps nearer and nearer to* SAUL, *fear, love and pity in his eyes. Timidly he kneels down far away from* SAUL, *but keeping anxious eyes fixed on him.*

He begins to play his harp—with one hand only—as though uncertain if this is the right thing to do. SAUL *does not stir. Slowly, without ever leaving off playing,* DAVID *creeps on his knees closer and closer. He begins to play a little more boldly. At last* SAUL *moves.* DAVID *holds his breath. Then, with great courage and determination, he draws quite close and plays his harp strongly—confidently, but never taking his eyes off* SAUL. *Listening,* SAUL *slowly raises his head and turns like one returning from another world. There is great danger in his expression when he recognises* DAVID *crouched, playing at his feet—smiling—radiantly happy. Then all tension leaves* SAUL *and he is merely listening to the music like one very far away.)*

ACT III

Scene I

IN A VISION OF THE NIGHT DAVID FORESEES HIS FUTURE, AND KNOWS IT NOT

The scene is the house of Jesse, as in Act I, except that the time is now late evening. The room is dimly lit by a lamp of the period. The fire is no longer in evidence. It is bed-time and the household of Jesse is about to retire to rest.

In those days the preparations were of the most primitive. The beds were merely mattresses or a skin on the floor, with seldom anything for a pillow, and were huddled together as suited the convenience of the household. There was scarcely any undressing beyond shoes or a coat, and they often added warmer garments instead of taking anything off.

Jesse and David and the four sons of Act I are to sleep here to-night as usual, and certain preparations have already begun. Three of the beds are already on the floor, including David's, which is down-stage.

(DAVID *is already in bed, placidly drinking his evening milk, dipping bread in it and licking his bowl. He wears a white garment not unlike a modern nightgown though of ancient days. The only other person present just now is his* MOTHER. *This little woman is of inexhaustible energy, and has a way of putting things in their place by butting her head at them. On rise of curtain she is climbing perilously to the window at back, carrying a board which is its shutter. She has difficulties with it but rams it cleverly in with one of those butts, just as it was about to fall. The characteristic of her butts is that she takes the object suddenly unawares, but there must be an avoidance of seeming to do it for stage effect ; it is all just part of*

1247

*the day's work. She finds a big lump in a bed and plays
sudden dab at it with her knees instead of her head. All
this is of the briefest. She is quick, vital, and an appall-
ingly active housewife, and in a few moments she is by the
side of* DAVID. *He, being accustomed to her ways, is
regardlessly drinking his milk. Having last seen him
holding his own in royal company, we now see him helpless
in the hands of this whirlwind of a woman.*

*All these silent scenes should be brief, with apparent
leisureliness.*)

MOTHER. Spilt again ! Never did I see such waste ! (*She
whirls him down, wipes him.*)

(*He submits placidly, as he knows he must.*)
(*She surveys him doggedly.*) Now sleep. At once ! One, two,
three ! He sleeps ! (*Suspiciously examining him, warningly.*)
He sleeps, I tell you.

DAVID (*quaking*). Not in the dark ! Mother, you promised
to give me a rush-light.

(*This woman is secretly proud of him now, but there is no
soft sentiment in her. She is still hopelessly perplexed
about what it all means.*)

MOTHER. No more talk of rush-lights. (*Sitting on his bed.*)
How it comes to be that you who are afraid to sleep in the dark
killed this Goliath . . . (*Despairingly*) I know not.

DAVID (*who easily loses faith in himself*). I did kill him,
mother, didn't I ?

MOTHER (*worried*). You *say* you did.

DAVID (*faltering*). When it is light, I know I did, but in
the dark I am not so sure.

MOTHER (*shaking her head*). Nor would I be sure if it were
not that we have the spear.

DAVID (*brightening*). Yes ! The spear ! Is it hid in a new
place to-night ?

MOTHER (*looking round cautiously*). H'sh ! Yes, another new
place. (*Scared*) David, when the news spreads to our neighbours, it will do the work of Bethlehem for days untold.

DAVID (*glorious*). My brothers will say we are the eight sons
of Jesse !

MOTHER. H'sh ! Not a word on your life to anyone until
Samuel comes again.

DAVID (*obediently*). No, oh no !

MOTHER. Unless the ass acquires speech we are safe. Yet, though none here knew it was you, reports are already circling round the well of Bethlehem that the giant was killed by some boy. They even say that he cut off Goliath's head.

DAVID. Do they ? (*He is promptly possessed by the grandeur of this idea.*) I remember now, I did cut off his head. I sawed it off with the spear !

MOTHER. Thou little liar ! (*Troubled*) What am I to think ? (*Gazing at* DAVID) How may I believe that a king had the heart to throw a javelin at your yellow head !

DAVID. My shepherd-man ! He did not mean to throw it at me, but at another, who was his enemy ; he was distraught because of that enemy and did mix us up. I do love him still.

MOTHER (*despairingly*). It is beyond me.

DAVID. Mother, I have lost my sling.

MOTHER. Careless boy !

DAVID. The sling I killed Goliath with ! (*He is in despair.*)

MOTHER (*relenting*). Your sling is safe. (*She shows it to him slung secretly round her neck and concealed in her bosom.*)

DAVID (*dumbfounded*). Why have you it there ?

MOTHER (*she becomes harsher, to get away from sentiment*). Sleep, I tell you, you confusion ! And no more of that dreaming of yours and hiding your head beneath the coverlet. Then do you look little like a champion !

DAVID (*quivering*). They were not as dreams, for lo, it was as if they lived.

MOTHER. They ? What mean you by they ?

DAVID (*huskily*). Do you think they are they that Saul spoke of—that which is to come to pass ?

MOTHER (*exasperated*). Some curse was on me when I bore you, boy.

> (*She treats him roughly and is going off with his bowl when* AMNON *enters at back with two nearly empty sacks flung over his shoulders. She speaks sharply.*)

You are late again, Amnon. (*Contemptuously*) The maidens at the well, I suppose.

AMNON. Ah me ! (*He is jealous of* DAVID'S *dress and speaks sarcastically*) Are these old eyes mistaken or do they see David in a coat of the night ?

(DAVID *displays himself vaingloriously.*)

MOTHER. You all had a coat of the night at his years. Moreover, it is the same coat. (*She goes out.*)

(AMNON *takes off his shoes, kneads his bed for bumps, finds another bed that he likes better and gets into it, rolling up his sacks as pillows.* AMINADAB *and* SHAMMAH *enter, carrying their beds, and place them ; neither uses a pillow, but both put on warm coats of wool as their one preparation for bed.* ELIAB *enters from back in a merry mood—but not at all intoxicated. The* MOTHER *returns.*)

AMNON. See Eliab roistering, mother. He has been boasting in the rest-house of his deeds at the camp of Saul.

MOTHER (*tartly*). It is high time that he returned thereto.

ELIAB. Ay, they need me. (*He makes a sort of dancing approach to his bed.*)

(*All are lying down or sitting on their beds when* JESSE *enters in his shirt-sleeves.*)

JESSE (*heavily*). Woman, I am disturbed about the ass. I notice some change in him. He is less compliant, and brays haughtily as if he thought himself a more notable ass than of old.

MOTHER. Can it be so ?

(*But she and* DAVID *exchange looks of subtle meaning.* JESSE *is putting on a thick coat.*)

Which bed for you to-night, Jesse ?

JESSE (*yawning*). Let me see. Where is Amnon ?

AMNON. I am here, father.

JESSE. Arise, Amnon. I will take your bed. Your choice is ever sound.

(AMNON *submits and they all get settled in their beds.*)

MOTHER (*now holding the lamp*). May good slumber be your hap, Jesse.

JESSE (*as his good-night greeting*). And yours. But it depends on that David, and his dreams. (*He holds up belt.*) This is for the first who breaks my rest to-night.

(*The* MOTHER, *after one glance round, goes off, carrying the lamp. The room is not quite plunged in darkness, as a little light comes from door, which she has not closed. There is a pause.*)

DAVID.　Father !

JESSE.　Quiet there !

DAVID.　Five minutes, father ?

JESSE.　No.

DAVID.　Two minutes, father ?

JESSE.　No.

DAVID.　One minute and a turn-round ?

JESSE.　Belt !

DAVID (*looking up after a pause*).　Is father asleep, Aminadab ?

AMINADAB.　He is—and so am I.

DAVID.　Eliab, was there more talk at the well about a boy having killed Goliath ?

AMNON (*yawning*).　Eliab sleeps.　But that story is a foolishness, David—it is more like the sort of thing you do make up yourself.

DAVID (*at once full of misgivings*).　Did I make it up, Amnon ?

(*Even* AMNON *is now asleep.*)

Amnon !　(*He is frightened at the stillness and pulls the blanket over his face.*)

(*A brief pause. Then the* MOTHER *is seen for a second pulling-to the door, and all is now black darkness. Other things unseen by audience have been happening since the darkness came. The back wall of the room has gone. It is really a change of scene without the curtain falling. There is perhaps low music, apparently to introduce the visions, but really to give* DAVID *time to change into a man. There is no other music throughout the visions. These visions begin with mysterious clouds and lights passing across the stage and gradually resolving themselves into the first vision. These visions can occupy all the stage from front to back.*

There are in all six of these visions, but as far as possible there should be no pause between them ; they should pass, slowly and dreamily, and without any jerks, the one into the other so that we are, as it were, looking upon one continuous picture. This can best be done, probably, by having no genuine scenery and the whole affair being a matter of curtains whose positions can be got by lighting, etc., as a vague scenic alteration has to be got from time to time. A sort of ghostly greyness is perhaps the best colour, and it should show grey not only in the curtains but in the clothing, and even to an extent in the faces of the characters, for it is a suggestion of ghost figures of the future that we should get. If necessary, there can be the drifting clouds, etc., after each vision.

Except the words they speak, no sound should come from these visions—for instance, we hear no footsteps. There is no furniture of any kind, unless specifically stated. In interiors there are no doors, or windows, or ' wings '; the characters are just there or not there. They come and go by the help of curtains insubstantially, as if vanishing or appearing from a mist. All this calls for adroitness from stage experts that is beyond the author's skill, who knows what he wants but not how to get it and has now given them enough to ponder over for one day. With a big stage, some of the scenes should attain a grandeur of effect.

The first vision shows the Cave of Adullam. It is a vague place with an opening at the back and rocks in it, made no doubt of velvet. The general effect of it should be wild, and here and elsewhere in the visions when they are out of doors, they should be reproductions of ancient places. Several Israelite soldiers, armed, appear among the rocks, evidently in search of DAVID. *They come without a sound, tracking him. They see indications that there has been a fire and draw their swords. The scene should be dim.* OPHIR *and* ABNER *are in command of these men.*)

OPHIR. Search the glade beyond. Tell them to put a ring of searchers round this and every cave.

ABNER. If you would be live men in the morning. For so Saul swears.

(*Only* OPHIR *and* ABNER *are now left. They crouch down by the fire.*)

ABNER. Truly there are evil shadows flitting through these caves to-night.

OPHIR. We seek but one of them—the son of Jesse.

ABNER. But again and again he avoids out of our presence. He is as one protected against such as Ophir and Abner.

OPHIR. But not against such a one as Saul.

ABNER. Saul has made the mountains drunk with the blood

of his enemies.   But still David escapes him.   So seems it to be again to-night.

(*In the opening at the back* SAUL *suddenly appears.*)

SAUL (*fiercely*).   You have not found mine enemy ?

OPHIR.   Every cave on the mountain is being searched.   We know by this fire that he was hiding here within the hour.

SAUL.   Ever within the hour !   What is this place called ?

OPHIR.   It is known as the Cave of Adullam.

ABNER.   We had hoped that the priests of the place called Nob would guide you to him.

SAUL (*savagely*).   There is now no place called Nob.

OPHIR.   But the priests of Nob.

SAUL.   There are no longer priests in Nob.

ABNER (*aghast*).   You cannot mean that——

SAUL.   When they refused to lead me to him I ordered my servants to smite them to the wall.

ABNER.   My King !   Priests !

SAUL.   Ay, so my servants cried and would not put forth their hands, but Doeg the Edomite was faithful and fell upon the priests, and four score and five who wore the linen ephod did he slay.

ABNER (*horrified*).   Sacrilege !

SAUL.   To that have I come.

OPHIR.   It was but excess of zeal.

SAUL.   The same zeal shall be apportioned to you—and you— if David is not delivered into my hands.   If again we fail I shall do as I have spoken of to you, Ophir !   I will make him my son-in-law so that my daughter may snare him.

OPHIR.   Not that, O King !

(*The second vision, which requires a much larger space of stage, shows* SAUL *and his troop asleep on a hillside.   His head is on a sort of kit-bag called a ' bolster,' and his javelin stands erect by him, stuck in the ground.   Near him lies* OPHIR, *and both are prominent down-stage.   The other sleeping figures are more vague.   It is a bright clear night.*

DAVID *appears at top on the hillside and we realise that his object is to reach* SAUL, *a very dangerous venture. Dagger in hand, ready to stab anyone who wakes, he descends, stepping over bodies.   He reaches the side of the*

*King. He is conscious of his remarkable position beside his
enemy. He raises his dagger threateningly and pauses,
indicating how easy it would be to do the deed. Then he
proceeds to mysterious, dangerous business, holding his
dagger in his teeth. He pulls the bolster inch by inch from
beneath* SAUL'S *head. Once* SAUL *moans a little and* DAVID
*holds the dagger ready to strike. Having got the bolster,
he takes out of it a leather cruse of water. He also wants*
SAUL'S *javelin, but* OPHIR'S *hand is on it. Pulling a hair
from his own head, he tickles* OPHIR'S *hand with it, ready
to kill if he wakes.* OPHIR *does not wake, but merely
removes his hand, scratches it, and sleeps on.*

DAVID *pulls the javelin out of the ground and, carrying
it and the water cruse, he goes up the incline across the
bodies. He stops and lays them down and, looking among
the bodies for something, finds it. It is a horn. He pulls
a hand across his brow, implying that now he has reached
the riskiest moment of his schemes. Then he boldly sounds
the horn—that is, though we hear no sound, the action
implies this. Possibly this one sound should be heard. As
if the sleepers had heard it, the horn wakens the* SOLDIERS
and they answer with cries and grasp their weapons.

DAVID *is now standing, a conspicuous figure, surrounded
by soldiers ready to pounce on him, his arms folded.* SAUL
and OPHIR *start up, and* ABNER *and others pointing at*
DAVID *add to his prominence.*)

OPHIR (*pointing*). My King, your enemy !

ABNER. Behold we deliver him into your hands.

DAVID (*speaking for the first time in the visions*). You deliver
me, Abner, son of Ner ! Asleep all of you, dastards, at your
posts ! What opportunity this night for men of evil intent to
have crept over your vile bodies and slain the Lord's anointed !

SAUL. He speaks true. Abner, Ophir, you are both worthy
of death.

OPHIR. His words are false, O King. Never were guards
more watchful. He knows he could not have come one step
nearer you and lived.

DAVID. I have wandered through you and over you and
stood by the side of the King.

SAUL. Nay, nay, that cannot have been, for I still live.

OPHIR. Not once did I close an eye, and my hand never failed to clutch thy javelin.

SAUL (*to* DAVID). Thou hearest?

DAVID. Where, then, my Ophir, is the javelin that your hand never failed to clutch?

(*Consternation when they find it has gone.*)

DAVID. Where, O King, is the cruse of water that was in the bolster on which you thought the head of Saul lay safe?

(*They find that it also has gone; increased astonishment.* DAVID *holds up, one in each hand, the cruse and the javelin. There are cries of wonder.*)

Now let one of the young men come up and fetch the King's javelin and the cruse that was in his bolster.

(*This is done.*)

OPHIR (*contrite*). My King!

(*His arms seek forgiveness, but* SAUL *strikes them down.*)

SAUL. Unworthy!

DAVID. Behold, Saul, I have taught these slovens that they should be a wall unto you by night and by day. Yet you have driven me from your service and hunted me through all Judah, seeking my life, and you came hither to tear it out of me on this mountain of the he-goats. You have chased me into serving other Lords whom I loved less than thee but trusted more. Now am I in thy grasp. Slay me as I stand if such is still your wish. Your young men's daggers are around me, and even Ophir and Abner are at last awake.

SAUL. Thou art bold of speech. Yet, my son David, I will no more do thee harm nor seek to pursue thee into the bowels of the earth or to snare thee like a pheasant on the mountains, but I will take thee back into my service because my soul was precious in thine eyes this night.

(DAVID *prostrates himself and the scene changes into a vague interior in the palace of Saul. There are no doors or windows to it. It is only an empty space with curtains but it has one piece of furniture, namely, a throne raised on two steps, and on the throne is sitting* SAUL *in kingly garments and with the crown on his head.* OPHIR *appears out of the nothingness.*)

SAUL. Well?

OPHIR.   My King, he has made the mountains drunk with the blood of thine enemies.

SAUL (*apprehensive*).   The son of Jesse ?

OPHIR.   The congregation of the people cry that we owe the day to him.   They are singing and dancing to his glory in the streets to the music of flute, hackbut, cornet and dulcimer.

SAUL (*dolefully*).   Ophir, it must be done—that of which I spoke to you.

(OPHIR *is reluctant.*)

It is the one way of breaking him that has not yet been tried. You spoke to him ?

OPHIR (*miserably*).   I gave him your words.   I said : ' Come you now, before the King, for Saul has delight in you.'

SAUL.   Delight !   How looked he at that ?

OPHIR.   He *eyed* me, O King.

SAUL.   Summon me my daughters.

(OPHIR *fades out, and in the same gradual way* MERAB *and* MICHAL, *two beautiful young women, daughters of* SAUL, *appear.   They are finely attired, and* MICHAL *is apparently high-spirited.*)

Merab——

(*She makes a sweeping obeisance.*)

Michal——

(*She does so also.*)

I have called you before the throne because I have a design to make one of you a snare unto the son of Jesse.

MERAB.   A snare.   Which one of us ?

SAUL (*sternly*).   Gainsay me not.

(DAVID *appears.   He is now handsomely attired as a captain, and is respectful but wary, and prepared for even an attempt upon his life.   He makes obeisance.*)

SAUL.   Rise, my captain.   The throne-room greets you.

DAVID.   O King, I am dazed by it.   Never have these eyes beheld the throne until this day.

SAUL.   Great has been your victory and I would reward you in a kingly way.

(*The two girls exchange puzzled glances.*)

This day shall you be my son-in-law.

(DAVID *bows but is still alert.*)

MERAB.   Father, which of us ?

SAUL (*to* DAVID).   Determine it between you.
   (*He moves away and is suddenly gone.*)

MERAB (*to* DAVID, *humbling herself before him*).   Noble captain, your fame grows apace.   You will be too great for me. I am for the simple Adriel.

MICHAL (*remaining erect*).   Never, captain, can you be great enough for me.   I am for a King.

   (*They see* DAVID *is staring at the throne with such interest that he is oblivious of their presence.   They look at each other bewildered and, moving away, they are gone.* DAVID *is unconscious of their going, and, drawn by something within him, he slowly moves forward and mounts the throne.* MICHAL *now returns softly and watches him from curtain, half in hiding.   Perhaps we only see her face.* DAVID *sits on the throne and we see that he likes it.*)

MICHAL (*in an intense murmur and holding out her arms*).   I am for a King !

   (*She withdraws into the background.   She goes.* DAVID, *left alone, still sits upon the throne, no longer fearfully but quite complacently.   Suddenly he claps his hand to his forehead as if hit by something.   He leaves the throne quickly, bewildered and as one who has done sacrilege.*

   The scene changes to SAUL'S *tent on the night before the battle of Gilboa.* SAUL *in armour is pacing the tent, raging at the shrinking* OPHIR *who is also armed.   Evidently* OPHIR *has brought bad news.   Though* SAUL *rages at first he is now less spirited than formerly ; he is a more saddened man.*)

SAUL (*fiercely*).   Again he has escaped me !   Sent I not you, with messengers, to compass his house and bring him up to me on his sick-bed that I may slay him ?

OPHIR (*at his heaviest, as one telling an astounding thing*).   Lo, when we were come in to where he lay there was an image on the bed, with a pillow of goat's hair for his bolster !——and it was Michal his wife who did this thing, and let him down from the window in a basket !

SAUL (*bitterly*).   Michal, the child of my bowels whom I had given to him to entice and to snare him !   Even his wife is on the side of this man. What murmur my soldiers against me because I drove him forth from the army of Israel ?

(OPHIR *hesitates*.)

The truth, Ophir.

OPHIR (*reluctantly*). Your Elders do proclaim that he was the wisest of your counsellors—and your Captains lament that you will not have him in to-morrow's battle, speaking of him as one who breaks upon an enemy like the breach of waters.

SAUL. And what says Ophir ?

OPHIR (*violently*). Ophir says he is the falsest in all Israel.

SAUL (*firmly though sadly*). So says not Saul. Mine enemy has ever fought me fair, and twice had he my life in his hands and returned it to me who slew four score and five of the priests of Nob because they would not deliver him unto me. I did wickedness that day. (*He shudders at himself*.) What say my people ?

(OPHIR *hesitates*.)

(*Harshly*) Answer me.

OPHIR. The more ignorant among the people cry : ' Saul has slain his thousands but David will slay his tens of thousands.'

SAUL. Ophir, I heard them ! And they were the bitterest words of all to me ! O fickle people ! Will this man give every one of you vines and fig-trees to sit under when the day's toil is done, as I have striven to do ? (*Honourably*) Ay, Ophir, he will, for I have that within me which knows he too does love the people. This man will make the earth shake and tremble, for he is a greater one than Saul. And now there is none of you sorry for me, no, not one.

OPHIR. My King ! (*On his knees to* SAUL.)

(SAUL, *who has been seated, rises and speaks quietly but with resolution*.)

SAUL. How long must I drag this chain of life—how long ? Now shall I seek Samuel, and know how long.

OPHIR (*startled*). My King, you know that Samuel's days are fulfilled and that he sleeps with his fathers at Ramah.

SAUL (*firmly*). I go to seek one who can bring him up.

OPHIR (*horrified*). Not the Woman of Endor ! (*Trembling*) King, it is impious to seek to bring up the dead.

SAUL. Leave me, Ophir, in the hour of my strait with the burden that is upon me. And hearken. Everyone now to his tent. I must be alone in this world to-night.

(OPHIR *goes.* SAUL *is left alone. After shivering once, he is firm of purpose. He peers out of the tent. The scene is now the cavern of the* WITCH OF ENDOR. *It should be specially vague and indeterminate, little more than blackness through which the ancient witch flits and is gone.* SAUL *appears in disguise. In the tent we have seen him a broken sorrowful man, but now he is of a noble and kingly bearing. He and the* WITCH *meet, but in such darkness that we see only their shapes.*)

SAUL (*as she shrinks back*). You know me not, I am not as you think. I am of this world. Divine unto me by the familiar spirit, and bring him up to me, the one whom I shall name unto thee.

(*The voices of both are pitched in a key to go with the solemnity of the occasion.*)

WITCH (*trembling*). Thou knowest what Saul has done. He has cut off those that have familiar spirits. Wherefore then layest thou a snare for my life to cause me to die ?

SAUL. There shall be no punishment happen to thee for this thing.

WITCH (*whose fears are in contrast to his firmness*). Whom shall I bring up unto thee ?

SAUL. Bring me up Samuel.

(*There is suddenly a torch in her hand and she is using it to peer at his face.*)

WITCH (*huskily*). Thou art Saul !

SAUL. Fear not. What see'st thou ?

WITCH. An old man cometh up and he is covered with a mantle.

(*She vanishes. Perhaps we see less the figure of* SAMUEL *than a thickness, and we know that someone is there. To that,* SAUL *addresses himself.*)

SAUL. Samuel ! (*He bows low to the unseen.*)

SAMUEL (*sternly*). Why hast thou disquieted me, Saul, to bring me up ?

SAUL (*firm*). I am sore distressed, for the Philistines make war against me, and the Lord answereth me no more. There-

fore I have called thee up that thou mayest make known to me
how long is my time—how long.

SAMUEL (*relentless*). The Lord is departed from thee, for
He rends the kingdom out of thy hand and gives it to thy neighbour. Because thou disobeyed'st Him He has done this thing
unto thee. To-morrow, after the battle with the Philistines,
thou and thy son shall no longer be of this world : you will be
in mine with me.

(SAUL *has listened without flinching. He again bows
lowly. He sways. The thickening fades. The scene
dissolves and changes to a mountain side on the next day,
where the Philistines gained their only great victory over
the Israelites and* SAUL *was slain. There is doubt as to
the exact site, but Mount Gilboa comes into the picture and
the battle might be called after it. The Israelites, who
always chose the higher ground because they were without
horses or chariots, were driven upward and dispersed with
great slaughter, but all we see is a last effort of* SAUL'S *after
the fight has been lost. In the background many dead of
both sides lie, seen vaguely as in mist.*

In the foreground, SAUL, *badly wounded, is hewing
down some of the enemy in the manner of a mighty warrior
of old ; but still we hear no sound. When they are killed
or driven off, he falls, shot by an arrow.* OPHIR, *equally
wounded, is by him.* SAUL *in the Old Testament was
wearing his crown.*)

SAUL.   Tell me, is it so with Jonathan—also ?

OPHIR.   Alas ! (*He bows his head.*)

SAUL.   Ophir, truly am I sore wounded by the archers.
Dispatch me now quickly. Thrust me through, lest the un-
circumcised Philistines come and abuse me.

OPHIR.   I cannot lift my hand against my King.

SAUL.   I forgive you, sweet Ophir.

(*He dies by his own hand and* OPHIR *falls back among the
slain. A figure appears on the battlefield and resolves
himself into the man* DAVID. *He comes down to the side
of* SAUL, *kneels, then rises and salutes him. He is again
in military rags, as in the second of the visions.*)

DAVID.   How are the mighty fallen ! Tell it not in Gath ;
publish it not in the streets of Ascalon, lest the daughters of the

Philistines rejoice. Ye mountains of Gilboa, let there be no dew, neither let there be rain, upon you, nor fields of offerings ; for here the shield of the mighty is vilely cast away, the shield of Saul, as though he had not been anointed with oil. From the blood of the slain, from the fat of the mighty, the bow of Jonathan turned not back, and the sword of Saul returned not empty. Saul and Jonathan were lovely and pleasant in their lives, and in their death they were not divided ; they were swifter than eagles, they were stronger than lions. Ye daughters of Israel, weep over Saul who clothed you in scarlet, with other delights. (*Now addressing a body which we do not distinguish*) O Jonathan, thou wast slain in thine high places. I am distressed for thee, my brother Jonathan ; very pleasant hast thou been unto me ; thy love to me was wonderful, passing the love of women. How are the mighty fallen, and the weapons of war perished ! (*He sinks down, mourning for* JONATHAN, *and is gone.*)

 (*The figure of* SAMUEL *comes to* SAUL. *Throughout the scene that follows they are as simple as two villagers gossiping about old times.*)

SAMUEL. Greeting, friend. Can I help you ?

 (SAUL *sits up.*)

SAUL. Do I know you ?

SAMUEL. I was called Samuel.

SAUL. I cannot remember such a one, but I like your face.

SAMUEL. And I yours—though it is unknown to me.

SAUL. Sit with me, good Samuel.

 (SAMUEL *sits beside him.*)

SAMUEL (*uncertain*). If your name should be Saul——

SAUL. It comes to me that such is my name.

SAMUEL. Then, to guide you, I was sent hither, as one who in a past time had, in some way now forgotten by me, been tied up with you in the bundle of life.

SAUL. Is it so ? (*Dropping unconsciously into* DAVID's *manner*) Now do you ask me what was my way of life, and I will tell you, and then shall I ask you what was your way of life, and, lo, you will tell me. (*Puzzled*) Was it you who used to say this to me ?

SAMUEL. I know not. But tell me, Saul, what was your way of life ?

SAUL. I was a shepherd. Now tell me what was yours.

SAMUEL. I see it not so clearly as you do, for I am farther away. All I bring back is that I had two troublesome sons. How one forgets the smaller things !

SAUL. Verily.

SAMUEL (*ruminating*). A shepherd ? It is as if I had known such a one—one who went out into far places to seek his asses which had strayed.

SAUL. Not my asses, my father's asses.

SAMUEL. It was you ?

SAUL. One forgets not such a thing as that.

SAMUEL (*his memory jogged*). Tell me, were you never a King ?

SAUL. What is that ?

SAMUEL. One who is lord-over-all.

SAUL (*quietly reproving*). Speak not blasphemy, friend. There is but One such.

SAMUEL. It is so. Nevertheless——

(*He prostrates before* SAUL, *whom it vaguely disturbs.*)

SAUL. What mean you ? Trouble me not.

SAMUEL. Thus did all your people.

SAUL. Who were my people ?

SAMUEL. They were called Israel.

SAUL. Israel. It is a beautiful word.

SAMUEL. Put all such vanity from you, friend.

SAUL. What happened, Samuel ? Was the Lord fair to me ? (*Giving it up contentedly*) Truly His ways are past finding out.

SAMUEL. Now are they to be made clear to you. Come with me.

SAUL. Israel.

(*They go away together. The scene darkens, and in the obscurity of the battlefield, we become aware of a small white figure wandering about on it. Only the white nightgown makes us realise that this is the boy* DAVID. *He is flitting about here and there, in search of* SAUL, *but does not find him. He calls :*)

Saul—Saul !

(*After a pause :*)

It is thy David seeking thee !

(*Again, after a pause :*)

Shepherd !

(Finally :)

Saul, Saul !

(His childishness is in strong contrast to the virility of the older DAVID. *The scene blacks out, and changes to the room of the sleepers, the back wall being replaced, and they are still lying there asleep.*

It should be noted that all sounds made in the room are now heard though none were heard in the visions. The room is still dark, but, as the MOTHER *enters, the grey light of early morning comes through the doorway which she has left open. It is now lighter in the room but only light enough to show the sleeping figures. The* MOTHER *is evidently the first up to meet the labours of the new day, and is carrying a broom. She comes to* DAVID'S *bed, expecting all to be as usual, and is startled to find that he is not in the bed. This should be unexpected to us also. She utters one alarmed cry.)*

MOTHER.   Jesse !

(And then realises that it is best not to waken the others. While she is pondering what to do, the back door opens and DAVID *comes in, still wearing his white garment, which is now bedraggled. He leaves the door open, which adds to the amount of light. His eyes are glassy and he moves like a sleep-walker. She murmurs his name, and she both goes to him and shrinks back, for she has a feeling that in his condition he ought not to be addressed. He does not see her, though she is in full view, but goes straight to his bed and lies on it like a log, in an extremity of sleep and exhaustion.*

She is no longer emotional, She is entirely practical. She takes off her shawl and puts it round his shoulders. She is startled to find his sling round his waist. She feels her own neck, thinking it is surely still there. She looks at door as a suspicion comes to her.)

MOTHER *(bewildered).*   Your sling ! Did you come in to where I lay and take it off me while I slept ? *(She finds his knee cut and bandages it. She says in awe)* David, where have you been ?

(He sleeps on.)

SCENE 2

DAVID AND JONATHAN

THE scene, which is pastoral, is the fields south-east of Bethlehem, and here David is found tending his sheep. It is early evening two days later and the setting sun lingers over its best achievement. We may see a suggestion of its rays, but not the sun itself. It should be an idyll of quiet rural loveliness, in contrast to the rest of the play. In the not far distance is the old walled town of Bethlehem on its hill, not conspicuous and yet vaguely dominating the landscape, which shows many of the wild flowers for which this place was famous, such as the white flower called the Star of Bethlehem, with masses of scarlet anemones. A half-cut field of barley is also prominent, shining at times in the sun. In the foreground is a large rock (practical) of limestone which slopes from right to left, beginning from ground and reaching at its highest point to nearly five feet. Thus it is really a small rock, though to David's eyes it is great. It extends back sufficiently far to contain a small cave just large enough to hold two people. It has moss growing on it, and there are similar smaller rocks here and there going into distance, for it is not rich ground for pasture but often stony. In the foreground there is a thick patch of long grass (practical), about half a dozen yards of it.

All the action of this scene of country life must take place down-stage. It really consists of a duologue between the two boys, and must not play much more than ten minutes. There are possibly some real sheep and black goats browsing here and there, but in any case most of them are artificial. There are bells round their necks, and at the opening of the scene (before any talk) the tinkle of the bells is heard, but this must not be overdone. It should be no louder than the hum of bees.

(DAVID *is discovered standing on the rock crest tending his sheep. A shepherd's staff with crooked handle is in his hand and it is much taller than himself; he has to reach to grasp the handle. He is wearing a long shepherd's mantle of linen, no doubt stitched together by his mother, though he thinks he is looking every inch a shepherd, and he should have the effect of a shepherd as seen in the pictures of the period. His hand is outstretched and he seems to be numbering the sheep. Seeing that all is well with his flock,* DAVID *sits on the rock pursuing a secret occupation. He has now a lump of soft clay in his hand on which he is laboriously writing a letter. This is done with a sharp instrument in his knife, and is really carving. His head is cocked in the effort and he is biting his tongue. The peaceful pastoral scene is interrupted by someone unseen throwing clods of earth at him. He evidently guesses who it is and he jumps down and hides in his cave.*

A whistle is heard off-stage. DAVID *whistles back and hides in cave. The voice of* JONATHAN *calls.)*

JONATHAN.   Son of Jesse !

(DAVID *thinks it all exceedingly funny.* JONATHAN *enters, not in armour, but well attired. He sees* DAVID *but politely pretends not to.)*

David ! Whither have you got ? I saw you on the rock like a he-goat.

DAVID *(like sentry).* Say the password.

JONATHAN.   Goliath.

DAVID.   Enter !

(JONATHAN *affects surprise to see him.* DAVID *and he point at each other gleefully.* DAVID *emerges on all-fours. He winces and limps and sits down on the ground.)*

JONATHAN.   Have you hurt yourself ?

DAVID *(emphatic).* No !

(JONATHAN *sits beside him.* DAVID *pulls bandage off his knee and shows bandage dramatically.)*

' Behold ! ' *(He then shows his knee badly scratched.)*

JONATHAN.   How then ? Have more strange things befallen *you* who killed Goliath but two days ago ?

DAVID.   Ay, truly ! *(Impressively)* Jonathan, hearken. My mother says I did wander from my home in the dark of the night, and whither I went no one knows ! *(He is rather scared.)* Jonathan, have you ever been at a dream ?

JONATHAN.   At a dream ? I have dreamed dreams, but you cannot be *at* a dream.

DAVID *(complacently, but uncomfortable).* I can !

JONATHAN. You are sure ?

DAVID. My mother is sure. When she sought me on my bed in the morning, I was not there, and then did I come in by the door and I saw her not, for my eyes were glassy. But my sling was in my hand and this knee did bleed, and she plucked from it thorns of the field. Jonathan, I had been at a dream !

JONATHAN (*awed*). You are a strange one, David.

DAVID (*also awed but pleased*). Am I not ?

JONATHAN. Show me your dream.

DAVID. It has now gone from me.

JONATHAN. Thus is it with dreams. (*With boyish eagerness*) Was I in it ?

DAVID (*reflecting*). I do not remember you in it.

JONATHAN. Then it interests me not.

DAVID. I think your father was in it.

JONATHAN. Tell me.

DAVID. Something about Saul and an enemy. (*Puzzled*) What enemy ? (*With excited glimpses of memory*) He was a ragged soldier seeking the hurt of Saul, and so I rose from my bed and went out with my sling to kill him. (*Realising*) Ay, that was why I went out into the dream.

JONATHAN. I am happy, David, that you do so love my father even in dreams.

DAVID. Also I do love you.

JONATHAN. And I you.

DAVID. Jonathan, I have made a gift for you.

JONATHAN. What is it ?

(DAVID *gets on to rock and lifts the lump of clay, covering it with his hand as a treasure.* JONATHAN *eagerly jumps up beside him and tries to open the hands of* DAVID. *They are sitting on rock.*)

DAVID (*putting it into* JONATHAN's *hand*). Now is it yours. Nay, be careful—it is now but soft clay, but when it is baked in the sun it will be . . . a brick !

JONATHAN. Only a brick ! (*Disappointed but polite.*) Truly a comely brick.

DAVID (*trying not to be lordly*). Jonathan, it is a letter !

(JONATHAN *examines it with wonder.*)

JONATHAN. You can write ?

DAVID (*swelling*). Behold ! (*Pointing to it.*)

JONATHAN. I cannot write. It is not for princes to practise such things.

(DAVID *offers it to him.*)

JONATHAN. Nor do we read. (*Eagerly*) How speaks it?

DAVID. It says: 'I, David, son of Jesse, am the one who slew Goliath, and none helped me, for I did it alone.' Thus, Jonathan, will my sons know 'twas I and no other who did it, and their sons and theirs and theirs down to for ever and a span will know, for such can be the life of a brick with writing on it.

JONATHAN. O excellent brick. (*Regally*) David, when I am King I will make you one of my guard.

DAVID. No, Jonathan, I have slain a lion and a bear and now is my great day ended.

JONATHAN. All things shall be as I direct. Sometimes you shall sit at my table.

DAVID. In my dream I saw the ragged one sit upon a throne.

JONATHAN. Was he anyone you know?

DAVID. No, he was a bad one. I can remember no more.

(JONATHAN *shivers.*)

JONATHAN. He sat upon a throne? David, I like not this.

DAVID. Then did I loose a pebble at him—and it struck him in the brow. Quickly did he leap from that throne! There was also a woman in the dream—(*Sadly, as if this were a phrase of portentous meaning*)—and, alas, she was fair to look upon. I think she was his wife, and he did call her Michal. . . . Here is another thing I do remember now. When he was old, he cried: 'O my son Absalom! Would that I had died for thee, O Absalom, my son, my son!' That time was I sorry for him—and I did vow never to call a son of mine Absalom. (*Dismissing the dream.*) Jonathan, come into my cave so that I may propose a hidden thing to you.

(*They sit in the cave.* DAVID *speaks rapturously.*) Jonathan, shall you and I make a covenant?

JONATHAN (*in the same spirit*). Let us! But what?

(*They are gleeful again.*)

DAVID. To be friends for ever and ever and a span!

JONATHAN. Whatever thy soul desireth, that will I do for thee, David.

DAVID. And so I swear I will do for thee. Behold now we have sworn.

JONATHAN. So we have ! Now, David, show me how you killed the lion and the bear.

DAVID. I will show you. Stand there and be the lion and I will come out of my cave and kill you. (*He goes into the cave.*)

(*JONATHAN gets ready to play the part of the lion.* DAVID *comes out of the cave and attacks* JONATHAN. *After a short fight* JONATHAN *throws* DAVID *to the ground.* DAVID *is bewildered.* JONATHAN, *very pleased with himself, laughs loudly.*)

DAVID. How shall I be able to kill you unless you roar ? Try again, foolish one. (*He goes back into the cave.*)

(*JONATHAN roars.* DAVID *rushes at him and, after a short struggle, he is thrown again.* JONATHAN *laughs.*)

JONATHAN. Now shall I be the bear ?

DAVID. Never, never, never ! (*He fetches brick and throws it down, battering it to pieces.*) Begone, thou lying brick !

JONATHAN (*bewildered*). Lying ?

DAVID (*now reaching the most tragic moment in his boyhood's story*). I wrote on my brick that I alone killed Goliath and that none helped me ; and that is false ; for *He* helped me !

JONATHAN (*completely at sea*). He ? Who ? David, these eyes saw your pebble that pierced the giant between the eyes.

DAVID. It was His pebble.

JONATHAN. Whose ?

(*After a moment* DAVID *whispers the terrible secret in his ear. When* JONATHAN, *who has looked upward, is able to speak, he says shakily :*)

Oh, David ! Are you not then so wonderful as I thought ?

DAVID (*mournfully*). No.

JONATHAN. But you did slay a lion and a bear, didn't you ?

DAVID (*in bitter humiliation*). 'Twas also He who slew the lion and the bear.

JONATHAN (*slightly drawing away from him*). Oh, David ! (*Eager to comfort*) But He let you help ?

DAVID (*in despair*). He did not need my help. (*With a cry*) I want to do something all by myself !

JONATHAN. Oh, David. Only kings can do things by themselves.

(DAVID *is sad for a moment.*)

Now must I seek the camp.

DAVID. And I my home. (*He lifts the staff.*) But first I must go round my fold and separate the sheep from the goats.

(*The dying sun is now bright over the scene, especially over the barley field.*)

JONATHAN. It is fair to look upon around Bethlehem.

DAVID. There is no place so fair as Bethlehem. So did Naomi think—and Ruth.

JONATHAN. Who were they?

DAVID. Naomi was of Bethlehem, and when she was old she did always want to come back here from a far land where she was wed. And Ruth was her daughter-in-law and said to her : 'Whither thou goest I will go, and where thou lodgest I will lodge : thy people shall be my people, and thy God my God, and where thou diest will I die, and there will I be buried' —and so, Jonathan, did it come to pass. But first she did glean in the field, for it was the time of the barley ; but the man Boaz did tell the reapers slyly to let fall handfuls so that she should get more than her share ! And thus did she wed Boaz, and became the mother of Obed, who begat Jesse, who begat me ! (*Pointing*) And that is the field in which he first saw her, and lo, it is again the time of the barley !

JONATHAN. The day groweth to an end. Whistle to me as I go, David, our whistle.

DAVID (*lying on his back*). None will harm you as you go, for those you may meet will be but poor shepherds that do lie in fields keeping their flocks by night. Such shall I be, Jonathan, through all the nights of my life.

JONATHAN (*he lifts the two biggest pieces of clay*). Alas, once proud brick.

DAVID (*taking them and dropping them in little pieces*). Its day has been shorter than we thought ! (*Swelling*) Nevertheless, I have still Goliath's spear.

JONATHAN. When you are a man, David, I will see to it that you carry that spear on your shoulder.

DAVID (*whispering*). Jonathan, *I can carry it on my shoulder now !*

JONATHAN. Not you ! Is that the secret ?

(DAVID *nods.*)

DAVID. Jonathan, it is something I did think out by myself.

(With a half-defiant, half-apprehensive look upwards) None helped me.

JONATHAN. Show me.

DAVID. Some day I will show you.

JONATHAN. Now am I gone. *(He starts to go, then turns and puts his hand on DAVID's shoulder.)* Remember the covenant. David and Jonathan friends for ever.

DAVID. And a span !

(They are not sentimental. They are gay and happy. JONATHAN goes off the way he had come. In the same moment DAVID gets on the rock, to look after him. JONATHAN does the whistle, unseen. DAVID, staff in hand, on the rock, whistles it. They whistle to each other till JONATHAN is too far away.

DAVID comes off the rock. He leaves his staff in the cave. He is sly and has some grand design on hand. He drags into view by both hands Goliath's spear, which so far has been hidden in the long grass in front. He drags it along the ground and up the sloping rock. Then, standing where the rock is highest, he pulls the spear on to him till it is balanced on his shoulder. With one glance upwards he goes off elatedly, with the spear over his shoulder. There is a slight accompaniment of sheep-bells.)

APPENDIX

COMPLETE LIST OF BARRIE'S PLAYS

Following is a complete list of Barrie's plays (excluding juvenilia and a number of trifles written for private entertainment and for charity performances) with the theatres and year of production. Those included in the present edition are indicated *.

	Theatre	Year
Becky Sharp (one act)	Terry's	1891
Ibsen's Ghost (one act)	Toole's	1891
Richard Savage (in collaboration with H. B. Marriott Watson)	Criterion	1891
*Walker, London	Toole's	1892
Jane Annie (written for D'Oyly Carte in collaboration with Conan Doyle) . . .	Savoy	1893
*The Professor's Love Story . . .	Comedy	1894
*The Little Minister	Haymarket	1897
*The Wedding Guest	Garrick	1900
*Quality Street	Vaudeville	1902
*The Admirable Crichton . . .	Duke of York's	1902
*Little Mary	Wyndham's	1903
*Peter Pan	Duke of York's	1904
*Pantaloon (one act)	,,	1905
*Alice Sit-by-the-Fire	,,	1905
Josephine (one act)	Comedy	1906
Punch (one act)	,,	1906
*What Every Woman Knows . . .	Duke of York's	1908
*Old Friends (one act)	,,	1910
*The Twelve-Pound Look (one act) . . .	,,	1910
A Slice of Life (one act)	,,	1910
*Rosalind (one act)	,,	1912

	Theatre	Year
*The Will (one act)	Duke of York's	1913
The Adored One (see *Seven Women, 1917) .	"	1913
*Half an Hour (one act)	Hippodrome	1913
The Dramatists Get What They Want (one act) .	"	1913
Der Tag (one act)	Coliseum	1914
*The New Word (one act)	Duke of York's	1915
Rosy Rapture, Pride of the Beauty Chorus . .	"	1915
*A Kiss for Cinderella . . .	Wyndham's	1916
*Seven Women (revised version of The Adored One, 1913)	New	1917
*The Old Lady Shows Her Medals (one act) .	New	1917
*Dear Brutus	Wyndham's	1917
*A Well-Remembered Voice (one act) . . .	"	1918
The Truth About the Russian Dancers (one act) .	Coliseum	1920
*Mary Rose	Haymarket	1920
*Shall We Join the Ladies ? (one act) . .	R.A.D.A.	1921
*Barbara's Wedding (one act) . . .	Savoy	1927
*The Boy David	His Majesty's	1936